Twelfth Edition

INTERNATIONAL BUSINESS
Environments and Operations

John D. Daniels
University of Miami

Lee H. Radebaugh
Brigham Young University

Daniel P. Sullivan
University of Delaware

Prentice Hall
Upper Saddle River, NJ 07458

Library of Congress Cataloging-in-Publication Data

Daniels, John D.
   International business : environments and operations/John D. Daniels, Lee H. Radebaugh,
   Daniel P. Sullivan.—12th ed.
      p. cm.
   ISBN-13: 978-0-13-602965-6 (hardcover)
   ISBN-10: 0-13-602965-5 (hardcover)
   1. International business enterprises.   2. International economic relations.   3. Investments,
Foreign.   I. Radebaugh, Lee H.   II. Sullivan, Daniel P.   III. Title.
HD2755.5.D35 2009
658.1'8—dc22

                                                                    2008005960

Editorial Director: Sally Yagan
Acquisitions Editor: Jennifer M. Collins
Product Development Manager: Ashley Santora
Editorial Assistant: Elizabeth Davis
Development Editor: Ron Librach
Director of Marketing: Patrice Lumumba Jones
Marketing Manager: Nikki Jones
Marketing Assistant: Ian Gold
Associate Managing Editor: Suzanne DeWorken
Project Manager, Production: Ann Pulido
Permissions Project Manager: Charles Morris
Senior Operations Supervisor: Arnold Vila
Creative Director: Leslie Osher
Senior Art Director: Janet Slowik
Interior Design: Ilze Lemesis
Cover Design: Ilze Lemesis
Illustration (Interior): Thistle Hill Publishing Services, LLC
Director, Image Resource Center: Melinda Patelli
Manager, Rights and Permissions: Zina Arabia
Manager, Visual Research: Beth Brenzel
Image Permission Coordinator: Kathy Gavilanes
Photo Researcher: Rachel Lucas
Composition: Integra
Full-Service Project Management: Thistle Hill Publishing Services, LLC
Printer/Binder: Quebecor World Color/Versailles
Typeface: 10/12 Palatino

Credits and acknowledgments borrowed from other sources and reproduced, with permission, in this
textbook appear on appropriate page within text.

Prentice Hall
is an imprint of

www.pearsonhighered.com

10 9 8 7 6 5 4 3 2 1
ISBN-13: 978-0-13-602965-6
ISBN-10:   0-13-602965-5

Brief Contents

Contents

Chapter Opening and Closing Cases

Maps

Designed to help improve students' geographic literacy, the book's many maps add interest and illustrate facts and topics discussed in the text. Many case maps zero in on the case company's home country to give students a close-up look at foreign locales. A complete atlas with index is available following Chapter 1.

Special Features

Point Counterpoint

LOOKING TO THE FUTURE

Does Geography Matter?

Preface

This textbook is one of the best-selling international business textbooks in both the United States and the rest of the world. Widely used in both undergraduate and MBA level courses, this text has had authorized translations into Spanish, Thai, and Russian, and unauthorized ones into some other languages such as Farsi. This textbook set the global standard for studying the environments and operations of international business. The elements of success that have driven this performance anchor our efforts to make this edition the best version yet. We believe these efforts result in a textbook that provides you and your students the best possible understanding of what is happening and is likely to happen in the world of business.

AUTHORITATIVE, RELEVANT, CURRENT

Students, faculty, and managers praise this book for its compelling balance between rigorous, authoritative theory and meaningful practice within the context of a fresh, current analysis of the international business environment. Indeed, this book not only describes the ideas of international business but also uses contemporary examples, scenarios, and cases to make sense of what managers do and should do. We include multiple insights and real-world examples, which we base on our research, discussions with managers and other stakeholders, opinions of students and professors, and observations from traveling the world. We believe no other textbook comes close to successfully blending a comprehensive review of international business theory with exhaustive attention to what happens in the many parts of the global market. We're confident that this new edition, by making international business ideas and practices more meaningful than ever before, will give students a comprehensive, current view of international business in the twenty-first century.

RELEVANT MATERIALS THAT ENGAGE STUDENTS

Author-Written Cases

An enduring strength of this text is its in-depth case profiles of cutting-edge issues in international business. This edition introduces new cases and updates and revises the remaining. (Please see pages xxi–xxiv for a complete list of cases.) All cases are unique and are personally written by the text's authors. As such, we believe they set the standard for integration of theory and practice in an international business textbook on the following three levels:

1. *Level of Analysis*: Cases engage an extensive range of topics from environmental, institutional, country, industry, company, and individual perspectives. No one perspective dominates; all are represented and, hence, create a meaningful representation of the world of international business.

2. *Scope of Geographic Coverage*: Cases cover topics in settings that span the globe; no region is left unaddressed, no major market is neglected.

3. *Scope of Company Coverage*: Cases look at various issues from a range of company perspectives, notably companies headquartered in all regions of the world, from large MNEs to small exporters, from old-line manufacturers to emergent cyber businesses, from companies that make products to those that deliver services.

Opening Business Case   Each chapter starts with a provocative case written to set the stage for the major issues covered in the chapter. Designed to grab the student's attention, these cases look at fascinating issues in a way that makes students want to understand the ideas and concepts of international business. These cases, by variously taking the point of view of individuals, companies, and institutions, give a great sense of the richness of the ensuing chapter. Material from the opening cases is then integrated with chapter discussions that we highlight in the text.

Closing Business Case   Each chapter closes with a rich, elaborate case that integrates the ideas and tools presented in the chapter. The closing cases aim to put the student into a situation that asks, given certain circumstances, what should be done. Called on to analyze issues and decisions for which the chapter prepares them, students can then grapple with many of the opportunities and challenges of international business.

NEW CASES IN THIS EDITION

We have updated *all* the cases from previous editions so that students will find them current. In addition, we have included several entirely new cases:

- Economic Conundrums and the Comeback of Emerging Economies
- Ecomagination and the Global Greening of GE
- The Fizz Biz: Coca-Cola
- Tommy Hilfiger: Clothes Make the Man and Vice Versa
- Ventus and Business Process Outsourcing
- Ericsson: The Challenges of Listing on Global Capital Markets and the Move to Adopt International Financial Reporting Standards
- GPS: In the Market for an Effective Hedging Strategy?
- Infosys: The Search for the Best and the Brightest

Looking to the Future

Each chapter offers future scenarios that are important to managers, companies, or the world. The topic of each *Looking to the Future* feature alludes to ideas discussed in the chapter in a way that prompts students to engage their imagination about the world in which they live.

LOOKING TO THE FUTURE

Which Countries Will Have the Jobs of the Future?

As capital, technology, and information grow more mobile among countries and companies, human resource development increasingly explains competitive differences. Consequently, companies' access to and retention of more qualified personnel grow more important as they face the challenge of recruiting and retaining highly skilled, highly valued workers.

Demographers are nearly unanimous in projecting that populations will grow much faster in emerging economies (China being the notable exception) than in

An increasing number of U.S. success stories from Taiwan, China, Korea, and India are returning to their native homes to start companies. Nonetheless, times of economic downturns will likely see unemployed workers in the wealthier countries blame foreign workers for their plight. Under this scenario, companies will have to spend more time getting work permits and integrating different nationalities into their workforces.

Another potential adjustment in wealthier countries is the continued push toward adopting robotics and other laborsaving equipment.[94] Although this may help solve some of the shortages in workers, it will inevitably

Point–Counterpoint

To reinforce our strong applications orientation, we have included a boxed theme in every chapter that brings to life a major debate in contemporary international business and globalization. We use a point–counterpoint style to highlight the diversity of perspectives that managers and policy makers use to make sense of vital issues. The give-and-take between two sides reinforces this textbook's effort to link theory and practice in ways that will undoubtedly energize class discussion.

Point | Counterpoint

Should Companies Forgo Investment in Violent Areas?

Point **Yes** As an executive of an MNE, I say they should. Companies have coincidently spread their operations internationally while violence has erupted against them. We're no longer concerned simply about being caught in the crossfire between opposing military groups. Antiglobalization groups want to harm our personnel and facilities. Groups see us as easy marks for extortion by threatening harm or kidnapping our personnel. Still others are against foreigners, regardless of the aims of the foreigners. For instance, such a group in Afghanistan killed five staff members from Médecins Sans Frontières, who were there to treat sick and injured people.

Counterpoint **No** Where there's risk, there are usually rewards. Companies should not shun areas with violence. Companies have always taken risks and employees have always gone to risky areas. As far back as the seventeenth century, migrants to what are now the United States, India, and Australia encountered disease and hostile native populations. Had companies and immigrants not taken chances, the world would be far less developed today.

You can't look at the risk from violence in isolation from other risks. Although we don't have historical data, risks are

Geography and International Business

In appropriate chapters, we have added "Does Geography Matter?" sections. Some of the geographic variables we include to help explain the chapters' content are country location, location of population and population segments within countries, natural resources and barriers, climate, natural disasters, and country size.

 **Does Geography Matter?**

Variety Is the Spice of Life

As you study this chapter, you'll see that geography plays a role in many of the theories and questions concerning trade. We pull them together in this discussion.

Part of a country's trading advantage is explained by its natural advantage—climate, terrain, arable land, and natural resources. Thus Saudi Arabia trades oil, a natural resource, for U.S. rice, which needs huge wet areas for production. Remember, however, that technology may often negate natural advantage, such as the development of substitutes (synthetic nitrate for natural nitrate) and development of different methods

incomes tend to depend little on trade because they produce and consume so little. Distance from foreign markets also plays a role. For instance, geographically isolated countries, such as Fiji, trade less than would be expected from their sizes because transportation costs increase the price of traded goods substantially.[25]

Conversely, Canada is a large high-income country, whose dependence on trade and trade per capita are not only among the world's highest but also much higher than we would expect from the theory of country size. This may be explained largely by Canada's population dispersion. Ninety percent of its population is within 100 miles of the U.S. border; thus shipping

New Topics and Chapter Changes

Although it is a tired cliché, every instructor of international business knows the world is changing in many and often unpredictable ways. We wake up to the same challenges you do, trying to make sense of what we read, hear, and see in the global press. Our effort to make sense of this leads to an unconditional effort to thoroughly update the text to reflect the latest knowledge and practice of international business. Most notably, this edition includes the following changes:

- **PART ONE: BACKGROUND FOR INTERNATIONAL BUSINESS**
- Differences between past and present globalization (Chapter 1)
- Country differences in degree of globalization (Chapter 1)
- Debate on the effects of globalization and offshoring (Chapter 1)
- Nobel economists' views on future challenges (Chapter 1)
- **PART TWO: COMPARATIVE ENVIRONMENTAL FRAMEWORKS**
- Integration of work from the World Values Survey (Chapter 2)
- Growth of groups that don't share their national cultures (Chapter 2)
- Emergence of a new class of managers with global cultures (Chapter 2)
- Expanded discussion of types of democracies (Chapter 3)
- Profile of third wave of democratization (Chapter 3)
- Coverage of the rule of law versus the rule of man (Chapter 3)
- Discussion of "freedom stagnation" (Chapter 3)
- Connection of intellectual property rights and legal philosophies (Chapter 3)
- Expanded coverage of the emerging economies, especially the BRICs (Chapter 4)
- Profile of the rubric markets (Chapter 4)
- Consideration of green measures of economic progress (Chapter 4)
- Tighter linkage of labor costs and productivity (Chapter 4)
- Expanded coverage of economic freedom (Chapter 4)
- Major ethical and social issues like global warming and child labor (Chapter 5)
- **PART THREE: THEORIES AND INSTITUTIONS: TRADE AND INVESTMENT**
- Relationship between interventionist and free trade theories (Chapter 6)
- Relationship between trade and factor mobility, especially issues concerning immigration (Chapter 6)
- Pros and cons of strategic trade policy (Chapter 6)
- Recent trade wars and retaliation (Chapter 7)
- Pros and cons of trade sanctions (Chapter 7)
- Strategy of Japanese car makers in Europe (Chapter 8)
- The struggles of the European Union to absorb into the EU more countries from Central and Eastern Europe (Chapter 8)
- The challenges facing countries from emerging markets to engage in regional integration when their most important markets lie in North America and Europe
- **PART FOUR: WORLD FINANCIAL ENVIRONMENT**
- Focusing more exclusively on foreign-exchange markets while moving capital markets to Chapter 19 in the broader discussion of the finance function and how managers must take advantage of capital markets around the world to expand their financial resource base (Chapter 9)

- Emerging factors influencing the value of a currency, especially with the rise in importance of the euro and the challenge of what to do with the Chinese yuan as the Chinese economy continues to grow (Chapter 10)
- Impact of domestic and international factors on exchange rate values (Chapter 10)
- **PART FIVE: GLOBAL STRATEGY, STRUCTURE, AND IMPLEMENTATION**
- Improved coverage of industry, strategy, and firm performance (Chapter 11)
- Coverage of emerging strategy types (Chapter 11)
- Discussion of intrinsic limits of strategy formulation (Chapter 11)
- National disasters and health problems as locational risk problems (Chapter 12)
- Qualitative factors that impact location decisions (Chapter 12)
- Effect of location on innovation (Chapter 12)
- Revamped export planning framework (Chapter 13)
- Updated profile of technology of trade (Chapter 13)
- Discussion of national security concerns on international trade (Chapter 13)
- Expanded coverage of Import Brokers (Chapter 13)
- Sharper focus on ideas of countertrade (Chapter 13)
- Debate on foreign control of key industries (Chapter 14)
- Greenfield versus acquisitions decisions (Chapter 14)
- How to make collaborative arrangements succeed (Chapter 14)
- Workplace trends and organization performance (Chapter 15)
- Contemporary organizational forms (Chapter 15)
- **PART SIX: MANAGING INTERNATIONAL OPERATIONS**
- Marketing regulation to third world countries (Chapter 16)
- Targeting international market niches rather than mass markets (Chapter 16)
- Marketing to low-income consumers (Chapter 16)
- Pros and cons of outsourcing innovation, as well as the importance of business process outsourcing to emerging economies (Chapter 17)
- The focus on new technologies to help track shipments of goods worldwide (Chapter 17)
- The importance of quality and lean manufacturing as strategies to attract more customers (Chapter 17)
- Adoption of International Financial Reporting Standards by the EU and other countries (Chapter 18)
- Global convergence of accounting standards between the IASB and national standards setters around the world, including the U.S. FASB (Chapter 18)
- Accounting performance evaluation practices by MNEs (Chapter 18)
- The impact of transfer pricing on performance evaluation (Chapter 18)
- The rise in global capital markets as an important source of debt and equity capital for MNEs (Chapter 19)
- The importance of hedging against financial risk to protect company assets (Chapter 19)
- Career standards and expatriate performance (Chapter 20)
- Role of English in international business (Chapter 20)
- Emerging expatriate selection criteria (Chapter 20)
- Trends in expatriate compensation (Chapter 20)

ENGAGING IN-TEXT LEARNING AIDS

We believe a powerful textbook must teach as well as present ideas. To that end, we use several in-text aids to make this book an effective learning tool. Most notably, each chapter uses all of the following features:

Chapter Objectives and Summary

Each chapter begins with learning objectives and ends with a summary that ties directly to the chapter material. This linkage helps students prepare for the major issues within each chapter, appreciate their general relationships, and reinforce the important lessons of the chapter material.

Concept Links

Throughout each chapter, as warranted by discussion in the corresponding text, we highlight how ideas from previous chapters link to the ideas being discussed. This cumulative series of concept links helps the student build an understanding of the connections among concepts across chapters.

Case Links

Another effort to help students better appreciate the connections among ideas and practices is our latest innovation. Specifically, as warranted by discussion in the corresponding text, we highlight with text shading and icons how those ideas being discussed elaborate ideas that were presented in the opening and closing cases of that chapter.

Key Terms and Points: Bolding, Marginal Notes, and Glossary

Every chapter highlights key terms; each key term is put in bold print when it first appears. Key learning points are also highlighted in the adjoining margin. These terms and others are then assembled in an end-of-chapter list and into a comprehensive glossary at the end of the book.

Case Questions

The closing case of each chapter stipulates several questions to guide how students apply what they have learned in the chapter to the reality of international business. We have found in our classes that the questions at the end of the case go a long way to putting the case into perspective for students. In addition, they make for great assignment activities, directing students to respond to questions with information presented in the specific case as well as the chapter.

Point–Counterpoint

This feature as we have already discussed, is compelling not only for class discussion, but also for specific assignments. These assignments may include requiring students to take sides in debates or to apply arguments to specific countries.

CURRENCY AND READABILITY

We have always prided ourselves on being current in the research and examples we cite in the chapters. The 12th edition is no exception; in fact, we believe our coverage goes beyond that of any other IB text. If you examine the endnotes for any chapter, you will see that we include both classic and the most up-to-date materials from both scholarly treatises and the popular press. If you examine the list of companies in the "Company Index and Trademarks," you will see that our citations are numerous and include large and small firms from a variety of industries based in countries throughout the world. These citations illustrate to students the practical reality of the theories and alternative operations we describe.

We have made a special effort in this edition to improve the readability of the extensive materials we present. First, we make a point of putting authors' names (except for classics such as Adam Smith) only in the reference section rather than in the chapters' prose. We have simply seen too many students try to remember names rather than concepts. Second, we have engaged both a developmental editor and copy editor to improve the language and flow of materials.

COMPANION WEBSITE

This text's Companion Website at **www.prenhall.com/daniels** contains valuable resources for both students and professors, including an interactive student study guide.

COURSESMART TEXTBOOKS ONLINE

CourseSmart Textbooks Online is an exciting new choice for students looking to save money. As an alternative to purchasing the print textbook, students can subscribe to the same content online and save up to 50 percent off the suggested list price of the print text. With a CourseSmart eTextbook, students can search the text, make notes online, print out reading assignments that incorporate lecture notes, and bookmark important passages for later review. For more information, or to subscribe to the CourseSmart eTextbook, visit **www.coursesmart.com.**

ACKNOWLEDGMENTS

Every author relies on the comments, critiques, and insights of reviewers. It is a tough task that few choose to support. Therefore, we want to thank the following people for their insightful and helpful comments on the eleventh edition of *International Business: Environments and Operations*, which helped guide us in preparing the twelfth edition.

RON ABERNATHY, University of North Carolina, Greensboro
YUSAF AKBAR, Southern New Hampshire University
BRENT ALLRED, William & Mary
DAVID ASTLES, Sierra Nevada College
DR. JUAN BARRERA, Elmhurst College
DON BEEMAN, The University of Toledo
BRIGITTE BOJKOWSZKY, University of Missouri, St. Louis
MICHAEL BARAN, South Puget Sound Community College
MARTIN BRESSLER, Houston Baptist University
BILL BRUNSEN, Eastern New Mexico University
MARK A. BUCHANAN, Boise State University
SANDRA CHRISTENSEN, Eastern Washington University
TREVA CLARK, York College of Pennsylvania

PHILLIP COHEN, San Jacinto College North Campus
ANGELICA CORTES, University of Texas Pan American
TIM CURRAN, University of South Florida, St. Petersburg
MADELINE DAMKAR, California State University, East Bay campus
ANNE DAVIS, University of St. Thomas
SHASHI DEWAN, Winona State University
DR. LAURA PORTOLESE DIAS, Shoreline Community College
MICHAEL FATHI, Georgia Southwestern State University
ADALBERTO FISCHMANN, Missouri Southern State University
JAN FLYNN, Georgia College & State University
MIKE GERINGER, California Polytechnic State University
DEBBIE GILLIARD, Metropolitan State College of Denver
LENORE GOLDBERG, Centenary College
J. TOMAS GOMEZ-ARIAS, Saint Mary's College of California
JORGE GONZALEZ, University of Wisconsin, Milwaukee
CHARLES M. GOODWIN, The State University of New York, Geneseo
KENNETH GRAY, Florida A&M University
DAVID GROSSMAN, Florida Southern College
JIAN (JAMES) GU, Salem State College
JAMES GUNN, Sage College of Albany
ALFRED J. HAGAN, Pepperdine University
DAVID HARRISON, University of South Carolina, Aiken
DONAL HEFFERNAN, Metropolitan State University
CHRISTINA HEISS, University of Missouri, Kansas City
FRED HOYT, Illinois Wesleyan University
PAUL HUDEC, Milwaukee School of Engineering
SAMIRA HUSSEIN, Johnson County Community College
BOYD JOHNSON, Indiana Wesleyan University
MERRILY KAUTT, University of Colorado at Denver
RAIHAN KHAN, The State University of New York, Oswego
KI HEE KIM, William Patterson University
CHRISTOPHER KORTH, Western Michigan University
SAL KUKALIS, California State University, Long Branch
BRUCE KUSCH, Brigham Young University, Idaho
ANN LANGLOIS, Palm Beach Atlantic University
JOSEPH LEONARD, Miami Unviersity
DEBORAH LITVIN, Merrimack College
RONALD LOCKLIN, Boston University
VIONCE LUCHSINGER, University of Baltimore
DENISE LUETHGE, University of Michigan, Flint
WLLIAM MACHANIC, University of New Hampshire
BARBARA MACLEOD, Ohio Wesleyan University
RAJIV MALKAN, Montgomery College
ERIC MARTIN, Eastern Connecticut State University
DAVID MCARTHUR, Utah Valley State College
MARLEEN MCCORMICK, University of Colorado at Denver and Health Sciences
    Center
JOHN ROBERT MCINTYRE, Georgia Institute of Technology
BOB MCNEAL, Alabama State University

MOHAN MENON, University of South Alabama
SAEED MORTAZAVI, Humboldt State University
VI NARAPAREDDY, University of Denver
LUCIARA NARDON, Vlerick Leuven Gent Management School
DENNIS NOAH, Towson University
JOSEPHINE OLSON, University of Pittsburgh
NORA PALUGOD, Richard Stockton College of New Jersey
JAMIE PAURUS, Valley City State University
JERRY PINOTTI, MacCormac College
MICHAEL J. PISANI, Central Michigan University
DANIEL POWROZNIK, Chesapeake College
CLINT RELYEA, Arkansas State University
CHRISTOPHER ROBERTSON, Northeastern University
JUAN ROBERTSON, Central Washington University Center
ROBERT ROBERTSON, Saint Leo University
AL ROSENBLOOM, Saint Xavier University
VARTAN SAFARIAN, Winona State University
ROBERT SANFORD, Salem State College
JESSE SAUCEDO, Syracuse University
LARRY SCHRAMM, Oakland University
EUGENE SEELEY, Utah Valley State College
NASIR SHEIKH, Portland State University
MARK SIPPER, La Roche College
ROBERT SPOHR, Montcalm Community College
DAVID STEPHEN, University of Colorado, Denver
JOHN STOVALL, Georgia Southwestern State University
DANTE SUAREZ, Trinity University
PEGGY TAKAHASHI, University of San Francisco
S. PETER TAN, Parkland College
KYLE USREY, Whitworth University
RAY VALADEZ, Pepperdine University
LOUIS WATANABE, Bellevue Community College
GARY WATERS, Hawaii Pacific University
CAROL WELLS, California National University
LARRY WILCH, Bob Jones University
WILLIAM WISE, Metropolitan State College of Denver
MARK WOODHULL, Schreiner University
ALAN WRIGHT, Henderson State University
WENDY WYSOCKI, Monroe County Community College
ANATOLY ZHUPLEV, Loyola Marymount University

In addition, we have been fortunate since the first edition to have colleagues who have been willing to make the effort to critique draft materials, react to coverage already in print, advise on suggested changes, and send items to be corrected. Because this is the culmination of several previous editions, we would like to acknowledge everyone's efforts. However, many more individuals than we can possibly list have helped us. To those who must remain anonymous, we offer our sincere thanks. In any event, special thanks go to the following faculty members who made detailed comments.

- ERVIN BLACK, Brigham Young University
- JEAN BODDEWYN, City University of New York
- MARY YOKO BRANNEN, San Jose State University
- ROBERT BUZZELL, George Mason University
- MICHAEL B. CONNOLLY, University of Miami
- STANLEY E. FAWCETT, Brigham Young University
- TOM FOSTER, Brigham Young University
- STANLEY FLAX, St. Thomas University
- ELDRIDGE T. FREEMAN, JR., Chicago State University
- RALPH GAEDEKE, California State University at Sacramento
- ROBERTO P. GARCIA, Indiana University
- ANDREW GROSS, Cleveland State University
- URNESH C. GULATI, East Carolina College
- MICHAEL J. HAND, United States Department of Commerce
- RALPH F. JAGODKA, Mt. San Antonio Community College
- R. BOYD JOHNSON, Indiana Wesleyan University
- TUNGA KIYAK, Michigan State University
- SEUNG H. KIM, Saint Louis University
- JEFFREY A. KRUG, Virginia Commonwealth University
- SUMIT K. KUNDU, Florida International University
- CHARLES MAHONE, Howard University
- BEHNAM NAKHAI, Millersville University
- MOONSONG DAVID OH, California State University at Los Angeles
- NAMGYOO K. PARK, Korean Advanced Institute of Science and Technology
- ANN PERRY, American University
- DOUGLAS K. PETERSON, Indiana State University
- LUCIE PFAFF, College of Mt. St. Vincent
- ASEEM PRAKASH, University of Washington
- FERNANDO ROBLES, George Washington University
- SAEED SAMIEE, University of Tulsa
- BILL SAWAYA, Brigham Young University
- KRISTIE SEAWRIGHT, Brigham Young University
- RICHARD A. STANFORD, Furman University
- ROBERT C. WOOD, San Jose State University
- CRAIG WOODRUFF, American Graduate School of International Management

We would also like to acknowledge people whom we interviewed in writing cases. These are Omar Aljindi (Java Lounge—Adjusting to Saudi Arabian Culture), Brenda Yester (Carnival Cruise Lines: Exploiting a Sea of Global Opportunity), and Ali R. Manbien (GPS: In the Market for an Effective Hedging Strategy?). Thank you to Joseph Ganitsky of the University of Miami, for his case suggestions. Additionally, others who helped with administrative and research matters are Melanie Hunter, Hongbin Hu, Melissa Okimoto, Julie Hales, Dirk Black, KC Johnston, and Exequiel Hernandez.

It takes a dedicated group of individuals to take a textbook from first draft to final manuscript. We would like to thank our partners at Pearson Prentice Hall for their tireless efforts in bringing the twelfth edition of this book to fruition. Our thanks go to Editorial Director, Sally Yagan; Acquisitions Editor, Jennifer M. Collins; Senior Managing Editor, Judy Leale; Associate Managing Editor, Suzanne DeWorken; Director of Development, Stephen Deitmer; Development Editor, Ron Librach; and Project Manager, Production, Ann Pulido.

About the Authors

From left to right: **Daniel Sullivan, Lee Radebaugh, John Daniels.**

Three respected and renowned scholars show your students how dynamic, how real, how interesting, and how important the study of international business can be.

John D. Daniels, the Samuel N. Friedland Chair of Executive Management at the University of Miami, received his Ph.D. at the University of Michigan. His dissertation won first place in the award competition of the Academy of International Business. Since then, he has been an active researcher. His articles have appeared in such leading journals as *Academy of Management Journal, Advances in International Marketing, California Management Review, Columbia Journal of World Business, International Marketing Review, International Trade Journal, Journal of Business Research, Journal of High Technology Management Research, Journal of International Business Studies, Management International Review, Multinational Business Review, Strategic Management Journal, Transnational Corporations,* and *Weltwirtschaftliches Archiv.* Professor Daniels recently co-edited with Jeffrey Krug three volumes, *Multinational Enterprise Theory,* and three volumes, *International Business and Globalization.* On its thirtieth anniversary, *Management International Review* referred to him as "one of the most prolific American IB scholars." He has also served as president of the Academy of International Business and dean of its Fellows. He also served as chairperson of the international division of the Academy of Management. Professor Daniels has worked and lived a year or longer in seven different countries, worked shorter stints in approximately thirty other countries on six continents, and has traveled in many more. His foreign work has been a combination of private sector, governmental, teaching, and research assignments. He was formerly a faculty member at the Pennsylvania State University, director of the Center for International Business Education and Research (CIBER) at Indiana University, and holder of the E. Claiborne Robins Distinguished Chair at the University of Richmond.

Lee H. Radebaugh is the KPMG Professor and Director of the Kay & Yvonne Whitmore Global Management Center at Brigham Young University. He received his M.B.A. and doctorate from Indiana University. He taught at Pennsylvania State University from 1972 to 1980. He also has been a visiting professor at Escuela de Administracion de Negocios para Graduados (ESAN), a graduate business school in Lima, Peru. In 1985, Professor Radebaugh was the James Cusator Wards visiting professor at Glasgow University, Scotland. His other books include *International Accounting and Multinational Enterprises* (John Wiley and Sons, 6th Edition) with S. J. Gray and Erv Black; *Introduction to Business: International Dimensions* (South-Western Publishing Company) with John D. Daniels; and seven books on Canada-U.S. trade and investment relations, with Earl Fry as co-editor. He has also published several other monographs and articles on international business and international accounting in journals such as the *Journal of Accounting Research, Journal of International Financial Management and Accounting, Journal of International Business Studies*, and the *International Journal of Accounting*. He is currently serving as editor of the *Journal of International Accounting Research* and area editor of the *Journal of International Business Studies*. His primary teaching interests are international business and international accounting. Professor Radebaugh is an active member of the American Accounting Association, the European Accounting Association, and the Academy of International Business, having served on several committees as the president of the International Section of the AAA and as the secretary treasurer of the AIB. He is a member of the Fellows of the Academy of International Business. He is also active with the local business community as past president of the World Trade Association of Utah and member of the District Export Council. In 2007, Professor Radebaugh received the Outstanding International Accounting Service Award of the International Accounting Section of the American Accounting Association, and in 1998, he was named International Person of the Year in the state of Utah and Outstanding International Educator of the International Section of the American Accounting Association. He is also Vice-President Communications of the International Association of Accounting Education and Research.

Daniel P. Sullivan, an Associate Professor of Management at the Alfred Lerner College of Business of the University of Delaware, received his Ph.D. from the University of South Carolina. He researches a range of topics, including globalization and business, international management, global strategy, competitive analysis, and corporate governance. His work on these topics has been published in leading scholarly journals, including the *Journal of International Business Studies, Management International Review, Law and Society Review,* and *Academy of Management Journal.* In addition, he serves on the editorial boards of the *Journal of International Business Studies* and *Management International Review.* Professor Sullivan has been honored for both his research and teaching, receiving grants and winning awards for both activities while at the University of Delaware and, his former affiliation, the Freeman School of Tulane University. He has been awarded numerous teaching honors at the undergraduate, M.B.A., and E.M.B.A. levels—most notably, he was voted Outstanding Teacher by the students of seven consecutive Executive M.B.A. classes at the University of Delaware and Tulane University. Professor Sullivan has taught, designed, and administered a range of graduate, undergraduate, and nondegree courses on topics spanning globalization and business, international business operations, international management, strategic perspectives, executive leadership, and corporate strategy. In the United States, he has delivered lectures and courses at several university sites and company facilities. In addition, he has led courses in several foreign countries, including China, Taiwan, Bulgaria, the Czech Republic, France, Switzerland, and the United Kingdom. Finally, he has worked with many managers and consulted with several multinational enterprises on issues of international business.

INTERNATIONAL BUSINESS
Environments and Operations

1
chapter one

Globalization and International Business

Objectives

- To define *globalization* and *international business* and show how they affect each other

- To understand why companies engage in international business and why international business growth has accelerated

- To discuss the major criticisms of globalization

- To become familiar with different ways in which a company can accomplish its global objectives

- To apply social science disciplines to understanding the differences between international and domestic business

The world is a chain, one link in another.

—Maltese proverb

CASE: The Global Playground

Even if you're an avid sports fan, you may not realize how avidly sports have entered the global arena.[1] Sports, according to one political historian, is now "the most globalized business in the world. The most lucrative," he admits, "is the drug trade, but for legitimate businesses, sports is probably number 1." Historically, players and teams in most sports competed only on their own home turf. There were, of course, some exceptions—notably the World Cup in soccer and the Grand Slams of tennis—but by and large, local fans used to be happy to cheer on local talent. Today, however, fans everywhere demand to see the best, and "best" has become a decidedly global standard.

How has sports managed to score so well with an international customer base? For one thing, satellite TV now brings live events from just about anywhere in the world to fans just about anywhere else in the world. With so many events transmitted to so many places, the key players in the sports-promotion business—team owners, league representatives, and sports associations—have broadened audience exposure, expanding fan bases and augmenting revenues, especially through advertising that cuts across national borders.

Likewise, because more and more fans tune into games expecting to see the best teams and players the world has to offer, the search for talent has become a worldwide phenomenon. Today, for example, you can find professional basketball scouts from the United States and Europe in remote areas of Nigeria looking for tall youngsters who can be trained to play a sport that's been imported from half a world away.

THE INTERNATIONAL JOB MARKET

Fortunately for foreign talent scouts, today's top-notch players are less constrained by allegiance to local fans, and they're willing to follow the money wherever it may take them. In the world of soccer—the world's most popular sport—the Fédération Internationale de Football Association (FIFA) boasts more member countries than the United Nations. Many of the best Brazilian players now play for European teams with much higher payrolls than their Brazilian counterparts, and in just about every sport, top players play for pay in foreign countries. British soccer star David Beckham, who's played for Spain's Real Madrid as well as for Manchester United and the British national team, is now competing in American Major League Soccer (MLS) as a member of the Los Angeles Galaxy.

Interestingly, fans continue to follow national favorites even after they've taken their talents elsewhere. About 300 million Chinese tuned in to watch the first game of local basketball legend Yao Ming when he took the court for the Houston Rockets of America's National Basketball Association (NBA). Many athletes, of course, maintain native ties by joining national teams for such international competitions as the Olympics and soccer's World Cup.

How the ATP Courts Worldwide Support

If you're a fan of individual (as opposed to team) sports, you've probably noticed that your favorite players are veteran globe hoppers. Take tennis, for example. Although tennis has grown in popularity in many countries, no single country boasts enough interested fans to keep players at home for year-round competition. In any case, there aren't very many top-ranked players who call any given country home; today's top-flight tennis pros come from every continent except Antarctica, and tennis fans everywhere want to see the top players compete on local courts.

Thus the Association of Tennis Professionals (ATP) not only sanctions 68 tournaments in 30 countries, but it also requires member pros to play in a certain number of events—and thus stop over in a number of countries—to maintain international rankings. Map 1.1, for example, traces the 2007 itinerary of Swiss tennis ace Roger Federer, who's competed everywhere from Cincinnati to Dubai.

By the same token, because no tennis pro can possibly play in every tournament, organizers must attract enough top draws to fill stadium seats and land lucrative TV contracts. Tournaments, therefore, compete for top-billed stars, not only with other tournaments but also with such regular international showcases as the Olympics and Davis Cup. How do tournaments compete? Your first guess is probably right: on the basis of money. Prizes for two weeks' worth of expert serving and volleying can be extremely generous (more than $7 million for the singles championships of the Australian Open).

Remember, too, that tournaments earn money through ticket sales, corporate sponsorship agreements, television contracts, and leasing of advertising space. The more people in the stadium attendance and the TV audience, the more sponsors and advertisers will pay to get their attention between tee shots and free throws. Moreover, international broadcast packages attract sponsorship from international companies. The sponsor list for the worldwide broadcast of the Australian Open tennis tournament includes a South

MAP 1.1
Roger Federer's 2007 Itinerary

In many sports, professional athletes spend a good part of the year traveling to the far reaches of the globe. All of the countries labeled here hosted tournaments sanctioned by the Association of Tennis Professionals (ATP) in 2007. The arrows trace the itinerary of Swiss pro Roger Federer over the course of the year.

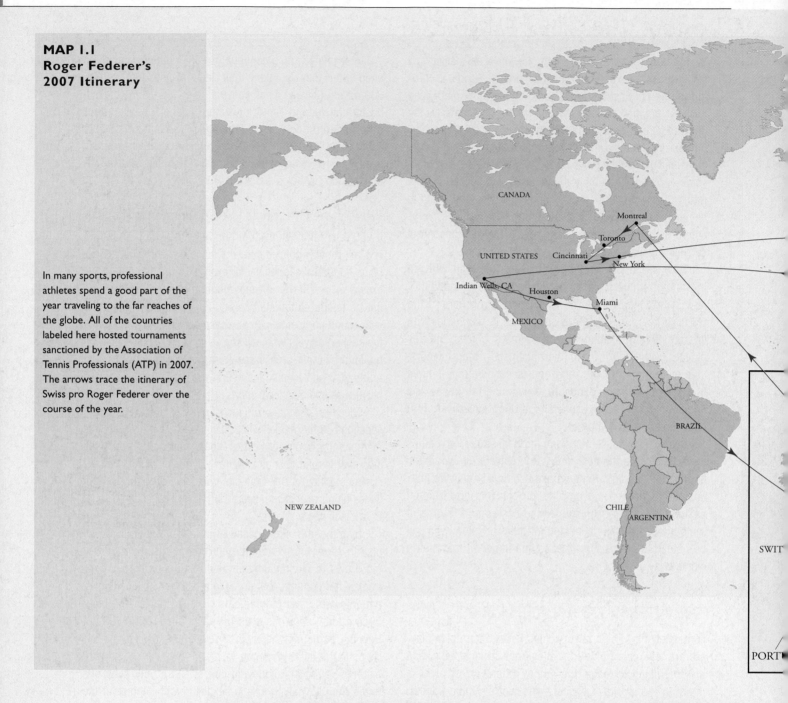

Korean automaker (Kia), a Dutch brewer (Heineken), a Swiss watchmaker (Rado), and a U.S. financial firm (American Express).

The International Pastime

Likewise, think about the emergence of baseball as an international pastime. The International Baseball Federation now has 112 member countries, but for most of its history, baseball was popular only among North Americans. As TV revenues flattened in these markets, Major League Baseball (MLB) began broadcasting games to international audiences. Increased exposure not only broadened the global fan base, but it also showed youngsters all over the world how the game was played. As late as 1986, about 86 percent of MLB players were U.S. born; by 2007, that number had dropped to 72 percent. The average MLB clubhouse is now a bastion of multilingual camaraderie, with players and coaches talking baseball in Spanish, Japanese, and Korean as well as English.

THE WIDE WORLD OF TELEVISED SPORTS

Not surprisingly, other professional sports groups have been quick to expand their global TV coverage (and marketing programs). Most viewers of Stanley Cup hockey watch from outside North America. Fans watch National Association for Stock Car Auto Racing (NASCAR) races in more than 120 countries and NBA games in about 200. If you lived in the North African nation of Tunisia and enjoyed simultaneous access to multiple TV channels, you could watch more hours of NBA action than there are hours in the year.

And TV isn't the only means by which sports organizations are building overseas fan bases and seeking to attract international player personnel. For several years, the National Football League (NFL) of the United States sponsored a now-defunct professional league in Europe. It continues to underwrite flag-football programs in Chinese schools and it will play some regular NFL games in Europe through 2011. With the growth of broadband, we'll soon enter the realm of thousand-channel TV, where we'll be able to tune into sporting events that currently appeal only to highly localized niche markets. Squash, anyone? How about Thai boxing?

The Top-Notch Pro as Upscale Brand

In a related development, many top players (and teams) have effectively become global brands. Golfer Tiger Woods and tennis star Maria Sharapova are so well known and widely followed by fans around the world that companies in the sports industry are willing to pay them millions for endorsing clothes and equipment. In fact, the most bankable sports stars are sought-after commodities among nonsports companies as well. You've probably seen tennis-star sisters Venus and Serena Williams plugging Avon cosmetics and bicyclist Lance Armstrong pitching Subarus. Many well-known sports stars augment their incomes by contracting the sale of photos and signing their names to memorabilia.

Promotion as Teamwork

A few teams, such as the New York Yankees in baseball and the New Zealand All Blacks in rugby, also have enough brand-name cachet to sell clothing and other items to fans around the world. Just about every team can get something for the rights to use its logo, and some teams have enough name recognition to support global chains of retail outlets.

What's the world's most valuable sports franchise? It's the British soccer team Manchester United (known to fans worldwide as "Man U"), whose Red Café sports-themed restaurants thrive in such faraway markets as Singapore. Similarly, companies both sponsor and seek endorsements from well-known teams. Nike, for instance, the U.S. maker of sports shoes and apparel, has fought hard to become the top sportswear and equipment supplier to European soccer teams, and the success of this campaign has had such a big influence on Nike's international sales efforts that it now takes in more money abroad than in the United States.

Many nonsports companies, such as Canon (cameras, office equipment), Sharp (consumer electronics), and Carlsberg (beer), sponsor teams mainly to get corporate logos emblazoned on uniforms. Still others, such as United Airlines in Chicago, pay for the naming rights to arenas and other venues. And, of course, teams themselves can be attractive investments. The CEO of Nintendo (Japan), for example, bought the Seattle Mariners baseball team (U.S.A.). In 2007, the owner of the Texas Rangers baseball team (U.S.A.) and the owner of the Montreal Canadiens hockey team joined forces to buy the Liverpool Football Club of the United Kingdom.

When did you first become a sports fan? Chances are—especially if you're a male—at one time you fantasized about going pro in some sport. You've probably given up that fantasy (perhaps to study international business) and settled into the role of avid fan. Now that pro sports has become a global phenomenon (and thanks to the advent of the Internet), you can enjoy a greater variety—and a higher level of competition—than any generation before you.

That's the upside, but we must point out that not everyone is happy with the unbridled globalization of sports—or at least with some of the effects. Brazilian soccer fans lament the loss of their best players, and U.S. fans and public officials protested the sale of the MLB Seattle Mariners to a foreigner.

Introduction

In its broadest sense, **globalization** refers to the broadening set of interdependent relationships among people from different parts of a world that happens to be divided into nations. The term sometimes refers to the integration of world economies through the reduction of barriers to the movement of trade, capital, technology, and people.[2]

Throughout recorded history, human contacts over ever wider geographic areas have expanded the variety of resources, products, services, and markets available to consumers. We've altered the way we want and expect to live, and we've become more deeply affected (positively and negatively) by conditions outside of our immediate domains.

Our opening case shows how far-flung global contact allows the world's best sports talent to compete, regardless of nationality, and fans to watch them, from almost anywhere. The changes that have led firms to consider ever more distant places as sources of supplies and markets affect almost every industry and, in turn, consumers. Although we may not always know it, we commonly buy products from all over the world. "Made in" labels may obscure product origins, and today so many different components or ingredients go into products that we're often challenged to say exactly where they were made.

Consider the findings of a Los Angeles restaurant that calculated the distance traveled by the ingredients in just one main course. The answer? The equivalent of more than two and a half trips around the world.[3] Here's another interesting example. Although we tend to think of the Kia Sorento as a Korean car, the Japanese firm Matsushita furnishes one of the car's features, the CD player. It makes the optical-pickup units in China, sends them to Thailand for mechanical structure and additional electronic components, transports the semifinished product to Mexico for final assembly, and trucks completed CD players to a U.S. port. Finally, they're shipped to Kia's South Korean factory, where they're installed in the vehicles that Kia markets around the world.[4]

WHAT IS *INTERNATIONAL BUSINESS*?

Globalization enables us to get more variety, better quality, or lower prices. Our daily meals, for instance, contain spices that aren't grown domestically and fresh produce that's out of season in one local climate or another. Our cars, like a Kia Sorento equipped with a CD player, cost less than if all the parts were made and the labor performed in one place. Remember, too, that all of these connections between supplies and markets result from the activities of **international business,** which consists of all commercial transactions—including sales, investments, and transportation—that take place between two or more countries. Private companies undertake such transactions for profit; governments may undertake them either for profit or for political reasons.

International business consists of all commercial transactions between two or more countries.

- The goal of private business is to make profits.
- Government business may or may not be motivated by profit.

The Study of International Business   Why should we study international business? A simple answer is that international business comprises a large and growing portion of the world's total business. Today, global events and competition affect almost all companies—large and small—because most sell output to and secure supplies from foreign countries. Many companies also compete against products and services that come from abroad. Thus most managers, regardless of industry or company size, need to approach their operating strategies from an international standpoint. Recall the NBA teams in our opening case. At first glance, you probably find it odd to think of basketball players as "inputs"; if so, remember that inputs are resources. NBA teams are looking globally for personnel resources—on-court talent—and they're also expanding their markets well beyond the confines of their home markets. As a manager in almost any industry, you'll need to consider both where to obtain the inputs you need of the quality you need and at the best possible price and where you can best sell the product or service that you've put together from them.

Understanding the Environment/Operations Relationship   At the same time, you'll need to understand that the best way of doing business abroad may not be the same as the best way at home. Why? Basically for two reasons. First, when your company operates internationally, it will engage in *modes* of business, such as exporting and importing, that differ from those in which it engages domestically. Obviously, you'll need to understand these different modes, which we discuss shortly. Second, the physical, social, and competitive conditions that affect the ways in which a country conducts business differ from country to country. Thus companies operating internationally have more diverse and complex operating environments than those that conduct business

FIGURE 1.1   Factors in International Business Operations

The conduct of a company's international operations depends on two factors: its objectives and the means by which it intends to achieve them. Likewise, its operations affect, and are affected by, two sets of factors: physical/social and competitive.

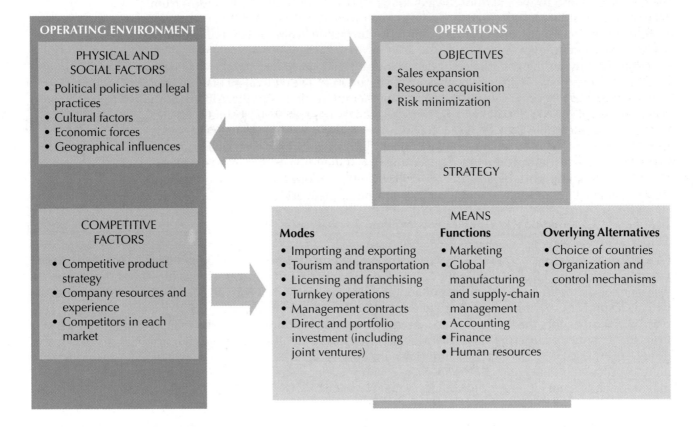

<table>
<tr><td colspan="2">OPERATING ENVIRONMENT</td><td colspan="3">OPERATIONS</td></tr>
</table>

OPERATING ENVIRONMENT

PHYSICAL AND SOCIAL FACTORS

- Political policies and legal practices
- Cultural factors
- Economic forces
- Geographical influences

COMPETITIVE FACTORS

- Competitive product strategy
- Company resources and experience
- Competitors in each market

OPERATIONS

OBJECTIVES

- Sales expansion
- Resource acquisition
- Risk minimization

STRATEGY

MEANS

Modes	Functions	Overlying Alternatives
• Importing and exporting	• Marketing	• Choice of countries
• Tourism and transportation	• Global manufacturing and supply-chain management	• Organization and control mechanisms
• Licensing and franchising		
• Turnkey operations		
• Management contracts	• Accounting	
• Direct and portfolio investment (including joint ventures)	• Finance	
	• Human resources	

Studying international business is important because

- Most companies either are international or compete with international companies.
- Modes of operations may differ from those used domestically.
- The best way of conducting business may differ by country.
- An understanding helps you make better career decisions.
- An understanding helps you decide what governmental policies to support.

only at home. Figure 1.1 outlines the complex set of relationships among conditions and operations that may occur when a firm decides to conduct some of its business on an international scale.

Even if you never have direct international business responsibilities, understanding some international business complexities may be useful to you. Both the nature of a company's international operations and the nature of governmental regulation of those operations affect profits, employment security and wages, consumer prices, and national security. A better understanding of international business will help you to make more informed operational and citizenry decisions, such as where you want to operate and what governmental policies you want to support.

The Forces Driving Globalization

Measuring globalization, especially for historical comparisons, is problematic. First, the degree of two countries' interdependence must be measured indirectly.[5] Second, when national boundaries shift (consider the breakup of the former Soviet Union or the reunification of East and West Germany), domestic business transactions can become international transactions or vice versa.

Nevertheless, various reliable indicators assure us that globalization has been increasing. Currently, about 25 percent of world production is sold outside its country of origin, as opposed to about 7 percent in 1950. Restrictions on imports have been decreasing, and foreign ownership of assets as a percentage of world production has been increasing. In almost every year since World War II, world trade has grown more rapidly than world production.

At the same time, however, globalization is less pervasive than you might suppose. Much of the world, for example (especially in rural Africa, Asia, and Latin America), lacks the resources to establish more than the barest connection with anyone beyond the outskirts of the isolated worlds.[6] Only a few countries—mainly very small ones—either sell over half their production abroad or depend on foreign output for over half their consumption. What this means is that most of the world's goods and services are still sold in the countries in which they're produced. Moreover, the principal source of capital in most countries is domestic rather than international.[7]

Granted, these measurements address only *economic* aspects of global interdependence. Various other studies have relied on different indicators for comparison.[8] One of the most comprehensive is the A.T. Kearney/Foreign Policy Globalization Index, which shows not only that some countries are more globalized than others but also that a given country may be highly globalized on one dimension and not on another. This index ranks 62 countries across four dimensions:

- *Economic*—international trade and investment
- *Technological*—Internet connectivity
- *Personal contact*—international travel and tourism, international telephone traffic, and personal transfers of funds internationally
- *Political*—participation in international organizations and government monetary transfers

In recent years, the index has ranked Singapore and Switzerland as the most globalized countries and India and Iran as the least globalized. The ranking of the United States shows how globalization can differ by dimension: The United States ranks first on the technological scale but only 58th on the economic.[9]

FACTORS IN INCREASED GLOBALIZATION

What factors have contributed to the increased growth in globalization in recent decades? Most analysts cite the following seven factors:

1. Increase in and expansion of technology
2. Liberalization of cross-border trade and resource movements
3. Development of services that support international business
4. Growing consumer pressures
5. Increased global competition
6. Changing political situations
7. Expanded cross-national cooperation

Needless to say, these factors are interrelated, and each deserves a closer look.

Increase in and Expansion of Technology　Many of the proverbial "modern marvels" that we take for granted have actually come about from fairly recent advances in technology. More than half the scientists who have ever lived are alive today. One reason, of course, is population growth, but another is economic growth: Today, a much larger portion of the total population is involved in *developing* new products rather than just *producing* them. Much of what we buy today didn't exist a decade or two ago, and the pace of new-product development is accelerating. Thus, as the base of our technology expands, we need more scientists and engineers to work on its potential applications.

Advances in Communications and Transportation   Strides in communications and transportation now permit us to learn about and want products and services developed in other parts of the world. Moreover, the costs of improved communications and transportation have risen more slowly than costs in general. A three-minute phone call from New York to London that cost $10.80 in 1970 costs less than $0.20 today.

Innovations in transportation mean that more countries can compete for sales to a given market. For example, the sale of foreign-grown flowers in the United States used to be impractical; today, however, flowers from as far away as Ecuador, Israel, the Netherlands, and New Zealand now compete in the U.S. market because growers can get them there, economically, the day after they've been picked. Imagine trying to export flowers (or any other perishable product) by a 13-mile-a-day caravan along the Silk Road between China and Europe—a method that, for centuries, accounted for an important share of world trade.

Or recall our opening case. Innovations in transportation and communications allow athletes and teams to go head to head at venues around the world and sports media to broadcast competitions to fans—and consumers—around the world. If it weren't for modern means of transportation, Roger Federer couldn't play in Monte Carlo right after finishing a tournament in Miami. If it weren't for modern means of advertising to fans around the globe, the prize money wouldn't be big enough to induce him to do all that traveling.

Not only do improved communications and transportation speed up interactions, but they also enhance a manager's ability to oversee foreign operations. Thanks to the Internet, even small companies can reach global customers and suppliers. Atlanta's Randy Allgaier, for example, sells lighting fixtures. Because he and his partner in Taiwan have contracted with a Chinese factory to manufacture fixtures for him, he's able to conduct his business without any costly onsite contact with people in either Taiwan or China.[10]

Liberalization of Cross-Border Trade and Resource Movements   To protect its own industries, every country restricts the movement across its borders not only of goods and services but also of the resources, such as workers and capital, needed to produce them. Such restrictions, of course, set limits on international business activities, and because regulations can change at any time, they also contribute to a climate of uncertainty. Over time, however, most governments have reduced restrictions on international movements of products and services. Why? Primarily for three reasons:

1. Their citizens want a greater variety of goods and services at lower prices.
2. Competition spurs domestic producers to become more efficient (see Figure 1.2).
3. They hope to induce other countries to lower their barriers in turn.

Development of Services That Support International Business   Companies and governments have developed a variety of services that facilitate the conduct of international business. Take the sale of goods and services in a foreign country and currency. Today, because of bank credit agreements, clearing arrangements that convert one currency into another, and insurance that covers such risks as damage en route and nonpayment, most producers can be paid relatively easily for goods and services sold abroad. What happens, for instance, when Nike sells sportswear to a French soccer team? As soon as the shipment arrives at French customs (probably from somewhere in Asia), a bank in Paris can collect payment in euros from the soccer team and pay Nike in U.S. dollars through a U.S. bank.

Such supporting services encompass much more than finance, and they're far too numerous for a comprehensive discussion. We will, however, mention one. Because of the Universal Postal Union, a specialized agency of the United Nations, you can send letters and packages any place in the world by paying postage only in the country from which you mail them and only in the local currency. It doesn't matter whether they pass

FIGURE 1.2 International Business as a Two-Edged Sword

Although global competition promotes efficiency, it obliges both companies and their employees to spend time and effort on a greater range of activities.

Source: © 1998 The New Yorker Collection, Roz Chast, from cartoonbank.com. All rights reserved.

through or over other countries. Or you can send them via any of the international package-service companies, such as UPS or DHL, simply by paying for transportation in your own currency.

Growing Consumer Pressures   Not only do consumers know more about products and services available in other countries, but also many more of them can afford to buy products that were once considered luxuries. Today, we want more, newer, better products, and we want them more finely differentiated. As usual, this greater affluence has been unevenly spread, both among and within countries, but more and more companies are now responding to those markets, such as China, in which incomes and consumption are growing most rapidly.

The availability of higher-income markets has also spurred companies to spend more heavily on research and development and to search worldwide—via the Internet, industry journals, trade fairs, and trips abroad—for innovations and products they can sell to ever-more-demanding consumers. By the same token, consumers are more proficient at scouring the globe for better deals; U.S. consumers, for instance, regularly search the Internet for lower-priced prescription drugs available from foreign sellers.

Increased Global Competition   The pressures, both present and potential, of increased foreign competition can persuade companies to buy or sell abroad. For example, they might introduce products into markets where competitors are already gaining sales or seek supplies where competitors are getting cheaper or more attractive products or the means to produce them.

In recent years, more companies have merged with or acquired foreign firms to gain operating efficiencies and larger global market shares. In addition, whereas a company such as Procter & Gamble took almost 100 years to go global, many companies today—so-called **born-global companies**—start out with a global focus (often because of founders' international experience).[11] Technological advances, especially in communications, give them a good idea of where global markets and supplies are and how they can realize competitive advantages by doing business in foreign countries.[12]

Regardless of industry, firms have to become more global to compete; in today's business environment, failure to do so can be catastrophic. Once a few companies have responded to foreign opportunities, others inevitably follow suit. *And* they learn from each other's foreign experiences. As our opening case suggests, for example, the early success of foreign-born baseball players in U.S. leagues undoubtedly spurred American basketball and football organizations to begin looking for and developing overseas talent. America's NBA, for instance, has begun to take advantage of the European system of developing basketball players, which allows them to join pro teams in their teens and train and practice against pros daily.[13]

Changing Political Situations   A major reason for growth in international business is the end of the schism between the non-Communist world and what was once the Communist world. For nearly half a century after World War II, business between the two camps was minimal. Moreover, even within the Communist bloc, countries strove to be as self-sufficient as possible. With the transformation of political and economic policies in the former Soviet Union, Eastern Europe, China, and Vietnam, trade now flourishes between those areas and the rest of the world.

Another political factor is the willingness of governments to support programs favorable to international trade. Merely by improving airport and seaport facilities, for example, governments have fostered travel efficiencies that speed the process and reduce the cost of delivering goods internationally. In addition, governments now provide an array of services to help domestic companies sell more abroad, such as collecting information about foreign markets, furnishing contacts with potential buyers abroad, and offering insurance against nonpayment in the home-country currency.

Expanded Cross-National Cooperation   Increasingly, governments have come to realize that their own interests can be addressed through international cooperation by means of treaties, agreements, and consultation. The willingness to pursue such policies is due largely to these three needs:

1. To gain reciprocal advantages
2. To attack problems jointly that one country acting alone cannot solve
3. To deal with areas of concern that lie outside the territory of any nation

Essentially, because companies don't want to be at a disadvantage when operating internationally, they aren't shy about petitioning home-country governments to act on their behalf. Thus governments join international organizations and sign treaties and agreements on a variety of commercial activities, such as transportation and trade. Treaties and agreements may be *bilateral* (involving only two countries) or *multilateral* (involving a few or many).

Countries commonly sign treaties that allow each other's commercial ships and planes to use certain seaports and airports in exchange for reciprocal port use. They enact treaties that cover commercial-aircraft safety standards and fly-over rights or treaties that protect property, such as foreign-owned investments, patents, trademarks, and copyrights. Countries also enact treaties for reciprocal reductions of import restrictions (remaining prepared, of course, to retaliate when another party interferes with trade flows by raising trade barriers or cutting diplomatic ties).

Multinational Problem Solving   Countries often act to coordinate activities along mutual borders, building highways and railroads or hydroelectric dams that serve the interests of all parties. They also cooperate to solve problems that they either cannot or will not solve by themselves—problems that usually reflect one or both of two problems:

1. The problem is too big or can best be solved by joint action.
2. The problem results from conditions that cross borders.

In the first case, the resources needed to solve the problem may be too great for one country to manage; likewise, sometimes no single country is willing to foot the bill for a project that will also benefit another country. Japan and the United States, for example, share the costs of ballistic-missile defense technology.[14] In any case, many problems are inherently global and can't easily be addressed by a single country. That's why we've seen the development of cooperative efforts to fight the spread of such diseases as malaria, to set warning systems against such natural disasters as tsunamis, and to take actions affecting environmental problems such as global warming.[15]

In the second case, one country's policies may affect those of others. High real-interest rates in one country, for example, can attract funds from countries with lower rates, thus creating a shortage of investment funds in the latter. In addition, because information can flow rapidly, particularly over the Internet, an event in one country can have almost instantaneous effects in another, such as companies' shifting of funds in response to slight interest rate changes.

Finally, many companies maintain knowledge networks that allow them to change suppliers in response to slight cost differences among suppliers' home countries, thus contributing to unemployment in the countries where they abandon suppliers.[16] To coordinate economic policies in these and other areas, eight economically important countries known as the *G8 countries*—Canada, France, Germany, Italy, Japan, Russia, the United Kingdom, and the United States—meet regularly to share information and pool ideas.[17]

Three areas of the globe belong to no single country—the noncoastal areas of the oceans, outer space, and Antarctica. Until their commercial viability was demonstrated, they excited little interest in either exploitation or multinational cooperation. The oceans, however, contain food and mineral resources, and they also constitute the surface over which much international commerce passes. Today, we need treaties to specify the amounts and methods of fishing to be allowed, to address questions of oceanic mineral rights, and to reach some consensus on dealing with pirates (yes, pirates are a problem in the twenty-first century).[18]

Likewise, there's disagreement on the commercial benefits to be reaped from outer space. Commercial satellites, for example, pass over countries that receive no direct benefit from them but argue they should. If that sounds a little far-fetched, remember that countries do charge foreign airlines for flying over their territory.[19]

Antarctica, with minerals and abundant sea life along its coast, attracts thousands of tourists each year and has thus been the subject of agreements to limit commercial exploitation. However, there is still disagreement about Antarctica's development— how much there should be and who does it. The photo on the next page shows one such controversial development.

(Much of the cooperation we've just described has been undertaken by such international organizations as the United Nations, the International Monetary Fund, the World Trade Organization, and the World Bank. We discuss these organizations in more detail in later chapters, especially in Chapter 8.)

The photo shows fuel tanks following construction on the road being built to Antarctica's South Pole. As an area lying outside the confines of any country, Antarctica, one of the last frontiers of globalization, elicited little interest from governments until its commercial viability became apparent. Now, there is much concern about the development. The number of visitors for 2007 was about 50,000.

What's Wrong with Globalization?

Critics of globalization claim

- Countries lose sovereignty.
- The resultant growth hurts the environment.
- Some people lose both relatively and absolutely.

Although we've discussed seven broad reasons for the increase in international business and globalization, we should remember that the consequences of these trends remain controversial. To thwart the globalization process, *antiglobalization* forces regularly protest international conferences (sometimes with attendant violence). There are many pertinent issues, but we focus on three broad categories: *threats to national sovereignty, growth and environmental stress,* and *growing income inequality.* We revisit each category in more depth in later chapters, and they furnish the issues for several of our "Point–Counterpoint" boxes.

THREATS TO NATIONAL SOVEREIGNTY

You've probably heard the slogan "Think globally, act locally." In essence, it means that the accommodation of local interests should prevail over global interests. Some observers worry that the proliferation of international agreements, particularly those that eliminate local restrictions on how goods are bought and sold, will diminish a nation's **sovereignty**—that is, a nation's freedom to "act locally" and without externally imposed restrictions.

The Question of Local Objectives and Policies   Let's look a little more closely at this argument. Countries seek to fulfill their own economic, political, and social objectives to maintain the well-being of their own citizens. To do this, they set rules that reflect a collective national priority, such as local rules governing worker protection and environmental practices. However, some critics argue that by opening borders to the movement of trade, the priorities of individual countries are undermined. For example, if regulations on labor conditions and clean production methods are stringent, companies may simply move production to where they can cut production costs because of less rigorous rules. The result may be that the strict country must forgo its priorities or face the downside of unemployment and tax loss because of the shift in production.

The Question of Local Overdependence   In addition, officials in small countries worry that overdependence on larger countries for supplies and sales will make them vulnerable to demands imposed by larger suppliers and sellers. What sort of demands?

Everything from supporting certain positions at the United Nations to supporting military or economic action against a developing country. They're also concerned that large international companies may become so powerful that they can either dictate the terms of their presence in weaker host countries (say, by threatening to relocate) or exploit legal loopholes to avoid political oversight and taxes. In some cases, a foreign government might force domestic companies to take actions abroad that are counter to a host country's best interests. Recently, for instance, Costa Rica blamed the closing of a Venezuelan-owned plant employing 400 people on political differences between the two countries.[20]

The Question of Cultural Homogeneity Finally, critics charge that globalization homogenizes products, companies, work methods, social structures, and even language. In Chapter 2, we'll see that, as international differences diminish, countries find it harder to maintain the traditional ways of life that unify and differentiate local cultures. Fundamentally, many critics feel helpless when it comes to stopping foreign incursion by such means as satellite television, newspapers, and Internet sites.[21] Globalization, they charge, undermines the cultural foundation of sovereignty.

ECONOMIC GROWTH AND ENVIRONMENTAL STRESS

Much antiglobalization criticism revolves around issues of economic growth. According to one argument, as globalization brings growth, it consumes more nonrenewable natural resources and increases environmental damage—despoliation through toxic and pesticide runoffs into rivers and oceans, air pollution from factory and vehicle emissions, and deforestation that can affect weather and climate.

The Argument for Global Growth and Global Cooperation Opponents of this position argue that globalization has positive results for both the sustenance of natural resources and the maintenance of an environmentally sound planet. Global cooperation, they say, fosters uniform standards for combating environmental problems. Consumer demand for foreign products and services encourages production in the cheapest locations, which usually involves use of fewer resources.

Finally, because more and more firms are producing for global markets, they're more reliant on resource-saving technologies, such as automobile engines that use less gas and emission systems that reduce pollution. However, unless the positive results of globalization outpace the negative consequences of growth, sustaining economic growth will remain a problem in the future.

The pursuit of global interests may even conflict with what a country's citizens think is best for themselves. Consider, for instance, the effect of global pressure on Brazil to curtail logging activity in the Amazon region. Brazil bowed to the pressure and arguments for the global good—but only temporarily. It resumed logging because of even stronger local pressure: Unemployed Brazilian workers demanded the restoration of jobs in the logging industry.

GROWING INCOME INEQUALITY

In measuring economic well-being, we must look not only at our absolute situations but also at how well we're doing compared to the economic well-being of others. We generally don't find our economic status satisfactory unless we're doing better *and* keeping up with others. When, for instance, a U.S. company shifts its computer programming to India, computer programmers in the United States may have to take lower-paying jobs.

The process of shifting production to a foreign country is called **offshoring,** and when it costs people (in this case, U.S. computer programmers) their higher-paying jobs, they lose in an absolute sense. In addition, the company offshoring achieves cost savings that may go in part to bonuses for the executives who thought up the cost savings.

This further increases the disparity of incomes within the company, causing those in lower-level jobs to lose more in relation to their bosses.

Finally, the shift in jobs speeds up the process by which India narrows its economic gap with the United States, thus causing the United States to lose relative to India.[22] In other words, even if overall worldwide gains from globalization are positive, there are bound to be some losers (who will probably become critics of globalization). The challenge, therefore, is to maximize the gains made possible by globalization while simultaneously minimizing the costs borne by the losers.

There are also certain repercussions of globalization fostering inequality that we can't measure in strictly economic terms. What about the stress imposed on the people who are losers in income-equality competition? There is in fact some evidence that the growth in globalization goes hand in hand not only with increased insecurity about job and social status but with increased terrorist activity as well.[23] Although few of the world's problems are brand new, it seems that we worry about them more because globalized communications can now bring exotic sagas of misery into living rooms everywhere.[24]

Moreover, one person's trivia is another person's trauma. Let's go back to our opening case, where we saw how globalization in the sports industry has enabled European teams to lure away Brazil's top soccer players with salary offers that local teams can't match. Brazilian soccer stars and European fans aren't complaining, but what about Brazilian fans, who gain nothing economically from the players' departure and who are deprived of the opportunity to watch home-grown talent in person?

Point Counterpoint

Is Offshoring Good Strategy?

Point **Yes** *If offshoring succeeds in reducing costs, it's good.* Take just one U.S. company: By shipping its programming work to China, IBM saves a tidy $40 an hour—which comes out to a very neat $168 million a year.[25] What good are cost savings? It's one of the things that you learn in your first business course: If you can cut your costs, you can cut your prices or improve your product. Ask another U.S. company: By offshoring work to India, Claimpower, a small medical-insurance billing company, cut costs, lowered the prices it charges to doctors, and quadrupled its business in two years.[26]

What's the main complaint about offshoring? Too many domestic jobs end up abroad. First of all, if a company can't survive without the cost savings it gets from outsourcing, it's going under otherwise, so in those cases, offshoring is the only way to *save* jobs. Moreover, when you become price competitive, you sell more abroad and thus *create* jobs in the process.[27] In fact, one study says that outsourcing has already increased the number of U.S. jobs. Again, it's basic business: Cost savings generate growth, and growth creates more jobs.[28]

And not just any jobs: This process lets companies create more *high-value* jobs at home—the ones done by people like managers, who draw the high salaries. When that happens,

Counterpoint **No** Some things are good for some of the people some of the time, and that's *almost* the case with offshoring, which, unfortunately, is only good for a *few* people but not for *most*. I keep hearing about the cost savings, but when I go into a store, I rarely find anything that's cheaper than it used to be. Companies like Ralph Lauren make almost all of their clothes in places where labor rates are low, but I see that they still charge the same upscale prices.

You point out that Claimpower cut prices to doctors, but when's the last time you visited *your* doctor? I know that mine hasn't cut any fees thanks to Claimpower. Moreover, I grant that Claimpower grew fast by keeping prices down, but Claimpower's growth had to be at the expense of other companies in the business, not because of growth in the economy: There are just so many insurance claims to go around. Here's another example. Fidelity Investments employs nearly 5,000 back-office workers in India. To do what? Fidelity says it's to cut the cost of industry research. But if offshoring is doing Fidelity so much good, why does it still charge me the same amount to manage my assets?

You refer to a study, so let's talk studies. I know of one that took a close look at 17 high-income countries, and demand for qualified people goes up, and in the United States, that process has already resulted in more buying power for *high-income* people—all as a result of sending *low-income* jobs to countries with lower labor costs.[29]

Admittedly, workers do get displaced, but *aggregate* employment figures show that they find other jobs. In a dynamic economy, people are constantly shifting jobs. So changing jobs because of outsourcing is no different from changing jobs for any other reason—say, because your company decided to invest in some laborsaving technology. In any case, because there are bound to be upper limits on the amount of outsourcing that a country can do, the direst predictions about job loss are exaggerated: There simply aren't enough unemployed people abroad who have the needed skills *and* who will work at a sufficiently low cost. In addition, outsourcing isn't for all companies or all types of operations.

Take U.S. Airways, which is bringing *back* jobs from overseas because the quality of the work wasn't good enough and because its technical resources weren't secure enough. In fact, about a fifth of the companies that have gone to outsourcing now say that the savings are less than they expected.[30] And that brings us back to what we said implicitly at the outset: Outsourcing works when you cut operating costs *effectively*. ●

here's what it found: In aggregate, the percentage of national income going to labor did in fact go down between 2000 and 2007. And profits? The percentage of national income going to profits also went up.[31]

Here's one of the key problems: When you replace jobs by offshoring, you're exchanging *good* jobs for *bad* ones. Most of the workers who wind up with the short end of the offshoring stick struggled for decades to get reasonable work hours and a few basic benefits, such as health care and retirement plans. More important, their incomes allowed them to send their kids to college, and the result was an upwardly mobile—and productive—generation.

Now, many of these employees have worked long and loyally for their employers, and what do they have to show for it in the offshoring era? Yes, I know the government subsidizes some health insurance costs, but very few of these displaced workers can come up with the 35 percent for cost-sharing their health-care bills when they've lost their jobs.[32] On top of everything else, they have no other usable skills, and at their ages, who's going to foot the bill for retraining them? The increase in what you call "high-value jobs" doesn't do *them* any good.

And while we're on the subject of job "value," what kind of jobs *are* we creating in poor countries? No doubt multinational enterprises (MNEs) pay workers in low-wage countries more than they could get otherwise, and I'll grant that some of these jobs—the white-collar and technical jobs—are pretty good. But for most people, the hours are long, the working conditions are barbaric, and the pay is barely enough to survive on.

And how much job security do they get out of MNEs? Not much, because big companies are always looking for some place where it's even cheaper to operate. Ask workers in the African country of Mauritius. For a while, they were a go-to source for cheap labor when clothing companies needed somebody to do their sewing, but as soon as Mauritians got it into their heads that they might expect a better way of life, MNEs discovered there were cheaper places to get the job done, and all those Mauritian workers who had started thinking about a better way of life found themselves out of work.[33]

Admittedly, in a dynamic economy, people have to change jobs more often than they would in a stagnant economy—*but not to the extent caused by offshoring*. I know that there's still some disagreement about the effects of offshoring on a country's employment rate. Researchers are still looking into the issue, but what they're finding are data like these: About 11 percent of U.S. jobs are at risk of being offshored—nearly 2 million of them in accounting-related fields alone.[34] Here's the bottom line: In countries like the United States, workers simply aren't equipped to handle the pace of change when it means that jobs can be exported faster than the average worker can retrain for different skills. ●

Why Companies Engage in International Business

We've already alluded to a few reasons why companies engage in international business. Basically, they're trying to create value for their organizations. At this point, let's focus on some of the specific ways in which firms can create value by going global. Start by taking another look at Figure 1.1 (page 8), where you'll see there are three major operating objectives that may induce companies to engage in international business:

- Expanding sales
- Acquiring resources
- Minimizing risk

Normally, these three objectives guide all decisions about whether, where, and how to engage in international business. Let's examine each of them in more detail.

EXPANDING SALES

Pursuing international sales usually increases the potential market and potential profits.

Foreign sources may give companies

- **Lower costs.**
- **New or better products.**
- **Additional operating knowledge.**

A company's sales depend on two factors: consumer interest in its products or services and consumer willingness and ability to buy them. For any product or service, then, there are more potential consumers and sales in the world than in any single country. Now, ordinarily, higher sales create value—but only if the costs of making the additional sales don't increase disproportionately. Recall, for instance, our opening case. Televising sports competitions to multiple countries increases costs only marginally. At the same time, the broadcasts generate advertising revenue far in excess of these marginally increased costs.

So increased sales are a major motive for a company's expansion into international markets, and in fact, many of the world's largest companies—including Volkswagen (Germany), Ericsson (Sweden), IBM (United States), Michelin (France), Nestlé (Switzerland), and Sony (Japan)—derive more than half their sales outside their home countries.[35] Bear in mind, however, that smaller companies (those with fewer than 20 employees) may also depend on foreign sales. Small companies make up nearly 97 percent of U.S. exporters and account for 29 percent of all exported U.S. goods.[36] Many small companies also depend on sales of components to large companies, which, in turn, install them in finished products slated for sale abroad.

ACQUIRING RESOURCES

Producers and distributors seek out products, services, resources, and components from foreign countries. Sometimes it's because domestic supplies are inadequate (as is the case with crude oil shipped to the United States). They're also looking for anything that will give them a competitive advantage. Sometimes this means acquiring a resource that cuts costs. Sporting goods companies like Rawlings, for example, rely largely on labor in Costa Rica, a country that hardly plays baseball, to produce baseballs.[37]

Sometimes firms gain competitive advantage by improving product quality or by differentiating their products from competitors' products; in both cases, they're potentially increasing market share and profits. Most automobile manufacturers, for example, hire one of several automobile-design companies in northern Italy to help with styling.[38] Many companies establish foreign research and development (R&D) facilities to tap additional scientific resources,[39] sometimes acquiring useful knowledge in the process. Avon, for instance, applies know-how from its Latin American marketing experience to help sell to the U.S. Hispanic market.[40]

MINIMIZING RISK

Operating in countries with different business cycles can minimize swings in sales and profits. The key is the fact that sales decrease or grow more slowly in a country that's in a recession and increase or grow more rapidly in one that's expanding economically. At one point early in the 2000s, for example, Nestlé experienced sluggish growth in Western Europe and the United States, but the trend was offset by faster growth in Asia, Eastern Europe, and Latin America.[41] In addition, by obtaining supplies of products or components from different countries, companies may be able to soften the impact of price swings or shortages in any one country.

Finally, companies often go into international business for defensive reasons. Perhaps they want to counter advantages gained by competitors in foreign markets that might hurt them elsewhere. By operating in Japan, for instance, Procter & Gamble (P&G) delayed foreign expansion on the part of potential Japanese competitors: P&G's presence in their home market hampered the efforts of Japanese companies to amass the necessary resources to expand into other international markets where P&G was active.

Similarly, British-based Natures Way Foods, which sells produce and prepared salads, followed a customer, the grocery chain Tesco, into the U.S. market. In so doing, it not only expanded sales but also strengthened its relationship with Tesco, effectively reducing the risk of Tesco's finding an alternative supplier who could turn around and threaten its sales to Tesco in the U.K. market.[42]

> International operations may reduce operating risk by
>
> - Smoothing sales and profits.
> - Preventing competitors from gaining advantages.

Modes of Operations in International Business

When pursuing international business, an organization must decide on one of the suitable *modes of operations* included in Figure 1.3. Among these modes we include *exports and imports* of both merchandise and service and *foreign investments,* both controlled and noncontrolled. Within these categories we include several subcategories, such as *joint ventures* and *management contracts.* In the following sections, we discuss each of these modes in some detail.

FIGURE 1.3   Modes of International Operations

In conducting international operations, a company may choose from among several operating modes, ranging from importing/exporting to direct and portfolio investment.

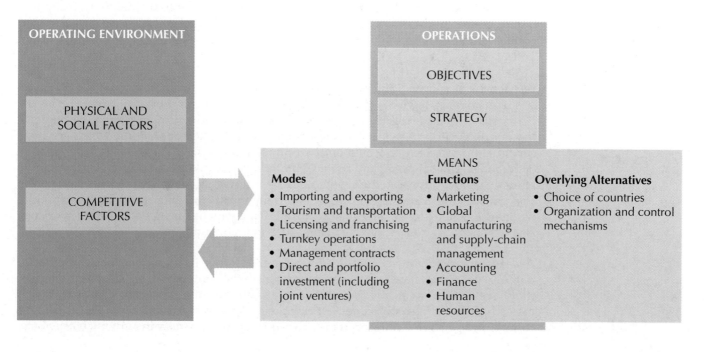

MERCHANDISE EXPORTS AND IMPORTS

Merchandise exports and imports usually are a country's most common international economic transaction.

Exporting and importing are the most popular modes of international business, especially among smaller companies. **Merchandise exports** are tangible products—goods—that are sent *out* of a country; **merchandise imports** are goods brought *into* a country. Because we can actually *see* these goods as they leave and enter the country, we sometimes call them *visible exports* and *imports*. When an Indonesian plant sends athletic shoes to the United States, the shoes are exports for Indonesia and imports for the United States. For most countries, the export and import of goods are the major sources of international revenues and expenditures.

SERVICE EXPORTS AND IMPORTS

Service exports and imports are international nonproduct sales and purchases.

- Examples of services are travel, transportation, banking, insurance, and the use of assets such as trademarks, patents, and copyrights.
- Service exports and imports are very important for some countries.
- They include many specialized international business operating modes.

Note that the terms *export* and *import* often apply only to *merchandise*, not to *services*. When we refer to products that generate *nonproduct international earnings*, we use the terms **service exports** and **service imports**. The company or individual that provides the service and receives payment makes a *service export*; the company or individual that receives and pays for it makes a *service import*. Currently, services constitute the fastest growth sector in international trade. Service exports and imports take many forms, and in this section, we discuss the most important:

- Tourism and transportation
- Service performance
- Asset use

Tourism and Transportation   Let's say that the Williams sisters, Venus and Serena, take Air France from the United States to Paris to play in the French Open tennis tournament. Their tickets on Air France and travel expenses in France are service exports for France and service imports for the United States. Obviously, then, tourism and transportation are important sources of revenue for airlines, shipping companies, travel agencies, and hotels.

The economies of some countries depend heavily on revenue from these sectors. In Greece and Norway, for example, a significant amount of employment and foreign-exchange earnings comes from foreign cargo carried on ships owned by domestically owned shipping lines. Tourism earnings are more important to the Bahamian economy than earnings from export merchandise. (As we'll see in our closing case, year-round good weather enables the Bahamas to cater to the cruise-line industry as an important port of call.)

Service Performance   Some services—including banking, insurance, rental, engineering, and management services—net companies earnings in the form of *fees*—payments for the performance of those services. On an international level, for example, companies may pay fees for engineering services rendered as so-called **turnkey operations,** which are often construction projects performed under contract and transferred to owners when they're operational. The U.S. company Bechtel currently has turnkey contracts in Afghanistan to rebuild facilities destroyed during the war to overthrow its Taliban leadership. Companies also pay fees for **management contracts**—arrangements in which one company provides personnel to perform general or specialized management functions for another. Disney receives such fees from managing theme parks in France and Japan.

Asset Use   When one company allows another to use its assets, such as trademarks, patents, copyrights, or expertise, under contracts known as **licensing agreements,** they receive earnings called *royalties*. On an international level, for example, sports teams license foreign companies to print their logos on shirts and caps. **Royalties** also come from franchise contracts. **Franchising** is a mode of business in which one party (the *franchisor*) allows another (the *franchisee*) to use a trademark as an essential asset of the franchisee's business. As a rule, the franchisor (say, McDonald's) also assists continuously in the operation of the franchisee's business, perhaps by providing supplies, management services, or technology.

INVESTMENTS

Dividends and interest paid on foreign investments are also considered service exports and imports because they represent the use of assets (capital). The investments themselves, however, are treated as different forms of service exports and imports. Note first of all that *foreign investment* means ownership of foreign property in exchange for a financial return, such as interest and dividends. Foreign investment takes two forms: *direct* and *portfolio*.

Direct Investment In **foreign direct investment (FDI),** sometimes referred to simply as *direct investment,* the investor takes a controlling interest in a foreign company. When, for example, Nintendo's CEO bought the Seattle Mariners, the baseball team became a Japanese FDI in the United States. Control need not be a 100 percent (or even a 50 percent) interest: If a foreign investor holds a minority stake and the remaining ownership is widely dispersed, no other owner may be able to counter the decisions of the foreign investor.

When two or more companies share ownership of an FDI, the operation is a **joint venture.** Recall the discussion in our opening case of the purchase by the owners of the Texas Rangers and Montreal Canadiens of the Liverpool Football Club. The agreement constitutes a joint venture between U.S. and Canadian owners.

Although the world's 100 largest international companies own 11 percent of all FDIs, the vast number of companies using FDI means that it's also common among smaller companies. Today, at least 61,000 companies worldwide control over 900,000 FDIs in every industry.[43]

Portfolio Investment A **portfolio investment** is a *noncontrolling* interest in a company or ownership of a loan made to another party. A portfolio investment usually takes one of two forms: stock in a company or loans to a company (or country) in the form of bonds, bills, or notes purchased by the investor. They're important for most companies with extensive international operations, and except for stock, they're used primarily for short-term financial gain—as a relatively safe means of earning more money on a firm's investment. To earn higher yields on short-term investments, companies routinely move funds from country to country.

Key components of portfolio investment are

- Noncontrolling interest of a foreign operation.
- Financial benefit (e.g., loans).

TYPES OF INTERNATIONAL ORGANIZATIONS

Basically, an "international company" is any company that operates internationally, but we have a variety of terms to designate different types of operations. Companies can work together on an international basis in any number of ways, including *joint ventures, licensing agreements, management contracts, minority ownership,* and *long-term contractual arrangements.* The term **collaborative arrangements** can be used to describe all of these types of operations. The term **strategic alliance** is sometimes used to mean the same thing, but it's often reserved to refer either to an agreement that's of critical importance to one or more partners or to an agreement that does not involve joint ownership.

Multinational Enterprises A **multinational enterprise (MNE)** takes a worldwide view of markets and production; in other words, it's willing to consider market and production locations anywhere in the world. The true MNE typically uses most of the modes of operation we've described in this chapter. However, because it isn't always easy to determine if a company really takes a "worldwide view," experts have devised some narrower

An MNE (sometimes called MNC or TNC) is a company that has a worldwide approach to markets and production *or* one with operations in more than one country.

definitions of an MNE. Some people argue, for instance, that an MNE must have direct investments in a minimum number of countries.

Does Size Matter?   Other definitions require a certain size—usually giant size. A small company, however, can take a worldwide view and adopt any of the operating modes that we've discussed, even while remaining within its resource capabilities. This is often the case with what we've called *born-global companies.* Take, for example, Vast.com, a U.S. search company founded in 2005. Within a year, it boasted 25 employees working in four countries on two continents.

Of course, successful small companies often become large ones. VistaPrint, which sells a variety of printed products such as business cards and stationery, is a born-global company founded in the late 1990s. It maintains two-thirds of its workforce outside the United States, sells in 120 countries, and has a capitalization of over a billion U.S. dollars.[44]

MNCs and TNCs   Today, most writers apply the term *MNE* to any company with operations in more than one country. This is the definition we use in this text. The term **multinational corporation (MNC)** is often used as a synonym for MNE, but, again, we prefer the MNE designation because many internationally involved companies (such as accounting partnerships) aren't organized as corporations. At the United Nations, the term **transnational company (TNC)** is sometimes used interchangeably with MNE.

Why International Business Differs from Domestic Business

Managers in international business must understand social science disciplines and how they affect all functional business fields.

Now that we've explained the modes by which companies operate internationally, let's turn to the conditions in a nation's *external environment* that may affect those operations. Smart companies don't form international strategies—or develop the means to implement them—without examining the dimensions of the external environment indicated in Figure 1.4. As you can see, we've organized these dimensions, or factors, into two broad categories:

- *Physical factors* (such as a country's geography) and *social factors* (such as its politics, law, culture, and economy)
- *Competitive factors* (such as the number and strength of a company's suppliers, customers, and rival firms)

FIGURE I.4   Physical and Social Factors Affecting International Business Operations

Every company that operates internationally both affects and is affected by the physical and social environments in which it conducts business.

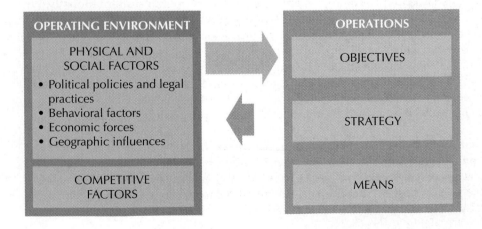

OPERATING ENVIRONMENT

PHYSICAL AND SOCIAL FACTORS
- Political policies and legal practices
- Behavioral factors
- Economic forces
- Geographic influences

COMPETITIVE FACTORS

OPERATIONS

OBJECTIVES

STRATEGY

MEANS

In examining both categories, we delve into the realm of the *social sciences*, which is extremely helpful in explaining how external conditions affect patterns of behavior in different parts of the world. If you're planning to get into some area of international management, we recommend you pay attention in your social science classes (which include everything from psychology and anthropology to political science and geography).

PHYSICAL AND SOCIAL FACTORS

All sorts of physical and social factors can affect the ways in which companies produce and market products, staff operations, and even maintain accounts. In the following sections, we focus on five key factors: *geographic, political, legal, behavioral,* and *economic.* Remember that, regardless of which factor is prominent, the amount of adjustment required of globally active businesses is determined in part by the extent to which home- and host-country environments are compatible.

Geographic Influences   Managers who know geography can better determine the location, quantity, quality, and availability of the world's resources, as well as the best way to exploit them. The uneven distribution of resources throughout the world accounts in large part for the fact that different products and services are produced in different parts of the world.

Again, take sports. Norway fares better in the Winter Olympics than in the Summer Olympics because of its climate, and except for the well-publicized Jamaican bobsled team (whose members actually lived in Canada), tropical countries don't even compete in the Winter Olympics. East Africans tend to dominate distance races because, at least in part, they can train at higher altitudes than most runners.

Geographic barriers—mountains, deserts, jungles, and so forth—often affect communications and distribution channels in many countries. And, the chance of natural disasters and adverse climatic conditions (hurricanes, floods, earthquakes, tsunamis) can make investments riskier in some areas than in others. (Again, we can look forward to our ending case. In truth, the weather in the Bahamas isn't always balmy; the islands are subject to hurricanes, which obviously puts a damper on the appeal for the cruise-line business.)

In addition, the same factors can affect both the availability of supplies and the prices of products. In New Zealand, for example, droughts in the early 2000s forced farmers to reduce stocks of sheep; in turn, global shortages of lamb and wool caused the prices of both to go up.[45] Finally, population distribution and the impact of human activity on the environment may exert strong future influences on international business, particularly if ecological changes or regulations force companies to move or alter operations.

Political Policies   It should come as no surprise that a nation's political policies influence the ways in which international business takes place within its borders (indeed, *whether* it will take place). Again, we can turn to the sports arena to see how politics can affect international operations in any industry. Did you know Cuba once had a minor-league baseball franchise? That arrangement went the way of diplomatic relations between Cuba and the United States back in the 1960s, but several Cuban baseball players are now members of professional U.S. teams. The big difference is that most of them had to defect from Cuba to play abroad. China permits NBA superstar Yao Ming to play basketball in the United States, but the Chinese government enforces restrictions on his salary and endorsement earnings. For many years, most countries barred athletes and teams from South Africa from international competition because of the country's racial policies.

Obviously, political disputes—particularly those that result in military confrontation—can disrupt trade and investment. Even conflicts that directly affect only small areas can have far-reaching effects. The terrorist bombing of a hotel in Indonesia, for instance, resulted in the loss of considerable tourist revenue and investment capital because both individuals and businesses abroad perceived the whole country as too risky an environment for safe and profitable enterprises.

Natural conditions affect where different goods and services can be produced.

Case Review Note

Case Review Note

Politics often determines where and how international business can take place.

Each country has its own laws regulating business. Agreements among countries set international law.

The interpersonal norms of a country may necessitate a company's alteration of operations.

Legal Policies   Domestic and international laws play a big role in determining how a company can operate overseas. *Domestic law* includes both home- and host-country regulations on such matters as taxation, employment, and foreign-exchange transactions. Singapore law, for example, determines how the local Manchester United Red Café is taxed, how its revenues can be converted from Singapore dollars to British pounds, and even the nationalities of the people it employs. Meanwhile, British law determines how and when the earnings from Man U's Singapore operations are taxed in the United Kingdom.

International law—in the form of legal agreements between the two countries—determines how earnings are taxed by *both* jurisdictions. Mainly as a function of agreements reached in international forums, international law may also determine how (and whether) companies can operate in certain places. As we point out in our closing case, for example, international agreement permits ships' crews to move about virtually anywhere without harassment. Many countries, however, restrict the activities of domestic companies in the Southeast Asian nation of Myanmar because of its dubious human-rights record.

Finally, the ways in which laws are *enforced* also affect a firm's overseas operations. Most countries, for example, have joined in international treaties and enacted domestic laws dealing with the violation of trademarks, patented knowledge, and copyrighted materials. Many, however, do very little to enforce either the treaties or their own laws. That's why companies must make a point not only of understanding treaties and laws but also of determining how fastidiously they're enforced in different countries.

Behavioral Factors   The related disciplines of anthropology, psychology, and sociology can help managers better understand values, attitudes, and beliefs in a foreign environment. In turn, such understanding can help managers make operational decisions in different countries.

Let's return once again to our opening case. In discussing the globalization of professional sports, we stressed certain commonalities in the national reception of sports, but we should remember that huge differences remain both in the popularity of different sports and in the way a single sport is played. Interestingly, these differences affect the way in which the U.S. film industry treats sports as subject matter. As a rule, U.S. producers spare no expense to ensure that big-budget movies generate the greatest possible international appeal (and revenue). When it comes to sports-themed movies, however, they typically cut costs. Why? Because people in one country usually don't care to see movies about other people's sports, movie-makers see no point in spending extra money trying to attract foreign audiences and revenues.[46]

While we're on the subject, we should point out that the Japanese *do* care about U.S. baseball. Japanese culture, however, values harmony more than U.S. culture does, and Americans tend to value competitiveness more than the Japanese do. This difference is reflected in different baseball rules: Whereas the best possible outcome of a baseball game in Japan is a tie, Americans prefer a game be played out until there's a winner.

Economic Forces   Among other things, economics explains why countries exchange goods and services, why capital and people travel among countries in the course of business, and why one country's currency has a certain value compared to another's. Recall from our opening case that the percentage of non-U.S.-born players on major-league rosters has been steadily increasing. Players from the Dominican Republic form the largest share of non-U.S.-born players, but even though baseball is quite popular in the Dominican Republic, the idea of putting a major-league baseball team there simply isn't feasible. Why? Because too few Dominicans can afford the ticket prices necessary to support a team. Obviously, higher incomes in the United States and Canada—in the case of baseball players, *much* higher incomes—attract Dominican players to major-league teams.

Economics also helps explain why one country can produce goods or services less expensively than another. In addition, it provides the analytical tools to determine the impact of an international company's operations on the economies of both host and home countries, as well as the impact of the host country's economic environment on a foreign company.

Economics explains country differences in costs, currency values, and market size.

THE COMPETITIVE ENVIRONMENT

In addition to its physical and social environments, every globally active company operates within a competitive environment. Figure 1.5 is thus a variation on Figure 1.4 that highlights the key competitive factors in the external environment of an international business—product strategy, resource base and experience, and competitor capability. Thus companies operate more easily in a country with similar physical and social conditions to those in their home country because they have less adjustment to make there.

Competitive Strategy for Products   Most products compete by means of *cost* or *differentiation strategies.* A successful differentiation strategy usually takes one of two approaches:

- Developing a favorable *brand image,* usually through advertising or from long-term consumer experience with the brand; or

- Developing *unique characteristics,* usually through R&D efforts.

Using either approach, a firm may mass-market a product or sell to a target market (the latter approach is called a *focus strategy*). Different strategies can be used for different products, but a firm's choice of strategy plays a big part in determining how and where it will operate. Take Fiat, an automobile brand that competes largely on a mass-market cost strategy. This strategy has determined the location of engine plants in China, where production costs are low, as well as production activities in India and Argentina, both of which are attractive but cost-sensitive markets.

Interestingly, Fiat also owns Ferrari, which competes on a differentiation basis to a targeted market of very high-income consumers. Whereas the competitive characteristics of the U.S. market aren't conducive to the Fiat brand strategy (there's no Fiat distribution in the United States), over a quarter of all Ferraris are sold in the United States.[47]

A company's situation may differ among countries by

- Its competitive ranking.
- The competitors it faces.

Company Resources and Experience   Another set of competitive factors is a company's size and resources compared to those of competitors. A market leader, for example—say, Coca-Cola—has resources for much more ambitious international operations than a

FIGURE 1.5   Competitive Factors Affecting International Business Operations

Depending on its products, its strategies, and the host-country environments (including rivals) in which it does business, every company faces its own set of competitive factors.

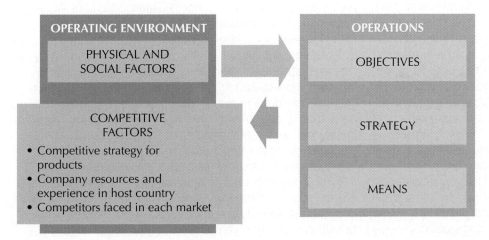

smaller competitor like Royal Crown. Royal Crown's resources, however, may be sufficient to gain national distribution on its own in small countries. In large markets (such as the United States), companies have to invest many more resources to secure national distribution. (And even then, they'll probably face more competitors: In European countries, for example, especially in retailing, a firm is likely to face three or four significant competitors, as opposed to the ten to twenty it will face in the United States.)[48]

Conversely, a company's national market share and brand recognition have a bearing on how it can operate in a given country. A company with a long-standing dominant market position uses operating tactics quite different from those employed by a newcomer. Remember, too, that being a leader in one country doesn't guarantee being a leader anywhere else. In most markets, Coca-Cola is the leader, with Pepsi-Cola coming in a strong second; in India, however, Coke is number three, trailing both Pepsi and a locally owned brand called Thums Up.[49]

Competitors Faced in Each Market   Finally, success in a market (whether domestic or foreign) often depends on whether your competition is also international or local. Commercial aircraft makers Boeing and Airbus, for example, compete only with each other in every market they serve. Thus what they learn about each other in one country is useful in predicting the other's strategies elsewhere. In contrast, the British grocery chain Tesco faces different competition in every foreign market it enters.

LOOKING TO THE FUTURE

Three Ways of Looking at Globalization

At this juncture, there's a good deal of difference of opinion on the future of international business and globalization. Basically, there are three major viewpoints:

- Further globalization is inevitable.
- International business will grow primarily along regional rather than global lines.
- Forces working against further globalization and international business will slow down both trends.

The view that globalization is inevitable reflects the premise that advances in transportation and communications are so pervasive that consumers everywhere will demand the best products for the best prices regardless of their origins. Those who hold this view also argue that because MNEs have so many international production and distribution networks in place, they'll pressure home governments to place fewer rather than more restrictions on the international movement of goods and the means of producing them.

Even if we accept this view, we must still meet at least one challenge in riding the wave of the future: Because the future is what we make of it, we must figure out how to spread the benefits of globalization equitably while minimizing the hardships placed on those parties—both people and companies—who suffer from increased international competition.

Not long ago, the *Wall Street Journal* posed one question to all living Nobel Prize winners in economics: "What is the greatest economic challenge for the future?" Robert Fogel said it's the problem of getting available technology and food to people who are needlessly dying. Milton Friedman argued for "holding down the size and scope of government." George Akerlof cited global warming. According to William Sharpe, we have to figure out how to finance health care and retirement. Both Vernon Smith and Harry Markowitz specified the need to bring down global trade barriers. Lawrence Klein called for "the reduction of poverty and disease in a peaceful political environment." John Nash felt we must address the problem of increasing the worldwide standard of living while the amount of the earth's surface per person is shrinking.[50] Clearly, each of these responses projects both challenges and opportunities for managers in the international arena.

The second view—that growth will be largely regional rather than global—is based on studies showing that almost all of the companies we think of as "global" conduct most of their business in home and neighboring countries.[51] In addition, most world trade is regional, and many treaties to remove trade barriers are regional agreements. Critics of this view hold that regionalization, whether of corporate or national business activity, may be merely a transition stage. In other words, companies may first promote international business in nearby countries and then expand their activities once they've reached certain regional goals.

The third view argues that the pace of globalization will slow down or may in fact already be in the process of collapse.[52] Even in Chapter 1, we've had occasion to cite a few antiglobalization sentiments, and it's easy to see that some people are adamant and earnest in voicing their reservations. The crux of the antiglobalization movement is the belief there's a growing schism between parties (including MNEs) who are thriving in a globalized environment and those who aren't.

Antiglobalists pressure governments to promote nationalism by raising barriers to trade and rejecting international organizations and treaties. Historically, such groups have often been successful (at least temporarily) in obstructing either technological or commercial advances that threatened their well-being. Recently, for example, antiglobalization interests in Australia and Austria succeeded in electing anti-immigration parties. In Brazil and South Africa, voters have authorized domestic companies to copy pharmaceuticals under global patent protection. Bolivia and Venezuela have nationalized some foreign investments, and the United States prevented China from purchasing a domestic oil company and Dubai from purchasing U.S. port operations. The sparring between pro- and antiglobalists is one of the reasons why the globalization process has so far progressed in fits and starts.

Finally, there is a view that for globalization to succeed, efficient institutions with clear-cut mandates are necessary; however, there is concern that neither the institutions nor the people working in them can adequately handle the complexities of an interconnected world.[53]

Going Forward

Only time will tell, but one thing seems certain from everything we've read in this chapter: If a company wants to capitalize on international opportunities, it can't wait too long to see what happens on political and economic fronts. Investments in research, equipment, plants, and personnel training can take years to pan out. Forecasting foreign opportunities and risks is always a challenge, but by examining different ways in which the future may evolve, a company's management has a better chance of avoiding unpleasant surprises. That's why each chapter of this book includes a box that shows how certain chapter topics can become subjects for looking into the future of international business. ■

Carnival Cruise Lines: Exploiting a Sea of Global Opportunity

CASE

I must go down to the seas again, for the call of the running tide

Is a wild call and a clear call that may not be denied

—John Masefield, *The Seekers*

In recent years, the call of the sea—or at least the prospect of a little deckboard relaxation—has made the cruise business one of the world's fastest growing industries.[54] Sea voyages, of course, have had an aura of mystique for centuries, but only in recent decades has the experience of the open sea and exotic ports of call been available to a mass market.

Historically, the recreational sea voyage has been an essentially elitist endeavor. Certainly, members of the lower classes occasionally found themselves on the open sea, but usually as displaced job seekers or crew members of luxury liners and tramp steamers. In recent years, however, the cruise industry has undergone a sea of change of sorts, and targeted demographic groups now include the working middle class as well as the idle rich. A 2006 survey indicated that only 50 percent of cruisers have annual household incomes above $75,000, with 46 percent falling into the $40,000 to $75,000 range.

What's a *Cruise*, and What Happened to the Cruise Industry?

A "cruise" is a sea voyage taken for pleasure (as opposed to, say, passage on a whaling ship, an assignment in the navy, or a ferry to get you from point A to point B). Typically, passengers enjoy cabin accommodations for the duration of a fixed itinerary that brings them back to their original point of embarkation.

MAP 1.2
Where Carnival Cruise Passengers Come From

Data come from the 2006 *Annual Report* of Carnival Corporation & PLC. Countries designated on the map denote headquarters locations of each company (e.g., five lines operate out of North America and four out of the U.K.). Percentage figures represent passenger capacity in each of the company's primary markets.

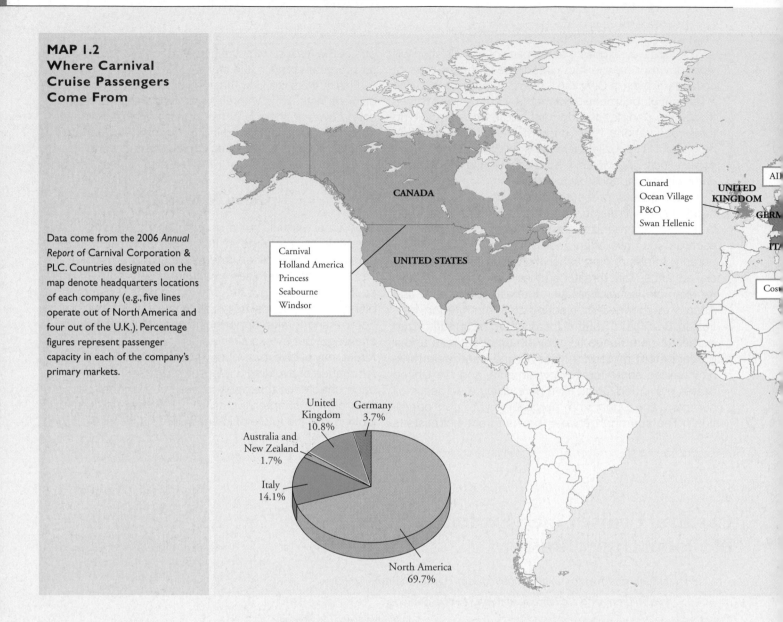

There was a time when ships (called *passenger liners*) transported a certain class of people across oceans and seas for business or pleasure, but the advent of transocean air service after World War II offered a speedier and less expensive alternative, and airlines captured passengers from ocean liners. The competitive balance tipped decisively in the 1960s, when advances in jet technology made air travel a viable option for a growing mass market of budget-minded international travelers. Converting more shipboard space to low-priced accommodations, shipping lines countered with the reminder that "getting there is half the fun," but one by one, the great luxury liners that had plied the seas for so many years were retired.

The Contemporary Cruise Industry

Today, the cruise industry is dominated by three companies—Carnival, Royal Caribbean, and Star—which command a combined 91 percent of the market. By far, the largest of the three is Carnival Corporation, which operates a number of lines that it calls *brands*. Map 1.2 shows the headquarters of these "brands," the primary markets served by each, and Carnival's percentage of passenger capacity represented by each geographic area. Carnival offers cruises to every continent on the globe, including Antarctica.

Carnival Corporation was born when Ted Arison, a former partner in Norwegian Cruise Lines, saw an opportunity to expand mass-market sea travel by promoting the idea of the "Fun Ship" vacation—an excursion on a pleasure craft designed to be a little less formal and luxurious than the traditional ocean liner. The timing was right. Sea travel still projected a certain aura, and Arison found that he could buy a retired liner at a good price. Moreover, there were more people in the world who could afford an ocean-borne vacation. On top of everything else, a lot of these vacationers gravitated to holidays—group tours, theme park visits, and sojourns in Las Vegas—that were compatible with the "Fun Ship" concept.

Arison bought a secondhand ship, refurbished it in bright colors, rigged it with bright lights, and installed discos and casinos. On its maiden voyage from Miami in 1972, the *Mardi Gras* ran aground with 300 journalists on board, but, fortunately, neither the ship nor Arison's business concept was severely damaged. Embarking from Miami to such destinations as Jamaica, Puerto Rico, and the U.S. Virgin Islands, the *Mardi Gras* soon became a successful fixture in the vacation industry.

Over time, Arison added not only ships but also whole cruise lines to his fleet. Today, each brand operates primarily in a designated area of the world and is differentiated from other Carnival brands in two different ways: (1) in terms of geographically pertinent themes (based in Italy, for instance, Costa boasts a Mediterranean flavor); and (2) in terms of cost per cruise (the cost per night on Cunard and Seabourne cruises is much higher than that on Carnival cruises).

Doing Business in International Waters

Given the nature of its business, it should come as no surprise that Carnival—indeed, the whole cruise-line industry—is international in scope. Take the nationality of competitors. Companies can obtain so-called *flags of convenience* from about 30 different countries. Here's how the process works. By registering as, say, a Liberian or Mongolian legal entity, a company can take advantage of the lower taxes and less stringent employment rules of those countries. Legally, Carnival is a Panamanian company, even though it's listed on the New York Stock Exchange, operates out of Miami, and caters mainly to passengers who set sail from the United States. Although cruise-line revenue is subject to neither Panamanian nor U.S. income taxes, Carnival does have to pay substantial "port fees" wherever its ships drop anchor.

Only a few cruise-line offerings—such as excursions along the Mississippi River, around the Hawaiian Islands, or among the Galapagos Islands—can be characterized as purely domestic. Even trips from the U.S. West Coast to Alaska are "international" because they stop in Canada. By far the most popular destination for cruise passengers is the Caribbean/Bahamas, largely because the area boasts balmy weather year round. During summer months, Carnival shifts some of its ships from Caribbean/Bahamas to Alaskan and Mediterranean routes.

Obviously, cruise ships go only where there are ports to call on, but that doesn't mean a cruise is nothing more than a series of dockside stopovers. Carnival, for instance, cooperates with (and owns some) tour operators who provide onshore excursions (for additional fees). Carnival estimates that half its passengers to the Caribbean take shore excursions to such sightseeing attractions as the Mayan ruins in Belize. Passengers on Carnival's Princess Lines, which serves Alaska, can helicopter to a glacier for a little dogsledding.

What It Takes to Operate a Cruise Line

Ship Shopping

Not surprisingly, ships constitute the biggest investment in the cruise-line industry. Shipyards in several countries—including Finland, France, Germany, Italy, Japan, and South Korea—are capable of building ships that meet cruise-industry needs, and to add to its global fleet, Carnival secures bids from all over the world. Because shipbuilding employs so many people and uses so much locally produced steel, governments often subsidize the industry—a practice that works to the benefit of the cruise-line industry by offering less expensive prices for ships. Recently, for instance, the Italian government awarded the shipyard Fincantieri about $50 million in subsidies to build five ships for Carnival to be delivered by 2010. The project is worth $2.5 billion to the Italian supplier.

Where to Find Able-Bodied Seamen

Shipping companies—including those that operate container vessels and other cargo ships as well as cruise lines—scour the world for able-bodied sailors who can not only perform specialized tasks but who are properly certified (by international agreement, a registered crew member can enter virtually any port in the world). Cruise lines, of course, have special staffing needs—notably, crew who can interact with passengers. About a third of all the world's ships' crews are from the Philippines, not only because of reasonable labor costs but because Filipinos are generally fluent in English. The next most prolific source is Eastern Europe, with China and Vietnam growing in importance. On a typical Carnival ship, crew members hail from over 100 countries, and Carnival maintains a range of employee-training programs, including instruction in English as a foreign language.

Casinos and Other Amenities

Although Carnival has thrived with the concept of cruises for a mass market, a Carnival cruise isn't necessarily a thoroughly informal experience. Each cruise offers one or two formal nights per week, theme-based dinners centering on national cuisines, and a variety of musical entertainment, games and contests, and spas and athletic facilities. Because cruises operate outside the jurisdiction of any national authority, they're not subject to any national laws restricting gambling. Casinos, therefore, are onboard fixtures.

Passengers can also shop for merchandise from all over the world. Indeed, art dealers occasionally hold shipboard auctions and seminars, and one dealer sells about 300,000 pieces of art per year on cruise ships. As you might expect, the pricier the cruise, the pricier the average objet d'art.

The Overseas Environment

Because Carnival operates around the world, it has the advantage of treating the whole world as a source of both customers and supplies. In addition, because its chief assets are ocean borne, Carnival can ship capital and other assets to places where they can best serve the company's needs. By the same token, however, it's also vulnerable to a wide range of environmental disturbances. Let's take a look at a few of these environmental demands.

Political Issues

After terrorists seized a cruise ship in the Mediterranean in 1985, the major cruise lines instituted a policy of strict security checks for boarding passengers. Even before 9/11, then, the cruise-line industry has had in place a security protocol that the airline industry didn't put in place until afterward.

In the wake of 9/11, when cancellations started to exceed bookings, Carnival increased the number of U.S. ports from which its ships embarked so passengers with a heightened fear of flying could reach points of departure by land. Carnival also redeploys cruises to avoid areas in which passengers might face danger from political upheaval. In 2002, it canceled cruises to St. Croix in the U.S. Virgin Islands because of a high crime rate. Further, Carnival does not stop in Cuba, a popular tourist destination, because the U.S. government limits travel there by U.S. citizens.

Health Issues

In 2006, almost 700 people on a Carnival transatlantic cruise were stricken with a virus that caused diarrhea and vomiting, a type of outbreak that had occurred sporadically in the past. Cruise operators have found these outbreaks hard to control because of the close contact among people on board a ship. More than once, Carnival has had to take an infected ship out of service to eradicate all traces of the virus; the process involves sanitizing every object on board, down to the poker chips. When the severe acute respiratory syndrome (SARS) epidemic hit, Carnival took such precautions as banning passengers who had recently been in infected areas.

Economic Issues

Buying a cruise is generally considered discretionary rather than priority spending. During recessions, people are more apt to take shorter cruises and to embark from nearby ports rather than flying to faraway points of departure. Interestingly, however, in comparison with other segments of the tourist industry, cruise lines have fared well during economic downturns. Why? In part because their all-inclusive per diem prices are often bargains when compared with the cost of travel to major cities and popular resorts. In addition, fixed cruise-line prices spare passengers the added risk of encountering unforeseen unfavorable exchange rates.

But there is some concern in the industry over rising gasoline prices and mortgage interest rates, which might leave even households earning $90,000 a year with too little discretionary income for taking cruises. In addition, oil price increases have forced up fuel costs at a time when many potential passengers want lower prices.

The Weather

In 2004, an unprecedented number of four hurricanes hit Florida, Carnival's main embarkation point. Hurricane Francis alone closed ports and canceled three cruises and abbreviated six others. Passengers on canceled trips received full refunds and those on shortened cruises partial refunds.

Concluding Remarks

Overall, the outlook for Carnival and the cruise-line industry is sunny. With incomes growing in many countries (such as China), more people will have discretionary income to spend on tourism. Only 16 percent of the U.S. population has yet to take a cruise—a potential two-edged sword. On the one hand, this number indicates growth potential. On the other hand, the remaining 18 percent continue to be repeat customers, and the percentage of first-time customers is in fact declining. On the downside, then, industry observers worry that experienced cruisers will tire of visiting one port that's pretty much like another and that noncruisers will still prefer such destinations as resorts to ports of call. ■

QUESTIONS

1. What global forces have contributed to the growth of the cruise-line industry?
2. What specific steps has Carnival Cruise Lines taken to benefit from global social changes?
3. What are some of the national differences that affect the operations of cruise lines?
4. Although most cruise-line passengers are from the United States, the average number of annual vacation days taken by U.S. residents is lower than that of workers in most other high-income countries (13 days, compared with 42 in Italy, 37 in France, 35 in Germany, and 25 in Japan). How might cruise lines increase sales to people outside the United States?
5. What threats exist for the future performance of the cruise-line industry and, specifically, of Carnival Cruise Lines? If you were in charge of Carnival, how would you (a) try to prevent these threats from becoming reality and (b) deal with them if they did become reality?
6. Discuss the ethics of cruise lines regarding the avoidance of taxes while buying ships built with governmental subsidies.

SUMMARY

- Globalization is the ongoing process that deepens and broadens the relationships and interdependence among countries. International business is a mechanism to bring about globalization.

- International business has been growing rapidly in recent decades because of technological expansion, the liberalization of government policies on cross-border movements (goods, services, and the resources to produce them), the development of institutions needed to support and facilitate international transactions, consumer pressures to buy foreign products and services, increased global competition, changing political situations, and cooperation in dealing with transnational problems and issues. Because of these factors, foreign countries increasingly are a source of both production and sales for domestic companies.

- Globalization has many critics, who feel it weakens national sovereignty, promotes growth that is detrimental to the earth's environment, and skews income distributions.

- Offshoring—the transferring of production abroad—is controversial in terms of who benefits when costs are reduced and whether the process exchanges good jobs for bad ones.

- Companies engage in international business to expand sales, to acquire resources, and to diversify or reduce their risks.

- A company can engage in international business through various operating modes, including exporting and importing merchandise and services, direct and portfolio investments, and collaborative arrangements with other companies.

- Multinational enterprises (MNEs) take a global approach to markets and production. Sometimes they are referred to as multinational corporations (MNCs) or transnational companies (TNCs).

- When operating abroad, companies may have to adjust their usual methods of carrying on business. This is because foreign conditions often dictate a more suitable method and the operating modes used for international business differ somewhat from those used on a domestic level.

- To operate within a company's external environment, its managers must have not only knowledge of business operations but also a working knowledge of the basic social sciences: geography, political science, law, anthropology, sociology, psychology, and economics.

- A company's competitive strategy influences how and where it can best operate. Likewise, from one country to another, a company's competitive situation may differ in terms of its relative strength and in terms of which competitors it faces.

- There is disagreement about the future of globalization—that it is inevitable, that it will be primarily regional, and that the growth will slow.

KEY TERMS

born-global company (p. 22)
collaborative arrangement (p. 21)
foreign direct investment (FDI) (p. 21)
franchising (p. 21)
globalization (p. 6)
international business (p. 7)
joint venture (p. 21)
licensing agreement (p. 20)

management contract (p. 20)
merchandise export (p. 20)
merchandise import (p. 20)
multinational corporation
(MNC) (p. 22)
multinational enterprise (MNE) (p. 21)
offshoring (p. 15)
portfolio investment (p. 21)

royalty (p. 20)
service export (p. 20)
service import (p. 20)
sovereignty (p. 14)
strategic alliance (p. 21)
transnational company
(TNC) (p. 22)
turnkey operation (p. 20)

ENDNOTES

1 *Sources include the following:* George Vecsey, "When the Game Absorbs the Globe," *New York Times*, April 1, 2007: A+; Steve McGrath, "Latest Private-Equity Triumph: U.K. Soccer," *Wall Street Journal*, February 7, 2007: C3; Matthew Graham, "Nike Overtakes Adidas in Football Field," *Financial Times*, August 19, 2004: 19; L. Jon Wertheim, "The Whole World Is Watching," *Sports Illustrated*, June 14, 2004: 73–86; Wertheim, "Hot Prospects in Cold Places," *Sports Illustrated*, June 21, 2004: 63–66; Grant Wahl, "Football vs. Fútbol," *Sports Illustrated*, July 5, 2004: 69–72; Wahl, "On Safari for 7-Footers," *Sports Illustrated*, June 28, 2004: 70–73; André Richelieu, "Building the Brand Equity of Professional Sports Teams," paper presented at the annual meeting of the Academy of International Business, Stockholm, Sweden (July 10–13, 2004); Brian K. White, "Seattle Mariners Justify Losing Streak as 'Cunning,' " GlossyNews.com, July 15, 2004 (accessed November 6, 2004); "Japanese Owners Don't Want MLB in Control of World Cup," SportsLine.com wire reports, July 8, 2004 (accessed November 6, 2004); Harald Dolles and Sten Söderman, "Globalization of Sports—the Case of Professional Football and Its International Challenges" (Tokyo: German Institute for Japanese Studies, working paper, May 1, 2005).

2 For a good discussion of the versatility of the term *globalization*, see Joyce S. Osland, "Broadening the Debate: The Pros and Cons of Globalization," *Journal of Management Inquiry* 10:2 (June 2003): 137–54.

3 Sara Dickerman, "Air Supply: How Many Frequent-Flier Miles Did Your Dinner Earn?" *New York Times Style Magazine* (Fall 2004): 30.

4 Sarah McBride, "Kia's Audacious Sorento Plan," *Wall Street Journal*, April 8, 2003: A12.

5 Günther G. Schulze and Heinrich W. Ursprung, "Globalisation of the Economy and the Nation State," *The World Economy* 22:3 (May 1999): 295–352.

6 Robert O. Keohane and Joseph S. Nye Jr., "Globalization: What's New? What's Not?" *Foreign Policy* 118 (Spring 2000): 104–19.

7 Martin Wolf, "Economic Globalisation," *Financial Times*, January 23, 2003: The World: 2003, section iii.

8 For example, see OECD, *Measuring Globalisation: OECD Economic Globalisation Indicators* (Paris: OECD, 2005); Pim Martens and Daniel Zywietz, "Rethinking Globalization: A Modified Globalization Index," *Journal of International Development* 18:3 (2006): 331–50.

9   "The Globalization Index," *Foreign Policy* (November–December 2006): 75–81.

10 Betty Liu, "Cross-Border Partnerships," *Financial Times*, March 14, 2003: 9.

11 See Rodney C. Shrader, Benjamin M. Oviatt, and Patricia Phillips McDougall, "How New Ventures Exploit Trade-Offs among International Risk Factors: Lessons for the Accelerated Internationalization of the 21st Century," *Academy of Management Journal* 43:6 (2000): 1227–47; Ian Fillis, "The Internationalization Process of the Craft Microenterprise," *Journal of Developmental Entrepreneurship* 7:1 (2002): 25–43; Michael Copeland, "The Mighty Micro Multinational," *Business 2.0 Magazine*, July 28, 2006, n.p.

12 S. Tamer Cavusgil, "Extending the Reach of E-Business," *Marketing Management* (March–April 2002): 24–29.

13 Dan McGraw, "The Foreign Invasion of the American Game," *The Village Voice*, May 28–June 3, 2003 (accessed June 4, 2007).

14 Kerry Gildea, "U.S., Japan Review Options for Future Sea-Based Missile Defense Work," *Defense Daily International*, July 12, 2002: 1–2.

15 Michael M. Phillips, "G-8 Nations Shape Plan to Fight Diseases," *Wall Street Journal*, February 13, 2006: A8.

16 Thomas L. Friedman, "Moving with the Herd," *Computerworld*, January 15, 2001: 41–43; Daniele Archiburgi and Bengt-Ake Lundvall, eds., *The Globalizing Learning Economy* (Oxford: Oxford University Press, 2001).

17 For a long time, the group was the *G7*; it became the *G8* when Russia started to attend meetings.

18 Robert Wright, "Pirates Still Proving Scourge of the High Seas," *Financial Times*, August 12–13, 2006: 4.

19 Susan Carey, "Calculating Costs in the Clouds," *Wall Street Journal*, March 6, 2007: B1+.

20 Adam Thomson, "Costa Ricans Blame Plant's Closure on Spat with Venezuela," *Financial Times*, February 23, 2007: 4.

21 Lorraine Eden and Stefanie Lenway, "Introduction to the Symposium Multinationals: The Janus Face of Globalization," *Journal of International Business Studies* 32:3 (2001): 383–400.

22 Steve Lohr, "An Elder Challenges Outsourcing's Orthodoxy," *New York Times*, September 9, 2004: C1+; Paul A. Samuelson, "Where Ricardo and Mill Rebut and Confirm Arguments of Mainstream Economists Supporting Globalization," *The Journal of Economic Perspectives* 18:3 (Summer 2004): 135–47.

23 Bernhard G. Gunter and Rolph van der Hoeven, "The Social Dimension of Globalization: A Review of the Literature," *International Labour Review* 143:1/2 (2004): 7–43.

24 Jagdish Bhagwati, "Anti-Globalization: Why?" *Journal of Policy Modeling* 26:4 (2004): 439–64.

25 William M. Bulkeley, "IBM Documents Give Rare Look at 'Offshoring,' " *Wall Street Journal*, January 19, 2004: A1+.

26 Craig Karmin, "Offshoring Can Generate Jobs in the U.S.," *Wall Street Journal*, March 16, 2004: B1.

27 N. Gregory Mankiw and Phillip Swagel, "The Politics and Economics of Offshore Outsourcing," NBR Working Paper No. 12398 (July 2006).

28 Matthew J. Slaughter, "Globalization and Employment by U.S. Multinationals: A Framework and Facts," *Daily Tax Report*, March 26, 2004: 1–12.

29 Robert C. Feenstra and Gordon H. Hanson, "The Impact of Outsourcing and High-Technology Capital on Wages: Estimates for the United States, 1979–1990," *Quarterly Journal of Economics* 114:3 (1999): 907–940.

30 Doug Cameron, "US Airways Repatriates Manila Call Centre Jobs after Problems," *Financial Times*, February 22, 2006: 20; Linda Tucci, "Offshoring Has Long Way to Go," *CIO News Headlines*, June 2, 2005: n.p.; Alexandra Harney, "Travel Industry," *Financial Times*, September 2, 2004: 11.

31 Marcus Walker, "Just How Good Is Globalization?" *Wall Street Journal*, January 25, 2007: A10, referring to data from Morgan Stanley Research.

32 Deborah Solomon, "Federal Aid Does Little for Free Trade's Losers," *Wall Street Journal*, March 1, 2007: A1+.

33 Carlos Tejada, "Paradise Lost," *Wall Street Journal*, August 14, 2003: A1+.

34 Alan S. Blinder, "Offshoring: The Next Industrial Revolution," *Foreign Affairs* 85:2 (March-April 2006): 113–22; David Wessel and Bob Davis, "Working Theory," *Wall Street Journal*, March 28, 2007: A1+ (discussing studies by Alan S. Binder).

35 United Nations Conference on Trade and Development, *World Investment Report 2001: Promoting Linkages* (New York and Geneva: United Nations, 2001): 90–92.

36 National Association of Manufacturers, "Profit from Exporting," www.nam.org/s_nam/sec.asp?CID= 201746&DID=230317, referring to a 2007 SBA study on exporting for small business.

37 Phillip Hersh, "Sewing Circles," *Chicago Tribune*, July 15, 2003: n.p.

38 "Invest Italy: Auto Components," www.investinitaly.com/context_sectorprofiles02.jsp?ID_LINK=398&area=18.

39 Heather Berry, "Leaders, Laggards, and the Pursuit of Foreign Knowledge," *Strategic Management Journal* 27 (2006): 151–68.

40 Nery Ynclan, "Avon Is Opening the Door to Spanglish," *Miami Herald*, July 23, 2002: E1.

41 Suzanne Kapner, "Nestlé Says Emerging Markets Help It Show Rise in Profits," *New York Times*, August 23, 2001: W1.

42 Jonathan Birchall, "Tesco to Bring Its Own Suppliers to US," *Financial Times*, November 24, 2006: 21.

43 United Nations Conference on Trade and Development, *World Investment Report 2004: The Shift towards Services* (New York and Geneva: United Nations, 2004); United Nations Conference on Trade and Development, *World Investment Report 2006: FDI from Developing and Transition Economies: Implications for Development* (New York and Geneva: United Nations, 2004): 30–31.

44 Copeland, "The Mighty Micro Multinational."

45 Terry Hall, "New Zealand Seeks Lost Sheep," *Financial Times*, March 28, 2002: 36.

46 Linn Hirschberg, "Is the Face of America That of a Green Ogre?" *New York Times Magazine*, November 14, 2004: 90–94.

47 Gabriel Kahn, "How to Slow Down a Ferrari: Buy It," *Wall Street Journal*, May 8, 2007: B1+.

48 John Willman, "Multinationals," *Financial Times*, February 25, 2003: Comment & Analysis, ii.

49 Edward Luce, "Hard Sell to a Billion Consumers," *Financial Times*, April 25, 2002: 14.

50 David Wessel and Marcus Walker, "Good News for the Globe," *Wall Street Journal*, September 3, 2004: A7+.

51 Alan M. Rugman and Cecelia Brain, "Multinational Enterprises Are Regional, Not Global," *Multinational Business Review* 11:1 (2004): 3.

52 John Ralston Saul, "The Collapse of Globalism," *Harpers*, March 2004: 33–43; James Harding, "Globalisation's Children Strike Back," *Financial Times*, September 11, 2001: 4; Bob Davis, "Wealth of Nations," *Wall Street Journal*, March 29, 2004: A1; Harold James, *The End of Globalisation: Lessons from the Great Depression* (Cambridge, MA: Harvard University Press, 2001).

53 On the schism between those who thrive in a globalized environment and those who don't, see Jagdish Bhagwati, "Anti-Globalization: Why?" *Journal of Policy Modeling* 26:4 (2004): 439–64; Roger Sugden and James R. Wilson, "Economic Globalisation: Dialectics, Conceptualisation and Choice," *Contributions to Political Economy* 24:1 (2005): 13–32; and J. Ørstrøm Møller, "Wanted: A New Strategy for Globalization," *The Futurist* (January–February 2004): 20–22.

54 *Sources include the following:* We'd like to acknowledge the invaluable assistance of Brenda Yester, vice president of Carnival Cruise Lines. Other sources include Tom Stieghorst, "Consumers Squeezed; Cruise Lines Feel Pain," *Knight Ridder Tribune Business News*, March 14, 2007: 1; Martha Brannigan, "Cruise Lines Aim for Wider Appeal," *Knight Ridder Tribune Business News*, March 14, 2007: 1; "Carnival Scrubs Ship after Virus Sickens Nearly 700 Passengers," *Wall Street Journal*, November 20, 2006: n.p.; Cruise Lines International Association, "Cruise Industry Overview," Marketing Edition 2006, at www.cruising.org/press/overview%202006.cfm (accessed May 9, 2007); Margot Cohen, "A New Source of Cheap Ocean Treasure," *Wall Street Journal*, September 22, 2004: A17; "Carnival Cruise Line Profile," at www.cruise2.com/Profiles/Carnival.html (accessed November 17, 2004); David F. Carr, "Royal Treatment," *Baseline*, August 1, 2004: 58; "Who's Who in Cruising," *Caterer and Hotelkeeper*, February 26, 2004: 77; Donald Urquhart, "Greed and Corruption Rooted in Flag of Convenience System," *The Business Times Singapore*, March 9, 2001: n.p.; "Fall 2003: Shipbuilding Back on Course?" at www.CruiseIndustryNews.com-Cruise (accessed November 19, 2004); Daniel Grant, "Onboard Art," *American Artist*, March 2003: 18; Nicole Harris, "Ditching the Cruise Director," *Wall Street Journal*, April 22, 2004: D1+; Douglas Frantz, "Sovereign Islands," *Miami Herald*, February 19, 1999: A1+; Rana Foroohar et al., "The Road Less Traveled," *Newsweek*, May 26, 2003: 40; Jonathan Adams, "Vacations: Cruising Nowhere," *Newsweek*, July 14, 2003: 64; Cruise Lines International Association, "The Overview, Spring 2004," at msword/reports/overviews/spring04OV.doc.

An Atlas

Satellite television transmission now makes it commonplace for us to watch events as they unfold in other countries. Transportation and communication advances and government-to-government accords have contributed to our increasing dependence on foreign goods and markets. As this dependence grows, updated maps are a valuable tool. They can show the locations of population, economic wealth, production and markets; portray certain commonalities and differences among areas; and illustrate barriers that might inhibit trade. In spite of the usefulness of maps, a substantial number of people worldwide have a poor knowledge of how to interpret information on maps and even of how to find the location of events that affect their lives.

We urge you to use the following maps to build your awareness of geography.

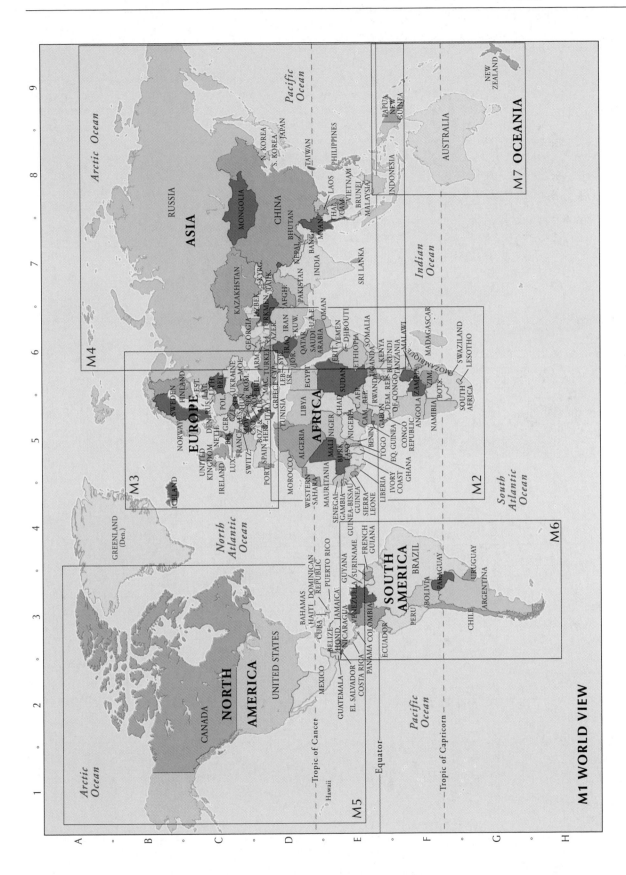

M1 WORLD VIEW

NORTH AMERICA

SOUTH AMERICA

EUROPE

AFRICA

ASIA

OCEANIA

M7 OCEANIA

Arctic Ocean

Pacific Ocean

North Atlantic Ocean

South Atlantic Ocean

Indian Ocean

Pacific Ocean

Arctic Ocean

Tropic of Cancer

Equator

Tropic of Capricorn

CANADA

UNITED STATES

MEXICO

GUATEMALA

EL SALVADOR

COSTA RICA

PANAMA

BELIZE

HOND.

NICARAGUA

BAHAMAS

CUBA

HAITI

JAMAICA

DOMINICAN REPUBLIC

PUERTO RICO

GREENLAND (Den.)

ECUADOR

COLOMBIA

VENEZUELA

GUYANA

SURINAME

FRENCH GUIANA

PERU

BOLIVIA

BRAZIL

PARAGUAY

CHILE

ARGENTINA

URUGUAY

ICELAND

NORWAY

SWEDEN

FINLAND

UNITED KINGDOM

IRELAND

NETH.

DEN.

GER.

POL.

BEL.

LUX.

FRANCE

SWITZ.

PORT.

SPAIN

ITALY

AUS.

CZE.

SLO.

HUN.

CRO.

BOZ.

HERZ.

MAC.

ROM.

GREECE

BUL.

MOL.

UKRAINE

EST.

LAT.

LITH.

BEL.

RUSSIA

GEORGIA

ARM.

AZER.

CYP.

TURKEY

SYR.

LEB.

ISR.

JOR.

IRAQ

IRAN

KUW.

QATAR

U.A.E.

SAUDI ARABIA

OMAN

YEMEN

KAZAKHSTAN

UZBEK.

KYRG.

TURKMEN.

TAJIK.

AFGH.

PAKISTAN

INDIA

NEPAL

BHUTAN

BANG.

MYAN.

SRI LANKA

CHINA

MONGOLIA

N. KOREA

S. KOREA

JAPAN

TAIWAN

THAI.

LAOS

VIETNAM

CAM.

PHILIPPINES

MALAYSIA

BRUNEI

INDONESIA

PAPUA NEW GUINEA

AUSTRALIA

NEW ZEALAND

MOROCCO

WESTERN SAHARA

ALGERIA

TUNISIA

LIBYA

EGYPT

MAURITANIA

MALI

NIGER

SENEGAL

GAMBIA

GUINEA-BISSAU

GUINEA

SIERRA LEONE

LIBERIA

IVORY COAST

BURK. FASO

GHANA

TOGO

BENIN

NIGERIA

CHAD

SUDAN

ERIT.

DJIBOUTI

ETHIOPIA

SOMALIA

C. AFR. REP.

CAM.

EQ. GUINEA

GABON

CONGO

DEM. REP. OF CONGO

UGANDA

KENYA

RWANDA

BURUNDI

TANZANIA

ANGOLA

ZAMBIA

MALAWI

MOZAMBIQUE

ZIM.

NAMIBIA

BOTS.

SOUTH AFRICA

SWAZILAND

LESOTHO

MADAGASCAR

Hawaii

M5

M3

M4

M2

M6

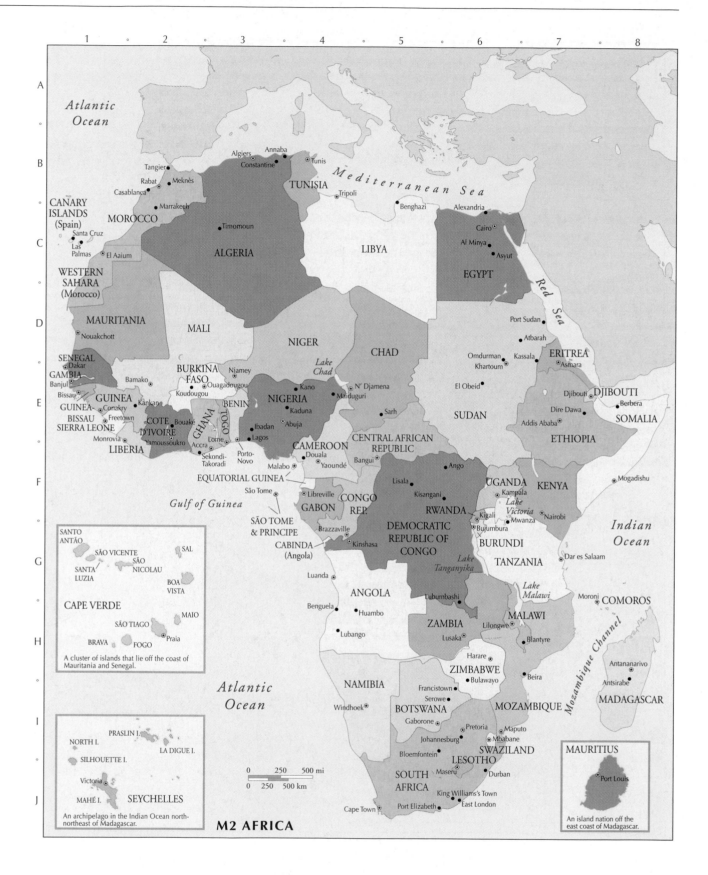

M2 AFRICA

M3 EUROPE

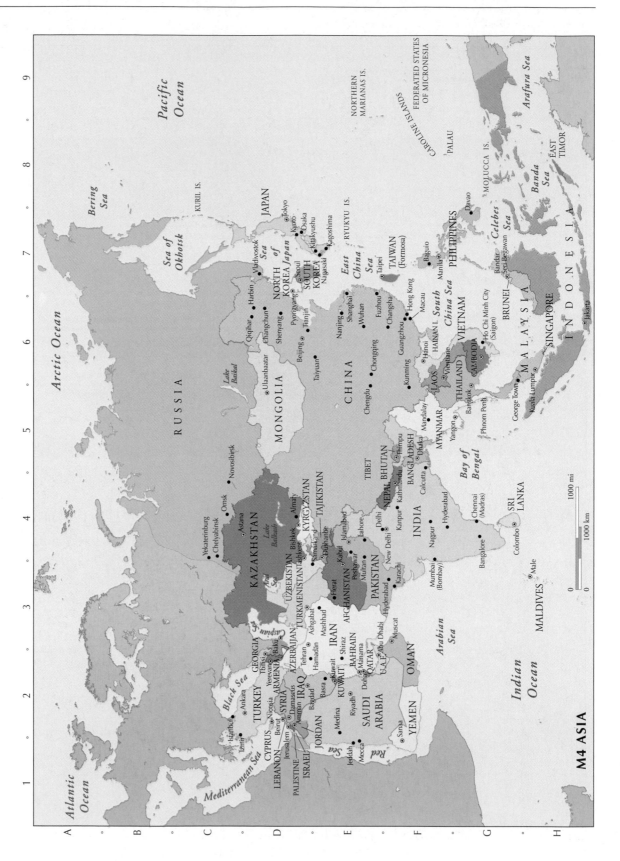

M4 ASIA

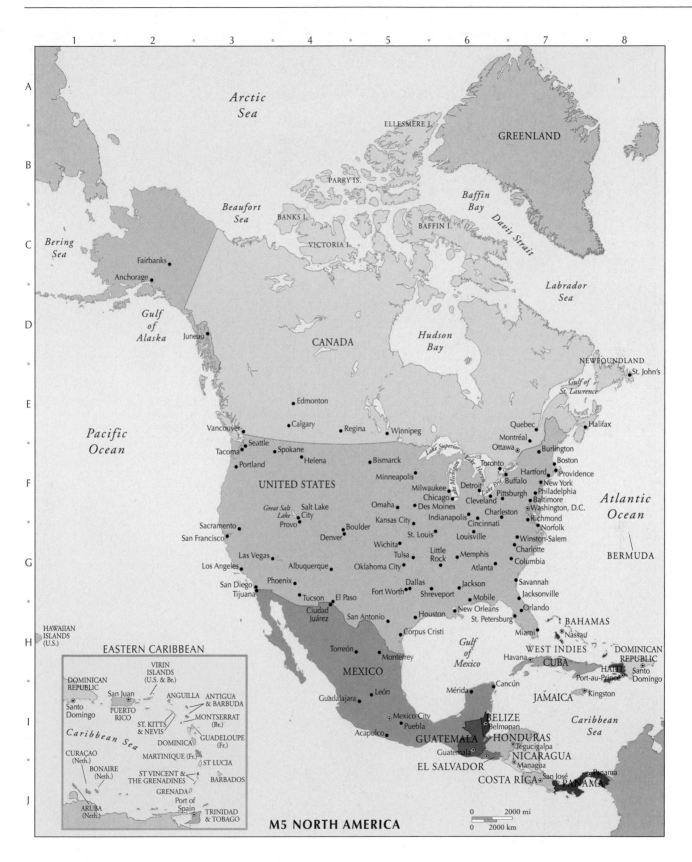

1 2 3 4 5 6 7 8

A

*Arctic
Sea*

ELLESMERE I.

GREENLAND

B

PARRY IS.

*Beaufort
Sea*

BANKS I.

*Baffin
Bay*

Davis Strait

BAFFIN I.

C

*Bering
Sea*

Fairbanks

Anchorage

VICTORIA I.

*Labrador
Sea*

D

*Gulf
of
Alaska*

Juneau

CANADA

*Hudson
Bay*

NEWFOUNDLAND
St. John's

E

*Pacific
Ocean*

Edmonton

Calgary

Regina

Winnipeg

*Gulf of
St. Lawrence*

Quebec

Halifax

Vancouver

Montréal

Burlington

Seattle

Spokane

Ottawa

Tacoma

Helena

Bismarck

Lake Superior

Toronto

Boston

Portland

Minneapolis

Lake Michigan

Lake Huron

Detroit

Lake Erie

Buffalo

Hartford

Providence

F

UNITED STATES

Milwaukee

Chicago

Pittsburgh

New York

Philadelphia

Cleveland

Baltimore

*Atlantic
Ocean*

Omaha

Des Moines

Washington, D.C.

*Great Salt
Lake*

Salt Lake
City

Charleston

Richmond

Sacramento

Provo

Kansas City

Indianapolis

Cincinnati

Norfolk

Boulder

St. Louis

Louisville

Winston-Salem

San Francisco

Denver

Wichita

Charlotte

BERMUDA

G

Las Vegas

Tulsa

Little
Rock

Memphis

Columbia

Los Angeles

Albuquerque

Oklahoma City

Atlanta

Savannah

San Diego

Phoenix

Dallas

Jackson

Jacksonville

Tijuana

Tucson

El Paso

Fort Worth

Shreveport

Mobile

Orlando

Ciudad
Juárez

San Antonio

Houston

New Orleans

St. Petersburg

BAHAMAS

H

HAWAIIAN
ISLANDS
(U.S.)

Corpus Cristi

Miami

Nassau

*Gulf
of
Mexico*

WEST INDIES

DOMINICAN
REPUBLIC

Torreón

Havana

CUBA

HAITI

Santo
Domingo

Monterrey

Port-au-Prince

EASTERN CARIBBEAN

VIRIN
ISLANDS
(U.S. & Br.)

Mérida

Cancún

JAMAICA

Kingston

DOMINICAN
REPUBLIC

San Juan

ANGUILLA

ANTIGUA
& BARBUDA

Guadalajara

León

I

Santo
Domingo

PUERTO
RICO

ST. KITTS
& NEVIS

MONTSERRAT
(Br.)

*Caribbean
Sea*

Mexico City

BELIZE

Belmopan

*Caribbean
Sea*

Caribbean Sea

DOMINICA

GUADELOUPE
(Fr.)

Acapulco

Puebla

GUATEMALA

HONDURAS

CURAÇAO
(Neth.)

MARTINIQUE (Fr.)

ST LUCIA

Tegucigalpa

NICARAGUA

BONAIRE
(Neth.)

ST VINCENT &
THE GRENADINES

BARBADOS

Guatemala

Managua

EL SALVADOR

GRENADA

ARUBA
(Neth.)

Port of
Spain

TRINIDAD
& TOBAGO

San José

PANAMA

COSTA RICA

Panama

M5 NORTH AMERICA

0   2000 mi

0   2000 km

MEXICO

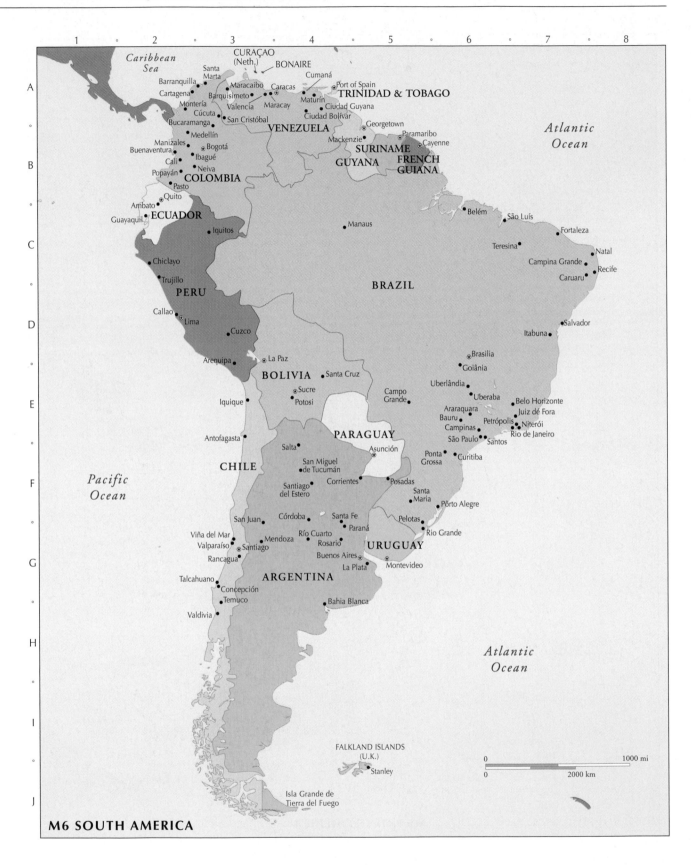

M6 SOUTH AMERICA

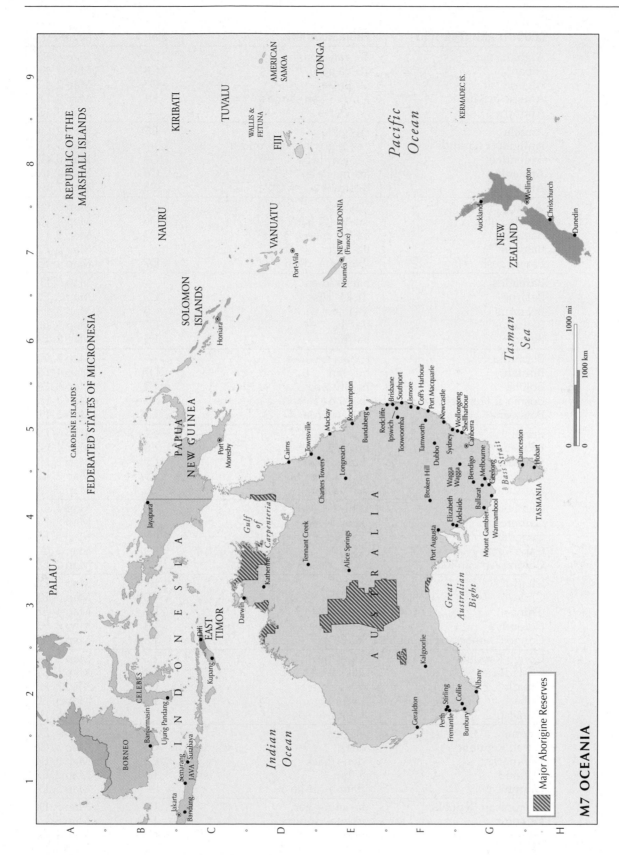

Major Aborigine Reserves

M7 OCEANIA

REPUBLIC OF THE
MARSHALL ISLANDS

KIRIBATI

TUVALU

NAURU

WALLIS &
FETUNA

FIJI

VANUATU

AMERICAN
SAMOA

TONGA

*Pacific
Ocean*

KERMADEC IS.

NEW CALEDONIA
(France)
Nouméa⊛

Port-Vila⊛

CAROLINE ISLANDS

FEDERATED STATES OF MICRONESIA

PALAU

M I C R O N E S I A

SOLOMON
ISLANDS

Honiara

PAPUA
NEW GUINEA

Port⊛
Moresby

Jayapura

M E L A N E S I A

I N D O N E S I A

BORNEO

CELEBES

Banjarmasin

Ujung Pandang

Jakarta
Bandung

Semarang

JAVA Surabaya

Kupang

Bali
EAST
TIMOR

*Indian
Ocean*

Darwin

Katherine

Tennant Creek

Alice Springs

*Gulf
of
Carpentaria*

A U S T R A L I A

Cairns

Townsville

Charters Towers

Longreach

Mackay

Rockhampton

Bundaberg

Redcliffe
Brisbane
Ipswich Southport
Toowoomba Lismore
Coff's Harbour
Port Macquarie
Tamworth Newcastle
Dubbo Sydney
Wollongong
Canberra⊛ Shellharbour
Wagga
Wagga
Broken Hill

Port Augusta

Geraldton

Perth Stirling
Fremantle Collie
Bunbury Albany

Kalgoorlie

*Great
Australian
Bight*

Elizabeth
Adelaide

Mount Gambier
Warrnambool

Ballarat
Bendigo
Geelong Melbourne

Bass Strait

Launceston
Hobart

TASMANIA

*Tasman
Sea*

NEW
ZEALAND

Auckland

Wellington⊛
Christchurch

Dunedin

1000 mi

1000 km

0

0

COUNTRY AND TERRITORY	PRONUNCIATION	MAP 1	MAPS 2–7
Afghanistan	af-ˈgan-ə-ˌstan	D7	Map 4, E3
Albania	al-ˈbā-nē-ə	C5	Map 3, I5
Algeria	al-ˈjir-ē-ə	D5	Map 2, C3
American Samoa	ə-merˈi-kən sə-mōˈə	F9	Map 7, D9
Andorra	an-ˈdȯr-ə	—	Map 3, H2
Angola	an-ˈgō-lə	E5	Map 2, G4
Antigua & Barbuda	an-ˈtē-g(w)ə / bär-ˈbüd-ə	—	Map 5, I3
Argentina	ˌˌär-jen-ˈtē-nə	G3	Map 6, G3
Armenia	är-ˈmē-ne-ə	C6	Map 4, D2
Australia	ȯ-ˈstrāl-yə	G8	Map 7, E4
Austria	ˈȯs-trē-ə	C5	Map 3, G4
Azerbaijan	ˈaz-ər-ˈbī-ˈjän	D6	Map 4, D2
Bahamas	bə-häˈ-məz	D3	Map 5, H7
Bahrain	bä-ˈrān	—	Map 4, E2
Bangladesh	ˈbänJ-glə-ˈdesh	D7	Map 4, F5
Barbados	bär-ˈbād-əs	—	Map 5, J3
Belarus	ˈbē-lə-ˈrüs	C5	Map 3, F6
Belgium	ˈbel-jəm	C5	Map 3, F3
Belize	bə-ˈlēz	D2	Map 5, I6
Benin	bə-ˈnin	E5	Map 2, E3
Bermuda	(ˈ)bər-ˈmyüd-ə	—	Map 5, G8
Bhutan	bü-ˈtan	D7	Map 4, F5
Bolivia	bə-ˈliv-ē-ə	F3	Map 6, E4
Bosnia & Herzegovina	ˈbäz-nē-ə / ˈhert-sə-gō-ˈvē-nə	D5	Map 3, H5
Botswana	bät-ˈswän-ə	F5	Map 2, I5
Brazil	brə-ˈzil	F3	Map 6, D6
Brunei	brōō-nīˈ	E8	Map 4, G7
Bulgaria	ˈbəl-ˈgar-ē-ə	D5	Map 3, H6
Burkina Faso	buˈr-ˈkē-nə-ˈfaˈ-sō	E5	Map 2, E2
Burundi	buˈ-ˈrün-dē	E6	Map 2, G6
Cambodia	kam-ˈbd-ē-ə	E7	Map 4, G5
Cameroon	ˈkam-ə-ˈrün	E5	Map 2, F4
Canada	ˈkan-əd-ə	C2	Map 5, E5
Cape Verde Islands	ˈvard	—	Map 2, G1
Central African Rep.		E5	Map 2, E5
Chad	ˈchad	E5	Map 2, D5
Chile	ˈchil-ē	G3	Map 6, F3
China	ˈchī-nə	D8	Map 4, E5
Colombia	kə-ˈləm-bē-ə	E3	Map 6, B3
Congo (Democratic Republic)	ˈkänJ(ˈ)gō	E5	Map 2, G5
Congo Republic	ˈkänJ(ˈ)gō	E5	Map 2, F4
Costa Rica	ˈkäs-tə-ˈrē-kə	E2	Map 5, J7
Croatia	krō-ˈā-sh(ē)ə	D5	Map 3, H5
Cuba	ˈkyü-bə	E3	Map 5, H7
Curaçao	ˈk(y)ür-ə-ˈsō	—	Map 5, J1
Cyprus	ˈsī-prəs	D6	Map 4, D2
Czech Republic	ˈchek	C5	Map 3, G5
Denmark	ˈden-ˈmärk	C5	Map 3, E4
Djibouti	jə-ˈbüt-ē	E6	Map 2, E7
Dominica	ˈdäm-ə-ˈnē-kə	—	Map 5, I3
Dominican Republic	də-ˈmin-i-kən	E3	Map 5, H8
Ecuador	ˈek-wə-ˈdȯ(ə)r	E3	Map 6, C2
Egypt	ˈē-jəpt	D5	Map 2, C6
El Salvador	el-ˈsal-və-ˈdȯ(ə)r	E2	Map 5, I6
Equatorial Guinea	ē-kwaˈ-tōr-ēal ˈgi-nē	E5	Map 2, F4
Eritrea	ˈer-ə-ˈtrē-ə	E6	Map 2, E6
Estonia	e-ˈstō-nē-ə	C5	Map 3, E6

COUNTRY AND TERRITORY	PRONUNCIATION	MAP 1	MAPS 2–7
Ethiopia	ˌē-thē-ˈō-pē-ə	E6	Map 2, E7
Falkland Islands	ˈfȯ(l)-klənd	—	Map 6, J4
Fiji	ˈfē-jē	—	Map 7, D8
Finland	ˈfin-lənd	B5	Map 3, C6
France	ˈfran(t)s	C5	Map 3, G3
French Guiana	gē-ˈan-ə	E3	Map 6, B5
Gabon	ga-ˈbōⁿ	E5	Map 2, F4
Gambia	ˈgam-bē-ə	E4	Map 2, E1
Georgia	ˈjȯr-jə	C6	Map 4, D2
Germany	ˈjerm-(ə-)nē	C5	Map 3, F4
Ghana	ˈgän-ə	E5	Map 2, E2
Greece	ˈgrēs	D5	Map 3, I6
Greenland	ˈgrēn-lənd	A4	Map 5, E7
Grenada	grə-nāˈdə	—	Map 5, J3
Guatemala	ˈgwät-ə-ˈmäl-ə	E2	Map 5, I6
Guinea	ˈgin-ē	E4	Map 2, E1
Guinea-Bissau	ˈgin-ē-bis-ˈauˈ	E4	Map 2, E1
Guyana	gī-ˈan-ə	E3	Map 6, B4
Haiti	ˈhāt-ē	E3	Map 5, H8
Honduras	hän-ˈd(y)uˈr-əs	E2	Map 5, I7
Hong Kong	ˈhänJ-ˈkänJ	—	Map 4, F6
Hungary	ˈhənJ-g(ə)rē	C5	Map 3, G5
Iceland	ˈī-slənd	B4	Map 3, B1
India	ˈin-dê-ə	D7	Map 4, F4
Indonesia	ˈin-də-ˈnē-zhə	E8	Map 4, H7; Map 7, B3
Iran	i-ˈrän	D6	Map 4, E3
Iraq	i-ˈräk	D6	Map 4, D2
Ireland	ˈī(ə)r-lənd	C5	Map 3, F1
Israel	ˈiz-rē-əl	D6	Map 4, D2
Italy	ˈit-əl-ē	D6	Map 3, H4
Ivory Coast	ˈīˈvə-rē	E5	Map 2, E2
Jamaica	jə-ˈmā-kə	E3	Map 5, I7
Japan	jə-ˈpan	D8	Map 4, D7
Jordan	ˈjȯrd-ən	D6	Map 4, D2
Kazakhstan	kə-ˈzak-ˈstan	D7	Map 4, D4
Kenya	ˈken-yə	E6	Map 7, F7
Kiribati	kîr-ì-bàsˈ	—	Map 7, B8
Korea, North	kə-ˈrē-ə	D8	Map 4, D7
Korea, South	kə-ˈrē-ə	D8	Map 4, D7
Kosovo	ˈKo-sō-vō	C5	Map M3, H6
Kuwait	kə-ˈwāt	D6	Map 4, E2
Kyrgyzstan	kîr-gē-stänˈ	D7	Map 4, D4
Laos	ˈlauˈs	D7	Map 4, F5
Latvia	ˈlat-vē-ə	C5	Map 3, E6
Lebanon	ˈleb-ə-nən	D6	Map 4, D2
Lesotho	lə-ˈsō-(ˈ)tō	F6	Map 2, J6
Liberia	lī-ˈbir-ē-ə	E5	Map 2, F2
Libya	ˈlib-ē-ə	D5	Map 2, C4
Liechtenstein	lìkˈtən-stīnˈ	—	Map 3, G4
Lithuania	ˈlith-(y)ə-ˈwā-nē-ə	C5	Map 3, E6
Luxembourg	ˈlək-səm-ˈbərg	C5	Map 3, G3
Macedonia	ˈmas-ə-ˈdō-nyə	D6	Map 3, I6
Madagascar	ˈmad-ə-ˈgas-kər	F6	Map 2, I8
Malawi	mə-ˈlä-wē	F6	Map 2, H6

COUNTRY AND TERRITORY	PRONUNCIATION	MAP 1	MAPS 2–7
Malaysia	mə-ˈlā-zh(ē-)ə	E8	Map 4, G6
Maldives	môlˈdīvz	—	Map 4, H3
Mali	ˈmäl-ē	D5	Map 2, D2
Malta	ˈmȯl-tə	—	Map 3, J5
Marshall Islands	märˈshəl	—	Map 7, A8
Mauritania	ˈmȯr-ə-ˈtā-nē-ə	D5	Map 2, D1
Mauritius	mȯ-ˈrísh'əs	—	Map 2, J8
Mexico	ˈmek-si-ˈkō	D2	Map 5, I5
Micronesia	mīˈkrō-nēˈzhə	—	Map 7, A5
Moldova	mäl-ˈdō-və	D6	Map 3, G7
Mongolia	män-ˈgōl-yə	D8	Map 4, D5
Morocco	mə-ˈräk-(ˈ)ō	D5	Map 2, B2
Mozambique	ˈmō-zəm-ˈbēk	F6	Map 2, H6
Myanmar	ˈmyän-ˈmär	E7	Map 4, F5
Namibia	nə-ˈmib-ē-ə	F5	Map 2, I4
Naura	näˈ-ü-rü	—	Map 7, B7
Nepal	nə-ˈpȯl	D7	Map 4, E4
Netherlands	ˈneth-ər-lən(d)z	C5	Map 3, F3
New Caledonia	ˈkal-ə-ˈdō-nyə	—	Map 7, E7
New Zealand	ˈzē-lənd	G9	Map 7, H7
Nicaragua	ˈnik-ə-ˈräg-wə	E3	Map 5, I7
Niger	ˈnī-jər	E5	Map 2, D4
Nigeria	nī-ˈjir-ē-ə	E5	Map 2, E4
Norway	ˈnȯ(ə)r-ˈwā	C5	Map 3, D3
Oman	ō-ˈmän	E6	Map 4, F2
Pakistan	ˈpak-i-ˈstan	D7	Map 4, E3
Palau	pä-louˈ	—	Map 7, A3
Palestine	pa-lə-ˈstīn	—	Map 4, D1
Panama	ˈpan-ə-ˈmä	E3	Map 5, J8
Papua New Guinea	ˈpap-yə-wə	F9	Map 7, C5
Paraguay	ˈpar-ə-ˈgwī	F3	Map 6, E4
Peru	pə-ˈrü	F3	Map 6, D2
Philippines	ˈfil-ə-ˈpēnz	E8	Map 4, F7
Poland	ˈpō-lənd	D5	Map 3, F5
Portugal	ˈpōr-chi-gəl	D5	Map 3, I1
Puerto Rico	ˈpōrt-ə-ˈrē(ˈ)kō	E3	Map 5, I2
Qatar	ˈkät-ər	D6	Map 4, E2
Romania	rō-ˈā-nē-ə	D5	Map 3, H6
Russia	ˈrəsh-ə	C7	Map 3, D7; Map 4, C5
Rwanda	ruˈ-ˈän-də	E6	Map 2, F6
St. Kitts & Nevis	ˈkits / ˈnē-vəs	—	Map 5, I3
St. Lucia	sānt-ˈlü-shə	—	Map 5, I3
St. Vincent and the Grenadines	grènˈə-dēnzˈ	—	Map 5, J3
San Marino	sàn mə-rēˈnō	—	Map 3, H4
São Tomé and Príncipe	soun tōə-mèˈprēnˈ-sēpə	—	Map 2, F3
Saudi Arabia	ˈsau'd-ē	E6	Map 4, E2
Senegal	ˈsen-i-ˈg'l	E4	Map 2, D1
Serbia & Montenegro	ˈsər-bē-ə / ˈmän-tə-ˈnē-grō	D5	Map 3, H2
Seychelles	sā-shèlzˈ	—	Map 2, J1
Sierra Leone	sē-ˈer-ə-lē-ˈōn	E4	Map 2, E1
Singapore	ˈsinJ-(g)ə-ˈpō(ə)r	—	Map 4, H6
Slovakia	slō-ˈväk-ē-ə	C5	Map 3, G5
Slovenia	slō-ˈvēn-ē-ə	C5	Map 3, H5
Solomon Islands	ˈsäl-ə-mən	—	Map 7, C6
Somalia	sō-ˈmäl-ē-ə	E6	Map 2, F8

COUNTRY AND TERRITORY	PRONUNCIATION	MAP 1	MAPS 2–7
South Africa	ˈa-fri-kə	F6	Map 2, J5
Spain	ˈspāpn	C5	Map 3, I1
Sri Lanka	(ˈ)srē-ˈlänJ-kə	E7	Map 4, G4
Sudan	sü-ˈdan	E6	Map 2, E6
Suriname	suˈr-ə-ˈnäm-ə	E3	Map 6, B5
Swaziland	ˈswäz-ē-ˈland	F6	Map 2, I6
Sweden	ˈswēd-ən	B5	Map 3, C5
Switzerland	ˈswit-sər-lənd	C5	Map 3, G4
Syria	ˈsir-ē-ə	D6	Map 4, D2
Taiwan	ˈtī-ˈwän	D8	Map 4, E7
Tajikistan	tä-ˈji-ki-ˈstan	D7	Map 4, E4
Tanzania	ˈtan-zə-ˈnē-ə	F6	Map 2, G6
Thailand	ˈtī-land	E8	Map 4, F5
Togo	ˈtō(ˈ)gō	E5	Map 2, E3
Tonga	ˈtän-gə	—	Map 7, D9
Trinidad & Tobago	ˈtrin-ə-ˈdad / tə-ˈbā-(ˈ)gō	—	Map 5, J3
Tunisia	t(y)ü-ˈnē-zh(ē-)ə	D5	Map 2, B4
Turkey	ˈtər-kē	D6	Map 4, D2
Turkmenistan	tûrkˈ-men-i-stànˈ	D6	Map 4, D3
Tuvalu	tüˈ-vä-lü	—	Map 7, C9
Uganda	(y)ü-ˈgan-də	E6	Map 2, F6
Ukraine	yü-ˈkrān	C6	Map 3, F7
United Arab Emirates	yoo-nīˈtid à rˈəb i-mîrˈits	D6	Map 4, E2
United Kingdom	kingˈdəm	C5	Map 3, F2
United States	yuˈ-ˈnīt-əd-ˈstāts	D2	Map 5, F5
Uruguay	ˈ(y)uˈr-ə-gwī	G3	Map 6, G5
Uzbekistan	(ˈ)uˈz-ˈbek-i-ˈstan	C6	Map 4, D3
Vanuatu	van-ə-ˈwät-(ˈ)ü	—	Map 7, D7
Vatican City	vàtˈ ì-kən	—	Map 3, H4
Venezuela	ˈven-əz(-ə)-ˈwā-lə	E3	Map 6, A4
Vietnam	vē-ˈet-ˈnäm	E8	Map 4, G6
Western Sahara	sə-hârˈə	D4	Map 2, C1
Yemen	ˈyem-ən	E6	Map 4, F2
Zambia	ˈzam-bē-ə	F5	Map 2, H5
Zimbabwe	zim-ˈbäb-wē	F6	Map 2, H6

chapter two

The Cultural Environments Facing Business

Objectives

- To understand methods for learning about cultural environments

- To analyze the major causes of cultural difference and change

- To discuss behavioral factors influencing countries' business practices

- To understand cultural guidelines for companies that operate internationally

To change customs is a difficult thing.

—Lebanese proverb

CASE: The Java Lounge—Adjusting to Saudi Arabian Culture

Saudi Arabia (see Map 2.1) is a land of contrasts and paradoxes.[1] It boasts supermodern cities, but strict religious convictions and ancient social customs often clash with the reality of the modern world. Granted, Saudi authorities sometimes allow some latitude in the enforcement of laws and customs. In addition, the observance of some customs has become more lax. Even so, because standards of enforcement

conservative than those of Saudi Arabia. All had experienced foreign restaurants and sampled foreign nightlife and reasoned there were perhaps enough Saudis like themselves to support a restaurant/lounge like those they knew abroad. However, because they weren't 100 percent sure, they hired a firm of Lebanese consultants to research their business concept.

MAP 2.1 Saudi Arabia and the Arabian Peninsula

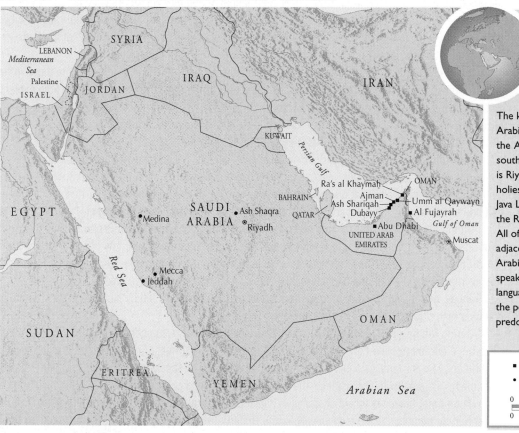

The kingdom of Saudi Arabia comprises most of the Arabian Peninsula in southwest Asia. The capital is Riyadh, and Mecca is the holiest city in Islam. The Java Lounge is located in the Red Sea port of Jeddah. All of the country's adjacent neighbors are also Arabic—that is, the people speak Arabic as a first language. All the nations on the peninsula are predominantly Islamic.

■ Emirates
● Major cities

0   400 mi
0   400 km

and observance vary substantially (whether by industry or geographic area), both Saudis and foreigners are often perplexed about acceptable personal and business behavior. Foreigners, moreover, often find Saudi laws and customs at odds with their own value systems.

Against this backdrop of cross-cultural uncertainty, four young Saudis wondered if the time was ripe for opening a restaurant/lounge catering to an affluent clientele. All four had lived and studied abroad, and three of them had ties to Arab countries whose customs were less

Ordinarily, market research can be difficult in Saudi Arabia. Researchers, for example, can't rely on family-focused interviews because of customs limiting male–female interaction. Saudis also view the home as private and regard questions about families as rude and invasive. In this case, researchers managed to interview Saudi families by getting permission to approach them in restaurants. How did they identify the best people to approach—namely, diners who appeared to be affluent and well traveled? Given that women must wear robes called *abayas* and men customarily wear robes called *thobes,* only people familiar with Saudi society were likely able to determine the economic status of people in restaurants.

Primarily, then, researchers noted people's *demeanor*—their manners and the general way in which they comported themselves. In addition, they distinguished between custom-made and off-the-rack robes and noted such things as the quality of wristwatches (which typically show beneath the long sleeves of traditional robes) and the care with which men keep their beards. When they were done, they concluded there was indeed sufficient market potential for the kind of business their clients had in mind.

As a result, the four partners opened the Java Lounge, an upscale 250-seat establishment, in 2003. They chose the city of Jeddah because it was a port and, as such, it enjoyed more contact with foreigners and was less conservative than much of the rest of the country. In the capital of Riyadh, for instance, women traditionally wear *garhas* that cover their faces; in Jeddah, where dress codes are more relaxed, they don't. All in all, the Java Lounge is not much different from modern first-class restaurants in any of the world's major cities. The French chef prepares the kinds of dishes found on the menus of the finest restaurants in Europe or North America.

But make no mistake about it: Operations at the Java Lounge differ considerably from those in restaurants outside Saudi Arabia. For one thing, the entire staff is male—a fact that may need a little explanation. In 2000, the Saudi government ratified an international agreement eliminating discrimination against women. Rules governing what women can and cannot do, however, remain quite rigid (especially when males are present), and to outsiders, they may also seem paradoxical. On the one hand, for example, although they are not permitted to drive (mobility increases the opportunity for improper behavior), women now outnumber men in Saudi universities (which are separate for men and women). Women also own about 20 percent of all Saudi businesses (most of which can sell only to female customers), and the CEO of one of the country's largest concerns, the Olayan Financing Company, is a woman.

On the other hand, while women comprise a large portion of Saudi teachers and doctors, they account for only about 7 percent of the total workforce. They cannot operate private law or architectural firms, nor can they be engineers. They can work alongside men in only a few professions, such as medicine and, more recently, the hotel and banking fields. If they work where men also work, they must use separate entrances, and they're separated from male coworkers by partitions. If they have to deal with male clerks, adult male relatives must serve as chaperones.

During the day, men coming to the Java Lounge without female accompaniment must use a separate entrance and sit upstairs, out of sight of families and female groups on the ground floor. In the evening, both floors are for families only. As a matter of fact, this sort of separation occurs in all Saudi retail establishments. Paradoxically, for instance, the sexes mix at the food court of Jeddah's largest shopping mall. At the same time, however, mixed shopping is allowed at upscale department stores like Saks Fifth Avenue and Harvey Nichols (based, respectively, in the United States and the United Kingdom) only on the lower floors, where all salespeople are men (even those specializing in such products as cosmetics and bras) and where there are no changing rooms or places to try cosmetics. On the upper floors, meanwhile, stores often maintain special floors for women only, where female shoppers can check their *abayas* and shop in jeans, spandex, or whatever they choose. One problem: Because male managers can visit these floors only when the store is closed, they are limited in their ability to observe operations.

If you're from a country that maintains more or less strict separation between religion and the state, you'll probably find the pervasiveness of religious culture in Saudi Arabia a little daunting. Religious proscriptions prevent the Java Lounge from serving pork products or alcohol, and live music is also prohibited. Because Saudi Arabia has an active black market for alcohol, employees must ensure that customers do not bring their own. If authorities detect consumption of alcohol on the premises, the Java Lounge stands to lose its operating license. During the holy period of Ramadan, when people fast during the day, the restaurant is allowed to serve customers only in the evening.

Other companies are also affected by the pervasive religious culture of Saudi Arabia. One importer, for example, was forced to halt sales of the children's game Pokémon because Saudi authorities feared it might encourage the un-Islamic practice of gambling. Starbucks franchisees had to remove part of the company logo because Saudi authorities objected to the public display of a woman's face. Coty Beauty does without the faces of models on point-of-purchase displays, and clothing retailers must remove the heads and hands of mannequins and keep them properly clad.

Many companies voluntarily adjust to Saudi rules as a matter of customer goodwill. Harvey Nichols, for example, has converted revenue-generating space into an area for prayer. During the five times per day when Muslim men are called to prayer, McDonald's dims its lights, closes its doors, and suspends service. During Ramadan, many stores shift operating hours to evenings.

Of course, not all business-related adjustments are due to religious principles. In most cultures, personal interactions are often tricky, and interactions between Saudis and non-Saudis are no exception. Here's an interesting example. British publisher Parris-Rogers International (PRI) dispatched two salesmen to Saudi Arabia. Because PRI paid them on commission, they adopted the strategy of moving aggressively, figuring they could make the same number of calls—and sales—per day as they made in Britain. Back home, they were also used to eight-hour workdays, the undivided attention of potential clients, and conversations devoted to business transactions. To them, in other words, time was money.

In Saudi Arabia, however, they soon found that appointments seldom began on time and most of them took place at local cafés over casual cups of coffee. As far as they were concerned, Saudis spent too much time on idle chitchat, and to make matters worse, they preferred talking to personal acquaintances to getting down to business. Eventually, both salesmen began showing their irritation at nonbusiness conversations and impromptu interruptions, and before long, their Saudi counterparts came to regard them as rude and impatient, and their employer had to recall them.

Foreign workers can also be traumatized by certain Saudi practices, especially when it comes to legal sanctions. Not only are there patrols to police female apparel, but hands and heads are occasionally cut off in public. Passersby are expected to observe the execution of these punishments, some of which are occasioned by crimes that don't constitute offenses in other countries (such as the public beheading, in 2002, of three homosexual men).

Rules of behavior may also be hard to comprehend because of the ways in which religious and legal rules have been rendered suitable to certain contemporary situations. Islamic law, for instance, forbids charging interest and the selling of accident insurance (strict Islamic doctrine holds there are no accidents, only preordained acts of God). In the case of mortgages, the Saudi government gets around the proscription by offering interest-free loans. This solution has worked well enough when the country is awash with oil revenue, but when oil prices fall, would-be homeowners must wait years for a loan. As for accident insurance, the government simply eliminated the prohibition because Saudi businesses, like businesses everywhere, need the coverage.

Such flexibility is particularly common when it comes to dealing with foreigners and foreign companies. Saudis, for instance, are more lenient toward visiting female executives than they are toward Saudi women. Whereas they don't allow Saudi women to work as flight attendants on Saudi Arabian Airlines (where they would have to work alongside men), they permit women from other Arab countries to do so. In foreign investment compounds, where almost everyone is a foreigner, religious patrols make exceptions to most strict religious prescriptions.

Before we leave Saudi Arabia, let's return to the Java Lounge, where we're happy to report the business has been successful from the start. Why? Primarily because the entrepreneurs who started it suspected that Saudi Arabia was home to an affluent niche of potential consumers who wanted a restaurant offering certain Western-style amenities—and who spent the time and money to do the research necessary to find out if they were right.

In fact, there are enough such people in the country to sustain a market for Parisian haute couture. Even though Saudi Arabia prohibits fashion magazines and movies, this clientele knows what is and isn't fashionable. Women buy items from designer collections, which they wear abroad or, if in Saudi Arabia, in front of husbands and other women. Underneath their *abayas,* they often sport expensive jewelry, makeup, and clothing. When traveling abroad, Saudi men also favor the latest high-end fashions. (Where do Saudi

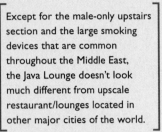

Except for the male-only upstairs section and the large smoking devices that are common throughout the Middle East, the Java Lounge doesn't look much different from upscale restaurant/lounges located in other major cities of the world.

men and women get their contemporary fashion sense? For one thing, although satellite dishes are also forbidden, it's estimated that two-thirds of Saudi homes have them. For another, Internet usage is widespread and growing among upper-income Saudis.)

Finally, the owners of the Java Lounge also realized that, as more Saudis interact with foreigners and the country strives for economic growth, there will be changes in domestic cultural and social values. At the 2004 Jeddah Economic Forum, for instance, a female Saudi delivered the keynote address—an event unthinkable only a few years earlier (and condemned by the nation's highest religious authority). Bear in mind, however, that such change tends to be sporadic, more so in some parts of the country and among people of certain income and educational levels. Right now, conditions are rewarding the foresight of the Java Lounge's entrepreneurs, but they remain carefully attuned to a variety of cultural and social norms that still characterize life in Saudi Arabia.

Introduction

Our opening case shows how important it is for companies to understand and adjust to ever-changing operating environments. Both the Java Lounge, a domestic company, and Harvey Nichols, a foreign company, operate successfully in Saudi Arabia because each is sensitive to the Saudi operating environment. Figure 2.1 shows how culture is an integral part of a nation's operating environment. **Culture** refers to learned norms based on the values, attitudes, and beliefs of a group of people. Culture is sometimes an elusive topic to study. Why? Because people belong to different groups with different "cultures"—groups based on nationality, ethnicity, religion, gender, work organization, profession, age, political party membership, and income level. (You've undoubtedly heard the term *youth culture*, which refers to a group designated by age.) In this chapter, we emphasize the nature of *national cultures*. At the same time, however, we also explore the importance of other cultural memberships, especially as they differ from country to country.

CONCEPT CHECK

In Chapter 1, we explain that, as *behavioral factors*, values, attitudes, and beliefs can be studied as keys both to cultural conditions and to ways of developing suitable business practices.

FIGURE 2.1 **Cultural Factors Affecting International Business Operations**

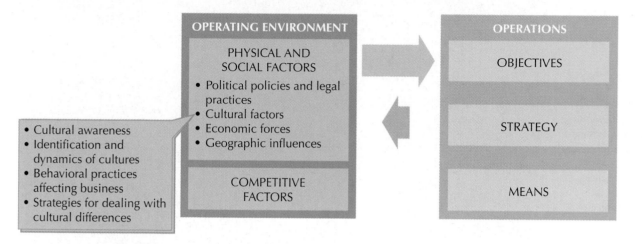

THE PEOPLE FACTOR

Business involves *people:* Every business employs, sells to, buys from, and is owned and regulated by people. International business, of course, involves people from different cultures. Every business function, therefore—managing a workforce, marketing and transporting output, purchasing supplies, dealing with regulators, securing funds—is subject to potential cultural differences.

Cultural Diversity In Chapter 1, we explained that companies become international to create value for their organizations and observed that one means to this end is the acquisition of foreign assets, including knowledge-based resources. Another means of gaining global competitive advantage is fostering cultural diversity. By bringing together people of diverse backgrounds and experience, companies often gain a deeper knowledge about products and services and ways in which to produce and deliver them. At companies like PepsiCo and IBM, executives report that much of their recent growth has been a result of greater workforce diversity.[2] As we see in the next few sections, however, the process of bringing together people with different backgrounds and perspectives is fraught with difficulties.

Cultural Collision **Cultural collision** occurs when divergent cultures come in contact. In international business, the major problems of *cultural collision* arise under two conditions:

* When a company implements practices that are less effective than intended
* When a company's employees encounter distress because of difficulty in accepting or adjusting to foreign behaviors

Sensitivity and Adjustment To predict and control its relationships and operations, an international firm must be sensitive to cultural differences. Thus it must realize that doing business as usual is not always the best way of doing things. When doing business in another country, a firm must determine which of that nation's business practices differ from its own and then decide what, if any, adjustments are necessary if it is to operate efficiently.

In this chapter, we start by examining *cultural awareness,* especially the need for building it. Then we discuss the causes of cultural differences, rigidities, and changes. Next, we describe the behavioral factors that affect the conduct of international business. Finally, we take a look at the reasons why some businesses—and some individuals—do or don't adjust well to other cultures.

CONCEPT CHECK

Keep in mind our definition of **international business** in Chapter 1, where we stress that it involves "all commercial transactions"—sales, investments, transportation, and so forth.

CONCEPT CHECK

Recall that, in Chapter 1, we identify two means of gaining useful knowledge from overseas activities: (1) learning from foreign operating experiences and (2) tapping into foreign intellectual competencies.

With globalization, the traditional often meets the modern. In the Mideast nation of Dubai, the traditional method of travel by camel is still preferred by many people. Today, however, the sights along the way may include a view of the world's tallest building, in the capital of Dubai City. The spire is visible from a distance of 95 miles.

Cultural Awareness

Almost everyone agrees that national cultures differ, but they disagree on what the differences are.

Problem areas that can hinder managers' cultural awareness are

- Subconscious reactions to circumstances.
- The assumption that all societal subgroups are similar.

Building your awareness of other cultures is not an easy task, and there's still no foolproof method for doing so.[3] Travelers remark on cultural differences, experts write about them, and international businesspeople find they affect operations. Even so, people tend to disagree on just what they are, whether they're widespread or limited in scope, and whether they're deep-seated or superficial.

Moreover, it's not easy to isolate "culture" from such factors as economic and political conditions. A survey, for instance, that measures people's attitudes toward risk taking in starting a new business may reflect current economic conditions or the fact that entrepreneurs are confident about governmental safety nets rather than spurred by basic values and beliefs.

Most cultural variables are universal. Every society, for example, has its own daily routines and rules, codes of social relations, language, and the show of emotions, and even concepts of luck. The forms of these variables, however, differ from culture to culture, and even within given cultures, not everyone responds to them in the same way. Every culture, for instance, features some form of dance, but types of dances vary among cultures, and in every culture, there are some nondancers.[4]

Some cultural differences, such as acceptable attire, are fairly obvious, and others aren't. Finally, people in every culture evince ingrained responses to given situations, and they often expect that people from other cultures will behave the same way they do. In our opening case, for example, the two British sales reps for PRI budgeted their time according to home-country guidelines and so regarded chatting about nonbusiness activities over coffee as a waste of time that should be devoted to conducting business. Averse to mixing business with pleasure, they got irritated when transactions were delayed by inopportune interruptions. In fact, their compensation system discouraged them from spending much time on each business transaction. Their Saudi counterparts, meanwhile, had no compulsion to wrap things up, regarded time spent in a café as worthwhile, and considered small talk a good way to determine if they could get along with potential business partners. They regarded business dealings as less urgent and personal relationships as more important.

A LITTLE LEARNING GOES A LONG WAY

Although some people seem to have an innate ability to say and do the right thing at the right time, others offend unintentionally or forget they're no longer on their home turf. Experts agree, however, that businesspeople can learn to improve awareness and sensitivity and, by educating themselves, they enhance the likelihood of succeeding on foreign soil. Gathering some basic research on another culture can be instructive, but it's usually just a start. For a variety of reasons, managers who plan to work abroad must assess the information they gather to determine if it perpetuates unwarranted stereotypes, covers only limited facets of a country and its culture, or relies on outdated information. They should also observe the behavior of those people who have garnered the kind of respect and confidence they themselves will need. (Incidentally, the best way to study a foreign culture is directly—go there and interact with the people.)

Of course, cultural variations are so numerous that no one can reasonably expect to memorize everything that he or she will need in every country (or, for that matter, in any country). Consider, for example, how many different ways there are to address people. Should you use a given name or a surname? If a surname, which surname? Does a wife take her husband's name? Some people find mistakes humorous, but if they perceive them as the result of ignorance or rudeness, you may have jeopardized your business deal. Fortunately, there are guidebooks for particular geographic areas, many of them based on the experiences of successful international managers. You can also consult with knowledgeable people at home and abroad, whether in a governmental or private capacity.

There is, however, another side to the cultural coin: Too often when we can't explain some difference—say, why the Irish like cold cereal more than the Spanish do—we tend to attribute it to culture without trying to understand it. (Perhaps the difference is simply that companies such as Kellogg's and General Mills have done a better job of marketing their cereals in Ireland.) Fortunately, we now have access to many recent studies designed to determine cross-cultural attitudes and preferences on a large number of issues concerning businesspeople.[5] Although we report major findings throughout the chapter, we should emphasize a few common shortcomings:

1. Comparing countries according to research findings can be risky. For one thing, what people say about their own attitudes (say, how satisfied they are with their working conditions) may be colored by the culture you're trying to understand (some groups of people, for example, may be happiest when they're complaining, or they respond with what they think you want to hear).

2. Specific variations within countries get overlooked when researchers are focused on national differences in terms of *averages*. As one observer puts it, for example: "Drivers are more likely to stop at a pedestrian crossing in the United Kingdom than in France, but it would be a grave mistake to step out into a British road in the expectation that every motorist will stop."[6] (And, of course, different people have different personalities, and certain personalities make people "outliers" in their own cultures; there's no certainty that they'll integrate and conform more regularly with cultural norms.[7])

3. Cultures evolve. Thus behavior reflecting "current" attitudes may well change in the future. Our opening case, for instance, details several ways in which Saudi attitudes toward women are changing. Interestingly, the Saudi government recently inaugurated a TV channel in which women with uncovered faces serve as anchors and interview men.

Taken together, major studies have thus far covered fewer than half the world's countries.

CONCEPT CHECK
We stress in Chapter 1 that understanding cultural values, attitudes, and beliefs is often crucial in deciding when and how to alter operations in foreign countries.

Case Review Note

The Idea of a "Nation": Delineating Cultures

In the following section, we begin by showing why the idea of a "nation" is a useful but imperfect cultural reference when we're talking about international business. Then we explain why cultures develop and change. Finally, we discuss the role of language and religion as influences on culture.

THE NATION AS A POINT OF REFERENCE

The nation is a useful definition of society because

- Similarity among people is a cause and an effect of national boundaries.
- Laws apply primarily along national lines.

Having said in Chapter 1 that international business includes all commercial transactions between two or more *nations,* we focus in this chapter on *national* cultures. The idea of a "nation" provides a workable definition of a "culture" because the basic similarity among people is often both cause and effect of national boundaries. The laws governing business operations also apply primarily along national lines. Within its borders a nation's people share such essential attributes as values, language, and race. There is a feeling of "we" that casts foreigners as "they." National identity is perpetuated through rites and symbols—flags, parades, rallies—and the preservation of national sites, documents, monuments, and museums promotes a common perception of history.

The Nation as Cultural Mediator   Obviously, the existence of shared attributes doesn't mean that everyone in a country is alike. Nor does it suggest that each country is unique in all respects. In fact, nations usually include various subcultures, ethnic groups, races, and classes, some of which transcend national boundaries (in many Asian countries, for example, ethnic Chinese embody a mixture of Chinese and local cultures).[8] Moreover, an individual's cultural makeup reflects not only different cultural memberships—such as gender and profession—but also a national culture that's flexible enough to accommodate the same diversity of memberships. In fact, the nation legitimizes itself by mediating the different interests,[9] and nations that fail in this role often dissolve.

The important thing is that every nation boasts certain human, demographic, and behavioral characteristics that constitute its national identity and affect the practices of any company that does business under its jurisdiction. Many people, regardless of nationality, for example, would object to being approached by marketing researchers in a restaurant, but as our opening case shows, Saudis additionally feel the need to exercise control over any male–female interaction that might result.

Remember, however, that certain cultural attributes can link groups from different nations more closely than groups within a given nation. No matter what country you're in, for instance, people in urban areas differ in certain attitudes from people in rural areas, and managers have different work attitudes than do production workers. Managers in Country A may hold values more similar to those of managers in Country B than to those of production workers in Country A.

Managers find country–by–country analysis difficult because

- Subcultures exist within nations.
- Similarities link groups from different countries.

When international businesspeople compare nations, they must be careful to examine *relevant groups*—differentiating, for example, between the typical attitudes of rural dwellers from those of urban dwellers. They should also remember, however, that the attitudes of these groups may differ for a variety of reasons. When, for example, scientists at Britain's Cambridge University and the United States' MIT set up a joint institute to improve the impact of teaching and research on economic success, the venture struggled—not because of differences in national or even professional cultures but because of different organizational cultures.

What was the problem? It seems that MIT scientists were accustomed to working closely with business to find research applications and generally hired separate administrators to deal with the business world. Cambridge scientists, in contrast, were not accustomed to seeking applications for basic research and preferred to handle administrative duties themselves rather than turning them over to professional administrators.[10]

HOW CULTURES FORM AND CHANGE

Culture is transmitted in various ways—from parent to child, teacher to pupil, social leader to follower, peer to peer. Developmental psychologists believe that by age 10 most children have their basic value systems: They've developed concepts of evil versus good, dirty versus clean, ugly versus beautiful, unnatural versus natural, abnormal versus normal, paradoxical versus logical, and irrational versus rational. At this point, these values are firmly in place and not easily changed.[11]

Cultural value systems are set early in life but may change through

- Choice or imposition.
- Contact with other cultures.

Sources of Change   Both individual and collective values and customs, however, may evolve over time. Examining this evolution may tell us something about the process by which a culture comes to accept (or reject) certain business practices, and this knowledge could be of use to international companies that would like to introduce changes into a culture. The important thing here is *change*, which may result from either *choice* or *imposition*.

Change by Choice   Change by choice may occur as a reaction to social and economic situations that present people with new alternatives. When, for example, rural people choose to accept factory jobs, they change some basic customs—notably, by working regular hours that don't allow the sort of work-time social interactions that farmwork allowed.

Change by Imposition   Change by imposition, sometimes called **cultural imperialism**, involves the imposed introduction into a culture of certain elements from an alien culture, such as the forced change in law by an occupying country which, over time, becomes part of the subject culture. The cartoon in Figure 2.2 gives a humorous twist to an unfortunate historical instance of change by imposition, and five centuries later, many people still have good reason to lament its occurrence.

As a rule, contact among countries brings change—a process known as *cultural diffusion*. When this change results in mixing cultural elements, the process is known as *creolization*. Some governments have tried to protect national cultures, but they have been less than fully successful because people travel more and access foreign information

FIGURE 2.2

"Not to worry. Diversity can only enrich our culture."

Source: Wall Street Journal, with permission from Cartoon Feature Syndicate.

through a variety of sources. As our opening case suggests, for example, fruitful interactions don't necessarily have to be of a strictly business nature: The founders of Java Lounge came up with their business idea because they had interacted as students in Western cultures.

LANGUAGE AS BOTH A DIFFUSER AND STABILIZER OF CULTURE

A common language within countries is a unifying force.

National boundaries and geographic obstacles limit people's contact with other cultures, and so does language. Map 2.2 shows the distribution of the world's major language groups. Not surprisingly, when people from different areas speak the same language, culture spreads more easily. That fact helps explain why there's greater cultural homogeneity among English-speaking countries or among Spanish-speaking countries than among English-speaking countries on the one hand and Spanish-speaking countries on the other.

Our map, by the way, omits most of the world's approximately 6,000 languages because they're spoken by only a few people. When people understand only one

MAP 2.2
Distribution of the World's Major Languages

The people of the world speak thousands of different languages, but only a few of them remain important in the dissemination of culture. A significant portion of the world, for example, speaks English, French, or Spanish. In those countries labeled "Regional," the predominant language is not dominant anywhere else; Japanese, for example, is dominant only in Japan. But take a look at China: It's the only place where people speak Mandarin, but it's important in international business because the population of China comprises a *lot* of people. The classification "Regional" actually takes in two categories: (1) countries in which the dominant language is not dominant anywhere else (e.g., Japan) and (2) countries in which several different languages are spoken (e.g., India).

Sources: www.udon.de/sprachk.htm. The number of native speakers is taken from *World Almanac and Book of Facts* (Mahwah, NJ: Primedia Reference, 2002).

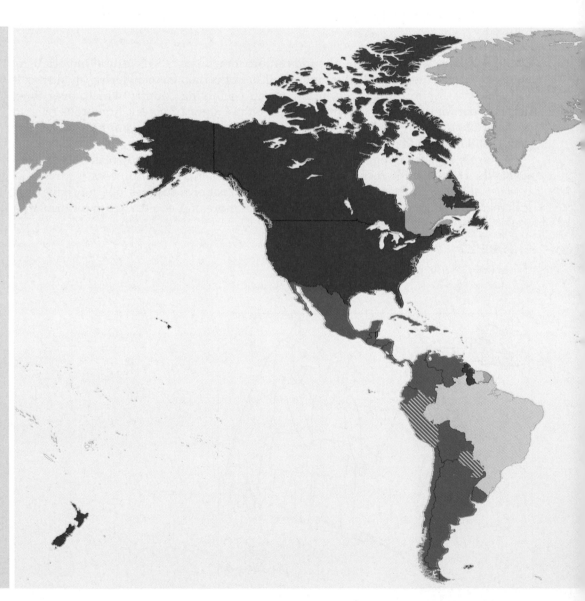

language that has relatively few users—especially if they're concentrated in a small geographic area—they tend to cling to their culture because they have little meaningful contact with others.

Such languages as English, French, and Spanish have such widespread acceptance (they're prevalent in 44, 27, and 20 countries, respectively) that, as a rule, native speakers don't feel the same need to learn other languages as do speakers of languages that, like Finnish or Greek, are found in only limited geographic areas. Among nations that share a same language, commerce is easier because translating everything (which can be both time consuming and expensive) isn't necessary. Thus when people study second languages, they usually choose the ones that are most useful in interacting with other countries, especially in the realm of commerce.

Why English Travels So Well   Take a look at Figure 2.3. The pie chart on the right shows portions of worldwide output by language. As you can see, English-speaking peoples account for over 40 percent of the world's production—a fact that goes a long way toward explaining why English is the world's most important *second*

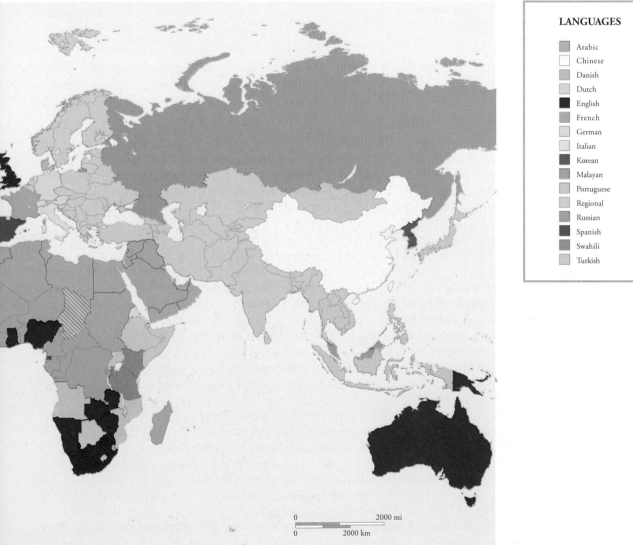

LANGUAGES

- Arabic
- Chinese
- Danish
- Dutch
- English
- French
- German
- Italian
- Korean
- Malayan
- Portuguese
- Regional
- Russian
- Spanish
- Swahili
- Turkish

| 0 | | 2000 mi |
| 0 | | 2000 km |

FIGURE 2.3   Major Language Groups: Population and Output

Native speakers of just a handful of languages—notably English—account for much more of the world's economic output than their total numbers would indicate. Only 6% of the world's people speak English as a native language, for example, but they account for 42% of its economic output, which helps to explain the prevalence of English as a second language in conducting international business.

Sources: Data for the chart on the left from the Central Intelligence Agency, *The World Factbook,* at www.cia.gov. Data for the chart on the right calculated from GDP figures supplied by the World Development Indicators database, World Bank (September 2004), and country language figures supplied by Wikipedia, at en.wikipedia.org.

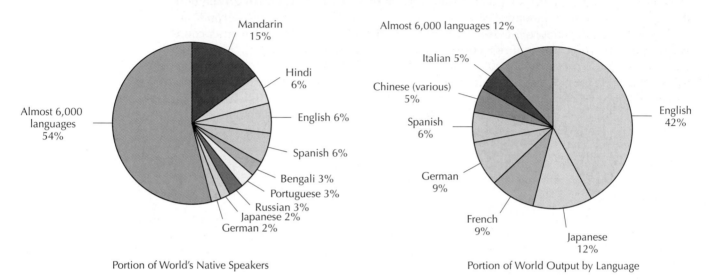

Portion of World's Native Speakers

Portion of World Output by Language

language. Remember, too, that MNEs—which are largely headquartered in English-speaking countries—decide on the functional language that will be used among their foreign subsidiaries. Not surprisingly, it's usually English, both because they tend to transfer English-only speakers as managers abroad and because they need a common means for managers from different countries to communicate with each other.

In addition, many MNEs from non-English-speaking countries, such as Nokia from Finland and Philips from the Netherlands, have adopted English as their operating language.[12] Thus you've probably heard that English is the "international language of business," but at least one prominent linguist predicts that monolingual English speakers will eventually experience more and more difficulty in communicating worldwide. Why? Because the percentage of people speaking English as a first language will decrease while the languages of such countries as China and India will grow very rapidly along with their economies.[13] As is so often the case, history may also have a thing or two to teach us in this matter: Latin once dominated as the language of scholarship and French as the language of diplomacy, but both have long since been supplanted.

Nevertheless, for some time now, English words—especially American-English words—have been entering into other languages. An estimated 20,000 English words, for example, have gone into the Japanese language. Why does English travel so well? In part because the U.S. media are so influential in promoting U.S. lifestyles. Our opening case offers a good example of this phenomenon: The name "Java Lounge" plays on the word *java* as English-language slang for "coffee"—a usage dating back to the time when the best coffees came from the Indonesian island of Java.

Of course, the United States also originates a healthy percentage of new technology and new products. When, for example, a new U.S. product enters a foreign market, it usually enters the language as well. Sometimes, it enters in its good old-fashioned English form. In Spanish-speaking countries, for instance, you might see a sign in the window of the clothing store announcing that *"Vendemos blue jeans en varios colores"* ("We sell various colors of blue jeans"). At other times, the local language gives it an Anglicized twist. Thus Russians call tight denim pants *dzhinsi* (pronounced "jeansy"), and the French call a self-service restaurant *le self.* Finally, the intrusion of English into another language may result in the development of a hybrid tongue, such as "Spanglish" (Spanish and English) or "Chinglish" (Mandarin Chinese and English), which may ultimately become a distinct language.[14]

Note, however, that some countries, such as Finland, prefer to coin their own new words rather than accept Anglicized items into their vocabularies, and because many countries see language as an integral part of the culture, they regulate linguistic changes. In the business arena, for example, they may require that all transactions be conducted and all "Made in" labels be printed in the local language.

Does Geography Matter?

Where Birds of a Feather Flock Together

Some groups of people are more isolated from the rest of the world than others, sometimes because of natural barriers (rugged terrain and geographic remoteness) and sometimes by culture (unique languages, outmoded transportation and communications, xenophobia). Obviously, the more isolated people are, the less likely they are to influence and be influenced by other people. Historically, natural barriers—and natural advantages—have been quite important in determining where people do and don't live. Take a quick look at any map, for instance, and you'll see that most big cities are situated where waterways facilitated the interaction of people and interchange of goods.

On the one hand, although airplanes and communications systems have rendered many natural barriers less formidable, they play a role in determining which people are harder to get to know than others. In Papua New Guinea, for example, the mutual isolation of tribal groups has resulted in about 800 different languages and permitted little cultural diffusion. Similarly, natural conditions continue to affect the different physical cultures that people have developed in different places. Nielsen ratings don't tell us how many native Inuits of the Arctic tune in to reruns of *Baywatch,* but it's pretty certain that, given the natural conditions of their habitat, they aren't likely to develop a taste for beachwear. Inuits, by the way, have more words for *snow* than any other language on the planet.

On the other hand, of course, some places have traditionally enjoyed more-than-average outside contact than other cultures. As we saw in our opening case, the Saudi port of Jeddah, having long experienced more external contact than the rest of Saudi Arabia, has borrowed much more liberally from outside cultures.

Then there's the effect of *proximity* on cultural diffusion: Not surprisingly, people generally have more contact with nearby groups than with those that are far away. Take a look, for instance, at Map 2.2 on pages 58–59. As you can see, most German-speaking countries, Arabic-speaking countries, and Spanish-speaking countries are more or less adjacent to each other. Likewise, Map 2.3 (pages 62–63) reveals that virtually all of the world's major religions—Christianity, Islam, and Buddhism—are geographically clustered. The notable exceptions to this rule have resulted from colonization and immigration. Both English and Spanish, for instance, spread to distant parts of the world during eras of European colonization.

Finally, cultural—and subcultural—clusters tend to confirm the old adage that "Birds of a feather flock together." Immigration patterns, for example, often reflect the influence of subcultural familiarity and even the formation of subcultural support groups. That's why there's a heavy concentration of Central American immigrants in the Los Angeles area. They feel comfortable locating there because, even if friends and family aren't already waiting, they'll find affinities in language, diet, and general customs. Globally, we find many such patterns, such as Hong Kong Chinese in Vancouver, Canada, and Algerians in Marseilles, France.●

RELIGION AS A CULTURAL STABILIZER

Many strong values are the result of a dominant religion.

Map 2.3 shows the approximate distribution of the world's major religions. In many countries, the practice of religion has declined significantly; indeed, a few nations in northern Europe are sometimes called "post-Christian" societies. At the same time, it is a cultural stabilizer because centuries of profound religious influence continue to play a major role in shaping cultural values even in these societies.[15] Among people with strong religious convictions, the role of religion in shaping behavior is even stronger.

Many of these religions—Buddhism, Christianity, Hinduism, Islam, and Judaism—influence specific beliefs that may affect business, such as inhibiting the sale of certain products or the performance of work at certain times. McDonald's, for example, serves neither beef nor pork in India so as not to offend either its Hindu or Muslim

**MAP 2.3
Distribution of
the World's Major
Religions**

Most countries are home to people of various religious beliefs, but a nation's culture is typically influenced most heavily by a dominant religion. The practices of the dominant religion, for instance, often shape customary practices in legal and business affairs.

Source: The numbers for adherents are taken from *World Almanac and Book of Facts,* Center for the Study of Global Christianity, Gordon-Conwell Theological Seminary. World Christian Database, at www.worldchristiandatabase.org (accessed September 2005). Reprinted with permission.

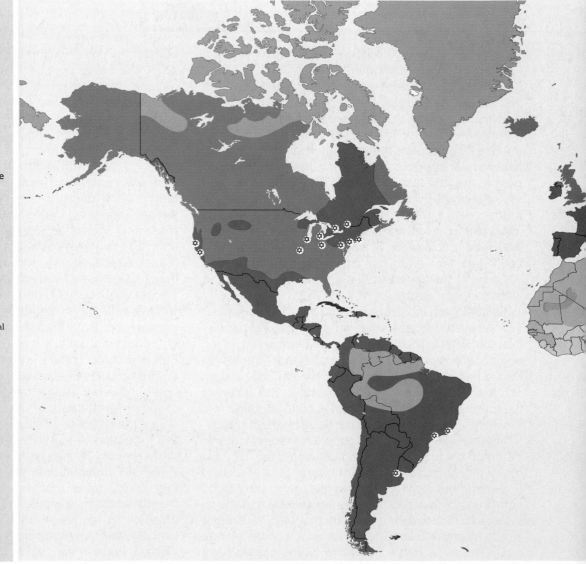

populations, and El Al, the Israeli national airline, does not fly on Saturday, the Jewish Sabbath.

Of course, not all nations that practice the same religion impose the same constraints on business. In predominantly Muslim countries, for example, Friday is a day of worship and a non-workday. In Turkey, however, a secular Muslim country that adheres to the Christian work calendar to keep in step with European business activity, Friday is a workday. In places where rival religions or factions are vying for political control, the resulting strife can cause so much upheaval that business activity suffers, whether from property damage, broken supply chains, or breaches in connections with customers. Unfortunately, the problem isn't rare: In recent years, religious-related violence has erupted in such countries as India, Iraq, Sudan, and Northern Ireland.

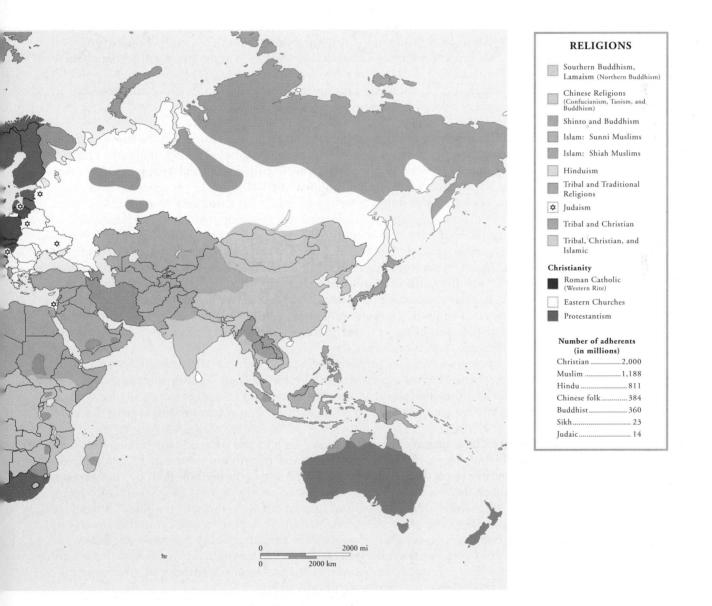

RELIGIONS

- Southern Buddhism, Lamaism (Northern Buddhism)
- Chinese Religions (Confucianism, Taoism, and Buddhism)
- Shinto and Buddhism
- Islam: Sunni Muslims
- Islam: Shiah Muslims
- Hinduism
- Tribal and Traditional Religions
- ✿ Judaism
- Tribal and Christian
- Tribal, Christian, and Islamic

Christianity

- Roman Catholic (Western Rite)
- Eastern Churches
- Protestantism

Number of adherents (in millions)

Christian	2,000
Muslim	1,188
Hindu	811
Chinese folk	384
Buddhist	360
Sikh	23
Judaic	14

0   2000 mi
0   2000 km

CONCEPT CHECK
In Chapter 1, we emphasize the importance of studying the *behavioral factors* that affect business conditions in helping managers decide why and how they may need to alter operations in different countries.

Behavioral Practices Affecting Business

It should come as no surprise that cultural attitudes and values affect business practices—everything from decisions about what products to sell to decisions about organizing, financing, managing, and controlling operations. Attitudes and values constitute *cultural variables,* and researchers define cultural variables differently, attaching different names to slightly different and sometimes overlapping concepts. Similarly, businesspeople define business functions differently. Because of all these nuances in terms and concepts, there are thousands of possible ways of relating culture to business—far too many to cover in one chapter. Thus we'll settle for hitting the highlights—the factors that, according to both international managers and academic researchers, have the most effect on different business practices in different countries. We also pursue the topic of cultural variables in later chapters.

ISSUES IN SOCIAL STRATIFICATION

Every culture values some people more highly than others, and such distinctions dictate a person's class or status within that culture. In business, this practice may entail valuing members of managerial groups more highly than members of production groups. The factors that determine rankings—or *social stratification*—vary substantially from country to country. Your ranking is determined by two sets of factors: (1) those pertaining to you as an individual and (2) those pertaining to your affiliation with or membership in certain groups. Let's focus for a moment on this second set.

Group affiliations can be

- Ascribed or acquired.
- A reflection of class and status.

Ascribed and Acquired Memberships   Affiliations determined by birth—known as **ascribed group memberships**—include those based on gender, family, age, caste, and ethnic, racial, or national origin. Other affiliations are called **acquired group memberships** and include those based on religion, political affiliation, and professional and other associations. Social stratification affects such business functions as marketing. Most advertisers, for example, prefer spokespeople who appeal to their target audience.

Social stratification also affects employment practices. One study of hiring, promotion, compensation, and staff-reduction practices at a number of banks showed that employers differed by nationality on all four functions. When, for example, they needed to make staff reductions, British banks were most prone to save costs by discharging on a performance-to-salary basis (targeting, say, a middle-aged manager with a high salary and average performance), whereas German banks were more concerned with minimizing personal hardship (targeting younger managers, regardless of performance, because they could find new jobs more easily).[16]

In the following sections, we focus on some of the individual characteristics and group memberships that influence a person's social ranking from country to country. We also touch on two additional factors that are often important: *education* (especially how much you have and where you got it) and *social connections* (who you know and in what places).[17]

Businesses reward competence highly in some societies.

Performance Orientation   In some nations, such as the United States, companies tend to base a person's eligibility for employment and promotion primarily on competence, thereby fostering work environments driven more by competition than by cooperation. In fact, some of these nations value competence so highly that they've actually taken regulatory steps (not always effective) to prevent discrimination against otherwise competent people on the basis of sex, race, age, and religion. In other countries, however, individual competence may be of secondary importance. A person's eligibility for employment or compensation may reflect some other factor. In Japan, for instance, where cooperation is stressed over competition in the workplace, seniority or "humaneness" (tolerance of mistakes) often carries significant weight.[18]

Open and Closed Societies   The more egalitarian, or "open," a society, the less the importance of ascribed group membership in determining rewards. In less open societies, however, laws may be designed either to reinforce or to undermine rigid stratification based on ascribed group membership. For example, laws requiring racial or ethnic quotas usually aim to weaken stratification by countering discrimination. Malaysia, for example, has long maintained employment quotas for three ethnic groups—Malays, Chinese, and Indians—primarily to upgrade the economic position of Malays because, at the time of Malaysia's independence, the Chinese and Indian minorities dominated business ownership and the professions, respectively.[19] The Malaysian system requires companies to maintain expensive record-keeping systems of their hiring practices. Likewise, Brazil, which has more than 300 terms to designate skin color, has proposed racial quotas in universities, government jobs, and even television soap operas.[20] (It plans no quotas for the national football team, where only competence counts.)

In other cases, ascribed group memberships deny large numbers of people equal access to the preparation needed to qualify for jobs. In much of sub-Saharan Africa, for instance, the literacy rate for women is much lower than that for men—in Niger and Mali, for example, 42 percent and 52 percent of the male literacy rate, respectively.[21] Consequently, prospective employers face quite different workforces in different countries.

Finally, even when individuals qualify for given positions and no legal barriers exist to hold them back, certain social obstacles—say, public opposition to the use of child labor in the employer's home country—may make a company wary of adopting certain practices in host countries. In some cases, opposition to certain groups may come from other workers, customers, local stockholders, or government officials. In addition, the old adage that "It's *who* you know, not *what* you know" has some validity just about everywhere. (This is a point we pursue in our chapter-ending case, which details a U.S. company's adventures in the African nation of Uganda. Here, we'll see not only that effective opposition can come from small ad hoc groups, but also that the people you need to know can sometimes be found in unexpected places.)

Gender-Based Groups   Country-specific differences in attitudes toward gender are sometimes quite pronounced. Some of these probably seem paradoxical, at least to the outsider. In both China and India, for example, the practice of aborting female fetuses (and even killing female newborns) certainly reflects an extreme attitude toward gender, but the practice has relatively little impact on the workplace: In both countries, women are prominent figures in both business and government.

"When Jobs Are Scarce . . ." (I)   In other countries, such as Egypt and Qatar, the traditional bias against gender equality is quite strong.[22] As we observed in our opening case, in most professions Saudi men and women must work separately. Moreover, women can't work at all in some professions, and they account for only 7 percent of the total Saudi workforce. There are, in other words, more than 13 employed men for every employed woman. Compare that figure with the United States, where only 1.2 men are employed for every woman.[23] Here's another interesting statistic. In Lithuania, more than 50 percent of both males and females agreed with the following statement: "When jobs are scarce, men have a better right to a job than women." In Sweden and Iceland, the number was under 10 percent.[24]

In many parts of the world, however, barriers to gender-based employment practices are coming down. In the United States, one noticeable change has been in the number of people of one gender employed in occupations previously dominated by the other. Nursing, for instance, was once a strictly female endeavor; today, however, about two fifths of students in U.S. nursing schools are male.[25] Developed nations have also witnessed a significant change in job composition: There's been a decrease in production jobs requiring brawn and an increase in jobs for people who need some formal education, as in such fields as X-ray technology and psychiatric casework. With these shifts, the relative demand for female employees has increased.

Egalitarian societies place less importance on ascribed group memberships.

Country–by–country attitudes vary toward

- Male and female roles.
- Respect for age.
- Family ties.

Age-Based Groups   All countries treat age-groups differently, and every country expresses its attitudes toward age in different ways. All countries, for instance, enforce age-related laws that reflect collective values. Typically, such statutes apply to employment, driving privileges, rights to obtain products and services (such as alcohol, cigarettes, certain pharmaceuticals, and bank accounts), and civic duty (voting, serving in the military or on juries). Sometimes, the logic of these laws—especially to outsiders but often to natives as well—seems quite contradictory. In the United States, for example, people can vote, marry, drive, and die for their country before they can legally buy alcohol.

National differences—both in laws and customs, and especially in employment practices—can be substantial. Both Finland and the Netherlands, for example, enforce mandatory retirement ages, but with few exceptions (say, airline pilots), U.S. law specifically prohibits the practice. In Britain, antidiscrimination laws apply to everyone, regardless of age, whereas U.S. law is designed to protect only people over age 40.[26] Laws regulating product sales and promotion also vary from country to country. In parts of Switzerland, you can legally buy alcohol at age 14, whereas U.S. law puts the age at 21.[27] Not surprisingly, every country specifies an age at which people can be licensed to drive, and in many cases, that age limit affects car sales. U.S. advertisers bombard children with TV advertisements, but Sweden prohibits ads targeted to children.

"When Jobs Are Scarce . . ." (II)   Finally, attitudinal differences concerning age can affect business operations in different countries. If, for example, you were to put the following proposition to people in different countries—"When jobs are scarce, people should be forced to retire early"—you'd find significant differences in the number of people who agree or disagree. Almost three quarters of Bulgarians will agree but only 10 percent of Japanese.[28] Why the difference? For one thing, Japanese hold much more strongly to the assumption there's a significant correlation between age and wisdom. That's why the seniority system, although now declining in importance, plays a key role in promotion and compensation decisions in Japan—much more so than in Western countries.[29] The United States, in contrast, is often characterized as a culture that favors youth. Indeed, U.S. TV writers claim they can't find jobs after age 30, and there's a booming market for products designed to make people look younger.

Family-Based Groups   In some cultures—say, China and southern Italy—the most important group membership is the family: An individual's position in society at large depends heavily on the family's social status or "respectability" rather than on individual achievement. Because family ties are so strong, there may also be a tendency to cooperate more closely within the family unit than in other relationships. In such cultures, not surprisingly, small family-run companies are quite successful; conversely, however, they often encounter difficulties in growing because owners are reluctant to share responsibility with professional managers hired from outside the family. When its business culture is hampered by this state of affairs, a country (or region) may lack the indigenously owned *large-scale* operations that are usually necessary for long-term economic development.[30]

Occupation   In every society, certain occupations are perceived as more prestigious than others. In turn, this perception usually affects the number and qualifications of people who seek employment in a given field. Most of these perceptions are fairly universal; dentists, for example, typically outrank street cleaners on the social-respectability scale. Generally speaking, higher-prestige jobs also pay better, in part because low-prestige jobs usually go to people whose skills are in low demand. In the United States, jobs such as babysitting, delivering newspapers, and bagging groceries traditionally go to teenagers, who leave them as they get older and gain additional training. In most poor countries, however, many low-prestige occupations are filled by adults who have very little opportunity to move on to more rewarding positions.

There are also national differences in the desire to be self-employed versus satisfaction in working for an employer. Americans have a higher preference for self-employment and worry less about the risk of failure than the Europeans. There are also differences within the European community: The Irish, for example, have a higher preference for self-employment and a higher tolerance for risk than Germans do.[31]

WORK MOTIVATION

Not surprisingly, motivated employees are normally more productive than those who aren't. On an aggregate basis, of course, this correspondence between motivation and productivity influences economic development positively. In studying why some areas of Latin America have attained higher levels of economic development than others, researchers trace some significant differences back to the early development of a strong work ethic.[32] Why are international companies concerned about attitudes toward work? Mainly because higher levels of motivation lead to higher levels of productivity and, in turn, to lower production costs. Studies show substantial differences in how and why people in different nations are motivated to work, and we devote the following discussion to summarizing the major differences.

Materialism and Motivation   Max Weber argued that predominantly Protestant countries were the most economically developed—a fact he attributed to a so-called Protestant ethic. According to Weber, this "ethic," as an outgrowth of the Protestant Reformation in sixteenth-century Europe, reflects the belief that work is a pathway to salvation and material success in the world is no impediment to salvation.

> The desire for material wealth is
> - A prime motivation to work.
> - Positive for economic development.

Although we no longer accept a strict distinction between Protestant and non-Protestant attitudes toward work and material gain, we do tend to adhere to the underlying values of Weber's concept—namely, that self-discipline, hard work, honesty, and a belief in a just world—foster work motivation and thus economic growth.[33] As a matter of fact, evidence indicates a positive correlation between the intensity of religious belief per se (regardless of specific belief systems) and adherence to attributes that lead to economic growth (say, confidence in the rule of law and belief in the virtue of thrift).[34] Moreover, there's strong evidence that the individual desire for material wealth is a prime incentive to perform the kind of work that leads to communitywide economic development.[35]

The Productivity/Leisure Trade-off   Some cultures place less value on leisure time than others, and as a result, people work longer hours, take fewer holidays and vacations, and, in general, spend less time and money on leisure activities. On average, for example, the Japanese take less time off than workers in any other developed country. In the United States, where the average income probably allows for more leisure time than most people use, there is still some disdain for people who fall on either end of the work–leisure spectrum: people of privilege who appear to contribute nothing to society and people who appear to be satisfied with a lifestyle that can be maintained by unemployment benefits. Americans, for instance, who give up work (primarily retirees) often complain they're no longer allowed to contribute anything useful to society.

In much of Europe, however, people appear to be more willing to trade added productivity for greater leisure rather than for extra income.[36] In parts of some poor countries, meanwhile, such as rural India, living "the simple life"—that is, without benefit of much material comfort—seems to be a desirable end in itself: When productivity gains afford them the choice, people tend to choose to work less rather than to earn and buy more.[37] By and large, however, today people in most countries, whether rich or poor, regard personal economic advancement as a worthwhile goal in life (although certainly not the only one).

Expectation of Success and Reward   One factor that motivates attitudes toward work is the perceived likelihood of success and reward. Generally, people have little enthusiasm for efforts that seem too easy or too difficult. Why? Because the probability of

People are more eager to work if

- Rewards for success are high.
- There is some uncertainty of success.

success on the one hand or failure on the other seems almost certain. Few of us, for instance, would care to run a race against either a snail or a racehorse; in either case, the outcome is too predictable. Our enthusiasm peaks when uncertainty is high—say, when we're challenged to race another human of roughly equal ability. Likewise, the reward for a successfully completed task—say, winning a fair footrace—may be high or low, and most of us usually work harder the more we expect to be rewarded.

Success and Reward Across Borders   Performed in different countries, the same tasks come with different probabilities of success, different rewards for success, and different consequences for failure. In cultures in which the probability of economic failure is almost certain and the perceived rewards of success are low, people tend, not surprisingly, to view work as necessary but unsatisfying, mainly because they foresee little benefit to themselves from their efforts. This attitude may prevail in harsh climates, in very poor areas, or in subcultures subject to discrimination. Take Cuba, for instance, where public policy allocates output from productive to unproductive workers; naturally, there's not much enthusiasm for work. We find the greatest enthusiasm for work when high uncertainty of outcome is combined with the likelihood of a positive reward for success and little or none for failure.[38]

Assertiveness: The Masculinity–Femininity Index   Average interest in career success varies substantially among countries. One study, for example, used a so-called **masculinity–femininity index** to compare the attitudes of employees in 50 countries toward work success and achievement. Employees with a high "masculinity score" admired successful achievers, harbored little sympathy for the unfortunate, and preferred to be better than others rather than on a par with them. They shared a money-and-things orientation rather than a people orientation, a belief that it's better "to live to work" than "to work to live," and a preference for performance and growth over quality of life and the environment. Countries with the highest masculinity scores were Japan, Austria, Venezuela, and Switzerland. Those with the lowest were Sweden, Norway, the Netherlands, and Denmark.[39]

Similarly, the degree to which individuals are assertive, confrontational, and aggressive in their relationships with others varies across borders. Such attitudinal differences help explain why local managers behave in different ways from country to country—sometimes in ways that international managers either don't expect or don't prefer. In a low-masculinity country, for instance, the typical purchasing manager probably has a high need for smooth social relationships and prefers amiable and continuing relationships with suppliers to, say, lower costs or faster delivery. Elsewhere, local managers may place such organizational goals as employee and social welfare ahead of a foreign parent's goals of growth and efficiency.

The ranking of needs differs among countries.

Hierarchies of Needs   According to the **hierarchy-of-needs theory** of motivation, people try to fulfill lower-level needs before moving on to higher-level needs.[40] As you can see from Figure 2.4, the most basic needs are *physiological*—the needs for food, water, and sex. You have to satisfy (or nearly satisfy) such needs before *security* needs—such as the need for a safe physical and emotional environment—become a sufficiently powerful set of motivators. Then you must satisfy your security needs before triggering the motivational effect of *affiliation* or social needs (such as the need for peer acceptance). Once you've satisfied your affiliation needs, you'll be motivated to satisfy your *esteem* needs—the need to bolster your self-image through recognition, attention, and appreciation. The highest-order need calls for *self-actualization*—self-fulfillment or (to quote Robert Lewis Stevenson) "becom[ing] all that we are capable of becoming." Finally, note that the hierarchy-of-needs theory also implies you'll typically work to satisfy a need, but once you've satisfied it, its value as a motivator diminishes.

What can hierarchy-of-needs theory tell us about doing business in foreign countries? For one thing, research has shown that people in different countries not only attach

FIGURE 2.4   The Hierarchy of Needs and Need-Hierarchy Comparisons

The pyramid on the left represents the five-level hierarchy of needs formulated by Maslow. The two block pyramids on the right (a, b) represent two different groups of people—say, the populations of two different countries. Note that the block representing affiliation needs (level 3) is wider in (b) than in (a); conversely, the block representing self-actualization needs (level 5) is wider in (a) than in (b). In other words, even if we rank various needs in the same order (or hierarchy), the people in one country may regard a given higher-order need as more important (wider) than people in another country.

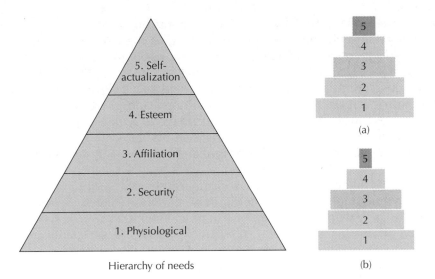

Hierarchy of needs

different degrees of importance to different needs, but also they even rank higher-order needs differently. Hierarchy-of-needs theory, then, can be helpful in differentiating among the reward preferences of employees in different countries. In very poor countries, for example, a company can motivate workers simply by providing enough compensation to satisfy their needs for food and shelter. Elsewhere, workers are motivated by other needs.

RELATIONSHIP PREFERENCES

So far, we've discussed two categories of behavioral practices affecting business: social stratification systems and work motivation. Among other things, we found that, within social stratification systems, reference-group members are not necessarily equal. We saw, too, that both work motivation and ways of motivating employees are influenced by different cultural norms. Next, we discuss some of the values underlying such differences.

Power Distance   From country to country, employees' preferences in interacting with bosses, subordinates, and peers vary substantially. Considerable anecdotal evidence indicates that people perform better when the nature of their interactions fits their preferences. That's why companies are well advised to align management styles with employee preferences for interacting with superiors.

There are national variations in the preference for autocratic or consultative management.

Power distance refers to this general relationship between superiors and subordinates. Where it's *high,* people prefer little consultation between superiors and subordinates: Employees usually prefer one of two management styles: *autocratic* (ruling with unlimited authority) or *paternalistic* (regulating conduct by supplying needs). Where power distance is *low,* they prefer "consultative" styles.[41] What might happen, therefore, if a Dutch company assigned domestic managers, who typically prefer low power distance, to improve productivity at a facility in Morocco, where workers typically prefer high power distance? The Dutch managers might consult with Moroccan subordinates in an attempt to improve employee productivity. Unfortunately, they may end up making subordinates feel so uncomfortable with the new management style that performance deteriorates even further rather than improves.

Interestingly, employees who prefer an autocratic style of superior–subordinate relationship are also willing to accept decision making by a majority of subordinates. What they don't accept is interaction between superiors and subordinates in decision making. Clearly, worker-participation methods are likely to be more effective in some countries than in others.

Individualism Versus Collectivism   Studies have also compared employee inclinations toward **individualism versus collectivism.** "Individualism" is characterized by low dependence on the organization for fulfilling leisure time, improving skills, and receiving benefits and a preference for personal decision making and on-the-job challenges. "Collectivism," in contrast, encourages dependence on the organization and a preference for thorough training, satisfactory workplace conditions, and good benefits. In countries typified by high individualism, self-actualization is a prime motivator because employees want challenges. In those characterized by high collectivism, the need for security—notably, the desire for a safe physical and emotional environment— is a prime motivator.[42]

> "Safe" work environments motivate collectivists. Challenges motivate individualists.

Degrees of individualism and collectivism also influence employee interactions. Japan, for instance, has a much more collectivist culture than the United States, especially concerning the role of work groups. Consider, for example, Levi Strauss, which once introduced team-based production into several U.S. plants because overseas managers had observed high productivity when the system was used in Asia. Unfortunately, U.S. employees—especially the most skilled workers—detested the system, productivity went down, and Levi returned to a system more suitable to its domestic workforce.

Situational Differences: The Family   Applying any measure of *individualism versus collectivism* is a complex and imprecise process.[43] In some cases, for example, the preference for individualism may vary according to circumstances. Although China and Mexico can be characterized as collectivist cultures, they differ from Japan to the extent that the preference for collectivism is based on kinship relationships and does not carry over into the workplace.[44] In both China and Mexico, moreover, the concept of family includes not only the *nuclear family* (consisting of husband, wife, and minor children) but also the *vertically extended family* (including members of several generations) and perhaps the *horizontally extended family* as well (encompassing aunts, uncles, and cousins).

Such differences can affect business in a variety of ways:

1. The material rewards to be gained from individual work may be less motivating when rewards are divided among members of a group.
2. Because relocation means that family members must also find new jobs, a worker's geographic mobility is limited. Even when extended families don't live together, mobility may be reduced because people prefer to remain near relatives.
3. Interrelated familial roles may complicate purchasing decisions.
4. Security and social needs may be met more effectively at home than in the workplace.

RISK-TAKING BEHAVIOR

People in various cultures differ in their willingness to accept things the way they are and in their feelings about their control over their destinies. The following discussion examines four types of *risk-taking behavior* that reflect these attitudes: *uncertainty avoidance, trust, future orientation*, and *fatalism*.

Uncertainty Avoidance   If you display **uncertainty avoidance,** you have a preference for known quantities. In countries where this preference is high, employees prefer set rules that are to be followed even if breaking them may be in the company's best interest. They also plan to stay with current employers for a long time, preferring the certainty of present positions over the uncertainty of potential advancement elsewhere.[45] When uncertainty avoidance is high, superiors may need to be more precise in their directions to subordinates, who typically aren't motivated to determine for themselves what they need to do to advance the company's interests.

In the same countries, fewer consumers are prepared to risk being first to try a new product—obviously an important consideration for firms trying to decide where to introduce new products. Gillette, for example, gets a large portion of its sales from recently introduced products. Thus it may be wise for Gillette to enter markets like Denmark and the United Kingdom, which rate low on uncertainty avoidance, before venturing into Belgium and Portugal, which rate high.

Trust   Surveys measure *trust* among countries by asking respondents to evaluate such statements as "Most people can be trusted" and "You can't be too careful in dealing with people." Findings indicate substantial international differences. Many more Norwegians than Brazilians, for example, regard most people as trustworthy.[46] Where trust is high, the cost of doing business tends to be lower because managers don't spend much time fussing over every possible contingency and monitoring every action for compliance with certain business principles. Instead, they can spend time investing and innovating.[47]

Future Orientation   Because cultures differ in their perceptions of the risks from delaying gratification by investing for the future, they also differ in the extent to which people live for the present rather than the future. Future orientation, for example, is more pronounced in Switzerland, the Netherlands, and Canada than in Russia, Poland, and Italy.[48] In the former cultures, companies may find it easier to motivate workers through such delayed-compensation programs as retirement plans.

Fatalism   If people believe strongly in self-determination, they may be willing to work hard to achieve goals and take responsibility for performance. But if they're *fatalistic*—if they believe every event in life is inevitable—they're less likely to accept the basic cause-and-effect relationship between work and reward. In countries that rate high on fatalism, people do less planning for contingencies. They may be reluctant, for example, to buy insurance. Religious differences play a significant role in levels of fatalism in a culture. Conservative or fundamentalist Christian, Buddhist, Hindu, and Muslim groups, for instance, tend to view occurrences as "the will of God." Likewise, they're less apt to be swayed by cause-and-effect logic than by such tactics as personal appeals and offers of rewards for complying with requests.[49]

INFORMATION AND TASK PROCESSING

"Beauty," we're often told, "is in the eye of the beholder." So, apparently, are perceptions and judgments, on cultural as well as personal levels. Both perception and judgment are based on what people perceive as accurate *information*, and different cultures handle information in different ways. The following discussion examines some of the ways in which different cultures perceive, obtain, and process information.

Perception of Cues   As a rule, we're selective in perceiving *cues*—features that inform us about the nature of something. We may identify things by means of any of our senses (sight, smell, touch, sound, or taste), and each sense can provide information in various ways; through vision, for example, we sense color, depth, and shape. The cues that people rely on differ among cultures. The reason is partly physiological. Genetic differences in eye pigmentation, for instance, allow some people to differentiate colors more precisely than others can.

Nationalities differ in

- Ease of handling uncertainties.
- Degree of trust among people.
- Future orientation.
- Attitudes of self-determination and fatalism.

Perceptual differences also reflect cultural factors. The richness of their descriptive vocabulary allows some people to note and express very subtle differences in color. This difference in perceptual faculties also allows some cultures to perceive certain subjects more precisely than others. Arabic, for example, has more than 6,000 different words for camels, their body parts, and the equipment associated with them,[50] and Arabic speakers can express nuances about camels that just about everybody else will probably overlook.

It helps managers to know whether cultures favor

- Focused or broad information.
- Sequential or simultaneous handling of situations.
- Handling principles or small issues first.

Obtaining Information: Low-Context Versus High-Context Cultures Researchers classify some countries (including the United States and most of northern Europe) as **low-context cultures:** cultures in which people generally regard as relevant only first-hand information that bears directly on decisions that need to be made. Businesspeople spend little time on small talk and tend to get to the point. In **high-context cultures** (for example, most countries in southern Europe), people tend to regard seemingly peripheral information as pertinent to decision making and to infer meanings from things that people say either indirectly or casually.

When people from the two types of cultures have to deal with each other, those from low-context cultures may perceive those from high-context cultures as inefficient in their use of time. Conversely, people from high-context cultures may perceive those from low-context cultures as too aggressive to be trusted. Recall from our opening case, for example, the problems encountered (and largely caused) by the low-context approach of two sales reps from Great Britain in the high-context business environment of Saudi Arabia.

Information Processing Insofar as all cultures categorize, plan, and quantify, information processing is a universal activity. At the same time, however, although every culture has its own systems for ordering and classifying information, they often vary widely from country to country. In U.S. telephone directories, for instance, entries appear in alphabetical order by last (family) name. In Iceland, they're organized by first (given) names. (Icelandic last names are derived from the father's first name: Thus Jon, son of Thor, is Jon *Thorsson*, and his sister's last name is *Thorsdottir* ["daughter of Thor"]). To perform efficiently and work amicably in a foreign environment, you need to understand such differences in processing systems. Perhaps more importantly, different processing systems create challenges in sharing global data. Even the use of global personnel directories is problematic because of different alphabets and alphabetizing systems.

Monochronic Versus Polychronic Cultures Cultural differences also affect the degree of multitasking with which people are comfortable. According to some researchers, for example, northern European cultures are **monochronic:** People prefer to work sequentially, such as finishing transactions with one customer before dealing with another. Conversely, **polychronic** southern Europeans are more comfortable when working simultaneously on a variety of tasks. One result of a polychronic attitude is a feeling of discomfort when unable to commence dealing immediately with all customers who need service.[51] Imagine the potential misconceptions if the two types of businesspeople try to get together: What if those from northern Europe perceive their southern European counterparts as uninterested in doing business with them because they don't bother to give them their undivided attention?

Idealism Versus Pragmatism Whereas some cultures tend to focus first on the whole and then on the parts, others do the opposite. Consider the following example. When asked to describe an underwater scene in which one large fish was swimming among some smaller fish and other aquatic life, most Japanese first described the overall picture. Most Americans, however, first described the large fish.[52]

Similarly, some cultures prefer to establish overall principles before they try to resolve small issues—an approach sometimes labeled **idealism.** Cultures in which people focus more on details than on abstract principles are said to be characterized by **pragmatism.** These different approaches to information processing can affect business in a number of ways. In a culture of pragmatists (as in the United States), for example, labor negotiations tend to focus on well-defined issues—say, hourly pay increases for a specific bargaining unit. In an idealist culture like that of Argentina, labor disputes tend to blur the focus on specific demands and workers tend to rely instead on mass action—such as general strikes or political activities—to publicize basic principles.

COMMUNICATIONS

Thus far, we've seen how language affects culture—and international business. We now look at problems in *communications*—that is, problems in translating spoken and written language. These problems occur not only when you must shift from one language to another, but also when you must communicate with someone from another country with the same official language. Next, we discuss communications that occur by means other than spoken and written language—by a so-called silent language.

Cross-border communications do not always translate as intended.

Spoken and Written Language   Translating one language directly into another is not as straightforward as it may seem. Some words simply don't have direct translations. Spanish, for example, has no single word for all people who work for businesses (i.e., *employees*). Instead, there is the word *empleados,* which means "white-collar workers," and another word, *obreros,* which means "laborers." This distinction reflects substantial class distinctions among different groups, and it could affect international business if miscommunication arises when Spanish-speaking managers deal with their English-speaking counterparts.

In addition, language, including common word meanings, is constantly evolving. Microsoft, for example, once purchased a thesaurus code for its Spanish version of Word, but by the time it had implemented the software, the connotations of many erstwhile synonyms had shifted; some, in fact, were transformed into outright insults, such as referring to people of mixed race by using the Spanish word for *bastard.* Only when newspapers and other media reports lambasted the program did Microsoft begin correcting the software, and then it was too late; it had already alienated untold numbers of potential Latin American customers.[53] Remember, too, that in any language, words mean different things in different contexts. One U.S. company, for instance, once described itself as an "old friend" of China. Unfortunately, the Chinese word it chose for *old* meant "former" instead of "long-standing."[54]

Finally, remember that grammar is complex and the seemingly slight misuse (or even placement) of a word can change the meaning of an utterance substantially. All of the following, each originally composed to assist English-speaking guests, have appeared on signs in hotels around the world:

FRANCE: "Please leave your values at the desk."

MEXICO (to assure guests about the safety of drinking water): "The manager has personally passed all the water served here."

JAPAN: "You are invited to take advantage of the chambermaid."

NORWAY: "Ladies are requested not to have children in the bar."

SWITZERLAND: "Because of the impropriety of entertaining guests of the opposite sex in the bedroom, it is suggested that the lobby be used for this purpose."

GREECE (at check-in line): "We will execute customers in strict rotation."

These examples offer a humorous look at language barriers, and in fact, slips of the tongue or word processor usually result in a little embarrassment. Poor translations, however, can have much graver consequences. Inaccurate translations have caused structural collapses in buildings and airplane crashes, such as the collision of Air Kazakhstan and Saudi Arabian Air aircraft over India.[55] When it comes to correspondence, negotiations, advertisements, conversations, and, especially, contracts, choose your words carefully. Although there's no foolproof way of ensuring translations, experienced international businesspeople rely on such rules as the following:

- Get references for the people who will do your translating.
- Make sure your translator knows the technical vocabulary of your business.
- For written work, do *back translations:* Have one person, for example, go from English to French and a second from French back to English. If your final message says the same thing that you said originally, it's probably satisfactory.
- Use simple words whenever possible (such as *ban* instead of *interdiction*).
- Avoid slang. American slang, especially words or phrases originating from sports, like *off base, out in left field, threw me a curve,* and *ballpark figure,* are probably meaningless to most businesspeople outside the United States.
- When either you or your counterpart is dealing in a language other than your first language, clarify communications in several ways (repeat things in different words and ask questions) to ensure that all parties have the same interpretation.
- Recognize the need for and budget from the start for the extra time needed for translation and clarification.

Be careful with humor. Although many jokes have universal appeal, a lot of humor does not. A Microsoft executive, for instance, once gave a speech to Indian executives in which he quipped that he really didn't have the qualifications to speak because he had never completed his M.B.A. The comment was badly received because Indians place high importance on education and on persevering rather than dropping out.[56]

Finally, even when all parties to a communication come from countries that share an official language, don't assume understanding will go smoothly. Table 2.1, for instance, lists just some of the approximately 4,000 words that have different meanings in British and American English. Here's a good example of what can go wrong. When Hershey's launched its Elegancita candy bar in Latin America, its expensive advertising campaign boasted about the *cajeta* in the product. Unfortunately, although *cajeta* means "goat's-milk caramel" in Mexico, in much of South America it's vulgar slang for a part of the female anatomy.[57]

Silent Language   Of course, spoken and written language isn't our only means of communicating. In fact, we constantly exchange messages through a host of nonverbal cues

TABLE 2.1   Dangers of Misspeaking the Language(s) of Business

Below are a couple of short lists containing words whose meanings are different in the United States and the United Kingdom—"two countries separated by a common language," as the British playwright G. B. Shaw once quipped. There are approximately 4,000 words with the potential to cause problems for people who—in theory—speak the same language.

United States	United Kingdom
turnover	*redundancy*
sales	*turnover*
inventory	*stock*
stock	*shares*
president	*managing director*
paperback	*limp cover*

that forms what has been called a "silent language."[58] Our opening case offers a good example. Recall that, in the process of evaluating local responses to an establishment like the Java Lounge, consultants found that cultural restrictions limited the number of Saudis they could interview; thus to select the most promising interviewees, they resorted to observing demeanor and certain physical cues.

Colors are an interesting aspect of a culture's "silent language" because they conjure up meanings derived from cultural experience. In most Western countries, for instance, black is associated with death. In parts of Asia, white has the same connotation; in Latin America, it's purple. For a product to succeed, its colors must obviously be consistent with the consumer's frame of reference. When, for example, United Airlines promoted a new passenger service in Hong Kong by giving white carnations to its best customers, the promotion backfired. Why? In Hong Kong, white carnations are given only in sympathy for a death in the family. On the spoken-language front, Motorola had difficulty assigning cell phone numbers in China because certain sounds in Mandarin came out wrong. If you give out a number ending in 54–7424, you'll sound as if you're saying, "I die, my wife dies, my child dies."[59]

> Silent language includes color associations, sense of appropriate distance, time and status cues, body language, and prestige.

Distance   Another aspect of silent language is the distance that people maintain during conversations. Our sense of appropriate distance is learned and differs among cultures. In the United States, for example, the customary distance for a business discussion is 5 to 8 feet; for personal business, it's 18 inches to 3 feet.[60] When the distance is closer or farther than what's customary for them, people tend to feel uneasy. Thus U.S. managers conducting business in Latin America may find themselves constantly moving backward to avoid the closer conversational distance to which their Latin American counterparts are accustomed. At the end of the discussion, both parties may well feel uneasy about each other without realizing why.

Time and Punctuality   Perceptions of time and punctuality also affect unspoken cues that differ by cultural context and may create confusion. U.S. businesspeople usually arrive early for business appointments, a few minutes late for dinner at someone's home, and a bit later for cocktail parties. In another country, the concept of punctuality in any or all of these situations may be different. U.S. businesspeople in Latin America may consider it discourteous if their Latin American counterparts do not arrive on time for a business meeting. Conversely, a Latin American host may find it equally discourteous if a U.S. guest arrives only a few minutes late for dinner.

Culturally speaking, there are different ways of looking at time. In English-speaking, Germanic, and Scandinavian countries, people tend to value time as a scarce commodity; if it's lost, it can't be recouped.[61] Thus they're prone not only to sticking to schedules but also to emphasizing short-term results, even if taking longer would yield better results.

In contrast, people who view time as an event prefer to take whatever time is necessary to complete the event. In one case, a U.S. company competing for a contract in Mexico with a French company drew up a presentation confident it would win on the basis of better technology. In fact, managers were so confident that they scheduled a tight one-day meeting in Mexico City, allowing what they thought was plenty of time for the presentation and questions. Unfortunately, the Mexican team arrived one hour late. Then, when one member of the Mexican team was called out of the room for an urgent phone call, the whole group got upset when the U.S. team tried to proceed without him. The French team, in contrast, allocated two weeks for discussions and won the contract even though its technology was clearly less sophisticated.[62]

Body Language   Body language, or *kinesics*—the way that people walk, touch, and move their bodies—also differs from culture to culture. Indeed, very few gestures are universal in meaning. A Greek, Turk, or Bulgarian, for example, indicates "yes" with a sideways movement of the head that resembles nothing so much as the shake of the head

FIGURE 2.5   Body Language Is Not a Universal Language

The fine line between approval and put-down: Very few gestures have universal meanings. In the United States, you'd probably be safe in approving of another person's statement by forming an *O* with your thumb and index finger (the so-called high sign). In Germany, Greece, and France, however, you'd be expressing a very different opinion.

Source: The meanings have been taken from decriptions in Roger E. Axtell, *Gestures* (New York: John Wiley, 1998). Reprinted by permission of John Wiley & Sons, Inc.

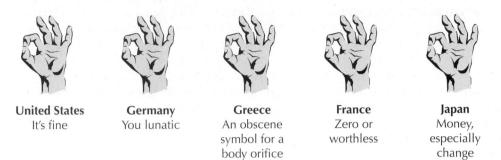

| **United States** | **Germany** | **Greece** | **France** | **Japan** |
| It's fine | You lunatic | An obscene symbol for a body orifice | Zero or worthless | Money, especially change |

that means "no" in the United States and much of Europe. As Figure 2.5 shows, certain gestures may have several—even contradictory—meanings.

Prestige   Another factor in silent language relates to a person's position in his or her organization. A U.S. businessperson who places great faith in objects as cues to prestige may underestimate the importance of foreign counterparts who don't value large plush offices on high floors. A foreigner may underestimate U.S. counterparts who perform their own services, such as opening their own doors, fetching their own coffee, and answering unscreened phone calls.

Dealing with Cultural Differences

After a company has identified key cultural differences in the country where it intends to do business, must it alter its customary practices to succeed there? Can people actually overcome culturally related adjustment problems when working abroad? There are no easy answers to these questions, but the following discussion highlights some of the variables that affect *degrees* of successful adjustment. Basically, we can break down these variables into four issues:

1. The extent to which a culture is willing to accept the introduction of anything foreign
2. Whether key cultural differences are small or great
3. The ability of individuals to adjust to what they find in foreign cultures
4. The general management orientation of the company doing business in a foreign culture

In the following sections, we address each of these issues in some depth.

ACCOMMODATION

Host cultures do not always expect foreigners to adjust to them.

Although our opening case illustrates the advantages of *adjusting* to a host country's culture, international companies sometimes succeed in introducing new products, technologies, and operating procedures with relatively little adjustment. How have they pulled off this feat? Primarily because the product, technology, or procedure they're introducing does not run counter to deep-seated attitudes or because the host culture is willing to accept the foreign product or practice as an agreeable trade-off. Bahrain, for instance, permits the sale of pork products (ordinarily prohibited by religious law) as long as transactions are limited to special grocery store departments in which Muslims can neither work nor shop.

Sometimes local society regards foreigners and domestic citizens differently. When staying overnight in Jeddah, for example, Western female flight attendants can wear jeans and T-shirts, but local women cannot.[63] At other times, local citizens may actually feel that their cultures are being mocked when foreigners bend over backwards to make adjustments.[64] But sometimes laws treat local and foreign citizens similarly. As we saw in our opening case, women in Saudi Arabia may be approached by patrols authorized to police female apparel, and this authority extends to foreigners as well as nationals.

CULTURAL DISTANCE: USEFULNESS AND LIMITATIONS

Obviously, some countries are much like other countries, usually because they share many cultural characteristics, such as language, religion, geographic location, ethnicity, and level of economic development. A Human Values study compared 43 societies on 405 dimensions,[65] and by averaging the *cultural distance* separating countries on each dimension (say, the number of countries apart for Sweden and Spain on each dimension), researchers could determine the *cultural proximity* of two countries. On this scale, the United Kingdom is culturally close to the United States and China is culturally distant.

Map 2.4 identifies 58 countries according to the findings of a study by GLOBE (Global Leadership and Organizational Behavior Effectiveness) designed to cluster countries on a fairly specific dimension—namely, the values and attitudes of middle managers toward leadership characteristics. When a company moves into a foreign country that's culturally close rather than culturally distant, or when it moves within a cluster of culturally similar countries, it should expect to encounter fewer cultural differences and to face fewer cultural adjustments. An Ecuadorian company doing business in Colombia, for instance, should expect to make fewer adjustments than if it wanted to do business in Thailand.

Even within clusters, however, there may still be significant cultural differences that could affect business dealings. Moreover, managers may assume that closely clustered countries are more homogeneous than they really are, and if they become too confident about the fit between their own and another nation, they may well overlook important subtleties. Women's roles and behavior, for example, differ substantially from one Arab country to another.

Companies should also consider the host country's perception of their role in its market. Disney, for instance, had much more success in opening a theme park in Japan than in France, even though France is culturally closer to the United States than Japan. Why? On the one hand, for a variety of reasons the Japanese were more receptive to Disney: (1) Both Japanese children and adults, familiar with the "Mickey Mouse Club" on TV, perceived Mickey Mouse as a wholesome, nonthreatening figure; (2) The Japanese had a tradition of buying souvenirs on family excursions; and (3) Disney's reputation for supercleanliness and smiling faces fit well with Japanese preferences for harmony and order. The French, on the other hand, knew Mickey Mouse only as a comic book conniver who'd been reformulated for the French market. They regarded Disney souvenirs as tacky and policies requiring personnel to dress uniformly and smile mindlessly as violations of personal dignity.[66]

CULTURE SHOCK

Any firm wanting to operate in a foreign country has to send personnel abroad for both short and long periods of time. These personnel are subject to the laws where they go, as well as to potential exposure to certain foreign practices they may find traumatic. Recall, for example, the severe forms of capital and corporal punishment in Saudi Arabia to which we alluded in our opening case. Tourists and business travelers should remember that Saudi laws—and penalties—apply to them as well as to Saudi nationals. In fact, there are cultural practices all over the world that many outsiders consider downright wrong, ranging from polygamy and child marriage to concubinage, slavery, and burning widows. Both companies and individuals must decide if they're ready to carry on business in places that countenance such practices.

When doing business in a similar culture, companies

- Usually have to make fewer adjustments.
- May overlook subtle differences.

MAP 2.4
A Synthesis of Country Clusters

As you can see, this map illustrates a key finding of the GLOBE study in the early 2000s of middle manager attitudes and values: namely, that managers in different countries share different ideas about the nature of *leadership*—ideas that, not surprisingly, tend to affect domestic business practices. Note that cluster labels (e.g., "Nordic Europe," "Confucian Asia") reflect the attitudes of *a majority of countries comprising each cluster.* Thus note the inclusion of Turkey— where Arabic is not the dominant language—in the "Arab" cluster and the inclusion of Costa Rica and Guatemala in the "Latin American" cluster even though attitudes there tend to be closer to those in countries grouped in the "Latin European" cluster.

Source: Reprinted from Vipin Gupta, Paul J. Hanges, and Peter Dorfman, "Cultural Clusters: Methodology and Findings," *Journal of World Business 37* (Spring 2002): 13. Reprinted with permission from Elsevier.

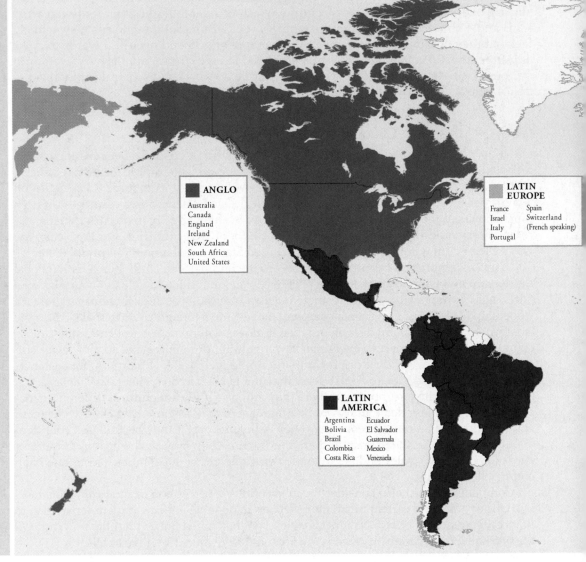

ANGLO
Australia
Canada
England
Ireland
New Zealand
South Africa
United States

LATIN EUROPE
France   Spain
Israel   Switzerland
Italy   (French speaking)
Portugal

LATIN AMERICA
Argentina   Ecuador
Bolivia   El Salvador
Brazil   Guatemala
Colombia   Mexico
Costa Rica   Venezuela

Some people get frustrated when entering a different culture.

In addition, even in countries whose practices aren't necessarily traumatic to them, workers who go overseas often encounter something called **culture shock**—the frustration that results from having to absorb a vast array of new cultural cues and expectations. Even such seemingly simple tasks as using a different type of toilet or telephone, getting a driver's license, or buying stamps can at first be taxing experiences.

According to some researchers, people working in a culture that's significantly different than their own may pass through certain stages in the process of adjustment. At first, much like tourists, they're delighted with quaint differences. Later, however, they grow depressed and confused (the *culture shock* phase) so their effectiveness in the foreign environment begins to suffer. Fortunately for most people, culture shock begins to ebb after a month or two as they grow more comfortable and experience greater job satisfaction.

Interestingly, some people experience culture shock when they go back home— a phenomenon known as **reverse culture shock.** What's happened? Basically, they've learned to accept the things they've encountered abroad—perhaps such seemingly simple things as more leisurely lunches—that were never common options back home.

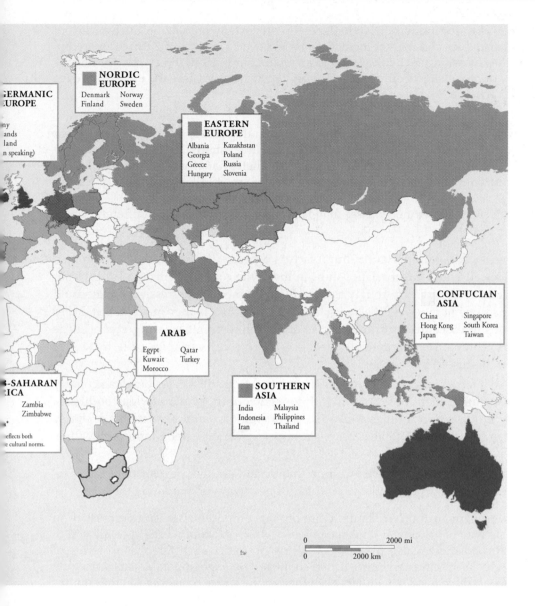

**GERMANIC
EUROPE**

ny
ands
land
n speaking)

**NORDIC
EUROPE**

Denmark   Norway
Finland   Sweden

**EASTERN
EUROPE**

Albania   Kazakhstan
Georgia   Poland
Greece   Russia
Hungary   Slovenia

**CONFUCIAN
ASIA**

China   Singapore
Hong Kong   South Korea
Japan   Taiwan

ARAB

Egypt   Qatar
Kuwait   Turkey
Morocco

**SOUTHERN
ASIA**

India   Malaysia
Indonesia   Philippines
Iran   Thailand

B-SAHARAN
ICA

Zambia
Zimbabwe

eflects both
e cultural norms.

0   2000 mi

0   2000 km

COMPANY AND MANAGEMENT ORIENTATIONS

Whether and how much a company and its managers adapt to a foreign culture depends not only on the host-country culture but also on the attitudes of home-country companies and managers. The following sections discuss three such attitudes or orientations—polycentrism, ethnocentrism, and geocentrism.

> Polycentrist management is so overwhelmed by national differences that it won't introduce workable changes.

Polycentrism   A *polycentric* organization or individual tends to believe business units in different countries should act like local companies. Given the unique problems that many companies have encountered in overseas ventures, it's not surprising that so many develop polycentric perspectives. In some respects, however, polycentrism may be an overly cautious response to cultural variety. How so? A firm whose outlook is too rigidly polycentric may shy away from certain countries or avoid transferring home-country practices or resources that will actually work well abroad.

Look at it this way. To compete effectively, an international company—and its local units—must usually perform some functions differently from the competitors it encounters

Ethnocentrist management
overlooks national differences
and

- Ignores important factors.
- Believes home-country
  objectives should prevail.
- Thinks change is easy.

Geocentric management often
uses business practices that are
hybrids of home and foreign
norms. Because people do not
necessarily accept change readily,
the management of change is
important.

CONCEPT CHECK

In Chapter 1, the sections on the
"Physical and Social Factors" that
influence a company's external
environment categorize a number
of constraints that may affect a
company's ability to conduct
global business. The section on
"The Competitive Environment"
discusses constraints that affect
another area of a company's
external environment.

abroad. They may, for instance, have to depend more heavily on new products or invent new ways to produce and market them. Because the overly polycentric firm is less receptive to the idea of risking such innovation in an unfamiliar market, it may rely too heavily on imitation of proven host-country practices and, in the process, lose the innovative edge it has honed at home.

Ethnocentrism   *Ethnocentrism* reflects the conviction that one's own culture is superior to that of other countries. In international business, it's usually applied to a company (or individual) strongly committed to the principle that what works at home will work abroad—so strongly that its overseas practices tend to ignore differences in cultures and markets.

Generally speaking, ethnocentrism may lead managers to take three different sets of practices:

1. Managers overlook important cultural factors because they've become accustomed to certain cause-and-effect relationships in the home country. Thus the British sales reps in our opening case wrongly assumed that by moving aggressively, they could make the same number of calls and sales in Saudi Arabia as they made in Britain. To check this ethnocentric attitude, and to ensure they aren't wearing ethnocentric blinders, companies can consult checklists of cultural variables (like those, for example, discussed in this chapter).

2. Although it recognizes environmental differences, a firm still focuses on home-country objectives rather than those that fit with foreign-country or worldwide conditions. Because it doesn't perform as well as local competitors—and because it's probably encountering opposition to its practices in overseas markets—long-term competitiveness may suffer.

3. Although recognizing differences, a firm underestimates the complexity of the problems involved in introducing new products or new ways of marketing them.

Before we go any further, we should point out that ethnocentrism isn't necessarily an inappropriate way of looking at things. Obviously, much of what works at home will in fact work abroad. Recall also that concentrating on national differences in terms of *averages* overlooks specific variations within countries. By engaging in a focus strategy, a company may be able to sell to outliers even though the *average* consumer in the country has strong cultural biases against the product. Pursuing such a strategy, for example, you could sell meat products to the minority of Indians who eat meat regularly or on occasion. Likewise, a company may identify partners, suppliers, and employees among the minority of population whose attitudes don't fit the cultural *average* (there are always individualists in even the most collectivist societies).

Geocentrism   Between the extremes of polycentrism and ethnocentrism, there is an approach to overseas business practices that integrates company practices, host-country practices, and some entirely new practices.[67] Both Saks Fifth Avenue and Harvey Nichols, for example, have adapted their customary merchandising practices in Saudi Arabia. As we saw in our opening case, however, they also adjust to Saudi customs (for instance, by setting aside women-only floors). At the same time, they've introduced entirely new practices, such as providing drivers' lounges for the chauffeurs of female customers.

Called *geocentrism*, this approach requires companies to balance informed knowledge of their own organizational cultures with both home- and host-country needs, capabilities, and constraints. Because it encourages innovation and improves the likelihood of success, geocentrism is the preferred approach of companies that conduct business in foreign cultures and markets.

Point Counterpoint

Does International Business Lead to Cultural Imperialism?

Point **Yes** The idea is pretty well accepted: International business influences globalization and globalization influences culture. Now, I have nothing against international business or globalization—at least part of it. What I don't like is *modern cultural imperialism*. What's *modern cultural imperialism?* It's what happens when the West, especially the United States, imposes its technical, political, military, and economic supremacy on developing countries.[68]

For years now, U.S. business has been in the business of exporting U.S. culture—mostly through tactics that are rarely in the best interests of the national cultures it's targeted for economic domination. Because U.S. companies monopolize the international entertainment media, people all over the world are stuck with CNN, MTV, and the Disney Channel and bombarded with U.S. movies. Moreover, the same viewers are barraged with ads for the products—everything from nonnutritious soft drinks to obesity-creating fast foods—that pop up in the TV shows and movies they can't escape, even in the privacy of their own homes.

And what about the hordes of U.S. tourists who plop down more for a night's lodging in a developing country than the hotel maid makes in a year? If you ask them, they'll tell you they're just taking a look at how the other half lives, but the fact is, they're selling the U.S. lifestyle to a target market that can't afford it and that's probably better off without a lot of it. Thanks to canned entertainment, nonstop advertising, and a sales force posing as tourists, culture shoppers in developing countries can sample U.S. possessions and practices to their hearts' content. Never mind that—at least according to TV and the movies—they come from a place that's populated mostly by the superwealthy and by cops and psychotic malcontents whose daily lives are taken up with bullet-spattered body parts, round-the-clock sex, and inane family relationships: It's seductive and promotes everything that's "Made in the U.S.A." That's why people everywhere are starting to behave and even talk like fictional Americans—after all, everyday speech from Manila to Managua is now peppered with U.S. slang. Along the way, people are letting their own cultural identities slip away.

Once they have a foot in the door, Western companies barge in to exploit the demand that they've created, further destabilizing local cultures. In Mexico, Wal-Mart thinks nothing of putting up a superstore virtually next door to ancient ruins—and in the process, by the way, eradicating the nearby street market. What's more, because international companies tend to cluster in urban markets, they drag

(continued)

Counterpoint **No** You imply that people in poor countries passively accept everything they see in movie theaters and on TV. I say they're not quite *that* naive. Granted, they drink Coca-Cola (and eat at McDonald's), but they've turned their backs on a lot of products that international companies have tried to foist on them. Like most of us, they pick and choose what they want and don't want based on their own needs and on their own cultural terms.[70] By the way, you also seem to assume that cultures in developing countries are the same. They aren't. They're different, and because of their differences, they interpret what they see and hear—and what they buy—quite differently.

You also suggest that cultural diffusion is a one-way process—from developing to developed. You even insinuate that developed countries can repel assaults from cultural invaders. Yes, France tries to protect its film industry in some quixotic plan to "maintain French culture," but the whole effort is probably misguided: Even in its so-called golden age, the French film industry wasn't above recruiting international stars to get in front of the camera and world-renowned directors to work behind it.

Like cultural purists everywhere, you've lost sight of how cultural diffusion works. Once contact has been made, culture heads in both directions and tends to survive—even evolve. Let's do a little time traveling. Way back, say, between 100 BC and AD 400, about 50 Mediterranean languages disappeared when people took up reading and writing in Latin and Greek.[71] Today, of course, very few of us converse in Latin, but that doesn't mean it's completely disappeared: It's *evolved*—namely, into the "Romance" languages—French, Italian, Spanish, and a few others.

Likewise, a lot of languages are in trouble today, and it's important to study them while they're still around. But the thing to remember is this: Not all of these languages are dying from the plague of international business. Most of them are indeed giving way to other languages, but in case you're interested, it's usually to some language other than English—Spanish, Mandarin, Arabic. Of course, American English is seeping into other languages, but Americans have recently added a lot of foreign words as well. Take Spanish. If you're a *macho* guy in charge of the whole *enchilada,* for example, you're probably called the head *honcho.*

Similarly, today you can find a McDonald's in the most remote corners of the globe, but as a matter of fact, you'd be hard-pressed to find any food items that U.S.-style fast food has entirely displaced. Because globalization works both ways, it tends to diffuse a culture in two directions, and when

(continued)

workers away from rural areas to work hours that don't even allow time to go home for lunch under managers who speak only English.[69]

I admit, if a country is rich enough, it can afford to resist cultural exploitation. Canada, for instance, says no to foreign investment in culturally sensitive industries and makes sure there's Canadian content in local entertainment media. Finland discourages architecture that runs counter to tradition, and in France, the government discourages languages other than French and subsidizes a national motion picture industry. In the developing world, however, where there's precious little cash for fighting off cultural extinction, people are at the mercy of foreign culture brokers (not to mention local politicians who are too busy siphoning off every extra rupee and peso to protect their own personal way of life).●

it comes to food, the result is greater diversity for everybody. And what we're witnessing is not "cultural imperialism" but rather cultural *hybridrization.* In most countries, U.S. hamburgers, Japanese sushi, Italian pizza, Mexican tacos, and Middle Eastern pita bread coexist with the local cuisine.

But let's assume for a moment that diffusion—the movement of media, advertising, and marketed products—is just one way. What's changed in the receiving culture other than the acceptance of certain *material* elements of the dominant culture? It doesn't necessarily follow that just because they've taken a liking to soft drinks and fast food, people all over the world have scrapped their traditional values. And until we can establish a link between these two phenomena, we can't assume that cultures are becoming homogenized.[72] Moreover, some evidence suggests that, although young people are most likely to adopt elements from a foreign culture, they tend to revert to traditional values and habits as they get older. If that's the case, it's hard to argue they're spearheading any permanent changes in their local cultures.[73]

Nobody is denying that having foreign products available creates new wants among consumers. Nor is anybody suggesting that, in fulfilling these new wants, people often have to make trade-offs. But here's the question: Are people (and societies) worse off because they give up, say, lunch with the family to be able to afford certain consumer goods that will satisfy the needs of a whole family? People have the right to make their own decisions about the needs they want to fulfill, and globalization gives them options they wouldn't otherwise have. And as for the impact of tourism, that's also a two-edged sword: You say that its effect on host cultures is primarily negative, but other people (myself included) would argue that, quite often, it has helped maintain certain features of a traditional culture. The art of traditional Balinese dancing, for example, is alive and kicking because tourists want to see it.

Let me close by saying that, yes, international companies often ignore local cultures (and worse). But look back at the opening case in this chapter: The story of the Java Lounge makes it clear that a successful business, whether locally or foreign owned, must accommodate itself to the culture in which it operates. In some cases, this means revising plans to respond to local demands. You neglected to mention, for instance, that before Wal-Mart finalized its construction plans in Mexico, executives consulted with anthropologists and agreed to reduce the store's height and to give it a stone facade in a subdued color: Now, like existing buildings in the area, it can be seen only from atop the pyramids. And while we're on the subject, you also failed to mention that the so-called traditional market in question was peddling imported plastic goods rather than indigenous Mexican handicrafts.●

STRATEGIES FOR INSTITUTING CHANGE

As we've seen, when companies want to establish competitive advantages in foreign markets, they may need to develop new products (such as veggie burgers in India) or operating methods (separate workstations for male and female employees in Saudi Arabia). Inevitably, however, they'll introduce some degree of change into the foreign markets in which they operate. Thus they need to bear in mind a fairly simple rule of thumb: People don't normally accept change very readily, either in the home- or host-country market. The methods that companies may choose for managing such changes are important for ensuring success.

Fortunately, we can gain a lot of insight into this issue by examining the international experiences of both for-profit and not-for-profit organizations. In addition, a great deal of material is available on potential methods and so-called *change agents*— people or processes that intentionally cause or accelerate social, cultural, or behavioral change—much of it dealing with overcoming resistance to change in the international arena. In the following sections, we discuss both experiences with and approaches to successful change. In particular, we focus on strategies in eight different areas:

- Value systems
- Cost-benefit analysis of change
- Resistance to too much change
- Participation
- Reward sharing
- Opinion leadership
- Timing
- Learning abroad

We conclude with a discussion on the importance of learning as a two-way process— one in which companies transfer knowledge to and from both domestic and foreign markets.

Value Systems   The more something contradicts our value system, the more difficulty we have accepting it. In Eritrea, for example, a poor nation in northeast Africa, people eat very modest amounts of seafood compared with people in a lot of other countries. This is noteworthy because Eritrea, whose economy is based on subsistence agriculture and that has suffered several periods of famine in recent years, boasts a long coastline rich in seafood. In trying to persuade Eritrean adults to eat more seafood, however, the Eritrean government and the United Nations World Food Program have faced formidable opposition, largely because of local value systems: There are religious taboos against eating fish without scales and insect-like sea creatures (including shrimp and crayfish), and most Eritreans grew up believing seafood has a foul taste. Among schoolchildren, however, whose value system and habits were still flexible, officials faced little opposition.[74]

Cost-Benefit Analysis of Change   Although some adjustments to foreign ways are inexpensive, others are quite costly. Some result in greatly improved performance, such as higher productivity or sales, whereas others improve performance only marginally. Thus a company must consider the expected *cost-benefit relationship* of any adjustments it makes abroad. On each December 12, for example, U.S.-based Cummins Engine shuts down its Mexican plant so workers may observe a religious holiday. Moreover, Cummins hosts a celebration for employees and families that includes a priest to offer the appropriate prayers. In this case, the cost to the employer is well worth the resulting renewal of employee commitment.

Resistance to Too Much Change   When the German magazine publisher Gruner + Jahr (G+J) bought U.S.-based *McCall's*, it immediately overhauled the magazine's format. The new owner changed editors, eliminated long stories and such features as advice columns, increased celebrity coverage, made layouts more robust, supplemented articles with sidebars, and refused discounts for big advertisers. Before long, as morale declined, employee turnover began to increase; more importantly, revenues fell because the change in format seemed too radical to advertisers.[75] According to most observers, G+J might have found it easier to obtain employee and advertiser acceptance had it instituted fewer changes at one time and phased in its plans for change a little more gradually.

Participation   One way to avoid problems like those encountered by G+J is to discuss proposed changes with stakeholders in advance. The company might perceive the strength of the resistance that it faces, stimulate stakeholders to recognize the need for change, and ease fears of the consequences of change. Employees may at least be satisfied that management has listened to them regardless of the decisions it ultimately makes.[76]

Companies sometimes make the mistake of thinking that stakeholder participation in decision making is effective only in countries with sufficiently educated people who are willing to speak up to make substantial contributions to the policy-making process. Anyone who's had to deal with foreign aid programs can tell you that participation may be extremely important even in countries where education levels are low and power distance and uncertainty avoidance high.

Reward Sharing   Sometimes a proposed change may have no foreseeable benefit for the people whose support must be obtained if it's to succeed. Production workers, for example, may have little incentive to try new work practices unless they see some more or less immediate benefit for themselves. What can an employer do? It might develop bonus or profit-sharing programs based on the new approach. In one case, a U.S.-Peruvian gold-mining venture won the support of skeptical Andean villagers by donating sheep.[77]

Opinion Leadership   By making use of local channels of influence, or *opinion leaders*, a firm may be able to facilitate the acceptance of change. Opinion leaders may emerge in unexpected places. When, for example, Ford wanted to instill U.S. production methods into a Mexican plant, managers relied on Mexican production workers, rather than on either Mexican or U.S. supervisors, to observe operations at U.S. plants. What was the advantage of this approach? The Mexican workers had more credibility than supervisors with the Mexican employees who would have to implement the new methods.[78] (Our closing case, which concerns a dam construction project in the African nation of Uganda, tells the story of a fairly unusual opinion leader—one whose leadership techniques include the performance of elaborate religious rituals.)

Timing   Many well-conceived changes fail simply because they're ill timed. A proposed laborsaving production method, for example, might under many circumstances make employees nervous about losing their jobs no matter how much management tries to reassure them. If, however, the proposal is made during a period of labor shortage, the firm is likely to encounter less fear and resistance.

In certain cases, of course, crisis precipitates the acceptance of change. In Turkey, for example, family members have traditionally dominated business organizations. Indeed, family members sometimes continue to exert substantial influence even after they no longer have any official responsibilities. In more and more instances, however, poor performance has stimulated a rapid change in this practice: Many families no longer "run" the business, but rather serve in "advisory capacities" (often on the board of directors).

Learning Abroad   Finally, remember that, as companies gain more experience in overseas operations, they may learn as well as impart valuable knowledge—knowledge that proves just as useful in the home country as in a host country. Companies such as Fuji and Kodak, for example, created the technology for while-you-wait photo development in Saudi Arabia. Why? Because Saudi customers were more insistent on retrieving photos without anyone else seeing them. Only later did processors transfer the technology to other countries.

LOOKING TO THE FUTURE

What Will Happen to National Cultures?

Scenario 1: New Hybrid Cultures Will Develop and Personal Horizons Will Broaden

International contact is, of course, increasing at a rate that no one could have imagined a few decades ago—a process that should lead to a certain mixing and greater similarity among national cultures. And at first glance, that's exactly what's happening.[79] The mixing seems evident when one sees, for example, a group of Japanese tourists listening to a Philippine band perform an American pop song in a British hotel in Indonesia. So, too, with the emergence of such combination languages as "Spanglish." The growing similarity seems evident when one sees people in every corner of the world wearing the same clothes and listening to the same recording stars. Similarly, competitors headquartered in far-flung areas of the globe are increasingly copying each other's operating practices, thus creating a competitive work environment that's now more global than national. As companies and people get used to operating internationally, they become more confident in applying the benefits of cultural diversity and globally inspired operating procedures to explore new areas in both workplace productivity and consumer behavior.

We'll also see people taking advantage of greater mobility and, in the process, broadening their concepts of what it means to enjoy global citizenship.[80] Historically, for example, most people who emigrated to foreign countries were able to return to their homelands perhaps once in their lives. They were thus compelled to accept the cultures of their adopted countries, in the process sacrificing much of their native cultural identity. Today, however, emigrés, most of whom come to high-income countries from low-income countries to find work, often obtain dual citizenship and maintain contact with their native cultures. Many of them find that, even though they're working thousands of miles away from home, it's becoming increasingly easier to

keep in contact with home. The important thing is that emigrés now tend to transfer culture in both directions, forcing both host and home countries to mediate a much greater level of cultural diversity than ever before. There has also emerged a class of international managers whose traditional ties to specific cultures are much looser than those of most people, even those involved in international business. Educated in France, for instance, CEO Carlos Ghosn of Japan's Nissan and France's Renault is a Brazilian of Lebanese extraction.[81]

Scenario 2: Although the Outward Expressions of National Culture Will Continue to Become More Homogeneous, Distinct Values Will Tend to Remain Stable

Beneath the surface of the visual aspects of culture (including most of the elements that we touched on in the previous section), people continue to hold fast to some of the basic things that make national cultures different from one another. In other words, although certain material and even behavioral facets of cultures will become more universal, certain fundamental values and attitudes—for example, ways in which people cooperate, in which they approach problem solving, and in which they're motivated—will remain much the same. Religious differences, for instance, are as strong as ever, and language differences still bolster ethnic identities. What's important is that differences in these areas are still powerful enough to fragment the world culturally and to stymie the standardization of products and operating methods that threaten to "globalize" cultures.

Scenario 3: Nationalism Will Continue to Reinforce Cultural Identity

If people didn't perceive the *cultural* differences among themselves and others, they'd be less likely to regard themselves as distinct *national* entities. That's why

(continued)

appeals to cultural identity are so effective in mobilizing people in defense of national identity. Typically, such efforts promote the "national culture" by reinforcing language and religion, subsidizing nationalistic programs and activities, and propagandizing against foreign influences on the national culture.

Scenario 4: Existing National Borders Will Shift to Accommodate Ethnic Differences

In several countries, we're seeing more evidence of the emergence of subcultural power and influence. Why? Basic factors include immigration and the rise of religious fundamentalism. Equally important seems to be the growing desire among ethnic groups for independence from the groups that dominate the nations in which they find themselves. In recent years, for

example, both Yugoslavia and Czechoslovakia have broken up for this reason, and in Sudan and Sri Lanka, ethnic groups are currently pitted against one another in bloody civil wars. Meanwhile, some subcultures—such as the Inuits in the Arctic and the Kurds in the Middle East—simply resist pigeonholing according to established national boundaries. Because they have less in common with their "countrymen" than with ethnic brethren in other countries, it's hard to assign them a national identity on the basis of (often unfortunate) geographic circumstances.

Regardless of the scenario that unfolds in any given arena, international businesspeople must learn to examine specific cultural differences if they hope to operate effectively in a foreign environment. In the future, analysis based only on national characteristics won't be sufficient: They'll have to pay attention to all the other myriad factors that contribute to distinctions in values, attitudes, and behavior. ■

CASE

Charles Martin in Uganda: What to Do When a Manager Goes Native

James Green, a vice president at U.S.-based Hydro Generation (HG), was pondering a specific question: Should he retain Charles Martin for the construction phase of a major dam project in the African nation of Uganda?[82] (See Map 2.5 for the location of Uganda in Africa and of the dam project in Uganda.) Martin had already completed his assignment on the preliminary phase of the project, and Green couldn't deny that Martin's results had been highly satisfactory—he'd finished every task on time and within budget.

Green, however, was a little concerned with the *means* by which Martin tended to achieve his ends. In Green's opinion, Martin was too eager to accommodate Ugandan ways of doing business, some of which ran counter both to HG's organizational culture and to its usual methods of operating in foreign environments. In particular, Green worried that some of Martin's accommodations with local stakeholders might have unforeseen repercussions for the company's presence in Uganda.

He also knew the philosophy and values of founder and current CEO Lawrence Lovell who had been instrumental in shaping HG's mission and culture. A devout Christian and regular attendee of the National Prayer Breakfast, Lovell believed strongly that business activities, though secular, should embody Christian values. As a manager, he believed subordinates should be given full responsibility in making and implementing decisions, but they should also be held accountable for the results.

Martin, however, wanted to stay in Uganda, and HG would be hard-pressed to find someone else with his combination of professional training, experience with HG, and familiarity

MAP 2.5   Uganda

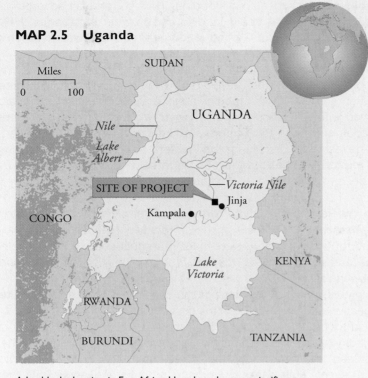

A land-locked nation in East Africa, Uganda embraces a significant portion of Lake Victoria, the largest lake on the continent. The capital Kampala (as well as several other major cities) is located near Lake Victoria, which is a source of the Nile, the world's longest river. As you can see, the site of the Hydro Generation dam-construction project is situated near the source of the river.

with the host country. (Martin, though only 29, had already proved effective in using his knowledge of local development issues to disarm critics of the power plant.)

Hiring Martin to handle all preconstruction operations represented a new approach for HG. In this capacity, Martin, who'd been transferred to Uganda a year and a half earlier as project liaison specialist, had been given a threefold task:

1. To gain local support for the project by working with both Ugandan authorities in the capital of Kampala and villagers in the vicinity of the construction site.

2. To set up an office and hire office personnel to take charge of local purchasing (including lower-level hiring), clearing incoming goods through customs, securing immigration permissions for foreigners attached to the project, overseeing the logistics of getting materials going from the airport in Kampala to the dam site, and keeping inventory and accounting records.

3. To help foreign personnel (mainly engineers) get settled and feel comfortable living and working in Uganda.

Martin was also responsible for establishing an operating structure that would spare incoming managers the hassles of such mundane start-up activities as obtaining licenses, installing telephones and utilities, and finding local people to hire for the wide range of jobs that would be needed. In addition, although HG specialized in power plants (it had built plants in 16 countries and retained ownership shares in about half of them), the Uganda project was its first African venture.

Now, dam construction anywhere requires huge amounts of capital, and projects often face opposition from groups acting on behalf of such local parties as the people who will need to move because of subsequent flooding. Thus to forestall adverse publicity and, more importantly, activity that could lead to costly work stoppages, HG needed as many local allies as it could get. Getting (and keeping) them was another key facet of Martin's job.

Martin, though still young by most standards, was well suited to the Ugandan project. After high school, he'd entered the University of Wisconsin, where he became fascinated with Africa through a course in its precolonial history. Graduating with a major in African studies, he served with the Peace Corps in Kenya, where he worked with small business start-ups and took side trips to Ethiopia and Tanzania. Although he loved working in Kenya, Martin developed a disdain for the Western managers and workers who isolated themselves in expatriate ghettos and congregated in the capital's first-class hotels. His own creed became "Don't draw attention to yourself and, above all, learn and respect the culture."

At the end of his Peace Corps stint, Martin was determined to return to and work somewhere in Africa. After earning an M.B.A. at the University of Maryland, he took a job with HG, where he worked for two years on project bidding and budgeting. Both when he was hired and when HG became involved in the Ugandan project, Martin made sure his superiors knew he wanted the African assignment.

Not surprisingly, HG saw the advantage of someone who possessed both a home-country corporate perspective and a knowledge of the host country's economics, politics, and culture. In Uganda, a country of about 25 million, English is the official language, but many people speak only an indigenous language, mainly Bantu or Nilotic languages of the Bugandas, Langos, Acholi, Teso, and Karamojong tribes. Although about two-thirds of Ugandans are Christians (about evenly split between Roman Catholics and Anglicans), there are large numbers of Muslims and adherents of various animistic religions.

Since gaining independence in 1962, Uganda has had a largely unhappy history. The ruthless dictatorship of Idi Amin included mass murder among its policies and, more recently, Uganda has been forced to absorb huge numbers of refugees fleeing bloodshed in Rwanda, Zaire, and the Sudan. Nepotism is the norm, and the government is considered one of the most corrupt in the world. On the positive side, foreign companies that want to do business in Uganda aren't heavily regulated, and because less than 5 percent of the population has access to electricity, the Ugandan government strongly favored the HG power plant project.

Now, 18 months later, Martin was completing his liaison assignment for the preconstruction phase of the project and Green was reviewing his performance. Specifically, he was concerned not only about some of Martin's business practices but also about certain aspects of his lifestyle, not the least of which was his participation in local tribal rituals. HG had no formal guidelines on the lifestyles of expatriate managers in its employ, but the company culture tended to encourage standards of living that were consistent with the values of a prosperous international company. With what HG paid him, Martin could certainly afford to live in one of the upscale neighborhoods that were home to most foreign managers working in and around Kampala. Martin, however, preferred a middle-class Ugandan neighborhood and declined to frequent the places where fellow expatriates typically gathered, such as churches and clubs.

As far as Green was concerned, not only was Martin's lifestyle inconsistent with HG culture, but also his preference for isolating himself from the expatriate community made him of little use in helping colleagues adapt to the kind of life that would be comfortable for them in the alien environment of Uganda.

As for Martin's business-related practices, Green was ready to admit that business in Uganda usually moved at a leisurely pace. It could take months to get a phone installed, supplies delivered, or operating licenses issued. Martin, however, had quickly learned he could speed things up by handing out tips in advance. Nor could Green argue that such payments were exorbitant: In a country where per capita GDP is about $1,300 a year, people tended to take what they could get.

It was also a fact of local life that unemployment was high and so-called job searches were generally conducted through word of mouth, especially among family members. Martin had developed the practice of mentioning openings to local people and then interviewing and hiring the relatives they recommended. In a country like Uganda, he reasoned, such family connections could come in handy. Hiring the niece of a high-ranking customs officer couldn't hurt when it came to getting import clearances.

To Green, however, although such practices were both normal and legal in Ugandan business dealings, they bordered on the unethical in a U.S. organization. He also worried about a variety of long-term practical consequences. For instance, what if word got out that HG was paying extra for everything (and, inevitably, it would)? Wouldn't *everyone* start to expect bonuses for every little service?

What's worse, if word reached the higher echelons of the Ugandan government, HG would probably find itself dealing with people in a position to demand large payments for such services as, say, not finding some excuse to delay the project. Not only would these payments start to get costly, but they might be illegal under U.S. law. What about adverse international publicity that could negatively affect HG's operations in other countries?

Finally, Green wasn't comfortable with Martin's hiring practices. He had no reason to doubt the competence of any given hiree, but nepotism comes with risks. An employee's close connection with some government official, for example, might encourage the employee to participate more actively in the extortion process. What if a woman hired to work on import clearances decided to go into business with her uncle the customs officer to charge a little extra for every import approval? In addition, given Uganda's history of political instability, the company ran the risk that today's friends in high places might be tomorrow's enemies of the state.

Then there was the issue of the tribal rituals. The dam would displace about 700 villagers, and during early negotiations with the Ugandan government (and before Martin's transfer to Uganda), HG assembled a resettlement package that included the renovation of schools and health centers in the new location. HG executives understood that the package, valued at millions of dollars, was acceptable to the people who were affected. Shortly after Martin's arrival, however, two tribes living close to the Bujagali Falls site of the dam proclaimed the river home to sacred spirits. One leader likened the site to the tribe's Mecca.

As news of the claims reached the international press, worldwide support for the tribes began to grow. With permission from HG headquarters, Martin hired a specialist in African religions, who advised HG to work with the religious caretakers of the falls to find a solution. When contacted, the official caretaker revealed that, although the spirits could not be moved, they could be appeased at the right price. For a fee of $7,500, he sacrificed a sheep, two cows, four goats, and a slew of chickens, pinning them down on hot coals while 40 diviners prayed and danced. For the finale, blood was sprinkled on some sacred trees. Unfortunately, the spirits were not appeased. It seems that Martin had not participated in the ceremony. So Martin paid another fee of about $10,000 to repeat the ceremony, in which he took part, evidently appeasing the spirits.

Green was concerned about Martin's part in the second ceremony, which he himself considered pagan and probably a sham. Granted, Martin's participation had allowed work to continue, but Green worried the episode could not only damage HG's image but also could offend Uganda's Christian majority and the many Christian missionaries in the country. On top of everything, Martin's participation might be construed in some quarters as a mockery of tribal customs, thereby contributing to a hostile environment for HG.

Having thoroughly considered the Charles Martin case, James Green now had to make decisions about staffing the next phase of the project. He knew he needed to transfer a number of technical personnel to Uganda, and he'd already begun interviewing senior HG managers for the position of project director. But he was still left with one critical question: How much would the new director benefit from the presence of an American who, like Martin, could be a valuable source of advice about Ugandan culture? And if he had to have someone in that role, was Martin still right for the part? ■

QUESTIONS

1. Describe Ugandan cultural attributes that might affect the operations of a foreign company doing business there.
2. How would you describe the respective attitudes of Martin and Green: ethnocentric, polycentric, or geocentric? What factors do you suspect of having influenced their respective attitudes?
3. Who was right, Green or Martin, about Martin's more controversial actions in facilitating the project? How might things have turned out if Martin had not been a member of the project team?
4. In the next phase of the project—constructing the dam itself—should HG employ someone whose main function is that of liaison between its corporate culture and the culture of its host country? If so, is Martin the right person for the job?

SUMMARY

- *Culture* includes norms based on learned attitudes, values, and beliefs. Almost everyone agrees there are cross-country differences in culture, but most experts disagree as to exactly what they are.

- International companies must evaluate their business practices to ensure that their behavior accords with national norms.

- In addition to being part of a *national* culture, people are simultaneously part of other cultures, such as a professional or organizational culture.

- Distinct societies are often found within a given country. People also may have more in common with similar groups in foreign countries than with groups in their own countries.

- Cultural change may take place as a result of choice or imposition. Isolation from other groups, especially because of language, tends to stabilize cultures.

- People fall into social-stratification systems according to their *ascribed* and *acquired group memberships*. These memberships determine an individual's level of access to economic resources, prestige, social relations, and power. An individual's affiliations may determine his or her qualifications and access to certain jobs.

- Some people work far more than is necessary to satisfy their basic needs for food, clothing, and shelter. They're motivated to work for various reasons, including the preference for material possessions over leisure time, the belief that work will bring success and reward, and the desire for achievement.

- There are national differences in norms that influence people's behavior. Such norms determine whether they prefer autocratic or consultative working relationships, whether they prefer their activities to follow set rules, and how much they prefer to compete or cooperate with fellow workers.

- There are national differences in norms determining such behavioral factors as trust, belief in fate, and confidence in planning for the future.

- Failure to perceive subtle distinctions in culturally determined behavior can result in misunderstandings in international dealings.

- People communicate through spoken, written, and silent language—all governed by culturally determined cues. Cultural background also plays a major role in the ways that people process information.

- Host cultures don't always expect foreign companies or individuals to conform to their norms. Sometimes they accommodate foreign companies, and sometimes they apply different standards to the behavior of foreigners.

- A company usually needs to make fewer adjustments when entering a culture that's similar to its own, but it must be quite careful to heed subtleties both in host-country behaviors and in host-country perceptions of foreigners' behaviors.

- People living and working in foreign environments should be sensitive to the dangers of excessive *polycentrism* and excessive *ethnocentrism*. As a rule, *geocentrism* is a safer approach.

- In deciding whether to make changes in either home- or host-country operations, a company should consider several factors—the importance of the proposed changes to every party involved, the cost and benefit to the company of each proposed change, the value of opinion leaders in implementing the changes, and the timing of changes.

KEY TERMS

acquired group membership (p. 64)
ascribed group membership (p. 64)
cultural collision (p. 53)
cultural imperialism (p. 57)
culture (p. 52)
culture shock (p. 78)
hierarchy-of-needs theory (p. 68)
high-context culture (p. 72)

idealism (p. 72)
individualism versus collectivism (p. 70)
low-context culture (p. 72)
masculinity–femininity index (p. 68)
monochronic (approach to multitasking) (p. 72)

polychronic (approach to multitasking) (p. 72)
power distance (p. 69)
pragmatism (p. 73)
reverse culture shock (p. 78)
uncertainty avoidance (p. 70)

ENDNOTES

1 *Sources include the following:* Karen Elliott House, "Pressure Points," *Wall Street Journal,* April 10, 2007: A1+; Karen Eliott House, "For Saudi Women, a Whiff of Change," *Wall Street Journal,* April 7, 2007: A1+; Rachel Miller, "How to Exploit Pop around the Globe," *Marketing,* August 8, 2002: point-of-purchase section, 27; Roula Khalaf, "Saudi Women Carve a Place in the Future of Their Country," *Financial Times,* January 25, 2002: 3; Steve Jarvis, "Western-Style Research in the Middle East," *Marketing News,* April 29, 2002: International section, 37; Nadim Kawach, "Job Nationalisation to Gain Peace," *Financial Times Global News Wire,* July 12, 2002; John A. Quelch, "Does Globalization Have Staying Power?" *Marketing Management* 11:2 (March–April 2002): 18–27; Andy Fry, "Pushing into Pan Arabia," *Haymarket Publishing Services,* June 8, 2001: worldwide advertising section, 21; Ali Kanso, Abdul Karim Sinno, and William Adams, "Cross-Cultural Public Relations," *Competitiveness Review* 11:1 (2001): 65; Edward Pilkington, "Like Dallas Policed by the Taliban," *The Guardian* [London], July 2, 2002: sec. G2, 2; Barbara Slavin, "U.S. Firms' Saudi Offices Face Manpower Issues," *USA Today,* May 13, 2002: 5A; Susan Taylor Martin, "Inside Saudi Arabia," *St. Petersburg* [FL] *Times,* July 21, 2002: 1A; Susan Taylor Martin, "Hanging Out at the Mall, Saudi Style," *St. Petersburg* [FL] *Times,* July 24, 2002: 8A; Colbert I. King, "When in Saudi Arabia . . . Do as Americans Do," *Washington Post,* February 2, 2002: A25; Donna Abu-Nasr, "Saudis Begin to Show Wear and Tear of Life under Feared Religious Police," *AP Worldstream,* April 28, 2002, n.p.; Cecile Rohwedder, "The Chic of Arabia," *Wall Street Journal,* January 23, 2004: A11+; Roula Khalaf, "Saudi's Grand Mufti Condemns Mixed Sexes at Economic Forum," *Financial Times,* January 22, 2004: 6; Joseph A. Kéchichian, "Jeddah Forum: A Step towards Reforms," *Gulf News,* January 22, 2004: n.p.; and Parris-Rogers International (PRI) case in John D. Daniels and Lee H. Radebaugh, *International Business: Environments and Operations,* 9th ed. (Upper Saddle River, NJ: Prentice Hall, 2001), pp. 45–46. We appreciate the help of Omar Aljindi, one of Java Lounge's owners, in providing information about the company's operations.

2 Jeanne Brett, Kristin Behfar, and Mary C. Kern, "Managing Multicultural Teams," *Harvard Business Review* 84 (November 2006): 84–91; Yaping Gong, "The Impact of Subsidiary Top

Management Team National Diversity on Subsidiary Performance: Knowledge and Legitimacy Perspectives," *Management International Review* 46:6 (2006): 771–98; and Carol Hymowitz, "Leadership," *Wall Street Journal,* November 14, 2005, R1.

3 Tomasz Lenartowicz and Kendall Roth, "The Selection of Key Informants in IB Cross-Cultural Studies," *Management International Review* 44:1 (2004): 23–51.

4 David E. Brown, "Human Universals, Human Nature and Human Culture," *Daedalus* 133:4 (Fall 2004): 47–54.

5 Three of the most significant are Geert Hofstede, *Cultures and Organizations: Software of the Mind* (New York: McGraw-Hill, 1997), which explores attitudes in 50 countries, primarily those concerning workplace relationships; Ronald Inglehart, Miguel Basañez, and Alejandro Moreno, *Human Values and Beliefs: A Cross-Cultural Sourcebook* (Ann Arbor: University of Michigan Press, 1998) analyzes political, religious, sexual, and economic norms in 43 countries; Robert J. House, Paul J. Hanges, Mansour Javidan, Peter W. Dorfman, and Vipin Gupta, eds., *Culture, Leadership, and Organizations* (Thousand Oaks, CA: Sage, 2004) examines leadership preferences in 59 countries.

6 Michael Skapinker, "The Myth of National Stereotypes," *Financial Times,* March 8–9, 2003: 6.

7 Geert Hofstede and Robert R. McCrae, "Personality and Culture Revisited: Linking Traits and Dimensions of Culture," *Cross-Cultural Research* 38:1 (February 2004): 52–88.

8 See Aihwa Ong, *Flexible Citizenship: The Cultural Logics of the Transnationality* (Durham, NC: Duke University Press, 1999); and Leo Paul Dana, *Entrepreneurship in Pacific Asia* (Singapore: World Scientific, 1999).

9 Robert J. Foster, "Making National Cultures in the National Acumen," *Annual Review of Anthropology* 20 (1991): 235–60, discusses the concept and ingredients of a national culture.

10 "The Lively Chemistry of Transatlantic Enterprise," *Financial Times,* November 1, 2001: 13.

11 Harry C. Triandis, "Dimensions of Cultural Variation as Parameters of Organizational Theories," *International Studies of Management and Organization* (Winter 1982–1983): 143–44.

12 Yadong Luo and Oded Shenkar, "The Multinational Corporation as a Multilingual Community: Language and Organization in a Global Context," *Journal of International Business Studies* 37 (2006): 321–39.

13 David Crystal, *English as a Global Language* (Cambridge: Cambridge University Press, 1997): 1–23; and Jon Boone, "Native English Speakers Face Being Crowded Out of Market," *Financial Times,* February 15, 2006: 8.

14 Evelyn Nien-Ming Ch'ien, *Weird English* (Boston: Harvard University, 2004).

15 Inglehart et al., *Human Values and Beliefs,* p. 21.

16 Michael Segalla, "National Cultures, International Business," *Financial Times,* March 6, 1998, mastering global business section, 8–10.

17 Fons Trompenaars, *Riding the Waves of Culture* (Burr Ridge, IL: Richard D. Irwin, 1994), pp. 100–16.

18 "When Culture Masks Communication: Japanese Corporate Practice," *Financial Times,* October 23, 2000: 10; and Robert House et al., "Understanding Cultures and Implicit Leadership Theories across the Globe: An Introduction to Project GLOBE," *Journal of World Business* 37 (2002): 3–10.

19 "Putting the Malaise into Malaysia," *Asia Times Readers Forum,* at forum.atimes.com/topic.asp?topic_ID=9002&whichpage=10 (accessed May 27, 2007).

20 Larry Rohter, "Multiracial Brazil Planning Quotas for Blacks," *New York Times,* October 2, 2001: A3; and "Out of Eden," *The Economist,* July 5, 2003: 31+.

21 *Women of the World 2005* (Washington, DC: Population Reference Bureau, 2005), p. 8.

22 Hayat Kabasakal and Muzaffer Bodur, "Arabic Cluster: A Bridge between East and West," *Journal of World Business* 37 (2002): 40–54.

23 "Labor Force Participation Trends for Women and Men," *Monthly Labor Review,* at www.bls.gov/opub/ted/2001/doc/wk3/art02.htm.

24 Inglehart et al., *Human Values and Beliefs,* question V128.

25 "The New Workforce," Economist.com (November 1, 2001; accessed March 12, 2005).

26 "The Employers Forum on Age," *Legal: Europe,* at www.efa.org.uk/legal/europe.asp (accessed May 27, 2007).

27 "Minimum Legal Ages for Alcohol Purchase or Consumption around the World," at www.geocities.jp/m_kato_clinic/mini-age-alcohol-eng-l.html (accessed May 28, 2007).

28 Inglehart et al., *Human Values and Beliefs,* questions V129.

29 Markus Pudalko, "The Seniority Principle in Japanese Companies: A Relic of the Past?" *Asia Pacific Journal of Human Resources* 44:3 (2006): 276–94.

30 Francis Fukuyama, *Trust: The Social Virtues and the Creation of Prosperity* (New York: Free Press, 1995).

31 Tobias Buck, "Europeans Balk at Starting Their Own Businesses," *Financial Times,* March 3, 2004: 4.

32 Everett E. Hagen, *The Theory of Social Change: How Economic Growth Begins* (Homewood, IL: Richard D. Irwin, 1962), p. 378.

33 For a good overview of the literature on the Protestant ethic, see Harold B. Jones Jr., "The Protestant Ethic: Weber's Model and the Empirical Literature," *Human Relations* 50:7 (1997): 757–86.

34 Luigi Guiso, Paola Sapienza, and Luigi Zingales, "People's Opium? Religion and Economic Attitudes," CRSP Working Paper No. 542, August 2002, accessed through Social Science Research Network Electronic Library, at papers.ssrn.com/sol13/papers.cfm?abstract_id331280.

35 See, for example, David S. Landes, *The Wealth and Poverty of Nations* (New York: Norton, 1998).

36 Martin Wolf, "Hard Work versus Joie de Vivre," *Financial Times,* February 20, 2002: 15.

37 David Gardner, "Indians Face 10m Rupee Question: Do You Sincerely Want to Be Rich?" *Financial Times,* July 15–16, 2000: 24.

38 Triandis, "Dimensions of Cultural Variation as Parameters of Organizational Theories," 159–60.

39 Geert Hofstede, *Cultures and Organizations.*

40 Abraham Maslow, *Motivation and Personality* (New York: Harper & Row, 1954).

41 Hofstede, *Cultures and Organizations,* pp. 49–78; and House et al., *Culture, Leadership, and Organizations.*

42 Hofstede, *Cultures and Organizations.*

43 Maxim Voronov and Jefferson A. Singer, "The Myth of Individualism-Collectivism: A Critical Review," *The Journal of Social Psychology* 142:4 (August 2002): 461–81.

44 See John J. Lawrence and Reh-song Yeh, "The Influence of Mexican Culture on the Use of Japanese Manufacturing Techniques in Mexico," *Management International Review* 34:1 (1994): 49–66; P. Christopher Earley, "East Meets West Meets Mideast: Further Explorations of Collectivistic and Individualistic Work Groups," *Academy of Management Journal* 36:2 (1993): 319–46.

45 Hofstede, *Cultures and Organizations.*

46 Inglehart et al., *Human Values and Beliefs,* question V94.

47 Srilata Zaheer and Akbar Zaheer, "Trust across Borders," *Journal of International Business Studies,* 37:1 (2006): 21–29.

48 Examples in this section come from the GLOBE (Global Leadership and Organizational Behavior Effectiveness) project. See Bakacsi et al., "The Germanic Europe Cluster: Where Employees Have a Voice," *Journal of World Business* 37 (2002): 55–68; and Jorge Correia Jesino, "Latin Europe Cluster: From South to North," *Journal of World Business* 37 (2002): 81–89.

49 Ping Ping Fu, Jeff Kennedy, Jasmine Tata, Gary Yuki, Michael Harris Bond, Tai-Kuang Peng, Ekkirala S. Srinivas, Jon P. Howell, Leonel Prieto, Paul Koopman, Jaap J. Boonstra, Selda Pasa, Marie-François Lacassagne, Hiro Higashide, and Adith Cheosakul, "The Impact of Societal Cultural Values and Individual Social Beliefs on the Perceived Effectiveness of Managerial Influence Strategies: A Meso Approach." *Journal of International Business Studies* 35:4 (2004): 284–304.

50 Benjamin Lee Whorf, *Language, Thought and Reality* (New York: Wiley, 1956), 13.

51 For an examination of subtle differences among northern European cultures, see Malene Djursaa, "North Europe Business Culture: Britain vs. Denmark and Germany," *European Management Journal* 12:2 (June 1994): 138–46.

52 Richard E. Nisbett et al., "Culture and Systems of Thought: Holistic versus Analytic Cognition," *Psychological Review* 108:2 (April 2001): 291–310.

53 Don Clark, "Hey, #@*% Amigo, Can You Translate the Word 'Gaffe'?" *Wall Street Journal,* July 8, 1996: B6.

54 René White, "Beyond Berlitz: How to Penetrate Foreign Markets through Effective Communications," *Public Relations Quarterly* 31:2 (Summer 1986): 15.

55 Mark Nicholson, "Language Error 'Was Cause of Indian Air Disaster,' " *Financial Times,* November 14, 1996: 1.

56 Manjeet Kripalani and Jay Greene, "Culture Clash," *Business Week,* February 14, 2005: 9.

57 Christina Hoag, "Slogan Could Offend Spanish Speakers," *Miami Herald,* March 8, 2005: C1+.

58 Much of the discussion on silent language is based on Edward T. Hall, "The Silent Language in Overseas Business," *Harvard Business Review* (May–June 1960). Hall identified five variables—time, space, things, friendships, and agreements—and was the first to use the term *silent language.*

59 Benjamin Fulford, "The China Factor," *Forbes,* November 13, 2000: 116–22.

60 Fulford, "The China Factor."

61 For an excellent explanation of four ways to view time, see Carol Saunders, Craig Van Slyke, and Douglas Vogel, "My Time or Yours? Managing Time Visions in Global Virtual Teams," *Academy of Management Executive* 18:1 (2004): 19–31. See also Lawrence A. Beer, "The Gas Pedal and the Brake: Toward a Global Balance of Diverging Cultural Determinants in Managerial Mindsets," *Thunderbird International Business Review* 45:3 (May–June 2003): 255–70.

62 Trompenaars, *Riding the Waves of Culture,* pp. 130–31.

63 Daniel Pearl, "Tour Saudi Arabia: Enjoy Sand, Surf, His-and-Her Pools," *Wall Street Journal,* January 22, 1998: A1.

64 June N. P. Francis, "When in Rome? The Effects of Cultural Adaptation on Intercultural Business Negotiations," *Journal of International Business Studies* 22:3 (1991): 321–22.

65 Inglehart *Human Values and Beliefs,* p. 16.

66 Mary Yoko Brannen, "When Mickey Loses Face: Recontextualization, Semantic Fit, and the Semiotics of Foreignness," *Academy of Management Review* 29:4 (2004): 593–616.

67 Mary Yoko Brannen and Yoko Salk, "Partnering across Borders: Negotiating Organizational Culture in a German-Japanese Joint Venture," *Human Relations* 53:4 (June 2000): 451–87; and Baruch Shimoni and Harriet Bergman, "Managing in a Changing World: From Multiculturalism to Hybridization—The Production of Hybrid Management Culture in Israel, Thailand, and Mexico," *Academy of Management Perspectives* (August 2006): 76–89.

68 John Tomlinson, *Globalization and Culture* (Chicago: University of Chicago Press, 1999).

69 "In Mexico, Ancient Life vs. Wal-Mart," *Miami Herald,* September 6, 2004: 6A.

70 Nader Asgary and Alf H. Walle, "The Cultural Impact of Globalisation: Economic Activity and Social Change," *Cross Cultural Management* 9:3 (2000): 58–76; Tyler Cowen, *Creative Destruction: How Globalization Is Changing the World's Cultures* (Princeton: Princeton University Press, 2002), pp. 128–52.

71 Clive Cookson, "Linguists Speak Out for the Dying Languages," *Financial Times,* March 26, 2004: 9.

72 Jonathan Xavier Inda and Renato Rosaldo, "A World in Motion," in Inda and Rosaldo, eds., *The Anthropology of Globalization* (Malden, MA: Blackwell Publishing, 2002), pp. 1–34;

73 Adrian Furnham and Stephen Bochner, *Culture Shock* (London: Methuen, 1986), p. 234.

74 Geraldine Brooks, "Eritrea's Leaders Angle for Sea Change in Nation's Diet to Prove Fish Isn't Foul," *Wall Street Journal,* June 2, 1994: A10.

75 Patrick M. Reilly, "Pitfalls of Exporting Magazine Formulas," *Wall Street Journal,* July 24, 1995: B1; James Bandler and Matthew Karnitschnig, "Lost in Translation," *Wall Street Journal,* August 19, 2004: A1+.

76 Mzamo P. Mangaliso, "Building Competitive Advantage from Ubuntu: Management Lessons from South Africa," *Academy of Management Executive* 15:3 (August 2001): 23–34.

77 Sally Bowen, "People Power Keeps Peru's Investors in Check," *Financial Times,* February 6, 1998: 6.

78 Roberto P. Garcia, "Learning and Competitiveness in Mexico's Automotive Industry: The Relationship between Traditional and World-Class Plants in Multination Firm Subsidiaries," unpublished Ph.D. dissertation (Ann Arbor: University of Michigan, 1996).

79 Philippe Rosinski, *Coaching across Cultures: New Tools for Leveraging National, Corporate & Professional Differences* (London: Nicholas Brealey, 2003).

80 Aihwa Ong, *Flexible Citizenship: The Cultural Logics of Transnationality* (Durham, NC: Duke University Press, 1999).

81 James Mackintosh, "A Superstar Leader in an Industry of Icons," *Financial Times,* December 16, 2004: 10.

82 *Sources include the following:* "AES Begins Compensation for the Bujagali Project Affected Residents," *The Bujagali Power Project Update* 1:3 (October 2001): 1+; Deepak Gopinath, "The Divine Power of Profit," *Institutional Investor* 35:3 (March 2001): 39–45; Probe International home page, "World Bank Campaign," at www.probeinternational.org (accessed November 3, 2004); Taimur Ahmad, "We Are Devo," *Project Finance,* 216 (April 2001): 39–44; "Give Us Freedom and Kampala: The Baganda on the March," *The Economist,* February 8, 2003: 64; "Uganda: Harnessing the Power of the Nile," *IrinNews.org* (March 21, 2003); Stephen Linaweaver, "A Case Study of the Bujagali Falls Hydropower Project, Uganda," Occasional Paper No. 42 (London: London School of Economics and Political Science, July 2002); "AAGM: Bujagali: A Dream That Ugandans Love to Hate," Financial Times Information, June 23, 2002; Charlotte Denny, "Nile Power Row Splits Uganda," The Guardian [London] (August 15, 2001), at www.guardian.co.uk; Marc Lacey, "Traditional Spirits Block a $500 Million Dam Plan in Uganda," *New York Times,* September 13, 2001: B1+; Mark Turner, "Uganda's Dam-Builders Search for Consensus," *Financial Times,* October 1, 2001: 15; "Appeasing the Spirits," *The Irish Times,* January 5, 2002: 62; "Face Music—History of Uganda," at www.music.ch/face/inform/history_uganda (accessed March 7, 2005); and "Uganda," Lonely Planet World Guide, at www.lonelyplanet.com/destinations/africa/uganda/culture.htm (accessed March 7, 2005). The people in the case are fictitious, but some of the incidents are based on the experiences of U.S.-based AES Electric, Ltd., the world's largest independent power producer, which contracted with the Ugandan government to build a $520 million dam on the Bujagali Falls of the Nile River in 2001. Citing diminishing returns, AES withdrew from the project in 2003. The Blackstone Group announced in 2007 that it would resume the project.

3

The Political and Legal Environments Facing Business

Objectives

- To discuss the goals and functions of a political system

- To profile trends in the emergence and diffusion of contemporary political systems

- To explain the idea of *political risk* and describe approaches to managing it

- To understand how political and legal systems affect the conduct of business

- To describe trends in the evolution and diffusion of contemporary legal systems

- To discuss the issue of the rule of law versus the rule of man

- To explain legal issues facing international companies

- To explain the idea of *intellectual property* and to discuss areas of concern and controversy

Every road has two directions.

—*Russian proverb*

CASE: China—Legal Growing Pains in a Land of Opportunity

Under the direct control of the Communist Party from 1949 to 1979, China's economy was *autarkic*: Adhering to the notion that contact with foreigners would corrupt the nation's political structure and pollute its cultural life, the government prohibited foreign investment and restricted foreign trade.[1] Near the end of the 1970s, however, Chinese leadership began to rethink its economic posture. Realizing by 1978 that it was economically lagging behind much of the rest of the world, the world's second largest economy, and it has joined the United States as one of the two locomotives powering the global economy; between 2001 and 2006, the two nations accounted for 60 percent of all global growth.

And here, perhaps, is an even more interesting fact: By the first quarter of 2007, the $12.5 trillion U.S. economy was sputtering while the $2.5 trillion Chinese economy was expanding at a rate of 11.1 percent. If this pace continues, China will

MAP 3.1   China: The Inscrutable Market

With more than 1.3 billion consumers and a labor force just over 800 million workers, China is attractive to foreign investors. One of every five people in the world lives in China, but the population is unevenly distributed: In fact, 50% of all Chinese live on 8.2% of the country's total land. Even so, maintaining centralized control over the nation's political and economic affairs has been traditionally almost impossible: The vast distances between seats of authority ensure that local officials are often free to run things the way they want to.

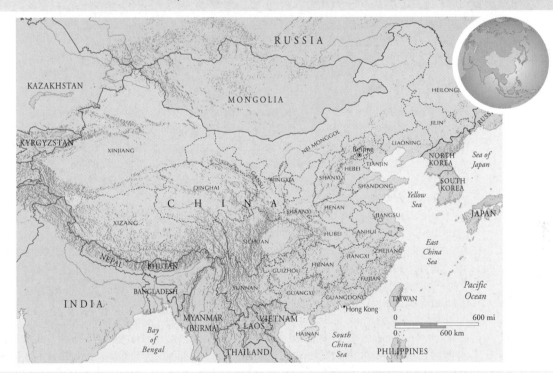

China took its first step toward economic modernization by enacting the Law on Joint Ventures using Chinese and Foreign Investment.

Since then, Chinese economic policy has been characterized by step-by-step liberalization and gradual entry into the world of foreign trade and investment. Now, make no mistake about it: The Communist Party maintains an absolute monopoly on political power. Today, however, the country's economy is shaped by free market principles. With a GDP that's been growing at more than 8 percent a year, China is now replace the United States as the world's largest economy, both in nominal and real terms, within the next two decades.

A LAND OF OPPORTUNITY

The incentives to invest in China are compelling. The 1980s witnessed a gold rush of investments by foreign companies, ranging from manufacturing ventures and export processing to licensing agreements and service relationships. Investment flows steadily accelerated through 2007, when total FDI in China, representing more than 600,000 ventures set up by companies from around the world, exceeded $800 billion.

Why have foreign companies been flocking to China? Typically, they've been anxious to take advantage of new opportunities in one or more of the following areas:

- *Market Potential.*   China (see Map 3.1) has just over 1.3 billion people, and economic growth has lifted many millions of them into the middle class. Hundreds of millions more, although desperately poor, appear to be looking at a brighter economic future. Moreover, many Chinese markets are still in the early- or mid-growth stage of the product life cycle.

- *Market Performance.*   Rapid economic growth has increased purchasing power, which has translated into increased consumer spending. Some economists note that, as America and Britain industrialized in the nineteenth century, they took 50 years to double real incomes per capita; essentially, China has achieved the same increase in just 9 years.

- *Infrastructure.*   China is in a multiyear program to build its infrastructure; it will invest trillions of dollars on highways, airports, seaports, dams, power plants, and communication networks.

- *Resources.*   China has a well-educated population and an immense pool of productive labor while wage rates remain far below those in many other countries—about 1/3 of the Mexican and 1/25 of the U.S. rate.

- *Strategic Positioning.*   More and more companies consider investment and operation in China as fundamental elements of their global strategies.

MARKET REALITIES

On the downside, China's attractiveness as a business destination continues to suffer from an array of political and legal complications that await any would-be entrepreneur or investor. In short, China's unique political and legal environments make local operations a complex and often frustrating process. Although many of these stumbling blocks are recent developments, all reflect the political and legal forces that have guided the modern transformation of the Chinese business environment and are deeply ingrained in the country's contemporary business landscape.

Some observers argue that, when it comes to doing business in China, the number one rule is to throw away the rule book. In particular, foreign investors are advised to abandon the notion that Western ideas will automatically work in China. In the West, for instance, a basic principle holds that you can form a corporation "for any valid business purpose." This principle does not exist in China. If you want to incorporate in China, the government wants to know—in excruciating detail—such basics as who you are, what you want to do, and, of course, how much you intend to invest.

Then your plans have to be officially approved before you're authorized to open. Traditionally, centralized authority has determined the path and pace of development—a situation that's hardly unique to China. As they undergo their own transitions, many once government-controlled economies around the world must deal with a tenacious tradition of centralized decision making. China, however, is a particularly tough case. According to aspiring foreign investors, China's political and legal systems foster time-consuming busywork and tend to stack the odds against foreigners who are bold enough to forge ahead in the face of an elaborate bureaucracy, a fledgling legal system, and a context of pervasive corruption.

POLITICS AND BUREAUCRACY

"If the great invention of European civilization was a legal system," quipped one observer, "then China's was bureaucracy." Many frustrated foreign investors put the blame for China's treacherous business terrain on a bureaucratic system that relies on political agendas rather than legal statutes as a means of regulating business activity.

Whereas Westerners have become accustomed to the principle of the "rule of law," China has long relied on another: the "rule of man" and its premise that legal rights derive from the will of the individual who has the power to enforce them. In the 1940s, with the ascendancy of Mao Zedong and the Communist Party, a new centralized leadership took over an already complicated civil service system and proceeded to add a further layer of bureaucratic authority by superimposing the hierarchy of the Communist Party. The result was a regulatory system more byzantine and daunting than ever.

Today, foreign investors still have to jump through hoops set up by one old-line bureaucracy or another. First, they report, you have to file an application—with multiple government ministries—detailing your investment and business plans, along with descriptions of business methods to be employed, products to be produced, and materials to be used; required infrastructure, staffing, and technology; and the skills and resources that you plan to transfer to China.

Next, you must seek the approval of the Ministry of Foreign Trade and Economic Cooperation (MOFTEC), which prioritizes industries according to those that it encourages, restricts, or prohibits. Finally, either MOFTEC or some provincial-level authority reviews each foreign investment application to determine whether it's in the best interest of China—that is, whether it encourages capital formation, promotes exports, creates jobs, or transfers technology.

Chinese officials typically subject each application to stringent criteria applied through a lengthy review process that reflects prevailing political goals and legal conditions. Typically, foreign investors endure long bouts of negotiation (often spanning several years) before their applications reach a government agency with the power to make a decision. Even then, they're not out of the woods, because MOFTEC has quite narrow criteria for determining what offers sufficient benefits to China.

The Mighty Dragon and the Local Snake

Complicating this already intricate process is a long-running conflict between central and local Chinese authorities. The vastness of the country means that local officials, whether headquartered in the smallest villages or the largest cities, are often left to govern according to their own preferences. "The centre," notes one observer, often "has no control over the provinces. When it sends people to investigate illegal pirating of CDs, local governors block access to the factories." Increasingly, for example, the central government makes efforts to lower trade barriers and increase competition by allowing foreign firms to control local operations, only to be thwarted by local officials who fear that such initiatives will result in hometown unemployment and instability.

That this power struggle has a long tradition is evident in a sixteenth-century Chinese saying: "The mightiest dragon cannot crush the local snake." What this means is that, even though the central government in Beijing may appear to be all powerful, its practical reach is limited by the politics of local bureaucracies.

THE LEGAL SYSTEM

Looking from the outside in, however, you can see that China has made great strides in stabilizing its legal environment. China had no formal legal system whatsoever in 1978, when it launched one of the greatest campaigns of legal reform in history. Unfortunately, the willingness to modernize doesn't ensure that all problems immediately disappear. China still faces some fundamental challenges, including legislative gaps, hazy interpretation, lax enforcement, and philosophical disagreement. Currently, for example, no comprehensive bankruptcy law protects businesses; recent draft legislation favors closing down debt-ridden enterprises rather than protecting creditors.

Nor is there any effective way of resolving contract disputes. If you want to challenge a local partner in a Chinese court, you'll probably end up ruining local business relationships. Why? Because suing an adversary violates Chinese tradition. You're better off working through international arbitration, a practice that's slowly gaining acceptance in China.

"Chinese legislation is chock-full of ambiguities," says one Beijing-based lawyer, who thinks it will take 10 to 15 years to iron out most of the wrinkles. Others are a little more pessimistic about the time frame, comparing the state of the present Chinese legal system with that of the United States in the 1920s—an antiquated composite of statutes and legal precursors that took over 80 years to modernize.

Other observers point out that, in the case of the Chinese system, even bigger problems reflect a fundamental difference in the conception of legality in a society. Unlike the West, where legal systems depend on the rule of law and the endorsement of systematic and objective laws executed by public officials who are held accountable for their administration, China, as we've seen, subscribes to a philosophy of the rule of man, and thus to a system that equates the decision of one man (or person), whether emperor, party, or local bureaucrat, with the law. Both bureaucrats and agencies are ceded the authority to make their own decisions without being subject to a transparent system of checks and balances.

The Matter of Intellectual Property

Not surprisingly, this approach to legal decision making, combined with the growing pains of fledgling legal institutions, creates problems for foreign companies. One area of controversy concerns *intellectual property*—the general term for intangible property rights resulting from intellectual effort and including such assets as patents, trademarks, and copyrights. Western companies in China often complain that China's industrial surge is being powered by the sophisticated theft of their intellectual property. For the past 40 years, explains one observer, "until China began putting intellectual-property laws in place, all patents were owned by the government, and could be shared by any company that was willing to use them. The Chinese government actually encouraged this, and that has left a deep impression on companies that intellectual property is there for anyone to use it." It's hard to pinpoint the precise extent of intellectual-property-rights violations in China, but aggressive estimates claim that nearly a third of the Chinese economy is pegged to traffic in counterfeit goods.

Collectively, political biases, legal shortcomings, and philosophical legacies have contributed to the weak or arbitrary enforcement of laws in China. Recalls Tim Clissold, who had a long business career in China, "I was dealing with a society that had no rules; or more accurately, plenty of rules, but they were seldom enforced. China appeared to be run by masterful showmen: appearances mattered more than substance, rules were there to be distorted, and success came through outfacing an opponent."

CORRUPTION

Take the pervasive role of government at all levels in business affairs, mix in an underdeveloped legal system with a habit of lax enforcement and the material temptations of an emerging capitalist society, and you have a prescription for corruption. As it stands, would-be investors in China still face many questions concerning property and procedures for which the Chinese government has furnished few solutions. Many foreign companies routinely battle bribes and attempts to steal property while struggling to establish clear titles to land and physical equipment.

In addition, embezzlement flourishes. "Tunneling," a scheme in which relatives or friends of managers of state-owned enterprises do business with the firms or their subsidiaries, is a popular method of embezzling that's spilled over into joint ventures with foreigners. In general, risks are everywhere. Prudent investors heed the failures of others; for example, the director of Subway Restaurant's China operations noted his Chinese joint-venture partner had cheated the company of $200,000 by various chicanery and misrepresentations. He warned that the lure of the Chinese market led "people [to] leave their heads at home when they come here. They forget all about due diligence. They meet a guy on the street, give him a ton of money to run something and six months later he absconds with it."

THE FUTURE

Opportunities in China will continue to attract foreign firms. Entrants have little doubt that the future of China's business environment will be determined by the play of internal political conditions. Still, they believe the influence of external institutions will spur Chinese officials to make the country's business environment more consistent, transparent, and fair. Many companies, for example, note China's membership in the World Trade Organization (WTO), a global institution that sets rules for international trade. China's membership in the WTO, effective since 2002, requires it to accept a system of global trading rules—rules on everything from tariffs and antidumping regulations to procedures for protecting trademarks and copyrights.

China has responded to many WTO regulations. State-owned enterprises, for example, no longer officially discriminate against foreigners by giving preferential treatment to local competitors. Now state-owned companies recognize commercial considerations in making purchasing decisions. China has also amended its legal code to conform to WTO stipulations on issues ranging from trade and investment to intellectual property protection.

No one, however, denies there are still problems, and some people have criticized China for its sluggishness in living up to its WTO obligations. In 2007, frustration with China's performance on protecting intellectual property provoked the United States to file complaints with the WTO of "inadequate enforcement." The United States argued that failure to curb piracy not only costs software, music, and book publishers billions of dollars in lost sales but also makes it unfairly hard for legitimate firms to operate in the Chinese market. Expressing "great regret and strong dissatisfaction at the decision," a Chinese official responded that the U.S. action was "not a sensible move."

Despite its uneven performance in internal economic reform and the persistence of external political tensions, foreign investors continue to pour money into China. Perhaps driven by optimism, perhaps by confidence in continued progress, or perhaps by desperation to get a foot in the Chinese market, businesses around the world are jockeying for the opportunity to take on the challenges posed by the business of doing business in China. Most of them seem to understand that, regardless of their motivations for getting in, once they *are* in, they'll face the often frustrating task of making sense of the Chinese marketplace.

Introduction

In Chapter 2, we showed that the cultural issues facing international businesses differ from those facing domestic firms. In this chapter, we carry this analysis forward, focusing on the fact that, once a company leaves its home country, it operates in markets with different political and legal systems. Certainly, the business environments of some countries are similar to those of others (U.S. companies won't find many surprises in Canada). In other cases, of course, the differences are profound (an unprepared Australian company will encounter quite a few surprises in Russia).

In either instance, political and legal factors contribute to the environment in which managerial decisions must be made. Indeed, our opening case on China shows how changes in a nation's political and legal environment force companies that want to operate there to think and rethink the best ways to acquire resources, minimize risk, and adapt operating modes. Figure 3.1 shows how political policies and legal practices are integral parts of a nation's operating environment. (You'll notice that Figure 3.1 is quite similar to Figure 2.1 [p. 53], which shows how *culture* is an integral part of a nation's operating environment.)

Obviously, its political and legal systems are vital parts of a country's business environment, and in navigating different markets, firms must understand how and where national business environments converge and diverge. Indeed, as we saw in our opening

Case Review Note

FIGURE 3.1 Political and Legal Factors Influencing International Business Operations

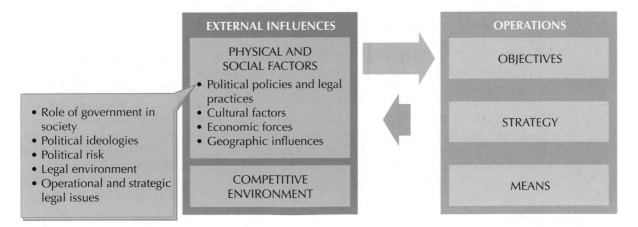

CONCEPT CHECK

In Chapter 2, we raise the question of how companies can determine the extent to which they should adapt their overseas operations to home-country cultures; as we suggest in our discussion of "Company and Management Orientations," this decision may result in the adoption of certain "attitudes or orientations"—**polycentrism, ethnocentrism**, or **geocentrism**.

case, determining precisely where, when, and how to adjust business practices, operating procedures, and strategies to meet the challenges posed by the local environment is a key to success in international business.

Not surprisingly, it's also more easily said than done. Successful international companies start by accepting the idea that, when it comes to politics and laws, countries have decidedly different ideas. They position themselves to compete by choosing to understand rather than to ignore—or, worse, resist—these intrinsic differences.

As we address this issue throughout the chapter, keep in mind that firms looking to operate in foreign countries must heed three points of view:

1. Discard the belief that firms can directly transfer to foreign environments the principles and practices they've developed in the home environment.

2. Accept the fact that political and legal systems vary among countries.

3. Acknowledge that these differences impact how firms capture opportunities and deflect threats.

In the first part of this chapter, we take a closer look at the political aspects of these issues; we devote the second part to analyzing the legal aspects.

The Political Environment

In our look at China in our opening case, we saw that the nation's reformed political and legal systems, while still struggling, have fostered an environment in which foreign investors can enter markets, establish operations, manage activities, and, ultimately, earn profits. At the same time, of course, we also saw how the Chinese political system imposed hardships for many companies while the legal system thwarted efforts to find remedies.

This situation is not unique. Consider the case of Russia. Its economy has grown rapidly since 2000; indeed, in 2007, it grew by 7.8 percent and attracted more than $30 billion in foreign investment. Even so, says an executive at Swedish retailer IKEA, the Russian political environment is "a bit of a roller coaster. . . . [Y]ou don't know exactly what will happen tomorrow."[2] The roster of horror stories features several well-known names: Products of communications- and information-technology giant Motorola were confiscated by import authorities, and the international professional-services firm PriceWaterhouseCooper was charged with tax evasion. (Arguably, these bumps in the road are minor when compared to the roadblock encountered by the Russian-owned gas and oil company Yukos, which was effectively expropriated.) If you want to do business in Russia today, you'd better be "big enough to defend yourself against bureaucratic attacks [and] . . . ready to hold your nose when elections are rigged and political opposition is crushed."[3] Ironically, although Russian president Vladimir Putin has promised a "dictatorship of the law," some see lawlessness on the upswing.[4]

Against such backdrops, firms must obviously study prospective political environments. They need to know, for example, how officials exercise authority. How are officials elected, monitored, and replaced? Do people respect the rule of law (and, if not, how do they go about challenging authority)?[5] Without answers to such questions, managers will be ill-prepared to take advantage of the trade-off between political risk and potential return on investment in a high-growth market.

The goal of the political system is to integrate the elements of a society.

Again, as we indicated in our opening case, a country's political system provides the context in which economic activity is carried out. What, exactly, is a **political system**? For our purposes, it includes the complete set of institutions, political organizations, and interest groups, as well as the relationships among institutions and the political norms and rules that govern their activities. Its purpose has been debated since Plato's *Republic* and Aristotle's *Politics* and, although different views persist, most analysts agree that a nation's political system must integrate different groups into a functioning, self-sustaining, self-governing society.

In other words, a political system ensures some level of stability in social relations, and it's usually effective when it's supported by a legitimate consensus of people who live under it. The acid test of a political system, therefore, is its ability to unite a society in the face of diverse and divisive viewpoints. When there are radically opposed views of government's role in the life of a society, a nation can (like the former Soviet Union) disintegrate. The resulting political instability jeopardizes companies currently trying to operate in the market as well as discouraging potential investors.

> The test of a political system: uniting a society in the face of diverse and divisive viewpoints.

INDIVIDUALISM VERSUS COLLECTIVISM

There are several ways to profile the similarities and differences between political systems. You might, for example, ask questions like the following about the government's role in a society:

> Individualism refers to the primacy of the rights and role of the individual. Collectivism refers to the primacy of the rights and role of the community.

- Should it endorse social equality or social hierarchy?
- Should it emphasize individual liberty or collective security?
- Should it have jurisdiction in some or all areas of society?
- What civil liberties should it grant to citizens?
- What remedies for redressing injustice should it allow citizens?

There's one central issue at the heart of all these (and any number of similar) questions: the issue of **individualism** versus **collectivism** in political systems. Simply put, then, a powerful question is: What is the general orientation within a society concerning the primacy of individual rights versus the needs of the larger community?

Philosophical Orientations   Philosophically, this debate has spanned centuries, beginning with Plato and continuing to attract the interest of such thinkers as Adam Smith, John Stuart Mill, and Milton Friedman. All have engaged the issue of how a political system can best serve the society that lives under it. Should it guarantee individual freedom in the pursuit of economic self-interest, or does society fare better when individual rights are subordinated to collective goals?

The Individualist Orientation   Probably the political system with the most pronounced individualistic orientation is that of the United States. A central tenet of this orientation is the principle that political officials and agencies play limited roles in social transactions. Economically, this tenet entails a series of related principles: The rule of law, for example, is generally supreme, and the recourse to regulations to correct market inefficiencies, such as insufficient consumer knowledge or excessive producer power, must be made fairly. Basically, countries with an individualistic orientation encourage business to support the good of the community by promoting fair and just competition. When competition is constrained or absent, government can ensure fair competition by instituting laws to regulate the marketplace. However, because government remains independent of day-to-day business practices, the relationship between government and business is often adversarial.

The Collectivist Orientation   Systems that feature a collectivist orientation, such as those of Japan and China, promote the principle that government may intervene in certain cases—namely, those involving the structure of industries, the conduct of companies, and the actions of managers—to ensure that business practices benefit society. We saw in our opening case, for example, that the Chinese bureaucracy now enforces certain policies we'd normally associate with an individualist system. At the same time, however, rather than relying on arm's-length transaction and regulation, Chinese officials prefer to establish both formal and informal relationships within the business community; the goal is to develop successful companies that will then boost national prestige and power. In other ways, China offers some clear examples of a collectivist orientation in a large society. By making the group rather than the individual the unit of political and economic analysis, a system with a collectivist orientation applies different standards to evaluate policies than does a system with an individualist orientation.

Governments that support other forms of collectivist societies, such as Sweden, are inclined to take actions that promote social equality, labor rights, and workplace democracy. Ultimately, government in a collectivist society is connected to and interdependent with business; relations between the two sectors are often cooperative.[6] In recent years, Asian countries like South Korea, Vietnam, Singapore, and Malaysia, which are keen to emulate aspects of Japan and China, have instituted collectivist principles and practices.[7]

POLITICAL IDEOLOGY

A **political ideology** is the system of ideas that expresses the goals, theories, and aims of a sociopolitical program. In the United States, the liberal principles of the Democratic Party and the conservative doctrines of the Republican Party reflect political ideologies. Most modern societies are *pluralistic*—different groups champion competing political ideologies. **Pluralism** can also arise when two or more groups in a country differ in language (Belgium), class structure (the United Kingdom), ethnic background (South Africa), tribal groups (Afghanistan), or religion (India).

In turn, such differences influence the conduct of the political system. Managers from the United States, for instance, where there are two primary political parties, would probably be puzzled by developments in a political environment in which several parties champion competing ideologies.

Figure 3.2 outlines a **political spectrum** of the various forms of political ideologies. It provides a way to profile their similarities and differences while figuring out where moderates fall between the two anchors. The key issue for any sort of spectrum analysis is specifying the ideas that anchor the ends. From a Western perspective, one commonly sees the endpoints defined as conservative versus liberal interpretations of democracy. Other endpoints command greater relevance in other contexts.

For example, a political spectrum in a modern Islamic country might be bounded by the poles of theocracy versus secularism to capture the role of the clergy in the government. Or, in the specific case of Taiwan, one could define the political spectrum in terms of parties that champion Chinese reunification versus those that endorse Taiwanese independence. Figure 3.2 respects such interpretations. However, it anchors the political spectrum with the broader-stroke constructs of democracy anchoring one pole and totalitarianism the other.

Democracy   Former British prime minister Winston Churchill endorsed the conviction that "democracy is the worst form of government except all those other forms that have

FIGURE 3.2
The Political Spectrum

In practice, purely democratic and totalitarian governments are extremes. Rather, looking around the world, one finds, there are variations to each approach. For example, democratic governments range from radical on one side (advocates of political reform) to reactionary (advocates of a return to past conditions). The vast majority of democratic political systems, however, lie somewhere in between.

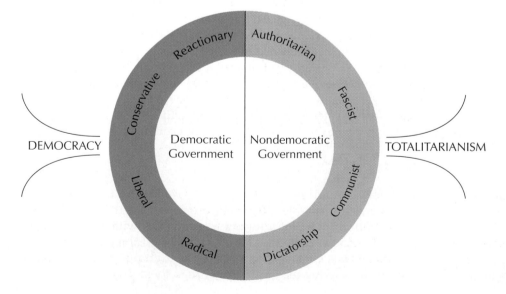

been tried from time to time."[8] Like Churchill, when most Westerners contemplate the ideals of "democracy," they usually think of the virtues of political freedom and civil liberty. Moreover, they generally equate greater degrees of political freedom and civil liberty with the virtues of greater democracy.

Furthermore, they tend to see modern-day democracies as the inheritors of an ancient legacy that goes back to the ancient Greeks. In this idealistic scheme, the Greeks pioneered the principles that all citizens are politically and legally equal, entitled equally to freedom of thought, opinion, belief, speech, and association, and equally enjoy sovereign power over legislators and executive governmental authority.

In the view of Abraham Lincoln, the sixteenth president of the United States, **democracy** is a government "of the people, by the people, and for the people." Practically speaking, a democracy is a political system that endorses the rule of law and grants the voting citizenry the power to alter the laws and structures of government, to make all decisions (either directly or through representatives), and to participate in elections that express their decisions. These are the principles and practices that enable a democracy to institutionalize political freedoms and civil liberties.

> Democratic systems involve wide participation by citizens in the decision-making process.

Bear in mind, however, that the scale and scope of modern society places practical limits on the practice of democracy. For one thing, the sheer population of most modern nations makes full participation by all eligible voters in the democratic process impossible. Thus many democratic countries practice various forms of representative democracy in which citizens elect representatives to make decisions on their behalf.

In some democracies, as in the United States, citizens directly elect executives and lawmakers. In others, such as in the United Kingdom, they vote for representatives or for a ruling party, which then selects a prime minister or some other figure to function as chief executive of the country. There are, of course, hybrids of each form. Israel, for example, has a parliamentary government like that of the United Kingdom, but Israelis vote directly for a chief executive called the prime minister. Because most democracies have only a few principal parties, forming a government even without a clear-cut electoral mandate is usually a reasonable task.

Types of Democracy   We can identify five prominent types of democracy:

- In a *parliamentary democracy,* citizens exercise political power by electing representatives to a legislative branch of government called a *parliament.* The executive branch typically consists of a cabinet headed by a prime minister regarded as the head of government. There is an independent judiciary but no formal separation of powers between the executive and legislative branches. Examples include India and Australia.

- A *liberal democracy,* as in Japan or New Zealand, originates in a constitution that specifically protects certain individual freedoms, such as freedom of speech, assembly, and religion, and certain individual liberties, such as the right to private property and privacy. All citizens, both public and private, are treated equally before the law and receive due process under it. All liberal democracies are representative democracies.

- When three or more political parties have the capacity to gain control of government, whether separately or as part of a coalition, the system is known as a *multiparty democracy.* The multiparty system prevents the leadership of a single party from setting policy without checks and balances imposed by opposition parties. Canada, Germany, Italy, and Israel all feature multiparty systems.

- As in the United States, a *representative democracy* is one in which the people's elected representatives hold ultimate sovereignty. Representatives are charged with the responsibility of acting in the people's interest, though not merely as their proxy representatives. In other words, they enjoy sufficient *authority* to deal directly and as they see fit with changing circumstances but not enough to act according to their own preferences.

- A *social democracy* advocates the use of democratic means to achieve a gradual transition from capitalism to socialism. Motivating this position is the belief that society must reform capitalism to remove its intrinsic injustices. The term *social democracy* is largely interchangeable with *democratic socialism.* Prime examples of social democracy are Norway and Sweden.

Notwithstanding nuances in terms and tenets, governments under virtually all democratic political systems endorse the theoretical legitimacy of the fundamental principles listed in Table 3.1.

The Issue of Centralization   The key difference among the world's democracies revolves around the issue of the appropriate degree of centralized government control of social activities. Although different countries practice the principle in different ways, central to democratic theory is the principle that the decentralization of power into the hands of the people must take precedence over the centralization of authority in the hands of public officials. Canada, for example, acts on this principle by vesting political authority in its provinces at the expense of its federal government. Similarly, the United States regards states' rights as a counterweight to policies laid down by the federal branch of government.

Ironically, we're back at the Chinese adage that we introduced in our opening case: "The mightiest dragon cannot crush the local snake." If all branches of a political system do not endorse the same theoretical principles, internal conflict threatens its integrity and operation. In China, the conflict between central and local authorities reflects inconsistent interpretations of basic theoretical principles, such as a fair and independent court system and a nonpolitical bureaucracy.

Case Review Note

The defining feature of democracy is freedom. Factors for evaluating freedom include political rights and civil liberties.

Assessing Democracy   The fundamental element of democracy is **freedom**—whether freedom of speech, freedom of association, freedom of belief, or freedom in any other walk of life. Since 1972, Freedom House, a nonprofit organization dedicated to the principles of political and economic freedom, has published an annual assessment of the state of political and civil freedom in 193 countries and 15 selected territories.[9] Freedom House derives its measures of freedom from the Universal Declaration of Human Rights enacted by the United Nations in 1948.[10] Applying these measures to each country, it computes an aggregate ranking that shows the relative performance of a particular country regarding the central measure of political and civil freedom. Map 3.2 shows a recent profile of the worldwide distribution of political and social freedom.

- *Free* in that it exhibits elected rule, competitive parties in which the opposition plays an important role and possesses actual power. There is widespread consensus on the intrinsic and inalienable freedoms of expression, assembly, association, education, and religion.
- *Partly free* in that it exhibits limited political rights and civil liberties. Such nations are characterized by political corruption, violence and terrorism, one-party dominance, and military influence on politics; elections are unfair, and the government practices censorship and political terror, frustrates free association, and discriminates against minorities.

TABLE 3.1   Fundamental Features of Democratic Political Systems

- Freedom of opinion, expression, press, religion, association, and access to information
- Exercise of citizen power and civic responsibility either directly or through elected representatives
- Citizen equality in opportunity and treatment before the law
- Free, fair, and regular elections
- Majority rule coupled with protection of individual and minority rights
- Fair and independent court system charged with protecting individual rights and property
- Subordination of government to the rule of law

- *Not free* in that it represses or denies basic rights and civil liberties through a political system ruled by autocrats, military juntas, one-party dictatorships, or religious hierarchies; the government allows only a minimal exercise of political rights, severely constrains religious and social freedoms, and highly regulates private business activity.

Totalitarianism In a **totalitarian system,** a single agent—whether an individual, group, or party—monopolizes political power and tries to mobilize the population toward two ends:

- Unquestioning support for the official state ideology
- Opposition to activities that run counter to the goals of the state

The ideological standards of totalitarianism require agents of the government to eliminate any dissent within the system. Toward this end, regimes typically rely on indoctrination, persecution, surveillance, propaganda, censorship, and violence.

In contrast to the democratic ideal of freedom, totalitarianism enforces restrictions that subordinate the day-to-day life of people—including occupation, income, personal interests, religion, and even family structure—to the interests of the state. In China, for example, a One Child Policy prohibits a family from having more than a single child; a couple that has a second child may be fined the equivalent of $1,300—a steep penalty in rural areas where most annual incomes are a fraction of that sum. In extreme situations, personal survival is linked to the regime's survival—a condition that forcibly merges the interests of individuals with those of the state. Not surprisingly, totalitarian states fall into Freedom House's "Not Free" category.

Types of Totalitarianism The term *totalitarianism* is a catchall for several forms of political systems, including the following:

- *Authoritarianism:* In an authoritarian form of government like that of North Korea, citizens are subject, at the expense of political and civil liberties, to state authority in many aspects of their lives. The regime tolerates no deviation from state ideology. Day-to-day life reflects unquestioning obedience to state authority, and resistance usually incurs severe punishment.
- *Fascism:* "The Fascist conception of the state," according to Benito Mussolini, the Fascist dictator of Italy from 1924 to 1943, "is all-embracing; outside of it no human or spiritual value may exist, much less have any value. Thus understood, Fascism is totalitarian and the Fascist State, as a synthesis and a unit which includes all values, interprets, develops, and lends additional power to the whole life of a people."[11] The fascist ideal, in other words, is control of people's minds and souls as well as their daily lives.
- *Secular totalitarianism:* Under such a system, leaders maintain power by wielding the authority of the state. A single political party forms a government in which only party members hold office; elections are controlled through unfair laws or other practices. In China, for example, the Communist Party (CPC) wields sole power, permitting eight other parties to participate in state affairs only under its recognized leadership. Similar conditions prevail in Vietnam and Singapore. Usually, the secular totalitarian state has no all-encompassing ideology; it grants individual freedoms only so long as ensuing activities threaten neither social stability nor political power. More pointedly, the Communist Party insists that its approximately 70 million members be atheists.
- *Theocratic totalitarianism:* Under this system, government is an expression of the preferred deity, with leaders often claiming to represent the deity's interests on earth. Operationally, the state relies on interpretation of ancient dogma in place of a modern legal code. Religious leadership, like the Taliban Party in Afghanistan, constitutes political leadership, with its interpretation of codified tenets for conducting personal and social affairs often resulting in political, legal, economic, and social regimentation.

CONCEPT CHECK

Recall our discussion in Chapter 2 of "Behavioral Factors Affecting Business": It's important to remember that these variables change as people change—or as some authority works to change them. In the effort to shape people's behavior to support the interests of the state, totalitarian systems work to manipulate behavioral norms governing work motivation, risk taking, and even communication practices.

A totalitarian system restricts decision making to a few individuals.

CONCEPT CHECK

Religion exerts a strong influence on people's values, and in Chapter 2, we note how it functions as a stabilizer of a country's **culture**. Similar forces are at play when countries mix religion and politics. The elements of religion that stabilize culture also regiment the political process.

MAP 3.2
Map of Freedom, 2007

If you live in a country classified as "Free," you enjoy a high level of political rights and civil liberties. If your homeland is "Not Free," you enjoy very few rights and liberties. If you're a citizen of a "Partly Free" nation, your share of rights and liberties ranges anywhere from average to just below average.

Source: Freedom House, "Map of Freedom 2007," at www.freedomhouse.org.

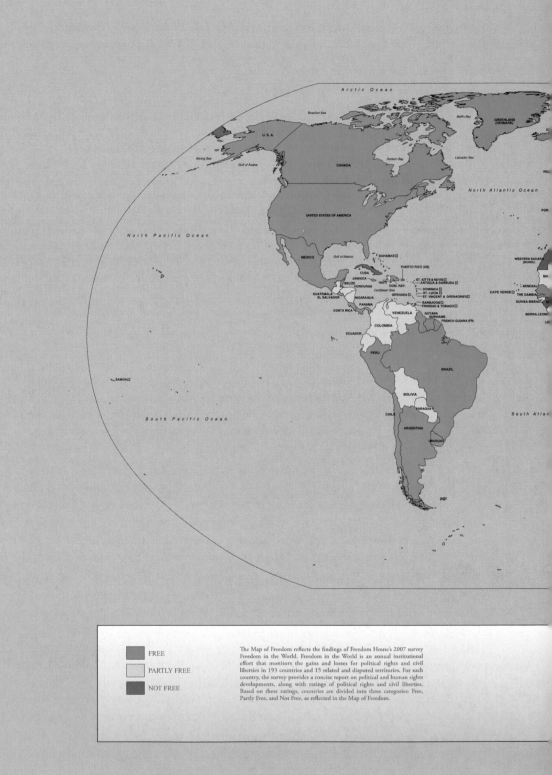

FREE

PARTLY FREE

NOT FREE

The Map of Freedom reflects the findings of Freedom House's 2007 survey Freedom in the World. Freedom in the World is an annual institutional effort that monitors the gains and losses for political rights and civil liberties in 193 countries and 15 related and disputed territories. For each country, the survey provides a concise report on political and human rights developments, along with ratings of political rights and civil liberties. Based on these ratings, countries are divided into three categories: Free, Partly Free, and Not Free, as reflected in the Map of Freedom.

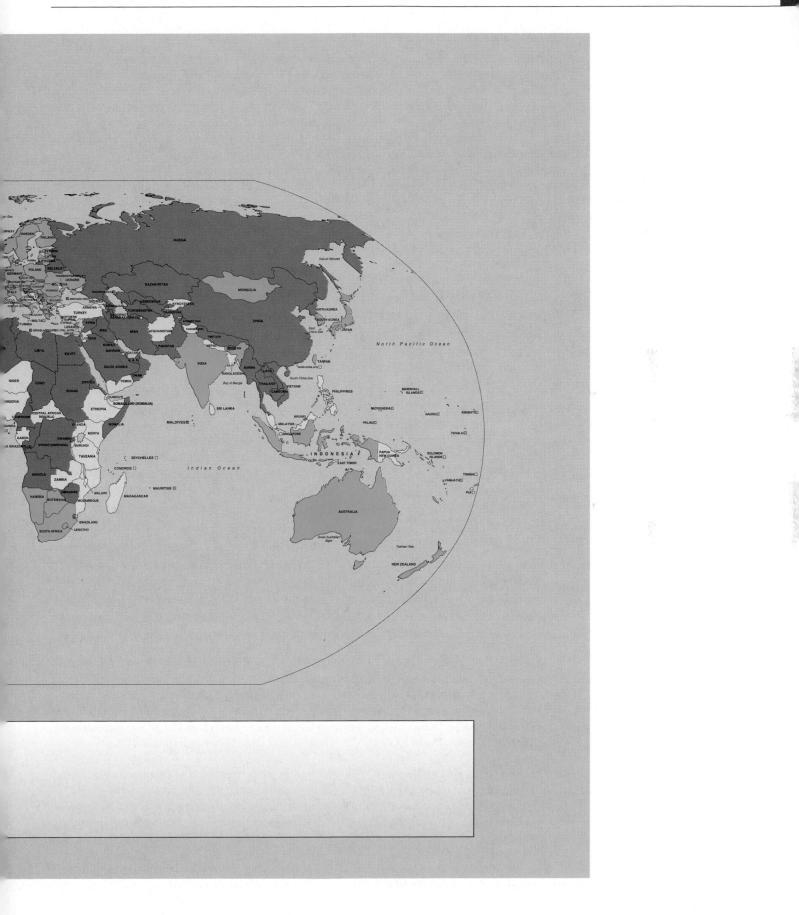

TRENDS IN POLITICAL SYSTEMS

The latter half of the twentieth century was characterized by a steady expansion of nations adhering to democratic political systems: Between 1950 and 2007, the number of democratic countries grew from 22 of 154 (14 percent) to 90 of 193 (47 percent). Indeed, the striking number of nations that made the transition from nondemocratic to democratic, particularly during the 1970s and 1980s, gave rise to the idea of a **third wave of democratization.**[12] The trend was worldwide: Countries from Africa, Asia, Latin America, South America, and Eastern Europe abandoned totalitarian systems. In their place emerged systems based on individual freedoms and civil liberties and boasting fairer civic institutions, more active media, objective judiciaries, and stronger property rights.[13] Today, as a result of this wave, more people live in countries with elected democratic governments than at any other time in history.

Engines of Democracy   Several engines powered this wave of democratization. We focus on three of the most important.

1. As the failure of many totalitarian regimes to deliver economic progress led to deepening legitimacy problems, citizens began challenging the right of governments to govern. The fall of the Berlin Wall and the disintegration of the Soviet bloc in 1989 highlighted this historical sea change. As formerly Communist countries adopted democratic principles and practices, they weakened links between new political practices and old economic habits.

2. Because democracy benefits from an informed public with access to media unfettered by restrictions on free speech, improved communications technology, largely via the Internet, eroded the ability of totalitarian states to control access to information. Widely publicized images of resistance and rebellion had a snowball effect on the worldwide campaign for democratic reform. For example, China regulates access to the Internet and has routinely blocked domestic access to international websites that report information counter to state standards. Still, the number of Internet users in China increased from 22 million in 2000 to more than 300 million in 2008.[14]

3. Many people championed democracy in the belief that political liberalization would lead to economic liberalization and, in turn, improved standards of living. The data show that freedom paid economic dividends. The median per capita gross domestic product (GDP) is almost seven times higher for the freest countries than for so-called not free countries. In many countries, economic advances fostered the emergence of increasingly prosperous middle and working classes. Their success led, in turn, to increased expectations and more vociferous calls for democratic reforms.

The powerful march toward greater political freedoms and more expansive civil liberties, beginning in the 1970s, strongly fueled a sense of the inevitability of democracy. Collectively, these trends stabilized operating conditions for companies worldwide and supported common rules for international competition (see Figure 3.3). As such, the increasing democratization of the world reinforced the foundation for the accelerating globalization of business.

The Momentum of Democracy   Recent events and trends raise questions about the momentum of democracy. Winston Churchill reasoned that although democracy is superior to its alternatives, it too suffers from imperfections. Some fledgling democracies that emerged in the past two decades, especially those in the former Soviet bloc countries, have struggled with domestic unrest and security threats that threaten to provoke the reappearance of state controls.

The terrorist attacks of September 11, 2001, also reset interpretations and standards of freedom as well. Resulting restrictions on freedoms and liberties raised questions about the legitimacy of leading democracies. Longitudinal data on the spread of democracy also give

---

CONCEPT CHECK

In profiling "The Forces Driving Globalization" in Chapter 1, we note the power of changing political situations. In particular, the past few decades have witnessed the spread of **democracy** and a decline in totalitarianism. The acceptance of the principles of democracy and their expression in a freer market has been a major reason for growth in **international business**.

CONCEPT CHECK

Another driving force behind **globalization** that we discuss in Chapter 1 is the "Expansion of Technology." Here, we focus on those forms of technology—such as the Internet—that have helped liberate the global flow of information. It's no secret that improvements in the technology for delivering information have contributed significantly to changing social and political attitudes in many countries.

Several indicators show slowing adoption of, if not growing backlash against, the principles of democracy.

FIGURE 3.3
**The Political Pull
of the Profit Motive**
Source: Copyright Harley Schwadron,
www.cartoonstock.com.

"MAKING A PROFIT WAS A LOT EASIER BEFORE SO MANY COUNTRIES ABANDONED SOCIALISM AND STARTED COMPETING!"

pause. In 1987, there were 66 electoral democracies in the world; in 1997, there were 118. But by 2006, the total had grown by only 5 countries, to a total of 123 (see Figure 3.4).[15] Recent data amplify these trends. Most directly, the *Freedom in the World 2008* report warned that "This year's results show a profoundly disturbing deterioration of freedom worldwide. A number of countries that had previously shown progress toward democracy have regressed, while none of the most influential Not Free states showed signs of improvement. As the second consecutive year that the survey has registered a global decline in political rights and civil liberties, friends of freedom worldwide have real cause for concern."

Other data corroborate this development. The Economist Intelligence Unit does in-depth studies of the texture of democracy, relying on 60 indicators that focus on the performance of free elections, civil liberties, government functioning, political participation, and political culture in a country.[16] Studying 165 countries it found that about half of the world's democracies are "democracies" in name only; just 28 are "full democracies," and almost twice as many (54) are "flawed democracies." Of the remaining 85 countries, 30 are classified as "hybrid regimes" (those that mix democratic and totalitarian practices), and 55 are outright authoritarian states. Finally, richer developed countries are more congenial to democratic systems of government; there are only two in Latin America, two in Central Europe, and one in Africa.

Public sentiment has also become more equivocal when it comes to the appeal and practicality of life in a democracy. In a Latinobarómetro poll conducted in 18 countries across Central and South America, only around half of the respondents are "convinced democrats" and just 37 percent of respondents pronounced themselves "satisfied with their democracies." Besides declining support for democracy, the poll reported growing support for an authoritarian government in half of the 18 countries.[17]

Finally, some observers have questioned the legitimacy of Western notions of democracy when applied to societies that don't have the same level of comfort with the ideas and institutions of Western parliamentary democracy. For example, Hu Jintao, China's president and Communist Party chief, speaks of "democracy" with a different meaning from the one understood by Westerners. In his view, calls for multiparty democracy are taboo, opposition cannot organize, reform must obey the "correct political orientation," and change must be in an "orderly" way that upholds the party's leadership.[18]

Similarly, consider the case of Russian president Vladimir Putin, who has, on the one hand, confirmed the allure of democracy with his contention that "I am a true democrat."

FIGURE 3.4   Tracking Electoral Democracies

According to the most recent Freedom House *Annual Survey of Political Rights and Civil Liberties*, there are now 123 electoral democracies in the world versus the 1987 total of 66. As you can see, however, the curve starts to flatten out in the mid-1990s: The present total of 123 constitutes a net gain of only 5 nations since 1997.

Source: Freedom House, "Freedom in the World 2007," at www.freedomhouse.org (accessed June 2007).

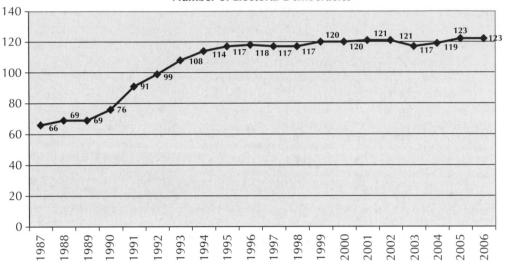

Number of Electoral Democracies

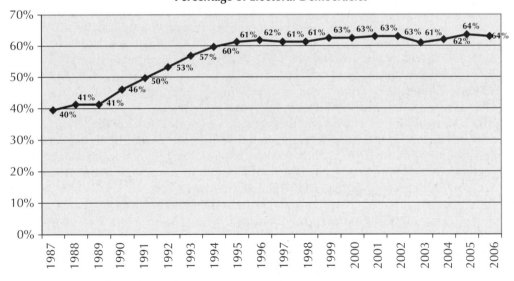

Percentage of Electoral Democracies

At the same time, however, Putin has argued that his country's application of authoritarian methods had been misinterpreted, and he's on record as charging that the "largest complexity today is that some of the participants in the international dialogue believe that their ideas [of democracy] are the ultimate truth."[19]

Charges of hypocrisy leveled against the United States because of its incursion in Iraq and other antiterrorist activities have raised the same question—namely, what constitutes democracy in action and what doesn't? Some people have even begun to wonder whether democracy—at least in the form espoused by the world's veteran democracies—has run its course as a preferred political system. And if so, as we consider in our Looking to the Future insert, what then might become of democracy?

LOOKING TO THE FUTURE

What Might Become of Democracy?

Routinely, managers wonder what a political map of the world will look like in the next decade. Will democracy continue to spread? Will totalitarianism make a comeback? Will new political ideologies arise? It's easy to regard these questions as purely speculative or as academic exercises. The latest data, however, suggest they're anything but. On a global scale, the fading momentum of freedom and democracy shows up in several indicators, notably the number of nations suffering a decrease in their degree of political freedom and the resurgence in authoritarian politics.

To some observers, this trend has ominous overtones. Why? For one thing, the overall imbalance in the political-freedom ledger spotlights the effect of growing threats to the expansion of political freedom—a trend that has in fact been building over the past decade. According to *Freedom in the World 2007*, the percentage of countries that can be designated "Free" has remained flat for nearly a decade—a fact that suggests the onset of what Freedom House director Jennifer Windsor calls a pattern of "freedom stagnation": "Although the past 30 years," she reports, "have seen significant gains for political freedom around the world, the number of 'Free' countries has remained largely unchanged since the high point in 1998. Our assessment points to a freedom stagnation that has developed in the last decade."[20]

The pattern is apparent worldwide. The cause of freedom has suffered setbacks in the Asia-Pacific region, declines in the Middle East, South America, and Africa, and the reacceptance of authoritarian rule in some of the nations of the former Soviet Union. Taken all together, these shifts raise the specter of a growing backlash against democracy.

For one thing, there is a variety of possible alternatives to democracy—something to appeal to a broad range of antidemocratic inclinations. Already, trends in just about every region of the world signal a reemergence of authoritarian regimes. Russia is a particularly noteworthy case—one which requires a very brief history. In 1991, following decades of Communist rule, Soviet President Mikhail Gorbachev lit the torch of freedom, building democratic institutions and acquainting the country with the rudiments of political and economic freedom. Boris Yeltsin, the first president of Russia, continued along the path blazed by Gorbachev. Today, however, under the direction of President Vladimir Putin, Russia has implemented programs designed to repress the practice of freedom in several areas, including freedom of expression and the press and the personal freedoms afforded by a genuine rule of law; the Russian government now boasts less transparency than at any time since the fall of communism, and corruption once again prevails. As a result, Freedom House has demoted Russia from the ranks of the "Partly Free" to those of the "Not Free."

Moreover, we see similar trends elsewhere. In Venezuela, populist president Hugo Chávez, who has initiated a program to nationalize foreign-owned assets, has steadily eliminated dissent, closing down organizations, movements, and media that have called for the expansion of democratic freedoms. Meanwhile, Iran has institutionalized overt hostility toward personal freedom and seems intent on enlisting other nations in its crusade against democracy. Put all these countries together, and you have a gallery of diverse models for imposing authoritarian governance on nations around the world.

Spreading democracy in the Arab world, which is regularly rated the world's least-free region, has been a U.S. foreign-policy goal since September 11, 2001. Progress, however, has been slow. U.S. involvement in Iraq has raised questions about the legitimacy of democratic ideals throughout the region. Too, faltering institutions and changes in political sentiments have combined to hinder the transition to democracy in several Islamic nations, including Bahrain, Egypt, Saudi Arabia, Jordan, and the Palestinian areas. Booming economies in the oil-rich Persian Gulf have also stalled the momentum toward democracy, which is not—or so it would appear—essential to economic prosperity. Today, leaders throughout the region are more apt than ever to fall back on the position that the transition from totalitarianism to democracy is "a slow process."[21]

Finally, some attitudes, by hindering the exchange of ideas, pose obstacles to democratization in the Arab world. These views, anchored in the historic reluctance of Islamic states to engage in democratic practice, lend credence to the "clash-of-civilizations" scenario that calls for irreconcilable cultural differences between Islam and the West to trigger a worldwide backlash against Western ideals of political rights and civil liberties.[22] Some experts even wonder if such an epic collision will usher in the age of a new political ideology.

Another potential model of antidemocratic governance is the emergent Chinese system of "totalitarian democracy." What is a **totalitarian democracy?** Essentially, it's a one-party system in which elected

(continued)

representatives, preapproved by the party, oversee a nominal democratic system whose citizens, though granted the right to vote, can't really participate in decision making.[23] The Chinese system was little more than a theoretical straw man for years, until the stunning economic performance of recent years lent it some credibility as a practical one-party alternative to liberal and multiparty democracies.

The advent of "freedom stagnation" throws into question long-cherished and presumably inalienable ideals of democracy. Today, as some countries abandon democracy and other political models emerge, more and more people debate the question of what's to become of democracy. Will it persist in the form of liberal democracy, as in the United States, or will it transmute into some form of single-party system like the one that now prevails in China? Will it simply be rejected in favor of authoritarianism, or will some apocalyptic "clash of civilizations" give rise to a brand-new conception of "freedom" and "liberty"?

Whatever the question, history will no doubt play a part in the answer. The first and second "waves of democratization" (1828–1926 and 1943–1962, respectively) were each followed by periods of "freedom stagnation" and antidemocratic backlash. Indeed, the end of the second wave witnessed a reversion to authoritarianism in more than 20 countries, and the question arises: Are we facing once again the same cycle of transitions, consolidations, and collapses?[24]

Whatever the answer to this question, there's little doubt that both politics and business as usual have gone by the boards. If orthodox democracy proves resilient, businesspeople face the task of adjusting operations to the growing pains of the countries that choose the democratic route. If democracy becomes something different than it is today, they face the challenge of rethinking the conduct of business in a world that champions economic growth at the price of freedom and liberty. If democracy as we know it changes because of a clash of civilizations, few signposts will be left standing as guides over the terrain of international business. Finally, if democracy actually falters in the face of an authoritarian resurgence, they'll face a new world of control and coercion. ∎

POLITICAL RISK

CONCEPT CHECK

In Chapter 1, we note that interest groups in some countries fear that the globalization of the local business environment will weaken national **sovereignty**— that is, a nation's freedom from external control and freedom to act in its own best interests. Here, we observe that this attitude itself contributes to political risk: Foreign companies and investors face greater problems when a host government becomes increasingly sensitive in matters of national sovereignty.

Investing overseas exposes companies to the risks that arise from the political quirks of the nations in which they invest. **Political risk** is the possibility that political decisions, events, or conditions will affect a country's business environment in ways that will cost investors some or all of the value of their investment or force them to accept lower-than-projected rates of return. As you can see in Table 3.2, which itemizes some of the more common types, a variety of factors contribute to political risks. As a result, experts identify several

TABLE 3.2   Sources and Consequences of Political Risk

Type	Outcome
Expropriation or nationalization	A government or political faction seizes a company's local assets. Compensation—if there is any—is usually trivial. More common in the 1960s and 1970s, expropriation is increasing in tandem with resurgent totalitarian political systems.
International war or civil strife	Military action damages or destroys a company's local assets.
Unilateral breach of contract	A government repudiates a contract negotiated with a foreign company. The company's profits are often reallocated to the host country. The foreign company also suffers when a government approves a local firm's repudiation of a contract.
Destructive government actions	By imposing unilateral trade barriers (say, in the form of revised local-content requirements), a government interferes with the transfer of goods or the distribution of goods to local consumers.
Harmful action against people	Action on the part of local agents—say, kidnapping, extortion, or terrorist activities—targets local employees of a foreign company.
Restrictions on repatriation of profit	A foreign government arbitrarily limits the amount of gross profit that a foreign company can remit from its local operations.
Differing points of view	A government's interpretations of such issues as labor rights or environmental obligations create problems for a foreign company in its home market.
Discriminatory taxation policies	A foreign company is saddled with a higher tax burden than a local competitor or other foreign firm that's treated favorably because of its nationality.

types of political risks, and in this section, proceeding from least to most disruptive, we examine four general categories of political risk: *systemic, procedural, distributive,* and *catastrophic.*

Systemic Political Risk As a rule, a country's political processes don't treat foreign operations unfairly. If they did, very few companies would hazard the investment. More often, the risks faced by investors—both domestic and foreign—result from shifts in public policy. New political leadership, for instance, may adopt an approach to social management that's quite different from its predecessor's—say, rejecting individualism in favor of collectivism. In that case, new regulations will alter the environment for all companies.

At other times, a government may target public-policy initiatives toward an economic sector that it regards as unduly dominated by foreign interests. In an effort to install what he calls a system of "Bolivarian socialism," for example, President Hugo Chávez of Venezuela has initiated a program to nationalize the local operations of foreign companies in several different sectors.[25]

In both situations, political change creates *systemic risks*—risks that impact all firms whose activities are affected by the political system. Bear in mind that systemic changes don't necessarily create political risks that reduce potential profits. In fact, elections and policy shifts can create opportunities for foreign investors. In the 1990s, for example, a newly elected government in Argentina initiated a radical program to deregulate and privatize the country's state-centered economy. Investors who accepted the risk and pursued the resulting opportunities prospered as Argentina became more democratic.

Our opening case traces the development of a similar pattern in China, where political change has created opportunities in several areas, including market potential and performance. The point is, of course, that taking advantage of such attractive opportunities entails taking risks in a country where political and legal complications still pose roadblocks to profitability.

> Political risk: the risk that political decisions or events in a country negatively affect the profitability or sustainability of an investment.

Procedural Political Risk Each day, people, products, and funds move from point to point in the global market. Each move creates a *procedural transaction* between the units involved, whether units of a company or units of a country. Political actions sometimes create frictions that interfere with these transactions. The repercussions, for example, of government corruption or a partisan judicial system can raise the costs of getting things done in a business environment. More specifically, a corrupt customs official might pressure a foreign firm to pay for "special assistance" if it wants to clear goods through customs in a timely fashion.

Distributive Political Risk Many countries see foreign investors as agents of prosperity. As foreign investors generate more and more profits in the local economy, the host country may begin to question the *distributive justice* of the rewards of operating in its market. In other words, as the business gets more successful over time, some officials question whether they are getting their "fair" share of the growing rewards. Occasionally, political officials decide that they aren't and launch a campaign of "creeping intervention" whose goal is to appropriate a greater share of the rewards—typically in ways that don't provoke the foreign profit center to pull up stakes and relocate. Common tactics include revising tax codes, regulatory structure, or monetary policy.

> The primary types of political risk, from least to most disruptive, are
>
> - Systemic
> - Procedural
> - Distributive
> - Catastrophic

A foreign firm may feel the pressure of distributive risk in quite subtle ways. Few people, for instance, think of the United States as a hotbed of distributive political risk. If you're in the cigarette business, however, you know the United States has perhaps the highest degree of political risk in the world. The U.S. government has long battled cigarette makers (both domestic and foreign) on matters of taxation, regulation, business practice, and liability. In the process, it has imposed direct costs of hundreds of billions of dollars and indirect costs that, according to some industry insiders, are incalculable.

Catastrophic Political Risk Catastrophic political risk includes random political developments that adversely affect the operations of every company in a country. Typically, it arises from specific flash points, such as ethnic discord, civil disorder, or war. It disrupts the business environment in a way that embroils every firm trying to do business in the country, and if such disruptions spiral out of control, they can devastate companies and even whole nations.

Today, corporate-risk officers and international bankers look increasingly to insurers to shield them from the financial consequences of political disorder. According to the Berne Union Group, which includes 30 of the largest public and private insurers in the world, members currently hold more than $113 billion in political-risk insurance policies. In 2006, the Berne Union Group wrote more than $44 billion in coverage, up from $37 billion the previous year.

Point | Counterpoint

Should Political Risk Management Be an Active Strategy?

Point **Yes** I think we can agree on a few points. First, it's no secret that the actions of the host government can have a huge effect on the success or failure of companies that want to operate under its jurisdiction. Second, this means every company doing business overseas faces *some* political risk, and that's why they all need strategies for *political risk management.*

Third, these strategies can take one of two approaches: *active* or *passive*. Naturally, those who advocate active political risk management believe it's the better way to go, and in my opinion, they're right: The more they're actively involved with local experts who can help them predict political problems, the better they're going to be at handling them in the long run.

Now, there's no denying you may be exposing yourself to political risk whenever you take an active approach to managing any facet of your overseas operations. This is why experienced overseas managers rely on not one, but two battle-tested tactics: They can turn to *statistical modeling* to quantify the *precise* degree of political risk they're facing, or they can solicit the judgment of local experts to estimate the *general* degree of political risk they'll have to deal with in a given country. When they rely on *either* of these approaches, they're operating on the perfectly valid assumption that neither positive nor negative political events in any country are independent or random events: They unfold in *observable patterns* that let managers make reasonable estimates of the odds of future events. That's why rigorous quantitative analysis and modeling aim to detect, measure, and predict future events reliably that may pose political risk.

If you support active political risk management, you're operating on the assumption that if you measure the right set of discrete events, then you should be able not only to calculate the degree of political risk you're running in a given country but also to estimate your odds of facing politically risky disruptions—civil strife, contract repudiation, financial control, regime change, ethnic tension, terrorism, and the like.

Counterpoint **No** Your proactive risk management position fails to observe that many companies abstain from managing political risk directly. Instead, they treat political risk as an *unpredictable hazard* of international business. They argue that no model, regardless of how systematically it's been specified, can predict political risk. Why? First and foremost, there is the difficulty of reliably measuring uncertain situations. This challenge is greatly aggravated by the range of variables that affect any country's political environment. They also contend that, because no one can accurately predict political risk, the strategically responsible thing to do is to find a cost-effective way to hedge their exposure.

This approach, they reason—and rightly, it seems to me—is all the more important in today's international business environment, in which the quest for growth lures many companies into emerging markets characterized by institutional and political peculiarities.

Typically, companies that favor passive risk management outsource the political-risk management process, largely because they reason that they're shielding themselves from political risk by buying **political risk insurance**. In addition, consider all the options that they give themselves by taking this approach. First, they have options to purchase coverage that protects operations from a wide array of political risks, including (but not limited to) government expropriation, involuntary abandonment, and damage to assets due to political violence. Second, they can purchase their political risk insurance from a variety of providers—government agencies, international organizations, and private companies. Here's a short list of reliable "insurers":

- *Overseas Private Investment Corporation* (OPIC) encourages U.S. investment projects overseas by offering political risk insurance, all-risk guarantees, and direct loans. OPIC insurance protects U.S. overseas investment ventures against civil strife and other forms

Granted, in taking this approach, you have to identify many valid indicators of political risk that can then be measured reliably—for example, the number of generals in political power, the pace of urbanization, the frequency and nature of government crises, the degree of literacy, and, of course, upsurges of ethnolingual fractionalization. But once you've collected the data for the right set of measures, there's no reason why you can't estimate—objectively—your exposure to political risk, not only within a given country, but across countries as well.

Generally, political risk indicators have proved valuable in helping global companies monitor developments in individual countries. Moreover, they can use the data that they've collected in one country to benchmark operations in another.

There's no doubt, then, that this approach to estimating political risk by means of cross-country, highly aggregated data is a powerful tool, but I won't go so far as to say there are no limitations to what you can do with it. That's why some companies opt to complement *quantitative* measures with certain in-depth, country-specific *qualitative* indicators of political risks.

How does this approach work? One tactic entails polling country experts to get their (presumably) insightful judgments. Of course, these people, too, consider quantitative factors when assessing a nation's political conditions. The best ones, however, bring something more personal to the table: They enrich their analyses by incorporating their own expertise—their sense of how things work in the targeted host country—that naturally involves certain subjective elements. If you want to integrate this tactic into your overall risk-assessment strategy, you could begin by running standardized interviews with experts to identify and evaluate key factors in a country's political environment over a specified period. Once you've done that, you can draw up likely scenarios and assign probabilities to any range of outcomes—currency manipulation, expropriation of assets, insurrection—that may occur over a finite period of time. ●

of violence, expropriation, and inconvertibility of currency. Recently, having reduced its role in the political-insurance end of the business, OPIC now focuses on investments in emerging markets that fit U.S. foreign-policy priorities.

- *Multilateral development banks (MDBs)* are international financial institutions (such as the African Development Bank, the Asian Development Bank, and the World Bank Group) that are funded and owned by member governments. Their goal is to promote progress in developing member countries by providing financial incentives that encourage firms to expand into politically risky environments.

- Several private insurance companies underwrite political risk—for a price. Many insurers, such as AIG, Chubb, and a cluster of syndicates at Lloyd's of London, cover "routine" political risks that involve property and income, such as contract repudiation and currency inconvertibility. By and large, however, they're reluctant to cover both the risk of political violence in the form of war or insurrection and the risk of nationalization and expropriation of assets.

In sum, given the difficulty of actively managing political risk coupled with the options to buy protection, why would one want to worry about it? ●

The Legal Environment

In highlighting investor concerns about the Chinese legal system, our opening case illustrates the importance of legal traditions and practices in a nation's ability to attract and retain foreign investment. For Western investors, for example, the purpose of bankruptcy laws is to protect creditors—and thus to encourage investment. In China, however, where this investment-oriented tradition has yet to take hold, prevailing legal tradition prescribes a certain degree of protection for debt-ridden firms.

We also saw in our opening case that the means by which it develops, interprets, and enforces its laws constitute a key aspect of a country's business environment and, from some views, society itself: "To distrust the judiciary," said the French writer Honoré de Balzac, "marks the beginning of the end of society." In degree, China may be an exception,

Case Review Note

A legal system is the mechanism for creating, interpreting, and enforcing the laws in a specified jurisdiction.

but all countries legislate a broad range of laws to regulate such business activities as the investment of capital, payment of dividends to foreign investors, and even decisions about internal structure and operations. Often, the same laws regulate such routine matters as customs procedures or document notarization. No matter the objective, the quality of legal governance is important for investment and growth.

LEGAL SYSTEMS

Modern legal systems exhibit elements of constitutional law, criminal law, and civil and commercial laws.

Legal systems differ from country to country, primarily because of differences in tradition, precedent, usage, custom, or religious precepts. Even so, the purpose of every legal system is to establish a comprehensive legal network to regulate social activities. By and large, modern **legal systems** share three components:

- A system of *constitutional law* designed to guarantee an open and just political order
- A system of *criminal law* designed to safeguard the social order
- A system of *civil and commercial laws* designed to ensure fairness and efficiency in business transactions

When it's functioning well, a legal system ensures that a society can pursue economic and social development and, when disagreements arise, resolve them without collapsing into anarchy.

Aspects of all three components bear on the decisions made by managers and foreign investors. Consider, for instance, the legal concept of *due diligence*, which requires the statements in a firm's security-registration forms be true and omit no material facts. The existence of such a statute demands that would-be investors take the responsibility for studying several issues: Does a country protect assets and ownership rights? What traditions and practices influence its regulations and their enforcement? Do its regulations create too many obstacles to doing business efficiently?

In this chapter, we focus on the ways in which a country's legal system specifies the methods that it uses to regulate business practices, to define acceptable practices for conducting business transactions, to specify the rights and obligations of parties engaged in business transactions, and to afford legal redress to those who believe they've been wronged in business transactions.

TYPES OF LEGAL SYSTEMS

Map 3.3 breaks down the world's various legal systems into five categories: *common law, civil law, theocratic law, customary law,* and *mixed systems.* Let's examine each of these categories more closely.

Common Law   A *common law system* is based on tradition, judge-made precedent, and usage, and it assigns a preeminent position to existing case law as a guide to dispute resolution. Judicial officials refer to statutory codes and legislation but only after they've considered the rules of the court, custom, judicial reasoning, prior court decisions, and principles of equity. The Anglo-American common law system prevails in countries such as Canada, the United States, England, New Zealand, and Australia.

Civil Law   A *civil law system* is based on a systematic and extensive codification of laws. Such systems often charge political officials—not government-employed judges—with responsibility for specifying accessible and written codes of law that apply to all citizens. Rather than create law, therefore, judges apply existing legal and procedural codes to resolve disputes. More than 70 countries, including Germany, France, and Japan, presently employ civil law systems.

Theocratic Law   A *theocratic law system* relies on religious and spiritual principles to define the legal environment. Ultimate legal authority is vested in religious leaders, who

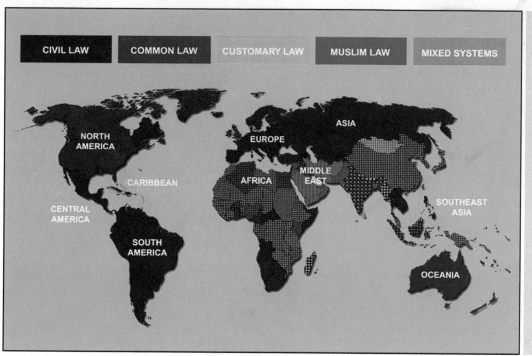

**MAP 3.3
The Wide World
of Legal Systems**

Despite the influence of globalized business practices—and despite the existence of overlap and covergence in systems—there's still considerable disparity in types of legal systems.

Source: University of Ottawa, "World Legal Systems," at www.droitcivil.uottawa.ca (accessed June 2007).

apply religious law to govern social transactions. The most prevalent theocratic system, Islamic law, or *Shari'a*, is based on a variety of sources: the Koran—the sacred text of Islam; the Sunnah—decisions and sayings of the Prophet Muhammad; the writings of Islamic scholars, who derive rules by analogy from the principles established in the Koran and the Sunnah; and the consensus of legal communities in Muslim countries.

Customary Law   A *customary law system* is anchored in the wisdom of daily experience or, for those who are more intellectually inclined, certain spiritual or philosophical traditions. Few countries in the world today operate under a legal system that is wholly customary. Still, in many countries with mixed legal systems, it sometimes plays a significant role in evaluating matters of personal conduct.[26]

Mixed System   A *mixed legal system* emerges when a nation's system engages two or more of the four legal systems we've just discussed. As you can see from Map 3.3, the majority of mixed legal systems can be found in Africa and Asia. Interestingly, although the legal system of the United States is categorized as a common law system, it contains aspects of a mixed system. Unlike its 49 counterparts, whose legal codes reflect a system of common law, the state of Louisiana relies largely on a system grounded in civil law. Similarly, theocratic law influences the basic civil law system of the Southeast Asian nation of Indonesia.

THE DIFFUSION OF LEGAL SYSTEMS

Businesspeople champion consistency in laws from country to country. They reason that, no matter where they're operating, a uniform set of rules makes it easier to plan and operate effectively. Still, differences in legal traditions and practices persist, and in the real world of international business, firms face different legal systems wherever they go. If we do have a sense of convergence of laws across borders, it's because of the way that both civil and common law systems have evolved and become diffused.

The Diffusion of Common Law   To get a sense of the evolution of common law systems, we need to start in England. Over a period of centuries, the English legal system has diffused to the United States, Canada (except for the province of Quebec), Australia,

CONCEPT CHECK

Recall that in discussing "Cultural Formation and Dynamics" in Chapter 2, we touch on the *transmission* of culture, including the method of transmission known as *cultural diffusion*. Here, we emphasize that a country's legal environment often reflects changes resulting from the diffusion of foreign principles and practices. In other words, the diffusion of legal systems, besides explaining why countries often have similar systems, also helps explain cultural formation and dynamics.

FIGURE 3.5   The Diffusion of Civil Law

The principles of *civil law*—which are based on the systematic codification of statutes—goes back to the Romans, from whom they were borrowed by countries in western Europe, notably France and Germany. From France they made their way to the New World; from Germany they were exported to central and eastern Europe and eastern Asia.

Source: Compiled from data reported in "Doing Business in 2004: Understanding Regulation," The World Bank.

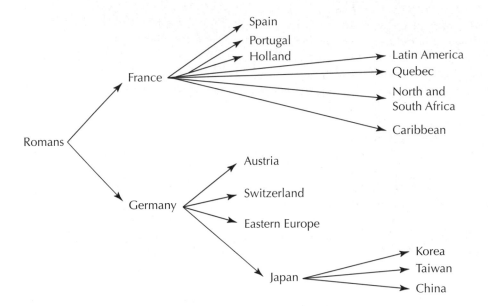

New Zealand, East Africa, large parts of Asia (including India), and most of the Caribbean. In this case, the primary means of diffusion was *colonization*. Figure 3.5 profiles the comparatively exotic diffusion of the civil law system.

Alternatives to democracy generally emphasize political and social stability at the expense of individual freedom and liberty.

The Diffusion of Civil Law   Elsewhere in Europe, meanwhile, France, Germany, and the Nordic countries adopted Roman law in developing civil law traditions. Eventually, France exported its version to Spain, Portugal, and Holland, all of which were conquered by Napoleon in the early nineteenth century. Coupled with colonization, *conquest* seems to have been the preferred French mode of diffusing its civil law system to Latin America, Quebec, large parts of Europe, parts of North and West Africa, parts of the Caribbean, and parts of Asia. The German civil law system influenced the development of legal codes in Switzerland and Austria, and the Austro-Hungarian Empire brought German commercial law to much of central and eastern Europe. Interestingly, Japan voluntarily adopted Germany's legal system and has steadily influenced the legal systems of the Republic of Korea, Taiwan, and China.

TRENDS IN LEGAL SYSTEMS

Earlier in this chapter, we discussed the evolution and diffusion of democracy throughout the world, and you no doubt recall our comments on the diffusion of and backlash against democratic principles in different parts of the world. It remains to be seen how this trend unfolds in the next 5 to 10 years. But, at this juncture, companies that want to do business overseas consider an array of legal implications. On the one hand, this situation forces them into a situation of uncertainty; on the other, however, the need to deal with uncertainty prompts firms to adopt perspectives from which they can better see marketplace trends and opportunities.

CONCEPT CHECK

As we see in Chapter 1, every company's *competitive environment* varies by company, industry, and country. Granted, there are points of convergence in all three areas, but conducting **international business** means recognizing the existence of fundamental *differences* across countries. Here, we stress the importance of legal differences and the need of foreign firms to make sure that their local activities comply with local laws.

The Preference for Stability   No one has yet reached a consensus on how best to take advantage of this situation, but there is some agreement on certain aspects. First, remember that the unfolding backlash against democracy tends to reveal a preference for some form of *authoritarian government* or *totalitarian democracy*. From the standpoint of the democratically inclined, this trend is unsettling, but the fact remains that the two preferred types of political system have something in common—namely, an emphasis on political and social stability at the expense of individual freedom and liberty. Step one, then, might be recognizing the fact that this preference will shape the ways in which government officials will use the legal system to regulate business activity.

The Influence of National Legacies   Here's another related trend that might help managers determine the way the wind is likely to blow in a given business environment. The timing of antidemocratic reaction coincides with the entry of developed countries into the global market: Countries like China, Venezuela, Thailand, Malaysia, Singapore, Vietnam, and Russia have enjoyed an acceleration of economic growth in the past few years.

Although we would normally regard the emergence of these countries as part of the larger phenomenon of international business growth, the suddenness of their economic emergence should caution us to assess their current legal behavior on the basis of particular national legal legacies. Thus although it's tempting to attribute to these newly developed nations certain principles of law that prevail in well-developed economies like those of the United States, Australia, France, or Sweden, we must remind ourselves that, in taking this internationalist perspective, we run the risk of misinterpreting nationalistic influences on legal systems in emerging economies.

The Recourse to Tradition in Dispute Resolution   Today, among the legal principles and practices on which virtually every developing and former communist nation relies are those that reflect the concerns and needs of agrarian societies. In agrarian societies, groups often appeal to senior individuals to mediate disputes for the simple reason that statutory codes for legal redress are either absent or regarded as illegitimate. Moreover, slight attention is paid in developing countries to philosophical issues in the nature, authority, and legitimacy of law.

Many legal theorists hold that these countries will eventually adopt the legal principles prevalent in developed economies. As Western economies evolved from agrarian to industrial, concern for property rights and product protection became more important. In turn, concerns such as these led to the development of modern legal systems that no longer appealed to those in power (whether the village elder or the local power broker) but rather to codes of written law.

UNDERSTANDING BASES OF RULE

For the time being, however, the freedom stagnation, coupled with the increasingly complex legal pressures faced by emerging economies, should remind firms of the need to understand exactly the *basis of rule* in any given country. Indeed, the key legal challenge today involves navigating between the danger of submitting to the "rule of man" and the danger of assuming that some form of the "rule of law" always prevails. Moreover, the assumptions that increase the danger in choosing one direction aren't the same as those that increase the danger in choosing the other.

The Rule of Man   On the one hand, the **rule of man** has been around for millennia. Indeed, for much of history, the ruler and the rule were synonymous: The law was the will of the ruler, whether in the person of the king, czar, raj, caliph, or emperor. Today, such titles have given way to others—chairman, general, supreme leader, and the like. Regardless of the title, the principle places ultimate power in the hands of one person, making his (or her) word and will (and whim) law, no matter how unfair, unjust, or nonsensical.

Because it grants inherent authority for the ruling party to act without being subject to checks and balances, the rule of man principle is a keystone of totalitarian government. As our opening case shows, however, the imposition of the rule of man (or party) doesn't necessarily eliminate sources of authority endorsed by long-standing traditions: In China, a byzantine civil service system is a hallowed tradition that's proved durable enough to often frustrate the will of the central Communist Party.

CONCEPT CHECK

As we observe in Chapter 2, the prevailing principles in a country's legal environment, including religious practices and other behavioral norms, are strongly influenced by its cultural orientation toward standards of accountability, equity, and fairness. In this case, as you can see, the prevailing legal principles reflect the needs of a culture oriented toward highly traditional standards of equity and fairness—standards carried forward by the wisdom derived by elders from experience.

In broad terms, totalitarian countries base their legal systems on the rule of man.

Case Review Note

The Rule of Law   The **rule of law,** however, is a hallmark of a democratic government. As a basis of rule, this principle holds that governmental authority is legitimately exercised in accordance with written, publicly disclosed laws that have been appropriately adopted and are enforced in keeping with established procedure.

Ideally, the rule of law institutes a just political and social environment, guarantees the enforceability of commercial contracts and business transactions, and safeguards personal property and individual freedom. Everyone who lives under it expects every legitimately enacted law, code, and statute to be grounded in and validated by the principles of the rule of law. No individual—whether public official or private citizen—stands above the law. Indeed, perhaps the primary purpose of the principle of the rule of law is to regulate and restrain the behavior of men and women, parties, juntas, clans, and dynasties that aspire to govern in its place.

IMPLICATIONS FOR MANAGERS

Like the ideal of democracy, the concept of the rule of law originated in the West. Thus there's little heritage of either in the legal traditions of many long developing, now emerging countries. If you take a close look at Map 3.4, you'll find that the rule of law flourishes in well-to-do developed countries—namely, the United States, Canada, Japan, New Zealand, Australia, and most of Europe. Indeed, the long crescent that begins in extreme northern Russia, cuts southward through China toward the Middle East, and

**MAP 3.4
The Rule of Law**

The principle of the *rule of law* holds that government authority is legitimate only when it's exercised according to written laws and established enforcement procedures. The coding of the map here is based on selected dimensions of governmental practice; percentiles reflect scores falling below the rating of a given country. So, for example, the classification of the United States at the 90th percentile indicates widespread support for the rule of law. Conversely, North Korea's classification at below the 10th percentile indicates its widespread support for the rule of man.

Source: World Bank, *Governance Matters VI: Governance Indicators for 1996–2006* (July 2007), at http://papers.ssrn.com (accessed December 15, 2007).

extends through Africa to South America indicates slight support for the rule of law. Conclusion? Presently, most emerging markets rely on the rule of man.

This situation is complicated by the acceptance of the rule of man in many emerging economies where political systems are more totalitarian than not. Uncertainty about the nature of law and the goals of government in so much of the world creates a perplexing situation for international businesses. Whereas operating in Western economies permits firms to rely on a consistent and systematic application of legal rules, operating in many emerging economies offers few such safeguards. In China, for example, legal action taken by foreign firms against local companies that counterfeit their products has proved virtually useless. Writs, threats, injunctions, and lawsuits get trapped in slow-grinding legal machinations, usually to be thrown out on technical grounds or simply to fail for such reasons as neglecting to register designs "properly."[27]

In consolation, firms keep waiting for the shift from agrarian to industrial economies to accelerate the adoption of the rule of law. They expect emerging economies, like their counterparts among the successful economies of the West, to recognize that the rule of law is the basis of a fair and just society. How long will they have to wait? In theory, emerging economies must first migrate from one basis of rule to another—that is, from the rule of man to "rule *by* law," which comes with the corollary notion that even a ruler is subject to the law. On fully adopting the principles and practices of model democracies, these societies will continue to evolve until their legal systems are anchored in the rule *of* law.

Uncertainty about the basis of law in a particular country creates challenging situations for managers.

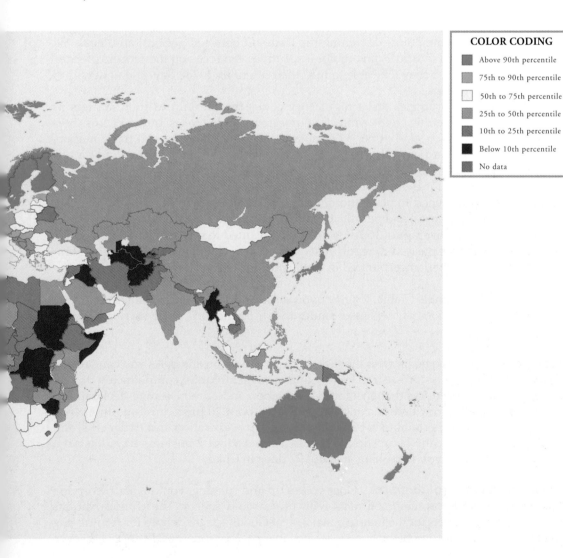

COLOR CODING

- Above 90th percentile
- 75th to 90th percentile
- 50th to 75th percentile
- 25th to 50th percentile
- 10th to 25th percentile
- Below 10th percentile
- No data

Unfortunately, recent trends complicate this scenario. For one thing, the backlash against democracy and social freedom has slowed the process. Quite simply, the principle of the rule of law is incompatible with an authoritarian political system, and because laws are made by politicians, firms now need to keep an eye out for signals indicating the direction of the "third wave of democratization," which may continue, slow down, or grind to a halt.

Legal Issues in International Business

The essential differences between our two bases of rule—the rule of law and the rule of man—are compounded by the fact that, regardless of its basic approach, any country can adopt any one of the five types of legal systems (common law, etc.) that we've described. Moreover, new forms of business activity, often coupled with changing patterns of trade and investment, may put firms in situations to which no clear legal standards apply. For our purposes, we can identify two noteworthy areas of importance: *operational concerns*, which involve the ways in which a business works on a day-to-day basis, and *strategic concerns*, which refer to a company's competitive position and long-term performance.

OPERATIONAL CONCERNS

Operational concerns that face managers worldwide include

- Starting a business.
- Entering and enforcing contracts.
- Hiring and firing local workers.
- Closing down the business.

Every company in every country must comply with local regulations regarding *operations*—starting, running, and closing down business activities. Obviously, then, firms study local legal systems to determine as well as possible their impact on day-to-day operations. At some point—assuming the trade-off between political and legal risk and potential financial returns is favorable—executives can focus on the process of starting up operations. Then they'll be able to turn their attention to the day-to-day details of running their businesses.

In general, host countries enact regulatory codes that pertain to such matters as employing workers, getting credit, protecting investors, paying taxes, trading across borders, enforcing contracts, and, if need be, closing the business. Although these matters are often straightforward in the firm's home market, managers must be prepared for different operating procedures when deciding to locate in a foreign country.

One entrepreneur, for example, recalls his experience in starting up his first company in Brazil (which happened to be his home country). He found that the task of securing the authorizations, licenses, and permits from seven different ministries needed to start a new business took an average of 150 days. When he wanted to start up a U.S.-based business, however, he was pleased to report that "within a week I had formed an LLC [limited liability corporation], incorporated in Delaware, and set up bank accounts."[28]

CONCEPT CHECK

In Chapter 1, we assume that democratic political systems grant firms the freedom to engage in their preferred "modes of international business." Note, however, that the backlash against democracy that we've detailed in this chapter creates uncertainty about operating in particular countries. When it comes to dealing with certain modes of **international business,** some nations simply prohibit them, whereas others control them by applying— sometimes arbitrarily and unpredictably—technicalities buried in their legal codes.

The Task of Compliance   Table 3.3 gives you an idea of how some countries regulate the day-to-day operations of businesses under their jurisdictions. We now turn to some of the specifics.

Getting Started   Let's begin with the task of starting up a business. As you can see, it's a relatively easy process in Australia and Canada, which require compliance with just two registration procedures that encompass tax, labor, and administrative declarations. In the African nation of Chad, in contrast, you face about 20 procedural requirements, including regulations pertaining to bank deposits, court registration, health benefits, and even your company seal. The upshot: Whereas it takes about 2 business days to start a business in Australia, you're looking at about 77 days in Chad.

Making and Enforcing Contracts   Once you're up and running, you can start worrying about entering and enforcing contracts with buyers and sellers. The United Nations Convention on Contracts for the International Sale of Goods sets guidelines for formulating and enforcing contracts among businesses located in signatory countries. Even so, however,

TABLE 3.3 The Regulation of Day-to-Day Operations in Various Countries

Country	Legal Origin	Starting a Business			Enforcing Contracts			Closing a Business	
		Number of Procedures[1]	Time (Days)	Cost (% of Income per Capita)	Number of Procedures[2]	Time[3] (Days)	Cost[4] (% of Claim)	Time to Insolvency (Years)	Cost[5] (% of Estate)
Australia	Common (English)	2	2	1.8	19	181	12.8	1	8
Canada	Common (English)	2	3	0.9	17	346	12.0	0.8	4
Chad	Civil (French)	19	77	226.1	52	743	54.9	10	63
China	Civil (German)	13	35	9.3	31	292	26.8	2.4	22
France	Civil (French)	7	8	1.1	21	331	11.8	1.9	9
Germany	Civil (German)	9	24	5.1	30	394	10.5	1.2	8
Guatemala	Civil (French)	13	30	52.1	36	1459	26.5	3	15
India	Common (English)	11	35	73.7	56	1420	35.7	10	9
Japan	Civil (German)	8	23	7.5	20	242	9.5	0.6	4
Korea	Civil (German)	12	22	15.2	29	230	5.5	1.5	4
Russia	Socialist	7	28	2.7	31	178	13.5	3.8	9
United Kingdom	Common (English)	6	18	0.7	19	229	16.8	1	6
United States	Common (English)	5	5	0.7	17	300	7.7	1.5	7

Source: Compiled from "Doing Business in 2007: How to Reform," The International Bank for Reconstruction and Development/The World Bank.

[1] Number of procedures that the entrepreneur must deal with in starting a business.

[2] Number of procedures mandated by law or court rules that demand interaction between the parties to the dispute or between them and the judge or court officer.

[3] The number of days from the moment the plaintiff files the lawsuit in court until the moment of settlement or actual payment.

[4] Cost incurred during dispute resolution, comprising court fees, attorney fees, and payments to other professionals.

[5] Cost of entire bankruptcy process, including court costs, insolvency practitioners' costs, and the costs of independent assessors, lawyers, and accountants.

there's considerable variation across types of legal systems and specific countries. As for legal systems, countries with common law systems tend to encourage precise, detailed contracts. In countries with civil law systems, where the civil code deals with many pertinent issues, the law encourages shorter and less specific contracts.

The same tendencies show up in contract-enforcement policies. Australia, Norway, and the United Kingdom require the fewest number of enforcement procedures; such countries as Burundi, Angola, Bolivia, Cameroon, El Salvador, Mexico, and Panama can subject firms to many times the number of procedures. Similarly, countries vary in the time span required to enforce a contract; the speediest enforcers, such as Australia, Russia, South Korea, and the United Kingdom, need around 200 days. Elsewhere—say, in Italy, Nigeria, Poland, or Guatemala—the same activities can stretch out to anywhere from 600 to 1,500 days.

Hiring and Firing   No matter where you're operating, you'll probably have to hire and, when necessary, fire local workers. In practice, of course, hiring should be relatively easy and firing extremely taxing. Singapore, New Zealand, and the United States are among the countries with the most flexible labor-regulations statutes. China enjoys not only the most flexibility in hiring and firing but also the greatest discretion in setting employment conditions (work hours, minimum wages, benefits). In contrast, Angola, Belarus, and Paraguay place rigid restrictions on firing: You have to provide documentation on the grounds for termination, establish detailed firing procedures, and furnish both generous prior notification and severance payments.

Going Under and Getting Out   Finally, many companies fail, and as if that isn't traumatic enough, some countries make the task of closing down quite difficult. The English bankruptcy law of 1732 was the first modern law to address this issue. The United States introduced its first bankruptcy law in 1800, essentially replicating the English law. France, Germany, and Spain adopted their first bankruptcy laws in the early nineteenth century. Today, these legacies still shape bankruptcy proceedings in their respective countries. Ireland, Japan, Canada, and Hong Kong make closing your doors both fast and cheap; procedures in India, the Philippines, Serbia, Chad, and Panama are among the slowest and most expensive.

General Relationships   The country profiles in Figure 3.4 (p. 110) reflect general tendencies in the regulation of commercial operations. You probably noticed in reading the preceding paragraphs an inverse relationship between a nation's per capita income and its tendencies in regulating business activity: Richer countries tend to regulate less and poorer countries to regulate more. In high-income countries (e.g., the United States, Italy, Japan), the average number of procedures to start a new business is 7; it's 10 in upper-middle-income countries (Mexico, Poland, Malaysia), 12 in lower-middle-income countries (Brazil, Jamaica, China), and 11 in low-income countries (Angola, Ghana, Vietnam).

In wealthy nations, furthermore, legal systems tend to be more consistent in regulating major operational activities than those in poorer countries. Those countries, for example, that make it easy to start a business also impose fewer and simpler regulations on both hiring and firing practices and bankruptcy procedures.

In summary, the top-ranked countries in Table 3.4 have in place legal codes that support the most favorable operating environments. In evaluating the likely impact of a given legal environment on their business activities, firms often consider such criteria in making their first cuts. Once the list of potential countries has been pared down, they refine relevant information by monitoring efforts to simplify business regulations, strengthen investor rights, ease tax burdens, facilitate access to credit, and improve employment practices. Combined, this information allows firms not only to forecast operating patterns but also to identify areas for improvement.

STRATEGIC CONCERNS

Successful companies develop **strategic plans** that describe their business goals and objectives. Because a country's legal system and basis of rule affect a company's operating

---

CONCEPT CHECK

In both Chapters 1 and 2, we discuss income and wealth as national resources; we also show how the availability of such resources impacts the actions that countries, both rich and poor, take to affect their business environments. We point out here that this influence can also be felt in the decisions that countries make when regulating the operations of foreign firms within their borders.

Strategic concerns that face managers worldwide include

- Product safety and liability.
- Marketplace behavior.
- Product origin and local content.
- Legal jurisdiction.
- Arbitration.

TABLE 3.4 Taking It Easier on Business: The Top 25 Countries

High ranking indicates a country whose legal code fosters a favorable operating environment including fair tax burdens, easy access to credit, and straightforward employment practices.

2007 RANK	ECONOMY
1	Singapore
2	New Zealand
3	United States
4	Canada
5	Hong Kong, China
6	United Kingdom
7	Denmark
8	Australia
9	Norway
10	Ireland
11	Japan
12	Iceland
13	Sweden
14	Finland
15	Switzerland
16	Lithuania
17	Estonia
18	Thailand
19	Puerto Rico
20	Belgium
21	Germany
22	Netherlands
23	Korea
24	Latvia
25	Malaysia

Source: "Doing Business in 2007: How to Reform," The International Bank for Reconstruction and Development/The World Bank.

decisions—where to make a product, how to market it, and how to protect its unique features—firms must take them into account when formulating their strategic plans. In the following sections, we discuss some of the key issues underlying the strategic plans developed by companies that want to do business abroad.

Product Safety and Liability International companies often customize products to comply with local legal standards. Sometimes these standards are higher than those in the home market, and sometime they're just different. *Product liability laws* are particularly stringent in the United States, the European Union, and many other wealthy countries; in many poorer countries, they're spotty, absent, or arbitrary. Product safety and liability cases brought to court in the United States can include sky-high punitive damages—a practice that's far less common in other countries.

Marketplace Behavior National laws also determine permissible practices in pricing, distributing, advertising, and promoting products and services. Many countries, for instance, prohibit TV cigarette advertising. In France, a manufacturer can't offer a product that it doesn't manufacture as an inducement to buy one that it does. Germany prohibits comparative advertising, and China prohibits comparisons if they reflect negatively on the competitor's product.

In countries where the rule of man is the basis of rule, acceptable marketplace behavior can be unpredictable. Outsiders have lodged complaints ranging from trumped-up legal charges and direct solicitation of bribes to blatant favoritism on behalf of local competitors. Especially controversial is the issue of the protection—or lack thereof—of intellectual property. We'll look at this issue in greater detail later.

Product Origin and Local Content In addition, national laws affect the flow of products across borders. To determine charges for the right to bring a product into the local market, for example, local governments often devise laws that depend on the product's place of origin. Product origin is also a common criterion for determining the proportion of the product that's produced by local competitors. The resulting proportion, called **local content,** is important to all nations, and most of them use some variation of local-content law to pressure foreign producers into making a greater share of a given product in the local market.

Legal Jurisdiction Each country specifies which laws should apply to which activities and the criteria for resorting to litigation when agents—whether legal residents of the same or of different countries—are involved. Moreover, a nation's courts have the final decision on any matter that falls within their jurisdiction. Usually, a company urges a home-country court to claim jurisdiction on the grounds that it's likely to receive more favorable treatment. That's why contracts typically contain *choice of law clauses* stipulating the country whose laws will apply to a dispute.

Arbitration More and more, companies are choosing to resolve disputes by means of *arbitration*, whereby both parties agree on an impartial third party to settle the matter. Most arbitration is governed by the New York Convention, a 1958 protocol that allows parties to choose their own mediators and resolve disputes on neutral ground. To render decisions more enforceable, the Convention limits appeal options to narrow circumstances. A small number of complaints against governments are arbitrated by the International Centre for Settlement of Investment Disputes. This body is closely linked to the World Bank, and a noncompliant government risks being cut off from bank funds.

INTELLECTUAL PROPERTY RIGHTS

The legal system of a country typically addresses such issues as product liability, product origin, and jurisdiction. Today, however, the most hotly contested battlefront in international law is the controversy over the protection of intellectual property. The way a country interprets its responsibility to protect intellectual property is a good test of the extent to which it's willing to foster a marketplace that's fair to both local and foreign investors. The growing power of ideas in the global economy also makes the protection of intellectual property a crucial issue in the development of a firm's international strategy.

Today, in other words, countries compete on the strength of their brainpower to create might, prestige, and wealth. We call the output of this brainpower **intellectual property**—the creative ideas, innovative expertise, or intangible insights that give an individual, company, or country a competitive advantage. Many observers contend that, without intellectual property protection, there's no incentive for innovation.

Here, in a nutshell, is the problem: Intellectual property, whether in the form of books, music, designs, brand names, or software, is tough to conceive but easy to copy. (In our closing case, we examine further the problems resulting from the fact that "digital" products, in particular, are ridiculously easy to copy—the main reason why the global software industry is so vulnerable to widespread piracy and counterfeiting.) Indeed, the range of products that get copied is mind boggling—books, music CDs, videotapes, aircraft parts, cigarettes, wristwatches, razor blades, batteries, motorcycles, automobiles, shampoo, pens, toys, wine, shoes, clothing, industrial equipment, luggage, medicines, foods, beer, perfume, and cleaning supplies; you name it.

CONCEPT CHECK

Recall from Chapter 2 our discussion of the ways in which **culture** influences attitudes toward the development and ownership of ideas. In this section, we show that certain attitudes—particularly attitudes toward workplace motivation and relationships—influence entrepreneurial behavior in a country; likewise, attitudes toward collective and individual priorities help shape numerous facets of a nation's competitive environment.

Intellectual property: the general term for creative ideas, innovation expertise, or intangible insights that give owners a competitive advantage.

The Chinese Connection; or, "We Can Copy Everything Except Your Mother"   Given its apparent popularity, it shouldn't be surprising that the costs of intellectual property theft—whether in terms of lost sales, ruined brand reputation, dangerous products, or the costs of policing and going to court—are high. The International Anti-Counterfeiting Coalition estimates that international trade in counterfeit products runs more than $500 billion a year—about 9 percent of the total value of world trade. Particularly noteworthy— as we suggested in our opening case—are intellectual-property violations in China. The European Union suggests that fully half of the 100 million fake items seized in Europe in 2004 came from China. In the United States, the FBI estimates that American companies lose up to $250 billion annually to counterfeiting, half of it conducted in China alone.

In frustration, the United States filed a complaint with the World Trade Organization (WTO), accusing the Chinese of counterfeiting or pirating software, videos, pharmaceuticals and other goods (sometimes with the open encouragement of Chinese officials), and of failing to stiffen punishments for perpetrators.[29] Nevertheless, on the city streets and country roads of China, counterfeiting is still business as usual. What accounts for China's status as the world's premier number-one counterfeiter? Most analysts point to four factors: cultural structure, the legacy of a rule-of-man basis, weak legal enforcement, and the country's sheer size.

"We have never seen a problem of this size and magnitude in world history," notes one observer. "There's more counterfeiting going on in China now than we've ever seen anywhere."[30] Estimates of the percentage of Chinese goods that are counterfeit range up to 30 percent. As they say in Shanghai, "We can copy everything except your mother."[31]

International Property Rights (IPRs)   Many countries have pushed for better protection of intellectual property, generally in the form of so-called **intellectual property rights (IPRs)** designed to give the registered owners of inventions, literary and artistic works, and symbols, names, images, or designs the right to determine the use of their property. In other words, the registered owner of a copyright would have the legal right to decide who may copy it or who may use it for another purpose (such as the manufacture of a product).

Technically, an IPR constitutes a legally enforceable but limited monopoly granted by a country to an innovator. Because an IPR specifies a period during which other parties may not copy an idea, the innovator can commercialize it to recoup initial investments

> Intellectual property rights refer to the right to control and derive the benefits from writing (copyright), inventions (patents), processes (trade secrets), and identifiers (trademarks).

Step right up and make an offer. Here we see a situation that takes place in market stalls throughout the developing world. Buyers and sellers at a display of pirated CDs and DVDs at the night market in Chinatown in Kuala Lumpur, Malaysia.

and capture potential profits. Naturally, companies safeguard potential sales and profits by protecting intangible assets through enforceable patents, trademarks, and copyrights.

Unfortunately, the extent of product piracy indicates just how hard it is to enforce such protections as IPRs. One obstacle is posed by poor compliance and enforcement in certain jurisdictions, and problems arise because not all countries formally support the various agreements developed to protect IPRs. The primary regulatory codes for intellectual property are the Paris Convention for the Protection of Industrial Property and the Berne Convention for the Protection of Literary and Artistic Works, both created in the 1880s and updated many times. More recently, the Trade-Related Aspects of Intellectual Property Rights (TRIPS) code of the World Trade Organization provides for stricter protection of intellectual property.

Naturally, most governments claim to abide by these agreements and to enforce intellectual property rights. Still, as the continuing spread of theft shows, an international company is taking a risk in introducing products based on intellectual property rights. The biggest problem remains jurisdiction: An IPR protected by, say, a U.S. patent, trademark registration, copyright, or design registration extends only to the United States and its territories and possessions. It confers no protection in a foreign country.

Furthermore, there's no shortcut to worldwide protection: There's no way to register some sort of "global" patent, trademark, or copyright (say, with TRIPS). Complicating matters is the fact that countries interpret and enforce agreements more or less arbitrarily. Indian patent law regarding pharmaceuticals, for example, protects only the "processes" by which drugs are made, not the drugs themselves. This means that, simply by using a process that's different from the innovator's process, Indian companies can manufacture drugs patented in other countries.

The Role of Local Attitudes   Most of these sorts of local legal issues pose reasonable challenges that can be met with improved international laws.[32] Unfortunately, we can't say the same for piracy, which is rooted in far more fundamental legal, economic, and cultural factors. To put it bluntly, not only are some countries less inclined to protect intellectual property but also certain local attitudes encourage violations. Let's take a closer look at a few elements of these local attitudes.

Legal Legacies   Most counterfeit goods come to us from emerging markets in which the basis of rule is the rule of man. Because many analysts cite its tradition of the rule of man as a main factor in China's propensity to make counterfeit goods and its reluctance to protect intellectual property more vigorously, we might as well begin our discussion with a return trip to China. (In addition, taking a closer look at conditions in China should put us in a better position to spot similar trends in other countries.)

Officially, China has passed a battery of laws confirming to international standards of market access, nondiscrimination, and transparency. The enduring legacy of the rule of man, however, means that neither a typical Chinese citizen nor a typical Chinese bureaucrat presently extends sufficient respect to laws that have been codified through foreign processes and are weakly enforced by domestic authorities. Recall from our opening case the view

expressed by one businessperson as a result of his experience in China, "I was dealing with a society that had no rules; or more accurately, plenty of rules, but they were seldom enforced. China appeared to be run by masterful showmen: appearances mattered more than substance; rules were there to be distorted; and success came through outfacing an opponent."[33]

The essence of the problem, then, is the discrepancy between domestic traditions and foreign standards, which tends to influence a lot of official decision making, both bureaucratic and legal. According to one Chinese judge, for example, Chinese intellectual property laws "exist to protect Chinese intellectual property from foreign intellectual property."[34] Aggressive calls for China to make greater concessions to the rule of law may one day prove successful, but the frustrating struggle against two millenniums of legal tradition has led more than one analyst to conclude that establishing rule of law in China may be "one of the largest social infrastructure projects in the history of mankind."[35]

Finally, this situation is not unique to China. Notwithstanding global pressure to improve along with domestic public statements to do so, countries struggle to adopt the principles that underlie justice and fairness. For example, the Asian Development Bank looked at the performance of Indonesia, Malaysia, the Philippines, South Korea, and Thailand, relative to the rest of the world, on measures of good governance (specifically, accountability, political stability, government effectiveness, regulatory quality, control of corruption, and the rule of law). Comparing 2005 with 1996, the scores for these East Asian countries deteriorated in 22 of the 30 comparisons (i.e., six measures for five countries). Moreover, using international rankings finds that these five countries have fallen in 28 of the 30 comparisons.[36]

Countries that observe the rule of man, as opposed to the rule of law, less aggressively protect intellectual property rights.

Level of Economic Development As we've already suggested, the vigor of its IPR protection often reflects a country's stage of economic development: Typically, poorer countries provide weaker legal protection than richer countries.[37] Why? Generally, developed countries contend that protecting ideas is the only way to energize the incentive to innovate. "If stuff you create can be misappropriated," explains one analyst, "your incentive for continuing to create valuable intellectual property diminishes significantly."[38] Poorer countries counter with three arguments against strict protection of intellectual property—namely, that it:

Generally, poorer countries provide weaker legal protection of intellectual property than do richer countries.

- Restricts the diffusion of new technologies
- Inflates the prices that poor nations pay for products that are available only from wealthy nations
- Inhibits economic development by constraining the use of existing knowledge

Furthermore, because few companies in poorer countries create or register intellectual properties, neither businesspeople nor officials have much reason for protecting them.

Finally, its proponents face the problem of extreme poverty in many of the countries that don't practice IPR protection. Consider the fact that people who have no wealth and little income have little money to spend for necessities, let alone for branded goods priced and distributed by corporations headquartered in wealthy countries. In the African nation of Kenya, for example, where the average income is about $1,500 and some people earn less than $200, it shouldn't come as a surprise that a lot of Kenyans "think you have to cheat to survive."[39]

Using TRIPS as a vehicle, the WTO continues to try to ease this ongoing tension. It gives wealthy countries, for instance, a year to comply with its latest rules on intellectual property but grants the poorest countries a 5- to 10-year grace period. Richer countries, however, hope that companies in such nations as China, Ukraine, and India will eventually be equipped to market products based on their own intellectual property; when that happens—or so the theory goes—they'll make the transition to the rule of law and recognize international intellectual property rights.

In fact, the booming economies of many emerging markets have encouraged observers in developed countries to expect the transition sooner rather than later. They reason that as developing countries progress from *using* to *inventing* intellectual property, they'll have a much more powerful incentive to protect it.[40]

Cultural Attitudes Cultural attitudes also help explain local differences in attitudes toward intellectual property. Countries with an *individualist* orientation, such as the United States, tend to regard the concept of individual ownership of an idea as intrinsically legitimate: It makes complete sense that if you create something, you have the right to say who can copy it or use it for any given purpose.

Cultural attitudes influence the protection of intellectual property rights. Notably, individualist societies are more vigilant than collectivist societies.

In contrast, countries with a *collectivist* orientation, such as China, extol the virtue of sharing over that of individual ownership; from this point of view, there's little reason to honor the idea of individual ownership. Asked about software piracy in his country, for instance, a South Korean diplomat explained, "[H]istorically, Koreans have not viewed intellectual discoveries or scientific inventions as the private property of the discoverers or inventors. New ideas or technologies [are] 'public goods' for everybody to share freely. Cultural esteem rather than material gain [is] the incentive for creativity."[41]

Finally, the rule of man, as we've already seen, appeals more to a collectivist society than to an individualist society. Members of collectivist societies hold that the value placed on cohesiveness and community helps create a "social contract" designed for the benefit of all parties. Many Chinese also adhere to the belief that social harmony is possible if every citizen acts in accord with the natural principles that define his or her position in society—or, as Confucius put it some 2,500 years ago, "Let the ruler be ruler, the minister minister, the father father, and the son son."[42]

CASE

Crime That Pays (and Pretty Well, Too)

I prowl the aisles of the software piracy mother lode, the Golden Shopping Arcade in Hong Kong's Sham Shui Po district. All around me in the basement of this dingy, block-long urban warehouse, eager shoppers paw through the bins and tables of the densely packed stalls. Inside a stall called the Everything CD shop, I buy the first of my installer discs, Volume 2. This tribute to pirate technology costs the same as all the other CD-ROMs at Golden Arcade, about nine bucks or three for $25. Incredibly, this disc has 86 programs on it, each compressed with a self-extracting installation utility. Volume 2 has a beta copy of Windows 95 as well as OS/2 Warp, CorelDraw! 5, Quicken 4.0, Atari Action Pack for Windows, Norton Commander, KeyCad, Adobe Premier, Microsoft Office, and dozens of other applications, including a handful written in Chinese. Connoisseurs of the genre compare the different versions of the installer discs like fine wines. Someone from Microsoft later tells me that the retail value of the disc is between $20,000 and $35,000.[43]

—One journalist's shopping trip to the software black market

Almost from its inception, software technology has been dogged by the problem of **digital piracy**—the illegal distribution and/or copying of software for personal or business use.[44] It's an explosive issue, and it cuts right to the perception, protection, and enforcement of IPRs. Presently, software pirates can be anyone from an individual making an unauthorized copy of a software product (for use, sale, or free distribution) to an entire crew of managers bent on mismanaging a company's own software licenses.

It's not that the rules against software piracy are ambiguous—quite the contrary. The United States, for example, stipulates that software is automatically protected by federal copyright law from the moment of its creation. Title 17 of the U.S. Copyright Act grants the copyright owner "the exclusive rights [to] reproduce the copyrighted work" and "to distribute copies" of it (Section 106). It also states that "anyone who violates any of the exclusive rights of the copyright owner . . . is an infringer of the copyright" (Section 501). The statute goes on to set forth specific penalties for violations.

Nor is ignorance of the law any excuse for piracy: As far as the United States is concerned, violators are liable for copyright infringement whether or not they know that they're violating U.S. federal law. This means that if you're a software user who's purchased a license from, say, Microsoft, you've purchased the right to load the product onto *one* computer and the right to make other copies for "archival purposes only." Furthermore, one illegal copy can land you a six-figure fine and jail time. In contrast, the corresponding "threshold laws" in China "let you have as many as 499 pirated DVDs without a criminal penalty. And if you get caught with those you get the equivalent of a parking ticket."

In 2006, industry groups reported that global software piracy—at national, regional, and worldwide levels—was rampant and showing few signs of letting up. News of this predicament shouldn't be surprising: The problem with software is that, like any "digital" product, it's extraordinarily easy to duplicate copies that are usually as good as the original (Table 3.5). And that, in short, is why piracy and counterfeiting continue to bedevil the global software industry.

TABLE 3.5   How to Pirate Software

End-user piracy	If you're simply a user, feel free to copy software (whether for personal or business use) without appropriate licensing; don't bother monitoring the number of licenses that you install, and don't worry about acquiring enough licenses to cover your needs.
Pre-installed software	If you manufacture computers, make operations more efficient by installing one copy of licensed software on a whole batch of computers.
Internet piracy	If you want to capitalize on the ability of the Internet to facilitate transactions, use it to download unauthorized copies of software.
Counterfeiting	If you are, say, an unscrupulous entrepreneur, make illegal copies of software, being sure to reproduce the manufacturer's packaging as well as his product; remember, too, that it's not much more trouble to counterfeit registration cards (and don't forget unauthorized serial numbers).
Online auction piracy	If you want to get into the distribution end of the business, you have two options: (1) resell software that's not authorized for resale, or (2) use the Internet to auction off counterfeit or unlawfully obtained software as "liquidated inventory" or as merchandise acquired through "bankruptcy sales."

Source: Adapted from Microsoft Corporation, "Piracy Basics" (2008), at www.microsoft.com/canada/sam/piracy/default.mspx (accessed December 15, 2007). Used with permission from Microsoft.

The Business Software Alliance (BSA) reports that, of all the packaged software installed on personal computers (PCs) worldwide in 2005, no less than 35 percent was acquired illegally—at a cost of $34 billion in losses to software makers and distributors; that figure is up from losses of $29 billion in 2003. Table 3.6 shows that, for many nations, 2005 piracy rates topped 75 percent. Where does most pirated software come from? Table 3.7 shows that—again, as of 2005—69 percent of all pirated software originated in Central/Eastern Europe, 68 percent in Latin America, 57 percent in the Middle East and Africa, and 54 percent in the Asia-Pacific region.

Waging a Multifront War

Obviously, several parties, including software makers, industry associations, and governments, have an interest in pursuing solutions to the piracy problem, usually by means of legislation and political cooperation. Until recently, an important front in the war against piracy was conducted by software makers, who relied on technical and business measures as a counteroffensive. In the 1980s and 1990s, for example, many companies integrated anticopying mechanisms into products.

Unfortunately, although such measures were fairly effective, consumers complained that they made software unduly difficult to use. Abandoning anticopying technologies, companies turned to other tactics, including distribution business models (e.g., requiring site and shrink-wrap licenses) and alternative technological protections (requiring passwords, registration numbers, and encrypting codes). This time, customers, though mildly annoyed, generally responded well, and for a while, it seemed as if the new measures might be effective in helping to control piracy.

At the same time, software companies began to lobby governments to enact laws supporting their IPRs. The United States, for example, elevated software piracy from a misdemeanor to a felony (if 10 or more illegal copies were made within a six-month period and if those copies were worth more than $2,500). The United States also became more vigorous in its enforcement efforts, threatening to sanction countries with especially "onerous and egregious" IPR violations, such as China, Russia, Argentina, India, Thailand, Turkey, and the Ukraine. As we noted in our opening case, one of the complications in China has been barely disguised government support of IPR violations: Besides reaping profits from outright piracy, putting intellectual property to commercial use often results in the birth and growth of whole industries whose emergence and ability to compete might otherwise be decades away. This is the main reason why the then U.S. Trade Representative declared that "we must defend ideas, inventions and creativity from rip-off artists and thieves"—not the simple need to protect naive tourists from the embarrassment of buying bogus Prada handbags.

TABLE 3.6   Software Piracy Rankings by Country

Scores refer to the percentage of installed software that was illegally acquired. In Vietnam, for example, of all the packaged software installed on PCs in 2005, 90% was illegally obtained by users. In the United States, which has the lowest rate of illegal installations, 1 out of every 5 installations involved pirated software.

20 COUNTRIES WITH THE HIGHEST PIRACY RATES

COUNTRY	2005	2004	2003
Vietnam	90%	92%	92%
Zimbabwe	90%	90%	87%
Indonesia	87%	87%	88%
China	86%	90%	92%
Pakistan	86%	82%	83%
Kazakhstan	85%	85%	85%
Ukraine	85%	91%	91%
Cameroon	84%	84%	81%
Russia	83%	87%	87%
Bolivia	83%	80%	78%
Paraguay	83%	83%	83%
Algeria	83%	83%	84%
Zambia	83%	84%	81%
Venezuela	82%	79%	72%
Botswana	82%	84%	81%
Ivory Coast	82%	84%	81%
Nigeria	82%	84%	84%
Senegal	82%	84%	81%
Serbia/Montenegro	81%	81%	
El Salvador	81%	80%	79%

20 COUNTRIES WITH THE LOWEST PIRACY RATES

COUNTRY	2005	2004	2003
United States	21%	21%	22%
New Zealand	23%	23%	23%
Austria	26%	25%	27%
Finland	26%	29%	31%
Denmark	27%	27%	26%
Germany	27%	29%	30%
Sweden	27%	26%	27%
Switzerland	27%	28%	31%
United Kingdom	27%	27%	29%
Japan	28%	28%	29%
Belgium	28%	29%	29%
Netherlands	30%	30%	33%
Norway	30%	31%	32%
Australia	31%	32%	31%
Israel	32%	33%	35%
Canada	33%	36%	35%
UAE	34%	34%	34%
South Africa	36%	37%	36%
Ireland	37%	38%	41%
Singapore	40%	42%	43%

Source: Business Software Alliance, *Fourth Annual BSA and IDC Global Software Piracy Study* (2007), at http://w3.bsa.org/globalstudy (accessed December 15, 2007).

In addition, industry associations, notably the BSA, the Software and Information Industry Association (SIIA), and the International Anti-Counterfeiting Coalition (IACC), spearhead efforts to spur governments to toughen laws. Normally, these multinational organizations provide global services in public policy, business development, corporate education, and intellectual property protection.

The BSA, for example, maintains programs in more than 80 countries. Each national unit works to promote a legal online world by negotiating with governments and consumers in the

TABLE 3.7   2005 Software Piracy Rankings by Region

Although 3 of the top 4 spots among national software pirates are occupied by countries in the Asia Pacific region, the Central/Eastern European region supplies more illegal software—68% of the worldwide total—than any other.

REGION	PERCENTAGE
North America	22
Western Europe	35
Asia Pacific	54
Middle East/Africa	57
Central/Eastern Europe	69
Latin America	68
European Union	36
Worldwide	35

Source: Adapted from Business Software Alliance, *Fourth Annual BSA and IDC Global Software Piracy Study* (2007), at http://w3.bsa.org/globalstudy (accessed December 15, 2007).

international software and Internet markets, especially working to educate consumers on software management and copyright protection, cybersecurity, e-commerce, and other Internet-related issues. BSA members include companies like Microsoft, Adobe, Dell, IBM, Intel, and Apple Computer.

Finally, software makers, governments, and associations, acting both singly and jointly, have successfully lobbied transnational institutions to help police piracy. In the early 2000s, for instance, the 184 member-nations of the World Intellectual Property Organization (WIPO) pledged to protect intellectual property worldwide by developing IPR treaties. WIPO then lobbied members to ratify an array of antipiracy treaties—namely, the World Copyright Treaty (WCT) and the WIPO Performances and Phonograms Treaty (WPPT). Similarly, the World Trade Organization (WTO) enacted an agreement on Trade-Related Aspects of Intellectual Property Rights (TRIPS), which is designed to regulate enforcement of copyright and counterfeiting violations. TRIPS requires all member-nations to protect and enforce IPRs according to global, not local, standards. Enacted in 1995, TRIPS was, at the time, the most comprehensive agreement on intellectual property.

Collectively, the action taken by companies, associations, governments, and other organizations produced some hope that global software piracy could be curtailed. By the late 1990s, moreover, software makers were encouraged by the fact that piracy rates appeared to be directly related to a country's rate of market growth. In other words, large and mature software markets, such as the United States and Canada, had low rates of piracy. This finding was promising because it suggested that, as software markets in other regions matured, piracy rates would decline there as well.

At this point, concerted political and commercial action seemed to be making headway. Some observers credited a host of promising antipiracy initiatives. Others argued that the war was being won because of a greater variety of factors, including the growing global reach of software companies, high-profile legal proceedings, increased government cooperation, the criminalization of software piracy, and tougher trade agreements. Still others pointed out that the significant decline in legal software prices was narrowing the gap between legal and illegal prices.

Piracy Persists

Today, those early hopes for the defeat of piracy seem fairly naive. As it turns out, it didn't matter which countries or regions were involved: Piracy rates, though not necessarily increasing, certainly weren't declining. Data for 2005 reported that, despite a constant global software piracy rate of 35 percent, total global losses had increased by another $1.6 billion. Moreover, the median piracy rate is now 64 percent: In other words, fully half the countries studied by the BSA have a piracy rate of 64 percent or higher.

Particularly given their recently rosy outlook, many analysts were especially alarmed by escalating piracy rates. Some even worried that piracy threatened to reach even higher levels. Finally, as more and more people entered the global software market—many of them eager to join the digital age despite income constraints—high-tech and law enforcement experts warned that the worldwide quest for lower prices could only fuel the growth of piracy.

In response, software makers stepped up their antipiracy efforts. Many, like Adobe and Symantec, ramped up campaigns to warn consumers that copying is illegal. Some, like Microsoft, hired former federal and police investigators, staged software stings, relayed information to prosecutors, and took legal action against thousands of technologically illicit websites. Most firms added security features, such as holograms and registration codes, to document the authenticity of their software. Others used search engines to prowl the Internet in search of sites that distributed or sold pirated software.

Governments also increased their efforts. In the United States, a number of initiatives were introduced. The Departments of Justice and Treasury and their primary investigative agencies, the FBI and the Customs Service, conducted worldwide raids against so-called warez groups that reproduced, modified, and distributed counterfeit software over the Internet. The Senate approved the Trade Promotion Authority, which gave the president more power to negotiate technology-related trade agreements.

As for industry associations, they reinforced their own programs and supported governmental efforts, working with authorities in many countries to develop legal procedures for promoting a law-abiding online world. The BSA continued pressuring officials in such countries as Mexico, Italy, Hong Kong, and Singapore to get tougher on piracy. Several software associations urged the United States to place certain countries—those without rules for protecting IPRs, those who fail to pursue vigorous enforcement policies, those who refuse to comply with TRIPS—on a list of high-profile offenders.

This barrage of harder-hitting measures has in fact produced some results. Between 2000 and 2004, for example, China—in connection with its admission to the WTO—amended its patent and trademark and copyright laws to make them more compliant with TRIPS. Officials in other countries, among them Costa Rica, Korea, Oman, and the Philippines, initiated or expanded antipiracy programs.

By 2005, the latest BSA reports showed that piracy rates had decreased, albeit moderately, in 51 of 97 countries surveyed, while increasing in only 19 countries. Significantly, some positive changes could be seen in the emerging markets of Russia, India, and China. Russia, for instance, showed a four-point drop in the piracy rate of PC software, India lowered its rate by two points. China, home to one of the fastest growing IT markets in the world, cut its software piracy rate from 90 percent in 2004 to 86 percent in 2005.

Despite renewed efforts and some successes, many observers believe the global cat-and-mouse game between software makers and pirates, far from winding toward a conclusion, is spiraling out of control, even as countries like China vow to protect IPR and others, such as Hong Kong, Malaysia, and Korea, sign major copyright treaties. Certainly, signs of official compliance seem like a step in the right direction, but a high-level IACC official points out that, "on paper, the laws and penalties are stiffer in many countries. The question now: Will those governments actually enforce those laws?" This official is "not optimistic."

To see why, let's take yet another look at China. Granted, the net piracy rate has dropped (albeit marginally). At the same time, however, China remains responsible for piracy losses of $3.9 billion, second only to losses in the United States of $6.9 billion. Along with a few other emerging markets—notably, Russia, Brazil, and India—China is still regarded as a haven for software pirates. The nations on this last list are particularly important because they're emerging markets—*big* emerging markets. As one analyst puts it, "If the piracy rate in emerging markets—where people are rapidly integrating computers into their lives and businesses—does not drop, the worldwide piracy rate will continue to increase." Data on piracy rates in developed versus emerging markets amplified this concern (see Table 3.8).

"The Bandits Are Everywhere"

Compounding all the problems we've mentioned so far is the fact that pirates have found it relatively easy to crack licensing codes, duplicate holograms, falsify e-mail headers, and set up anonymous post office boxes. "Like drug trafficking," notes one observer, "the counterfeiting problem is so massive [that] you don't know how to get a handle on it. The bandits are everywhere."

Worse still, counterfeiters are becoming sophisticated entrepreneurs. "When you are dealing with high-end counterfeits," explains Microsoft senior attorney Katharine Bostick, "you are talking about organizations that have a full supply chain, a full distribution chain, full manufacturing tools all in place, and it is all based on profits." Ironically, piracy gets a boost

Table 3.8   Software Piracy by Market Type: Developed versus Emerging Economies

Not surprisingly, developed countries constitute a more profitable market for pirated software than emerging countries. The latter group, however, includes many nations—some of them, like Russia and India, very large—in which people are just beginning to integrate computers into their daily activities.

	2005 PAID FOR ($ BILLIONS)	2005 PIRATED VALUE ($ BILLIONS)
Developed World	$54	$22
Emerging Countries	6	12

Source: Third Annual BSA and IDC Global Software Piracy Study (May 2006); Business Software Alliance, www.bsa.org/globalstudy.

from the increasing availability of pirated software through various Internet channels, like spam, P2P file-sharing sites, and mail-order or auction sites.

The pervasiveness and tenacity of software piracy continue to pose profound questions for IPRs in general and the software industry in particular. Some people worry that the variety of national legal traditions among countries stands in the way of agreement on some of the most basic issues—such as the definition of the problem. TRIPS was supposed to settle such troublesome issues, but its most glaring shortcoming—its failure to deal with the impact of the Internet to ease the distribution of pirated software—made it, at least from the point of view of Microsoft, "woefully outdated."

Others fear that the antipiracy war may already be lost: All over the world, they argue, consumers and businesses have been seduced by low-priced pirated software for so long that they don't see anything wrong with it. Similarly, many in collectivist cultures reason that software makers should allow everyone to share the informational and technical wealth by openly sharing software codes with customers and other stakeholders. Finally, there are those who regard piracy as simply the most effective way of dealing with Western monopolists who charge exorbitant prices for the necessary tools of economic development. In response to this last point—and in an effort to curb piracy—Microsoft has offered to supply Asian countries with a simpler, cheaper version of its Windows operating system.

Microsoft also plans to offer low-income consumers, both in the United States and around the world, heavily discounted versions of Windows XP Starter Edition and Office 2007 Home and Student. Programs that typically cost consumers about $150 in new PC bundles will run about $3 on PCs that will typically cost $300 or less. To qualify, you must be in the lowest 15 percent of the population financially. In the United States, that means an annual income under $15,000. Computers sold through the program will typically reach consumers through local, state, or national governments. Analysts, however, are skeptical: How, they ask, can the offer of a cheaper and simpler version of Windows curb piracy when full-scale copies are available—illegally—for the same price or less?

In particular, the conundrum posed by Microsoft's approach suggests that curbing piracy is going to be a long, hard battle. In addition, constant innovation in technology, coupled with growing market development in poorer parts of the world, will likely perpetuate the struggle. ■

QUESTIONS

1. What is the relationship among governments, institutions, organizations, and companies in developing legal codes to fight software piracy?
2. Should software companies, industry associations, home governments, or transnational institutions take the lead in dealing with the governments of countries with high piracy rates? Why?
3. Can the software industry expect to control software piracy without relying on governments? Why would the software industry dislike greater government regulation?
4. How do you think consumers in high-theft countries justify software piracy? Similarly, what ideas or conditions lead consumers in low-theft countries to respect IPRs?

SUMMARY

- Political and legal systems across countries both converge and vary. The cultural (profiled in Chapter 2), political and legal, and economic (profiled in Chapter 4) systems create the potential benefits, costs, and challenges of the business environment in a country.

- Political systems can be assessed according to two dimensions: the degree to which they emphasize collectivism as opposed to individualism, and the degree to which they are democratic as opposed to totalitarian.

- Collectivism reasons that the needs of society take precedence over the needs of the individual. Collectivism encourages state intervention in society in the belief that government's role is to define the needs and priorities of a country.

- Political officials and agencies have a limited role in an individualistic society, whereas they have an extensive role in a collectivist society.

- Individualism sees the primacy of the individual's freedoms in the political, economic, and cultural realms. Individualism endorses minimal intervention in the economy by the government.

- Democracy and totalitarianism are the polar ends of the political spectrum. In a representative democracy, there is wide participation in the decision-making process. In totalitarian regimes, few citizens participate.

- The measure of political freedom looks at the degree to which fair and competitive elections occur, the extent to which individual and group freedoms are guaranteed, and the existence of freedom of the press.

- Recent data, in suggesting a situation of freedom stagnation, may signal a backlash against democracy and a resurgence of authoritarianism.

- Political risk occurs because of changing opinions of political leadership, civil disorder, or external relations between the host country and the foreign investor's home country.

- The type of legal system used in a country determines many elements of the business environment.

- The rule of law endorses systematic and objective laws applied by public officials who are held accountable for their administration, whereas the rule of man holds that legal rights derive from the will of the individual who has the power to enforce them.

- A common law system is based on tradition, precedent, custom and usage, and interpretation by the courts, a civil law system is also called a codified legal system, a theocratic legal system is based on religious precepts, a customary legal system follows the wisdom of daily experience, and a mixed legal system combines elements of other systems.

- Primary legal issues in international business include product safety and liability, marketing practice, rule of origin, jurisdiction, and intellectual property protection.

- Patents, trademarks, trade names, copyrights, and trade secrets are referred to as intellectual properties.

- The protection of intellectual property rights within a country is moderated by its particular legal legacies, level of economic development, and cultural orientation toward individualism versus collectivism.

KEY TERMS

collectivism (p. 101)
democracy (p. 103)
digital piracy (p. 130)
freedom (p. 104)
individualism (p. 101)
intellectual property (p. 126)
intellectual property rights (IPR) (p. 127)

legal systems (p. 116)
local content (p. 126)
pluralism (p. 102)
political ideology (p. 102)
political risk (p. 112)
political spectrum (p. 102)
political system (p. 100)

rule of law (p. 120)
rule of man (p. 119)
strategic plans (p. 124)
third wave of democratization (p. 108)
totalitarian democracy (p. 111)
totalitarian system (p. 105)

ENDNOTES

1 **Sources include the following:** Michael Sylvester, "Flaming Hoops," *Corporate Counsel: Market Report China* 11:10 (2004):171; Mure Dickie, "A Call for More Chinese Walls: Foreign Companies Are Angered by Beijing's Inability to Tackle Piracy," *The Financial Times,* September 21, 2004: 9; Kevin Honglin Zhang, "What Attracts Foreign Multinational Corporations to China?" *Contemporary Economic Policy* (July 2001): 336; Jiang Xueqin, "Letter from China," *The Nation* (March 4, 2002): 23; "A Disorderly Heaven," *The Economist,* March 20, 2004: 12, US; "Bulls in a China Shop," *The Economist* (March 20, 2004): 10; Howard French, "Whose Patent Is It, Anyway?" *New York Times,* March 5, 2005; Philip Bowring, "China's Middle Class: Not What You Think It Is," *The Asian Sentinel,* April 11, 2007; "China Slams US Piracy Complaint," *BBC News,* April 10, 2007. The pace of change in China's business environment makes any discussion of it hazardous and tentative. Regard this case as a set of educated generalizations about the kinds of problems encountered by would-be foreign investors in China from the 1990s to date.

2 "Business in Russia: Dancing with the Bear," *The Economist*, February 1, 2007.

3 "Business in Russia: Dancing with the Bear."

4 "Crocodile Tears," *The Economist*, April 28, 2007.

5 Daniel Kaufmann; Aart Kraay; and Massimo Mastruzzi, "Governance Matters IV: Governance Indicators for 1996–2004" (May 2005). World Bank Policy Research Working Paper Series No. 3630.

6 Samuel Huntington, "Democracy for the Long Haul," *The Strait Times*, September 10, 1995: 1. Nexis Library: News.

7 Audrey T. Sproat and Bruce R. Scott, "Japan: A Strategy for Economic Growth," Harvard Business School Case 9–378–106: 1–35.

8 "Politics Brief: Is There a Crisis?" *The Economist*, July 17, 1999: 49.

9 Adrian Karatnycky, *Freedom in the World 2001–2002: The Democracy Gap* (New York: Freedom House, 2002), at www.freedomhouse.org.

10 On December 10, 1948, the General Assembly of the United Nations adopted the Universal Declaration of Human Rights and has since called on all member countries to publicize the text and "to cause it to be disseminated, displayed, read and expounded principally in schools and other educational institutions, without distinction based on the political status of countries or territories." For the full text of the Declaration, go to www.un.org/Overview/rights.html.

11 Jaroslaw Piekalkiewicz and Alfred Wayne Penn, *Politics of Ideocracy* (Albany: State University of New York Press, 1995): 4.

12 Samuel P. Huntington, *The Third Wave: Democratization in the Late Twentieth Century* (Norman: University of Oklahoma Press, 1991).

13 Francis Fukuyama, in *The End of History and the Last Man* (Penguin, 1992).

14 See "Internet World Stats" at www.internetworldstats.com/asia/cn.htm (accessed May 20, 2007).

15 *Freedom in the World: The Annual Survey of Political Rights and Civil Liberties* (2006), at ww.freedomhouse.org/template.cfm?page=15 (accessed May 20, 2007).

16 Laza Kekic, "A Pause in Democracy's March," *The Economist*, The World in 2007: 59–60.

17 "The Democracy Dividend," *The Economist*, December 7, 2006.

18 "Democracy? Hu Needs It," *The Economist*, June 28, 2007. "A Warning for Reformers," *The Economist*, November 17, 2007.

19 " 'I am a True Democrat': G-8 Interview with Vladimir Putin," *Spiegel Online*, June 4, 2007, at www.spiegel.de/international/world/0,1518,486345,00.html.

20 "Freedom in the World: The Annual Survey of Political Rights and Civil Liberties" (2006), at www.freedomhouse.org/template.cfm?page=15 (accessed May 20, 2007).

21 Hassan Fattah, "Democracy in the Arab World, a U.S. Goal, Falters," *New York Times*, April 10, 2006.

22 Samuel Huntington, *The Clash of Civilizations and the Remaking of World Order* (New York: Simon & Schuster, 1996); Huntington, *Who Are We? The Challenges to America's National Identity* (New York: Simon & Schuster, 2004).

23 Jacob Talmon, *The Origins of Totalitarian Democracy* (London: Secker & Warburg,1952).

24 Laza Kekic, "A Pause in Democracy's March," *The Economist*: The World in 2007.

25 "Venezuelan Bluster? Hugo Chávez Threatens to Seize Banks and a Steel-Maker," *The Economist Intelligence Unit*, May 8, 2007.

26 Presently, the tiny nation of Andorra and Guernsey and Jersey Islands, both of which belong to the United Kingdom, apply customary law only. The codification of civil law developed out of legal customs that developed in particular communities and, over time, were collected and recorded by local jurists.

27 "The Sincerest Form of Flattery," *The Economist*, April 4, 2007.

28 Geoff Lewis, "Who in the World Is Entrepreneurial?" *Fortune: Small Business*, June 1, 2007.

29 Steven Weisman, "Before Visit to China, a Rebuke," *New York Times*, December 12, 2006.

30 "The World's Greatest Fakes," *60 Minutes*, August 8, 2004; quote by Dan Chow, at www.cbsnews.com/stories/2004/01/26/60minutes/main595875.shtml.

31 "The Sincerest Form of Flattery."

32 "India: Cipra Launches 3-in-1 AIDS Pill," *Clinical Infectious Diseases*, September 15, 2001: ii.

33 "A Disorderly Heaven," *The Economist*: 1.

34 Veronica Weinstein and Dennis Fernandez, "Recent Developments in China's Intellectual Property Laws," *Chinese Journal of International Law* 3:1 (2004): 227.

35 Zhenmin Wang, "The Developing Rule of Law in China," *Harvard Asia Quarterly* 4:4 (2000).

36 "Gold from the Storm," *The Economist*, June 28, 2007.

37 Robert L. Ostergard Jr., "The Measurement of Intellectual Property Rights Protection," *Journal of International Business Studies* 31 (Summer 2000): 349.

38 Stephanie Sanborn, "Protecting Intellectual Property on the Web—the Internet Age Is Making Digital Rights Management Even More Important," *InfoWorld*, June 19, 2000: 40.

39 "Going Up or Down?" *The Economist*, June 7, 2007.

40 A Gathering Storm," *The Economist*, June 7, 2007.

41 "A High Cost to Developing Countries," *New York Times*, October 5, 1986: D2.

42 "The Rectification of Names," *Analects* 13, iii.

43 A. Lin Neumann, "Information Wants to Be Free—But This Is Ridiculous," *Wired*, November 22, 2002, at www.wired.com/wired/archive.

44 *Sources include the following:* Third Annual BSA and IDC Global Software Piracy Study, May 2006; Business Software Alliance, April 29, 2007, at http://bsa.org; International Anti-Counterfeiting Coalition Recording Industry, April 29, 2007, at www.iacc.org; Recording Industry Association of America, April 29, 2007, at www.riaa.com; Motion Picture Association of America, April 29, 2007, at www.mpaa.org/home.htm; Bryan W. Husted, "The Impact of National Culture on Software Piracy," *Journal of Business Ethics* 26 (August 2000): 197–211; Jennifer Lee, "Pirates on the Web, Spoils on the Street," *New York Times*, July 11, 2002: E1; Suzanne Wagner and G. Lawrence Sanders, "Considerations in Ethical Decision-Making and Software Piracy," *Journal of Business Ethics* (January 2001): 161; Steve Lohr, "Software by Microsoft Is Nearly Free for the Needy," *New York Times*, April 19, 2007: C5; Brad Stone and Miguel Helft, "New Weapon in Web War over Piracy," *New York Times*, February 19, 2007: C1; "U.S. Puts 12 Nations on Copyright Piracy List," The Associated Press, April 30, 2007; John Dvorak, "Inside Track," *PC Magazine*, July 17, 2007.

4

The Economic Environments Facing Businesses

Objectives

- To understand the importance of economic analysis of foreign markets

- To identify the major dimensions of international economic analysis

- To compare and contrast macroeconomic indicators

- To profile the characteristics of the types of economic systems

- To discuss the idea of economic freedom

- To profile the idea, drivers, and constraints of economic transition

Poverty does not destroy virtue, nor does wealth bestow it.

—Spanish proverb

CASE: Economic Conundrums and the Comeback of Emerging Economies

In the world of globalization, one often struggles to separate the hype from reality. Some view it in the extreme, as in the transformation of everything.[1] Others see it as simply the latest stage in the evolution of the business environment. Despite far-ranging opinions, most agree that the ongoing integration of national economies into the global market has changed the business environment.

Discussion of the economic environment of globalization has taken on a far more dramatic tone since 2001. Some commentators see trends that indicate a flattening of the world whereby advances in institutions, communications, and technology fundamentally change the economics of globalization. They speak of "distributed tools of innovation and connectivity empowering individuals from anywhere to compete, connect, and collaborate."

Other analysts emphasize the entry of billions of people into the global marketplace. They reason that the world is in the "middle of a two-part revolution. Three billion new people—billion and a half Chinese, billion Indians, half a billion people from former Soviet bloc—have suddenly come into the global economy all at one time. Within these three billion people is a population as big as the United States, bigger than anybody in Europe or Japan, who are every bit as skilled and can do anything that could be done in the U.S. or Japan or any of the developed countries for ten cents on the dollar." The combination of low wages and billions of skilled workers changes how we interpret capital and labor in the production of goods and services.

Provocative in their own right, these interpretations suggest that, in the first years of the twenty-first century, globalization

MAP 4.1   Leading Emerging Markets, 2008

Source: Compiled from *The Economist* and the Morgan Stanley Emerging Markets Index.

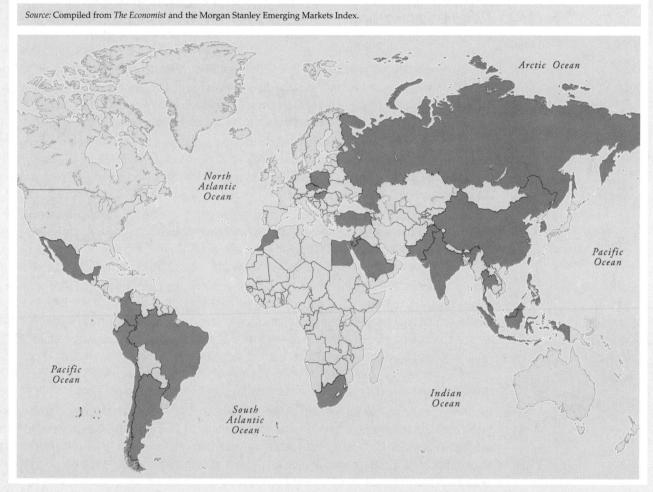

has introduced developments and initiated trends that challenge economic orthodoxy. Some say that combined, these developments and trends will powerfully impact one's job, company, future, and even one's country. The possibility that globalization has reached an inflection point, namely, a time where old strategic patterns are giving way to the new, signals the need for managers to rethink their understanding of economics.

Adding urgency to this task is the fact that many long-established market patterns took unexpected twists and turns during the first years of the new century. As a result, there is now a rash of puzzling economic developments that defy conventional explanation. Among these is performance data on inflation, interest rates, wages, productivity, distribution of rewards, income equality, poverty, balance of payments, and capital flows that run counter to precedent. More specifically:

- *Wages:*   Since 2000, world gross domestic product per capita has grown by an average of 3.2 percent a year. If this pace continues, the first decade of the twenty-first century will see the fastest growth in average world income in history. At the same time, however, the average real wages of workers are flat or falling around the world. Workers' share of national income in many countries has fallen to its lowest level in decades. The fall in real wages is especially confusing given the rising productivity of workers. Historically, wages tended to track average productivity growth, but now it appears that wages are decoupling from productivity. In the United States, for instance, worker productivity rose 16.6 percent from 2000 to 2005 while total compensation for the median worker rose 7.2 percent.

- *Distribution of rewards:*   It appears that the middle class bears a disproportionate loss of benefits relative to the top and bottom sectors of the workforce. Workers in America, Britain, and Germany, at the bottom as well as at the top, have done better than those in the middle-income group. The real median wage of college graduates in the United States, for example, has fallen by 6 percent since 2000.

- *Corporate profits:*   Around the world, companies are reporting astounding profits, accounting for a record share of national income. In the United States, corporate profits, as a share of national income, increased from 7 percent in mid-2001 to 13 percent in 2007. So, whereas workers' share of national income has fallen to its lowest level in decades, companies' share of profits has surged to all-time highs.

- *Capital flows:*   Presently, the poorer countries of the world are financing the lifestyles of those in richer countries. This flow of capital is exactly the opposite of that predicted by economic theory. Capital should flow from rich countries with abundant capital, such as the United States, to poorer ones, such as China, where capital is relatively scarce. In doing so, this generates higher returns. Today, however, borrowing by the United States soaks up more than two-thirds of the combined excess savings of all the surplus countries in the world. The transfer of wealth from poor countries to the United States, said one analyst, arguably qualifies as the "biggest foreign-aid program in world history."

- *Income inequality:*   While workers are being squeezed, high-wage earners have pocketed ever bigger portions of gains in personal income. Consequently, income inequality has widened to levels not seen in decades. In 2005, the top 1 percent of Americans received their largest share of national income since 1928. They owned around 40 percent of America's wealth—the highest proportion since 1929—up from just 20 percent in the 1970s.

- *Inflation:*   Despite growing demand for goods as well as rising commodity prices, the average monthly consumer price inflation rates at the global level rate have declined from an annual average of close to 25 percent in the early 1990s to about 4 percent in 2006. The average inflation rate in industrial economies have fallen more than 300 percent over the past decade. In developing countries, the decline has been even steeper. In the early 1990s, the average inflation rate in developing countries has been around 80 percent; that had declined to 5.4 percent by 2005 and may fall below 5 percent in 2007.

- *Savings and borrowing:*   In the mid-1990s, the poorer countries of the world relied on money borrowed from their richer counterparts to finance their growth plans. Now, however, the growing wealth and savings of poorer countries have flip-flopped, and they are now exporting capital to and financing consumption of richer countries. For example, in 2006, the U.S. savings rate reached its lowest point since 1933. That year, it reached a negative 1 percent, meaning that Americans on average spent all they earned and also either borrowed or spent part of their savings. In contrast, the savings rate in China has gone from almost 20 percent of GDP in 1981 to 30 percent in 1988 and currently stands near 50 percent.

- *Interest rates:* Global interest rates are still historically low, despite strong growth and heavy government borrowing. For example, the Bank of Japan set its interest rates to 0.5 percent in mid-2007, up from 0 percent one year earlier. In 2005, then-U.S. Federal Reserve Board Chairman Alan Greenspan faced what he called a "conundrum" in the international bond market: Yield curves had inverted whereby long-term yields were below short-term rates.

- *Input prices:* The past few years have seen the sharpest rise in commodity prices in history. Prices for products like copper, nickel, platinum, palladium, gold, silver, corn, sugar, uranium, and other raw materials have shot up in just five years. Specifically, since 2001, the prices of precious metals and industrial metals like copper, silver, and gold have nearly tripled while crude oil, heating oil, and natural gas prices have risen by more than 700 percent. Still, the prices of many manufactured goods have tracked inflation or have even fallen (such as those in the consumer electronics market).

Individually significant, each of these economic factors is part of a larger puzzle. Combined, they create uncertainty that calls into play assumptions about economic variables and relationships.

The quest to understand where the economic environment might be heading pushes executives to look at where the world is coming from. Initially, attention turned toward how the world economy had changed between 1950 and 2000. During this time, the diffusion of democracy and free-market principles encouraged growing trade among prominent nations to spill over to include most countries around the world.

However, in terms of helping managers interpret the confusing economic puzzles they face, precedents from this era fell short of providing meaningful explanations. As one analyst suggests, "What this means for the global economy is that looking at growth rates, economic slack, inflation or monetary conditions in the developed world alone would result in a fairly distorted picture of the global economy."

As economic trends unfolded, an increasingly dominant scenario gained attention. This scenario emphasized the epochal shift in the center of gravity of the global economy. By 2050, four of the six largest economies in the world—Japan, China, India, and Russia—will be in greater Asia. Their growth will likely create a second tier of powerful economies among their Asian neighbors, such as South Korea, Indonesia, Taiwan, Vietnam, and Thailand, that will correspondingly become more prominent.

Although 2050 may seem far off, these countries are quickly developing economic policies that will lay the foundation for future growth. And although extrapolation is always risky, hard data point to their growing success in transforming the global economy. For instance, the combined output of emerging economies reached an important milestone: It accounted for more than half of total world GDP in 2006 (as measured in terms of purchasing power parity). Similarly, their share of world exports is now 43 percent, up from 20 percent in 1970, and their share of the world's foreign-exchange reserves is now 70 percent, up from net deficits in the mid-1990s.

Analysis of the economic environment in emerging economies suggests the revolution has only just begun. Their ambition to improve infrastructure, increase productivity, create jobs, and alleviate poverty has put into motion what will likely be the biggest economic stimulus in history. The last transformation of similar magnitude—the Industrial Revolution—involved far fewer people in far fewer nations. The revolution unfolding today covers nearly the entire globe and involves billions of people. As expected, analysts see emerging economies powering, if not steering, global growth. The transfer of the growth baton from rich countries to emerging markets shows increasing odds of resetting the nature, and our interpretation, of the economic environment of international business.

The search for anchors to guide analysis leads some to seek precedent further back in history. Some say one need only review the last millennium to put the current economic drama into perspective. From roughly 1000 until the mid-1880s, China and India were the world's two biggest economies. Before the steam engine and the power loom drove the transfer of economic might from Asia to the West, today's emerging economies dominated world output. However, these countries "temporarily" lost their lead as internal failure, spurred by closing borders, forced them to retreat into isolationism. The penalty for this policy was the missed opportunity to participate in the Industrial Revolution.

FIGURE 4.1   Emerging Markets Make a Comeback

About 1,000 years ago, today's emerging economies, most notably China and India, accounted for about 80% of the global economic output. By the twentieth century, today's developed economies such as the United States and France, generated more than half of global economic output. Current market trends suggest that emerging economies will account for more than 70% of global economic output by 2050.

Source: The World Economy: A Millennial Perspective. By Angus Maddison. Paris: OECD Development Centre Studies, 2001; IMF; *The Economist;* data reported in *Purchasing Power Parity.*

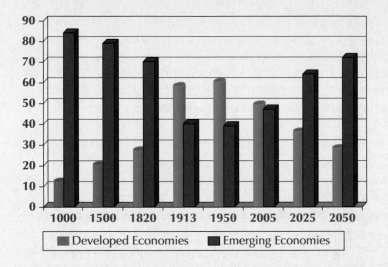

Reports indicate that in the eight centuries leading up to 1820, today's emerging economies produced, on average, 70 to 80 percent of world output (see Figure 4.1). By 1950, emerging economies' share of global output had fallen to 40 percent. The ambition of their current economic policies highlights their intention to return to their historic stature. Since 2001, their annual growth has averaged nearly 7 percent, the fastest pace in recorded history; in contrast, the rich economies have growth rates just above 2 percent. The International Monetary Fund (IMF) forecasts that in the next five years emerging economies will grow at an average rate of 6.8 percent a year, whereas the developed economies may hit 2.7 percent. If both groups continue in this way, in 30 years' time today's emerging economies will complete their comeback and once again account for more than 70 percent of global output.

The shrinking role of today's leading rich economies, coupled with the accelerating scope of emerging economies, has begun triggering fundamental shifts in investment, trade, consumption, wealth, poverty, and fiscal and monetary policy. These shifts create opportunities and challenges for international companies. Put differently, strategic inflection points do not necessarily lead to disaster. Change in the way business is conducted creates prospects for players, whether newcomers or incumbents, who are adept at operating in the new economy. Policymakers, executives, workers, and investors will wrestle with making sense of the shift in the global economic environment.

Therefore, we now turn to specifying the frameworks that will be brought to bear on the economic environment, identifying the elements that will anchor analysis and the logic that managers will use to interpret the results.

Introduction

Earlier chapters looked at how cultural, political, and legal systems influence a company's decisions on where and how to do business internationally. This chapter completes this profile by presenting the perspectives and tools that managers use to evaluate economic environments.

The importance of this chapter follows from the fact that different countries have different levels of economic development, performance, and potential. For instance, in absolute terms, world economic output more than tripled between 1975 and 2006, reaching $47 trillion. In relative terms, many countries prospered but some more than others and, in a few cases, some not at all. Thus estimating the attractiveness of a country as a place to do business and then, once there, making prudent investment and operational decisions depends on how well managers understand economic performance and trends.

When a company wants to do business in another country, it must answer standard questions about wealth, income, stability, poverty, and the like. The dynamic nature of political and economic events means it also must prepare for new questions. Besides assessing the foreign markets in which they operate, managers also need to monitor those in which they do not. Globalization connects countries in many ways; change in one country likely has economic consequences in other countries. Companies must also watch economic changes in those countries where they may not operate but where their competitors do. Improving economic performance or revised economic policies in a particular country, such as is happening in Brazil, China, India, and Russia, may unexpectedly strengthen their rivals' competitiveness.

Company managers study economic environments to estimate how trends affect their performance.

Although the pace varies from country to country, national economic environments around the world are continually changing. We have seen over the past decade tremendous change in economic opportunities as more and more countries have adopted the principles and practices of free markets. Indeed, a country's economic policies give a clear indication of the government's goals and the economic tools and market reforms it must adopt. Managers aim to spot those small changes in a country's economic environment that promise to have big market impact. Therefore, we conclude this chapter by looking at processes of economic development and market transition.

A country's economic policies are a leading indicator of government's goals and its planned use of economic tools and market reforms.

Finally, economic development is a vital topic to citizens, managers, policymakers, and institutions. The evident triumph of free markets over controlled economies has spurred countries to unleash ambitious economic programs. To some degree, economic development efforts have helped countries improve their standard of living. Then again, the bold development programs of some countries have fallen short. A fuller understanding of the process of economic transition and development helps managers make better decisions that benefit their companies, their countries, and the world.

Economic development directly impacts citizens, managers, policymakers, and institutions.

The impact of economic change has a variety of characteristics. Some are direct and clearly linked to environments, companies, or competitors. Others exert a subtle influence on a firm's activities and its ultimate performance. Carly Fiorina, CEO of Hewlett-Packard in 2001, gave a good sense of the range of economic factors and relationships that bear on the international company in her Annual Letter to Shareholders. Specifically, she explained:

CONCEPT CHECK

In discussing "The Forces Behind Globalization" in Chapter 1, we explain how an economic environment responds to technology, trade, competition, consumer attitudes, and cross-border relationships. Here we point out that the scope of the connections among these conditions spurs companies to examine them as both discrete and interdependent factors.

> *In terms of economic growth and stability, 2001 was one of the toughest years on record, particularly for the IT [information technology] industry. Triggered in part by the collapse of the hyper-inflated dot-com sector, in Q3 of calendar [year] 2001, the U.S. economy softened considerably. A dramatic slowdown in business investment, compounded by the events of September 11, tipped the United States into its first recession in a decade. During 2001, the world's three leading economies slowed simultaneously for the first time since 1974. The European economy stalled, and Japan struggled to fight deflation and recession. Information technology spending plummeted. The telecommunications and manufacturing industries—two of HP's largest customer sectors—were hit especially hard by the global economic slowdown. These factors had a significant impact on HP's fiscal 2001 results.[2]*

In summary, understanding the economic environments of a country helps managers better apprise how developments and trends have and will likely affect their companies' performance.

INTERNATIONAL ECONOMIC ANALYSIS

The World Bank reports 208 discrete economic environments in the world today—194 countries and 14 other economies with populations of more than 30,000.[3] Inevitably, managers must ask which of those countries warrant their attention and investment. Unfortunately, there is no universal scheme to assess the performance and potential of a country's economic environment. Granted, there are many useful approaches. Still, two conditions hamper specifying a universal method:

1. It's difficult to specify the definitive set of economic indicators that precisely estimates the performance and predicts the potential of a country's economy. The distribution of income, for example, is a fundamental issue in Brazil but a minor concern in Sweden.

2. On specifying a set of estimators, new challenges emerge when interpreting their relationship with other elements of the economic environment.

Meaningful Dimensions and Systemic Relationships   Figure 4.2, which shows some of the economic conditions that create unique market, physical, and social factors in a country, gives a sense of the challenge. Importantly, it also suggests a way to solve it. Research has isolated important elements of an economic environment. These include factors like income, purchasing power, market size, market type, and economic freedom. This chapter shows that reducing the idea of an economic environment to its elemental components lets us then determine how they shape the market.

In addition, Figure 4.2 highlights the importance of applying a systems perspective to our analyses. That is, the configuration and connection of various elements show that a change in one element in the economy can affect other parts of the market. The key to understanding how an economic environment works is also a function of making sense of the interactions of the parts with one another.

More precisely, Figure 4.2 suggests managers assess an economic environment of a country by first looking at meaningful dimensions of its economy. Then, confident these elements make sense, managers assess their systemic relationship and estimate the path of transition and potential performance for that country's economy. Managers often adjust their interpretation for risks that might alter current activity or future performance. This chapter follows this scheme. It starts by profiling important features of an economic environment, moves on to types of economic systems, and closes with a look at processes of economic transitions.

Key economic forces include

- Price stability.
- Capital markets.
- Factor endowments.
- Market size.
- Public policy.

FIGURE 4.2   Economic Factors Affecting International Business Operations

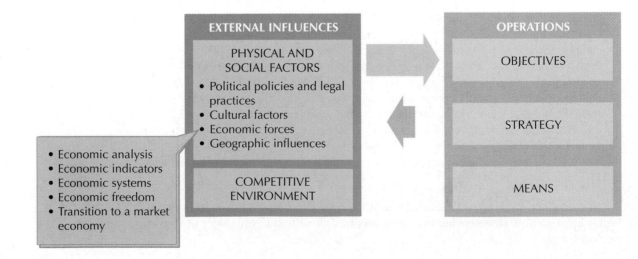

Elements of the Economic Environment

Managers use different economic measures to assess a country's level of performance and potential. Some may be informal or idiosyncratic indicators in a country—for example, the number of wireless phones or circulation patterns of newspapers. In practice, managers usually begin their analyses by looking at the monetary value of the total flow of goods and services in the economy of a nation. They refine this analysis by considering issues like growth rates, income distribution, inflation, unemployment, wages, productivity, debt, and the balance of payments. We now examine these factors.

GROSS NATIONAL INCOME

Gross national income (GNI) measures the income generated both by total domestic production as well as the international production activities of national companies. GNI is the value of all production in the domestic economy plus the net flows of factor income (such as rents, profits, and labor income) from abroad during a one-year period. Technically, GNI is the market value of final goods and services newly produced by domestically owned factors of production.[4] So, for example, the value of a Ford sports utility vehicle (SUV) that is built in the United States and the portion of the value of a Ford SUV made in Mexico using U.S. capital and management get counted in the GNI of the United States. Conversely, the portion of the value of a Japanese Toyota SUV built in the United States using Japanese capital and management would count in the GNI of Japan, not the United States. Table 4.1 identifies the 10 largest economies in the world in terms of GNI.

Gross Domestic Product   GNI is the broadest measure of economic activity for a country. An essential part of GNI is **gross domestic product (GDP)**—the total value of all goods and services produced within a nation's borders over one year, no matter whether domestic or foreign-owned companies make the product.[5] As such, GDP is especially useful for assessing countries in which the output of the multinational sector is a significant share of activity; for example, almost 90 percent of Irish exports are made by foreign-owned firms.

> **CONCEPT CHECK**
>
> In discussing "Growing Consumer Pressures" among the drivers of **globalization**, we report in Chapter 1 that worldwide consumption grew sixfold in the second half of the twentieth century—a trend that will likely accelerate throughout the twenty-first century. Here we stress the importance of such information for managers of global companies, who, in order to make a variety of decisions, estimate how much income consumers in a given market have now and will have in the future.

TABLE 4.1   The 10 Largest Economies by GNI, 2005*

Rank	Country	GNI (US$, millions)
1	United States	12,912,889
2	Japan	4,976,464
3	Germany	2,875,640
4	United Kingdom	2,272,716
5	China	2,269,745
6	France	2,169,169
7	Italy	1,772,942
8	Spain	1,095,876
9	Canada	1,052,563
10	India	804,967

*Data calculated with the *Atlas method*, which smooths exchange rate fluctuations by using a three-year moving average, price-adjusted conversion factor.

Source: The World Bank, at www.worldbank.org. World Bank development indicators 2005 by World Bank. Copyright 2007 by the World Bank. Reproduced with permission of the World Bank in the format textbook via Copyright Clearance Center.

Technically, GDP plus the income generated from exports, imports, and the international operations of a nation's companies equals GNI. So both a Ford and a Toyota truck manufactured in the United States would be counted in U.S. GDP, but the truck made in Mexico by Ford would not.

The absolute size of GNI reveals a lot about the market opportunity in a country. For example, Paraguay and Brazil are neighbors in South America. Paraguay had a GDP of $31 billion in 2006, whereas Brazil clocked in at $943 billion. Consequently, foreign companies are more inclined to build operations in Brazil and then export to Paraguay.

Managers improve the usefulness of gross national income (GNI) by adjusting it for the number of people, growth rate, and the cost of living in a country.

Improving the Power of GNI   GNI is a robust estimator of an economy's absolute performance. However, GNI can mislead managers when they compare countries. For example, economic powers, like the United States, Japan, and Germany, consistently claim the top spots on rankings of countries by GNI. As such, a quick look at these rankings might give the impression that these top-ranked countries are far richer than countries like Ireland or Luxembourg. Therefore, managers improve the usefulness of GNI by adjusting it for the number of people in a country, growth rate, the local cost of living, and economic sustainability.

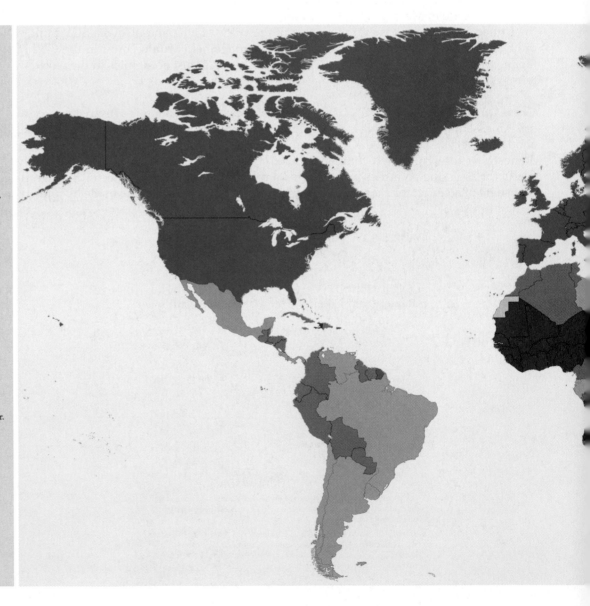

MAP 4.2
GNI per Capita, 2005

GNI is a raw number that refers to the market value of the final products produced by domestically owned factors of production. *GNI per capita* measures a country's performance in terms of its population. Thus a nation might have a very high rank on the basis of GNI (e.g., Germany or France) but rank only in the middle on the basis of GNI per capita. In fact, China, which is the world's fifth largest economy according to GNI, ranks in the bottom tier of countries according to GNI per capita.

Source: "Economy Statistics," *NationMaster.com*, at www.nationmaster.com (accessed October 12, 2007).

Per Capita Conversion Managers transform GNI, as well as many other economic indicators, by the number of people who live in a country. This conversion leads to a per capita estimator that measures a country's relative performance. Technically, we compute the per capita GNI by taking the GNI of a country and converting it into a standard currency—say, the U.S. dollar, at prevailing market rates—and then dividing this sum by its population.

This, along with other per capita indicators, helps explain an economy's performance in terms of the number of people who live in that country (see Map 4.2). For example, GNI may be low in absolute terms, such as is the case for Luxembourg, which ranks among the smaller economies of the world. But Luxembourg ranks first in the world by GNI per capita.

Officially, the World Bank reports that worldwide GNI per capita was $7,011 in 2005, up from $5,500 in 2003.[6] Technically, the World Bank's classification scheme orders the countries of the world into one of four categories on the basis of their per capita GNI. Respectively, the cutoffs for GNI per capita for the 52 low-income countries is $905 or less, $906 to $3,595 for the 54 lower-middle countries, $3,596 to $11,115 for the 41 upper-middle countries, and $11,116 or more for the 59 high-income countries.

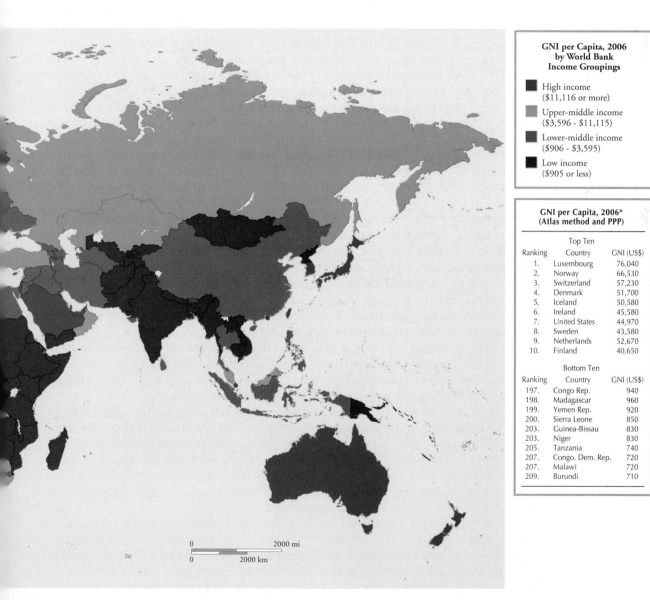

GNI per Capita, 2006 by World Bank Income Groupings

- ■ High income ($11,116 or more)
- ▨ Upper-middle income ($3,596 - $11,115)
- ▦ Lower-middle income ($906 - $3,595)
- ■ Low income ($905 or less)

GNI per Capita, 2006* (Atlas method and PPP)

Top Ten

Ranking	Country	GNI (US$)
1.	Luxembourg	76,040
2.	Norway	66,530
3.	Switzerland	57,230
4.	Denmark	51,700
5.	Iceland	50,580
6.	Ireland	45,580
7.	United States	44,970
8.	Sweden	43,580
9.	Netherlands	52,670
10.	Finland	40,650

Bottom Ten

Ranking	Country	GNI (US$)
197.	Congo Rep.	940
198.	Madagascar	960
199.	Yemen Rep.	920
200.	Sierra Leone	850
203.	Guinea-Bissau	830
203.	Niger	830
205.	Tanzania	740
207.	Congo. Dem. Rep.	720
207.	Malawi	720
209.	Burundi	710

0   2000 mi
0   2000 km

The World Bank refers to low- and middle-income countries as *developing countries* (although, as we saw in our opening case, many analysts prefer *emerging countries* or *emerging economies*). They comprise the largest number of countries and highest number of inhabitants in the world. High-income countries are often called developed countries, richer nations, or industrial countries.

Map 4.2 also shows that high-income countries are clustered in a few regions and include primarily Japan, Australia, New Zealand, Canada, the United States, and Western Europe. High-income countries presently account for less than 15 percent of the world's population but over 75 percent of world GNI. Lower-income countries are spread throughout the world, from Asia to Africa to South America and to the Pacific Region. They account for a small share of the world's GNI and report GNI per capita figures from the low hundreds to low thousands (in U.S. dollars).

Rate of Change   Gross figures are a snapshot of one year of activity and cannot measure the rate of change in an indicator. Interpreting present and predicting future economic performance requires pinpointing the rate of change. So, for example, looking at the countries in terms of their growth rate for GNI per capita, we find a wide range in growth. For example, between 1998 and 2002, Ireland was the fastest growing economy in the world, expanding more than 8 percent per annum. Japan, in contrast, grew by only 0.2 percent over that period.

Generally, the GNI growth rate also indicates its economic potential—if GNI grows at a higher (or *lower*) rate than the population, standards of living are said to be rising (or *falling*). The GNI growth rate highlights likely business opportunities. For example, China has been one of the fastest growing economies over the past 25 years, averaging high single-digit growth for the past several years. This growth, in turn, has resulted in the swiftest, most extensive rise out of poverty any nation has ever seen, a rise that has attracted immense amounts of foreign investment. In addition, as we saw in our opening case, the so-called comeback of emerging economies foreshadows accelerating standards of living. Figure 4.3 compares the real GDP growth rates for a sample of developed and developing economies.

Purchasing Power Parity   Managers, when comparing markets, often convert the GNI figure in one nation in terms of the currency of their home market. This simple conversion greatly refines economic analysis. Comparing countries in terms of GNI per capita requires translating each currency into a common currency unit at the prevailing rate to trade one currency for another (the so-called exchange rate). So, converting Indian rupees to U.S. dollars at official exchange rates, we estimate Indian GNI per capita at just over $700. This gap would suggest tremendous differences between the two countries. Some managers then might wrongly decide to look no further at the Indian market.

This simple conversion can create a systematic distortion. Exchange rates tell us how many units of one currency it takes to buy one unit of another—for example, how many Indian rupees one needs to buy one U.S. dollar. However, exchange rates do not tell us what that unit of local currency can buy in its home country.

More directly, the calculation of GNI per capita does not consider the differences in cost of living from one country to another. Instead, it presumes that a dollar of income in Minneapolis has the same "purchasing power" of a dollar of income in Mumbai (formerly, Bombay), even though the cost of living between the United States and India differs. Consequently, GNI per capita is unable to tell us much about how many goods and services someone can buy with a unit of income in one country relative to how much someone can buy with a unit of income in another country.

Managers adjust GNI per capita for a particular country in terms of its local **purchasing power parity (PPP).** Technically, PPP is the number of units of a country's currency required to buy the same amounts of goods and services in the domestic market that one unit of income would buy in the other country. Specifically, one calculates PPP by estimating the value of a universal "basket" of goods (like soap, bread, and clothing) and services (like telephone, electricity, and energy) that can be purchased with one unit

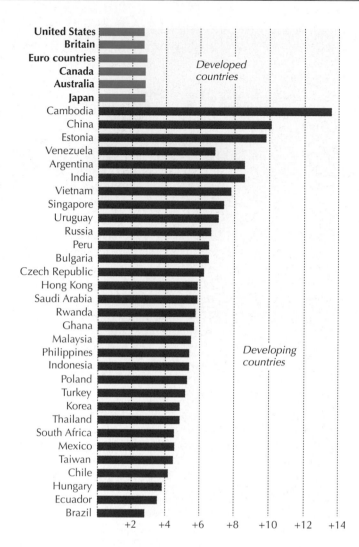

FIGURE 4.3
GDP—Real
Growth Rate

GDP increases from year to year partly because a country produces more goods and services and partly because prices go up. Measuring annual growth against price levels in a designated year, *real* GDP—as opposed to *nominal* GDP—keeps prices constant. What's left is annual growth in the actual production of goods and services. This conversion, by stripping out price effects, shows that the economies of developing countries are growing much faster than those of the developed countries.

Sources: Central Intelligence Agency, *The World Factbook*, at www.cia.gov (accessed October 12, 2007).

of a country's currency. The resulting estimate of the GNI per capita in terms of its local purchasing power in a country lets us see what local consumers can buy with one unit of income. The most common PPP exchange rate comes from comparing a basket of goods and services in a country with an equivalent basket in the United States.

So let's return to the comparison of the United States and India. Whereas India's GNI per capita in 2007 is $820, it is actually, in terms of its local purchasing power, just under $3,800.[7] Effectively, then, GNI per capita in terms of relative PPP is higher in India because of the lower cost of living. This means that it costs far less to buy the same basket of goods in India than it does in the United States.

The opposite effect occurs in the case of Switzerland. Because the cost of living is higher in Switzerland than in the United States, Switzerland's GNI per capita falls from $55,230 to $38,610 when expressed in terms of PPP. On a broader scale, recall the gap in GNI per capita between low-income countries ($585) and high-income countries ($35,264). Expressing these income data in terms of PPP, we find that low-income countries increase to $2,470 and high-income countries decrease to $32,824. Map 4.3 profiles the countries of the world in terms of GNI adjusted for purchasing power.

Degree of Human Development   GNI, including its expression in terms of per capita, growth rate, and PPP, profiles growth and development in an economy. Some argue that these indicators, by focusing on growth only as measured by monetary indicators, misrepresent the scale and scope of a country's level of development. Managers can deal with these concerns by looking at a country's degree of human development—in terms of both economic and social factors—to estimate its current

MAP 4.3
GNI per Capita and PPP

Assume for a moment that income in every country has been converted to U.S. dollars. In countries like Canada and Australia, the average person has more than US$30,000 with which to purchase goods and services over the course of a year. In countries like Bolivia, Sudan, and Pakistan, the average person would have only US$1,000–$3,000 to spend. Bear in mind that, because the *cost of living* is lower in the developing countries, each U.S. dollar will go a little further. The income disparity between nations, even after adjustment remains quite glaring.

Source: International Monetary Fund, GDP PPP per Capita World Map, at http://en.wikipedia.org (accessed October 15, 2007); World Bank, World Development Indicators Database, May 1, 2007.

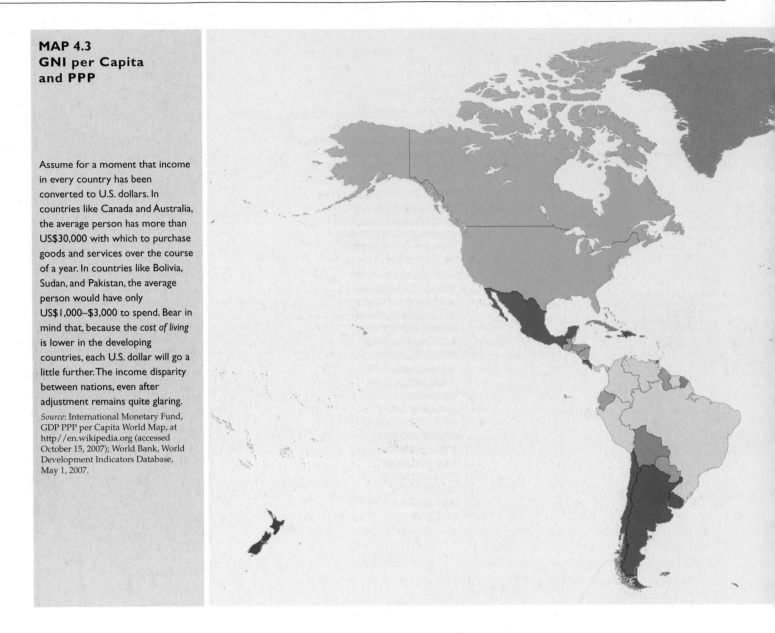

and future economic activity. Jointly considering economic and social indicators enables managers to more fully measure development in terms of the capabilities and opportunities that people enjoy.

These conditions might not show up immediately in income or growth figures but they will ultimately. More specifically, the reasoning goes like this:

> *The basic purpose of development is to enlarge people's choices. In principle, these choices can be infinite and can change over time. People often value achievements that do not show up at all, or not immediately, in income or growth figures: greater access to knowledge, better nutrition and health services, more secure livelihoods, security against crime and physical violence, satisfying leisure hours, political and cultural freedoms and sense of participation in community activities. The objective of development is to create an enabling environment for people to enjoy long, healthy, and creative lives.[8]*

The Human Development Index combines indicators of real purchasing power, education, and health to give a more comprehensive measure of economic development.

Economic indicators certainly identify the potential consumption in a country. Still, their monetary basis risks missing the underlying effects of human development and capabilities that are, in due course, instrumental in increasing GNI. To that end, managers

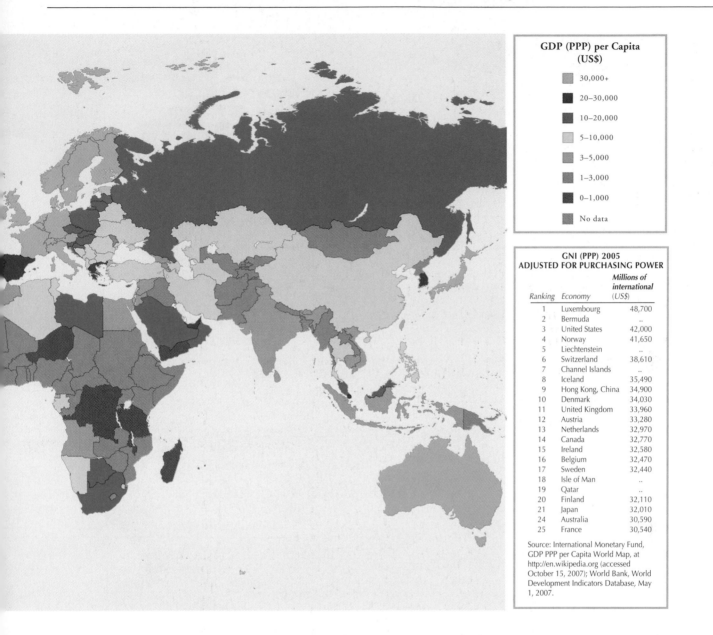

GDP (PPP) per Capita (US$)	
	30,000+
	20–30,000
	10–20,000
	5–10,000
	3–5,000
	1–3,000
	0–1,000
	No data

GNI (PPP) 2005 ADJUSTED FOR PURCHASING POWER

Ranking	Economy	Millions of international (US$)
1	Luxembourg	48,700
2	Bermuda	..
3	United States	42,000
4	Norway	41,650
5	Liechtenstein	..
6	Switzerland	38,610
7	Channel Islands	..
8	Iceland	35,490
9	Hong Kong, China	34,900
10	Denmark	34,030
11	United Kingdom	33,960
12	Austria	33,280
13	Netherlands	32,970
14	Canada	32,770
15	Ireland	32,580
16	Belgium	32,470
17	Sweden	32,440
18	Isle of Man	..
19	Qatar	..
20	Finland	32,110
21	Japan	32,010
24	Australia	30,590
25	France	30,540

Source: International Monetary Fund, GDP PPP per Capita World Map, at http://en.wikipedia.org (accessed October 15, 2007); World Bank, World Development Indicators Database, May 1, 2007.

can complement economic indicators by also analyzing the economic environment in terms of the overall quality of life in a country: measuring how well a country does in terms of social liberties, life expectancy, and literacy rates.

THE U.N. HUMAN DEVELOPMENT INDEX   The United Nations has translated this view into its Human Development Report and its principal indicator, the **Human Development Index (HDI).**[9] Specifically, the HDI measures the average achievements in a country on three dimensions:

- *Longevity,* as measured by life expectancy at birth
- *Knowledge,* as measured by the adult literacy rate and the combined primary, secondary, and tertiary gross enrollment ratio
- *Standard of living,* as measured by GNI per capita expressed in PPP for U.S. dollars

By design, the HDI aims to capture long-term progress in human development rather than short-term changes. Map 4.4 shows countries' HDI performance.

MAP 4.4
Human Development Index, 2006

Measures such as GNI, PPP, and growth rate express "development" in strictly economic terms. The purpose of the HDI is to present a broader and more accurate picture of a country's development; thus it supplements *economic* factors with *social* factors—namely, *longevity* (life expectancy), *knowledge* (literacy, school enrollments), and *standard of living* (GNI per capita in PPP).

Source: United Nations, *Human Development Index* (2006), at http://en.wikipedia.org (accessed October 15, 2007); United Nations, *Human Development Report 2005*, at http://hdr.undp.org (accessed October 15, 2007).

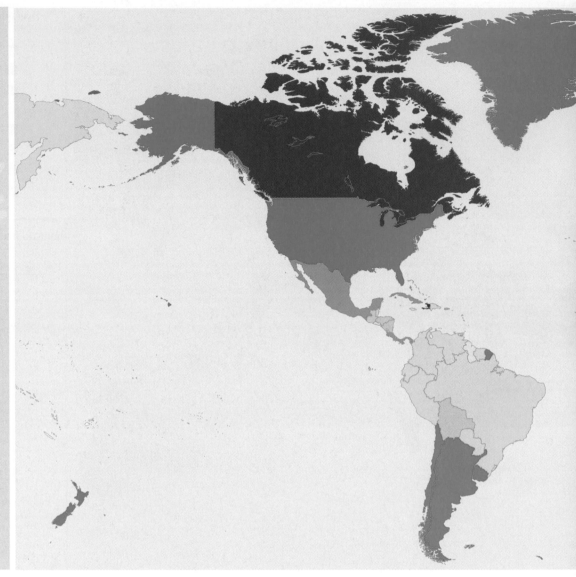

CONCEPT CHECK

After pointing out in Chapter 1 that not all interested parties unconditionally support **globalization**, in Chapters 2 and 3, we discuss several of the cultural and political reasons for opposition in various quarters. Here we round out this discussion by adding that much of this opposition comes from critics who charge that too many people pay too much attention to economic measures of performance; to understand growth, progress, and prosperity fully, they contend, we should focus more sharply on "green" measures of economic performance.

OTHER PROPOSED INDEXES   The United Nations refines the HDI to better assess gender and poverty in development. Specifically, it proposed the following indexes:

- *Gender-Related Development:*   Adjusts for gender inequalities; measures the inequalities between men and women in terms of a long and healthy life, knowledge, and standard of living.

- *Gender Empowerment:*   Assesses a woman's opportunities in a country by looking at inequalities in political participation and decision making, economic participation and decision making, and power over economic resources.

- *Human Poverty:*   Estimates the standard of living in a country by measuring human deprivations and the denial of choices and opportunities for living a life one has reason to value.[10]

Collectively, these indicators improve managers' sense of a country's achievements in longevity, knowledge, and a decent standard of living.

Green Measures of GNP   Growing concern for the ecological welfare of the world spurs calls for green measures of GNP. Green economics hold that a country's economy is a component of, and dependent on, the natural world within which it resides. As such,

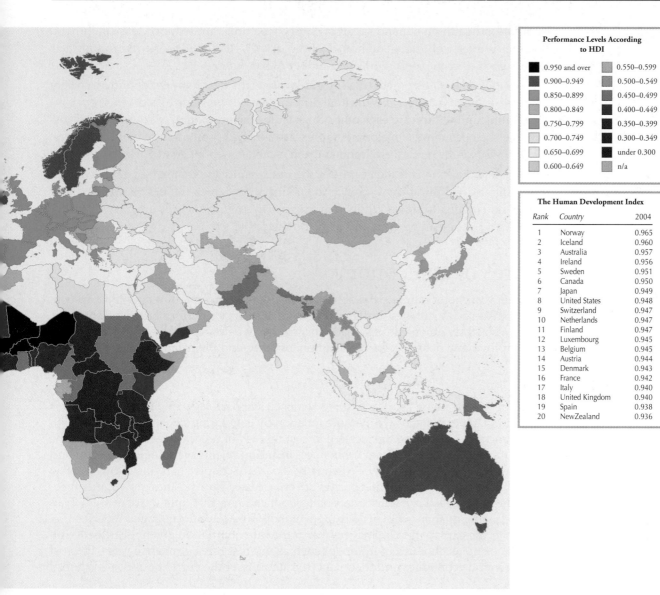

Performance Levels According to HDI	
■ 0.950 and over	0.550–0.599
0.900–0.949	0.500–0.549
0.850–0.899	0.450–0.499
0.800–0.849	0.400–0.449
0.750–0.799	0.350–0.399
0.700–0.749	0.300–0.349
0.650–0.699	under 0.300
0.600–0.649	n/a

The Human Development Index

Rank	Country	2004
1	Norway	0.965
2	Iceland	0.960
3	Australia	0.957
4	Ireland	0.956
5	Sweden	0.951
6	Canada	0.950
7	Japan	0.949
8	United States	0.948
9	Switzerland	0.947
10	Netherlands	0.947
11	Finland	0.947
12	Luxembourg	0.945
13	Belgium	0.945
14	Austria	0.944
15	Denmark	0.943
16	France	0.942
17	Italy	0.940
18	United Kingdom	0.940
19	Spain	0.938
20	NewZealand	0.936

the standard measures of GDI and GNP are misleading indicators of a country's long-term economic health and performance.

More specifically, measuring the quantity of market activity without accounting for the associated social and ecological costs results in mismeasuring economic performance. Moreover, ensuring sustainable development requires managers to heed the idea that economic activity must ultimately "meet the needs of the present without compromising the ability of future generations to meet their own needs."[11] Therefore, **green economics** calls for a wider view of what qualifies as economic growth and progress in studying a country's economy.

Presently, there is no consensus on how to adjust GDP for green concerns. Current candidates include the following:

- *Green Net National Product:*   Calls for measuring GNP to account for the corresponding depletion of natural resources and degradation of the environment (much the same way a company must depreciate both its tangible and intangible assets in making a product). The resulting indicator, net national product (NNP), adjusts for the depreciation of the country's physical assets.[12]

- *Genuine Progress Indicator:*   This measure starts with the same accounting framework used to calculate GDP but then adjusts for values assigned to environmental quality,

Green measures of gross national production aim to gauge economic performance in terms of long-term sustainability.

population health, livelihood security, equity, free time, and educational attainment. It values unpaid voluntary and household work as well as paid work. It also subtracts factors such as crime, pollution, and family breakdown.

- *Gross National Happiness:*   This measure holds that true development of human society takes place when material and spiritual development occurs side by side, thereby complementing and reinforcing each other. It measures the promotion of equitable and sustainable socioeconomic development, preservation and promotion of cultural values, conservation of the natural environment, and establishment of good governance.

- *Happy Planet Index:*   This idea captures the utilitarian view that most people want to live long and fulfilling lives. Hence the country that does the best is the one that allows its citizens to do so while avoiding infringing on the opportunity of future people, and people in other countries, to do the same.

Features of an Economy

GNI and its variations estimate the absolute and relative income of a country. As such, these data create powerful, first-order indicators of a country's performance and potential. Managers also study other features of an economy. As we now see, they often study inflation, unemployment, debt, income distribution, poverty, and the balance of payments.

INFLATION

Inflation is a measure of the increase in the cost of living.

A general, sustained rise in prices measured against a standard level of purchasing power is called inflation. Operationally, we measure inflation by comparing two sets of goods at two points in time and computing the increase in cost that is not reflected by an increase in the quality of the good. In mainstream economics, **inflation** results when aggregate demand grows faster than aggregate supply—essentially, too many people are trying to buy too few goods, thereby creating demand that pushes prices up faster than incomes grow. Other theories, notably the so-called Austrian School of Economics, holds that inflation of overall prices is the consequence of an increase in the supply of money by central banking authorities.[13]

Whatever the explanation, managers watch the rate of inflation given its influence on many parts of the economic environment such as interest rates, exchange rates, the cost of living, general economic confidence, and the stability of the current political system.[14]

Inflation and the Cost of Living   Consider the impact of inflation on the cost of living. Rising prices make it more difficult for consumers to buy products unless their incomes rise at the same or faster pace. Sometimes this is practically impossible. For example, during periods of rapid or "hyperinflation" (for example, in Brazil in the early 1990s or Turkmenistan in the mid-1990s), consumers have to spend their money as fast as they get it or else watch it turn worthless.

More pointedly, in Zimbabwe over the past few years, prices have been rising 1 to 20 percent per day, and by mid-2007, the inflation rate hit 3,714 percent. Upon reflection, the chairman of the Combined Harare Residents Association in Zimbabwe noted, "There's a surrealism here that's hard to get across to people. If you need something and have cash, you buy it. If you have cash you spend it today, because tomorrow it's going to be worth 5 percent less. Normal horizons don't exist here."[15]

Certainly, these are extreme cases. Still, history shows that chronic inflation, essentially annual inflation rates of 10 to 30 percent, erodes confidence in a country's currency and spurs people to search for better ways to store value.

Implications of Chronic Inflation   Chronic or hyperinflation has bleak implications for companies. Neither they nor their customers can effectively plan long-term investments, they have no incentive to save, and ordinary investment instruments like insurance policies, pensions, and long-term bonds become speculative. Inflation also puts great pressure on governments to control it. Often, governments try to reduce inflation by raising interest rates, installing wage and price controls, or imposing protectionist trade policies and currency controls. Either alone or together, these measures slow or stop economic growth.

Price Indexes and Problems in Measuring Inflation   Finally, the measurement of inflation highlights a commonplace difficulty—namely, what a country is measuring when it reports data on an economic variable. Specifically, price indexes are sensitive to decisions about their scope, the formulas by which they are calculated, and other factors decided by the agencies that disseminate them.

For instance, in the United States, the **Consumer Price Index (CPI)** is the official measure of inflation. In the European Union, it is the Harmonized Index of Consumer Prices (HICP). The CPI differs from the HICP in two major respects: First, the HICP includes the rural population in its scope and, second, the HICP excludes owner-occupied housing. Consequently, managers must be mindful of the process by which institutions report economic data.[16]

UNEMPLOYMENT

The *unemployment rate* is the number of unemployed workers who are seeking employment for pay divided by the total civilian labor force. Countries that are unable to create jobs for their citizens create a risky business environment. Generally, people out of work and unable to find jobs depress economic growth, create social pressures, and provoke political uncertainty. As such, the proportion of unemployed workers in a country shows how well a country productively uses it human resources.

Some economists suggest managers can refine their assessment by estimating the *misery index,* which is the sum of a country's inflation and unemployment rates. The higher the sum, the greater the economic misery, and the more likely consumers and companies will curtail spending and investment.

The Working-Age Population   Presently, the wealthier countries of the world are watching their working-age population shrink from approximately 740 million to 690 million people between 2000 and 2025. However, over the same time, the working-age population will increase across poorer countries from about 3 billion to 4 billion people. In China alone, the population above the age of 16 will grow by 5.5 million annually on average in the next 20 years. The total population of working-age Chinese will reach 940 million by 2020. Presently, the youth of the world suffer the highest rates of unemployment in most countries, with rates twice that of adult (ages 25 to 65) unemployment. China, for example, sees the age structure of its population creating severe employment pressure within the next two decades.[17]

> Unemployment is a measure of the number of workers who want to work but do not have jobs.

Labor Regulation   Emerging economies also face challenges from excessive labor regulation that aggravates unemployment. For example, India's labor laws, little changed since they were enacted after the country's independence in 1947, make it difficult to lay off employees even if a company's fortunes hit hard times or the economy slows. Consequently, companies are reluctant to hire workers at the risk of being unable to fire them if need be. "[C]ompanies think twice, 10 times, before they hire new people," explained, the chairman of the Hero Group, one of the world's largest manufacturers of inexpensive motorcycles.[18]

Problems in Measuring Unemployment   Again, as in the case of inflation, measuring the number of unemployed workers actually seeking work in various countries is difficult given various assumptions and exclusions. In the United States, the unemployment rate may misestimate the impact of the economy on people. Specifically, the unemployment figures indicate how many are not working for pay but seeking employment for pay; they do not count the number of people who are actually not working at all, working without pay, have stopped looking for work, or are working illegally.

Moreover, the unemployment rate means different things in different countries given different social policies and institutional frameworks.[19] Some countries, such as France and Germany, provide generous unemployment protection, whereas other countries, like China, Kenya, or Jordan, offer little to no support. Hence managers must be careful in evaluating the implications of unemployment rates for consumption and growth.

Finally, unemployment estimates throughout many poorer nations routinely underestimate the true degree of joblessness and, more significantly, the productivity of those who work. Many countries in Asia, Africa, and South America face more difficult problems because of widespread underemployment. That is, even though officially employed, people work only part time, which results in reduced productivity, low incomes, and social unease.

DEBT

Debt, the sum total of a government's financial obligations, measures the state's borrowing from its population, from foreign organizations, from foreign governments, and from international institutions. The larger the total debt becomes, the more uncertain a country's economy becomes, both in the present, as interest expenses divert money from more productive uses, and the future, as people worry about the ability of future generations to pay back the debt.

Presently, the national debt for many countries is growing. For example, the U.S. national debt has grown from $1 trillion in 1980 to $9.4 trillion in early mid-2008. On a per capita basis, each citizen's share of this debt is just about $30,800.[20] In comparison, the corresponding figures for Canada's debt are about $740 billion, resulting in a per capita share of roughly $22,600.

Some caution against emphasizing the absolute amount of debt. Instead, they look at the size of a nation's debt as a percentage of its GDP as the best measure of its severity. Based on this relationship, the national debt of the United States in 2007 is about 65 percent of its GDP; France is just about the same, and Germany comes in at 67 percent. Furthermore, some experts warn that comparing the balance of debt between years does not account for inflation, which makes balances from later years appear larger. Taking the U.S. national debt as a percentage of nominal GDP (which is not adjusted for inflation) drops it to under 60 percent.

A country has two types of debt:

- Internal: Portion of the government debt that is denominated in the country's own currency and held by domestic residents.

- External: Debt owed to foreign creditors and denominated in foreign currency.

Internal and External Debt   A country's debt has two parts: internal and external. Internal debt results when the government spends more than it collects in revenues. Internal deficits occur for any number of reasons, including when an imperfect tax system prevents the government from collecting revenue, when the costs of security and social programs exceed available tax revenues, and when state-owned enterprises run deficits. Consequently, every government struggles with setting spending priorities, better controlling expenses, improving budget management, and refining tax policy. The resulting pressure to revise government policies, in the face of growing internal debt, can create economic uncertainties for investors and companies.

External debt results when a government borrows money from foreign lenders. Presently, much of the debt burden in low-income countries dates back to the 1970s and 1980s when high oil prices pushed countries to borrow a great deal of money to fund domestic projects (in the belief that high prices and export earnings would be sustained) or domestic programs (in the necessity of offsetting the costs of oil price shocks, high interest rates, and low commodity prices).

Some countries recovered, but many did not. Current programs, such as the Heavily Indebted Poor Countries (HIPC) initiative, try to alleviate debt for the poorest countries that have severe external debt burdens. Growing understanding of the hardship of extreme debt has led creditors, mostly the world's wealthiest countries, to cancel many debt obligations. So far, debt reduction packages have been approved for 30 countries, 25 of them in Africa, which provided $35 billion in debt relief.[21]

More recently, many countries have borrowed from international lenders to finance their movement to freer markets, a process of economic transition we look at later in the chapter. Many countries that began with this ambition but eventually failed then had to rely on foreign debt. Governments in countries with high debt burdens, like Liberia and Zambia, must often slow the rate of economic growth or else try to borrow more money. Foreign investors monitor debt levels to gauge debt and put pressure on the government to revise its economic policies.

INCOME DISTRIBUTION

GNI or PPP, even when weighted by the size of the population, can misestimate the relative wealth of a nation's citizens: That is, GNI or PPP per capita reports, on average, how much income the average person earns. Because not everyone is average, neither indicator tells us what share of income goes to what segments of the population.

For example, Brazil's GNI is $1.4 trillion, a performance that ranks well in the world. Similarly, its GNI per capita is nearly $3,550, a strong regional accomplishment (its neighbors, like Guyana and Bolivia, report GNI per capita just over $1,000). However, Brazil's economic performance looks questionable when we consider that the richest fifth of Brazilians (about 35 million people) receive about 65 percent of total income while the poorest fifth of Brazilians receive only 2.2 percent.[22] The situation is worse in countries such as India, where over 80 percent (more than 800 million people) of the population live on less than $2 per day and over 40 percent live on less than $1 per day.

> Income distribution is a description of the fractions of a population that are at various levels of income.

The Gini Coefficient Managers estimate income distribution in a particular country by examining its Gini coefficient. This measure assesses the degree of inequality in the distribution of family income in a country. The more nearly equal a country's income distribution, the lower its Gini coefficient (for example, Finland, with an index of 26.9). The more unequal a country's income distribution, the higher its Gini coefficient (for example, Brazil, with an index of 56.7).

Income Distribution Among Wealthy Nations Uneven income distribution is not a problem for poorer nations. The United States has the largest inequality gap between rich and poor compared to other industrialized nations. For example, the top 1 percent receives more income than the bottom 40 percent; this gap is the widest it has been in 70 years.

Furthermore, in the last 20 years, the share of income going to the top 1 percent has increased, but it has decreased for the poorest 40 percent. This skewed distribution pattern spans the world. In 1960, the wealthiest 20 percent of the world's population had 30 times the income of the poorest 20 percent. This grew to 32 times in 1970, 45 times in 1980, 60 times in 1990, and 75 times in 2000. In addition, the richest 1 percent of the population of the world gets as much income as the bottom 57 percent—in other words, the 50 million richest people received as much income as did the 2.7 billion poorest people. Widening inequality can threaten economic growth if it fans social unrest.

Urban Versus Rural Income Distribution Similarly, there is a strong relationship between skewed income distributions and the split between those who live in urban settings versus those who live in rural areas. For example, the booming urban centers of China—such as Beijing, Shanghai, Hong Kong, Shenzhen, and Guangzhou—saw their per capita income pass $1,200 in 2006, about 3.22 times as much as that of the typical rural dweller. Current models forecast this ratio hitting 4 to 1 by 2020.

Furthermore, China projects that urban income will be seven times as much as rural income in 2020.[23] So although one sees Lexus, Porsche, and Mercedes-Benz dealerships in Beijing, many in rural China still rely on bicycles and animals for transportation. Rising income disparities between the nation's booming cities and vast, impoverished countryside, if not resolved, will undermine social stability as early as 2010.[24]

Similar situations unfold elsewhere. The median years of schooling in Vietnam is 8.1 for urban residents versus 5.4 for rural residents. And 73 percent of urban households in India have access to adequate sanitation versus 14 percent of rural households.

A Note on Income Equality   Finally, the historical record adds an important perspective to this discussion. Specifically, dramatic income equality is a recent phenomenon. In 2002, Jeffery Sachs of the Earth Institute observed:

> *The world is more unequal than at any time in world history. There's a basic reason for that which is that 200 years ago everybody was poor. A relatively small part of the world achieved what the economists call a modern economic growth. Those countries represent only about one-sixth of humanity, and five-sixths of humanity is what we call the developing world. It's the vast majority of the world. The gap can be 100–1, maybe a gap of $30,000 per person and $300 per person. And that's absolutely astounding to be on the same planet and to have that extreme variation in material well-being.*[25]

CONCEPT CHECK

As we suggest in Chapters 1 and 3, both income inequality and poverty should diminish as **international business** activity drives greater efficiency through trade and greater opportunities through democratization. Here we reiterate the principle that more efficient trading relationships and more productive use of liberated capital helps create job opportunities and fosters income growth among greater segments of the global population.

In sum, managers hone their sense of the economic potential of a country by adjusting their analyses to reflect the distribution of income. Moreover, managers realize that income inequality is not just bad for social justice; it is also bad for economic efficiency. Left to persist, it can fan crime, corruption, and risks that limit growth and erode stability in an economy.

POVERTY

The distribution of income is important to understand a market's performance and potential. Still, its reliance on central tendencies in income distributions presumes there actually is a reasonable income within a country. If not, then this statistic misreads an economy if unchecked by an assessment of the scale and scope of poverty in a country. And, as noted above, despite long-running efforts by many groups, organizations, and institutions, poverty prevails in every part of the world.

What Is Poverty?   **Poverty** has many dimensions. In general terms, it is a condition in which a person or community is deprived of, or lacks the essentials for, a minimum standard of well-being and life. These essentials can be life-sustaining material resources such as food, safe drinking water, and shelter; they may be social resources such as access to information, education, health care, and social status; they may be the opportunity to develop meaningful connections with other people in society.

This text takes an income perspective in which a person is defined as being poor when his or her income is below the threshold considered a minimum to satisfy specific needs and wants.

There is a growing gap between the rich and poor in virtually every country in the world.

Poverty According to the World Bank   The World Bank reports that the world population is about 78 percent poor (average PPP income less than $3,470 annually), 11 percent middle income, and 11 percent rich (average PPP income more than $8,000 annually). However, great attention is paid to more stark assessments of poverty. The World Bank defines *extreme poverty* as living on less than $1 per day (PPP) and *moderate poverty* as less than $2 per day (PPP). This standard shows that in 2004, 986 million people lived on less than $1 a day and some 2.6 billion, or almost half of the developing world's population, lived on less than $2 a day.

Critics contend that the World Bank's standards underestimate the pervasiveness of poverty. The standard of $1 per day (PPP) does not apply equally to all regions. The Economic Commission for Latin America and the Caribbean (ECLAC) puts the threshold for extreme poverty at $2 per day, whereas in the United States it is estimated at around $12 per day. Hence integrating World Bank standards with national definitions of poverty suggests that more than 3 billion people, of the 6.45 billion on planet Earth in early 2008, live in moderate to extreme poverty.[26]

Finally, poverty appears to be growing worldwide. Granted, estimates of the number of people in extreme poverty have fallen by approximately 200 million since 1990. However, this reduction has been concentrated in a few countries. Excluding China and India from the estimates finds that the number of poor people in the world has actually increased. More precisely, more than 80 countries had lower per capita GNI at the end of the 1990s than they had at the end of the 1980s.

Poverty and the Economic Environment Poverty of this scale and scope impacts economic environments. Throughout the world, people struggle for food, shelter, clothing, clean water, and health services, to say nothing of safety, security, and education. Failure results in suffering, malnutrition, mental illness, death, epidemics, famine, and war. For example, 100 percent of Canadians have access to clean water, whereas only 13 percent of the people in Afghanistan do; per capita dietary protein supply in the United States is 121 grams but just 32 grams in Mozambique; the average life expectancy in Japan is 81 years yet only 31 years in Botswana.[27] International companies facing such situations must deal with their implications for virtually every feature of the economic environment. In the face of extreme poverty, market systems may not exist, national infrastructures may not work, criminal behavior may be pervasive, and governments may be unable to regulate society consistently or adopt prudent economic policies. The growth of worldwide business activity and economic progress ultimately depend on alleviating poverty.

The Potential of the Poor Despite this daunting gap, managers must keep in mind the immense potential of today's poor consumers. For example, in 2002, India had just under 15 million mobile phone subscribers. By 2006, it had 136 million subscribers. India's government projects 500 million phone subscribers by 2010. Powering the penetration of mobile phones is the fact that Indian companies offer the cheapest mobile services in the world yet still earn attractive profits.

Similar developments with computers (e.g., the US$100 One Laptop per Child Project) and automobiles (the development of functional cars priced between US$2,000 and $3,000) highlight the importance of looking at poverty as an opportunity. More dramatically, one manager noted, "A billion customers in the world are waiting for a $2 pair of eyeglasses, a $10 solar lantern and a $100 house."[28]

LABOR COSTS

Companies continually scrutinize where it makes the most sense to locate particular activities. Also, changing economic environments mean companies look at cost structures in current terms as well as estimate cost structure five to ten years down the road. North American footwear makers, like Nike, for example, once made shoes in the United States, but over a 30-year span, they moved production from Taiwan, to the Philippines, Thailand, Korea, Vietnam, and China in the quest for the lowest possible production costs. Despite the growing uniformity of many markets, cost structures vary from country to country.

Labor and Total Cost For many goods and services, the cost of labor is a key element of total costs. Consequently, companies scan the world, looking for the best deal with the difference between low-cost and high-cost countries. For example, a factory worker in the United States typically costs between $15 and $30 per hour; factory wages in Mexico are about 11 percent of the U.S. level; in China, factory wages are 3 percent of the U.S. level.[29] For service employees, such as phone center employees, the cost differentials are also striking. The labor cost savings a company realizes by outsourcing a service job to India can be as much as 60 percent. More significantly, current projections see the average wage range in the United States moving to a bit over $25, to about $1.30 in China, and $0.70 in Indonesia.

Consider the case of Wonder Auto of China. A maker of auto parts, it calculates that it cost $4 million to set up an assembly line employing 20 workers in Jinzhou, a city of 800,000 in northeastern China. The combined wages of these 20 workers are $40,000 a year—a sum that's roughly the annual base pay for one unionized auto-parts worker or two nonunion auto-parts workers in the United States.[30]

Notably, a factory job at Wonder Auto and its top wage of $170 a month are a ticket to the middle class. In Jinzhou, a basic apartment without amenities like a refrigerator rents for about $40 a month, and a large meal at the restaurant of the city's best hotel costs less than $3. As such, jobs at Wonder Auto are much sought after, and turnover is almost zero; said

Sun Shaohua, 30, a factory line worker who strips copper wires for alternators, "Many people come, but nobody ever leaves."[31] Expectedly, companies in other countries see this situation, do their comparative cost calculations, and typically opt to open operations in China.

PRODUCTIVITY

Productivity measures the efficiency with which goods and services are produced.

Companies refine their interpretation of labors costs by considering *productivity*—specifically, the amount of output created per unit input used. In terms of labor, productivity is the quantity produced per person per labor hour.[32] Beginning in the first half of the 1990s, emerging markets have accelerated global productivity (see Figure 4.4). China's sustained performance has been notably impressive, yet productivity growth has also been strong throughout Asia and Eastern Europe and is showing signs of accelerating in Africa and South America.

This level of performance has reversed the productivity differential between workers in the richer countries versus those in emerging economies. The Conference Board pegs China's annual productivity growth from 2000 through 2007 at 10.4 percent. In the United States, productivity grew an average of 2.5 percent a year in the late 1990s and over 3 percent a year between 2002 and 2004. By 2006, it was 1.4 percent, the lowest in more than a decade, despite a strong business cycle. Similarly, the European Union saw modest productivity gains of only 1.5 percent in 2006.[33]

The Impact of Technology   Most immediately, the continuing diffusion of management methods and technology among many low-cost markets will power further productivity gains. Productivity worldwide has benefited from a powerful combination of technological progress, an increasingly open global trading system, rising cross-country capital flows, and more resilient macroeconomic policy frameworks and financial systems.[34] The forces driving globalization, as we discussed in Chapter 1, fortify these conditions.

THE BALANCE OF PAYMENTS

A country's **balance of payments (BOP),** officially known as the *Statement of International Transactions,* is the statement of the balance of a country's trade and financial transactions as conducted by individuals, businesses, and government agencies located in that nation with the rest of the world over a specific period (usually one year).

FIGURE 4.4   Global Productivity Performance*

Beginning in 1992, the productivity-growth rate of developing countries began accelerating. Then, in the 1995-1997 period, it surpassed that of advanced economies. The IMF estimates that a widening productivity gap between developing countries and advanced economies is largely due to the former's improving communications systems and transportation infrastructures.

*Rates indicate annual percentage increases as three-year moving average; output is measured as real GDP divided by working-age population.

Sources: World Bank, *World Development Indicators* (2006); IMF, *World Economic and Financial Surveys* (2007), at www.imf.org (accessed October 15, 2007).

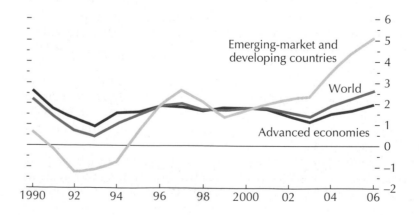

Current and Capital Accounts   The BOP has two main accounts:

- The **current account,** which tracks all trade activity in merchandise
- The **capital account,** which tracks both loans given to foreigners and loans received by citizens

Table 4.2 lists the components of each account.

The first few years of the twenty-first century directed attention toward countries' current accounts. Mechanically, exports generate positive sales abroad while imports generate negative sales domestically. Positive net sales, done simply by exporting more than importing, results in current account surplus; likewise, importing more than exporting results in a current account deficit. Table 4.3 lists the 10 countries with the greatest current account surpluses and, likewise, the 10 countries with the greatest current account deficits.[35]

The notion of *balance* means that all BOP transactions have an offsetting receipt. For instance, a country might have a surplus in **merchandise trade** (indicating it is exporting more than it is importing) but may then report a deficit in another area, such as its investment income. In other words, because the current account and the capital account add up to the total account, which is necessarily balanced, a deficit in the current account is always accompanied by an equal surplus in the capital account and vice versa. A deficit or surplus in the current account cannot be explained or evaluated without simultaneous explanation and evaluation of an equal surplus or deficit in the capital account.

BOP and Economic Stability   Managers use the BOP to assess a country's economic stability. By measuring a country's transactions with the rest of the world, the BOP estimates a country's financial stability in the world market. For example, a deficit in merchandise trade means the supply of that country's currency is increasing throughout the world, given that its consumers are using it to buy the imports that then cause a trade deficit. Unless the government revises its economic policies, the market will do so by proxy and depreciate the value of its currency.

BOP and Company Strategy   Monitoring trends in the BOP gives managers one more piece of data in deciding whether or not to do business in a country. More generally, it confirms the importance of the connection between a company's strategy and the implications of BOP data to economic activities and government policy. For example, some say the solution to the U.S. deficit would come from faster growth overseas, decline in the value of the U.S. dollar, slower growth in consumer spending, and a higher U.S. savings rate. Any one of these factors would change important elements of the economic environment of the United States as well as trigger change in economic policies in countries around the world.

> Companies monitor the balance of payments to watch for factors that could lead to currency instability or change in government policy.

TABLE 4.2   Components of a Country's Balance of Payments

Current Account

- Value of exports and imports of physical goods, such as oil, grain, or computers (also referred to as *visible trade*)
- Receipts and payments for services, such as banking or advertising, and other intangible goods, such as copyrights and cross-border dividend and interest payments (also referred to as *invisible trade*)
- Private transfers, such as money sent home by expatriate workers
- Official transfers, such as international aid, on which the government expects no returns

Capital Account

- Long-term capital flows (i.e., money invested in foreign firms as well as profits made by selling those investments and returning the money home)
- Short-term capital flows (i.e., money invested in foreign currencies by international speculators as well as funds moved around the world for business purposes by companies with international operations)

TABLE 4.3   Current Account Balances: The Top 10 and The Bottom 10

Rank Top 10	Country	Current Account Balance (in millions of US$)
1	China	$ 179,100
2	Japan	174,400
3	Germany	134,800
4	Russia	105,300
5	Saudi Arabia	103,800
6	Norway	63,330
7	Switzerland	50,440
8	Netherlands	50,170
9	Kuwait	40,750
10	Singapore	35,580
Bottom 10		
153	South Africa	−12,690
154	Portugal	−16,750
155	Greece	−21,370
156	Italy	−23,730
157	Turkey	−25,990
158	India	−26,400
159	France	−38,000
160	Australia	−41,620
161	United Kingdom	−57,680
162	Spain	−98,600
163	United States	−862,300

Source: Central Intelligence Agency, "Rank Order—Current Account Balance," *The World Factbook* (2007), at www.cia.gov (accessed October 15, 2007).

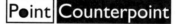

Is a Trade Deficit an Advantage?

Point **Yes** The phrase *balance of trade* has an innocent sound to it. Operationally, it is straightforward—simply the amount of exports sent by Country A to other countries less the amount of imports brought into Country A from other countries. This statistic is widely reported as a leading indicator of the state of health of a country's economy.

However, adding the term *deficit* to the balance of trade turns it into a politically charged phrase that prompts different interpretations. Some people reason that a trade deficit is a sign of a strong economy; others counter it is a leading indicator of crisis. Events in the United States help put this debate into perspective.

In the first week or so of each month, the U.S. Department of Commerce announces the country's trade balance. The monthly announcement of the U.S. balance of trade increasingly gains greater prominence in light of its dramatic growth—indeed, beginning in 2001, the trade deficit has set new records for five consecutive years.[36] In January 2008 payday,

Counterpoint **No** Some see the growing U.S. trade deficit as a crisis waiting to happen. Said one observer, "We now have the Grand Canyon of trade deficits. Actually, deficit is really a misnomer. Chasm, gorge, black hole, infinitely deep well all fit the description better."[40]

Though extreme, this view fits historic interpretations—technically, the trade deficit is a negative in the Commerce Department's estimates of GDP because of the assumption that imports replace U.S. products and thus, when they are growing, signal a weakening domestic economy.

Senator Byron L. Dorgan, a Democrat representing North Dakota, claims the deficit figure is reaching "dangerous levels that are hurting this country's future. This deficit manifests itself in the lives of American families every day with the loss of jobs overseas, lower wages, and a feeling of less security."[41]

He and others called on President Bush to convene an emergency meeting of key government policymakers to avert the Commerce Department reported that the U.S. trade deficit, on a monthly basis, was $63.1 billion for November 2007.

Despite a significant increase in American exports to expanding overseas economies due to the falling value of the U.S. dollar, Americans' appetite for foreign goods charges on. Moreover, so far this year, the trade deficit is running at an annual rate of $702 billion versus the record of $765.3 billion set in 2006. Each report reignites the debate about the implication of the U.S. trade performance.

One perspective sees the U.S. trade deficit as an indicator of the strength of the U.S. economy. Prominently, free-market economists argue that the deficit does not really matter—it is mostly a benign side effect of America's faster economic growth and its appeal as a destination for foreign investment. Trade imbalances are nothing to worry about, these economists say, because they merely measure private transactions that happen to take place across national borders.[37]

Furthermore, a current account deficit is not, in itself, a sign of bad economic policy or of bad economic conditions. If the United States has a current account deficit, all this means is that the United States is importing capital from overseas lenders. In addition, the inflow of foreign capital that accompanies the current account deficit may lead some to fear that foreigners are increasingly "owning" the United States; in theory, capital inflows increase the domestic capital pool.

The Bush administration agrees, noting that the trade deficit should be seen as testimony to the strength of the American economy and its role as an engine of global growth. Put simply, our economy is growing, expanding, creating jobs and disposable income, and that shows up in our growing demand for imports.[38] A spokesperson for the Treasury Department concurred: "We view these figures [the U.S. trade deficit] as an affirmation that we're growing faster than our trading partners by as much as two percent and we need them to take steps so they can grow and buy our products."[39]

Effectively, then, the U.S. trade deficit shows the strength of American consumer confidence and, due to their inability to buy enough U.S.-made goods and services, the weakness of U.S. trading partners. According to this analysis, the responsibility for altering the trade imbalance lies not with the United States but with its trade partners. Once America's trade partners get their act together, their economies will grow and they will then have the resources to buy American products and consume more of what they produce domestically. At that time, the U.S. trade deficit will shrink as fast as the economies of its trading partners grow.

Others echo these thoughts, noting that the trade deficit is an unimportant bookkeeping record because trade actually benefits all—successful foreign firms will invest more capital in the United States (such as by buying U.S. Treasury bills) and we need only return the favor by buying more of their exports. ●

disaster. Similarly, as the president of the Federal Reserve Bank of Boston notes, "Unavoidable economic logic suggests that eventually this situation will prove unsustainable."[42]

In theory, a country can sustain a trade deficit for many years without its economy suffering—as long as the trade deficit is trivial compared with the country's gross national income and wealth. As such, some claim that a wealthy country like the United States can endure a trade deficit for many years. However, they concede that no nation can endure a trade deficit forever simply because it cannot borrow endlessly from others without sooner or later eroding the foundations of its economy.

Furthermore, theory suggests that a trade deficit is a positive economic indicator, provided the deficit is due to firms importing technology and other capital goods from abroad that they then use to improve their productivity and international competitiveness.

Increasingly, the view of the deficit due to growing consumption of foreign-made consumer goods led many to fret that the United States is heading toward a balance of payments crisis. First, the U.S. trade deficit is no longer trivial; at $765 billion for 2006, the deficit was nearly 6.5 percent of the GDP for the United States.[43] That was a record for the United States both in absolute dollars and as a relative share of the GNP.

Most economists argue that this level is unsustainable. Paul Volcker, former chairman of the Federal Reserve, has become worried enough to call these circumstances as "dangerous and intractable" as any he can remember.[44] Peril follows from the fact that the growing trade deficit pushes the United States to rely increasingly on foreign credit to finance its investment and consumption.

Finally, say some, our trade deficit shows that people in the United States are collectively undersaving and overconsuming. Extreme consumerism in the United States—on average, Americans spend more than twice as much as anyone in any other country in the world per year—means people are living beyond their means. In the end, for the United States to balance its trade, American consumers must spend less on imports and, ideally, foreign consumers will buy more of its exports. ●

Integrating Economic Analysis

Case Review Note

The preceding overview of economic development, in highlighting divergence among countries, spotlights the dilemma for international companies. The high-income countries are the logical place to do business because of the quality of labor and quantity of consumer demand. As we saw in our opening case, however, emerging economies exhibit improving skills, accelerating growth, and astounding market potential. The sheer size of the total population—about 80 percent of all countries and 85 percent of the world's population—spurs companies to rethink many economic measures.

Dealing with this dilemma leads international companies to estimate a country's growth potential by gauging its current economic policies and practices. This requires that managers go from examining individual elements of the economic environment to analyzing how a country's economic environment works. Managers handle this task from two perspectives. The first looks at the type of current economic system in the country. The second looks at the transition process by which a country has moved or is moving from one type of economic system to another.

TYPES OF ECONOMIC SYSTEMS

An economic system is a mechanism that deals with the production, distribution, and consumption of goods and services.

An **economic system** is the set of structures and processes that guides the allocation of resources and shapes the conduct of business activities in a country. Spectrum analysis, as we saw applied in Chapter 3 with regard to political systems, gives a sense of the range of economic systems in the world today. One end of the spectrum of economic systems is anchored by the idea of capitalism, the other with that of communism. Major differences between these ideas exist in terms of their implications for economic matters such as the ownership and control of factors of production and also the freedom of price to balance supply and demand.

Capitalism is a free-market system built on private ownership and control. This philosophy holds that owners of capital have inalienable property rights that give them the right to earn a profit in return for their effort, investment, and risk. In contrast, **communism** champions a centrally planned system built on state ownership of all economic factors of production and control of all economic activity.

Here we have a panorama of Shanghai, China, from the mid-1990s. At the time, Shanghai, along with China, was making the transition from a command economy to a market economy.

Flash forward a decade and we have a far more dramatic panorama of Shanghai. The successful adoption of free market principles has powered a dramatic transformation of Shanghai, to say nothing of many other parts of China. Many see in Shanghai's towering skyscrapers and storied waterfront the emergence of the world's premier city.

There are few instances of the pure expression of either capitalism or communism. Instead, managers use the principles of capitalism and communism to analyze prevailing types of economic systems—a market economy, a command economy, and a mixed economy—that define economic environments across the world. We now look at each.

Market Economy   A **market economy** is a system in which individuals, rather than government, make the majority of economic decisions. A market economy gives individuals the freedom to decide where to work doing what, how to spend or save money, and whether to consume now or later.

This view is anchored in the principle of laissez-faire and its notion that a market is best left to its own dynamics. Free of government regulation, a free market efficiently determines the relationships among price, quantity, supply, and demand. This principle is credited to Adam Smith and his proposition that in a market economy, producers, spurred by the profit motive, efficiently make products that consumers want. In turn, consumers, by virtue of what they do and do not buy, ensure that producers put capital and labor to the best possible use.

Private Ownership of Resources   Because individuals make economic decisions, a market economy depends on individuals and companies owning and controlling resources rather than the government. Only with private ownership can a market economy allocate factors of production as if, Adam Smith wrote, an "invisible hand" were guiding the efficient actions of self-interested individuals. Hence consumer sovereignty, whereby consumers influence the allocation of resources through their demand for products, is the cornerstone of a market economy.

Role of Government Intervention   A market economy depends on as few government restrictions as possible—the less invisible the "hand" becomes due to government intervention, the less efficiently the market will work. Nonetheless, the invisible hand is not

A market economy encourages open exchange of goods and services between producers and consumers.

In a command economy, all dimensions of economic activity are determined by a central government plan.

In discussing "totalitarianism" in Chapter 3, we observe that a totalitarian system seeks to subordinate all aspects of people's day-to-day lives—including their behavior in and attitudes toward the marketplace. Here we explain how domination of the national economy works to reinforce this overriding policy: Such control enables a government to influence attitudes toward risk and return, economic motivation, and means of communicating with other agents in the marketplace.

infallible, given the need for some public goods (like traffic lights or national defense) and precautions (such as environmental regulations) that preempt those inclined to maximize personal gain in unfair ways. Therefore, a free market needs government action to enforce contracts, protect property rights, ensure fair and free competition, regulate certain sorts of economic activities, and provide general safety and security.

Hong Kong, Great Britain, Canada, and the United States are examples of contemporary market economies. Strictly speaking, none of them is a "pure" market economy because their governments do intervene in the marketplace. Nonetheless, these economies are closer to the pure market economy model than are others.[45]

Command Economy   A **command economy,** also known as a *centrally planned economy,* describes the economic system whereby the government owns and controls all resources. Hence the government commands the authority to decide what goods and services a country will produce, the quantity in which they are produced, and the price at which they are sold. For example, in a market economy, if the government wants more cars, it collects taxes and then buys cars at market prices. In a centrally planned economy, the explicitly visible hand of the government orders state-owned and state-controlled carmakers to make more cars with no concern for price.[46]

Centrally planned economies have telltale features. The government owns the means of production—land, farms, factories, banks, stores, hospitals, and so forth—that are then managed by employees of the state. Consequently, the prices of goods and services do not often change in a command economy because government officials, not consumers, determine them. Quality, however, tends to vary dramatically, often getting worse over time, for at least three reasons:

- Most products are usually in short supply.
- Consumers typically have few or no alternatives.
- There's not much incentive for companies to innovate and little profit to invest in upgrades.

Command economies can appear to perform well for short periods of time, especially in terms of growth rates, because by controlling everything and everybody, the state has a tremendous ability to mobilize unemployed or underemployed resources to generate growth. Impressive growth rates can be achieved as long as the main source of growth is putting unemployed resources (principally labor) to work. Similarly, command economies typically develop large-scale, capital-intensive production that often achieves marginal rates of efficiency while making acceptable products that are not competitive with global standards.

Mixed Economy   In reality, there is no pure version of a market economy or a command economy. Instead, most economies, broadly labeled **mixed economies,** fall in the middle of the capitalism–communism spectrum. A mixed economy is a system in which economic decisions are largely market driven and ownership is largely private, but the government intervenes in private economic decisions.

Thus the mixed economic system has elements of market and central-planning economies—the government owns key factors of production, yet consumers and private producers still influence price and quantity.[47] For example, the government may own companies that manufacture cars. But rather than telling managers how much to sell each car for, the government permits the market forces of supply and demand to set prices. Countries commonly classified as mixed economies include South Africa, Japan, South Korea, France, Brazil, Germany, and India.

Inevitably, this question emerges: Why would a country not opt for one of the pure economic types, betting on either free markets or state control to maximize economic performance? In response, the proponents of mixed economies concede that an economic system should aspire to achieve the efficiencies endemic to free markets. But an economic system must also, at the least, protect society from the excesses of unchecked individualism and greed, and ideally, apply policies needed to achieve low unemployment, low poverty, steady economic growth, and an equal distribution of wealth. Consequently, the fact that the pure forms of market and command economies are theoretically unable to achieve both of these goals without violating their basic principles motivates many countries to mix elements of each type.

> A mixed economic system combines elements of the market and command economic systems, whereby both the government and private enterprise influence production, consumption, investment, and savings.

Forms of Government Intervention   Operationally, government intervention in the mixed economy takes various forms:

- Central, regional, or local governments may actually own some means of production, such as the Tennessee Valley Authority in the United States that generates electricity for several states, or Airbus Industries, which is jointly owned by several European governments.
- The government can influence private production or consumption decisions such as by buying goods and services or by subsidizing or taxing certain activities.
- The government can redistribute income and wealth in pursuit of some equity objective, such as socialized medicine and other welfare programs.

The extent and nature of government intervention, besides differing from country to country, change over time based on a country's political, social, cultural, and institutional traditions and trends.

ECONOMIC FREEDOM AND MARKET TRANSITIONS

The past two decades have seen widespread adoption of free-market principles. Countries have reshaped economic environments by deferring to the laws of supply and demand, instead of the visible hand of political officials, to regulate price and quantity. Countries that adopted greater degrees of freedom outperformed those that did not on a range of dimensions. In 2006, free economies had per capita GNI of $29,219, more than twice that of countries that were mostly free, and more than four times that of countries that had mostly nonfree economies.

Similar patterns exist regarding income levels, growth rates, price stability, and employment. In addition, reports find positive correlations between **economic freedom** and higher average income per person, higher income for the poor, higher life expectancy, higher literacy, lower infant mortality, and less corruption. Collectively, these indicators confirm the long-running trend that countries freer of high taxes, regulations, and other government controls achieve the greatest economic growth and the highest standards of living (see Figure 4.5).

> **CONCEPT CHECK**
> Recall from Chapter 1 our inclusion of "Increased Global Competition" among the forces behind **globalization**. Then we showed how **international business** activity depends on competitive environments that recognize the sanctity of property rights. Here we reinforce the same principle: If you can't be sure you can compete on the basis of your effectively protected intellectual property, you're a lot less likely to innovate and invest.

Economic Freedom Index   Since 1995, the Heritage Foundation and the *Wall Street Journal* have annually reported the **Economic Freedom Index**. Officially, *economic freedom* is defined as the "absence of government coercion or constraint on the production, distribution, or consumption of goods and services beyond the extent necessary for citizens to protect and maintain liberty itself. In other words, people are free to work, produce, consume, and invest in the ways they feel are most productive."[48]

Operationally, this index estimates the extent to which the government of a country intervenes with the principles of free choice and free enterprise for reasons that go beyond the basic need to protect property, liberty, citizen safety, and market efficiency. Practically, this survey rates countries in terms of 50 independent indicators that are

> Countries with the freest economies have had the highest annual growth and a greater degree of wealth creation.

FIGURE 4.5
The Correlates of Economic Freedom

These charts highlight the relationship between economic freedom and key macroeconomic indicators. The data show that the higher the degree of economic freedom in a country, the stronger the performance of its economy. Technically, those countries that are considered to be the most economically free are placed within the top quintile; those countries that are considered to be the least economically free fall into the fifth quintile. The remaining countries are distributed among the second, third, and fourth quintiles.

Source: The Heritage Foundation and the *Wall Street Journal, The 2007 Index of Economic Freedom* (2007), at www. heritage.org (accessed October 15, 2007). Reprinted by permission of The Heritage Foundation.

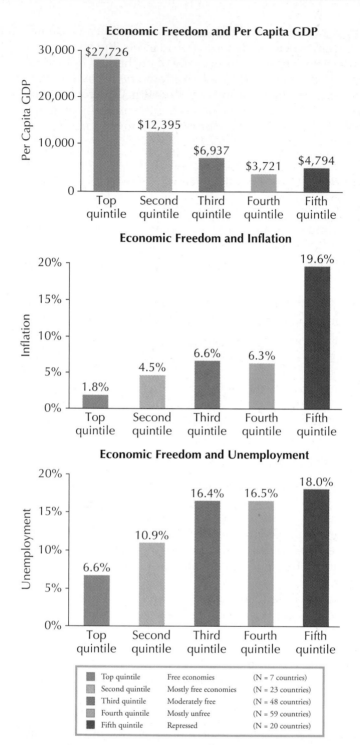

organized into the 10 dimensions listed in Table 4.4. Operationally, the higher the score on a factor, within the range of 0 to 100 percent, the lower the level of government interference in the economy.

Now look at Map 4.5, which reports the classification of 157 countries in terms of their degree of economic freedom in 2006. These data show that 7 countries have free economies, 23 are rated mostly free, 48 are moderately free, 59 are mostly nonfree, and 20 are repressed. In terms of head counts, the bulk of the world's population lives in mostly nonfree economies (4.16 billion).

TABLE 4.4 **Dimensions of the Economic Freedom Index**

Dimension	Definition
Business freedom	The ability to create, operate, and close an enterprise quickly and easily. Burdensome, redundant regulatory rules are the most harmful barriers to business freedom.
Trade freedom	A composite measure of the absence of tariff and nontariff barriers that affects imports and exports of goods and services.
Monetary freedom	Combination measure of price stability and assessment of price controls. Both inflation and price controls distort market activity. Price stability without microeconomic intervention is the ideal state for the free market.
Freedom from government	Assessment of all government expenditures—including consumption and transfers—and state-owned enterprises. Ideally, the state will provide only true public goods, with an absolute minimum of expenditure.
Fiscal freedom	A measure of the burden of government from the revenue side. It includes both the tax burden in terms of the top tax rate on income (individual and corporate separately) and the overall amount of tax revenue as a portion of GDP.
Property rights	An assessment of the ability of individuals to accumulate private property secured by clear laws that are fully enforced by the state.
Investment freedom	An assessment of the free flow of capital, especially foreign capital.
Financial freedom	A measure of banking security as well as independence from government control. State ownership of banks and other financial institutions, such as insurer and capital markets, is an inefficient burden, and political favoritism has no place in a free-capital market.
Freedom from corruption	The application of quantitative data that assesses the perception of corruption in the business environment, including levels of governmental, legal, judicial, and administrative corruption.
Labor freedom	A composite measure of the ability of workers and businesses to interact without restriction by the state.

Source: The Heritage Foundation and the *Wall Street Journal, The 2007 Index of Economic Freedom* (2007), at www.heritage.org (accessed October 15, 2007). Reprinted by permission of The Heritage Foundation.

The other categories are less uneven. There are 381 million inhabitants in free economies, and 647 million, 792 million, and 271 million living in mostly free, moderately free, and repressed economies, respectively. The distribution of economic systems, in raw numbers, evenly falls into two camps: 78 of the 157 countries studied qualify as free, mostly free, or moderately free, whereas 79 countries are mostly not free or repressed. Again, in terms of population counts, the former set has 1.82 billion inhabitants versus 4.28 billion in the latter.

In 2006, the average economic freedom score was 60.6 percent, the second highest level since the index began in 1995 but down by 0.3 percentage point from the previous year. In a general parallel to freedom stagnation discussed in Chapter 3, the freedom scores of 65 countries increased between 2005 and 2006, but the scores of 92 countries decreased. In contrast, from 2004 to 2005, of the 155 countries studied, 86 countries adopted more economic freedoms, compared with 57 countries that imposed more state controls.

MAKING THE TRANSITION TO A MARKET ECONOMY

Although recent economic freedom surveys suggest possible stagnation in the adoption of free-market principles, the longer-term trend shows positive momentum. Between 1985 and 2006, 89 percent of the sampled countries increased their economic freedom score, 6 percent reduced it, and 5 percent were unchanged. The average score has increased from 5.17 in 1985 to 6.4 in the most recent available year. Critics point out, though, that this original set of countries sampled 105 nations. The current set samples 157 countries, many of which are former totalitarian states that operated command economies. As such, despite promising indications, the data are presently equivocal about the strength of the long-term trend in economic freedom.

Economic Freedom and Economic Development   The economic freedom index has straightforward implications to the origins and causes of economic development. For the past few decades, countries with the most economic freedom have had higher rates of long-term economic growth and enjoyed more prosperity than those with less economic freedom. Most significantly, those countries ranking highest on economic

MAP 4.5
Global Distribution of Economic Freedom

The concept of *economic freedom* is based on the proposition that all citizens in every country have the right to work, produce, consume, and invest in the way that they prefer. At present, the Index of Economic Freedom classifies *economic freedom* into five categories: *free, mostly free, moderately free, mostly unfree,* and *repressed*. Classification criteria revolve around the degree to which governments influence people's economic choices.

Source: The 2007 Index of Economic Freedom (The Heritage Foundation and *Wall Street Journal*, 2007) www.heritage.org.

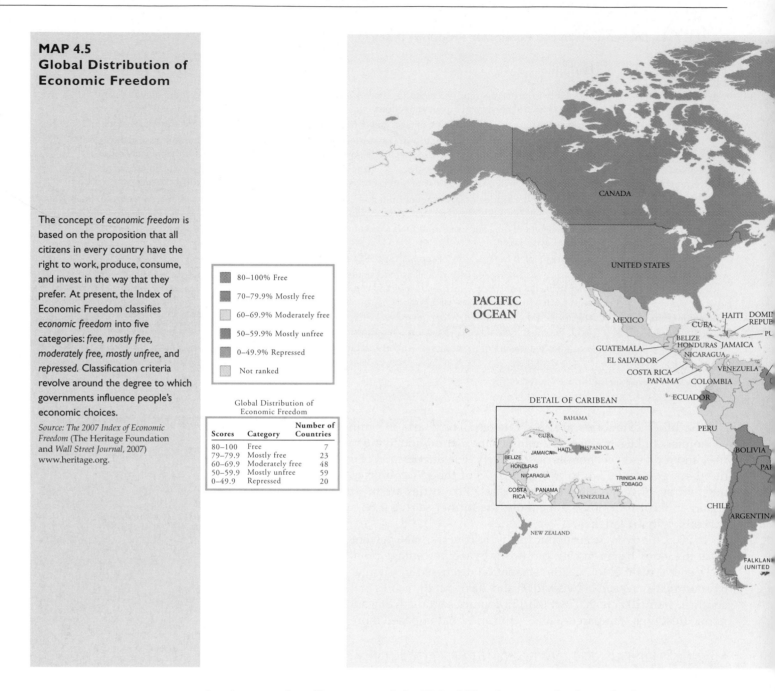

80–100% Free

70–79.9% Mostly free

60–69.9% Moderately free

50–59.9% Mostly unfree

0–49.9% Repressed

Not ranked

Global Distribution of
Economic Freedom

Scores	Category	Number of Countries
80–100	Free	7
79–79.9	Mostly free	23
60–69.9	Moderately free	48
50–59.9	Mostly unfree	59
0–49.9	Repressed	20

freedom—such as Singapore and the United Kingdom—tend to have the fastest economic growth and highest living standards.

In addition, countries with low levels of freedom scored far worse two decades ago. A case in point is China. Like many other emerging economies, China has high growth rates (10 percent plus) but relatively low economic freedom (index score of 54 percent in 2007). Applying today's economic freedom measures to China 30 years ago would have resulted in an index value near zero. Since beginning its transition to a free market, China's degrees of economic freedom, along with its economic growth, has steadily increased and likely will continue to do so. Still, others point out that China's economic freedom score has increased marginally from 1995 through 2007, going from 52.1 to 54 percent. Then again, India saw its economic freedom score rise from 46.4 to 55.6 over the same time span.

More pointedly, few doubt that the choice to slow economic reforms jeopardizes growth. The past few decades have shown that market economies outperformed their mixed and command counterparts largely because, in the case of the latter, government

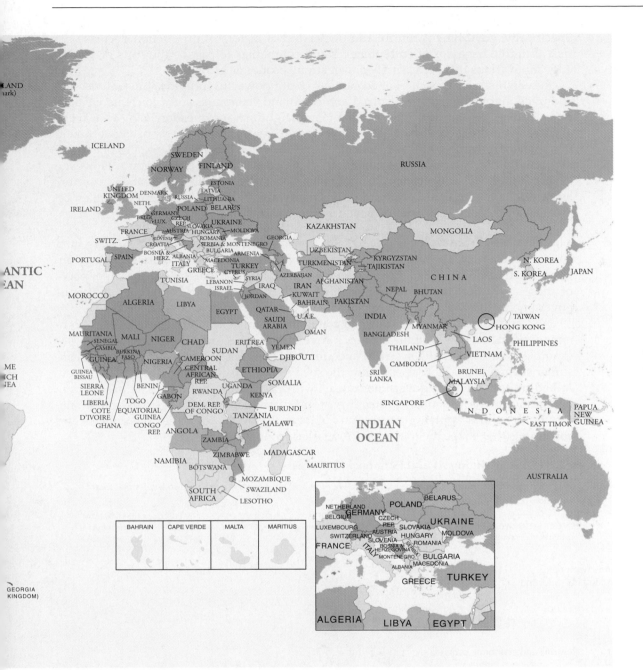

ownership and control of the factors of production constrained growth. Certainly, government ownership and control has some benefits, such as lower unemployment and far-reaching social programs. Still, case after case shows that it tends to create conditions of operational inefficiency and strategic ineffectiveness in the economic environment.

The Future of Market Economies Regarding strategic ineffectiveness, many mixed and command economies, besides dealing with tough challenges here and now, face challenging futures. Granted, we noted earlier that government-directed economies often can perform well. Over time, however, the power of their typical advantages—cheap labor, large-scale production facilities, artificially cheap capital, low R&D investment—fade as management systems and production processes in other countries improve.

Furthermore, the growing connections among countries, as the scope of international business expands, permit the freer flow of products, people, and ideas. Together, these developments aggravate a fundamental limitation of mixed and command economies.

Specifically, government control and ownership of factors of production decrease the risk-affinitive behavior of entrepreneurs and companies to pursue the sorts of knowledge innovations that increasingly power strong economic growth.

Research shows that market economies create powerful individual incentives that stimulate innovation, whereas mixed and command economies seem to create weak or no incentives. Essentially, it boils down to a straightforward question: Why work hard and risk everything on a new idea if whatever you create is the property of a government that will not reward you for your sacrifice? Until recently, the cost of low rates of innovative activity did not erode the foundations of a mixed or command economy. However, as global markets move from industrial to intellectual enterprises, innovation in sectors as varied as health care, communications, software, and entertainment has taken on greater significance as engines of a country's long-run growth.

Transition to a market economy involves liberalizing economic activity, reforming business activity, and establishing legal and institutional frameworks.

The Means of Transition   The process of transition to a market economy differs from country to country. The steps taken in Ireland, Thailand, and Mexico are different from those taken in China, Brazil, Estonia, Vietnam, or Ukraine. Nonetheless, the experiences of these and other countries confirm the quest to create freer economies that spur governments to adopt common principles and practices.

First and foremost, the shift from a command or mixed economy to a market economy depends on how well the country's government can dismantle certain features (for example, central planning systems) and create certain other features (for example, consumer sovereignty). More specifically, the success of transition appears to be intricately linked to how well the government deals with privatizing the means of production, deregulating the economy, protecting property rights, reforming fiscal and monetary policies, and applying antitrust regulation. Figure 4.6 identifies the policies and constraints that shape the transition to a market economy.

FIGURE 4.6   Reforms and Economic Progress

There are several reforms that are necessary to achieve economic progress, but there are also factors that retard economic progress.

Source: Finance & Development, June 1999, Volume 36, Number 2. FINANCE AND DEVELOPMENT by IMF. Copyright 1999 by INTERNATIONAL MONETARY FUND. Reproduced with permission of INTERNATIONAL MONETARY FUND in the format textbook via Copyright Clearance Center.

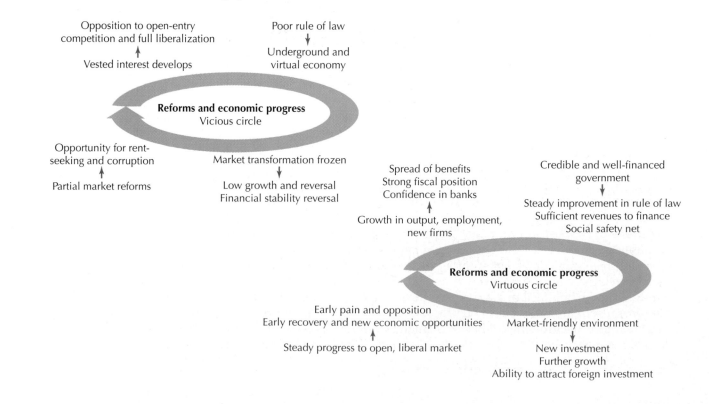

Privatization   A necessary, but by no means sufficient, condition of creating a market economy is that the state transfers its ownership and control of factors of production to private owners via the process of **privatization** (the sale and legal transfer of government-owned resources to private interests). Privatization is essential, not just for the sake of improving general market efficiency but also because only a robust private sector can shape the relationship between supply and demand so it leads to better production and consumption decisions. Hence the ambition to move toward a market economy requires the government to disengage from the economy by privatizing state-owned enterprises.

Most immediately, privatization reduces government debt by eliminating the need to subsidize typically inefficient, money-losing, state-owned enterprises. In the longer term, privatization increases market efficiency in light of the expectation that private owners will more aggressively upgrade technologies, improve business practices, and create innovations than state-appointed administrators will. Perhaps the key motivator is the fact that privatized companies must compete in open markets for material, labor, and capital. Hence private enterprises succeed or fail on their own merits (and, as Figure 4.7 suggests, answer one way or another to their shareholders).

Deregulation   Deregulation involves relaxing or removing restrictions on the free operation of markets and business practices. Doing so then allows businesses to be more productive by saving the time and money previously spent complying with regulations.

FIGURE 4.7

Privatization can be a headache if directors aren't used to answering to shareholders

—or owners—who have a vested interest in their policies and practices.

Source: Copyright John Morris, Cartoonstock.com.

"This is the part of privatisation I don't like."

Also, the reasoning goes, the resulting freedom and savings encourage managers to make investments into the innovations that then lead to economic growth.

Property Rights Protection   Protection of property rights means that entrepreneurs who come up with an innovation can legally claim the present and future rewards of their idea, effort, and risk. This protection also supports a competitive economic environment by assuring investors and entrepreneurs that they, not the state, will prosper from their hard work. If this protection is lacking or rarely applied, as in the case of a legal system anchored in the principles of the rule of man, companies face a high risk of contract or property rights violations.

Fiscal and Monetary Reform   Economic decision making by political officials often leads governments to adopt tax or spending polices that slow growth and increase interest rates, inflation, and unemployment. Adopting free-market principles requires a government to rely on market-oriented instruments for macroeconomic stabilization, set strict budget limits, and use market-based policies to manage the money supply. Often, these measures create temporary economic hardships. For instance, using the market to enforce fiscal and monetary discipline leads to economic environments that, in turn, attract the investors, companies, and capital needed to start and finance growth.

Antitrust Legislation   Markets can create situations in which a single seller or producer supplies a good or service. When one company is able to control a product's supply and, therefore, its price, it is considered a monopoly. The anticompetitive practices of monopolies are antithetical to a free market. Consequently, liberalizing an economic system requires a government to legislate antitrust laws that encourage the development of industries with as many competing businesses as the market will sustain. In such industries, prices are kept low by the forces of competition. By enforcing antitrust laws, governments can prevent monopolies from exploiting consumers and restraining market growth.

LOOKING TO THE FUTURE

Is There a Move to Push Back Economic Freedom?

The 2007 Economic Freedom Index reported that the freedom scores of 65 countries increased from 2005 to 2006, but the scores of 92 countries decreased. Just as the apparent pushback against democracy discussed in Chapter 3 has provoked debate, some wonder whether there may be an analogous push back against economic freedom.

Unquestionably the success stories of countries that have migrated from command and mixed economies to market economies are impressive. For instance, China's transition has generated great economic success. It has been the fastest growing economy over the past 30 years and, in the process, is managing the swiftest, most extensive rise out of poverty any nation has ever seen. Other countries, such as Ireland, Brazil, and India, have also seen free-market reforms translate into greater wealth and higher standards of living.

On the basis of these success stories, one would think all countries would aspire to do the same. In actuality, some individuals, officials, and policymakers question the ultimate benefit of moving from a mixed or command economy toward a market economy. Few expect an easy transition process. Several countries aiming to transition toward a market economy have run into difficulties. These hardships have pushed them to ratchet down their economic forecasts as well as deal with growing political and social unrest. Consequently, some now question whether a market economy is truly the best bet for future prosperity.

Critics of freer markets believe a market economy cannot protect social values and skews income distribution. They add that a market economy also encourages the accumulation of vast wealth and powerful self-interests that threaten social liberties and political rights. Hence, they argue, the costs of a market economy, when fully measured, greatly exceed the benefits provided by a strong, active government in a mixed economy.

For example, the French government has sold more than $30 billion worth of state-owned enterprises to private investors. These sales have proven politically unpopular and competitively questionable. Surveys find that the French electorate continues to endorse state-led economic programs as well as extensive social welfare programs. One poll, for instance, reported that 66 percent of French citizens preferred France's combination of rich benefits and high unemployment to the option of low jobless rates and a smaller social safety net found in market economies like the United States and Hong Kong. Ernest-Antoine Seillière, president of the French conglomerate CGIP, states, "Here, social security and social solidarity weigh more than efficiency."[49]

Furthermore, the proper role for government in a market economy remains controversial. Certainly, most advocates of a market economy believe that government has a legitimate role in defining and enforcing the rules of the market. More contentious is the question of how strong a role the government should have in both guiding the economy and addressing the inequalities the market produces.

For example, there is no universal agreement on issues such as protectionist tariffs, federal control of interest rates, and welfare programs. In addition, the less involved government becomes in the economic environment, the greater the need to try to establish market institutions, such as central banks and stock markets, to stabilize macroeconomic conditions. Countries in transition must deal with other issues, such as environmental damage and the development of human capital. Dealing with these complicated issues calls for more government involvement in the economic affairs of the state, not less, goes the reasoning.

Slowing, if not stopping, the transition from a command to market economy is the challenge of privatization. Selling state assets, critics argue, is a political as well as an economic process. They point out that political objectives do not always result in the best economic results. Many state-owned enterprises, such as Pemex, the state-owned oil company in Mexico, are seen as the crown jewels of a country. Countries struggle with the dismal prospect of selling them to private investors, especially foreign buyers, to continue privatizing the economy.

Complicating matters are various political impediments, such as the typically uncooperative attitudes of existing managers and employees of state-owned enterprises.[50] In Bolivia, Peru, Venezuela, and Ecuador, there has been growing backlash against free-market changes—largely fueled by the locals' sense that they were promised more benefits than were eventually delivered by foreign companies. Instead of higher-quality products at lower prices, they are offered overpriced, often inconsistent services from the now-private companies. The ensuing social turmoil has made their governments reverse privatization and nationalize companies.[51]

Finally, some raise the suggestion that a mixed economy does not necessarily condemn a country to poor economic performance that can then only be fixed by disengaging the state and dismantling social welfare programs. Rather, they advocate fine-tuning the government's economic role and modernizing social welfare institutions to meet the competitive standards of the global marketplace. Austria, the Netherlands, and Sweden are taking this route. In the Netherlands, for example, labor unions and the government agreed on wage restraints, shorter working hours, budget discipline, and the trimming of social benefits. As a result, Dutch unemployment is about half that in neighboring countries and the country enjoys macroeconomic stability.

Looking at just a few examples highlights the multifaceted challenge of economic transition around the world. Some countries, like those in Central and Eastern Europe and Russia, are simultaneously undergoing political and economic reforms that call for many new economic freedoms. Others, such as Cuba, Vietnam, and China, focus on economic transition but are emphatically uninterested in commensurate political change. Some, such as Poland, Hungary, and the Czech Republic, are liberalizing their economies at a rapid rate while trying to maintain some sense of political and social stability.

So, although free markets appear to provide a compelling ideal, marketplace trends are far from set. Countries in transition must figure out how to maintain political and macroeconomic stability, boost economic growth, improve legal and institutional policies, and resolve a host of social issues, such as health care, security, poverty, and child welfare. If successful, a reasonable projection is the spread of economic and political freedom around the world. If not, then we may likely see growing demands to return to greater state ownership and control of the economic environment. ■

CASE

Meet the BRICs

The opening case for this chapter highlighted the accelerating success of emerging economies.[52] The focus of attention is now squarely on the vanguard of emerging economies, the so-called BRICs: Brazil, Russia, India, and China. The BRIC countries, although much larger in scale and scope than other emerging markets, symbolically represent trends that are developing throughout the world. Many presume that where the BRICs go, others will follow. As we look at the emergence of the BRICs, we discuss the implications for the economic environment as well as individual company activity. Then, to close, we'll see what threats to the BRICs might make them crumble.

At current trends and with reasonable projections, over the next few decades Brazil, Russia, India, and China will become a larger, more powerful force in the world economy. By 2050, the BRICs will eclipse most of the current richest countries of the world, will encompass over 40 percent of the world's population, and hold a combined PPP-adjusted GDP of nearly $15 trillion. Consequently, the rankings of national economies will change dramatically (see Figure 4.8).

In terms of specifics, China and India will be the dominant global suppliers of manufactured goods and services, respectively, while Brazil and Russia will become the principal suppliers of raw materials. Collectively, on almost every scale, they will become the largest entity on the global stage.

The unfolding influence of the BRICs as engines of new growth and spending power leads some to argue that these transitions may happen even sooner, especially given the

FIGURE 4.8   The Largest Economies in the World: 2050

Current projections see the national economic order of the world changing dramatically over the next few generations. By midcentury China will likely claim the top rank, followed by the United States and India.

Source: Dominic Wilson and Roopa Purushothaman, "Global Economics Paper No. 99: Dreaming with BRICs: The Path to 2050" (Goldman Sachs, 2005), at www.gs.com (accessed October 15, 2007).

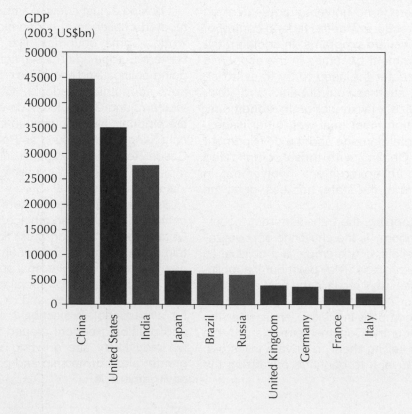

GDP
(2003 US$bn)

aging working populations and falling productivity rates in richer nations. Experts forecast that the most dramatic transition will take place over the next 20 to 30 years.

By 2016, China's economy will be larger than those of Japan, the United Kingdom, Germany, France, Italy, and Canada, with an eye to passing the United States as the world's largest economy soon thereafter. India's economy will pass Japan's by 2030, making it the third largest in the world. Of the premier economic powers of the twentieth century, only the United States and Japan will be among the largest economies in 2050.

This trend has also shaped relationships between parties. India and China, the world's two most populous countries, agreed to form a strategic partnership to end a border dispute and boost trade in a deal marking a major shift in relations between the Asian giants. The agreement, signed by the premiers of both countries, eases decades of mutual distrust between the nations as a result of a war in 1962. "India and China can together reshape the world order," Indian prime minister Manmohan Singh proclaimed at a ceremony for his Chinese counterpart, Premier Wen Jiabao, at India's presidential palace.

Similarly, bilateral Sino-Russian trade was $33 billion in 2006, up from $20 billion in 2005, and it is expected to reach $70 billion by 2010. China is Russia's fourth-largest trading partner; Russia is China's eighth. They are the leading members of the Shanghai Cooperation Council, one of the most influential economic centers in the world. Indications show a strengthening of ties between these nations. In many people's eyes, Russia, by rolling back democracy and reviving its imperialist past, is more politically aligned with the one-party state of China.

As of early 2008, no text was made public of any formal agreement to which all four BRIC nations are signatories. Still, change was afoot. BRIC leaders knew that a multilateral alliance would amplify their political, legal, economic, and strategic influence. Spearheading these efforts was President Putin of Russia with his goal to build "a new world economic architecture" that would reflect the rising power of emerging economies and the decline of the old heavyweights of the United States, Japan, and many European countries.

At a recent G8 summit, a forum for leading market economies, Putin condemned existing global organizations as archaic and undemocratic. "The world is changing before our very eyes," he said. "Countries that seemed hopelessly backward only yesterday are becoming the world's fastest-growing economies today." Emerging economies, led by the BRICs, no longer wanted simply to be part of the world's outdated architecture—instead, they wanted to go forward into a brave new world largely unencumbered by the past.

The diffusion of commodities, work, technology, and companies outward from the United States and fellow rich countries has changed the game of globalization. Furthermore, improving sophistication of information technology enables reorganizing production across borders, thereby opening up new production frontiers for previously nontradable services. The steadily shrinking role of the prominent economies of the twentieth century will trigger fundamental shifts in firm strategy, consumption, and investments.

Regarding firm strategy, companies from richer countries are scrambling to reorient their operations to the BRICs. For many, there seems to be a tentative consensus that just being there, no matter the shape or form of investment, is more crucial than the product the company actually offers. Others are further along in their reorientation, some motivated by the opportunity, many motivated by the realization that "companies that don't take a vigorous approach to China and India will face threats to their very existence in coming years."

For example, GM is going great guns in China even though it is struggling in the United States. In 2005, its sales rose 35.2 percent to a record 665,390 vehicles and by 2007, it was the biggest carmaker in China. Russia is McDonald's fastest growing market. Although McDonald's had only 128 outlets in Russia by 2005, it plans to add hundreds more in the next few years. Similarly, Wal-Mart and Bharti Enterprises, a leading Indian cell phone operator, plan to open hundreds of Wal-Mart superstores across India by 2010.

Other tales amplify the strategic significance of the BRICs. Cisco Systems has decided that 20 percent of its top talent should be in India within five years. In 2007, it moved one of its highest-ranking executives to Bangalore with the title of chief globalization officer. More dramatically, IBM is slowly making India the company's center of gravity. From a local labor force of 9,000 in 2003, IBM now employs 73,000 in India—meaning that almost one in five IBM workers now is in India. Having invested US$2 billion in its Indian operation from 2003 through 2006, IBM announced it would invest an additional $6 billion by 2008. Symbolizing the growing primacy of its Indian operations is IBM's historic decision to hold its annual Investors Day in 2007 on the grounds of the Bangalore Palace; this event had never before been held outside of the United States. But this change made perfect sense given that "India is at the epicenter of the flat world," explained Michael J. Cannon-Brookes, vice president for business development in India and China at IBM.

In terms of consumption, the BRICs are on the verge of rapid growth in consumer products. Economic analyses advise companies to start capitalizing on this coming wave of consumption given that consumer demand takes off when GNI per capita income is between $3,000 and $10,000.

The first economy to hit those levels was Russia. China, India, and Brazil are steadily heading there. China and India, in particular, have rapidly growing middle classes whose demand aspirations are changing quickly. Analysts predict the middle class will expand from 50 million to 583 million people by 2025. More immediately, between 2005 and 2015, over 800 million people in the BRICs will cross the annual income threshold of $3,000. At this point people move from consuming necessities to consuming higher-priced branded goods.

By 2025, approximately 200 million people in these economies will have annual incomes above $15,000. For example, there are only 2 cars for every 100 people in China, as opposed to 50 cars per 100 Americans. By 2040, China's car ownership will likely rise to 29 cars per 100 people. The total number of cars in China and India combined could rise from around 30 million today to 750 million by 2040, more than all the cars on the world's roads today. Even then, however, car ownership rates in those two countries will be half those in the United States today.

Notwithstanding the spectacular economic performance and potential of the BRICs, there is some skepticism. In principle, observers note the endemic problem of "recency bias," which is the dubious expectation that the current trend will continue into the future. Repeatedly, companies, executives, investors, and officials extrapolating the present into the future have made mistakes.

There are also several practical threats. Despite high-octane economic growth, the BRICs face futures of widespread poverty and distorted income distributions. By 2025, the income per capita in today's richer countries will exceed $35,000 for more than a billion people. In contrast, only about 24 million people out of the nearly 3 billion folks in the BRIC economies will hit that threshold.

Long term, income per capita in the United States is projected to reach $80,000 by 2050 while China will likely be just over $31,000, Brazil about $26,600, and India just $17,400. With the possible exception of Russia, hundreds of millions of people in the BRICs will be far poorer on average than individuals in Germany, France, Japan, Italy, Canada, and the United States. Consequently, for the first time in history the largest economies in the world will no longer be the richest when measured by GNI per capita.

Inevitably, many ask if the BRICs could turn into bricks in their march to miracle economies. Unquestionably, governments in each country have developed economically sensible policies, opened trade and domestic markets, and begun building institutions that support free markets. Still, there is more than a passing chance that conditions in one economy, if not all, will fall out of sync for the simple fact that the transition from command-controlled economies to freer markets rests on a difficult set of accomplishments. Basically four instrumental conditions must occur, more or less concurrently, for a market economy to grow consistently:

1. Sound macroeconomic policies and a solid macroeconomic background, as seen in low inflation, prudent public finances, and supportive government policy
2. Strong political institutions that endorse transparency, fairness, and the rule of law
3. Openness to trade, capital flows, and foreign direct investment
4. High levels of education at both the primary and secondary levels

The failure to achieve these standards jeopardizes current economic performance and long-term growth potential.

In addition, political uncertainties and social assumptions in each country limit their economic potential. Brazil's economic potential has been anticipated for decades, but it has struggled to achieve expectations due to problems in income equality, productivity, and education. Likewise, the population count of Russia is declining, and the country's uncertain government, environmental degradation, and crumbling infrastructure confound growth projections. India, in addition to other pressing economic and political challenges, has many poor people. China's particular interpretation of the rule of law, rights of citizens, environmental sustainability, and principles of democracy poses problems. Too, China faces a closing window of opportunity; by 2020 China will have the largest number of both old and very old people on earth.

Finally, so-called green constraints shadow the bright futures of all. The emergence of the BRICs will challenge the well-being and sustainability of the global environment. Global warming, diminishing raw materials, and escalating pollution suggest there is a finite limit to how much the BRICs can develop before exceeding the capacity of the global economy to supply them and of the environment to support them. More worrisome is the Worldwatch Institute report that if China and India, to say nothing about Russia and Brazil, were to consume resources and produce pollution at the current U.S. per capita level, it would require two planet Earths just to sustain their two economies.

In summary, the emergence of the BRICs suggests that the next generation of economic development of the global economy will be a fascinating yet bumpy ride. No matter what, coming anywhere close to reaching their apparent potential will redefine the structure of economic environments, patterns of growth, and dynamics of economic activity worldwide. ∎

QUESTIONS

1. Map the proposed sequence of evolution of the economy of the BRICs. What indicators might companies monitor to guide their investments and organize their local market operations?
2. What are the implications of the emergence of the BRICs for careers and companies in your country?
3. Do you think recency bias has led to overestimating the potential of the BRICs? How would you, as a manager for a company assessing these markets, try to control this bias?
4. How might managers interpret the potential for their product in a market that is, in absolute economic terms, large but, on a per capita basis, characterized by a majority of poor to very poor consumers?
5. In the event that one BRIC country, if not all, fails to meet its projected performance, what would be some of the implications for the economic environment of international business?
6. Compare and contrast the merits of GNI per capita versus the idea of purchasing power parity, human development, and green economics as indicators of economic potential in Brazil, Russia, China, and India.

SUMMARY

- The economic environment of a country plays a significant role in establishing its attractiveness to foreign investors.

- Managers assess economic environments and forecast market trends in the effort to make better investment choices, operating decisions, and competitive strategies.

- Understanding the economic environments of foreign companies and markets can help managers predict how trends and events in those environments might affect their company's future performance.

- Economic analysis looks at several indicators of an economic environment with emphasis given to how local conditions require adjusting analysis and interpretation.

- Managers recognize that the power of economic analysis is a function of identifying the best possible indicators and then understanding how they work in isolation and interactively.

- Important economic dimensions are GNI, GNI per capita, purchasing power parity (PPP), growth rate, distribution of income, and degree of human development.

- The benefits of doing business in a country are directly influenced by the size of the market (GNI or PPP), the present wealth (either GNI or PPP per capita) of consumers, and the likely future wealth of consumers (in terms of income distribution and human development).

- Gross national product is a broad measure of national income that is the market value of final goods and services produced by domestically owned factors of production. Per capita GNP is used to rank countries in terms of their individual wealth.

- The wide range in the cost of living worldwide spurs managers to pinpoint the true purchasing power of a nation. A country with low GNI per capita may, when considered in terms of PPP, have a vibrant economy.

- Balance of payments is a record of a country's international transactions. Key elements are (1) current account—trade in goods and services and income from assets abroad, (2) capital account—transactions in real or financial assets between countries, such as the sale of real estate to a foreign investor, and (3) merchandise trade balance—the net balance of exports minus imports of merchandise.

- Managers refine their sense of economic performance and potential by evaluating the state of inflation, unemployment, poverty, debt, and balance of payments.

- Economic freedom is the degree to which governments intervene in the economic environment. Free countries tend to have higher economic growth, higher standards of living, and greater macroeconomic stability than do less free or repressed countries.

- The type of economic system is a strong predictor of a country's present economic performance and future economic prospects.

- The economic system determines who owns and controls factors of production and, by extension, the price and quantity of goods and services.

- In a pure market economy, the goods and services that a country produces, and the quantity in which they are produced, are not planned by anyone. Rather, price and quantity are determined by the invisible hand of supply and demand.

- In a pure command economy, the government plans what goods and services a country produces, the quantity in which they are produced, and the price at which they are sold.

- A mixed economy includes some elements of a market and command economy. Market forces as well as the government play a significant role in directing the investment activities of private enterprise and consumption activities of individuals.

- The transition to a market economy takes place when command and mixed economies liberalize their economic policies and transfer more ownership and control of the economy to market forces.

KEY TERMS

balance of payments (BOP) (p. 160)	Economic Freedom Index (p. 167)	inflation (p. 154)
capital account (p. 161)	economic system (p. 164)	market economy (p. 165)
capitalism (p. 164)	green economics (p. 153)	merchandise trade (p. 161)
command economy (p. 166)	gross domestic product	mixed economy (p. 166)
communism (p. 164)	(GDP) (p. 145)	privatization (p. 173)
Consumer Price Index (CPI) (p. 155)	gross national income (GNI) (p. 145)	poverty (p. 158)
current account (p. 161)	Human Development Index	purchasing power parity
economic freedom (p. 167)	(HDI) (p. 151)	(PPP) (p. 148)

ENDNOTES

1 *Sources include the following:* Thomas Friedman, "The World Is Flat: A Brief History of the Twenty-first Century," Farrar, Straus, and Giroux, 2005. Clyde Prestowitz, "Three Billion New Capitalists," video transcript, *News Hour*, August 15, 2005, at www.pbs.org/newshour/bb/economy/july-dec05/prestowitz_8–15.html; Steven Greenhouse and David Leonhardt, "Real Wages Fail to Match a Rise in Productivity," *New York Times*, August 28, 2006; David Autor, Lawrence Katz, and Melissa Kearney, "The Polarisation of the U.S. Labour Market," *NBER Working Paper No. 11986*, January 2006; Autor, Katz, and Kearney, "Trends in U.S. Wage Inequality: Re-Assessing the Revisionists," *NBER Working Paper No. 11627*, September 2005; Kenneth Rogoff, "Betting with the House's Money," *Project Syndicate*, at www.project-syndicate.org/commentary/rogoff27 (accessed May 7, 2007); Anne O. Krueger, "Stability, Growth, and Prosperity: The Global Economy and the IMF," at www.imf.org/external/np/speeches/2006/060706.htm (accessed June 7, 2006); Nick Beams, "Global Interest Rate 'Conundrum' Recalls the 1930s," *WSWS*, at www.wsws.org/articles/2005/jun2005/bond-j14.shtml (accessed June 14, 2005); Floyd Norris, "Maybe Developing Nations Are Not Emerging But Have Emerged," *New York Times*, December 30, 2006; Angus Maddison, *The World Economy, 1–2030 AD* (London: Oxford University Press, 2007); *The World Economy: Volume 1: A Millennial Perspective* (Paris: Development Centre, 2001); *Volume 2: Historical Statistics* (Paris: Development Centre, 2003).

2 *Hewlett-Packard Annual Report 2001* (2002), at www.hp.com/hpinfo/investor/financials/annual/2001/text_only_10k.pdf, 2001.

3 The World Bank Group, at www.worldbank.org/data/databytopic/class.htm. See also "How Many Countries Are in the World?" at http://geography.about.com/cs/countries/a/numbercountries.htm.

4 Andrew B. Abel and Ben S. Bernanke, *Macroeconomics* (Reading, MA: Addison-Wesley, 1992), p. 30.

5 Abel and Bernanke, *Macroeconomics*, pp. 32–33. Historically, GNI was commonly referred to as gross national product. The definition and measurement of GNI and GNP are identical, but institutions such as the World Bank, the International Monetary Fund, and the Central Intelligence Agency now use the term GNI.

6 The World Bank, using its Atlas method, divides national economies according to 2003 GNI per capita. The groups are low income, $765 or less; lower-middle income, $766 to $3,035; upper-middle income, $3,036 to $9,385; and high income, $9,386 or more. For the record, the World Bank explains the Atlas method as follows:

   In calculating gross national income (GNI—formerly referred to as GNP) and GNI per capita in U.S. dollars for certain operational purposes, the World Bank uses the Atlas conversion factor. The purpose of the Atlas conversion factor is to reduce the impact of exchange rate fluctuations in the cross-country comparison of national incomes. The Atlas conversion factor for any year is the average of a country's exchange rate (or alternative conversion factor) for that year and its exchange rates for the two preceding years, adjusted for the difference between the rate of inflation in the country, and through 2000, that in the G-5 countries (France, Germany, Japan, the United Kingdom, and the United States). For 2001 onwards, these countries include the Euro Zone, Japan, the United Kingdom, and the United States. A country's inflation rate is measured by the change in its GDP deflator.
   (For more information, go to www.worldbank.org/data/aboutdata/working-meth.html.)

7 World Bank, *2003 Survey* (Atlas methodology for GNI per capita). Typically, the prices of many goods are considered and weighted according to their importance in the economy of the particular country.

8 Statement by Dr. Mahbub ul Haq, Pakistani, economist and key founder, with Dr. Amartya Sen, of the theory of human development.

9 The index was developed in 1990 by Pakistani economist Mahbub ul Haq and has been used since 1993 by the United Nations Development Programme in its annual report. The HDI is comparable over time when it is calculated based on the same methodology and comparable trend data. HDR 2003 presents a time series in HDI for 1975, 1980, 1985, 1990, 1995, and 2001. This time series uses the latest HDI methodology and the most up-to-date trend data for each component of the index.

10 The gender-related development index (GDI) is a composite indicator that measures the average achievement of a population in the same dimensions as the HDI while adjusting for gender inequalities in the level of achievement in the three basic aspects of human development. It uses the same variables as the HDI, disaggregated by gender. The gender empowerment measure (GEM) is a composite indicator that captures gender inequality in three key areas:

   • *Political participation and decision making,* as measured by women's and men's percentage-shares of parliamentary seats

   • *Economic participation and decision-making power,* as measured by two indicators: women's and men's percentage-shares of positions as legislators, senior officials, and managers; and women's and men's percentage-shares of professional and technical positions

   • *Power over economic resources,* as measured by women's and men's estimated earned income (PPP in U.S. dollars)

11 *Process of Preparation of the Environmental Perspective to the Year 2000 and Beyond.* General Assembly Resolution 38/161, December 19, 1983, at www.un.org/documents/ga/res/38/a38r161htm (accessed: May 27, 2007).

12 Joseph Stiglitz, "Good Numbers Gone Bad: Why Relying on GDP as a Leading Economic Gauge Can Lead to Poor Decision-Making," *Fortune,* September 25, 2006.

13 Murray N. Rothbard, "Ludwig von Mises (1881–1973)," at www.mises.org/content/mises.asp (accessed May 27, 2007).

14 Economists use different types of indexes to measure inflation, but the one they use the most is the *Consumer Price Index (CPI).* The CPI measures a fixed basket of goods and compares its price from one period to the next. A rise in the index indicates inflation.

15 Michael Wines, "How Bad Is Inflation in Zimbabwe?" *New York Times,* May 2, 2006.

16 For instance, as of 2003, only three countries had annual inflation rates in excess of 40 percent, the level above which it is generally considered to be acutely damaging. All major industrial countries had inflation under 3 percent (and in Japan, deflation persisted). Moreover, inflation in many middle- and lower-income countries, once stuck with extreme inflation pressure, had fallen well into single digits in the early twenty-first century. Many credited the fall in inflation to a combination of the price pressures of globalization along with more vigilant central bankers and economic policymakers. See Kenneth Rogoff, "The IMF Strikes Back," *Foreign Policy* (January/February 2003): 39–48.

17 "Working Age Population to Hit 940m by 2020," *Xinhua* [China], April 26, 2004.

18 Keith Bradsher, "A Younger India Is Flexing Its Industrial Brawn," *New York Times,* September 1, 2006.

19 See Constance Sorrentino, "International Unemployment Rates: How Comparable Are They?" *Monthly Labor Review* (June 2000), at www.bls.gov/opub/mlr/2000/06/art1exc.htm.

20 See U.S. National Debt Clock, at www.brillig.com/debt_clock.

21 "Debt Relief Under the Heavily Indebted Poor Countries (HIPC) Initiative," *International Monetary Fund,* at www.imf.org/external/np/exr/facts/hipc.htm.

22 See "Gap Between Rich and Poor: World Income Inequality," at www.infoplease.com/ipa/A0908770.html.

23 Zhao Huanxin, "Closing Farm-Urban Income Gap 'Top' Goal," *China Daily,* February 1, 2005: 1.

24 "Chinese Scholars Warn Growing Wealth Gap Likely to Trigger Social Instability," Associated Press, July 8, 2005.

25 "Transcript, Chapter 18, Episode Three: The New Rules of the Game," *Commanding Heights: The Battle for the World Economy,* at www.pbs.org/wgbh/commandingheights/lo/index.html.

26 "Impossible Architecture," *Social Watch Report 2006,* at www.socialwatch.org/en/portada.htm (accessed May 27, 2007).

27 The Food and Agriculture Organization (FAO) of the United Nations (UN) translates the food commodities available for human consumption in a country into their protein equivalent. This measure compensates for differences in protein supplied by different foods across countries. (Go to www.fao.org.)

28 Donald McNeil Jr., "Design That Solves Problems for the World's Poor," *New York Times,* May 29, 2007.

29 Paul Krugman, "Divided over Trade," *New York Times,* May 14, 2007.

30 Calculated at the exchange rate of 7.65 yuan to the dollar, as of June 12, 2007.

31 Bradsher, Keith, "Chinese Auto Parts Enter the Global Market," *New York Times,* June 7, 2007.

32 Productivity growth has two components: a long-term trend (set by the quality of the workforce, the pace of capital investment, and the speed of innovation) and more volatile short-term fluctuations driven by the business cycle. Early in an expansion, for instance, productivity takes off temporarily as firms squeeze their existing staff harder before hiring new workers. As an economy slows, it decelerates givens firms' reluctance to fire workers immediately.

33 "U.S. Labor Productivity Growth in 2006 Was the Lowest in More Than a Decade," *Conference Board,* January 23, 2007; "Making Less with More," *The Economist,* April 12, 2007.

34 "World Economic Outlook: Spillovers and Cycles in the Global Economy," *International Monetary Fund,* April 2007, at www.imf.org/external/pubs/ft/weo/2007/01.

35 Go to www.cia.gov/library/publications/the-world-factbook/rankorder/2187rank.html.

36 "U.S. Trade Deficit Rises to Six-Month High," *MSNBC,* May 10, 2007.

37 Eduardo Porter and Mark Landler, "Trade Deficit Stubbornly Defies the Dollar's Slide," *New York Times,* January 20, 2007.

38 Reported in Elizabeth Becker, "U.S. Trade Deficit Hit Highest Figure Ever in November," *New York Times,* January 12, 2005.

39 Becker, "U.S. Trade Deficit Hits $58.3 Billion as Chinese Imports Surge," *New York Times,* March 11, 2005.

40 "U.S. Trade Deficit Soars to All-Time High," *Forbes,* January 12, 2005, quoting Joel Naroff.

41 Reported in "US Trade Deficit Soars," *Australian Times,* January 13, 2005.

42 "U.S. Trade Gap Widened to Record $60.3 Billion in Nov," *Bloomberg,* January 12, 2005, quoting Cathy Minehan.

43 Bo Nielsen, "Weak Dollar? Currency, at 10-Year Low, May Fall More," at *Bloomberg.com* (accessed May 13, 2007).

44 David Leonhardt, "Gambling against the Dollar," *New York Times,* November 1, 2006.

45 Some experts suggest characterizing the United States and a number of other similar countries as *established market economies (EMEs),* the term referring both to their high levels of per capita income and to the well-developed and relatively stable nature of those institutions that support the efficient operation of sophisticated markets.

46 Companies in centrally planned economies exhibited a particular quirk. The absence of competition and bankruptcy in this sort of economic system meant that once an enterprise was up and running, it survived indefinitely, irrespective of performance.

47 Michael P. Todaro, *Economic Development,* 6th ed. (Reading, MA: Addison Wesley, 1996), p. 705.

48 William W. Beach and Marc A. Miles, "Explaining the Factors of the Index of Economic Freedom," *2005 Index of Economic Freedom,* at www.heritage.org/research/features/index.

49 Frank Vanden Broucke, "The EU and Social Protection: What Should the European Convention Propose?" The Foreign Policy Centre, at http://fpc.org.uk/articles/175.

50 International Finance Corporation, *Privatization Principles and Practice* (Washington, DC: Author, 1995).

51 Juan Forero, "Latin America Fails to Deliver on Basic Needs," *New York Times,* February 22, 2005.

52 *Sources include the following:* Dominic Wilson and Roopa Purushothaman, "Global Economics Paper No. 99: Dreaming with BRICs: The Path to 2050," Goldman Sachs, at www.gs.com/insight/research/ reports/report6.html; "Bric by Bric—How the World Will Change," at www.rediff.com/money/2003/ oct/16guest1.htm; "The BRICs Are Coming—Fast," *Business Week,* October 27, 2003; Pratap Ravindran, "Global Economy Will Be Built by BRICs," *The Hindu Business Line,* Wednesday, January 12, 2005, at www.thehindubusinessline.com/bline/2005/01/12/stories/2005011200310900.htm; James F. Hoge Jr., "A Global Power Shift in the Making—Is the United States Ready?" *Foreign Affairs* (July–August 2004): 2; Daniel Gross, "The U.S. Is Losing Market

Share. So What?" *New York Times,* January 28, 2007; Anand Giridharadas and Saritha Rai, "Wal-Mart to Open Hundreds of Stores in India," *New York Times,* November 27, 2006; Nirmala George, "India, China to Form Strategic Partnership," Associated Press, April 11, 2004; Andrew Kramer, "Putin Wants New Economic 'Architecture,' " *International Herald Tribune,* June 10, 2007; "Chilling Time," *The Economist,* June 14, 2007; Anil Gupta and Haiyan Wang, "How to Get China and India Right,"

Wall Street Journal, April 28, 2007: 4; Anand Giridharadas, "India's Edge Goes Beyond Outsourcing," *New York Times,* April 4, 2007; Stephen Roach, "Unstable, Unbalanced, Uncoordinated, and Unsustainable," *Morgan Stanley Global Economic Forum,* March 19, 2007; see www.morganstanley.com/views/gef/archive/2007/20070319-Mon.html; State of the World 2006: China and India Hold World in Balance, Worldwatch Institute; see/www.worldwatch.org.

5

Globalization and Society

Objectives

- To identify problems in evaluating the activities of multinational enterprises (MNEs)

- To evaluate the major economic effects of MNEs on home and host countries

- To understand the foundations of responsible corporate behavior in the international sphere

- To discuss some key issues in the social activities and consequences of globalized business

- To examine corporate responses to globalization

There is no shame in not knowing; the shame lies in not finding out.

—*Russian proverb*

CASE: Ecomagination and the Global Greening of GE

As noted in Map 5.1, a recent TV ad opens by inviting viewers to take up the perspective of a small green frog as it does a little globe hopping from one exotic location to another.[1] The frog, however, doesn't seem intent on hitting the usual tourist spots: He prefers stopovers at such places as a solar farm in South Korea, a water-purification plant in Kuwait, and a wind farm in Germany. To begin the second leg of his tour, he hops a GE90 Aircraft engine flying over China and, from there, takes viewers to a "clean" coal-powered facility somewhere in

"GREEN IS GREEN"

The ad is part of a major promotional campaign by General Electric Company (GE) for its Ecomagination Initiative. Announced in 2005 by CEO Jeffrey Immelt, Ecomagination is an ambitious strategy designed to demonstrate that an ecologically conscious conglomerate can cultivate the bottom line while doing its duty toward the global environment. Hence the campaign motto "Green Is Green."

MAP 5.1   Global Travels of GE's "Green Frog," Its Symbol of Commitment to the Environment

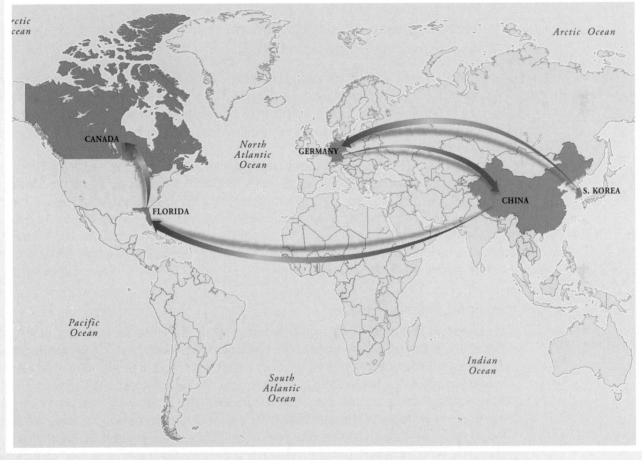

Florida. As he boards a GE Evolution locomotive in the Canadian Rockies, a voiceover explains the point of all this seemingly mundane sightseeing: "At GE, we're combining imagination with advanced technology around the world to make it a better place to live for everyone." Journey's end finds our frog in the lush—and very green—midst of a tropical rain forest.

Based in Fairfield, Connecticut, GE is the world's second-largest corporation (in terms of market capitalization) and operates in over 100 countries through six core businesses: commercial finance, consumer finance, industrial manufacturing, infrastructure, health care, and communications. It sells, among other things, appliances, aircraft engines, consumer electronics, energy-related products such as solar panels and wind generators, and locomotive engines and owns NBC Universal in its media division.

When the company announced its plan to launch an internal green revolution, GE surprised both investors and industrial customers who had long seen the firm as an ally in the struggle against environmental activists and lobbyists. But as more and more evidence piles up to support the claim that carbon dioxide emitted from human-made sources is heating up average global temperatures, GE has decided to take a more conciliatory stance, allying itself with a growing number of companies that regard investor and environmental interests as intrinsically interlocked rather than diametrically opposed.

Commitments and Goals

Its new initiative represents three basic commitments on the part of GE:

1. Reducing greenhouse emissions
2. Doubling investment in the research and development of "clean" technologies
3. Increasing revenues from those same technologies

GE now evaluates business-unit managers not only on profitability and return on capital but also on success in reducing emissions of carbon dioxide, the chief greenhouse gas (GHG) attributed to global warming. Energy-intensive divisions, such as those catering to the power and industrial sectors, are responsible for the largest cuts, but even the financial-services and communications units are required to reduce whatever emissions they produce.

The company's overall target is a 1 percent reduction from 2004 levels by 2012. At first glance, that goal doesn't seem overly ambitious, but that number represents a significant improvement if you take into account the fact that, given GE's projected growth, levels would otherwise soar to *40* percent above 2004 levels. Immelt has also committed the company to reducing the *intensity* of GHG emissions—its level of emissions in relation to the company's economic activity—30 percent by 2008 and to improving energy efficiency 30 percent by 2012. To ensure that these goals are met, Immelt has assembled a cross-business, cross-functional team to oversee planning and monitor progress.

A Little Consensus Seeking

In addition to instituting the internal changes necessary to curb GHG emissions, Immelt has taken a close look at GE's global political environment. He's traveled to Brussels and Tokyo to enlist the Belgian and Japanese governments in the global ecological discussion, and he's allied GE with other environmentally minded corporations to lobby American lawmakers on such matters as mandatory GHG reductions, essentially calling for regulations similar to those endorsed by the Kyoto Protocol, which calls for member countries to reduce emissions by 8 percent below 1990 levels by 2012. Working with the Environmental and Natural Resources Defense Council and the Pew Center on Global Climate Change, GE has also joined the likes of BP, DuPont, and Duke Energy to form the U.S. Climate Action Partnership, which seeks to help shape the international political debate over global warming.

Now, bear in mind that neither GE nor its corporate allies claim to be acting strictly from civic-minded motives: As usual—and as to be expected—they're pursuing their own best interests, particularly the idea that ecologically proactive firms are fashioning a strategic advantage over companies that are still dragging their feet. With other countries already enforcing limits stipulated by the Kyoto Protocol, and with other jurisdictions, such as the state of California, preparing to set their own limits, global corporations have much more to consider when it comes to developing forward-looking strategies and making long-term investments in an increasingly fragmented regulatory environment. With half of its markets located outside of the United States, GE is already under the jurisdiction of foreign governments that are more active than the United States in addressing environmental issues.

TECHNOLOGICAL TACTICS AND ECO-FRIENDLY PRODUCTS

Under Immelt's direction, GE is also gearing up to double R&D investment in clean technologies, including renewable-energy and water-purification processes and fuel-efficient products, from $700 million in 2005 to $1.5 billion in 2010. In turn, GE expects significant revenue growth. Its Ecomagination products earned $6 billion in 2004, $12 billion in 2006, and $14 billion in 2007. The company hopes to increase that total to $20 billion by 2010, and the way things are going, its projections appear to be on track.

Back in 2005, when the Ecomagination initiative was first launched, GE marketed only 17 products that met its own Ecomagination criteria; by 2007, there were 45 such products. It is interesting to see how GE positions its eco-friendly products on its corporate Web site. On its Ecomagination site, it discusses some of its products. It has developed auxiliary power units for trucks to help reduce gasoline burn when a truck is idling. It has also developed a new combustion system for gas turbines that reduces emissions, and a new diesel engine is being used on locomotives in Kazakhstan that generates the same horsepower using less fuel than its predecessor engines.

On its main corporate Web site, it also discusses how its other standard products, such as clothes washers, refrigerators, and lightbulbs, are energy efficient too. GE also intends to establish itself as an "energy-services" consultant and to bid on contracts for maintaining water-purification plants and wind farms—a venture that could be five times as lucrative as simply manufacturing the products needed for such projects.

"Solving Environmental Problems Is Good Business"

GE insists the markets for such products and services are both growing and profitable, and Immelt is convinced that taking advantage of them not only helps the environment but also strengthens GE's strategic position with major profit opportunities. As one GE executive puts it, "Solving environmental problems is good business . . . and constitutes a significant growth strategy for the company."

GE also regards its Ecomagination strategy as a necessary response to customer demand. Before embarking on this initiative, GE spent 18 months working with industrial customers, inviting managers to two-day "dreaming sessions" to imagine life in 2015 and to discuss the kinds of products they'd need in such an environment. The result? GE came out of the talks with the indelible impression that both its customers and the social and political environments in which it conducted business would be demanding more environmentally "clean" products.

Going on the Offensive

"This is not just GE jamming environment down their throats," admonished former GE vice chairman David Calhoun. "We decided that if this is what our customers want, let's stop putting our heads in the sand, dodging environmental interests, and go from defense to offense." In fact, many of GE's Asian and European competitors had already begun investing in cleaner technologies, and GE knew it couldn't risk falling behind. Currently, the company is focusing on burgeoning markets in such developing countries as China and India, where rapid economic growth has spurred the need for expanded infrastructures, such as water and sewage systems, and for means of curbing appallingly high levels of pollution. China alone, which is home to no fewer than 16 of the world's 20 most-polluted cities, has already earmarked $85 billion for environmental spending.

New Evolution™ locomotives, on order by Kazakhstan, reduce fuel consumption by 3 to 5 percent or roughly 189,000 fewer gallons of fuel in the engine's lifetime.

The products in GE's Ecomagination line run the gamut from long-lasting, energy-efficient Diamond Precise lightbulbs to the reduced-emissions, energy-efficient Evolution locomotive.

MIXED REACTIONS

Not surprisingly, GE has received its share of praise for its efforts to go green. It claimed the top spot on *Fortune* magazine's list of the "Most Admired Companies" for 2007, and it's earned a place on the Dow Jones Sustainability Index, which identifies the 300 firms that perform best according to combined environmental, social, and financial criteria.

At the same time, however, the company has generated a certain amount of skepticism. What happens, for example, if the markets that it's betting on don't materialize fast enough (or at all)? Back in the 1980s and 1990s, for instance, a number of firms, including DuPont and such British and French water companies as Suez, predicting double-digit growth in clean-technology markets, invested heavily in the area, only to be forced to scale back considerably when demand didn't take off as expected.

Another potential risk revolves around the participation of developing nations in the clean-technology push. In particular, will they be willing to pay prices that developed countries pay for the technology that reaches the market? Even GE's Calhoun admitted that, at least in the key Chinese market, margins were already tight. And GE is still faced with the challenge of implementing the internal changes entailed by its fledgling green strategy. Traditionally, GE's culture has become accustomed to strategies of incremental change in time-tested products and services. In fact, its highly touted Six Sigma program, championed by ex-CEO Jack Welch, inherently discourages radical deviation and unnecessary risk taking. Management may have its work cut out when it comes to persuading marketing, sales, and production teams that untested early-stage Ecomagination products are worth the risk.

Then, of course, there are clients and shareholders. Many of GE's customers work out of the utility sector, which has assumed a leadership role in disregarding warnings of climatic change and opposing eco-friendly regulation. In 2007, GE was presented with a shareowner resolution calling for top management to document the projected costs, benefits, and profits of the Ecomagination initiative. Investors seemed particularly concerned about the company's newfound activism and the potential of newly instituted greening initiatives to alienate industrial customers.

The question essentially comes down to whether GE's green strategy will bring about sufficient ecological and economic results to satisfy a worldwide constituency of customers, shareholders, governments, and societies.

Introduction

CONCEPT CHECK

A definition refresher: In Chapter 1, we define a **multinational enterprise (MNE)** as a company with a worldwide approach to markets and production or one with operations in more than one country. In the same chapter, we define **foreign direct investment (FDI)** as a form of investment that gives the investor a controlling interest in a foreign company.

As we learned in Chapter 1, there are three major criticisms of the globalization of business: the threat to sovereignty, the threat to growth, and the threat of increasing inequality. The MNE, whose greatest impact on host countries involves its strategies of foreign direct investment (FDI), is constantly confronted with questions issuing from this set of criticisms and must answer for the effects of its activities, both in the home and the host country.

Figure 5.1, which outlines the major relationships between global companies and both home and host countries, reminds us that government policies can either encourage or restrict FDI. In most respects, this ambiguity isn't hard to understand. Every country can use the money that comes with FDI, but many worry the global orientation of the MNE may render it insensitive to local interests and concerns.

Likewise, although not all MNEs are huge, many of them are indeed immense, and sheer size bothers a lot of countries. Let's face it: If you're a country doing business with an MNE whose sales exceed your GDP, you have a right to worry about potential imbalance in the relationship. And make no mistake about it: Colossal MNEs wield considerable power in negotiating business arrangements with small governments, and in bargaining over the terms under which they'll operate in a foreign jurisdiction, top MNE executives often expect to deal directly with heads of state.

Not surprisingly, then, various groups in the host country (as well as in the home country) frequently pressure governments to adopt policies that regulate the activities of

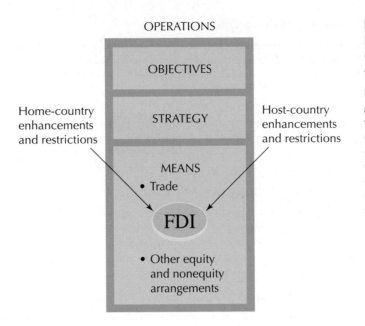

OPERATIONS

OBJECTIVES

Home-country
enhancements
and restrictions

STRATEGY

Host-country
enhancements
and restrictions

MEANS
• Trade

FDI

• Other equity
and nonequity
arrangements

FIGURE 5.1
Home- and Host-Country Influences on the Allocation of FDI

In both home and host countries, governmental policies can either foster or restrict the FDI policies of MNEs. In both countries, for example, a variety of groups work to regulate the impact of giant companies, which can exercise considerable power in negotiating the terms of FDI allocation.

MNEs. Growth in worldwide FDI makes it likely that such groups will monitor MNEs even more closely in the future.

In this chapter, we analyze the impact of FDI on both home and host countries and then examine a series of issues pertaining to the social responsibilities of MNEs whose strategies include penetrating foreign markets or sourcing merchandise from abroad.

Evaluating the Impact of FDI

Although some countries respond with suspicion to FDI and any potential strings with which it may come attached, other countries, such as Vietnam, have eagerly replaced obstacles with incentives. In the first four months of 2007, foreign companies invested $1.43 billion in Vietnam, with the government issuing licenses for 298 new projects valued at nearly $3 billion during the same period. The Southeast Asian country hopes to bring the total to $12 billion by the end of the year.

Likewise, both developing and industrialized countries have deregulated markets, privatized national enterprises, liberalized private ownership, and encouraged regional integration in an effort to create more favorable climates for foreign investment. FDI flows slowed in the aftermath of September 11, 2001, but they picked up again beginning in 2003. Although developed countries are still the major beneficiaries of worldwide FDI, many developing countries, notably China, now receive healthy doses. Recent trends in FDI include increased FDI inflows into services and natural resources, increased participation by firms from developing countries and countries in economic transition, a burgeoning number of cross-border mergers and acquisitions, and continued liberalization of government policies.[2]

The result, as you can see from Figure 5.2, is the emergence of FDI as a major contributor to global growth and development, spreading the benefits of capital, technology, management expertise, jobs, and wealth to just about every corner of the world. As we've already seen, however, FDI activities still attract controversy.[3] Many countries that have opened their markets to FDI have suffered economic and social disruption; others have seen how MNE investment can impede the progress of domestic companies.

On the other side of the coin, MNEs themselves have also run into problems. In particular, many major investments in overseas ventures have performed poorly. In an effort to optimize performance, companies often allocate resources among various countries, but allocations are often influenced by different governments' interpretations of the relative costs and benefits of FDI. For example, if a government feels an MNE exerts too

CONCEPT CHECK

In Chapter 4, we observe that a country's economic policies are among the leading indicators of its government's goals, its planned use of economic tools, and any projected market reforms; we also point out that, because changes in policy can strengthen a rival's competitiveness, companies need to monitor policy changes in countries where industry rivals do business.

Pressure groups push to restrict the activities of MNEs at home and abroad.

The effort to create favorable investment environments has led many countries to replace obstacles to FDI with incentives for FDI.

The growing prevalence of FDI requires a better understanding of the views of home and host countries.

FIGURE 5.2   What MNEs Have to Offer

Their sheer size means that many MNEs have vast stores of resources in several areas that can be applied to the pursuit of a host country's economic and social objectives. Critics, however, wonder if these assets are always adequately applied to the economic and social tasks at hand.

Source: Adapted from *World Investment Report 1992: Transnational Corporations: Engines of Growth: An Executive Summary* by Transnational Corporations and Management Division © 1992. United Nations. Reprinted with permission of the publisher.

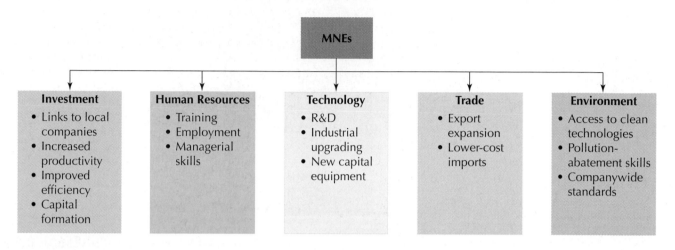

CONCEPT CHECK

Recall from Chapter 3 our admonition that, like any investment, **FDI** is subject to **political risk**—the risk that political decisions or events in a country may negatively affect an investor's profitability or sustainability.

---

much economic power in the country, it may decide the costs of that power exceed the benefits of receiving capital and technology, and it may place restrictions on the activities of the MNE. If that happens, the MNE may decide to allocate fewer resources in that particular country. Global businesspeople must be aware of these variations and, whenever possible, try to clarify them. Citizens, whether of the host or home country, need to press for government policies that will enhance the national interest.

CONSIDERING THE LOGIC OF FDI

Both sets of responsibilities require an understanding of why, under varying circumstances, countries may react to FDI in a spirit of opposition, suspicion, or cooperation. This effort means that we must examine the relationship between two factors:

- The decisions of those who make foreign investments (typically, MNEs)
- Their possible effects on the countries on the receiving end of FDI

To get a better understanding of the various ways in which this relationship can affect FDI activities, we look at three areas in which we can see it at work and in which we can assess its effects: *stakeholder trade-offs, cause-and-effect relationships,* and *individual and aggregate effects.* As you'll see, in each of these areas, we also encounter certain typical pitfalls in logic that we need to be aware of when we're trying to assess the outcomes of this relationship.

Companies must satisfy

- Shareholders.
- Employees.
- Customers.
- Society.

Stakeholder Trade-Offs   To prosper (indeed, to survive), a company must satisfy different groups of **stakeholders** including shareholders, employees, customers, suppliers, and society at large. Obviously, this juggling act is often quite tricky. In the short term, for example, group aims often conflict. *Stockholders* want additional sales and increased productivity (which result in higher profits and returns). *Employees* want safer workplaces and higher compensation. *Customers* want higher-quality products at lower prices. *Society* would like to see increased corporate taxes, more corporate support for social services, and more trustworthy behavior on the part of corporate executives.

In the *long* term, all of these aims must be adequately met. If they aren't, there's a good chance that none of them will, especially if each stakeholder group is powerful enough to bring operations to a standstill. In addition, as we've already suggested, pressure groups—which may reflect the interests of any stakeholder group—lobby governments to regulate MNE activities both at home and abroad.

As we noted in our opening case, for example, GE's Ecomagination initiative has generated pressure from various constituencies, including clients and shareholders concerned about profitability; various governments concerned with drafting regulations; employees concerned about changes in the company's strategies and goals; and environmental lobbyists, NGOs, and fellow businesses concerned with preserving the environment. Each of these groups has a powerful influence on how GE does business and on how successful it is in the marketplace.

Unfortunately, although a firm's management must take all of these competing interests into consideration, it must, *at any given period*, give them unequal attention. Under one set of circumstances, management may divert gains to consumers; under another, it may target shareholders. In short, the process entails *trade-offs*, but making trade-offs is difficult even in the home environment. Abroad, inadequate familiarity with customs or stakeholders themselves complicates the challenge of choosing the group that needs the most attention, particularly if dominant interests differ among the countries in which a firm does business.

The effects of an MNE's activities may be simultaneously positive for one national objective and negative for another.

It's also important to understand that for consumers to win, for example, it does not necessarily mean that shareholders must lose. That may be the case, but it is also possible for both customers and shareholders to win. If customers receive higher-quality products at a lower price, total sales may rise, leading to a possible rise in profits and, therefore, gains to shareholders.

FDI may result in a win-win, win-lose, or lose-lose situation for both countries involved.

The Question of Cause-and-Effect Relationships   Let's say that, when a decision has been made, two factors—for example, level of unemployment and level of FDI investment—are simultaneously affected, with the two effects reflecting an apparently predictable pattern—when one, for example, goes up, the other goes down. Can we conclude that they're interdependent? Not necessarily. A simultaneous increase in a nation's overall unemployment and its FDI doesn't mean that increased FDI *caused* increased unemployment. Nevertheless, opponents of FDI persist in trying to link MNE activities to such problems in recipient countries as inequitable income distribution, political corruption, environmental debasement, and social deprivation.[4]

In contrast, proponents of MNE activities tend to assume a (positive) link between those activities and such effects in recipient countries as higher tax revenues, increased levels of employment and exports, and greater innovation. As a rule, both sides are more active during periods in which a local government is considering proposals either to restrict or to encourage FDI. In many cases, both groups present accurate and convincing data in support of their claims, but we're still faced with a problem: Our input is always incomplete because we can never know what would have happened had an MNE made a different decision—had located elsewhere, for instance, or instituted different practices.

It is hard to determine whether the actions of MNEs cause societal conditions.

Individual and Aggregate Effects   MNEs, according to one astute observer, are like animals in a zoo: "Multinationals (and their affiliates) come in various shapes and sizes, perform distinctive functions, behave differently, and make their individual impacts on the environment."[5] Obviously, then, it doesn't make much sense to fall back on generalizations about the investment activities of MNEs and their effects on the nations in which they choose to invest.

Some countries evaluate MNEs and their activities on individual or case-by-case bases. Granted, this approach may foster greater fairness and tighter control, but it's time consuming and costly. Other nations, therefore, prefer to apply the same policies and control mechanisms to all MNEs, even though this approach risks missing some good opportunities while steering clear of dubious ones. Moreover, it's hard to choose between these two approaches because the governments that have applied one or the other have been far from perfect in predicting the future impact of FDI activities in their jurisdictions.

The philosophy, actions, and goals of each MNE are unique.

The Economic Impact of the MNE

FDI can be positive for the shareholder wealth of MNEs, especially in emerging economies undergoing market liberalization and structural reform.

MNEs may affect many facets of a country's economy—balance of payments, growth, employment objectives, and so forth. Under different conditions, these effects may be positive or negative, either for the host country or the home country. In addition, the same can be said for the impact of foreign investment on MNEs themselves. In one instance, for example, research showed that an announcement about the expansion of U.S. MNEs abroad resulted in significant positive changes in shareholder wealth, especially in the transition economies of Central and Eastern Europe and the former Soviet Union. In addition, returns to MNEs were highest when investments were made in countries with the best records on market liberalization and structural reform.

The effect of an individual FDI may be positive or negative.

Although our discussion centers more on the impact of foreign direct investment (and of certain other entry modes) on home and host countries, it's important to realize that such activity is also strategically important to MNEs themselves. In addition, potential gains to host countries go up as local environments become more attractive for FDI.

BALANCE-OF-PAYMENTS EFFECTS

CONCEPT CHECK

Recall that, in Chapter 4, we examine the **balance-of-payments effect** from the perspective of companies looking to invest in foreign countries. Ironically, because its own actions influence a host country's **balance of payments**, a firm doing business overseas is well advised to monitor that country's balance of payments, being particularly on the lookout for developments that could prompt a government to take actions intended to correct an imbalance.

Why do countries want capital inflows? Because such inflows give them the foreign exchange they need to import goods and services and to pay off foreign debt. Remember, however, that FDI brings both capital inflows and capital outflows. Many countries, therefore, are concerned about the net **balance-of-payments effect** and about the possibility that, when the books are ultimately balanced, the effect of their net balance of payments may be negative.

Effect of Individual FDI   To appreciate better why countries must evaluate the effect of each investment on their balance of payments, we can examine two extreme hypothetical scenarios reflecting the effects of FDI on a nation's balance of payments:

- *Scenario 1:*   Depositing funds in a Bermudan bank, a Mexican MNE makes an FDI when purchasing a Haitian-owned company. Because the MNE makes no changes in management, capitalization, or operations, profitability remains the same. Dividends, however, now go to the foreign owners rather than remaining in Haiti. There is thus a drain on Haiti's foreign exchange and a corresponding inflow to Mexico.

- *Scenario 2:*   A Mexican MNE purchases idle resources (land, labor, materials, equipment) in Haiti and converts them to the production of formerly imported goods. Rising consumer demand leads the MNE to reinvest its profits in Haiti, where the import substitution increases the host country's foreign-exchange reserves.

The formula to determine the balance-of-payments effect is simple, but the data used must be estimated and are subject to assumptions.

Most FDI falls somewhere between these two extreme examples. That's why they're hard to evaluate, particularly when policymakers try to apply regulations to all in-bound investments. There is, however, a basic equation for analyzing the effect of FDI on a host country's balance of payments:

$$B = (m - m_1) + (x - x_1) + (c - c_1)$$

where

B = balance-of-payments effect

m = import displacement

m_1 = import stimulus

x = export stimulus

x_1 = export reduction

c = capital inflow for other than import and export payment

c_1 = capital outflow for other than import and export payment

Calculating Net Import Effect   Now, even though the equation itself is pretty straight-forward, determining *the value for each variable* can be a challenge. Let's try our hand at it by evaluating the effect of the decision to locate a Toyota automobile plant in Brazil—an instance of FDI by a Japanese MNE. First, to calculate the *net import effect* $(m - m_1)$, we need to know *how much Brazil would import if the Toyota plant were not built*.

We must, of course, consider the amount that Toyota makes and sells in Brazil, but that would be only a rough indication of how much Brazil would import. Why? Because the selling price and product characteristics of the Brazilian-made cars may differ from those of the cars that Brazil would otherwise import from Japan. Moreover, sales of the Brazilian-made Toyota cars may come at the expense either of cars from other plants in Brazil or of imported foreign cars other than Toyotas. Note, too, that by definition, the value of m_1 should include the equipment, components, and materials brought by Toyota into Brazil. Remember, for example, that Toyota buys a lot of parts from suppliers that import them from other countries.

Finally, the value of m_1 should also include estimates of the increase in Brazilian imports due to increases in national income caused by the capital inflow from Japan. Assume, for instance, that, because of the Toyota investment, Brazilian national income rises R\$50 million (50 million reals). At this point, we have to consult the *marginal propensity to import principle*, which defines the fraction of a change in imports due to a change in income and states that the recipients of that income will spend some portion of it on imports. If we calculate this portion as 10 percent, imports should rise by R\$5 million (that is, 10 percent of R\$50 million).

The net export effect is the *export stimulus* minus the *export reduction* $(x - x_1)$, but bear in mind that this figure is particularly controversial. Why? Because different evaluators, starting out with different assumptions, regularly arrive at widely varying conclusions.

Let's go back to our Toyota example. In this case, we can make the assumption that the Brazilian plant merely substitutes for imports from and production in Japan. If in fact we proceed on this assumption, we get *no net export effect* for Brazil. For Japan, we arrive at a *negative net export effect* because of Toyota's export reduction (it's now selling cars made in Brazil to Brazilian consumers instead of exporting Japanese-made cars to Brazil). Toyota, however, might well defend itself on the grounds that its moves abroad are (largely) defensive. How so? Under this assumption, Toyota can argue it's capturing sales that would otherwise go to non-Japanese carmakers in Brazil. In that case, Toyota's export reduction from Japan amounts only to the *export replacement* (loss) resulting from the decision to build a production plant in Brazil.

In some cases, MNEs have argued that their overseas investments stimulate home-country exports of complementary products (say, in Toyota's case, auto parts) that they can sell in host countries through foreign-owned facilities. Again, to appreciate the amount of these exports, we must make assumptions about the amount that *could* have materialized had the overseas subsidiaries *not* been established.

Calculating Net Capital Flow   Net capital flow $(c - c_1)$ is the easiest figure to calculate because of controls maintained by most central banks. There are, however, a few sticking points. Basing your evaluation on a given year for evaluation is problematic because there's a time lag between a company's outward flow of investment funds and the inward flow of remitted earnings. Because companies eventually plan to take out more capital than they originally put in, what appears at a given time to be a favorable (or unfavorable) capital flow may prove, over a longer period, to be the opposite. The time it takes Toyota to recoup its capital outflow in Brazil depends on such factors as the need to reinvest funds in the host country, the ability to borrow locally, and estimates of future exchange rates.

As a rule, MNE investments are initially favorable to the host country and unfavorable to the home country. After some time, however, the situation usually reverses.[6] Why? Because nearly all foreign investors plan eventually to have their subsidiaries remit dividends back to the parent company in excess of the amount they sent abroad. If the net value of the FDI continues to grow through retained earnings, dividend payments for a given year may ultimately exceed the total amount of capital transfers comprising the initial investment.

On the import side, the balance-of-payments effect is positive if the FDI results in a substitution for imports and negative if it results in an increase in imports.

On the export side, the balance-of-payments effect is positive if the FDI results in generating exports in the host country and negative if it produces only for the local market and stops exports.

The balance-of-payments effects of FDI are usually

- Positive for the host country initially and negative for the home country.
- Positive for the home country and negative to the host country later.

GROWTH AND EMPLOYMENT EFFECTS

In contrast to balance-of-payments effects, MNE effects on growth and employment don't necessarily amount to *zero-sum games* (games in which gains must equal losses) between home and host countries. Classical economists assumed that production factors were always at full employment; consequently, any movement of any of these factors from home to abroad would result in an increase in foreign output abroad and a decrease in domestic output. Even if this assumption were realistic, it's still possible that gains in the host country will be greater or less than the losses in the home country.

The argument that both home and host countries may gain from FDI rests on two assumptions:

1. Resources aren't necessarily being fully employed.
2. Capital and technology can't easily be transferred from one industry to another.

Let's say, for example, that a soft-drink maker is producing at maximum capacity for the domestic market but is limited (say, by high transportation costs) in generating export sales. In addition, moving into other product lines or using its financial resources to increase domestic productivity aren't viable options.

But what about setting up a foreign production facility? This move is appealing because it would allow the company to develop foreign sales without reducing resource employment in its home market. In fact, it may wind up hiring additional domestic managers to oversee international operations; perhaps it will also end up earning dividends and royalties from the foreign use of its capital, brand, and technology.

Ultimately, the argument cuts two ways: Although stakeholders in both home and host countries may gain from FDI, some observers maintain that stakeholders in one country or the other are destined to end up with the short end of the economic stick. In the following sections, we look at some of the arguments advanced to support this position.

Home-Country Losses   In recent years, many U.S. and European garment manufacturers have moved production operations to low-wage countries to realize cost advantages. In the process, they've shut down—or at least declined to expand—home-country operations. Thus overseas FDI in the garment-making industry has resulted in a loss of jobs in home countries while creating jobs abroad. The situation may be unfortunate, but the fact that it did come about may mean it was inevitable. In the absence of serious protection, argue some experts, home-country operations would have closed down because of competition from abroad, and jobs would have been lost anyway. (As Figure 5.3 suggests, many industries are subject to the same phenomenon.)

Host-Country Gains   Conversely, of course, host countries gain through the transfer of capital and technology. If that capital is used to acquire host-country operations that are going out of business, then the foreign investor may very well save host-country jobs and, through the import of technology and managerial ability, even create new jobs. In 2002, for example, U.S. carmaker General Motors (GM) paid $400 million for an interest in Korean carmaker Daewoo Motors. Without this infusion of capital (and the managerial expertise that GM brought to the deal), Daewoo might have gone bankrupt.

In many cases, FDI provides foreign firms with increased capacity or enhanced capabilities. In China, for instance, foreign investors have done so much to improve the capabilities of Chinese automakers that China is now beginning to export cars. Sometimes, however, local politics can complicate FDI and compromise its potential advantages.

A case in point is the South American nation of Venezuela, which decided for such U.S. companies as ExxonMobil Corp., Chevron Corp., and British-owned BP PLC to reduce the ownership of operations in Venezuela and give more control to the Venezuelan government as part of a program to assume more control over its valuable oil fields. In the process, Venezuelan officials exposed certain deficiencies in the capabilities of the domestic industry: They had sacrificed the expertise they needed to develop their

FIGURE 5.3
Santa's Workshop
Moves to Mexico

When a company uses FDI to move resources from the home country to a foreign host country, certain stakeholders—notably, employees, who are both resources and stakeholders—can become concerned about the consequences of the policy.

Source: © The New Yorker Collection 1992, Dana Fradon, Cartoonbank.com. All rights reserved. Reprinted by permission.

"Great. You move to Mexico, and we all end up working at McDonald's."

own crude-oil resources. Ultimately, to retain access to needed management experience and process technologies, the Venezuelan government had to ask expelled foreign companies to maintain minority shares in local ventures.[7]

Host-Country Losses   Critics, however, contend that MNEs often make investments that domestic companies could otherwise make, thereby locking out local entrepreneurs. Likewise, they say, foreign investors often bid up prices when competing with local companies for labor and other resources. In the United States, for example, local firms complained that Toyota was monopolizing the best workers in the northern Indiana area by paying them higher wages.[8]

Critics also claim that FDI destroys local entrepreneurship in ways that affect national development. Because entrepreneurs are inspired by the reasonable expectation of success, the collapse in several countries of small cottage industries, especially in the face of MNE efforts to consolidate local operations, may have played a role in undermining the competitive confidence of local businesspeople.

Not everyone, of course, accepts this claim.[9] The presence of MNEs, say pro-MNE analysts, may actually increase the number of local companies operating in host-country markets. How? By serving as role models for local talent to emulate. Avid entrepreneurs, they add, will regard MNEs not as obstacles but as challenges.

> Host countries may lose if investments by MNEs
>
> - Replace local companies.
> - Take the best resources.
> - Destroy local entrepreneurship.
> - Decrease local R&D undertakings.

The Foundations of Ethical Behavior

In addition to worrying about balance of payments, growth, and employment, MNEs, regardless of how they enter a foreign business environment, must act *responsibly* wherever they go. In this section, we concentrate on the cultural and legal foundations of ethical behavior and then look at some specific examples of the sort of ethical dilemmas faced by globalizing companies.

> Many actions elicit universal agreement on what is right or wrong, but other situations are less clear.

WHY DO COMPANIES CARE ABOUT ETHICAL BEHAVIOR?

First, however, let's take a brief look at a preliminary but fairly important question: Why should companies worry about ethical behavior at all? As we discuss later, there are cultural and legal reasons to behave ethically. Also, individuals may have high standards of ethical behavior that can be translated into company policy. Here's one way to look at this question: From a business standpoint, ethical behavior can be instrumental in achieving one or both of two possible objectives:

1. To develop competitive advantage
2. To avoid being perceived as irresponsible

As for the first objective, some analysts argue that responsible behavior contributes to strategic and financial success because it fosters trust, which, in turn, encourages commitment.[10] As we indicate in our opening case, for instance, GE's Ecomagination program reflects the belief of top managers that by proactively responding to social concerns about global warming, GE can gain a strategic advantage over competitors; in particular, the company hopes to develop an edge in emerging markets facing severe environmental problems.

As for the second objective, companies are aware that more and more nongovernmental organizations are becoming active in monitoring—and publicizing—international corporate practices. The Interfaith Center on Corporate Responsibility (ICCR), for example, is a nongovernmental organization (NGO) that represents about 275 religious institutions. In the past, it has sponsored shareholder resolutions and even threatened to withdraw investments from its $110 billion in pension funds from companies whose practices it considers irresponsible.[11] It has also prodded many companies to change their practices, encouraging U.S.-based ExxonMobil, for example, to get serious on the issue of global warming.[12] These efforts fall under the twofold mission of ICCR's Global Warming Working Group to educate businesses about the environmental and economic threats posed by their operations and to urge companies to increase shareholder value by addressing these issues proactively.

THE CULTURAL FOUNDATIONS OF ETHICAL BEHAVIOR

During the early part of the twenty-first century, several U.S. companies faced severe financial problems and even dissolution because of their managers' unethical or illegal actions. Some of these companies hid their illicit actions for a number of years through their international operations. The upshot of these revelations included public outrage, investor anxiety, and, in general, a heightened interest in the activities of companies and the people who run them. (See Figure 5.4.)

Relativism Versus Normativism   Today, just about everyone agrees the actions in question were wrong (although a couple of defendants still argue otherwise), and, indeed, there's almost universal agreement on what's right and wrong when it comes to ethical and socially responsible behavior in business.[13] In the real world, however, managers face many situations in which the difference between right and wrong is less than crystal clear. For one thing, people have different ideas about right and wrong. Beliefs about what's right and wrong are influenced by family and religious values, laws and social pressures, our own observations and experiences, and even our economic circumstances. Because ethical convictions tend to be deep-seated, people tend to be avid in defending their views.

In addition, even within a given country are found starkly contrasting views on ethical matters, and to complicate things even more, our own personal values may differ from our employers' policies, from prevalent social norms, or both. Finally, everything that complicates dilemmas in the domestic business environment tends to complicate them even further in the international environment.

Relativism   On the one hand, **relativism** holds that ethical truths depend on the values of the groups propounding and practicing them and that outside *intervention* is inherently unethical. One thing to remember is the fact that the idea of accepting or adopting alien cultural values is a uniquely Western notion—one that goes back at least as far as St. Ambrose's fourth-century suggestion that "When in Rome, do as the Romans do."

NGOs are active in prodding companies to comply with certain standards of ethical behavior.

Values differ from country to country and sometimes between employees and companies.

Relativism—Ethical truths depend on the groups holding them.

Normativism—There are universal standards of behavior that all cultures should follow.

CONCEPT CHECK

Recall from Chapter 2 our discussion of "Cultural Awareness" and the various ways in which social and cultural distinctions can characterize a country's population. We also observe that companies doing business overseas need to be sensitive to internal diversity: They should remember that people in most nations are often members of multiple **cultures** and in some cases share more with certain foreign groups than with domestic groups.

FIGURE 5.4
No Ethics for Old Men

Sometimes businesspeople face ethical dilemmas: They must consider cultural, moral, legal, and political factors in choosing between acceptable but opposing alternatives. On the other hand, of course, there are questions of right versus wrong—whether or not to do something that's unethical or downright illegal.

Source: The New Yorker, March 24, 1975, Dana Fradon, Cartoonbank.com.

"Miss Dugan, will you send someone in here who can distinguish right from wrong?"

Normativism   **Normativism,** on the other hand, holds there are indeed universal standards of behavior, which although influenced differently by different cultural values, should be accepted by people everywhere. From this perspective, *nonintervention* is unethical. Not surprisingly, then, global firms are always struggling with the problem of how to implement their own ethical principles in foreign business environments: Should they consider their principles as reflections of universally valid "truths" (the normative approach), or should they be willing to adapt to local conditions on the assumption that every place has its own "truths" and needs to be treated differently (the relative approach)?

Walking the Fine Line Between Relativism and Normativism   Often a company faces certain pressures to opt for this second choice—to comply with local norms. Such pressures may take the form of laws that permit—or even require—only certain practices that grant competitive advantages to firms that accept local norms or throw up roadblocks in front of companies that try to impose home-country practices in the local arena. Conversely, firms may face certain pressures *not* to comply. These pressures can come from the company's own internal values, from its home-country government, or even from constituencies that threaten retaliatory action if it buckles under to objectionable foreign practices.

Many individuals and organizations have laid out minimum levels of business practices that they say a company (domestic or foreign) must follow regardless of the legal requirements or ethical norms prevalent where it operates.[14] One could consider this as behavior based on principles of honesty and fairness, or what can be called "ordinary decency."[15] Many argue that legal permission for some action may be given by uneducated or corrupt leaders who either do not understand or do not care about the consequences. They argue further that MNEs are obligated to set good examples that may become the standard for responsible behavior.

Negotiating Between Evils   Another potential complication derives from the fact that both societies and companies must often choose between the lesser of two evils. Consider the following illustration. As most of us know by now, the pesticide DDT is dangerous to the environment (especially to birds), and high-income countries have banned its use. At the same time, companies headquartered in those countries have subsequently been chided for selling DDT to lower-income countries that need it to fight malaria, one of the

CONCEPT CHECK

In discussing ways of "Dealing with Cultural Differences" in Chapter 2, we demonstrate that successful accommodation to a host country's **culture** depends not only on that culture's willingness to accept anything foreign but also on the extent to which foreign firms and their employees are able to adjust to the culture in which they find themselves.

Managers need to exhibit ordinary decency—principles of honesty and fairness.

Managers need to create competitive advantages through ethical behavior and avoid being perceived as irresponsible.

CONCEPT CHECK

As we point out in Chapter 2, **international business** on any scale increases interactions among countries, and any level of interaction is apt to introduce cultural change. We list a few types of cultural influence—namely, *creolization*, *indigenization*, and *cultural diffusion*—which, though introducing only certain elements of a foreign culture, have been known to cause concern about cultural identity in the host country.

Social responsibility requires human judgment, which is subjective and ambiguous.

CONCEPT CHECK

Note that in Chapter 3, we define a country's *legal system* as the fundamental institution that creates a comprehensive legal network to regulate social interaction; its purpose is to stabilize political and social environments as well as to ensure a fair, safe, and efficient business environment.

CONCEPT CHECK

Recall our explanation in Chapter 3 of a **civil law system** as one based on a systematic and extensive codification of laws.

Legal justification for ethical behavior may not be sufficient because not everything that is unethical is illegal.

world's worst diseases.[16] Or take the production of ethanol, an alternative energy source that's less damaging to the environment than petroleum. It turns out that a Brazilian company that produces ethanol has been forcing workers to toil 14-hour days under horrific conditions to harvest the sugarcane needed to produce ethanol.[17]

Obviously, issues of ethical and social responsibility can be—and often are—ambiguous, and responsible behavior requires a little judgment. Granted, a number of multilateral agreements simplify some ethical decisions, mostly in the areas of employment practices, consumer protection, environmental protection, political activity, and human rights. Nevertheless, despite a growing body of treaties, pacts, agreements, and codes, there is still no set of universally accepted guidelines. In our opening case, for example, we saw how GE has had to adjust to environmental regulations in both the United States and Europe, where opinions on how to approach environmental issues sometimes diverge significantly.

Respecting Cultural Identity   Some international business practices, although they don't exactly "clash" with certain national values, may nevertheless work to undermine the long-term cultural identity of a host country. Think about the use of a company's home-country language or cultural artifacts and the introduction of products and work methods that cause changes in social relationships. Host countries have sometimes reacted negatively to such use. The Finns, for example, aren't happy with MNEs that have introduced non-Finnish architecture in their Finnish facilities, and France even fined BodyShop for using English in French stores.[18]

THE LEGAL FOUNDATIONS OF ETHICAL BEHAVIOR

Dealing with *ethical dilemmas* is often a balancing act: a problem of balancing *means*—the actions that we take and which may be right or wrong—and *ends*—the results of our actions, which may also be right or wrong. Ethics, according to one student of its role in business affairs, teaches that "people have a responsibility to do what is right and to avoid doing what is wrong."[19] Now, as we've already seen, proponents of cultural relativism suggest there are no universally reliable standards for deciding whether any behavior is ever appropriate. In this book, however, we're going to take up the position that it is indeed possible to judge whether behavior is appropriate. For one thing, we must point out that individuals tend to seek justification for their behavior and, in so doing, raise issues concerning both cultural values (many of which are universal) and principles sanctioned by the legal system.

Legal Justification: Pro and Con   Indeed, some experts suggest the legal justification for ethical behavior is the only important standard. According to this theory, an individual or company can do anything that isn't illegal. Opponents respond that there are five good reasons why this is inadequate:

1. Because some things that are *unethical* are not *illegal*, the law is not an appropriate standard for regulating *all* business activity. Some forms of interpersonal behavior, for example, can clearly be wrong even if they're not against the law.

2. The law is slow to develop in emerging areas of concern. It takes time to legislate laws and test them in courts. Moreover, because laws are essentially responses to issues that have already surfaced, they can't always anticipate dilemmas that will arise in the future. Countries with well-developed systems of civil law rely on specificity in the law, and it isn't feasible to enact laws dealing with every possible ethical issue.

3. The law is often based on imprecisely defined moral concepts that can't be separated from the legal concepts they underpin. In other words, we must in any case consider moral concepts whenever we're considering legal ones.

4. The law often needs to undergo scrutiny by the courts. This is especially true of case law, in which the courts create law by establishing precedent.

5. The law simply isn't very efficient. "Efficiency" in this case implies achieving ethical behavior at a very low cost, and it would be impossible to solve every ethical behavioral problem with an applicable law.[20]

Unfortunately, things aren't that simple. Proponents of the legal-justification standard reply there are also several good reasons for complying with it:

1. Because the law embodies many of a country's moral principles, it is in fact an adequate guide for proper conduct.

2. The law provides a clearly defined set of rules, and following it at least establishes a good precedent for acceptable behavior.

3. The law contains enforceable rules that apply to everyone.

4. Because the law represents a consensus derived from widely shared experience and deliberation, it reflects careful and wide-ranging discussions.[21]

> The law is a good basis for ethical behavior because it embodies local cultural values.

> As countries tackle similar ethical issues, laws will become more similar.

Extraterritoriality   When, however, you're trying to use the law to govern behavior in different countries, you'll soon run into a very basic problem—namely, the fact that laws vary from country to country. Recall, for instance, the challenges faced by GE in its efforts to deal with international variations in environmental laws. GE has actually lobbied the U.S. government to enact legislation more closely aligned to Europe's, reasoning that having to deal with a shifting array of regulations and limitations will not only impede its strategy but also become unnecessarily costly.

Interestingly, this fact brings us directly back to the relationship between ethics and moral concepts: Laws vary from country to country because moral values vary from country to country. In addition, strong home-country governments may adopt a practice known as **extraterritoriality**: That is, they may impose domestic legal and ethical practices on the foreign subsidiaries of companies headquartered in their jurisdictions.

Ethics and Corporate Bribery

Granted, we've gone from con to pro and back again in our introduction to the relationship between ethics and the law. Nevertheless, let's return once more to a pro-law argument. Why? Because in spite of all the problems that arise, considering the law is still a good place to start when studying ethics. The reason shouldn't be surprising: As countries find themselves searching for common solutions to common problems (problems like the ones we discuss in the following sections), they find themselves taking common legal steps. In addition, in the effort to tackle important problems, they encounter certain **externalities** that must be solved in the public arena—certain by-products of activities that affect the well-being of people or the health of the environment even if those effects don't show up in market prices.

Now that we've discussed the cultural and legal foundations of ethical behavior—and now that we have some tools for assessing worldwide corporate behavior—we should be prepared to examine some key ethical issues that companies must confront in doing business in foreign countries.

> **CONCEPT CHECK**
> As we explain in Chapter 3, the trend toward the harmonizing of legal procedures and rules is known as the *diffusion of legal systems*—a process that's been ongoing for centuries.

CORRUPTION AND BRIBERY

The first of these issues is *bribery*, which is actually one facet of the much bigger issue of *corruption*. The multifaceted determinants of corruption include cultural, legal, and political forces.[22]

Congressional investigations of U.S. MNEs in the 1970s yielded anecdotal information indicating that questionable payments to foreign government officials by U.S. firms had

Bribery of public officials takes place to obtain government contracts or to get officials to do what they should be doing anyway.

long been business as usual in both industrial and developing countries. How much money was involved, both in payouts from U.S. MNEs and from those based in other countries? Recent data give us some idea of the cost of doing business on a global scale. The U.S. government reported that, between 1994 and 2001, it learned of cases in which foreign firms from more than 50 countries offered bribes to buyers in more than 100 countries; these cases involved more than 400 competitions for contracts valued at $200 billion.[23]

Figure 5.5 also offers some interesting insight into the propensity of companies from various countries to participate in schemes involving bribes.[24] Although it is true that no country is free of corruption, it is obvious that corruption is higher in countries that are also high in poverty. In addition, it is important to note that corruption requires someone to give a bribe in order for someone to take a bribe, and intermediaries are also necessary to facilitate the transactions, from bankers to accountants.

Bribes are payments or promises to pay cash or anything of value.

The Consequences of Corruption What's wrong with bribes? A number of things. First, bribery affects both the performance of companies and the economies of countries. Higher levels of corruption, for instance, correlate strongly with lower national growth rates and lower levels of per capita income.[25] Corruption can also erode the authority of governments that condone it. Over the years, bribery-based scandals have led to the downfall of numerous heads of state; many government officials have been jailed for accepting bribes, and numerous business executives and government officials have been forced to resign, fined, imprisoned, or even, as in the case of China's former head of the State Food and Drug Administration, who was convicted of accepting bribes in return for approving certain medicines, executed.[26] Moreover, disclosures of corruption not only damage the reputations of companies and whole countries, but also they compromise the legitimacy of MNEs in the eyes of local and global communities.[27] Finally, corruption is expensive, inflating a company's costs and bloating its prices.

The Foreign Corrupt Practices Act is U.S. legislation that makes bribery illegal. It applies to domestic or foreign operations and to company employees as well as their agents overseas.

What's Being Done About Corruption? Multilateral efforts are currently under way to slow the pace of bribery as an international business practice. In issuing *Business Principles for Countering Bribery* in 2003, a nonprofit organization called Transparency International hastened to point out its principles were consistent with such existing initiatives as the Organization for Economic Cooperation and Development (OECD) Convention on Combating Bribery of Foreign Public Officials in International Business Transactions, the International Chamber of Commerce (ICC) Rules of Conduct to Combat Extortion and Bribery, and the antibribery provisions of the revised OECD Guidelines for Multinationals. Let's take a brief look at each of these accords.

FIGURE 5.5 Where Bribes Are (and Are Not) Business as Usual

Transparency International asked 835 business experts in 15 countries the following: "In the business sectors with which you are most familiar, please indicate how likely companies from the following countries are to pay or offer bribes to win or retain business in [your home country]." The scale runs from 1 to 10, with higher scores indicating a lower propensity to pay or offer bribes.

Source: Transparency International, "TI Corruption Perceptions Index" (2006), at http://transparency.org (accessed October 16, 2007).

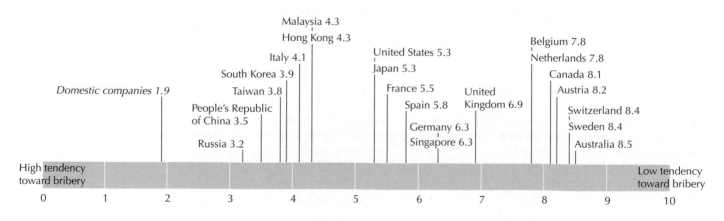

Cross-National Accords: The OECD, the ICC, and the UN   A number of cross-national accords, as well as efforts in various nations at the national level, have also proved somewhat effective in fighting corruption. Interestingly, research shows that countries that rank low on masculinity on the Hofstede scale tend to foster less corruption than those that are high on masculinity, as do nations that rate high on economic development and political and economic freedom. Research also shows that as information, including Internet communication, becomes more accessible, corruption tends to decline.[28]

The OECD Convention was initially signed in 1997 by the member nations of the Organisation for Economic Co-operation and Development. In 2007, South Africa became the 37th signatory and first African member to enact antibribery laws based on the OECD Convention, which targets the supply side of corruption (the activities of bribe seekers) in cross-border deals.[29]

The ICC issued a code of rules against corrupt practices in 1999 and has since been active in supporting other multilateral approaches to combating bribery, including codes of conduct issued by the OECD, the World Trade Organization (WTO), and the United Nations (UN). Originally founded in 1945 to foster global cooperation in international law, security, economic development, and social equity,[30] the UN is currently involved in addressing a number of issues that affect MNEs, including not only corruption but also climate change (a topic we take up shortly). Whereas the OECD Convention targets the supply-side machinations of corruption in the public sector, the ICC is particularly interested in the private sector and the demand side of cross-border economics, where extortion by public officials is a favorite criminal practice.[31]

The U.S. Foreign Corrupt Practices Act   In the United States, international accords on anticorruption efforts are implemented by the **Foreign Corrupt Practices Act (FCPA)**, which outlaws bribery payments by U.S. firms to foreign officials, political parties, party officials, and political candidates. In 1998, FCPA coverage was extended to include bribery by foreign firms operating in U.S. territory. The FCPA applies not only to companies registered in the United States but also to any foreign company quoted on any stock exchange in the United States.

There's an apparent inconsistency in the provisions of the FCPA—namely, the fact that, although it's legal to make payments to officials to expedite otherwise legitimate transactions—a practice officially called *facilitation payments* but sometimes referred to as *speed money* or *grease money*—they can't be made to officials who aren't directly responsible for the transactions in question. In 1988, an amendment to the FCPA actually excluded facilitation payments from the definition of *bribery*. Now, for example, payment to a customs official to clear legitimate merchandise is legal, whereas a payment to a government minister to influence a customs official is not. What's the difference? The FCPA allows payment in the former case because it recognizes that officials can delay legal transactions indefinitely or until they receive payments.

The U.S. government, however, continues to step up anticorruption efforts both at home and abroad. As of 2007, the government was conducting 43 investigations into corporate bribery—not an extremely high number of cases until you realize that, in the first three decades following the passage of the FCPA, it pursued a grand total of only 60.[32] Additional legislation has been enacted since the FCPA that indirectly affects corruption. Most notable, perhaps, is the Sarbanes-Oxley Act (SOX).[33] Passed in 2002, SOX was a response to an epidemic of well-known corporate scandals involving such companies as Enron and Tyco International. SOX toughened standards with regard to corporate governance, financial disclosure, and oversight of accounting and auditing practices.

Industry Initiatives   Finally, various industries have recently stepped up their own efforts against bribery and corruption. In 2005, for example, in conjunction with the World Economic Forum, nearly 50 multinational construction and natural-resources companies, representing at least $300 billion in annual revenues, signed a "zero-tolerance" pact against extortion by bribery. This voluntary effort, called the Partnering Against Corruption Initiative, calls for member firms to set up "extensive internal programs to

---

Margin notes:

International multilateral accords to combating bribery include those by the OECD, the International Chamber of Commerce, and the United Nations.

Sarbanes-Oxley legislation in the United States is helpful in combating corruption through more effective corporate governance, financial disclosure, and public accounting oversight.

A zero-tolerance pact against bribery was signed by companies at the 2005 World Economic Forum.

educate and oversee company officials and business partners and also [to] prohibit political contributions and charitable gifts designed to curry favor."[34] Although many firms still adhere to their own antibribery standards, participants hope that the PACT Initiative will encourage companies within the industry to monitor each other.

Relativism, the Rule of Law, and Responsibility   Obviously, avoiding bribe payments when they're regarded as business as usual is a challenge, especially when business is being held up by foreign government officials. Although it might be easier to fall back on the standard of cultural *relativism* (and, say, simply pay bribes where they're accepted and/or expected), the international initiatives we've described in this section have made some headway in introducing the rule of law into more and more international business activity. Companies are now freer to establish policies and procedures that are consistent both with their own domestic laws and those of other countries. As the principles laid down by the OECD and UN are incorporated into national statutes, companies are finding that laws and practices that once varied radically from country to country have become more uniform and easier to implement.

Clearly, the international community is serious about dealing with the problem of corruption, but companies need to remember they're still responsible for complying with the laws of the nations in which they conduct business. According to a recent survey, however, few firms undertake necessary precautions and preventive measures. Although nearly a third of U.S. companies, for instance, conduct background investigations on their overseas investments, only 30 percent of them actually check for evidence of bribery and other forms of corruption. Such lack of due diligence could land a negligent MNE on the wrong side of a law that's in force in one place or another.[35]

Point | Counterpoint

Are Top Managers Responsible When Corruption Is Afoot?

Point **Yes** Let's start by taking a trip back in time to the real world. In November 2006, German police raided the offices of the giant electrical engineering and electronics company Siemens AG. They netted nearly 36,000 documents to support allegations that Siemens regularly diverted funds filed under bogus consulting contracts into a network of "black accounts" for bribing officials in countries like Italy, Greece, Argentina, and Saudi Arabia, where Siemens was seeking lucrative public-sector contracts. Following the raid, the company itself announced that it had uncovered over €420 million ($570 million) in suspicious payments going back as far as the early 1990s. Several of the managers caught up in the probe insisted that corruption was endemic to the company's culture and that they had acted with the knowledge—and even the approval—of CEO Klaus Kleinfeld and board chief (and former CEO) Heinrich von Pierer.[36]

Now, nobody's going to deny that what Siemens employees did was misguided and wrongheaded, but let's be realistic: Step 1 in every textbook on foiling fraud is *follow the money*, and in this case you can follow the money back to a culture that condones financial shenanigans. That means

Counterpoint **No** Granted, Siemens was up to its corporate neck in a culture of corruption. But is that fact supposed to excuse the actions of the individual grown-ups who were directly involved in the present case? Or to put it in more legal-sounding Latinate terms: Does it mitigate their culpability? At the end of the business day, the actions of individuals, more than the official codes and theoretical due diligence of top managers, actually shape a company's culture.

Even so, back when he was CEO, von Pierer not only authorized a strict companywide code of conduct, but also he hired a few hundred compliance officers to enforce it.[42] When his turn came, Kleinfeld instituted a "zero-tolerance" policy toward corruption.[43] But more importantly, in Siemens's case, in which you're talking about a far-flung, highly decentralized conglomeration with 11 business units run by separate boards as virtually independent operating entities, it's hardly reasonable to expect top executives back home in Munich to know everything that's going on from Siemens Turkey to Siemens Taiwan. Former CEO von Pierer is absolutely right in arguing that under such circumstances, "deducing a political responsibility" would be that the real blame for the company's current mess rests with top management.

Here's a little background on the business world in which Siemens is a leading corporate citizen. In comparison with some other countries (say, the United States), Germany was slow to enact laws prohibiting bribery. In fact, up until 1999, German law allowed you to write off overseas bribes as legitimate business expenses, and up until 2002, it was still legal to bribe employees of foreign companies if you were willing to absorb the cost without the tax break.[37] And even when the laws began to change, German businesses were slow to catch on. In 2005 alone, they racked up roughly 90,000 corporate crimes.[38]

The point? Like a lot of other companies in Germany, Siemens was hanging on to a corporate culture that was perfectly comfortable with bribery and other forms of corrupt behavior. One senior executive says that Siemens even had an encryption code for itemizing bribe payments. (If you're interested, it involved juggling letters standing for "Make Profit.") The same exec says that he himself got a call from a Saudi contractor demanding $910 million in commission payments or else he'd send a bunch of incriminating documents about Siemens's business practices to certain U.S. authorities. When he alerted his superiors—including Kleinfeld and von Pierer—they replied that $910 million was perhaps a little high but went on to suggest that a deal for $17 million in "past obligations" and $33 million in "hush money" wasn't beyond reason. According to this insider, most of his colleagues tossed off bribe payments as mere "peccadilloes" because, after all, "it was all for the good of the company."[39]

All of this transpired on the watches of von Pierer and Kleinfeld (who, by the way, was directly in charge of the telecommunications unit that handled most of the bribery). To say all of these goings-on completely escaped their notice is ridiculous. It's top management's responsibility to lay out the ethical boundaries at a company and to see no one crosses them. Siemens management wasn't guarding its own ethical borders.

On top of everything else, Kleinfeld's "management style"—which boiled down to "fix, sell, or close"[40]—was hardly the right approach for a company that already had a dirty-tricks chapter in its playbook. Once he became CEO, Kleinfeld immediately set high profit targets and started spinning off divisions that apparently weren't sufficiently inspired by the profit motive. His motto was "Go for Profit & Growth," and when a team of managers failed to deliver, he just took an axe to the whole division. You did what you had to do to show a profit that satisfied Kleinfeld or your whole division was out on the street.[41] Under top-down pressure like that, what other choice did anyone whose job depended on Kleinfeld really have? If the answer is "none," you have to admit that ultimate responsibility for companywide behavior rests in the executive suite. ●

absurd. As most of us learned in business school, the job of senior executives is strategic planning; it doesn't involve auditing the books and double-checking every suspicious double entry.[44]

And while we're on the subject of top-level managers, it's true that a bunch of former employees who are in trouble with the law claim that top Siemens managers knew all about the bribery and other underhanded activities. So far, however, no one, including an independent law firm that's looking into the matter, has found any solid evidence that they're telling the truth. Plus, neither Kleinfeld nor von Pierer has been officially accused of any wrongdoing.

As for the question of whether dragging its governmental feet on antibribery legislation has anything to do with the resilience of corruption in Germany, there's little question that adapting to new laws may take some time (or that *passing* them may take a *long* time). But that doesn't justify breaking them until you're good and ready to obey them. Regardless of the *company's* approach to adapting to a new legal environment, those of its employees who perpetuated the practice of paying bribes fully understood what the law said and had to be fully aware they were violating it. Besides, creating false consulting contracts and diverting company money into slush funds has come under the heading of legally dubious behavior for a long time and just about everywhere. Furthermore, no matter when a law goes into effect, it always comes with a pretty clear list of *do's* and *don'ts*, and it's obvious that certain individuals at Siemens took it on themselves to ignore those guidelines.

Finally, what about the argument that employees had no choice but to violate the law because they had to protect their jobs? The fact that many of them now face criminal charges and jail time with no hope of continuing their careers at Siemens or anywhere else attests to the faulty logic of that claim. Meanwhile, their former employer, which is still responsible for nearly half a million paychecks worldwide, has already paid out €63 million ($85.7 million) to outside auditors and investigators and still faces a court-ordered fine of €38 million ($51.4 million) following the conviction of just one finance officer and one consultant.[45] Siemens also risks being banned from contract bidding in any one of the 190 countries where it does business and generates wealth. ●

Ethics and the Environment

If for no other reason, environmental problems are important because they're a matter of life or death (either now or in the future). As we saw in our opening case, for example, GE has come to see environmental responsibility as a matter of protecting not only the future of the environment but also the future of GE. Like GE, companies contribute to environmental damage in a variety of ways. Some, for example, endanger the environment by contaminating the air, soil, or water during manufacturing processes or by manufacturing products, such as automobiles or electricity, that release fossil-fuel contaminants into the environment.

In extracting natural resources, other companies also have a direct and unmistakable impact on the environment. But even in these cases, the issue isn't necessarily clear-cut. Granted, although some resources, such as minerals and gas and oil, may not be renewable, others, such as timber, are, and some observers even suggest that resources can never really become scarce. Why? Because as they become less available, prices go up and technology or substitutes compensate for the scarcity. (See Figure 5.6.)

Companies that extract natural resources, generate air or water waste, or manufacture products such as autos that generate pollution need to be concerned with their environmental impact.

WHAT IS "SUSTAINABILITY"?

Sustainability means meeting the needs of the present without compromising the ability of future generations to meet their own needs, and proponents of the concept argue that sustainability considers what's best for both people and the environment.[46] Nevertheless, it remains a controversial concept—one that's subject to different interpretations by environmentalists and businesspeople—neither of which groups can settle on their own definition of the term. It is important, however, that, regardless of how they feel about the principle of sustainability, businesses that impact the environment establish policies for responsible behavior toward the environment—a responsibility that has both cultural and legal ramifications.

Sustainability involves meeting the needs of the present without compromising the ability of future generations to meet their own needs while taking into account what is best for the people and the environment.

GLOBAL WARMING AND THE KYOTO PROTOCOL

To illustrate some of the challenges faced by these companies, we start by examining the issue of *global warming*, including the role of the *Kyoto Protocol* and its potential impact

A man paddles a canoe past floating logs near a sawmill on the banks of Marajo Island in the Amazon River, where logging is destroying the Brazilian rain forest and reducing the world's capacity to absorb greenhouse gases.

FIGURE 5.6

Q. Is this really an ethical *dilemma*—at least as it's defined in Figure 5.4?

A. Technically, no—unless you consider destroying the ozone an acceptable alternative.

Source: Copyright John Morris, CartoonStock.com.

"Gentlemen, we have a dilemma. Pollution scientists say it will destroy the ozone - however, Market Research predict it will sell like hot cakes."

on corporate behavior. Global warming has certainly captured the attention of the world, even in the entertainment industry. Twentieth Century Fox's hit movie, *The Day After Tomorrow,* shows the potentially devastating impact of global warming; Michael Crichton's book, *State of Fear,* examines the dangers of politicizing science. Although there was mild criticism of *The Day After Tomorrow,* there was a vigorous debate over Crichton's book and its thesis that critics of global warming are being suppressed.

> Global warming results from the release of greenhouse gases that trap heat in the atmosphere rather than allowing it to escape.

The Kyoto Protocol   At the core of the international treaty called the Kyoto Protocol is the theory that global warming is a result of an increase in carbon dioxide and other gases that act like the roof of a greenhouse, trapping heat that would normally be radiated back into space and warming the planet. If carbon dioxide emissions aren't reduced and controlled, rising temperatures could have catastrophic consequences, including the melting of the polar ice cap, flooding in coastal regions, shifting storm patterns, reduced farm output, drought, and even plant and animal extinctions.[47] Even though most observers agree the world is warming, however, there's no clear consensus on the cause or scope of the problem, much less the solution.[48]

It's clear that something can and must be done to reduce the carbon dioxide emissions from the burning of fossil fuels and methane, and that's why the Kyoto Protocol came about. Signed in 1997, the **Kyoto Protocol,** an extension of the UN Framework Convention on Climate Change of 1994, commits signatory countries to reducing greenhouse gas emissions to 5.2 percent below 1990 levels between 2008 and 2012.

> The Kyoto Protocol was signed in 1997 to require countries to cut their greenhouse gas emissions to 5.2 percent below 1990 levels between 2008 and 2012. Some countries have adopted stricter requirements, and others, such as the United States, China, and India, are not part of the compliance.

As of June 2007, 175 nations and regional economic organizations had ratified the Protocol.[49] The United States, which generates 25 percent of the world's greenhouse gases, initially signed the agreement in 1998 but withdrew in 2001, citing concerns about domestic economic growth and exemptions for rapidly expanding developing countries like China and India.[50] (Together, these two nations account for about 14 percent of the world's total emissions, but because they're regarded as developing countries, they aren't required to make reductions.) Why is the United States reluctant to get on board? Basically, it's banking on the development of low-carbon technologies to solve the problem and would prefer not to meet mandatory reductions for fear that reduced economic growth would create domestic employment problems.

U.S.-based MNEs must comply with the Kyoto Protocol in compliance countries where they may have operations.

National and Regional Initiatives   Meanwhile, companies operating in countries that have adopted the protocol are under pressure to take one of two steps: reduce emissions or buy credits from companies that have reduced emissions below target levels. The choice isn't terribly attractive because they'll have to invest in new technologies, change the way they do business, or pay for someone else to clean up their acts. In addition, MNEs (such as GE) are now forced to reconsider their global strategies, particularly because firms with operations in countries that have adopted the Kyoto Protocol are required to adhere to the same standards as local companies. The European Union (EU) has set a target of an 8 percent reduction from 1990 levels—a figure that's more aggressive than Protocol target levels. The Germans went one step further, setting a target of 21 percent (based on the assumption they'd be able to close down coal-fired power plants still operating in the former East Germany).[51]

Company-Specific Initiatives   As a result, of course, U.S. companies operating in Europe share the same stringent requirements with European-based firms. Not surprisingly, many U.S.-based MNEs, though not bound by Protocol targets at home, are preparing for what they believe is the inevitable. Between 2000 and 2005, for example, when GM took part in a voluntary emissions-reduction program, it achieved a 10 percent reduction in North American plant emissions. GM is now trying to determine what it needs to do to make its 11 European plants comply with EU standards.[52] DuPont has cut emissions by 65 percent since 1990, and Alcoa has set a target of 25 percent reductions by 2010.[53] Thus companies are clearly changing the way they do business, whether or not they're bound by Protocol standards. Our opening case provides a good example: Recall that GE set a target of reducing greenhouse gas emissions at all levels of its operations to 1 percent below 2004 levels.

Finally, bear in mind that many MNEs, based in the United States or otherwise, also face the task of adapting to different standards in different countries. A European-based MNE with operations in, say, the United States, Germany, and China and a U.S.-based MNE with plants in the same countries are faced with a smorgasbord of regulatory environments. On the one hand, the *legal* approach to responsible corporate behavior says an MNE can settle for operating in accord with local laws. The *ethical* approach, on the other hand, urges companies to go beyond the law to do whatever is necessary and economically feasible to reduce greenhouse gas emissions.

LOOKING TO THE FUTURE

How to See the Trees in the Rain Forest

When it comes to the emission of carbon dioxide (and other gases), the whole world is one big greenhouse. From Pago Pago to Peoria, it doesn't matter where you live—you're affected by greenhouse gas emissions. So what difference does it make if greenhouse gas emissions also affect, say, the city of Porto Velho in southwestern Brazil? Porto Velho, situated on the Madeira River, a major tributary of the Amazon River, happens to be in the Amazon rain forest, which accounts for a third of the world's remaining tropical forest. Covering about 60 percent of Brazil, it's home to no less than 30 percent of the world's animal and plant species. As forests go, it's quite large—roughly the size of Western Europe and just slightly smaller than the United States (including Alaska and Hawaii).

Rain forests may provide a key to solving the problem of global warming. The reason's simple: Trees absorb carbon dioxide. That's why one of the approaches to the reduction of greenhouse gas emissions proposed by the Kyoto Protocol involves reforestation. Given its size, the Amazon rain forest is obviously key to the success of any reforestation project, but, unfortunately, it's currently under a twofold human-made assault: logging and burning. Logging is an important source of revenue for Brazil, which suffers from high rates of unemployment and underemployment. In addition, Brazilians are cutting down and burning large tracts of rain forest to make room for farming and cattle ranching. In some cases, ranchers turn around and sell their land to agricultural interests, clear additional land for pastures, and sell the lumber to the timber industry.

Not only does the burning of rain forest land add to the volume of carbon dioxide emissions, but also the destruction of the forests eliminates a vast carbon dioxide "sink" that could benefit the rest of the world by disposing of an immense amount of greenhouse gas emissions. Brazil, then, is a major front in the war against greenhouse gas pollution.

Burning alone accounts for 75 percent of Brazil's greenhouse gas emissions (5.38 percent of the world's total), making Brazil one of the world's top 10 polluters). Moreover, the huge timber potential has already attracted heavy investment from many multinational logging firms that plan to harvest even more trees in the future. ■

Ethical Dilemmas and Business Practices

Now that we have a foundation of ethical dilemmas and socially responsible behavior, let's look at a few industries and issues. Sometimes the dilemmas are industry specific, such as the pharmaceutical industry. Other times the dilemmas are not exactly industry specific but deal with issues that cross industries, such as with labor conditions in developing countries. We have chosen two examples—ethical dilemmas and the pharmaceutical industry and ethical dimensions of labor conditions—to demonstrate how companies have to examine their ethical conduct as they spread internationally. There are others we could have chosen, but we think these two, which are prominent in the news, will give you an idea of what you might face and how you can resolve the conflicts in a satisfactory way. We finish this section and the chapter by discussing the importance of corporate codes of conduct.

ETHICAL DILEMMAS AND THE PHARMACEUTICAL INDUSTRY

GlaxoSmithKline (GSK), one of the largest research-based pharmaceutical companies in the world, focuses on two lines of business: pharmaceuticals (prescription drugs and vaccines) and consumer health-care products. With revenues of $23 billion annually, the U.K.-based company operates in 117 countries and sells in more than 140. It employs more than 100,000 people, with 35,000 working at 80 manufacturing sites in 37 countries, more than 15,000 of them in R&D.

To continue developing new products, GSK spends 14.5 percent of its revenues on R&D[54] and, like most research-based pharmaceutical companies, it is involved in the R&D, manufacturing, and sales ends of the patented-pharmaceuticals industry. To fund its large R&D budget and because so many of the drugs it tries to develop never make it to market and because other drugs take so long to get to market, the companies sell their successful drugs at a high price as long as they are covered by a patent.

After the patent expires, the drug becomes generic and is sold at a much lower price. Generic manufacturers specialize in selling drugs that are no longer patent protected. Although patent laws vary from country to country, branded pharmaceuticals are protected by U.S. patent for 17 years. Because generic drug manufacturers do not have to engage in R&D and are only selling proven products, their costs are much lower, and they are able to sell the drugs at a lower price.

Tiered Pricing and Other Price-Related Issues There are some exceptions to this pricing structure. Only 3 percent of GSK's revenues, for instance, come from the Middle East and Africa, where GSK offers preferential prices for vaccines. This practice is known as *tiered pricing*, in which consumers in industrial countries pay higher prices and those in developing countries, especially low-income developing countries, pay lower subsidized prices.

If a governmental buyer is still unsatisfied with the high cost of patented drugs, it may resort to substituting so-called generics (whose production is a major industry in

Tiered pricing for pharmaceuticals means that companies charge a market price for products sold in industrial countries and a discounted price for products sold in developing countries.

such countries such as India, Brazil, and China). Generics are legitimate *if* the countries in which they're produced extend patent protection to patent holders.

Here's an example of the kinds of problems that can arise when the cost of pharmaceuticals becomes a point of contention in the marketplace. AIDS is a major health problem in Brazil, where the government, at substantial cost, distributes AIDS drugs to anyone who needs them. In 2007, when the drugmaker Merck offered to provide an AIDS drug at a 30 percent discount, the Brazilian government said thanks but no thanks and, instead, made it lawful for Brazilian firms to manufacture or buy generic versions of the drug while paying Merck only nominal royalty fees.[55]

Brazil has also resorted to the tactic of *reverse engineering* certain key drugs so they can be produced at lower prices. (One more point about generics: Often they're simply pirated versions of the real thing, and pirated versions—about 10 percent of medicines sold worldwide, according to the World Health Organization [WHO]—often lack key ingredients.[56])

Our closing case includes a similar illustration, which involves the efforts of GlaxoSmithKline to offer steep discounts on AIDS drugs to a MNE attempting to provide free treatment to workers in South Africa.

Taking TRIPS for What It's Worth   The WTO Agreement on Trade-Related Aspects of Intellectual Property Rights (TRIPS) allows poor countries to counter the high cost of patented drugs by doing either of two things: (1) producing generic products *for local consumption* or (2) importing generic products from other countries *if they themselves don't have the capacity to produce generics*. In both cases, the developing nation is compelled to license patented drugs from legal patent holders so the patent holders generate revenue on the drugs they developed as opposed to buying the drug from pirated sources. However, in claiming that health problems such as HIV/AIDS and heart disease are "national emergencies," Brazil and Thailand have permitted local companies to make *unlicensed* generics and thus take advantage of a TRIPS clause that allows them to avoid paying the royalties, even though some companies and countries dispute that decision.[57]

Not surprisingly, this tactic is a major concern for pharmaceutical companies. For one thing, they worry that these generic products will find their way back into the developed countries where they generate the majority of patent holders' revenues. They also worry about fakes for the same reason. Interestingly, the German pharmaceutical company Boehringer Ingelheim has decided to accommodate the needs of low-income nations like Brazil: It plans to slash all of its HIV-drug prices and to allow generic manufacturers to produce low-cost copies. Why such a seemingly costly strategy? The answer is twofold, partly ethical and partly financial. First, the company believes it's the only ethically reasonable response to the AIDS crisis. Second, it calculates that the principle of *preferential pricing*, which entails charging higher prices in developed countries, will still allow it to cover its R&D costs.[58]

R&D and the Bottom Line   With the Boehringer Ingelheim strategy, we're back to the bottom line in the issue of ethics and pharmaceutical sales: Drugs are *very* expensive to develop. Moreover, developing them is a lot more expensive in developed countries than in developing countries. It's estimated, for example, that the price for developing a new drug is close to $1 billion in the United States but as little as $100 million in a country like India.

As it happens, India, which is now home to a thriving industry in *unlicensed* generic drugs, once enjoyed hefty FDI in pharmaceuticals. But when it refused to secure patents on drugs made there by foreign companies, those companies chose to leave the country rather than give away all their secrets to local competitors. Today, however, a new patent-protection law (which went into effect in 2005) has brought India into line with WTO guidelines and fostered a whole new environment for pharmaceuticals. Many Indian R&D facilities have sprung up to develop new drugs that

Case Review Note

CONCEPT CHECK

In Chapter 3, we define *intellectual property rights (IPRs)* as intangible property rights resulting from intellectual effort. Note, however, that an IPR registered in one country doesn't necessarily confer protection in another.

Legal generic products allow countries to purchase drugs at lower costs and comply with drug patents, whereas illegal generic products are fakes that may or may not be of high quality.

Countries with health crises, such as African countries with people suffering from AIDS, are allowed by TRIPS to manufacture or import generic drugs.

India is a major manufacturer of generic drugs and is now moving to R&D of new drugs.

can be legitimately produced and sold by Indian companies, and foreign pharmaceutical firms are now looking at different strategies for penetrating the Indian market, from FDI to licensing agreements with generic manufacturers. Now home to 74 FDA-approved pharmaceutical manufacturing facilities—more than any country outside the United States—India now sells $1.15 billion worth of generic drugs annually in the United States and Europe.[59]

In this arena, then, the issue of social responsibility comes down to developing ways in which drug makers can generate enough revenues to create new products (which is, after all, their major source of competitive advantage) while at the same time responding to the needs of developing countries that are long on diseases and short on funds. Is finding solutions the responsibility of drug makers or the responsibility of developing nations, perhaps in conjunction with industrial countries in such global forums such as the WHO? Should drug makers encourage the development of generic products long before patents expire, or will they thereby run the risk of promoting a flood of cheaper products that will come back to haunt them in their home markets?

Governments and private foundations are attempting to solve the problem of developing country access to drugs and vaccines through an International Finance Facility for Immunization and/or advance-purchase contracts.

ETHICAL DIMENSIONS OF LABOR CONDITIONS

A major challenge facing MNEs today is the twofold problem of globalized supply chains and the working conditions of foreign workers. Labor issues—which involve companies, governments, trade unions, and nongovernmental organizations alike—include wages, child labor, working conditions, working hours, and freedom of association. They're especially critical in retail, clothing, footwear, and agriculture—industries in which MNEs typically outsource huge portions of production to independent companies abroad, usually located in the developing countries of Asia, Latin America, and Africa.

As an introduction to this section, look at Figure 5.7, which highlights the multiple pressures placed by external stakeholders on companies to adopt responsible employment practices in their overseas operations. A more specific listing of worker issues was developed by the Ethical Trading Initiative (ETI), a British-based organization that focuses on the ethical employment practices of MNEs. Its members include representatives from Gap Inc., Levi Strauss & Co., Marks & Spencer, The Body Shop International, and other companies, as well as from trade union organizations, NGOs, and governments.

Major labor issues that MNEs get involved in through FDI or purchasing from independent manufacturers in developing countries are fair wages, child labor, working conditions, working hours, and freedom of association.

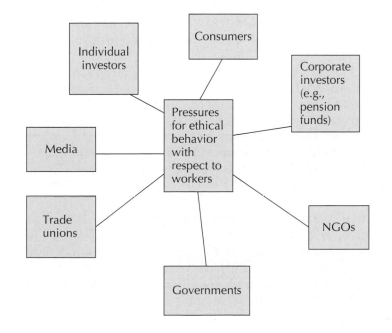

FIGURE 5.7
Sources of Worker-Related Pressures in the Global Supply Chain

The objective of ETI is to get companies to adopt ethical employment policies and then monitor compliance with their overseas suppliers. ETI's trading initiative base code identifies the following issues:

1. Employment is freely chosen.
2. Freedom of association and the right to collective bargaining are respected.
3. Working conditions are safe and hygienic.
4. Child labor shall not be used.
5. Living wages are paid.
6. Working hours are not excessive.
7. No discrimination is practiced.
8. Regular employment is provided.
9. No harsh or inhumane treatment is allowed.[60]

Although all issues identified by ETI are important, we focus on the one that, for a variety of good reasons, receives the most attention: *child labor*.

The Problem of Child Labor   Let's start by considering a couple of very brief cases:

- There are two arguments for the use of children in the Indian carpet industry: (1) They're better suited than adults to perform certain tasks, and (2) if they weren't employed, they'd be even worse off. In fact, children in India are often put to work because parents don't earn enough to support families, and if they don't make enough to pay off debts, children are often *indentured* to creditors.

- In the 1990s, the impoverished Asian nation of Bangladesh was pressured to stop employing thousands of child workers or face U.S. trade sanctions. In this case, the plight of the children did in fact go from bad to worse. Between 5,000 and 7,000 young girls, for example, went from factory work to prostitution.[61]

An estimated 250 million children between 5 and 17 years old are working, but only about 5 percent of child labor is involved in export industries.

Some companies avoid operating in countries where child labor is employed, whereas others try to establish responsible policies in those same countries.

MNEs may not be willing to hire local workers who want to work long hours due to concerns about exploitation.

According to the International Labor Organization (ILO), a UN institution, 250 million children between the ages of 5 and 17 are working worldwide. Of those, according to one report, 180 million are "young children or in work that endangers their health or well-being, involving hazards, sexual exploitation, trafficking, and debt bondage."[62] According to ILO guidelines, children who are at least 13 years old may be employed in "light" work that's not harmful to their health and doesn't interfere with school. All children under the age of 18 should be protected against the most abusive labor conditions.

For MNEs, the basic challenge is negotiating a global labyrinth of business environments with different cultural, legal, and political rules than those they're used to at home. In addition, they typically rely on local suppliers who are subject to specifically local pressures. Under these conditions, MNEs clearly can't solve all the problems revolving around child labor, especially given the fact that only about 5 percent of child labor worldwide occurs in industries supported by MNEs.[63] Most underage workers can be found in the informal sectors of an economy, especially agriculture, in which it's difficult to protect them.

What MNEs Can and Can't Do   This doesn't mean, however, that MNEs are powerless when it comes to labor-related matters in overseas facilities. The Swedish retailer IKEA, for example, ran into trouble in India because it was buying carpets from local companies that relied heavily on extensive child labor. Rather than trying to force suppliers to stop using child labor, IKEA identified and tackled two different problems. First, it helped working mothers increase family earning power so they could escape the clutches of the

A young boy assembles filter-tipped cigarettes while sitting cross-legged on the floor in a factory in Bangladesh.

loan sharks to whom they were putting up their children as collateral. Second, IKEA set up "bridge schools" to enable working children to enter mainstream education channels within a year.[64]

Sometimes, of course, there's little that companies can do. In some cases, for instance, local law constitutes the biggest impediment to progress. In Thailand, the law "permits" people to work 84 hours a week in seven 12-hour shifts. Naturally, some MNEs are hesitant to allow workers that many hours, in part because they don't want to be accused of exploitation. Thus Nike instituted a maximum workweek of 60 hours in Thailand.

Most of us, of course, tend to see this cap as a benefit to workers, but as it's turned out, Nike has found it harder to retain workers under its 60-hour maximum. Why? Because workers need the money and want to work as many hours as possible. Even offering higher wages didn't alleviate the problem. To complicate matters, because several different MNEs (not to mention local companies) often subcontract with the same local suppliers, subcontractors have trouble managing workforces when some workers can work for 84 hours and others for only 60.

Frequently, MNEs operating in countries where labor policies vary widely from those at home succumb to the pressure simply to leave the market. Usually, it turns out to be a shortsighted decision. Research shows, for instance, that companies like Nike have substantially improved the conditions of workers in overseas facilities. Granted, MNEs are in no position to revolutionize the employment practices of the countries in which they operate, but they can improve conditions at subcontract facilities and even influence the guidelines set by other foreign investors.

In any case, if they don't invest in developing countries at all, they'd certainly have no leverage whatsoever. Chinese labor practices, for example, have come in for a good deal of criticism in the West, but today, thanks in large part to the amount of business being done in China by foreign firms, wages are going up and conditions are getting better. Moreover, as China gradually implements WTO rules, it's opening up more of the country to FDI. One result is that many young female workers from the interior are now able

CONCEPT CHECK

In discussing "Legal Issues in International Business" in Chapter 3, we enumerate certain "operational concerns" of which overseas managers should be conscious: In particular, they need to accept three facts: (1) They may need to jettison any plan to transfer directly principles and practices that work in the domestic business environment, (2) political and legal systems differ among countries, and (3) these differences affect the ways in which firms can exploit opportunities and deflect threats.

to find work closer to home, and the resulting shortage of workers in industrial areas has pushed up wages there.

CORPORATE CODES OF ETHICS: HOW *SHOULD* A COMPANY BEHAVE?

So far, we've discussed numerous issues related to the impact of globalization on business, the role of businesses in the globalization process, and the impact of international businesses on society. But now we come to a qualitatively different question: *How* should *a company behave?* Granted, it's a highly abstract question, but a quick glance at Figure 5.7 (p. 209) will serve to remind you that companies themselves don't pose it in a vacuum: MNEs do in fact face many very real pressures to act responsibly. They aren't all applied with the same consistency, nor do they all carry the same weight; at various times, however, companies must acknowledge and respond to all of them.

Motivations for Corporate Responsibility   Generally speaking, companies experience four strong motivations for acting responsibly:

1. Unethical and irresponsible behavior can result in *legal headaches*, especially in such areas as financial mismanagement and product safety.

2. Such behavior could also result in *consumer action*, such as boycotts, but we hasten to add there's little evidence of the effectiveness of boycotts in effecting change. Nike, for example, has occasionally come under media scrutiny over the employment practices of subcontractors in developing countries, but adverse publicity has never cut into sales. In fact, a U.K. study found that although 30 percent of consumers surveyed claimed to be ethical shoppers, so-called fair-trade products (products certified by an organization called the Fairtrade Labelling Organizations International as meeting certain criteria such as fair prices, fair labor conditions, and environmental sustainability) enjoyed only a 3 percent market share.[65]

3. Unethical behavior can affect *employee morale*. And, conversely, responsible behavior can have a positive influence on a workforce, both at corporate headquarters and at overseas facilities. For example, XanGo LLC, a privately held network-marketing company whose product is based on the mangosteen fruit found in Asia, has contributed profits and employee time to a number of different charitable projects worldwide under the banner of "Charitable Goodness," and the project has proved to be a strong rallying point for employees who think their employer should be active in the communities in which it does business.[66]

4. You never know when *bad publicity* is going to cost you sales. Perhaps this concern is one reason why Nike and other apparel and clothing companies responded so quickly to criticism about allegedly unfair employment practices in developing countries.

Developing a Code of Conduct   A major component of most companies' strategies for ethical and socially responsible behavior is a **code of conduct.** In the context of international operations, we can take up two perspectives on codes of conduct: external and internal. An *external code of conduct* is a set of "guidelines, recommendations and rules issued by entities within society with the intent to affect the behavior of international business entities within society in order to enhance corporate responsibility."[67]

Bear in mind that external codes of conduct are useful only insofar as they give companies some general guidance on how to operate. The practical challenge for the company is familiarizing itself with the codes of many different organizations and, although codes will undoubtedly vary widely, use them to fashion its own *internal code of conduct.*

Companies need to act responsibly because unethical and irresponsible behavior

- *Could result in legal sanctions.*
- *Could result in consumer boycotts.*
- *Could lower employee morale.*
- *Could cost sales because of bad publicity.*

A major component in a company's strategy for ethical and socially responsible behavior is a code of conduct.

What Makes a Good Internal Code of Conduct? In this section, we focus on four criteria for designing an effective internal code of conduct:

1. *It sets global policies with which everyone working anywhere for the company must comply.* A good example is the code promulgated by the Finnish cell-phone company Nokia, which discusses how its code was set, who approved it, how it is communicated to its employees, and what its foundation values are. A portion of the code is as follows:

   Nokia has always recognized that its own long-term interests and those of its various stakeholders depend on compliance with the highest standards of ethical conduct and applicable law. The Code of Conduct has been approved by Nokia's Group Executive Board and is introduced and reinforced to Nokia employees through induction, training and internal communications. The Nokia Values are embedded in this Code, and every Nokia employee is expected to conduct himself or herself, and his or her business, in line with this Code without exception. Stricter guidelines or more detailed instructions may be appropriate for certain regions or countries, but they should not contradict this Code. Nokia periodically reviews this Code and is committed to making changes in its content and implementation when changes or further clarification so demand. . . .

   Nokia is strongly committed to the highest standards of ethical conduct and full compliance with all applicable national and international laws. This includes, for example, those relating to antitrust and promoting fair competition, corporate governance, preventing bribery, illicit payments and corruption, publicly traded securities, safety in the intended use of the products and services Nokia delivers to customers, labor laws and practices, the environment, human rights laws and internationally recognized standards, and protecting copyright, company assets and other forms of intellectual property. Nokia's goal is not mere minimum legal compliance, but as an industry leader to be among the world's best in corporate responsibility, practicing good corporate citizenship wherever it does business.[68]

2. *It communicates company policies not only to all employees but to all suppliers and subcontractors as well.* Gap, for example, maintains an education program to help subcontractors develop their own compliance programs that meet the objectives of Gap's own code.[69]

3. *It ensures that the policies laid out in the code are carried out.* There are a variety of ways to approach this task:

   - GSK requires employees to confirm in writing that they've read and understand the company's code of conduct.

   - Syngenta, an Anglo-Swiss agrochemicals group, found out through press reports that child labor was being used in its supply chain. To ensure that suppliers were adhering to its policies in the matter, the company arranged with the Fair Labor Association, a nonprofit NGO, to submit its operations to external monitoring.[70]

   - A company can hire a major auditing firm, such as KPMG, to conduct *compliance audits.*

   - Sometimes firms act as their own watchdogs. Nike maintains a large staff of compliance officers in Thailand, where they regularly visit subcontractor facilities and work with them on workforce-related issues. Adhering to a similar program, in 2003 Gap revoked the contracts of 136 factories because of persistent or severe violations of its code of conduct.

4. *It reports the results to external stakeholders.* This can be a complicated and sometimes tricky process. Up until a few years ago, for instance, Nike was willing to provide a lot of information about its labor practices. In 1998, however, when a lawsuit charged that the

Codes of conduct involve four dimensions:

- Setting a global policy that must be complied with wherever the company operates.
- Communicating the code to employees, suppliers, and subcontractors.
- Ensuring that policies are carried out.
- Reporting results to external stakeholders.

report constituted false advertising, Nike was forced to pay $1.5 million to the Fair Labor Association. Ever since the ruling came down in 2001, the giant shoe and apparel company has been less forthcoming about labor-related activities. Gap, however, has begun providing *more* information about its worldwide monitoring activities, including details about its code of conduct and practices; the Gap report also discusses its challenges—and failures—in getting subcontractors to act in accord with company policies.[71]

There's no reason to believe that in the future, governments won't continue to compete for larger shares of the wealth and other benefits to be gained from the activities of MNEs. In the short term, most countries will probably work to create more favorable environments for foreign investors, and there are several good reasons why. On the one hand, investment inflows provide developing countries with ways to deal with debt burdens and capital-accounts problems. Meanwhile, industrial nations struggling with trade-deficit problems, like the United States, are more inclined to welcome FDI. The European Union, for example, will probably continue to welcome foreign investment as a means of fueling the growth that it hopes to attain through unification.

The long term, however, may tell a different story. Historically, attitudes toward FDI have tended to fluctuate, with governments tending to favor restrictions when economies are thriving and incentives when they're struggling. But according to some observers, if they don't experience the rate of rapid growth they're expecting from the substantial FDI that they've already attracted, developing countries may make the same about-face that such nations as Russia and Iran have already made—that is, place new restrictions on the flow of foreign investment.

Worse still, growing disappointment with the net results of foreign investment may lead some nations to attribute such problems as weakened sovereignty, increasing poverty, and cultural disintegration to overdependence on FDI. If this reaction to foreign investment is paired with growing criticism from NGOs and other external stakeholders, the ability of companies to operate globally will be further compromised.

CASE

Anglo American PLC in South Africa: What Do You Do When Costs Reach Epidemic Proportions?

By now it should be obvious that, regardless of where it chooses to do business, an MNE is going to face quite a variety of threats and disruptions—ranging from bureaucratic corruption and political instability to terrorism and even war—to its plans and operations. In 2007, Anglo American PLC, the world's largest gold miner, found itself facing a threat that, although by no means new, defies most traditional categories of things that complicate business overseas—an HIV/AIDS epidemic in South Africa, the world's largest gold producer.[72]

In 2002, Anglo American made a landmark decision to provide free antiretroviral therapy (ART) to HIV-infected employees at its South African operations. Surprisingly, however, this commitment has met with mixed reactions from various constituencies and achieved only controversial results, and the U.K.-based company is now asking itself, "Where do we go from here?"

AIDS in South Africa

How bad does a disease have to be to be accorded the status of an "epidemic"? Here's some background information. Sub-Saharan Africa, the portion of Africa lying south of the Sahara Desert, is home to just over 10 percent of the world's population and to 60 percent of all people infected with HIV, the virus that causes AIDS. Located at the southernmost tip of the African continent, the nation of South Africa suffers one of the world's highest rates of HIV infection—approximately 5.5 million cases in a population of 45 million. Every day 1,000 South Africans contract HIV and another 800 die. Moreover, say the UN and the WHO, the epidemic has a long way to go before it reaches its peak.

Needless to say, the spread of the disease has, over the past decade, had a profound impact on both the people of South Africa and their economy. Life expectancy is 42.45 years, compared to, say, 75.19 years in Poland, a country with a similar population size and GDP per capita.

AIDS has also had a devastating effect on the country's economy. Between 1992 and 2002, the South African economy lost $7 billion annually—around 2 percent of GDP—as a result of AIDS-related worker deaths. Experts predict that, as AIDS spreads throughout sub-Saharan Africa, it will continue to reduce per capita growth by 1 percent to 2 percent per year and, in the worst affected countries, cut annual GDP growth by as much as 0.6 percent by 2010. The consequences include both diminishing populations and shrinking economies, with GDPs deflating anywhere from 20 to 40 percent of the sizes they would have reached in the absence of AIDS.

Anglo American Operations in South Africa

Anglo American PLC is a mining conglomerate operating in 61 countries to produce gold, platinum, and other metals (base, ferrous, and industrial), diamonds, coal, forest products, and financial and technical services. Founded in 1917 as the Anglo American Corporation of South Africa, it was South Africa's first home-based public limited company. Although it's now a multinational firm headquartered in London, the company still dominates South Africa's domestic economy: With interests in about 1,300 South African companies, Anglo American employs 80,000 people in its main operations and another 44,000 at regional subsidiaries. Through majority-share ownership of subsidiaries and associate companies, Anglo American controls over 25 percent of all shares traded on the South African stock market.

Anglo American and ART

With such a huge investment in South Africa, Anglo American has been hit hard by the HIV/AIDS epidemic that's descended on the country. Having recognized the threat as far back as the early 1990s, Anglo American was one of the first corporations to develop a comprehensive, proactive strategy to combat the ravages of the disease on its workforce and the repercussions for its operations.

Originally, the program consisted of prevention initiatives aimed at education and awareness, the distribution of condoms, financial and skill-related training to alleviate poverty, and a survey system to monitor the prevalence of the infection. Eventually, these policies were expanded to include voluntary counseling, testing, and care-and-wellness programs, and the services of all programs were extended to cover not only the families of employees but also the populations of surrounding communities. Anglo American also became a member of the Global Business Council on HIV/AIDS, an organization of multinational companies that focuses on alleviating the effects of AIDS throughout the world and on protecting the rights of infected workers.

By adopting these strategies so early, Anglo American became a de facto leader in the private-sector fight against HIV/AIDS in Africa. Many other MNEs—including Coke, Ford, Colgate-Palmolive, and Chevron Texaco—soon followed Anglo American's example and initiated prevention, education, and wellness programs of their own. Even then, however, the majority of companies operating in South Africa still hesitated, and that's why Anglo American's announcement that it would provide ART to its South African workforce (at company expense) was met with a good deal of excited approval from such interested parties as the WHO, the Global Business Council on HIV/AIDS, and a host of other NGOs.

The Costs of Operating in an Epidemic

The incentive for Anglo American's ART program largely came from the failure of its AIDS-prevention efforts to make much headway in stemming the spread of the disease. By 2001, according to Brian Brink, senior VP of the firm's medical division, the prevalence of

HIV-positive workers had risen to an average of 21 percent across all operations—a figure that was climbing steadily at a rate of 2 percent annually. Bobby Godsell, CEO and chairman of the subsidiary AngloGold, reported that HIV/AIDS was adding as much as $5 to the cost of producing 1 ounce of gold, thereby tacking on $11 million a year to the company's production costs in addition to the $7 million it was spending annually to combat such AIDS-related illnesses as tuberculosis (which was five times as prevalent as it had been just a decade earlier).

Finally, in addition to losses in productivity, the company had to bear the costs entailed by high levels of absenteeism, the constant retraining of replacement workers, and burgeoning payouts in health, hospitalization, and death benefits. Studies conducted at the time indicated not only that the costs of AIDS could reach as much as 7.2 percent of the company's total wage bill but also that the costs of leaving employees untreated would be even higher than those of providing ART.

Five years after it rolled out its ART program, Anglo American now finds itself struggling to please various constituencies and to determine whether all of its efforts are making a difference in the underlying problem or merely masking its effects. By the end of 2006, for instance, although 4,600 employees—approximately 65 percent of those in need of treatment—were receiving ART, nearly a third of those who'd began treatment had dropped out (for reasons such as death or termination of employment). By 2007, 23 percent of the company's South African workforce was infected with the deadly virus—a disappointing increase of 2 percent over levels in 2001, before the program was implemented.

On top of everything else, Anglo American also faces the problem of spiraling costs for the program itself. Even though the prices of most of the necessary drugs have been decreasing, the cost of distributing them remains high, and the treatment regime costs the company an estimated $4,000 per year per employee—quite expensive, especially when compared with the wages and benefits that Anglo American typically offers mineworkers. (Average monthly wages in the South African mining industry are about 5,100 rand, or $830.) Meanwhile, as Anglo American officials continue to remind investors that treating workers ultimately serves the bottom line, recent estimates project a total cost to the company of $1 billion or more over 10 years.

On the upside, cost per patient should decrease as the number of workers participating in the program increases. Unfortunately, one of the biggest challenges facing Anglo American is encouraging participation among a migrant and largely ignorant workforce laboring under harsh conditions in an unstable environment. In South Africa, HIV/AIDS still carries a severe stigma, and many South Africans refuse to be tested or to admit they've been infected for fear of discrimination by managers, fellow employees, and even society at large.

Moreover, many of those who had agreed to participate were confused by rumors and misinformation into assuming they could stop using condoms once they were on the drugs—a situation, of course, that only exacerbated the prevalence of unsafe behavior. ART is in fact a lifelong regimen that can lead to various side effects and needs to be administered under strict supervision. Anglo American, however, continues to struggle with high levels of nonadherence. At one point, for example, supervisors were reporting that all workers undergoing treatment were taking medications as directed; urine tests, however, revealed that only 85 percent were actually doing so. By 2006, the company was forced to report that 10.5 percent of participants had dropped out because of inability or unwillingness to adhere to the regimen. Now physicians have to worry that extensive patterns of nonadherence pose a risk of fostering new drug-resistant strains of the virus.

In addition, harsh working conditions often make it hard for workers to take medications on time or to deal with certain side effects. Finally, migrant workers—about four-fifths of the total workforce—come from isolated villages located hundreds of miles away. They're 2.5 times more likely to contract the disease, which they take with them back to their villages.

Constituencies and Critics

Then there's the problem of pressure from various constituencies. Anglo American has come under fire for failing to provide free treatment to dependents of its employees, and the National Union of Mineworkers has been hesitant to voice its support, citing the company's limitations on health-insurance benefits and lack of cooperation with national agencies. The union has also accused the company of helping to foster working conditions that exacerbate the problem. Even then-CEO Brian Gilbertson of BHP Billiton, another large mining concern operating in South Africa, charged Anglo American with merely trying to contain the problem instead of attacking its underlying causes: "You don't approach the problem by just throwing drugs at it," said Gilbertson.

Anglo American has countered many of these criticisms by insisting that it's beyond the resources and capacity of a single company to combat the overall problem and has called for more involvement on the part of the South African government. Instead of cooperation, however, the company has encountered outright opposition from political leaders. Indeed, the South African government has proved to be one of Africa's least committed to a program of effective intervention. Over the course of two years, the government diverted only 0.6 percent of the national budget to the HIV/AIDS crisis and has even resisted the wide distribution of antiretroviral drugs on the grounds it's too expensive and too difficult to implement.

Matters weren't helped any when President Thabo Mbeki publicly questioned the link between the HIV virus and the onset of AIDS. Then the country's health minister decried the Anglo American initiative as a "vigilante" move designed to place unreasonable burdens on the government, which would, after all, have to pick up the tab for treatments once workers had retired or left the company's employment.

In addition, dealing with pharmaceutical companies has proved a tricky proposition. On the one hand, Anglo American has a deal with GlaxoSmithKline allowing it to purchase antiretroviral drugs at a tenth of the market price in the industrialized world (the same that GSK charges not-for-profit organizations). At the same time, however, other drug makers have been hesitant and unreliable at best, promising price cuts and then reneging over fears of violating intellectual property rights. As a matter of fact, several of these companies, complaining that cheap generic drugs made available in Africa will eventually be resold by profiteers on higher-priced Western markets, have put their energies into suing the South African government for what they claim to be generally poor enforcement of their patent rights.

Given the many challenges it's faced, not to mention the opposition from unexpected quarters, some observers have gone so far as to suggest that Anglo American would be better off by simply pulling back on its HIV/AIDS treatment program rather than to pouring more resources into the effort to make it work. In the long run, however, the company must consider the continued pressure it will get from ethically minded shareholders as well as its own sense of moral responsibility.

There are also indications that the future may not be as bleak as it often appears. Of the workers who faithfully adhere to the drug regime, 95 percent have responded well to treatment and are working productively. The South African government may also be undergoing a gradual change of heart, having recently launched a National Strategic Plan for combating HIV/AIDS, which includes the aggressive goal of cutting the number of HIV infections in half by 2011. ■

QUESTIONS

1. What are the pros and cons of Anglo American's adoption of an aggressive strategy in combating HIV/AIDS among its South African workforce? What recommendations would you give the company concerning its HIV/AIDS policy?

2. Because such a large percentage of its workforce consists of migrant workers who are more likely to acquire and spread HIV/AIDS, should Anglo American adopt the policy of not hiring migrant workers? Should the South African government close the doors to migrant workers?

3. What role do pharmaceutical companies play in responding to the HIV/AIDS epidemic in South Africa? What policies or courses of action would you recommend to a company that produces HIV/AIDS drugs?

4. Elsewhere in the chapter, we described the more aggressive policies of the Brazilian and Thai governments in the battle against HIV/AIDS. Should the South African government adopt a similarly aggressive approach? Why or why not?

SUMMARY

- FDI is a major source of capital and expertise, but it is also the center of a controversy over the costs and benefits to home and host countries.

- MNEs must balance the interests of different constituencies that have different objectives.

- The economic and political effects of MNEs are difficult to evaluate because of conflicting influences on different countries' objectives, intervening variables that obscure cause-and-effect relationships, and differences among MNEs' practices.

- MNEs may affect countries' balance of payments, growth, and employment objectives. Under different conditions, these effects may be positive or negative for the host or home country.

- The balance-of-payments effects of FDI involve import stimulus versus import displacement, export stimulus versus export displacement, and capital inflows versus capital outflows. In the latter case, capital flows might be positive initially for the host country but negative later as the investor sends returns back to the home market.

- FDI creates jobs and economic growth in the host country. Given that resources are not fully employed, FDI may or may not have an adverse impact on jobs and economic growth in the home market.

- Relative behavior implies that we act according to the norms of the countries where we operate. Normative behavior implies there are universal standards for ethical conduct that should be followed everywhere.

- The law is an important basis for ethical behavior, but not all unethical behavior is illegal. Thus ethical behavior must go beyond the law to include common decency.

- Bribery is a form of unethical behavior being addressed at the multilateral level, such as at the UN and OECD, and at the national level, such as with the Foreign Corrupt Practices Act in the United States.

- Environmental concerns are raised with extractive industries and industries that generate air and water pollution or that produce products such as automobiles that use fossil fuels.

- The Kyoto Protocol, which requires the reduction of the emission of greenhouse gases, has not been adopted by all countries and is therefore still limited in its total global impact. However, companies must adapt to countries that have implemented the Kyoto Protocol.

- Pharmaceutical companies face challenges on how to make enough money to fund the R&D into new drugs and how to help provide critical drugs to developing countries at lower prices.

- A major challenge facing MNEs is the globalization of the supply chain and the impact on workers, especially in the areas of fair wages, child labor, working conditions, working hours, and freedom of association.

- Companies respond to the pressures for greater corporate social responsibility by establishing codes of conduct, distributing them to suppliers and subcontractors internationally, and ensuring compliance with the codes through effective training and auditing programs.

KEY TERMS

balance-of-payments effect (p. 192)
code of conduct (p. 212)
externality (p. 199)
extraterritoriality (p. 199)

Foreign Corrupt Practices Act (FCPA)
(p. 201)
Kyoto Protocol (p. 205)
normativism (p. 197)

relativism (p. 196)
stakeholder (p. 190)
sustainability (p. 204)

ENDNOTES

1   *Sources include the following:* General Electric Co. home page, at www.ge.com/en/company (accessed May 21, 2007); GE Ecomagination home page, at http://ge.ecomagination.com/site/index.html (accessed May 21, 2007); "A Lean, Clean Electric Machine," *The Economist*, December 10, 2005: 77–79; *GE 2006 Annual Report*, General Electric Co. (2007); Alan Murray, "Business: Why Key Executives Are Warming to Legislation on Climate Change," *Wall Street Journal*, February 7, 2007: A10; Rachel Pulfer, "Gambling on Green," *Canadian Business*, April 24, 2006: 35; Kara Sissell, "Major Corporations Form Advocacy Group to Curb Climate Change," *Chemical Week*, January 31, 2007: 12; "Safety, Health & the Environment at GE," *ASSE Professional Safety*, December 2006, online edition, at www.asse.org; Anne Fisher, "America's Most Admired Companies," *Fortune*, March 19, 2007: 88–94; Neal St. Anthony, " 'Green' Strategy Has GE Investor Seeing Red," Minneapolis-St. Paul (MN) *Star Tribune* (February 3, 2006): 1.; Brendan Murray and Kim Chipman, "Bush Opposes Limits on Pollution Linked to Global Warming," *Pittsburgh Post-Gazette*, January 23, 2007: A5; John Teresko, "Technology of the Year: Connection Profits and Preservation," *Industryweek.com*, December 2005.

2   *World Investment Report 2006: FDI from Developing and Transition Economies: Implications for Development* (United Nations Council on Trade and Development, 2006).

3   See Gavin Boyd and John Dunning, eds., *Structural Change and Cooperation in the Global Economy* (Northampton, MA: Edward Elgar, 1999); Joseph E. Stiglitz, *Globalization and Its Discontents* (New York: W. W. Norton, 2002).

4   Mohsin Habib and Leon Zurawicki, "Corruption and Foreign Direct Investment," *Journal of International Business Studies* 33 (Summer 2002): 291–308.

5   John H. Dunning, "The Future of Multinational Enterprise," *Lloyds Bank Review* (July 1974): 16.

6   Ravi Ramamurti, "The Obsolescing 'Bargaining Model'? MNE-Host Developing Country Relations Revisited," *Journal of International Business Studies* 32 (Spring 2001): 23.

7   "Venezuela Takes Operations from Big Oil Companies," *New York Times*, May 1, 2007, online edition (accessed May 1, 2007).

8   Timothy Aeppel, "Scaling the Ladder," *Wall Street Journal*, April 6, 1999: A1.

9   On the argument that MNEs contribute to host-country gains, see William Keng and Mun Lee, "Foreign Investment, Industrial Restructuring and Dependent Development in Singapore," *Journal of Contemporary Asia* 27 (March 1997): 58–71. On the opposite view, see Brian J. Aitken and Ann E. Harrison, "Do Domestic Firms Benefit from Direct Foreign Investment? Evidence from Venezuela," *American Economic Review* 89:3 (1995): 605.

10 David J. Vidal, *The Link Between Corporate Citizenship and Financial Performance* (New York: Conference Board, 1999).

11 Interfaith Center on Corporate Responsibility, at www.iccr.org.

12 Elizabeth Wine, "Ethical Crusaders Resolve to Redeem the Corporate Sinners," *Financial Times*, March 30–31, 2002: 24.

13 Ronald Berenbeim, "The Search for Global Ethics," *Vital Speeches of the Day* 65:6 (1999): 177–178.

14 S. Prakash Sethi, "Standards for Corporate Conduct in the International Arena: Challenges and Opportunities for Multinational Corporations," *Business and Society Review* (Spring 2002): 20–39.

15 "The Ethics of Business," in "A Survey of Corporate Social Responsibility," *The Economist*, January 22, 2005: 20.

16 See "Indonesia's Plague," *Far Eastern Economic Review*, July 12, 2001: 8; John Danley, "Balancing Risks: Mosquitos, Malaria, Morality, and DDT," *Business and Society Review* (Spring 2002): 145–70.

17 "Brazil Authorities Raid Plantation over Labor Conditions," *CNN News*, at www.cnn.com/2007/ WORLD/americas/07/03/brazil.labor.ap/index.html (accessed July 3, 2007).

18 See Pirkko Lammi, "My Vision of Business in Europe," in Jack Mahoney and Elizabeth Vallance, eds., *Business Ethics in a New Europe* (Dordrecht, Netherlands: Klüwer Academic, 1992), 11–12; Andrew Jack, "French Prepare to Repel English Advance," *Financial Times*, January 7, 1997: 2.

19 Alfred Marcus, *Business & Society: Ethics, Government, and the World Economy* (Homewood, IL: Irwin, 1996).

20 John R. Boatright, *Ethics and the Conduct of Business* (Upper Saddle River, NJ: Prentice Hall, 1993), 13–16.

21 Boatright, *Ethics and the Conduct of Business*, 16–18.

22 See A. M. Ali and I. H. Saiad, "Determinants of Economic Corruption," *Cato Journal* 22:3 (2003): 449–66; H. Park, "Determinants of Corruption: A Cross-National Analysis," *Multinational Business Review* 11:2 (2003): 29–48.

23 "The Short Arm of the Law—Bribery and Business," *The Economist*, March 2, 2002: 78.

24 For an even more detailed listing, go to the Web site of Transparency International at www.transparency.org and take a look at the *Corruption Perceptions Index (CPI)*.

25 See The World Bank, *World Development Report 2002: Building Institutions for Markets*; M. Habib and L. Zurawicki, "Country-Level Investments and the Effect of Corruption—Some Empirical Evidence," *International Business Review* 10:6 (2001): 687–700.

26 "China Execution Warning to Others," *Aljazeera.net*, Wednesday, July 11, 2007, at http://english.aljazeera.net (accessed August 20, 2007).

27 S. Ghoshal and P. Moran, "Towards a Good Theory of Management," in J. Birkinshaw and G. Piramal, eds., *Sumantra Ghoshal on Management: A Force for Good* (Financial Times/Prentice Hall, Upper Saddle River, NJ, 2005): 1–27.

28 Cassandra E. DiRienzo, Jayoti Das, Kathryn T. Cort, and John Burbridge Jr., "Corruption and the Role of Information," *Journal of International Business Studies* 38:2 (2007): 320–32.

29 OECD, "South Africa Joined the OECD's Anti-Bribery Convention," January 28, 2005, at www.oecd.org/topic/0,3373,en_2649_37447_1_1_1_1_37447,00.html (accessed July 3, 2007).

30 United Nations home page, at www.un.org (accessed July 7, 2007).

31 International Chamber of Commerce, "Extortion and Bribery in International Business Transactions," 1999 revised version, at www.iccwbo.org/home/statements_rules/rules/1999/briberydoc99.asp. (accessed April 23, 2005).

32 "Battling Bribery Abroad," *ABA Journal* 93:3 (2007): 48–54.

33 OECD, "Steps Taken and Planned Future Actions by Participating Countries to Ratify and Implement the Convention of Combating Bribery of Foreign Public Officials in International Business Transactions," March 10, 2005, at www.oecd.org/topic/0,2686,en_2649_37447_1_1_1_1_37447,00.html (accessed April 23, 2005).

34 Glenn R. Simpson, "Multinational Companies Unite to Fight Bribery," *Wall Street Journal*, January 27, 2005, at http://online.wsj.com.

35 "Survey Shows Few Checks for Bribery," *Financial Times*, April 13, 2007: 26.

36 Colleen Taylor, "U.S., Japan Authorities Join in Siemens' 'Black Money' Probe," *Electronic News*, February 12, 2007: 7; David Crawford and Mike Esterl, "Room at the Top: German Giant Siemens Faces Leadership Crisis," *Wall Street Journal*, April 26, 2007; Crawford and Esterl, "Widening Scandal: At Siemens, Witnesses Cite Pattern of Bribery," *Wall Street Journal*, January 31, 2007: A.1.

37 "The Hollow Men," *The Economist*, March 17, 2007: 71.

38 Michael Connolly, "Germany Inc. Under a Cloud," *Wall Street Journal*, November 24, 2006.

39 Crawford and Esterl, "Widening Scandal."

40 Konstantin Richter, "The House of Siemens," *Wall Street Journal*, April 27, 2007: 13.

41 Jack Ewing, "Siemens' Culture Clash: CEO Kleinfeld Is Making Changes, and Enemies," *Business Week*, January 29, 2007: 42–46.

42 Richter, "The House of Siemens," 13.

43 David Crawford and Mike Esterl, "Siemens to Decide if New Leader Is Needed amid Widening Probes," *Wall Street Journal*, April 25, 2007: A.3.

44 Ewing, "Siemens' Culture Clash," 42–46; Richter, "The House of Siemens," 13.

45 G. Thomas Sims, "Siemens Struggles to Regain Equilibrium," *New York Times* online edition, April 27, 2007; Sims, "Two Former Siemens Officials Convicted for Bribery," *New York Times* online edition, May 15, 2007.

46 For information on the concept of *sustainability*, go to www.afsc.org/trade-matters/learn-about/glossary.htm and http://en.wikipedia.org/wiki/Sustainability.

47 John Carey, "Global Warming," *Business Week*, August 16, 2004: 60–69.

48 "Hotting Up," *The Economist*, February 5, 2005: 73–74.

49 UNFCC home page, at http://unfcc.int/files/kyoto_protocol/background/status_of_ratification/Application/pdf/kp_ratification.pdf (accessed July 3, 2007).

50 Alison Graab, "Greenhouse Gas Market to Slow Global Warming," *CNN.com* (accessed April 12, 2005).

51 Mark Lander, "Mixed Feelings as Kyoto Pact Takes Effect," *New York Times*, February 16, 2005.

52 Lander, "Mixed Feelings as Kyoto Pact Takes Effect."

53 Carey, "Global Warming," 62.

54 *GlaxoSmithKline 2006 Annual Report*, various pages, at www.gsk.com/index.htm.

55 Miriam Jorda, "Brazil to Stir Up AIDS-Drug Battle," *Wall Street Journal*, September 5, 2003: A3; "Brazil to Break Merck AIDS Drug Patent," Associated Press story on MSNBC Web site, May 4, 2007.

56 Frederik Balfour, "Fakes!" *Business Week*, February 7, 2005: 56.

57 "A Gathering Storm: Pharmaceuticals," *The Economist*, June 9, 2007: 73.

58 Andrew Jack, "Companies Europe: HIV Drug Price Slashed," *Financial Times*, May 15, 2007: 27.

59 Manjeet Kripalani, "India: Copycats No More," *Business Week*, April 18, 2005: 51.

60 Ethical Trading Initiative, at www.ethicaltrade.org (accessed August 20, 2007).

61 Ans Kolk and Rob van Tulder, "Child Labor and Multinational Conduct: A Comparison of International Business and Stakeholder Codes," *Journal of Business Ethics* (March 2002).

62 Frances Williams, "Economic Case Made for Ending Child Labour," *Financial Times*, February 4, 2004: 5.

63 Kolk and van Tulder, "Child Labor and Multinational Conduct."

64 Edward Luce, "Ikea's Grown-Up Plan to Tackle Child Labour," *Financial Times*, September 15, 2004: 7.

65 Michael Skapinker, "Cost Cuts and False Economics," *Financial Times*, November 24, 2003: 5.

66 Global Goodness Initiatives, at www.xangogoodness.org (accessed August 20, 2007).

67 A. Kolk, R. vanTulder, and I. Sloekers, "International Codes of Conduct and Corporate Social Responsibility: Can Transnational Corporations Regulate Themselves?" *Transnational Corporations* 8 (2001): 143–80.

68 Nokia Web site, at www.nokia.com/link?cid=EDITORIAL_64678 (accessed July 31, 2007).

69 Amy Merrick, "Gap Offers Unusual Look at Factory Conditions," *Wall Street Journal*, May 12, 2004: A1.

70 "Syngenta Opens Up to Independent Scrutiny," *Financial Times*, May 12, 2004: 8.

71 Sarah Murray and Alison Matiland, "The Trouble with Transparent Clothing," *Financial Times*, May 12, 2004: 8.

72 *Sources include the following:* Mark Schoofs, "Anglo American Drops Noted Plan on AIDS Drugs," *Wall Street Journal*, April 16, 2002: A19; World Health Organization/AFRO, "Southern African Health Challenges Intensify," press release, September 13, 2004: 1–2; Schoofs, "New Challenges in Fighting AIDS—Enlisting Multinationals in Battle," *Wall Street Journal*, November 30, 2001: B1; "AIDS in the Workplace," *Business Africa*, July 1, 2001: 1–2; "The Corporate Response," *Business Africa*, September 1, 2001: 4; Schoofs, "South Africa Reverses Course on AIDS Drugs," *Wall Street Journal*, November 20, 2003: B1; "Anglo American to Provide HIV/AIDS Help for Workers," *American Metal Market*, August 7, 2002: 4; Bruce Einhorn and Catherine Arnst, "Why Business Should Make AIDS Its Business—Multinationals Are Taking Baby Steps to Control the Disease in Their Workforce," *Business Week*, August 9, 2004: 83; "Digging Deep," *The Economist*, August 10, 2002: 55; James Lamont, "Anglo's Initiative," *Financial Times*, August 8, 2002: 10; "Anglo American to Give Mineworkers AIDS Drugs Free," *Wall Street Journal*, August 7, 2002: A13; Matthew Newmann, Scott Hensley, and Scott Miller, "U.S. Reaches Patent Compromise to Provide Drugs to Poor Nations," *Wall Street Journal*, August 28, 2003: A3; Statistics South Africa, "Labour Statistics Survey of Average Monthly Earnings," *Statistical Release P0272*, February 2002: 3; UNAIDS, UNICEF, WHO, "South Africa—Epidemiological Fact Sheets," *Treat 3 Million by 2005* (2004); Anglo American PLC, "Safety, Health, and Environment Report 2001" (2001), at www2.coca-cola.com/citizenship/africa_employee_program.html; Anglo American PLC, "Report to Society 2002" (2002): 4–6, 33 at www.angloamerican.co.uk/about/businesses.asp; Anglo American PLC "Annual Report 2002" (2002), at http://galenet.galegroup.com.erl.lib.byu.edu/

servlet/BCRC?vrsn=137&locID=byu_main&srchtp=glbc&
cc=1&c=2&mode=c&ste=74&tbst=tsCM&tab=4&ccmp=
Anglo+American+PLC&mst=Anglo+American+PLc&n=
25&docNum=I2501307472&bConts=4911; Integrated Regional
Information Network (IRIN), "South Africa—Antiretroviral
Therapy Is Cost-Effective, Says Report," *News Report*,
September 15, 2004, at www.cia.gov/cia/

publications/factbook/geos/sf.html#people; Integrated
Regional Information Network (IRIN), "Africa—Greater
Commitment, More Funding Urged for Treatment,"
News Report, September 21, 2004, at www.cia.gov/cia/
publications/factbook/geos/pl.html; "South Africa AIDS/
HIV Statistics, at www.avert.org/safricastats.htm
(accessed May 20, 2005).

6

International Trade and Factor-Mobility Theory

Objectives

- To understand theories of international trade

- To explain how global efficiency can be improved through free trade

- To identify factors affecting national trade patterns

- To explain why a country's export capabilities are dynamic

- To understand why production factors, especially labor and capital, move internationally

- To explain the relationship between foreign trade and international factor mobility

A market is not held for the sake of one person.

—*African (Fulani) proverb*

CASE: Costa Rica: Using Foreign Trade to Trade Up Economically

As you can see from Map 6.1, Costa Rica, a Central American country of slightly more than 4 million people, borders the Pacific Ocean and the Caribbean arm of the Atlantic. Its name, "Rich Coast," refers to its fertile soil and bountiful biodiversity.[1] The World Bank classifies Costa Rica as *upper middle income* because it possesses some attributes we associate with developed countries and some that we associate with developing countries. With a per capita GDP of $12,500 (based on purchasing price parity in 2006), Costa Rica is highly dependent

movement of goods, services, and production factors across borders—to pursue its economic objectives. In any country, these two sets of policies are closely intertwined with the nature and quantity of the products that the country produces. Naturally, they also change over time, as both domestic and foreign conditions evolve, and they're politically sensitive, especially when it comes to the economic priorities and judgments of the nation's leadership.

MAP 6.1 Costa Rica

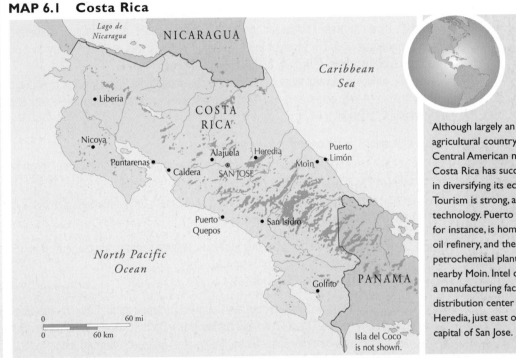

Although largely an agricultural country, the Central American nation of Costa Rica has succeeded in diversifying its economy. Tourism is strong, as is technology. Puerto Limón, for instance, is home to an oil refinery, and there's a petrochemical plant in nearby Moin. Intel operates a manufacturing facility and distribution center in Heredia, just east of the capital of San Jose.

Isla del Coco is not shown.

on agricultural commodities—primarily bananas, coffee, pineapples, and sugar—for its export earnings; it has a fairly high level of external debt, a literacy rate of 96 percent, a life expectancy at birth of 77.21 years, and fairly even income distribution (the highest 10 percent of the population earns about 37 percent of its income). It has also enjoyed a long history of democracy and political stability.

FOUR ERAS

Like all countries, Costa Rica relies on *international trade* and *factor-mobility policies*—strategies related to the

In Costa Rica as elsewhere, therefore, these policies have evolved continuously, but in the case of Costa Rica, it's convenient to trace that evolution through four historical periods, each of which tends to be characterized by a particular set of policies regarding international trade and factor mobility:

- *1800s–1960: Liberal trade*—a policy calling for minimal government interference in trade and investment
- *1960–1982: Import substitution*—a policy calling for the local production of goods and services that would otherwise have to be imported

- *1983–early 1990s: Liberalization* of imports, export promotion, and incentives for foreign investments
- *Early 1990s–present: Strategic trade and investment*—a policy calling for the production of specific types of products—and openness to imports

1800s–1960

In the latter part of the 1800s, most nations adopted policies permitting goods, capital, and people to move with relative freedom from one country to another. Governments tended to interfere only minimally (usually in support of certain industries), and the result, generally speaking, was an economic environment in which individual producers determined what to produce and where to produce it. Under the sway of such liberal policies, trade flourished and countries tended to specialize in selling what they could best produce.

Most Latin American countries specialized in either a single or a few commodities (raw materials or agricultural products), which they exported in exchange for both other commodities and manufactured goods. Not only was Costa Rica no exception, but it also managed to adhere to this regime until the early 1960s. Costa Rican farmers specialized, first, in coffee and, later, after the development of refrigerated ships, in bananas as well. For most of the period, the country was well served by this policy, primarily because commodity prices, especially coffee prices, remained high.

Eventually, however, several factors combined to convince Costa Rican leaders to encourage diversified production and economic self-sufficiency. These factors arose principally out of three sets of circumstances both external and internal:

- Trade disruptions occasioned by two world wars
- A drop in coffee and banana prices relative to the prices of manufactured products, particularly as new commodity producers (especially in Africa) entered world markets
- The fact that Latin American countries with less open international markets had insulated themselves more from adverse international conditions

As a result of these developments, Costa Rica turned to policies centered on the idea of import substitution.

1960–1982

Import substitution is a policy calling for the development of products that would otherwise be imported. Beginning in the early 1960s, Costa Rican authorities reasoned that if they limited imports (say, by taxing them heavily), they'd provide both Costa Rican and foreign investors with an incentive to produce more things domestically for sale to Costa Rican consumers. They also realized that, unfortunately, the Costa Rican market was too small to support investments requiring large-scale production.

To address this problem, Costa Rica joined with four other countries—El Salvador, Guatemala, Honduras, and Nicaragua—to form the Central American Common Market (CACM), which allowed goods produced in any member country to enter freely into the market of any other member. Under this arrangement, a company located in a member country would be in a position to serve a five-country market rather than a one-country market.

Miscalculations and Mixed Results

The results were mixed. On the one hand, by rendering itself less dependent on agriculture (which accounted for 25.2 percent of GDP in 1960 versus 18 percent in 1980), Costa Rica did in fact diversify its economy. Unfortunately, the same shift had been even more pronounced in the period between 1950 and 1960, when, with little government interference in the economy, agricultural production had dropped from 40.9 percent to 25.2 percent of GDP.

Likewise, although some foreign investment was attracted to the local manufacturing sector, most of it was earmarked for the Costa Rican market and not the larger CACM market. In the pharmaceutical industry, for example, the strategy of import substitution was indeed effective in helping domestic producers increase sales and revenue, but the availability of a larger market was not the primary reason; in this case, the strategy worked basically because small-scale packaging and processing are efficient strategies in the pharmaceuticals industry.

So why was the strategy of import substitution, even coupled with a complementary regional trade agreement, less successful than CACM leaders had hoped? Quite simply, neither local nor foreign investors were convinced that the CACM was destined to last, and as it turned out, they were right. By the late 1970s, civil wars in both El Salvador and Guatemala stifled those economies, and a new regime in Nicaragua was ideologically committed to complete governmental control of all aspects of the economy, including trade; El Salvador and Honduras even went to war with each other.

In some cases, import substitution led to increased exports. Costa Rica found new markets, both local and export, for processed coffee and cotton seeds. Many economists and prospective investors, however, began to worry that policies designed to protect local production—including price controls, import prohibitions, and subsidies—were channeling the country's resources away from areas of production in which it had long been most efficient. Costa Rica, for example, had become nearly self-sufficient in rice production, but only because government policies kept lower-cost foreign-produced rice out of the market.

Moreover, the government managed to hold down consumer rice prices only by subsidizing domestic producers. And where did the money for these subsidies come from? In part, from higher taxes on efficient industries—industries that, in turn, found it hard to expand because they were strapped for cash. Finally, some inefficient producers survived not because they received subsidies but because they reaped the benefits of the high prices being paid by consumers—who were thus left with less disposable income to spend on any products, domestic or foreign.

At this point, Costa Rican policymakers reached the conclusion that the country must emphasize the production of goods that could compete in international markets. For one thing, they had the example of Asian countries that were achieving rapid growth by competing internationally. In 1983, therefore, Costa Rica shifted to a policy of promoting exports.

1983–EARLY 1990s

First, to help ensure that only internationally competitive companies and industries were likely to survive in the newly projected business environment, the government began removing import barriers. Rice imports, for example, rose substantially as the government removed the protective barriers it had erected around domestic production.

CINDE

Policymakers also decided to seek more outside capital and expertise to support economic reforms. As luck would have it, the United States launched its Caribbean Basin Initiative, which allowed products originating in the Caribbean region (including Costa Rica) to enter the United States at lower tariff, or import-tax, rates than those originating elsewhere. To capitalize on this new opportunity, Costa Rica formed CINDE (la Coalición Costarricense de Iniciativas de Desarrollo), a private organization funded by the government and grants from the U.S. government. The purpose of CINDE was to aid in economic development, and one of its top priorities was attracting foreign direct investment.

To augment CINDE's work, Costa Rica established an export processing zone (EPZ) that allowed companies exporting finished output to import all inputs and equipment tax free. They were also exempted from paying Costa Rican income tax for eight years and allowed to pay at a 50 percent discount for the next four years. By 1989, 35 companies—mainly textile and footwear producers seeking to take advantage of Costa Rica's pool of inexpensive labor—had located in the EPZ.

By this time, however, CINDE officials were beginning to worry about two potential problems facing its ambitious new initiatives:

1. That Costa Rica could not remain cost competitive in the type of products exported from the EPZ because other countries (mainly Mexico) were benefiting from even lower U.S. tariffs

2. That Costa Rica's highly skilled and educated workforce was not being utilized to the best advantage by the types of industries attracted to the EPZ

CINDE officials decided to work with the Costa Rican government to identify and attract investors who matched up better with Costa Rican resources.

EARLY 1990s–PRESENT

This approach—identifying and targeting industries for international competition—is often called a *strategic trade policy* (or an *industrial policy*). Which industries did the Costa Rican government target? Mainly ones that promised high growth potential and, like medical instruments and appliances, electronics, and software, could pay higher wages and salaries than most of those that had already invested in the EPZ.

Costa Rican officials also took a close look at the characteristics of developing countries that were attracting significant amounts of foreign investment: a highly educated, largely English-speaking workforce (especially the availability of engineers and technical operators), political and social stability and relatively high levels of economic freedom, and a quality of life that would appeal to the managers and technical personnel that foreign investors would bring in to work in the facilities. The conclusion? In its targeted industries, Costa Rica should be able to compete on the international market.

WHAT CINDE RECOMMENDED

CINDE also hired the Foreign Investment Advisory Service (FIAS) of the International Finance Corporation (an arm of the World Bank) to study the feasibility of attracting companies in these industries and the best means of attracting them to Costa Rica. FIAS concluded that attracting the right number of the right companies was well within Costa Rica's reach.

It also suggested areas within this selection of targeted industries, such as power technologies, that best fit with Costa Rica's main advantage—a labor force that was well educated in relation to its cost—and recommended that officials target industries that supported the electronics and computer industries, such as plastics and metalworking. Finally, FIAS noted areas in which Costa Rica needed to improve, such as the protection of intellectual property rights and English proficiency among technicians and engineers. In response, Costa Rica revised the curriculum for training midlevel technicians and set up Spanish-language training for the personnel brought in by foreign investors.

Progress Report

Setting out to attract investments in electronics and software, Costa Rica landed such high-tech investors as Reliability, Protek, Colorplast, and Sensortronics. By far the largest investment, however, has been by Intel. What did CINDE officials do to make Costa Rica attractive to the computer-chip giant? By drawing up a list of all the questions and concerns that Intel might have, they were prepared to respond to them quickly and knowledgeably. They also involved top governmental and company leaders in meetings with Intel executives, who were even piloted by President José Figueres on a helicopter survey of plant sites.

Since then, Costa Rica has turned its attention to medical devices, an area in which it has attracted investments by such companies as Abbott Laboratories, Baxter, and Procter & Gamble. Although exports of coffee and bananas are still important to the nation's economy, as of 2005, about two-thirds of Costa Rica's exports have been manufactured goods, with high-tech products now constituting the backbone of the economy and export earnings.

> Trade theory helps managers and government policymakers focus on these questions:
>
> • What products should we import and export?
>
> • How much should we trade?
>
> • With whom should we trade?

Introduction

The preceding case shows how Costa Rica has used trade and factor mobility (movement of capital, technology, and people) to help it achieve its economic objectives. Like Costa Rica, other countries wrestle with the questions of what, how much, and with whom their country should import and export. These questions are intertwined with considerations of what they can produce efficiently and if and how they can improve their competitiveness by increasing the quality and quantity of capital, technical competence, and worker skills.

LAISSEZ-FAIRE VERSUS INTERVENTIONIST APPROACHES TO EXPORTS AND IMPORTS

Once countries make decisions, officials enact policies to achieve the desired results. These policies have an impact on business because they affect which countries can produce given products more efficiently and whether countries will permit imports to compete against their own domestically produced goods and services. Some countries take a more *laissez-faire* approach, one that allows market forces to determine trading relations because they believe government programs lead to inefficiency. Whether taking interventionist or laissez-faire approaches, countries rely on trade theories to guide policy development. Figure 6.1 shows that trade in goods and services and the movement of production factors are means by which countries are linked internationally.

In this chapter, we look first at trade theories that address the complex issue of whether a government should intervene directly to affect a country's trade with other countries and, if so, how to go about what can be a fairly tricky task. In effect, these theories cover opposite ends of the spectrum. At one end are *mercantilism* and *neomercantilism*, which prescribe a great deal of government intervention to affect trade. At the other end are *free-trade theories* (absolute advantage and comparative advantage), which prescribe that governments should not intervene directly to affect trade.

THEORIES OF TRADE PATTERNS

From there, we examine theories that help explain trade patterns (how much countries depend on trade, what products they trade, and with whom they primarily trade). These include theories of *country size, factor proportions,* and *country similarity*. Then we consider theories dealing with the dynamics of countries' trade competitiveness for particular products. These theories include the *product life cycle theory* and the *Porter diamond*.

Factor-Mobility Theory Because the stability and dynamics of countries' competitive positions depend largely on the quantity and quality of their production factors (land, labor, capital, technology), we conclude the chapter with a discussion of factor mobility. Table 6.1 summarizes the major theories and their emphases. A check mark indicates that the theory deals with this question, and a dash indicates it does not. The "yes" and "no" apply only to the question, "Should government control trade?" because the other theories don't deal with the question.

CONCEPT CHECK

Compare Figure 6.1 with Figure 1.1, which outlines certain conditions that may affect a firm's operations when it decides to do business on an international scale. Here the graphic focuses in on operational adjustments that a company faces when it takes specific strategic actions to go international—namely, to trade and transfer means of production.

Some trade theories prescribe that governments should influence trade patterns; others propose a laissez-faire treatment of trade.

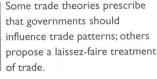

OBJECTIVES

STRATEGY

MEANS OF OPERATIONS
- Importing and exporting goods and services (trade)
- Transferring production factors, such as labor and capital, internationally

Country A ⟷ Country B

FIGURE 6.1
International Operations and Economic Connections

To meet its international objectives, a company must gear its strategy to trading and transferring its means of operation across borders— say, from (Home) Country A to (Host) Country B. Once this process has taken place, the two countries are connected economically.

TABLE 6.1   What Major Trade Theories Do and Don't Discuss: A Checklist

A check mark indicates that a theory of trade concerns itself with the question asked at the head of the column; if there's a dash, it doesn't. In column 4, you can see how each theory responds to the specific question; again, a dash indicates that the theory does not address the question.

Theory	Description of Natural Trade			Prescription of Trade Relationships			
	How Much Is Traded	What Products Are Traded?	With Whom Does Trade Take Place?	Should Government Control Trade?	How Much Should Be Traded?	What Products Should Be Traded?	With Whom Should Trade Take Place?
Mercantilism	—	—	—	yes	✓	✓	✓
Neomercantilism	—	—	—	yes	✓	—	—
Absolute advantage	—	✓	—	no	—	✓	—
Comparative advantage	—	✓	—	no	—	✓	—
Country size	✓	✓	—	—	—	—	—
Factor proportion	—	✓	✓	—	—	—	—
Country similarity	—	✓	✓	—	—	—	—
Product life cycle (PLC)	—	✓	✓	—	—	—	—
Porter diamond	—	✓	—	—	—	—	—

These different theories provide insights about favorable locales for exports as well as potentially successful export products. They also help companies determine where to locate their production facilities because, in the absence of government trade restrictions, exports of given products move from lower-cost to higher-cost production locations. However, trade restrictions may diminish export capabilities and cause companies to locate some production in the restricting countries. The theories also increase understanding about government trade policies and predict how those policies might affect companies' competitiveness.

Interventionist Theories

We begin our discussion with theories prescribing government intervention because one of these, mercantilism, is the oldest trade theory, out of which neomercantilism has more recently emerged. These are not the only reasons for governmental intervention. In fact, the subject is so large, especially protectionism and methods to bring it about, that it is the subject of the next chapter.

MERCANTILISM

According to mercantilism, countries should export more than they import.

Mercantilism is a trade theory holding that a country's wealth is measured by its holdings of "treasure," which usually means its gold. This theory formed the foundation of economic thought from about 1500 to 1800.[2] According to the theory, countries should export more than they import and, if successful, receive gold from countries that run deficits. Nation-states were emerging during the period from 1500 to 1800, and gold empowered central governments that invested it in armies and national institutions. These nation-states sought to solidify the people's primary allegiances to the new nation and lessen their bonds to such traditional units as city-states, religions, and guilds. One can see why mercantilism flourished.

Governmental Policies   To export more than they imported, governments imposed restrictions on most imports, and they subsidized production of many products that could otherwise not compete in domestic or export markets. Some countries used their colonial possessions to support this trade objective. Colonies supplied many commodities that the colonizing country might otherwise have had to purchase from a nonassociated country. Second, the colonial powers sought to run trade surpluses with their own colonies as an additional way to obtain revenue. They did this not only by monopolizing colonial trade but also by preventing the colonies from engaging in manufacturing.

The colonies had to export less highly valued raw materials and import more highly valued manufactured products. Mercantilist theory was intended to benefit the colonial powers. The imposition of regulations based on this theory caused much discontent in colonies and was one cause of the American Revolution.

As the influence of the mercantilist philosophy weakened after 1800, the governments of colonial powers seldom aimed directly to limit the development of industrial capabilities within their colonies. However, their home-based companies had technological leadership, ownership of raw material production abroad, and usually some degree of protection from foreign competition. This combination continued to make colonies dependent on raw material production and to tie their trade to their industrialized mother countries. In fact, we still see vestiges of these relationships.

The Concept of *Balance of Trade* Some terminology of the mercantilist era has endured. A **favorable balance of trade,** for example, still indicates that a country is exporting more than it is importing. An **unfavorable balance of trade** indicates the opposite, which is known as a deficit. Many of these terms are misnomers. For example, the word *favorable* implies "benefit," and the word *unfavorable* suggests "disadvantage." In fact, it is not necessarily beneficial to run a trade surplus nor is it necessarily disadvantageous to run a trade deficit. A country that is running a surplus, or a favorable balance of trade, is, for the time being, importing goods and services of less value than those it is exporting.[3]

> Running a favorable balance of trade is not necessarily beneficial.

In the mercantilist period, the difference was made up by a transfer of gold, but today it is made up by holding the deficit country's currency or investments denominated in that currency. In effect, the surplus country is granting credit to the deficit country. If that credit cannot eventually buy sufficient goods and services, the so-called favorable trade balance actually may turn out to be disadvantageous for the country with the surplus.

Neomercantilism Recently, the term **neomercantilism** has emerged to describe the approach of countries that try to run favorable balances of trade in an attempt to achieve some social or political objective. For instance, a country may try to achieve full employment by setting economic policies that encourage its companies to produce in excess of the demand at home and to send the surplus abroad. Or a country may attempt to maintain political influence in an area by sending more merchandise to the area than it receives from it, such as a government granting aid or loans to a foreign government to use for the purchase of the granting country's excess production.

> A country that practices neomercantilism attempts to run an export surplus to achieve a social or political objective.

Free Trade Theories

Thus far, we have intentionally ignored the question of why countries need to trade at all. Why can't Costa Rica (or any other country) be content with the goods and services produced within its own territory? In fact, many countries, following mercantilist policy, did try to become as self-sufficient as possible through local production of goods and services. In this section, we discuss two theories supporting *free trade: absolute advantage* and *comparative advantage.*

Both hold that nations should neither artificially limit imports nor promote exports.[4] The so-called *invisible hand* will determine which producers survive as consumers buy those products that best serve their needs. Both free trade theories imply *specialization.* Just as individuals and families produce some things that they exchange for things that others produce, national specialization means producing some things for domestic consumption and export while using the export earnings to buy imports of products and services produced abroad.

> **CONCEPT CHECK**
>
> In Chapter 1, we observe that nations are currently in the mood to reduce barriers to the movement of trade, capital, technology, and people; we also explain that this policy reflects a couple of key facts—namely, that consumers want a greater variety of goods and services at lower prices and that competition spurs efficiency.

THEORY OF ABSOLUTE ADVANTAGE

In 1776, Adam Smith questioned the mercantilists' assumption that a country's wealth depends on its holdings of treasure. Rather, he said, the real wealth of a country consists of the goods and services available to its citizens. Smith developed the theory of **absolute advantage,** which holds that different countries produce some goods more efficiently than other countries; thus global efficiency can increase through free trade. Based on this theory, he questioned why the citizens of any country should have to buy domestically produced goods when they could buy those goods more cheaply from abroad.

Smith reasoned that if trade were unrestricted, each country would specialize in those products that gave it a competitive advantage. Each country's resources would shift to the efficient industries because the country could not compete in the inefficient ones. Through specialization, countries could increase their efficiency because of three reasons:

1. Labor could become more skilled by repeating the same tasks.
2. Labor would not lose time in switching from the production of one kind of product to another.
3. Long production runs would provide incentives for the development of more effective working methods.

A country could then use its excess specialized production to buy more imports than it could have otherwise produced. But in what products should a country specialize? Although Smith believed the marketplace would make the determination, he thought that a country's advantage would be either *natural* or *acquired.*

Natural Advantage   A country may have a **natural advantage** in producing a product because of climatic conditions, access to certain natural resources, or availability of certain labor forces. The country's climate may dictate, for example, which agricultural products it can produce efficiently. As we saw in our opening case, Costa Rica's climate supports the production of coffee, bananas, and pineapples. Interestingly, climate is also a factor in the country's success in exporting services: Its thriving eco-tourism industry attracts tourists to its network of tropical national parks. Costa Rica imports wheat. If it were to increase its production of wheat, for which its climate and terrain are less suited, it would have to use land now devoted to the cultivation of coffee, bananas, or pineapples or to convert some of its national park areas to agricultural production, thus reducing the earnings from these products or services.

Conversely, the United States could produce coffee (perhaps in climate-controlled buildings), but at the cost of diverting resources away from products such as wheat, for which its climate and terrain are naturally suited. Trading coffee for wheat and vice versa is a goal more easily achieved than if these two countries were to try to become self-sufficient in the production of both. The more the two countries' climates differ, the more likely they will favor trade with one another.

Most countries must import ores, metals, and fuels from other countries. No one country is large enough or sufficiently rich in natural resources to be independent of the rest of the world except for short periods. Costa Rica, for example, has very few minerals. The United States is self-sufficient in coal but not in petroleum. Another natural resource is soil, which, when coupled with topography, is an important determinant of the types of products a country can produce most efficiently.

Variations among countries in natural advantages also help explain in which countries certain manufactured or processed products might be best produced, particularly if by processing an agricultural commodity or natural resource prior to exporting, companies can reduce transportation costs. Processing coffee beans into instant coffee reduces bulk and is likely to reduce transport costs on coffee exports. Producing canned latte could add weight, lessening the industry's internationally competitive edge.

Acquired Advantage   Most of the world's trade today is of services and manufactured goods rather than agricultural goods and natural resources. Countries that produce

According to Adam Smith, a country's wealth is based on its available goods and services rather than on gold.

Natural advantage considers climate, natural resources, and labor force availability.

manufactured goods and services competitively have an **acquired advantage,** usually in either product or process technology. An advantage of *product technology* is that it enables a country to produce a unique product or one that is easily distinguished from those of competitors. For example, Denmark exports silver tableware, not because there are rich Danish silver mines but because Danish companies have developed distinctive products.

Acquired advantage consists of either product or process technology.

An advantage in process technology is a country's ability to produce a homogeneous product (one not easily distinguished from that of competitors) efficiently. For example, Japan has exported steel in spite of having to import iron and coal, the two main ingredients for steel production. A primary reason for Japan's success is that its steel mills encompass new laborsaving and material-saving processes. Thus countries that develop distinctive or less expensive products have acquired advantages, at least until producers in another country emulate them successfully.

Acquired advantage through technology has created new products, displaced old ones, and altered trading-partner relationships. The most obvious examples of change are new products and services, such as computers and software, which make up a large portion of international business. Products that existed in earlier periods have increased their share of world trade because of technological changes in the production process. For example, early hand-tooled automobiles reached only elite markets, but a succession of manufacturing innovations—from assembly lines to robotics—has enabled automobiles to reach an ever-widening mass market.

In other cases, companies have developed new uses for old products, such as the use of aloe in sunscreen. Other products have been at least partially displaced by substitutes, such as cotton, wool, and silk by artificial fibers, and hydrogen fuel cell technology may displace much of the world's petroleum trade in the future. Finally, technology may overcome natural advantages. Iceland now exports tomatoes grown near the Arctic Circle, and Brazil now exports quality wine produced near the equator; in both cases these were impossible until the development of fairly recent technology.[5]

How Does Resource Efficiency Work?   We demonstrate absolute trade advantage here by examining two countries (Costa Rica and the United States) and two commodities (coffee and wheat). Because we are not yet considering the concepts of money and exchange rates, we define the cost of production in terms of the resources needed to produce either coffee or wheat. This example is realistic because real income depends on the output of goods compared to the resources used to produce them.

Free trade will bring

- Specialization.
- Greater efficiency.
- Higher global output.

Start with the assumption that Costa Rica and the United States are the only existing countries and each has the same amount of resources (land, labor, and capital) to produce either coffee or wheat. Using Figure 6.2, let's say that 100 units of resources are available in each country. In Costa Rica, assume it takes 4 units to produce a ton of coffee and 10 units per ton of wheat. This is shown with the red Costa Rican production possibility line, whereby Costa Rica can produce 25 tons of coffee and no wheat, 10 tons of wheat and no coffee, or some combination of the two.

In the United States, it takes 20 units per ton of coffee and 5 units per ton of wheat. This is shown in the blue U.S. production possibility line, whereby the United States can produce 5 tons of coffee and no wheat, 20 tons of wheat and no coffee, or some combination of the two. Costa Rica is more efficient (that is, takes fewer resources to produce a ton) than the United States in coffee production, and the United States is more efficient than Costa Rica in wheat production.

To demonstrate how production can be increased through specialization and trade, we need first to consider a situation in which the two countries have no foreign trade. We could start from any place on each production possibility line; for convenience, however, we assume that if Costa Rica and the United States each devotes half of its 100 resources, or 50, to producing coffee and half, or 50, to producing wheat, Costa Rica can produce 12.5 tons of coffee (divide 4 into 50) and 5 tons of wheat (divide 10 into 50). These values are shown as point A in Figure 6.2. The United States can produce 2.5 tons of coffee (divide 20 into 50) and 10 tons of wheat (divide 5 into 50). These are shown as point B in Figure 6.2.

FIGURE 6.2   Production Possibilities Under Conditions of Absolute Advantage

In short, specialization increases output.

ASSUMPTIONS
for Costa Rica
1. 100 units of resources available
2. 10 units to produce a ton of wheat
3. 4 units to produce a ton of coffee
4. Uses half of total resources per product
   when there is no foreign trade

ASSUMPTIONS
for United States
1. 100 units of resources available
2. 5 units to produce a ton of wheat
3. 20 units to produce a ton of coffee
4. Uses half of total resources per product
   when there is no foreign trade

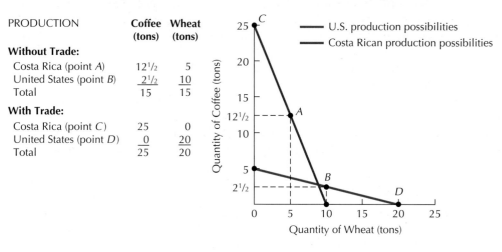

PRODUCTION	Coffee (tons)	Wheat (tons)
Without Trade:		
Costa Rica (point *A*)	12½	5
United States (point *B*)	2½	10
Total	15	15
With Trade:		
Costa Rica (point *C*)	25	0
United States (point *D*)	0	20
Total	25	20

Because each country has only 100 units of resources, neither one can increase wheat production without decreasing coffee production, or vice versa. Without trade, the combined production is 15 tons of coffee (12.5 + 2.5) and 15 tons of wheat (5 + 10). If each country specialized in the commodity for which it had an absolute advantage, Costa Rica then could produce 25 tons of coffee and the United States 20 tons of wheat (points *C* and *D* in the figure).

You can see that specialization increases the production of both products (from 15 to 25 tons of coffee and from 15 to 20 tons of wheat). By trading, global efficiency is optimized, and the two countries can have more coffee and more wheat than they would without trade.

THEORY OF COMPARATIVE ADVANTAGE

Gains from trade will occur even in a country that has absolute advantage in all products because the country must give up less efficient output to produce more efficient output.

We have just described absolute advantage, which is often confused with and called *comparative advantage*. In 1817, David Ricardo examined this question: "What happens when one country can produce all products at an absolute advantage?" and developed the theory of **comparative advantage**. This theory says that global efficiency gains may still result from trade if a country specializes in those products it can produce more efficiently than other products—regardless of whether other countries can produce those same products even more efficiently.

Comparative Advantage by Analogy   Although this theory may seem initially incongruous, an analogy should clarify its logic. Imagine that the best physician in town also happens to be the best medical secretary. Would it make economic sense for the physician to handle all the administrative duties of the office? Definitely not. The physician can earn more money by working as a physician, even though that means having to employ a less skilled medical secretary to manage the office. In the same manner, a country gains if it concentrates its resources on producing the commodities it can produce most efficiently. It then trades some of those commodities for those commodities it has relinquished. The following discussion clarifies why this theory is true.

Production Possibility   In this example, assume the United States is more efficient in producing both coffee and wheat than Costa Rica is.[6] The United States has an absolute advantage in the production of both products. Take a look at Figure 6.3, which, as in our earlier example of absolute advantage, assumes that there are only two countries and each has a total of 100 units of resources available. In this example, it takes Costa Rica 10 units of resources to produce either a ton of coffee or a ton of wheat, whereas it takes the United States only 5 units of resources to produce a ton of coffee and 4 units to produce a ton of wheat.

As in our production possibility example for absolute advantage, we can start from any place on each production possibility line. However, once again for convenience, we assume that if each country uses half (50) of its resources in the production of each product, Costa Rica can produce 5 tons of coffee and 5 tons of wheat (point *A* on the red line), and the United States can produce 10 tons of coffee and 12.5 tons of wheat (point *B* on the blue line). Without trade, neither country can increase its production of coffee without sacrificing some production of wheat, or vice versa.

Although the United States has an absolute advantage in the production of both coffee and wheat, it has a comparative advantage only in the production of wheat. This is because its advantage in wheat production is comparatively greater than its advantage in coffee production. Thus, by using the same amounts of resources, the United States can produce 2.5 times as much wheat as Costa Rica but only twice as much coffee. Although Costa Rica has an absolute disadvantage in the production of both products, it has a comparative advantage (or less of a comparative disadvantage) in the production of coffee. Why? Because Costa Rica is half as efficient as the United States in coffee production and only 40 percent as efficient in wheat production.

Without trade, the combined production is 15 tons of coffee (5 in Costa Rica plus 10 in the United States) and 17.5 tons of wheat (5 in Costa Rica plus 12.5 in the United States). Through trading, the combined production of coffee and wheat within the two

FIGURE 6.3   Production Possibilities Under Conditions of Comparative Advantage

There are advantages to trade even if one country enjoys an absolute advantage in the production of all products.

ASSUMPTIONS
for Costa Rica

1. 100 units of resources available
2. 10 units to produce a ton of wheat
3. 10 units to produce a ton of coffee
4. Uses half of total resources per product
   when there is no foreign trade

ASSUMPTIONS
for United States

1. 100 units of resources available
2. 4 units to produce a ton of wheat
3. 5 units to produce a ton of coffee
4. Uses half of total resources per product
   when there is no foreign trade

PRODUCTION	Coffee (tons)	Wheat (tons)
Without Trade:		
Costa Rica (point *A*)	5	5
United States (point *B*)	10	12½
Total	15	17½
With Trade (increasing coffee production):		
Costa Rica (point *C*)	10	0
United States (point *D*)	6	17½
Total	16	17½
With Trade (increasing wheat production):		
Costa Rica (point *C*)	10	0
United States (point *E*)	5	18¾
Total	15	18¾

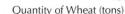

Quantity of Wheat (tons)

countries can be increased. For example, if the combined production of wheat is unchanged from when there was no trade, the United States could produce all 17.5 tons of wheat by using 70 units of resources (17.5 tons times 4 units per ton). The remaining 30 U.S. resource units could be used for producing 6 tons of coffee (30 units divided by 5 units per ton). This production possibility is point *D* in Figure 6.3. Costa Rica would use all its resources to produce 10 tons of coffee (point *C*). The combined wheat production has stayed at 17.5 tons, but the coffee production has increased from 15 tons to 16 tons.

If the combined coffee production is unchanged from the time before trade, Costa Rica could use all its resources to produce coffee, yielding 10 tons (point *C* in Figure 6.3). The United States could produce the remaining 5 tons of coffee by using 25 units of resources. The remaining 75 U.S. units could be used to produce 18.75 tons of wheat (75 divided by 4). This production possibility is point *E*. Without sacrificing any of the coffee available before trade, wheat production has increased from 17.5 tons to 18.75 tons.

If the United States were to produce somewhere between points *D* and *E*, both coffee and wheat production would increase over what was possible before trade took place. Whether the production target is an increase of coffee or wheat or a combination of the two, both countries can gain by having Costa Rica trade some of its coffee production to the United States for some of that country's wheat output.

Don't Confuse Comparative and Absolute Advantage   Most economists accept the comparative advantage theory, and it's influential in promoting policies for freer trade. Nevertheless, many government policymakers, journalists, managers, and workers confuse comparative advantage with absolute advantage and do not understand how a country can simultaneously have a comparative *advantage* and absolute *disadvantage* in the production of a given product. This misunderstanding helps explain why managers face uncertain government trade policies that affect where they choose to locate their production.

THEORIES OF SPECIALIZATION: SOME ASSUMPTIONS AND LIMITATIONS

Both absolute and comparative advantage theories are based on specialization. They hold that output will increase through specialization and that countries will be best off by trading the output from their own specialization for the output from other countries' specialization. However, these theories make assumptions, some of which are not always valid.

Full employment is not a valid assumption of absolute and comparative advantage.	**Full Employment** The physician/secretary analogy we used earlier assumed the physician could stay busy full time practicing medicine. If we relax this assumption, then the advantages of specialization are less compelling. The physician might, if unable to stay busy full time with medical duties, perform secretarial work without having to forgo a physician's higher income. The theories of absolute and comparative advantage both assume that resources are fully employed. When countries have many unemployed or unused resources, they may seek to restrict imports to employ or use idle resources.
Countries' goals may not be limited to economic efficiency.	**Economic Efficiency** Our physician/secretary analogy also assumed that the physician who can do both medical and office work is interested primarily in maximization of profit, or maximum economic efficiency. Yet there are a number of reasons why physicians might choose not to work full time at medical tasks. They might find administrative work relaxing and self-fulfilling. They might fear that a hired secretary would be unreliable. They might wish to maintain secretrial skills in the somewhat unlikely event that administration, rather than medicine, commands higher wages in the future. Countries also often pursue objectives other than output efficiency. They may avoid overspecialization because of the vulnerability created by changes in technology and by price fluctuations.

Division of Gains   Although specialization brings potential benefits to all countries that trade, the earlier discussion did not indicate how countries will divide increased output. In the case of our wheat and coffee example, if both the United States and Costa Rica receive some share of the increased output, both will be better off economically through specialization and trade. However, many people, including government policymakers, are concerned with relative as well as absolute economic growth, relative meaning in comparison to trading partners. If they perceive a trading partner is gaining too large a share of benefits, they may forgo absolute gains for themselves so as to prevent relative losses.[7]

Two Countries, Two Commodities   For simplicity's sake, both Smith and Ricardo originally assumed a simple world composed of only two countries and two commodities. Our example makes the same assumption. Now, although this simplification is unrealistic, it does not diminish the usefulness of either theory: Economists have applied the same reasoning to demonstrate efficiency advantages in multiproduct and multicountry trade relationships.

Transport Costs   If it costs more to transport the goods than is saved through specialization, the advantages of trade are negated. In other words, in our example of Costa Rica and the United States, the countries would need to divert workers from coffee or wheat production to ship coffee and wheat between them. However, as long as the diversion reduces output by less than what the two countries gain from specialization, there are still gains from trade.

Statics and Dynamics   The theories of absolute and comparative advantage address countries' advantages by looking at them at one point in time. Thus the theories view the advantages statically. However, the relative conditions that give countries advantages or disadvantages in the production of given products are dynamic (constantly changing). For example, the resources needed to produce coffee or wheat in either Costa Rica or the United States could change substantially because of advancements in genetically modified crops.[8]

In addition, as we show in our opening case, when Costa Rica decided to focus on goods that could compete in international markets, it turned to a few promising high-tech industries—industries in which it has since developed and enhanced a competitive advantage. Thus we should not assume that future absolute or comparative advantages will remain as they are today. We return to this theme later in the chapter as we examine theories to explain the dynamics of the location of production and export sources.

Services   The theories of absolute and comparative advantage deal with products rather than services. However, an increasing portion of world trade is in services. This fact does not render the theories obsolete because resources must go into producing services, too. For instance, some services that the United States sells extensively to foreign countries are education (many foreign students attend U.S. universities) as well as credit card systems and collections. However, the United States buys more foreign shipping services than foreigners buy U.S. shipping services. To become more self-sufficient in international shipping, the United States might have to divert resources from its more efficient use in higher education or in the production of competitive products.

Production Networks   Both theories deal with trading one product for another. Increasingly, however, we see divisions by component and function as well within a company's value chain network. For instance, a company may conduct R&D in Country A, secure components in Countries B and C, assemble final products in Country D, manage finances in Country E, and carry out call-center services in Country F. Although this type of development adds complexity to the analysis, it fits well with the concept of advantages through specialization. In other words, activities take place in those countries where there is an absolute or comparative advantage for their production.

CONCEPT CHECK

Recall from Chapter 2 our discussion of "Work Motivation," in which we explain that in **cultures** ranking high on so-called masculinity, people tend to value economic achievement over certain other values; we also observe, however, that, in other cultures, quality of life is valued over economic performance.

Bigger countries differ in several ways from smaller countries. They

- Tend to export a smaller portion of output and import a smaller part of consumption.
- Have higher transport costs for foreign trade.

Case Review Note

CONCEPT CHECK

As we point out in discussing the ramifications of **globalization** in Chapter 1, although any given product may carry a "made-in" label (as in "Made in Taiwan"), such labels may actually obscure rather than clarify the origins of products, which nowadays often include components or ingredients from a surprising variety of countries.

Mobility   The theories of absolute and comparative advantage assume that resources can move domestically from the production of one good to another—and at no cost. But this assumption is not completely valid. For example, a steelworker in the eastern part of the United States might not move easily into a software-development job on the West Coast. That worker probably would have difficulty working in such a different industry and might have trouble moving to a new area. The theories also assume that resources cannot move internationally. Increasingly, however, they do. It is estimated, for example, that between 500,000 and a million Nicaraguans are now living in Costa Rica,[9] and U.S. companies have transferred both personnel and capital to support their Costa Rican investments. The movement of resources such as labor and capital is clearly an alternative to trade, a topic we discuss later in the chapter. However, it is safe to say that resources are more mobile domestically than they are internationally.

Trade Pattern Theories

The free trade theories of absolute and comparative advantage demonstrate how economic growth occurs through specialization and trade; however, they do not deal with issues such as how much a country will depend on trade if it follows a free trade policy, what types of products countries will export and import, and with which partners countries will primarily trade. In this section, we discuss the theories that help explain these patterns.

HOW MUCH DOES A COUNTRY TRADE?

Although free trade theories deal with specialization, they do not imply that only one country should or will produce a given product or service. To begin with, there are **nontradable goods**—products and services that are seldom practical to export, primarily because of high transportation costs, regardless of production cost and efficiency differences among countries. For instance, many services fall into this category, such as haircuts and retail distribution of groceries. Apart from nontradable goods, we find that country size is a factor helping to explain why some countries depend more on trade than others and why some countries account for larger portions of world trade than others.

Theory of Country Size   The **theory of country size** holds that large countries usually depend less on trade than small countries. Countries with large land areas are apt to have varied climates and an assortment of natural resources, making them more self-sufficient than smaller countries. Most large countries, such as Brazil, China, India, the United States, and Russia, import much less of their consumption needs and export much less of their production output than do small countries, such as Uruguay, the Netherlands, and Iceland.

Furthermore, transport costs in trade affect large and small countries differently. Normally, the farther the distance, the higher the transport costs. Further, in addition to the direct costs of transportation, distance creates indirect costs of tying up inventory for longer periods and of adding to the uncertainty and unreliability of timely delivery. Among countries that border each other, the smaller country tends to depend more on trade than the larger country because of transportation costs.

Assume, for example, that the normal maximum distance for transporting a given product is 100 miles because prices increase too much at greater distances. Although almost any location in Belgium is within 100 miles of a foreign country, the same isn't true for two of its larger neighbors, France and Germany. Thus Belgium's trade involves a higher percentage of its production and consumption than the comparable figures in either France or Germany.

Size of the Economy   Although land area is the most obvious way of measuring a country's size, countries also can be compared on the basis of economic size. Although

TABLE 6.2   Shares of World Merchandise Trade, 2005

"Value" is measured in billions of dollars; "share" indicates a percentage of total worldwide trade.
With the exception of China, every country listed is regarded as a *developed* country.

Rank	Exporters	Value	Share of World Trade	Rank	Importers	Value	Share of World Trade
1	Germany	969.9	9.3	1	United States	1,732.3	16.6
2	United States	904.4	8.7	2	Germany	773.8	7.4
3	China	767.0	7.3	3	China	660.0	6.3
4	Japan	594.9	5.7	4	Japan	514.9	4.9
5	France	460.2	4.4	5	United Kigdom	510.2	4.9
6	Netherlands	402.4	3.9	6	France	497.9	4.7
7	United Kingdom	382.8	3.6	7	Italy	379.8	3.6
8	Italy	367.2	3.5	8	Netherlands	359.1	3.4
9	Canada	359.4	3.4	9	Canada	320.0	3.1
10	Belgium	334.3	3.2	10	Belgium	318.7	3.1
	Total		53.0		Total		58.0

Source: World Trade Organization, *International Trade Statistics, 2006* (Geneva: 2006), pp. 195–208.

percentage of output and consumption are ways of comparing countries, so is the absolute amount of their trade. Table 6.2 shows that of the world's top 10 exporters and importers are all developed countries except for China. China, although not a developed country, has a very large economy by virtue of its large population. In fact, these 10 countries account for over half the world's exports and imports.

We return momentarily to why these countries are so dominant in world trade, but one reason is that these countries produce so much that they have more to sell—both domestically and internationally. In addition, because these countries produce so much, incomes are high and people buy more from both domestic and foreign sources. At the same time, little of the trade of developing countries is with other developing countries.

WHAT TYPES OF PRODUCTS DOES A COUNTRY TRADE?

In our discussion of absolute advantage, we indicated this advantage might be either natural or acquired. In this section, we discuss theories that help explain what types of products result from these natural and acquired advantages. We won't delve again into those factors we've already discussed (climate and natural resources) that give a country a natural advantage; however, we will examine the factor endowment theory of trade. For acquired advantage, we discuss the importance of production and product technology.

Factor-Proportions Theory   Eli Heckscher and Bertil Ohlin developed **factor-proportions theory,** which is based on countries' production factors—land, labor, and capital (funds for investment in plant and equipment). This theory said that differences in countries' endowments of labor compared to their endowments of land or capital explain differences in the cost of production factors. These economists proposed that if labor were abundant in comparison to land and capital, labor costs would be low relative to land and capital costs. If labor were scarce, labor costs would be high in relation to land and capital costs. These relative factor costs would lead countries to excel in the production and export of products that used their abundant—and, therefore, cheaper—production factors.[10]

> According to the factor-proportions theory, factors in relative abundance are cheaper than factors in relative scarcity.

People and Land   Factor-proportions theory appears logical. In countries in which there are many people relative to the amount of land—for example, Hong Kong and the Netherlands—land price is very high because it's in demand. Regardless of climate and soil conditions, neither Hong Kong nor the Netherlands excels in the production of goods requiring large amounts of land, such as wool or wheat. Businesses in countries such as Australia and Canada produce these goods because land is abundant compared to the number of people.

Manufacturing Locations   Casual observation of manufacturing locations also seems to substantiate the theory. For example, the most successful industries in Hong Kong are those in which technology permits the use of a minimum amount of land relative to the number of people employed: Clothing production occurs in multistory factories where workers share minimal space. Hong Kong does not compete in the production of automobiles, however, which requires much more space per worker.

| Production factors are not homogeneous, especially labor.

Capital, Labor Rates, and Specialization   In countries where little capital is available for investment and where the amount of investment per worker is low, managers might expect to find cheap labor rates and export competitiveness in products that require large amounts of labor relative to capital. These managers can anticipate the opposite when labor is scarce. For example, Iran (where labor is abundant in comparison to capital) excels in the production of handmade carpets that differ in appearance as well as in production method from the carpets produced in industrial countries by machines purchased with cheap capital.

However, because the factor-proportions theory assumes production factors to be homogeneous, tests to substantiate the theory have been mixed.[11] Labor skills in fact, vary within and among countries because people have different training and education. Training and education require capital expenditures that do not show up in traditional capital measurements, which include only plant and equipment values. When the factor-proportions theory accounts for different labor groups and the capital invested to train these groups, it seems to explain many trade patterns.[12] For example, because exports from high-income countries embody a higher proportion of professionals such as scientists and engineers than in low-income economies' exports, those countries are using their abundant production factors to maintain their lead in exports. Exports of low-income economies, though, show a high intensity of less skilled labor.[13]

This variation in labor skills among countries has led to more international specialization by task to produce a given product. For example, a company may locate its research activities and management functions primarily in countries with a highly educated population, and it may locate its production work in countries where less skilled—and less expensive—workers can be employed.

| Companies may substitute capital for labor depending on the cost of each.

Process Technology   Factor-proportions analysis becomes more complicated when the same product can be produced by different methods, such as with labor or capital. Thus production technology helps explain where products are made. For instance, Bangladesh produces rice by using a smaller number of machines in comparison to its abundant and cheap labor. In contrast, Italy produces rice with a capital-intensive method (high expenditure on machinery per worker) because of its abundance of low-cost capital relative to labor. This contrast is shown in photos below, which show the same task being performed by a capital-intensive method in Italy and a labor-intensive method in the much poorer Asian nation of Bangladesh. In the final analysis, the optimum location of production depends on comparing the cost in each locale based on the type of production that minimizes costs there.

| Bigger countries depend more on products requiring longer production runs.

Large economies are more likely to produce goods that use technologies requiring long production runs. Why? Because these countries develop industries to serve their large domestic markets, which, in turn, tend to be competitive in export markets.[14] However, companies may locate long production runs in small countries if they expect few barriers in other countries to the export of their output.[15] In industries where long production runs are important for gaining competitive advantages,

In the top photo, rice production in Bangladesh is labor intensive because of lower labor costs. The opposite is true for production in Italy, which is shown in the bottom photo.

companies tend to locate their production in few countries, using these locations as sources of exports to other countries. Where long production runs are less important, we find a greater prevalence of multiple production units scattered around the world in different countries so as to minimize the cost of transportation through exporting. In addition, high expenditures on research and development create high fixed costs for companies.

Therefore, the technologically intensive company from a small nation may have a more compelling need to sell abroad than would a company with a large domestic market. In turn, this pulls resources from other industries and companies within the company's domestic market, causing more national specialization than in a larger nation.[16]

FIGURE 6.4   Worldwide Trade of Major Manufactured Products

As a percentage of total world trade, manufactured products are more important than products in any other category. Services, however, constitute the fastest-growing category.

Source: From World Trade Organization, *Annual Report* (Geneva, various years).

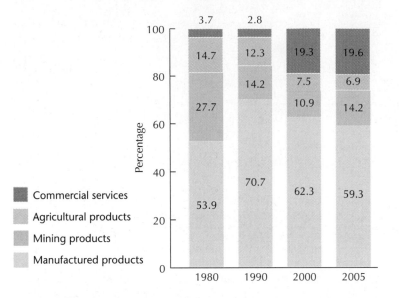

Most new products originate in developed countries.

Product Technology   Figure 6.4 shows the changing composition of world trade. Manufacturing is by far the largest sector, with commercial services the fastest-growing sector. Manufacturing is a sector that depends on acquired advantage, largely technology, which depends, in turn, on a large number of highly educated people (especially scientists and engineers) and a large amount of capital to invest in research and development.

Because developed countries have an abundance of these features, they originate most new products and account for most manufacturing output and trade. Developing countries depend much more on the production of primary products; thus they depend more on natural advantage. Although these primary products may encompass large amounts of process technology, the products themselves involve little change from year to year.

WITH WHOM DO COUNTRIES TRADE?

We have already noted that developed countries account for the bulk of world trade. They also primarily trade with each other, whereas developing countries mainly export primary products and labor-intensive products to developed countries in exchange for new and technologically advanced products. In this section we discuss the roles of similarity among countries in terms of economic, cultural, and political levels and interests. Then we examine the role that distance plays in the determination of trading partners.

Developed countries primarily trade with each other because they

- Produce and consume more.
- Emphasize technical breakthroughs in different industrial sectors.
- Produce differentiated products and services.

Country-Similarity Theory   Thus far in this chapter, the theories explaining why trade takes place have focused on the differences among countries in terms of natural conditions and factor endowment proportions. At the same time, we showed that most trade takes place among developed countries, a pattern that can be further explained by **country-similarity theory.** This theory says that once a company has developed a new product in response to observed market conditions in its home market, it turns to markets it sees as most similar to those at home.[17]

Specialization and Acquired Advantage   Markets in developed countries can support the development and sale both of new products and variations of existing ones. Trade occurs because *countries* specialize to gain acquired advantage—for example, by apportioning their research efforts more strongly to some sectors than to others. Germany is traditionally strong in machinery and equipment, Switzerland in pharmaceutical products, and Denmark in food products.[18] Even developing countries have gained advantages through specialization whereby they concentrate successfully on very narrow product segments. For instance, Bangladesh has been successful at exporting shirts, trousers, and hats but not bed linens or footballs, whereas Pakistan has been successful at exporting bed linens and footballs.[19]

Product Differentiation   Trade also occurs because *companies* differentiate products, thus creating two-way trade in similar products. For example, the United States is both a major exporter and a major importer of tourist services, vehicles, and passenger aircraft because different companies from different countries have developed product variations that appeal to different consumers. For instance, both Boeing from the United States and Airbus Industrie from Europe produce aircraft that fly people from point *A* to point *B*, but U.S. and European airlines buy both Boeing's and Airbus Industrie's aircraft because their models differ in such features as capacity, flying range, fuel consumption, and perceived reliability.[20] The two companies sell them primarily within their own and each other's markets because these markets have higher economic purchasing power.

The Effects of Cultural Similarity   Cultural similarity also helps explain much of the direction of trade. Importers and exporters find it easier to do business in a country they perceive as being culturally similar to their home countries because they speak a common language. Likewise, historic colonial relationships explain much of the trade between specific high-income and low-income economies. For instance, the colonial history of France in Africa has given an edge to Air France in serving those former colonies' international air passenger markets.[21] Similarly, the lack of extensive trade among nations in the Southern Hemisphere is due partly to the absence of historic ties. Importers and exporters find it easier to continue business ties than to develop new distribution arrangements in countries where they are less experienced.

The Effects of Political Relationships and Economic Agreements   Political relationships and economic agreements among countries may discourage or encourage trade between them. An example of trade discouragement is the political animosity between the United States and Cuba that has caused mutual trade to be almost nonexistent for the last four decades. The United States replaced Cuban sugar imports with imports from such countries as Mexico and the Dominican Republic. An example of trade encouragement is the agreement among many European countries to remove all trade barriers with each other. This agreement has caused a greater share of the countries' total trade to be conducted within the group.

The Effects of Distance   Although the theories regarding country differences and similarities help explain broad world trade patterns, such as those that link developed countries and developing countries, they are incomplete in explaining specific pairs of trading relationships. Aside from the degree of cultural and political affinity among countries, why does a country buy more from one country than from another? Although no single answer explains all product flows, the geographic distance between two countries accounts for many of these world trade relationships.

In essence, greater distances usually mean higher transportation costs; that's why Intel's cost to ship semiconductors from Costa Rica to the United States is lower than if it had to bring them from, say, Argentina. For example, Finland is a major exporter to Russia because its transport costs are cheap and fast compared to transport costs to major Russian markets from other countries. Acer, a Taiwanese computer maker, built a plant in Finland to serve Russia because it realized savings by shipping from Finland rather

Trading partners are affected by

- Distance.
- Cultural similarity.
- Relations between countries.

CONCEPT CHECK

In discussing "Cultural Distance" in Chapter 2, we show that "distance" is an index of similarities between countries based primarily on such shared cultural attributes as language, ethnicity, or values. We indicate that, by and large, a company from one country should expect fewer adjustments when moving to a country whose culture is close to that of its home base, but we also caution that, even in these cases, executives should be aware of subtle cultural differences.

than from Asia and because a Finnish plant provided more secure storage and ease of operations than a Russian one.[22]

Overcoming Distance   But transport cost is not the only factor in trade partner choice. For example, New Zealand competes with Chile, Argentina, and South Africa for out-of-season sales of apples to the Northern Hemisphere—but with a disadvantage in freight costs to the United States and Europe. It has countered this disadvantage by increasing yields, developing new premium varieties, bypassing intermediaries to sell directly to supermarkets abroad, and consolidating efforts through a national marketing board. However, such methods to overcome distance disadvantages are difficult to maintain. For example, both Chinese and Chilean orchardists have smuggled new strains of apple tree cuttings out of New Zealand.[23]

Does Geography Matter?

Variety Is the Spice of Life

As you study this chapter, you'll see that geography plays a role in many of the theories and questions concerning trade. We pull them together in this discussion.

Part of a country's trading advantage is explained by its natural advantage—climate, terrain, arable land, and natural resources. Thus Saudi Arabia trades oil, a natural resource, for U.S. rice, which needs huge wet areas for production. Remember, however, that technology may often negate natural advantage, such as the development of substitutes (synthetic nitrate for natural nitrate) and development of different methods of production (Chile is not using traditional bogs for the successful growing of cranberries). Nevertheless, a country's geography, particularly ease of moving goods to markets in other countries, may give it an advantage or disadvantage. For instance, landlocked countries have a considerable cost disadvantage relative to countries with seacoasts.[24]

Factor-proportions theory helps explain where certain goods may be more efficiently produced, such as labor-intensive goods where labor is plentiful in relation to capital and land. Thus Bangladesh excels in the production of clothing requiring lots of labor in relation to either capital or land. However, these factors can change in both quantity and quality. Hong Kong has a very high population density, and it used to excel in production of labor-intensive goods. But as Hong Kong has accumulated capital and upgraded the education of its workforce, its competitive production and exports encompass more capital intensity and more skilled labor.

Usually, small countries need to trade more than large countries, primarily because they are apt to have less variety of natural advantages, but there are exceptions. Small countries that also have low incomes tend to depend little on trade because they produce and consume so little. Distance from foreign markets also plays a role. For instance, geographically isolated countries, such as Fiji, trade less than would be expected from their sizes because transportation costs increase the price of traded goods substantially.[25]

Conversely, Canada is a large high-income country whose dependence on trade and trade per capita are not only among the world's highest but also much higher than we would expect from the theory of country size. This may be explained largely by Canada's population dispersion. Ninety percent of its population is within 100 miles of the U.S. border; thus shipping goods between, say, Vancouver and Seattle or Toronto and Cleveland is often more feasible than between Vancouver and Toronto.

Although distance helps us understand the importance of pairs of trading partners, political relationships and cultural similarity are important factors as well. For example, there is a large amount of trade within regional trading organizations and between former colonizers and their former colonies. Of most importance, though, is the preponderance of world trade among developed countries. These countries produce and consume more. Further, they engage in technological specialization and product differentiations to fit market niches.

However, this begs the question of why some countries are developed and others are not. This is a very complex issue that we cannot hope to answer. Nevertheless, some of the factors affecting income levels, and thus trade, are geographic. For instance, one study showed that 70 percent of the difference among countries in per capita income can be accounted for by four factors—malaria, hydrocarbon endowments, coastal access, and transportation cost—all of which relate to geography.[26] ●

The Statics and Dynamics of Trade

Although we've alluded to the fact that trading patterns change, for example, because of political and economic relations among countries and the development of new product capabilities, we now discuss two theories, the product life cycle theory and Porter's diamond, that help explain how countries develop, maintain, and lose their competitive advantages.

> According to the PLC theory of trade, the production location for many products moves from one country to another depending on the stage in the product's life cycle.

PRODUCT LIFE CYCLE (PLC) THEORY

The international **product life cycle (PLC) theory** of trade states that the location of production of certain kinds of products shifts as they go through their life cycles, which consist of four stages: *introduction, growth, maturity,* and *decline.*[27] Table 6.3 highlights these stages.

Changes over the Cycle   Companies develop new products primarily because there is an observed need and market for them nearby. This means a U.S. company is most apt to develop a new product for the U.S. market, a French company for the French market, and so on. At the same time, almost all new technology that results in new products and production methods originates in developed countries.[28] They have most of the resources to develop new products and most of the income to buy them.

Introduction   Once a company has created a new product, theoretically it can manufacture that product anywhere in the world. In practice, however, the early-production

TABLE 6.3   Life Cycle of the International Product

During its life cycle, focus on a product's production and market locations often shifts from industrial to developing markets. The process is accompanied by changes in the competitive factors affecting both production and sales, as well as in the technology used to produce the product.

	Life Cycle Stage			
	1: Introduction	**2: Growth**	**3: Maturity**	**4: Decline**
Production location	• In innovating (usually industrial) country	• In innovating and other industrial countries	• Multiple countries	• Mainly in developing countries
Market location	• Mainly in innovating country, with some exports	• Mainly in industrial countries • Shift in export markets as foreign production replaces exports in some markets	• Growth in developing countries • Some decrease in industrial countries	• Mainly in developing countries • Some developing country exports
Competitive factors	• Near-monopoly position • Sales based on uniqueness rather than price • Evolving product characteristics	• Fast-growing demand • Number of competitors increases • Some competitors begin price cutting • Product becoming more standardized	• Overall stabilized demand • Number of competitors decreases • Price is very important, especially in developing countries	• Overall declining demand • Price is key weapon • Number of producers continues to decline
Production technology	• Short production runs • Evolving methods to coincide with product evolution • High labor input and labor skills relative to capital input	• Capital input increases • Methods more standardized	• Long production runs using high capital inputs • Highly standardized • Less labor skill needed	• Unskilled labor on mechanized long production runs

The introduction stage is marked by

- Innovation in response to observed need.
- Exporting by the innovative country.
- Evolving product characteristics.

stage called the *introductory stage* generally occurs in a domestic location so the company can obtain rapid market feedback as well as save on transport costs. At this stage, export markets are small and mainly to other developed countries because more customers in those countries can afford the new products.

The production process is apt to be more labor intensive in the introductory stage than in later stages to permit response to market feedback dictates and because machinery to produce on a large scale using few workers may be introduced only when sales begin to expand rapidly. Although the early production is most apt to occur in developed countries with high labor rates, the education and skills make their labor efficient on non-standardized production. Even if production costs are high because of expensive labor, companies can often pass costs on to consumers who are unwilling to wait for possible price reductions later.

Growth is characterized by

- Increases in exports by the innovating country.
- More competition.
- Increased capital intensity.
- Some foreign production.

Growth   As sales grow, competitors enter the market. During the *growth stage,* demand may justify producing in some foreign countries (usually developed ones) to reduce transport charges. At this stage sales are likely to stay almost entirely in the countries producing the product. Let's say, for example, that the innovator is in the United States and the additional manufacturing unit is in Japan. The producers in Japan sell mainly in Japan for several reasons:

1. There is increased demand in the Japanese market for the product.
2. Producers need to introduce unique product variations for Japanese consumers.
3. Japanese costs may still be high because of production start-up problems.

Sales growth at home and abroad creates incentives for companies to develop process technology, but this incentive is partially countered by product variations by competitors and for different countries. Thus the capital intensity, though growing, is less than will come later. The original producing country will increase its exports in this stage but lose certain key export markets in which local production commences.

Maturity is characterized by

- A decline in exports from the innovating country.
- More product standardization.
- More capital intensity.
- Increased competitiveness of price.
- Production start-ups in emerging economies.

Maturity   In the *maturity stage*, worldwide demand begins to level off, although it may be growing in some countries and declining in others. There often is a shakeout of producers such that product models become highly standardized, making cost an important competitive weapon. Longer production runs reduce per unit cost, thus creating more demand in developing economies. Because markets and technologies are widespread, the innovating country no longer commands a production advantage. Producers have incentives to shift production to developing economies where they can employ less skilled and less expensive labor efficiently for standardized (capital-intensive) production. Exports decrease from the innovating country as foreign production displaces it.

Decline is characterized by

- A concentration of production in developing countries.
- An innovating country becoming a net importer.

Decline   As a product moves into the *decline stage,* those factors occurring during the mature stage continue to evolve. The markets in developed countries decline more rapidly than those in developing economies as affluent customers demand ever-newer products. By this time, market and cost factors have dictated that almost all production is in developing economies, which export to the declining or small-niche markets in developed countries. In other words, the country in which the innovation first emerged—and exported from—then becomes the importer.

Verification and Limitations of PLC Theory   The PLC theory holds that the location of production facilities that serve world markets shifts as products move through their life cycle. Such products as ballpoint pens and hand calculators have followed this pattern. They were first produced in a single developed country and sold at a high price. Then production shifted to multiple developed country locations to serve those local markets. Finally, most production is located in developing countries, and prices have declined.

However, if transportation costs are very high, there is little opportunity for export sales, regardless of the stage in the life cycle.

In addition, there are many types of products for which shifts in production location do not usually take place. In these cases, the innovating country may maintain its export ability throughout the product's life cycle. These exceptions include the following:

Not all products conform to the dynamics of the PLC.

- Products that, because of very rapid innovation, have extremely short life cycles—a factor that makes it impossible to achieve cost reductions by moving production from one country to another. Some fashion items fit this category.

- Luxury products for which cost is of little concern to the consumer. In fact, production in a developing country may make the product seem less luxurious than it really is.

- Products for which a company can use a differentiation strategy, perhaps through advertising, to maintain consumer demand without competing on the basis of price.

- Products that require specialized technical labor to evolve into their next generation. This seems to explain the long-term U.S. dominance of medical equipment production and German dominance in rotary printing presses.

Regardless of the product type, there has been an increased tendency on the part of MNEs to introduce new products at home and abroad almost simultaneously. In other words, instead of merely observing needs within their domestic markets, companies develop products and services for observable market segments that transcend national borders. In so doing, they eliminate delays as a product is diffused from one country to another, and they choose an initial production location that will minimize costs for serving markets in multiple countries. This production location may or may not be in the innovating company's home market.

THE PORTER DIAMOND

Why do specialized competitive advantages differ among countries—for example, why do Italian companies have an advantage in the ceramic tile industry and Swiss companies have one in the watch industry? The **Porter diamond** is a theory showing four conditions as important for competitive superiority: demand conditions; factor conditions; related and supporting industries; and firm strategy, structure, and rivalry. We have already discussed all four of these conditions in the context of other trade theories, but how they combine affects the development and continued existence of competitive advantages.

The framework of the theory, therefore, is a useful tool for understanding how and where globally competitive companies develop and sustain themselves. Usually, but not always, all four conditions need to be favorable for an industry within a country to attain global supremacy.

Facets of the Porter Diamond   Both PLC theory and country-similarity theory show that new products (or industries) usually arise from companies' observation of need or demand, which is usually in their home country.

Demand Conditions   *Demand conditions* are the first condition in the theory. Companies then start up production near the observed market. This was the case for the Italian ceramic tile industry after World War II: There was a postwar housing boom, and consumers wanted cool floors because of the hot Italian climate.

Factor Conditions   The second condition of the Porter diamond—*factor conditions* (recall natural advantage within absolute advantage theory and the factor-proportions theory)—influenced both the choice of tile to meet consumer demand and the choice of Italy as the production location. Wood was less available and more expensive than tile,

According to the Porter diamond theory, companies' development of internationally competitive products depends on their domestic

- Demand conditions.
- Factor conditions.
- Related and supporting industries.
- Firm strategy, structure, and rivalry.

and most production factors (skilled labor, capital, technology, and equipment) were available within Italy on favorable terms.

Related and Supporting Industries

The third condition—the existence of nearby *related and supporting industries* (enamels and glazes)—was also favorable. Recall, for instance, our discussions of the importance of transport costs in the theory of country size, in assumptions of specialization, and in the limitation factors of PLC theory.

Firm Strategy, Structure, and Rivalry

The combination of three conditions—demand, factor conditions, and related and supporting industries—influenced companies' decisions to initiate production of ceramic tiles in postwar Italy. The ability of these companies to develop and sustain a competitive advantage required favorable circumstances for the fourth condition: *firm strategy, structure, and rivalry.*

Barriers to market entry were low in the tile industry (some companies started up with as few as three employees), and hundreds of companies initiated production. Rivalry became intense as companies tried to serve increasingly sophisticated Italian consumers. These circumstances forced breakthroughs in both product and process technologies, which gave the Italian producers advantages over foreign producers and enabled them to gain the largest global share of tile exports.

Limitations of the Porter Diamond Theory

The existence of the four favorable conditions does not guarantee that an industry will develop in a given locale. Entrepreneurs may face favorable conditions for many different lines of business. In fact, comparative advantage theory holds that resource limitations may cause companies in a country to avoid competing in some industries even though an absolute advantage may exist. For example, conditions in Switzerland would seem to have favored success if companies in that country had become players in the personal computer industry. However, Swiss companies preferred to protect their global positions in such product lines as watches and scientific instruments rather than to downsize those industries by moving their highly skilled people into a new industry.

A second limitation concerns the increased ability of companies to attain market information, production factors, and supplies from abroad. We can actually break down this complex issue into four separate considerations:

1. Observations of foreign or foreign plus domestic, rather than just domestic, demand conditions have spurred much of the recent growth in Asian exports. In fact, such Japanese companies as Uniden and Fujitech target their sales almost entirely to foreign markets.[29]
2. Companies and countries are not dependent entirely on domestic factor conditions. For example, capital and managers are now internationally mobile.
3. If related and supporting industries are not available locally, materials and components are now more easily brought in from abroad because of advancements in transportation and the relaxation of import restrictions. In fact, many MNEs now assemble products with parts supplied from a variety of countries.
4. Companies react not only to domestic rivals but also to foreign-based rivals they compete with at home and abroad. Thus the absence of any of the four conditions from the diamond domestically may not inhibit companies and industries from becoming globally competitive.

Using the Diamond for Transformation

As we saw in our opening case, Costa Rica diversified its economy from agricultural products to modern high-tech products, and it did so by satisfying the market entry conditions of the diamond. This transformation

CONCEPT CHECK

In discussing the concept of the **market economy** in Chapter 4, we explain that such a system encourages an open exchange of goods and services among producers and consumers, both of which groups consist of "individuals" who make their own economic decisions; in this respect, then, the interaction among producers and consumers determines what products will be produced and in what quantities.

could not have occurred had Costa Rica looked only at what was available within its own borders. It was possible because the country adopted a global view. In Costa Rica itself, there was (and still is) very little demand for the high-tech products, such as microchips and medical devices, that it now produces; good transportation, however, makes efficient export possible. Similarly, Costa Rica initially lacked some of the factor conditions necessary for producing high-tech products, especially trained personnel. Eventually, however, it altered its educational system to fit human resource development to production needs and allowed companies to bring in foreign managers and technicians to fill human resource gaps. Finally, it developed local factors, such as additional power and metal-working expertise, and it attracted enough high-tech companies to ensure a vibrant competitive environment. Thus understanding and having the necessary conditions to be globally competitive is important, but these conditions are neither static nor purely domestic.

Case Review Note

Point | Counterpoint

Should Nations Use Strategic Trade Policies?

Point | **Yes** What's so important about acquiring advantage in world trade? For one thing, if you're a country that wants to compete in today's globalized business environment (and you have to), you obviously have to develop and maintain some industries that will *be competitive*. But there's more: Those industries must also grow and *earn sufficient revenues to keep your domestic economy performing as well as the economies of other countries*. What's the role of your government in the process of going global? It should be central to your whole effort; after all, we're talking about *national economies* here.

For one thing, a government's role is rarely neutral. A government may claim its economic policies don't affect the performance of specific domestic industries on the world stage, but a lot of those policies are bound to have precisely that effect. For instance, who's going to argue that the U.S. government's efforts to "improve agricultural productivity" and "enhance defense capabilities" have nothing to do with the fact that the United States does a healthy business in the export of farm and aerospace products?

Moreover, just about every government policy designed to help one industry is going to have the opposite effect on another one. European airlines, for example, complain (with some justification) that government support for high-speed rail traffic in Europe deprives them of the revenue they need to compete with U.S. overseas carriers, which don't have much to worry about from railroad passenger traffic at home. In other words, national policymakers everywhere are faced with trade-offs. Therefore, if every government policy is going to help one party while hurting another one anyway,

(continued)

Counterpoint | **No** Why would anyone who's paying attention disagree that countries should try to become most competitive in the industries that promise the best returns? And who'd deny that emerging growth industries are a country's most promising bet for going global? Obviously, they're the ones most likely to add value (in the form of high profits and good wages) to national production.

Nor would any reasonable observer deny the obvious fact that the earlier your own industry gets into the global arena, the faster it will acquire the marketing and production advantages it needs to fight competition from abroad. Here's my problem with the pro-strategic-trade policy argument: Strategic trade policy is *not* the best way to achieve the goals on which just about everybody agrees.

I'll start by making a concession: There are indeed (limited) circumstances under which a targeting program will work, particularly for small countries. In 2006, for example, Costa Rica's GDP of $21.4 billion amounted to less than 10 percent of the value of Wal-Mart's annual sales. What this says to me is that a targeting program is indeed feasible when the scale of policy-making is manageable—when most of the parties involved have worked with one another for years and can count on reaching mutually beneficial agreements with minimal frustration. But in a large economy? Impossible.

As a matter of fact, even in a small country like Costa Rica, it's debatable just how much of the country's economic success is due to strategic trade policy and how much goes back to conditions that existed *before* the government started the whole process of targeting industries

(continued)

why shouldn't a country's game plan call for taking special care of the players that give the home team the best competitive advantage?

In fact, executing a game plan like this one can be pretty simple. First, target a growth *industry* and figure out what factors make it competitive (or potentially competitive). Next, identify your *country's* comparative advantages (and make sure you know why you have them). Finally, develop a little synergy between the strong points that you've uncovered during both processes: Target the resources needed to support the *industries* that fit best with your *country's* comparative advantages.

This program—which comes under the general heading of *strategic trade policy*—is particularly effective if you're a developing country. Why? Because you've probably decided already that (1) you need to integrate yourself into the global economy and that (2) you need to figure out the best way of getting into the international game. So far, so good, but you need to remember that simply opening up your borders to foreign competition doesn't necessarily mean that domestic producers are going to have an easier time competing, either abroad or even at home.

When you throw open your borders, the first companies to take you up on the invitation will be foreign competitors with considerable advantages over the homegrown industries you're trying to develop: They've had a head start that's allowed them to develop not only certain internal efficiencies but cozy relations with everybody in the international distribution channel.

Moreover, no matter how promising your targeted industries may be, and no matter how carefully you've tried to match up your industries with your competitive advantages, as a developing country, you probably don't have the technology and marketing skills you'll need to compete with more experienced players.[30]

Which brings us back to the reason why strategic trade policy—as opposed to adopting a policy of laissez-faire and hoping for the best—is your optimal choice if you're a developing country: Your government *must* protect your local industries—say, by helping them get the skills and technology they're going to need. You could also focus your foreign-investment efforts on companies that have the marketing and technical skills you need; that's one good way of bringing home the *kind* of production you need. And it wouldn't hurt to be liberal in extending credit to the industries you're counting on.

If you're looking for some evidence that strategic trade policy is effective in helping developing nations go global, look at Singapore, which not only managed to attract companies with experience in consumer-electronics production but eventually emerged as a global competitor because it also had the comparative advantage of low wages.[31] By the same token, we have ample evidence that laissez-faire often

and attracting high-tech foreign investors. Lest we forget, Costa Rica already had a well-educated workforce, a relatively high level of economic freedom, a large population of English-speaking workers, a quality of life that had some appeal to foreign personnel, and, last but not least, more than an average quotient of Latin American political stability. Yes, Costa Rica landed Intel, but it's only fair to point out that Intel had already decided to put a plant *somewhere* in Latin America. Costa Rica's job, then, was basically convincing Intel it was a better choice than certain countries, such as Brazil and Chile, which were at a distance disadvantage when it came to sending output to the United States.

Moreover, laissez-faire—"just sitting back and hoping for the best"—is not the only alternative policy to strategic trade schemes: What if a country opted to focus on conditions affecting its attractiveness to profitable companies *in general* instead of targeted industries *in particular*? There's no good reason why a government can't alter conditions affecting, say, factor proportions, efficiency, and innovation. Why couldn't it upgrade production factors by improving human skills, providing an adequate infrastructure, encouraging consumers to demand higher-quality products, and promoting an overall competitive environment for any industry that's interested in doing business within its borders?

I wouldn't be surprised if—despite the institutional inadequacies that you so indiscriminately attribute to the region—this approach could work even in sub-Saharan Africa. I'll even make another concession: Institutional inertia is indeed a way of life in the area, and there's no reason to expect that it will go away any time soon.[34]

But what if we looked at things from another perspective? Wouldn't all of these bureaucratic agencies and ministries, rather than trying to focus on a specific industry in, say, the global high-tech universe, find it easier to review (and enforce) their own laws; take steps to stabilize their populations and rectify their most glaring economic, social, and gender inequities; and support entrepreneurial activity in the informal sectors of their economies? Wouldn't they find it more productive (in every sense of the word) to foster an environment of trust—one in which, say, the government helps cut transaction costs so local firms will be willing to work with other companies, domestic and foreign, to acquire a little of the knowledge and a few of the resources they need to be competitive?[35]

To repeat: Instead of picking (and haggling over) special industries, wouldn't they be better advised to improve the investment environment in which, after all, everybody's ultimately going to have to operate in anyway?

At this point, I might as well take the offensive in this debate. Let me point out that, as a matter of fact, strategic trade policies typically result in no more than small payoffs—primarily because, not surprisingly, most governments find it difficult to identify and target the right industries.[36] What if *doesn't* work in developing countries. In sub-Saharan Africa, for example, government institutions are so deeply rooted that it's almost impossible for anyone—either individuals or multinational conglomerates—to make a move without getting entangled in the bureaucratic undergrowth.[32]

Moreover, because no single institution has much in the way of resources, all of them are better off focusing their collective efforts on specific industries that have some potential for international competitiveness; otherwise, all you have is a bunch of underresourced agencies and ministries aiming at markets scattered all over the economic landscape.[33]●

a country targets an industry in which global demand never quite lives up to expectations? That's what happened to the United Kingdom and France—hardly newcomers to the world of international commerce—when they got together to underwrite supersonic passenger planes.

Or what if the domestic companies in a targeted industry simply fall short at the task of competing? That's what happened when Thailand decided to get into the steel business even though local steel companies suffered from such disadvantages as high production costs because of poorly trained managers and higher labor costs than neighboring competitors with similar ideas.[37]

What if too many nations tend to target the same global industries, thereby committing themselves to excessive competition and inadequate returns?[38] What if two countries compete to support the same industry, as happened when both Brazil and Canada decided to produce regional jets in the same hemisphere?[39] Finally, what if a country successfully targets an industry only to have unexpected conditions arise? Should it stay the course despite the fact that it's probably reacting to various pressures, such as the pressue to support employment in a distressed industry?[40]

Finally, even if a government can identify a future growth industry in which a domestic firm is likely to succeed—a very big *if*, in my opinion—it doesn't follow that it a company deserves public assistance merely because it happens to be engaged in the chosen industry. History recommends that nations permit their entrepreneurs to do what they do best (and what's most pressing under the circumstances): take risks that don't jeopardize whole sectors of the economy. The upshot will probably be the same as always: Some will fail, but the successful ones will survive and thrive competitively.●

Factor-Mobility Theory

In the preceding discussions, we indicated that factor conditions change in both quantity and quality. As they do, the relative capabilities of countries also change. The change may come about because of internal circumstances. For instance, if savings rates increase, countries have more capital relative to their factors of land and labor. If they spend relatively more on education, they improve the quality of the labor factor.

Currently, one of the biggest changes underway concerns relative population change. At present rates, 33 countries are projected to have smaller populations in 2050 than today primarily because of low fertility rates, such as a projected decrease of 14 percent and 22 percent in Japan and Italy, respectively. The same countries with projected decreases or slow population growth are also encountering an aging population, leaving a smaller portion of the population to provide output. They will need large increases in immigration just to maintain the present ratios of employed people relative to retirees. Concomitantly, eight countries are expected to account for half of the world's population increase, with India, Pakistan, and Nigeria leading the pack.[41]

These changes, of course, are important in understanding and predicting changes in export production and import market locations. At the same time, the mobility of capital, technology, and people affect trade and relative competitive positions. In this section, we discuss the **factor-mobility theory** of trade patterns, which focuses on the reasons why production factors move, the effects that such movement has in transforming factor endowments, and the effect of international factor mobility (especially people) on world trade.

WHY PRODUCTION FACTORS MOVE

CONCEPT CHECK

As we explain in Chapter 1, a **foreign investment** is an interest in a company or ownership of a loan made to another party; such a transaction can take place between countries, of course, and companies typically use some form of portfolio investment for short-term financial gain. We also point out that to earn higher yields on short-term investments, firms routinely move funds from country to country.

Capital   Capital, especially short-term capital, is the most internationally mobile production factor. Companies and private individuals primarily transfer capital because of differences in expected return (accounting for risk). They find information on interest rate differences readily available, and they can transfer capital by wire instantaneously at a low cost. Short-term capital is more mobile than long-term capital such as direct investment because there is more likely to be an active market through which investors can quickly buy foreign holdings and sell them if they want to transfer capital back home or to another country.

Political and economic conditions affect investors' perceptions of risk and where they prefer to put their capital. At the same time, companies invest long term abroad to tap markets and lower operating costs, as illustrated humorously in Figure 6.5. However, businesses do not make all the international capital movements. Governments give foreign aid and loans. Not-for-profit organizations donate money abroad to relieve worrisome economic and social conditions. Individuals remit funds to help their families and friends in foreign countries. Regardless of the donor or motive, the result affects factor endowments.

People   People are also internationally mobile, but less so than capital. Of course, some people travel to another country as tourists, students, and retirees; however, this travel does not affect factor endowments because they do not work there. Unlike funds that can be cheaply transferred by wire, people must usually incur high transportation costs to

FIGURE 6.5

The cosmoeconomic question of the day: Will foreign galaxies prove to be sources of less expensive labor?

Source: 1997 Joel Pett, *Lexington Herald-Leader.* Reprinted by permission.

work in another country. If they move legally, they must get immigration papers, and most countries give these documents sparingly.

Finally, such people may have to learn another language and adjust to a different culture away from their families and friends who serve as their customary support groups. During the latter part of the nineteenth and early part of the twentieth centuries, migration was the major engine of globalization, and at present, it is important again. About 3 percent of the world's population (about 200 million people) has migrated to another country.[42] Because this 3 percent is spread unevenly, the impact is much greater on some countries than on others, such as about 11 percent of the U.S. population.[43]

Of the people who go abroad to work, some move permanently and some move temporarily. For example, on the one hand, some people emigrate to another country, become citizens, and plan to reside there for the rest of their lives. On the other hand, MNEs assign people to work abroad for periods ranging from a few days to several years (usually to a place where they also transfer capital), and some countries allow workers to enter on temporary work permits, usually for short periods. For instance, about two-thirds of the population in the United Arab Emirates are temporary workers.[44] In many cases, workers leave their families behind in the hope of returning home after saving enough money while working in a foreign country. Some move legally and others move illegally (that is to say, they are undocumented).

Economic Motives   People, whether professionals or unskilled workers, largely work in another country for economic reasons. For example, Indonesian laborers work in Malaysia because they can make almost 10 times as much per day as they can at home.[45] State-enterprise hotels in China entice Western executives to work for them in China to improve the hotels' economic performance.[46]

Political Motives   People also move for political reasons—for example, because of persecution or war dangers, in which case they are known as refugees. However, once they are refugees, they usually become part of the labor pool where they live. Sometimes it is difficult to distinguish between economic and political motives for international mobility because poor economic conditions often parallel poor political conditions. For example, in the early twenty-first century, hundreds of thousands of Colombians left the country, fleeing both a civil war and unemployment.[47] Map 6.2 highlights recent global immigration.

EFFECTS OF FACTOR MOVEMENTS

Neither international capital nor population mobility is a new occurrence. For example, had it not been for historical masses of immigration, Australia, Canada, and the United States would have a greatly reduced population today. Further, many immigrants brought human capital with them, thus adding to the base of skills that enabled those countries to be newly competitive in an array of products they might otherwise have imported. Finally, these same countries received foreign capital to develop infrastructure and natural resources, which further altered their competitive structures and international trade.

What Happens When People Move   Recent evidence is largely anecdotal. Nevertheless, factor movements are substantial for many countries and insignificant for others. For example, the foreign-born population as a percentage of total population is over 20 percent for Luxembourg, Australia, Switzerland, New Zealand, and Canada, but it is no more than 2 percent in South Korea, the Slovak Republic, Hungary, and Japan.[48]

The United States is currently an example of a country whose recent immigration is largely concentrated at the high and low ends of human skills. For instance, over a third of all people with doctoral degrees in the United States are foreign born. At the other extreme, although the United States classifies all people without a high school education as "low skilled," Mexican low-skilled workers in the United States average three years

---

Capital and labor move internationally to

- Gain more income.
- Flee adverse political situations.

Factor movements alter factor endowments.

MAP 6.2
Global Immigration

Net gain and loss figures are in thousands and reflect annual average numbers of immigrants. Note that movement is primarily from developing to developed countries and that movement *into developing nations* consists largely of immigrants from neighboring countries. All in all, about 3% of the world's population—nearly 200 million people—live outside their nation of birth.

Source: Adapted from "Snapshots: Global Migration," *New York Times,* June 24, 2007: 8. Data from United Nations Population Division, The World Bank, and the International Monetary Fund.

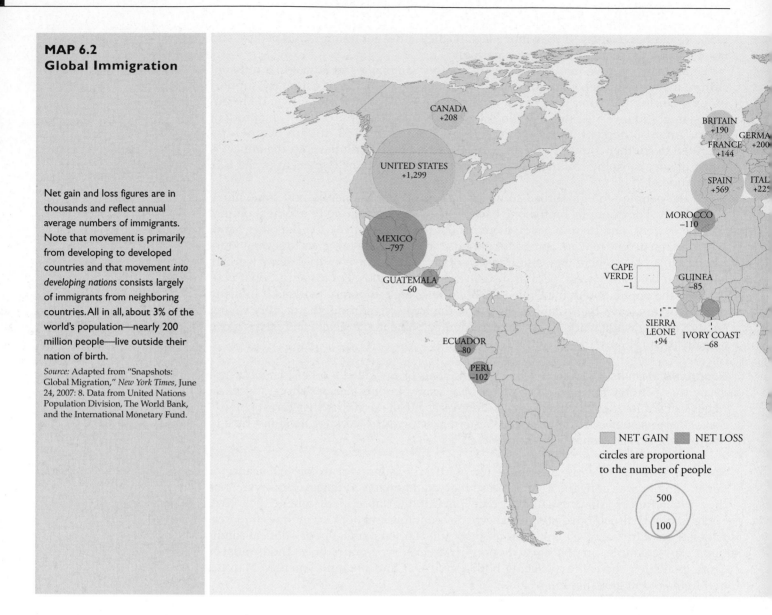

less formal education than their U.S. counterparts.[49] At both extremes, the United States has shortages of native-born workers, which is partially alleviated through immigration.

Isolating a particular aspect of labor mobility is fraught with difficulty. Although labor and capital are different production factors, they are intertwined. For instance, Singapore has transformed itself from a labor-intensive and low-wage country to a capital-intensive and high-wage country largely because of capital accumulation that has come from abroad.[50] For example, much of Singapore's capital accumulation has been in human capital—that is, in the import of skilled foreigners and the education of its own workforce.

Further, countries lose potentially productive resources when educated people leave, a situation known as a *brain drain,* but they may gain from the foreign earnings on those factors. For example, Ecuador lost almost 5 percent of its population between 1999 and 2001, including 10,000 teachers and many other people with substantial work skills. However, many of these people are now sending remittances back to Ecuador. El Salvador and the Dominican Republic receive much more income from remittances that their citizens working abroad send home than they receive from their exports. Overall, Latin American and Caribbean countries are receiving more from remittances than from foreign aid and foreign investment combined.[51]

Finally, countries receiving productive human resources also incur costs of social services and for acculturating people to a new language and culture. Further, the unskilled

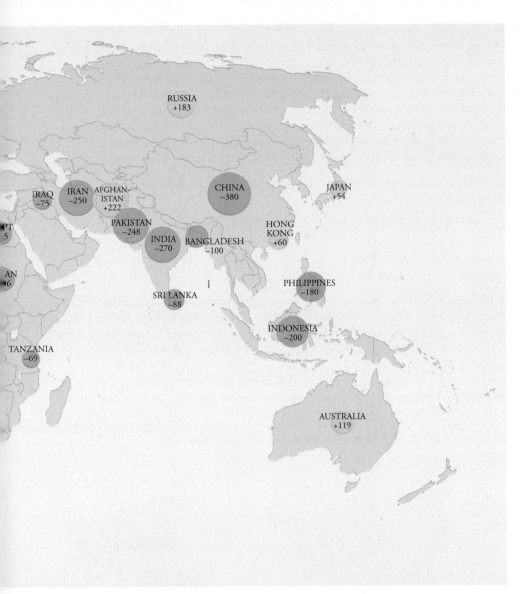

workers who take jobs that native-born workers don't want—like dishwashing, maintaining grounds, and picking agricultural produce—have children who eventually enter the workforce. If these children are also unskilled, the country is perpetuating a long-term class of "have-nots." If these children become skilled, then there is a need to bring in even more unskilled workers from abroad.

THE RELATIONSHIP BETWEEN TRADE AND FACTOR MOBILITY

Factor movement is an alternative to trade that may or may not be a more efficient allocation of resources.[52] We now discuss how free trade when coupled with freedom of factor mobility internationally usually results in the most efficient allocation of resources.

Substitution   When the factor proportions vary widely among countries, pressures exist for the most abundant factors to move to countries with greater scarcity—where they can command a better return. In countries where labor is abundant compared to capital, laborers tend to be unemployed or poorly paid. If permitted, these workers go to countries that have full employment and higher wages.

Similarly, capital tends to move away from countries in which it is abundant to those in which it is scarce. For example, Mexico gets capital from the United States, and the

There are pressures for the most abundant factors to move to an area of scarcity.

United States gets labor from Mexico.[53] If finished goods and production factors were both free to move internationally, the comparative costs of transferring goods and factors would determine the location of production.

However, as is true of trade, there are restrictions on factor movements that make them only partially mobile internationally, such as both U.S. immigration restrictions that limit the legal and illegal influx of Mexican workers and Mexican ownership restrictions in the petroleum industry that limit U.S. capital investments in that industry.

A hypothetical example, shown in Figure 6.6, should illustrate the substitutability of trade and factor movements under different scenarios. Assume the following:

- The United States and Mexico have equally productive land available at the same cost for growing tomatoes.
- The cost of transporting tomatoes between the United States and Mexico is $0.75 per bushel.
- Workers from either country pick an average of 2 bushels per hour during a 30-day picking season.

The only differences in price between the two countries are due to variations in labor and capital cost. The labor rate is $20.00 per day, or $1.25 per bushel, in the United States and $4.00 per day, or $0.25 per bushel, in Mexico. The capital needed to buy seeds, fertilizers, and equipment costs the equivalent of $0.30 per bushel in the United States and $0.50 per bushel in Mexico.

If neither tomatoes nor production factors can move between the two countries (see Figure 6.6[a]), the cost of tomatoes produced in Mexico for the Mexican market is $0.75

FIGURE 6.6   Unrestricted Trade, Factor Mobility, and the Cost of Tomatoes

Costs are lowest when trade is unrestricted and production factors are mobile.

Assumptions, cost per bushel:

1. U.S. labor = $1.25
2. Mexican labor = $0.25
3. Mexican labor in the United States (including incremental costs) = $1.15
4. U.S. capital = $0.30
5. Mexican capital = $0.50
6. U.S. capital in Mexico = $0.40
7. Transport for exports = $0.75
8. Transport of Mexican workers to the United States = $0.90

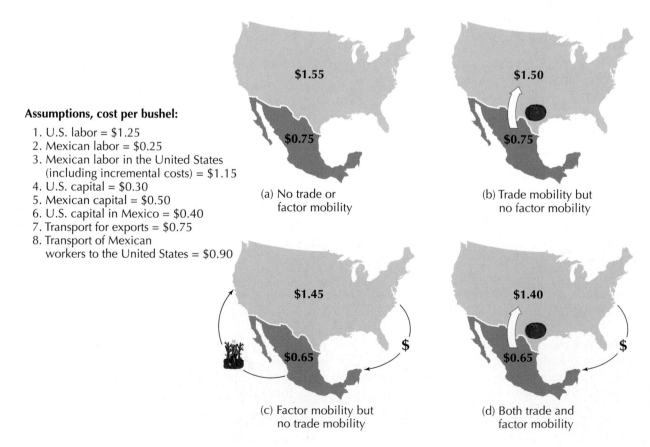

(a) No trade or factor mobility $1.55 $0.75

(b) Trade mobility but no factor mobility $1.50 $0.75

(c) Factor mobility but no trade mobility $1.45 $0.65

(d) Both trade and factor mobility $1.40 $0.65

per bushel ($0.25 of labor plus $0.50 of capital), whereas those produced in the United States for the U.S. market cost $1.55 per bushel ($1.25 of labor plus $0.30 of capital). If the two countries eliminate trade restrictions on tomatoes between them (Figure 6.6[b]), the United States will import from Mexico because the Mexican cost of $0.75 per bushel plus $0.75 for transporting the tomatoes to the United States will be $0.05 less than the $1.55 per bushel cost of growing them in the United States.

Consider another scenario in which neither country allows the importation of tomatoes but both allow certain movements of labor and capital (Figure 6.6[c]). Mexican workers can enter the United States on temporary work permits for an incremental travel and living expense of $14.40 per day per worker, or $0.90 per bushel. At the same time, U.S. companies will invest capital in Mexican tomato production, provided the capital earns more than it would earn in the United States—say, $0.40 per bushel, which is less than the Mexican going rate.

In this scenario, Mexican production costs per bushel will be $0.65 ($0.25 of Mexican labor plus $0.40 of U.S. capital) and U.S. production costs $1.45 ($0.25 of Mexican labor plus $0.90 of travel and incremental costs plus $0.30 of U.S. capital). Each country would reduce its production costs—from $0.75 to $0.65 in Mexico and from $1.55 to $1.45 in the United States—by bringing in abundant production factors from abroad.

With free trade *and* the free movement of production factors (Figure 6.6[d]), Mexico will produce for both markets by importing capital from the United States. According to the three assumptions just stated, doing this will be cheaper than sending labor to the United States. In reality, because neither production factors nor the finished goods they produce are completely free to move internationally, slight changes in the extent of restrictions can greatly alter how and where goods may be produced most cheaply.

> The lowest costs occur when trade and production factors are both mobile.

In some cases, however, the inability to gain sufficient access to foreign production factors may stimulate efficient methods of substitution, such as the development of alternatives for traditional production methods. For example, U.S. tomato farmers in California depended almost entirely on Mexican temporary workers (*braceros*) until the *bracero* program terminated in 1964. Since then, the tomato harvests have quadrupled while labor has dropped 72 percent through mechanization.

However, not all harvesting jobs can be reasonably mechanized. For instance, because cantaloupes ripen at different times, pickers go through a field about 10 times. A robot would have to be able to distinguish colors so as to leave green cantaloupes behind.[54] At the same time, many other jobs are largely filled by unskilled immigrants in developed countries that defy the imagination for mechanization, such as bussing tables at restaurants and changing beds in hotels.

> Both finished goods and production factors are partially mobile internationally.

Complementarity   In our tomato example for the United States and Mexico, we showed that factor movements may substitute for or stimulate trade. When companies invest abroad, the investments often stimulate exports from their home countries. As we show in our closing case, for example, the giant Russian oil company LUKOIL has been making investments abroad not only to stimulate its exports but also to pursue a strategy of forward integration into the ownership of foreign distribution outlets. About a third of world trade (exports) is among controlled entities, such as from parent to subsidiary, subsidiary to parent, and subsidiary to subsidiary of the same company.

Case Review Note

Many of the exports would not occur if overseas investments did not exist. One reason is that a company may export capital equipment as part of the value of its investment when building a facility abroad. It may have more confidence in this equipment than in equipment built locally, and it may want maximum worldwide uniformity. Still another reason is that domestic operating units may export materials and components to their foreign facilities for use in a finished product. For example, Coca-Cola exports concentrate to its bottling facilities abroad. A foreign facility may produce part of the product line while serving as sales agent for exports of its parent's complementary products.

> Factor mobility through foreign investment often stimulates trade because of
>
> - The need for components.
> - The parent's ability to sell complementary products.
> - The need for equipment for subsidiaries.

LOOKING TO THE FUTURE

In What Direction Will Trade Winds Blow?

When countries have few restrictions on foreign trade and factor mobility, companies have greater latitude in reducing operating costs. For example, fewer trade restrictions give them opportunities to gain economies of scale by servicing markets in more than one country from a single base of production. Fewer restrictions on factor movements give them opportunities to combine factors for more efficient production. However, government trade and immigration restrictions vary from one country to another, from one point in time to another, and under different circumstances.

Nevertheless, it's probably safe to say that trade restrictions have been diminishing, primarily because of the economic gains that countries foresee through freer trade. Further, restrictions on the movement of capital and technology have become freer, but whether restrictions on the movement of people are freer is questionable.

However, there are uncertainties as to whether the trend toward the freer movement of trade and production factors will endure. Groups worldwide question whether the economic benefits of more open economies outweigh some of the costs, both economic and noneconomic. Although the next chapter discusses import restrictions (protectionism) in detail, it is useful at this point to understand the overall evolution of protectionist sentiment.

One key issue is the trade between developed and developing economies. At the same time that trade barriers are being lowered, many developing economies, in which wage rates are very low, are growing economically more rapidly than are developed countries. Concomitantly, shifts in production to developing economies may cause the displacement of many jobs within developed countries.

There is uncertainty as to how fast new jobs will replace old ones in developed countries and how much tolerance these countries will have for employment shifts that would be less likely to occur within protected markets. Regardless of whether freer trade or protectionism prevails in the future, companies must try to predict what will happen to those industries in which they operate.

If present trends continue, relationships among factor endowments (land, labor, and capital) will continue to evolve. For example, the population growth rate is much higher in developing economies than in developed countries. Three possible consequences of this growth are continued shifts of labor-intensive production to developing economies, shifts of agricultural production away from densely populated areas, and pressures on the developed countries to accept more immigrants.

At the same time, the finite supply of natural resources may lead to price increases for these resources, even though oversupplies have often depressed prices. The limited supply may work to the advantage of developing economies because supplies in developed countries have been more fully exploited.

Even as population grows rapidly in developing countries, so does the pace of urbanization, which largely has already taken place in developed countries. Considerable evidence now indicates that productivity increases with urbanization because firms can more likely find people with the exact skills they need, there are economies in moving supplies and finished products, and knowledge flows more easily from one company and industry to another. Thus we might expect higher growth in some developing countries undergoing urbanization. This should also lead to these countries' accounting for a larger share of world trade.

We will probably see the continued trend toward a more finely tuned specialization of production among countries to take advantage of specific country conditions. Although part of this will be due to human differences, such as wage and skill differences that cause low-skilled jobs to migrate to developing countries, other factors are important as well. For instance, differences in protection of property rights may cause technologically intensive companies either to locate more activities within countries that offer much protection or to specialize component production in different countries, thus making it more difficult for people in any single country to gain the full picture needed to pirate the production process.

Four factors are worth monitoring because they could cause product trade to become relatively less significant in the future:

1. There are some indications that protectionist sentiment is growing. For example, major trading countries have recently squabbled over trade for a number of products, including genetically altered agricultural products, bananas, steel, and passenger aircraft. These sorts of disputes could prevent competitively produced goods from entering foreign countries.

2. As economies grow, efficiencies of multiple production locations also grow, which may allow

country-by-country production to replace trade in many cases. For example, most automobile producers have moved into China and Thailand or plan to do so as a result of China's and Thailand's growing market size.

3. Flexible, small-scale production methods, especially those using robotics, may enable even small countries to produce many goods efficiently for their own consumption, thus eliminating the need to import those goods. For example, steel production used to take larger capital outlays that needed

enormous markets before the development of efficient minimills that can produce on a small scale.

4. Services are growing more rapidly than products as a portion of production and consumption within high-income countries. Consequently, product trade may become a less important part of countries' total trade. Further, many of the rapid-growth service areas, such as home building and dining out, are not easily traded, so trade in goods plus services could become a smaller part of total output and consumption. ■

C A S E

LUKOIL: Trade Strategy at a Privatized Exporter

In 2006, Russia's GDP grew by almost 7 percent, its eighth straight year of significant growth.[55] That growth has been fueled by the oil and gas sector, which currently accounts for about 25 percent of GDP and 40 percent of all exports. Today, Russia consumes about 27 percent of its oil production and exports the other 73 percent, and so lucrative is its business in gas and oil that petroleum export taxes have allowed the current government to pay off all foreign debt incurred by its Soviet predecessor. On the downside, of course, its dependence on petroleum exports makes Russia quite vulnerable to fluctuations in global petroleum markets. If the price per barrel of oil shifts by so much as $1, Russian revenues shift by about $1.4 billion in the same direction.

In recent years, so much oil has been discovered in Russia that the country now has 15 percent more proven reserves than Saudi Arabia. In addition, as a result of diplomatic negotiations to enlist Russian support for the war against the Taliban and al Queda in Afghanistan, Russia also controls petroleum exports from the former Central Asian Soviet republics of Azerbaijan and Kazakhstan, both of which, like Russia itself, are oil rich. In fact, Russia's supplies are so plentiful that, according to one Moscow-based energy-intelligence expert, it's "choking on the crude it produces."

Because of fierce competition in the global oil industry, however, even control of such vast supplies is no guarantee Russia can sell its output at an acceptable margin. In addition, Russia depends on oil exports to pay for the imports, primarily machinery, needed to sustain the present pace of economic development—a top priority for the Russian government for two reasons:

1. At a purchasing price parity of $12,200 in 2006, Russian GDP per capita is still well below that of any other G8 country.

2. The oil sector—which is a capital- rather than labor-intensive industry—employs less than 1 percent of the country's population.

The Role of LUKOIL

As Russia's largest oil company, LUKOIL is the second-largest owner (and the largest private owner) of proven reserves in the world. (In some of the world's biggest oil producers, such as Saudi Arabia and Venezuela, reserves are government owned.) Although it has gradually reduced its holdings in LUKOIL for fairly obvious reasons, the Russian government maintains close ties with LUKOIL: Controlling about 19 percent of all Russian production and refining, LUKOIL racked up sales of US$67.7 billion in 2006, and in addition to huge investments in Russia itself, it has been busy investing some of its capital abroad (see Map 6.3, which locates and identifies the company's foreign operations). In the United States, for instance, it acquired

MAP 6.3
LUKOIL: Expands Its Operations

LUKOIL has expanded its operations internationally, not only by exporting (notably to the United States) but also by investing in foreign production, exploration, and refining operations and marketing efforts. Note that the preponderance of the company's expansion has taken place in nearby countries.

Source: Information taken from the LUKOIL *Annual Report* (2006).

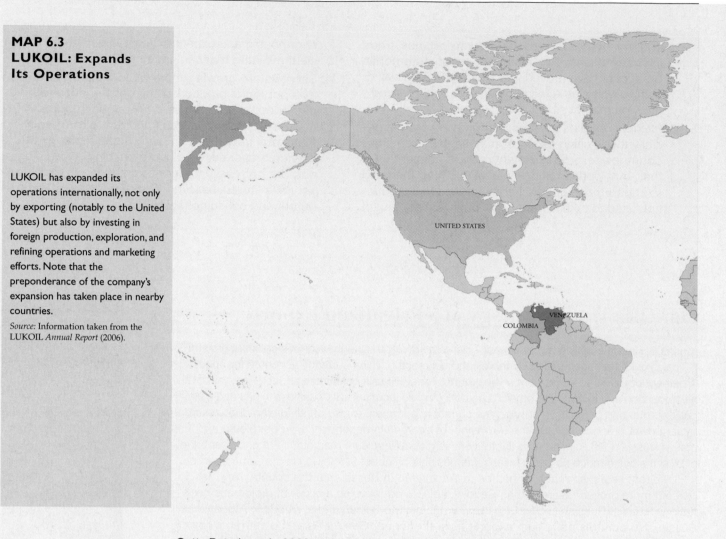

Getty Petroleum in 2000 and, in 2004, a string of gasoline stations owned by ConocoPhillips—acquisitions whereby it now controls a U.S. retail network of nearly 2,000 outlets.

What's LUKOIL's Strategy?

As we've already seen, Russia has a lot of oil but desperately needs capital; we've also explained that both Russia and its premier oil company are highly dependent on export revenues. Given this situation, you might well ask why a Russian company sees any advantage in investing abroad. To answer this question, we first need to take a closer look at both LUKOIL's competitive situation and its strategy for dealing with it.

We know that LUKOIL has to sell in foreign markets, both to make adequate use of its capacity and to earn sufficient profits. We should also point out that, since the beginning of the twenty-first century, Russia's export position has been generally quite favorable. Between January 1999 and September 2000, for example, a combination of factors caused oil prices to triple—namely, bad weather, strong demand, and production cutbacks by the Organization of Petroleum Exporting Countries (OPEC), of which Russia is not a member. In the wake of economic uncertainty following 9/11, prices gave back about half this gain, but since then they've increased to all-time highs, again as a result of a combination of factors—political unrest in Venezuela, the war in Iraq, Chinese economic expansion, and further production curtailments by OPEC.

As a general result, LUKOIL has been able to sell more oil, at higher prices, outside Russia than it could just a few years earlier. Thus favorable market conditions have for several years enabled LUKOIL to amass a substantial store of capital that could be channeled into foreign investment—if, of course, management concluded that such investment would enhance the firm's strategic position.

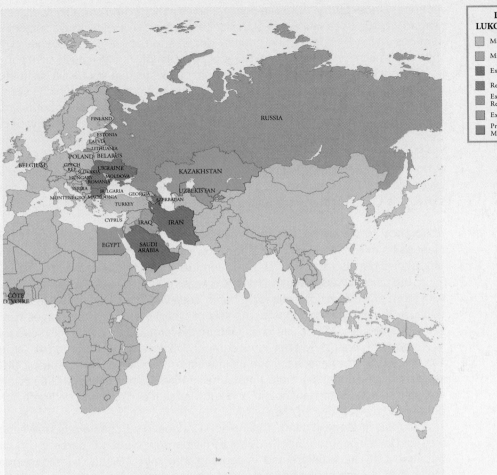

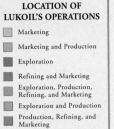

LOCATION OF LUKOIL'S OPERATIONS

- Marketing
- Marketing and Production
- Exploration
- Refining and Marketing
- Exploration, Production, Refining, and Marketing
- Exploration and Production
- Production, Refining, and Marketing

Why LUKOIL Went the Foreign Investment Route   In addition to its reliance on exporting as a means of using the firm's capacity, LUKOIL management has long wanted to use foreign expansion as a means both of earning bigger margins and of ensuring more reliable full on-time payment than it can get in Russia. The question, however, still remains: Why doesn't LUKOIL simply export rather than risk foreign investment? The answer lies in the following combination of factors.

Fluctuating Oil Prices   In spite of a general upward trend since the beginning of the century, oil prices—and, with them, the marketability of Russian oil abroad—have in the past been known to fluctuate widely. On more than one occasion, prices have surged over 100 percent and, in one year, plummeted to levels lower than those at which the boom began.

Thus, in the late 1990s, when a global oil glut and depressed prices combined to take a deep cut out of its profits, LUKOIL decided to emulate its larger Western competitors by venturing on a strategy of forward integration into the ownership of foreign distribution outlets. Its first foreign investments had been made no farther from home than the former Soviet satellite countries—and close longtime customers—of Bulgaria and Romania, where it bought up some formerly state-owned production facilities. Since then, however, LUKOIL has ventured farther afield, almost exclusively by means of purchasing existing operations.

It's a sound strategy. Why? To put it simply, when oil producers invest in distribution, they strengthen their ties to markets in which they may be better able to sell crude oil in times of global oversupply. Moreover, integrating into distribution can potentially reduce operating costs, primarily because a producer doesn't have to rely on negotiating and enforcing a network of agreements by which it sells oil to intermediaries in other countries.

Political Uncertainty   Despite huge reserves at home and enviable success as an exporter abroad, LUKOIL was well aware of the fact that export sales are always subject to political disruptions. What if an importing country decides to reduce its purchases of Russian oil to protest some internal Russian political policy (or simply to diversify its own supply sources)?

Or consider another problem that's more or less unique to LUKOIL's situation. As it turns out, the Russian government owns the pipeline system through which virtually all Russian oil exports must pass, allocating access to the system by means of quotas among domestic oil companies. What if a competitor manages to gain sufficient influence with certain political decision makers to siphon off part of LUKOIL's quota?

Finally, LUKOIL can never forget that, although it has itself been almost completely privatized, the Russian government still owns some of its domestic competitors and has often given its own firms preferential treatment in various matters. That's just one reason why LUKOIL is trying to increase foreign oil supplies to about 20 percent of its total.

Efficiency Imperatives   To be a major global competitor, LUKOIL must become as efficient as its major Western competitors. Toward that end, it must not only achieve operating efficiencies but also acquire state-of-the-industry technology and marketing skills.

In the past, LUKOIL's administrative expenses and cost of capital have been high compared with those of Western competitors. At home, such inefficiencies resulted in only minor problems because the competition consisted solely of other Russian oil companies hampered by the same operational inefficiencies inherited from the former state-owned oil monopoly.

Even in Russia, however, new competitive threats are starting to emerge (BP and TotalFinaElf, for instance, have bought interests in Russian oil companies). LUKOIL, however, sees them as something more than stiffer domestic competition: They're also potentially valuable sources of the technology and knowledge that it needs to compete not only at home but abroad as well.

With this strategy in mind, it has placed independent directors from Western oil companies on its board. In addition, ConocoPhillips now owns 20 percent of LUKOIL, in part because LUKOIL is interested in tapping into the U.S. firm's management expertise. Meanwhile, foreign acquisitions, such as Getty in the United States, present another source of experienced personnel, technology, and competitive know-how. ■

QUESTIONS

1. What theories of trade help explain Russia's position as an oil exporter? Why? Which ones don't? Why not?
2. How do global political and economic conditions affect global oil markets and prices?
3. Discuss the following statement as it applies to Russia and LUKOIL:
   Regardless of the advantages a country may gain by trading, international trade will begin only if companies within that country have competitive advantages that enable them to be viable traders—and they must foresee profits in exporting and importing.
4. In LUKOIL's situation, what is the relationship between factor mobility and exports?
5. Reviewing the opening case of this chapter, compare the role assumed by the Costa Rican government in using trade to meet national economic objectives with that of the Russian government.

SUMMARY

- Some trade theories examine what will happen to international trade in the absence of government interference. Other theories prescribe how governments should interfere with trade flows to achieve certain national objectives.

- Trade theory is useful because it helps explain what might be produced competitively in a given locale, where a company might go to produce a given product efficiently, and whether government practices might interfere with the free flow of trade among countries. Other theories address the explanation of trade patterns.

- Mercantilist theory proposed that a country should try to achieve a favorable balance of trade (export more than it imports) to receive an influx of gold. Neomercantilist policy also seeks a favorable balance of trade, but its purpose is to achieve some social or political objective.

- The theory of absolute advantage proposes specialization through free trade because consumers will be better off if they can buy foreign-made products that are priced more cheaply than domestic ones.

- According to the theory of absolute advantage, a country may produce goods more efficiently because of a natural advantage (e.g., raw materials or climate) or because of an acquired advantage (e.g., technology or skill for a product or process advantage).

- Comparative advantage theory also proposes specialization through free trade because it says that total global output can increase even if one country has an absolute advantage in the production of all products.

- Policymakers have questioned some of the assumptions of the absolute and comparative advantage theories. These assumptions are that full employment exists, output efficiency is always a country's major objective, countries are satisfied with their relative gains, there are no transport costs among countries, advantages appear to be static, and resources move freely within countries but are immobile internationally. Although the theories use a two-country analysis of products, the theories hold for multicountry trade and for services as well.

- The theory of country size holds that because countries with large land areas are apt to have varied climates and natural resources, they are generally more self-sufficient than smaller countries. A second reason for this greater self-sufficiency is that large countries' production and market centers are more likely to be located at a greater distance from other countries, raising the transport costs of foreign trade.

- The factor-proportions theory holds that a country's relative endowments of land, labor, and capital will determine the relative costs of these factors. These factor costs, in turn, determine which goods the country can produce most efficiently.

- According to the country-similarity theory, most trade today occurs among high-income countries because they share similar market characteristics and because they produce and consume so much more than emerging economies.

- Much of the pattern of two-way trading partners may be explained by cultural similarity between the countries, political and economic agreements, and by the distance between them.

- Manufactured products comprise the bulk of trade among high-income countries. This trade occurs because countries apportion their research and development differently among industrial sectors. It also occurs because consumers from high-income countries want and can afford to buy products with a greater variety of characteristics than are produced in their domestic markets.

- The international product life cycle (PLC) theory states that companies will manufacture products first in the countries in which they were researched and developed. These are almost always developed countries. Over the product's life cycle, production will shift to foreign locations, especially to developing economies as the product reaches the stages of maturity and decline.

- The Porter diamond shows that four conditions are important for competitive superiority: demand conditions; factor conditions; related and supporting industries; and firm strategy, structure, and rivalry.

- Production factors and finished goods are only partially mobile internationally. The cost and feasibility of transferring production factors rather than exporting finished goods internationally will determine which alternative is better.

- Although international mobility of production factors may be a substitute for trade, the mobility may stimulate trade through sales of components, equipment, and complementary products.

KEY TERMS

absolute advantage (p. 230)
acquired advantage (p. 231)
comparative advantage (p. 232)
country-similarity theory (p. 240)
factor-mobility theory (p. 250)

factor-proportions theory (p. 237)
favorable balance of trade (p. 229)
mercantilism (p. 228)
natural advantage (p. 230)
neomercantilism (p. 229)

nontradable goods (p. 236)
Porter diamond (p. 245)
product life cycle (PLC) theory (p. 243)
theory of country size (p. 236)
unfavorable balance of trade (p. 229)

ENDNOTES

1 *Sources include the following:* World Trade Organization, "Trade Profiles: Costa Rica," at http://stat.wto.org/CountryProfile/WSDBCountryPFView.aspx?Language=E&Country=CR (accessed July 16, 2007); Debora Spar, *Attracting High Technology Investment: Intel's Costa Rican Plant* (Washington, DC: The World Bank, Foreign Investment Advisory Service Occasional Paper 11, 1998); CIA Factbook, at http://CIA.GOV/CIA/publications/factbook/geos/cs.html (accessed July 16, 2007); Gail D. Triner, "Recent Latin American History and Its Historiography," *Latin American Research Review* 38:1 (2003): 219–38; John Weeks, "Trade Liberalisation, Market Deregulation and Agricultural Performance in Central America," *The Journal of Development Studies* 35:5 (June 1999): 48–76; Niels W. Ketelhöhn and Michael E. Porter, "Building a Cluster: Electronics and Information Technology in Costa Rica," *Harvard Business School Case 9703422* (November 7, 2002); John Schellhas, "Peasants Against Globalization: Rural Social Movements in Costa Rica," *American Anthropologist* 103:3 (2001): 862–63; Jose Itzigsohn, *Developing Poverty: The State, Labor Market Deregulation, and the Informal Economy in Costa Rica and the Dominican Republic* (University Park: Pennsylvania University Press, 2000); Roy Nelson, "Intel's Site Selection Decision in Latin America," *Thunderbird, The American Graduate School of International Management Case A06–99–0016*; and Andrés Rodríguez-Clare, "Costa Rica's Development Strategy Based on Human Capital and Technology: How It Got There, The Impact of Intel, and Lessons for Other Countries," *United Nations Human Development Report 2001* (New York: United Nations Development Programme, 2001).

2 For a good survey of mercantilism and the mercantilist era, see Gianni Vaggi, *A Concise History of Economic Thought: From Mercantilism to Monetarism* (New York: Palgrave Macmillan, 2002).

3 For reviews of the literature, see Jordan Shan and Fiona Sun, "On the Export-Led Growth Hypothesis for the Little Dragons: An Empirical Reinvestigation," *Atlantic Economic Review* 26:4 (1998): 353–71; and George K. Zestos and Xiangnan Tao, "Trade and GDP Growth: Causal Relations in the United States and Canada," *Southern Economic Journal* 68:4 (2002): 859–74.

4 For a good discussion of the history of free trade thought, see Leonard Gomes, *The Economics and Ideology of Free Trade: A Historial Review* (Cheltenham, UK: Edward Elgar, 2003).

5 "Year Round Production of Tomatoes in Iceland," at www.freshplaza.com/news_detail.asp?id=3791 (accessed July 16, 2007); "The History of Wine Production in Brazil," at www.brazilian-wines.com/en/brazilie_histoire.asp (accessed July 16, 2007).

6 For simplicity's sake, both Smith and Ricardo originally assumed a simple world composed of only two countries and two commodities. Our example makes the same assumption. Now, although this simplification is unrealistic, it does not diminish the usefulness of either theory: Economists have applied the same reasoning to demonstrate efficiency advantages in multiproduct and multicountry trade relationships. Smith's seminal treatise remains abundantly in print; for a reliable recent edition, see *An Inquiry into the Nature and Causes of the Wealth of Nations* (Washington: Regnery Publishing, 1998). Like

Smith's Wealth of Nations, Ricardo's seminal work on comparative advantage, originally published in London in 1817, is continuously reprinted; see, for example, *On the Principles of Political Economy and Taxation* (Amherst, NY: Prometheus Books, 1996).

7 For a good discussion of this paradoxical thinking, see Paul R. Krugman, "What Do Undergraduates Need to Know About Trade?" *American Economic Review Papers and Proceedings* (May 1993): 23–26. For a discussion of some developing countries' views that monopolistic conditions keep them from gaining a fair share of gains from international trade, see A. P. Thirwell, *Growth and Development*, 6th ed. (London: Macmillan, 1999).

8 See David Adams, "UN Attempts to Boost Biosafety in Developing World," *Nature*, January 24, 2002: 353; Hemel Hempstead, "Worldwide Project to Assess Safety of GM Crops," *Appropriate Technology* 29:1 (January–March 2002): 37–38.

9 "Nicaraguan Protest," *Tiquicia's Blog*, April 26, 2006, at http://tiquicia-cr.blogspot.com/2006/04/nicaraguan-protest.html (accessed July 17, 2007).

10 Eli J. Heckscher, *Heckscher-Ohlin Trade Theory* (Cambridge, MA: MIT Press, 1991).

11 For a discussion of ways in which the theory does not fit the reality of trade, see Antoni Estevadeordal and Alan M. Taylor, "A Century of Missing Trade?" *The American Economic Review* 92:1 (2002): 383–93. For a study supporting the theory, see Yong-Seok Choi and Pravin Krishna, "The Factor Content of Bilateral Trade: An Empirical Test," *The Journal of Political Economy* 112:4 (2004): 887–915.

12 See, for example, Donald R. Davis and David E. Weinstein, "An Account of Global Factor Trade," *The American Economic Review* 91:5 (2001): 1423–53; Oner Guncavdi and Suat Kucukcifi, "Foreign Trade and Factor Intensity in an Open Developing Country: An Input-Output Analysis for Turkey," *Russian & East European Finance and Trade* 37:1 (2001): 75–88.

13 See, for example, P. Krugman and A. J. Venables, "Globalization and the Inequality of Nations," *Quarterly Journal of Economics* 110 (1995): 857–80.

14 See Paul Krugman, "Scale Economies, Product Differentiation, and the Patterns of Trade," *The American Economic Review* 70 (1980): 950–59; James Harrigan, "Estimation of Cross-Country Differences in Industry Production Functions," *Journal of International Economics* 47:2 (1999): 267–93.

15 Drusilla K. Brown and Robert M. Stern, "Measurement and Modeling of the Economic Effect of Trade and Investment Barriers in Services," *Title Review of International Economics* 9:2 (2001): 262–86, discuss the role of economies of scale and trade barriers.

16 See Gianmarco I. P. Ottaviano and Diego Puga, "Agglomeration in the Global Economy: A Survey of the 'New Economic Geography,'" *The World Economy* 21:6 (1998): 707–31; Ottaviano, Takatoshi Tabuchi, and Jacques-François Thisse, "Agglomeration and Trade Revisited," *International Economic Review* 43:2 (2002): 409–35.

17 Stefan B. Linder, *An Essay on Trade Transformation* (New York: Wiley, 1961).

18 Dirk Pilat, "The Economic Impact of Technology," *The OECD Observer* 213 (August–September 1998): 5–8.

19 Anthony J. Venables, "Shifts in Economic Geography and Their Causes," *Economic Review—Federal Reserve Bank of Kansas City* 91:4 (2006): 61–85, referring to work by R. Hausmann and D. Rodrik, "Economic Development as Self Discovery" (2003), Harvard Kennedy School working paper.

20 Two discussions of intraindustry trade are Don P. Clark, "Determinants of Intraindustry Trade between the United States and Industrial Nations," *The International Trade Journal* 12:3 (Fall 1998): 345–62; H. Peter Gray, "Free International Economic Policy in a World of Schumpeter Goods," *The International Trade Journal* 12:3 (Fall 1998): 323–44.

21 Daniel Michaels, "Landing Rights," *Wall Street Journal*, April 30, 2002: A1+.

22 "That's Snow-Biz," *The Economist*, April 13, 1996: 58.

23 Terry Hall, "NZ Finds Pirated Varieties in Chile," *Financial Times*, January 21, 1999: 24.

24 Anthony J. Venables, "Shifts in Economic Geography and Their Causes," *Economic Review—Federal Reserve Bank of Kansas City* 91:4 (2006): 61–85.

25 Jeffrey A. Frankel and David Romer, "Does Trade Cause Growth?" *The American Economic Review* 89:3 (June 1999): 379–99.

26 J. L. Gallup and J. Sachs, "Geography and Economic Development," in B. Pleskovic and J. E. Stiglitz, eds., *Annual World Bank Conference on Development Economics* (1998).

27 See Raymond Vernon, "International Investment and International Trade in the Product Life Cycle," *Quarterly Journal of Economics* (May 1996): 190–207; David Dollar, "Technological Innovation, Capital Mobility, and the Product Cycle in North–South Trade," *American Economic Review* 76:1 (1986): 177–90.

28 This is true according to various indicators. See, for example, International Bank for Reconstruction and Development, "Science and Technology," *The World Development Indicators* (Washington, DC: 2000), p. 300.

29 Kiyohiko Ito and Vladimir Pucik, "R&D Spending, Domestic Competition, and Export Performance of Japanese Manufacturing Firms," *Strategic Management Journal* 14 (1993): 61–75.

30 Hubert Schmitz, "Reducing Complexity in the Industrial Policy Debate," *Development Policy Review* 25:4 (2007): 417–28.

31 James Kynge and Elisabeth Robinson, "Singapore to Revise Trade Priorities," *Financial Times*, January 21, 1997: 6.

32 Sonny Nwankwo and Darlington Richards, "Institutional Paradigm and the Management of Transitions: A Sub-Saharan African Perspective," *International Journal of Social Economics* 31:1/2 (2004): 111.

33 Jeffrey Sachs, "Institutions Matter, But Not Everything," *Finance and Development* (June 2003): 38–41.

34 Nwankwo and Richards, "Institutional Paradigm and the Management of Transitions," 111.

35 Andrés Rodríguez-Clare, "Clusters and Comparative Advantage: Implications for Industrial Policy," *Journal of Development Economics* 82 (2007): 43–57.

36 Paul Krugman and Alasdair M. Smith, eds., *Empirical Studies of Strategic Trade Policies* (Chicago: University of Chicago Press, 1993); Howard Pack and Kamal Saggi, "Is There a Case for Industrial Policy?" *The World Bank Research Observer* 21:2 (2006): 267.

37 Paul M. Sherer, "Thailand Trips in Reach for New Exports," *Wall Street Journal*, August 27, 1996: A8.

38 Richard Brahm, "National Targeting Policies, High-Technology Industries, and Excessive Competition," *Strategic Management Journal* 16 (1995): 71–91.

39 Andrea E. Goldstein and Steven M. McGuire, "The Political Economy of Strategic Trade Policy and the Brazil-Canada Export Subsidies Saga," *The World Economy* 27:4 (2004): 541.

40 Theresa M. Greaney, "Strategic Trade and Competition Policies to Assist Distressed Industries," *The Canadian Journal of Economics* 32:3 (1999): 767.

41 UN Population Division, at www.un.org/esa/population/unpop.

42 International Organization for Migration, *World Migration Report 2000*, at www.iom.int.

43 Ron Hutcheson, "Defining 'American,' " *Miami Herald*, April 2, 2006: 16A.

44 Richard B. Freeman, "People Flows in Globalization," *Journal of Economic Perspectives* 20:2 (2006): 145–70.

45 John Salt, "The Future of International Labor Migration," *Migration Review* 26:4 (2002): 1077.

46 Ben Dolven, "China Recruits Foreign Talent," *Wall Street Journal*, April 15, 2004: A13.

47 "Making the Most of an Exodus," *The Economist*, February 23, 2002: 41–42.

48 *Trends in International Migration*, at oecd.org/dataoecd/7/49/24994376 (accessed March 18, 2005).

49 Freeman, "People Flows in Globalization."

50 See C. Chris Rodrigo, "East Asia's Growth: Technology or Accumulation?" *Contemporary Economic Policy* 18:2 (2000): 215–27; Paul Krugman, "The Myth of Asia's Miracle," *Foreign Affairs* 73:6 (1994): 62–78.

51 Richard Lapper, "Latin Americans Scale Summit of the Remittance League," *Financial Times*, March 26, 2004: 2, using data from the Inter-American Development Bank.

52 Keith Head and John Ries, "Exporting and FDI as Alternative Strategies," *Oxford Review of Economic Policy* 20:3 (2004): 409–29.

53 See Frank D. Bean et al., "Circular, Invisible, and Ambiguous Migrants: Components of Differences in Estimates of the Number of Unauthorized Mexican Migrants in the United States," *Demography* 38:3 (2001): 411–22; United Nations Conference on Trade and Development, *World Investment Report 2000: Cross-Border Mergers and Acquisitions and Development* (New York and Geneva: United Nations, 2000), p. 312.

54 June Kronholtz, "Immigrant Labor or Machines?" *Wall Street Journal*, December 19, 2006: A4.

55 *Sources include the following:* "Alliances, Acquisitions Key to LUKOIL Ambitions," *International Petroleum Finance*, June 8, 2007: 1; Sabrina Tavernise and Peter S. Green, "Oil Concerns in Russia Branch Out," *New York Times*, April 2, 2002: W1; Bhushan Bahree, "Western Oil Flirts with Russia Firms, Insider Says," *Wall Street Journal*, April 29, 2002: A13; Reuters, "Mobius and Chevron Exec Nominated for LUKOIL Board," January 17, 2002, at http://biz.yahoo.com/rf/020117/117507998_1.html; Paul Starobin, "LUKOIL Is Lonesome," *Business Week Online*, April 24, 2000, at www.businessweek.com:2000/00_17/b3678229.htm?scriptFramed; "LUKOIL Oil Company," at www.lukoil.com; "LUKOIL Expands at Home and Abroad," *Hart's European Fuels News*, March 7, 2001; "Focus, the Russians Are Coming," *Petroleum Economist*, December 31, 2000; Andrew Jack and Arkady Ostrovsky, "LUKOIL in U.S. Petro Deal," *Financial Times*, November 4, 2000: 8; David Ignatius, "The Russians Are Pumping," *Pittsburgh Post-Gazette*, December 28, 2001: A-21; Tina Obut, "Perspective on Russia's Oil Sector," *Oil & Gas Journal*, February 1, 1999: 20; *LUKOIL Annual Report*, various years; "Event Brief of September 30: ConocoPhillips and LUKOil," *CCBN Wire Service*, September 30, 2004; "LUKOIL Leading Peers in Adding to Production outside Russia," *Platts Oilgram News*, April 13, 2004: 1; "World Oil Price Chronology," March 2005, at www.eia.doe.gov/emeu/cabs/chron (accessed March 8, 2005); and "Russia" www.cia.doe.gov/cabs/russia (accessed July 21, 2007).

7

Governmental Influence on Trade

Objectives

- To explain the rationales for governmental policies that enhance and restrict trade

- To show the effects of pressure groups on trade policies

- To describe the potential and actual effects of governmental intervention on the free flow of trade

- To illustrate the major means by which trade is restricted and regulated

- To demonstrate the business uncertainties and business opportunities created by governmental trade policies

A little help does a great deal.

—French proverb

CASE: Making the Emperor's (and Everyone Else's) New Clothes: Textile and Clothing Trade

Most countries have a long history of protecting their production of textiles and clothing because these are essential products for all their citizens.[1] This production also employs lots of people, and employment is a politically sensitive issue. As early as the 1950s, the United States and European countries negotiated voluntary export restraints with China, Hong Kong, India, Japan, and Pakistan. Although these countries "voluntarily" limited their exports, there was really nothing voluntary about the agreements. Had they not agreed, the United States and European countries would certainly have limited the imports of a number of products from these countries.

provided for importing countries (mainly developed economies) to negotiate quotas (quantitative restrictions) with exporting countries (mainly developing economies).

In addition to quotas, developed countries also placed tariffs (taxes) on imported textiles and clothing that, by adding to their prices, made them less competitive. The tariff rates were, and still are, very complex and vary by product origin and by minute product descriptions. For instance, a current U.S. schedule specifies a separate tariff rate (ranging from 7.7 percent to 21.7 percent depending on origin) on "bleached satin or twill weave fabrics, containing 85 percent or more cotton by weight and weighing not more than 200 grams per square meter."

However, in the decades following the MFA enactment, developed countries became more concerned about two conditions in developing countries: (1) the piracy of intellectual property rights, and (2) trade protection in services, such as banking.

MAP 7.1   Winners and Losers from the MFA Demise

THE MULTIFIBER ARRANGEMENT

These agreements led to further agreements, which culminated in the Multifiber Arrangement (MFA) of 1974 that included over 40 countries and lasted until the beginning of 2005. The MFA

FIGURE 7.1   Market Shares of Imported Clothing in the United States

The pie chart on the left shows the distribution of market share while the Multifiber Agreement of 1974 remained in force (until early 2005). Subsequent projected distribution is shown in the pie chart on the right—that is, once the safeguard clause of the MFA was no longer in effect.

Source: Data were taken from WTO Secretariat, Discussion Paper No. 5, Hildegunn Kyvik Nordås, "The Global Textile and Clothing Industry Post the Agreement on Textiles and Clothing," 2004.

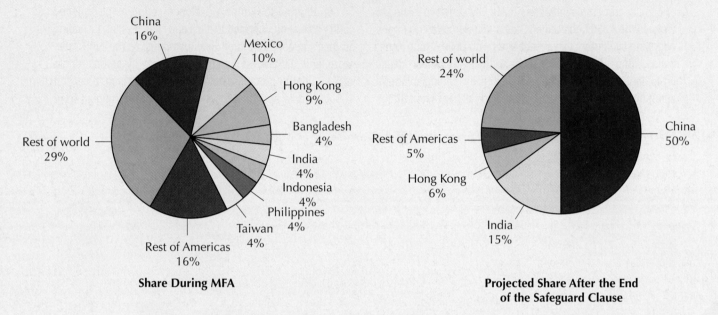

Share During MFA

Projected Share After the End of the Safeguard Clause

Thus, in exchange for developing countries' concessions to curtail piracy and to allow entry of investments in services, developed countries agreed to dismantle the MFA over 10 years commencing in 1995.

However, there was a safeguard clause whereby importing countries limited Chinese imports through 2008 to no more than 8 percent above the figure for the previous year. Because China is considered the most formidable competitor, there has been concern about market share after 2008. One such projection is shown in Figure 7.1 along with figures at the end of the MFA.

REPERCUSSIONS: SINCE 1995

The production of clothing is well suited for developing economies because of the industry's high labor intensity, employment of about five times as many unskilled workers as skilled workers, and the availability of the latest machinery and technology at relatively low cost. The production of textiles requires more capital and technology, but developing countries have a location advantage because of benefits deriving from having textile production near clothing production.

Thus developing countries have felt they have much to gain through increased access to markets in developed countries. In fact, a number of such countries (such as Bangladesh, Macao, Cambodia, Pakistan, El Salvador, Mauritius, Sri Lanka, and Dominican Republic) have depended on textiles and clothing for over half their merchandise exports. Map 7.1 highlights these countries along with China and India, the expected big gainers from the MFA's demise.

In the meantime, producers in developed countries have worried that they cannot survive without protection. By 2006, foreign production had already captured 32 percent of the U.S. textile market and 71 percent of the clothing market. Between 1980 and 2006 U.S. employment in textiles and clothing fell from 2.1 million to 610,000. Although some of this drop was because of productivity gains, much can be attributed to the displacement of U.S. production with imports.

The Strategy of the NCTO

The National Council of Textile Organizations (NCTO), which represents the U.S. textile and clothing industries, has been most concerned with Chinese competition, and it was instrumental in getting the

U.S. government to invoke the safeguard clause against Chinese imports. To bring about protection, the NCTO has taken a three-pronged attack:

1. To demonstrate that the U.S. industries are in jeopardy
2. To convince decision makers that their protection is in the national interest
3. To build allies to support the need for protection

The NCTO quickly pointed out the industries' job losses—12,200—during the first month after the MFA demise and before invoking the safeguard clause. Further, the United States recorded the largest trade deficit ever with a single country, China. Finally, the NCTO publicized what had happened in other U.S. industries—bicycles, lighting, toys, Christmas decorations, appliances, and rubber footwear—where Chinese production claimed more than half the U.S. market.

Three Arguments of the NCTO   The NCTO focused on three arguments to justify that protection would be in the national interest: unemployment, unfairness of Chinese competition, and the role of the industry in national security. The NCTO used the unemployment argument not only in terms of likely displacements (estimating a loss of over 600,000 jobs) but also because many workers in this industry have few skills and little ability to train for new jobs. Thus the loss of jobs would create greater social and welfare problems than loss of jobs in many other industries.

Interestingly, the NCTO has not claimed that cheap Chinese labor has an unfair advantage. Indeed, it has illustrated that producers in a number of countries have lower labor rates, closer proximity to the United States, and lower tariffs when exporting to the United States than Chinese producers. Instead the NCTO has shown that the Chinese government is the main owner of its industry, is willing and able to sustain losses to secure markets, and has spent over $600 million to bail out its largest producer. The NCTO has further argued that China has kept prices low by purposely undervaluing its currency in violation of agreements within the International Monetary Fund.

Finally, the NCTO has pointed out the industry's role in supplying the U.S. military with everything from uniforms to high-tech protective clothing. When individual sizes are factored in, it supplies over 30,000 different items. It has implied that the country should not depend on foreign supplies for its military uniforms.

Mixed Results   Efforts to secure allies have had mixed results. On the one hand, because the estimated job loss is highly concentrated geographically, it is significant enough to some congressional members to support protection. It has also had success in building allies among groups that would be disadvantaged by a smaller U.S. clothing and textile industry, such as U.S. cotton growers.

On the other hand, some traditional supporters have been less supportive. For example, the U.S. furniture industry no longer depends as much on U.S. textiles because it has offshored so much of its production to China. In addition, although the U.S. textile and clothing producers were historically united in pushing for protection against imports, they have not always supported one another recently. One reason is that many U.S. clothing producers believe textile imports give them cost savings and variety that make them more competitive. Some high-end fashion producers also feel their design work makes them immune from price competition.

Furthermore, many U.S. clothing companies have already turned to production in foreign locations such as Asia and Latin America. U.S. clothing retailers have openly fought to promote imports because they feel lower prices will improve their sales. Finally, some economic sectors, such as the container shipping industry, have publicly stated they will downsize if trade restrictions reduce Chinese exports substantially.

Unlikely Allies Against the Chinese Threat   Surprisingly, the NCTO has built some of its staunchest allies among developing economies that had quotas to sell in the United States during the MFA era. Many of these had already seen their markets decline during the 10-year phaseout period of the MFA. For instance, El Salvador lost nearly 6,000 clothing jobs in 2004. Thus these countries' main concern was that they would be unable to compete against China.

More than 50 nations have lobbied for the United States and EU to enact new restrictions to prevent the market takeover by Chinese producers. This lobbying has been taken seriously because both the United States and EU often need the political support of these countries and use economic measures to gain such support. For instance, the United States offered Turkey more access to the U.S. textile market in an attempt to get Turkey to cooperate in the invasion of Iraq.

At the same time, there has been some concern in the United States that it could not push China too far without China retaliating. Retaliation could be economic, such as buying passenger aircraft from Airbus Industrie rather than from Boeing or selling much of its holdings of U.S. Treasury bonds, which the United States needed to sell to foreigners because of its budget and trade deficits. Retaliation could also be political, such as not cooperating with sanctions against Iranian and North Korean nuclear activities.

Introduction

CONCEPT CHECK

As we demonstrate in Chapter 6, *specialization* (coupled with trade) can increase a country's output of certain products; we also observe that the theories of both **absolute** and **comparative advantage** support the contention that free trade encourages specialization and more efficient output. Here we point out that **protectionist** policies, though sometimes warranted, can impede the process that revolves around specialization.

At some point, you may work for or own stock in a company whose performance, or even survival, depends on governmental trade policies. These policies may affect the ability of foreign producers to compete in your home market. They may limit or enhance your facility to sell abroad, such as by prohibiting or subsidizing the export of certain products to certain countries, or by making it more difficult or easy for you to buy what you need from foreign suppliers. Collectively, these governmental restrictions and competitive support actions are known as **protectionism.**

The restrictions illustrated in the opening case are not atypical: All countries regulate the flow of goods and services across their borders. Figure 7.2 illustrates the pressures on governments to regulate trade and the subsequent effect of regulation on companies' competitive positions. This chapter begins by reviewing the economic and noneconomic rationales for trade protectionism and follows by explaining the major forms of trade controls and their effects on companies' operating decisions.

FIGURE 7.2   Physical and Social Factors Affecting the Flow of Goods and Services

In response to a variety of *physical and social* (i.e., political/legal, behavioral, economic, and geographic) *factors,* governments enact measures designed either to enhance or restrict international trade flows. These measures invariably affect the *competitive environment* in which companies operate, either enhancing or hindering their capacity to compete on an international scale. To an extent, of course, the converse is also true: Companies influence government trade policies that affect their activities.

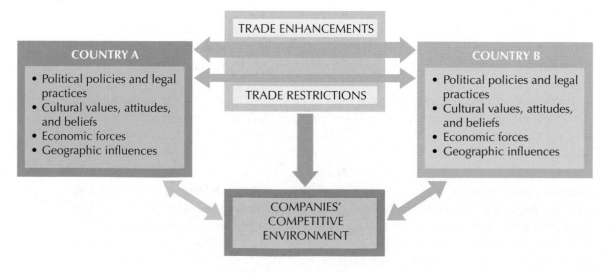

Conflicting Results of Trade Policies

Despite the benefits from free trade, governments intervene in trade to attain economic, social, or political objectives. Governmental officials apply trade policies that they reason have the best chance to benefit their nation and its citizens—and, in some cases, their personal political longevity. Determining the best way to influence trade is complicated by frequent conflicts in the outcomes of policies. For example, two of the original purposes of the MFA were to help workers in developing countries and to maintain employment in a sensitive industry at home; in actuality, it helped the workers in some developing countries while disadvantaging those in others, and it helped home-country U.S. clothing and textile workers while passing on additional costs to consumers.

In general, governments would also like to help their struggling companies and industries without penalizing those that are doing well. But this goal is often impossible, especially if other countries retaliate against their protectionist actions. For example, additional U.S. import restrictions on Chinese clothing and textiles could cause China to take actions against U.S. companies operating in China, a worry expressed by the director of Procter & Gamble's global trade policy.[2]

All countries seek to influence trade, and each has economic, social, and political objectives:

- Conflicting objectives.
- Interest groups.

THE ROLE OF STAKEHOLDERS

Proposals for trade regulation reform often spark fierce debate among people and groups that believe they will be affected—so-called *stakeholders*. Of course, those most directly affected are most apt to speak out. For example, U.S. stakeholders whose livelihood depends on a U.S. base of clothing production (workers, owners, suppliers, and local politicians) are fighting to limit imports of clothing and textiles. Displaced workers see themselves as being forced to take new jobs in new industries, perhaps even in new towns. They fear prolonged unemployment, reduced incomes, uncertain work conditions, and unstable social surroundings. People threatened in this way tend to object often and loudly.

The Role of Consumers In contrast, consumers (who are stakeholders) typically buy the best product they can find for the price, often without knowing or caring about the product's origin. They often don't realize how much retail prices rise in aggregate because of import restrictions. Further, because the consumer costs are typically spread out among many people and throughout the year, consumers take little notice. For example, EU restrictions on banana imports cost EU consumers about $2 billion a year because of higher banana costs, a significant amount in total but trivial for each banana or for each consumer.

Similarly, U.S. import restrictions on peanuts and sugar add to the price of peanut butter and confectionary products in the United States.[3] Even if consumers knew about this surcharge, they would likely not see enough incentive to band together and push their governmental leaders to rectify the situation.

CONCEPT CHECK

In Chapter 5, we define **stakeholders** as all the groups—shareholders, employees, customers, society at large—among which a company must make satisfactory trade-offs if it is to survive.

Economic Rationales for Governmental Intervention

Governmental intervention in trade may be classified as either economic or noneconomic, as shown in Table 7.1. Let's begin by analyzing some leading *economic rationales*.

TABLE 7.1 Why Governments Intervene in Trade

Economic Rationales	Noneconomic Rationales
Preventing unemployment	Maintaining essential industries
Protecting infant industries	Dealing with unfriendly countries
Promoting industrialization	Maintaining or extending spheres of influence
Improving comparative position	Preserving national identity

FIGHTING UNEMPLOYMENT

The unemployed can form an effective pressure group for import restrictions.

There's probably no more effective pressure group than the unemployed; no other group has the time and incentive to protest publicly, contact governmental representatives, and confront organizations. The photo below shows an example of a group protesting freer trade. Displaced workers are often the ones who are least able to find alternative work at a comparable salary. On average, trade-displaced workers in the United States have earned about 13 percent less in their new job than they did on their old job—more than a third have suffered a 30 percent drop in wages.[4]

Similar effects have been found in Germany, Canada, and France.[5] In addition, displaced workers often spend their unemployment benefits on living expenses rather than on retraining in the hope they will be recalled to their old jobs. When they do seek retraining, many workers, especially older ones, lack the educational background necessary to gain required skills. Worse still, some train for jobs that do not materialize.

Import restrictions to create domestic employment

- *May lead to retaliation by other countries.*
- *Are less likely retaliated against effectively by small economies.*
- *Are less likely to be met with retaliation if implemented by small economies.*
- *May decrease export jobs because of price increases for components.*
- *May decrease export jobs because of lower incomes abroad.*

What's Wrong with Full Employment as an Economic Objective?   Although every country has full employment as an economic objective, using trade policy to achieve this is problematic. From a practical standpoint, gaining jobs by limiting imports may not fully work as expected. Even if successful, the costs may be high and need to be borne by someone.

The Prospect of Retaliation   One difficulty with restricting imports to create jobs is that other countries normally retaliate with their own restrictions. That is, trade restrictions designed to support domestic industries typically trigger a drop in production in some foreign countries, and they react. For example, the EU, Brazil, and Japan threatened to restrict purchases of U.S. products, such as oranges, when the United States imposed import restrictions on their steel. This was one factor in the U.S. decision to rescind its steel protection.[6]

However, two factors can affect the impact of retaliation. First, small trading countries are less important in the retaliation process. For example, if the United States were to limit clothing imports further, China would have more power to retaliate than Mauritius. Further, the United States is less apt to retaliate against Mauritian trade restrictions than against Chinese ones because the latter affect the U.S. economy more. Second, retaliation that decreases employment in a capital-intensive industry may not affect employment as much as the value of the trade loss would imply.

For example, if the United States restricts imports of apparel from China, a labor-intensive good, any resultant Chinese retaliation against U.S. exports of the same value

Farmers protest in Cairns, Australia. The farmers gathered peacefully outside the venue in a demonstration demanding greater protection for their industry.

in a capital-intensive industry, say U.S.-produced semiconductors, would threaten fewer U.S. jobs than would be gained from maintaining apparel production. In addition, the highly skilled semiconductor workers might more easily find alternative employment than the semiskilled workers can.

Even if no country retaliates, the restricting country may gain jobs in one sector only to lose jobs elsewhere. Why? There are three factors to consider:

1. *Fewer imports of a product mean fewer import-handling jobs.*
2. *Import restrictions may cause lower sales in other industries because they must incur higher costs for components.* For example, U.S. import restrictions on steel created competitive problems for automobile manufacturing in the United States, and GM, Ford, DaimlerChrysler, Toyota, Honda, and Nissan banded together and successfully convinced authorities to remove the restrictions.[7]
3. *Imports stimulate exports, although less directly, by increasing foreign income and foreign-exchange earnings, which are then spent on new imports by foreign consumers.* Thus restricting earnings abroad will have some negative effect on domestic earnings and employment.

Analyzing Trade-Offs   In deciding whether to restrict imports to create jobs, governments should compare the costs of higher prices by limiting imports with the costs of unemployment and displaced production that would result from freer trade. In addition, they must consider the costs of policies to ease the plight of displaced employees, such as for unemployment benefits or retraining.

| Possible costs of import restrictions include higher prices and higher taxes. Such costs should be compared with those of unemployment.

These are challenging tasks that involve not only difficult economic but also social questions. For example, it is hard to put a price on the distress suffered by people who lose their jobs due to import competition. It is also difficult for working people to understand they may be better off financially (because of lower prices) even if they must then pay higher taxes to support unemployment or welfare benefits for people who lost their jobs to rising imports.

In summary, persistent unemployment pushes many groups to call for protectionism. However, evidence suggests that efforts to reduce unemployment through import restrictions are usually ineffective.[8] Unemployment, in and of itself, is better dealt with through fiscal and monetary policies. If import restrictions do increase domestic employment, fellow citizens will have to bear the costs of higher prices or higher taxes. In addition, if managers believe trade protection is a long-term policy, they may see no competitive urgency to invest in technological innovation, thus further depriving consumers of higher-quality products at lower prices.

PROTECTING "INFANT INDUSTRIES"

In 1792, U.S. treasury secretary Alexander Hamilton presented what has become one of the oldest arguments for protectionism. The **infant-industry argument** holds that a government should shield an emerging industry from foreign competition by guaranteeing it a large share of the domestic market until it is able to compete on its own. Many developing countries use this argument to justify their protectionist policies.

| The infant-industry argument says that production becomes more competitive over time because of
| • Increased economies of scale.
| • Greater worker efficiency.

Underlying Assumptions   The infant-industry argument presumes that the initial output costs for a small-scale industry in a given country may be so high as to make its output noncompetitive in world markets. Eventual competitiveness is not the reward for endurance but the result of the efficiency gains that take time. Therefore, the host government needs to protect an infant industry long enough for its fledgling companies to gain economies of scale and their employees to translate experience into higher productivity. These achievements will enable a company to produce efficiently, thereby positioning it to compete internationally. At this point, the government can then recoup the costs of trade protection through benefits like higher domestic employment, lower social costs, and higher tax revenues.

Risks in Designating Industries   Although it's reasonable to expect production costs to decrease over time, there is a risk that costs never fall enough to create internationally competitive products. This risk poses two problems.

Determining Probability of Success   First, governments must identify those industries that have a high probability of success. Some industries grow to be competitive because of governmental protection; automobile production in Brazil and South Korea are good examples. However, in many other cases—such as automobile production in Malaysia and Australia—the protected industries remain inefficient even after years of government aid.

If infant-industry protection goes to an industry that fails to reduce costs enough to compete against imports, chances are its owners, workers, and suppliers will constitute a formidable pressure group that may prevent the importation of competing lower-priced products. Also, the security of government protection against import competition may deter managers from adopting the innovations needed to compete globally and to provide their own consumers with high-quality products at a low price.

Identifying Qualified Industries   Second, even if policymakers can determine those infant industries likely to succeed, it does not necessarily follow that companies in those industries should receive governmental assistance. There are many examples of entrepreneurs who endured early losses to achieve future benefits without any public help. Still, some policymakers regularly contend that governments should assist new companies facing high entry barriers and efficient foreign rivals because local entrepreneurs may lack the means to become competitive without assistance.

Infant-industry protection requires some segment of the economy to incur the higher cost when local production is still inefficient. Typically, consumers end up paying higher prices for the protected industries' products. An alternative is for a government to subsidize companies so consumer prices do not increase, in which case taxpayers pay this subsidy. In addition, production subsidies reduce the amount that governments can spend elsewhere, such as on education and infrastructure, a serious consideration in improving overall competitiveness. Ultimately, the validity of the infant-industry argument rests on the expectation that the future benefits of an internationally competitive industry will exceed the costs of the associated protectionism.

DEVELOPING AN INDUSTRIAL BASE

Countries seek protection to promote industrialization because that type of production

- Brings faster growth than agriculture.
- Brings in investment funds.
- Diversifies the economy.
- Brings more income than primary products do.
- Reduces imports and promotes exports.
- Helps the nation-building process.

Countries with a large manufacturing base generally have higher per capita incomes than those that do not. Moreover, a number of countries, such as the United States and Japan, developed an industrial base while largely restricting imports. Many developing countries try to emulate this strategy, using trade protection to spur local industrialization. Specifically, they operate under the following set of assumptions:

1. Surplus workers can more easily increase manufacturing output than agricultural output.
2. Inflows of foreign investment in the industrial area promote sustainable growth.
3. Prices and sales of agricultural products and raw materials fluctuate very much, which is a detriment to economies that depend on few of them.
4. Markets for industrial products grow faster than markets for agricultural products.
5. Local industry reduces imports and promotes exports.
6. Industrial activity helps the nation-building process.

In the sections that follow, we review each of these assumptions in some detail.

Surplus Workers   A large portion of the population in many developing countries lives and farms in rural areas. Usually, there is disguised unemployment in these areas inasmuch as some people are effectively contributing little, if anything, to the agricultural output. Consequently, many people can shift from the agricultural to industrial sector without significantly reducing total agricultural output. Like the infant-industry argument, the **industrialization argument** presumes the unregulated importation of lower-priced products prevents the development of a domestic industry. However, unlike the infant-industry argument, the industrialization rationale asserts that industrial output will increase, even if domestic prices do not become globally competitive, because local consumers must buy goods from local producers.[9]

Shifting people out of agriculture, however, can create at least three problems:

1. Workers' high expectations of industrial jobs may be unfulfilled, leading to increasing demand for social services. A major problem facing developing countries is the migration to urban areas of people who then cannot find suitable jobs, housing, and social services. For example, China's move toward industrialization has spurred millions of people to move to cities; most have prospered but many have not. Some estimate China's urban unemployment rate runs three to five times the officially reported rate.[10]

2. Improved agriculture practices, not a drastic shift to industry, may be a better means of achieving economic success. Typically, few developing countries farm their land efficiently—doing so can create great benefits at low cost.[11] Equally, industrialization is not the only means of growth. The United States, Canada, and Argentina grew during the nineteenth century, largely through their comparative advantage in agricultural exports. They continue to profit from exports of food products. Similarly, Australia, New Zealand, and Denmark maintain high per capita income with a mix of industry and agricultural specialization.

3. Rapid migration from rural to urban areas may abruptly reduce agricultural output, further jeopardizing a country's self-sufficiency. Interestingly, most of the world's agricultural production and exports come from developed countries because their efficient and capital-intensive agricultural sectors enable the transfer of resources into the manufacturing sector without decreasing agricultural output.

> When a country shifts from agriculture to industry
> - Demands on social and political services in cities may increase.
> - Output increases if the marginal productivity of agricultural workers is very low.
> - Development possibilities in the agricultural sector may be overlooked.

Investment Inflows   Import restrictions, applied to spur industrialization, also may increase foreign direct investment, which provide capital, technology, and jobs. Barred from an attractive foreign market by trade restrictions, foreign companies may transfer manufacturing to that country to avoid the loss of a lucrative or potential market. For example, Thailand's automobile import restrictions prompted foreign automakers to invest there.

> If import restrictions keep out foreign-made goods, foreign companies may invest to produce in the restricted area.

Diversification   Export prices of many primary products fluctuate markedly. For instance, coffee prices fell about two-thirds between 2000 and 2002 and then regained half the loss the next year.[12] Price variations due to uncontrollable factors—such as weather affecting supply or business cycles abroad affecting demand—can wreak havoc on economies that depend on the export of primary products. This is especially true when an economy must rely on only a few commodities, a situation facing many developing countries. Frequently, they are caught in a feast or famine cycle, as it were: able to afford foreign luxuries one year but unable to find the funds for replacement parts for essential equipment the next. Contrary to expectation, a greater dependence on manufacturing does not guarantee diversification of export earnings. The GDPs of many developing economies are small; a move to manufacturing may shift dependence from one or two agricultural commodities to one or two manufactured products.

Growth in Manufactured Goods   **Terms of trade** refers to the quantity of imports that a given quantity of a country's exports can buy—that is, how many bananas Country A must sell to Country B to purchase one refrigerator from Country B. Historically, the prices of raw materials and agricultural commodities do not rise as fast as the prices of finished products, although they may rise faster during short periods. Over time, therefore, it takes more low-priced primary products to buy the same amount of high-priced

> Terms of trade for emerging economies may deteriorate because
> - Demand for primary products grows more slowly.
> - Production cost savings for primary products will be passed on to consumers.

manufactured goods. In addition, the quantity of primary products demanded does not rise as rapidly, so developed nations that depend on primary products have become increasingly poorer relative to developed countries.

The declining terms of trade for developing countries is partly explained by a decreased percentage of expenditures on food as incomes rise and by changes in technology that have reduced the need for many raw materials. A further explanation is that competitive rivalry transfers many of the benefits of lower production costs of primary products to consumers. In contrast, cost savings for manufactured products go mainly to higher profits and wages.

Import Substitution and Export-Led Development   Traditionally, developing countries promoted industrialization by restricting imports to boost local production for local consumption of products they would otherwise import. If the protected industries do not become efficient, an all-too-frequent outcome, local consumers may have to support them by paying higher prices or higher taxes. In contrast, some countries, such as Taiwan and South Korea, have achieved rapid economic growth by promoting the development of industries that export their output. This approach is known as **export-led development.** In reality, it's not easy to distinguish between import substitution and export-led development. Industrialization may result initially in import substitution, yet export development of the same products may be feasible later.

Nation Building   The performance of free markets suggests a strong relationship between industrialization and aspects of the nation-building process. Industrialization helps countries build infrastructure, advance rural development, and boost the skills of the workforce. For example, Ecuador and Vietnam maintain that industrialization has helped them move from feudal economies suffering chronic food shortages to nations with improved food security and budding export competitiveness.[13]

ECONOMIC RELATIONSHIPS WITH OTHER COUNTRIES

Every nation monitors its absolute economic welfare and compares its performance to that of other countries. Thus governments may impose trade restrictions to improve their relative trade positions. They might buy less from other countries than those countries buy from them. They might try to charge higher export prices while keeping import prices low—though not so low as to penalize their domestic producers. Among the many motivations, four stand out: making balance-of-trade adjustments, gaining comparable access to foreign markets, using restrictions as a bargaining tool, and controlling prices.

Balance-of-Trade Adjustments   A trade deficit creates problems for nations with low foreign exchange reserves—the funds that help a nation finance the purchase of priority foreign goods and maintain the trustworthiness of its currency. So, if balance-of-trade difficulties arise and persist, a government may take action to reduce imports or encourage exports to balance its trade account. Basically, it has two options that affect its competitive position broadly:

1. Depreciate or devalue its currency—an action that makes all of its products cheaper in relation to foreign products
2. Rely on fiscal and monetary policy to bring about lower price increases in general than those in other countries

Both of these options, however, take time. Furthermore, they aren't selective; for instance, they make both foreign essentials and foreign luxury products more expensive. Thus a country may use protection more effectively so as to affect only certain products. This is really a stop-gap measure that gives the country time to address its fundamental economic situation that is causing its residents to buy more abroad than they are selling.

For example, since the 1970s the United States has imported more from Japan than it has exported there. Trade in automobiles makes up most of the imbalance. At times, the

CONCEPT CHECK

In the opening case of Chapter 6, we explain *import substitution* as a policy of calling for the local production of goods and services that would otherwise have to be imported. We also demonstrate why this policy failed to achieve certain goals of one country's long-term trade strategy.

Industrialization emphasizes either

- Products to sell domestically
  or
- Products to export.

CONCEPT CHECK

In the "Point–Counterpoint" box in Chapter 4, we explain why a *trade deficit* usually indicates that a country's currency—along with its debt—is piling up around the world; we go on to explain why a country afflicted with a burgeoning trade deficit needs to reconsider key areas of its economic policy.

U.S. government has tried to correct the imbalance by regulating the value and number of Japanese vehicles imported into the United States, persuading Japanese automotive companies to locate more production within the United States and negotiating with the Japanese government to ease the entry of U.S.-made cars into Japan. Nevertheless, the United States is still running trade deficits with Japan.

Comparable Access or "Fairness"   Companies and industries often argue they are entitled to the same access to foreign markets as foreign industries and companies have to their markets. Economic theory supports this idea for industries where increased production leads to steep cost decreases (that is to say, there are substantial cost decreases through economies of scale). Companies that lack equal access to a competitor's market will struggle to gain enough sales to be cost competitive. The **comparable-access argument** has been used in the semiconductor, chemicals, aircraft, softwood lumber, energy, and telecommunications industries.[14]

> Domestic producers may be disadvantaged if their access to foreign markets is less than foreign producers' access to their market.

The argument for comparable access also is presented as one of fairness. For example, the U.S. government permits foreign financial service companies to operate in the United States, but only if their home governments allow U.S. financial service companies equivalent market access. There are, however, at least two practical reasons for rejecting the idea of fairness:

1. Tit-for-tat market access can lead to restrictions that may deny one's own consumers lower prices.
2. Governments would find it impractical to negotiate and monitor separate agreements for each of the many thousands of different products and services that might be traded.

Restrictions as a Bargaining Tool   We have already discussed how countries retaliate to other countries' trade restrictions. Thus the imposition of import restrictions may be used as a means to persuade other countries to lower their import barriers. The danger in this is that each country escalates its restrictions so, in effect, we have a trade war that impacts all the countries' economies negatively.

Nevertheless, to use restrictions successfully as a bargaining tool, you need to be very careful in targeting the products you threaten to restrict. In particular, you need to consider two criteria:

- *Believability:*   Either you have access to alternative sources for the product or your consumers are willing to do without it. For instance, in trade retaliations between the United States and the EU, the EU has threatened to impose trade restrictions on U.S.-grown soybeans when Brazil had surplus production.
- *Importance:*   Exports of the product you're restricting are significant to certain parties in the producer country—parties who are sufficiently influential to prompt changes in their own country's trade policy. This consideration was emphasized after the United States had placed restrictions on the importation of steel. The EU threatened to place restrictions on the importation of apples from the state of Washington and oranges from Florida. Given the importance of these two states in a close presidential election, the decision to remove the steel import restrictions was hastened by this threat.

Price-Control Objectives   Countries sometimes withhold goods from international markets in an effort to raise prices abroad. This action is most feasible when a few countries hold a monopoly or a near-monopoly control of certain resources. They can then limit supply so consumers must pay a higher price. However, this policy often encourages smuggling, such as of emeralds and diamonds.

This policy may also encourage other countries to develop technology that will provide either substitute products, such as synthetic rubber in place of natural rubber, or different ways of producing the same product, such as the aquaculture production of sturgeons to produce caviar in the United States in response to high Russian prices for caviar from wild sturgeon.[15] Export controls are especially ineffective if a product can

> Export restrictions may
> - Keep up world prices.
> - Require more controls to prevent smuggling.
> - Lead to substitution.
> - Keep domestic prices down by increasing domestic supply.
> - Give producers less incentive to increase output.
> - Shift foreign production and sales.

be digitized—such as music, video, and texts—because they are easily copied abroad. In addition, if prices are too high or supplies too limited, people will seek substitutes.

A country may also limit exports of a product that is in short supply worldwide to favor domestic consumers. Typically, greater supply drops local prices beneath those in the intentionally undersupplied world market. Argentina, for instance, has pursued this strategy by limiting exports of natural gas, and Canada has considered doing it with patented prescription drugs.[16] Favoring consumers usually disfavors producers so they lack an incentive to maintain production when prices are low.

Countries also fear that foreign producers will price their exports so artificially low that they will drive domestic producers out of business. If foreign producers are successful, there are two potential adverse consequences for domestic producers:

1. As the U.S. clothing and textile industries have been arguing for some time, China is simply shifting its potential unemployment to the United States.

2. If there are high entry barriers, surviving foreign producers can charge exorbitant prices abroad once the foreign competition goes out of business.

However, competition among producers from different countries usually limits anyone's ability to charge exorbitant prices. For example, low import prices have eliminated most U.S. production of consumer electronics. Still, the United States has some of the lowest prices in the world for consumer electronics because so many companies produce them in so many countries, and there seems to be little prospect that these prices will become exorbitant in the future.

Import restrictions may

- Prevent dumping from being used to put domestic producers out of business.
- Get foreign producers to lower their prices.

Dumping Companies sometimes export below cost or below their home-country price, a practice called **dumping**. Most countries prohibit imports of dumped products, but enforcement usually occurs only if the imported product disrupts domestic production. If there is no domestic production, then host-country consumers get the benefit of lower prices. Companies may dump products because they cannot otherwise build a market abroad—essentially, a low price encourages consumers to sample the foreign brand.

Companies can afford to dump products if they can charge high prices in their home market or if their home-country government subsidizes them. They may also opt to incur short-term losses abroad, presuming they can recoup those losses after they eliminate their rivals or gain brand loyalty and then raise their prices. Ironically, home-country consumers or taxpayers seldom realize that paying high prices locally results in lower prices for foreign consumers.

An industry that believes it's competing against dumped products may appeal to its government to restrict the imports. U.S. companies in such industries as shrimp, candles, and furniture have done so in recent years.[17] However, determining a foreign company's cost or domestic price is difficult because of limited access to the foreign producers' accounting statements, fluctuations in exchange rates, and the passage of products through layers of distribution before reaching the end consumer. The result is that governments allegedly restrict imports arbitrarily through antidumping provisions of their trade legislation and are slow to dispose of the restrictions if pricing situations change. Companies caught in this situation often lose the export market they labored to build.

Optimum-Tariff Theory Another price argument for governmental influence on trade is the **optimum-tariff theory**. This theory states that a foreign producer will lower its prices if the importing country places a tax on its products. If this occurs, benefits shift to the importing country because the foreign producer lowers its profits on the export sales.

Let's examine a hypothetical situation. Assume an exporter has costs of $500 per unit and is selling to a foreign market for $700 per unit. With the imposition of a 10 percent tax on the imported price, the exporter may choose to lower its price to $636.36 per unit, which, with a 10 percent tax of $63.64, would keep the price at $700 for the importer. The exporter may feel a price higher than $700 would result in lost sales and a profit of

$136.36 per unit instead of the previous $200 per unit is better than no profit at all. Consequently, an amount of $63.64 per unit has thus shifted to the importing country.

As long as the foreign producer lowers its price by any amount, some shift in revenue goes to the importing country and the tariff is deemed an optimum one. There are many examples of products whose prices did not rise as much as the amount of the imposed tariff; however, it is difficult to predict when, where, and which exporters will voluntarily reduce their profit margins.

Noneconomic Rationales for Government Intervention

Economic rationales help explain many government actions on trade. However, governments sometimes use noneconomic rationales, such as the following:

- Maintaining essential industries (especially defense)
- Preventing shipments to unfriendly countries
- Maintaining or extending spheres of influence
- Preserving national identity

Let's look at each rationale.

In protecting essential industries, countries must

- Determine which ones are essential.
- Consider costs and alternatives.
- Consider political consequences.

MAINTAINING ESSENTIAL INDUSTRIES

Governments apply trade restrictions to protect essential domestic industries during peacetime so a country is not dependent on foreign sources of supply during war. This is called the **essential-industry argument.** For example, the U.S. government subsidizes the domestic production of silicon so domestic computer chip producers will not need to depend on foreign suppliers. Because of nationalism, this argument has much appeal in rallying support for import barriers. However, in times of real (or perceived) crisis or military emergency, almost any product could be deemed essential. In our opening case, for example, we pointed out that, in the United States, the NCTO has proposed a variation on this argument, citing the industry's role in supplying the U.S. military with everything from uniforms to high-tech protective clothing.

Because of the high cost of protecting an inefficient industry or a higher-cost domestic substitute, the essential-industry argument should not be (but frequently is) accepted without a careful evaluation of costs, real needs, and alternatives. It is difficult to remove protection, once given, because the protected companies and their employees support politicians who support their continued protection—even when the rationale for the subsidies long ago disappeared. This is why the United States, for example, continued to subsidize its mohair producers more than 20 years after mohair was deemed no longer essential for military uniforms.[18]

PREVENTING SHIPMENTS TO "UNFRIENDLY" COUNTRIES

Groups concerned about security often use national defense arguments to prevent the export, even to friendly countries, of strategic goods that might fall into the hands of potential enemies or that might be in short supply domestically. For example, the United States prevented exports of data-encryption technology (data-scrambling hardware and software) until a group of U.S. high-tech companies allied themselves with privacy advocacy groups to convince the U.S. government to relax the export curbs. Now U.S. companies can export any encryption product to the members of the EU and other European and Pacific Rim allies without first getting permission.[19]

Countries levy trade restrictions to coerce other countries to change their policies.

Export constraints may be valid if the exporting country assumes there will be no retaliation that prevents it from securing even more essential goods from the potential importing country. Even then, the importing country may find alternative supply sources or develop a production capability of its own. In this situation, the country limiting exports is

Case Review Note

the economic loser. (Our ending case discusses U.S. barriers to trade with Cuba—including prohibitions on all unlicensed financial transactions and any direct or indirect import-export transactions—as a means of weakening the Communist nation's economy.)

Trade controls on nondefense goods also may be used as a weapon of foreign policy to try to prevent another country from meeting its political objectives. For example, the United States imposed trade sanctions on nine Chinese companies and an Indian businessman it found had sold technology to Iran that was then put to use by that country's chemical and conventional weapons programs. The sanctions barred these firms from doing business with the U.S. government, forbade them to export goods into the United States, and prevented U.S. companies from exporting certain items to them.[20]

Still, there is potential for gains from trade as countries become friendlier. For example, the United States lifted trade sanctions against Libya in 2004, and three U.S. oil companies (Occidental Petroleum, Amerada Hess, and ChevronTexaco) received licenses to explore for Libyan oil in 2005.[21]

Point | Counterpoint

Should Governments Forgo Trade Sanctions?

Point **Yes** Every time I turn around, I see my government imposing a new sanction. Although some don't affect my business, others do. When they do, I lose business that took me years to develop. For instance, a few years back, my company had worked hard to develop a market for office machinery in Iraq. Then, suddenly, we could not export to Iraq and were left holding inventory we had on the loading dock ready to ship. Thus the trade sanctions were aimed at hurting the government of Iraq, but we were the ones who were hurt even though we had never engaged in any objectionable behavior.

Besides, I really question whether these sanctions even work. For example, the United States maintained a 20-year trade embargo on Vietnam. Still, Vietnamese consumers were able to buy U.S. consumer products, such as Coca-Cola, Kodak film, and Apple computers, through other countries that did not enforce the sanctions.[22] The U.S. trade embargo with Panama only made Panama's Noriega government more adamant in its opposition to the United States, and it took a military invasion to depose him. Oil embargos against South Africa because of its racial policies merely spurred South African companies to become leaders in converting coal to oil.[23]

Furthermore, even if trade sanctions are successful at weakening the targeted countries' economy, who really suffers in that economy? You can bet that the political leaders still get whatever they need, so that the costs of sanctions are borne by innocent people. This occurred in Iraq, where there were widespread reports of children's deaths because of inadequate supplies of food and medicine from the sanctions. Moreover, the people adversely affected usually blame their suffering, not on their internal regime, but rather on the countries carrying on the sanctions. Despots are very good at manipulating public opinion.[24]

Counterpoint **No** As I've said so many times before, let's face it: We're now living in a global society where actions in one country can spill over and affect people all over the world. For instance, the development of a nuclear arsenal in one country can escalate the damage that terrorists can do elsewhere. The failure of a country to protect endangered species can have long-term effects on the whole world's environment. We simply can't sit back and let things happen elsewhere that will come back to haunt us.

At the same time, some pretty dastardly things occur in some countries, and most of the world community would like to see them stopped. These include human rights violations in Myanmar, the use of child slaves to harvest cocoa in the Ivory Coast, and the use of diamond production in Sierra Leone to finance revolutions.

Even if we can't stop these occurrences, we have a moral responsibility not to participate even if it costs us. If I can draw an analogy, I may get some economic benefits by buying from a criminal, and I may not stop that criminal's activity by withholding my business. However, I refuse to deal with the criminal because, in effect, that makes me a criminal's associate.

Although not all trade sanctions have been successful, many have at least been influential in achieving their objectives. These included UN sanctions against Rhodesia (now Zimbabwe), U.K. and U.S. sanctions against the Amin government of Uganda, and Indian sanctions against Nepal.[25]

At the same time, it is difficult to assess the full result of a trade sanction. For instance, although there were multiple factors opposing the Duvalier regime in Haiti and apartheid in South Africa, few doubt that trade sanctions on Haiti and South Africa significantly damaged their political regimes.[26] Further, although the nearly five decades of sanctions against Cuba have not brought down communism there, they may have slowed Cuba's ability to create revolutions elsewhere.

Finally, governments sometimes seem to impose trade sanctions based on one issue rather than on a country's overall record. For instance, some critics have suggested using trade policies to press Brazil to restrict the cutting of Amazon forests, even though its overall environmental record, particularly its limiting of adverse exhaust emissions by converting automobile engines to use methanol instead of gasoline, is quite good. ●

Finally, when a nation breaks international agreements or acts in unpopular ways, what courses of action can other nations take? Between 1827 and World War I, nations mounted 21 blockades, but these are now considered to be too dangerous. Military force has also been used, such as for the overthrow of the Saddam regime in Iraq, but such measures have little global support. Thus nations may take such punitive actions as withholding diplomatic recognition, boycotting athletic and cultural events, seizing the other country's foreign property, and eliminating foreign aid and loans. These may be ineffective in and of themselves without the addition of trade sanctions. In addition, countries may give incentives rather than taking punitive actions. This has occurred, for example, with North Korea to curb its nuclear program and has been suggested for Iran for the same purpose.[27] ●

MAINTAINING OR EXTENDING SPHERES OF INFLUENCE

There are many examples of governmental actions on trade designed to support their spheres of influence. Governments give aid and credits to, and encourage imports from, countries that join a political alliance or vote a preferred way within international bodies. The EU and the 77 members of the African, Caribbean, and Pacific Group of States signed the Cotonou Agreement to formalize preferential trade relationships by offering members of the latter group privileged access to European markets.[28] Venezuela has been exporting oil at low cost and with long-term financing to targeted Latin American countries to gain influence in the region.[29]

A country's trade restrictions may coerce governments to follow certain political actions or punish companies whose governments do not. For example, China delayed permission for Allianz, a German insurance group, to operate in China after Germany gave a reception for the Dalai Lama, the exiled Tibetan spiritual leader.[30]

PRESERVING NATIONAL IDENTITY

Countries are held together partially through a unifying sense of identity that sets their citizens apart from those in other nations. To sustain this collective identity, countries limit foreign products and services in certain sectors. For many years, Japan, South Korea, and China maintained an almost total ban on rice imports, largely because rice farming has been a historically cohesive force in each nation. Recent pressures from the WTO have led them to relent.[31] Canada relies on a "cultural sovereignty" argument to prohibit foreign ownership or control of publishing, cable TV, and bookselling.[32] Korea requires theaters to show Korean films a certain number of days per year.[33] Despite these efforts, consumers generally seek out the best products and services they can buy for the best price, a situation characterized in Figure 7.3.

Instruments of Trade Control

Governments use many rationales and seek a range of outcomes when they try to influence exports or imports. We now review the instruments that governments use to try to do so. Because a country's trade policy has repercussions abroad, retaliation from foreign governments looms as a potential obstacle to achieve the desired objectives. Therefore, the choice of the instrument of trade control is crucial because each type may incite

CONCEPT CHECK

We observe in Chapter 2 that a primary function of **culture** is to support a nation's sense of its uniqueness and integrity. We also explain that—especially in developing countries—many people fear the escalation and influence of global business interaction is a prelude to another era of **cultural imperialism** in which weaker nation-states will be weakened even further. Finally, we note that similar concerns are raised by the prospect of *cultural diffusion*—a process by which elements of a foreign culture may insinuate themselves into a local culture.

**FIGURE 7.3
Import-Fickle
Consumers**

Workers in industries favorably affected by trade policy are (relatively) easily motivated to support those policies—at least compared to *consumers*, who prefer the freedom to seek out the best products for the best prices.

Source: Mike Thompson, *The Detroit Free Press.*

different responses from domestic and foreign groups. One way to understand trade-control instruments is by distinguishing between two types that differ in their effects:

* Those that indirectly affect the amount traded by directly influencing the *prices* of exports or imports.
* Those that directly limit the *amount* of a good that can be traded.

TARIFFS

Tariffs may be levied

* On goods entering, leaving, or passing through a country.
* For protection or revenue.
* On a per unit or a value basis.

When it comes to explaining tariffs, we need to start by distinguishing tariff barriers (which directly affect prices) and *nontariff barriers* (which may directly affect either price or quantity). A **tariff** (also called a **duty**) is the most common type of trade control and a tax that governments levy on a good shipped internationally. That is, governments charge a tariff on a good when it crosses an official boundary—whether it be that of a nation, say Mexico, or a group of nations, like the EU, that have agreed to impose a common tariff on goods entering their bloc.

Tariffs collected by the exporting country are called **export tariffs;** if they're collected by a country through which the goods have passed, they're **transit tariffs;** those collected by importing countries are called **import tariffs.** Because import tariffs are by far the most common, we discuss them in some detail.

Import Tariffs   Unless they're *optimum tariffs* (which we discussed earlier in the chapter), import tariffs raise the price of imported goods by placing a tax on them that is not placed on domestic goods, thereby giving domestically produced goods a relative price advantage. A tariff may be protective even though there is no domestic production in direct competition. For example, a country that wants its residents to spend less on foreign goods and services may raise the price of some foreign products, even though there are no close domestic substitutes, to curtail demand for imports.

Tariffs as Sources of Revenue   Tariffs also serve as a source of governmental revenue. Import tariffs are of little importance to developed countries, usually costing more to collect than they yield.[34] Tariffs, however, are a major source of revenue in many developing countries. This is because government authorities in these countries may have more control over determining the amounts and types of goods crossing their borders and collecting a tax on them than they do over determining and collecting individual and corporate income taxes. Although revenue tariffs are most commonly collected on imports, some countries charge export tariffs on raw materials.[35] Transit tariffs were once a major source of revenue for countries, but governmental treaties have nearly abolished them.

Criteria for Assessing Tariffs   A government may assess a tariff on a per unit basis, in which case it is applying a **specific duty.** It may assess a tariff as a percentage of the value of the item, in which case it is an **ad valorem duty.** If it assesses both a specific duty and an ad valorem duty on the same product, the combination is a **compound duty.** A specific duty is straightforward for customs officials to assess because they do not need to determine a good's value on which to calculate a percentage tax.

A tariff controversy concerns developed countries' treatment of manufactured exports from developing countries that seek to add manufactured value to their exports of raw materials (like instant coffee instead of coffee beans). Raw materials frequently enter developed countries free of duty; however, if processed, developed countries then assign an import tariff. Because an ad valorem tariff is based on the total value of the product, meaning the raw materials and the processing combined, developing countries argue that the **effective tariff** on the manufactured portion turns out to be higher than the published tariff rate.

For example, a country may charge no duty on coffee beans but may assess a 10 percent ad valorem tariff on instant coffee. If $5 for a jar of instant coffee covers $2.50 in coffee beans and $2.50 in processing costs, the $0.50 duty is effectively 20 percent on the manufactured portion because the coffee beans could have entered free of duty. This anomaly further challenges developing countries to find markets for their manufactured products. At the same time, the governments of developed countries cannot easily remove barriers to imports of developing countries' manufactured products, largely because these imports are more likely to displace workers who are least equipped to move to new jobs.

NONTARIFF BARRIERS: DIRECT PRICE INFLUENCES

Now that we've shown how tariffs raise prices and limit trade, let's turn to a discussion of the ways in which governments alter the prices of products to limit their trade.

Subsidies   **Subsidies** are direct assistance to companies, making them more competitive. Although this definition is straightforward, there are trade frictions because of disagreement on what constitutes a subsidy. Again, consider our opening case, which discusses the contention of the NCTO that China's policy of subsidizing its clothing and textile industries—which includes government funds to underwrite the country's largest producer—is forcing many U.S. competitors out of both U.S. and global markets.

However, not everyone agrees that companies are being subsidized just because they lose money, nor that all types of government loans or grants are subsidies. One long-running controversy involves commercial aircraft. Airbus Industrie and the EU claim that the U.S. government subsidizes Boeing through research and development contracts for military aircraft that also have commercial applications. Boeing and the U.S. government claim the EU subsidizes Airbus Industrie through low-interest government loans.[36]

Agricultural Subsidies   The one area in which everyone is in agreement that subsidies exist is agricultural products in developed countries. The official reason for granting subsidies to farmers is that food supplies are too critical to be left to chance. Although subsidies lead to surplus production, surpluses are preferable to the risk of food shortages.

Although this official reason seems compelling, there is an unofficial reason as well. Within the EU, Japan, and the United States, rural areas have a disproportionately high representation in government decision making. For instance, in the United States, there is one senator per 300 thousand people in Vermont, a state with a 68 percent rural population, and one senator per 18 million in California, a state with a 93 percent urban population. The result is that internal politics effectively prevents the dismantling of such instruments as price supports for farmers, government agencies to improve agricultural productivity, and low-interest loans to farmers.

Governmental subsidies may help companies be competitive when

- Subsidies to overcome market imperfections are least controversial.
- There is little agreement on what a subsidy is.
- There has been a recent increase in export-credit assistance.

And the effect? Developing countries are disadvantaged in serving the developed country markets with competitive agricultural products. Further, much of the surplus production from developed countries is exported at prices below those in the products' domestic markets, thus distorting trade and disadvantaging production from developing countries.[37]

Overcoming Market Imperfections   There is another subsidization area that is less contentious. Most countries offer potential exporters many business development services, such as market information, trade expositions, and foreign contacts. From the standpoint of market efficiency, these sorts of subsidies are more justifiable than tariffs because they seek to overcome, rather than create, market imperfections. There are also benefits to disseminating information widely because governments can spread the costs of collecting information among many users.

Aid and Loans   Governments also give aid and loans to other countries. If the recipient is required to spend the funds in the donor country, which is known as *tied aid* or *tied loans*, some products can compete abroad that might otherwise be noncompetitive. Tied aid helps win large contracts for infrastructure, such as telecommunications, railways, and electric power projects.

However, there is growing skepticism about the value of tied aid because it requires the recipient to use suppliers in the donor country that may not be the best. Further, tied aid can slow the development of local suppliers in developing countries and shield suppliers in the donor countries from competition. These concerns led the members of the OECD to untie financial aid to developing countries, no longer obliging aid recipient countries to purchase equipment from suppliers in the donor country.[38] However, China is using tied aid for nearly all its foreign projects.[39]

Because it is difficult for customs officials to determine the honesty of import invoices

- They may arbitrarily increase value.
- Valuation procedures have been developed.
- They may question the origin of imports.

Customs Valuation   Tariffs for imported merchandise depend on the product, price, and origin. The temptation exists for exporters and importers to declare these wrongly on invoices to pay less duty. Generally, most countries have agreed to use the invoice information unless customs officers doubt its authenticity. Agents must then assess on the basis of the value of identical goods. If not possible, agents must assess on the basis of similar goods arriving in or about the same time.

For example, there is no sales invoice when imported goods enter for lease rather than purchase. Customs officials must then base the tariff on the value of identical or similar goods. If this basis cannot be used, officials may compute a value based on final sales value or on reasonable cost. Similarly, sometimes agents use their discretionary power to assess the value too high, thereby preventing the importation of foreign-made products.[40]

Valuation Problems   The fact that so many different products are traded creates valuation problems. It is easy (by accident or intention) to misclassify a product and its corresponding tariff. The differences among products in tariff schedules are minute. For example, the United States has a different tariff on athletic footwear than on sports footwear. On each of these, there are different tariffs depending on whether the sole overlaps the upper part of the shoe or not. Each type of accessory and reinforcement of the shoes' uppers have different tariffs. In another example, U.S. Customs charged the French company Agatec a higher duty than for the product (laser leveling device) indicated on the invoice because the product would be used primarily indoors (higher duty) than both indoors and outdoors (lower duty), even though the promotional material indicated it was for use in both areas.[41]

Administering more than 13,000 categories of products means a customs agent must use professional discretion to determine if, say, silicon chips should be considered "integrated circuits for computers" or "a form of chemical silicon." Marvel fought a six-year court battle to win a verdict that its X-Men Wolverines were toys (at a 6.8 percent duty) and not dolls (at a 12 percent duty). The difference in duty may seem trivial, but it amounted to millions of dollars. Similarly, the U.S. Customs Service had to determine whether sport utility vehicles, such as the Suzuki Samurai and the Land Rover, were cars or trucks. It assessed the 25 percent duty on trucks instead of the 2.5 percent duty on cars. Later, a federal trade court ruled them to be cars.

Because countries assess different duties and have different import controls for different countries, customs must also determine a product's origin. This is neither cheap nor easy. However, U.S. and EU officials have uncovered instances of transshipping such products as shoes, cigarette lighters, garlic, and lightbulbs, primarily from China through Cambodia to overcome quantity limitations as well as higher duties.[42] Otherwise, exporters and importers could misstate the origin to pay a lower duty.

Other Direct Price Influences   Countries use other means to affect prices, including special fees (such as for consular and customs clearance and documentation), requirements that customs deposits be placed in advance of shipment, and minimum price levels at which goods can be sold after they have customs clearance.

NONTARIFF BARRIERS: QUANTITY CONTROLS

Governments use other nontariff regulations and practices to affect directly the quantity of imports and exports. Let's take a look at the various forms that such regulations and practices typically take.

Quotas   The **quota** is the most common type of quantitative import or export restriction, limiting the quantity of a product that can be imported or exported in a given time frame, typically per year. *Import quotas* normally raise prices for two reasons: (1) They limit supply, and (2) they provide little incentive to use price competition to increase sales. A notable difference between tariffs and quotas is their effect on revenues. Tariffs generate revenue for the government. Quotas generate revenues only for those companies that are able to obtain a portion of the intentionally limited supply of the product that they can then sell to local customers. (Sometimes governments allocate quotas among countries based on political or market conditions. Recall from our opening case, for example, the creation of the Multifiber Arrangement, by which a group of developed nations agreed to negotiate quotas on textile imports from a group of developing countries.)

To circumvent quotas, companies can sometimes convert the product into one for which there is no quota. For instance, the United States maintains sugar import quotas that result in U.S. sugar prices averaging about double the world market price for sugar. As a result, many U.S. candy producers (e.g., Fanny May, Brach's, Mars, Tootsie Roll, Hershey) have moved plants to Mexico where they can buy lower-cost sugar and import the candy duty-free to the United States. This has resulted in a loss of about 10,000 U.S. jobs in the candy industry.[43]

Finally, import quotas are not necessarily imposed to protect domestic producers. Japan has maintained quotas on many agricultural products that are not produced within the country. It has then allocated import rights to competing suppliers as a means of bargaining for sales of Japanese exports as well as preventing excess dependence on any one country for essential foods in the event that adverse climatic or political conditions abruptly cut off supply.

Voluntary Export Restraint   A variation of an import quota is the so-called **voluntary export restraint (VER)**. Essentially, the government of Country A asks the government of Country B to reduce its companies' exports to Country A voluntarily. The term *voluntarily* is somewhat misleading; typically either Country B volunteers to reduce its exports or else Country A may impose tougher trade regulations. For example, we illustrated examples of VERs in the opening case on the textile and clothing trade. Procedurally, VERs have unique advantages. A VER is much easier to switch off than an import quota. In addition, the appearance of a "voluntary" choice by a particular country to constrain its shipments to another country tends not to damage political relations between those countries as much as an import quota does.

A country may establish *export quotas* to assure domestic consumers of a sufficient supply of goods at a low price, to prevent depletion of natural resources, or to attempt to

A quota may

- Set the total amount to be traded.
- Allocate amounts by country.

Case Review Note

raise export prices by restricting supply in foreign markets. To restrict supply, some countries band together in various commodity agreements, such as those for coffee and petroleum, which then restrict and regulate exports from the member countries.

Embargoes   A specific type of quota that prohibits all forms of trade is an **embargo.** As with quotas, countries—or groups of countries—may place embargoes on either imports or exports, on whole categories of products regardless of origin or destination, on specific products with specific countries, or on all products with given countries. Governments impose embargoes in the effort to use economic means to achieve political goals. As we explain in our closing case, for instance, the U.S.-imposed embargo on Cuba was conceived to weaken the Cuban economy and thus induce a demoralized populace to overthrow the Communist regime. The reasoning has been straightforward for nearly five decades—the Cuban economy was so weak that a demoralized population would overthrow Castro if economic conditions deteriorated just a little more.

"Buy Local" Legislation   Another form of quantitative trade control is so-called *buy local legislation*. Government purchases are a large part of total expenditures in many countries; typically, governments favor domestic producers. Sometimes governments specify a domestic content restriction—that is, a certain percentage of the product must be of local origin. Sometimes they favor domestic producers through price mechanisms. For example, a government agency may buy a foreign-made product only if the price is at some predetermined margin below that of a domestic competitor. For example, the U.S. Congress passed legislation in 2005 that required the Department of Homeland Security to buy only products that had at least 50 percent U.S. content.[44]

Standards and Labels   Countries can devise classification, labeling, and testing standards to allow the sale of domestic products but obstruct that of foreign-made ones. Take product labels, for instance. The requirement that companies indicate on a product where it is made provides information to consumers who may prefer to buy products from certain nations. In addition, countries may dictate content information on packaging that is not required elsewhere. These technicalities add to a firm's production costs, particularly if the labels must be translated for each export market.

In addition, raw materials, components, design, and labor increasingly come from many countries, so most products today are of such mixed origin that they are difficult to sort out. For example, the United States stipulated that any cloth "substantially altered" (woven, for instance) in another country must identify that country on its label. Consequently, designers like Ferragamo, Gucci, and Versace must declare "Made in China" on the label of garments that contain silk from China.[45]

The professed purpose of standards is to protect the safety or health of the domestic population. However, some foreign companies argue that standards are just another means to protect domestic producers. For example, some U.S. and Canadian producers have contended that EU regulations and labeling requirements on genetically engineered corn and canola oil are merely means to keep out the products until their own technology catches up.[46]

In another case, following publicity about contaminated foods from China in the United States, China upped its rejection of foodstuffs from the United States—citing contamination with drugs and salmonella.[47] In reality, there's no way of knowing to what extent products are kept out of countries for legitimate safety and health reasons versus arbitrarily to protect domestic production. Nevertheless, Table 7.2 shows that, for the United States, the rejection of foreign food shipments is significant.

Specific Permission Requirements   Some countries require that potential importers or exporters secure permission from governmental authorities before conducting trade transactions. This requirement is known as an **import or export license.** A company may have to submit samples to government authorities to obtain an import license. This procedure can restrict imports or exports directly by denying permission or indirectly because of the cost, time, and uncertainty involved in the process.

Case Review Note

Through "buy local" laws

- Government purchases give preference to domestically made goods.
- Governments sometimes legislate a percentage of domestic content.

Other types of trade barriers include

- Arbitrary standards.
- Licensing arrangements.
- Administrative delays.
- Reciprocal requirements.
- Service restrictions.

TABLE 7.2 Food Refused at the U.S. Border

Foreign products—edible or otherwise—may be denied access to a local market for a variety of health and safety reasons. They can also be refused because local policy is designed to protect local production. Technically, there's no way of knowing which is the case, but the volume of food products denied at the U.S. border by the FDA is significant and reflects a range of regulatory violations.

Food Refused at the Border

An analysis of food imports denied by the FDA in the last year reveals the variety and extent of violations.

Countries with the most FDA refusals *July '06 to June '07*	Number of refused food shipments *July '06 to June '07*	Most frequent food violation and counts *July '06 to June '07*		Total value of food imports *2006*
India	1,763	Salmonella (mostly on spices, seeds, shrimp)	256	$1.2 billion
Mexico	1,480	Filth (candy, chilis, juice, seafood, cheese)	385	9.8
China (mainland)	1,368	Filth (produce, seafood, bean curd, noodles)	287	3.8
Dominican Republic	828	Pesticide (produce)	789	0.3
Denmark	543	Problems with nutrition label (candy)	85	0.4
Vietnam	533	Salmonella (seafood, black pepper)	118	1.1
Japan	508	Missing documentation (drinks, soups, beans)	143	0.5
Italy	482	Missing documentation (beans, jarred foods)	138	2.9
Indonesia	460	Filth (seafood, crackers, candy)	122	1.5

Source: Andrew Martin and Griff Palmer, "China Not Sole Source of Delicious Food," *New York Times*, July 12, 2007: C1+. Data from Food and Drug Administration, U.S. International Trade Commission.

A **foreign-exchange control** is a similar type of control. It requires an importer of a given product to apply to a governmental agency to secure the foreign currency to pay for the product. As with an import license, failure to grant the exchange, not to mention the time and expense of completing forms and awaiting replies, obstructs foreign trade.

Administrative Delays Closely akin to specific permission requirements are intentional administrative delays, which create uncertainty and raise the cost of carrying inventory. For example, United Parcel Service provisionally suspended its ground service between the United States and Mexico because of burdensome Mexican customs delays. Competitive pressure, however, moves countries to improve their administrative systems. Chinese trade authorities, for example, cut the time taken for goods manufactured by Hong Kong firms in Guangdong to pass through internal customs checks from one week to one day. Improved processes, such as electronic submission of cargo manifests, affected 68,000 nonmainland firms and reduced administrative costs more than US$70 million.[48]

Reciprocal Requirements Governments sometimes require exporters to take merchandise in lieu of money or to promise to buy merchandise or services, in place of cash payment, in the country to which they export. This requirement is common in the aerospace and defense industries—sometimes because the importer does not have enough foreign currency. For instance, Indonesia bought Russian jets in exchange for commodities such as rubber.[49]

Countertrade More frequently, however, reciprocal requirements are made between countries with ample access to foreign currency that want to secure jobs or technology as part of the transaction.[50] For example, McDonnell Douglas sold helicopters to the British government but had to equip them with Rolls-Royce engines (made in the United Kingdom) as well as transfer much of the technology and production work to the United Kingdom.[51] Such transactions are called **countertrade** or **offsets.**

Countertrade often requires exporters to find markets for goods outside their lines of expertise or to engage in complicated organizational arrangements that require they relinquish some operating control. All things being equal, companies avoid countertrade.[52] However, some companies have developed competencies in these types of arrangements.

Restrictions on Services   Services are the fastest-growing sector in international trade. In deciding whether to restrict trade in services, countries typically consider three factors: *essentiality*, *standards*, and *immigration*.

Essentiality   Countries judge certain service industries to be essential because they serve strategic purposes or because they provide social assistance to their citizens. They sometimes prohibit private companies, foreign or domestic, in some sectors because they feel the services should not be sold for profit. In other cases, they set price controls for private competitors or subsidize government-owned service organizations, creating disincentives for foreign private participation.

Not-for-Profit Services   Mail, education, and hospital health services are often not-for-profit sectors in which few foreign firms compete. When a government privatizes these industries, its customary preference for local ownership and control of essential services may preclude foreign firms from competing. For example, most countries, including the United States, restrict foreign companies from transporting cargo and passengers over their domestic routes. Other essential services in which foreign firms are sometimes excluded are media, communications, banking, and utilities.

Standards   Governments limit foreign entry into many service professions to ensure practice by qualified personnel. The licensing standards of these personnel vary by country and include such professionals as accountants, actuaries, architects, electricians, engineers, gemologists, hairstylists, lawyers, physicians, real estate brokers, and teachers.

At present, there is little reciprocal recognition in licensing from one country to another because occupational standards and requirements differ substantially. This means, for example, that an accounting or legal firm from one country faces obstacles in another country, even to service its domestic clients' needs. The company must hire professionals within each foreign country or else try to earn certification abroad. The latter option can be difficult because examinations will be in a foreign language and likely emphasize materials different from those in the home country. Furthermore, there may be lengthy prerequisites for taking an examination, such as internships, time in residency, and course work at a local university.

Immigration   Satisfying the standards of a particular country is no guarantee that a foreigner can then work there. In addition, governmental regulations often require that an organization—domestic or foreign—search extensively for qualified personnel locally before it can even apply for work permits for personnel it would like to bring in from abroad. Even if no one is available, hiring a foreigner is still difficult.[53]

Dealing with Governmental Trade Influences

Government intervention in trade affects the flow of imports and exports of goods and services between countries. When companies face possible losses because of import competition, they have several options to deal with this situation, four of which stand out:

1. Move operations to another country.
2. Concentrate on market niches that attract less international competition.
3. Adopt internal innovations, namely, greater efficiency or superior products.
4. Try to get governmental protection.

There are costs and risks with each option. Nevertheless, the record of many companies shows that success is possible. For example, competition from Japanese imports spurred the

CONCEPT CHECK

In Chapter 1, we define **service exports** and **imports** and discuss the significance of services for some companies and countries. We also divide them into three categories: tourism and transportation, service performance, and asset use.

Three main reasons for restricting trade in services are

- Essentiality.
- Standards.
- Immigration.

CONCEPT CHECK

In discussing "Factor Mobility" in Chapter 6, we explain the effect of the increasing reliance on people as an internationally mobile production factor. In particular, we observe that most countries hand out immigration papers only sparingly and that many others allow workers to enter for only short periods of time.

When facing import competition, companies can

- Move abroad.
- Seek other market niches.
- Make domestic output competitive.
- Try to get protection.

U.S. automobile industry to move some production abroad (such as to subcontract with foreign companies to supply cheaper parts), develop niche markets through the sale of minivan and sport utility vehicles (SUVs) that initially had less international competition, and adopt innovations such as lean-production techniques to improve efficiency and product quality.

TACTICS FOR DEALING WITH IMPORT COMPETITION

Granted, these methods are not realistic for every industry or every company. Companies may lack the managerial, capital, or technological resources to shift production abroad. They may not be able to identify more profitable product niches. In addition, even if they manage to develop product niches or improve efficiency, foreign competitors may quickly copy their innovation. In such situations, companies often ask their governments to restrict imports or open export markets. In the case of automobiles, the U.S. industry sought and received protection from Japanese imports in the form of VERs. And as our opening case shows, textile and clothing producers are lobbying to restrict imports into the United States, even though some companies have successfully pursued one of the first three options.

Locating Decision Makers   Governments cannot try to help every company that faces tough international competition. Likewise, helping one industry may hurt another. Thus, as a manager, you may propose or oppose a particular protectionist measure. Inevitably, the burden falls on you and your company to convince governmental officials that your situation warrants particular governmental policies. You must identify the key decision makers and convince them. Trade policies in the United States, for example, are often championed by members of Congress who are especially sensitive to employment and company conditions in their home districts.[54] In any situation, companies must convey to public officials that voters and stakeholders support their position. Managers can and do use the economic and noneconomic arguments presented in this chapter.

Involving the Industry and Stakeholders   Companies improve the odds of success if they can ally most, if not all, domestic companies in their industry. Otherwise, officials may feel that a particular company's problems are due to its specific inefficiencies rather than the general challenge of imports or difficulty in gaining export sales. Similarly, it helps to involve many stakeholders. When the U.S. auto industry sought relief from Japanese auto competition, for example, company managers and union representatives worked together.

Managers may also identify other groups that may have a common objective, even though for different reasons. For example, the International Brotherhood of Teamsters worried about U.S. job losses because of citrus imports from Brazil. It then allied with activist groups concerned about the use of child labor in Brazil to get support for citrus import restrictions.[55] Companies often build public support by advertising their position to stakeholders. Finally, companies can lobby decision makers and endorse the political candidates who are sympathetic to their situation.

Preparing for Changes in the Competitive Environment   Companies can take different approaches to deal with changes in the international competitive environment. Frequently, companies' attitudes toward protectionism are a function of the investments they have made to implement their international strategy. Companies that depend on freer trade and those that have integrated their production and supply chains among countries tend to oppose protectionism. In contrast, companies with single or multidomestic production facilities, such as a plant in Japan to serve the Japanese market and a plant in Taiwan to serve the Taiwanese market, tend to support protectionism.

Companies also differ in their perceived abilities to compete against imports. In nearly half the cases over a 60-year period in which U.S. firms proposed protecting a U.S. industry, one or more companies in that industry opposed it. The latter typically commanded competitive advantages in terms of scale economies, supplier relationships, or differentiated products. Thus they reasoned that not only could they successfully battle international rivals, but they also stood to gain even more as their weaker domestic competitors failed to do so.[56]

CONCEPT CHECK

As we point out in Chapter 3, although representative democracies tend to share many features, the process whereby citizens select representatives to make decisions on their behalf varies from country to country, especially when it comes to the *centralization* or *decentralization* of authority. Among other things, the task of locating decision makers for business purposes thus differs from one country to another.

LOOKING TO THE FUTURE

Dynamics and Complexity

While some groups and companies are pushing for freer trade, others are clamoring for greater protectionism. It's probably safe to say that we'll see mixtures of the two stances as barriers come down for some products in some countries but go up for some products in other countries. Our opening case on the textile and clothing trade is indicative of the complexity of trade protection and promotion, which exists for an array of other products as well. When trade restrictions change, there are winners and losers among countries and among companies and workers within them.

In addition, gains to consumers may be at the expense of some workers. People who see themselves as big losers are not apt to take the change without a struggle; that is, they'll garner as much support for their positions as they can, and they may win. This support may well come from alliances that cross national borders, such as the alliances among clothing companies in various nations that are uniting to push governments to enact new quota agreements. Thus if you are a manager in an industry that may be affected by changes in governmental protection, you must watch closely to predict how the politics may affect your own economic situation.

Finally, the international regulatory situation is becoming more, rather than less, complex—a situation that challenges companies to find the best locations to produce. New products are coming onto the market regularly, thus making the task of tariff classification more complex. Services available over the Internet, such as international online gambling, challenge governments to find means of regulation and collection of taxes. Heightened concerns about terrorism and product safety compound considerations of what should or should not be traded.

In Chapter 8, we discuss the trade agreements that countries are reaching; nevertheless, it's useful at this point to say a word or two about the impact these have on decision making. Every time countries negotiate a trading agreement (and these agreements are proliferating), there is the possibility that a new optimum production location emerges. For instance, the United States and Mexico negotiated a free trade pact, which caused some U.S. imports to shift from Taiwan to Mexico. However, with an additional free trade agreement between the United States and Central America, some of the production that developed in Mexico might now shift to a Central American country. Another free trade agreement might cause another shift in the future. All of this creates uncertainties for companies' operations. ■

CASE

U.S.–Cuban Trade: When Does a Cold War Strategy Become a Cold War Relic?

The U.S. embargo of Cuba has been a resilient foreign policy, able to weather a variety of political leaders, economic events, and historical eras.[57] In 2008, Fidel Castro ceded Cuban leadership to his younger brother Raúl (age 76), which led to speculation about Fidel's future behind-the-scenes influence and whether Raúl would make economic and political reforms.

Shortly before this, the United States tightened economic relations with Cuba by requiring any export sales to Cuba to be paid in cash in advance of shipment, reducing the maximum remittances that people in the United States could send to family in Cuba and restricting visits to Cuba by Cuban Americans to once in three years instead of once a year. The reasoning was straightforward and similar to one that had prevailed over nearly five decades: The Cuban economy was so weak that a demoralized population would overthrow Castro if economic conditions deteriorated just a little more. Many observers agreed and many disagreed, but let's first look at the history of the situation.

After the Revolution

In the 1950s, more than two-thirds of Cuban foreign trade took place with the United States. After Castro overthrew the Batista government in 1959, he threatened to incite revolutions elsewhere in Latin America. The United States countered by canceling its agreements to buy

Cuban sugar, and Cuba retaliated by seizing U.S. oil refineries. The oil companies refused to supply Cuba with crude oil. Cuba then turned to the Soviet Union for replacement supplies.

The Cold War Sets In

This conflict occurred at the height of the Cold War tension between the United States and the Soviet Union. In 1962, the United States severed diplomatic relations and initiated the full trade embargo of Cuba. In 1963, the Treasury Department set forth regulations that prohibited all unlicensed financial transactions, forbade direct or indirect imports from Cuba, and imposed a total freeze on Cuban government assets held in the United States. Trade between the United States and Cuba stopped.

The incidents that strained relations during the next decades are too numerous to detail. Some threatened peace; others bordered on the absurd. They included the U.S. sponsorship of an invasion by Cuban exiles at the Bay of Pigs, the placement and removal of Soviet missiles in Cuba, the deployment of Cuban forces to overthrow regimes the United States supported (such as in Nicaragua and Angola), and exposés that the CIA had tried to airlift someone to assassinate Castro and had tried to develop a powder to make his beard fall out. Figure 7.4 gives a timeline of major events in U.S.-Cuban relations.

Enacting the Embargo

During this period, the U.S. trade embargo endured as originally set. Despite the collapse of communism in most of the world in the early 1990s, the U.S. Congress passed the Cuban Democracy Act in 1992. This policy codified the ban on American travel to Cuba and extended the embargo to the foreign subsidiaries of U.S. companies operating abroad—there would be no trade, direct or otherwise, between the United States and Cuba. The act also required Cuba to hold democratic elections before the U.S. executive branch could repeal the embargo.

The Helms-Burton Act in 1996 reinforced many of these provisions as well as added stipulations for penalizing foreign companies that did business in Cuba. This act provided for legal action (to seize assets in the United States) against non-U.S. companies using expropriated property in Cuba that U.S. citizens (including Cuban exiles) had owned. It prohibited executives of these companies and their families from visiting the United States and forbade normal U.S. relations with any future Cuban government that included Fidel Castro.

Shifting Sympathies

Over time, the U.S. role in the Cuban drama has played to a less sympathetic audience worldwide. Initially, many countries supported the U.S. embargo. All members of the Organization of American States except Mexico agreed in 1964 to endorse it. Gradually, countries began trading with Cuba anyway. In 1995, the United Nations voted 117 to 3 against the U.S.

FIGURE 7.4   The Saga of U.S.-Cuba Relations

Relations between the United States and the island nation of Cuba have been embroiled in the vicissitudes of international politics for more than a century—and especially since the advent of a Communist government in Cuba in 1961.

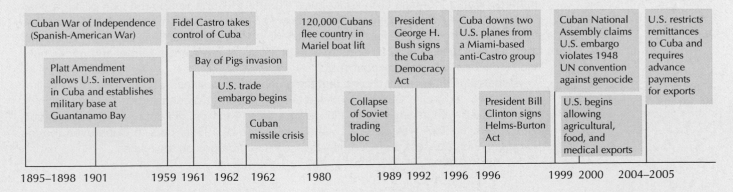

embargo. Only Israel and Uzbekistan voted with the United States, and both of these countries traded with Cuba. By 2001, some 150 nations had normal trade relations with Cuba.

The Cold War Thaws

Events increasingly created questions about the rationale for continuing the embargo. The fall of the Berlin Wall and the end of the Cold War in the early 1990s triggered many changes. The attendant collapse of the Soviet Union deprived Cuba of the estimated $3.5 to $4.5 billion in annual subsidies that sustained its feeble economy. Before long, the export of revolution from Cuba seemed less of a threat.

In fact, Cuba's staggering economy seemed on the brink of collapse. On the one hand, in 2000 U.S. Secretary of State Colin Powell ruled out the possibility of completely lifting the Cuban embargo until Castro departed. On the other hand, in the same year, congressional legislation allowed certain exports of U.S. agricultural, food, and medical products. After the passage of this act, Cuba quickly became the 21st-largest agricultural market for the United States with sales exceeding $400 million in 2004. In 2006, the United States was the fourth largest exporter to Cuba after China, Spain, and Canada.

The Debate in the United States

The U.S. public has been increasingly divided on the usefulness of the embargo on Cuba. A poll in 2007 showed that 62 percent of Americans favored establishing diplomatic relations with Cuba. Hardliner policies had failed for more than 40 years to dislodge Castro from power while causing adversity for over 11 million Cubans. Advocates of normal relations with Cuba argued that tighter restrictions on U.S. firms and reprisals on foreign companies would not weaken Castro's political power. In fact, they pointed to Castro's retaliation against the Cuban people in reprisal against new U.S. economic policies. These included the raising of prices in Cuba for foreign-produced goods and the elimination of the U.S. dollar as an official currency.

Moreover, they warned that Cuban economic downturns would likely invite retaliation and aggravate U.S. immigration tensions with Cuba. A growing number of leaders in the United States (including heads of major firms, Democratic and Republican members of Congress, and labor leaders) publicly favored normalization of U.S.-Cuban trade rather than tightening the economic noose. For example, former U.S. Secretary of State Lawrence Eagleburger reasoned that U.S. trade actions gave Castro something, other than his inept policies, to blame for his economic blunders. "The worst thing that could happen [to Castro]," said Eagleburger, "would be for the U.S. to open the gates of trade and travel." Increasing exposure to the United States, not the embargo, seemed to be a more promising force of change.

Some Pros and Cons of Doing Business with Cuba   Repealing the embargo would help many U.S. industries and companies. Cuba had already attracted investments from many businesses from other countries, largely drawn by its highly qualified workforce, near-perfect literacy rate, and demand for foreign products and services. Groups in the United States noted the market potential of Cuba; a Texas A&M study projected that lifting the trade embargo would increase U.S. agricultural exports to Cuba to about $1.24 billion a year. Others cited the potential gains for U.S. tourism and transportation companies. At the same time, there are bright spots for the Cuban economy. Venezuela has been supplying Cuba with about 98,000 barrels per day of petroleum products at preferential terms, and prices have been high for its nickel and cobalt exports.

At the same time, many argued that the potential for business with Cuba was highly limited. Cuba's per capita GDP in 2006 was about $4,000 at purchasing power parity, which when coupled with its small population (a little over 11 million) did not amount to much purchasing power. This was evident by the prevalence of 1950s' cars in Cuba even though European and Japanese auto companies faced no embargos on their sales.

In addition, Cuba had to export enough to pay for imports. Cuba depends heavily on commodity exports—sugar, nickel, tobacco, citrus, coffee—for which the United States has ample alternative supplies. In fact, the U.S. sugar quota system with a number of countries would surely cause a political backlash in those countries if part of their sugar quotas were given to Cuba. Certainly, there is the possibility of tourism, but the hotels in Cuba are already booked fairly full with tourists from Europe and Canada.

Is the Embargo a Cold War Relic?   Finally, there was debate over the basis for the pro-embargo position. Some argued that, in an age when China is a member of the WTO and nations like Vietnam are trading with the United States, the Cuban embargo looked like a Cold War relic. Moreover, besides being far tougher than the U.S. economic sanctions against Iran and North Korea, the Cuban embargo is the longest and harshest embargo by one state against another in modern history. In addition, some questioned the politics of U.S. policy. But there seemed to be a strong personal dimension; U.S. Vice President Cheney observed that "as soon as [Fidel] Castro is gone from the scene, there is no reason in the world why we can't have a really first-class normalized set of relationships with Cuba." ■

QUESTIONS

1. Should the United States seek to tighten the economic grip on Cuba? If so, why?
2. Should the United States normalize business relations with Cuba? If so, should the United States stipulate any conditions?
3. Assume you are Cuba's leader. What kind of trade relationship with the United States would be in your best interest? What type would you be willing to accept?
4. How does the structure and relationships of the U.S. political system influence the existence and specification of the trade embargo?

SUMMARY

- Despite the documented benefits of free trade, no country permits an unregulated flow of goods and services across its borders.

- It is difficult to determine the effect on employment from protecting an industry due to the likelihood of retaliation and the fact that imports as well as exports create jobs.

- Policymakers continue to struggle with the problem of income redistribution due to changes in trade policy.

- The infant-industry argument for protection holds that governmental prevention of import competition is necessary to help certain industries evolve from high-cost to low-cost production.

- Governmental interference is often argued to be beneficial if it promotes industrialization, given the positive relationship between industrial activity and economic development.

- Trade controls are used to improve economic relations with other countries. Their objectives include improving the balance of payments, raising prices to foreign consumers, gaining fair access to foreign markets, preventing foreign monopoly prices, assuring that domestic consumers get low prices, and lowering profit margins for foreign producers.

- Considerable governmental interference in international trade is motivated by political rather than economic concerns, including maintaining domestic supplies of essential goods and preventing potential enemies from gaining goods that would help them achieve their objectives.

- Trade controls that directly affect price and indirectly affect quantity include tariffs, subsidies, arbitrary customs-valuation methods, and special fees.

- Trade controls that directly affect quantity and indirectly affect price include quotas, VERs, "buy local" legislation, arbitrary standards, licensing arrangements, foreign-exchange controls, administrative delays, and requirements to take goods in exchange.

- A company's development of an international strategy will greatly determine whether it will benefit more from protectionism or from some other means for countering international competition.

KEY TERMS

ad valorem duty (p. 281)
comparable-access argument (p. 275)
compound duty (p. 281)
countertrade (p. 285)
dumping (p. 276)
duty (p. 280)
effective tariff (p. 281)
embargo (p. 284)
essential-industry argument (p. 277)

export-led development (p. 274)
export tariffs (p. 280)
foreign-exchange control (p. 285)
import tariff (p. 280)
import (or export) license (p. 284)
industrialization argument (p. 273)
infant-industry argument (p. 271)
offsets (p. 285)
optimum-tariff theory (p. 276)

protectionism (p. 268)
quota (p. 283)
specific duty (p. 281)
subsidy (p. 281)
tariff (or duty) (p. 280)
terms of trade (p. 273)
transit tariff (p. 280)
voluntary export restraint
   (VER) (p. 283)

ENDNOTES

1 *Sources include the following:* Hildegunn Kyvik Nordås, "The Global Textile and Clothing Industry Post the Agreement on Textiles and Clothing" (Geneva: WTO Secretariat Discussion Paper No. 5, 2004); Scott Miller and Charles Hutzler, "Poor Nations Seek WTO Textile Aid," *Wall Street Journal,* October 1, 2004: A2+; Christopher Swann, "US Textile Makers to Sue over Imports," *Financial Times,* September 2, 2004: 6; Frances Williams, "Textile Producers Weave a Web to Restrict China," *Financial Times,* October 22, 2004: 7; "U.S. Government Accepts Five More Special Textile Safeguard Petitions for Consideration" (November 3, 2004), at www.ncto.org/newsroom/pr200413.asp; United States International Trade Commission, at http://dataweb.usitc.gov/scripts/tariff2005.asp; Mei Fong and Dan Morse, "Backlash Is Likely as Chinese Exports Surge," *Wall Street Journal,* March 28, 2005: A3+; Ginger Thompson, "Fraying of a Latin Textile Industry," *New York Times,* March 25, 2005: 1; Rebecca Buckman, "Navigating China's Textile Trade," *Wall Street Journal,* September 10, 2004: A10.

2 The opinion is by Scott Miller in John McCary and Andrew Batson, "Politics & Economics," *Wall Street Journal,* June 23, 2007: A4.

3 Hans S. Nichols, "Taking the Fix Out of Farm Subsidies," *Insight on the News,* August 13, 2001: 20.

4 Lori Kletzer, *Job Loss from Imports: Measuring the Costs* (Washington, D.C.: Institute for International Economics, 2001).

5 Kenneth A. Couch, "Earnings Losses and Unemployment of Displaced Workers in Germany," *Industrial and Labor Relations Review* 54 (2001): 559; David Margolis, "Worker Displacement in France," mimeograph (Paris: Université de Paris, Pantheon-Sorbonne, 1999).

6 Alan M. Field, "WTO Approves Sanctions Against U.S." *Journal of Commerce—Online,* August 31, 2004: WP.

7 Greg Hitt, Paul Glader, and Mike Spector, "Trade Ruling on Steel May Boost Auto Industry," *Wall Street Journal,* December 15, 2006: A3.

8 Fuat Sener, "Schumpeterian Unemployment, Trade and Wages," *Journal of International Economics* 54 (2001): 119.

9 This argument is most associated with the writings of Raul Prebisch, Hans Singer, and Gunnar Myrdal in the 1950s and 1960s.

For a recent discussion, see John Toye and Richard Toye, "The Origins and Interpretation of the Prebisch-Singer Thesis," History of Political Economy 35:3 (2003): 437–57.

10 Jiang Xueqin, "Letter from China," *The Nation,* March 4, 2002.

11 Steve Padgittm, Peggy Petrzelka, Wendy Wintersteen, and Eric Imerman, "Integrated Crop Management: The Other Precision Agriculture," *American Journal of Alternative Agriculture* 16 (January 2001): 16.

12 Kevin Morrison and Deborah Hargreaves, "Commodities Are Big New Theme," *Financial Times,* September 18, 2003: 15, and Sergio Lence and Dermot Hayes, "U.S. Farm Policy and the Volatility of Commodity Prices and Farm Revenues," *American Journal of Agricultural Economics* 84 (2002): 335–52.

13 Hou Hexiang, "Vietnam to Accelerate Industrialization and Modernization of Rural Areas," *Xinhua News Agency*[China], June 2, 2002: 1008; "Pushing Ecuador into the 21st Century," *Latin Finance,* March 2002: 30, at http://web.lexis-nexis.com/universe (accessed July 17, 2002); "Is Inequality Decreasing? Debating the Wealth and Poverty of Nations," *Foreign Affairs* (August 2002): 178.

14 Gerald K. Helleiner, "Markets, Politics, and Globalization: Can the Global Economy Be Civilized?" *Global Governance* (July–September 2001): 243; Marina Murphy, "EU Chemicals Need Flexibility: A Level Playing Field Should Be Established between the EU and US Chemicals Industries," *Chemistry and Industry,* July 1, 2002: 9; Lisa Schmidt, "How U.S. Sees Trade Rows," *Calgary Herald* [Canada], June 25, 2002: A2.

15 Annie Gowen, "U.S. Caviar with a Russian Accent," *Washington Post,* December 31, 2004: Metro, B1.

16 Adam Thomson, "Argentina Cuts Gas Exports to Avert a Crisis," *Financial Times,* March 27–28, 2004: 5; Randall Palmer, "Canada Mulls Nonprescription-Drug Tactic," *Seattle Times,* February 19, 2005: A13.

17 Edward Alden and Raphael Minder, "EU and Canada Impose Retaliatory Duties on U.S. Imports," *Financial Times,* April 1, 2005: 6.

18 Stephen Moore, "Tax Cut and Spend: The Profligate Ways of Congressional Republicans," *National Review,* October 1, 2001: 19.

19 George Leopold, "U.S. Eases Regulations on Cryptography Exports," *Electronic Engineering Times*, July 24, 2000: 43.

20 James Dao, "U.S. to Punish 10 Businesses for Iran Sales," *New York Times*, July 20, 2002: D1.

21 Doug Cameron and Kevin Morrison, "U.S. Groups Win Libyan Oil Exploration Permits License Auction," *Financial Times*, January 31, 2005: 9.

22 Philip Shenon, "In Hanoi, U.S. Goods Sold But Not by U.S.," *New York Times*, October 3, 1993: A1.

23 Patrick Barta, "Black Gold," *Wall Street Journal*, August 16, 2006: A1+.

24 Jacob Weisberg, "Sanctions Help to Sustain Rogue States," *Financial Times*, August 3, 2006: 11.

25 Lance Davis and Stanley Engerman, "Sanctions: Neither War Nor Peace," *Journal of Economic Perspectives* 17:2 (Spring 2003): 187–97.

26 Scott Erickson, "Low-Level Trade Sanctions," *Global Competitiveness* 7 (Annual 1999): 375.

27 "Leaders: A Grand Bargain with the Great Satan? Testing Iran's Nuclear Intentions," *The Economist*, March 12, 2005: 10.

28 "EU/Latin America/Caribbean: Leaders Aim to Revive Ties," *European Report*, May 15, 2002: 501.

29 Vanessa Bauza, "In Struggle for Influence, It's Better to Give," *Knight Ridder Tribune Business News*, March 24, 2007: 1.

30 Tony Walker, "China Warns Australia over Dalai Lama Visit," *Financial Times*, September 18, 1996: 1; Ying Ma, "China's America Problem," *Policy Review* (February 2002): 43–57.

31 Gail L. Cramer, James M. Hansen, and Eric J. Wailes, "Impact of Rice Tariffication on Japan and the World Rice Market," *American Journal of Agricultural Economics* 81 (1999): 1149.

32 Matthew Fraser, "Foreign Ownership Rules Indefensible: And There Appears to Be Appetite for Change," *Financial Post*, May 28, 2001: C2.

33 John Larkin, "Now Playing: Korea's Movie Industry Prevents Investment Pact with the U.S.," *Wall Street Journal*, March 20, 2002: A19.

34 "Futile Fortress," *Financial Times*, August 26, 2003: 16.

35 Bernard Hoekman and Kym Anderson, "Developing-Country Agriculture and the New Trade Agenda," *Economic Development & Cultural Change* 49 (October 2000): 171.

36 Neil King, Jr., Scott Miller, Daniel Michaels, and J. Lynn Lunsford, "U.S., Europe Sue Each Other at WTO over Aircraft Subsidies," *Wall Street Journal*, October 7, 2004: A2+.

37 G. Chandrashekhar, "Should India Demand Farm Subsidy Cuts by Developed Nations?" *Businessline*, January 4, 2006: 1.

38 Chi-Chur Chao and Eden S. H. Yu, "Import Quotas, Tied Aid, Capital Accumulation, and Welfare," *Canadian Journal of Economics* 34 (2001): 661; Mark Rice, "Australia Must Join Other Countries in Untying Overseas Aid," *Australian Financial Review*, April 4, 2002: 59.

39 Jamil Anderlini, "China 'Ties' 5 B[illio]n Aid to Africa," *Financial Times*, June 26, 2007: 8.

40 Mohsin Habib and Leon Zurawicki, "Corruption and Foreign Direct Investment," *Journal of International Business Studies* 33 (2002): 291–308.

41 "National Import Specialist Addresses Outreach to the Public," *U.S. Customs Border Protection Today*, October–November 2006, at www.customs.ustreas.gov/xp?CustomsToday/2006/october_november/import_article (accessed July 13, 2007); *Customs Bulletin and Decision*, June 27, 2007: 58.

42 John W. Miller, "Why Some China Exports Are Taking Illegal Detours," *Wall Street Journal*, May 25, 2007: B1+.

43 Jeremy Grant, "Signs of Decay as Companies Desert the U.S. Candy Capital," *Financial Times*, January 21, 2004: 14; Christopher Swann, "Shielding Sugar Industry 'Costs Thousands of Jobs,' " *Financial Times*, February 15, 2006: 6.

44 Ed Fruenheim, " 'Buy American' Legislation Draws Fire," *C/Net News*, May 20, 2005, at http://news.com.com/Buy+American+legislation+draws+fire/2100–1022_3–5715486.html (accessed July 13, 2007).

45 Blaise J. Bergiel and Erich B. Bergiel, "Country-of-Origin as a Surrogate Indicator: Implications/Strategies," *Global Competitiveness* 7 (1999): 187.

46 Jeremy Grant and Ralph Minder, "Comment & Analysis: Agribusiness," *Financial Times*, February 1, 2006: 11.

47 Anita Chang, "Food Safety," *Miami Herald*, July 15, 2007: 18A.

48 Peggy Sito, "Guangdong to Slash Internal Customs Delays," *South China Morning Post*, May 16, 2002: 1.

49 Devi Asmarani, "MPs Criticise Jakarta for Buying Pricey Russian Jets," *The Straits Time* [Singapore], June 19, 2003.

50 Chong Ju Choi, Soo Hee Lee, and Jai Boem Kim, "A Note on Countertrade: Contractual Uncertainty and Transaction Governance in Emerging Economies," *Journal of International Business Studies* 30 (Spring 1999): 189.

51 "McDonnell and Partner Win $4 Billion British Copter Deal," *New York Times*, July 14, 1995: C5.

52 Choi et al., "A Note on Countertrade," 189.

53 Sara Robinson, "Workers Are Trapped in Limbo by I.N.S.," *New York Times*, February 29, 2000: A12.

54 Ralph G. Carter and Lorraine Eden, "Who Makes U.S. Trade Policy?" *International Trade Journal* 13:1 (1999): 53–100.

55 Matt Moffett, "Citrus Squeeze," *Wall Street Journal*, September 6, 1998: A1.

56 Eugene Salorio, "Trade Barriers and Corporate Strategies: Why Some Firms Oppose Import Protection for Their Own Industry," unpublished DBA dissertation, Harvard University, 1991.

57 *Sources include the following:* Anne Gearan, "U.S. Public's Feelings Mixed on Castro," *Miami Herald*, February 8, 2007: 12A; "CIA World Factbook—Cuba," at www.cia.gov/library/publications/the-world-factbook/geos/cu.html (accessed July 13, 2007); Pascal Fletcher, "US Anti-Cuba Law Feeds Businessmen's Paranoia," *Financial Times*, July 2, 1996: 5; William M. Leo Grande, "From Havana to Miami: U.S. Cuba Policy as a Two-Level Game," *Journal of Interamerican Studies and World Affairs* 40:1 (1998): 67–86; Albert R. Hunt, "End the Anachronistic Embargo Against Cuba," *Wall Street Journal*, April 22, 1999: A23; Daniel P. Erikson, "The New Cuba Divide," *The National Interest* (Spring 2002); Kathleen Parker, "Exposure, Not Embargoes, Will Free Fidel's Cuba," *The Seattle Times*, March 14, 2001: B6; Albor Ruiz, "Shifts Start in U.S.-Cuban Relations," *Daily News*, January 14, 2002: 3; Keith Suter, "U.S. Should Lift Failed Sanctions on Cuba," *Canberra Times* [Australia], May 23, 2002; Michael Doyle, "State Eyeing Cuban Trade: Lawmakers Are Seeking to Lift the Longtime Embargo," *Sacramento Bee*, July 30, 2002; Timothy Ashby, "Who's Really Being Hurt?" *Journal of Commerce*, January 31, 2005; "The Web Site of Cuban Industry," at www.cubaindustria.cu/English; Theresa Borden, "Cubans Feel Pinch from Dollar Ban," *Atlanta Journal-Constitution*, November 10, 2004: 6F.

8

Cross-National Cooperation and Agreements

Objectives

- To identify the major characteristics and challenges of the World Trade Organization

- To discuss the pros and cons of global, bilateral, and regional integration

- To describe the static and dynamic impact of trade agreements on trade and investment flows

- To define different forms of regional economic integration

- To compare and contrast different regional trading groups, including but not exclusively the European Union (EU), the North American Free Trade Agreement (NAFTA), the Southern Common Market (MERCOSUR), and the Association of Southeast Asian Nations (ASEAN)

- To describe other forms of global cooperation, such as the United Nations and the Organization of Petroleum Exporting Countries (OPEC)

Marrying is easy, but housekeeping is hard.

—*German proverb*

CASE: Toyota's European Drive

Anna Kessler put the key into the ignition of her brand-new Toyota Yaris, started the engine, and began to navigate her way home from work through the crowded streets of Berlin, Germany.[1] Having owned the car for just over a week, she was already satisfied with her decision. She liked the car's distinctive European look, the generous warranty it had come with, and its low fuel consumption.

categories of a recent quality survey and the Yaris had achieved an outstanding four-star Euro NCAP safety rating, which led her to investigate the car more thoroughly.

With her purchase, Anna became another one of the millions of Toyota vehicle owners located around the globe, contributing to the Japanese automaker's rapid growth over the past decade. In 1990, the company possessed 20 production

MAP 8.1 Toyota has Sales, Production, and Design Facilities Scattered Throughout Europe

Her decision the previous week marked the first time Anna had ever owned a vehicle manufactured by an Asian company; in fact, it was the first time she had considered one. When she had made her last car purchase, the thought of buying a car from Toyota—then known for its lackluster designs, limited options, and seven-month-long waiting lists—had not even entered her mind. However, as she was researching different vehicles, she found that Toyota had ranked the highest in several

facilities in 14 countries; now it has 52 facilities in 27 countries, including nine located in Western and Eastern Europe that employ 55,000 people and produce over 800,000 vehicles annually.

Known for its low-cost, efficient production operations and with global annual sales in 2006 of around 8.52 million units and a net income of over $14 billion, Toyota Motor Corp. is not only the world's second largest manufacturer of automobiles in unit sales, but it is also the world's most profitable. And recently, nowhere is Toyota's market power more apparent than in Europe (Map 8.1), where it and other major Asian automakers have been experiencing marked success compared with their European counterparts.

In 2004, while Europe's five largest manufacturers lost 1.2 percent market share, Asia's five largest manufacturers gained 1 percent. Toyota's sales increased 2.3 percent in the region while Volkswagen, Mercedes-Benz, and French carmakers Renault SA and PSA Peugeot-Citroën SA were down 4 percent, 6.6 percent, 5.2 percent, and 8.3 percent, respectively. Other Asian manufacturers, including Honda, Hyundai, and Mazda, recorded gains ranging from 12 to 30 percent. The trend has continued for Toyota. Its market share has grown steadily, from 5.0 percent in 2004 to 5.8 percent in 2006, and in the early months of 2007, it saw a 13 percent rise in new car registration at a time when overall registrations in Europe fell 2.5 percent. European rivals, such as Renault and BMW, saw losses or only marginal gains.

Given these details, it's hard to believe that before 2002, Toyota had not posted a profit for its European operations for three decades and had suffered from consistently low market share and growth in the region. So why has it taken Toyota so long to crack into the competitive European market, and why are European companies only now beginning to feel the pressure from Asian manufacturers? Many analysts have pointed to an agreement between the Japanese government and the European Community (EC)—the predecessor to the European Union (EU)—in which each year the two negotiated a quota for the number of Japanese cars imported into Europe. The quota amounts agreed on each year depended on such factors as the level of consumer demand and sales growth in the region and were fixed at 11 percent of the European market.

The arrangement was set up to allow European carmakers to become more competitive as the EC made the transition to a common market; previously, several independent European nations possessed their own import and registration restrictions on Japanese cars. Italy, for example, limited the number of imported Japanese vehicles to 3,000 while France kept them at a 3 percent share of its market. Britain, Spain, and Portugal imposed similar restrictions. This policy goes back to the end of World War II when the Japanese government asked the European automakers to curtail exports to Japan to help Japan rebuild its industry. The Europeans reciprocated by limiting their market to Japanese autos. At the time, that wasn't a problem. However, when the Japanese auto companies became export conscious, they wanted access to the European markets. The quota system helped protect the domestic industry.

Under the new system, these countries had to abandon their individual policies, but French carmakers fought to include an 80 percent local-content rule and an allowance to export 500,000 cars a year to Japan, five times the current level. In the end, the EC disregarded these additional requests, and in the first year of the agreement, 1.089 million Japanese cars were allowed to be imported.

The quota, however, also fixed separate caps for each participating country and then divided this amount among the Japanese automakers according to their historic market shares. The caps essentially prevented the Japanese from being able to transfer their excess imports from countries where their quotas weren't being met to ones where they were unable to meet demand due to their having already reached the maximum limits. It was primarily for this reason that they actually never met their quota for the EC, and during the seven years the quota system was in effect, Toyota was held to a 2 to 3 percent market share in most EU countries.

Although the system seemed to be having the desired effect, even some French auto officials admitted that the eventual opening of the market was inevitable. One noted, "Can we put off change for years? Officially, yes. But honestly, I don't think so." That statement proved prophetic when the EU lifted the import quota in 1999 and additionally made it easier for the Japanese auto manufacturers to expand distribution and to sign up dealers. Although this move did not necessarily cause the Japanese to flood the European market with their products, it did open the way for them to invest more heavily in design and manufacturing facilities in the EU, to broaden the range of products they marketed there, and to customize their offerings to better appeal to European tastes.

Toyota responded to the drop in barriers by introducing a new strategy of designing vehicles targeted specifically at European customers. The new strategy involved setting up a European Design and

Development center in southern France and allowing design teams across the globe to compete for projects. The Yaris, Toyota's best-selling vehicle in the EU, was designed by a Greek and was the first to be developed within the region. It subsequently was named Car of the Year 2000 in both Europe and Japan.

As another key element of its European strategy, Toyota has also set up additional production centers in the region and now manufactures all of its best European-selling vehicles in Europe. The new-generation Toyota Corolla, voted 2002 European Car of the Year, and the Avensis, the first Toyota vehicle to be exported from Europe to Japan, were both designed and built in Europe.

In December 2006, Toyota celebrated its one millionth made-in-Europe Yaris at its Valenciennes plant in France. Additionally, manufacturing facilities in Eastern Europe allow the Japanese automaker to lower production costs due to lower wages. For example, workers in Toyota's plant in Turkey earn only $3.60 an hour, giving Toyota a distinct cost advantage over European competitors, such as Volkswagen, which pays as much as $40.68 per hour to the workers in its plants in Germany.

The difference in wages, in addition to its efficient operations, has allowed Toyota to remain profitable while others are undergoing layoffs and industrywide restructuring. Volkswagen cut nearly 20,000 jobs and introduced longer shifts in its German factories. GM's European unit cut 13,000 jobs to help it reduce costs and restore profitability after seven consecutive years of losses in the region. Additionally, Ford, Fiat SpA, and Volkswagen have undergone substantial management changes as they've sought to rein in operations to keep costs from running over in the new competitive market in which they are slowly losing market share.

The situation seems even bleaker as Japanese competitors continue to open up facilities in the Eastern bloc countries recently admitted to the EU as well as other low-wage areas, such as China. Toyota has already set up state-of-the-art production plants in the Czech Republic and Poland—the one in the Czech Republic being established in cooperation with France's PSA Peugeot-Citroën to develop good relationships with PSA's local suppliers. Because of the elimination of internal tariffs in the EU, Toyota can manufacture automobiles anywhere within the EU and ship them to all markets duty-free. Before the reduction in tariff barriers, this would not have been possible.

Other recent trends in the EU have also favored Toyota since the quotas were eliminated. In light of a sluggish European economy facing high unemployment and low growth, Europeans are becoming less loyal to European brands in their search for more economical, higher-quality vehicles. In recent J. D. Power customer surveys in the United Kingdom and Germany, Toyota ranked first overall and scored the highest in three of seven categories; Ford, Renault, and Volkswagen all ranked below average. In addition, Toyota's environmentally friendly hybrid vehicle, the Prius, was voted the 2005 European Car of the Year. In light of its growing presence in Europe, the company's application to become a full member of the European Automobile Manufacturers' Association has been accepted.

Riding on its success in Europe and its growth internationally, Toyota has ambitious goals for the future. With confidence in its profitability, even in the competitive European market, and in its financial flexibility, it is driving to capture a 15 percent share of the global market by 2010 and recently overtook GM in terms of quarterly sales volume. Considering that its European operations account for approximately 13.2 percent of its worldwide sales, coming in third only to its North American and domestic operations, would Toyota ever have been able to achieve its worldwide goals if the EU had not loosened its restrictions on imported Japanese cars?

Introduction

In some respects, the United States is the perfect example of economic integration—the largest economy in the world composed of 50 states in the continental United States, Alaska, and Hawaii, a common currency, and labor and capital mobility. However, it is just one country. What about the rest of the world? Economic integration is the political

CONCEPT CHECK

Recall from Chapter 6 our discussion of the ways in which the mobility of capital, technology, and people affects a country's trade and the relative competitive positions of domestic firms and industries. Imbalances in such **factor mobility** are often addressed in strategies for cross-national integration.

Approaches to economic integration—political and economic agreements among countries that give preference to member countries in the agreement—may be

- Bilateral.
- Regional.
- Global.

Case Review Note

and economic agreements among countries that give preference to member countries to the agreement. There are three ways to approach economic integration:

- Global integration through the World Trade Organization.
- **Bilateral integration,** where two countries decide to cooperate more closely together, usually in the form of tariff reductions.
- **Regional integration,** where a group of countries located in the same geographic proximity decide to cooperate, such as is the case with the European Union.

In the mid- to late 1940s, countries decided that if they were going to emerge from the wreckage of World War II and promote economic growth and stability within their borders, they would have to assist—and get assistance from—nearby countries. This chapter discusses some of the important forms of economic cooperation.

Why do you need to understand the nature of these agreements? Trading groups, whether bilateral or regional, are an important influence on the strategies of MNEs. Such groups can define the size of the regional market and the rules under which companies must operate. In fact, an increase in market size is the single most important reason for trading groups.[2] Companies in the initial stages of foreign expansion must be aware of the regional economic groups that encompass countries with good manufacturing locations or market opportunities. As companies expand internationally, they must change their organizational structure and operating strategies to take advantage of regional trading groups. As we noted in our opening case, Toyota has been able to find success in Europe by taking advantage of changes in EU policy that allow it to adjust its design and production strategies to meet the unique needs of European consumers.

MNEs are interested in regional trade groups because the MNEs themselves tend to be regional as well. Although we often think of MNEs as companies that do business in all of the **triad** regions of the world—Europe, North America, and Asia—current research demonstrates that most MNEs generate a majority of their revenues in their home regions. Using a sample of the top 500 companies in the world, which tend to generate most of the world's trade and foreign direct investment, it was found that 320 MNEs generate at least 50 percent of their revenues from their home region, 25 MNEs are biregional (at least 20 percent of their revenues from two regions but less than 50 percent from any single region), 11 MNEs are host region oriented (more than 50 percent of their revenues from a region outside of their home region), and only 9 MNEs are truly global (at least 20 percent of their revenues from each of three triad regions and with less than 50 percent of their sales from one region).[3]

However, that does not minimize the importance of different regions for MNEs. For example, RC Willey, the regional furniture, electronics, and appliances store in the United States owned by Berkshire Hathaway, does not generate any foreign sales. However, it imports products from all over the world. Managers of the company are very interested in trade agreements because such agreements could have an impact on where they source their purchases to reduce costs and improve quality.

The World Trade Organization (WTO)

Governments often actively cooperate with each other to remove trade barriers. The following discussion looks at the **World Trade Organization (WTO),** the successor to the General Agreement on Tariffs and Trade and the major multilateral forum through which governments can come to agreements and can settle disputes regarding trade.

GATT: THE PREDECESSOR TO THE WTO

In 1947, 23 countries formed the **General Agreement on Tariffs and Trade (GATT)** under the auspices of the United Nations to abolish quotas and reduce tariffs. By the time the WTO replaced GATT in 1995, 125 nations were members. Many believe that GATT's contribution to trade liberalization made possible the expansion of world trade in the second half of the twentieth century.

CONCEPT CHECK

In Chapter 7, we explain that, in principle, no country allows an unregulated flow of goods and services across its borders; rather, governments routinely influence the flow of imports and exports. We also observe that governments directly or indirectly *subsidize* domestic industries to help them compete with foreign producers, whether at home or abroad. (In Chapter 1, we list the motivations for governments to engage in cross-national agreements—indeed, to cooperate at all.)

Trade Without Discrimination   The fundamental principle of GATT was that each member nation must open its markets equally to every other member nation—any sort of discrimination was prohibited. The principle of "trade without discrimination" was embodied in GATT's **most-favored-nation (MFN) clause**—once a country and its trading partners had agreed to reduce a tariff, that tariff cut was automatically extended to every other member country irrespective of whether they were a signatory to the agreement. GATT held several major conferences (eventually referred to as "rounds") from 1947 to 1993 to address trade issues. These sessions led to many multilateral reductions in tariffs and nontariff barriers.

Over time, GATT grappled with the issue of nontariff barriers in terms of industrial standards, government procurement, subsidies and countervailing duties (duties in response to another country's protectionist measures), licensing, and customs valuation. In each area, GATT members agreed to apply the same product standards for imports as for domestically produced goods, treat bids by foreign companies on a nondiscriminatory basis for most large contracts, prohibit export subsidies except on agricultural products, simplify licensing procedures that permit the importation of foreign-made goods, and use a uniform procedure to value imports when assessing duties on them.

GATT slowly ran into problems. Its success led some governments to devise craftier methods of trade protection. World trade grew more complex, and trade in services—not covered by GATT rules—grew more important. Procedurally, GATT's institutional structure and its dispute settlement system seemed increasingly overextended. In addition, GATT could not enforce compliance with agreements. These market trends and organizational challenges made trade agreements harder to work out. Restoring an effective means for trade liberalization led officials to create the WTO in 1995.

WHAT DOES THE WTO DO?

The WTO adopted the principles and trade agreements reached under the auspices of GATT but expanded its mission to include trade in services, investment, intellectual property, sanitary measures, plant health, agriculture, and textiles, as well as technical barriers to trade. Currently, the WTO has 150 members, including China, that collectively account for more than 97 percent of world trade. The entire membership makes significant decisions by consensus. However, there are provisions for a majority vote in the event of a nondecision by member countries. Agreements then must be ratified by the governments of the member nations.

The highest-level decision-making body in the WTO's structure is the Ministerial Conference; it meets at least once every two years. The next level is the General Council (usually ambassadors and the director of a country delegation) that meets several times a year. The General Council also meets as the Trade Policy Review Body and the Dispute Settlement Body. At the next level are the Council for Trade in Goods, the Council for Trade in Services, and the Council for Trade-Related Aspects of Intellectual Property Rights (TRIPS). Specialized committees, working groups, and working parties deal with the individual agreements and other areas, such as the environment, development, membership applications, and regional trade agreements. WTO members deal with these areas separately and on an ongoing basis.

Normal Trade Relations   The WTO replaced the MFN clause of GATT with the concept of **normal trade relations.** The WTO restricts this privilege to official members. Still, governments have made the following exceptions:

1. Developing countries' manufactured products have been given preferential treatment over those from industrial countries.
2. Concessions granted to members within a regional trading alliance, such as the EU, have not been extended to countries outside the alliance. (Recall from our opening case, for instance, that, although EU members can export and import cars from other EU nations without limitations, Japanese carmakers must comply with strict import tariffs.)

Exceptions are made in times of war or international tension.

> **CONCEPT CHECK**
>
> In Chapter 7, we define a **tariff** as the most common type of trade control and describe it as a "tax" that governments levy on goods shipped internationally. Here we emphasize the fact that tariff barriers affect the prices of goods that cross national borders.

> **CONCEPT CHECK**
>
> In discussing "Nontariff Barriers" as instruments of *trade control* in Chapter 7, we include **subsidies,** which we describe as direct government payments made to domestic companies, either to compensate them for losses incurred from selling abroad or to make it more profitable for them to sell overseas.

> The World Trade Organization is the major body for
>
> - Reciprocal trade negotiations.
> - Enforcement of trade agreements.

> **CONCEPT CHECK**
>
> We explain *TRIPS* in Chapter 5 as an agreement that allows poor countries either to produce generic products for local consumption or to import them from countries other than patent holders' home countries.

> Normal trade relations—same as MFN under GATT but with trade privileges restricted to official members.

Case Review Note

CONCEPT CHECK

In Chapter 7, we show how the imposition of import restrictions can be used as a means of persuading other countries to lower import barriers. Here we point out that the same practice can also be used to punish nations whose policies fail to comply with provisions of the WTO or other agreements.

Dispute Settlement   Countries may bring charges of unfair trade practices to a WTO panel, and accused countries may appeal. There are time limits on all stages of deliberations, and the WTO's rulings are binding. If an offending country fails to comply with the panel's judgment, its trading partners have the right to compensation. If this penalty is ineffective, then the offending country's trading partners have the right to impose countervailing sanctions.

Doha Round   Perhaps the most complex set of issues the WTO is currently faced with, however, is those it is trying to address through the Doha Round, which commenced in Doha, Qatar, in 2001 and is focused on giving a boost to developing countries on the world scene. The largest of the disputes has essentially resulted in a split between developed members, such as the United States, Japan, and the EU, and developing nations, led by Brazil and India, over the large agricultural subsidies maintained by the richer nations and the industrial subsidies enforced by developing nations.

As we see later in the chapter, the challenges facing a resolution at Doha go beyond the typical developed/developing country differences and include differences between different groups of developing countries. Despite continued trade talks, the parties have remained deadlocked on the issue, with Brazil and India—representing their alliance of developing nations known as the "Group of 22"—walking out of negotiations in frustration on several occasions.

Despite these advances, deadlines to conclude the round in both 2005 and 2006 were missed, and fears of further prolonged negotiations and pressure to reach an agreement have been steadily increasing. Following the failure in recent talks, WTO negotiators in Geneva who are overseeing the agricultural negotiations have begun drawing up draft proposals on the subsidies in hopes of providing a viable framework to bring the round to a successful conclusion.[4] Still, the Doha Round's effectiveness and the WTO's ability to handle the large number of interests and issues presented in it have been called into question, and many countries have even begun looking for alternative methods of reaching their trade goals.

The Rise of Bilateral Agreements

Bilateral agreements can be between two individual countries or may involve one country dealing with a group of other countries.

As the negotiations over the Doha Round broke down, Brazil and the EU announced a proposed strategic alliance between them. The agreement would give Brazil the same trading status that China and Russia have with the EU and would initiate discussions in other areas, such as energy, climate change, and human rights. In a similar fashion, South Korea signed a free trade pact with the United States, and India began negotiating a deal with the EU.[5] These examples highlight the increasing willingness of individual countries to circumvent the multilateral system and engage in bilateral agreements, also known as *preferential trade agreements* (PTAs) or *free trade agreements* (FTAs), with each other to meet their global trade objectives.

The term *bilateral* is a little misleading. In most cases, the treaties involve two countries, such as a treaty between the United States and Australia. In other cases, the bilateral treaties involve one country with several other countries linked together in a free trade agreement. Because the EU negotiates trade as one trading block, its agreements with other countries, such as between the EU and Brazil, are technically bilateral agreements.

Another example of a bilateral agreement is the agreement between the United States and the Central American Free Trade Agreement–Dominican Republic (CAFTA-DR), even though the agreement really involves seven countries.[6] Bilateral agreements are relatively easier for countries to pursue than are agreements in the WTO because it is easier to resolve issues in a smaller setting.

In the capital of Bucharest, Romanian workers pass by the symbol of the European Union. After Romania joined the EU on January 1, 2007, citizens were permitted to travel among member nations using only national ID cards. Romanian workers, however, face work restrictions in some EU countries.

Regional Economic Integration

Going beyond the bilateral approach is the regional approach, called *regional trade agreements,* or RTAs. Not all are in force, but as of July 2007, 205 of the 380 registered RTAs were currently in operation. Taking into account RTAs that are enforced but have not yet been registered, those signed but not enforced, those being currently negotiated, and those in the proposal stage, nearly 400 RTAs are scheduled to be implemented by 2010.[7]

It's logical that most trade groups contain countries in the same area of the world. Neighboring countries tend to ally for several reasons:

- The distances that goods need to travel between such countries are short.
- Consumers' tastes are likely to be similar, and distribution channels can be easily established in adjacent countries.
- Neighboring countries may have a common history and interests, and they may be more willing to coordinate their policies.[8]

As also noted earlier, the major reason to establish a regional trade group is to increase market size. There are two basic types of regional economic integration from the standpoint of tariff policies:

- *Free Trade Agreement (FTA)*   The goal of an FTA is to abolish all tariffs between member countries. Free trade agreements usually begin modestly by eliminating tariffs on goods that already have low tariffs, and there is usually an implementation period during which all tariffs are eliminated on all products. In addition, each member country maintains its own external tariff against non-FTA countries.

> Regional trade agreements—integration confined to a region and involving more than two countries.

> Geographic proximity is an important reason for economic integration.

CONCEPT CHECK

In discussing *geographic distance* in Chapter 6, we observe that because greater distances ordinarily mean higher transportation costs, geographic proximity usually encourages trade cooperation. In the same chapter, we explain **country-similarity theory** by showing that, once a company has developed a new product in response to conditions in its home market, it will probably try to export it to those markets that it regards as most similar to its own.

Major types of economic integration:

• Free trade area—no internal tariffs.

• Customs union—no internal tariffs plus common external tariffs.

• Common market—customs union plus factor mobility.

Regional integration has social, cultural, political, and economic effects.

Static effects of integration—the shifting of resources from inefficient to efficient companies as trade barriers fall.

Dynamic effects of integration—the overall growth in the market and the impact on a company caused by expanding production and by the company's ability to achieve greater economies of scale.

CONCEPT CHECK

In Chapter 6, we define **comparative advantage** as the theory that global efficiency gains may result from trade *if* a country specializes in those products it can produce more efficiently than other products (regardless of whether other countries can produce the same products even more efficiently).

Trade creation—production shifts to more efficient producers for reasons of comparative advantage.

• *Customs Union*   In addition to eliminating internal tariffs, member countries levy a common external tariff on goods being imported from nonmembers. For example, the EU established a common external tariff in 1967. It had begun to remove internal tariffs in 1959, and that process was completed in 1967 at the same time the common external tariff was established. Now the EU negotiates as one region in the WTO rather than as separate countries. (Thus, as we observed in our opening case, when it came to import quotas on cars shipped to EU members, Japan had to negotiate with the EU as a whole, rather than with individual countries.) However, most trade gains come from membership in a free trade agreement, not a customs union, which is driven more by political than economic reasons.[9]

Common Market   Beyond the reduction of tariffs and nontariff barriers, countries can enhance their cooperation in a variety of other ways. The EU, for example, also allows free mobility of production factors such as labor and capital. This means that labor, for example, is free to work in any country in the common market without restriction. This type of cooperation where free mobility of factors of production is added to a customs union results in a **common market.** In the absence of the common market arrangement, workers from member countries would have to apply to immigration for a visa, and that might be difficult to come by.

In addition, the EU has harmonized its monetary policies through the creation of a common currency complete with a central bank. This level of cooperation creates a degree of political integration among member countries, which means they lose a bit of their sovereignty. Thus PTAs and RTAs generally start as free trade agreements and progress to customs unions, and then move to common market status as they add free trade in services and investment.

THE EFFECTS OF INTEGRATION

Regional economic integration can affect member countries in social, cultural, political, and economic ways. Initially, however, our focus is on the economic rationale for regional integration. As we noted in Chapter 7, the imposition of tariff and nontariff barriers disrupts the free flow of goods, affecting resource allocation.

Static and Dynamic Effects   Regional economic integration reduces or eliminates those barriers for member countries. It produces both *static effects* and *dynamic effects*. **Static effects** are the shifting of resources from inefficient to efficient companies as trade barriers fall. **Dynamic effects** are the overall growth in the market and the impact on a company caused by expanding production and by the company's ability to achieve greater economies of scale. As shown in Figure 8.1, free trade agreements result in static and dynamic effects on trade and investment flows.

Static effects may develop when either of two conditions occurs:

1. *Trade creation:*   Production shifts to more efficient producers for reasons of comparative advantage, allowing consumers access to more goods at a lower price than would have been possible without integration. Companies protected in their domestic markets face real problems when the barriers are eliminated and they attempt to compete with more efficient producers.

   The strategic implication is that companies that might not have been able to export to another country—even though they might be more efficient than producers in that country—are now able to export when the barriers come down. Thus there will be more demand for their products, and the demand for the protected, less efficient products will fall. Also, it is possible that investment might shift to countries that are more efficient or that have a comparative advantage in one or more of the factors of production.

2. *Trade diversion:*   Trade shifts to countries in the group at the expense of trade with countries not in the group, even though the nonmember companies might be more efficient in the absence of trade barriers.

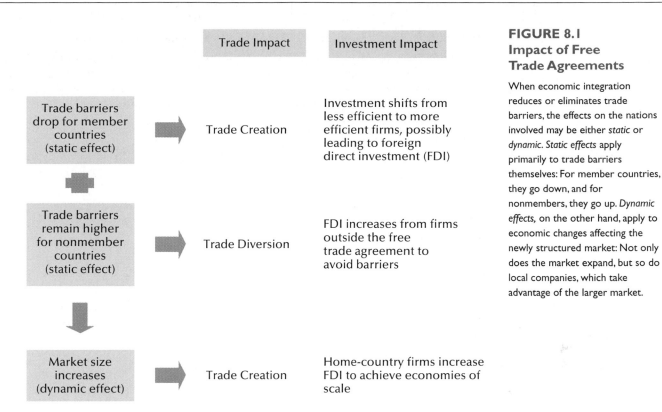

	Trade Impact	Investment Impact
Trade barriers drop for member countries (static effect)	Trade Creation	Investment shifts from less efficient to more efficient firms, possibly leading to foreign direct investment (FDI)
Trade barriers remain higher for nonmember countries (static effect)	Trade Diversion	FDI increases from firms outside the free trade agreement to avoid barriers
Market size increases (dynamic effect)	Trade Creation	Home-country firms increase FDI to achieve economies of scale

FIGURE 8.1
Impact of Free Trade Agreements

When economic integration reduces or eliminates trade barriers, the effects on the nations involved may be either *static* or *dynamic. Static effects* apply primarily to trade barriers themselves: For member countries, they go down, and for nonmembers, they go up. *Dynamic effects,* on the other hand, apply to economic changes affecting the newly structured market: Not only does the market expand, but so do local companies, which take advantage of the larger market.

For example, assume that U.S. companies are importing the same product from Mexico and Taiwan. If the United States enters into an FTA with Mexico but not with Taiwan, these companies might be more likely to import goods from Mexico than from Taiwan due to lower tariffs. Also, MNEs from countries outside the FTA might consider investing in the FTA countries to service the market more effectively.

Trade diversion—trade shifts to countries in the group at the expense of trade with countries not in the group.

Economies of Scale   Dynamic effects of integration occur when trade barriers come down and the size of the market increases. Because of the larger size of the market, companies can increase their production, which will result in lower costs per unit, a phenomenon we call **economies of scale.** Companies can produce more cheaply, which is good because they must become more efficient to survive. This could result in more trade between the member countries (trade creation) or an increase in FDI as the market increases and it becomes feasible for MNEs to invest in the larger market.

Economies of scale—the average cost per unit falls as the number of units produced rises; occurs in regional integration because of the growth in the market size.

Increased Competition   Another important effect of the FTA is the increase in efficiency due to increased competition. Many MNEs in Europe have attempted to grow through mergers and acquisitions to achieve the size necessary to compete in the larger market. Companies in Mexico were forced to become more competitive with the passage of NAFTA due to competition from Canadian and U.S. companies. This could result in investment shifting from less efficient to more efficient companies, or it could result in existing companies becoming more efficient.

Major Regional Trading Groups

The two ways to look at different trading groups are by location and by type. Major trading groups exist in every region of the world. It is impossible to cover every group in every region, so we discuss a few of the major groups. Each regional group is either a free trade agreement or a customs union, but several, such as the EU, are also common markets that are organized for political as well as economic reasons.

Companies are interested in regional trading groups for their markets, sources of raw materials, and production locations. The larger and richer the new market, the more likely it is to attract the attention of the major investor countries and companies.

European Union:

- Changed from the European Economic Community to the European Community to the European Union.
- The largest and most successful regional trade group.
- Free trade of goods, services, capital, and people.
- Common external tariff.
- Common currency.

THE EUROPEAN UNION

The largest and most comprehensive regional economic group is the **European Union.** It began as a free trade agreement with the goal to become a customs union and to integrate in other ways. The formation of the European Parliament and the establishment of a common currency, the euro, make the EU the most ambitious of all the regional trade groups.[10] Table 8.1 summarizes the key milestones for the EU, and Map 8.2 identifies the members of the EU and other key European groups.

TABLE 8.1   European Union Milestones

From its inception in 1957, the EU has been moving toward complete economic integration. However, it is doubtful that its initial adherents ever dreamed that European cooperation would have achieved such integration as to move to a common currency.

1946	Winston Churchill calls for a United States of Europe.
1948	The Organization for European Economic Cooperation (OEEC) is created to coordinate the Marshall Plan.
1951	The Six (Belgium, France, Germany, Italy, Luxembourg, the Netherlands) sign the Treaty of Paris establishing the European Coal and Steel Community (ECSC) to begin in 1952.
1957	The Six sign the Treaties of Rome establishing the European Economic Community (EEC) and the European Atomic Energy Community (Euratom or EAEC). They become effective on January 1, 1958.
1959	The first steps are taken in the progressive abolition of customs duties and quotas within the EEC.
1960	The Stockholm Convention establishes the European Free Trade Association (EFTA) among seven European countries (Austria, Denmark, Norway, Portugal, Sweden, Switzerland, the United Kingdom). The OEEC becomes the Organization for Economic Cooperation and Development (OECD).
1961	The first regulation on free movement of workers within the EEC comes into force.
1962	The Common Agricultural Policy is adopted.
1965	A treaty merging the ECSC, EEC, and Euratom is signed. The treaty enters into force on July 1, 1967.
1966	Agreement is reached on a value-added tax (VAT) system; a treaty merging the Executives of the European Communities comes into force; and the EEC changes its name to European Community (EC).
1967	All remaining internal tariffs are eliminated, and a common external tariff is imposed.
1972	The currency "snake" is established in which the Six agree to limit currency fluctuations between their currencies to 2.25 percent.
1973	Denmark, Ireland, and the United Kingdom become members of the EC.
1979	European Monetary System comes into effect; European Parliament is elected by universal suffrage for the first time.
1980	Greece becomes the tenth member of the EC.
1985	Commission sends the Council a White Paper on completion of internal market by 1992.
1986	Spain and Portugal become the eleventh and twelfth members of the EC. Single European Act (SEA) is signed, improving decision-making procedures and increasing the role of the European Parliament; comes into effect on July 1, 1987.
1989	Collapse of the Berlin Wall; German Democratic Republic opens its borders.
1990	The first phase of European Monetary Union (EMU) comes into effect. Unification of Germany.
1992	European Union signed in Maastricht; adopted by member countries on November 1, 1993.
1993	The Single European Market comes into force (January 1, 1993).
	Council concludes agreement creating European Economic Area, effective January 1, 1994.
1995	Austria, Finland, Sweden become the thirteenth, fourteenth, and fifteenth members of the EU.
1996	An EU summit names the 11 countries that will join the European single currency with all EU countries joining but Britain, Sweden, Denmark (by their choice), and Greece (not ready).
1999	The euro, the single European currency, comes into effect (January 1, 1999).
2001	Greece becomes the twelfth country to adopt the euro (January 1, 2001).
2002	The euro coins and notes enter circulation (January 1, 2002).
	The EU announces 10 new countries to join the EU in May 2004 (October 2002).
	All 15 member states ratify the Kyoto Protocol.
2004	Admission of Cyprus, the Czech Republic, Estonia, Hungary, Latvia, Lithuania, Malta, Poland, Slovakia, Slovenia, bringing number of member states to 25.
2007	Bulgaria and Romania join, bringing number of member states to 27. Candidate countries are Croatia, Former Yugoslav Republic of Macedonia, and Turkey.

Source: European Union, "The History of the European Union," at http://europe.eu.int (accessed July 2007). © European Communities, 1995–2007. Reprinted with permission.

MAP 8.2 European Trade and Economic Integration

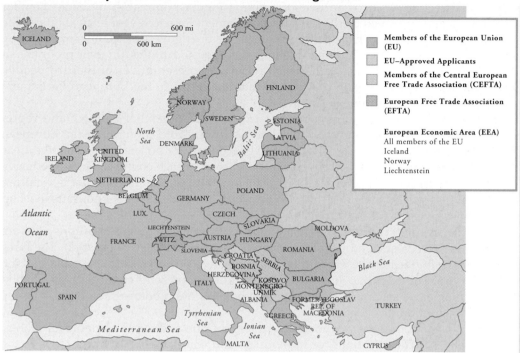

Legend:
- Members of the European Union (EU)
- EU–Approved Applicants
- Members of the Central European Free Trade Association (CEFTA)
- European Free Trade Association (EFTA)

European Economic Area (EEA)
All members of the EU
Iceland
Norway
Liechtenstein

Although the 27-member EU is easily the dominant trading bloc in Europe, it's not the only one. Founded in 1960, the four-member European Free Trade Association (EFTA) also maintains joint free trade agreements with several other countries. The European Economic Area (EEA) includes three members of the EFTA and all members of the EU. The Central European Free Trade Agreement (CEFTA) was originally formed to integrate Western practices into the economics of former Soviet bloc nations, two of whom have already been admitted into the EU.

Predecessors Because of the economic and human destruction left by World War II, European political leaders realized that greater cooperation among their countries would help speed up recovery. Many organizations were formed, including the European Economic Community (EEC), which eventually emerged as the organization that would bring together the countries of Europe into the most powerful trading bloc in the world. Several other countries, including the United Kingdom, formed the European Free Trade Association (EFTA) with the limited goal of eliminating internal tariffs, but most of those countries eventually became part of the EU, and those that have decided not to leave EFTA (Iceland, Liechtenstein, Norway, and Switzerland) are linked together with the EU as a customs union.

The EEC, later called the European Community (EC) and finally the European Union (EU), set about to abolish internal tariffs to integrate European markets more closely and ideally allow economic cooperation to help avoid further political conflict.

Organizational Structure The EU encompasses many governing bodies, among which are the European Commission, the Council of the European Union, European Parliament, the European Court of Justice, and the European Central Bank. Details about all of the governing bodies can be found on the official EU Web site at http://europa.eu, so we focus briefly on only the key bodies just mentioned. The European Central Bank, an important institution governing certain financial activities in the EU, is discussed briefly in Chapter 10.

In Chapter 3, we noted how important it is for MNE management to understand the political environment of every country where it operates. The same is true for the EU. To be successful in Europe, MNEs need to understand the governance of the EU, just as they need to understand the governance process of each of the individual European countries in which they are investing or doing business. These institutions set parameters under which companies must operate, so management needs to understand the institutions and how they make decisions that could affect corporate strategy. Recall from our opening case, for example, how EU policies shaped Toyota's corporate strategy in the region, inducing it to shift from limited exporting to the establishment of full design and manufacturing facilities.

CONCEPT CHECK

In Chapter 6, we discuss the **theory of country size,** which holds that large countries usually depend less on trade than small countries. The same principle tends to be true of economic blocs, and here we point out that **regional integration** is one way to achieve the size necessary to reduce members' dependence on trade.

European Free Trade Association—FTA involving Iceland, Liechtenstein, Norway, and Switzerland with close ties to the EU.

Case Review Note

The European Commission provides political leadership, drafts laws, and runs the various daily programs of the EU.

The Council of the European Union or European Summit is composed of the heads of state of each member country.

The three major responsibilities of the European Parliament are legislative power, control over the budget, and supervision of executive decisions.

The European Court of Justice ensures consistent interpretation and application of EU treaties.

The Single European Act was designed to eliminate the remaining nontariff barriers to trade in Europe.

The Treaty of Maastricht sought to foster political union and monetary union.

The euro

- Is a common currency in Europe.
- Is administered by the European Central Bank.
- Was established on January 1, 1999.
- Resulted in new bank notes in 2002.
- Does not include the United Kingdom, Denmark, Sweden, or the 11 new entrants to the EU as of 2007.

The EU expanded from 15 to 25 countries in 2004 with countries from mostly Central and Eastern Europe. In 2007 it admitted Romania and Bulgaria, bringing the number to 27.

Key Governing Bodies   The European Commission provides the EU's political leadership and direction. It is composed of commissioners nominated by each member government and approved by the European Parliament for a five-year term of office. The president of the commission is nominated by the member governments and approved by the European Parliament. The commission is designed to run the different programs of the EU on a day-to-day basis rather than serve as representatives of their respective governments. The commission drafts laws that it submits to the European Parliament and the Council of the European Union.

The council is composed of representatives of each member country and represents the interests of the country. The council is responsible, along with the European Parliament, for passing laws and making and enacting major policies, including the areas of security and foreign policy. The respective ministers of each country meet periodically to discuss the issues facing those ministries. For example, the ministers of agriculture meet to discuss issues facing agriculture. The presidents and/or prime ministers meet up to four times a year to set broad policy.

The Parliament is composed of 785 members from all 27 member nations who are elected every five years, and its membership is based on country population. The three major responsibilities of the Parliament are legislative power, control over the budget, and supervision of executive decisions. The commission presents community legislation to the Parliament. Parliament must approve the legislation before submitting it to the council for adoption.[11]

The Court of Justice ensures consistent interpretation and application of EU treaties. Member states, EC institutions, or individuals and companies may bring cases to the Court. The Court of Justice is an appeals court for individuals, firms, and organizations fined by the commission for infringing treaty law.[12] The Court of Justice is relevant to MNEs because it deals mostly with economic matters, especially in the area of possible antitrust violation.

The Single European Act   The passage of the Single European Act of 1987 was designed to eliminate the remaining barriers to a free market, such as customs posts, different certification procedures, rates of value-added tax, and excise duties. In addition, the Single European Act resulted in closer cooperation in trade (the EU has one negotiator for the WTO who negotiates for all members of the EU), foreign policy, and the environment.

Monetary Union: The Euro   In 1992, the members of the EU signed the Treaty of Maastricht in part to establish a monetary union. The decision to move to a common currency in Europe, the **euro,** has eliminated currency as a barrier to trade for the member countries that have adopted it. However, not all have adopted the euro. In fact, as of June 2007, only 13 of the 27 members of the EU had adopted the euro (on July 10, 2007, Malta and Cyprus were approved by the EU to adopt the euro in January 2008).

The countries that adopted the euro at its launch were Austria, Belgium, Germany, Finland, France, Ireland, Italy, Luxembourg, the Netherlands, Portugal, and Spain. Greece adopted the euro on January 1, 2001. All these countries introduced the euro in cash form at the beginning of 2002. Of the 15 members of the EU prior to the expansion in 2004, only the United Kingdom, Denmark, and Sweden elected not to adopt the euro. On January 1, 2007, Slovenia became the first of the new members that joined in 2004 to adopt the euro. The other new members (except for Malta and Cyprus) have not yet qualified, but they can after meeting certain criteria.

Expansion   One of the EU's major challenges is that of expansion. The May 2004 expansion has been its largest and included Cyprus, the Czech Republic, Estonia, Hungary, Latvia, Lithuania, Malta, Poland, the Slovak Republic, and Slovenia. Bulgaria and Romania were admitted at the beginning of 2007, and candidates for future membership currently include Turkey, the former Yugoslav Republic of Macedonia, and Croatia. However, Turkey has been put on hold while it continues to improve its human rights record.

Old and New Members The acquisition of the 12 new countries increased the EU's population and added economic output, but the expansion added countries that are poor, have fledgling democracies, and depend greatly on agriculture—as much as 10 percent of GDP, compared with only 2.6 percent on average in the EU. They will thus strain the EU's financial resources. The new member states are coming in with lower wages and lower taxes, but with two to four times the growth rates of the original 15 members.

In spite of the growth rates, many people from the new countries are trying to immigrate to the higher-income countries, creating some real challenges. People from the new member countries are denied unlimited freedom to work anywhere they want in the EU until 2010, giving the older member countries time to gear up for the rise in immigration. The United Kingdom, Ireland, and Sweden are the only EU countries that have given guest workers from the 12 new countries permission to work inside their national boundaries. For the United Kingdom alone, this has resulted in an influx of nearly 638,000 immigrants from the 12 recently added members.[13]

Table 8.2 illustrates the differences in the old and new members of the EU in terms of population and per capital GNI. The four most powerful members of the EU—France, Germany, Italy, and the United Kingdom—have 53.6 percent of the population and generate 66.6 percent of the GNI. However, the new countries already rely heavily on the EU for trade. For example, 84.1 percent of the Czech Republic's exports and 77.2 percent of Poland's exports go to EU countries. This compares with 63.4 percent for Germany, 56.6 percent for the United Kingdom, 65 percent for France, and 75 percent for the Netherlands.

Again, this points out earlier how important regional trade groups are to the member countries and how much that affects trade and investment decisions of MNEs and other companies doing business in the EU. As noted in Table 8.2, the continued expansion of the EU has increased its size and importance relative to NAFTA, which is dominated economically by the United States and discussed later.

Bilateral Agreements In addition to the reduction of trade barriers for member countries, the EU has signed numerous bilateral free trade agreements with other countries outside of the European region. As mentioned earlier, in 2007 the EU announced a proposal for a strategic partnership with Brazil. Similar partnerships and free trade agreements have been signed with other countries.

Closer to home, the EU entered into an agreement with the members of the European Free Trade Association, with the exception of Switzerland, to form the European Economic Area (EEA). The three EFTA countries participate in the basic four freedoms with the EU: freedom of movement of goods (excluding agriculture and fisheries, which are included in the agreement only to a very limited extent), persons, services, and capital. The difference between the EEA and the expansion of the EU is that the members of the EFTA are not interested in complete membership in the EU but just want to take advantage of the free flow of food, labor, services, and capital.

How to Do Business with the EU: Implications for Corporate Strategy The EU is a tremendous market in terms of both population and income, and so it is one that companies cannot ignore. In addition, the EU is a good example of how geographic proximity and the removal of trade barriers can influence trade. As noted earlier, more than half of the merchandise exports and imports of EU countries are considered to be intrazonal trade.

Doing business in the EU can influence corporate strategy, especially for non-EU MNEs, in these three ways:

1. *Determine where to produce products.* One strategy is to produce products in a central location in Europe to minimize transportation costs and the time it takes to move products from one country to another. However, the highest costs are in central Europe. As we saw in our opening case, for instance, manufacturing wages in the German auto industry top $40 per hour, compared with much lower wages in Eastern European members of the EU. That's why Toyota opted to set up operations in lower-wage countries such as the Czech Republic and Poland.

CONCEPT CHECK

In Chapter 6, we point out that, in countries where *labor* is abundant compared to *capital*, many workers (not surprisingly) tend to be either unemployed or poorly paid. If permitted, they will migrate to countries that enjoy full employment and higher wages— a form of **factor mobility** that governments in the latter group of countries often restrict.

CONCEPT CHECK

As you'll recall from Chapter 6, trade restrictions may diminish export capabilities and induce companies to locate some production in countries imposing the restrictions; the absence of trade barriers gives them more flexibility not only in deciding where to locate production but also in determining how to service different markets.

Case Review Note

TABLE 8.2   Comparative Statistics by Trade Group

EU Member Countries	Population in Millions (2005)	GNI Billions of $(2005)	Per Capita GNI in $(2005)
Austria	8	303.6	36,980
Belgium	10	373.8	35,700
Denmark	5	256.8	47,390
Finland	5	196.5	37,460
France	61	2,177.7	34,810
Germany	82	2,852.3	34,580
Greece	11	218.1	19,670
Ireland	4	166.6	40,150
Italy	57	1,724.9	30,010
Luxembourg	0.5	35.1	76,040
Netherlands	16	598.0	36,620
Portugal	11	170.0	16,170
Spain	43	1,100.1	25,360
Sweden	9	370.5	41,060
United Kingdom	60	2,263.7	37,600
Cyprus	1	13.6	18,430
Czech Republic	10	109.2	10,710
Estonia	1	12.2	9,100
Hungary	10	101.2	10,030
Latvia	2	15.1	6,760
Lithuania	3	24.1	7,050
Malta	0.4	5.5	13,610
Poland	38	271.4	7,110
Slovakia	5	42.8	7,950
Slovenia	2	34.7	17,350
Bulgaria	8	26.7	3,450
Romania	22	82.9	3,830
Turkey	73	342.2	4,710
Macedonia FYR	2	5.8	2,830
Croatia	4	35.8	8,060
E-15	382.5	12,807.7	36,640
E-10 2004 Admits	72.4	629.8	10,810
E-2 2007 Admits	30	109.6	3,640
E-27 (E-15, E-2, E-10)	484.9	13,547.1	17,030
E-30	563.9	13,930.9	8,158
NAFTA Member Countries			
Canada	32	1,051.9	32,600
Mexico	103	753.4	7,310
United States	296	12,969.6	43,740
Total	431	14,774.9	27,883
MERCOSUR Member Countries			
Argentina	39	173.0	4,470
Brazil	186	644.1	3,460
Paraguay	6	7.9	1,280
Uruguay	3	15.1	4,360
Venezuela*	27	127.8	4,810
Total	261	967.9	3,676

*As of October 1, 2007, the congresses of Uruguay and Argentina have voted to accept Venezuela, but the congresses of Brazil and Paraguay have not.

Source: Emmanual Y. Jimenez, *World Bank Development Report.* © The International Bank for Reconstruction and Development/The World Bank, 2006. Reproduced with permission of The World Bank in the format textbook via Copyright Clearance Center.

2. *Determine whether to grow through new investments, through expanding existing invest-ments, or through joint ventures and mergers.*   As we've seen, Toyota, in order to take advantage of the European carmaker's supplier network, has entered into a joint venture with PSA Peugeot-Citroën to build a new factory in the Czech Republic. However, mergers and acquisitions have really picked up in Europe. The market in Europe is still considered fragmented and inefficient compared with the United States, so most experts feel that mergers, takeovers, and spinoffs will continue in Europe for years to come. U.S. companies are buying European companies to gain a market presence and to get rid of competition.

3. *Balance "common" denominators with national differences.*   There are wider national differences in the EU than in the different states in the United States, mostly due to language and history. But there are also widely different growth rates in the EU. Many smaller nations, such as Ireland and Belgium, are experiencing unprecedented growth because their membership in the EU has increased their attractiveness for FDI, helped them develop global perspectives, and sheltered them from economic risks.

Meanwhile, the larger countries of Germany, Europe's biggest economy and histori-cally the engine for economic growth in Europe, and France have been faced with stag-nant growth and high unemployment.[14] And what about Toyota? In terms of products, Toyota is busy designing a European car, but for which Europe? Tastes and preferences—not to mention climate—vary greatly between northern and southern Europe. Toyota, however, is attempting to use production location and design to facilitate a pan-European strategy.

Companies will always struggle with the degree to which they develop a European strategy versus different national strategies inside Europe. In spite of the challenges, there are many opportunities for companies to expand their markets and sources of supply as the EU grows and encompasses more of Europe.

THE NORTH AMERICAN FREE TRADE AGREEMENT (NAFTA)

The **North American Free Trade Agreement (NAFTA),** which includes Canada, Mexico, and the United States, went into effect in 1994. The United States and Canada historically have had various forms of mutual economic cooperation. They signed the Canada-U.S. Free Trade Agreement effective January 1, 1989, which eliminated all tariffs on bilateral trade by January 1, 1998. In February 1991, Mexico approached the United States to estab-lish a free trade agreement. The formal negotiations that began in June 1991 included Canada. The resulting North American Free Trade Agreement became effective on January 1, 1994.

Why NAFTA?   NAFTA has a logical rationale, in terms of both geographic location and trading importance. Although Canadian–Mexican trade was not significant when the agreement was signed, U.S.–Mexican trade and U.S.–Canadian trade were. The two-way trading relationship between the United States and Canada is the largest in the world. As we indicate in Table 8.2 (p. 308), NAFTA is a powerful trading bloc with a combined pop-ulation greater than the 15-member EU and GNI greater than the 27-member EU. What is significant, especially when compared with the EU, is the tremendous size of the U.S. economy in comparison with those of Canada and Mexico. In addition, Canada has a much richer economy than that of Mexico, even though its population is about a third that of Mexico.

Even though NAFTA is a free trade agreement instead of a customs union or a com-mon market, its cooperation extends far beyond reductions in tariff and nontariff barriers, including provisions for services, investment, and intellectual property. In addition, the agreement establishes a new dispute resolution process.

Implications of the EU for corporate strategy:
* Companies need to determine where to produce products.
* Companies need to determine what their entry strategy will be.
* Companies need to balance the commonness of the EU with national differences.

The North American Free Trade Agreement
* Includes Canada, the United States, and Mexico.
* Went into effect on January 1, 1994.
* Involves free trade in goods, services, and investment.
* Is a large trading bloc but includes countries of different sizes and wealth.

NAFTA rationale:
* U.S.-Canadian trade is the largest bilateral trade in the world.
* The United States is Mexico's and Canada's largest trading partner.

Mexico made significant strides in tariff reduction after joining GATT in 1986. At that time, its tariffs averaged 100 percent. Since then, it has reduced tariffs dramatically. As a result of NAFTA, most tariffs on originating goods traded between Mexico and Canada were eliminated immediately or phased in over a 10-year period that ended on December 31, 2003. In a few exceptions, the phaseout period will be completed by the end of 2008. Tariffs between the United States and Mexico were, in general, either eliminated immediately or over a 5- or 10-year period that ended on December 31, 2003. In the first five years after passage of the agreement, Mexico trimmed its average tariff on U.S. goods from 10 percent to 2 percent, and U.S. tariffs on Mexican products dropped to less than 1 percent.[15]

Static and Dynamic Effects   NAFTA provides the static and dynamic effects of economic integration discussed earlier in this chapter. For example, Canadian and U.S. consumers benefit from lower-cost agricultural products from Mexico, a static effect of economic liberalization. U.S. producers also benefit from the large and growing Mexican market, which has a huge appetite for U.S. products—a dynamic effect.

NAFTA is a good example of trade diversion; some U.S. trade with and investment in Asia have been diverted to Mexico.

Trade Diversion   In addition, NAFTA is a good example of trade diversion. Many U.S. and Canadian companies have established manufacturing facilities in Asia to take advantage of cheap labor. Now, U.S. and Canadian companies can establish manufacturing facilities in Mexico rather than in Asian countries to take advantage of relatively cheap labor. For example, IBM is making computer parts in Mexico that were formerly made in Singapore. In five years, IBM boosted exports from Mexico to the United States from $350 million to $2 billion. Had the subassemblies not been made in and exported from Mexico, they would have been made in Singapore and other Asian locations and exported to the United States.

Gap Inc. and Liz Claiborne are increasingly buying garments from Mexican contractors, who can offer faster delivery than Asian contractors. RC Willey, the U.S. furniture retailer, also imports furniture from Mexico as well as from China rather than importing everything from China because of the reduction of tariff barriers and close proximity to Mexico.[16]

Rules of Origin and Regional Content   An important component of NAFTA is the concept of rules of origin and regional content. Because NAFTA is a free trade agreement and not a customs union, each country sets its own tariffs to the rest of the world. That's why a product entering the United States from Canada must have a commercial or customs invoice that identifies the product's ultimate origin. Otherwise, an exporter from a third country would always ship the product to the NAFTA country with the lowest tariff and then reexport it to the other two countries duty-free.

Rules of origin—goods and services must originate in North America to get access to lower tariffs.

Rules of Origin   "Rules of origin" ensure that only goods that have been the subject of substantial economic activity within the free trade area are eligible for the more liberal tariff conditions created by NAFTA. This is a major contrast with the European Union, which is a customs union rather than just a free trade agreement. When a product enters France, for example, it can be shipped anywhere in the EU without worrying about rules of origin because tariffs are the same for all EU member countries. If NAFTA was a customs union instead of a free trade agreement, a product entering Mexico from Japan, for example, and shipped to the United States would enter duty-free into the United States because the United States and Mexico would have the same duty on imports.[17]

Regional content:

- The percentage of value that must be from North America for the product to be considered North American in terms of country of origin.
- 50 percent for most products; 62.5 percent for autos.

Rules of Regional Content   According to regional content rules, at least 50 percent of the net cost of most products must come from the NAFTA region. The exceptions are 55 percent for footwear, 62.5 percent for passenger automobiles and light trucks and the engines and transmissions for such vehicles, and 60 percent for other vehicles and automotive parts.[18] For example, a Ford car assembled in Mexico could use parts from Canada, the United States, and Mexico, as well as labor and other factors from Mexico. For the car to enter Canada and the United States according to the preferential NAFTA duty, at least 62.5 percent of its value must come from North America.

Special Provisions Most free trade agreements in the world are based solely on one goal: to reduce tariffs. However, NAFTA is a very different free trade agreement. Because labor unions and environmentalists strongly objected to the agreement, two auxiliary agreements covering those issues were included in NAFTA. When first debating NAFTA, opponents worried about the potential loss of jobs in Canada and the United States to Mexico as a result of Mexico's cheaper wages, poor working conditions, and lax environmental enforcement.

NAFTA opponents, particularly U.S. union organizers, thought companies would close down factories in the north and set them up in Mexico. As a result, the labor lobby in the United States forced the inclusion of labor standards, such as the right to unionize, and the environmental lobby pushed for an upgrade of environmental standards in Mexico and the strengthening of compliance. This is a challenge internationally because not all countries care about labor and environmental standards. The United States often uses trade agreements to advance political and moral objectives. When China enters into a preferential trade agreement with other countries, it does not include labor, environmental, or moral objectives in the agreements, so it is easier for countries to enter into trade agreements with China than with the United States.[19] As the cartoon in Figure 8.2 suggests, however, the prospect of unrestricted trade with a partner as productive as China may not be as rosy as some nations would like.

The Impact of NAFTA There are pros and cons to any trade agreement, and NAFTA is no exception. It is obvious that trade and investment in NAFTA have increased significantly since the agreement was signed in 1994. The trading relationship between the United States and Canada is the largest bilateral flow between two countries of goods, services, and income in the world, reaching nearly $533 billion. Canada is the largest export market for U.S. goods, and Mexico is number two, although the EU as a whole is the second largest destination for U.S. goods after Canada. Canada, China, and Mexico are the top three exporters to the United States, although the EU as a whole exports more to the United States than Canada does.

FIGURE 8.2
Fortune Cookies Love Trade with China

Once China joined the WTO, Chinese marketers were ready to make overtures to consumers around the world. (The Chinese, by the way, don't make or eat many fortune cookies, which are regarded as foreign. They actually import some, but hardly enough to threaten the country's massive trade surplus.)

Source: The New Yorker, July 18, 1994, Mick Stevens, the Cartoonbank.

It's important to note the importance of the United States to both Canada and Mexico. Canada exports 83.9 percent of its merchandise to the United States and imports 56.5 percent of its merchandise from the United States. Mexico exports 85.8 percent of its merchandise to the United States and imports 53.6 percent of its merchandise from the United States. Although trade between Canada and Mexico has increased since the implementation of NAFTA, the U.S. market still remains the most significant market for Canadian and Mexican firms because of its size.

Wages, Investment, and Labor   The United States is more diversified in terms of its trade relationships, but it still relies on its NAFTA partners for 36.7 percent of its merchandise exports and 26.8 percent of its merchandise imports.[20] As noted earlier in the chapter, this is in contrast with the EU, where intrazonal trade is above 50 percent for all countries.

Because of low wages in Mexico, U.S. companies invested significantly in Mexico. It is complicated to determine wage rates, however, due to factors such as exchange rates and trying to identify comparable wage rates. The Bureau of Labor Statistics reported that the hourly compensation costs in U.S. dollars for production workers in manufacturing in 2005 was $2.63 for Mexican workers, compared with $23.65 for U.S. workers and $23.82 for Canadian workers.[21] Whether or not the numbers are accurate, it is easy to see the magnitude of the difference. As MNEs assess where to locate production facilities, they can't ignore the wage differences.

FDI from the United States to Mexico has averaged around $12 billion per year since the passage of NAFTA, and the United States has accounted for about 62 percent of all FDI into Mexico during that period.[22] Not only has that resulted in the inflow of capital, but it has also brought with it technology, management skill, and access to international markets. The rise of FDI and the increase in Mexican exports has helped raise Mexico's per capita income as well. Mexico's per capita income rose to $7,310 in 2005, compared with only $1,740 in China, and was higher than in any other country in Latin America, including Brazil.[23]

The investment and employment pictures are complicated. One concern for U.S. workers when the agreement was being debated was that investment would move to Mexico because of that country's lower wages and lax environmental standards. When NAFTA was signed, companies like IBM and Canon began investing in Mexico instead of Asia for certain types of manufacturing. They could enjoy many tax and tariff exemptions, labor was plentiful and cheap, and high U.S. demand was just miles away. Foreign investment in Mexico rose from $4 billion per year in 1993 to $11.8 billion per year in 1999.[24]

In 2001, however, when NAFTA required Mexico to strip the *maquiladoras* (companies on the Mexican border) of their duty-free status, foreign companies started looking elsewhere. This was also compounded by the weakening U.S. economy and the stronger peso. Companies like Sanyo, Canon, and French battery producer Saft left Mexico and relocated to China, Vietnam, and Guatemala, where labor is cheaper.[25] In addition, now that China has opened up its market to more foreign investment as it becomes a part of the WTO, Mexicans are concerned that foreign investment is being diverted to China to take advantage of even lower manufacturing wages and generous incentives.

Even though employment in the *maquiladora* factories has dropped by more than 20 percent since 2000, Mexico is still an attractive market for investment. Although U.S. FDI to Mexico dropped after 1999 and 2000, Mexico still had the largest stock of FDI of any country in Latin America or Asia, except for Japan. As you'll see in the case at the end of the chapter, Wal-Mart is investing significantly in Mexico and is now the largest employer in Mexico.

Immigration   A major challenge to NAFTA is immigration. As trade in agriculture increased with the advent of NAFTA, it is estimated that 1.3 million farm jobs disappeared in Mexico due to competition from the United States. Many of these farmers ended up as illegal immigrants in the United States working in the agricultural and other sectors, sending home more money in wire transfers (see the opening case in Chapter 9) than Mexico receives in FDI. This has become a major political issue in both the United States and Mexico, especially as the United States tries to figure out how to stop the flow of illegal immigration and what to do with illegal immigrants already in the United States.

Additional NAFTA provisions:

• Workers' rights.

• The environment.

• Dispute resolution mechanism.

Case Review Note

A major challenge to NAFTA is illegal immigration.

How to Do Business with NAFTA: Implications for Corporate Strategy   Although NAFTA has not expanded beyond the original three countries due to political obstacles, each member of NAFTA has entered into bilateral agreements with other countries.

Predictions and Outcomes   Several predictions were made when NAFTA was signed. One prediction was that companies would look at NAFTA as one big regional market, allowing companies to rationalize production, products, financing, and the like. That has largely happened in a number of industries—especially in automotive products and in electronics (e.g., in computers). Each country in NAFTA ships more automotive products, based on specialized production, to the other two countries than any other manufactured goods. Employment has increased in the auto industry in the United States since NAFTA was established, even as it has declined in Mexico because of productivity.[26]

Rationalization of automotive production has taken place for years in the United States and Canada, but Mexico is a recent entrant. Auto manufacturing has moved into Mexico from all over the world. Over 500,000 Mexicans make parts and assemble vehicles for all of the world's major auto producers. NAFTA's rules of origin requiring 62.5 percent regional content have forced European and Asian automakers to bring in parts suppliers and set up assembly operations in Mexico.

In one case, a Canadian entrepreneur established a metal-stamping plant in Puebla, Mexico, to supply Volkswagen, the German auto manufacturer. The VW plant assembles the revitalized Beetle that is being supplied to the U.S. market.[27] DaimlerChrysler is producing 45,000 cars and 200,000 trucks in Mexico; between 80 and 90 percent of them are being exported to the United States and Canada. DaimlerChrysler began producing the PT Cruiser in Toluca, Mexico, for export to Canada, the United States, and Europe. It is using that one plant to manufacture one model for the entire world.

The story of DaimlerChrysler's production in the United States is similar. In 1993, Chrysler exported only 5,300 vehicles to Mexico. The following year, after the signing of NAFTA, it exported 17,500, and in 2000 it exported 60,000.[28] Because barriers to trade are next to zero in the NAFTA zone, companies can set up operations wherever it makes the most sense for them to do so and then easily ship their goods to any of the three countries.

The examples indicate how production is intertwined among the member countries. However, some companies are simply leaving the United States and Canada and moving to Mexico. This is happening in the apparel and furniture industries. Initially, NAFTA rules on apparel caused the Mexican textile industry to bring jobs back from Asia, and U.S. textile companies set up operations in Mexico to supply both the Mexican and U.S. apparel markets.

This is a good example of trade diversion being applied to investment—investment being diverted from Asia to NAFTA countries, especially Mexico. However, the labor cycle is turning again. Just as some companies left Asian countries like Malaysia and Singapore as labor rates increased, so too will they leave Mexico as wages increase. This is especially true because the apparel industry is moving to China to take advantage of the elimination of textile quotas by the WTO. Mexico hopes that the benefits of a closer U.S. market due to NAFTA will keep companies interested in investing, but the competition for investment will be fierce.

A second prediction was that sophisticated U.S. companies would run Canadian and Mexican companies out of business once the markets opened up. That has not happened. In fact, U.S. companies along the border of Canada are finding that Canadian companies are generating more competition for them than low-wage Mexican companies. Also, many Mexican companies have restructured to compete with U.S. and Canadian companies. The lack of protection has resulted in much more competitive Mexican firms. NAFTA has forced companies from all three countries to reexamine their strategies and determine how best to operate in the market.

However, as was discussed in the context of agriculture, some industries have been hard hit by U.S. competitors. And as we show in the Wal-Mart case at the end of the chapter, Mexican retailers have had a difficult time adjusting to giant competitors like Wal-Mart, Target, Costco, and Carrefour.

A final prediction had to do with looking at Mexico as a consumer market rather than just a production location. Initially, the excitement over Mexico for U.S. and Canadian

Case Review Note

companies was the low-wage environment. However, as Mexican income continues to rise—which it must do as more investment enters Mexico and more Mexican companies export production—demand is rising for foreign products. But U.S. and Canadian companies need to make the transition to Mexico as a significant final consumer market.

REGIONAL ECONOMIC INTEGRATION IN THE AMERICAS

If you look at Map 8.3 and Map 8.4, you'll see there are six major regional economic groups in the Americas. They can be divided into Central American and South American. In Central America (not including NAFTA member Mexico) are the Caribbean Community (CARI-COM), the Central American Common Market (CACM), and the Central American Free Trade Agreement (CAFTA-DR), which includes the members of CACM but also adds Honduras and the Dominican Republic, along with the United States. The two major groups in South America are the Andean Community (CAN) and the Southern Common Market (MERCOSUR). In addition, there's the proposed South American Community of Nations.

The major reason for these different groups in Central and South America entering into collaboration was market size. The post–World War II strategy of import substitution to resolve balance-of-payments problems in many of the markets in Latin America was doomed because of Latin America's small national markets. Therefore, some form of economic cooperation was needed to enlarge the potential market size so Latin American companies could achieve economies of scale and be more competitive worldwide.

CARICOM: Benchmarking the EU Model   The **Caribbean Community (CARICOM)** is working hard to establish an EU-style form of collaboration, complete with full movement of goods and services, the right of establishment, a common external tariff, free movement of capital, a common trade policy, free movement of labor, and so on. Many of these initiatives have come about through an initiative called the CARICOM single market and economy (CSME).

MAP 8.3   Economic Integration in Central America and the Caribbean

Throughout Central America and the Caribbean, the focus on economic integration has shifted from the concept of the *free trade agreement* (whose goal is the abolition of trade barriers among members) to that of the *common market* (which calls for internal factor mobility as well as the abolition of internal trade barriers). The proposed structure of the Caribbean Community and Common Market (CARICOM) is modeled on that of the EU.

MAP 8.4   Latin American Economic Integration

ANDEAN GROUP (CAN)
Bolivia
Colombia
Ecuador
Venezuela

MERCOSUR
Argentina
Brazil
Paraguay
Uruguay
Venezuela (Associate member)

SOUTH AMERICAN COMMUNITY OF NATIONS (CSN)
Argentina
Bolivia
Brazil
Chile
Colombia
Ecuador
Guyana
Paraguay
Peru
Suriname
Uruguay
Venezuela

The proposed structure of the South American Community of Nations (CSN), which combines the countries of MERCOSUR and those of the Andean Group (CAN), is modeled on that of the European Union: Plans call eventually for a common currency, legislature, and passport.

In some ways, the changes in the Caribbean Community mirror what has happened in the EU, although on a smaller scale. The entire population of the Caribbean Community is only 6.5 million people, and 60 percent of them live in only two countries: Jamaica and Trinidad and Tobago. That would put the entire Caribbean Community on the level of EU-member Bulgaria in terms of population. However, it is important for the Caribbean Community to succeed in order to expand market size and attract more investment and jobs.

The Challenge of Export Reliance   The problem is that Latin countries rely heavily on countries outside of the region for trade. For example, Jamaica, a member of the Caribbean Community, relies on the EU for 32 percent of its exports and the United States for 21.5 percent of its exports. Although Trinidad and Tobago is the second major source of imports into Jamaica, no other member of the Caribbean Community is significant to Jamaica as either a destination or a source for its exports. The United States buys 58.6 percent of the exports of Trinidad and Tobago, another member of the Caribbean Community, whereas its major sources of imports are the United States, Brazil, and the EU.

The same could be said for most of Latin America. The United States and EU represent significant markets for most countries in Latin America. A notable exception is in South America, where Brazil and Argentina, members of MERCOSUR, are major trading partners with each other.

MERCOSUR   The major trade group in South America is **MERCOSUR,** which was established in 1991 by Brazil, Argentina, Paraguay, and Uruguay. Its major goal is to become a customs union with free trade within the bloc and a common external tariff. Venezuela has

CONCEPT CHECK

In Chapter 6, we observe that little of the trade of low-income countries is conducted with other low-income countries. By and large, emerging economies rely heavily on trade with high-income countries, typically exporting primary and labor-intensive products in exchange for new and technologically advanced products.

Regional integration in Latin America has not been very successful, and countries rely more on the United States for trade than members of their own groups.

since joined, although by mid-2007, the governments of Brazil and Paraguay had not approved Venezuela's membership, meaning it is a full member but not quite approved.

Although both Map 8.4 and Table 8.2 (pp. 315 and 308, respectively) include Venezuela as a member of MERCOSUR, that could change in the future. In addition, Chile, Bolivia, Ecuador, and Peru have been added as associate members, meaning they have duty-free access to the MERCOSUR markets without getting involved in negotiations to complete the customs union phase of MERCOSUR.

MERCOSUR is a partial customs union among Argentina, Brazil, Paraguay, and Uruguay.

Size   MERCOSUR is significant because of its size: It has around 250 million people, a GDP of $1.1 trillion, and generates 75 percent of South America's GDP. That makes MERCOSUR the fourth largest trading bloc in the world after the EU, NAFTA, and the Association of Southeast Asian Nations (ASEAN). Progress has been slow in implementing the programs of MERCOSUR. It has neither eliminated internal barriers to trade nor completed the implementation of a common external tariff.

CONCEPT CHECK

Recall from Chapter 3 our admonition that political instability does more than merely complicate regional cooperation: It also contributes to **political risk**—the chance that political decisions, events, or conditions in a country will affect its business environment in ways that will cost investors some or all of the value of their investments.

Political Instability   As we mentioned earlier, economic and political instability in the region and poor political relations among the countries have complicated the process of achieving free trade and customs union status. Argentina's economic crisis in 2002 spilled over into Brazil and Uruguay and threatened the stability of the entire region. The dramatic fall in the value of the Argentine peso changed the trading structure in MERCOSUR, making Argentine products cheaper but making it more difficult for Argentine tourists to travel to the resort areas in Brazil or purchase Brazilian products. In addition, Brazilian President Lula da Silva has been increasingly visible on the world stage, trying to become the leader of the developing countries, and this has created strong resentment in Argentina.

The addition of Venezuela has altered the dynamic as Venezuela's president, Hugo Chávez, has voiced strong interest in solving the issues of the poor while not seeming to be very interested in trade and investment issues. Chávez's anti-American stance has the potential of turning MERCOSUR into a divisive political voice in the Americas.

The Andean Community is one of the original regional economic groups but has not been successful in achieving its original goals.

Andean Community (CAN)   Although the **Andean Community (CAN)** is not as significant economically as MERCOSUR, it is the second most important regional group in South America. CAN has been around since 1969. However, its focus has shifted from one of isolationism and statism (placing economic control in the hands of the state—the central government) to being open to foreign trade and investment. If Venezuela is finally approved as a member of MERCOSUR, it will have to leave CAN because members of MERCOSUR cannot be parties to other agreements. If other CAN nations, such as Bolivia, decide to join MERCOSUR, CAN will be further weakened and may eventually disappear.

The South American Community of Nations was organized in 2004 in an attempt to bring together CAN, MERCOSUR, Chile, Suriname, and Guyana.

South American Community of Nations (CSN)   In 2004, the members of CAN and MERCOSUR got together with other countries in South America to launch the 12-nation **South American Community of Nations (CSN)**, whose goals are to liberalize trade and eventually have a common currency, parliament, and passport. CSN will begin by phasing out tariffs between the member countries (CAN and MERCOSUR plus Chile, Suriname, and Guyana) and then moving to other areas of cooperation.[29]

Besides opening up more trade opportunities and linking the two major trade groups in South America, it is hoped that CSN will give the South American countries a larger voice in global trade talks. However, the heads of state of several countries, including Argentina, didn't even attend the organizational meeting, and most observers are not very optimistic about the success of CSN given that no other trade agreement in South America has been that successful to this point.

Note that Mexico, one of the major countries in Latin America, is not a part of CSN. This is largely because of Mexico's membership in NAFTA, which aligns it more closely with Canada and the United States, whereas CSN is trying to distance itself from the United States. Also, it would not be in Mexico's best interests to sour its relationship with the United States to align itself with CSN.

Point Counterpoint

Is CAFTA-DR a Good Idea?

Point **Yes** CAFTA-DR is a *great* idea. The Central American Free Trade Agreement and Dominican Republic will link together the United States with six other countries in a free trade agreement: five countries in Central America plus the Dominican Republic in the Caribbean. CAFTA-DR is an agreement that holds enormous benefits for both the United States and the nations that have signed it.

It will open the door for increased trade between the United States and the region and will stimulate economic growth in the region by encouraging foreign direct investment and by offering shorter international supply chains that CAFTA-DR companies will be able to more easily participate in. Furthermore, it will encourage not only economic reform but also political reform in an area historically plagued by Marxism, dictatorships, and civil wars.

One of the biggest benefits the United States has to gain is reciprocal tariff treatment from the participating nations. Due to temporary trade-preference programs and other regional agreements that are currently in place, 80 percent of the products from at least five Central American nations already enter the United States duty free. U.S. manufactured exports are subject to tariffs that average 30 to 100 percent higher than the tariffs Central American exports face when entering the United States.[30]

CAFTA-DR will allow the Central American nations to maintain these favorable gains but will level the playing field for the United States to benefit in a similar way by reducing restrictions on 80 percent of U.S. industrial exports and on more than 50 percent of its agricultural exports to the region. CAFTA-DR is now the second largest export market in Latin America for U.S. goods after Mexico and the tenth largest U.S. export market in the world.[31]

There's fear that the freer inflow of Central American agricultural products will undercut U.S. agricultural prices. However, as mentioned before, the United States is already largely open to these products, and although the heavily subsidized U.S. sugar industry adamantly opposed CAFTA-DR, the sugar deal will set a quota that will amount to only 1.7 percent of U.S. production in 15 years.

Many critics argue that the benefits certain CAFTA-DR countries gain will come at the expense of other participating countries, but in truth the gains will be mutual. For example, the growth that CAFTA-DR will foster in Central American industries, particularly its apparel industry, will also benefit exporters in the United States whose products are used in their manufacturing processes.

Fifty-six percent of the apparel exports from the Central American region are produced from textiles exported from

(continued)

Counterpoint **No** CAFTA-DR is *not* a good idea at all—not for the United States or for the impoverished nations it is allegedly supposed to help. Recently, much has been said about how the accord will boost trade between the two regions, support constructive economic and political reforms in Central America, create thousands of jobs, and demonstrate the benefits of free trade and open competition. However, there is neither the evidence to bear out these claims nor consideration for the consequences of the results.

The agreement will open the participating Central American countries to more duty-free exportation on behalf of U.S. manufacturers and farmers, but will this really translate into benefits for either side? The U.S. agricultural industry already can sell pretty much all the products it wants on the worldwide market; what it really needs is an increase in the worldwide market prices, but Central America's economies are too small to even affect world prices. Plus, the increased flow of U.S. corn and rice into Central America will devastate the region's own farm economies.

The idea that it will benefit the region by allowing increased imports to the United States is also faulty. Due to its giant deficit, the United States really cannot afford to tolerate many more imports, and the value of these imports to the United States is also expected to decrease in value, which means Central America will gain little economic advantage from them anyhow, especially given the concessions it must make in return.

In addition, CAFTA-DR will actually be increasing some barriers to free trade. For example, the accord may make it harder for countries such as Guatemala to obtain access to affordable lifesaving medicines because of stringent intellectual property clauses included in the agreement.

CAFTA-DR is also a bad move for labor and workers' rights. It will most likely trigger the loss of manufacturing jobs in the United States and agricultural jobs in Central America. Although proponents of the deal assert that it will stem illegal immigration from these poorer nations, the shift in jobs will most likely increase immigration, as it did with NAFTA.

Furthermore, it will trigger a "race to the bottom" when it comes to wages. The accord will open up U.S. labor markets to competition against a low-wage area, which will drive down the current wage level. NAFTA and other trade agreements currently in place have already stymied wage growth, which has grown a meager 9 percent over the last 30 years compared to an increase of 80 percent in worker productivity. And this depression of wages and shift of jobs created

(continued)

the United States; 40 percent of yarn exports and about 25 percent of fabric exports from the United States are purchased by these nations. By working together through CAFTA-DR, the United States and Central America will prevent the loss of Central American apparel jobs to China, whose products contain little or no input from the United States. The National Council of Textile Organizations, which represents more than 75 textile companies, strongly supports CAFTA-DR.

Another argument that critics make is that CAFTA-DR will create shifts in the job market that will lead to thousands of job losses in the manufacturing and agricultural sectors. However, predictions from the U.S. Chamber of Commerce don't bear out this claim. For example, it predicts that in North Carolina alone, CAFTA-DR will increase industrial output by $3.9 billion and create 28,913 jobs over nine years. Other sources have stated that 250,000 jobs in Central America depend on CAFTA-DR being approved. And although labor organizations have decried the lack of worker-protection clauses in the agreement, a report from the International Labor Organization actually praises Central American labor laws and standards.[32]

If the United States would have decided to opt out of CAFTA-DR, it would have seriously hurt its position as the leading champion of global free trade and open competition, possibly damaging its position in the WTO and its relationships with other nations with which it wishes to establish bilateral agreements. ●

by current agreements has done little to improve the economic conditions of the developing Central American nations, where wages have grown only 12 percent since 1980, compared with 80 percent during the period between 1960 and 1979. Furthermore, no clauses in the agreement address the protection of workers or the banning of child labor.[33]

Because the accord involves developing countries with vastly different interests than the United States, it will be hard to please all parties. Although it signed CAFTA-DR, Costa Rica is currently showing hesitance in ratifying it. The country is faced with opposition from trade unions, farm groups, and even businesses and fears the accord's stringent intellectual-property clauses and the chance that it might force the country to privatize its free universal health-care system. Costa Rica's hesitancy undermines the argument posed by Washington that CAFTA-DR is something earnestly sought after by struggling Central American countries.[34] ●

REGIONAL ECONOMIC INTEGRATION IN ASIA

The WTO recognizes seven different RTAs in Asia. As is the case in Latin America, regional integration in Asia has not been as successful as the EU or NAFTA because most of the countries in the region have relied on U.S. and EU markets for as much as 20 to 30 percent of their exports, which is not as extensive as in Latin America but still significant. However, the Asian financial crisis of 1997 and 1998 demonstrated that weakness in one country resulted in contagion throughout the region.

Association of Southeast Asian Nations (ASEAN)   The **Association of Southeast Asian Nations (ASEAN),** organized in 1967, comprises Brunei, Cambodia, Indonesia, Laos, Malaysia, Myanmar, the Philippines, Singapore, Thailand, and Vietnam (see Map 8.5). It possesses a combined GDP of over $1 trillion, total trade of $1.44 trillion, and a population of 567 million people.[35]

ASEAN promotes cooperation in many areas, including industry and trade. Because of its large size, ASEAN is the third largest free trade agreement in the world after the EU and NAFTA and above MERCOSUR. Member countries are protected in terms of tariff and nontariff barriers, yet they hold promise for market and investment opportunities because of their large market size.

The ASEAN Free Trade Area is a successful trade agreement among countries in Southeast Asia.

ASEAN Free Trade Area   On January 1, 1993, ASEAN officially formed the ASEAN Free Trade Area (AFTA). AFTA's goal was to cut tariffs on all intrazonal trade to a maximum of 5 percent by January 1, 2008. The weaker ASEAN countries would be allowed to phase in their tariff reductions over a longer period. By 2005, most products traded among the AFTA countries were subject to duties from 0 to 5 percent, so AFTA has been successful in its free trade objectives.

MAP 8.5   The Association of Southeast Asian Nations

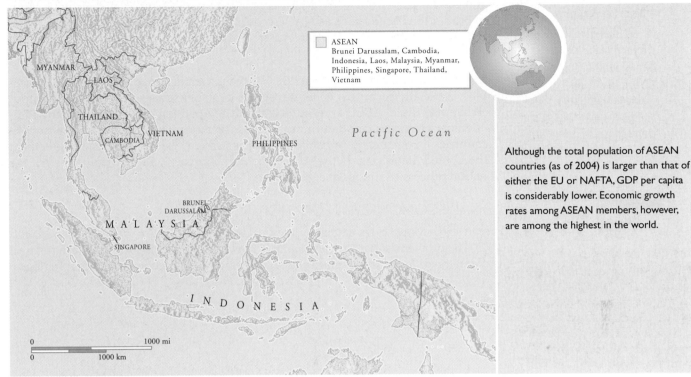

ASEAN
Brunei Darussalam, Cambodia,
Indonesia, Laos, Malaysia, Myanmar,
Philippines, Singapore, Thailand,
Vietnam

Although the total population of ASEAN
countries (as of 2004) is larger than that of
either the EU or NAFTA, GDP per capita
is considerably lower. Economic growth
rates among ASEAN members, however,
are among the highest in the world.

Calls for Closer Cooperation   Many MNEs are hoping that ASEAN countries will work harder to loosen their borders. Companies such as BMW, Matsushita Electrical Industrial, Honda Motor, and Procter & Gamble have operations in the ASEAN countries but aren't able to expand to their full potential because ASEAN countries aren't cooperating with each other.

Malaysia, Singapore, Thailand, and the Philippines are still passing protectionist measures, which downgrade the effectiveness of AFTA and shrink trade. General Motors expanded heavily into Thailand in 1996, but in 2001 it built only 52,000 cars in a plant designed to build 130,000. Most of these cars were sent to the European market because barriers within ASEAN are too large.

Unless ASEAN nations start cooperating, MNEs will move their operations to China. GM's sales doubled in China in 2001, and as GM's ASEAN chief put it, "It is growth like that, that makes it imperative for ASEAN nations to put aside their differences and embrace free trade."[36]

Other companies, however, have been able to take advantage of AFTA. Dell Computer, for example, established computer assembly operations in Malaysia to take advantage of Malaysia's location-specific advantages, such as the Multimedia Supercorridor, which is like a little Silicon Valley and links Dell with its suppliers, offers favorable tax rates, and provides a good workforce. In addition, Malaysia's membership in AFTA gives Dell duty-free access to the other ASEAN countries.

Asia Pacific Economic Cooperation (APEC)   APEC, the **Asia Pacific Economic Cooperation,** was formed in November 1989 to promote multilateral economic cooperation in trade and investment in the Pacific Rim.[37] It's composed of 21 countries that border the Pacific Rim—both in Asia as well as the Americas. To accomplish its objectives, APEC leaders committed themselves to achieving free and open trade in the region by 2010 for the industrial nations (which generate 85 percent of the regional trade) and by 2020 for the rest of the members.[38]

> APEC is composed of 21 countries that border the Pacific Rim; progress toward free trade is hampered by size and geographic distance between member countries and the lack of a treaty.

Challenges to Solidity   The difference between APEC and other regional trade groups is that there are no binding treaties. Although the group is huge, accounting for approximately 41 percent of the world's population (2.6 billion people), 56 percent of world GDP

(US$19,254 billion), and about 49 percent of world trade, it operates by consensus and does not have the same teeth as the RTAs recognized by the WTO. It also includes countries that border the Pacific, such as NAFTA countries, Chile, Russia, China, Hong Kong, Taiwan, many members of AFTA, and Australia and New Zealand. It is more than an Asian trade bloc, but it is not a very solid bloc.

The Goal of "Open Regionalism" APEC has the potential to become a significant economic bloc, especially because it generates such a large percentage of the world's output and merchandise trade. APEC is trying to establish "open regionalism," whereby individual member countries can determine whether to apply trade liberalization to non-APEC countries on an unconditional, MFN basis or on a reciprocal, free trade agreement basis. The United States prefers the latter approach. The key will be whether or not the liberalization process continues at a good pace.[39]

There are several African trade groups, but they rely more on their former colonial powers and other developed markets for trade than they do on each other.

REGIONAL ECONOMIC INTEGRATION IN AFRICA

As you can see in Map 8.6, several major regional trade groups in Africa are registered with the WTO. The problem is that African countries have been struggling to establish a political identity, and the different trade groups have political as well as economic underpinnings.

MAP 8.6 Regional Integration in Africa

Although African nations have joined to form several groups for the purpose of economic integration, total amount of trade among members remains relatively small. African nations tend to rely heavily on trading relationships with countries elsewhere in the world—notably with industrialized nations.

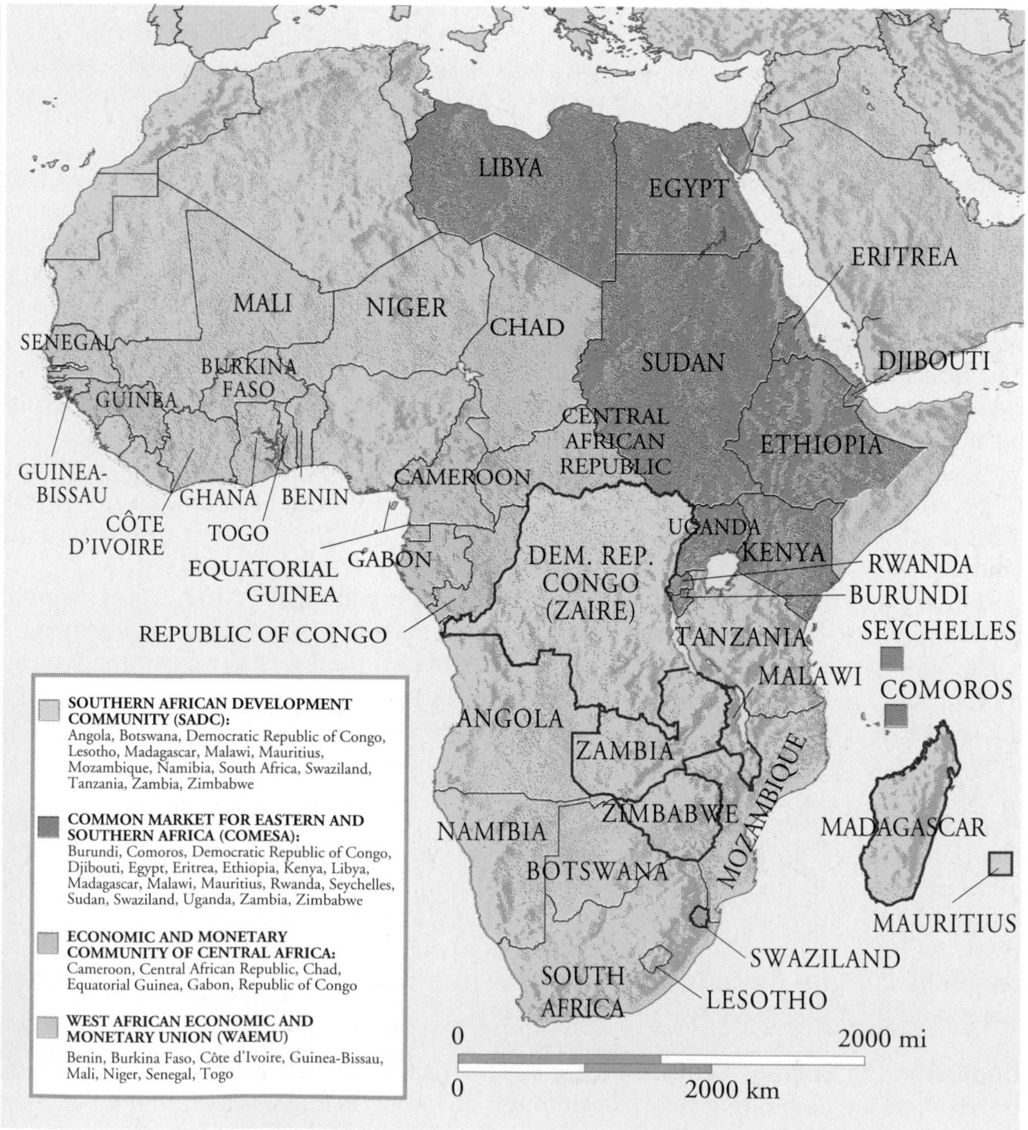
LIBYA
EGYPT
ERITREA
MALI
NIGER
CHAD
SENEGAL
SUDAN
DJIBOUTI
BURKINA FASO
GUINEA
CENTRAL AFRICAN REPUBLIC
ETHIOPIA
GUINEA-BISSAU
CAMEROON
GHANA
BENIN
CÔTE D'IVOIRE
TOGO
UGANDA
KENYA
RWANDA
BURUNDI
EQUATORIAL GUINEA
GABON
DEM. REP. CONGO (ZAIRE)
REPUBLIC OF CONGO
TANZANIA
SEYCHELLES
MALAWI
COMOROS
ANGOLA
ZAMBIA
MOZAMBIQUE
ZIMBABWE
NAMIBIA
MADAGASCAR
BOTSWANA
MAURITIUS
SWAZILAND
SOUTH AFRICA
LESOTHO
SOUTHERN AFRICAN DEVELOPMENT COMMUNITY (SADC):
Angola, Botswana, Democratic Republic of Congo, Lesotho, Madagascar, Malawi, Mauritius, Mozambique, Namibia, South Africa, Swaziland, Tanzania, Zambia, Zimbabwe
COMMON MARKET FOR EASTERN AND SOUTHERN AFRICA (COMESA):
Burundi, Comoros, Democratic Republic of Congo, Djibouti, Egypt, Eritrea, Ethiopia, Kenya, Libya, Madagascar, Malawi, Mauritius, Rwanda, Seychelles, Sudan, Swaziland, Uganda, Zambia, Zimbabwe
ECONOMIC AND MONETARY COMMUNITY OF CENTRAL AFRICA:
Cameroon, Central African Republic, Chad, Equatorial Guinea, Gabon, Republic of Congo
WEST AFRICAN ECONOMIC AND MONETARY UNION (WAEMU)
Benin, Burkina Faso, Côte d'Ivoire, Guinea-Bissau, Mali, Niger, Senegal, Togo
0
2000 mi
0
2000 km

The African Union One group not shown on Map 8.6 is the African Union, created by 53 African countries in 2002 to take the place of the Organization of African Unity (OAU). The OAU was established in 1963 to focus on political issues in Africa, notably colonialism and racism. However, the new AU is modeled loosely on the EU, although that type of integration will be extremely difficult in Africa. Civil war, corruption, diseases such as AIDS, and poor government infrastructures have hampered African countries and their ability to progress economically.

Because most African countries rely more on trade links with former colonial powers than with each other, intrazonal trade is not significant. African markets, with the notable exception of South Africa, are relatively small and undeveloped, making trade liberalization a relatively minor contributor to economic growth in the region. However, any type of market expansion through regional integration will help these small countries.

LOOKING TO THE FUTURE

Will the WTO Overcome Bilateral and Regional Integration Efforts?

Will regional integration be the wave of the future, or will the WTO become the focus of global economic integration? The WTO's objective is to reduce barriers to trade in goods, services, and investment. Regional groups attempt to do that and more. Although the EU has introduced a common currency and is increasing the degree of cooperation in areas such as security and foreign policy, the WTO will likely never engage in those issues. Regional integration deals with the specific problems facing member countries, whereas the WTO needs to be concerned about all countries in the world.

However, regional integration might actually help the WTO achieve its objectives in three major ways:

1. Regionalism can lead to liberalization of issues not covered by the WTO.
2. Regionalism, given that it typically involves fewer countries with more similar conditions and objectives, is more flexible.
3. Regional deals lock in liberalization, especially in developing countries.

NAFTA and the EU are the key regional groups in which significant integration is taking place. In the future, these groups will continue to develop stronger linkages, and then they will expand to include other countries. The key for NAFTA will be whether or not the U.S. Congress can avoid getting caught up in protectionist sentiment and allow expansion to take place. If it does not, Canada and Mexico will continue to engage in bilateral agreements with non-NAFTA countries in the region along the lines of the NAFTA agreement. The EU will continue to expand east until it meets Russia, and then its expansion will either stop or take on a whole new character.

In addition, the EU faces a real dilemma as it tries to figure out what to do with Turkey, which has applied for entrance into the EU. However, Turkey has a larger population than every country in the EU except for Germany and would be the only country in the EU with a predominantly Muslim population. Although the country is officially secular as opposed to religious, the ruling Islamist party, the Justice and Development Party, won 46.6 percent of the vote in national elections in 2007. Given the concerns with radical Islam and the fact that EU members have a common passport and full mobility of labor, it has to be a security nightmare for the other members of the EU.

That being said, the Islamist party appears to follow the secular tradition in Turkey and is pro-business, pro-EU. It will be interesting to see how the EU deals with the possible admission of Turkey as a new member.

Regional integration in Africa will continue at a slow pace due to the existing political and economic problems there, but Asian integration, primarily in AFTA, will pick up steam as the economies of East and Southeast Asia recover and open up. Since the beginning of the decade, Asian countries have signed over 70 FTAs among themselves. In a matter of months, Japan alone ratified free trade agreements with Singapore, Malaysia, and the Philippines, and it began negotiating agreements with ASEAN, Australia, and Thailand.[40] However, the key to their growth may be China and its rapidly growing influence in Asia and the rest of the world.

The challenges to the WTO come not only from the growing strength of regional groups but also from the strong divisions between developed and developing countries within the WTO. As we noted earlier in the chapter, the Doha agreement has been a disaster so far. After several rounds of negotiations, member countries cannot agree on how to solve the substantive issues surrounding agriculture and manufactured products. Initially, it appeared that the problem was the resistance

(continued)

of rich countries such as the United States and members of the EU to reduce farm subsides and the hesitancy of developing countries to reduce tariffs on manufactured goods. However, it now appears there are problems within the developing countries as some countries, like Brazil and India, favor reducing tariffs on manufactured goods to 25 to 30 percent because of their fear of being swamped by imports from China.

Other developing countries would prefer a lower level of tariffs on manufactured goods and are irritated that larger developing countries like Brazil and India are speaking on their behalf. The poorest African nations feel like they have no voice at all.[41] Will the developing countries develop a common voice in current and future trade negotiations, or will the dialogue involve the developed countries (with the United States and EU not always agreeing on issues), the rapidly growing and large developing countries, China, and the less developed countries? If the current trend continues, it will become increasingly difficult for countries to agree on multilateral trade agreements, pushing more of the substantive effort to bilateral and regional talks. ■

OTHER FORMS OF INTERNATIONAL COOPERATION

Up to this point, the chapter has focused on treaties between nations designed to reduce trade and investment barriers and increase trade and investment among member nations. We moved from the global—the WTO—to the bilateral and the regional. However, there are other forms of cooperation worth mentioning that could have an influence on the strategies of MNEs.

The United Nations   The first form of cooperation worth exploring is the United Nations. The UN was established in 1945 in response to the devastation of World War II to promote international peace and security and to help solve global problems in such diverse areas as economic development, antiterrorism, and humanitarian actions. If the UN performs its responsibilities, it should improve the environment in which MNEs operate around the world, reducing risk and providing greater opportunities.

> The UN was established in 1945 following World War II to promote international peace and security. It deals with economic development, antiterrorism, and humanitarian movements.

Organization and Membership   The UN family of organizations is too large to list, but it includes organizations such as the World Trade Organization discussed earlier in the chapter and the International Monetary Fund and the World Bank, which are discussed in subsequent chapters. These organizations are all part of the UN Economic and Social Council, one of six principal organs of the UN System, which also includes the General Assembly, the Security Council, and the International Court of Justice.

There are 192 member states in the UN represented in the General Assembly, including 15 member states that comprise the Security Council. There are five permanent members of the Security Council—China, France, the Russian Federation, the United Kingdom, and the United States—and 10 other members elected by the General Assembly to serve two-year terms.[42]

> UNCTAD was established to help developing countries participate in international trade.

Focus on Developing Nations: UNCTAD   As noted, the UN is involved in a variety of social, political, and economic activities. In addition, the UN tends to focus on the problems of the developing countries in an attempt to resolve major issues facing them. One of the most important organizations in the UN that affects MNEs is the UN Conference on Trade and Development, or UNCTAD, a program authorized by the General Assembly and established in the 1960s to tackle the problems of the developing countries in international trade.

UNCTAD is involved in a variety of different activities, such as trade and commodities; investment, technology, and enterprise development; and macroeconomic policies and debt and development financing. Obviously, these are just a few activities of UNCTAD. It has also been active conducting in the so-called North-South dialogue (between the developed and the developing countries), in formulating international commodities agreements, in developing codes of conduct, in working to resolve the debt crisis, and a variety of other projects.

Nongovernmental Organizations (NGOs) Nongovernmental, nonprofit voluntary organizations are all lumped under the category of NGOs. They refer to private institutions that are independent of the government. Some NGOs operate only within the confines of a specific country, whereas other NGOs are international in scope. The International Red Cross is an example of an international NGO. It is concerned with humanitarian issues around the world, not just in one country.

Many NGOs, such as Doctors Without Borders, are like the Red Cross in that they are concerned about humanitarian issues. Other NGOs came about as a response to what is perceived as the negative side of globalization. Many of these NGOs were discussed in Chapter 5 with respect to the environment and labor issues. For example, in that chapter we discussed the U.K.-based Ethical Trading Initiative, or ETI.

Several NGOs concerned about workers' rights, such as Africa Now, Anti-Slavery International, Quaker Peace and Social Witness, Save the Children, and Working Women Worldwide, are members of ETI. NGOs perform an important role in bringing potential abuses to light and tend to be very narrowly focused, usually on a specific issue. There is a Committee on Non-Governmental Organizations that is a part of the Economic and Social Council (ECOSOC) of the UN that meets to discuss issues of importance to general and specific NGOs.

Commodity Agreements

Commodities refer to raw materials or primary products that enter into trade, such as metals or agricultural products. Primary commodity exports, such as crude petroleum, natural gas, copper, tobacco, coffee, cocoa, tea, and sugar, are still important to the developing countries. "[O]ut of 141 developing countries," notes a UN report, "95 depend on more than half of their export earnings on commodities. For 70 of them, these revenues were generated by only three commodities"—a fact that "makes these countries very vulnerable to price declines and volatility."[43] African countries in general depend on commodities for about 80 percent of their exports.[44]

> **CONCEPT CHECK**
> *Commodities* often represent *natural advantages*, which we define in Chapter 6 as advantages in producing products resulting from climatic conditions, access to certain natural resources, or availability of certain labor forces.

> **CONCEPT CHECK**
> Remember from Chapter 6 the fact that lower-income countries depend much more on the production of *primary products* than do wealthier nations; consequently, they depend more heavily on **natural advantage** as opposed to the kinds of **acquired advantage** that involve more advanced technologies and processes.

The sign reads "Create Opportunities. Support the Free Trade Agreement." In support of the U.S.-CAFTA-DR in 2005, thousands of Costa Rican workers demonstrate in front of the presidential palace in the capital of San José.

NGOs: Private nonprofit institutions that are independent of the government.

The attempts of countries to stabilize commodity prices through producer alliances and commodity agreements have been largely unsuccessful.

Many commodity agreements now exist for the purpose of

- Discussing issues.
- Disseminating information.
- Improving product safety.

COMMODITIES AND THE WORLD ECONOMY

Both long-term trends and short-term fluctuations in commodity prices have important consequences for the world economy. On the demand side, commodity markets play an important role in industrial countries, transmitting business cycle disturbances to the rest of the economy and affecting the rate of growth of prices. On the supply side, primary products account for about half, on average, of developing countries' export earnings, and many developing countries derive the bulk of their export earnings from one or two commodities.

CONSUMERS AND PRODUCERS

Primary commodities are important to both consumers and producers. The slowdown in global growth in 2001 caused demand to fall for commodities, resulting in a fall in prices. The low commodity prices were a boon to consumer countries because they helped companies keep down costs and, therefore, prices. But producer countries, especially developing countries, suffered because of low commodity revenues. However, the resurgence of the economies of China and India and their strong demand for commodities, including oil, in 2004–2005 raised the prices for commodities again.

For many years, countries tried to ban together as producer alliances or joint producer/consumer alliances to try to stabilize commodity prices. However, these efforts—with the exception of OPEC, which we discuss later—have not been very successful. UNCTAD established a Commodities Branch to attempt to deal with the issues facing developing countries because of high dependence on commodities, especially agricultural commodities, for export revenues.

The most important international commodity organizations and bodies, such as the International Cocoa Organization, the International Coffee Organization, and the International Copper Study Group, take part in UN-led discussions to help commodity-dependent countries establish effective policies and strategies. However, each organization, such as the International Coffee Organization (ICO), has its own organizational structure independent of the UN. For example, the ICO is composed of 45 exporting countries and 32 importing countries. All of the exporting countries are developing countries, and most of the importing countries are developed countries.

Whereas many of the original commodity agreements were designed to influence price through a variety of market-interfering mechanisms, most of the existing commodity agreements are established to discuss issues, disseminate information, improve product safety, and so on. Very little can be done outside of market forces to influence price.

Finally, because commodities are the raw materials used in the production process, it is important for managers of companies that use commodities to understand the factors that influence their prices. Investment and pricing decisions must be based on the cost of inputs, and it is difficult to forecast those costs when the commodities markets are highly volatile.

THE ORGANIZATION OF PETROLEUM EXPORTING COUNTRIES (OPEC)

OPEC is a producers' alliance in oil that has been successful in using quotas to keep oil prices high.

The **Organization of Petroleum Exporting Countries (OPEC)** is an example of a producer cartel that relies on quotas to influence prices. It is a group of commodity-producing countries that have significant control over supply and band together to control output and price. OPEC is part of a larger category of energy commodities, which also includes coal and natural gas. OPEC is not confined to the Middle East. The members are Algeria, Angola, Ecuador, Indonesia, Iran, Iraq, Kuwait, Libya, Nigeria, Qatar, Saudi Arabia, the United Arab Emirates, and Venezuela.

Price Controls and Politics   OPEC controls prices by establishing production quotas on member countries. Saudi Arabia has historically performed the role of the dominant supplier in OPEC that can influence supply and price. Periodically—at least annually—OPEC oil ministers gather together to determine the quota for each country based on estimates of supply and demand.

Politics are also an important dimension to OPEC deliberations. OPEC member countries with large populations need large oil revenues to fund government programs. As a result, they are tempted to exceed their export quotas to generate more revenues. A major reason for Iraq's invasion of Kuwait in 1990 was that Kuwait was producing more than its quota, which depressed world oil prices. Former Iraqi president Saddam Hussein blamed Kuwait for low world oil prices, which reduced the amount of revenue Iraq could earn with its oil exports. Thus he felt justified in invading Kuwait to gain control of its oil supplies so he could increase his own oil revenues.

Output and Exports OPEC member countries produce about 43 percent of the world's crude oil and 18 percent of its natural gas. However, OPEC's oil exports represent about 51 percent of the oil traded internationally.[45] Therefore, OPEC can have a strong influence on the oil market, especially if it decides to reduce or increase its level of production.[46]

Sometimes OPEC policies work; sometimes they don't. In addition, events beyond OPEC's control can influence prices. The rapidly escalating price of crude oil in recent years is a mixture of rising demand worldwide, especially in China, a shortage of refining capacity and environmental rules in some countries that preclude the building of new refineries, and political instability in the Middle East.

The Downside of High Prices Keeping oil prices high has some downside for OPEC. Competition from non-OPEC countries increases because the revenues accruing to the competitors are higher. Because some OPEC countries are putting up roadblocks to production, major producers like BP, ExxonMobil, and Shell are investing heavily in areas like the Caspian Basin, the Gulf of Mexico, and Angola and are trying to enter areas like the Russian Federation. Production in these areas is expected to grow significantly.

Another problem is that higher oil prices could depress growth worldwide and thus lower demand for oil. Also, because of OPEC's power, for the most part its countries have been able to avoid competitive pressures to improve their industries—and some are, therefore, decades out of date.[47]

Political and social forces are also affecting oil prices. High oil prices have permitted President Hugo Chávez of Venezuela to spend millions on domestic poverty programs and foreign aid while underinvesting in Venezuela's oil infrastructure. As long as prices are high, he has no incentive to balance his priorities between spending and investment. If prices were to fall, he could face the twin problems of deteriorating production and social unrest.

The downside of high oil prices for OPEC:

- Producers investing in countries outside of OPEC.
- Depression of worldwide growth and demand.
- Lack of competitive pressures to improve industries.
- Complication of balancing social, political, and economic objectives.

Wal-Mart Goes South

C A S E

Comercial Mexicana S.A. (Comerci), one of Mexico's largest retail chains, is faced with a serious dilemma.[48] Since Wal-Mart's aggressive entry into the Mexican retail market, Comerci has found it increasingly difficult to remain competitive. Wal-Mart's strong operating presence and low prices since NAFTA's lifting of tariffs have put pressure on Comerci, and now management must determine if Comerci's recent participation with the purchasing consortium Sinergia will be sufficient to compete against Wal-Mart.

What's caused this intense competitive pressure on Comerci, and what is likely to be its future? Mexico's retail sector has benefited greatly from the increasing trade liberalization the government has been pushing. After decades of protectionism, Mexico joined GATT in 1986 to help open its economy to new markets. In 1990, with Mexico's economy on the upswing and additional free trade negotiations with the United States and Canada taking place, the founder of Wal-Mart, Sam Walton, met with the president of Cifra, Mexico's leading retail store. Their meeting resulted in a 50/50 joint venture in the opening of Mexico's first Sam's Club, a subsidiary of Wal-Mart, in 1991 in Mexico City.

It only took a couple of months after the opening to prove the store's success—it was breaking all the U.S. records for Sam's Club. The joint venture evolved to incorporate all new stores, and by 1997, Wal-Mart purchased enough shares to have a controlling interest in Cifra. In 2000, it changed the name to Wal-Mart de Mexico, S.A. de C.V., and the ticker symbol to WALMEX.

Prior to 1990, Wal-Mart had never made moves to enter Mexico or any country other than the United States. Once Wal-Mart started growing in Mexico, management created the Wal-Mart International Division in 1993. The company has expanded internationally to 14 countries through new-store construction and acquisitions. It now operates in Argentina, Brazil, Canada, China, Costa Rica, El Salvador, Guatemala, Honduras, Japan, Mexico, Nicaragua, Puerto Rico, and the United Kingdom. Wal-Mart serves 49 million customers weekly through its international operations.

With growth stalling in the United States, Wal-Mart is looking to international expansion for growth. It currently has over 2,700 retail units worldwide and employs 500,000 people. In December 2005 alone, it acquired 545 new stores and increased its personnel by 50,000 in Japan and South America. In fiscal year 2007, the international division increased sales over the previous year by 30.2 percent—to $77.1 billion—and operating profit increased 21.5 percent—to $4.2 billion. The division accounts for approximately 22 percent of sales and 37.5 percent of profits.

Some forecasters believe Wal-Mart's growth outside of the United States will grow by an average of 26 percent for the foreseeable future and estimate that its holdings could double by the end of the decade. These predictions hold with the company's recent acquisitions of local retailers in both Brazil and China that have dramatically increased its market presence in the two countries.

Nevertheless, Wal-Mart's success internationally has varied by country. It has struggled to match consumer preferences and work successfully with suppliers in Japan, encountered trouble in the United Kingdom, and failed to turn profits in Germany and South Korea, forcing it to withdraw completely from both markets. However, it has flourished in Canada and, most notably, in Mexico. Wal-Mart's operations in Canada began in 1994 with the acquisition of 122 Woolco stores. It now has more than 277 stores, 6 Sam's Clubs, and 7 Supercenters and enjoys strong partnerships with Canadian suppliers. In Mexico, Wal-Mart operates 912 units, including Sam's Clubs, Bodegas (discount stores), Wal-Mart Supercenters, Superamas (grocery stores), Suburbias (apparel stores), and VIPS restaurants, and it has become the largest retailer in the country.

Given its hit-and-miss success rate on the international scene, it is natural to wonder how much of Wal-Mart's triumph in Canada and Mexico has stemmed from its internal processes, international strategies, and geographic proximity and how much can be attributed to the close economic ties shared by the United States with the two countries through NAFTA.

Wal-Mart's Competitive Advantage

Much of Wal-Mart's international success comes from the tested practices on which the U.S. division bases its success. Wal-Mart is known for the slogan "Every Day Low Prices." It has expanded that internally to "Every Day Low Costs" to inspire employees to spend company money wisely and work hard to lower costs. Because of its sheer size and volume of purchases, Wal-Mart can negotiate with suppliers to drop prices to agreeable levels.

It also works closely with suppliers on inventory levels using an advanced information system that informs suppliers when purchases have been made and when Wal-Mart will be ordering more merchandise. Suppliers can then plan production runs more accurately, thus reducing production costs, which are passed on to Wal-Mart and eventually to the consumer.

Wal-Mart also has a unique distribution system that reduces expenses. It builds super warehouses known as Distribution Centers (DCs) in central locations that receive the majority of merchandise sold in Wal-Mart stores. It sorts and moves the merchandise via a complex system of bar codes and its inventory information system then transports it to the various stores, using its company-owned fleet or a partner. The central distribution center helps Wal-Mart negotiate lower prices with its suppliers because of the large purchasing volumes.

These strategies have resulted in great success for Wal-Mart. In 2001, it passed GE and ExxonMobil to become the largest company in the world, with sales of $344.9 billion. It has the largest private-sector workforce, with 1.9 million people in 6,995 facilities throughout the world. And it even uses the second most powerful computer in the world—behind the Pentagon's—to run its logistics.

Wal-Mart in Mexico

Despite its current success in the region, Wal-Mart encountered some difficulties with its opening in Mexico prior to the passage of NAFTA. One of the biggest challenges it faced was import charges on many of the goods sold in its stores, thus preventing Wal-Mart from being able to offer its "Every Day Low Prices."

Unsure of local demand, Wal-Mart stocked its shelves with things like ice skates, fishing tackle, and riding lawnmowers—all unpopular items in Mexico. Rather than informing headquarters that they wouldn't need those items, local managers heavily discounted the items, only to have the automatic inventory system reorder the products when the first batch sold. Wal-Mart also encountered logistics problems due to poor roads and the scarcity of delivery trucks. Yet another problem was the culture clashes between the Arkansas executives and the local Mexican managers.

Some of these problems were solved by trial and error, but the emergence of NAFTA in 1994 helped solve most of the problems. Among other things, NAFTA reduced tariffs on American goods sold to Mexico from 10 percent to 3 percent. Prior to NAFTA, Wal-Mart was not much of a threat to companies like Comerci, Gigante, and Soriana, Mexico's top retailers. But once the agreement was signed, the barriers fell and Wal-Mart was on a level playing field with its competitors—all it needed to become number one.

NAFTA encouraged Mexico to improve its transportation infrastructure, thus helping to solve Wal-Mart's logistical problems. The signing of NAFTA also opened the gates wider to foreign investment in Mexico. Wal-Mart was paying huge import fees on goods shipped to Mexico from areas like Europe and Asia. Foreign companies knew that if they built manufacturing plants in Mexico, they could keep costs low with Mexican labor but ship to NAFTA's free trade zone—Mexico, the United States, or Canada.

As companies began to build manufacturing plants in Mexico, Wal-Mart could buy these products without paying the high import tariffs. An example of this tactic is Sony's flat-screen television line, Wega. Sam's Clubs in Mexico imported Wega TVs from Japan with a 23 percent import tariff plus huge shipping costs, resulting in a $1,600 retail price at Sam's Club. In 1999, Sony built a manufacturing plant in Mexico, thus allowing Sam's Club to purchase the Wegas without import tariffs; this tactic also yields much lower shipping fees. Sam's Clubs passed on the savings to customers—with a retail price of only $600.

The benefits of NAFTA, such as lower tariffs and improved infrastructure, helped not only Wal-Mart but also its competitors, like Comerci. But Wal-Mart used the advantages of NAFTA better than anyone else. Rather than pocketing the differences the lower tariffs made, Wal-Mart reduced its prices. In 1999, it closed one of its Supercenters for a day to discount up to 6,000 items by 14 percent.

Comerci and others have combated Wal-Mart's tactics by lowering their own prices, but on many items, they can't get the prices as low. Wal-Mart's negotiating power with its suppliers is large enough that it can get the better deal. Also, most of Mexico's retailers priced goods differently. They were used to putting certain items on sale or at deep discount, a strategy known as "high and low," rather than lowering all prices. They have been trying to adjust their pricing structure to match Wal-Mart's, but they are still frustrated with the continued cost cutting of Wal-Mart. Competitors and certain suppliers are so angry that they have gone to Mexico's Federal Competition Commission (known in Mexico as CoFeCo) with complaints of unfair pricing practices.

Formation of Sinergia

Unable to compete with Wal-Mart under the new conditions, Comerci has been faced with extinction. Wal-Mart is the largest retailer in Mexico and owns about 55 percent of the market share in Mexico's supermarket sector, with $15.4 billion in sales and $585 million in profit in the country during 2005. In 2007 alone, Wal-Mart added 120 new stores in Mexico. In contrast, Comerci realized only $3.6 billion in sales and $167.5 million in net profit and has seen its market share drop to 15 percent.

Fear over the giant retailer's predominance and over its unexplained withdrawal from the Mexican National Association of Department Stores (ANTAD) in 2004 prompted Comerci to band with two other struggling homegrown supermarket chains, Soriana and Gigante, to form a purchasing consortium that would allow them to negotiate better bulk prices from suppliers.

The collaboration, known as *Sinergia*, was initially rejected by CoFeCo and met resistance from the Consumer Product Council of Mexico, a 46-member organization representing major consumer goods companies, which feared that Sinergia would use its purchasing power to force unreasonably low prices on suppliers. However, after its second presentation to CoFeCo, the consortium was at last approved, provided that it issue regular reports to CoFeCo outlining the nature of its purchasing agreements and that it sign confidentiality agreements with the participating chains to prevent price-fixing and monopolistic behavior. As a representative body with no assets, Sinergia's purchases are currently limited to only local suppliers, and its future is still uncertain.

Should Sinergia fail to improve the situation, Comerci could still look for possible foreign buyers, like France's Carrefour, or it could duplicate the efforts of its Sinergia partner Soriana, which is attempting, with some notable success, to differentiate itself from Wal-Mart by offering products and a store atmosphere that appeal more to Mexicans' middle-class aspirations.

The government may give Comerci a break if it rules against Wal-Mart's aggressive pricing, but as one analyst put it, "We do not believe the CFC will end up penalizing Wal-Mart for exercising its purchasing power in an attempt to get the best deals available in the marketplace, which is the goal of every retailer in the world, especially when [these savings] are ultimately passed on to consumers." One thing is certain, however—Comerci cannot afford to sit still. ∎

QUESTIONS

1. How has the implementation of NAFTA affected Wal-Mart's success in Mexico?
2. How much of Wal-Mart's success is due to NAFTA, and how much is due to Wal-Mart's inherent competitive strategy? In other words, could any other U.S. retailer have the same success in Mexico post-NAFTA, or is Wal-Mart a special case?
3. What has Comerci done in its attempt to remain competitive? What are the advantages and challenges of such a strategy, and how effective do you think it will be?
4. What else do you think Comercial Mexicana S.A. should do, given the competitive position of Wal-Mart?

SUMMARY

- The General Agreement on Tariffs and Trade (GATT), begun in 1947, created a continuing means for countries to negotiate the reduction and elimination of trade barriers and to agree on simplified mechanisms for the conduct of international trade.

- The World Trade Organization (WTO) replaced GATT in 1995 as a continuing means of trade negotiations that aspires to foster the principle of trade without discrimination and to provide a better means of mediating trade disputes and of enforcing agreements.

- Efforts at regional economic integration began to emerge after World War II as countries saw benefits of cooperation and larger market sizes. The major types of economic integration are the free trade area and the customs union, followed by broader economic and political integration in the common market.

- Free trade agreements result in trade creation and trade diversion as barriers drop for member countries but remain higher for nonmember countries. There are static effects of the reduction of trade barriers. The static effects of economic integration improve the efficiency of resource allocation and affect both production and consumption. The dynamic effects are internal and external efficiencies that arise because of changes in market size.

- Once protection is eliminated among member countries, trade creation allows MNEs to specialize and trade based on comparative advantage.

- Trade diversion occurs when the supply of products shifts from countries that are not members of an economic bloc to those that are.

- Regional, as opposed to global, economic integration occurs because of the greater ease of promoting cooperation on a smaller scale.

- The European Union (EU) is an effective common market that has abolished most restrictions on factor mobility and is harmonizing national political, economic, and social policies. It is composed of 27 countries, including 12 countries from mostly Central and Eastern Europe that joined since 2004. The EU has abolished trade barriers on intrazonal trade, instituted a common external tariff, and created a common currency, the euro.

- The North American Free Trade Agreement (NAFTA) is designed to eliminate tariff barriers and liberalize investment opportunities and trade in services. Key provisions in NAFTA are labor and environmental agreements.

- There are key trade groups in other parts of the world, including Latin America, Asia, and Africa.

- The United Nations is composed of representatives of most of the countries in the world and influences international trade and development in a number of significant ways.

- Many developing countries rely on commodity exports to supply the hard currency they need for economic development. Instability in commodity prices has resulted in fluctuations in export earnings. OPEC is an effective commodity agreement in terms of attempting to stabilize supply and price.

KEY TERMS

Andean Community (CAN) (p. 316)
Asia Pacific Economic Cooperation (APEC) (p. 319)
Association of Southeast Asian Nations (ASEAN) (p. 318)
bilateral integration (p. 298)
Caribbean Community (CARICOM) (p. 314)
common market (p. 302)
dynamic effect (p. 302)

economic integration (p. 298)
economy of scale (p. 303)
euro (p. 306)
European Union (EU) (p. 304)
General Agreement on Tariffs and Trade (GATT) (p. 298)
MERCOSUR (p. 315)
most-favored-nation (MFN) clause (p. 299)
normal trade relations (p. 299)

North American Free Trade Agreement (NAFTA) (p. 309)
Organization of Petroleum Exporting Countries (OPEC) (p. 324)
regional integration (p. 298)
South American Community of Nations (CSN) (p. 316)
static effect (p. 302)
triad (p. 298)
World Trade Organization (WTO) (p. 298)

ENDNOTES

1 *Sources include the following:* Stephen Power, "EU Auto Industry Faces Overhaul as Japanese Gain in Market Share," *Wall Street Journal*, October 14, 2004: A1; Jathon Sapsford, "Toyota Aims to Rival GM Production," *Wall Street Journal*, November 2, 2004: A3; Mari Koseki, "Quota on Auto Exports to EC Curbed at 1.089 Million in '93," *Japan Times*, April 12–18, 1993: 14; Nick Maling, "Japan Poised for EU Lift of Export Ceiling," *Marketing Week*,

May 6, 1999: 26; Todd Zaun and Beth Demain, "Leading the News: Ambitious Toyota, Buoyed by Europe, Sets Global Goals," *Wall Street Journal*, October 22, 2002: A3; Mark M. Nelson, Thomas F. O'Boyle, and E. S. Browning, "International—The Road to European Unity—1992: EC's Auto Plan Would Keep Japan at Bay—1992 Unification Effort Smacks of Protectionism," *Wall Street Journal*, October 27, 1988: A1; Sapsford, "Toyota Posts 3.5% Profit Rise,

Boosts Sales Forecast for Year," *Wall Street Journal*, February 4, 2005: A3; Gail Edmondson and Chester Dawson, "Revved up for Battle," *Business Week*, January 10, 2005: 30; Joe Guy Collier, "Toyota Posts Record $14-Billion Profit," *Knight Ridder Tribune Business News*, May 9, 2007: 1; "ACEA Board of Directors Recommends Accepting Toyota Motor Europe Membership Application," *PR Newswire Europe Including UK Disclose*, May 4, 2007; Toyota Motor Corp. home page, "Toyota—Joining Europe," at www.toyota-europe.com/experience/the_ company/ toyota-in-europe.aspx (accessed May 10, 2007); Toyota Motor Corps. home page, "Toyota: Company > Company Profile," at www.toyota.co.jp/en/about_toyota/outline/index.html (accessed May 10, 2007); Christoph Rauwald, "Leading the News: Toyota Sales in Europe Jump as Market Stalls," *Wall Street Journal*, March 16, 2007: 2; "World Business Briefing Europe: Germany: Sale of Unit Helps VW," *New York Times*, February 21, 2007: C10; Mark Milner, "Financial: Car Boss Calls on EU to Tackle Yen," *The Guardian* [UK], March 30, 2007: 32.

2 Peter J. Buckley, Jeremy Clagg, Nicolas Forsans, and Kevin T. Reilly, "Increasing the Size of the 'Country': Regional Economic Integration and Foreign Direct Investment in a Globalised World Economy," *Management International Review* 41:3 (2001): 251–75.

3 Alan M. Rugman and Alain Verbeke, "A Perspective on Regional and Global Strategies of Multinational Enterprises," *Journal of International Business Studies* 35 (2004): 7.

4 Sandra O'Malley, "Thawing Trade Iceberg," *The Cairns Post* (Canada), July 7, 2007: 39.

5 John W. Miller, "Brazil and Others Push outside Doha for Trade Pacts," *Wall Street Journal*, July 5, 2007: A6; "EU Proposes 'Strategic Partner' Status for Brazil," *CNN.com* (accessed July 6, 2007).

6 Neil King, Jr., and Scott Miller, "Cancun: Victory for Whom?" *Wall Street Journal*, September 16, 2003: A4.

7 Peter Sutherland, "The Future of the WTO Chapter II—The Erosion of Non-Discrimination," WTO, 2005, at www.wto.org/ english/thewto_e/10anniv_e/future_wto_chap2_e.pdf.

8 Bela Balassa, *The Theory of Economic Integration* (Homewood, IL: Richard D. Irwin, 1961), p. 40; Panjak Ghemawat, "Distance Still Matters: The Hard Reality of Global Expansion," *Harvard Business Review* (September 2001): 3–11.

9 Buckley et al., "Increasing the Size of the 'Country.' "

10 For more information on the EU, check out its Web site at http://europa.eu.int/index_en.htm.

11 "The European Parliament," 2005, at http://europa.eu.int/ institutions/parliament/index_en.htm.

12 "The European Court of Justice," 2002, at http://europa.eu.int/ inst/en/cj.htm.

13 Damien Henderson, "8000 New Workers Arrive after EU Expansion," *The* (Miami, FL) *Herald*, May 23, 2007: 2.

14 Tom Hundley, "How Uniting Europe Helped Small Nations," *Seattle Times*, March 24, 2007: 7.

15 Richard Lawrence, "NAFTA at 5: Happy Birthday?" *Journal of Commerce*, February 1, 1999.

16 Geri Smith and Elisabeth Malkin, "Mexican Makeover: NAFTA Creates the World's Newest Industrial Power," *Business Week*, December 21, 1998: 50–52.

17 "OAS Overview of the North American Free Trade Agreement: Chapter 4: Rules of Origin," 2003, at www.sice.oas.org/ summary/nafta/nafta4.asp.

18 "OAS Overview of the North American Free Trade Agreement."

19 "OAS Overview of the North American Free Trade Agreement: Chapter 20: Institutional Arrangements and Dispute Settlement Procedures," 2003, at www.sice.oas.org/summary/nafta/ nafta20.asp.

20 Data from the WTO Web site, at www.wto.org. Updated information can be found by searching the WTO Statistics Database for each member country.

21 Bureau of Labor Statistics, "International Comparisons of Hourly Compensation Costs for Production Workers in Manufacturing, 2005," Table 2, at www.bls.gov/news.release/ichcc.t02.htm (accessed July 21, 2007).

22 Jesus Cañas, Roberto Coronado, and Robert W. Gilmer, "U.S.-Mexico Deepen Economic Ties," *Southwest Economy* (January/February, 2006), Federal Reserve Bank of Dallas, at www.dallasfed.org/research/swe/2006/swe0601c.html (accessed July 21, 2007).

23 Geri Smith and Cristina Lindblad, "Mexico: Was NAFTA Worth It?" *Business Week*, December 22, 2003, online version.

24 Smith and Malkin, "Mexican Makeover," 51.

25 "The Decline of the Maquiladora," *Business Week*, April 29, 2002: 59.

26 Sydney Weintraub, "A Politically Unpopular Success Story," *Los Angeles Times*, February 7, 1999: 2.

27 Smith and Malkin, "Mexican Makeover," 51.

28 Robert B. Zoellick, "Speech on NAFTA Before the Foreign Trade Council," *USTR* (July 26, 2001): http://www.ustr.gov/speech-test/zoellick/zoellick_7.PDF.

29 Go to http://en.wikipedia.org/wiki/ South_American_Community_of_Nations.

30 Alan M. Field, "Showdown for CAFTA-DR," *Journal of Commerce*, April 11, 2005: 1.

31 Harold McGraw and Mark Weisbrot, "Is CAFTA-DR a Good Thing?" *Miami Herald*, April 16, 2005: 25A.

32 Field, "Showdown for CAFTA-DR," 1.

33 McGraw and Weisbrot, "Is CAFTA-DR a Good Thing?" 25A.

34 John Lyons, "Costa Rica Balks at Free-Trade Pact," *Wall Street Journal*, May 3, 2005: A2.

35 ASEAN, "Selected Basic ASEAN Indicators," May 15, 2007, at www.aseansec.org/19226.htm (accessed July 2007).

36 Jason Booth, "Southeast Asia Moves Haltingly toward Single Consumer Market," *Wall Street Journal*, April 1, 2002, at www.wsj.com.

37 Asia-Pac Paul Cashin, Hong Liang, and C. John McDermott, "Do Commodity Price Shocks Last Too Long for Stabilization Schemes to Work?" *Finance & Development* 36:3 (Summer 1999); Pacific Economic Cooperation, 2003, at www.apecsec.org.sg.

38 Go to www.apecsec.org.sg/apec/about_apec.html (accessed May 23, 2005).

39 Go to www.apecsec.org.sg/apec/about_apec.html (accessed May 23, 2005).

40 "Asia: The Japan Syndrome; Free-Trade Agreements," *The Economist*, May 12, 2007: 65.

41 Steven R. Weisman, "After Six Years, the Global Trade Talks Are Just That: Talk," *New York Times*, July 21, 2007, online edition.

42 The United Nations, at www.un.org. Go to "Main Bodies" for more information about the principal organs of the UN and the different organizations that make up the UN system.

43 United Nations Press Release DSG/SM/210/GA/10202, "Developing Country Dependence on Commodities Must be Addressed for Any Chance at Meeting Anti-Poverty Goals," March 11, 2003, at www.un.org/News/Press/docs/2003/ dsgsm210.doc.htm.

44 "Trade to Pick Up Sharply in 2002 After Sharp Drop in 2001," *World Trade Organization News*, May 2, 2002, at www.wto.org/english/news_e/pres02_e/pr288_e.htm.

45 OPEC, "Does OPEC Control the Oil Market?" at www.opec.org/library/FAQs/aboutOPEC/q13.htm (accessed July 2007); *OPEC Annual Statistical Bulletin* (2003).

46 "Frequently Asked Questions About OPEC," 2003, at www.opec.org.

47 "Does OPEC Have Sand in Its Eyes?" *Business Week*, July 1, 2002: 60.

48 ***Sources include the following:*** Gabriela Lopez, "Mexico Probes Retail Competition as Walmex Dominates," *Reuters Company News*, May 29, 2002; Lopez, "Mexico's Retailers Launch Price War," *Forbes*, June 24, 2002, at www.forbes.com/newswire/ 2002/06/24/rtr641092.html; "Wal-Mart Around the World," *The Economist*, December 6, 2001, at www.economist.com/ displayStory.cfm?Story_ID=895888; David Luhnow, "Crossover Success: How NAFTA Helped Wal-Mart Reshape the Mexican Market," *Wall Street Journal*, August 31, 2001: A1; Alexander Hanrath, "Mexican Stores Wilt in the Face of US Group's Onslaught," *Financial Times*, August 14, 2002, at www.ft.com; Richard C. Morais, "One Hot Tamale," *Forbes*, December 27, 2004: 134–47; Mike Troy, "Wal-Mart International," *DSN Retailing Today*, December 13, 2004: 20–22; Ricardo Castillo Mireles, "Taking It to the Competition, Mexican Style," *Logistics Today*, December 2004: 10; Wal-Mart Stores, "International Data Sheet," at http://walmartstores.com/GlobalWMStoresWeb/ navigate.do?catg= 371 (accessed July 16, 2007); *Wal-Mart 2007 Annual Report*, Wal-Mart (2007); Matthew Boyle, "Wal-Mart v. the world," *CNNMoney*, December 19, 2007; Kate Linebaugh, "Wal-Mart to Buy Grocer-Retail Chain in China," *Wall Street Journal*, October 17, 2006: p. A3; "Wal-Mart Buys Brazil Biz for $757M," *CNNMoney*, December 14, 2005; Martin Fackler, "Wal-Mart Doubles Down on Its Investment in Japan," *New York Times*, October 29, 2005; "CATALYST: Wal-Mart's Distribution Juggernaut," *Businessline*, June 14, 2007: 1; "Same Store Sales of Mexico's Antad Retail Association Down 2.5% in April," *Noticias Financieras*, May 16, 2007: 1.

9
chapter nine

Global Foreign-Exchange Markets

Objectives

- To learn the fundamentals of foreign exchange

- To identify the major characteristics of the foreign-exchange market and how governments control the flow of currencies across national borders

- To describe how the foreign-exchange market works

- To examine the different institutions that deal in foreign exchange

- To understand why companies deal in foreign exchange

All things are obedient to money.

—*English proverb*

CASE: Going Down to the Wire in the Money-Transfer Market

Long known as "the fastest way to send money," U.S.-based Western Union controls nearly 80 percent of the money-transfer market and is widely acknowledged as the world leader in *wire transfers*—electronic transfers of funds from one financial institution to another.[1] In this case, it's a transfer from one Western Union office to another. However, Western Union is now facing stiff competition from banks threatening to encroach on its market share of the electronic money-transfer business.

Customers have many different options when sending money through Western Union. Money can be sent in person at an agent location, over the phone, or online, and senders may use cash, debit cards, or credit cards. For example, to send money to Ukraine using a Western Union agent location, the customer must fill out a "Send Money" form. He or she then receives a receipt, which includes a Money Transfer Control number. This number must be given to the person receiving the funds. The

MAP 9.1 Most of Western Union's Outbound Remittances are Sent to Mexico by Mexican Emigrants

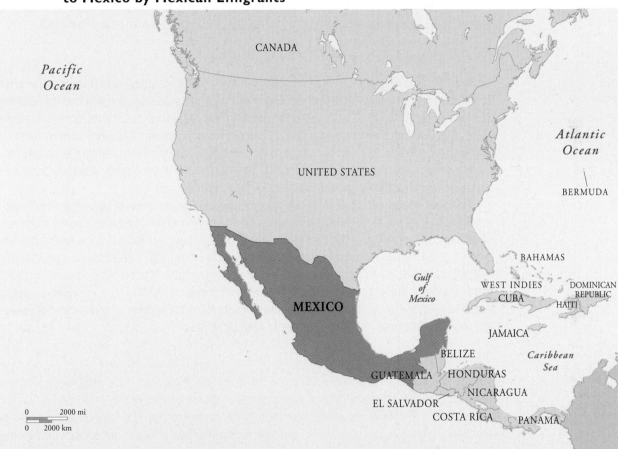

Western Union was started in 1851 when a group of businessmen in Rochester, New York, formed a printing telegraph company. The name of the company was changed to Western Union in 1861 when it completed the first transcontinental telegraph line. Western Union introduced its money-transfer service in 1871 and started offering this service outside North America in 1989. Today, over 275,000 Western Union agent locations are found in over 200 countries and territories around the world. Money transfers account for 80 percent of Western Union's revenues, and about $50 billion is transferred annually through Western Union.

receiver fills out a "Receive Money" form and presents the Money Transfer Control number along with valid identification at a Western Union agent location in Ukraine to receive the money.

CONVERTING CURRENCY

The funds are converted into the foreign currency using an exchange rate set by Western Union. The transfer fees for sending money are determined based on how much money is sent, in what form it is sent (cash or debit/credit card), and where it is going. For example, sending $500 to Mexico from

California costs $15; sending $500 to the Philippines from California costs $32. Part of Western Union's attractiveness is its speed and anonymity. Western Union can move cash from one location of the world to another in just minutes and requires no ID, background check, or bank account.

The Mexican Connection (I)

It's estimated that each year over 80 million migrant workers send more than $100 billion to their native countries. Most of Western Union's wire transfer business in the United States comes from Mexican emigrants who send part of their paycheck home to support their families (Map 9.1). In 2006, Mexico received at least $23 billion in remittances, making it the largest host country in Latin America for remittances, followed by Brazil. The Inter-American Development Bank estimates that remittances to Latin America and the Caribbean could rise from $62.3 billion in 2006 to $100 billion by 2010. Remittances already exceed foreign direct investment and overseas aid as sources of foreign exchange. Annual remittance income has passed tourism to become the second-largest source of foreign-exchange income in Mexico after oil revenues.

EXCHANGE RATES AND COMPETITION

A class-action lawsuit was filed against Western Union in 1997 charging that Western Union offered its customers lower exchange rates than the market exchange rates without informing them of the difference. The lawsuit was settled in 2000, and Western Union is now required to state on its receipts and advertisements that it uses its own exchange rate on transactions and that any difference between the company rate and the market rate is kept by the company. For example, the market exchange rate on May 16, 2007, for Mexican pesos was 10.8012 pesos/USD (US$500 = 5,400.60 pesos); Western Union's offered exchange rate was 10.54 pesos/USD (US$500 = 5,270 pesos).

Financial institutions such as banks have pressured Western Union to use better exchange rates. Profit margins in the money-transfer business can reach 30 percent, and many banks have started to offer their own money-transfer services in an attempt to take advantage of the continued expected growth of the foreign money-transfer industry. For example, in 2001, Wells Fargo agreed to accept a consular identification card from Mexican immigrants who want to open a bank account but lack a U.S. driver's license. This card verifies Mexicans' identities without revealing their immigration status. After Wells Fargo began accepting the consular identification card, the number of bank accounts opened with the consular ID jumped by over 500 percent within three years.

The Mexican Connection (II)

Wells Fargo and other U.S. banks, including Citi and Bank of America, have established alliances with Mexican banks to offer remittance accounts to the emigrant workers in the United States. Workers can now open a U.S. bank account with their consular ID and ask for two ATM cards. They can then deposit remittance money in the U.S. account, and their family members at home can withdraw the money from the associated Mexican bank.

In 2005, the Federal Reserve teamed up with Mexico's central bank to create a new program that facilitates remittances made from the United States to Mexico. This program allows U.S. commercial banks to make money transfers for Mexican workers through the Federal Reserve's own automated clearinghouse, which is linked to Banco de Mexico, the Mexican central bank.

Even the wire transfer fees at banks are cheaper than Western Union's. For example, Wells Fargo charges a $5 fee to send $500 to Mexico compared with Western Union's $15 fee for the same transaction. Many banks are moving toward eliminating exchange-rate spreads (the difference between the market rate and the rate they use for the wire transfer) and transfer fees to Mexico to provide more attractive alternatives to migrant workers.

This new onslaught of competition by banks has forced Western Union to cut its fees and offer new services, including a home-delivery service, where money is delivered directly to the recipient's door. Western Union is also moving into countries such as China and India to increase its market share. The increased competition has driven down remittance fees around the world. In Ukraine, for example, Western Union was forced to drop its fee from $43 to $20.

The Mexican Connection (III)

Migrant workers complain about the high transfer fees and exchange-rate spread associated with Western Union, but many continue to use this service instead of the lower-cost method of remitting money through banks. Mexico has a history of unstable currencies and widespread inflation, resulting in a traditional mistrust of banks. Other emigrants base their choice on word of mouth or convenience and location. Many are simply unaware of the variety of choices available for sending money and do not know how to get the best deal.

Another reason why many continue to use Western Union is its worldwide availability. For thousands of tiny villages, Western Union is the main link to the outside world. For example, Coatetelco is a small Mexican village south of Mexico City with no bank. A few people grow maize, chilies, and fruit, but remittances—mostly from agricultural or construction workers in Georgia and the Carolinas—account for 90 percent of the villagers' incomes. Patricio, 49, says that at the end of each month, he gets a call from his two sons, who are working illegally in Georgia. They give him a code number, and he drives or rides his horse 4 miles to the nearest Western Union office, located in a government telegraph office, to pick up the $600 they spent $40 to wire to him. Less expensive remittance services are available at the nearby Banamex bank in Mazatepec, but so far, Patricio and his neighbors are not willing to travel the 8 miles to get there. Besides, he says, "we do not trust the banks, and they make everything more difficult."

Introduction

Changing money from one currency to another and moving it around to different parts of the world is serious business, both on a personal and a company level. To survive, both MNEs and small import and export companies must understand foreign exchange and exchange rates. In a business setting, there is a fundamental difference between making a payment in the domestic market and making a payment abroad. In a domestic transaction, companies use only one currency. In a foreign transaction, companies can use two or more currencies. For example, a U.S. company that exports skis to a French distributor may ask the French store that buys skis to remit payment in dollars, unless the U.S. company has some specific use for euros (the currency France uses), such as paying a French supplier.

Assume you're a U.S. importer who has agreed to purchase a certain quantity of French perfume and to pay the French exporter €4,000 for it. Assuming you had the money, how would you go about paying? First, you would go to the international department of your local bank to buy €4,000 at the going market rate. Let's assume the euro/dollar exchange rate is €0.7276 per dollar. Your bank then would charge your account $5,498 ($4,000/€0.7276) plus the transaction costs and give you a special check payable in euros made out to the exporter. The exporter would deposit it in a French bank, which then would credit the exporter's account with €4,000. Then the foreign-exchange transaction would be complete.

WHAT IS *FOREIGN EXCHANGE*?

Foreign exchange is money denominated in the currency of another nation or group of nations.[2] The market in which these transactions take place is the **foreign-exchange market.** Foreign exchange can be in the form of cash, funds available on credit and debit cards, traveler's checks, bank deposits, or other short-term claims.[3] As our opening case illustrates, for example, Mexican migrant workers in the United States often use Western Union to convert dollars to pesos and then wire the pesos to offices in Mexico where relatives can retrieve the cash.

An **exchange rate** is the price of a currency. It is the number of units of one currency that buys one unit of another currency, and this number can change daily. For example, on July 26, 2007, €1 could purchase US$1.3744. Exchange rates make international price and cost comparisons possible.

CONCEPT CHECK

When we introduced the idea of a **multinational enterprise (MNE)** in Chapter 1, we emphasized that MNEs are firms that take a global approach to production and markets. Here we add that the need to deal with **foreign exchange** is one of the important factors in the environment in which MNEs must conduct business.

Foreign exchange—money denominated in the currency of another nation or group of nations.

Exchange rate—the price of a currency.

Case Review Note

The Bank for International Settlements divides the foreign-exchange market into reporting dealers (also known as dealer banks or money center banks), other financial institutions, and nonfinancial institutions.

CONCEPT CHECK

In discussing "The Political Environment" in Chapter 3, we observe that the relationships comprising a country's political system—relationships among its institutions, organizations, and interest groups—depend on the "political norms and rules" over which its government exercises control. As we'll see in Chapter 10, these strictures include rules for trading currency; moreover, governments are active traders of foreign currency through money center banks.

Dealers can trade foreign exchange

- Directly with other dealers.
- Through voice brokers.
- Through electronic brokerage systems.

Reuters, EBS, and Bloomberg facilitate foreign-exchange trades on automated trading systems.

Foreign exchange market

- Over-the-counter (OTC) commercial and investment banks.
- Securities exchanges.

PLAYERS ON THE FOREIGN-EXCHANGE MARKET

The foreign-exchange market is made up of many different players. The **Bank for International Settlements (BIS),** a central banking institution in Basel, Switzerland, owned and controlled by 55 member central banks, divides the market into three major categories: *reporting dealers,* other *financial institutions,* and *nonfinancial institutions.*

Who Are the Players? *Reporting dealers,* also known as *money center banks,* include large banks, such as Deutsche Bank, UBS, Citi, RBS, Barclays Capital, and HSBC. (In our closing case, we show how one money center bank, HSBC, dealt with a financial crisis in Argentina.) Because of the volume of transactions that the money center banks engage in, they are influential in setting prices and are the market makers. Other financial institutions include commercial banks other than the money center banks (local and regional banks), hedge funds, pension funds, money market funds, currency funds, mutual funds, specialized foreign-exchange trading companies, and so forth. Western Union, whose current activities are detailed in our opening case, is a good example of a nonbanking financial institution that deals in foreign exchange.

Whom Do the Players Serve? Nonfinancial customers include governments and companies (MNEs as well as small- and medium-size corporations and companies). The BIS reported in its 2007 survey of reporting dealers that 43 percent of their counterparties were other reporting dealers, 40 percent were other financial institutions, and 17 percent were nonfinancial institutions. In comparison with prior surveys, the share of reporting dealers declined somewhat, whereas the share of other financial institutions rose somewhat.[4]

What Do Players Do? Dealers, at whatever level, can operate on a proprietary basis where they trade currencies to generate profit from those transactions, or they can provide a wide range of foreign-exchange services for their customers. In the interbank market, or the market between dealer banks, banks either deal directly with each other or they operate through foreign-exchange brokers. The trades can be conducted by voice or electronically; however, the trend is clearly moving to and dominated by electronic trades.

Electronic Services Dealers, whether in the money center banks or other financial institutions, use one or a combination of electronic services to trade currencies. Three of the most widely used are Reuters, EBS (bought by UK-based ICAP in 2006), and Bloomberg. Reuters is also a U.K.-based firm, whereas Bloomberg is a U.S.-based firm. A bank or other customer gets access to the automated system by purchasing the service from one of the providers and paying a monthly fee to receive a link through telephone lines to the bank's computers. Then the bank can use the automated system to trade currency. The automated system is efficient because it lists bid and sell quotes, allowing the bank to trade immediately.

Also, the services provide a great deal of market data, news, quotes, and statistics about different markets around the world. It is not uncommon for a trading room to have more than one electronic service and for traders to have different preferences within the same office. For example, one trader may prefer Reuters, whereas another may provide Bloomberg, even though both work in the same trading room.

SOME ASPECTS OF THE FOREIGN-EXCHANGE MARKET

The foreign-exchange market has two major segments: the over-the-counter market (OTC) and the exchange-traded market. The OTC market is composed of commercial banks as just described, investment banks, and other financial institutions. The exchange-traded market is composed of securities exchanges, such as the CME Group, the Philadelphia Stock Exchange, and London International Financial Futures and Options Exchange (LIFFE) CONNECT, where certain types of foreign-exchange instruments, such as exchange-traded futures and options, are traded.

Some Traditional Foreign-Exchange Instruments   Several different types of foreign-exchange instruments are traded in these markets, but the traditional foreign-exchange instruments that comprise the bulk of foreign-exchange trading are *spot transactions, outright forwards,* and *FX swaps:*

- **Spot transactions** involve the immediate exchange of currency, which is generally made on the second business day after the date on which the two foreign-exchange dealers agree to the transaction. The rate at which the transaction is settled is the **spot rate.** (Our opening case, which discusses Western Union's policies on currency conversion, gives a good idea of how individuals can trade foreign exchange on the spot market.)

- **Outright forward transactions** involve the exchange of currency on a future date. It is the single purchase or sale of a currency for future delivery. The rate at which the transaction is settled is the forward rate and is a contract rate between the two parties. The forward transaction will be settled at the forward rate no matter what the actual spot rate is at the time of settlement.

- In an **FX swap,** one currency is swapped for another on one date and then swapped back on a future date. Most often, the first leg of a FX swap is a spot transaction, with the second leg of the swap a future transaction. For example, assume that IBM receives a dividend in British pounds from its subsidiary in the United Kingdom but has no use for British pounds until it has to pay a British supplier in pounds in 30 days. It would rather have dollars now than hold on to the pounds for 30 days. IBM could enter into an FX swap in which it sells the pounds for dollars to a dealer in the spot market at the spot rate and agrees to buy pounds for dollars from the dealer in 30 days at the forward rate. Although an FX swap is both a spot and a forward transaction, it is accounted for as a single transaction.

Derivatives   In addition to the traditional instruments, there are **derivatives,** such as currency swaps, options, and futures.[5] Currency swaps are OTC instruments, options are traded both OTC and on exchanges, and futures are exchange-traded instruments.

- **Currency swaps** deal more with interest-bearing financial instruments (such as a bond), and they involve the exchange of principal and interest payments. As we observe in our closing case, HSBC is involved in a variety of foreign currency transactions, including all OTC derivatives; Western Union, the subject of our opening case, is more directly involved in spot transactions and in transferring funds from one country to another.

- **Options** are the right but not the obligation to trade foreign currency in the future.

- A **futures contract** is an agreement between two parties to buy or sell a particular currency at a particular price on a particular future date, as specified in a standardized contract to all participants in that currency futures exchange.

Size, Composition, and Location of the Foreign-Exchange Market   Before we examine the market instruments in more detail, let's look at the size, composition, and geographic location of the market. Every three years, the BIS conducts a survey of foreign-exchange activity in the world. In the 2007 survey, it estimated that $3.2 trillion in foreign exchange is traded every day.[6]

Foreign-exchange activity increased substantially in 2007 by 71 percent compared with the 2004 survey. This increase more than reversed the fall in global foreign-exchange activity from 1998 to 2001. Some of the reasons for the increase are the growing importance of foreign exchange as an alternative asset and a larger emphasis on **hedge funds**— funds typically used by wealthy individuals and institutions that are allowed to use aggressive strategies that are unavailable to mutual funds.

Figure 9.1 illustrates the trends in foreign-exchange trading beginning with the 1989 survey. The $3.2 trillion daily turnover includes traditional foreign-exchange market activity only—spots, outright forwards, and FX swaps. In the OTC derivatives market,

---

Traditional foreign-exchange instruments

- Spot.
- Outright forward.
- FX swap.

The spot rate is the exchange rate quoted for transactions that require delivery within two days.

Outright forwards involve the exchange of currency beyond three days at a fixed exchange rate, known as the forward rate.

An FX swap is a simultaneous spot and forward transaction.

Three other important foreign-exchange instruments:

- Currency swaps.
- Options.
- Futures.

Size of the foreign-exchange market—$3.2 trillion daily.

FIGURE 9.1   Foreign-Exchange Markets: Average Daily Volume, 1992–2007

The data compiled by the BIS include traditional foreign-exchange activity, such as spots, outright forwards, and FX swaps, as well as the volume of derivatives, such as hedge funds, traded in the OTC. In fact, the growth in hedge fund trading is one factor in the significant increase in activity between 2001 and 2007.

Source: Bank for International Settlements, *Central Bank Survey of Foreign Exchange and Derivatives Market Activity,* 2007 (Basel, Switzerland: BIS, December 2007), 2. Reprinted by permission of the Bank for International Settlements.

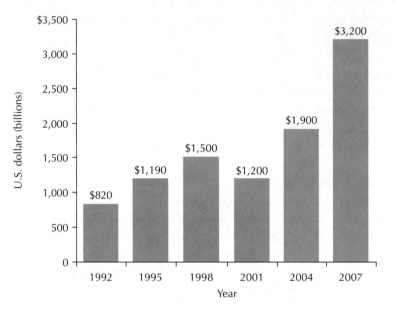

CONCEPT CHECK

It's interesting (though not necessarily surprising) to note that the most widely traded currencies in the world are those issued by countries that enjoy high levels of political freedom (see Chapter 3) and economic freedom (see Chapter 4).

daily activity increased by 74 percent to $4.2 trillion. This is also a significant escalation in activity compared with the period 1998 to 2001, when activity increased by 10 percent. Some of the derivatives just described are traded in both the OTC and exchange markets, but the BIS data only count the derivatives traded in the OTC market.

Using the U.S. Dollar on the Foreign-Exchange Market   The U.S. dollar is the most important currency in the foreign-exchange market; in 2007, it comprised one side (buy or sell) of 86.3 percent of all foreign currency transactions worldwide, as Table 9.1 illustrates. This means that almost every foreign-exchange transaction conducted on a daily basis has the dollar as one leg of the transaction. Numbers in the table are percentages and add up to 200 percent because there are two sides to each transaction.

TABLE 9.1   Global Foreign Exchange: Currency Distribution

The US$ is involved in a whopping 86.3% of all worldwide foreign-exchange transactions. Because it's so readily available, it's a popular choice for exchanges between two countries other than the United States, and it's involved in four of the seven most frequently traded currency pairs (the $/€ is number one, the $/¥ number two).

Currency	April 1992	April 1995	April 1998	April 1998	April 2001	April 2007
U.S. dollar	82.0%	83.3%	87.3%	90.3%	88.7%	86.3%
Euro	—	—	—	37.6	37.2	37.0
Japanese yen	23.4	24.1	20.2	22.7	20.3	16.5
Pound sterling	13.6	9.4	11.0	13.2	16.9	15.0
Swiss franc	8.4	7.3	7.1	6.1	6.1	6.8
All others	72.6	75.9	74.4	30.1	30.8	38.4

Source: Bank for International Settlements, *Central Bank Survey of Foreign Exchange and Derivatives Market Activity,* 2007 (Basel, Switzerland: BIS, December 2007), p. 11. Reprinted by permission of the Bank for International Settlements.

There are five major reasons why the dollar is so widely traded:[7]

1. It's an investment currency in many capital markets.
2. It's a reserve currency held by many central banks.
3. It's a transaction currency in many international commodity markets.
4. It's an invoice currency in many contracts.
5. It's an intervention currency employed by monetary authorities in market operations to influence their own exchange rates.

Because of the ready availability of U.S. dollars worldwide, this currency is important as a vehicle for foreign-exchange transactions between two countries other than the United States. An example of how the dollar can be used as a vehicle currency for two other countries is when a Mexican company importing products from a Japanese exporter converts Mexican pesos into dollars and sends them to the Japanese exporter, who converts the dollars into yen. Thus the U.S. dollar has one leg on both sides of the transaction—in Mexico and in Japan.

There may be a couple of reasons to go through dollars instead of directly from pesos to yen. The first is that the Japanese exporter might not have any need for pesos, whereas it can use dollars for a variety of reasons. The second is that the Mexican importer might have trouble getting yen at a good exchange rate if the Mexican banks are not carrying yen balances. However, the banks undoubtedly carry dollar balances, so the importer might have easy access to the dollars. Thus the dollar has become an important vehicle for international transactions, and it greatly simplifies life for a foreign bank because the bank will not have to carry balances in many different currencies. (And, not surprisingly, some currencies are harder to find than others—see the cartoon in Figure 9.2.)

Frequently Traded Currency Pairs   Another way to consider foreign currency trades is to look at the most frequently traded currency pairs. The top seven currency pairs involve the U.S. dollar, with the top two pairs being the euro/dollar (EUR/USD) (27 percent of total) and the dollar/yen (USD/JPY).[8] This reinforces the idea that the dollar is a vehicle currency for trading between other currencies, which is known as *cross-trading*.

The trade between the dollar and yen is very sensitive politically because the exchange rate is often a function of trade negotiations between Japan and the United States.[9] The Japanese yen is an important currency in Asia because its value reflects the competitive positions of other countries in the region and because it is freely traded, unlike the Chinese yuan, which is more tightly controlled by the government.

THE EURO   The euro is also in four of the top ten currency pairs. Although the dollar is still more popular in most emerging markets, the euro is gaining ground, particularly in Eastern European countries like the Czech Republic and Hungary. Prior to the introduction of the euro, the German mark or Deutsche mark was one of the most important trading currencies in the world. In the 1998 BIS survey, the Deutsche mark represented 30.1 percent of the average daily turnover in foreign exchange (down from a high of 39.6 percent in the

> The dollar is the most widely traded currency in the world:
>
> - An investment currency in many capital markets.
> - A reserve currency held by many central banks.
> - A transaction currency in many international commodity markets.
> - An invoice currency in many contracts.
> - An intervention currency employed by monetary authorities in market operations to influence their own exchange rates.

> The dollar is part of four of the top seven currency pairs traded:
>
> - The dollar/euro is number one.
> - The dollar/yen is number two.

FIGURE 9.2
The Challenge of Pricing Exotic Currencies

Even if the exchange rate were readily available, there's no guarantee that your bank carries the currency in question. You're probably better off making your exchange in US$.

Source: Copyright Werner Wejp-Olsen, Cartoonstock.com.

FIGURE 9.3   Foreign-Exchange Markets: Geographical Distribution, April 2007

The United Kingdom handles a little over 34% of all world foreign-exchange activity (compared to just over 16.6% by the United States). Location is a big factor in the United Kingdom's popularity: London is close to all the capital markets of Europe, and its time zone makes it convenient for making trades in both the U.S. and Asian markets.

Source: Bank for International Settlements, *Central Bank Survey of Foreign Exchange and Derivatives Market Activity, 2007* (Basel, Switzerland: BIS, December 2007), p. 11. Reprinted by permission of the Bank for International Settlements.

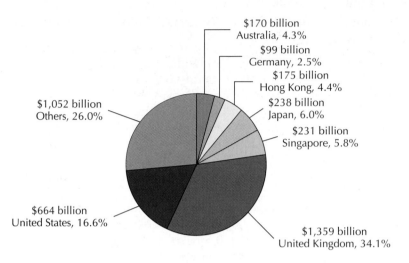

1992 survey), but as noted in Table 9.1, the euro represented only 37.0 percent of the average daily turnover in the 2007 survey. That shows how important the Deutsche mark was and how influential Germany is as a member of the European Monetary System.

Given that the dollar is clearly the most widely traded currency in the world, you'd expect the biggest market for foreign-exchange trading would be in the United States. As Figure 9.3 illustrates, however, the biggest market by far is in the United Kingdom. The four largest centers for foreign-exchange trading (the United Kingdom, the United States, Japan, and Singapore) account for 62.5 percent of the total average daily turnover. The U.K. market is so dominant that more dollars are traded in London than in New York.[10]

The biggest market for foreign exchange is London, followed by New York, Tokyo, and Singapore.

Does Geography Matter?

Foreign-Exchange Trades

Given that the U.S. dollar is the most widely traded currency in the world, why is London so important as a trading center? There are two major reasons for London's prominence. First, London, which is close to the major capital markets in Europe, is a strong international financial center where a large number of domestic and foreign financial institutions have operations. Thus London's geographic location relative to significant global economic activity is key.

Second, London is positioned in a unique way because of the time zone where it is located. In Map 9.2 (p. 342), note that at noon in London, it is 7 in the morning in New York and evening in Asia. The London market opens toward the end of the trading day in Asia and is going strong as the New York foreign-exchange market opens up. London thus straddles both of the other major markets in the world.

Another way to illustrate the importance of geography is to note the daily volume of market activity that takes place in different markets around the world, especially in North America and Europe. Figure 9.4 illustrates the average number of electronic conversations per hour as monitored by Reuters. It illustrates how market activity is concentrated on the time period when Asia and Europe are open or when Europe and the United States are open, even though the market is really open 24 hours a day. Because the U.S. dollar is the most widely traded currency in the world and London is the major market center for dollars traded outside of the United States, it makes sense that most market activity would take place during the hours that the U.S. and London markets are open. A better price for currencies can be had when the markets are active and liquid. ●

FIGURE 9.4   The Circadian Rhythms of the Foreign-Exchange Market

Peak periods for foreign-exchange activity occur between about 0600 and 1200 hours (when both European and U.S. markets are open for business) and 1200 and 1800 hours (when both U.S. and Asian markets are active). Time (0100–2400) is Greenwich Mean Time.

Source: Reuters.

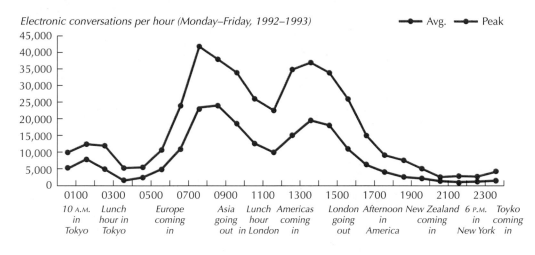

Electronic conversations per hour (Monday–Friday, 1992–1993)   ● Avg.   ● Peak

Major Foreign-Exchange Markets

THE SPOT MARKET

Foreign-exchange dealers are the ones who quote the rates. The dealers always quote a *bid (buy)* and *offer (sell) rate.* The **bid** is the price at which the dealer is willing to buy foreign currency; the **offer** is the price at which the dealer is willing to sell foreign currency. In the spot market, the **spread** is the difference between the bid and offer rates, and it is the dealer's profit margin. In our opening case, we explained how Western Union quotes exchange rates for the purpose of trading dollars for pesos. Its rates are often different from those quoted by commercial banks, but some people prefer to use Western Union, pay higher fees, and get lower exchange rates. Why? In part, because of a lack of trust in the banking system.

Direct and Indirect Quotes   Let's look at an example of how a bid and offer rate might work. The rate a dealer quotes for the British pound might be $2.0267/69 (assume the dealer is U.S. based). This means the dealer is willing to buy pounds at $2.0267 each and sell them for $2.0269 each. Obviously, a dealer wants to buy low and sell high. In this example, the dealer quotes the foreign currency as the number of U.S. dollars for one unit of that currency. This method of quoting exchange rates is called the **direct quote,** also known in the foreign-exchange industry as **American terms.** It represents a quote from the point of view of someone in the United States.

The other convention for quoting foreign exchange is known as **European terms,** which is the direct quote for someone located in Europe. Using the example of the British pound and U.S. dollar, that means the direct quote in Europe would be the number of British pounds per dollar. This is also sometimes called the **indirect quote** in the United States. In Table 9.2, the direct quote for the U.K. pound is $2.0489, and the indirect quote is £0.4881.

Base and Term Currencies   When dealers quote currencies to their customers, they always quote the **base currency** (the denominator) first, followed by the **terms currency** (the numerator). This seems backward, but that is the convention dealers use. A quote for

Case Review Note

Key foreign-exchange terms:

- Bid—the rate at which traders buy foreign exchange.
- Offer—the rate at which traders sell foreign exchange.
- Spread—the difference between bid and offer rates.
- American terms or direct quote—the number of dollars per unit of foreign currency.
- European terms or indirect quote—the number of units of foreign currency per dollar.

MAP 9.2
International Time Zones and the Single World Market

The world's communication networks are now so good that we can talk of a single world market. It starts in a small way in New Zealand at around 9:00 a.m. (local time), just in time to catch the tail end of the previous night's market in New York (where it's about 4:00 p.m. local time). Two or three hours later, Tokyo opens, followed an hour later by Hong Kong and Manila, and then half an hour later by Singapore. By now, with the Far East market in full swing, the focus moves to the Near and Middle East. Mumbai (formerly Bombay) opens two hours after Singapore, followed after an hour and a half by Abu Dhabi and Athens. By this stage, trading in the Far and Middle East is usually thin as dealers wait to see how Europe will trade. Paris and Frankfurt open an hour ahead of London, and by this time Tokyo is starting to close down, so the European market can judge the Japanese market. By lunchtime in London, New York is starting to open up, and as Europe closes down, positions can be passed westward. Midday in New York, trading tends to be quiet because there is nowhere to pass a position to. The San Francisco market, three hours behind New York, is effectively a satellite of the New York market, although very small positions can be passed on to New Zealand banks. (Note that in the former Soviet Union, standard time zones are advanced an hour. Also note that some countries and territories have

"dollar/yen" means the dollar is the base currency and the yen is the terms currency. If you know the dollar/yen quote, you can divide that rate into 1 to get the yen/dollar quote. In other words, the exchange rate in American terms is the reciprocal or inverse of the exchange rate in European terms. For example, using the rates for the Japanese yen in Table 9.2, 1/.008420 = ¥118.76.

In a dollar/yen quote, the dollar is the denominator and the yen is the numerator. By tracking changes in the exchange rate, managers can determine whether the base currency is strengthening or weakening. For example, on February 10, 2007, the dollar/yen rate was ¥121.73/$1.00, and on April 28, 2005, the rate was ¥118.51/$1.00.

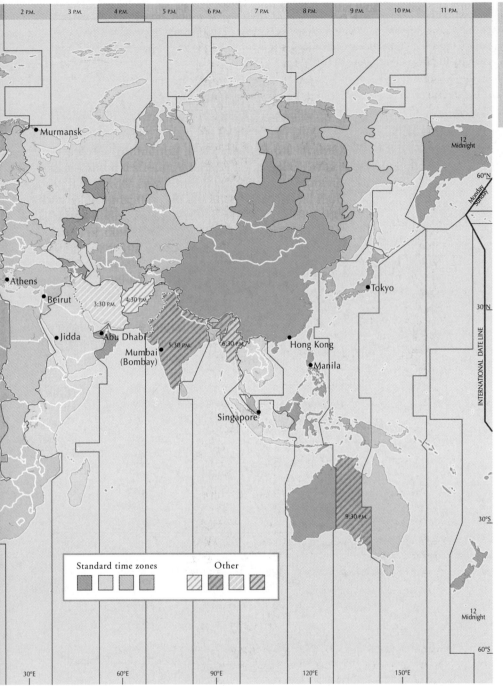

adopted half-hour time zones, as shown by hatched lines.)

Source: Adapted from Julian Walmsley, *The Foreign Exchange Handbook* (New York: John Wiley, 1983), 7–8. Reprinted by permission of John Wiley & Sons, Inc. Some information taken from *The Cambridge Factfinders*, 3rd ed., ed. David Crystal (New York: Cambridge University Press, 1998), 440.

As the numerator falls, the base currency—the dollar—is weakening or getting less expensive. Conversely, the terms currency, or the yen in this case, is strengthening or getting more expensive from a dollar perspective.

Most large newspapers, especially those devoted to business or those having business sections, quote exchange rates daily. Because most currencies constantly fluctuate in value, many managers check the values daily. For example, the *Wall Street Journal* provides quotes in American terms (US$ equivalent) and European terms (currency per US$), as shown in Table 9.2. All quotes, except those noted as one-month, three-month, and six-month forward, are spot quotes.

TABLE 9.2 Foreign-Exchange Markets, July 26, 2007

The *direct* quote—the price of the foreign currency in terms of the home-country currency—is given in the column headed "In US$"; the *indirect* quote—the price of the home-country currency in terms of the foreign currency—is given in the column headed "Per US$." Thus, the direct quote for the Japanese yen (¥) is $.008420/¥1 and the indirect quote ¥118.75/$1.

Currencies

U.S.-dollar foreign-exchange rates in late New York trading

July 26, 2007

Country/currency	Thurs In US$	Thurs Per US$	US$ vs, YTD chg (%)	Country/currency	Thurs In US$	Thurs Per US$	US$ vs, YTD chg (%)
Americas				**Europe**			
Argentina/peso*	.3185	3.1397	2.6	Czech Rep./koruna**	.04913	20.354	−2.3
Brazil/real	.5203	1.9220	−10.0	Denmark/krone	.1847	5.4142	−4.2
Canada/dollar	.9491	1.0536	−9.6	Euro area/euro	1.3744	.7276	−3.9
1-mos forward	.9498	1.0529	−9.6	Hungary/forint‡	.005462	183.08	−3.9
3-mos forward	.9508	1.0517	−9.6	Malta/lira	3.1961	.3129	−3.8
6-mos forward	.9517	1.0508	−9.4	Norway/krone	.1713	5.8377	−6.4
Chile/peso	.001908	524.11	−1.5	Poland/zloty	.3598	2.7793	−4.3
Colombia/peso	.0005020	1992.03	−11.0	Russia/ruble‡	.03926	25.471	−3.2
Ecuador/U.S. dollar	1	1	unch	Slovak Rep/koruna	.04111	24.325	−6.8
Mexico/peso*	.0912	10.9697	1.5	Sweden/krona	.1484	6.7385	−1.6
Peru/new soil	.3159	3.166	−0.9	Switzerland/franc	.8309	1.2035	−1.3
Uruguay/peso	.04240	23.58	−3.3	1-mos forward	.8329	1.2006	−1.2
Venezuela/bolivar***	.000466	2145.92	unch	3-mos forward	.8365	1.1955	−1.1
Asia-Pacific				6-mos forward	8414	1.1885	−1.0
				Turkey/lira**	.7683	1.3015	−8.1
Australian/dollar	8719	1.1469	−9.5	UK/pound	2.0489	.4881	−4.4
China/yuan	1322	2.5654	−3.1	1-mos forward	2.0480	.4883	−4.4
Hong Kong/dollar	1278	7.8232	−0.6	3-mos forward	2.0458	.4888	−4.3
India/rupee	.02477	40.371	−8.5	6-mos forward	2.0413	.4899	−4.1
Indonesia/rupiah	.0001094	9141	1.6	**Middle East/Africa**			
Japan/yen	.008420	118.76	−0.2				
1-mos forward	.008454	118.29	−0.2	Bahrain/dinar	2.6526	.3770	unch
3-mos forward	.008518	117.40	−0.2	Egypt/pound*	.1768	5.6561	−1.0
6-mos forward	.008610	116.14	−0.1	Israel/shekel	.2317	4.3059	2.4
Malaysia/ringgits §	.2908	3.4388	−2.6	Jordan/dinar	1.4114	.7085	−0.1
New Zealand/dollar	.7833	1.2767	−10.1	Kuwait/dinar	3.5410	.2824	−2.3
Pakistan/rupee	.01653	60.496	−0.5	Lebanon/pound	.0006612	1512.40	unch
Philippines/peso	.0221	45.310	−7.6	Saudi Arabia/riyal	.2666	3.7509	unch
Singapore/dollar	.6598	1.5156	−1.1	South Africa/rand	.1414	7.0721	1.1
South Korea/won	.0010890	918.27	−1.3	UAE/dirham	.2723	3.6724	unch
Taiwan/dollar	.03045	32.841	0.8				
Thailand/baht	.03373	29.647	−16.4	SDR††	1.5324	.6526	−1.8

*Floating rate.
†Financial.
§Government rate.
‡Russian Central Bank rate.
**Rebased as of Jan. 1, 2005.
††Special Drawing Rights (SDR); from the International Monetary Fund, based on exchange rates for U.S., British, and Japanese currencies.
*** Changed to bolívar fuerte on January 1, 2008, at a new ratio of 1 Bs. F to 1000 bolívares.
Note: Based on trading among banks of $1 million and more, as quoted at 4 p.m. by Reuters.

A man in Tel Aviv, Israel, counts his money after exchanging U.S. dollars for Israeli shekels (ILS, formerly NLS). The money-changer prominently displays the current *buy spot rate* (ILS4.82/US$) and *sell spot rate* (ILS4.94/US$). The *spread* (ILS4.94 − ILS4.82 = ILS0.12) is the trader's profit on the exchange of U.S. dollars for Israeli shekels.

Interbank Transactions   The spot rates are the selling rates for interbank transactions of $1 million and more. **Interbank transactions** are transactions between banks. Retail transactions, those between banks and companies or individuals, provide fewer foreign currency units per dollar than interbank transactions. Similar quotes can be found in other business publications and online. However, these are only approximations, and exact quotes are available through the dealers.

THE FORWARD MARKET

As noted earlier, the spot market is for foreign-exchange transactions that occur within two business days, but in some transactions, a seller extends credit to the buyer for a period longer than two days. For example, a Japanese exporter of consumer electronics might sell television sets to a U.S. importer with immediate delivery but payment due in 30 days. The U.S. importer is obligated to pay in yen in 30 days and may enter into a contract with a currency dealer to deliver the yen at a forward rate—the rate quoted today for future delivery.

> The forward rate is the rate quoted for transactions that call for delivery after two business days.

In addition to the spot rates for each currency, Table 9.2 shows the forward rates for the British pound, Canadian dollar, Japanese yen, and Swiss franc. These are the most widely traded currencies in the forward market. However, forward contracts are available in many other currencies as well. The more exotic the currency, the more difficult it is to get a forward quote out too far in the future, and the greater the difference is likely to be between the forward rate and the spot rate.

Forward Discounts and Premiums   Building on what we said earlier, we now can say that the difference between the spot and forward rates is either the **forward discount** or the **forward premium.** An easy way to understand the difference between the forward rate and the spot rate for U.S. companies is to use currency quotes in American terms. If the forward rate for a foreign currency is less than the spot rate, then the foreign currency is selling at a forward discount. If the forward rate is greater than the spot rate, the foreign currency is selling at a forward premium. Using the direct quotes in Table 9.2 for the

> A forward discount exists when the forward rate is less than the spot rate.

A premium exists when the forward rate is greater than the spot rate.

Swiss franc for a six-month forward contract, the premium or discount would be computed as follows:

$$\frac{.8414 - .8309}{.8309} \times \frac{12}{6} = .025 \text{ or } 2.5\%$$

The premium percentage is annualized by multiplying the difference between the spot and forward rates by 12 months divided by the number of months forward, or six months in this example. Because the forward rate is greater than the spot rate, the Swiss franc is selling at a premium in the forward market by 2.5 percent over the spot market.

OPTIONS

An option is the right but not the obligation to trade a foreign currency at a specific exchange rate.

An *option* is the *right*, but not the *obligation*, to buy or sell a foreign currency within a certain time period or on a specific date at a specific exchange rate. An option can be purchased OTC from a commercial or investment bank, or it can be purchased on an exchange. For example, assume a U.S. company purchases an OTC option from a commercial or investment bank to buy 1,000,000 Japanese yen at ¥118.76 per US$ ($0.008420 per yen)—or $8,420. The writer of the option will charge the company a fee for writing the option. The more likely the option is to benefit the company, the higher the fee. The rate of ¥118.76 is called the *strike price* for the option. The fee or cost of the option is called the *premium.*

On the date when the option is set to expire, the company can look at the spot rate and compare it with the strike price to see what the better exchange rate is. If the spot rate were ¥125 per US$ ($0.00800 per yen)—or $8,000—it would not exercise the option because buying yen at the spot rate would cost less than buying them at the option rate. However, if the spot rate at that time were ¥96 per US$ ($0.01042 per yen)—or $10,417—the company would exercise the option because buying at the option rate would cost less than buying at the spot rate.

The option provides the company flexibility because it can walk away from the option if the strike price is not a good price. In the case of a forward contract, the cost is usually cheaper than the cost for an option, but the company cannot walk away from the contract. So a forward contract is cheaper but less flexible than an option.

FUTURES

A futures contract specifies an exchange rate in advance of the actual exchange of currency, but it is not as flexible as a forward contract.

A foreign currency futures contract resembles a forward contract insofar as it specifies an exchange rate some time in advance of the actual exchange of currency. However, a future is traded on an exchange, not OTC. Instead of working with a banker, companies work with exchange brokers when purchasing futures contracts. A forward contract is tailored to the amount and time frame the company needs, whereas a futures contract is for a specific amount and specific maturity date.

The futures contract is less valuable to a company than a forward contract. However, it may be useful to speculators and small companies that cannot enter into a forward contract. Table 9.3 summarizes the differences between forward contracts, which are traded OTC, and exchange-based contracts, such as futures and options.

The Foreign-Exchange Trading Process

When a company sells goods or services to a foreign customer and receives foreign currency, it needs to convert the foreign currency into the domestic currency. When importing, the company needs to convert domestic to foreign currency to pay the foreign supplier. This conversion usually takes place between the company and its bank.

TABLE 9.3 **Foreign-Exchange Markets: Exchange-Based and OTC Options**

	Exchange-Based (Options and Futures)	OTC (Forward Contracts)
Contract specifications	Standardized and customized	Customized
Regulation	Securities and Exchange Commission (SEC)	Self-regulated
Type of market	Open outcry, auction market	Dealer market
Counterparty* to every transaction	"AAA"-rated Options Clearing Corporation (OCC)	Bank on the contraside
Transparency/visible prices	Yes	No
Margin required for short positions**	Yes	No[†]
Orders anonymously represented in the market	Yes	No
Required to mark positions daily	Yes	No[†]
Audit trail	Complete sequential and second-by-second audit trail of each transaction	No
Participants	Public customers, as well as corporate and institutional users	Corporate and institutional users

*The *counterparty* is the party on the other end of the transaction. If, for instance, IBM were to enter into an OTC option with Citibank, the bank would be the counterparty; if it entered into an option on the Philadelphia Stock Exchange (PHLX), the counterparty would be a registered broker.

**A *margin* is a percentage of the value of the investment contract that a firm must pay in order to enter the contract. At day's end, the exchange adjusts the margin for the investor's gain or loss against the current market price—a process called *marking*. Marking is not required in the OTC market.

[†]Not a requirement but available.

Source: Philadelphia Stock Exchange, *A User's Guide to Currency Options* (1995–2006), at www.phlx.com (accessed July 28, 2007). Reprinted by permission of the Philadelphia Stock Exchange.

Originally, the commercial banks provided foreign-exchange services for their customers. Eventually, some of these commercial banks in New York and other U.S. money centers, such as Chicago and San Francisco, began to look at foreign-exchange trading as a major business activity instead of just a service. They became intermediaries for smaller banks by establishing correspondent relationships with them. They also became major dealers in foreign exchange.

The left side of Figure 9.5 shows what happens when U.S. Company A needs to sell euros for dollars. This situation could arise when U.S. Company A receives payment in euros from a German importer. The right side of the figure shows what happens when U.S. Company A needs to buy euros with dollars. This situation could arise when a company has to pay euros to a German supplier.

In either case, the U.S. company would contact its bank for help in converting the currency. If the company is a large MNE, such as a Fortune 500 company in the United States or a Global Fortune 500 company, it will probably deal directly with a money center bank (as shown on the top arrow in Figure 9.5) and not worry about another financial institution. Generally, because the MNE already has a strong banking relationship with its money center bank (or several different money center banks), the bank trades foreign exchange for the client as one of the services it offers. Companies below the Fortune 500 level operate through other financial institutions, such as local or regional banks or other financial institutions that can facilitate foreign-exchange trades. In that case, Financial Institution A and Financial Institution B still operate through a money center bank to make the trade because those institutions are too small to trade on their own. They typically have correspondent relationships with money center banks to allow them to make the trades.

Large MNEs go through their money center banks to settle foreign-exchange balances, but other firms use local banks or other financial institutions.

CONCEPT CHECK

In explaining "The Forces behind Globalization" in Chapter 1, we observe that although many barriers to the cross-border movement of commercial resources—including capital—are being removed, they have by no means completely disappeared. One reason for maintaining cordial relations with one's banker is the fact that these barriers make conducting international business more expensive than conducting domestic business. As we also explain in Chapter 6, conducting international business, especially on a large scale, requires high levels of capital mobility.

FIGURE 9.5   The Foreign-Exchange Trading Process

Let's say that you're U.S. Company A, that you've received euros in payment for goods, and that you want to sell your euros in return for dollars. To make the exchange, you may contact your local bank or go directly to a money center bank.

On the other hand, perhaps you're U.S. Company B and you expect to receive euros as a future payment. To protect yourself against fluctuations in the exchange rate, you want to buy euros that you can subsequently trade back for dollars. You could choose, say, a forward or a swap, and your path would be essentially a mirror image of Company A's.

Finally, either Company A or Company B could choose to convert by such means as an option or a futures contract—in which case the trade could be made by an options/future exchange, either directly or through a broker.

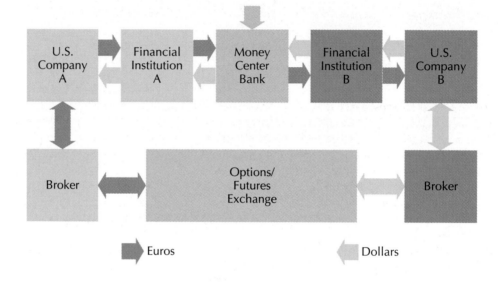

Assume that U.S. Company B is going to receive euros in the future. Because it cannot convert in the spot market until it receives the euros, it can consider a forward, swap, options, or futures contract to protect itself until the currency is finally delivered. Financial Institution B can do a forward, swap, or options contract for Company B. However, Company B can also consider an options or futures contract on one of the exchanges, such as the CME Group, the Philadelphia Stock Exchange, or LIFFE CONNECT. The same is true for Company A, which will need euros in the future.

BANKS AND EXCHANGES

At one time, only the big money center banks could deal directly in foreign exchange. Regional banks had to rely on the money center banks to execute trades on behalf of their clients. The emergence of electronic trading has changed that, however. Now even the regional banks can hook up to Reuters, EBS, or Bloomberg and deal directly in the interbank market or through brokers. In spite of this, the greatest volume of foreign-exchange activity takes place with the big money center banks. Because of their reach and volume, they are the ones that set the prices in global trading of foreign exchange.

Top Foreign-Exchange Dealers   There is more to servicing customers in the foreign-exchange market than size alone. Each year, *Euromoney* magazine surveys treasurers, traders, and investors worldwide to identify their favorite banks and the leading dealers in the interbank market. In addition to examining transaction volumes and quality of services, the criteria for selecting the top foreign-exchange dealers include the following:

- Ranking of banks by corporations and other banks in specific locations, such as London, Singapore, and New York
- Capability to handle major currencies, such as the U.S. dollar and euro
- Capability to handle major cross-trades—for example, those between the euro and pound or the euro and yen
- Capability to handle specific currencies
- Capability to handle derivatives (forwards, swaps, futures, and options)
- Capability to engage in research and analytics.[11]

For this reason, large companies may use several banks to deal in foreign exchange, selecting those that specialize in specific geographic areas, instruments, or currencies. In the past, for example, AT&T used Citibank for its broad geographic spread and wide coverage of different currencies, but it also used Deutsche Bank for euros, Swiss Bank Corporation for Swiss francs, NatWest Bank for British pounds, and Goldman Sachs for derivatives.

Table 9.4 identifies the top banks in the world in terms of foreign-exchange trading. They are the key players in the OTC market and include both commercial banks (such as Deutsche Bank and Citi) and investment banks (such as UBS—the London-based investment banking division of Union Bank of Switzerland and Swiss Bank Corporation). Whether one is looking at overall market share of foreign-exchange trading or the best banks in the trading of specific currency pairs, these top-10 banks are usually at or near the top in every category.

In addition to the OTC market, there are a number of exchanges in which foreign-exchange instruments, mostly options and futures, are traded. Three of the best-known exchanges are the **Chicago Mercantile Exchange (CME) Group,** the Philadelphia Stock Exchange (PHLX), and LIFFE, which is part of NYSE Euronext.

The top banks in the interbank market in foreign exchange are so ranked because of their ability to

- Trade in specific market locations.
- Engage in major currencies and cross-trades.
- Deal in specific currencies.
- Handle derivatives (forwards, options, futures, swaps).
- Conduct key market research.

CONCEPT CHECK

In Chapter 11, we explain why companies work so hard to establish and maintain effective **value chains**—frameworks for dividing value-creating activities into separate processes. For one thing, a reliable value chain permits a firm to focus on its **core competencies**—the unique skills or knowledge that make it better at something than its competitors. Because managing currencies and cross-trades is typically not among a firm's core competencies, its bankers are key components of its value chain.

TABLE 9.4 Foreign-Exchange Trades: Top Commercial and Investment Banks, 2007

Rankings from *Euromoney* magazine, which annually rates the top foreign-exchange banks in the world. Key criteria include location of trades and types of currency traded.

Trading Bank	Estimated Market Share %	Best in Euro/$	Best in $/Pounds	Best Euro/Pounds	Best in $/Yen
1. Deutsche Bank	19.3	1	5	1	2
2. UBS	14.85	4	4	3	3
3. Citi	9.0	2	3	5	1
4. RBS	8.90	6	6	6	6
5. Barclays Capital	8.80	5	2	2	5
6. Bank of America	5.29	8	7	9	8
7. HSBC	4.36	3	1	4	4
8. Goldman Sachs	4.14	—	—	—	9
9. JPMorgan	3.33	10	8	10	7
10. Morgan Stanley	2.86	—	—	—	—

Source: "FX Poll 2007: Overall Market Share," *Euromoney* (May 2007) and "FX Poll 2007: Best for Currencies," *Euromoney* (May 2007).

Firms can also use securities exchanges for derivatives trade in foreign exchange.

CME Group   The CME Group was formed on July 9, 2007, as a merger between the CME (Chicago Mercantile Exchange) and the Chicago Board of Trade. The CME operates according to so-called open outcry: Traders stand in a pit and call out prices and quantities. The platform is also linked to an electronic trading platform, which is increasing in popularity. The CME Group trades many different commodities. In terms of foreign exchange, it trades a variety of futures and options contracts in numerous currencies against the dollar as well as in cross rates—such as the euro against the Australian dollar.

In 2005, CME entered into an agreement with Reuters to have its futures contracts quoted, which should increase the access of trades to futures contracts.[12] In March 2007, CME and Reuters teamed up again to launch the world's first centrally cleared global foreign-exchange platform called FXMarketSpace. The basic idea behind the model is to establish a centrally cleared global platform that allows customers to buy and sell currencies anonymously. The new venture is targeting hedge funds, which are using computer-driven trading models to trade foreign exchange.[13]

Major exchanges that deal in foreign currency derivatives are the CME Group, the Philadelphia Stock Exchange, and LIFFE.

Philadelphia Stock Exchange   The Philadelphia Stock Exchange was one of the pioneers in trading currency options. It has also partnered with the Philadelphia Board of Trade to expand its offerings in currency futures. Options are currently offered in the Australian dollar, the British pound, the Canadian dollar, the euro, the Japanese yen, and the Swiss franc. Futures are offered in British pounds and the euro.[14]

London International Futures and Options Exchange   The London International Futures and Options Exchange was founded in 1992 to trade a variety of futures contracts and options. It was subsequently bought in 2002 by Euronext, then a European stock exchange based in Paris but with subsidiaries in other European countries, and it became known as Euronext.liffe. Beginning in 2003, the electronic platform where its derivatives products traded on member exchanges was known as LIFFE CONNECT. In 2007, Euronext merged with the New York Stock Exchange to create NYSE Euronext. Their futures and options contracts on the U.S. dollar/euro and euro/U.S. dollar are still traded on LIFFE CONNECT as part of LIFFE.

LOOKING TO THE FUTURE

Where Are Foreign-Exchange Markets Headed?

Significant strides have been made and will continue to be made in the development of foreign-exchange markets. The speed at which transactions are processed and information is transmitted globally will certainly lead to greater efficiencies and more opportunities for foreign-exchange trading. The impact on companies is that costs of trading foreign exchange should come down, and companies should have faster access to more currencies.

In addition, exchange restrictions that hamper the free flow of goods and services should diminish as governments gain greater control over their economies and as they liberalize currency markets. Capital controls still impact foreign investment, but they will continue to become less of a factor for trade in goods and services.

The introduction of the euro has allowed cross-border transactions in Europe to progress more smoothly. As the euro solidifies its position in Europe, it will reduce exchange-rate volatility and should lead to the euro taking some of the pressure off the dollar, so it is no longer the only major vehicle currency in the world.

Technological Developments

Technological developments may not cause the foreign-exchange broker to disappear entirely, but they will certainly cause foreign-exchange trades to be executed more quickly and cheaply. The advent of technology clearly has caused the market to shift from phone trades to electronic trades.[15]

It is hard to know how extensive online trading will become. Numerous companies now advertise online trading for investors, but that is not where most of the trades take place. The growth of Internet trades in currency will take away some of the market share of dealers and allow more entrants into the foreign-exchange market. Internet trade will also increase currency price transparency and increase the ease of trading, thus allowing more investors into the market. It is interesting to note that Barclays Capital, the fifth largest bank in foreign-exchange trades, is trying to build its online trading portal by offering automated exchange tools to financial and nonfinancial clients. One idea is to offer the system to their correspondent banks who can then offer the system to their corporate clients. This is a response to the fact that foreign-exchange trading is shifting from telephone trades to online trades.[16] This will force the banks to offer more services to clients. ∎

How Companies Use Foreign Exchange

Companies enter the foreign-exchange market to facilitate their regular business transactions and/or to speculate. The treasury department of a company is responsible for establishing policies for trading currency and for managing banking relationships to make the trades. From a business standpoint, companies first of all trade foreign exchange for exports or imports and the buying or selling of goods and services.

For example, when Boeing sells the new 787 Dreamliner commercial airplane to LAN, the largest airline in South America, it has to be concerned about the currency in which it will be paid and how it will receive payment. In this case, the sale is probably denominated in dollars, so Boeing will not have to worry about the foreign-exchange market (nor, in theory, will its employees—see the cartoon in Figure 9.6). However, LAN will have to worry about the market. Where will it come up with the dollars, and how will it pay Boeing?

CONCEPT CHECK

In Chapter 19, we discuss the functions of a company's CFO, not only in managing its cash flows but in managing its *foreign-exchange exposure*—the extent to which fluctuations in currencies can affect the costs of its international transactions.

FIGURE 9.6   The Working Man's Foreign-Exchange Dilemma

Source: Copyright John Morris, Cartoonstock.com.

"Last week I had pesetas in my wage packet, this week it's escudos - that's the trouble with working for a multi-national company."

BUSINESS PURPOSES (I): CASH FLOW ASPECTS OF IMPORTS AND EXPORTS

When a company must move money to pay for purchases or receives money for sales, it has an option on the documents it can use, the currency of denomination, and the degree of protection it can ask for. Obviously, if Boeing wanted the greatest security possible, it could ask LAN to pay for the Dreamliner before LAN takes title to the aircraft. That is not very practical in this case, but sometimes it happens when the seller has all of the control in the transaction. More common is the use of commercial bills of exchange and letters of credit.

> With a draft or commercial bill of exchange, one party directs another party to make payment.

Commercial Bills of Exchange   When an individual or a company pays a bill in a domestic setting, it can pay cash, but it typically uses a check, often electronically transmitted. The check is also known as a **draft** or a **commercial bill of exchange.** A draft is an instrument in which one party (the *drawer*) directs another party (the *drawee*) to make a payment. The drawee can either be a company like the importer or a bank. In the latter case, the draft would be considered a bank draft.

Documentary drafts and documentary letters of credit are often used to protect both the buyer and the seller. They require that payment be made based on the presentation of documents conveying the title, and they leave an audit trail identifying the parties to the transactions. If the exporter requests payment to be made immediately, the draft is called a **sight draft.** If the payment is to be made later—for example, 30 days after delivery—the instrument is called a **time draft.**

> A sight draft requires payment to be made when it is presented. A time draft permits payment to be made after the date when it is presented.

> A letter of credit obligates the buyer's bank to honor a draft presented to it and assume payment; a credit relationship exists between the importer and the importer's bank.

Letters of Credit   With a bill of exchange, it is always possible the importer will not be able to make payment to the exporter at the agreed on time. A **letter of credit (L/C),** however, obligates the buyer's bank in the importing country to honor a draft presented to it, provided the draft is accompanied by the prescribed documents. However, the exporter still needs to be sure the bank's credit is valid as well. The letter of credit could be a forgery issued by a "nonexistent bank." The exporter, even with the added security of the bank, still needs to rely on the importer's credit because of possible discrepancies that could arise in the transaction. The L/C could be denominated in the currency of the exporter or of the importer. If it is denominated in the currency of the importer, the exporter will still have to convert the foreign exchange into their currency through their commercial bank.

> A revocable letter of credit is one that can be changed by any of the parties. An irrevocable letter of credit is one that cannot be adjusted without consent of all parties.

Revocable and Irrevocable Letters of Credit   When an exporter requires a letter of credit, the importer is responsible for arranging for it at the importer's bank. Figure 9.7 explains the relationships among the parties to a letter of credit. A letter of credit (L/C) can be revocable or irrevocable. A **revocable letter of credit** can be changed by any of the parties. However, both exporter and importer may prefer an **irrevocable letter of credit,** which is a letter that cannot be canceled or changed in any way without the consent of all parties to the transaction. With this type of L/C, the importer's bank is obligated to pay and is willing to accept any drafts (bills of exchange) at sight, meaning these drafts will be paid as soon as the correct documents are presented to the bank.

As noted earlier, an L/C can also be issued at any time. The exporter must adhere precisely to all of the conditions on the letter of credit, such as the method of transportation and the description of the merchandise. Otherwise, the letter of credit will not be paid without approval of all parties to an elimination of the discrepancies. Again, a key issue related to this chapter is that the L/C needs to specify the currency of the contract. If the L/C is not in the exporter's currency, the exporter will have to convert the foreign exchange into their currency as soon as it is received.

Confirmed Letters of Credit   A letter of credit transaction may include a confirming bank in addition to the parties mentioned previously. With a **confirmed letter of credit,** the

FIGURE 9.7 **Letter-of-Credit Relationships**

A *letter of credit* guarantees an exporter (seller) that the importer's (buyer's) bank will pay for the imported products. The credit relationship exists between the importer and the importer's bank (the opening bank). A *confirmed letter of credit* bears an additional guarantee: If the importer's bank defaults, the exporter's bank will pay the exporter.

Source: Adapted from *Export and Import Financing Procedures* (Chicago: The First National Bank of Chicago), p. 22.

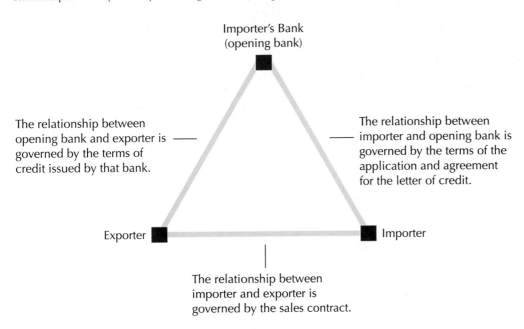

Importer's Bank
(opening bank)

The relationship between opening bank and exporter is —— governed by the terms of credit issued by that bank.

The relationship between —— importer and opening bank is governed by the terms of the application and agreement for the letter of credit.

Exporter   Importer

The relationship between importer and exporter is governed by the sales contract.

exporter has the guarantee of an additional bank, sometimes in the exporter's home country, sometimes in a third country. It rarely happens that the exporter establishes the confirming relationship. Usually, the opening bank seeks the confirmation of the L/C with a bank with which it already has a credit relationship. If this letter of credit is irrevocable, none of the conditions can be changed unless all four parties to the L/C agree in advance.

> A confirmed letter of credit adds the obligation of the exporter's bank to pay the exporter.

BUSINESS PURPOSES (II): OTHER FINANCIAL FLOWS

Companies may have to deal in foreign exchange for other reasons. For example, if a U.S. company has a subsidiary in the United Kingdom and the subsidiary sends a dividend to the parent company in British pounds, the parent company has to enter into the foreign-exchange market to convert pounds to dollars. If the parent company lends dollars to the British subsidiary, the British subsidiary has to convert the dollars into pounds. When they pay principal and interest back to the parent company, they have to convert pounds into dollars.

> Companies also deal in foreign exchange for other transactions, such as the receipt or payment of dividends or the receipt or payment of loans and interest.

Speculation Sometimes companies deal in foreign exchange for profit. That is especially true for some banks, traders, and investors, but sometimes corporate treasury look at its foreign-exchange operations as profit centers and also buy and sell foreign exchange with the objective to earn profits.

Investors can use foreign-exchange transactions to speculate for profit or to protect against risk. **Speculation** is the buying or selling of a commodity, in this case foreign currency, that has both an element of risk and the chance of great profit. For example, an investor could buy euros in anticipation that the euro will strengthen against other currencies. If it strengthens, the investor earns a profit; if it weakens, the investor incurs a loss. Speculators are important in the foreign-exchange market because they spot trends and try to take advantage of them. They can create demand for a currency by purchasing it in the market, or they can create a supply of the currency by selling it in the market.

> Speculators take positions in foreign-exchange markets and other capital markets to earn a profit.

Arbitrage is the buying and selling of foreign currencies at a profit due to price discrepancies.

Arbitrage   One type of profit-seeking activity is **arbitrage,** which is the purchase of foreign currency on one market for immediate resale on another market (in a different country) to profit from a price discrepancy. For example, a dealer might sell U.S. dollars for Swiss francs in the United States, then Swiss francs for British pounds in Switzerland, and then the British pounds for U.S. dollars back in the United States, with the goal to end up with more dollars.

Here's how the process might work. Assume the dealer converts 100 dollars into 150 Swiss francs when the exchange rate is 1.5 francs per dollar. The dealer then converts the 150 francs into 70 British pounds at an exchange rate of 0.467 pounds per franc and finally converts the pounds into 125 dollars at an exchange rate of 0.56 pounds per dollar. In this case, arbitrage yields $125 from the initial sale of $100. Given the transparency of exchange rate quotes globally, it is difficult to make a lot of money on arbitrage, but it is possible for an investor who has a lot of money and can move quickly.

Interest arbitrage involves investing in interest-bearing instruments in foreign exchange in an effort to earn a profit due to interest rate differentials.

Interest arbitrage is the investing in debt instruments, such as bonds, in different countries. For example, a dealer might invest $1,000 in the United States for 90 days or convert $1,000 into British pounds, invest the money in the United Kingdom for 90 days, and then convert the pounds back into dollars. The investor would try to pick the alternative that would yield the highest return at the end of 90 days.

Is It Ok to Speculate on Currency?

Point **Yes** People trade in foreign exchange for a number of reasons, and one of them is speculation, which is not illegal or necessarily bad. Just as stockbrokers invest people's money to try to earn a return that is higher than the market average, foreign currency brokers invest people's money in foreign exchange to make a profit for the investor. Speculation is merely taking a position in a currency in order to profit from market trends.

The electronic trading of foreign exchange has made it easier for a variety of different kinds of investors to speculate in foreign exchange. Hedge funds are an important source of foreign exchange speculation. There is no one specific strategy hedge fund managers follow to speculate in foreign exchange. However, the transparency in trading has driven the smaller players out of the market and allowed the large institutions and traders to earn profits on small margins that require large volumes of transactions. Hedge funds generally deal in minimum investments that are quite large, so the hedge fund managers that trade in foreign exchange trade in very large volumes. They might make long-term bets on a currency based on macroeconomic conditions, or they might try to balance off buy and sell strategies in currencies so that one side offers protection against the other side. In either case, the hedge fund manager is betting on the future position of a currency to earn money for the investors in the fund.

However, speculation is not for the faint of heart. Political and economic conditions outside of the control of the speculators can quickly turn profits to losses, and probably

Counterpoint **No** There are plenty of opportunities for a dealer, whether in foreign exchange or securities, to make money illegally or contrary to company policy. The culture of banks trying to make money off trading foreign exchange combined with lax controls contributes greatly to these scandals.

One of the most publicized events in the derivatives markets in recent years involved 28-year-old Nicholas Leeson and the 233-year-old British bank Barings PLC. Leeson, a dealer for Barings PLC, went to Singapore in the early 1990s to help resolve some of the bank's problems. Within a year, he was promoted to chief dealer. The problem was that he was responsible for trading securities and booking the settlements. This meant there were no checks and balances on his trading actions, thus opening the door to possible fraud.

When two different people are assigned to trade securities and book settlements, the person booking the settlements can confirm independently whether or not the trades were accurate and legitimate. In 1994, Leeson bought stock index futures on the Singapore International Monetary Exchange, or SIMEX, on the assumption that the Tokyo stock market would rise. Most dealers watching Leeson's feverish trading activity assumed Barings had a large client that Leeson was trading for, but it turns out he was using the bank's money to speculate. Because the Japanese economy was recovering, it made sense to assume the market would continue to rise, thus generating more profits for Leeson and Barings. Unfortunately, something happened quicker than is the case in the stock market. Currencies are inherently unstable. Consider the problems of the U.S. dollar in 2007 and 2008 where the dollar was quite weak against the euro and Japanese yen. What should hedge fund managers do? Their expectation of the future might be that the dollar will continue to weaken. But what if it strengthens? Conversely, they might think the dollar has reached its floor and is ready for a rise. That would argue that the managers should buy dollars. But when will the dollar rise and by how much? By mid-March 2008, the dollar had declined by 15 percent in the prior 12 months, but by May 2008, many experts felt like the dollar had reached a low point and was expected to rise. This was based on the market expectations that interest cuts by the Fed were expected to stop and that the credit crisis was beginning to soften. Now the speculators have to decide what to do with those expectations.

Sometimes speculators can buy a currency on the basis of good economic fundamentals, or they can buy or sell currency because they feel governments are following poor economic policies. When speculators looked at the economic fundamentals behind the economy of Thailand in 1997, they felt like the government was making poor choices and that the Thai baht could not continue to trade at its existing level. So they sold Thai baht on the assumption that the currency would have to fall. Is there anything wrong with that? Was the subsequent fall in the Thai baht because of evil speculators, or was it because the speculators profited on the inevitable? As long as markets are free and information is available, traders ought to be able to make some money on their predictions of the future.

The key is that currency speculation is a different way to invest money and allows investors to diversify their portfolios from traditional stocks and bonds. Just as foreign exchange can be traded for speculative purposes, trading in shares is also speculation. Even though we call such trades "investments," they are just another form of speculation hoping to gain a return that is higher than the market average and certainly higher than what a CD can yield.●

that nobody could predict—the January 17, 1995, earthquake that hit the port city of Kobe.

As a result of the devastation and uncertainty, the market fell, and Leeson had to come up with cash to cover the margin call on the futures contract. A *margin* is a deposit made as security for a financial transaction that is otherwise financed on credit. When the price of an instrument changes and the margin rises, the exchange "calls" the increased margin from the other party—in this case Leeson.[17]

However, Leeson soon ran out of cash from Barings, so he had to come up with more cash. One approach he used was to write options contracts and use the premium he collected on the contracts to cover his margin call. Unfortunately, he was using Barings' funds to cover positions he was taking for himself, not for clients, and he also forged documents to cover his transactions.

As the Tokyo stock market continued to plunge, Leeson fell further and further behind and eventually fled the country, later to be caught and returned to Singapore for trial. Barings estimated that Leeson generated losses in excess of $1 billion, which put Barings into bankruptcy. Eventually, the Dutch bank ING purchased Barings. Leeson's activities in the derivatives market were illegal and a violation of solid internal controls.

Finally, Leeson went to prison in Singapore (where he was treated for colon cancer as well). On July 3, 1999, Leeson was released from prison, and he returned to his native Britain.[18]

Since the collapse of Barings, measures have been put into place in banks to prohibit such consequences, yet negative outcomes of rogue trading continue to happen. In February 2002, Allied Irish Banks discovered that an employee, John Rusnak, at its U.S. subsidiary, Allfirst Bank, lost nearly $700 million from trading foreign-exchange derivatives, the fourth largest foreign-exchange scandal on record. At the end of 2000, Rusnak's trading showed a gain of $224 million, but the profit was not investigated by the bank because it was making a great deal of money off his trades. But because of the volatility of the U.S. market at that time, Rusnak's leveraged gains quickly turned to huge losses. AIB suspects Rusnak was involved with fictitious trades and collusion inside or outside of Allfirst Bank. Rusnak was subsequently sentenced to $7\frac{1}{2}$ years in prison.

Sometimes fraud involves several traders at a bank rather than just a rogue trader as was the case with Barings. Between October 2003 and January 2004, several traders colluded to enter into illegal and fictitious foreign-exchange trades in the foreign currency options desk for National Australia Bank, resulting in an estimated loss of $160 million. Four different bank officers were involved in the scandal, all of whom were sentenced to prison, and two of the key perpetrators were found guilty of influencing other dealers to process deceptive and fictitious foreign-exchange trades.[19]●

CASE

Banking on Argentina

In the first half of 2007, HSBC Holdings PLC saw profits soar to new records as it expanded aggressively in Asia, Latin America, and other emerging markets.[20] HSBC is counting on its investments in emerging markets, especially China, Brazil, Argentina, and Vietnam, to pick up market share and increase profits. However, only six years prior, HSBC was struggling in Argentina and gambled that the peso crisis would pass and Argentina would be a key emerging market for them in the future.

Was their strategy successful? Are there dangers lurking in the emerging markets, especially in Argentina? Argentina's economy collapsed at the end of 2001, leaving both local and foreign companies suffering from a shortage of cash, a devaluing peso, and a burden of growing debt. HSBC lost $1.1 billion in 2001 because of Argentina's problems. At the height of the crisis, the situation in Argentina was so unstable that HSBC employees came to work in casual clothes, entering and exiting their headquarters in Buenos Aires at odd times and using any entrance but the front door to avoid demonstrators and violence.

A Little Background on HSBC

London-based HSBC derives its name from its founding member, the Hong Kong and Shanghai Banking Corporation Limited, which was established in 1865 to permit trade between China and Europe. Until the early twentieth century, Hong Kong and Shanghai Banking Corporation set up offices and branches mainly in China and Southeast Asia—but also in India, Japan, Europe, and North America.

Acquisitions and Diversification

After World War II, Hong Kong and Shanghai Banking Corporation expanded and diversified its business with acquisitions and alliances. Through the 1980s, it expanded into Canada, Australia, and the United States, and in the 1990s, it moved into Brazil and Argentina. In 1991, its member companies came together to form HSBC Holdings PLC.

HSBC pursues a balance of opportunities in developed economies and emerging markets and now has over 10,000 offices in 83 countries and stock market listings in London, Hong Kong, New York, and Paris. Its main lines of business are personal banking; corporate, investment banking, and markets; and private banking. Its foreign-exchange operations fall under the markets organization.

Foreign-Exchange Trading

Although HSBC is involved in a wide range of banking activities and ranked as the 18th-largest bank in the world in total assets, it is one of the top banks in the world in foreign-exchange trading. HSBC trades foreign exchange in 75 of their treasury sites worldwide in 60 countries and territories. They provide market information, trades, and consulting in the area of risk exposure and how to minimize the impact of market volatility on its clients.

As we noted in Table 9.4 (p. 349), it is the seventh-largest bank in the world in market share in foreign-exchange trading. However, it is in the top five in terms of most currency trades, and it ranks third in trading Latin American currencies after Citi and Deutsche Bank. In addition to being the third-largest foreign-exchange trader in South America, HSBC is ranked number one for trades in Asian currencies, holding the number-one position for trading Chinese yuan.

HSBC Ventures into Argentina

HSBC's entry into Argentina began in 1997 when the bank acquired Roberts S.A. de Inversiones, changing its name to HSBC Argentina Holdings S.A. Along with the banking arm, HSBC bought into a general insurance agency with the purchase of Roberts. In 1994, HSBC united with New York Life to form a life and retirement insurance company, so the acquisition of Roberts was a strategic fit in both banking and insurance. HSBC Argentina has also acquired companies in pension fund management and medical care, thus creating a diversified portfolio in Argentina.

The outlook for HSBC in Argentina looked good when it entered the country. In 1998, its first full year of operations, the bank had a pretax loss of $13 million but earned a profit of $67 million in 1999 and expected profits to continue growing at 100 percent.

Argentina: A Little Economic History

To understand the problems facing HSBC in Argentina, we must take a look at Argentina's economic history. Argentina's economy flourished in the beginning of the twentieth century, growing at an annual rate of 5 percent for three years. It attracted a flood of British and Spanish capital and was rated as one of the world's 10 richest countries—even ahead of France and Germany.

However, it has been downhill since then. When Juan Perón ruled the country from 1946 to 1955, he instituted protectionist measures and printed money to finance generous benefits for workers. State intervention in all sectors led to poor productivity and structural weakness in the economy. Inflation plagued the country; there were two bouts of hyperinflation in the 1980s and two banking collapses. As a result, Argentines lost trust in the peso and invested in U.S. dollars or shipped their capital abroad.

The Advent of the Currency Board

In 1989, Carlos Menem took control of the country and set out to implement free market reforms and to restructure monetary and economic policies. He privatized many state-run companies, tightened fiscal management, and opened up the country's borders to trade. Probably the most important policy he established was the Convertibility Law, which pegged the Argentine peso 1:1 with the U.S. dollar and restricted the money supply to its hard dollar currency reserves. This monetary arrangement, called a *currency board,* was established to impose discipline on the central bank.

Successes   The new currency board accomplished what it set out to do: It halted inflation and attracted investment. Investors felt there was little risk now in investing in the peso because it was pegged to the dollar. The sentiment that "the peso is as good as the dollar" was strong throughout the country. Because there was a stable money supply, this reduced inflation to nearly 0 percent through the rest of the 1990s and kept the exchange rate at a constant value. Real GDP grew by 6.1 percent from 1991 to 1997 compared with 0.2 percent from 1975 to 1990.

Shortcomings   In spite of these positive developments, the currency board also had its drawbacks. It reduced the Argentine government's ability to respond to external shocks by allowing its exchange rate and monetary policy to be determined de facto by the United States. Interest rates were in reality set by the U.S. Federal Reserve; plus there was a risk margin for investing in Argentina.

This arrangement was put to the test in 1995 when the Mexican peso devalued. Investors got nervous about Latin America in general and pulled investments out of Argentina. Its economy shrank by 4 percent, and many banks collapsed. The government responded by tightening bank regulation and capital requirements, and some of the larger banks took over weaker ones. Argentina increased exports and investment, and the country returned to 5.5 percent growth.

Unfortunately, the government was not so lucky with its results at the end of the 1990s. Commodity prices, on which Argentina heavily relied, declined; the U.S. dollar strengthened against other currencies; Argentina's main trading partner, Brazil, devalued its currency; and emerging economies' cost of capital increased. Argentina soon fell into a recession, with GDP falling to 3.4 percent in 1999 and unemployment increasing into the double digits. Argentina, because of its hard link to the dollar, was unable to compete internationally, especially in Brazil, because of its high prices.

One way to correct this problem would be to devalue the currency to bring the value closer to its fundamental value. Argentina could not devalue unless it canceled the currency board, a move it did not want to make because of the currency board's popularity and past success. The only way for Argentina to become more competitive was for prices to fall. As deflation set in, the government (and some private companies) found it difficult to pay off debt because it was not collecting as much revenue. Banks had been lending dollars at 25 percent interest rates even though the risk was supposed to be low.

The Burden of Debt   Argentina was acquiring a burgeoning public debt. When the recession hit, tax revenue fell and spending increased to pay for such things as higher unemployment. Tax evasion is extremely high in Argentina, but the government did little to tackle the problem. The budget went from a surplus of 1.2 percent of GDP in 1993 to a deficit of 2.4 percent in 2000. Increased interest rate payments also added to the increasing budget deficit. From 1991 to 2000, the amount of interest rate payments increased from $2.5 billion to $9.5 billion annually. This drained the economy more as most of this money went to overseas investors. This currency "mismatching," meaning most of the debt is taken out in one currency but assets are held in another, was large in Argentina and would later prove disastrous.

Political Perplexities and Monetary Problems   Politicians found little they could do to help the struggling economy. They fiddled with tariffs and finally the currency board. They pegged the peso half to the dollar and half to the euro for exporters. The idea of devaluation scared investors and caused interest rates to rise even more. Unable to pay its interest payments and unwilling to declare a debt default, the government turned to the banks.

The Menem government had strengthened the banking system, particularly the central bank, but its successor, Fernando de la Rua, sent a crushing blow to the sector. He strong-armed the banks into buying government bonds. This triggered a bank run, and Argentines withdrew over $15 billion between July and November 2001. In a desperate attempt to save the industry, de la Rua imposed a ceiling of $1,000 a month on bank withdrawals on December 1. Within days, the country defaulted on $155 million in public debt, the largest such default in world history. As rioters and looters took to the streets, de la Rua resigned.

Argentina struggled to find a president who was fit for the job. It went through a total of five presidents in four months, ending finally with Eduardo Duhalde. The government abandoned the currency board in January 2002 and let the peso float against the dollar. The peso began falling quickly, so the government spent around $100 million a day—to a total of $1.2 billion—to prop up the value. More money was leaking out of the banking system too (around $50 million a day) because the courts had overturned the freeze on withdrawals.

In March 2002, Duhalde imposed new restrictions on the foreign-exchange market. Individuals could buy no more than $1,000 a day and companies no more than $10,000 a day. Banks and businesses had restrictions on the number of dollars they could hold and on how much money could be shipped abroad. Currency exchanges could only operate three to four hours each day—versus the typical seven hours.

However, the courts kept overturning policies set by the government and had police arrest bank managers who did not follow their rulings. Still unable to prevent the increasing flow of money out of the system, Duhalde closed all banks for a week. In the meantime, he proposed to forcibly convert billions of dollars in bank deposits into low-interest bonds. The senate refused the president's bond proposal, thus sending him back to the drawing board.

To repair its economy, Argentina sought help from the International Monetary Fund (IMF). However, the IMF continued to turn down Argentina's requests for help until it implemented some sweeping changes in its exchange-rate policy, fiscal policy, and banking system. In an attempt to find someone to blame, Duhalde started criticizing foreign-owned banks, such as HSBC, for not infusing more cash into the system from their headquarters.

The Peso Crisis   The central bank printed pesos to keep banks solvent, but this led to increased inflation. The national and provincial governments also used bond notes, quasi currency, to pay many of their debts. This note was swapped in everyday transactions and surprisingly held its value against the peso. Almost a year after the initial freeze on bank deposits, the government lifted the remaining restrictions on withdrawing cash from banks, further easing the financial strain on the banking system.

In May 2003, Nestor Kirchner became the new president of Argentina, replacing Duhalde. Under the guidance of Kirchner and his economic minister, Roberto Lavagna, Argentina's economy has rebounded significantly. Although the country experienced hyperinflation after the abandonment of the peso's peg to the dollar, the devaluated peso is now one of the causes of the economic recovery. The peso was trading at 0.9920 pesos per dollar on December 31, 2001, but it fell to 3.39 pesos on December 31, 2002.

In the next few years, the peso strengthened to just under 2.8 pesos per dollar, but it has gradually weakened since mid-2003 and was trading at 3.12260 on July 31, 2007. The peso is nearly 70 percent cheaper against the dollar than it was in the 1990s, resulting in increased exports of farm products and other commodities. The devaluation has also resulted in new foreign direct investment and increased business with Brazil.

Negotiations with the IMF   Despite the economic growth stimulated by the devaluated peso, Argentina was still burdened by its huge debt to private creditors and the IMF. From the middle of 2002 to spring 2003, Argentina and the IMF disagreed on conditions of IMF aid. Argentina defaulted on debt payments to both the IMF and the World Bank, saying it would not make payments without a guarantee of aid from the IMF. The IMF, however, refused to grant that aid to Argentina without implementation of certain economic reforms, including spending cuts and restructuring in the banking sector. Four months after his victory, Kirchner and the IMF agreed on a deal that would allow Argentina to pay interest only on its $21 billion debt over the next three years.

To repay most of its debt, including overdue interest, Argentina proposed a plan to its creditors, asking them to write off 70 percent of the present net value of their government bonds. The majority of creditors reluctantly agreed, and in February 2005, Argentina closed on the biggest debt restructuring in history. However, Argentina still has debts worth nearly 75 percent of its annual economic output, and the country must agree on a new loan deal with the IMF as soon as possible.

HSBC's Reaction

HSBC's reaction to the crisis was similar to that of other banks in the country. It was forced to rethink loans and to decide if the political and economic instability of the country was worth the risk of continued operations. Due in part to the depreciation of the peso, HSBC lost $977 million in 2001 in Latin America, compared with a profit of $324 million in 2000. Overall, HSBC Holdings doubled its bad debt charges to $2.4 billion, and pretax profits fell by 14 percent in 2001.

The Problem with Pesification

Because of the *pesification* instituted by the Argentine government, loan repayments to HSBC were deeply discounted. In June 2002, HSBC refused a loan payment by Pérez Companc, an energy holding company, because the payment was in pesos. The original loan was for $101 million and Pérez's offered payment of 104.57 pesos only equaled about $28 million at market rates. HSBC argued that debt was not covered by pesification.

Despite early losses after the initial economic collapse, HSBC has remained in Argentina throughout its financial crisis and tumultuous recovery. HSBC paid on all its external obligations and has continued to capitalize its Argentine subsidiary to maintain its stability. However, after the initial crisis, HSBC refused to infuse new capital in the Argentine operations, forcing HSBC to operate on funds generated in Argentina. After suffering a $210 million loss in 2002, the Argentine subsidiary of HSBC recorded profits of $48 and $156 million in 2003 and 2004, respectively. ■

QUESTIONS

1. What are the major factors that caused the peso to fall in value against the dollar? What has the government done to reverse the recession?
2. What has been Argentina's experience with the IMF? Has the IMF been helpful or not?
3. How has the fall in the value of the peso affected business opportunities for companies doing business in Argentina and in exporting and importing?
4. Should HSBC invest more money in its operations in Argentina? What factors should they monitor as they make their decision?

SUMMARY

- Foreign exchange is money denominated in the currency of another nation or group of nations. The exchange rate is the price of a currency.

- The foreign-exchange market is dominated by the money center banks, but other financial institutions, such as local and regional banks, and nonfinancial institutions, such as corporations and governments, are also players in the foreign-exchange market.

- Dealers can trade currency by telephone or electronically, especially through Reuters, EBS, or Bloomberg.

- The foreign-exchange market is divided into the over-the-counter market (OTC) and the exchange-traded market.

- The traditional foreign-exchange market is composed of the spot, forward, and foreign-exchange swap markets. Other key foreign-exchange instruments are currency swaps, options, and futures.

- Spot transactions involve the exchange of currency on the second day after the date on which the two dealers agree to the transaction.

- Outright forward transactions involve the exchange of currency three or more days after the date on which the dealers agree to the transaction. A foreign-exchange swap is a simultaneous spot and forward transaction.

- Approximately $3.2 trillion in foreign exchange is traded every day. The dollar is the most widely traded currency in the world (on one side of 86.3 percent of all transactions), and London is the main foreign-exchange market in the world.

- Foreign-exchange dealers quote bid (buy) and offer (sell) rates on foreign exchange. If the quote is in American terms, the dealer quotes the foreign currency as the number of dollars and cents per unit of the foreign currency. If the quote is in European terms, the dealer quotes the number of units of the foreign currency per dollar. The numerator is called the *terms currency* and the denominator the *base currency*.

- If the foreign currency in a forward contract is expected to strengthen in the future (the dollar equivalent of the foreign currency is higher in the forward market than in the spot market), the currency is selling at a premium. If the opposite is true, it is selling at a discount.

- An option is the right, but not the obligation, to trade foreign currency in the future. Options can be traded OTC or on an exchange.

- A foreign currency future is an exchange-traded instrument that guarantees a future price for the trading of foreign exchange, but the contracts are for a specific amount and specific maturity date.

- Companies work with foreign-exchange dealers to trade currency. Dealers also work with each other and can trade currency through voice brokers, electronic brokerage services, or directly with other bank dealers. Internet trades of foreign exchange are becoming more significant.

- The major institutions that trade foreign exchange are the large commercial and investment banks and securities exchanges. Commercial and investment banks deal in a variety of different currencies all over the world. The CME Group and the Philadelphia Stock Exchange trade currency futures and options.

- Companies use foreign exchange to settle transactions involving the imports and exports of goods and services, for foreign investments, and to earn money through *arbitrage* or *speculation*.

KEY TERMS

American terms (p. 341)
arbitrage (p. 354)
Bank for International Settlements (BIS) (p. 336)
base currency (p. 341)
bid (p. 341)
Chicago Mercantile Exchange (CME) Group (p. 349)

confirmed letter of credit (p. 352)
currency swap (p. 337)
derivative (p. 337)
direct quote (p. 341)
draft (or commercial bill of exchange) (p. 352)
European terms (p. 341)
exchange rate (p. 335)

foreign exchange (p. 335)
foreign-exchange market (p. 335)
forward discount (or forward premium) (p. 345)
futures contract (p. 337)
FX swap (p. 337)
hedge fund (p. 337)
indirect quote (p. 341)

interbank transaction (p. 345)
interest arbitrage (p. 354)
irrevocable letter of credit (p. 352)
letter of credit (L/C) (p. 352)
offer (p. 341)

option (p. 337)
outright forward transactions (p. 337)
revocable letter of credit (p. 352)
sight draft (p. 352)
speculation (p. 353)

spot rate (p. 337)
spot transaction (p. 337)
spread (p. 341)
terms currency (p. 341)
time draft (p. 352)

ENDNOTES

1 *Sources include the following:* "Immigrants Sent 3.7 Billion Euros from Spain to Latin America in 2006, Says IDB Fund," press release, Inter-American Development Bank, June 5, 2007; "Remittances to Latin America and the Caribbean to Top $100 Billion a Year by 2010, IDB Fund Says," press release, Inter-American Development Bank, March 18, 2007; Marla Dickerson, "Cash Going to Mexico Likely to Start at a Bank," *Los Angeles Times*, February 14, 2007: 21; Miriam Jordan, "U.S. Banks Woo Migrants, Legal or Otherwise," *Wall Street Journal* (Eastern Edition), October 11, 2006: B1; Ioan Grillo, "Wired Cash," *Business Mexico*, 12:12/13:1 (2003): 44; Julie Rawe, "The Fastest Way to Make Money," *Time*, June 23, 2003: A6; Rosa Salter Rodriguez, "Money Transfers to Mexico Peak as Mother's Day Nears," *The* (Fort Wayne, IN) *Journal Gazette*, May 1, 2005: 1D; Deborah Kong, "Mexicans Win Back Fee on Money They Wired," *Grand Rapids* (MI) *Press*, December 19, 2002: A9; Karen Krebsbach, "Following the Money," *USBanker*, September 2002: 62; Tyche Hendricks, "Wiring Cash Costly for Immigrants," *San Francisco Chronicle*, March 24, 2002: A23; Nancy Cleeland, "Firms Are Wired into Profits," *Los Angeles Times*, November 7, 1997: 1; David Fairlamb, Geri Smith, and Frederik Blafour, "Can Western Union Keep On Delivering?" *Business Week*, December 29, 2003: 57; Heather Timmons, "Western Union: Where the Money Is—In Small Bills," *Business Week*, November 26, 2001: 40.

2 Sam Y. Cross, *All About the Foreign Exchange Market in the United States* (New York: Federal Reserve Bank of New York, 1998), p. 9.

3 Cross, *All About the Foreign Exchange Market*, p. 9.

4 Bank for International Settlements, "Central Bank Survey of Foreign Exchange and Derivatives Market Activity in 2007" (Basel: BIS, December 2007): 5–8.

5 Cross, *All About the Foreign Exchange Market*, p. 31.

6 Bank for International Settlements, "Central Bank Survey," p. 1.

7 Cross, *All About the Foreign Exchange Market*, p. 19.

8 Bank for International Settlements, "Central Bank Survey," p. 10.

9 Brian Dolan, "Tailoring Your Technical Approach to Currency Personalities," July 26, 2007: www.forex.com/currency_pairs.html.

10 Cross, *All About the Foreign Exchange Market*, p. 12.

11 See "Foreign Exchange Poll 2007: Methodology," *Euromoney*, May 2007.

12 Deborah Kimbell, "E-FX Takes Another Step Forward," *Euromoney*, February 2005: 1.

13 Peter Garnham, "Reuters Reveals Ambitions on Launch of FXMarketSpace," *Financial Times*, March 26, 2007: 21.

14 PHLX News Release, "The Philadelphia Stock Exchange and the Philadelphia Board of Trade to Expand World Currency Product Line with Launch of Options and Futures on Major Currencies," April 27, 2007: http://phlx.com/news/pr2007/07pr042707.htm.

15 Steve Bills, "State St.'s Forex Deal a Lure for Hedge Funds," *American Banker*, January 23, 2007: 10.

16 Steve Bills, "Barclays Seeking Forex Boost via Online Offerings," *American Banker*, October 10, 2006: 17.

17 More specifically, Leeson did not actually buy the contracts outright but rather paid a certain percentage of the value of the contract, known as the *margin*. When the stock market fell, the index futures contract became riskier, and the broker who sold the contract required Leeson to increase the amount of the margin.

18 The Collapse of Barings: A Fallen Star," *The Economist*, March 4, 1995: 19–21; Glen Whitney, "ING Puts Itself on the Map by Acquiring Barings," *Wall Street Journal*, March 8, 1995: B4; John S. Bowdidge and Kurt E. Chaloupecky, "Nicholas Leeson and Barings Bank Have Vividly Taught Some Internal Control Issues," *American Business Review*, January 1997: 71–77; "Trader in Barings Scandal Is Released from Prison," *Wall Street Journal*, July 6, 1999: A12; Ben Dolven, "Bearing Up," *Far Eastern Economic Review*, July 15, 1999: 47; "Nick Leeson and Barings Bank," *bbc.co.uk*, at www.bbc.co.uk/crime/caseclosed/nickleeson.shtml (accessed May 19, 2005); Nick Leeson and Edward Whitley, *Rogue Trader* (London: Little Brown: 1996), p. 272.

19 "The Ogre Returns," *The Economist*, February 14, 2002: www.economist.com; Conor O'Clery and Siobahn Creation, *Panic at the Bank: How John Ruskak Lost AIB $700,000,000* (Dublin: Gill & Macmillan, 2002), p. 256; Darin Tyson-Chan, "NAB Rogue Traders Jailed," *Money Management*, July 13, 2006: 14.

20 *Sources include the following:* HSBC website: www.hsbc.com; Dean Baker and Mark Weisbrot, "What Happened to Argentina," *Center for Economic and Policy Research*, January 31, 2002: www.cepr.net/ IMF/what_happened_to_argentina.htm; "A Decline Without Parallel," *The Economist*, February 28, 2002: www.economist.com; "HSBC/Argentina—2: To Work with the Argentine Govt.," *Dow Jones*, March 4, 2002: http://216.239.37.100/search?q=cache:Nmw7jFQFeREC:sg.biz.yahoo.com/020304/15/2k8tv.html+hsbc+argentina&hl=en&ie=UTF-8; "Argentina Hits HSBC Profits," *BBC News*, March 4, 2002: http://news.bbc.co.uk/1/hi/business/1853342.stm; Larry Rohter, "Peso Down Steeply, Argentines Strengthen Currency Curbs," *New York Times*, March 26, 2002: www.nytimes.com; "Sympathy, But No Cash," *The Economist*, April 22, 2002: www.economist.com; Rohter, "Argentine President Unveils Crisis Legislation," *New York Times*, April 23, 2002: www.nytimes.com; "Scraping Through the Great Depression," *The Economist*, May 30, 2002: www.economist.com; "Spoilt for Choice," *The Economist*, May 31, 2002: www.economist.com; "HSBC Rejects Perez Companc Peso Debt Payment," Reuters, June 21, 2002: www.reuters.com; "Carving Up the Scraps of Power," *The Economist*, September 5, 2002: www.economist.com; "Duhalde Sifts Budget Priorities, Raising Federal Wages,

Benefits," *Wall Street Journal*, September 10, 2002: www.wsj.com; Andrew B. Abel and Ben S. Bernanke, *Macroeconomics* (Reading, MA: Addison-Wesley, 2003), pp. 20–22; Colin Barraclough, "Reversal of Fortune," *Business Week*, May 9, 2005: 56; "Menem Pulls Out of Argentina Race," *BBC News*, May 15, 2003: http://news.bbc.co.uk/1/hi/world/americas/3025841.stm; "Argentina Wins Vital IMF Deal,"

BBC News, September 11, 2003: http://news.bbc.co.uk/1/hi/business/3098590.stm; "Argentina Takes Hard Line on IMF," *BBC News*, February 28, 2005: http://news.bbc.co.uk/1/hi/business/4304317.stm; "Top 50 Banks in the World," *Bankers Almanac*: http://www.bankersalmanac.com/addcon/infobank/wldrank.aspx.

10

chapter ten

The Determination
of Exchange Rates

Objectives

- To describe the International Monetary Fund and its role in the determination of exchange rates

- To discuss the major exchange-rate arrangements that countries use

- To explain how the European Monetary System works and how the euro became the currency of the euro zone

- To identify the major determinants of exchange rates

- To show how managers try to forecast exchange-rate movements

- To explain how exchange-rate movements influence business decisions

A fair exchange brings no quarrel.

—*Danish proverb*

CASE: El Salvador Adopts the U.S. Dollar

El Salvador, a country of 6.5 million people, is the smallest and most densely populated country in Central America (see Map 10.1) and about the size in area of the U.S. state of Massachusetts.[1] El Salvador has been a member of the Central American Common Market (CACM), which also includes Costa Rica, Guatemala, Honduras, and Nicaragua, since its inception in 1960. It was also the first of the Central American countries to sign on to the CAFTA-DR Agreement as of March 1, 2006, linking it closer to trade relations with the United States.

America have adopted the dollar as their currency—Panama, which adopted the dollar when it gained independence from Colombia over a century ago, and Ecuador, which dollarized its economy in 2000 as a means of eliminating hyperinflation.

Why the Dollar?

Why did El Salvador adopt the dollar? The economy of El Salvador is closely tied to the U.S. economy. At the time

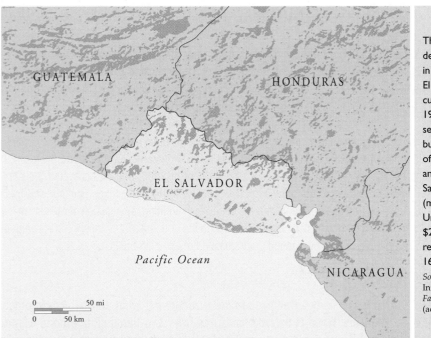

MAP 10.1   El Salvador

GUATEMALA

HONDURAS

EL SALVADOR

Pacific Ocean

NICARAGUA

0   50 mi
0   50 km

The smallest and most densely populated country in Central America, El Salvador pegged its currency to the US$ in 1994. The decision made sense: The United States buys more than two-thirds of the country's exports, and some 2 million Salvadorans living abroad (most of them in the United States) remit about $2 billion annually to relatives at home—roughly 16% of El Salvador's GDP.

Source: Data from Central Intelligence Agency, *World Factbook,* at www.cia.gov (accessed October 19, 2007).

PEGGING THE COLÓN TO THE DOLLAR

In 1994, the government of El Salvador decided to peg the colón, the country's currency, to the U.S. dollar (USD). In 2001, the government decided to do away with the colón and adopt the dollar as its currency. El Salvador is now one of 41 countries that have entered into an exchange arrangement in which they do not have their own currency. Among the other countries that do not have their own currency are the members of the European Union, which have adopted the euro, as discussed briefly in Chapter 8 and in more detail later, as well as 14 African countries that are members of the CFA franc zone.

El Salvador is one of nine countries that use another currency as their legal tender. Two other countries in Latin

of the switch to the dollar, the United States imported over two-thirds of El Salvador's exports. In addition, over 2 million Salvadoreans lived in the United States and wired home nearly $2 billion a year to relatives. This is over four times the total merchandise exports of El Salvador and nearly a seventh of El Salvador's GDP. By switching to the dollar, companies and the government in El Salvador were able to get access to cheaper interest rates because dollarization eliminated, or at least reduced, the risk of devaluation, thereby infusing more confidence in foreign banks to lend to El Salvador. Corporate borrowing rates are among the lowest in Latin America, and consumer credit rose as lower interest rates made it more attractive to borrow.

CONCEPT CHECK

In Chapter 8, we introduce the Central American Free Trade Agreement–Dominican Republic (CAFTA-DR) as a free trade agreement designed to reduce tariffs between the United States on the one hand and six Latin American countries on the other. We also note that, despite a membership of seven, it's actually a *bilateral agreement*.

CONCEPT CHECK

In Chapter 3, we discuss the importance of the role of government in influencing the *economic environment* in which companies, both domestic and foreign, must operate. Here, we cite an instance of unforeseeable change in a country's economic environment: Although a government usually tries to build a consensus to support important political decisions, unexpected policy shifts are also a significant fact of life in the international business environment.

Ecuador: The Test Case

Ecuador's situation was a little different from that of El Salvador, but it tied its currency to the dollar in 2000. Ecuador has a population double the size of and a GNI a little less than twice that of El Salvador. In addition, it doesn't rely on the U.S. market as much as El Salvador does. When Ecuador decided to dollarize its economy, the president was in the midst of a political crisis, and the announcement to dollarize was totally unexpected. In 1999, Ecuador's consumer price inflation was 52.2 percent, the highest in Latin America. Until February 1999, the Central Bank had maintained a crawling peg exchange-rate system. However, pressure on the currency forced the Central Bank to leave the peg and allow the currency to float freely. It promptly devalued by 65 percent in 1999.

At that time, Panama was the only country in Latin America that had dollarized, although Argentina had officially linked its currency to the dollar, so Ecuador was seen as a test case that many thought would spread to other countries in Latin America, especially El Salvador. A World Bank official, discussing the rationale for Ecuador's decision, noted that "most countries have a large amount of their debt in dollars, maintain a large percent of their reserves abroad in dollars, and write contracts indexed to the dollar."

In addition, Ecuador, a member of OPEC, generates most of its foreign-exchange earnings from oil, which is also priced in dollars. One difference between Ecuador and El Salvador is that Ecuador maintains its currency, the sucre (ESC), but it pegs the currency to the dollar at ESC 25,000 per USD (recently adjusted to ESC 25,050). El Salvador no longer uses its currency but instead uses the dollar.

Test Results   Ecuador's experiment with dollarization has been successful, but it has not been easy. When dollarization became official in 2000, inflation rose to 96.1 percent. But it dropped back to 29.2 percent in 2001, less than 20 percent in 2002, less than 7 percent in 2003, and an estimated 3.4 percent in 2006. However, with 70 percent of the population living below the poverty level, Ecuador still has political and economic problems that dollarization alone will not cure. In addition, the election of radical left-wing President Rafael Correa, who took office on January 1, 2007, and the appointment of a new central bank president who is not very supportive of the dollarization program could result in changes.

THE DOWNSIDE OF DOLLARIZATION

As we noted, there are many advantages to dollarization, but what are the disadvantages? Consider El Salvador's neighbors. When El Salvador dollarized, over two-thirds of its exports went to the United States. By 2003, that had changed: 19.4 percent of El Salvador's exports went to the United States, putting the latter in the number-two spot after Guatemala. Four of the top five destinations for Salvadorean products were CACM countries. On the import side, the United States was the largest supplier to El Salvador, with 34.2 percent of the market. The top-five countries of origin for El Salvador's imports were the United States, Guatemala, the EU, Mexico, and Ecuador.

Of these countries, Mexico is closely linked to the dollar due to NAFTA, Ecuador is dollarized, and Guatemala's currency is also very closely linked to the dollar, although officially it is considered to have a free-floating currency. But from January 1, 2002, until December 31, 2004, the Guatemalan quetzal had actually strengthened by about 3 percent against the dollar. Thus 55.8 percent of El Salvador's imports were from countries that were closely tied to the USD.

Crawling Pegs and Crawling Bands

El Salvador's other neighbors in Central America had different exchange-rate regimes. Costa Rica and Nicaragua had *crawling pegs,* which means that their currencies were adjusted periodically in response to selected indicators, such as relative rates of inflation in comparison with major trading partners. However, the change is not as extreme as would be the case of an independently floating regime. Since 2002, the Costa Rican colón has fallen 43.9 percent against the dollar, and the Nicaraguan cordoba has fallen 26.5 percent against the dollar.

The Honduran lempira was officially classified by the International Monetary Fund as an exchange rate within a *crawling band,* which means the lempira maintains a value plus or minus 1 percent from a central rate. It gives a little more flexibility to its currency value, and the lempira has fallen about 15 percent against the dollar since 2002. The only currency that has stayed quite close to the value of the dollar since 2002 is the Guatemalan quetzal.

SURVIVING DOLLARIZATION

The problem this creates for Salvadorean companies is that they are increasingly having difficulty in export markets due to the strength of their currency against those of its Central American neighbors. How can they possibly compete against companies from Nicaragua and Honduras when those currencies have fallen against the dollar? That means Nicaraguan and Honduran companies are reaping a huge cost advantage in export markets. El Salvador has had to move into new sources of growth, such as shipping, tourism, and communications, to avoid having its economy hollowed out due to higher costs relative to its neighbors.

Case: Fresco Group S.A.   Many Salvadorean companies have had to change the way they do business. Fresco Group S.A., a family-owned textile company in El Salvador, has struggled to compete. Although the company was able to get low-cost loans to fund an expansion of facilities, it has had to move away from simple stitching of garments to creating designs, procuring materials, and manufacturing clothing based on a single sketch.

Basically, Fresco Group has had to move upscale and leave the lower-end manufacturing to other Central American companies that have benefited from weak currencies. In addition, Fresco Group is concerned about its ability to compete with textile companies from India and China because textile and garment quotas were eliminated in 2005. Management wonders if they can move upscale fast enough and convince customers that their small size and better flexibility will overcome their cost disadvantage due to the strong dollar relative to other currencies in Central America.

The Future of Dollarization in El Salvador

Should El Salvador continue to use the dollar as its currency? Is it possible that the other members of CACM should move to a dollar-based economy as they move to closer integration and membership in CAFTA-DR? El Salvador is hoping that remittances by Salvadoreans living abroad, increased foreign direct investment, and the reduction of trade barriers with other countries will help stimulate the economy and offset any downsides to dollarization.

With the advent of CAFTA-DR, El Salvador's trade with the United States picked up again. By the end of 2006, 57.1 percent of El Salvador's exports went to the United States, and 40.5 percent of its imports came from the United States. Will this closer linkage with the United States be a good thing in the long run, or does it need to diversify its trade as it did with the initial advent of the dollarization program?

> **CONCEPT CHECK**
>
> When we get to Chapter 11, we'll point out that when a country initiates a comprehensive policy change over which businesses (whether domestic or foreign) have no control, they should re-examine each link in their *value chains*—the collective activities required to move products from materials purchasing through operations to final distribution. Here we observe that a change in a nation's exchange-rate regime is just one of the changes in economic conditions that foreign firms can't control.

Introduction

As we learned in Chapter 9, an exchange rate represents the number of units of one currency needed to acquire one unit of another currency. Although this definition seems simple, managers must understand how governments set an exchange rate and what causes the rate to change. Such understanding can help them both anticipate exchange-rate changes and make decisions about business factors that are sensitive to those changes, such as the sourcing of raw materials and components, the placement of manufacturing and assembly, and the choice of final markets.

The International Monetary Fund

In 1944, toward the close of World War II, the major Allied governments met in Bretton Woods, New Hampshire, to determine what was needed to bring economic stability and growth to the postwar world. As a result of the meetings, the **International Monetary Fund (IMF)** came into official existence on December 27, 1945, and began financial operations on March 1, 1947.[2]

ORIGIN AND OBJECTIVES

Twenty-nine countries initially signed the IMF agreement, and there were 185 member countries by the middle of 2008.[3] These are the IMF's major objectives:

- To promote international monetary cooperation, exchange stability, and orderly exchange arrangements
- To foster economic growth and high levels of employment
- To provide temporary financial assistance to countries to help ease balance-of-payments adjustment[4]

Bretton Woods and the Principle of Par Value   The **Bretton Woods Agreement** established a system of fixed exchange rates under which each IMF member country set a **par value** for its currency based on gold and the U.S. dollar. Because the value of the dollar was fixed at $35 per ounce of gold, the par value would be the same whether gold or the dollar was used as the basis. This par value became a benchmark by which each country's currency was valued against other currencies. Currencies were allowed to vary within 1 percent of their par value (extended to 2.25 percent in December 1971), depending on supply and demand. Additional moves from par value and formal changes in par value were possible with IMF approval. As we see later, par values were done away with when the IMF moved to greater exchange-rate flexibility.

Because of the U.S. dollar's strength during the 1940s and 1950s and its large reserves in monetary gold, currencies of IMF member countries were denominated in terms of gold and U.S. dollars. By 1947, the United States held 70 percent of the world's official gold reserves. Therefore, governments bought and sold dollars rather than gold. The understanding—though not set in stone—was that the United States would redeem dollars for gold. The dollar became the world benchmark for trading currency, and it has remained so, in spite of the move away from fixed rates to flexible exchange rates.

THE IMF TODAY

The Quota System   When a country joins the IMF, it contributes a certain sum of money, called a **quota,** based on its economic position relative to other countries. It takes into account its GDP, current account transactions, and official reserves.[5] The quota is a pool of money that the IMF can draw on to lend to countries, and it is the basis of how much a country can borrow from the IMF. It is also the basis on which the IMF allocates special drawing rights (SDRs), discussed later.

Finally, the quota determines the voting rights of the individual members. At the end of March 2007, the total quota held by the IMF was SDR 217 billion (US$327 billion).[6] The United States has the largest quota, comprising 16.79 percent of the total. The next four countries are Japan (6.02 percent), Germany (5.88 percent), France (4.86 percent), and the United Kingdom (also 4.86 percent), so it is easy to see how much power the United States has and how dominating in general the developed countries are. This is a major source of contention with developing countries, which rely on the IMF to help out in times of monetary crisis.

The board of governors, the IMF's highest authority, is composed of one representative from each member country. The number of votes a country has depends on the size of its quota. The board of governors is the final authority on key matters, but it leaves day-to-day authority to a 24-person board of executive directors.[7]

Assistance Programs   In addition to identifying exchange-rate regimes, the IMF provides a great deal of assistance to member countries. The IMF negotiates with a country to provide financial assistance if the country agrees to adopt certain policies to stabilize its economy. This arrangement is presented in a letter of intent to the executive board of the fund, and as soon as the board accepts the arrangement, it releases the funds in different phases, which allows it to monitor progress before releasing all of the funds.

> The IMF lends money to countries to help ease balance-of-payments difficulties.

In Chapter 9, we discussed how the IMF helped Argentina initially during the currency crisis of 2002. For over a year, Argentina and the IMF argued over the "Arrangement," before Argentina finally defaulted on its debt payments to the IMF and the World Bank. However, they finally worked out a concession while Argentina continued to work with its private creditors. As all of this was going on, the IMF issued a report criticizing some of Argentina's decisions that helped lead to the crisis. As it defended Argentina's dollarization of the peso, the government was forced to pile up a lot of debt to support the currency. Eventually, this debt was not sustainable, and the crisis ensued.[8]

Special Drawing Rights (SDRs)   To help increase international reserves, the IMF created the **special drawing right (SDR)** in 1969. Basically, the IMF printed money—the SDR—to support the fixed exchange-rate system that existed at that time. For a country to support its currency in foreign-exchange markets, it could only use U.S. dollars or gold to buy it currency. However, there was not enough gold and dollars to do that, so the IMF created the SDR to give member countries instant reserve assets to supplement dollars and gold.[9]

> The SDR is
> * An international reserve asset given to each country to help increase its reserves.
> * The unit of account in which the IMF keeps its financial records.

Thus the SDR is an international reserve asset created to supplement members' existing reserve assets (official holdings of gold, foreign exchange, and reserve positions in the IMF). SDRs serve as the IMF's unit of account and are used for IMF transactions and operations. By unit of account, we mean the unit in which the IMF keeps its records. So instead of the IMF keeping its records in U.S. dollars or another currency, it keeps its records in terms of SDRs.

For example, we noted earlier that the total quota the IMF holds is SDR 217 billion, which at current exchange rates (i.e., in the first quarter of 2007) was about $327 billion. The value of the SDR is based on the weighted average of four currencies. On January 1, 1981, the IMF began to use a simplified basket of four currencies for determining valuation. At the beginning of 2007, the U.S. dollar made up 44 percent of the value of the SDR; the euro, 34 percent; the Japanese yen, 11 percent; and the British pound, 11 percent.[10] These weights were chosen because they broadly reflect the importance of each particular currency in international trade and payments.

> Currencies making up the SDR basket are the U.S. dollar, the euro, the Japanese yen, and the British pound.

Unless the executive board decides otherwise, the weights of each currency in the valuation basket change every five years. The board determined this rule in 1980. A new value was established in 2000 for the period 2001 to 2005, and then again in 2005 for the period 2006 to 2010. It will be interesting to see how the IMF decides to weight the currencies in 2010 if the dollar continues to weaken against the euro.

In addition, as we'll see in our closing case, although the Chinese yuan is not a part of the SDR basket, it will continue to gain in importance as the Chinese economy grows and as the yuan eventually becomes less controlled by the government and more subject to market forces. Also, it is hard to ignore that China has the largest foreign-exchange reserves in the world.

EVOLUTION TO FLOATING EXCHANGE RATES

The IMF's system was initially one of fixed exchange rates. Because the U.S. dollar was the cornerstone of the international monetary system, its value remained constant with respect to the value of gold. Other countries could change the value of their currency against gold and the dollar, but the value of the dollar remained fixed.

On August 15, 1971, as the U.S. balance of trade deficit continued to worsen, U.S. president Richard Nixon announced that the United States would no longer trade dollars for gold unless other industrial countries agreed to support a restructuring of the international monetary system. He was afraid that the United States would lose its large gold reserves if countries worried about holding so many dollars resulting from the large U.S. trade deficit turned in their dollars to the U.S. government and demanded gold in return.

The Smithsonian Agreement   The resulting **Smithsonian Agreement** of December 1971 had several important aspects:

Exchange-rate flexibility was widened in 1971 from 1 percent to 2.25 percent from par value.

- An 8 percent devaluation of the dollar (an official drop in the value of the dollar against gold)
- A revaluation of some other currencies (an official increase in the value of each currency against gold)
- A widening of exchange-rate flexibility (from 1 percent to 2.25 percent on either side of par value)

This effort did not last, however. World currency markets remained unsteady during 1972, and the dollar was devalued again by 10 percent in early 1973 (the year of the Arab oil embargo and the start of fast-rising oil prices and global inflation). Major currencies began to float (i.e., each one relied on the market to determine its value) against each other instead of relying on the Smithsonian Agreement.

The Jamaica Agreement   Because the Bretton Woods Agreement was based on a system of fixed exchange rates and par values, the IMF had to change its rules to accommodate floating exchange rates. The **Jamaica Agreement** of 1976 amended the original rules to eliminate the concept of par values and permit greater exchange-rate flexibility. The move toward greater flexibility can occur on an individual country basis as well as on an overall system basis. Let's see how this works.

The Jamaica Agreement of 1976 resulted in greater exchange-rate flexibility and eliminated the use of par values.

Exchange-Rate Arrangements

The Jamaica Agreement formalized the break from fixed exchange rates. As part of this move, the IMF began to permit countries to select and maintain an exchange-rate arrangement of their choice, provided they communicate their decision to the IMF. The IMF has a surveillance program that allows it to monitor the economic policies of countries that would affect those countries' exchange rates. As noted earlier in the case with Argentina, sometimes the surveillance program doesn't work as effectively as it should.

The IMF also consults annually with countries to see if they are acting openly and responsibly in their exchange-rate policies. Each year, the countries notify the IMF of the exchange-rate arrangement they will use, and then the IMF uses the information provided by the country and evidence of how the country acts in the market to place each country in a specific category. Table 10.1 identifies the different exchange-rate arrangements and the countries that belong to each one. The arrangements described in the table are ranked primarily on their degree of flexibility, from least to most flexible. It is also important to note that the classifications are based on each country.

In addition, the IMF requires countries to identify their specific monetary policy framework. For example, most countries that select a fixed or pegged exchange rate use what is called an *exchange-rate anchor* for its monetary policy. That means that it buys or sells foreign exchange at a given exchange rate to maintain the value of its currency. The target is the exchange rate. In addition, countries can adopt a monetary policy that uses

The IMF surveillance and consultation programs are designed to monitor exchange-rate policies of countries and to see if they are acting openly and responsibly in exchange-rate policies.

The IMF allows countries to classify their currency regimes according to the degree of flexibility—or lack thereof.

TABLE 10.1 Exchange-Rate Arrangements and Anchors

Exchange-Rate Regime (Number of Countries)	Monetary Policy Framework				Monetary Aggregate Target	Inflation-Targeting Frame-Work	IMF-Supported or other Monetary Program	Other[2]
	Exchange-Rate Anchor							
Exchange arrangements with no separate legal tender (41)	Another currency as legal tender (9)	ECCU (6)[3]	CFA franc zone (14)					Euro area (12)
			WAEMU	CAEMC				
	Ecuador El Salvador[4] Kiribati Marshall Islands Micronesia, Fed. States of Palau Panama San Marino Timor-Leste, Dem. Rep. of	Antigua and Barbuda Dominica* Grenada* St. Kitts and Nevis St. Lucia St. Vincent and the Grenadines	Benin* Burkina Faso* Côte d'Ivoire Guinea-Bissau Mali* Niger* Senegal Togo	Cameroon* Central African Rep. Chad* Congo, Rep. of* Equatorial Guinea Gabon				Austria Belgium Finland France Germany Greece Ireland Italy Luxembourg Netherlands Portugal Spain
Currency-board arrangements (7)	Bosnia and Herzegovina Brunei Darussalam Bulgaria* Hong Kong SAR Djibouti Estonia[5] Lithuania[5]							
Other conventional fixed-peg arrangements (52)	Against a single currency (47)							Pakistan[+7]
	Aruba Bahamas, The[9] Bahrain, Kingdom of Barbados Belarus[7] Belize Bhutan Bolivia[7,10] Cape Verde China[+6] Comoros[11] Egypt[7] Eritrea Ethiopia[7] Guyana*[7,8] Honduras*[+7] Iraq*[7] Jordan[7] Kuwait Latvia[5] Lebanon[7] Lesotho Macedonia, FYR*[7] Maldives		Malta[5] Mauritania[7] Namibia Nepal* Netherlands Antilles Oman Pakistan[+7] Qatar Rwanda* Saudi Arabia Seychelles[7] Sierra Leone*[7] Solomon Islands[7] Suriname[7,8,9] Swaziland Syrian Arab Rep.[9] Trinidad and Tobago[7] Turkmenistan[7] Ukraine[7] United Arab Emirates Venezuela, Vietnam[7] Zimbabwe[9]		China[+6] Guyana*[7,8] Sierra Leone*[7] Suriname[7,8,9]			

(Continued)

TABLE 10.1   Exchange-Rate Arrangements and Anchors (continued)

Exchange-Rate Regime (Number of Countries)	Monetary Policy Framework					
	Exchange-Rate Anchor		Monetary Aggregate Target	Inflation-Targeting Frame-Work	IMF-Supported or other Monetary Program	Other[2]
	Against a composite (5)					
	Fiji Libyan Arab Jamahiriya Morocco	Samoa Vanuatu				
Pegged exchange rates within horizontal bands (6)[12]	**Within a cooperative arrangement (4)** Cyprus[5] Denmark[5] Slovak Rep.[†5] Slovenia[5]	**Other band arrangements (2)** Hungary[†] Tonga		Hungary[†] Slovak Rep.[†5]		
Crawling pegs (5)	Azerbaijan[7] Botswana[9] Costa Rica Iran, I.R. of[7,13] Nicaragua[*]		Iran, I.R. of[7,13]			
Managed floating with no predetermined path for the exchange rate (51)			Argentina Bangladesh[*] Cambodia Gambia, The[7] Ghana[*7] Haiti[7] Jamaica[7] Lao P.D.R.[9] Madagascar[*7] Malawi[*] Mauritius Moldova[*] Mongolia Sri Lanka[7] Sudan Tajikistan Tunisia Uruguay[*] Yemen, Rep. of[7] Zambia[*]	Colombia[*] Czech Rep. Guatemala[7] Peru[*] Romania Serbia, Rep. of[14] Thailand	Afghanistan, I.R. of[*] Armenia[*7] Georgia[*] Kenya[*] Kyrgyz Rep.[*] Mozambique[*7]	Algeria Angola Burundi[*] Croatia[*] Dominican Rep.[*] Guinea[7] India Kazakhstan Liberia[7] Malaysia Myanmar Nigeria[7] Papua New Guinea[7] Paraguay[*] Russian Federation São Tomé and Príncipe[*] Singapore Uzbekistan[9]

(Continued)

growth in the money supply (called the *monetary aggregate anchor*), a targeted rate of inflation, or something else that they feel is important.

FIXED VERSUS FLEXIBLE CURRENCIES

As mentioned earlier, the IMF requires countries to classify their currencies into one of seven different categories, moving from the least to the most flexible. In reality, you could say that currencies are either *fixed* or *flexible*. If they are fixed, they lock their value on to something and don't change. If they are flexible, they move up and down in value against market forces. Their value is based on supply and demand.

TABLE 10.1 Exchange-Rate Arrangements and Anchors (continued)

Exchange-Rate Regime (Number of Countries)	Monetary Policy Framework				
	Exchange-Rate Anchor	Monetary Aggregate Target	Inflation-Targeting Framework	IMF-Supported or other Monetary Program	Other[2]
Independently floating (25)		Albania* Congo, Dem. Rep. of Indonesia Uganda	Australia Brazil Canada Chile Iceland Israel Korea Mexico New Zealand Norway Philippines Poland South Africa Sweden Turkey* United Kingdom	Tanzania*[7]	Japan Somalia[9,15] Switzerland United States

[1]An asterisk (*) indicates the country has an IMF-supported or other monetary program. A dagger (†) indicates the country adopts more than one nominal anchor in conducting monetary policy. (Note, however, that it would not be possible, for practical reasons, to include in this table which nominal anchor plays the principal role in conducting monetary policy.)

[2]Includes countries that have no explicitly stated nominal anchor but rather monitor various indicators in conducting monetary policy.

[3]The ECCU has a currency board arrangement.

[4]The printing of new colones, the domestic currency, is prohibited, but the existing stock of colones will continue to circulate along with the U.S. dollar as legal tender until all colón notes wear out physically.

[5]The member participates in the ERM II.

[6]On July 21, 2005, China announced a 2.1% revaluation of the renminbi-U.S. dollar exchange rate and a change in its exchange-rate arrangement to allow the value of the renminbi to fluctuate based on market supply and demand with reference to an undisclosed basket of currencies. To permit a greater role for market forces in determining the renminbi exchange rate, steps have been taken since July 2005 to liberalize and develop China's foreign-exchange markets, including the establishment of an over-the-counter spot foreign-exchange market and markets for currency swaps and futures. From end-July 2005 to end-July 2006, the renminbi exchange rate was more flexible, but the fluctuation in the renminbi-U.S dollar exchange rate was less than the 2% range (for a three-month period) used in the IMF's de facto exchange rate classification system as an indicator for a conventional fixed-peg exchange-rate arrangement.

[7]The regime operating de facto in the country is different from its de jure regime.

[8]There is no evidence of direct intervention by the authorities in the foreign-exchange market.

[9]The member maintains an exchange arrangement involving more than one foreign-exchange market. The arrangement shown is that maintained in the major market.

[10]This is a de facto classification. The Bolivian authorities consider their regime as a crawling peg and have not committed to the current level of the exchange rate.

[11]Comoros has the same arrangement with the French Treasury as the CFA franc zone countries.

[12]The bands for these countries are as follows: Cyprus ±15%, Denmark ±2.25%, Hungary ±15%, Slovak Republic ±15%, Slovenia (undisclosed), and Tonga ±5%.

[13]The rial crawls vis-à-vis an unannounced basket of currencies.

[14]While the current monetary framework is anchored by the announcement of core inflation objectives, the National Bank of Serbia is preparing the transition to full-fledged inflation targeting.

[15]Insufficient information on the country is available to confirm this classification, and so the classification of the last official consultation is used.

Source: Adapted from the International Monetary Fund, *IMF Annual Report 2006* (Washington, DC: IMF, 2006), pp. 145–46. Data as of July 31, 2006.

But what does that actually mean? Take the euro, for example. In Table 10.1, France, a member of the euro zone, fits in the category "exchange arrangements with no separate legal tender." Does France have a fixed or flexible exchange rate? On one dimension, you could say that France has a fixed exchange rate because the old French franc has been eliminated, and the euro has now replaced it. On another dimension, you could say that France has a floating exchange rate because the euro exchange rate varies according to market forces.

Furthermore, the footnote to the euro says that the "countries have no explicitly stated monetary anchor, but rather monitor various indicators in conducting monetary policy." As we see later, the monetary authority that monitors the value of the euro is the European Central Bank, not the central bank of any one country in the European Union.

EXCHANGE ARRANGEMENTS WITH NO SEPARATE LEGAL TENDER

In the first category in Table 10.1, countries lock the value of their currency on to another currency. As we explained in our opening case, the Central American nations of Ecuador and El Salvador fall into the first category. Fourteen countries in Africa have adopted a new currency called the CFA franc as their common currency. The French Treasury guarantees the value of the CFA franc in euros.[11]

Dollarization   That same concept was being considered in Latin America, and it is called the *dollarization* of the currency, as illustrated in the opening case. The idea would be to take all of their currency out of circulation and replace it with dollars. Basically, the U.S. Federal Reserve Bank (the Fed) would have greater control over monetary decisions instead of the governments of the local countries. Prices and wages would be established in dollars instead of in the local currency, which would disappear.

The concern is that this would result in a loss of sovereignty and could lead to severe economic problems if the United States decided to tighten monetary policy at the same time those countries needed to loosen policy to stimulate growth. Unfortunately, this is exactly what happened in Argentina in 2002. Although Argentina's exchange-rate regime did not go to the extreme of dollarization, its currency board regime was just a step away. The currency board tied the peso closely enough to the dollar and to the decisions the U.S. Fed made that the government's ability to use monetary policy to strengthen its stalling economy was limited. As a result of the experiences in Argentina and the low popularity of the U.S. government, most countries in Latin America have decided not to go the route of dollarization.[12]

CURRENCY BOARD ARRANGEMENTS

The second category is *currency board arrangements*, which is what Argentina used to have. Now, however, only seven countries have currency boards. A currency board is an organization generally separate from a country's central bank. Its responsibility is to issue domestic currency that is typically anchored to a foreign currency. If it does not have deposits on hand in the foreign currency, it cannot issue more domestic currency.

The currency board in Argentina used the U.S. dollar as its anchor before it abandoned its currency board. The Hong Kong (HK) currency board also uses the U.S. dollar as its anchor currency. Even though the HK dollar is locked onto the U.S. dollar, it moves up and down against other currencies as the dollar changes in value. Thus the HK dollar is both fixed (against the U.S. dollar) and flexible (because the U.S. dollar is an independently floating currency).

CONVENTIONAL FIXED-PEG ARRANGEMENTS

In a *conventional fixed-peg arrangement*, a country pegs its currency to another currency or basket of currencies and allows the exchange rate to vary plus or minus 1 percent from that value. It is more similar to the original fixed exchange-rate system used by the IMF.

This is the largest category of all, with 52 countries, or 27.8 percent of the total. Although most countries fix the value of their currency against another currency, some fix the value against a composite of currencies. As we'll see in our closing case, for example, China fixes its currency against a basket of currencies but does not disclose their relative proportions. (In fact, it doesn't say which currencies it uses.) This category is slightly more flexible than the first two categories, but it is still not as flexible as the floating-rate categories described later.

PEGGED EXCHANGE RATES WITHIN HORIZONTAL BANDS

This category contains only a few countries, and it is a slight variation of the first three categories. The countries in this category simply have a wider band of fluctuation but are still locked on to something else, such as the euro for Denmark, Cyprus, and Hungary, three of the countries in this category.

MORE FLEXIBLE ARRANGEMENTS

The last three categories have a much wider degree of flexibility.

Crawling Pegs   In the case of a *crawling peg*, which has the smallest number of countries of all of the different arrangements, the country maintains the value of the currency within a very tight margin, but it changes the value of the currency as needed. Thus it tries to maintain the value of the currency but does not hold rigidly to that value as economic conditions change. We note in our opening case that, whereas El Salvador has adopted the dollar as its currency, Costa Rica and Nicaragua, two of the countries with which it competes in CAFTA-DR, have adopted crawling pegs. As a result, the currencies of both countries move against the dollar.

> Flexible exchange-rate regimes include crawling pegs, exchange rates within crawling bands, managed floating rates, and independently floating rates.

Managed Float   This is the second largest category and officially called "managed floating with no predetermined path for the exchange rate." Countries in this category allow their currencies to float, but they also intervene as necessary based on economic conditions. This is far more flexible than countries that peg their currency and intervene in markets to keep their currencies at a set level, but it is not as flexible as the countries whose currencies are independently floating.

Argentina is an example of a country that has adopted a managed floating regime. As noted earlier, Argentina used to operate through a currency board, but it changed to a managed float after the peso crisis in 2002. Even though the currency is floating, Argentina still watches its value carefully and intervenes where needed, based on what is happening to the domestic money supply. Thailand, in contrast, also uses a managed floating regime, but it targets inflation to determine when to intervene in the markets.

Independently Floating   "Independently floating" is the final category and the one adopted for some of the key currencies in the world: the U.S. dollar, the Swiss franc, the Japanese yen, and the British pound. In addition, many developing countries, such as Brazil, Mexico, and Chile, have independently floating currencies. This means that the currency floats according to market forces without Central Bank intervention to determine a rate, although there may be some intervention to moderate rates of change in the value of the currency. As noted earlier, the euro should be classified as an independently floating currency, but Table 10.1 is organized by country, not currency, and the European Union is not considered a country.

EXCHANGE RATES: THE BOTTOM LINE

What is really the bottom line in the preceding discussion, and why should managers be concerned about these issues? In the first place, the world can be divided into countries that basically let their currencies float according to market forces with minimal or no Central Bank intervention and those that do not but rely on heavy Central Bank intervention and control. Although it appears from Table 10.1 that fewer countries have floating currencies, that is a little misleading. As we noted earlier, on the one hand, the countries in the euro area have given up control of their national currencies in favor of the euro, and the euro itself independently floats as does the U.S. dollar. On the other hand, most currencies that lock on to another currency, such as the U.S. dollar, don't float, but their currencies move against other currencies as the dollar moves. It is just that they depend on the value of the dollar, irrespective of what is going on in their own countries.

Second, anyone involved in international business needs to understand how the exchange rates of countries with which they do business are determined because

> Countries may change the exchange-rate regime they use, so managers need to monitor country policies carefully.

exchange rates affect marketing, production, and financial decisions, as we discuss at the end of the chapter. Note that sometimes countries change their approach to managing or not managing their currency, as Argentina did in 2002 when it moved from a currency board to managed floating currency. Chile was listed in a prior IMF survey as a country that kept its exchange rate within a crawling band, adjusting the exchange rate periodically according to inflation. But in late 1999, Chile suspended the trading bands, which it had established around the peso, and moved to a floating-rate regime in an effort to stimulate export-led economic growth, and it is still in that category. Likewise, in 2001, Iceland moved from a pegged regime, within a horizontal band, to a free-floating regime. Brazil did the same thing in early 1999; so did Turkey in 2001.[13]

Map 10.2 identifies the countries that fit into each category listed in Table 10.1 (p. 371). Because a country's classification is subject to change constantly, managers should consult the IMF frequently for updates. In addition, it is necessary to supplement the IMF information with current events, as illustrated in the earlier examples of regime changes in Chile and Iceland.

**MAP 10.2
Exchange-Rate
Arrangements, 2006**

About half of the nations in the world have opted for floating exchange rates (e.g., Russia, India, Argentina); only about one-fourth allow their currencies to float independently (e.g., the United States, Brazil, Australia). Like El Salvador, several countries have chosen the most flexible arrangement: They've abandoned their own currencies in favor of another currency. Most of these nations are quite poor (e.g., Chad, Gabon) or quite small (e.g., Grenada, San Marino).

Source: IMF Annual Report 2006 (September 25, 2006). Annual Reports by IMF. Copyright 2006 by International Monetary Fund. Reproduced by permission of International Monetary Fund in the format *textbook* via Copyright Clearance Center.

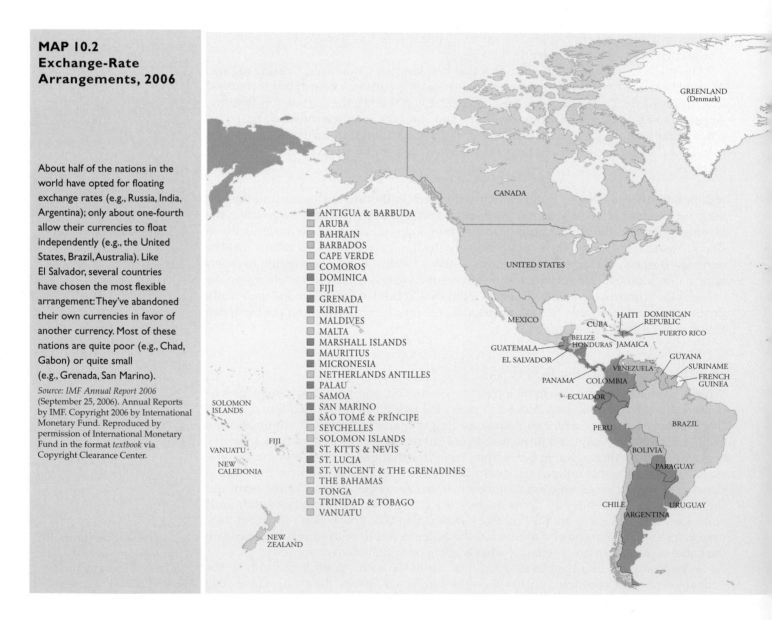

It is important for MNEs to understand the exchange-rate arrangements for the currencies of countries where they are doing business so they can forecast trends more accurately. It is much easier to forecast a future exchange rate for a relatively stable currency pegged to the U.S. dollar, such as the Hong Kong dollar, than for a currency that is freely floating, such as the Japanese yen.

THE EURO

One of the most ambitious examples of an exchange arrangement with no separate legal tender is the creation of the euro. Not content with the economic integration envisaged in the Single European Act, the EU nations signed the Treaty of Maastricht in 1992, which set steps to accomplish two goals: political union and monetary union. The decision to move to a common currency in Europe has eliminated currency as a barrier to trade. To replace each national currency with a single European currency called the euro, the countries had to converge their economic policies first. It is not possible to have different monetary policies in each member country and one currency.

CONCEPT CHECK

Each of these commitments to greater economic cooperation represents a step in the direction of **regional integration**, a form of **economic integration** that we define in Chapter 8 as the elimination of economic discrimination among geographically related nations. Here we emphasize that the **EU** has introduced a common currency to its already existing free trade internally and a common external tariff policy.

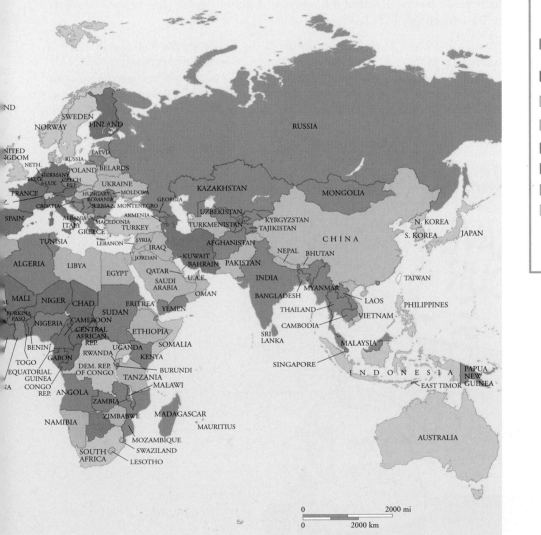

EXCHANGE-RATE ARRANGEMENTS

- Managed floating with no predetermined path for exchange rate (51)
- Exchange arrangements with no separate legal tender (41 countries)
- Independently floating rates (25)
- Other conventional fixed-peg arrangements (52)
- Currency board arrangements (7)
- Crawling pegs (5)
- Pegged exchange rates within horizontal bands (6)
- No data available

The European Monetary System and the European Monetary Union   European monetary union did not occur overnight. The roots to the system began in 1979, when the **European Monetary System (EMS)** was put into place. The EMS was set up as a means of creating exchange-rate stability within the European Community (EC) at the time. A series of exchange-rate relationships linked the currencies of most members through a parity grid. As the countries narrowed the fluctuations in their exchange rates, the stage was set for the replacement of the EMS with the Exchange Rate Mechanism (ERM) and full monetary union.

According to the Treaty of Maastricht, countries had to meet certain criteria to comply with the ERM and be part of the **European Monetary Union (EMU).** Termed the Stability and Growth Pact, the criteria outlined in the treaty, which continue for euro applicants today, are the following:

> The criteria that are part of the Growth and Stability Pact include measures of deficits, debt, inflation, and interest rates.

- Annual government deficit must not exceed 3 percent of GDP.
- Total outstanding government debt must not exceed 60 percent of GDP.
- Rate of inflation must remain within 1.5 percent of the three best performing EU countries.
- Average nominal long-term interest rate must be within 2 percent of the average rate in the three countries with the lowest inflation rates.
- Exchange-rate stability must be maintained, meaning that for at least two years, the country concerned has kept within the "normal" fluctuation margins of the European Exchange Rate Mechanism.[14]

After a great deal of effort, 11 of the 15 countries in the EU joined the EMU on January 1, 1999. Greece joined on January 1, 2001. The Republic of Slovenia joined on January 1, 2007.[15] Those of the original 15 countries not yet participating in the euro are the United Kingdom (see the cartoon in Figure 10.1), Sweden, and Denmark (by their choice). Sweden announced in July 2002 that it had met all the criteria for joining the EMU,[16] but voters' rejection of the

> The United Kingdom, Sweden, and Denmark are the only members of the original 15 EU countries that opted not to adopt the euro.

FIGURE 10.1
The Brits Love Their Pound

The pound sterling has been around for more than 900 years, and a lot of Britons are reluctant to abandon it—though not simply for sentimental reasons. Many politicians and economists are wary of the effects of the euro itself. Warns one anti-euro ad campaign: "The euro is forever—if it's a disaster, we can't leave."

Source: Copyright Clive Goddard, Cartoonstock.com.

euro in 2003 has placed its entry on hold for the time being.[17] As of 2008, 5 of the 27 countries in the EU have adopted the euro. The euro is being administered by the **European Central Bank (ECB),** which was established on July 1, 1998. The ECB has been responsible for setting monetary policy and for managing the exchange-rate system for all of Europe since January 1, 1999.

> The European Central Bank sets monetary policy for the adopters of the euro.

The ERM is important in converging the economies of the EU. Because the ECB is an independent organization like the U.S. Federal Reserve Board, it can focus on its mandate of controlling inflation. Of course, different economies are growing at different rates in Europe, and it is difficult to have one monetary policy that fits all. Countries might be tempted to use an expansion fiscal policy to stimulate economic growth, but the deficit requirements of the ERM keep countries from stimulating too much.

Pluses and Minuses of the Conversion   In its first year of operation, the euro fluctuated in value between a high of $1.1827 per euro to a low of nearly $1.00 per euro. It fell in value compared to the U.S. dollar for most of 2000 and 2001 and began rising again in 2002. The euro has risen almost steadily against the dollar since then, rising slightly above $1.5 to the euro in May 2008.

The move to the euro has been smoother than predicted. It is affecting companies in a variety of ways. Banks had to update their electronic networks to handle all aspects of money exchange, such as systems that trade global currencies, buy and sell stocks, transfer money between banks, manage customer accounts, or print out bank statements. Deutsche Bank estimated that the conversion process cost several hundred million dollars.[18]

However, many companies also believe the euro will increase price transparency (the ability to compare prices in different countries) and eliminate foreign-exchange costs and risks. Foreign-exchange costs are narrowing as companies operate in only one currency in Europe, and foreign-exchange risks between member states are also disappearing, although there are still foreign-exchange risks between the euro and nonmember currencies, such as the U.S. dollar, British pound, Swiss franc, and so on.

The euro has some challenges, however. Three of the original 15 members have opted not to join, as already mentioned, and the United Kingdom is experiencing higher growth, lower inflation, and lower unemployment than most other members of the euro zone. In addition, several members of the euro zone, notably Germany, France, and Italy, have exceeded the government deficit requirement and/or public debt and as a percentage of GDP of the ERM, forcing the EU to back down on its implementation of fines for noncompliance.

Finally, 9 of the 12 new members of the EU still need to qualify for membership in the euro area, which will take time. Some will be able to join fairly soon, but others will delay while they attempt to meet the convergence criteria. In the meantime, they will try to narrow the fluctuation between their currencies and the euro.

Point Counterpoint

Should Africa Develop a Common Currency?

Point   **Yes** The success of the euro and the deep economic and political problems in Africa have caused many experts to wonder if African nations should attempt to develop one common currency in Africa with a central bank to set monetary policy.[19] In 2003, the Association of African Central Bank Governors of the African Union (AU) announced it would work to create a common currency by 2021. The 53-member AU was created as a successor to the African Economic Community and the Organization of African Unity.

(continued)

Counterpoint   **No** There is no way that the countries of Africa will ever establish a common currency, even though the African Union hopes to do so by 2021. The institutional framework in the individual African nations is not ready for a common currency. Few of the individual central banks are independent of the political process, so they often have to stimulate the economy to respond to political pressures. If the process is not managed properly and the currency is subject to frequent devaluation,

(continued)

The development of a common currency would be great for Africa because it would hasten economic integration in a continent that desperately needs to increase market size to achieve more trade and greater economies of scale. A common currency would lower transaction costs and make it easier to engage in trade among countries.

There are several degrees of economic cooperation in Africa already, including three forms of currency cooperation. These three regional monetary unions are the Common Monetary Area (CMA), including Lesotho, Namibia, South Africa, and Swaziland, based on the South African rand; the Economic and Monetary Community for Central Africa (CAEMC), including Cameroon, Central African Republic, Chad, Republic of Congo, Equatorial Guinea, and Gabon; and the West African Economic and Monetary Union (WAEMU), including Benin, Burkina Faso, Côte d'Ivoire, Guinea-Bissau, Mali, Niger, Senegal, and Togo. The latter two monetary unions are part of the CFA franc zone, designated by the IMF as an exchange arrangement with no separate legal tender. All of the countries in the CFA franc zone are former colonies of France and maintain French as the official language except for Guinea-Bissau and Equatorial Guinea, which were ruled by Portugal and Spain, respectively. The two groups of countries in the CFA franc zone each have central banks that monitor the value of the CFA franc.

The CFA franc zone has been successful in delivering low inflation, but it has not necessarily delivered high growth. The CMA is controlled by South Africa because of the size of its economy and the fact that the currency of the CMA is the South African rand. The members of the CMA are classified as "other conventional fixed-peg arrangements," with the exception of South Africa, which has an independently floating currency.

In addition to the three regional monetary unions, there are five existing regional economic communities: Arab Monetary Union, Common Market for Eastern and Southern Africa, Economic Community of Central African States, Economic Community of West African States, and Southern African Development Community. These groups are working hard to reduce trade barriers and increase trade among member countries, so all these groups would have to do is combine into one large African economic union, form a central bank, and establish a common monetary policy as the EU does.

A major advantage of establishing a central bank and common currency is that institutions in each African nation will have to improve, and the central bank may be able to insulate the monetary policy from political pressures, which often create inflationary pressures and subsequent devaluations. ●

there will be no pride in the region or clout on the international stage.

Further, each country will have to give up monetary sovereignty and will have to rely on other measures, such as labor mobility, wage and price flexibility, and fiscal transfers, to weather the shocks. Even though there is good labor mobility in Africa, it is difficult to imagine that the African countries will be able to transfer tax revenues from country to country to help stimulate growth. In addition, it is difficult to transfer goods among the different countries in Africa because of transportation problems that are not an issue in the EU.

The establishment of the euro in the EU was a monumental task, but it took years to establish, following a successful customs union and a gradual tightening of the ERM in Europe. For Africa to establish a common currency, there needs to be closer economic integration first, so it is important to be patient and give Africa a chance to move forward. Maybe one way to move to a common currency is to strengthen the existing regional monetary unions and then gradually open up the unions to neighboring countries until there are three huge monetary unions. Then the three unions can discuss ways to link together into a common currency in Africa. ●

Determining Exchange Rates

One of the first steps in being able to forecast future values of a currency is to understand how exchange rates change in value. The exchange-rate regimes described earlier are either fixed or floating, with fixed rates varying in terms of how fixed they are and floating rates varying in terms of how much they actually float. However, currencies change in different ways depending on whether they are in floating-rate or fixed-rate regimes. First we examine how supply and demand determine currency values in a floating world in the absence of government intervention. Then we show how governments can intervene in markets to help control the value of a currency.

NONINTERVENTION: CURRENCY IN A FLOATING-RATE WORLD

Currencies that float freely respond to supply and demand conditions free from government intervention. This concept can be illustrated using a two-country model involving the United States and Japan. Figure 10.2 shows the equilibrium exchange rate in the market and then a movement to a new equilibrium level as the market changes. The demand for yen in this example is a function of U.S. demand for Japanese goods and services, such as automobiles, and yen-denominated financial assets, such as securities.

The supply of yen in this example is a function of Japanese demand for U.S. goods and services and dollar-denominated financial assets. Initially, the supply of and demand for yen in Figure 10.2 meet at the equilibrium exchange rate e_0 (for example, 0.00926 dollar per yen, or 108 yen per dollar) and the quantity of yen Q_1.

Assume demand for U.S. goods and services by Japanese consumers drops because of, say, high U.S. inflation. This lessening demand would result in a reduced supply of yen in the foreign-exchange market, causing the supply curve to shift to S'. Simultaneously, the increasing prices of U.S. goods might lead to an increase in demand for Japanese goods and services by U.S. consumers. This, in turn, would lead to an increase in demand for yen in the market, causing the demand curve to shift to D' and finally leading to an increase in the quantity of yen and an increase in the exchange rate.

Demand for a country's currency is a function of the demand for that country's goods and services and financial assets.

The new equilibrium exchange rate would be at e_1 (for example, 0.00943 dollar per yen, or 106 yen per dollar). From a dollar standpoint, the increased demand for

Three Masai tribesmen exchanging foreign currency in Stone Town, Zanzibar, Tanzania, East Africa.

FIGURE 10.2
The Equilibrium Exchange Rate and How It Moves

Let's say that inflation in the United States is comparatively higher than in Japan. In that case (and assuming that Japanese consumers are buying U.S. goods and services), the *demand* for the Japanese yen will go up, but the *supply* will go down. What if Japan wants to keep the dollar-to-yen exchange rate at e_0? It can increase the supply of yen in the market—and therefore lower the exchange rate—by selling yen for dollars.

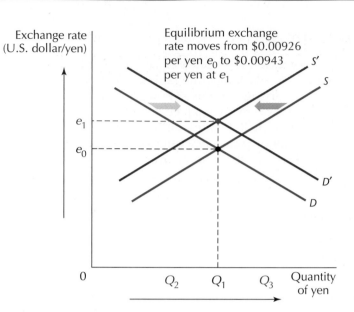

Japanese goods would lead to an increase in supply of dollars as more consumers tried to trade their dollars for yen, and the reduced demand for U.S. goods would result in a drop in demand for dollars. This would cause a reduction in the dollar's value against the yen.

INTERVENTION: CURRENCY IN A FIXED-RATE OR MANAGED-FLOATING-RATE WORLD

In the preceding example, Japanese and U.S. authorities allowed supply and demand to determine the values of the yen and dollar. That does not occur for currencies that fix their exchange rates and do not allow them to move according to market forces. There can be times when one or both countries might not want exchange rates to change.

Assume, for example, that the United States and Japan decide to manage their exchange rates. Although both currencies are independently floating currencies, their respective governments could intervene in the market. The U.S. government might not want its currency to weaken because its companies and consumers would have to pay more for Japanese products, which would lead to more inflationary pressure in the United States. Or the Japanese government might not want the yen to strengthen because it would mean unemployment in its export industries.

A government buys and sells its currency in the open market as a means of influencing the currency's price.

But how can the governments keep the values from changing when the United States is earning too few yen? Somehow the difference between yen supply and demand must be neutralized. To understand this process, let's first examine the role of central banks in foreign-exchange markets.

THE ROLE OF CENTRAL BANKS

Each country has a central bank responsible for the policies affecting the value of its currency, although countries with currency boards independent from the central bank use the currency board to control the value of the currency. The central bank in the United States is the Federal Reserve System (the Fed), a system of 12 regional banks. The New York Fed, in close coordination with and representing the Federal Reserve System and the U.S. Treasury, is responsible for intervening in foreign-exchange markets to achieve dollar exchange-rate policy objectives and to counter disorderly conditions in foreign-exchange markets. The U.S. Treasury is responsible for setting exchange-rate

Central banks control policies that affect the value of currencies; the Federal Reserve Bank of New York is the central bank in the United States.

policy, whereas the Fed is responsible for executing foreign-exchange intervention. Further, the Federal Reserve Bank of New York serves as a fiscal agent in the United States for foreign central banks and official international financial organizations.[20]

In the European Union, the European Central Bank now coordinates the activities of each member country's central bank to establish a common monetary policy in Europe, much as the Federal Reserve Bank does in the United States.

Central Bank Reserve Assets   Central bank reserve assets are kept in three major forms: foreign-exchange reserves, IMF-related assets (including SDRs), and gold. According to the annual report of the IMF, foreign exchange comprises about 88 percent of total reserves worldwide, with U.S. dollars representing about 67 percent of the total, followed by the euro at about 25 percent of the total. Other currencies, such as the Japanese yen, British pound, and Swiss franc, are also reserve assets but at relatively small percentages. Clearly the U.S. dollar and the euro are the two main reserve asset currencies. Their percentage of total varies from year to year depending on their relative strengths, and their relative position for different countries also varies.[21]

Having strong central bank reserve assets is essential to the financial strength of a country. When the financial crises in Asia, Russia, and South America hit in the late 1990s, very few countries had strong central bank reserve assets. As a result, they had to borrow a lot of U.S. dollars, which turned out to be devastating when they finally had to devalue their currencies. Since 2000, however, the picture has changed. Due to strong commodity prices, expanding exports, and restraint in incurring dollar debt, many of those same countries have strengthened their financial position by increasing their reserves.

> Central bank reserve assets are kept in three major forms: gold, foreign-exchange reserves, and IMF-related assets. Foreign exchange is 85.5 percent of reserve assets worldwide.

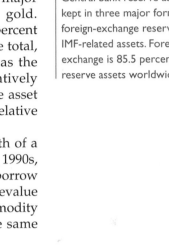

Eurotower Building Headquarters of the Central European Bank, Frankfurt-Am-Main, Germany.

Take Brazil, for example. Its foreign-exchange reserves are expected to reach $170 billion by the end of 2007, leading the way for the rest of Latin America, where reserves have increased fourfold since 2000.[22] However, this is relatively small compared with China, which had $1.33 trillion in reserves by mid-2007. They were followed by Japan with $924 billion and the euro zone with $439 billion. In spite of that, Brazil's reserves were greater than every country in the world except for China, Japan, Russia, and Korea, exceeding the reserves of both the United Kingdom and Germany.[23]

Central banks intervene in currency markets by buying and selling currency to affect its price.

How Central Banks Intervene in the Market   A central bank can intervene in currency markets in several ways. The U.S. Fed, for example, usually uses foreign currencies to buy dollars when the dollar is weak or sells dollars for foreign currency when the dollar is strong. Depending on the market conditions, a central bank may do any of the following:

- Coordinate its action with other central banks or go it alone
- Enter the market aggressively to change attitudes about its views and policies
- Call for reassuring action to calm markets
- Intervene to reverse, resist, or support a market trend
- Announce or not announce its operations, be very visible or very discreet
- Operate openly or indirectly through brokers[24]

Case: The U.S. Dollar and the Japanese Yen   Although the U.S. dollar is an independently floating currency, let's continue with the example illustrated in Figure 10.2 (p. 382) and show how a central bank could intervene. In a managed fixed-exchange-rate system, the New York Federal Reserve Bank would hold foreign-exchange reserves, which it would have built up through the years for this type of contingency. It could sell enough of its yen reserves (make up the difference between Q_1 and Q_3 in Figure 10.2) at the fixed exchange rate to maintain that rate. Or the Japanese central bank might be willing to accept dollars so that U.S. consumers can continue to buy Japanese goods. These dollars would then become part of Japan's foreign-exchange reserves. Although this is a two-country example, sometimes several central banks coordinate their intervention to support a currency rather than just have two countries involved.

The fixed rate could continue as long as the United States had reserves or as long as the Japanese were willing to add dollars to their holdings. Sometimes governments use monetary policy, such as raising interest rates to create a demand for their currency and to keep the value from falling. Unless something changed the basic imbalance in the currency supply and demand, however, the New York Federal Reserve Bank would run out of yen and the Japanese central bank would stop accepting dollars because it would fear amassing too many, similar to what happened to South Korea in early 2005 and Thailand in 2007. At this point, it would be necessary to change the exchange rate to lessen the demand for yen.

If a country determines that intervention will not work, it must adjust its currency's value. If the currency is freely floating, the exchange rate will seek the correct level according to the laws of supply and demand. However, a currency pegged to another currency or to a basket of currencies usually is changed on a formal basis—in other words, through a devaluation (a weakening of the currency) or revaluation (a strengthening of the currency), depending on the direction of the change.

Different Approaches to Intervention   Government policies change over time, depending on economic conditions and the attitude of the prevailing administration in power, irrespective if the currency is considered to be freely floating or not. The United States is a good example of how policies change. The George H. W. Bush administration, in 1989 alone, bought and sold dollars on 97 days and sold $19.5 billion. In the first two and a half years of the first Clinton administration, the Fed intervened in the market by buying dollars on only 18 days, spending about $12.5 billion in the process.[25]

During the first term of office of President George W. Bush, the Fed rarely intervened in the market despite a decline in the value of the dollar against the euro and the yen. In fact, from August 1995 to December 2006, spanning the presidencies of Bill Clinton and George W. Bush, the U.S. Fed intervened only twice in foreign-exchange markets.[26] Due to the large U.S. trade deficit, the administration of President George W. Bush has preferred to let the market determine the value of the U.S. dollar, hoping a weakening of the dollar will lead to an expansion of exports and reduction of imports, thus improving the trade balance.

From the beginning of 2003 until the end of 2004, the dollar continued to weaken against both the euro and the yen. In an attempt to strengthen the dollar, the Japanese central bank spent a record 20 trillion yen in 2003 and 10 trillion yen in the first two months of 2004. Despite the efforts of the Japanese authorities, the yen rose 11 percent against the dollar in 2003 and continued to strengthen through 2004. The Japanese finance ministry stopped its foreign-exchange intervention in March 2004, but the dollar's continued weakening against both the euro and yen at the end of 2004 sparked new threats of intervention by the Japanese and Europeans. A senior Japanese finance ministry official said, "It is natural for Japan and Europe to act when the dollar alone is falling. If the (dollar's) movement affects the European economy and the Japanese economy, we should defend ourselves."[27]

In 2005, the Central Bank of South Korea intervened heavily in currency markets to try to slow down the rise in the Korean won against the dollar by selling won and buying dollars. From 2002 to 2005, the won appreciated 30 percent against the dollar, 17 percent of which occurred in 2004. However, the cost of intervention was high, and South Korea decided to stop when its foreign-exchange reserves reached $206 billion, the fourth highest in the world at that time.[28]

U.S. Attitude Toward Intervention   In general, the United States disapproves of foreign-currency intervention. The reason is that it is very difficult, if not impossible, for intervention to have a lasting impact on the value of a currency. Given the daily volume of foreign-exchange transactions, no one government can move the market, unless its movements can change the psychology of the market. Intervention may temporarily halt a slide, but it cannot force the market to move in a direction it doesn't want to go, at least for the long run. For that reason, it is important for countries to focus on correcting economic fundamentals instead of spending a lot of time and money on intervention. Even when the dollar was falling from 2003 to 2007, the government decided not to intervene because the dollar was simply coming back to the level it was at before the run-up of the dollar from 1995 to 2002.[29]

Revisiting the BIS   Coordination of central bank intervention can take place bilaterally or multilaterally. The Bank for International Settlements (BIS) in Basel, Switzerland, links together the central banks in the world. As we noted in Chapter 9, the BIS was founded in 1930 and is owned and controlled by the major central banks in the world. The major objective of the BIS is to promote the cooperation of central banks to facilitate international financial stability. Although only 55 central banks or monetary authorities are shareholders in the BIS—11 of which are the founding banks and are from the major industrial countries—the BIS has dealings with some 140 central banks and other international financial institutions worldwide.[30]

The BIS acts as a central banker's bank. It gets involved in swaps and other currency transactions between the central banks in other countries. It also is a gathering place where central bankers can discuss monetary cooperation and is increasingly getting involved with other multilateral agencies, such as the IMF, in providing support during international financial crises.[31] In addition, the BIS conducts the triennial central bank

---

Sidebar notes:

Governments vary in their intervention policies by country and by administration.

The Bank for International Settlements in Basel, Switzerland, is owned by and promotes cooperation among a group of central banks.

CONCEPT CHECK

In Chapter 9, we discuss the importance of the **BIS** in collecting information about the massive volume of activity on the global **foreign-exchange market**. Here we add that the BIS may also help coordinate the policies of central banks in matters of foreign-exchange intervention.

survey of foreign exchange and derivatives market activity that is the basis for much of the trading data provided in Chapter 9.

BLACK MARKETS

A black market closely approximates a price based on supply and demand for a currency instead of a government-controlled price.

In many of the countries that do not allow their currencies to float according to market forces, a black market could parallel the official market and be aligned more closely with the forces of supply and demand than is the official market. The less flexible a country's exchange-rate arrangement, the more likely there will be a thriving black market. A **black market** exists when people are willing to pay more for dollars than the official rate. In March 2005, the government of Zimbabwe arrested 10,000 people, who were charged with black market activities, including selling foreign exchange.

Authorities blamed foreigners for a thriving foreign currency informal market where the Zimbabwe dollar was trading at up to 25,000 to the U.S. dollar against an official rate of 9,000. However, many experts feel that the reason for the black market activities is poverty in Zimbabwe and government crackdowns will simply drive the black market activities deeper. Until the government loosens controls on the currency, foreign exchange will continue to command a hefty premium in the black market.[32]

Zimbabwe's official currency regime is a fixed-peg arrangement and is pegged to the U.S. dollar. However, things didn't improve much. With inflation hitting around 4,500 percent in 2007, the highest in the world, the currency continued to fall. A loaf of bread in 2007 cost 44,000 Zimbabwean dollars, which was only 18 cents at black market rates or $176 at the official exchange rate.[33] The movement to a floating rate would eliminate the need for a black market. However, as is the case with Zimbabwe, it is impossible to move to a floating exchange rate without controlling inflation and other aspects of the economy.

FOREIGN-EXCHANGE CONVERTIBILITY AND CONTROLS

Some countries with fixed exchange rates control access to their currencies. *Fully convertible currencies* are those that the government allows both residents and nonresidents to purchase in unlimited amounts.

A hard currency is a currency that is usually fully convertible and strong or relatively stable in value in comparison with other currencies.

Hard and Soft Currencies   **Hard currencies,** such as the U.S. dollar, euro, British pound, and Japanese yen, are currencies that are fully convertible. They also are relatively stable in value or tend to be strong in comparison with other currencies over time. In addition, they are desirable assets. Currencies that are not fully convertible are often called **soft currencies,** or **weak currencies.** They tend to be the currencies of developing countries. A major reason why countries restrict convertibility of their currencies is because they are short on foreign-exchange reserves and try to use them for essential transactions. That's why soft currencies tend to be from developing countries where foreign-exchange reserves are low. The higher the reserves, the less a country has to resort to restricting convertibility.

A soft currency is one that is usually not fully convertible and is also called a weak currency.

Most countries today have *nonresident,* or *external, convertibility,* meaning that foreigners can convert their currency into the local currency and can convert back into their currency as well. For example, travelers to Zimbabwe can convert U.S. dollars (USD) into Zimbabwe dollars (ZWD) and convert ZWD back into USD when they leave. However, they have to show receipts of all conversions into or from ZWD inside the country to make sure that all transactions took place on the official market.

Controlling Convertibility   To conserve scarce foreign exchange, some governments impose exchange restrictions on companies or individuals who want to exchange money. The devices they use include *import licensing, multiple exchange rates, import deposit requirements,* and *quantity controls.* As we discussed in Chapter 9, Argentina's government placed exchange restrictions on individuals and companies at the beginning of 2002 to keep individuals and companies from sending money out of Argentina.

In 2007, for instance, the Thai baht was rising in value, approaching a 10-year high against the U.S. dollar. The baht is a managed floating currency that is loosely tied to the dollar. Given that the Thai government had limited the convertibility of the baht in some areas, they decided it might be best to loosen controls and encourage an outflow of currency to try to reduce the value of the baht. On June 25, 2007, the government announced several measures to reduce controls: "Among the measures, effective immediately, was approval for Thai-listed companies to purchase foreign exchange of up to $100 million a year for foreign investment. Institutional investors no longer need central bank approval to invest in deposits with foreign institutions, and individuals may now send up to $1 million a year overseas as transfers to expatriate relatives, as donations or to buy real estate."[34] The quote serves to illustrate ways that governments institute foreign-exchange controls to preserve a currency's value.

Licenses Government licenses fix the exchange rate by requiring all recipients, exporters, and others who receive foreign currency to sell it to its central bank at the official buying rate. Then the central bank rations the foreign currency it acquires by selling it at fixed rates to those needing to make payment abroad for essential goods. An importer may purchase foreign exchange only if that importer has obtained an import license for the goods in question.

> Licensing occurs when a government requires that all foreign-exchange transactions be regulated and controlled by it.

Multiple Exchange Rates Another way that governments control foreign-exchange convertibility is by establishing more than one exchange rate. This restrictive measure is called a **multiple exchange-rate system.** The government determines which kinds of transactions are to be conducted at which exchange rates. Countries with multiple exchange rates often have a floating exchange rate for luxury goods and financial flows, such as dividends. Then they have a fixed, usually lower, exchange rate for other trade transactions, such as imports of essential commodities and semimanufactured goods.

> In a multiple exchange-rate system, a government sets different exchange rates for different types of transactions.

Import Deposits Another form of foreign-exchange convertibility control is the **advance import deposit.** In this case, the government tightens the issue of import licenses and requires importers to make a deposit with the central bank, often for as long as one year and interest free, covering the full price of manufactured goods they would purchase from abroad.

> Advance import deposit—a government requires deposit of money prior to the release of foreign exchange to pay for imports; varies to as long as a year in advance.

Quantity Controls Governments also may limit the amount of exchange through quantity controls, which often apply to tourism. A quantity control limits the amount of currency that a local resident can purchase from the bank for foreign travel. The government sets a policy on how much money a tourist is allowed to take overseas, and the individual is allowed to convert only that amount of money.

> Quantity controls—the government limits the amount of foreign currency that can be used in a specific transaction.

In the past, currency controls have significantly added to the cost of doing business internationally, and they have resulted in the overall reduction of trade. However, the liberalization of trade in recent years has eliminated a lot of these controls to the point that they are found to be a minor impediment to trade.[35] In addition, the move from fixed to flexible exchange rates has also eliminated the need for controls in many countries.

EXCHANGE RATES AND PURCHASING POWER PARITY

Purchasing power parity (PPP) is a well-known theory that seeks to define relationships between currencies. In essence, it claims that a change in relative inflation (meaning a comparison of the countries' rates of inflation) between two countries must cause a change in exchange rates to keep the prices of goods in two countries fairly similar. According to the PPP theory, if, for example, Japanese inflation was 2 percent and U.S. inflation was 3.5 percent, the dollar would be expected to fall by the difference in inflation rates. Then the dollar would be worth fewer yen than before the adjustment, and the yen would be worth more dollars than before the adjustment.

> Purchasing power parity from the standpoint of exchange rates seeks to define the relationships between currencies based on relative inflation.

The "Big Mac Index"   An interesting illustration of the PPP theory for estimating exchange rates is the "Big Mac index" of currencies used by *The Economist* each year. Since 1986, the British periodical *The Economist* has used the price of a Big Mac to estimate the exchange rate between the dollar and another currency (see Table 10.2). Because the Big Mac is sold in over 120 countries, it is easy to compare prices. PPP would suggest that the exchange should leave hamburgers costing the same in the United States as abroad. However, the Big Mac sometimes costs more and sometimes less, demonstrating how far currencies are under- or overvalued against the dollar.

The Big Mac price in dollars is found by converting the price of a Big Mac in the local currency into dollars at the current exchange rate. For example, in Table 10.2 the U.S. dollar equivalent of a Big Mac in China is $1.45, which is the price of the Big Mac in China (which happens to be 11 yuan as provided separately by *The Economist* but not included in the table) converted into dollars at the actual exchange rate (which was 7.586 yuan per dollar). The price of the Big Mac and the exchange rate were determined by *The Economist* when the editors did their survey. Unfortunately, they don't provide us with the local prices and exchange rates for the other countries in the survey or the date at which they made the determination. However, you can see from Table 10.2 that it is much cheaper to buy a Big Mac in China than it is in the United States.

The second column tries to show what the exchange rate should be if the price in dollars equals the price in the local currency. Continuing with China as the example, if you divide 11 yuan by $3.41 (the prices of the Big Mac in China and in the United States), you get 3.23 yuan per dollar, which is what the exchange rate should be for a Big Mac to cost the same in the two countries. Column 3 shows how much the currency1 is under- or overvalued against the dollar. For the Chinese yuan, you take $(3.24 - 7.586)/7.586 = -.5742$, or the yuan is undervalued against the dollar by about 57.4 percent or 58 percent according to the table.

As you can see from Table 10.2, several European currencies, including the euro, are significantly overvalued against the dollar. That makes it easier for U.S. companies to export to Europe and harder for European countries to export to the United States. However, many currencies in Asia, including China, are undervalued against the dollar, so it is easier for Asian companies to export to the United States and harder for U.S. companies to export to Asia. However, consider that the euro is overvalued by 22 percent against the dollar according to the Big Mac index, whereas the Chinese yuan is undervalued by 58 percent against the dollar. That means that the euro is overvalued by 80 percent against the yuan, making their trade relationship even more complicated.[36]

There are supporters of the Big Mac index, also known as "McParity," but there also are detractors. Even though McParity may hold up in the long run, as some studies have shown, there are short-run problems that affect PPP:

- The theory of PPP falsely assumes there are no barriers to trade and that transportation costs are zero.

- Prices of the Big Mac in different countries are distorted by taxes. European countries with high value-added taxes are more likely to have higher prices than countries with low taxes.

- The Big Mac is not just a basket of commodities; its price also includes nontraded costs, such as rent, insurance, and so on.

- Profit margins vary by the strength of competition: The higher the competition, the lower the profit margin and, therefore, the price.[37]

Despite the PPP theory flaws, most economists agree that PPP measures provide a more realistic picture of the relative size of economies than market exchange rates.

> If the domestic inflation rate is lower than that in the foreign country, the domestic currency should be stronger than that of the foreign country.

TABLE 10.2 The Big Mac Index

In order to estimate the exchange rate between the dollar and another currency, the index converts into US$ the price of a Big Mac in the second currency. To appreciate the difference in prices in US$ made by differences in currency valuations, compare the data for the euro area with the data for Switzerland. Note, too, that, of the countries on the list, you can get the best deals on a Big Mac in China and Hong Kong.

	Big Mac Prices in Dollars*	Implied PPP[†] of the Dollar	Under (−)/ Over (+) Valuation Against the Dollar, %
United States[‡]	3.41	–	–
Argentina	2.67	2.42	−22
Australia	2.95	1.01	−14
Brazil	3.61	2.02	+6
Britain	4.01	1.71[§]	+18
Canada	3.68	1.14	+8
Chile	2.97	459	−13
China	1.45	3.23	−58
Czech Republic	2.51	15.5	−27
Denmark	5.08	8.14	+49
Egypt	1.68	2.80	−51
Euro area**	4.17	1.12[††]	+22
Hong Kong	1.54	3.52	−55
Hungary	3.33	176	−2
Indonesia	1.76	4,663	−48
Japan	2.29	82.1	−33
Malaysia	1.60	1.61	−53
Mexico	2.69	8.50	−21
New Zealand	5.89	1.35	+73
Peru	3.00	2.79	−12
Philippines	1.85	24.9	−46
Poland	2.51	2.02	−26
Russia	2.03	15.2	−41
Singapore	2.59	1.16	−24
South Africa	2.22	4.55	−35
South Korea	3.14	850	−8
Sweden	4.86	9.68	+42
Switzerland	5.20	1.85	+53
Taiwan	2.29	22.0	−33
Thailand	1.80	18.2	−47
Turkey	3.66	1.39	+7
Venezuela	3.45	2,170	+1

*At current exchange rates

[†]Purchasing power parity; local price divided by price in United States

[‡]Average of New York, Chicago, Atlanta, and San Francisco

[§]Dollars per pound

**Weighted average of prices in euro area

[††]Dollars per euro

Source: "The Big Mac Index: Sizzling," *The Economist,* July 7, 2007: 74.

EXCHANGE RATES AND INTEREST RATES

Although inflation is the most important long-run influence on exchange rates, interest rates are also important. To understand this interrelationship between interest rates and exchange rates, we need to understand two key finance theories: the *Fisher Effect* and the *International Fisher Effect.*

The nominal interest rate is the real interest rate plus inflation. Because the real interest rate should be the same in every country, the country with the higher interest rate should have higher inflation.

The Fisher Effect   The first theory links inflation and interest rates, and the second links interest rates and exchange rates. The **Fisher Effect** is the theory that the nominal interest rate r in a country (the actual monetary interest rate earned on an investment) is determined by the real interest rate R (the nominal rate less inflation) and the inflation rate i as follows:

$$(1 + r) = (1 + R)(1 + i) \text{ or } r = (1 + R)(1 + i) - 1$$

According to this theory, if the real interest rate is 5 percent, the U.S. inflation rate is 2.9 percent, and the Japanese inflation rate is 1.5 percent, then the nominal interest rates for the United States and Japan are computed as follows:

$$r_{US} = (1.05)(1.029) - 1 = 0.08045, \text{ or } 8.045 \text{ percent}$$

$$r_{J} = (1.05)(1.015) - 1 = 0.06575, \text{ or } 6.575 \text{ percent}$$

So the difference between U.S. and Japanese interest rates is a function of the difference between their inflation rates. If their inflation rates were the same (zero differential) but interest rates were 10 percent in the United States and 6.575 percent in Japan, investors would place their money in the United States, where they could get the higher real return.

The IFE implies that the currency of the country with the lower interest rate will strengthen in the future.

The International Fisher Effect   The bridge from interest rates to exchange rates can be explained by the **International Fisher Effect (IFE),** the theory that the interest-rate differential is an unbiased predictor of future changes in the spot exchange rate. For example, the IFE predicts that if nominal interest rates in the United States are higher than those in Japan, the dollar's value should fall in the future by that interest-rate differential, which would be an indication of a weakening, or depreciation, of the dollar. That is because the interest-rate differential is based on differences in inflation rates, as we discussed earlier. The previous discussion on purchasing power parity also demonstrated that the country with the higher inflation should have the weaker currency. Thus the country with the higher interest rate (and the higher inflation) should have the weaker currency.

Of course, these issues cover the long run, but anything can happen in the short run. During periods of general price stability, a country (such as the United States) that raises its interest rates is likely to attract capital and see its currency rise in value due to the increased demand. However, if the reason for the increase in interest rates is because inflation is higher than that of its major trading partners and if the country's central bank is trying to reduce inflation, the currency will eventually weaken until inflation cools down. Although the interest-rate differential is the critical factor for a few of the most widely traded currencies, the expectation of the future spot rate also is very important. Normally, a trader will automatically estimate the future spot rate using the interest-rate differential and then adjust it for other market conditions.

Other key factors affecting exchange-rate movements are confidence and technical factors, such as the release of economic statistics.

OTHER FACTORS IN EXCHANGE-RATE DETERMINATION

Various other factors can affect currency values. One factor not to be dismissed lightly is confidence. In times of turmoil, people prefer to hold currencies considered safe. In addition to basic economic forces and confidence, exchange rates may be influenced by such technical factors as the release of national economic statistics, comments by a central bank, seasonal demands for a currency, and a slight strengthening of a currency following a prolonged weakness, or vice versa.

Four Brief Cases In August 2007 when the U.S. economy was hit by the subprime mortgage problems, the U.S. Fed reduced interest rates to stimulate the economy. In the foreign-exchange markets, investors were closely watching the statements of Federal Reserve officials to see if they could pick up information to help them figure out the direction exchange rates and other financial markets would take.[38]

Similarly, early in 2005, the global currency markets experienced shocks due to some misinterpreted comments by the Bank of Korea's governor. Reports that the Bank of Korea wanted to "diversify" its holdings were construed as a decision to cut dollar holdings. As a result, the dollar dropped against other currencies, rebounding only after Korean officials stated their statements had been misunderstood.[39] Similarly, some South Korean government officials in July 2007 released statements that the Korean won was overvalued, causing instability in the market. However, after the won weakened several days in a row, another government official announced that the South Korean government wasn't trying to direct the value of the won in the markets, hoping to make it clear that the government was committed to a freely floating exchange rate.

Yet another example of how currency markets react strongly to news occurred in the spring of 2005. A reporter for the China News Service wrote an article about the impact of a possible appreciation of the Chinese yuan. Her story was translated by the *People's Daily* online newspaper as fact, and it changed significantly as it moved from one news market to the other. In response to the article, currency traders and fund managers panicked, thinking the news story reflected the intentions of the Chinese government, and the U.S. dollar plunged in value. Only after the story was revealed to be inaccurate did the dollar rise again in value.[40]

Finally, in the run-up to Brazil's presidential election of 2002, the *real* (Brazil's currency) hit all-time lows because of high poll ratings for a left-wing candidate whom investors feared would not be able to control the country's finances.[41] However, when the candidate, Lula da Silva of the Worker's Party, won the election and established a conservative fiscal and monetary policy, the real strengthened again.

Forecasting Exchange-Rate Movements

The preceding section looked at the effect of the law of supply and demand on exchange rates, showed how governments intervene to manage exchange-rate movements, and explained how inflation and interest rates can be important determinants of exchange rates. This section identifies factors that managers can monitor to get an idea of what will happen to exchange rates.

Because various factors influence exchange-rate movements, managers must be able to analyze those factors to formulate a general idea of the timing, magnitude, and direction of an exchange-rate movement. However, prediction is not a precise science, and many things can cause the best of predictions to differ significantly from reality.

FUNDAMENTAL AND TECHNICAL FORECASTING

Managers can forecast exchange rates by using either of two approaches: fundamental forecasting or technical forecasting. **Fundamental forecasting** uses trends in economic variables to predict future rates. The data can be plugged into an econometric model or evaluated on a more subjective basis.

Technical forecasting uses past trends in exchange rates themselves to spot future trends in rates. Technical forecasters, or *chartists,* assume that if current exchange rates reflect all facts in the market, then under similar circumstances, future rates will follow the

Fundamental forecasting uses trends in economic variables to predict future exchange rates. Technical forecasting uses past trends in exchange-rate movements to spot future trends.

same patterns.[42] However, all forecasting is imprecise. A corporate treasurer who wants to forecast an exchange rate—say, the relationship between the British pound and the euro—might use a variety of sources, both internal and external to the company. Many treasurers and bankers use outside forecasters to obtain input for their own forecasts. Forecasters need to provide ranges or point estimates with subjective probabilities based on available data and subjective interpretation.

Dealing with Biases   There are, however, some biases that can skew forecasts:

- Overreaction to unexpected and dramatic news events
- Illusory correlation, that is, the tendency to see correlations or associations in data that are not statistically present but are expected to occur on the basis of prior beliefs
- Focusing on a particular subset of information at the expense of the overall set of information
- Insufficient adjustment for subjective matters, such as market volatility
- The inability to learn from one's past mistakes, such as poor trading decisions
- Overconfidence in one's ability to forecast currencies accurately[43]

Good treasurers and bankers develop their own forecasts of what will happen to a particular currency and use fundamental or technical forecasts of outside forecasters to corroborate them. Doing this helps them determine whether they are considering important factors and whether they need to revise their forecasts in light of outside analysis.

However, it is important to understand that no matter how carefully prepared a forecast is, it is still an educated guess. As the *Wall Street Journal* stated,

> But after a benign period when global trends seemed relatively predictable, confusion now rages over many critical issues that shape trading strategies: the pace of the Federal Reserve's interest-rate increases; the direction of oil prices; the timing of a Chinese currency revaluation; uncertainty over whether the U.S. economy is slowing or merely in a soft patch—to name a few. . . . As currency managers lose conviction over the direction of global trends, they have found it harder to decide which criterion matters most when valuing currencies. "[There have been] times this year when people shift their theme within the week, and then back again."[44]

Managers need to be concerned with the timing, magnitude, and direction of an exchange-rate movement.

Timing, Direction, and Magnitude   Forecasting includes predicting the timing, direction, and magnitude of an exchange-rate change or movement. For countries whose currencies are not freely floating, the timing is often a political decision, and it is not so easy to predict. Although the direction of a change probably can be predicted, the magnitude is difficult to forecast. Toyota Motor Corporation has operations in the United States, and it has to forecast the yen value of its dollar results each year. At the beginning of 2002 when the yen was trading at 131 per dollar, Toyota forecast that the dollar would weaken to 125 yen. However, the dollar ended up weakening to 116 yen. They guessed the direction correctly, but they missed the magnitude of the change. That resulted in a loss of 150 billion yen, or $1.3 billion, more than anticipated.[45] It forecast the direction correctly, but it missed the magnitude.

It is hard to predict what will happen to currencies and to use those predictions to forecast profits and establish operating strategies. The problem with predicting the value of a freely floating currency like the yen is that you never know what could happen to its value. You might be tempted to think that a currency linked to the dollar, like the Hong Kong dollar, would be much easier to predict. But since political control of

Hong Kong was handed over to China in 1997, there have been discussions concerning Hong Kong's adoption of the Chinese yuan. Even rumors of this change spooked the region's financial markets. Hong Kong officials vowed to stick with the 19-year-old currency system, but many economists think it makes more sense for Hong Kong to change to the yuan.[46] But 10 years later, the Hong Kong dollar had continued to maintain its independence while widening the trading range with the U.S. dollar. Again, experts were predicting it was just a matter of time before Hong Kong switched to the yuan. Which prediction is correct? How should a company position itself in these two different scenarios?

FACTORS TO MONITOR

For freely fluctuating currencies, the law of supply and demand determines market value. However, very few currencies in the world float freely without any government intervention. Most are managed to some extent, which implies that governments need to make political decisions about the value of their currencies. Assuming governments use a rational basis for managing these values (an assumption that may not always be realistic), managers can monitor the same factors the governments follow to try to predict values:

Key factors to monitor—the institutional setting, fundamental analysis, confidence factors, events, and technical analysis.

- *Institutional Setting*

  - Does the currency float, or is it managed—and if so, is it pegged to another currency, to a basket, or to some other standard?

  - What are the intervention practices? Are they credible? Sustainable?

- *Fundamental Analyses*

  - Does the currency appear undervalued or overvalued in terms of PPP, balance of payments, foreign-exchange reserves, or other factors?

  - What is the cyclical situation in terms of employment, growth, savings, investment, and inflation?

  - What are the prospects for government monetary, fiscal, and debt policy?

- *Confidence Factors*

  - What are market views and expectations with respect to the political environment, as well as to the credibility of the government and central bank?

- *Circumstances*

  - Are there national or international incidents in the news; the possibility of crises or emergencies; governmental or other important meetings coming up?

- *Technical Analyses*

  - What trends do the charts show? Are there signs of trend reversals?

  - At what rates do there appear to be important buy and sell orders? Are they balanced? Is the market overbought? Oversold?

  - What are the thinking and expectations of other market players and analysts?[47]

Business Implications of Exchange-Rate Changes

Why do we need to bother with predicting exchange-rate changes? As illustrated in the Toyota example, exchange-rate changes can dramatically affect operating strategies as well as translated overseas profits. We now look briefly at how exchange-rate changes can affect companies' marketing, production, and financial decisions.

MARKETING DECISIONS

Marketing managers watch exchange rates because they can affect demand for a company's products at home and abroad. If Panasonic was selling its 58-inch plasma high-definition TV set for 605,000 yen, it would cost $5,500 in the United States when the exchange rate was 110 yen to the dollar. At a forecast rate of 108 yen, the TV would cost $5,601. Suppose the yen rises even more—to 105—thus increasing the price of the TV to $5,762. At this point, would consumers be willing to pay $5,762 for a new TV set, or would they wait for the cost to come down? Should Panasonic pass on the new price to consumers or sell at the same price and absorb the difference in its profit margin? If the yen continues to strengthen beyond 105 yen, what can Panasonic do?

Strengthening of a country's currency value could create problems for exporters.

PRODUCTION DECISIONS

Exchange-rate changes also can affect production decisions. A manufacturer in a country where wages and operating expenses are high might be tempted to relocate production to a country with a currency that is rapidly losing value. That is one option for Panasonic to consider. The company's currency would buy lots of the weak currency, making the company's initial investment cheap.

Further, goods manufactured in that country would be relatively cheap in world markets. For example, BMW made the decision to invest in production facilities in South Carolina because of the unfavorable exchange rate between the Deutsche mark (now the euro) and the dollar. However, the company announced plans to use the facilities not only to serve the U.S. market but also to export to Europe and other markets.[48] The issue worsened in 2004 when the euro rose significantly against the dollar. The devaluation of the Mexican peso came shortly after the introduction of NAFTA. Although companies had already begun to establish operations in Mexico to service North America, the cheaper peso certainly helped their manufacturing strategies.

Companies might locate production in a weak currency country because

- *Initial investment there is relatively cheap.*
- *Such a country is a good base for inexpensive exportation.*

FINANCIAL DECISIONS

Finally, exchange rates can affect financial decisions, primarily in the areas of sourcing of financial resources, the remittance of funds across national borders, and the reporting of financial results. In the first area, a company might be tempted to borrow money in places where interest rates are lowest. However, recall that interest-rate differentials often are compensated for in money markets through exchange-rate changes.

In deciding about cross-border financial flows, a company would want to convert local currency into its own home-country currency when exchange rates are most favorable so it can maximize its return. However, countries with weak currencies often have currency controls, making it difficult for MNEs to do so.

Finally, exchange-rate changes can influence the reporting of financial results. A simple example illustrates the impact that exchange rates can have on income. If a U.S. company's Mexican subsidiary earns 2 million pesos when the exchange rate is 9.5 pesos per dollar, the dollar equivalent of its income is $210,526. If the peso depreciates to 10.2 pesos per dollar, the dollar equivalent of that income falls to $196,078. The opposite will occur if the local currency appreciates against that of the company's home country. This is the problem that Toyota faced in the earlier example. The yen equivalent of Toyota's dollar earnings in the United States continues to fall as the dollar falls against the yen.

Exchange rates can influence the sourcing of financial resources, the cross-border remittance of funds, and the reporting of financial results.

CONCEPT CHECK

In Chapter 18, we'll explain how companies factor in **foreign exchange** in preparing financial statements. In Chapter 19, we'll show how **exchange rates** influence financial flows and describe some of the strategies that companies enlist to protect themselves against exchange-rate risk.

It is important to learn about exchange rates and the forces that affect their change. Several years ago, a large U.S.-based telephone company was preparing a bid for a major telecommunications project in Turkey. The manager preparing the bid knew nothing about the Turkish lira, and he prepared his bid without consulting with the company's foreign-exchange specialists. He figured out the bid in dollars, then turned to the foreign-exchange table in the *Wall Street Journal* to see what rate he should use to convert the bid into lira. What he didn't realize was that the lira at that time was weakening against the dollar. By the time he received the bid, he had lost all of his profit to the change in the value of the lira against the dollar, and by the time he had finished the project, he had lost a lot of money. If he had talked to someone who knew anything about the lira, he could have forecast the future value and maybe entered into a hedging strategy to protect his receivables in lira. If managers don't understand how currency values are determined, they can make serious, costly mistakes.

LOOKING TO THE FUTURE

In Which Direction Is Exchange-Rate Flexibility Headed?

The international monetary system has undergone considerable change since the early 1970s when the dollar was devalued the first time. New countries have been born with the breakup of the Soviet empire, and with them have come new currencies. As those countries have gone through transition to a market economy, the currencies have adjusted as well. The countries will continue to change over to a floating-rate system as they get their economies under control.

It will be interesting to see what will happen to the currencies of Latin America. Since the collapse of the Argentine peso, economists across all ideologies have stepped up to the plate to predict what will happen with Argentina's exchange-rate regime. Although the Brazilian real has strengthened against the dollar since the election of President da Silva, political and economic uncertainty argues for a long-term weakening of the real. Another question is prompted by our opening case: Will the members of the Central American Common Market follow the lead of El Salvador by dollarizing their currencies, or will they continue the policy of stepwise devaluations? One thing is clear at this point: South American currencies have strengthened with the rise in commodity prices. Many observers still wonder, however, what will happen if commodity prices weaken.

The euro will continue to succeed as a currency and will eventually take away market share from the dollar as a prime reserve asset. In addition, its influence will spread throughout Europe as non–euro zone countries adopt the euro or at least come into harmony with it. The countries that joined the EU since 2004 have been pushing the EMU to allow them to switch to the euro. Slovenia was recently allowed to adopt the euro as its currency. The EU will allow other countries to adopt the euro as the countries come into convergence with the ERM. Increasing trade links throughout Europe with non–euro zone countries will dictate closer alliance with the euro.

For Asia, no Asian currency can compare with the dollar in the Americas and the euro in Europe. The yen is too specific to Japan, and the inability of the Japanese economy to reform and open up will keep the yen from wielding the same kind of influence as the dollar and the euro, even though the yen is one of the most widely traded currencies in the world. In fact, it is far more likely that the dollar will continue to be the benchmark in Asia insofar as Asian economies rely heavily on the U.S. market for a lot of their exports.

However, the real wild card in Asia is the Chinese yuan. The Chinese decided to de-link the yuan to dollar peg in 2005 and widened the trading band in 2007. These adjustments have had very little impact, and many countries insist that China is still practicing currency manipulation. Further changes will probably have to be made to the currency to avoid a major trade war with Europe and the United States. The trend will continue to lead to greater flexibility in exchange-rate regimes, whether as managed floats or as freely floating currencies. Even countries that lock on to the dollar will float against every other currency in the world as the dollar floats. Capital controls will continue to fall, and currencies will move more freely from country to country. ■

The Chinese Yuan: Be Careful of the Dragon's Tail

On January 7, 1994, the Chinese government, after debating what to do with its currency, decided to fix the value of the *yuan* (CNY) (also known as the *renminbi*, or RMB) to the U.S. dollar at a rate of 8.690 per dollar, and over 10 years later, it had settled in at 8.2765.[49] But pressure began to build in 2005, as both the European Union and the United States faced strong competition from imports from China as well as from Chinese exports to developing markets. That pressure culminated in the Chinese government slightly loosening control over the yuan so it began to rise against the U.S. dollar, settling in at 7.5 to 7.6 yuan per dollar by mid-2007. But is that enough? (The cartoon in Figure 10.3 implies another question: When will fluctuations trickle down to consumers?)

Pressures for Change

When China fixed the value of its currency in 1994, it was not considered a major economic powerhouse, but by 2005, things had changed. In 1999, China was the largest country in the world in population and seventh largest in GNI. By 2003, it was the sixth largest country in the world in GNI, exceeded only by the United States, Japan, Germany, the United Kingdom, France, and Italy. It was also growing faster than any of the top six countries. In the decade of the 1990s, China grew by an annual average of 9.5 percent and was above 8 percent every year in the first half of the 2000s.

Because of China's low manufacturing wages, it was exporting far more to the United States than it was importing. In 2004, China had a trade surplus of $155 billion with the United States, compared with a surplus of only $86 billion with the EU. However, between

FIGURE 10.3   What Happens When Exchange-Rate Fluctuations Trickle Down

Source: Copyright Harley Schwadron, Cartoonstock.com.

"Of course I know the value of the dollar. That's why I'd like my allowance in Chinese Yuan."

FIGURE 10.4   The Yuan Versus the Euro and the Dollar

The Chinese yuan (CNY) is pegged to the US$—that is, its exchange rate is fixed in terms of the US$. Thus as the euro (€), beginning in early 2002, grew by 45% against the US$, it grew at the same rate against the CNY. Because the euro therefore bought more CNY, it was also worth more when it came to buying products made in China. In the process, Chinese products became cheaper and more attractive to EU consumers, and by mid-2007, the EU's trade deficit with China had doubled.

Source: Based on "FXHistory®:Historical Currency Exchange Rates," *Oanda.com: The Currency Site,* at www.Oanda.com. End-of-quarter rates cited.

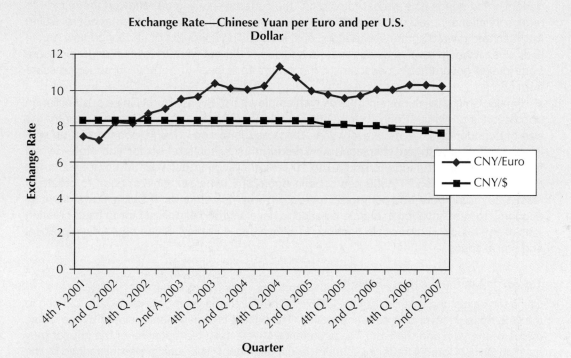

2002 and 2004, China's surplus with the EU doubled, whereas it grew by a little over a half with the United States. The major problem with the EU is that, during that time period, the euro had grown by 45 percent against the dollar, which meant it had also grown by 45 percent against the yuan, which was fixed against the dollar (see Figure 10.4). In effect, Chinese exports had gotten cheaper against European products both in the euro zone as well as in Europe's export markets.

However, the competitive pressure of China in Asia was not the same. Because most Asian currencies were also locked onto the dollar, the yuan traded in a narrow range against those currencies. Most of the Asian countries were using China as a new market for their products, and they were not anxious to have anything upset the Chinese economy and reduce demand for their products.

Critics from the United States and EU argued that the yuan was undervalued by 15 to 40 percent and the Chinese government needed to free the currency and allow it to seek a market level. Even the Big Mac PPP demonstrated how undervalued the yuan is against the U.S. dollar.

The pressures for and against change were both political and economic. The U.S. government had been working with the Chinese for an extended period of time to get them to revalue their currency, but the Chinese government had found plenty of excuses not to do that. Finally, many members of the U.S. Congress decided to force the issue, and they announced they would push to pass steep tariffs on Chinese exports if the Chinese didn't loosen their currency. The U.S. administration, concerned about possible protectionist threats by Congress, announced it would give the Chinese until October 2005 to revalue its currency, or it would consider that China's exchange-rate policy was, in fact, currency manipulation to improve its export position, forcing the government to negotiate sanctions against Chinese exports. The United States took the exchange-rate issue so seriously in 2005 that the U.S. treasury secretary named a special envoy to work with China on the issue.

Political Pressures at Home

China had its own political pressures. For one thing, a lot of people had been moving currency into China in anticipation of a revaluation of the yuan, which was creating inflationary pressures in China. The Chinese government was forced to buy the dollars and issue yuan-denominated bonds as a way of "sterilizing" the currency—taking currency off the market to reduce inflationary pressures. The Chinese government was not very excited about revaluing the yuan and rewarding the speculators, so it kept saying it would not announce how much, if, or when it would revalue its currency. In addition, it did not want to revalue under pressure from foreign governments because it did not want to appear to be bowing under pressure from abroad.

Finally, China has serious problems with employment. Even though China's 1.3 billion in population is growing at only 1 percent a year, it adds the equivalent of a new country the size of Ecuador or Guatemala every year. China needs to add enough jobs to keep up with its population growth and displaced workers from its agricultural sector and state-owned firms. That means it needs to add 15 to 20 million new jobs per year. In comparison, the United States created 275,000 new jobs in April 2005, whereas China needs to create at least 1.25 million new jobs per month to keep up with its demands. If China slows down its economy to keep inflation in check, it needs to have a strong export sector to keep creating jobs. If the export sector cools because of a revalued currency, China could have political and social chaos.

The Advent of the Currency Basket

China took a historic step on July 21, 2005, and de-linked the yuan from its decade-old peg to the U.S. dollar in favor of a currency basket. The basket is largely denominated by the dollar, the euro, the yen, and the won. These currencies were selected because of the impact they have on China's foreign trade, investment, and foreign debt. The yuan is also influenced by the currencies of several other countries, including Singapore, Britain, Malaysia, Russia, Australia, Thailand, and Canada.

The central bank of China in Beijing decides a central parity rate daily and then allows a trading band on either side of the decided point. The move to the currency basket increased the yuan-to-dollar rate by 2.1 percent. Before the peg was de-linked, the yuan was kept around 8.28 dollars, and immediately following it traded around 8.11 dollars. The United States, Europe, and Japan thought the change was too small and continued to assert that the yuan was undervalued.

By the end of 2006, the yuan had appreciated by 5.68 percent since the peg to the U.S. dollar was dropped in 2005. This had little affect on the U.S. trade deficit because the first quarter 2007 trade deficit reached $56.9 billion, an increase of 35.8 percent over the $41.9 billion deficit in the first quarter of 2005. Pressures from the international community continued to be heaped on China.

The central bank of China responded to the pressures by widening the trading band of the yuan on May 18, 2007. The move came a week before the Chinese delegation was to meet for a second round of strategic economic talks with senior U.S. officials led by Treasury Secretary Henry Paulson and while the Treasury Department was preparing its semiannual report on the currency market. Many believed China would be cited as a currency manipulator in the Treasury Department report.

Some experts believe China is gradually moving in the right direction; others believe they made an insignificant adjustment to gain goodwill in the international community before their trading partners made changes that would negatively affect them. Despite the widening of the trading band, pressure continues to mount on China to revalue its currency as the U.S. Senate is contemplating a bill that would take punitive actions against China.

What's Next?

What if the Chinese currency continues to rise in small increments? What difference would it make? Critics in the United States assume a yuan revaluation would solve the U.S. trade deficit. But Chinese exports are only 10 percent of total U.S. imports, so it would take a massive revaluation to have much impact on U.S. imports. Even a 10 percent revaluation would only reduce the trade-weighted value of the dollar by 1 percent, which is minor. One expert argued that even a 25 percent revaluation would reduce the current-account deficit by less than 5 percent.

However, one could argue that the revaluation could also improve U.S. exports to other markets where exporters were facing competition from Chinese exports. Europe has a much bigger problem because it is doubtful that the Chinese will allow their currency to revalue by the amount the euro has risen against the dollar and the yuan since early 2002. European companies will still be uncompetitive, especially given China's low wages.

If the yuan rises too much, China's U.S. dollar foreign-exchange reserves will fall by the amount of the revaluation. That is a major disincentive for a revaluation. In addition, the Chinese have basically invested their reserves in U.S. Treasury bills. If the Chinese decide that T-bills are a bad investment in a weaker dollar world, they might decide to invest in something else, like euros. The United States might be forced to raise interest rates, which could slow down the U.S. economy, which could reduce the demand for Chinese goods—which would now be more expensive anyway—which could lead to a rise in unemployment in China. Not a good idea!

Taking SAFE Steps

Until the yuan began its ascent against the dollar, it was very easy to deal in foreign exchange in China because the rate was fixed against the U.S. dollar. It doesn't take a lot of judgment for a trader to operate in a fixed-rate world. In June 2005, the State Administration of Foreign Exchange (SAFE) in China decided to allow banks in Shanghai to trade and quote prices in eight currency pairs, including the dollar-sterling and euro-yen. Prior to that, licensed banks were only allowed to trade the yuan against four currencies—the U.S. dollar, the Hong Kong dollar, the euro, and the yen.

However, all the trades were at fixed rates, and they did not involve trades in non-yuan currency pairs. SAFE also decided to open up trading to seven international banks (HSBC, Citigroup, Deutsche Bank, ABN AMRO, ING, Royal Bank of Scotland, and Bank of Montreal) and two domestic banks (Bank of China and CITIC Industrial Bank).

Some argue that the steps being taken by SAFE are designed to build capability in trading before opening up the yuan to greater flexibility. Clearly, it is necessary to build capability in the banking sector as well as the regulatory sector. SAFE is responsible for establishing the new foreign-exchange trading guidelines as well as for managing China's foreign-exchange reserves.

Options

What did the Chinese government consider in 2005? It could widen the trading band against the U.S. dollar, it could peg the yuan to a larger basket of currencies, or it could allow the yuan to float freely.

Widening the Trading Band   The first option, widening the trading band against the dollar, was a possibility, at least in the short run. In 2002, the yuan was trading within the 0.3 percent band of around 8.277 to the U.S. dollar, but by 2005, the band disappeared, and the yuan was trading at a fixed 8.2765. How much should it widen the band, and how quickly should it be widened? Before permitting floating exchange rates, the IMF allowed countries to trade their currencies within a band of 2.25 percent above or 2.25 percent below par value. If the Chinese allowed their currency to float up by 2.25 percent, would that take off the pressure?

Pegging the Yuan to a Bigger Basket   The second option, pegging the yuan to a larger basket of currencies and possibly managing the value of the currency, would free the yuan from relying on the U.S. dollar as its main peg. This would also result in less volatility because some currencies in the basket might be strong and others weak. If China picked the currencies of its four major trading partners, it would pick the U.S. dollar, the euro, the yen, and the South Korean won. It might also want to include the British pound as well. The first challenge would be picking the currencies to include in the basket, the second would be to weight those currencies, and the third would be to determine how much the yuan would float against the basket.

Letting the Yuan Float   The third option is to allow the yuan to float freely. That is a big risk because there is no way of knowing how much the yuan will rise against the dollar. If it rises too far, too fast, it could choke off economic growth in China and create political and social problems. In addition, it might be difficult for an emerging foreign-exchange market in China to handle the volatility. However, that is the system used for the U.S. dollar and the euro. ∎

QUESTIONS

1. Evaluate the three choices that China faces in determining what to do with its currency value. Which choice would you choose, and why?
2. On July 23, 2005, China revalued the yuan by 2.1 percent. Given that the exchange rate was 8.2725 prior to the revaluation, look at the exchange rate today. How much has the yuan revalued against the dollar since then? Do you think this is enough to take the pressure off China? Why or why not?
3. Using Table 10.1 (p. 371), which exchange-rate arrangement is China using now? Be sure to read the footnotes.
4. Assume you are a Chinese exporter. Would you prefer a Chinese export tariff on selected garment and textile exports as a way to relieve pressure against the yuan or a revaluation of the currency? Why?
5. China has the largest foreign-exchange reserves in the world at $1.33 trillion by the end of the second quarter in 2007. This is compared with foreign-exchange reserves of about $165.6 billion in 2000. Why do you think China's reserves have grown so much in less than seven years? How can that large reserve position help China manage the value of the yuan? Most of China's foreign-exchange reserves are in U.S. dollars, especially U.S. Treasury bills. If you were an adviser to China's central bank, would you recommend China continue that course, or are there alternatives?

SUMMARY

- The International Monetary Fund (IMF) was organized in 1945 to promote international monetary cooperation, to facilitate the expansion and balanced growth of international trade, to promote exchange-rate stability, to establish a multilateral system of payments, and to make its resources available to its members who are experiencing balance-of-payments difficulties.

- The special drawing right (SDR) is a special asset the IMF created to increase international reserves.

- The IMF started out with fixed exchange rates but now allows countries to choose how fixed or flexible they want their exchange rates to be.

- The euro is a common currency in Europe that has been adopted by 12 of the first 15 members of the EU, and it is slated to be adopted by the 10 countries added to the EU in 2004 as soon as they meet convergence criteria.

- African countries are committed to establishing a common currency by 2021, but many obstacles may prevent them from accomplishing this objective.

- Currencies that float freely respond to supply and demand conditions free from government intervention. The demand for a country's currency is a function of the demand for its goods and services and the demand for financial assets denominated in its currency.

- Fixed exchange rates do not automatically change in value due to supply and demand conditions but are regulated by their central banks.

- Central banks are the key institutions in countries that intervene in foreign-exchange markets to influence currency values.

- The Bank for International Settlements (BIS) in Switzerland acts as a central banker's bank. It facilitates communication and transactions among the world's central banks.

- A central bank intervenes in money markets by increasing a supply of its country's currency when it wants to push the value of the currency down and by stimulating demand for the currency when it wants the currency's value to rise.

- Many countries that strictly control and regulate the convertibility of their currency have a black market that maintains an exchange rate more indicative of supply and demand than the official rate.

- Fully convertible currencies, often called *hard currencies,* are those that the government allows both residents and nonresidents to purchase in unlimited amounts.

- Currencies that are not fully convertible are often called *soft currencies* or *weak currencies.* They tend to be the currencies of developing countries.

- To conserve scarce foreign exchange, some governments impose exchange restrictions on companies or individuals who want to exchange money, such as import licensing, multiple exchange rates, import deposit requirements, and quantity controls.

- Some factors that determine exchange rates are purchasing power parity (relative rates of inflation), differences in real interest rates (nominal interest rates reduced by the amount of inflation), confidence in the government's ability to manage the political and economic environment, and certain technical factors that result from trading.

- Major factors that managers should monitor when trying to predict the timing, magnitude, and direction of an exchange-rate change include the institutional setting (what kind of exchange-rate system the country uses), fundamental analysis (what is going on in terms of the trade balance, foreign-exchange reserves, inflation, etc.), confidence factors (especially political factors), events (like meetings of the G8 group of countries to discuss exchange rates), and technical analysis (trends in exchange-rate values).

- Exchange rates can affect business decisions in three major areas: marketing, production, and finance.

KEY TERMS

advance import deposit (p. 387)
black market (p. 386)
Bretton Woods Agreement (p. 368)
European Central Bank (ECB) (p. 379)
European Monetary System (EMS) (p. 378)
European Monetary Union (EMU) (p. 378)
Fisher Effect (p. 390)

fundamental forecasting (p. 391)
hard currency (p. 386)
International Fisher Effect (IFE) (p. 390)
International Monetary Fund (IMF) (p. 368)
Jamaica Agreement (p. 370)
multiple exchange-rate system (p. 387)
par value (p. 368)

purchasing power parity (PPP) (p. 387)
quota (p. 368)
Smithsonian Agreement (p. 370)
soft (or weak) currency (p. 386)
special drawing right (SDR) (p. 369)
technical forecasting (p. 391)

ENDNOTES

1 *Sources include the following:* "El Salvador Learns to Love the Greenback," *The Economist,* September 26, 2002; John Lyons, "Squeezed by Dollarization," *Wall Street Journal,* March 8, 2005: A18; Bureau of Economic and Business Affairs, U.S. Department of State, "2001 Country Reports on Economic Policy and Trade Practices," February 2002, at www.state.gov/documents/organization/8202.pdf (accessed May 30, 2005); U.S. Department of State, "Background Note—El Salvador," at www.state.gov/r/pa/ei/bgn/2033.htm (accessed May 30, 2005); U.S. Department of State, "Background Note—Ecuador," www.state.gov/r/pa/ei/bgn/35761.htm (accessed May 30, 2005); Juan Forero, "Ecuador's President Vows to Ride Out Crisis over Judges," *New York Times,* April 18, 2005.

2 International Monetary Fund, "IMF Chronology," at http://imf.org/external/np/exr/chron/chron.asp (accessed August 22, 2007).

3 IMF, "The IMF at a Glance." *International Monetary Fund* (June 11, 2007), at http://imf.org/external/np/exr/facts/glance.htm.

4 IMF, "About IMF," at http://imf.org/external/about.htm (accessed August 22, 2007).

5 IMF, "Glossary of Selected Financial Terms" (updated October 31, 2006), at http://imf.org/external/np/exr/glossary/showTerm.asp#64 (accessed August 22, 2007).

6 IMF, "The IMF at a Glance."

7 IMF, "Organization," at http://imf.org/external/np/obp/orgcht.htm (accessed August 22, 2007).

8 Todd Benson, "Report Looks Harshly at IMF's Role in Argentine Debt Crisis," *New York Times,* July 30, 2004: W1.

9 IMF, "Special Drawing Rights (SDRs): A Factsheet," at http://imf.org/external/np/exr/facts/sdr.htm (accessed August 21, 2007).

10 IMF, "Special Drawing Rights (SDRs)."

11 IMF, *IMF Annual Report 2006* (Washington, DC: IMF, September 14, 2006), p. 144. A more detailed description of the exchange-rate arrangements in this section can be found at this source.

12 See Guillermo A. Calvo and Carmen M. Reinhart, "Capital Flow Reversals, the Exchange Rate Debate, and Dollarization," *Finance & Development* 36:3 (1999): www.imf.org/external/pubs/ft/fandd/1999/09/calvo.htm; "No More Peso?" *The Economist,* January 23, 1999: 69; Steve H. Hanke, "How to Make the Dollar Argentina's Currency," *Wall Street Journal,* February 19, 1999: A19; Michael M. Phillips, "U.S. Officials Urge Cautious Approach to Dollarization by Foreign Countries," *Wall Street Journal,* April 23, 1999: A4; "A Decline without Parallel," *The Economist,* February 28, 2002: www.economist.com.

13 Craig Torres, "Chile Suspends Trading Band on Its Peso," *Wall Street Journal,* September 7, 1999: A21; "IMF Welcomes Flotation of Iceland's Krona," *IMF News Brief,* March 28, 2001: www.imf.org/external/np/sec/nb/2001/nb0129.htm.

14 "Convergence Criteria for European Monetary Union," *Bloomberg News,* August 9, 2002: www.bloomberg.com.

15 "Slovenia, Welcome to the Euro Area!" *Europa,* June 11, 2007: http://ec.europa.eu/economy_finance/euro/slovenia/main_en.htm.

16 "Prime Minister Says Sweden Fulfills Criteria to Adopt Euro," *Dow Jones Newswires,* August 19, 2002: www.wsj.com.

17 Christopher Rhoads and G. Thomas Sims, "Rising Deficits in Europe Give Euro Its Toughest Challenge Yet," *Wall Street Journal,* September 15, 2003: A1.

18 Edmund L. Andrews, "On Euro Weekend, Financial Institutions in Vast Reprogramming," *New York Times,* January 2, 1999: www.nytimes.com.

19 Paul Masson and Catherine Patillo, "A Single Currency for Africa?" *Finance & Development* (December 2004): 9–15; "History of the CFA Franc," at www.bceao.int/internet/bcweb.nsf/pages/umuse1 (accessed May 30, 2005); IMF, "The Fabric of Reform—An IMF Video," at www.imf.org/external/pubs/ft/fabric/backgrnd.htm (accessed May 30, 2005).

20 "Welcome to the Federal Reserve Bank: International Operations," at www.ny.frb.org/aboutthefed/whatwedo.html (accessed August 25, 2007).

21 IMF, *IMF Annual Report 2006,* pp. 127–28.

22 Joanna Slater and John Lyons, "Emerging Markets Lose a Little of their Resilience—Now Face Stress Test," *Wall Street Journal,* July 17, 2007: C1.

23 IMF, "Time Series Data on International Reserves and Foreign Currency Liquidity": www.imf.org/external/np/sta/ir/8802.pdf.

24 Sam Y. Cross, *All About the Foreign Exchange Market in the United States* (New York: Federal Bank of New York, 2002), pp. 92–93.

25 David Wessel, "Intervention in Currency Shrinks under Clinton," *Wall Street Journal,* September 14, 1995: C1.

26 Federal Reserve Bank of New York, "U.S. Foreign Exchange Intervention," at www.newyorkfed.org/aboutthefed/fedpoint/fed44.html (accessed August 25, 2007).

27 See Jamie McGeever, "Dollar Gets Battered Across the Board," *Wall Street Journal,* December 9, 2003: C17; Sebastian Moffett, "Japan's Yen Strategy Offers Economic Relief," *Wall Street Journal,* January 12, 2004: A2; Miyako Takebe, "Japan Plans to Keep Intervening in Markets to Hold Down the Yen," *Wall Street Journal,* March 17, 2004: B4E; Alan Beattie, "Japan and ECB Consider Joint Currency Move as Dollar Falls," *Financial Times,* December 2, 2004: 11.

28 "South Korea to Stop Currency Intervention: Report," *Yahoo! News* (May 18, 2005), at http://news.yahoo.com/s/afp/20050518/bs_afp/forexusskorea_050518191953 (accessed May 30, 2005).

29 Callan Eoin and Peter Garnham, "Bill Would Allow U.S. Currency Intervention," MSNBC [London], May 9, 2007, at www.msnbc.msn.com/id/18945598/(accessed May 30, 2007).

30 Bank for International Settlements, "About BIS: Organisation and Governance," at www.bis.org/about/orggov.htm (accessed August 25, 2007).

31 Bank for International Settlements, "About BIS: BIS History," at www.bis.org/about/history.htm (accessed August 25, 2007).

32 "Zimbabwe Arrests 10,000 in Black Market Crackdown," at www.stuff.co.nz/stuff/0,2106,3292209a12,00. html (accessed May 30, 2005).

33 Sheridan Prasso, "Zimbabwe's Disposable Currency," *Fortune,* August 6, 2007 (accessed on *CNNMoney.com,* August 25, 2007).

34 Phisanu Phromchanya, "Thai Currency Controls Eased in Bid to Cool Baht," *Wall Street Journal,* July 25, 2007.

35 Natalia T. Tamirisa, "Exchange and Capital Controls as Barriers to Trade," *IMF Staff Papers* 46:1 (1999): 69.

36 "The Big Mac Index: Sizzling," *The Economist,* July 7, 2007: 74.

37 "The Big Mac Index: Food for Thought," *The Economist,* May 27, 2004; quoting Michael Pakko and Patricia Polland, "For Here or to Go? Purchasing Power Parity and the Big Mac" (St. Louis: Federal Reserve Bank of St. Louis, January 1996).

38 Riva Froymovich, "Yen Eases on Dollar, Euro as Risk Appetite Returns," *Wall Street Journal,* August 25, 2007: B14.

39 "More 'Distorted' Comments Roil Markets," *Wall Street Journal,* May 20, 2005: www.wsj.com.

40 "How a News Story, Translated Badly, Caused Trading Panic," *Wall Street Journal,* May 12, 2005: www.wsj.com.

41 "Race against Time," *The Economist*, September 26, 2002: www.economist.com.

42 "Forecasting Currencies: Technical or Fundamental?" *Business International Money Report*, October 15, 1990: 401–2.

43 Andrew C. Pollock and Mary E. Wilkie, "Briefing," *Euromoney* (June 1991): 123–24.

44 "Currency Game Is Plenty Big, Plenty Tough," *Wall Street Journal*, May 6, 2005: www.wsj.com.

45 Akio Hayashida and Junichi Maruyama, "Recovery Hopes Hit by Fall in U.S. Dollar," *Daily Yomiuri*, July 25, 2002: www.globalpolicy.org/socecon/crisis/2002/0725yomiuri.htm.

46 Dominic Lau, "Market Jitters Making HK Currency Peg Debate Taboo," *Reuters News Service*, September 24, 2002: http://asia.news.yahoo.com/.

47 Cross, *All About the Foreign Exchange Market*, p. 114.

48 Oscar Suris, "BMW Expects U.S.-Made Cars to Have 80% Level of North American Content," *Wall Street Journal*, August 5, 1993: A2.

49 ***Sources include the following:*** Andrew Batson, "China's Currency Reserves Expand as Economy Continues to Surge," *Wall Street Journal*, July 12, 2007: A11; Natasha Brereton, "Revaluing the Yuan May Not Fix Imbalances," *Wall Street Journal*, July 17, 2007; Andrew Browne, "China's Reserves Near Milestone, Underscoring Its Financial Clout," *Wall Street Journal*, October 17, 2006: A1; "China's Yuan, Softly, Softly," *The Economist*, March 31, 2005: www.economist.com/agenda/PrinterFriendly.cfm?Story_ID=3819927; Craig Karmin, "Dollar Rebound Builds on Stronger Economic Data," *Wall Street Journal*, May 16, 2005: A1; "Easing Prices Bolster Beijing's Currency Stance," *Wall Street Journal*, May 17, 2005: A10; Marcus Walker, "Euro Zone Suffers from China Syndrome," *Wall Street Journal*, May 17, 2005: A10; "Putting Things in Order," *The Economist*, March 17, 2005: www.economist.com/agenda/PrinterFriendly.cfm?Story_ID=3764776; "What Do Yuant from Us?" *The Economist*, May 18, 2005; Edmund L. Andrews, "Toughening Its Line, U.S. Warns China on Currency," *New York Times*, May 18, 2005; Keith Bradsher, "China's Growth Ebbs, a Deterrrent to Revaluation," *New York Times*, May 19, 2005; Andrew Browne, "U.S., China Press Yuan Row," *Wall Street Journal*, May 19, 2005: A2; Greg Hitt, "U.S. Picks Envoy to Engage China on Exchange Rates," *Wall Street Journal*, May 20, 2005: C3.

11

chapter eleven

The Strategy of International Business

Objectives

- To examine the idea of industry structure, firm strategy, and value creation

- To profile the features and functions of the value chain framework

- To appreciate how managers configure and coordinate a value chain

- To identify the dimensions that shape how managers develop strategy

- To profile the types of strategies firms use in international business

*A man must put grain
in the ground before
he can cut the harvest.*

—Gypsy proverb

CASE: Value Creation in the Global Apparel Industry

Strategy in the global apparel industry is based on a combination of production, buying, and distribution forces.[1] Historically, large national retailers outsourced apparel production, via global brokers, to literally tens of thousands of small apparel makers. The typical apparel manufacturer, almost always located in a low-wage market, is a small-scale operation that employs a few to a few dozen workers. In a highly labor-intensive process, workers make specific pieces of clothing, often in a narrow range of sizes and colors. These pieces are then integrated with the output of hundreds of other such companies spread across dozens of countries. As more countries make more specialized products—for example, one factory makes only zippers, one

overseas factories to increase the speed and flexibility of responses to market shifts. By planning assortments closer to the selling season, testing the market, placing smaller initial orders, and reordering more frequently, retailers can avoid forecast errors and inventory risks.

The final links in this chain are markets and customers. Although there is overlap among countries, local customers' preferences had traditionally varied. For example, the British seek out stores based on social sensitivities, Germans are price sensitive, and shoppers in the United States look for a mix of variety, quality, and price. Collectively, these conditions create a buyer-driven chain in the global apparel industry that

MAP 11.1   Spain

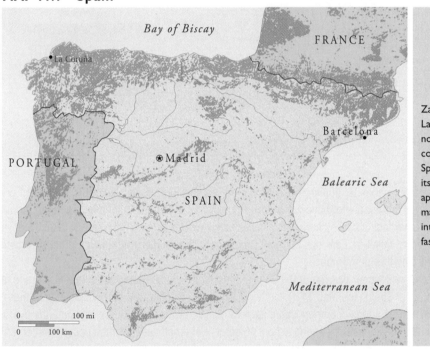

Zara is headquartered in La Coruña, in the extreme northwest corner of the country. Contemporary Spain increasingly looks to its growing textile and apparel industry, which has made the country an international center for the fashion business.

makes only linings—multinational trading companies step in to become vital cross-border intermediaries.

Once assembled, finished goods are supplied to apparel retailers, many of which traded independence for the security of national chains. In 2005, the top-five national chains accounted for more than half of apparel sales in many countries. Despite growing national concentration, retailing activities remain quite local. The top-10 retailers worldwide operated in an average of 10 countries in 2000, deriving less than 15 percent of their total sales from outside their home markets.

No matter the home base, apparel retailers push trading companies to improve coordination between themselves and

links fragmented factories, global brokers, national retailers, and local customers.

The growing globalization of markets is changing the operational decisions of apparel firms. Conventional wisdom suggests that firms should choose a "sliver" of a particular activity—make only zippers, manage logistics, focus on store design, or cater to precise customer segments—instead of trying to create value across several different activities. Many advocate a strategy of "do what we do best" and outsource the rest. Today, reductions in tariff barriers, integration of markets, and improving communications have changed the market, creating new strategic choices.

FIGURE 11.1
Cycle Time in the Global Apparel Industry

In the apparel industry, as in many other industries, globalization has brought changes that opened up new strategic options for players in the market. For example, innovations in technology, sourcing, and production let apparel makers steadily compress by several weeks the *cycle time* required by activities within a company's buyer chain.

Source: Zara Company documents.

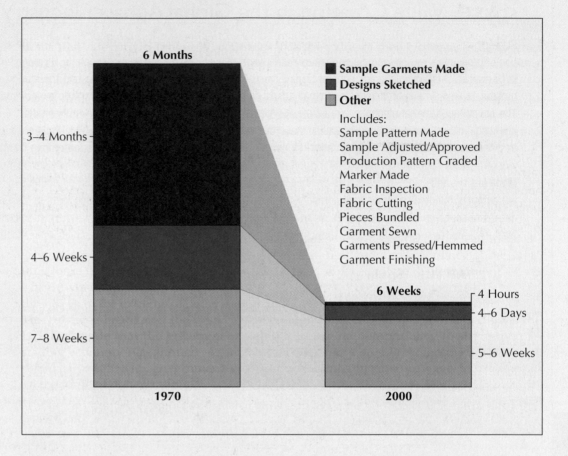

Regarding change, nothing provides a more compelling example than the significant compression of cycle times in the apparel-buyer chain (see Figure 11.1). In the 1970s, getting a garment from the factory to the customer took six months. Now it takes about six weeks. For one firm, Zara, it takes 15 days. By rejecting conventional wisdom, Zara has set new standards in the relationship among industry structure, company strategy, and firm performance.

Zara, the premier division of the Spanish firm Inditex, is headquartered near La Coruña, a midsize city in northwest Spain (see Map 11.1). Inditex Group employs about 60,000 people, half of them in Spain and the rest in the various countries where it operates. The Group's workforce is young (the average age is 26) and female (besides representing almost 86 percent of employees, women occupy 54 percent of the executive, technical, and managerial positions).

The first Zara shop opened its doors in 1975 in La Coruña; it now has a network of 1,026 stores across 64 countries. Although revenues place it behind the U.S.-based Gap and Swedish clothier H&M, its performance is stellar. The parent, Inditex, was recently named Global Retailer of the Year by the World Retail Congress. Inditex's net sales increased 22 percent and its net income rose 25 percent in 2006. From June 2004 through December 2007, Inditex's stock price appreciated more than 80 percent while that of the Gap fell nearly 10 percent.

Zara uses an innovative strategy to power its global performance. It has redefined the idea of infotech and fashion through its integration of design, speed, production, responsiveness, technology, and e-business methods to make and move sophisticated fashion at moderate prices. Operationally, Zara can translate the latest fashion trend from a catwalk in Paris to its store shelves in New York in as little as two weeks versus the industry standard of six months. Moreover, Zara can create new designs in between fashion seasons to accommodate the tastes of fickle customers. In so doing, its strategy threw into question the historic standard of creating value in the global apparel industry.

Zara's success stems from a number of competencies that span design, production, logistics, distribution, and retailing.

DESIGN

Zara rejects the idea of conventional spring and autumn clothing collections in favor of "live collections" that can be designed, manufactured, distributed, and sold almost as quickly as their customers' fleeting tastes—no style lasts more than four weeks. Zara's 300 or so designers continuously track market events, fashion trends, and customer preferences in designing about 11,000 distinct items per year compared with 2,000 to 4,000 items by rivals.

Designers get ideas from store managers, industry publications, TV, Internet, film content, and trend spotters who focus on university campuses and nightclubs. Zara's so-called slaves-to-fashion staff is quick to snap digital pictures at couture shows and immediately reproduce the looks for the mass market.

Zara does not develop products to respond to a particular country's requirements. Management believes the convergence of fashion and taste across national boundaries endorses its strategic bias toward standardization. However, some product designs do cater to physical, cultural, or climate differences—smaller sizes in Japan, special women's clothing in Arab countries, and different seasonal weights in South America. Still, 85 to 90 percent of the basic designs sold in Zara stores tend to be common from country to country.

SOURCING

Zara sources from external suppliers with the help of purchasing offices in Beijing, Barcelona, Hong Kong, along with headquarters staff. Zara also acquires fabric, other inputs, and finished products from numerous suppliers in Spain, India, Morocco, and the Far East. Linked with Zara's network, suppliers can coordinate their production with Zara's projections. About half of the fabric purchased is "gray" (not yet dyed) to update designs quickly during a season. José Maria Castellano, Inditex's CEO, explains, "We have the ability to scrap an entire production line if it is not selling. We can dye collections in new colors, and we can create a new fashion line in days."

PRODUCTION

Like its rivals, Zara sources many finished garments from suppliers in Europe, North Africa, and Asia. But unlike its rivals, Zara employs more than 14,000 people to make about 40 percent of its finished garments in any of its 20 fully owned factories, 18 of them clustered around its headquarters in La Coruña. Zara makes its most time- and fashion-sensitive products internally. Its factories are automated, specialize by garment type, and focus on the capital-intensive parts of the production process—pattern design and cutting—as well as final finishing and inspection.

Although it has been making garments since the 1980s, Zara solicited the help of Toyota of Japan to install a just-in-time system in the early 1990s. The company spent some 20 to 40 percent more to make garments in Spain and Portugal than rivals spent in China, mainly due to labor costs. Zara compensates for higher costs by minimizing advertising, cutting inventory expenses, and adjusting to fashion trends quickly.

Despite technology, many garments cannot be made by machine. In response, Zara has built a network of about 450 workshops, located primarily in Galicia, the home state of La Coruna, and across the border in northern Portugal, that perform the labor- and scale-sensitive activity of sewing the garment pieces that were cut at the factories. These workshops are small operations averaging about 20 to 30 employees that specialize by product type. Zara accounts for most, if not all, of their business, providing them with tools, technology, logistics, and financial support while paying them standard rates per finished garment.

Zara's factories cut and color fabric of a particular garment. It then sends these pieces to the workshop workers, who then return the finished garments to Zara. Upon return, they are inspected, ironed, folded, bagged, and electronically tagged before traveling on hanging rails along 125 miles of underground tracks that link the various production sites to the logistics center.

LOGISTICS

All garments, both internally made and externally contracted, flow into Zara's massive distribution center in La Coruña or smaller satellite centers in Brazil and Mexico. Equipped with a mobile tracking system that docks hanging garments in the appropriate bar-coded area, and with carousels capable of handling

45,000 folded garments per hour, they have the mission to move inventory as fast as possible from the warehouse to stores around the world.

Driving the process are the twice-weekly deliveries to every Zara store triggered by real-time inventory data collected through a network of Web-connected handheld computers. Lorena Alba, Inditex's director of logistics, regards the warehouse as a place to move merchandise rather than store it. According to her, "The vast majority of clothes are in here only a few hours," and none stay at the distribution center for more than three days. Third-party delivery services manage the transfer of preprogrammed lots to stores. This fancy digital footwork has dropped Inditex's inventory to 7 percent of annual revenues, compared with the mid- to high teens of its rivals.

MARKETING

Zara's trailblazing particularly challenges age-old retail marketing practices. Its product policy emphasizes reasonable-quality goods, rapidly changing product lines, and a relatively high fashion image. The company uses little advertising or promotion—it spends less than 1 percent of its revenue on media advertising, compared with 3 to 4 percent for most specialty retailers. Instead, it relies on word of mouth among its legions of loyal shoppers.

Its pricing strategy, in the words of one analyst, is "Armani at moderate prices." Interestingly, management adjusts pricing for the international market, thereby making customers in foreign markets bear the costs of shipping products from Spain: generally, Zara's prices are 40 percent higher in northern European countries, 10 percent higher in other European countries, 70 percent higher in the Americas, and 100 percent higher in Japan.

STORE OPERATIONS

Zara's stores have two primary purposes: present the company's face to the world and function as grass-roots marketing research agents. The stores are put in high-profile slots, most often premier shopping streets in markets such as the Champs-Elysées in Paris, Regent Street in London, and Fifth Avenue in New York. Zara takes great care to make sure it puts its best face forward. Regional teams of window dressers and interior coordinators visit each store every three weeks, making sure the window displays and interior presentations convey the targeted message.

Back at headquarters, designers wander the mock store space and test possible themes, color schemes, and product presentation. These same standards apply to the staff: Store employees wear Zara clothes while working. Store managers and staff choose which merchandise to order, which to discontinue, and which to propose. Zara equips all salespeople with wireless handheld organizers that let them punch in trends, customer comments, and orders. Networked stores transfer data on which merchandise is selling, along with customer requests, to Zara's design teams, factories, and logistics center in La Coruña. The availability of store managers capable of handling these responsibilities, according to CEO Castellano, is the single most important constraint on Zara's global expansion.

FIRM INFRASTRUCTURE

The infrastructure that Zara has built to support these operations is a point of particular competency for the company. There are many aspects, but two stand out: managers' sense of customers and markets and their ability to coordinate activity worldwide. Managers believe the allure of Zara is the freshness of its offerings, the creation of a sense of exclusiveness, an attractive in-store ambience, and positive word of mouth.

These ideas led to the notion of rapid product turnover, with new designs arriving in each twice-weekly shipment. Zara's fans soon learn which days of the week goods are delivered and shop accordingly. About three-quarters of the merchandise on display is changed every three to four weeks. This corresponds to the average time between visits given estimates that the average Zara shopper visits the chain 17 times a year. This compares to an average figure of just three to four visits a year at competing apparel chains.

Attractive stores, both inside and out, are an asset. As Luis Blanc, a director at Inditex, explains, "We invest in prime locations. We place great care in the presentation of our storefronts. That is how we project our image. We want our clients to enter a beautiful store where they are offered the latest fashions. But most important, we want our customers to understand that if they like something, they must buy it now, because it won't be in the shops the following week. It is all about creating a climate of scarcity and opportunity."

Rapid turnover also fans a sense of "buy now because you won't see this item later." Zara reinforces the sense of scarcity with small shipments, display shelves that are sparsely stocked, and a limit of one month on how long individual items can be displayed. Rapid turnover means that consumers visit Zara three or four times a season rather than just one. These policies also keep Zara's shops looking fresh and reduce markdowns; the number of items that it puts on clearance sale is about half the industry average.

Managers' adept coordination of the overlapping activities among its designers, workers, salespeople, and plants testifies to the power of this strategy. Presently, no other company can ship new fashion designs to stores as quickly as Zara. Still, the company has achieved the same profit margins with higher sales per square foot than its rivals. Steadily, Zara's strategy and business design leave rivals with less time to integrate design, manufacturing, and distribution systems within their own global chains.

Some believe that firms have little option but to follow Zara's strategic lead. If they don't, warns a leading retail analyst, they "won't be in business in 10 years." Nonetheless, some rivals downplay these cautions. A few of the big clothing retailers prefer to maintain the power of their conventional strategy to create value. "We have over 900 suppliers and we see a lot of advantages in working that way, such as flexibility, larger-volume capability, etc.," says an H&M spokeswoman. "This system has worked for us for a long time." It remains to be seen if this strategy can rival Zara's.

Introduction

The first half of this text explains that international companies operate in an environment shaped by economic, political, legal, cultural, market, trade, monetary, governmental, and institutional forces (see Figure 11.2). In theoretical terms, these forces make

FIGURE 11.2   The Role of Strategy in International Business

In Chapter 1, we introduced the term *operating environment* to encompass the factors—physical/social and competitive—that influence the external environment in which an international business conducts its operations. Among these operations, we included *strategy*—the means by which managers establish and sustain the company's competitive position within its industry. Beginning with this chapter, we focus on the way that a firm's strategy responds to—and shapes—the physical/social and competitive factors in its external environment.

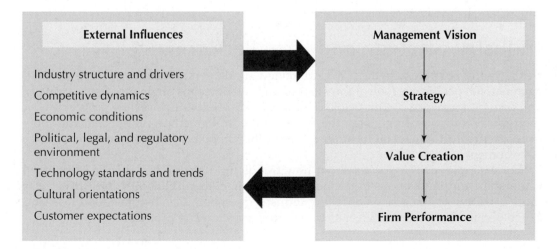

up the environment of international business. In applied terms, these forces represent the system outside the international firm's boundaries that influences the actions of its managers. It is this latter perspective, what managers do to enable their companies to compete more effectively as international businesses, that anchors this chapter and the remainder of the text.

Specifically, this chapter looks at how managers, as agents of their firms, devise strategies to engage international markets in ways that boost current performance and sustain long-term growth. The first half of the text shows that although the many commonalities that unite countries create opportunities for companies, substantial differences endure that constrain their actions. This chapter takes this cumulative understanding as the point of departure and moves into identifying the environmental factors that influence managers' strategic analyses. Among them are the managers' evaluation of strategy, the tools that support their strategic choices, and the processes they use to convert their analyses into actions.

Ensuing chapters elaborate the framework we build in this chapter. That is, the perspective of strategy we develop guides our analysis of subsequent issues, including how firms choose to enter which foreign markets, which companies they opt to ally with, and how they build organizations to govern their worldwide activities. In the final section of the text, these ideas anchor our discussions of how MNEs design and implement their marketing, manufacturing, supply, accounting, finance, and human resources strategies.

> **Strategy is the framework that managers apply to determine the competitive moves and business approaches that run the company.**

Revisiting Zara   Our opening profile of Zara previews many of these issues. When Zara began its global expansion, for instance, the conventional strategy in the apparel business was defined by the structure of the industry—a structure that was largely inefficient (it took too much time to design and deliver clothing) and ineffective (both apparel makers and sellers were plagued by an array of planning and inventory problems). Figure 11.1 (p. 406) shows how Zara rejected the strategic imperatives dictated by prevailing industry structure and, over the next decade, developed a strategy for improving both operational efficiency and effectiveness.

Zara's strategy changed the nature of the apparel industry in ways that redefine ideas of global integration and national responsiveness. More specifically, Zara changed how a company in the apparel business created value in design, manufacturing, logistics, export, marketing, and service. In addition, it introduced novel standards regarding how a company builds the internal infrastructure to coordinate the various business functions that generate value both for the consumer and company.

Most importantly, Zara's long-running series of seemingly distinct choices in production, manufacturing, staffing, logistics, and so on, highlight the fundamental value of strategy for the international company—managing the tension between global integration and local responsiveness in a way that converts a unique strategy into superior value.

> **Strategy is management's idea on how to best**
> - Attract customers.
> - Operate efficiently.
> - Compete effectively.
> - Achieve goals.
> - Create value.

Industry, Strategy, and Firm Performance

Before profiling strategy in the MNE, we review fundamental features of strategic management. In specific, we look at the ideas of and relationships among industry, strategy, and firm performance. We first look at industry because it influences the profitability of the typical company. In general, the forces in the MNE's environment that routinely have the greatest impact on its strategy are in its immediate industry and competitive environment.

For example, BMW worries about how trends in interest rates, change in political leadership, and innovations in technologies will affect its profitability. But BMW is far more sensitive to the actions of fellow industry members like Toyota, Goodyear, and Bosch because they directly affect its competitive position and profitability.

> **CONCEPT CHECK**
> Recall that, in Chapter 3, we rely on the dichotomy between **democracy** and **totalitarianism** and the idea of political freedom as a framework for integrating information about international business. In Chapter 4 we use the differences among **free**, **mixed**, and **command economies** and the notion of economic freedom to build a similar framework. An underlying framework in this chapter concerns the different ways in which managers regard **strategy** within the context of industry structure.

INDUSTRY ORGANIZATION PARADIGM LEADING STRATEGY PERSPECTIVES

A prominent model of strategy in a market of perfect competition, the **industry organization (IO) paradigm**, captures this thesis. First off, the IO paradigm presumes that markets are perfectly competitive; that is, there are large numbers of fully informed buyers and sellers of a homogeneous product and there are no obstacles to the entry or exit of firms into the market. In this sort of market structure, risk-adjusted rates of return should be constant across firms and industries—effectively, over time, no one firm or industry should consistently outperform others.[2] Those industries that do will eventually attract firms that freely enter that market. New entrants create more competition that then lowers prices and lowers firms' profits.

The IO view holds that the performance of a firm is a function of its market conduct, which in turn is determined by the structure of its industry. Research supports this view, finding that industry effects explain up to 75 percent of the difference in average returns for companies in an industry.[3]

Beginning in the 1980s, other studies reported that over time different companies in different industries sustained different levels of profitability in ways that were moderated, but not determined, by the particular structure of their industry.[4] Unquestionably, within the theoretical context of **perfect competition,** the performance of any firm is largely determined by industry characteristics. However, the IO paradigm's predictability was constrained by the fact that many industries exhibited imperfect competition. Among these were the presence of entry barriers that deterred new firms; the presence of a few large sellers who behaved like oligarchs; or many buyers, whether intermediate or end consumers, who were passive price takers. Moreover, studies identified firms that were outstanding performers, year in and year out, in their industry. Some examples quickly come to mind, such as General Electric in jet turbines, Toyota in automobiles, and Goldman Sachs in capital markets.

These two anomalies—markets are not always perfectly competitive and some firms consistently outperform industry averages—suggest industry structure is not necessarily deterministic of firm performance. Instead, firm performance is influenced by the presence of bright, motivated managers and their keen sense of innovative products or processes. Essentially, as seen in the notion of seeking alpha in finance, industry matters, but so too does the quality of managers.[5]

This realization qualifies the IO paradigm for the potential that great managers who develop better strategies and build better companies outperform their counterparts. Effectively, then, innovative strategic thinking prepares managers to achieve and maintain competitive advantages despite the structure of an industry. As we saw in our opening case, for example, Zara's strategy of making and moving sophisticated, moderately priced fashions demanded tighter integration of design, speed, responsiveness, and information technology; managers thus worked to develop a repertory of competencies spanning design, production, logistics, distribution, and retailing. (In our closing case, we'll see how a similar process has contributed to the success of eBay.)

In summary, strategic management research reports two important relationships:

1. Although competition may not be necessarily perfect, industry structure directly influences a company's performance.

2. The reality that competition may not be necessarily perfect creates the potential for a company to convert an innovative strategy into superior competitiveness.

Therefore, the strong relationships among industry structure, strategy, and performance means managers must understand what strategy is, the tools they can use to make it, and the implication of their choices to the performance of their company. The first part of this chapter develops these ideas, first profiling how managers assess industry structure and then discussing how they develop strategy for international business.

Perfect competition presumes

- Many buyers and sellers such that no individual affects price or quantities.
- Perfect information for both producers and consumers.
- Few, if any, barriers to market entry and exit.
- Full mobility of resources.

Bright managers find innovative ways to create value that are not easily matched or cheaply copied by rivals.

THE IDEA OF INDUSTRY STRUCTURE: THE FIVE-FORCES MODEL

The idea of industry structure helps explain the functions, form, and interrelationships among

- Suppliers of inputs.
- Buyers of outputs.
- Substitute products.
- Potential new entrants.
- Rivalry among competing sellers.

The idea of **industry structure** has well-defined concepts that specify the means to assess its character.[6] Often managers anchor analysis of industry structure by modeling the strength and importance of the so-called five fundamental forces of an industry. This model, shown in Figure 11.3, holds that the nature of competition in an industry is the combined outcome of the competitive pressures generated by

- The moves of rivals battling for market share
- The entry of new rivals seeking market share
- The efforts of other companies outside the industry to convince buyers to switch to their own substitute products[7]
- The push by input suppliers to charge more for their inputs
- The push by output buyers to pay less for products

Collectively, the **five-forces model** develops a representation of the structure and competition in an industry that prepares managers to figure out what forces shape strategic conduct, how strong each force is, what forces are driving changes in the industry, what strategic moves rivals are likely to make next, and what the key factors are for future competitive success. Common to each issue is the question of whether the current or future outlook suggests that firms in the industry have no, some, or great potential to make profits.

Analysis of industry structure provides the basis for estimating the kinds of strategic moves that companies are likely to use. For example, companies operating in an industry characterized by steep scale economies, as in the liquid screen display industry, will likely face rivals who are keenly intent on exploiting the cost-saving economies of larger-scale standardization. The fact that this objective depends on increasing sales volumes,

FIGURE 11.3
Five-forces Model of Industry Structure

From the strategists' perspective, analysis of these five forces—and of the ways in which they interact—is important because it spurs them to focus on a number of strategic questions. For example, which forces are driving industrywide change? Which forces are likely to determine the strategic moves of competitors? Which forces will be particularly important in the future?

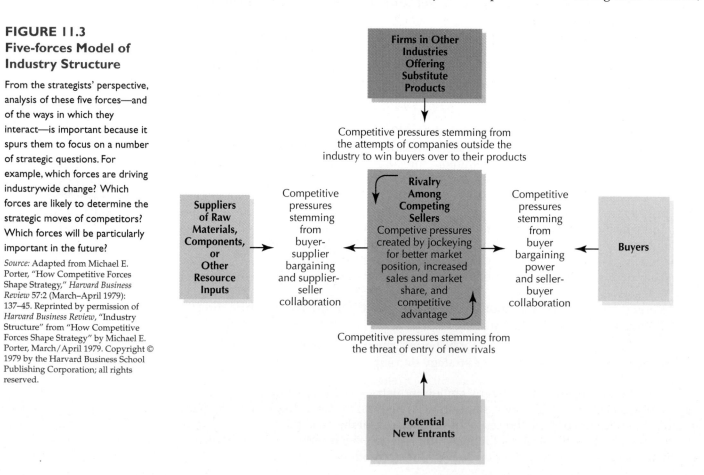

typically at the expense of existing rivals, means that less efficient and smaller-scale companies face tremendous pressure to compete and, ultimately, survive.

By contrast, industries marked by a continuous stream of product innovations, as in the digital camera industry, create different imperatives. Now, creating value rests on how well a company can fund R&D, translate ideas into innovations, and get its products to market quickly. Product innovation, not cost control, becomes the basis for sustainable value creation.

The Five-Forces Model in the Financial Services Industry   A look at globalization in the financial services industry demonstrates the interpretative power of the five-forces model. The opening of new markets and the advent of new technologies have spurred many companies to rethink how they run operations in their evolving industry. Most notably, the financial services industry is now one in which firms must compete in world markets to prosper. This evolution means a firm's competitive advantage depends on how well it can achieve economies of scale and economies of scope across countries. Greatly influencing these trends has been the potential for offshoring to create a global operating model for financial services.

> A global industry is one in which a firm's competitive position in one country is significantly affected by its position in other countries.

These developments have prompted companies to change the way they compete. Some, like HSBC and Bank of America, have prospered; others, like Citibank and Deutsche Bank, Germany's largest bank, have been scrambling. On a different front, the growing profits of the global financial services industry attract new entrants. These companies launch new strategies and products that change the nature of competition in the industry. For example, ING Direct, part of the Dutch financial giant ING, became the fastest growing savings and loan association in the United States through a new approach to banking. The emergence of new markets in Asia and Central Europe has brought many new buyers and suppliers of all sorts of financial products.

Finally, the increasing sophistication of buyers gives them incentive to sort through the growing number of options in the search for the best deal. Collectively, these forces have changed the structure of the global financial services industry as well as the potential for profitability for industry members. We see similar scenarios in a wide cross section of industries, such as textbook publishing, credit cards, mobile phones, automobiles, steel, oil, and business services.

INDUSTRY CHANGE

The structure of industries is continually in flux. New products, new firms, new markets, and new managers trigger new developments in rivalry, pricing, substitutes, buyers, and suppliers. These developments often change a minor feature of the industry, such as the expansion of an existing distribution channel. Minor changes leave industry members the option of continuing to operate as they have.

Occasionally, though, a change redefines one or more of the five fundamental forces in an industry, such as what the merger of market leaders Deutsche and Dresdner or JPMorgan Chase did to intra-industry rivalry in financial services. At this time, managers identify the force of the particular change, estimate the impact it may have on their industry and company, and determine an effective response.

Forces That Can Change Industry Structure   The types of forces that can transform an industry's structure include the following:

- Changes in the long-term industry growth rate
- New technologies, like containerization and wireless communications
- New consumer buying and usage patterns, such as buying music online or renting, receiving, and returning DVDs via the mail
- Manufacturing innovations that revise cost and efficiency frontiers, like Six Sigma programs

> Industry structure changes because of events like
> - Competitors' moves.
> - Government policies.
> - Changes in economics.
> - Shifting buyer preferences.
> - Technological developments.
> - Rate of market growth.

- The diffusion of business, executive, and technical expertise across countries, such as the transfer of the Western management approach to emerging Asian companies
- Change in government regulation, such as the privatization of state assets
- The entry or exit of major firms, such as the emergence of large-scale foreign companies

Some industries are affected by certain forces more so than others. The ball bearings industry, for instance, is more likely to change due to rapid escalation of pricing pressures, whereas the insurance business is more likely to change to reflect the emergence of international and online rivals. Although many forces of change may be in play in a given industry, generally no more than a few command the power to reset the industry. Hence managers separate major factors from minor ones and best position the firm to compete.

STRATEGY AND VALUE

Earlier, we profiled the view that great managers make great strategies that make great companies that outperform their industry rivals; much has been done to specify the principles and practices of each dimension of this relationship. Perhaps the most notorious task is setting the standards of a great strategy. A quick look through any library finds thousands of views of the standards of a great strategy.

Still, there are some common denominators. A great strategy defines the perspectives and tools managers use to appraise the company's present situation, identifies the direction the company should go, and determines how the company will get there. These issues, challenging for any firm, are especially so for the international company because it must deal with the contingencies created by dealing with different consumers, markets, industries, institutions, and environments.

> Strategy helps managers assess the company's present situation, identify the direction the company should go, and determine how the company will get there.

These issues are vital aspects of strategy. Ultimately, though, each one references the fundamental principle of strategy: creating value. The idea of value can be defined in a variety of ways, including economic value, market value, pro forma value, book value, insurance value, use value, par value, and replacement value—or, as we see in Figure 11.4, the value of victory. Value can also be defined from a number of perspectives, such as those of customers, employees, stakeholders, or shareholders.

FIGURE 11.4
When Executives Enter the War Room

Source: Copyright Mike Shapiro, Cartoonstock.com.

MIKE SHAPIRO

"REMEMBER OUR STRATEGY. YOU DIVIDE, I'LL CONQUER."

For our purposes, we define **value** as the measure of a firm's capability to sell what it makes for more than the costs incurred to make it. Therefore, **strategy** is the efforts of managers to build and strengthen the company's competitive position within its industry to create value.

CREATING VALUE

The importance of creating value spurs the firm to develop a compelling value proposition that specifies its targeted customer markets, whether on a nation-by-nation or worldwide basis, and how it sees itself making and selling a product that exceeds customers' expectations. The more successfully the company does so, the greater the profits it earns. Operationally, companies create value either by making their products for a lower cost than any other firm in their industry (the strategy of low-cost leadership) or making those products that consumers are willing to pay a premium price for (the strategy of differentiation).

Low-Cost Leadership   Firms that choose this strategy strive to be the low-cost producer in an industry for a given level of quality. This strategy pushes a firm to sell its products either at average industry prices to earn a profit higher than that of rivals or below the average industry prices to capture market share. Companies incur different costs because of differences in such matters as the prices they pay for raw materials and component parts, wage rates and productivity of their employees, scale of their production, and promotion and distribution expenses.

A cost-leadership strategy is a key advantage in highly competitive industries. In the event of a price war, the low-cost leader can cut its prices, thereby imposing losses on competitors, yet still earn some profits. Even without a price war, as the industry matures and prices decline, the firm that makes products more cheaply will earn profits longer than its rivals. The cost-leadership strategy usually targets a broad market. Presently, many Chinese companies are using this approach. They have combined efficient manufacturing operations, inexpensive labor, and efficient distribution channels to undercut global rivals on price.[8]

Differentiation   Firms that choose this strategy aspire to develop products that offer unique attributes that they reason are highly valued by customers and which customers perceive to be better than or sufficiently different from products offered by other companies. The value added by the uniqueness of the product allows the firm to charge a higher price that more than offsets the added costs of making and marketing it.

Companies like Apple, LVMH, and Rolex, for example, create value via differentiation strategies. Each has been able to convert customer insights, skilled and creative product development, persuasive marketing programs, and premier reputations for quality into superior value creation.

Companies that engage a differentiation strategy must continually find ways to develop products that have unique features that, in turn, lead buyers to prefer their goods and services versus those provided by rivals. Perhaps most importantly, the differentiation strategy demands that a company develop points of uniqueness that rivals find hard, if not impossible, to match or copy, such as the prestige of a Rolex watch, the quality of a Lexus sedan, the superior service at a Ritz-Carlton, the fashion of a Zara suit, or the one-of-a-kind system of eBay.

The Firm as Value Chain

No matter whether a firm opts for low-cost leadership or differentiation, the value creation potential of its strategy is a function of the amount of value, whether actual or perceived, that customers attribute to its products and the cost the firm incurs to make it. For both the low-cost leadership or differentiation strategies, the firm earns higher profits than its rivals when it creates more value for its customers and is able to charge them a

Value is what remains after expenses have been deducted from the revenues of a firm.

CONCEPT CHECK
In Chapter 2, we explain how **globalization** reveals the need for a variety of managerial approaches to business operations. Similarly, in Chapters 3 and 4, we emphasize how companies in the process of globalizing encounter an array of **political/legal systems** and **economic environments**. Here we likewise engage the notion that although globalization trends support an increasingly homogeneous market, there is little agreement on the single best international business strategy.

Cost leadership emphasizes high production volumes, low costs, and low prices.

Differentiation spurs the company to provide a unique good or service that its rivals find hard, if not impossible, to match or copy.

price that rewards it. Understanding this relationship, and then determining how to sustain it, is the basis for superior strategy.[9]

Eventually, managers move from the ambition of a low-cost or high-differentiation strategy to the reality of achieving their goals. Countless questions then pop up. As we saw in our opening case, executives at Zara make and continually test their decisions on a variety of key issues: Where should we design the product? Where should we make it? What's the best way to get it to customers in other countries? What are the most effective marketing tools? What kind of people should we hire to staff retail outlets? What should be headquarters' role in decision making?

Common to each of these questions are fundamental concerns about creating value: how the company will design, make, move, and sell products; how it will find efficiencies in doing so; and how it will coordinate the decisions in one part of the business with those made in other parts.[10]

> The value chain is the set of linked value-creating activities the company performs to design, produce, market, deliver, and support a product.

WHAT IS THE VALUE CHAIN?

Thinking of the firm as a value chain helps deal with these challenges. The **value chain** represents a straightforward framework that lets managers deconstruct the general idea of "create value" into a series of discrete activities that their company actually does to create value. So, on specifying their company's value chain, managers can then target their insights and investments toward those activities that create value and avoid those that do not.

> Value chain analysis helps the manager understand the behavior of costs and the existing and potential sources of differentiation.

Moving from the general idea of value creation to banking the profits from a sale requires a firm to complete a series of discrete activities. Managers decide how the firm will handle the functions and business processes that move a product from its conception, through its design, sourced raw materials and intermediate inputs, marketing, distribution, and support, to the end consumer.

Figure 11.5 shows the organization of the value chain.

FIGURE 11.5
The Value Chain Framework

Creating value is a powerful idea in the business world. Managers often use the *value chain* to focus on activities that must be performed to convert their plans into actions.

Source: Adapted with permission of The Free Press, a Division of Simon & Schuster Adult Publishing Group, from *Competitive Advantage: Creating and Sustaining Superior Performance* by Michael E. Porter. Copyright © 1985, 1998 by Michael E. Porter. All rights reserved.

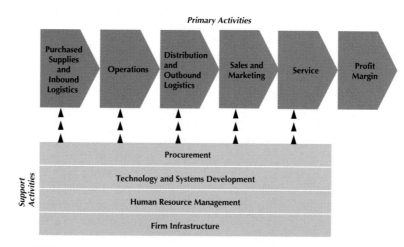

Primary Activities
Inbound Logistics Receiving, warehousing, and controlling inventory of production inputs from suppliers.
Operations Processes that transform inputs into finished product.
Outbound Logistics Moving the finished product into the supply chain from factory to wholesalers, retailers, or the final consumer.
Sales and Marketing Getting buyers to buy the product by using the marketing mix and advertising.
Service Customer support in terms of installation, after-sales service, complaints handling, training, and so on.

Support Activities
Procurement Purchasing the raw materials, components, and other inputs used throughout the value chain.
Technology and Systems Development Research and development, process automation, telecom and wireless systems, and other technology used to support value activities.
Human Resource Management Recruiting, developing, compensating, and retaining employees as well as labor relations activities.
Firm Infrastructure Activities related to general management, accounting and finance, legal and regulatory affairs, safety and security, management information systems, and other "overhead" functions.

Dimensions of the Value Chain   A value chain has four organizing dimensions:

A value chain disaggregates a firm into

- Primary activities that create and deliver the product.
- Support activities that aid the individuals and groups engaged in primary activities.

- *Primary activities* are those involved in the physical movement of raw materials and finished products, the production of goods and services, and the marketing, sales, and subsequent services of the outputs of the business. We identify primary activities with functional labels, such as in-bound logistics, operations, marketing, and so on. Hence the primary activities reflect classical managerial functions of the firm where there is an organizational entity with a manager in charge of a specific task that has clear lines of functional demarcation.

- *Support activities* make up the managerial infrastructure of the firm that supports carrying out the primary activities. The support activities include the processes and systems installed to coordinate decision making among the various value activities.

- *Profit margin:* The purpose of the value chain—to show how a firm creates value—is captured in "profit margin." Placed at the end of the value chain, the profit margin reports the difference between the total revenue generated by sales and the total cost of the activities that led to those sales.[11]

- *Upstream and downstream:* The final element of a value chain is orientation—namely, whether the particular activity takes place upstream or downstream. Upstream refers to those activities, such as inbound logistics, research and development, and manufacturing, which gather and process the inputs that the company uses to make a product. Downstream refers to those activities, such as outbound logistics, marketing, and service, which deal more directly with the end customer.

USING THE VALUE CHAIN

How well a company designs and manages its value chain determines its competitiveness. The value chain helps managers integrate the knowledge and skills of employees around the world in the way that lets them best leverage the company's global reach. As such, value chain analysis anchors managers' effort to build expertise in those activities that reduce costs or improve differentiation.

Value chains identify the format and interactions between different activities of the company.

Operationally, managers deal with the matters of configuration and coordination in setting up and running a value chain. Dispersing discrete activities of the value chain to those locations around the globe where perceived value is maximized or where the costs of value creation are minimized defines the matter of configuration. Integrating the discrete activities of the globally dispersed stages of the value chain into a cohesive, coherent whole defines the matter of coordination. Configuration and coordination are intrinsically related, but each has unique features.

Configuration   No matter how small or large, every MNE looks to establish elements of its value chain in the best spots in the world. The option to go anywhere in the world to do any activity gives MNEs tremendous choice in where to locate value activities. MNEs improve their competitiveness by configuring value activities to exploit **location economies**—namely, the economies that arise from performing a value activity in the optimal location given prevailing economic, political, legal, and cultural conditions.

Configuration is the way that managers arrange the activities of the value chain.

Thus, if the best industrial designers are in Germany, a firm should base its design operations there. If the most productive labor force for assembly operations is in China, that's where the firm should base assembly operations. If the most creative advertising minds are in Italy, then the firm should create its advertising campaign there. The manager's task is to find those locations, resources, and markets that best support the company's vision of creating a competitive value chain.

The key caveat for location decisions is the notion that configuration should be optimized "given prevailing economic, legal, political, and cultural conditions." The complexity of this challenge has frustrated many MNEs. At one point, following

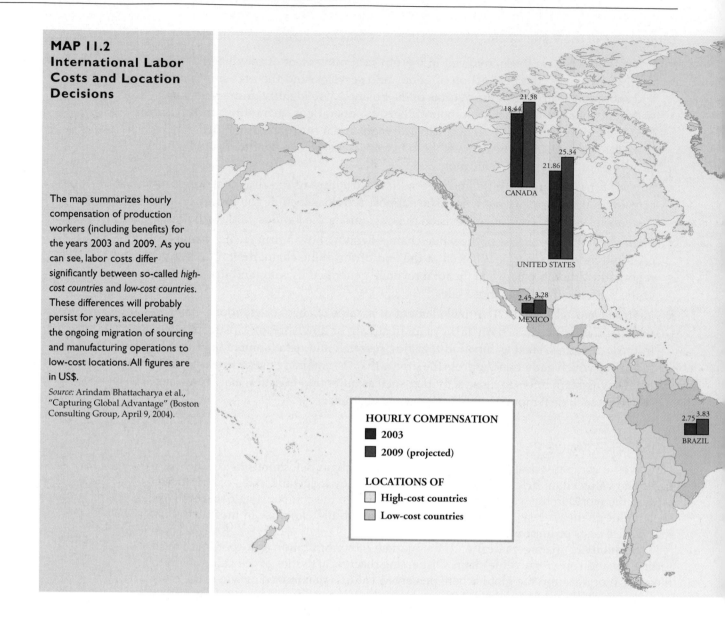

**MAP 11.2
International Labor Costs and Location Decisions**

The map summarizes hourly compensation of production workers (including benefits) for the years 2003 and 2009. As you can see, labor costs differ significantly between so-called *high-cost countries* and *low-cost countries*. These differences will probably persist for years, accelerating the ongoing migration of sourcing and manufacturing operations to low-cost locations. All figures are in US$.

Source: Arindam Bhattacharya et al., "Capturing Global Advantage" (Boston Consulting Group, April 9, 2004).

HOURLY COMPENSATION
■ 2003
■ 2009 (projected)

LOCATIONS OF
□ High-cost countries
□ Low-cost countries

CONCEPT CHECK

In discussing "The Elements of the Economic Environment" in Chapter 4, we describe information on such factors as labor costs, wage rates, and productivity as tools for assessing cost factors as part of a company's strategy for operating in foreign countries. In Chapter 6, we discuss methods of interpreting the relative economic performance of different countries. Here we underscore the importance of these processes in helping managers determine optimal locations for overseas operations.

another change in the international business environment, Jack Welch, former chairman and CEO of General Electric, thought the best location decision for GE factories was a mobile platform, explaining, "Ideally, you'd have every plant you own on a barge, to move with currencies and changes in the economy."[12]

Earlier chapters showed that countries vary on many dimensions and these differences directly affect business costs in a particular country. Moreover, we also saw from international trade theory that relative differences in cost factors give certain countries a comparative advantage in performing certain activities of a value chain. Therefore, managers configure value chains worldwide based on cost factors, business environments, cluster effects, logistics, degree of digitization, economies of scale, and buyers' needs.

Cost Factors   Differences in wage rates, worker productivity, inflation rates, and government regulations create significant variations in production costs from country to country. Consider, for example, labor costs. In 2003, the average hourly compensation (including benefits) for production workers in China was $0.80 versus $25.34 in the United States.[13] By 2007, wages in Mexico were about 11 percent of the U.S. level; in China, wages were 3 percent of the U.S. level.[14] Relative productivity performances did

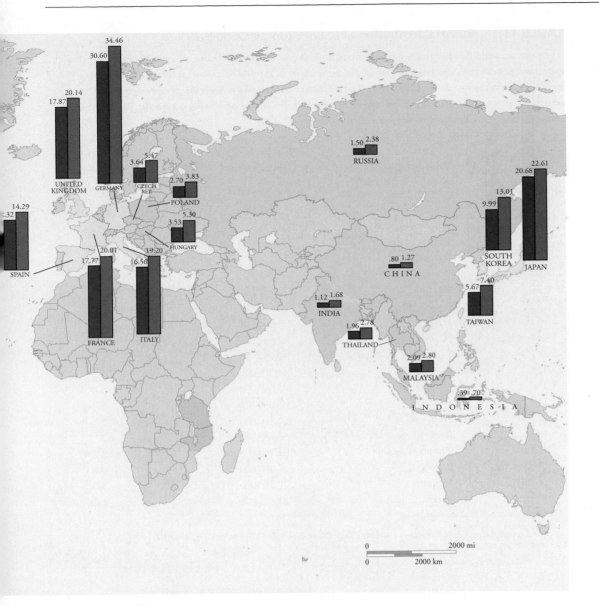

not neutralize these differences. Consequently, footwear companies, like Nike or Reebok, locate upstream activities (sourcing and manufacturing) of their value chain in Mexico or China and downstream activities (marketing and service) in the United States.

Map 11.2 displays the current and projected wages for various countries that have tremendous implications for value creation and value chain configuration at many companies. For instance, thousands of MNEs from around the world have started operations in China in the past few years in the quest for productive, low-cost labor. Furthermore, these data suggest the global migration of sourcing and manufacturing operations from high-cost to rapidly developing low-cost countries in Southeast Asia, Central and Eastern Europe, and South America will likely accelerate.

Table 11.1 rank-orders countries with the largest labor forces. As such, it provides a sense of where companies might go in the search for labor. Notably, just two countries—China and India—account for more than 43 percent of the total labor in the world. In the longer term, we expect to see many companies look to India for investment opportunities. Between 2004 and 2050, India's population will increase more than 500 million, whereas China's will rise about 79 million while that in and the United States will grow about 98 million.

Factors that influence value chain configuration include

- Cost factors.
- Business environments.
- Cluster effects.
- Logistics.
- Economies of scale.
- Buyers' needs.

TABLE 11.1   Global Distribution of Labor: Top 20 Countries

From the standpoint of primary cost factors, China and India are attractive sources for firms seeking abundant, productive, and low-cost labor. As such, China and India help demonstrate the idea of location economies—specifically those economies that companies achieve by performing value chain activities, such as manufacturing and assembly, in countries where prevailing economic, political, and cultural conditions create optimal operating conditions.

Rank	Country	Labor Force	Share of Total World Labor Pool[1]
1	China	798,000,000	26.6
2	India	509,300,000	16.9
3	European Union	222,700,000	7.4
4	United States	151,400,000	5.0
5	Indonesia	108,200,000	3.1
6	Brazil	96,340,000	3.2
7	Russia	73,880,000	2.5
8	Bangladesh	68,000,000	2.3
9	Japan	66,440,000	2.2
10	Nigeria	48,990,000	1.6
11	Pakistan	48,290,000	1.6
12	Vietnam	44,580,000	1.5
13	Germany	43,660,000	1.5
14	Mexico	38,090,000	1.3
15	Thailand	36,410,000	1.2
16	Philippines	35,790,000	1.2
17	United Kingdom	31,100,000	1.0
18	Burma	28,490,000	.096
19	France	27,880,000	.092
20	Turkey	24,800,000	.082

[1]The total labor count for the world is approximately 3,001,000,000 workers.

Source: Excerpted from Central Intelligence Agency, "Rank Order—Labor Force," *The World Factbook 2007,* at www.cia.gov (accessed January 7, 2008).

> Manufacturing costs vary from country to country because of wage rates, worker productivity, resource availability, and fiscal and monetary policies.

Auguste Comte, a nineteenth-century social scientist, reasoned that "demography is destiny." So too, in large degree, with the configuration of value chains. Executives everywhere are rethinking the implications of the cost structures in emerging economies to their idea of value creation. As we saw in Chapter 4 in regard to the responses of McDonald's, Cisco, and IBM to the BRICs, this process has moved many companies to reconfigure their value chains.

Cluster Effects   A peculiarity of value creation is the so-called *cluster effect,* in which a particular industry gradually clusters more and more related value creation effects in a specific location.[15] For example, London is a center for global finance, Baden-Württemberg for cars and electrical engineering, Silicon Valley for technology, Hollywood for mass media, and Mumbai for business process outsourcing.

Each economic cluster creates unique location advantages that offer firms in that locale access to specialized resources that improve the potential for innovation. The power of cluster effects led the Taiwanese to build Hsinchu, outside of Taipei, into a tech ecosystem to make gadgets designed in California; likewise, Chinese and Indians are doing the same to Shanghai and Bangalore, respectively, to make microchips and software.

> Logistics entails how companies obtain, produce, and exchange material and services in the proper place and in proper quantities for the proper value activity.

Logistics   At some point in every transaction along a value chain, the potential arises for a product transfer. In some situations, the value-to-weight ratio of that transaction makes a huge difference in configuration decisions. For example, the greater the value of a product to its weight, the less storage and transportation costs matter. Therefore, the decision of where to manufacture computer chips, software, or aircraft (unlike tractor axles, carpets, or furniture) need not pay much attention to the distance between the factory and the consumer. In addition, as we observed in our opening case on Zara, if a company builds a value chain in which just-in-time inventory practices are key to both inbound and outbound logistics, then it makes sense to locate design, production, and warehousing activities in the same area.

Degree of Digitization   The process of *digitization* involves converting an analog product into a string of zeros and ones. The degree of difficulty of this process influences how a company configures its value chain. Increasingly, products like software, music, and books and services like call centers, application processing, and financial consolidation can be done virtually anywhere. Equipped with a networked computer, workers can send goods and services anywhere in the world at negligible cost and complication.

For example, many activities that could only be done in a few specialized places, such as the due diligence process in mergers and acquisitions that once took place largely in New York City, are now offshored to Indian firms.[16] Efforts to narrow the digital divide—the gap between those with regular, effective access to digital and information technology and those without this access—expand configuration options.

Economies of Scale   The reduction in unit cost achieved by producing a large volume of a product is called **economies of scale.** Generally, economies of scale occur in industries with high capital costs that can be distributed across a large number of units of production, thereby resulting in lower per-unit costs. The cost of setting up a research center, production facility, and logistics hub can be substantial for some companies.

For example, building a production site to make flat panel displays exceeds $4 billion, whereas outfitting a plant to make furniture might run a few million dollars.[17] Therefore, steep up-front costs create high potential for scale economies. This relationship leads managers to design value chains that exploit the efficiencies of a few large centralized plants rather than operating several smaller, less efficient plants scattered across the world.

Scale economies refers to the decrease in the unit cost of production associated with the increase in total output.

Business Environment   Production costs alone do not determine location decisions. Companies also configure their value chain to access or avoid a country based on its business environment. Governments of many countries recruit foreign investments. They promise business-friendly market climates that offer lower corporate tax rates, more flexible operating requirements, and public policies that are responsive to industry.

On the flip side, governments can create risky environments that deter local operations. For example, governments that support the rule of man, versus the rule of law, as the basis of their legal environment deter firms fearful of intellectual property theft.

Chapter 3 discussed the growing importance of intellectual property to companies' long-term competitiveness. Today, no matter where in the world one operates, innovation has pushed itself to the top of policy-making and senior executive agendas. Moreover, some see technological change only accelerating: One view holds that "in the first 20 years of the 20th century, we saw more advancement than in all of the 19th century. And we won't experience 100 years of progress in the 21st century—it will be more like 20,000 years of progress at the current rate."[18] Maximizing the potential for innovative ideas, products, and services pushes managers to configure value chains with an eye toward locating activities in knowledge-intensive, technology-enabled business environments.

Table 11.2 rank-orders the most innovative countries in the world—as determined by their performance in promoting leading-edge technologies, expanded human capacities, better organizational and operational capability, and improved institutional performance.[19] The United States tops the rankings, reflecting its superior environment for

TABLE 11.2   Global Innovation Index, 2007

The importance of innovation has spurred efforts to estimate the degree to which countries develop business environments that support knowledge creation, increased competitiveness, and greater wealth generation. The following index values measure the relative performance of various countries in generating ideas and leveraging them for innovative products and services.

Rank	Country	Index Value[a]
1	United States	5.80
2	Germany	4.89
3	United Kingdom	4.81
4	Japan	4.48
5	France	4.32
6	Switzerland	4.16
7	Singapore	4.10
8	Canada	4.06
9	Netherlands	3.99
10	Hong Kong	3.97
11	Denmark	3.95
12	Sweden	3.90
13	Finland	3.85
14	United Arab Emirates	3.81
15	Belgium	3.77
16	Luxembourg	3.72
17	Australia	3.71
18	Israel	3.68
19	South Korea	3.67
20	Iceland	3.66
21	Ireland	3.66
22	Austria	3.64
23	India	3.57
24	Italy	3.48
25	Norway	3.48
26	Malaysia	3.47
27	Spain	3.38
28	New Zealand	3.35
29	China	3.21
30	Kuwait	3.14
31	Estonia	3.12
32	Czech Republic	3.10
33	Chile	3.03
34	Thailand	3.01
35	Slovak Republic	2.97
36	Hungary	2.88
37	Mexico	2.88
38	South Africa	2.87
39	Portugal	2.86
40	Brazil	2.84

[a]Index value ranges from 1 to 7; a higher index value indicates better performance.

Source: Based on Soumitra Dutta and Simon Caulki, "The World's Top Innovators," *The World Business/INSEAD Global Innovation Index 2007* (January 2007), at www.worldbusinesslive.com (accessed June 18, 2007).

innovation and superior effectiveness in exploiting it. Still, critics note that the United States risks its edge given its reliance on attracting scientists and engineers from overseas to offset shortcomings of its primary and secondary education.

Presently, though, the United States leads the second most innovative nation (Germany) by almost a full point. European nations claim 5 of the 10 spots—the United Kingdom, France, Switzerland, and the Netherlands alongside Germany—and 11 in the top 20. The data suggest, however, rising innovation in Asia. Japan, Singapore, Hong Kong, and South Korea place high and India and China are moving up. Collectively, Asia appears to be moving from relying on polices and practices that optimized efficiency and quality to optimizing its environment for innovation.[20]

Customer Needs   Buyer-related activities, such as distribution to dealers, sales and advertising, and after-sale service, usually take place close to buyers. This can press a company to locate the capability to perform such activities in every country physically where it has major customers. For example, the leading management consulting and accounting firms have many international offices to service the foreign operations of their globally dispersed clients.

Coordination   The discrete activities of the value chain, as elements of a larger system, require managers to figure out how to coordinate decisions and transactions both within and across value activities. The task of coordinating the different activities that go into making and moving a product around the world, though sounding ordinary, has emerged as the basis of the superior performance that separates good from great MNEs.

For example, Zara's strategy of rapid response to ever-changing fashion trends demands a high degree of coordination. First, managers must coordinate the efforts of salespeople who double as wired grassroots market researchers responsible for punching in trends, customer comments, and orders. Data are then transferred daily to headquarters, where they're used to coordinate design, production, and delivery. The task for managers at headquarters can be brutal: They must coordinate material flows from dozens of suppliers and then transmit orders to factories and delivery status to a thousand-plus storefronts.

Core Competencies   Coordinating value activities has been part of international operations since companies began venturing abroad. Managers work to coordinate linkages between value activities in the belief that weaving them into a coherent whole achieves the synergy of international operations. This goal has assumed greater importance in the past few years given the growing appreciation of the performance and competitive benefits of better coordinating so-called *core competencies* throughout a value chain.[21]

Technically, a **core competency** is a special outlook, skill, capability, or technology that creates unique value for the firm by creating an acknowledged thread that runs through all of the firm's value activities. Well-known examples of core competencies include Wal-Mart's sophisticated information management and product distribution systems, 3M's legacy of product innovation, Intel's design of complex semiconductors, Honda's expertise in engine technology, Toyota's insight into management systems, Procter & Gamble's marketing-distribution skills, and Apple's eye for product design.

A core competency effectively gives everyone in the MNE, not just a few executives at headquarters, a principle or practice that helps them coordinate activities. Finally, the fact that rivals cannot easily match or replicate it serves as a powerful source of competitive advantage for a company—as seen in, for example, Apple's or Toyota's ability to capitalize on innovation that led to superior profitability and premier industry positions.

Understanding the interactions and overlaps among value activities and linking them to the firm's core competency is instrumental to making a value chain work. Doing so spurs managers to see particular activities not as ends unto themselves but as the means of creating superior value. For example, a country in a remote location that offers the

Case Review Note

Coordination is the way that managers connect the activities of the value chain.

A company's core competency is

• The unique skills and/or knowledge that it does better than its competitors.

• Essential to its competitiveness and profitability.

A core competency can emerge from various sources, including

• Product development.

• Employee productivity.

• Manufacturing expertise.

• Marketing imagination.

• Executive leadership.

CONCEPT CHECK

In discussing the worldwide "Increase and Expansion of Technology" in Chapter 1, we note the role of technology in fostering new ways of communicating and transmitting information among operations spread throughout the world. What we want to underscore here is the impact of new technologies on the ability of companies to experiment with options—many of them unprecedented—for coordinating the geographically dispersed parts of their **value chains.**

Several factors influence value chain coordination:

- Operational obstacles.
- National cultures.
- Learning effects.
- Subsidiary networks.

maximum value creation for manufacturing but results in higher logistics costs actually reduces the value for marketing and possibly the entire value chain. Thus managers' capability to associate activities, assets, costs, and revenues directly helps them understand how the firm creates value—both in specific activities as well as overall.

Both UPS and Federal Express are expanding their operations into all parts of the world, most recently reinforcing their beachheads in China with the expansion of local hubs. Similarly, General Electric, Microsoft, and Accenture have opened research and development facilities in India, reasoning that the high productivity of the local scientific community will create new points of value creation for them. As each of these companies disperses greater portions of their value chain over greater territory, they must develop coordination tools that enable them to transfer their extensive and unique knowledge.

The global elaboration of a company's value chain leads to the question of how managers will coordinate the greater dispersion of value activities. Coordinated well, MNEs can leverage their core competencies, using them to boost sales and profits. Coordinated poorly, MNEs can fail to leverage their core competencies from country to country. In the case of the latter, for example, breakthroughs at the John F. Welch Technology Center in Bangalore, India, will not make it to GE's operations in Hungary, Brazil, or the United States. Therefore, managers develop value chains with an eye to how they will coordinate activities that may span anywhere from one to many nations. Several factors moderate managers' analyses of how to coordinate value activities: *operational obstacles, national cultures, learning effects, and subsidiary networks.*

Operational Obstacles   MNEs run into problems when trying to get the various links of their global value chain to deal with each other. Communication challenges arise when trying to synchronize languages; parts flowing from the Far East to South America to their ultimate stop in the United States generate possible points of miscommunication.

In principle, companies can insist that staff rely on browser-based communications. However, this option still has a way to go. European companies, for instance, have widely adopted EDIFACT as the basis of their electronic communication interface. In the United States, this interface is largely limited to large manufacturers and their first-tier suppliers, such as the relationship between Wal-Mart and Procter & Gamble.

Some groups champion the language protocol of the World Wide Web, specifically hypertext markup language (HTML), or XML, as the best global standard. So far, though, there is no agreement on the standards of business exchange. Beside communications, currency exchange and measurement systems (metric versus decimal) can create weak links among globally dispersed activities. In sum, well-planned coordination preempts these threats, thereby letting workers worry less about what is supposed to happen with material transfers and product delivery and more about creating value.

CONCEPT CHECK

In Chapters 2, 3, and 4, we show how different national cultures influence the social, workplace, political, legal, and economic contexts of business around the world. It's important to remember that differences in cultural conditions can have a significant effect on the range of strategic options available to companies overseas, shaping such choices as where to locate an operation and even who to hire to run it.

National Cultures   The globalization of a company's value chain, such as design done in Finland, inputs sourced from Brazil, production done in China, distribution organized in the United States, and service done in Mexico, presses managers to understand how foreign cultures influence coordination. For example, the performance of even the simplest value chain depends on each link meeting a specified timetable. Companies in Western countries generally see deadlines as firm promises of delivery. Some cultures, however, see deadlines as guidelines with flexible end dates.

Trying to run value chains worldwide without preparing for these sorts of operational gaps can undermine coordination. National cultures can also impose higher hurdles in coordinating a transaction from one stage of the value chain with another. Units anchored in different cultures may disagree over how much information they should share or who should take lead responsibility. Coordination can then suffer from conflict.

Learning Effects   Learning effects refer to cost savings that come from learning by doing. Managers, for example, learn by recurrence how to transfer best practices from one country to another, such as innovative ways to improve internal and external customer service. Successfully transferred, an MNE can convert higher productivity into lower costs or higher customer satisfaction into higher prices.

The Experience Curve   The information about steps in the value chain that managers learn can then help them to better plan, execute, evaluate, and leverage performance. In this way, they can gain new insights into managing the value chain as a whole instead of as a collection of parts. Similarly, companies can often cut costs by 20 to 30 percent each time their cumulative output doubles, a phenomenon known as the **experience curve**.[22] A reduction may occur when a company covers fixed costs over more units of output, becomes more efficient as it gains operating experience, or secures quantity discounts on materials and transportation.

The matter of learning shapes how both manufacturing and service MNEs coordinate value chains. In the case of the former, MNEs must prepare production activities for different attitudes and approaches to manufacturing across countries. For example, an MNE may have factories in different parts of the world, such as Japan and Mexico, that manufacture the same product but with different production philosophies. The Mexican factory might adopt a traditional assembly-line operation given the local conditions of inexpensive labor, poor transportation infrastructure, and limited exposure to high technology. The company's Japanese factory, in contrast, might install a lean production system to take advantage of local labor competency, manufacturing expertise, and efficient logistics.

The different capital structures and productivity of each type of system complicate how managers keep both plants working in harmony with the other. If ignored, MNEs can suffer production crunches that lead to high overtime costs, reduced quality, disappointed customers, and lost sales.

Coordinating Services   Service industries run into similar challenges in coordinating the sharing of specialized knowledge across their globally dispersed value chains. Management consulting firms like McKinsey & Company, Boston Consulting Group, and Bain & Company exemplify a successful approach. Their strategic asset is the consistent performance of their highly qualified people; their clients are confident that whoever is assigned to them, he or she will perform well. Crafting and sustaining such consistency across global operations has led these firms to ensure that their staff learns the client company's preferred principles and practices.

Subsidiary Networks   The current culmination of globalization trends is a world marked by real-time connectivity among the subsidiaries of an MNE. Subsidiaries around the world can exchange information freely, whether done systematically within an enterprise resource planning (ERP) context or tacitly via e-mails. Moreover, an astounding number of companies and affiliates engage in international business. The UN reports that more than 200,000 MNEs have established nearly 650,000 subsidiaries worldwide. These two trends, growing connectivity and growing populations of MNEs with dispersed subsidiary networks, result in an integrated market where ideas can emerge from and easily travel to subsidiaries around the world. Skills, ideas, and technologies can be created anywhere within an MNE's global network of subsidiaries.

An increasingly vital task for managers, then, is to coordinate the company's value chain so it can leverage the competencies developed within any subsidiary and apply them wherever they can create value within the firm's global network. For example, managers from Canada GE identified a New Zealand appliance maker, Fisher & Paykel, producing a broad range of products very efficiently in its small low-volume plant. When the Canadians used the flexible job-shop techniques to increase productivity in their high-volume factory, the U.S. appliance business became interested. A group of managers and employees from GE's Louisville plant went to Montreal to study the accomplishments. Convinced of its potential, they systematized the program and transferred it to their operation. They soon reported that they had cut their production cycle in half and reduced inventory costs by 20 percent. Immediately, GE's Appliance Park in Louisville became a

CONCEPT CHECK
As we explained in the closing case in Chapter 4, the emergence of the so-called *BRIC markets*—Brazil, Russia, India, and China—has spurred fundamental shifts in global investment and company strategy. Here we observe that one of these shifts moves companies to explore strategies for operating in different environments with a keen eye toward leveraging innovations across subsidiary networks.

"must see" destination for other GE units, and within a year, other managers had leveraged this knowledge into the value chains for the locomotive and jet engine businesses.

CHANGE AND THE VALUE CHAIN

Once built, a firm's value chain is not etched in stone. Because the features and functions of products that consumers judge most critical change over time—as we see in financial services, clothing, entertainment, electronics, and so on—the basis of value creation in an industry evolves. Some firms, like Zara and eBay, anticipate market situations and begin operations with a value chain that is well configured and well coordinated. Far more common, though, are firms that must rethink their value chains in the face of adverse market trends and industry situations.

> The configuration and coordination of value chains respond to changes in customers, competitors, industries, and environments.

A Case in Point   In 1997, Sony Corporation, Japan's premier electronics company, took little notice of the Samsung Electronics Company, a South Korean television maker then snared in a life-or-death struggle to endure the Asian currency crisis. A decade later, Samsung had nearly twice the market capitalization of Sony and now commands the role once claimed by Sony—the competitor with the breadth of cool products and the appeal of a premium brand.

Samsung powered its rise by reconfiguring its value chain. In 1997, Samsung was a back-of-the-store brand with bulky low-quality televisions. Since then, Samsung has upgraded its product lines to compete directly with Sony for the premium market. In terms of R&D, Samsung has been one of the world's "top 10" in U.S. patents for several years, relying on more than 13,000 researchers to come up with tomorrow's products. Too, Samsung's quest to being "World Best" involved, in 2007, $8.7 billion in capital spending, the largest for any information technology company in the world. Samsung has turned this investment into a manufacturing capacity that can build raw components for its many products, like memory chips and display panels, at some of the lowest production costs in the world.

Similarly, Samsung has annually invested billions of dollars in advertising. By 2005, the change was complete: For the first time, Samsung's $14.6 billion brand value exceeded Sony's value of $10.7 billion.[23] As one observer noted, "Samsung is like the old Sony. . . . [I]t has much of the spirit of Sony 10 years ago." Sony, looking to revive its operations, took the unprecedented step, for a major Japanese MNE, of naming an American as its chairman in mid-2004.[24]

> Here we see Vietnamese workers putting the finishing touches on a recent run of Nike shoes at a production facility on the outskirts of Ho Chi Minh City (formerly Saigon). The powerful economics of low-cost, productive labor, whether in Vietnam, India, or China, for instance, directly shapes how companies configure their value chains.

Caveat: A Limitation of Strategy Interesting in its own right, the Sony-Samsung contest spotlights a fundamental limitation of strategy. The strategy literature holds that a decisive sense of purpose anchors short-term competitiveness and long-term advantages. However, this outlook can also stifle creativity and erode the effectiveness of decision making.[25] Again, think back to Sony's experiences. As Samsung steadily encroached on its territory, Sony's management feverishly worked to improve its products, serve its customers, and anticipate new markets. Ultimately, though, these efforts fell far short of management's vision.

Consequently, no matter how highly tuned the company's strategic compass, executives' limitations, along with marketplace uncertainty, can quickly turn prized core competencies into strategic liabilities. Many companies face this quandary as they figure out how to adjust the value creation tools of the twentieth century with the opportunities and challenges of the twenty-first century. Our look at the contest between real versus virtual value chains highlights this situation.

P●int Counterpoint

Are Value Chains Real?

P●int **Yes** The concept of the *value chain* has a strong historical basis. Analysts conceived it in the 1960s and 1970s by charting a path of development for mineral-exporting economies.[26] It was then adopted in French planning literature as a *filière* (literally, a "thread") to describe the perceived need for French industrial capability to span the complete thread of a value chain.[27] According to French planning exercises, the idea of *filière* suggests that the full chain of activities that goes into a product should take place within national boundaries.

So, for a country intent on developing the leading capabilities in color TVs, it would need to set industry policies that create expertise in picture tube technology, printed circuit board design and manufacturing, design and production of integrated circuits and other electronic components, and metal- and plastic-forming technologies.

Since French adaptation, value chain analysis has become widely used. Today, the value chain serves as a powerful business system concept that helps managers do a number of things efficiently. First, it evaluates the company's strengths and weaknesses. It then interprets the determinants of the internal cost structure, the basis of core competencies, and relationships with customers. Finally, it links the internal features and functions of a competitor to the content of its marketplace strategy. Applying this analysis enables managers to identify how well the firm's present strategy works and the strategic issues it faces in the marketplace.

The value chain, however, does impose some analytical restrictions. Managers applying value chain analysis follow the model's template in data collection, interpretation, and strategic decision making. This template is defined by the

(continued)

Counterpoint **No** The recent emergence of the Internet has given rise to the alternative idea of the virtual value chain as the basis of superior value creation and competitive advantage.[28] This view reasons that the Internet creates a new basis for value creation via virtual means, which has already proven successful in industries as diverse as agrochemicals, biotech, and furniture.[29]

Virtuality calls for managers to rethink their traditional focus on static, internally focused "chains" to consider the potential of virtual value networks that arrange value activities in terms of dynamic "webs," both within and outside the company. These sorts of value networks, as seen at companies like eBay, Alibaba, and Google, form open, interconnected environments that enable a company to configure value activities in ways that let them fully leverage their core competencies.

The premise of virtuality is that companies can create value with information: Developing, codifying, and sharing information among the members of an organization lie at the heart of virtuality. A company's ability to leverage its information advantage enables it to generate new products to serve new markets, much in the way Google has evolved from a search engine to a diversified media company offering an expanding range of services.

The idea for the virtual value chain builds on the communications technology of the Internet and its capacity to support a new business architecture that challenges the industrial-age notion of a series of sequential steps as the basis for value creation. Virtual value chains open new paths for value creation, allowing managers to rethink how best to capture the benefits of lower search, coordination,

(continued)

real activities, functions, and business processes the firm performs in moving a product from conception, through its various stages of design, production, marketing and distribution, and, finally, to the end consumer. In theory, anchoring analysis and making decisions based on the orderly progression of value chain activities allow managers to formulate profitable strategies and coordinate operations.

Some contend that dealing with the "hard realities" of international operations, whether by expanding into conventional markets or heading to distant and different territories, is best done within the context of the "real" value chain—business is business and every firm must deal with traditional primary and support activities. Others believe that "virtual" value chains are the most effective way to branch out globally.

However, the dazzle of virtuality itself may lead some companies to lose sight of intrinsic difficulties when configuring and coordinating value chains for international business operations. Granted, the idea of virtual companies operating in cyberspace, free of the bounds of national borders and the constraints of geography, may eventually come to pass. Presently, though, international business takes place within a world marked by geographic borders and populated by companies running real value chains. This is why proponents of real value chains believe their system better equips an MNE to deal with the global market. ●

contracting, and other transaction costs among people, agents, firms, and institutions.

Virtuality has provocative implications as to how managers decide what to do and where to do it. For example, Nike has limited production facilities and Reebok owns no plants whatsoever. Both companies contract their entire footwear production virtually to footwear makers in China, Vietnam, and other low-cost labor countries. Although nominally independent, these companies enable Nike and Reebok to create virtual production capability. It also allows them to leverage their core competencies in design and marketing while relying on the suppliers' expertise of rapidly retooling for the manufacturing of new products to keep pace with changing tastes. Similar situations are occurring at Dell, Corning, Li Fung, and Acer.

In the end, the relative importance of a real versus virtual value chain depends on the characteristics of a particular company's products and services. The potential of virtuality has important implications for eBay's global expansion, as we see in our closing case, but middling implications for companies such as Nestlé that deal with physical situations in many different geographies. Still, the combined theoretical context of "real versus virtual" opens up new paths of analysis that promise to help international companies better understand the configuration and coordination of activities and the creation of value. ●

Global Integration Versus Local Responsiveness

Global and local pressures challenge how the firm configures and coordinates its value chain.

Companies that operate internationally face two asymmetric forces: pressures for **global integration** and pressures for **local responsiveness.** The asymmetry puts contradictory demands on how the firm configures and coordinates its value chain. Should it standardize all activities of its value chain to achieve economies of scale? Conversely, should it customize all local activities to the particular demands of each country? Over time, research has uncovered a straightforward relationship: the higher the pressure for global integration, the greater the need to maximize efficiency; and, conversely, the higher the pressure for responsiveness to local conditions, the greater the need to maximize market sensitivity.

Navigating between these two demands requires the international firm face a range of macro pressures that affects how its managers identify and interpret the best way to configure and coordinate a value chain. This section looks at the pressures for global integration and local responsiveness. We then discuss the implications of their interaction to the types of strategies an MNE can engage.

PRESSURES FOR GLOBAL INTEGRATION

The convergence of national markets and quest for production efficiency push for global integration of value activities.

A theme of this text is the growing globalization of business. Presently, global markets now produce and consume more than 20 percent of world output and are projected to multiply 12-fold, to more than 80 percent of world output, by 2025. Similarly, more economic integration will take place in the next 30 years than occurred in the previous 10,000 or more.

Managers, companies, and industries react accordingly, as seen in the ongoing formation of global markets in chemicals, credit cards, financial services, accounting, food, health care, mass media, forest products, information technology, automobiles, telecommunications, and so on. Earlier chapters identified many contributing factors. We highlight two pressures for global integration: the *globalization of markets* and the *efficiency gains of standardization*.

Globalization of Markets   A provocative thesis, increasingly supported by global buying patterns and companies' strategies, suggests that consumers seek and accept standardized global products—whether they are Apple iPods, Samsung plasma screens, Starbucks' espressos, or Zara blouses.[30] Two conditions compel the globalization of markets. On one hand are the intrinsic functions of money—it is hard to acquire, difficult to save, and always in scarce supply. These functions mean that consumers worldwide seek to maximize their purchasing power by buying the highest quality good for the lowest possible price. Ultimately, the theory goes, consumers do not care who provides the product, as long as it meets their needs and delivers superior value.

On the flip side, communication technologies steadily strengthen the infrastructure that converge consumer preferences across countries with improving transportation logistics necessary to ensure the availability of standardized products worldwide. Coupled together, the quest to maximize individual purchasing power, along with the growing exposure and access to higher-quality goods at lower prices, compels the increasing homogeneity of the global market. In so doing, this relationship spurs companies to maximize global integration and standardize activities.

Our opening case chronicles one company's response to these imperatives. As you'll recall, Zara realized that by offering standardized fashion styles at reasonable prices, it could leverage fixed design, manufacturing, and retail costs across its global retail network and thereby achieve economies of scale. When it ran into stubborn local preferences, Zara soon found that it could get by with minor customization—provided its products offered superior value. The firm's entire value chain thus reflects several responses to the imperatives discussed in this section.

Case Review Note

Commodities   There are many goods—so-called **commodities**—that serve a universal need (think of oil, steel, sugar, or wheat). The preferences of consumers in different countries, if not identical, are highly similar for many sorts of commodities. Hence companies can standardize their product to remarkable degrees. Pressures for global integration in such markets are absolute, given that product differentiation is difficult and competition tends toward price wars.

Efficiency Gains of Standardization   Worldwide standardization of an MNE's products, purchases, methods, and policies can significantly reduce the costs of its operations. For example, if an MNE standardizes machinery in the production stage of its value chain, it can often negotiate quantity discounts on raw material purchases as well as streamline the stockpiling of inventories. The company can also realize economies in other value activities such as R&D (single product design) or advertising (universal message). Therefore, standardization, by pushing a company to mass-produce a standardized product at the optimal location in the world, helps exploit location economies.

Always a factor in international business, standardization pressures have increased as more countries have joined the global economy in general and the WTO in particular. As we saw in earlier chapters, virtually every country in the world is a member of, or waiting to join, the WTO.

The liberalization of trade has spurred the emergence of many competitors who anchor their value chains in low-cost locations without forsaking access to markets worldwide—for example, business process outsourcing firms in India, steel producers in China, chip designers in Taiwan, and orange growers in Brazil. In addition, emergent companies

CONCEPT CHECK

In earlier chapters, we stress the increasing efficiency of international business, noting that political systems have migrated toward democratization (Chapter 3), economic systems toward freer markets (Chapter 4), national markets toward regional trade agreements (Chapter 8), and local capital markets toward global capital markets (Chapter 9). All of these shifts are, in one form or another, conducive to standardization, and here we emphasize that standardization is conducive to efficiently configured value chains.

around the world steadily add more efficient production capacity to global supply and, in an effort to capture market share, they often use price as their means. These new entrants escalate cost pressure in an industry that then compels companies to minimize their costs by standardizing components of their value chain via global integration.

PRESSURES FOR LOCAL RESPONSIVENESS

International companies face several pressures to tailor their operations to local market conditions. Thus far in the text, we have looked at the influence of the external environment, government influence on trade, and regional economic integration. Later chapters profile the implication of issues like product standards, financial regulations, distribution channels, and human resources. At this point, though, we want to emphasize two primary pressures for local responsiveness: *consumer divergence* and *host-government policies*.

Consumer Divergence   Contrary to the globalization of markets thesis, some maintain that fundamental divergences in consumer tastes and preferences across countries will continue to exert strong pressure for local responsiveness. Indeed, the thesis of the globalization of national markets is often painted as an extreme view that is more the exception than an enduring trend.

No matter the moderating functions of money or technologies, differences in consumer tastes and preferences across countries emerge and endure due to several factors, including cultural predisposition, historical legacy, emergent nationalism ("buy local" campaigns), and economic prosperity.[31] Regardless of the cause, the outcome is the same: Consumers prefer goods that are sensitive to their way of life.

Cross-national divergence presses international companies to side with local responsiveness, doing such things as designing and making a product that local customers prefer (large cars in the United States, smaller cars in Europe), adopting marketing practices that speak to their situation (heavy print and media promotion in the United States, greater personal salesmanship in Brazil), and using marketing practices that address their consumption patterns (large package sizes in Australia, smaller sizes in Japan). Adapting to local consumer tastes and preferences can require a company to reconfigure its entire value chain, moving from a global to a national orientation.

In some industries, a globally oriented value chain offers minimal benefits simply because the products are unsuitable for standardization. For example, not much incentive exists for food processors like Nestlé to integrate their value chains across countries because food inputs are generally commodities, production has limited potential for scale economies, widespread distribution faces high costs given the low product value-to-weight ratio, and marketing is best done locally given that tastes, competitors, and retail channels differ at the local level.

Host-Government Policies   There is great variability of political, legal, and economic situations in markets around the world. The sources of many of these variations are the policies, or the lack thereof, mandated by host-country governments. We saw in earlier chapters that widespread movement toward privatization, economic freedom, legal uniformity, and deregulation reduces the variability among countries. Still, exceptions emerge as the international company moves from country to country. These exceptions typically push the firm to determine how to best configure and coordinate its value chain so it provides the necessary degree of local responsiveness without jeopardizing its capability to create value.

A Case in Point   A salient example of this relationship is found in health care. The pharmaceutical industry, for example, has a strong need for integration. The typical pharmaceutical company sells undifferentiated products (aspirin, e.g.) that, in turn, make the efficient scale of production vital to offset the costs of product development. Nonetheless, almost every country has installed a unique administrative system to regulate the development, practice, and delivery of health care.

CONCEPT CHECK

In Chapter 1, we discuss opposition to globalization from critics who argue that it creates high costs, which are, in turn, passed on as economic penalties to local consumers. **Globalization**, we observe, though a powerful force, isn't necessarily an inevitable outcome of current business trends, and in Chapter 3, we reinforce this argument by pointing out that freer markets and democratic systems are not inevitable outcomes of current political trends. Here we add that, for reasons such as these, both consumer needs and government pressures continue to prompt companies to tailor value chains to local conditions.

Consequently, pharmaceutical firms usually manufacture their product in several locations in several countries despite the fact that making pills is most economically done in a few centralized plants. Moreover, cost concerns do not dictate which production locations pharmaceutical companies choose. Rather, many plant sites are chosen to comply with the clinical testing, registration procedures, pricing restrictions, and marketing regulations mandated by a particular government.

In theory, a pharmaceutical company could opt to reject conventional industry practice as Zara did in apparel. Health care, as a heavily regulated industry, constrains this option. At the least, different government authorities approve each product in each country where those companies sell. Also, most governments fund significant shares of the national health-care budget. They can, therefore, insist that any company that would like local support also demonstrate a high level of local responsiveness.

Host governments also have a range of aggressive tools to ensure that an MNE's value chain is locally responsive. These tools can be broad policy directives calling for economic nationalism, explicit threats or acts of trade protectionism to encourage local production, local content rules that require a specified percentage of a product be made locally, or simply national product standards that can be met only by local operations.

WHEN PRESSURES INTERACT

The interaction of global integration and local responsiveness, in terms of how they bear on an MNE, is expressed in the **integration-responsiveness (IR) grid.** Figure 11.6 illustrates this interaction by placing particular industries in their respective quadrants. The IR grid expresses how a company's choice of strategy is a function of the particular relationship the company sees between its idea of value creation and the corresponding pressures for global integration or local responsiveness in its industry.[32]

Essentially, as we see in the next section, one gets a sense of the trade-offs that a company faces by plotting the company's position in terms of the pressures for global integration and those for local responsiveness. So, for example, firms like Huawei or Mittal

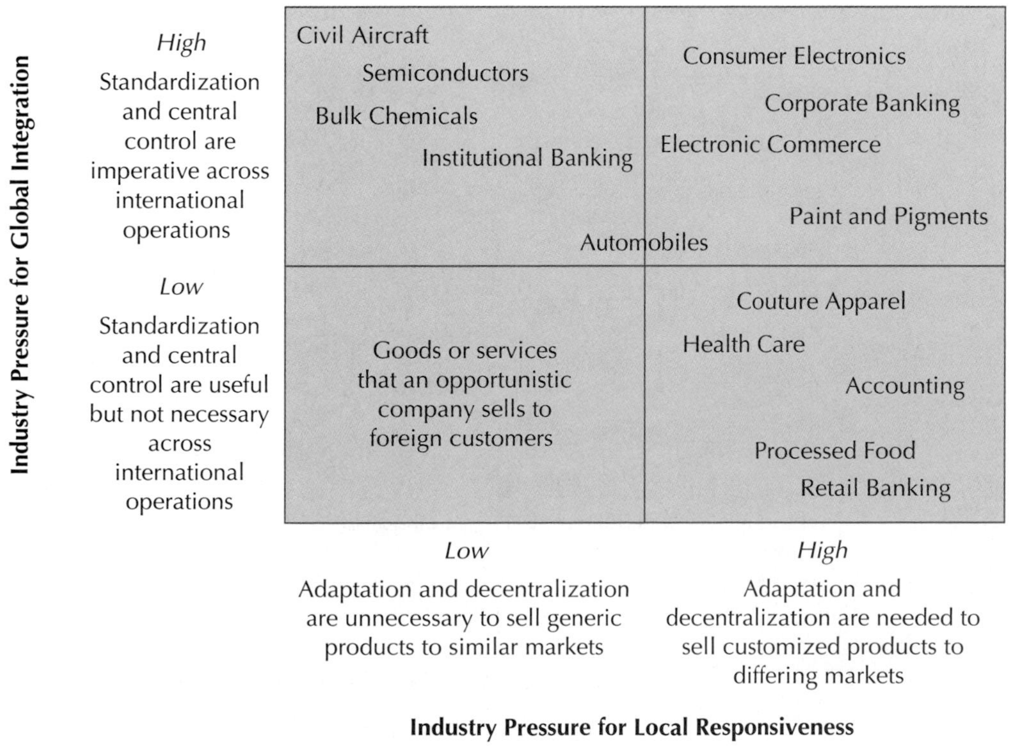

Integration is the process of combining differentiated parts into a standardized whole. Responsiveness is the process of disaggregating a standardized whole into differentiated parts.

Industry Pressure for Global Integration		Low Adaptation and decentralization are unnecessary to sell generic products to similar markets	High Adaptation and decentralization are needed to sell customized products to differing markets
High Standardization and central control are imperative across international operations		Civil Aircraft Semiconductors Bulk Chemicals Institutional Banking	Consumer Electronics Corporate Banking Electronic Commerce Paint and Pigments Automobiles
Low Standardization and central control are useful but not necessary across international operations		Goods or services that an opportunistic company sells to foreign customers	Couture Apparel Health Care Accounting Processed Food Retail Banking

Industry Pressure for Local Responsiveness

FIGURE 11.6 Integration-Responsiveness (IR) Grid (I): Industry Types

Every company's strategy embodies its concept of *value creation.* To what extent do its strategic decisions reflect its response to two sources of industrywide pressure: pressure toward global integration versus pressure toward local responsiveness? The answer to this question almost invariably entails *trade-offs.*

Steel face pressures for standardized products in a global market; there is little need or reward to respond to local market conditions with, respectively, specialized ethernet switches or stainless steel. Others, such as Nestlé, see scant benefits from global integration but high return from responding to the features of particular markets.

Finally, most companies, from Procter & Gamble to Infosys to LVHM, do not have such clarity. Rather, they face high pressures for global integration and local responsiveness. Configuring and coordinating the value chain to deal with this dilemma is an enduring challenge for managers.

Types of Strategy

When defining their strategy, MNEs look to international markets for growth opportunities, cost reductions, and risk diversification within a context of satisfying the competing demands of global integration and local responsiveness.[33] Figure 11.7 identifies conditions that shape the decision of when to use which type of strategy within the context of the integration-responsiveness grid. MNEs use a variety of perspectives to decide how they run their operations, to reach goals and deal with challenges.

Generally, MNEs choose from four basic strategies to guide how they will enter and compete in the international environment: an international strategy, a multidomestic strategy, a global strategy, or a transnational strategy. Each of these strategies differs fundamentally regarding where managers put value activities and how they try to run them. We now define each strategy, identifying its implications for configuring and coordinating a value chain, and discuss its particular benefits and drawbacks.

INTERNATIONAL STRATEGY

Companies adopt an **international strategy** when they aim to leverage their core competencies by expanding opportunistically into foreign markets. International firms include the likes of McDonald's, Kellogg, Google, Haier, Wal-Mart, and Microsoft. The international model relies on local subsidiaries in each country to administer business as instructed by headquarters. Some subsidiaries may have freedom to adapt products to local conditions as well as to set up some light assembly operations or promotion

CONCEPT CHECK

When managers design a **strategy** for a foreign environment, they consider numerous factors, ranging from local culture to global trade theory. The perspectives that managers themselves introduce into the equation can ultimately be characterized as versions of what, in Chapter 1, we explain as **ethnocentrism**, **polycentrism**, or **geocentrism**.

The international strategy leverages a company's core competencies in foreign markets. It allows limited local customization.

FIGURE 11.7 Integration-Responsiveness (IR) Grid (II): Strategy Types

What factors enter into a firm's strategic decisions about dealing with the competing pressures toward integration and localization? Again, it's a matter of *trade-offs*, and decisions usually reflect a choice from among four types of strategy.

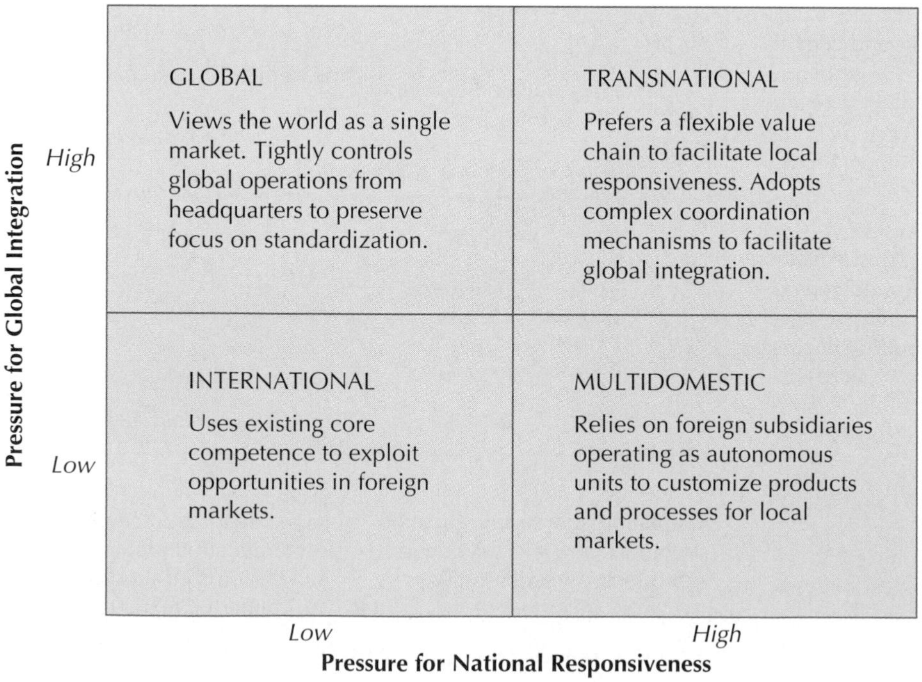

	Pressure for National Responsiveness — Low	Pressure for National Responsiveness — High
Pressure for Global Integration — High	GLOBAL — Views the world as a single market. Tightly controls global operations from headquarters to preserve focus on standardization.	TRANSNATIONAL — Prefers a flexible value chain to facilitate local responsiveness. Adopts complex coordination mechanisms to facilitate global integration.
Pressure for Global Integration — Low	INTERNATIONAL — Uses existing core competence to exploit opportunities in foreign markets.	MULTIDOMESTIC — Relies on foreign subsidiaries operating as autonomous units to customize products and processes for local markets.

programs. Still, ultimate control resides with managers at headquarters who reason they best know the basis and potential extension of the company's core competencies.

International Strategy and the Value Chain Historically, critical elements of the company's value chain, such as research and development or branding, have been centralized at headquarters. Yahoo!, for example, develops the core architecture underlying its Web products in San Jose, California. This site is also home to many of the people who develop its Web functions and online services. However, Google does allow national subsidiaries to customize minor aspects of its Web pages to deal with local differences in language and alphabet. Ultimately, though, headquarters is the source for new products, processes, and ideas for its overseas operations.

Firms that pursue an international strategy try to create value by transferring core competencies and unique products to those foreign markets where rivals are unable to develop, match, or sustain them. The international strategy, therefore, facilitates the transfer of skills, expertise, and products from the parent company to its subsidiaries. Headquarters can translate their expertise in and control over important activities into powerful positions to command foreign operations to follow their lead.

This expertise and control can take place in manufacturing processes or general management skills. The latter, for example, explains the growth of international hotel chains such as Hilton International, Four Seasons, and Sheraton. In summary, an international strategy makes sense if a firm has a core competence that local competitors in other markets lack and if industry conditions do not push the firm to improve its cost controls or local responsiveness. In such circumstances, an international strategy creates moderate operational costs and, often, high profits.

Liability of International Strategy Under an international strategy, however, the central role of headquarters often hinders identifying and responding to local conditions. Headquarters' ethnocentric orientation—a one-way view from the home office to the rest of the world—can lead to missed market opportunities and a realization among foreign operations that international activity is secondary to the home market.

These limitations become costly when other companies emphasize customizing their goods and services to local conditions. Carrefour, for instance, ran into this problem in the United States. Carrefour tried shifting its strategy to deal better with local tastes and preferences, but this eventually proved too costly and the company shut down its U.S. operations.

MULTIDOMESTIC STRATEGY

A *multidomestic company*, sometimes called a *locally responsive company*, follows a strategy that allows each of its foreign-country operations to act fairly independently. The company's subsidiaries in their respective local markets have the authority to design, make, and market products that directly respond to local customers' preferences. Johnson & Johnson is an example of a company that follows a **multidomestic strategy** to great success. Our close-up look at this company in Chapter 15 shows how it differentiates value chain activities to meet local markets and adapts policies to conform to host-government regulation.

> The multidomestic strategy adjusts products, services, and business practices to meet the needs of individual countries and regions.

Multidomestic Strategy and the Value Chain Firms applying a multidomestic strategy design a value chain that gives each country's operations the discretion to respond to its local cultural, legal-political, and economic environments. So, for example, if a government is offering incentives for local manufacturing, then the local unit can build its own plant; if local consumers prefer to deal directly with people in the sales process rather than rely on mass media for information, the local company can build a sales force; if the country has an unfavorable work environment, then the local operation can opt to import products made elsewhere.

Companies applying a multidomestic strategy customize their products, marketing, and service programs to local conditions. These decisions require the multidomestic company to decentralize decision making from headquarters to subsidiary operations so local executives have the authority to manage their responsibilities.

Basically, managers in a multidomestic company hold a polycentric point of view that people who are close to the market (philosophically, culturally, and physically) ought to run the business. Thus, for example, the managers of a backpack factory in Singapore have the right to decide what sort of backpack they want to make—even if the size, shape, and style differ from those made in the United States, Mexico, or Ukraine.

Management that chooses the multidomestic strategy believes in responding to the unique conditions prevailing in different markets.

Benefits of Multidomestic Strategy   A multidomestic strategy makes great sense when the company faces a high need for local responsiveness and low need to reduce costs via global integration. It has other benefits, such as minimizing political risk given the local standing of the company, lower exchange rate risk given the low need to repatriate funds to the home office, greater prestige given its national prominence, higher potential for innovative products from local R&D, and higher growth potential due to entrepreneurial spirit.

For example, Procter & Gamble has followed a multidomestic strategy. The R&D unit at its Japanese subsidiary, responding to the low storage space in the typical Japanese home, invented technology that reduced the thickness of an infant's diaper without any loss of absorbency. This innovation created value for Procter & Gamble in Japan and, eventually, for Procter & Gamble worldwide.

Limitations of Multidomestic Strategy   These benefits do come with costs. The multidomestic strategy leads to duplication of management, design, production, and marketing activities. Each local subsidiary builds value chain operations to meet local demands. Hence the multidomestic strategy is often economically impossible in industries that have intense cost pressures.

Too, decentralizing control of value activities to local managers can create powerful subsidiaries that behave as autonomous units. On any given matter, they may opt not to follow headquarters' policy, instead maintaining that it does not work with their particular situation and/or that it must be adjusted to fit their local market.

Whatever the explanation, the fact that the subsidiary is a virtual stand-alone operation means headquarters must resort to persuasion in lieu of command to effect change. Persuasion can lead to costly struggles. For example, Johnson & Johnson launched Tylenol in 1960 as an over-the-counter pain reliever in the United States. Although it was available to local operating units shortly thereafter, the Japanese unit did not begin selling it until 2000.

GLOBAL STRATEGY

A global strategy champions worldwide consistency and standardization.

The company adopting a **global strategy** chooses to maximize integration. This decision spurs a company to make and market a standardized product, such as razor blades, or service, such as package delivery, for a specific global market segment. The global strategy pushes companies to think in terms of creating products for a world market, manufacturing them on a global scale in a few highly efficient plants, and marketing them through a few focused distribution channels. Thus, companies that adopt the global strategy see the world as one market and assume there are either no differences among countries with regard to consumer tastes and preferences or, if there are, then consumers will sacrifice them if given the opportunity to buy a comparatively higher-quality product for a lower price.

Operationally, MNEs that adopt a global strategy aim to become the low-cost player in their industry. Failing to do so can lead to a weak competitive position against the firm that does. Low-cost leadership entails building global-scale production facilities in a few low-cost locations that create the platforms for efficient operations—whether it is a sneaker factory in Vietnam, an auto-parts maker in China, or a service call center in India. In other words, managers aim to convert the gains of efficient operations into cost reductions that drive profitability.

Global Strategy and the Value Chain The efficiency goals of the global strategy have plain implications for configuring a value chain. R&D, production, and marketing activities are concentrated in the most favorable locations. These locations need not be in the same country; a fully optimized global value chain conceivably will locate each activity in the best possible place. The dispersed activities of the resulting value chain are then coordinated by formal linkages. Making sure the worldwide system works efficiently is the responsibility of executives at the centralized world headquarters who standardize practices and processes. Little if any strategic decision-making authority exists at the local level.

What then of pressures to respond to current or future local preferences? As a rule, the cost sensitivity of a global strategy gives MNEs little latitude to customize their products or systems to local conditions. Customizing a product or process to particular market situations increases costs at each stage in the value chain. Different product designs require different materials, production runs become shorter, marketing programs must be adjusted, new distribution channels must be developed, and various organizational functions must be replicated in each market. Instead, global firms strive to make, market, and service a standardized product worldwide that lets them convert global efficiency into price competitiveness and value creation.

> Firms that choose the global strategy face strong pressures for cost reductions but weak pressure for local responsiveness.

Strengths of Global Strategy Generally, the global strategy is best suited for those industries that put strong pressures on efficient operations and where local responsiveness needs are either nonexistent or can be neutralized by offering a high-quality product for a lower price than the local substitute. Increasingly, these conditions prevail in many industries, both in the manufacturing and service sectors. The wireless industry, for example, endorses global standards that create enormous demand for standardized global products in every country.[34]

Similarly, the credit card industry has specified a range of standards and rules for electronic payment protocols that supports customers using and merchants accepting this form of payment around the world. In both cases, firms act accordingly; in wireless, Nokia and Texas Instruments, and in credit cards, American Express, all pursue a global strategy.

Finally, a global strategy also can drive a onetime transaction that exploits a worldwide distribution network, standardized financial controls, and universal messages. There are limits to the use of a global strategy. Many consumer goods and health-care markets, where demands for local responsiveness remain high, give companies little latitude to standardize operations.

TRANSNATIONAL STRATEGY

The **transnational strategy** is arguably the most direct response to the growing globalization of business. It holds that today's environment of interconnected consumers, industries, and markets requires an MNE to find ways to configure a value chain that exploits location economies, coordinate value activities to leverage core competencies effectively, and ensure that the value chain deals directly with pressures for local responsiveness.

> A transnational strategy simultaneously exploits location economies, leverages core competencies, and pays attention to local responsiveness.

The MNE applying a transnational strategy differentiates capabilities and contributions from country to country, finding ways to learn systematically from its various environments, and then ultimately integrating and diffusing this knowledge throughout its global operations. The transnational concept of strategy, therefore, endorses an integrated framework of technology, financial resources, creative ideas, and people that move it fundamentally beyond the ideas of the international, multidomestic, or global strategy types.

Transnational Strategy and "Global Learning" The first-order conditions of the transnational strategy—combine the market sensitivity of local responsiveness with the competitive efficiency of global integration—integrates characteristics of the multinational and global strategies.

However, the transnational strategy has a unique aspect that theoretically distinguishes it from the other strategy types. Specifically, the transnational strategy champions the cause of interactive "global learning" by which an MNE develops valuable skills in any of its worldwide operations, uses them to improve its core competencies, and then diffuses these innovations throughout its global operation. So, rather than the top-down (headquarters to foreign subsidiary) or bottom-up (foreign subsidiary to headquarters) flow of ideas, the transnational strategy champions a flow from the idea generator to idea adopters, no matter where one or the other happens to be.

A transnational strategy aims to make the relentless renewal, enhancement, and exchange of ideas across borders the basis of value creation.

The global learning capability has many benefits. For example, managers can develop internal capabilities that can respond in a multitude of ways to changing environments, leverage internal resources with external networks of other companies, and integrate subsidiaries without imposing more bureaucracy. Ultimately, these capabilities let an MNE standardize some links of the value chain to maximize efficiency as well as adapt other links to meet pressures for local responsiveness but in a way that does not sacrifice the benefits of one for the other.

Transnational Strategy: A Case in Point   Can a firm effectively pursue a transnational strategy? Some clues can be seen in the case of GE. In the 1980s, growing competitive threats from emergent low-cost competitors in Asia pushed GE to look to global markets to sell products, reasoning that expanding sales volumes would lead to greater scale economies. At the time, Jack Welch declared, "the idea of a company being global is nonsense. Businesses are global, not companies."

In 1987, GE redefined its outlook toward globalization, elevating it to a dominant strategic theme. Beginning in 1981, the performance standard for each business had been to "be either number 1 or 2" in its domestic industry or else face divestment. In 1987, the standard was raised to the business's position in its global industry. Soon thereafter, GE's sense of globalization moved from finding new markets to finding new worldwide sources that could provide higher-quality resources for lower costs.

GE Becomes a "Boundaryless Company"   Around this time, Jack Welch articulated his vision of the boundaryless company, explaining it was an "open, anti-parochial environment, friendly toward the seeking and sharing of new ideas, regardless of their origins." More specifically, Welch explained that the "boundaryless company we envision will remove the barriers among engineering, manufacturing, marketing, sales, and customer service; it will recognize no distinctions between domestic and foreign operations—we'll be as comfortable doing business in Budapest and Seoul as we are in Louisville and Schenectady."

Soon, a score of boundarylessness success stories emerged within GE: increased efficiency in its appliance business; productivity solutions in lighting; transaction effectiveness in GE capital; cost-reduction techniques in aircraft engines; and global account management in plastics. In addition, careers were halted if managers refused to share ideas with others. Welch explained, "We take people who aren't boundaryless out of jobs. If you're turf-oriented, self-centered, don't share with people, and aren't searching for ideas, you don't belong here."

GE Globalizes Its "Intellect"   Soon thereafter, GE moved to phase three of its globalization evolution. Besides emphasizing global markets and global sources, Welch now called on his managers to "globalize the intellect of the company," seeking best practices and compelling ideas from anyone, anywhere, and then diffusing them throughout GE.

By 1999, at the end of Welch's tenure, GE was again named the most respected company in the world by the *Financial Times* and Jack Welch was judged the CEO of the twentieth century. His successor, Jeffrey Immelt, has continued these efforts, explaining that success in international business is "truly about people, not about where the buildings are. You've got to develop people so they are prepared for leadership jobs and then promote them. That's the most effective way to become more global."[35]

GE's performance speaks to principles of the transnational strategy. GE made ideas—constantly renewed, enhanced, and exchanged within the expanding context of globalization—the basis of its value creation. As such, GE shows that the more its managers translated their knowledge, ideas, and innovations into better production methods, designs, and marketing programs anywhere in the world, the more they made profitable decisions. As knowledge flowed from one manager in one part of the value chain to counterparts in far-flung parts of the company, integration happened more efficiently, responsiveness happened more effectively, and new ideas emerged more regularly.

Limitations of Transnational Strategy The transnational type, although appearing to offer many advantages, is difficult to build, poses serious challenges (especially in coordinating value activities), and is prone to shortfalls. For every GE, there are Philipses, Matsushitas, and Acers that struggle to apply a transnational strategy.

Which sorts of firms, then, should aspire to adopt it? Generally, a transnational strategy makes sense when a firm faces high pressures for cost reductions, high pressures for local responsiveness, and where there are opportunities to leverage core competencies extensively throughout the company's global network. In the 1990s, this mandate applied to few companies. Increasingly, competitive conditions and environmental trends spur more companies to reset their value chains to enact a transnational strategy.

LOOKING TO THE FUTURE

What's New in the World of Strategy Types?

The strategy gamut of "international-multidomestic-global-transnational" has prevailed for several years in international business theory. An increasingly provocative issue, given unfolding trends toward greater globalization, is this: *What types of strategies might international companies follow in the future?*

Evolution of the Multinational Corporation

Some see an evolutionary dynamic playing out. In this scenario, the emergent standards of a multinational corporation respond to the cues of accelerating globalization. The person with perhaps the best views regarding this scenario is Sam Palmisano, the CEO of IBM. Reflecting on the evolution of IBM, he contends that the company has passed through three distinct phases on its way to its current status as a global powerhouse.

- First there was the nineteenth-century "international model, whereby the company was headquartered both physically and mentally in its home country; it sold goods, when it was so inclined, through a scattering of overseas sales offices." Although one could consider this "international," IBM was actually more focused on its business dealings in its home country.
- Phase two of the evolution ushered in the classic, multinational firm of the late twentieth century. This model is based on the parent company creating smaller versions of itself in countries around the

world. These smaller companies are run by home country expatriates, so, in a sense, the only thing multinational about them is their location.

- The third phase, the "globally integrated enterprise," begins with the realization that emerging economies are seen as an opportunity. But the fast-growing fledgling companies of this emerging economy represent a threat to established global firms. To continue to thrive, or even survive, global firms must find a way to turn this threat into opportunity.

The changing context of competing worldwide eliminates the "mini-me's" option. Instead, some declare that a company must integrate global operations in such a way that it can shape its strategy, develop its management, and run its operations as a single global entity. Strategically, the company must look to put people, jobs, and investments anywhere in the world "based on the right cost, the right skills and the right business environment. And it integrates those operations horizontally and globally." In this approach, "work flows to the places where it will be done best, that is, most efficiently and to the highest quality."[36]

A Few Concepts for the Future

In contrast, others trumpet a world where a dynamic ecology of locations and firms pushes beyond the historic division of local firms versus global companies to make sense of strategy in international business.[37] This view provides a wide scope of the many different types of companies following many types of strategies. In a sense, these companies become part of a natural

(continued)

ecology of various companies that all react to, and interact with, their different environments.

The diversity of these strategies and companies in this global ecology creates a business world populated by a variety of local firms, regional firms, firms that operate in a few countries or many countries, centralized firms, and networks of firms. Against this backdrop, questions about the co-location of different places with different types of firms mean strategy will emerge from the interplay among firms and places. Ultimately, companies will more or less remain the same, although the context with which they create value will change.

The "Metanational" Company

Still others call for the emergence of a new type of global corporation, the so-called metanational company, which thrives on the process of seeking out uniqueness that it can exploit elsewhere or that complements its own existing operations. More precisely, the metanational company is seen as a "company that builds a new kind of competitive advantage by discovering, accessing, mobilizing, and leveraging knowledge from many locations around the world."[38]

Some believe metanational companies will conquer international markets by developing value chains with three core competencies:

- The ability to prospect for and access untapped pockets of technology and emerging consumer trends from around the world.
- The ability to leverage knowledge scattered throughout its local subsidiaries.
- The ability to mobilize fragmented knowledge to generate innovations that produce, market, and deliver value on a global scale.

Some point to MNEs like Shiseido and PolyGram as emergent metanationals already showcasing the capacity to mobilize scattered knowledge to create global-dominant innovations.

"Micro-Multinationals"

Others argue that the evolutionary frontier for multinational corporations is a matter of size. We have long assumed that multinationals must be big, essentially large colossuses that straddle the globe. And although the number of multinational corporations in the United States continues to grow (currently, there are more than 60,000), their average size is falling. Evidence links this anomaly to the growing rise of so-called micro-multinationals, basically clever small companies that are born global and, hence, operate worldwide from day one.[39]

Unlike their bigger corporate counterparts that expanded internationally by gradually entering new markets, so-called micro-multinationals are global immediately, able to now expand beyond the United States for nations where customers and productive labor are plentiful. Indeed, nearly 40 percent of start-ups in the United States employ engineers, marketers, analysts, and others in jobs created in India and other nations. The proliferation of micro-multinationals suggests they may represent a new form of value creation in international business.

The "Cybercorp"

Finally, there is the idea of the *cybercorp,* a form of company that was beyond imagination a decade ago but plausible today.[40] To this type of MNE, national boundaries are no longer a useful proxy for market segments, operational zones, or location options. The cyberspace created by evolving Internet technologies, not the physical geography of lines on a map, defines the boundaries of the cybercorp.

Strategically, the cybercorp seeks to develop competencies that prepare it to react in real time to changes in its customers, competition, industry, and environment. The cybercorp, therefore, engages perspectives and strategies that bias its value chain toward virtuality to develop the flexibility to link competencies dynamically from ever-changing networks of allies and associates. Some believe the cybercorp, built for speed and able to engage strategies that learn, evolve, and transform as required, will become the new international company.

The next global model to emerge is still more a matter of speculation than stipulation. But no matter what specific type emerges, we expect it to utilize the historic markers of great strategy: superior value creation, superb core competencies, and bright people who can articulate clear visions and practical goals while developing the organizational capability to redefine the play of ideas with real or virtual boundaries. ∎

The Globalization of eBay

On Labor Day 1995, Pierre Omidyar launched eBay—an online trading platform that permits peer-to-peer trading in an auction format.[41] Essentially a Web-based forum, it provides an efficient market for buyers and sellers to connect. That is, eBay helps individuals and businesses buy and sell items in categories including antiques and art, books, business and industrial, cars, CDs & DVDs, clothing and accessories, coins, collectibles, computers and electronics, home furnishings, real estate, sporting goods and memorabilia, stamps, tickets, toys, and travel.

eBay discovered that buyers were seeking used or vintage items that sellers were eager to supply, hoping to make a profit. The way eBay was structured naturally placed it in the position of intermediary; it acted like a sophisticated software program running on a bunch of networked Web servers that left much of the work to sellers and buyers.

Operationally, then, eBay created an efficient distribution system that demanded virtually little supervision. Sellers paid eBay for the opportunity to design, set up, monitor, and supervise their particular auctions while buyers used eBay's software to search for products and place bids. After the auction clock ran out, the seller contacted the winning bidder to negotiate payment and shipping terms. For this matchmaking service, eBay charges between 7 and 18 percent of the closing auction price. In 1999, net revenues topped $225 million. By 2006, revenues grew to $6 billion with net income of $1.1 billion. The company projects revenue near $7.5 billion in 2007.

eBay linked its initial success to its core vision: to support interaction in the eBay community by providing a useful online platform to value-oriented buyers and sellers; to uphold the principles of trust and safety, guaranteeing low fraud losses and high transaction protection to its community; and to focus on market efficiency by delivering state-of-the-art information technology. Depicted as a Venn diagram, eBay saw its competitive advantage residing in the overlapping center zone whereby it could pioneer new communities around the world built on commerce, sustained by trust, and inspired by opportunity.

eBay's value proposition hasn't changed since its inception. Management confesses surprise at how extensible its strategy has been to new products, services, and markets. eBay's users generated a total of 588 million listings in the first quarters of 2007; these listings summed to a gross merchandise value of $14.28 billion. eBay's users totaled more than 100 million and were spread among more than 150 nations; these users included individual buyers and sellers, small businesses, and even large-scale enterprises.

From the buyer who shops on eBay for practical needs or for fun, to the seller who relies on eBay as a primary source of income, eBay has become a part of many users' lives. As such, eBay's platform is a leading general shopping destination on the Internet in virtually every market where it operates. Few dispute eBay's self-characterization that its array of buyer and seller services makes it a driving force of global e-commerce.

The success of eBay as an online trading platform relies on delivering network benefits. A host of companies are developing services to support trading on the eBay platform, such as Square Trade, a dispute-resolution service, and Auctionwatch, an automated item listing service. Adding to its success, more companies are building businesses that extend from eBay's platform. As Meg Whitman, president and CEO, notes, "the thing is, we're not the only source of innovation. We're so well-served by letting others think about how to make this platform even more powerful."

Where gaps remained, eBay quickly found solutions. For example, early on, the single biggest friction point in the buyer-to-seller link was the lack of an efficient way for the buyer to pay the seller. To remedy this, in 2002, eBay acquired PayPal, an online financial service, to enable any individual or business with an e-mail address to send and receive payments online securely, easily, and quickly.

Similarly, eBay believed buyers and sellers would increasingly prefer to speak to each other. So, in late 2005, it acquired Skype, a software protocol that enables free Voice over Internet Protocol (VoIP) calls between Skype users online as well as low-cost connectivity to traditional fixed-line and mobile telephones.

Global Expansion

The success of U.S. operations had, by the turn of the century, inspired eBay to define its mission as providing a global trading platform where practically anyone, anywhere, could trade practically anything at anytime. By 2007, eBay's growing global reach meant its members could rely on local sites that served customers in such countries as Australia, Austria, Belgium, Canada, France, Germany, India, Ireland, Italy, South Korea, Singapore, Spain, Sweden, Switzerland, Taiwan, and the United Kingdom.

Once eBay was firmly established in the United States, management looked to the overseas market as the best opportunity to sustain growth; eBay's international markets had more than twice as many Internet users. In terms of market potential, eBay estimated it had less than 10 percent penetration of the combined annual $30 trillion-plus global merchandise market. International expansion then became the goal.

eBay quickly assembled a program to promote its global strategy: AAA—Acquisition, Activation, and Activity. eBay eventually acquisitioned the leading auction Web sites in 23 countries, mixed the acquisition and activation components in the United Kingdom, Korea, and Hong Kong, and applied all three components in Canada, Germany, and India.

Challenges and Solutions

Skeptics questioned eBay's outlook, deeming its plan of convenient e-commerce worldwide an overwhelming task. It also cited many challenges, among them translation software, the digital divide, cultural attitudes about e-commerce, government regulations, and the pace of international expansion.

Translation Software

Early on, many people zeroed in on the challenge posed by translation software. Developing a global trading community meant that eBay had to let sellers in any country post their auction description in their native language and then rely on software to translate that post into the native language of potential buyers—no matter what language they preferred.

Early editions of translation software struggled to handle the nuances of regional colloquialisms, informal shorthand, and slang—all of which were commonly used to describe items listed on eBay. Although newer software came with memory banks that stored complex sentences to translate them more accurately, many programs simply translated word for word, irrespective of the structural differences between languages.

eBay believed the limitations in translation software were minor setbacks to its globalization strategy. It conceded that translation software was imperfect and admitted that possible nuances, idioms, and secondary meanings created problems. However, translation programs were steadily improving. eBay held steadfast in its belief that the global market was ready for person-to-person auctions, with or without completely accurate translation. Whitman reinforced this stance when she stated, "The great thing about eBay is that this doesn't have to be perfect. This is not diplomatic relations. This is not military secrets. This is trading items between 50 and 100 dollars. Our users have expressed a willingness to work with 'pretty good'—not 'perfect,' but 'pretty good.'"

Steadily, eBay applied increasingly sophisticated software, thereby making it easier to post auctions in more and more foreign markets. Available software let companies cater their Web sites more readily to international markets by automating the translation and localization of content. In eBay's case, that meant that auction pages not only read correctly in local languages but also were worded to conform to local customs.

Moreover, related software upgrades steadily introduced new features such as a vendor-management tool, improved integration with content repositories and formats, better search functionality, and more flexibility in applying security policies, all of which improved the global functionality of eBay's platform.

Government Regulations

Critics noted that government trade regulations would inevitably stymie eBay's global strategy. Many countries outlaw the exportation of native fossils, historical artifacts, plants, and animals. Some countries, such as Cuba, outlaw exportation of any item not sanctioned by the government. In addition, eBay could encounter legal and political hassles if it enabled sellers to export native herbs or medicines, rare currencies, anthropological relics, political memorabilia, or other sensitive goods.

Complicating matters, each country presents unique cultural and legal challenges. For instance, in France it's illegal to exhibit or sell objects with racist overtones. A few years earlier, a French judge ordered Yahoo! to deny Web surfers access to sales of Nazi memorabilia because such items are "an offense to the collective memory of the country."

eBay believed it had a solution. Noting the legal challenge Yahoo! faced in France, eBay stated, "What we are going to do in France is try to help the government by putting up warning signs that say, 'We are a U.S.-based site that does not conform to the rules about Nazi memorabilia.' We're going to bend over backward to work with the French government and French political groups to try to enable a solution that is French. . . . We've taken a 'work really closely, let's be best friends' approach with local governments and political groups."

The Digital Divide

Some say that no matter what eBay trumpets, the world is far from technologically ready for its vision of Web-connected buyers and sellers. Especially ominous is the digital divide—the gap between the haves and have-nots in access to technology. Many countries that eBay is targeting are years, if not decades, away from convenient, affordable Internet access. Rex Bird, CEO of Body Trends, notes, "Guatemala is not going to dig trenches for conventional lines so that villages can be wired to the Internet. It'd be a great project for the Peace Corps to come in and set up a computer with Internet access but it's going to be a very, very slow process."

eBay faces more immediate problems in existing markets. At the end of 2007, India had more than 1 billion people but just over 9 million landline Internet connections. Although many Indians who do not own computers visit cybercafés to browse the Internet, relatively few consumers have credit cards. Many believe China is in a similar predicament.

eBay remains undaunted in finding solutions to enable more people to connect to its sites as well as each other. Chief Financial Officer Rajiv Dutta posits, "Do many of the markets we've entered recently have lower per capita income and lower Internet penetration? Yes, but that will increase. . . . Our management philosophy is to build for the long-term. What's a small portion of the business today may well be a very large percentage in the future."

Cultural Attitudes About E-Commerce

Data suggest that many people, such as those in India, China, and greater Asia, are intrinsically distrustful of e-commerce transactions. For example, a study of cross-cultural comparisons of online information usage, interpretation, and reaction revealed significant differences between a country's culture and uncertainty avoidance. Online participants in high uncertainty-avoidance cultures, such as Japan, exhibit drastic behavioral changes when faced with limited information within an ambiguous decision context compared to those consumers in the same situation in Germany and the United States.

The American origins of eBay pose problems of their own. Nicolas Dufourcq, director of multimedia at France Telecom, said, "Sometimes when you are on an American portal, you feel imprisoned in a family that's clearly not yours." A European user also added that the "global scale of the site appears an arrogant claim to Europeans . . . because of its global approach, the structure of the site is like a maze. Every time a change is made, the site becomes more complex and less self-explanatory. Any near-monopoly—and eBay has become one because of the number of visitors to its site—will eventually be shown the exit by innovative new entries to the market that cater more to local customers."

Because of these differences in cultural attitudes, eBay ceased operations in Japan in early 2002. At the time, Yahoo! Japan held 95 percent of the $2 billion online-auction market, a feat many linked to their partnership with the local company Softbank. Officially, eBay stated that it found Japanese consumers more interested in new goods rather than used goods or collectibles. Similar events later unfolded in China. In late 2006, eBay announced plans to shut down its main Web site in China and enter into a joint venture with a Chinese company.

Pace of International Expansion

Finally, some suggest eBay's ambition spurred a risky rush to globalize. Difficulties for each acquisition began to arise. Increasingly, eBay had to pay steep premiums to acquire foreign operations. Some analysts doubt that future results will justify the high acquisition costs. eBay believes otherwise, noting the early law of Internet strategy: "Get Big Fast." They predict that by helping transform developing nations into virtual marketplaces with buyers in place eager to snatch up native handicrafts, they will be infusing remote villages with cash that will improve locals' standard of living. Whitman enthused,

> It's fascinating. There is a real frontier here that would truly make global trading a reality. You think about the third world, villagers in Guatemala and Africa who have handicrafts to sell, who could list in their currency and their language and sell to the industrialized world. As that seller community makes more money for their town or village, they then have more purchasing power to buy more products and services from the more developed world. . . . Certainly it has the power to transform countries and cities and villages and empower people to make a living in ways they could not before . . . eBay is creating new trade on a global basis that the world has never seen—that's what gets us up in the morning.

Some remain skeptical that eBay can transform the international business marketplace in ways that will create legions of exporters and importers, help impoverished nations, balance the world's supply and demand, and significantly improve the efficiency of the global market. In the back of everyone's mind, though, are the staggering potential of global e-commerce and the stunning performance of eBay's global strategy thus far. Steven Weinstein, Pacific Crest e-commerce analyst, summed it up when he said, "A total transformation may be slightly fanciful. But, then again, look at what eBay did to small business. It certainly transformed that."

No matter what the critics say, Meg Whitman remains undeterred: "The fun thing about eBay is that we're pioneering a whole new marketplace. . . . It's going to be tremendous." ∎

QUESTIONS

1. What is eBay's core competency? How does it relate to its chosen strategy?
2. Explain how eBay has decided to configure and coordinate its value chain.
3. Would you characterize eBay's value chain as virtual or real? Why?
4. Consider again your description of eBay's strategy. Is it different from what it was 10 years ago? Why? How might it look in 10 years?
5. What are the implications to the challenges identified in the case regarding eBay's strategy—today and in the future?

SUMMARY

- Managers, as agents of their firms, devise strategies to engage international markets in ways that sustain the company's growth and boost its profitability.

- Strategy is defined as the efforts of managers to build and strengthen the company's competitive position within its industry to create superior value.

- Value is the measure of a firm's ability to sell what it makes for more than the cost it incurred to make it.

- Firm performance is influenced by both the structure of the company's industry and the insight of managers' strategic decision making. Estimates vary on the degree of influence for both factors. Managers need to be familiar with industry- and firm-level conditions in making strategy.

- Managers typically anchor analysis of industry structure by modeling the strength and importance of the so-called five fundamental forces.

- Firms create value either through a low-cost leadership strategy or a differentiation strategy.

- Interpreting the firm within the context of the value chain provides a strong tool to improve the accuracy of strategic analyses and decisions.

- The value chain lets managers deconstruct the general idea of "create value" into a series of discrete activities.

- The value chain is shaped by how managers opt to configure and then coordinate discrete value activities.

- Firms pay close attention to location economics when configuring their value chain.

- Competitive rivalry presses companies to coordinate value chain activities so that they leverage core competencies.

- Companies that operate internationally face the asymmetric pressures of global integration versus local responsiveness.

- Change, whether in managers, competencies, industries, or environments, often spurs companies to rethink and reset their value activities.

- The firm entering and competing in foreign markets can adopt either an international, multidomestic, global, or transnational strategy.

- Firms often use a mix of these four types due to company, industry, and environmental situations.

KEY TERMS

commodity (p. 429)
core competency (p. 423)
economies of scale (p. 421)
experience curve (p. 425)
five-forces model (p. 412)
global integration (p. 428)
global strategy (p. 434)

industry organization (IO) paradigm (p. 411)
industry structure (p. 412)
integration-responsiveness (IR) grid (p. 431)
international strategy (p. 432)
local responsiveness (p. 428)

location economies (p. 417)
multidomestic strategy (p. 433)
perfect competition (p. 411)
strategy (p. 415)
transnational strategy (p. 435)
value (p. 415)
value chain (p. 416)

ENDNOTES

1 *Sources include the following:* Frank DuBois, "Globalization Risks and Information Management," *Journal of Global Information Management* (April–June 2004): 3; A. R. Bonnin, "The Fashion Industry in Galicia: Understanding the 'Zara' Phenomenon," *European Planning Studies* 10 (2002): 519; "The Stars of Europe— Armancio Ortega, Chairman, Inditex," *Business Week,* June 11, 2001; "Rapid Response Retail," *Marketing,* April 3, 2003: 20; Richard Heller, "Galician Beauty," *Forbes,* May 28, 2001: 98; Patrick Byrne, "Closing the Gap Between Strategy and Results," *Logistics Management* (March 2004); Rachel Tiplady, "Zara: Taking the Lead in Fast-Fashion," *Business Week,* June 4. 2006; "Shining Examples," *The Economist,* June 15, 2006.

2 In general, the higher the risk, the higher the return. Therefore, riskier projects and investments must be evaluated differently from their riskless counterparts. By discounting risky cash flows against less risky cash flows, risk-adjusted rates account for changes in the profile of the investment.

3 Jens Boyd, "Intra-Industry Structure and Performance: Strategic Groups and Strategic Blocks in the Worldwide Airline Industry," *European Management Review* 1 (2004): 132–45. Schmalensee (1985) tested for evidence of business-specific differences through a single, exogenous measure of market share. His analysis also included corporate-parent effects, which he called "firm effects." Industry effects accounted for about 20 percent of variance,

market-share effects accounted for less than 1 percent of variance, and corporate-parent effects did not significantly contribute to variance. Managerial influences were not important compared to differences in industry structure. R. Schmalensee, "Do Markets Differ Much?" *American Economic Review* (1985): 341–51.

4 See B. Wernerfelt, "A Resource-Based View of the Firm," *Strategic Management Journal* 5 (1984): 171–80. In addition, Rumelt (1991) found that corporate-parent effects contributed to the variance in firm performance (Richard Rumelt, "How Much Does Industry Matter?" *Strategic Management Journal* 6 (1985): 167–86). McGahan and Porter (2002) found similar evidence of corporate-parent effects: see "What Do We Know About Variance in Accounting Profitability?" *Management Science* 48 (2002): 834–51.

5 See Jenkins Wyn, "Competing in Times of Evolution and Revolution: An Essay on Long-Term Firm Survival," *Management Decisions,* January 1, 2005: 26; Belen Villalonga, "Intangible Resources, Tobin's Q, and Sustainability of Performance Differences," *Journal of Economic Behavior & Organization* 54 (June 2004): 205. Determining whether a money manager outperforms a market index relies on separating the returns available from market movements (beta in the jargon) and managerial skill (alpha). Like great product managers, great money managers find innovative ways to earn in excess of what would be predicted by an equilibrium model like the *capital asset pricing model* (CAPM). More specifically, we can compare the performance of investment managers by allowing for portfolio risk with the so-called Jensen index, also called Alpha. This measure uses the CAPM as its basis for determining whether or not a money manager outperformed a market index. The sum of the outperformance is known as alpha.

6 Michael Porter, *Competitive Advantage* (New York: Free Press, 1985).

7 The threat of substitute comes from products outside the bounds of a particular industry. For example, the price of glass bottles, steel cans, and plastic containers influences the price of aluminum beverage cans. These substitute types of containers are not direct rivals to can makers in the aluminum can industry. Still, they influence the conduct of the aluminum can industry.

8 "Special Report: The China Price," *Business Week,* December 6, 2004.

9 Michael E. Porter, "What Is Strategy?" *Harvard Business Review* (November–December 1996): 61–79.

10 Managers may make decisions that they strongly reason support the firm's strategy but, in actuality, more often do not. Challenges emerge because often few managers understand the full demands of the company's strategy and its implications for international operations. More worrisome, managers are far more likely to make the wrong than right decision. See Dan Lovallo and Daniel Kahneman, "Delusions of Success: How Optimism Undermines Executives' Decisions," *Harvard Business Review* (July 2003): 56.

11 The former follows from measuring the total revenues collected by buyers' payments for business output. The latter follows from summing the total cost the firm incurs to complete the activities that make up its value chain. Added value is created whenever the buyer's contribution exceeds the total cost.

12 Janet C. Lowe, *Welch: An American Icon* (New York: Wiley and Sons, 2002).

13 See Arindam Bhattacharya et al., "Capturing Global Advantage: How Leading Industrial Companies Are Transforming Their Industries by Sourcing and Selling in China, India, and Other Low-Cost Countries," *Boston Consulting Group Publications,* April 9, 2004, esp. Exhibit 7.

14 Paul Krugman, "Divided Over Trade," *New York Times,* May 14, 2007.

15 George Norman and Lynne Pepall, "Knowledge Spillovers, Mergers and Public Policy in Economic Clusters," *Review of Industrial Organization* 25 (September 2004): 155–75.

16 "Offshoring has created a truly global operating model for financial services, unleashing a new and potent competitive dynamic that is changing the rules of the game for the entire industry. . . . There has never been an economic discontinuity of this magnitude in the history of the world," said Bain's Mark Gottfredson. "These powerful forces are allowing companies to rethink their sourcing strategies across the entire value chain." Financial firms are expanding into other areas like insurance claims processing, mortgage applications, equity research, diligence, valuation, and accounting. Deloitte forecasts that by 2010, the 100 largest global financial institutions will move $400 billion of their work offshore for $150 billion in annual savings. (Quotes reported in "Financial Firms Hasten Their Move to Outsourcing," *New York Times,* August 18, 2004.)

17 "A Grim Picture," *The Economist,* November 2, 2006.

18 Ray Kurzweil, "The Law of Accelerating Returns," at www.kurzweilai.net/articles/art0134.html?printable=1 (accessed June 18, 2007).

19 Soumitra Dutta and Simon Caulki, "The World's Top Innovators," *The World Business/INSEAD Global Innovation Index* 2007, at www.worldbusinesslive.com/article/625441/the-worlds-top-innovators (accessed June 18, 2007).

20 Dutta and Caulki, "The World's Top Innovators."

21 *Synergy* is defined as the combination of parts of a business such that the sum is worth more than the individual parts. It is often expressed in the equation 2 + 2 = 5, with the additional unit of value the result of synergy. Research reports a relationship between a firm's performance and managers' sophistication in diffusing core competencies throughout the value chain. See David Collis and Cynthia Montgomery, "Competing on Resources: Strategy in the 1990s," *Harvard Business Review* (July–August 1995): 118–28.

22 For instance, with a 20 percent cost reduction and an initial cost of $100 per unit, the second unit produced will cost $80, the fourth $64, and so on. In this example, the average cost per unit goes from $100 to $90 to $81.33, and so on.

23 "Top 100 Global Brands Scoreboard," *Business Week,* at http://bwnt.businessweek.com/brand/2005/ and http://bwnt.businessweek.com/brand/2006 (accessed May 19, 2007).

24 James Brooke and Saul Hansel, "Samsung Is Now What Sony Once Was," *New York Times,* March 9, 2004.

25 Dan Lovallo and Daniel Kahneman, "Delusions of Success: How Optimism Undermines Executives' Decisions," *Harvard Business Review* (July 2003): 56.

26 N. Girvan, "Transnational Corporations and Non-Fuel Primary Commodities in Developing Countries," *World Development* 15 (1987): 713–40.

27 Raphael Kaplinsky and Mike Morris, "A Handbook for Value Chain Research," at www.seepnetwork.org/files/2303_file_Handbook_for_Value_Chain_Research.pdf.

28 Richard T. Pascale, "Surfing the Edge of Chaos," *Sloan Management Review* (Spring 1999): 83; Eric Beinhocker, "Strategy at the Edge of Chaos," *McKinsey Quarterly* 1 (1997): 25; Mary J. Cronin, *Unchained Value: The New Logic of Digital Business* (Harvard Business School Press, 2001).

29 See Andreas Hinterhuber, "Value Chain Orchestration in Action and the Case of the Global Agrochemical Industry," *Long Range Planning* 35 (2002): 615; G. D. Bhatt and A. F. Emdad, "An Analysis of the Virtual Value Chain in Electronic Commerce," *Logistics*

Information Management, January 17, 2001: 78; S. Winter, John McIntosh, and David May, "Survival in the Korean Furniture Industry: Value-Chain Networking," *Journal of Managerial Issues* 15 (2003): 450.

30 Theodore Levitt, "The Globalization of Markets," *Harvard Business Review* 61 (1983): 92–102.

31 Regarding cultural predisposition, Japanese doctors disfavor the American-style, high-pressure sales force. Pharmaceutical sales representatives, therefore, adapt their marketing practices in that country. Regarding historical legacy, people drive on the left side of the road in England, thereby creating demand for right-hand-drive cars, whereas people in Italy drive on the right side of the road, thereby creating demand for left-hand-drive cars. Similarly, consumer electrical systems are based on 110 volts in the United States, whereas many European countries use a 240-volt standard.

32 C. Prahalad and Y. Doz, *The Multinational Mission: Balancing Local Demands and Global Vision* (New York: Free Press, 1987).

33 The term *multinational corporation* (MNC) is also commonly used in the international business arena and often is a synonym for MNE. We prefer the *MNE* designation because there are many internationally involved companies, such as accounting partnerships, that are not organized as corporations.

34 "A World of Connections," *The Economist,* April 26, 2007.

35 Direct quotes from the following: Jack Welch and John A. Byrne, *Jack: Straight from the Gut* (New York: Warner Business Books, 2001); Chris Bartlett and Meg Wozny, "GE's Two-Decade Transformation: Jack Welch's Leadership," *Harvard Business School Case* 399150 (1999); Lowe, *Welch: An American Icon.*

36 "Hungry Tiger, Dancing Elephant: How India Is Changing IBM's World," *The Economist,* April 4, 2007.

37 Joan Ricart, Michael J. Enright, Pankaj Ghemawat, Stuart L. Hart, and Tarun Khanna, "New Frontiers in International Strategy," *Journal of International Business Studies* 35 (May 2004): 175.

38 Yves Doz, Jose Santos, and Peter Williamson, *Global to Metanational: How Companies Win in the Knowledge Economy* (Cambridge, MA: Harvard Business School Press, 2001).

39 Michael V. Copeland, How Startups Go Global, *Business* 2.0, July 28, 2006; Jim Hopkins, "The Rise of the Micro-Multinationals," *USA Today,* February 11, 2005.

40 Marc Singer, "Beyond the Unbundled Corporation," *The McKinsey Quarterly* (Summer 2001): 4; Remo Hacki and Julian Lighton, "The Future of the Networked Company," *The McKinsey Quarterly* (Summer 2001): 26; James Martin, "Only the Cyber-Fit Will Survive," *Datamation* (November 1996): 60.

41 *Sources include the following:* eBay, at ebay.com/corporatehome and ebay.com/investosrelations; Rachel Konrad, "eBay's Whitman Touts International Plans," *CNET News.com,* August 15, 2000; Konrad, "CEO Whitman Looks Overseas, Ponders Peer-to-Peer," *CNET News.com,* August 17, 2000; "Global Reach? eBay Isn't There Yet," *Business Week,* April 9, 2001: 8; "Q&A with eBay's Meg Whitman," *Business Week,* March 24, 2003; Rimin Dutt, "eBay Picks Up Top Indian Trading Site for $50M," *Industrial Business Journal,* July 15, 2004; Tony Kontzer, "Software Helps eBay's Global Expansion Efforts," *InformationWeek,* December 1, 2003; Bob Tedeschi, "eBay Lends Hand to Drop-Off Stores," *New York Times: E-Commerce Report,* August 30, 2004; Konrad, "International Sales Boost eBay," *Information Week,* July 21, 2004; "How Yahoo! Japan Beat eBay at Its Own Game," *Business Week,* June 4, 2001: 58; Katie Hafner and Brad Stone, "eBay Is Expected to Close Its Auction Site in China," *New York Times,* December 19, 2006; Brad Stone, "Stirring Up the Cubicles at eBay," *New York Times,* February 21, 2007.

12

Country Evaluation and Selection

Objectives

- To grasp company strategies for sequencing the penetration of countries

- To see how scanning techniques can help managers both limit geographic alternatives and consider otherwise overlooked areas

- To discern the major opportunity and risk variables a company should consider when deciding whether and where to expand abroad

- To know the methods and problems when collecting and comparing information internationally

- To understand some simplifying tools for helping decide where to operate

- To consider how companies allocate emphasis among the countries where they operate

- To comprehend why location decisions do not necessarily compare different countries' possibilities

CASE: Carrefour: Finding Retail Space in All the Right Places

Carrefour, which opened its first store in 1960, is now the largest retailer in Europe and Latin America and the second largest worldwide.[1] By 2007, it had more than 12,500 stores and 456,000 employees. Its stores depend on food for about 60 percent of their sales and on a wide variety of nonfood items for the rest. In 2006, Carrefour derived 52 percent of its sales and 47 percent of its profits outside of France, its home country. The Institute of Grocery Distribution ranks Carrefour as the world's most global retailer, based on foreign sales, number of countries with operations, and ratio of foreign sales to total sales. It operates in about twice the number of countries as the world's largest retailer, Wal-Mart.

Carrefour plans to continue growing; thus management must decide which countries to emphasize in its expansion and where in each country to locate the new stores. Concomitantly, it must decide what to do with underperforming stores and countries. It sells stores and moves from countries that offer less potential profits than if capital is placed elsewhere. For instance, in 2006, it sold its operations in South Korea and Slovakia while expanding heavily in Poland. It also announced plans in 2007 to enter the Indian and Russian markets.

Carrefour sells in five types of stores: hypermarkets, supermarkets, hard discount stores, cash-and-carry stores, and convenience stores. Hypermarkets account for the largest portion of Carrefour's sales and retail space and are in more countries than Carrefour's other types of retail operations. Carrefour invented and opened the first hypermarket, an enormous commercial establishment that combines a department store and a supermarket. Whereas a typical supermarket might have 40,000 square feet, a hypermarket might have 330,000. A vice president of the magazine *Progressive Grocer* explained the size difference: "A grocery store is like a family farm, a supermarket is like a big corporate farm, and a hypermarket is like the whole state of Iowa."

As a rule of thumb, a hypermarket requires 500,000 households within a 20-minute drive to derive sufficient business. Carrefour's supermarkets carry less variety than its hypermarkets, and its hard discount stores and cash-and-carry stores carry even less. The cash-and-carry stores cater strictly to the trade, such as restaurant owners and hoteliers. Its convenience stores (more than 95 percent are franchise operations) are still smaller and carry fewer items. One of Carrefour's key contributions to franchisees is selecting locations for their stores.

Carrefour's French hypermarket operation was a success from the beginning, and by 2006, Carrefour operated 218 hypermarkets in France. The timing for introducing the hypermarket concept was perfect. Supermarket operations were not yet well developed in France, and French consumers generally shopped for food items in different outlets—for example, bread, meat, fish, cheese, and fresh vegetables in different specialty stores or open markets. Few retailers had convenient or free parking, so customers had to shop long hours and make frequent trips to stores.

However, Carrefour began when more French families had cars, more had refrigerators large enough to store a week's supply of fresh products, and more had high disposable incomes that they could spend on nonfood items. Further, more women were working, and they wanted one-stop shopping. Thus French consumers flocked to Carrefour's suburban hypermarkets, which offered free parking and discounted prices on a very wide selection of merchandise.

However, Carrefour and other hypermarket operators have faced obstacles to French expansion. Government authorities at times have restricted new hypermarket permits to safeguard town centers, protect small businesses, and prevent visual despoliation of the countryside. As a consequence, Carrefour decided to expand internationally. Map 12.1 shows the countries in which Carrefour operates wholly owned stores and those in which it relies on partnerships or franchising. Figure 12.1 provides a chronology of Carrefour's expansion into foreign markets via company-owned outlets. Its first foreign entry, with a partnership, was to Belgium, and its first wholly owned foreign store was in Spain. Both are neighboring countries, and both entries were with hypermarkets.

Carrefour managed these ventures without difficulty because its French suppliers initially provided much of the stores' stock and because its managers from France could travel easily to oversee the operations. When Carrefour entered Belgium and Spain, the consumers there were going through lifestyle changes similar to those that helped assure the company's earlier success in France. Since then, one of the principal factors guiding Carrefour's international expansion has been countries' economic evolution. Its former CEO, Daniel Bernard, said, "We can start with a developing country at the bottom of the economic curve and grow within the country to the top of the curve."

Nevertheless, Carrefour has not always followed this location strategy, and the deviation has influenced its failure

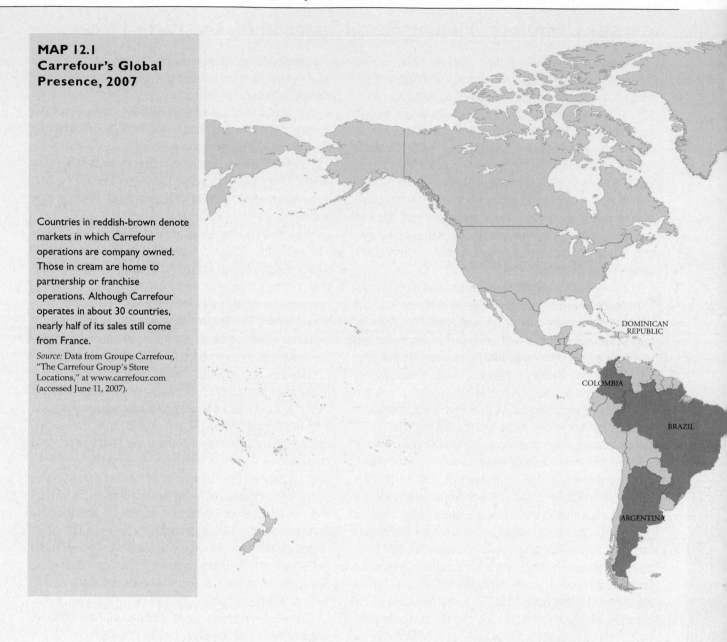

**MAP 12.1
Carrefour's Global
Presence, 2007**

Countries in reddish-brown denote markets in which Carrefour operations are company owned. Those in cream are home to partnership or franchise operations. Although Carrefour operates in about 30 countries, nearly half of its sales still come from France.

Source: Data from Groupe Carrefour, "The Carrefour Group's Store Locations," at www.carrefour.com (accessed June 11, 2007).

FIGURE 12.1   Where and When Carrefour Entered Foreign Markets

Data refer to company-owned outlets and do not include partnerships and franchises. Expansion into new markets has accelerated significantly since 1989, but note, too, that during the same period, Carrefour has also entered and exited no fewer than nine overseas markets, including the United Kingdom, the United States, Japan, and China.

Source: Based on data from Groupe Carrefour, "The Carrefour Group's Store Locations," at www.carrefour.com (accessed June 11, 2007).

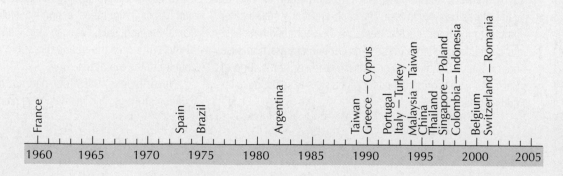

CARREFOUR'S GLOBAL
PRESENCE, 2007

■ Company-Owned Operations

□ Partnership and Franchising
Operations

in some markets. It expanded into the United States and the United Kingdom in the mid-1980s after both of these countries had gone through the economic transitions that helped assure success in other locales and after other distributors had satisfied the changed consumer needs. Carrefour later pulled out of both markets.

Carrefour also entered the Mexican, Japanese, Korean, and Chilean markets late and had little success before selling the operations there. Bernard said later, "To go global, you need to be early enough. Generally, in new countries you need to be the first in for the first win. When you arrive as number three or four, it is too late."

However, some additional factors caused problems for Carrefour in markets it has abandoned. In the United States distributors have had scant success with hypermarkets. U.S. customers have simply not wanted to spend the time it takes to shop in a hypermarket. For example, Carrefour's Philadelphia store had 61 checkout counters, and customers had to pass all of them before they even reached the first aisle. In the United Kingdom, Carrefour did well on sales of food items but not on durables; consumers preferred to shop for these in city centers where they could compare the products offered by different distributors.

In Mexico, Carrefour met an established Wal-Mart, which could integrate buying and distribution with its successful U.S. operations. In Japan, consumers were disappointed not to find a French shopping experience. In both Hong Kong and Chile, Carrefour was unable to build enough stores to gain the economy of distribution it needed to compete with existing retailers.

Another factor influencing Carrefour's choice of country has been the ability to find a viable partner familiar with local operating needs until its own management learned local operations sufficiently. Carrefour teamed with the Maus group in Switzerland, President Enterprise in Taiwan, the Sabanci group in Turkey, and Harbor Power Equipment in China.

However, Wal-Mart's entry into Mexico well before Carrefour enabled it to team with the best local partner, Cifra. A few years later, Carrefour partnered with Gigante, but the latter lacked sufficient resources to expand as rapidly as Carrefour desired, so Carrefour ultimately bought Gigante's interest in the joint operation and later sold the whole operation.

In Japan, Carrefour established operations without a partner. In essence, management felt no need for a partner because its traditional operating costs were so much lower than those of Carrefour's Japanese rivals. At the time, a retail analyst prophetically said, "Their [Carrefour's] chances of success are zero." Carrefour lasted only four years before selling out.

Why would another company want to partner with Carrefour? Aside from financial resources, Carrefour brings to a partnership expertise on store layout, clout in dealing with global suppliers (for example, it runs a global sales campaign, "Most Awaited Month," in which the largest manufacturers of global consumer goods provide its stores worldwide with lower prices for a one-month sale), direct e-mail links with suppliers that substantially reduce inventories and the number of buyers, and the ability to export unique bargain items from one country to another.

Carrefour also considers whether a national or regional location can justify sufficient additional store expansion to gain economies of scale in buying and distribution. To help gain these economies, Carrefour and some of its competitors have recently been expanding via acquisition. However, some analysts have felt that Carrefour may be expanding retail operations to too many countries and will not be able to build sufficient presence in each to gain necessary economies of scale. For example, Tesco, a British retailer, is expanding to fewer countries but is building a large presence in each one. In the six countries where both Tesco and Carrefour operate, Tesco is bigger in four of them.

In addition, in 2005, Carrefour replaced its CEO, largely because too little attention was being paid to its biggest market, France. Its new CEO announced that the major short-term emphasis would be to protect positions in France and Spain while growing in China.

Carrefour depends primarily on locally produced goods, using manufacturers' trademarks or no trademarks at all. This strategy contrasts with such retailers as Tesco and Marks & Spencer, another British retailer, which depend heavily on own-label products. Thus consumers can easily compare prices of most Carrefour products with those of competitors because few of its products have unique labels.

Nevertheless, Carrefour has recently been pushing global purchasing. For example, when stores in one country find an exceptional supplier, the management passes on the information to Carrefour's merchandising group in Brussels, which then seeks markets within Carrefour stores in other countries. The Malaysian operation, for example, found a good local supplier of disposable gloves, and Carrefour now sells them in its stores worldwide.

Mass retailers sell most of their consumer goods in high-income countries and much less in developing countries. For example, chain stores probably account for less than 3 percent of retail sales in China and India. Nevertheless, Carrefour moved early into the Chinese market and is the undisputed leader there. China now has a middle class that totals at least 100 million. A market research study indicated that the top factors influencing where these people shop are convenience, spaciousness and comfort of stores, and selection. Price ranks only sixth.

However, in spite of the success in many markets, analysts feel that Carrefour will never become the world's largest retailer without a significant presence in the United States and the United Kingdom. Its only presence in either is a minority interest in Costco in the United States.

Introduction

The old adage that "location, location, and location" are the three most important factors for business success rings quite true for international business. Countries offer different opportunities for companies to create value from increasing sales or acquiring competitively useful assets. They also differ in the risk that companies face. Furthermore, because all companies have limited resources, they must be careful in making the following decisions:

1. In which countries to locate sales, production, and administrative and auxiliary services
2. The sequence for entering different countries
3. The amount of resources and efforts to allocate to each country where they operate

Committing human, technical, and financial resources to one locale may mean forgoing or delaying projects in other areas. So managers must be choosy. In our opening case, for instance, we saw that Carrefour, although the world's second largest retailer, has taken over 40 years to move into roughly only 15 percent of the world's countries, and its presence in some of those countries is still quite small. So to become a significant player in more than a few countries, managers usually need to take time. Even after companies are well established in most countries, they still need to allocate resources by emphasizing some countries more than others. Thus picking the right locations affects companies' ability to gain and sustain competitive advantage.[2]

Figure 12.2 highlights the importance of location decisions in companies' international business strategy. By examining the external environment and comparing this

> Companies lack resources to take advantage of all international opportunities.

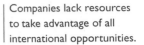

> Companies need to
> - Determine the order of country entry.
> - Set the rates of resource allocation among countries.

FIGURE 12.2   Location Decisions Affecting International Operations

In choosing locations for international operations, a company should begin by analyzing three factors: its *objectives*, its *competencies*, and its comparative *environmental fit* with conditions in the countries under consideration.

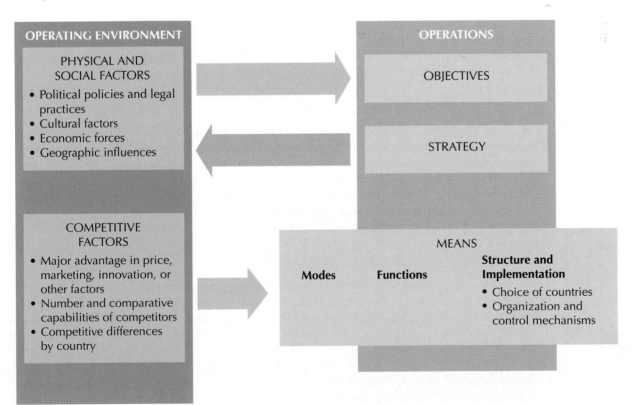

environment with the company's objectives and capabilities, managers might ask, "Where can we best leverage our existing competencies?" and "Where can we go to best sustain, improve, or extend our competencies?"

To answer those questions, managers need to answer two more: "Which markets should we serve?" and "Where should we place production (including administration and auxiliary functions) to serve those markets?" On the one hand, the answers to these questions can be one and the same, particularly if transport costs or government regulations mean that companies must produce in the countries where they sell. Many service industries, such as hotels, construction, and retailing (such as Carrefour), must locate facilities near their foreign customers.

On the other hand, companies' large-scale production technology may favor producing in only a few countries and exporting to others, such as occurs for companies in the capital-intensive automobile and steel industries. Finally, companies' location decisions may be more complex, such as using multiple countries for sourcing raw materials and components that go into one finished product. Or they may divide operating functions, such as having headquarters in the United States, a call center for handling service in India, and an R&D facility in Switzerland.

Flexibility in locations is important because country and competitive conditions change. Thus a company needs to respond to new opportunities and withdraw from less profitable ones. There is no one-size-fits-all theory for picking operating locations because product lines, competitive positions, resources, and strategies make each company unique.

To further complicate matters, companies must make assumptions about the uncertain future, such as political conditions in the foreign environment, costs and prices, competitors' reactions, and technology. Nevertheless, our forthcoming discussion relies on the experiences and considerations of a large number of companies that have expanded internationally. Figure 12.3 shows the major steps international business managers must take in making these decisions. The following discussion examines these steps in depth.

> In choosing geographic sites, a company must decide
>
> • Where to sell.
>
> • Where to produce.

How Does Scanning Work?

Managers use scanning techniques to compare countries on broad indicators of opportunities and risks. Scanning is like seeding widely and then weeding out—it is useful insofar as a company might otherwise consider too few or too many possibilities.

> Without scanning, a company may
>
> • Overlook opportunities and risks.
>
> • Examine too many or too few possibilities.

MANAGING THE ALTERNATIVES

There are approximately 200 countries, so many that managers might easily overlook some good opportunities, zeroing in instead on those that first come to mind. The former vice chairman of DaimlerChrysler summed up this problem by saying, "The chief executive who gets asked repeatedly by the press and Wall Street analysts the same question—'Why are you so slow on your China strategy?'—quickly gets the idea he's missing something and orders a China strategy. These 'forced' actions, taken because of 'peer pressure,' almost always result in disaster."[3]

SCANNING VERSUS DETAILED ANALYSIS

Furthermore, managers may lump certain countries together—such as Latin American countries—and reject all of them without examining individual ones sufficiently. For instance, they might not consider Costa Rica because they think "Latin America is too risky" based on what they've read recently about, say, Bolivia or Venezuela. (As we'll see in our chapter-ending case, South Africa came under such secondhand scrutiny when, with the end of white-minority rule in 1994, observers predicted the advent of political instability and an antibusiness environment.) Yet a detailed analysis of 200 countries would be overly expensive and time consuming.

Case Review Note

FIGURE 12.3   The Location-Decision Process

Location, location, location: Committing resources to an overseas location may entail a risky trade-off—say, delaying or abandoning projects elswhere. The decision-making process is essentially twofold: examining the external environments of proposed locations and comparing each of them with the company's objectives and capabilities.

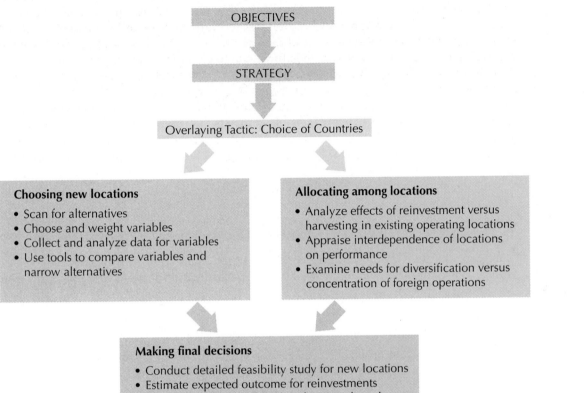

OBJECTIVES

STRATEGY

Overlaying Tactic: Choice of Countries

Choosing new locations

- Scan for alternatives
- Choose and weight variables
- Collect and analyze data for variables
- Use tools to compare variables and narrow alternatives

Allocating among locations

- Analyze effects of reinvestment versus harvesting in existing operating locations
- Appraise interdependence of locations on performance
- Examine needs for diversification versus concentration of foreign operations

Making final decisions

- Conduct detailed feasibility study for new locations
- Estimate expected outcome for reinvestments
- Make location and allocation decisions based on company's financial decision-making tools

Scanning as Step 1   Scanning allows managers to examine most or all countries broadly and then narrow them to the most promising ones. In scanning, managers compare country information that is readily available, inexpensive, and fairly comparable— usually without having to incur the expense of visiting foreign countries. Instead they analyze publicly available information, such as from the Internet, and they communicate with experienced people. They compare countries on a few conditions that could significantly affect the success or failure of their business and that fit with the company's resources and objectives. Because of using fairly easy-to-find information, managers may consider a large group of countries at this point, such as all the countries within a global region.

Detailed Analysis as Step 2   Once managers narrow their consideration to the most promising countries, they need to compare the feasibility and desirability of each. At this point, unless they are satisfied to outsource all their production and sales, they almost always need to go on location to analyze and collect more specific information.

   Take a situation in which managers need to decide where to place their sales efforts. They will likely need to visit the countries shortlisted through scanning, to conduct, for example, market research and visit with distributors before making a final decision. Or take a situation in which managers need to decide where to locate production of a

On-site visits follow scanning and are part of the final location decision process.

finished product or component. If they plan to outsource this production, they may want to inspect potential contractors' facilities. If they plan to own facilities themselves, they will need to collect such specific on-site information as availability of land and suppliers before committing significant resources.

Intel's manufacturing expansion into Latin America offers an illustrative example. Intel used scanning techniques to limit visits to a few Latin American countries. The follow-up visitations sought much more detailed information, even the availability of suitable housing, medical services, and food products for the personnel it would need to transfer. The visits also allowed the visiting team to gain qualitative information, such as their impressions of the welcome they might get from local government officials and business leaders.

The more time and money companies invest in examining an alternative, the more likely they are to accept it regardless of its merits, a situation known as an *escalation of commitment*. A feasibility study should have clear-cut decision points, which are points where managers can cut the commitment before they invest too much time and money.

What Information Is Important in Scanning?

Managers should consider country conditions that could significantly affect success or failure. These conditions should reveal both opportunities and risks, which we discuss in the coming section.

OPPORTUNITIES

We divide the section on opportunities into sales expansion and resource acquisition, although some conditions affect both, given the relationship between decisions of where to sell and where to produce.

Sales Expansion   Expansion of sales is probably the most important factor motivating companies to engage in international business because they assume that more sales will lead to more profits. Thus it is vital for them to decide where best to make those sales.

Of course, managers would like to have figures on past and current sales by country for the type of product they want to sell, but such information may not be available, especially if the product is a new one. In such instances, one way they can make rough estimates of market potential is to base projections on what has happened to sales for a similar or complementary product. For instance, they might project flat-screen television sales potential based on figures for DVD equipment sales.

However, such complementary figures may not be available either. So what can they do? They can use economic and demographic data as sales potential, particularly historical data on other countries. For instance, Figure 12.4 shows an example of aluminum per capita consumption among a sample of countries. Management may make a rough estimate that aluminum demand for all countries will increase along the trend line as GDP per capita increases.

Similarly, Korean demand for apparel, cosmetics, and automobiles has grown in close parallel with what happened when GDP per capita grew in other countries in earlier years. In fact, companies expand heavily into markets experiencing high economic growth because they expect that the demand for their products will increase along with that growth.

Of course, you should examine indicators related directly to the products you wish to sell. For example, if you're trying to sell luxury products, GDP per capita may tell you very little. Instead, you need to know how many people have income above a certain

FIGURE 12.4 Aluminum Consumption vs. GDP per Capita

By plotting a line based on GDP per capita, you can get a fairly good estimate of demand per capita for aluminum.

Source: From a presentation by Paul Thomas, North American Fabricated Products of Alcoa, April 20, 2004: "Globalization and the Aluminum Market—Opportunities and Challenges," The Aluminum Association Inc. (2004), at www. aluminum.org (accessed October 29, 2007).

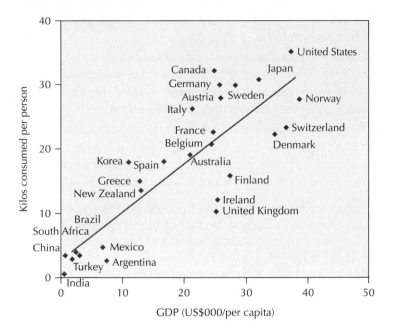

level. For instance, India's GDP per capita is low, but it has enough millionaires to support the sale of high-end products by companies like LMVH that sell Tag Heuer watches.

Furthermore, although your product or service may not appeal to the average customer, you may seek out niches within that market. Pollo Campero, a Guatemalan-based fast-food chain, and Gigante, Carrefour's former Mexican partner, have both successfully entered the United States by going only to cities with large Central American and Mexican populations.[4]

Examining Economic and Demographic Variables Here are some of the main things to consider when examining economic and demographic variables:

- *Obsolescence and leapfrogging of products.* Consumers in developing economies do not necessarily follow the same patterns as those in higher-income countries. In China, for example, consumers have leapfrogged the use of landline telephones by jumping from having no telephones to using cellular phones almost exclusively.[5]

- *Prices.* If prices of essential products are high, consumers may spend more on these products than what one would expect based on per capita income, thus having less to spend on discretionary purchases. The expenditures on food in Japan are higher than would be predicted by either population or income level because food is expensive and work habits promote eating out.

- *Income elasticity.* A common tool for predicting total market potential is to divide the percentage of change in product demand by the percentage of change in income in a given country. The more that demand changes in relation to income changes, the more elastic is the demand. Demand for necessities, such as food, is usually less elastic than is demand for discretionary products, such as flat-screen TVs.

- *Substitution.* Consumers in a given country may more conveniently substitute certain products or services than consumers in some other countries. For example,

> Companies must consider variables other than income and population when estimating potential demand for their products in different countries.

there are fewer automobiles in Hong Kong than one would expect based on income and population because the crowded conditions make the efficient mass transit system a desirable substitute for automobiles.

- *Income inequality.*   Where income inequality is high, the per capita GDP figures are usually low because many people have little to spend. This masks the fact that there are middle- and upper-income people who have substantial income to spend, like in our example of luxury product sales in India.

- *Cultural factors and taste.*   Countries with similar per capita incomes may have different preferences for products and services because of values or tastes. For example, the large Hindu population in India reduces per capita meat consumption there. However, there is a large niche market of Indians who are neither Hindu nor vegetarian.

- *Existence of trading blocs.*   Although a country may have a small population and GDP, its presence in a regional trading bloc gives its output access to a much larger market. For instance, Uruguay has a small domestic market, but its production has duty-free access to three other countries in the Southern Common Market (MERCOSUR).[6]

Given all of the factors just cited, managers cannot project potential demand perfectly. However, by considering factors that may influence the sale of their products, they can make workable estimates that help them narrow detailed studies to a reasonable number.

Resource Acquisition   Companies undertake international business to secure resources that are either not sufficiently available or are too expensive in their home countries. They may purchase these resources from another organization or they may establish foreign investments to exploit them. In either case, they must prioritize where they can best secure what they want.

If they want to acquire a scarce resource, they are obviously limited to those locales that have it, such as securing petroleum only in those countries that have reserves. However, even when the resource is limited to a few countries, there are better opportunities in some countries than in others. In the case of petroleum reserves, for example, there are cost differences in extraction, transportation, and taxes. Although cost differences are of utmost importance to companies seeking to compete primarily on a low-cost basis, cost differences are important for companies following differentiation strategies as well.

When considering cost differences, a particular resource may be overriding for specific industries or companies, such as the low-cost sugar that has led U.S. candy companies to produce in Mexico or the low-cost water power that has led aluminum companies to process in the northwestern United States and southwestern Canada.

Cost Considerations   However, the total cost is made up of numerous subcosts that need to be considered. Many of these are industry or company specific, which must be examined in the detailed on-site visitations. Nevertheless, there are several—*labor, infrastructure, ease of transportation and communications,* and *government incentives*— that apply to a large cross section of companies. We discuss these next.

LABOR   Although capital intensity is growing in most industries, labor compensation remains an important cost for most companies. In the scanning process, you can examine such factors as labor market size, labor compensation, minimum wages, customary and required fringe benefits, and unemployment rates to compare labor cost and availability.

Labor, however, is not homogeneous. For example, if you want to establish a low-cost call center, you may need to find people with specific language skills. For this reason, call centers to serve the U.S. market are frequently located in the Philippines, where there are many English speakers, but not in Senegal, where many French companies locate call centers to serve French-language markets. Or you may wish to establish an R&D facility where figures on the number of science and engineering graduates can give you a rough idea where needed skills are available. In fact, many

CONCEPT CHECK

Recall our discussion of "Regional Economic Integration" in Chapter 8, where we explain the **dynamic effects** of integration: As we point out, when trade barriers come down within a regional bloc, the size of the market available to small member nations typically increases quite dramatically.

CONCEPT CHECK

In Chapter 11, we explain *differentiation* as a **strategy** of offering a product with unique attributes that make it valuable to customers and for which they're willing to pay a higher price. That price, of course, is designed to cover the *costs* of making the product, but the strategy continues to work only as long as its attributes make a product sufficiently valuable to justify both its cost and its price.

Costs—especially labor costs—are an important factor in companies' production-location decisions.

New recruits attend a call-center training session in the Philippines, a favorite location for companies whose customers need responses in English. Locating call centers in developing countries has proved to be a cost-saving strategy, but labor costs can't be a company's only consideration. Language competence is also an important factor.

companies have recently set up R&D facilities in China, Hungary, India, and Israel because of the availability of technical talent at low cost.[7]

If a country's labor force lacks the specific skill levels required, a company may have to train, redesign production, or add supervision—all of which are expensive. Keep in mind also that there may be sector and geographic differences in wage rates within countries. For example, Mexican tire wages are much higher than the average Mexican industrial wage, and wages in the capital and other large cities are higher than elsewhere.[8]

In addition, you should look for conditions that can cause changes in labor availability and cost. In our closing case, for example, we'll learn that in South Africa, which is attractive for foreign direct investment (FDI) in many respects, about 21.5 percent of the adult population is infected with HIV—a problem that may drastically reduce the country's labor force over the next 10 to 15 years.

When companies move into developing countries because of labor-cost differences, their advantages may be short-lived for one or more of three reasons:

- Competitors follow leaders into low-wage areas.
- There is little first-mover advantage for this type of production migration.
- The costs rise quickly as a result of pressure on wage or exchange rates.

Case Review Note

Infrastructure problems add to operating costs.

INFRASTRUCTURE   Poor internal infrastructure and social services may easily negate cost differences in labor rates. In many developing countries, infrastructure is both poor and unreliable, which adds to companies' cost of operating.

An interesting example of this is the case of Cadbury Schweppes in Nigeria. Its workers spend extra hours each day just getting to and from work on congested bottlenecked roads, which makes them less productive. The company, like many others in Nigeria, uses its own power generators at two and a half times the cost of the unreliable publicly provided power. This is necessary not only to assure continuance of assembly lines but also to prevent spoilage of the food products it makes. Because phone lines are often unavailable for days at a time, Cadbury Schweppes must send people out to visit customers and suppliers. When goods are ready for delivery, they must again face the slow roads and congestion. When they go outside the city, these roads are in poor condition, thus further slowing the delivery process.[9]

The need to coordinate product, process, production, and sales influences location decisions.

EASE OF TRANSPORTATION AND COMMUNICATIONS   Related to infrastructure is the advantage for companies to locate near customers and suppliers For example, companies with rapidly evolving technologies need to connect product, process, and production technologies. Generally, they seek to locate production in places that allow them to tightly coordinate these activities to speed new products to market and to diminish competitors' opportunity to copy them.[10] This tends to push more production for this type of company into developed countries, where they conduct most of their R&D.

Two other factors affect location when companies need to have tight connections among these functions. First, there is distance, which roughly correlates with time and cost of shipments; thus a geographically isolated country, such as New Zealand, does not fit as easily into a company's global integration strategy because supplies to and production from such locations may be untimely and costly.[11] There are also advantages in locating activities in countries with few trade restrictions because of lowering tariff costs and better assuring a continuous flow of components where they are needed.[12]

Finally, when companies produce far from their markets, they may have fewer satisfactory transportation options. For example, U.S. toy companies such as Hasbro and

An overloaded truck makes its way to market in the east African nation of Somalia. For companies looking to do business overseas, poor infrastructure can result in substantial costs in production and distribution.

Mattel depend on Asian production and ocean freight. However, they cannot afford to use air freight in the event of a prolonged shipping strike.[13]

Companies may find advantages in being near specialized private and public institutions such as banks, financing firms, insurance groups, public accountants, freight forwarders, customs brokers, and consular offices, all of which handle international functions. In this respect, some companies have moved their headquarters to another country to be nearer their markets and centers of finance.[14]

For instance, Halliburton relocated its CEO and corporate headquarters from the United States to Dubai in 2007 to be closer to its customers and employees. If a company is looking for a production location that will serve sales in more than one country, the ease of moving goods into and out of the country is very important; thus it is useful to consider the efficiency of port facilities along with trade liberalization agreements with other countries.[15]

GOVERNMENTAL INCENTIVES AND DISINCENTIVES   Most countries at this writing seek foreign investment because of the jobs it will create, the competitiveness it will enhance, and the impact it will have on their trade balance. For example, Japan took out full-page ads in the *Wall Street Journal* and *Financial Times* in mid-2007 to entice foreign companies to consider Japan as a location for their investments.[16]

> Government practices may increase or decrease companies' costs.

Because countries compete to attract investors, many offer incentives, through regulations or negotiations, that lower companies' costs of operating. These incentives include such things as lower taxes, training of employees, loan guarantees, low-interest loans, exemption of import duties, and subsidized energy and transportation. Differences in tax rates are particularly important when deciding where to produce within a regional trading bloc inasmuch as companies can serve the entire region from any country within the bloc. This factor helps explain the recent popularity of Ireland as a location within the European Union.

At the same time, companies may begin operating more quickly and with fewer steps in some countries than in others. World Bank studies show that countries differ in terms of the ease or difficulty of starting a business, entering and enforcing contracts, hiring and firing workers, getting credit, and closing a business.[17] Governmental actions may delay or prevent companies from bringing in expatriate personnel and from timely clearing needed for imports through customs.

In addition, countries differ in both legal transparency and corruption. A disincentive occurs when companies must spend excessive time in satisfying government agencies on such matters as taxes, labor conditions, and environmental compliance when they are unsure of the legal consequences of their actions and when they may be required to pay bribes to be competitive.[18]

A CAVEAT   The continuous development of new production technologies makes cost comparisons among countries more difficult. As the number of ways to make the same product increases, a company might have to compare the cost of labor-intensive production in a low-wage country with that of capital-intensive production in a high-wage country. For example, Volkswagen moved some production from Germany to Slovakia and switched from a highly automated, capital-intensive assembly line to a labor-intensive plant because the low Slovakian wages and high productivity cut costs from those in Germany.[19] A company should also compare the cost from large-scale production that reduces fixed costs per unit by serving multicountry markets with the cost from multiple smaller-scale production units that reduce transport and inventory costs.

> **CONCEPT CHECK**
> We show in Chapter 6 that, in applying **factor-proportions theory** to determine the best place to locate a manufacturing facility, a company may compare the amount (and cost) of machinery that it will need in one place to the number (and cost) of people that it will need in another.

RISKS

Any decision by companies (or that matter, any of our personal decisions) involves weighing opportunity against risk. For example, a sales-seeking company may not necessarily go to the country showing the highest sales potential. Nor will an asset-seeking company necessarily go where the assets are cheapest. In both cases, this is because decision makers may perceive that the risks in those locales are too high.

Factors to Consider in Analyzing Risk   Keep in mind several factors as we discuss specific types of risk:

1. *Companies and their managers differ in their perceptions of what is risky, how tolerant they are in taking risk, what they expect returns should be for the risk they take, and the portion of their assets they are willing to put at risk.*[20]

2. *One company's risk may be another's opportunity.*   For example, companies offering security solutions (e.g., alarm systems, guard services, insurance, weapons) may find their biggest sales opportunities where other companies find only operating risks.

3. *There are means by which companies may reduce their risks other than avoiding locations, such as by insuring, but all these options incur costs that decision makers should take into account.*

4. *There are trade-offs among risks.*   For instance, avoidance of a country where political risk is high may leave a company more vulnerable to competitive risk if another company earns good profits there. Finally, returns are usually higher where risk is higher.

Although the preceding discussion emphasizes the individual nature of risk assessment, there are a number of factors that large numbers of companies consider important. We have grouped these into three categories—political, monetary, and competitive—which we'll now discuss.

CONCEPT CHECK

Recall from Chapter 3 our definition of **political risk** as the possibility that political decisions, events, or conditions will affect a country's business environment in ways that will cost investors some or all of the value of their investment or force them to accept lower-than-projected rates of return.

Political Risk   Political risk may occur because of changes in political leaders' opinions and policies, civil disorder, and animosity between the host and other countries, particularly with the company's home country. It may cause the loss or damage of property, disrupted operations, and the need to adjust to changes in the rules governing business. The result may be expensive for companies.

Recently, for example, Unilever has encountered difficulty in attracting foreign executives to work in Pakistan because of security concerns; Chiquita Brands paid money to terrorists in Colombia to protect its employees there; oil companies, such as Total, had their investments expropriated in Venezuela; Marriott had a hotel bombed in Indonesia; and Coca-Cola has had interrupted services (police protection of its trucks and telephone connections) in Angola.[21]

Managers use three approaches to predict political risk: *analyzing past patterns, analyzing opinions,* and *examining the social and economic conditions that might lead to such risk.*

Companies should

- Examine views of government decision makers.
- Get a cross section of opinions.
- Use expert analysts.

Analyzing Past Patterns   Although companies are influenced by past patterns of political risk, predicting risk on that basis is problematic because situations may change for better or worse as far as foreign companies are concerned. Further, a country's overall situation masks political risk differences within countries. For example, with few exceptions, government takeovers of companies have been highly selective, primarily affecting operations that have a visible widespread effect on the country because of their size or monopoly position. Similarly, unrest that leads to property damage and disruption of supplies or sales may not endanger the operations of all foreign companies.

This may be because of the limited geographic focus of the unrest. For example, during the civil war that led to the breakup of Yugoslavia, companies operating in Slovenia escaped the damage that companies incurred in other parts of the country.

Asset takeover or property damage does not necessarily mean a full loss to investors. Governments have preceded most takeovers with a formal declaration of intent and have followed with legal processes to determine the foreign investor's compensation.

Companies may examine past settlement patterns as an indicator of whether and how they may be compensated.

In addition to the investment's book value, other factors may determine the adequacy (or not) of compensation. On the one hand, the compensation may earn a lower return elsewhere. On the other hand, other agreements (such as purchase and management contracts) may create additional benefits for the former investor. In analyzing political risk, managers should predict the likely loss if political problems occur.

Analyzing Opinions Because influential people may sway future political events that affect business, managers should access statements made by political leaders both in and out of office to determine their philosophies on business in general, foreign input to business, the means of effecting economic changes, and their feelings toward given foreign countries. They should also access polls showing different leaders' likelihood of gaining political office. Modern technology has improved access to newspapers and television from major parts of the world, and reports are sometimes available almost simultaneously with the original publications or broadcasts.

Managers should eventually visit the short-listed countries to listen to a cross section of opinions. Embassy officials and foreign and local businesspeople are useful sources of opinions about the probability and direction of change. Journalists, academicians, middle-level local government authorities, and labor leaders usually reveal their own attitudes, which often reflect changing political conditions that may affect the business sector.

Companies may determine opinions more systematically by relying on analysts with experience in a country. These analysts might rate a country on specific political conditions that could lead to problems for foreign businesses, such as the fractionalization of political parties that could cause disruptive changes in government.

A company also may rely on commercial risk-assessment services, of which there are many. In fact, companies have been relying more on these services rather than generating their own risk analyses because these services offer concise reports that management decision makers view as credible.[22]

Examining Social and Economic Conditions Countries' social and economic conditions may lead to unrest if large sectors of the population have unmet aspirations. Frustrated groups may disrupt business by calling general strikes and destroying property and supply lines. For example, this has been the recent experience in the Niger delta region of Nigeria where groups have attacked foreign oil companies' property and kidnapped their employees.[23] Frustrated groups might also replace government leaders.

Moreover, political leaders might harness their support by blaming problems on foreigners and foreign companies. This may lead to boycotts or rule changes for foreign companies or even expropriation of their properties. However, there is no general consensus as to what constitutes dangerous conditions or how such instability can be predicted. The lack of consensus is illustrated by the diverse reactions of companies to the same political situations.

Rather than political stability itself, the direction of change in government seems to be very important. But even if a company accurately predicts the direction of change in government that will affect business, it will still be uncertain as to the time lag between the change and its actions.

Monetary Risk Companies may be affected by either changes in exchange rates or ability to move funds out of a country. We now examine these two types of risks.

Exchange Rate Changes The change in value of a foreign currency is a two-edged sword depending on whether you are going abroad to seek sales or resources. If you are seeking sales, say, a U.S. company selling to India, then a deterioration in the value of the Indian rupee will make your exports to that country less competitive because it will cost more rupees to buy the U.S. products or services.

Under this scenario, if the U.S. company produces within India to serve the Indian market, the same rupee profits from India will buy fewer U.S. dollars, thus adversely affecting the U.S. company's profits. If, however, the U.S. company is seeking assets from India, say Indian personnel to staff a call center, a fall in the rupee value lowers the U.S. dollar cost of the personnel. In Chapter 10, we explained major ways of forecasting exchange-rate changes. Some factors that companies may use for roughly comparing countries are trends in exchange rates, inflation, and foreign trade deficits.

Mobility of Funds   If a company is to invest abroad, then the ability to get funds out of the country is a factor when comparing countries. A theory that helps to explain this is **liquidity preference,** which is much like option theory, in that it states that investors usually want some of their holdings to be in highly liquid assets on which they are willing to take a lower return. They need liquidity in part to make near-term payments, such as paying out dividends; in part to cover unexpected contingencies, such as stockpiling materials if a strike threatens supply; and in part to be able to shift funds to even more profitable opportunities, such as purchasing materials at a discount during a temporary price depression.[24] The comparative liquidity among countries varies because of the activity of capital markets and because of governmental exchange control.

Sometimes companies want to sell all or part of their equity in a foreign facility so that the funds may be used elsewhere. However, the ability to find buyers depends in part on the existence of a local capital market, particularly if the investor wishes to sell shares on a local exchange. For example, the Mexican conglomerate, Grupo Carso, spun off its U.S. stake in CompUSA, a process facilitated not only by CompUSA's potential profits but also by the developed U.S. capital market. Thus when comparing countries, you may wish to include the existence of an active stock market as a favorable variable.

If the government restricts the conversion of funds (at this writing, for example, such countries as China, India, Thailand, and Venezuela have various degrees of exchange control), the foreign investor will be forced to spend some profits or proceeds from share sale in the host country. Thus it's not surprising that, if other things are equal, investors prefer projects in strong currency countries, where there is little likelihood of exchange controls.

Does Geography Matter?

Don't Fool with Mother Nature

A major tsunami hit southern Asia in late 2004. Soon after, there was an outbreak of the deadly Marburg virus in Angola. These events publicized global vulnerability to natural disasters and communicable diseases. Each year about 130 million people are exposed to earthquake risk, 119 million to tropical cyclone hazards, 196 million to catastrophic flooding, and 220 million to drought. On average, there are 184 deaths per day from natural disasters. In addition, they cause physical damage to industrial plants, crops, inventories, and infrastructure that all have negative effects on business.

These natural disasters are spread unevenly around the world. For instance, Iran, Afghanistan, and India are heavily exposed to earthquakes, and some African states have the highest vulnerability to drought. The United Nations Development Programme has published a disaster risk index (DRI) that shows the relative level of physical exposure to natural disaster hazards by country.[25]

Although only 11 percent of the people exposed to these disasters live in the poorest countries of the world, these countries account for 55 percent of the deaths because of having so many people in poor housing without adequate medical assistance. Likewise, as rural dwellers have migrated to urban areas in developing countries, many have settled in dangerous mountainsides and ravines that are ill equipped to deal with earthquakes and cyclones. For instance, when Hurricane Mitch hit Honduras in 1998, it left 10,000 dead, 20,000 missing, and 2.5 million needing emergency aid.[26] The disturbing prognosis is that the fastest urban growth is taking place in developing countries.

What does this have to do with companies' international locations? Catastrophic events upset markets, infrastructure, and production while damaging companies' property and injuring their personnel. Although they are most devastating in the world's poorer areas, events in high-income areas can play havoc with global supplies as well. For instance, the Kobe earthquake in Japan upset the world computer industry's production because it created semiconductor shortages.[27]

Thus natural events create additional operating risks and additional costs to insure against them. In turn, insurance companies are challenged to estimate the likelihood and cost of these events.

The World Health Organization has developed global atlases of infectious diseases.[28] Many of these diseases are where medical facilities are weakest because of these diseases' association with poverty.

They are also associated with natural disasters. For instance, cholera and malaria outbreaks are most apt to occur after flooding. Thus they tend to follow geographic patterns. For example, malaria kills about 2 million people a year, mainly in Africa, where Sasol Petroleum had to set up a clinic in Mozambique to treat its workers.[29]

The debilitating effects impact labor force participation and life expectancy. In turn, they are costly to companies. Companies also hesitate to send their personnel to epidemic areas. For example, during the Asian severe acute respiratory syndrome (SARS) outbreak, a number of companies (such as Wal-Mart, Gap, Liz Claiborne, and Kenneth Cole) banned employee travel to affected countries, thus hindering their buying and quality-assurance programs.[30] ●

Competitive Risk   The comparison of likely success among countries is largely contingent on competitors' actions. We now examine four competitive factors you should consider when comparing countries: *making operations compatible, spreading risk, following competitors or customers*, and *heading off competitors*.

Making Operations Compatible   Companies operating abroad usually encounter environments with which they are less familiar, thus creating operating risks relative to local companies. Thus companies prefer to operate in environments they perceive as being more familiar to them. As a company gains experience in operating in a particular country or in similar countries, it improves its assessments of consumer, competitor, and government actions—thereby reducing its uncertainty.

In fact, foreign companies have a lower survival rate than local companies for many years after they begin operations—a situation known as the **liability of foreignness.** However, those foreign companies that learn about their new environments and manage to overcome their early problems have survival rates comparable to those of local companies in later years.[31]

This concept helps explain why, for instance, U.S. companies put earlier and greater emphasis on Canada and the United Kingdom than would be indicated by the opportunity and risk variables we've discussed thus far. In short, managers feel more comfortable doing business in a similar language, culture, and legal system.[32] Language and cultural similarities may also keep operating costs and risks low because of greater ease in understanding employees and customers.

Finally, economic similarity influences where initial foreign operations will reside. Both Canada and the United Kingdom have high per capita GDPs, similar to those in the United States, which indicate a likely demand for products first created for the U.S. market. Thus, in comparing countries, you might consider their similarity to your country in terms of culture and economic level.

Managers should also try to assure that countries' policies and norms allow them to use their competitive advantages effectively. For example, Blockbuster failed in Germany because it could not duplicate the successful formula it used elsewhere where it depended on evening, Sunday, and holiday rentals when people make last-minute rental decisions. Laws in Germany prevented Blockbuster from operating at these times. Further, Blockbuster creates a store environment to attract the whole family. However,

---

Companies are highly attracted to countries that

- Are located nearby.
- Share the same language.
- Have market conditions similar to those in their home countries.

CONCEPT CHECK

In discussing "Cultural Distance" in Chapter 2, we observe that when two countries are culturally close, a company usually expects fewer differences—and must make fewer adjustments—when moving operations from one to the other. Here we point out that economic similarity often fosters the same conditions of compatibility.

consumers in Germany preferred to see family entertainment in a movie house and sought pornographic films from video stores.[33]

Companies may also give preference to locales that will permit them to operate with product types, plant sizes, and operating practices familiar to their managers. When examining locales, teams that include personnel with backgrounds in each functional area—marketing, finance, personnel, engineering, and production—will more likely uncover the best fits with their companies' resources and objectives.

Companies also consider local availability of resources in relation to their needs. Many foreign operations require local resources, a requirement that may severely restrict the feasibility of given locales. For example, the company may need to find local personnel or a viable local partner who understands its type of business and technology. Or it may need to add local capital to what it is willing to bring in.

Spreading Risk   By operating in diverse countries, companies may be able to smooth their sales and profits, which may give them a competitive advantage in raising funds. Such a practice reduces their risks without necessarily reducing shareholder value.[34] Such a strategy is in many ways opposite of what we just discussed about preferring countries similar to the home country. This is because geographic diversification leads companies to countries whose economies are the least correlated.

Companies may further guard against the effects of currency value changes by locating in countries whose exchange rates are not closely correlated.[35] They may further reduce the risk in loss of key suppliers or customers by extending the geographic scope of either or both. Finally, companies may balance operations in low-return and low-risk countries with operations in high-return and high-risk countries, thereby improving their performance.

In terms of competition, some different strategies are to go

- First where local firms are most apt to enter the market as competitors.
- Into markets that competitors have not entered.
- Where there are clusters of competitors.

Following Competitors or Customers   Managers may purposely crowd a market to prevent competitors from gaining advantages therein that they can use to improve their competitive positions elsewhere, a situation known as **oligopolistic reaction**.[36] For example, China now has more automobile producers than any other country, far more than automobile market analysts believe the market can sustain.[37]

At the same time, companies may gain advantages by locating where competitors are. To begin with, the competitors may have performed the costly task of evaluating locations, so followers may get a so-called free ride. In doing so, they avoid the pitfall that "the first to land on the beach gets shot." Moreover, there are clusters of competitors (sometimes called *agglomeration*) in various locations—think of all the computer firms in California's Silicon Valley. More recently, hundreds of high-tech computer companies from all over the world are located in Dubai.[38]

These clusters attract multiple suppliers and personnel with specialized skills. They also attract buyers who want to compare potential suppliers but don't want to travel great distances between them. Companies operating in the cluster area may also gain better access to information about new developments because they frequently come in contact with personnel from the other companies.[39]

There are also advantages of following customers into a market. For example, Bridgestone Tires was a major supplier to Japanese auto companies in Japan. When those auto companies established U.S. manufacturing facilities, Bridgestone moved into the U.S. market as well. First, Bridgestone's track record with Japanese auto companies, such as Toyota, gave it an advantage over other tire manufacturers in the United States. Second, if another tire manufacturer was to develop a strong relationship with Toyota in the United States, it might use this experience as a successful springboard to undermine Bridgestone's position elsewhere.

Heading Off Competition   A company may try to reduce competitive risk by either getting a strong foothold in markets before competitors do or by avoiding strong competitors

FIGURE 12.5   Where No Competitor Has Gone Before

Source: Copyright Martha Murphy, CartoonResource.com.

"Maybe there's a good reason why
no one else has broken into this market."

altogether. A company's innovative advantage may be short lived. Even when it has a substantial competitive lead time, the time may vary among markets.

One strategy for exploiting temporary innovative advantages is known as the **imitation lag,** whereby a company moves first to those countries where local competitors are most likely to catch up to the innovative advantage.[40] Those countries apt to catch up more rapidly are the ones whose companies invest a great deal in technology and whose governments offer little protection for the foreign innovator's intellectual property rights.

Companies also may develop strategies to avoid significant competition, rather than going where the competition is located. For example, PriceSmart, a discount operator, has all its warehouse stores outside its home country (the United States), and it has been successful by targeting locations in Central America, the Caribbean, and Asia that are considered too small to attract competitors like Wal-Mart and Carrefour.[41] As Figure 12.5 suggests, however, competitors tend to note whether locations are good or not.

In our opening case, we showed how Carrefour tries to enter growth markets before its major competitors. The reasons, as we saw, are fairly obvious: By being the first major competitor in a market, Carrefour can more easily gain the best partners, best locations, and best suppliers—a strategy to gain **first-mover advantage.** Another advantage of being first into a market is the potential of gaining strong relations with the government, such as Volkswagen in China and Lockheed with Russia.[42]

Information is needed at all levels of control.

Collecting and Analyzing Data

Companies undertake business research to reduce outcome uncertainties from their decisions and to assess their operating performance. The research includes finding answers to questions like these: "Can we hire qualified personnel?" "Will the economic and political climate allow us to reasonably foresee our future?" "Are our distributors servicing sufficient accounts?" and "What is our market share?"

Clearly, information helps managers improve their companies' performance. However, they can seldom get all the information they want because of time and cost constraints. Thus managers should compare the estimated costs of information with the probable payoff the information will generate in revenue gains or cost savings.

Companies should compare the cost of information with its value.

SOME PROBLEMS WITH RESEARCH RESULTS AND DATA

The lack, obsolescence, and inaccuracy of data on many countries make much research difficult and expensive to undertake. Although there are problems everywhere, the problems are most acute in developing countries. We now discuss the two basic problems: inaccurate information and noncomparability in information from different countries.

Inaccurate Information   For the most part, there are five basic reasons why reported information may be inaccurate:

1. Governmental resources may limit accurate data collection.
2. Governments may purposely publish misleading information.
3. Respondents may give false information to data collectors.
4. Official data may include only legal and reported market activities.
5. Poor methodology may be used.

Limited Resources   Developing countries may have such limited resources that other projects necessarily receive priority in the national budget. Why collect precise figures on the literacy rate, the leaders of a poor country might reason, when the same outlay can be used to build schools to improve that rate? Even if they place an emphasis on collecting accurate information, economic factors also hamper record retrieval and analysis because funds may be short for buying the latest computer equipment and training the people to use it. The result is that there may be gaps in reliable and timely information.

False or Misleading Data   Of equal concern to the researcher is the publication of false or purposely misleading information designed to mislead government superiors, the country's rank and file, or companies and institutions abroad. For example, an in-house investigation in China's National Bureau of Statistics found over 60,000 cases of statistical misrepresentations that distorted such important figures as GDP, economic growth, and energy use.[43]

Even if government and private organizations do not purposely publish false statements, many organizations may be so selective in the data they include that they create false impressions. Therefore, it is useful for managers to consider carefully the source of such material in light of possible motives or biases.

Cultural factors affect responses. Mistrust of how the data will be used may lead respondents to answer incorrectly, particularly if questions probe financial details or anything else that respondents may consider private. For example, many government figures are collected through questionnaires, such as those in the United States to estimate international travel and tourism expenditures. People may misstate their actual expenditures, particularly if they had not reported the true value of foreign purchases on incoming customs forms.

Reliance on Legally Reported Market Activities   Further distortions may occur because nationally reported income figures include only legal and reported market activities. Thus illegal income from such activities as the drug trade, theft, bribery, and prostitution is not included in national income figures, or it appears in other economic sectors because of money laundering. Contraband figures do not appear in official trade statistics and may be substantial. For instance, it is estimated that about $3 billion of Nigerian oil per year is stolen and shipped abroad. Finally, many economic activities, such as payments in cash for illegal immigrants' services or to avoid tax payments on the income, may also be substantial.[44]

Poor Research Methodology   Finally, many inaccuracies are due to poor collection and analysis by researchers both within and outside the government. Too often, broad generalizations are drawn from too few observations, on nonrepresentative samples, and on poorly designed questionnaires.

Noncomparable Information   Countries publish censuses, output figures, trade statistics, and base-year calculations for different time periods. So companies need to compare country figures by extrapolating from those different periods.

There also are numerous definitional differences among countries. For example, a category as seemingly basic as "family income" may include only the nuclear family—parents and children—in some countries, but it may include the extended family—the nuclear family plus grandparents, uncles, and cousins—elsewhere. Even using the same definition, differences in family size distort comparisons.

Similarly, some countries define literacy as some minimum level of formal schooling, others as attainment of certain specified standards, and still others as simply the ability to read and write one's name. Further, percentages may be published in terms of either adult population (with different ages used for adulthood) or total population. Accounting rules such as depreciation also differ, resulting in noncomparable net national product figures.

National income figures are particularly noncomparable because of differences in activities taking place outside the market economy—for example, within the home, which do not show up in income figures. The extent to which people in one country produce for their own consumption (for example, grow vegetables, prepare meals at home, sew clothes, or cut hair) distorts comparisons with other countries where different portions of people buy these products and services.

Another comparability problem concerns exchange rates, which must be used to convert countries' financial data to some common currency. A 10 percent appreciation of the Japanese yen in relation to the U.S. dollar will result in a 10 percent increase in the GDP per person of Japanese residents when figures are reported in dollars. Does this mean the Japanese are suddenly 10 percent richer? Obviously not, because they use about 85 percent of their yen income to make purchases in yen in the Japanese economy; thus they have no additional purchasing power for 85 percent of what they buy. Even if changes in exchange rates are ignored, purchasing power and living standards are difficult to compare because costs are so affected by climate and habit. Exchange rates, even when using purchasing power parity (PPP), are a very imperfect means of comparing national data on income.

> Problems in information comparability arise from
>
> • Differences in definitions and base years.
> • Distortions in currency conversions.

EXTERNAL SOURCES OF INFORMATION

Although information is needed for making good location decisions, there are simply too many sources for us to include a comprehensive list. Chances are, at least for scanning purposes, you will use the Internet to collect most of your information simply by using search engines to find information on key variables by entering words or phrases. Some searches will lead you to free information, and others will lead you to services for which you must pay. The following discussion highlights the major types of information sources in terms of their completeness, reliability, and cost.

Individualized Reports   Market research and business consulting companies conduct studies for a fee in most countries. They generally are the most costly information source because the individualized nature restricts prorating among a number of companies. However, the fact that a company can specify what information it wants often makes the expense worthwhile.

Specialized Studies   Research organizations prepare and sell fairly specific studies at costs much lower than those for individualized studies. These specialized studies sometimes are directories of companies that operate in a given locale, perhaps with financial or other information about the companies. They also may be about business in certain locales, forms of business, or specific products.

Service Companies Most companies providing services to international clients—for example, banks, transportation agencies, and accounting firms—publish reports. These reports usually are geared toward either the conduct of business in a given area or some specific subject of general interest, such as tax or trademark legislation. Because the service firms intend to reach a wide market of companies, their reports tend to be fairly general, although they give useful background information. Some service firms also offer informal opinions about such things as the reputations of possible business associates and the names of people to contact in a company.

Government Agencies Governments and their agencies are another source of information. Different countries' statistical reports vary in subject matter, quantity, and quality. When a government or government agency wants to stimulate foreign business activity, the amount and type of information it makes available may be substantial. For example, the U.S. Department of Commerce compiles news about and regulations in individual foreign countries. It disseminates specific information on product location in the National Trade Data Bank, and its representatives also help set up appointments with businesspeople abroad.

International Organizations and Agencies Numerous organizations and agencies are supported by more than one country. These include the United Nations (UN), the World Trade Organization (WTO), the International Monetary Fund (IMF), the Organisation for Economic Co-operation and Development (OECD), and the European Union (EU). All of these organizations have large research staffs that compile basic statistics as well as prepare reports and recommendations concerning common trends and problems. However, keep in mind that these organizations depend on national governments to supply them with the data they use. Many of the international development banks even help finance investment-feasibility studies.

Trade Associations Trade associations connected to various product lines collect, evaluate, and disseminate a wide variety of data dealing with technical and competitive factors in their industries. Many of these data are available in the trade journals published by such associations; others may or may not be available to nonmembers.

Information Service Companies A number of companies have information-retrieval services that maintain databases from hundreds of different sources, including many of those already described. For a fee, or sometimes for free at public libraries, a company can obtain access to such computerized data and arrange for an immediate printout of studies of interest.

INTERNALLY GENERATED DATA

Multinational enterprises (MNEs) may have to conduct many studies abroad themselves. Sometimes the research process may consist of no more than observing keenly and asking many questions. Investigators can see what kind of merchandise is available, see who is buying and where, and uncover the hidden distribution points and competition.

In some countries, for example, the competition for ready-made clothes may be from seamstresses working in private homes rather than from retailers. The competition for vacuum cleaners may be from servants who clean with mops rather than from other electrical appliance manufacturers. Surreptitiously sold contraband may compete with locally produced goods. Traditional analysis methods would not reveal such facts.

In many countries, even bankers have to rely more on clients' reputations than on their financial statements. Shrewd questioning may yield very interesting results. But such questioning is not always easy. For example, political unrest and the lack of telephones may inhibit the sampling of people.[45]

Often a company must be extremely imaginative, extremely observant, or both. For example, one soft drink manufacturer wanted to determine its Mexican market share relative to that of its competitors. Management could not make reliable estimates from the final points of distribution because sales were so widespread. So the company hit on two alternatives, both of which turned out to be feasible: The bottle cap manufacturer revealed how many caps it sold to each of its clients, and customs supplied data on each competitor's soft drink concentrate imports.

Point Counterpoint

Should Companies Forgo Investment in Violent Areas?

Point **Yes** As an executive of an MNE, I say they should. Companies have coincidently spread their operations internationally while violence has erupted against them. We're no longer concerned simply about being caught in the crossfire between opposing military groups. Antiglobalization groups want to harm our personnel and facilities. Groups see us as easy marks for extortion by threatening harm or kidnapping our personnel. Still others are against foreigners, regardless of the aims of the foreigners. For instance, such a group in Afghanistan killed five staff members from Médecins Sans Frontières, who were there to treat sick and injured people.

At the same time, getting caught in the crossfire has become a bigger risk. Arms trafficking has increased and has lowered prices, not only to revolutionaries but also to drug and alien smugglers and to criminals involved in money laundering.[46] As MNEs, we can't help being visible, and this visibility makes us vulnerable.

In essence, if we have direct investments where risk of violence is great, we put our personnel at risk, especially those who are foreigners in the countries. Although local personnel may be at a lesser risk of say, kidnapping, experience shows they are not immune either.

Furthermore, to operate in these risky areas, we have to send foreign personnel there. Some go as managers or technicians on long assignments. Others must go on business trips, such as to audit books, assure quality control, and offer staff advice that must involve on-site visits. The dangers are not inconsequential. There are about 8,000 reported kidnappings per year, many targeting foreign workers and their families. For instance, there were more than 200 reported Nigerian kidnappings of foreign workers in the year and a half before mid-2007.[47]

It's simply unethical to put our employees in such situations. Of course, we don't force people to go to dangerous

(continued)

Counterpoint **No** Where there's risk, there are usually rewards. Companies should not shun areas with violence. Companies have always taken risks and employees have always gone to risky areas. As far back as the seventeenth century, migrants to what are now the United States, India, and Australia encountered disease and hostile native populations. Had companies and immigrants not taken chances, the world would be far less developed today.

You can't look at the risk from violence in isolation from other risks. Although we don't have historical data, risks are probably lower today. Disease is still a bigger risk than violence, but medical advances against a number of historical killers (such as polio, measles, smallpox, and tuberculosis) have lessened the risk from disease. Further, evacuation in case of a *real* emergency situation is much faster.

But let's assume for a moment that we decide we should avoid countries with the potential for violence against our facilities and employees. Is there any such place? The opinions we get from so-called risk experts are certainly conflicting. One said, "It's an even playing field around the world. You can go to London, Caracas, Madrid, or New York, and from a terrorism standpoint, the risk is the same."[49] Another intelligence provider placed the United States as riskier for terrorism than Iraq and placed Britain as riskier than Nepal.[50]

Although these analyses seem intuitively wrong, bombings in London and Oklahoma City, along with school and university shootings in the United States, certainly make me wonder. The deputy assistant director of the FBI said, "We are dealing every single day with a variety of domestic terrorism threats that are alive and well and in this country [United States]."[51] About the only places that everyone agrees are low risk are Greenland and Iceland.

(continued)

places, and we can get enough people to work in these areas. However, our experience is that there are three types of people who want or are willing to work in these areas, and none of these types are ideal. First, you get the people who simply want the high compensation and big insurance policies, some of whom are experienced in military or undercover activities. However, these people tend to be highly independent and hard to control. Second, you get the naive, who because of not really understanding the danger are difficult to safeguard through training and security activities. Third, you get the thrill seekers, who find that adrenaline is like an addictive drug. These are most at risk because of the thrill of danger and the reluctance to leave when situations worsen.[48]

High risk to individuals is indicative of a political situation out of control. Thus it is a harbinger of additional risks that may occur through governmental changes, falls in consumer confidence, and a general malaise that affects revenues and operating regulations negatively. This is not the kind of country in which to conduct operations. ●

In addition, some industries don't have the luxury of deciding on any country in the world to put their operations. Take the petroleum industry. The companies have to go where there is a high likelihood of finding petroleum. Although it would be great to find all the petroleum in places like Iceland and Switzerland, this is not the reality. Most of the realistic alternatives are in areas that have had recent bombings, kidnappings, or organized crime—the Middle East, West Africa, the Central Asian former Soviet republics, Ecuador, and Venezuela.[52] If we did not go to these places, we'd be out of business.

In effect, we'll keep operating anywhere that there are opportunities. If a place seems physically risky, we'll take whatever precautions we can. We'll share intelligence reports, put people through safety training courses (there are plenty of these available now), take security actions abroad, and perhaps not transfer spouses and children to risky areas. We do this latter practice so we do not have to be on top of what is happening with as many people. ●

Country Comparison Tools

Once companies collect information on possible locations through scanning, they need to analyze the information. Two common tools for analysis are *grids* and *matrices*. In preparing either, it is useful to use a team made up of people from different functions so production, marketing, finance, human resource, and legal factors are all considered. However, once companies commit to locations, they need continuous updates. We now discuss grids and matrices.

GRIDS

Grids are tools that

- May depict acceptable or unacceptable conditions.

- Rank countries by important variables.

A company may use a grid to compare countries on whatever factors it deems important. Table 12.1 is an example of a grid with information placed into three categories. The company may eliminate certain countries immediately from consideration because of characteristics it finds unacceptable. (Companies vary in what they consider unacceptable.) These factors are in the first category of variables, in which Country I is eliminated. The company assigns values and weights to other variables so it ranks each country according to the relative importance of attributes to it. In this hypothetical example, we've attached more weight to the size of investment needed than to the tax rate. For example, the table graphically pinpoints Country II as high return–low risk, Country III as low return–low risk, Country IV as high return–high risk, and Country V as low return–high risk.

Both the variables and the weights differ by product and company depending on the company's internal situation and its objectives. The grid technique is useful even when a company does not compare countries because it can set the minimum score needed for either investing additional resources or committing further funds to a more detailed feasibility study. Grids do tend to get cumbersome, however, as the number of

TABLE 12.1 Simplified Market-Penetration Grid

This table is simply an example: In the real world, a company chooses the variables that it regards as most important and may weight some as more important than others. Here managers rate Country II the most attractive because it's regarded as high return–low risk. Country IV also promises a high return and Country III low risk. Note that Country I is eliminated immediately because the company will go only where 100 percent ownership is permitted.

Variable	Weight	Country I	II	III	IV	V
1. Acceptable (A), Unacceptable (U) factors						
a. Allows 100 percent ownership	—	U	A	A	A	A
b. Allows licensing to majority-owned subsidiary	—	A	A	A	A	A
2. Return (higher number = preferred rating)						
a. Size of investment needed	0–5	—	4	3	3	3
b. Direct costs	0–3	—	3	1	2	2
c. Tax rate	0–2	—	2	1	2	2
d. Market size, present	0–4	—	3	2	4	1
e. Market size, 3–10 years	0–3	—	2	1	3	1
f. Market share, immediate potential, 0–2 years	0–2	—	2	1	2	1
g. Market share, 3–10 years	0–2	—	2	1	2	0
Total			18	10	18	10
3. Risk (lower number = preferred rating)						
a. Market loss, 3–10 years (if no present penetration)	0–4	—	2	1	3	2
b. Exchange problems	0–3	—	0	0	3	3
c. Political-unrest potential	0–3	—	0	1	2	3
d. Business laws, present	0–4	—	1	0	4	3
e. Business laws, 3–10 years	0–2	—	0	1	2	2
Total			3	3	14	13

variables increases. Although they are useful in ranking countries, they often obscure interrelationships among countries.

MATRICES

To show more clearly the opportunity and risk relationship, managers can plot values on a matrix such as the one shown in Figure 12.6. In this particular example, Countries E and F are high-opportunity and low-risk countries in comparison with Countries A, B, C, and D. Thus Countries E and F are better candidates for detailed analysis than the other countries.

In reality, however, managers may sometimes have to choose between two countries, one with a high risk and high opportunity and another with a low risk and low opportunity. They are apt to make their decision based on their tolerance for risk and on the portfolio of countries where the company is already operating. Further, although A, B, C, and D are less appealing than E and F, the company may nevertheless find opportunities in A, B, C, and D without necessarily making a large commitment. For example, they may be ideal candidates for licensing or shared ownership arrangements.

But how can managers plot values on such a matrix? They must determine which factors are good indicators of their companies' risk and opportunity and weight them

With an opportunity-risk matrix, a company can

- Decide on indicators and weight them.
- Evaluate each country on the weighted indicators.

FIGURE 12.6   Opportunity–Risk Matrix

Countries E and F are the most desirable because they boast a combination of a high level of opportunity and a low level of risk. But what if the decision came down to Countries A and B? The level of opportunity in Country A may not be as high as a company would like, but the low level of risk may be attractive. Country B, on the other hand, promises a high level of opportunities but also threatens a high level of risk. A decision between Countries A and B will probably take the firm's *risk tolerance* into consideration.

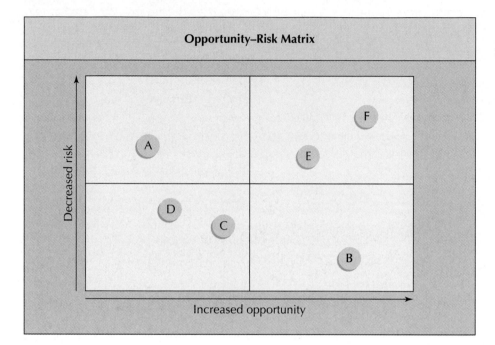

to reflect their importance. For instance, on the risk axis they might give 20 percent (0.2) of the weight to expropriation risk, 25 percent (0.25) to foreign-exchange controls, 20 percent (0.2) to civil disturbances and terrorism, 20 percent (0.2) to natural disasters, and 15 percent (0.15) to exchange-rate change, for a total allocation of 100 percent.

They would then rate each country on a scale of 1 to 10 for each variable (with 10 indicating the best score and 1 the worst) and multiply each variable by the weight they allocate to it. For instance, if they give Country A a rating of 8 on the expropriation-risk variable, the 8 would be multiplied by 0.2 (the weight they assign to expropriation) for a score of 1.6. They would then sum all of Country A's risk-variable scores to place it on the risk axis. They would plot the location of Country A on the opportunity axis similarly.

Once they determine the scores for each country, they can ascertain the average scores for all countries' risks and opportunities and divide the matrix into quadrants based on the average risk and average opportunity score among the countries they compare.

A key element of this kind of matrix, and one that managers do not always include in practice, is the projection of where countries will be in the future. Such a projection is obviously useful. Thus managers may rely on forecasters who are knowledgeable not only about the countries but also about forecasting methods.

Some types of information are more important to one company or for one product than another. For example, managers in a company selling a low-priced consumer product might heavily weigh population size as an indicator of market opportunity, whereas those in a company selling tire retreading services might heavily weigh the number of vehicles registered. In terms of production location, managers in one company may be most concerned about the wage rates of low-skilled workers and managers in another with the local availability of supplies.

Allocating Among Locations

The scanning tools we have just discussed are useful for narrowing alternatives among countries. They are also useful in allocating operational emphasis among countries, but there are other factors companies need to consider. We now discuss three of them: alternative gradual commitments, geographic diversification versus concentration, and reinvestment versus harvesting.

ALTERNATIVE GRADUAL COMMITMENTS

We discussed that because of risk perceptions, companies favor operations in countries similar to their home countries. Nevertheless there are alternative means of risk-minimization expansion patterns they can undertake. We show these in Figure 12.7, and

Companies may reduce risks from the liability of foreignness by

• Going first to countries with characteristics similar to their home countries.

• Having experienced intermediaries handle operations for them.

• Operating with forms requiring commitment of fewer resources abroad.

• Moving initially to one or a few, rather than many, foreign countries.

FIGURE 12.7   The Usual Pattern of Internationalization

The farther that a company moves outward along any of the axes (A, B, C, D), the deeper its international commitment. Most companies move at different speeds along different axes.

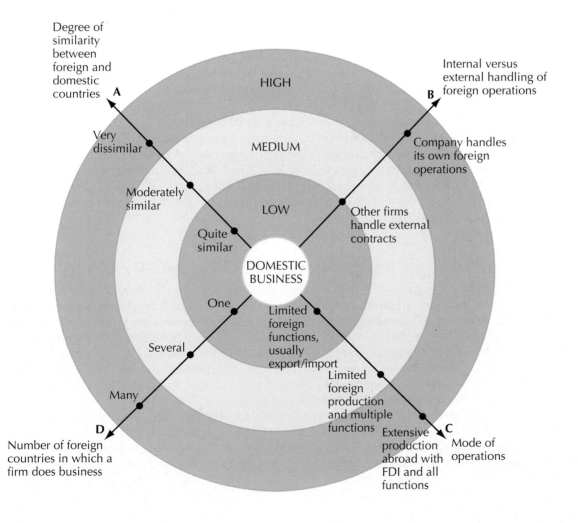

as you examine this figure, note that the farther a company moves from the center on any axis, the deeper its international commitment becomes.

However, a company does not necessarily move at the same speed along each axis. In fact, it may jump over some of the steps on an axis. A slow movement along one axis may free up resources that allow faster expansion along another. For example, a company may find the best growth opportunities in countries that are dissimilar to those in its home country, so it may go first to those countries but limit the resources it puts at risk. Let's now examine Figure 12.7 more closely.

Axis A shows that companies generally move gradually from a purely domestic focus to one that eventually encompasses operations in multiple countries, some of which are quite dissimilar from one's own country. However, an alternative when moving quickly along the A axis is to move slowly along the B axis, especially for dissimilar countries. The B axis shows that a company may use intermediaries to handle foreign operations during early stages of international expansion because it minimizes the resources it puts at risk and its liability of foreignness.

Thus a company can then commit fewer resources to both international endeavors, instead relying on intermediaries that already know how to operate in the foreign market. But if the business grows successfully, the company may want to handle the operations with its own staff. This is because it has learned more about foreign operations and the countries where the intermediaries have secured business, considers them less risky than at the onset, and realizes the volume of business may justify the development of internal capabilities such as hiring trained personnel to maintain a department for foreign sales or purchases.

Axis C shows that importing or exporting is usually the first international mode a company undertakes. At an early stage of international involvement, importing and exporting require the least placement of a company's resources abroad. In fact, it may involve the least need to invest more resources if the company can use excess production capacity to produce more goods, which it would then export. Thus moving along the C axis is a means to minimize the risk of the liability of foreignness because of forgoing such functions as managing a foreign workforce for production.

Later, the company might, in addition to exporting, make an even higher commitment through foreign direct investments to produce abroad. Its infusion of capital, personnel, and technology is highest for these operations. Axis D shows that companies can move internationally one country at a time, thus not having to become overwhelmed by learning about many countries at the same time. However, as we discuss in the next section, there may be a competitive impulse to move to a number of countries almost simultaneously.

GEOGRAPHIC DIVERSIFICATION VERSUS CONCENTRATION

Strategies for ultimately reaching a high level of commitment in many countries are

- Diversification—go to many fast and then build up slowly in each.
- Concentration—go to one or a few and build up fast before going to others.
- A hybrid of the two.

Ultimately, a company may gain a sizable presence and commitment in most countries; however, there are different paths to that position. Although any move abroad means some geographic diversification, the term **diversification strategy** when used for location decisions describes a company's movement rapidly into many foreign markets, gradually increasing its commitments within each one. A company can do this, for example, through a liberal licensing policy to ensure sufficient resources for the initial widespread expansion. The company eventually will increase its involvement by taking on activities that it first contracted to other companies.

At the other extreme, with a **concentration strategy** the company will move to only one or a few foreign countries until it develops a very strong involvement and competitive position there. There are, of course, hybrids of these two strategies—for example, moving rapidly to most markets but increasing the commitment in only a

TABLE 12.2   To Diversify or to Concentrate: The Role of Product and Market Factors

If a company determines that "Product or Market Factors" satisfy the conditions in the column headed "Prefer Diversification," it may benefit from moving quickly into several markets simultaneously. If the same factors satisfy the conditions under "Prefer Concentration," it may decide to enter and work initially to develop a substantial presence in just one or a few markets.

Product or Market Factor	Prefer Diversification if:	Prefer Concentration if:
1. Growth rate of each market	Low	High
2. Sales stability in each market	Low	High
3. Competitive lead time	Short	Long
4. Spillover effects	High	Low
5. Need for product, communication, and distribution adaptation	Low	High
6. Program control requirements	Low	High

Source: "Marketing Expansion Strategies in Multinational Marketing," from *Journal of Marketing*, Vol. 43, Spring 1979, p. 89. Reprinted by permission of the American Marketing Association © 1979.

few. Table 12.2 sums up the major variables that a company should consider when deciding which strategy to use.[53] We discuss each of these variables in the following sections.

Growth Rate in Each Market   When the growth rate in each market is high or needs to be high, a company should usually concentrate on a few markets because it will cost a great deal to expand output sufficiently in each market. In our opening case, for instance, we point out that to be cost effective in an overseas market, Carrefour focuses on building a sufficient distribution presence in target countries. However, slower growth or need for growth in each market may result in the company's having enough resources to build and maintain a market share in several different countries.[54]

Sales Stability in Each Market   As we have discussed, a company may smooth its earnings and sales because of operations in various parts of the world. The more stable that sales and profits are within each market, the less advantage there is from a diversification strategy. Similarly, the more correlated markets are, the less smoothing is achieved by selling in each.

Competitive Lead Time   We have discussed why Carrefour has wanted to gain first-mover advantages. If a company determines it has a long lead time before competitors are likely to be able to copy or supersede its advantages, then it may be able to follow a concentration strategy and still beat competitors into other markets. Otherwise, it may need either to cede leadership in some countries to competitors or follow a diversification strategy.

Spillover Effects   **Spillover effects** are situations in which the marketing program in one country results in awareness of the product in other countries. These effects are advantageous because additional customers may be reached with little additional cost. This can happen if the product is advertised through media sent cross-nationally, such

Case Review Note

as U.S. television ads that reach Canadians. When marketing programs reach many countries, such as by satellite television or the Internet, a diversification strategy has advantages.

Need for Product, Communication, and Distribution Adaptation   Companies may have to alter products and their marketing to sell abroad, a process that, because of cost, favors a concentration strategy. The adaptation cost may limit the resources the company has for expanding in many different markets. Further, if the adaptations are unique to each country, the company cannot easily spread the costs over sales in other countries to reduce total unit costs. For example, Ben & Jerry's took a concentration strategy by moving into the British market with as rapid an increase in distribution as possible so it could cover the high fixed costs of its local adaptations in ice cream production and advertising.[55]

Program Control Requirements   The more a company needs to control its operations in a foreign country, the more favorable a concentration strategy is. This is because the company will need to use more of its resources to maintain that control. Its need for more control could result from various reasons, including the fear that collaboration with a partner will create a competitor or the need for highly technical assistance for customers.

REINVESTMENT VERSUS HARVESTING

So far, we've discussed the sequencing of countries to enter. In addition, once a company is operating abroad, it must evaluate how much effort to place on each location. If a company uses contract arrangements to sell or obtain resources abroad, such as selling to an independent distributor or buying from a foreign contractor, these contracts may more easily be severed than if the company wants to eliminate ownership in foreign direct investments.

With foreign direct investments, the company transfers capital abroad and has physical capital in place abroad. If the investment is successful, the company will earn money that it may remit back to headquarters or reinvest to increase the value of the investment. Over time, most of the value of a company's foreign investment comes from reinvestment. If the investment is unsuccessful or if its outlook is less favorable than possible investments in other countries, the company may consider using the earnings elsewhere or even to discontinue the investment.

A company may have to make new commitments to maintain competitiveness abroad.

Reinvestment Decisions   Companies treat decisions to replace depreciated assets or to add to the existing stock of capital from retained earnings in a foreign country somewhat differently from original investment decisions. Once committed to a given locale, a company may find it doesn't have the option of moving a substantial portion of the earnings elsewhere—to do so would endanger the continued successful operation of the given foreign facility. The failure to expand might result in a falling market share and a higher unit cost than that of competitors.

Aside from competitive factors, a company may need several years of almost total reinvestment and allocation of new funds in one area to meet its objectives. Over time, a company may use the earnings to expand sales and production. Another reason a company treats reinvestment decisions differently is that once it has experienced personnel within a given country, it may believe those workers are the best judges of what is needed for that country, so headquarters managers may delegate certain investment decisions to them. In fact, managers within those countries will most likely submit capital budget requests that include proposals to expand their operations.

Harvesting   Companies commonly reduce commitments in some countries because those countries have poorer performance prospects than do others, a process known as

harvesting (or divesting). Carrefour, for example, sold off underperforming operations in Korea and Slovakia to have funds for more promising ventures into the Chinese, Indian, and Russian markets. There are other reasons as well. For instance, J. Sainsbury withdrew from the Egyptian market because its management did not expect a turn-around in its poorly performing operation there.[56] Dana sold its U.K. facility to use funds to concentrate on developing different automotive technologies.[57] Goodyear sold its Indonesian rubber plantation because of its decision to no longer produce rubber itself.[58]

Some indications suggest that companies might benefit by planning divestments better and by developing divestment specialists. Companies have tended to wait too long before divesting, trying instead expensive means of improving performance. Local managers, who fear losing their positions if the company abandons an operation, propose additional capital expenditures. In fact, this question of who has something to gain or lose is a factor that sets decisions to invest apart from decisions to divest. Both types of decisions should be highly interrelated and geared to the company's strategic thrust.

Ideas for investment projects typically originate with middle managers or with managers in foreign subsidiaries who are enthusiastic about collecting information to accompany a proposal as it moves upward in the organization. After all, the evaluation and employment of these people depend on growth. They have no such incentive to propose divestments. These proposals typically originate at the top of the organization after upper management has tried most remedies for saving the operation.[59]

Companies may divest by selling or closing facilities. They usually prefer selling because they receive some compensation. A company that considers divesting because of a country's political or economic situation may find few potential buyers except at very low prices. In such situations, the company may try to delay divestment, hoping the situation will improve. If it does, the firm that waits out the situation generally is in a better position to regain markets and profits than one that forsakes its operation.

A company cannot always simply abandon an investment either. Governments frequently require performance contracts, such as substantial severance packages to employees, that make a loss from divestment greater than the direct investment's net value. Further, the length of time to go through insolvency (up to 10 years) alters the percentage of value recovered from a divestment. For example, in Japan, Singapore, and Finland, investors recover on average of over 90 percent of the value, whereas in Brazil, Cambodia, and Madagascar, they typically recover nothing.[60] Finally, many MNEs fear adverse international publicity and difficulty in reentering a market if they do not sever relations with a foreign government on amicable terms.

Companies must decide how to get out of operations if

- *They no longer fit the overall strategy.*
- *There are better alternative opportunities.*

Noncomparative Decision Making

Because companies have limited resources at their disposal, it might seem they maintain a storehouse of foreign operating proposals that they may rank by some predetermined criteria. If this were so, management could simply start allocating resources to the top-ranked proposal and continue down the list until it could make no further commitments. This is often not the case, however. They make *go–no-go* decisions by examining one opportunity at a time and pursuing it if it meets some threshold criteria.

To begin with, companies sometimes need to respond quickly to prospects they had not anticipated. For example, many companies need to respond to unsolicited proposals to sell abroad or sign joint venture or licensing contracts. Similarly, undertakings may be one-time possibilities because a government or another company publishes a request for proposals. For example, when the government of India announced that foreign companies could invest in Indian newspapers, foreign publishers had to react quickly.[61]

Most companies examine proposals one at a time and accept them if they meet minimum-threshold criteria.

Or there may be a chance to buy properties that another company divests. For instance, when Enron faced bankruptcy, it needed to sell many of its foreign facilities; thus companies such as Tractebel from Belgium and Royal Dutch/Shell bid on its Korean facilities.[62] Further, we have discussed the competitive advantages of following customers' and competitors' moves into foreign markets, and we cannot always foresee when they will make them.

Another factor inhibiting the comparison of country operations is that they may be so interdependent that one cannot meaningfully evaluate country operations separately. Profit figures from individual operations may obscure the real impact those operations have on overall company activities. For example, if a U.S. company were to establish an assembly operation in Australia, the operation could either increase or reduce exports from the United States, thus affecting U.S. profit figures. Alternatively, the same company might build a plant in Malaysia to produce a product using cheaper labor; however, doing that would necessitate more coordination costs at headquarters.

Or perhaps by building a plant in Brazil to supply components to Volkswagen of Brazil, the company may increase the possibility of selling to Volkswagen in other countries. As a result of the Australian, Malaysian, or Brazilian projects, management would have to make assumptions about the changed profits in the United States and elsewhere. Finally, interdependence occurs because much of the sales and purchases of foreign subsidiaries are among units of the same parent company. The prices the company charges on these transactions will affect the relative profitability of one unit compared to another.

In sum, three factors inhibit companies from comparing investment opportunities: cost, time, and the interrelation of operations on global performance. Clearly, some companies cannot afford to conduct very many feasibility studies simultaneously. Even if they can, the studies are apt to be in various stages of completion at a given time. For example, suppose a company completes its study for an Australian project while continuing studies on New Zealand, Japan, and Indonesia. Can the company afford to hold off on making a decision about Australia? Probably not. Waiting would likely invalidate much of the Australian study, thus necessitating added expense and further delays to update it.

LOOKING TO THE FUTURE

Will Prime Locations Change?

Demographers expect a slowing in the growth of global population through 2050. In fact, a number of high-income countries, Japan and Italy for example, should have declining populations. At the same time, population growth should remain robust in many developing economies, particularly those in sub-Saharan Africa. The result of this is that the percentage of people living in currently developed countries is expected to fall to 13.7 percent from a 2000 figure of 19.7 percent. The least developed countries will have the biggest population increase.

Further, because the world's population will continue to age, the share of what we now consider the working-age population should fall for developed countries and increase in many developing countries. Because there is a positive relationship between the changes in the size of the working-age population and per capita GDP, the growth in per capita GDP should be higher in today's developing economies than in today's developed countries.[63] These demographic changes, if they materialize, will have implications both for the location of markets and the location of labor forces.

An intriguing future possibility is the near officeless headquarters for international companies. Technology may permit some people to work from anywhere as they e-mail and teleconference with their colleagues, customers, and suppliers elsewhere. Thus they could live anywhere in the world and work from their homes. The use of offices at home is already occurring within some professions.[64]

However, if people can work from their homes, they may move their homes where they want to live rather than living where their employers are now headquartered. Because we're talking here about highly creative and highly innovative self-motivated people, they can usually get permission to live in almost any country of the world.

A leading researcher on urbanization and planning has shown that beginning at least as early as the Roman Empire, these types of people have been drawn to certain cities that were the centers of innovation. He says that this attraction is due to people's improvement through interchange with others like themselves, like "a very bright class in a school or a college. They all try to score off each other and do better." Thus, if he's correct, the brightest minds may work more at home but still need the face-to-face interaction with their colleagues.[65]

His arguments are provocative, particularly because we now have technology to allow people to communicate without traveling as much, yet business travel continues to increase. Hence people need face-to-face interaction. He further suggests that these people will be drawn to the same places that attract people to visit as tourists. Concomitantly, another view is that in leading Western societies, the elite made up of intellectuals and highly educated people is increasingly using its capability to delay and block new technologies. If successful, their efforts will result in the emergence of different countries at the forefront of technological development and acceptance.[66] ■

FDI in South Africa

CASE

Since 2002, South Africa has given incentives to foreign investors through its Strategic Industrial Project (SIP), which includes such provisions as tax reductions between 50 and 100 percent for approved investment, export marketing assistance, relief from various import taxes, and removal or reduction of virtually all restrictions on the form or extent of foreign investment.[67] There are still some restrictions, such as on foreign ownership of the media. These incentives seem to have helped South Africa attract more FDI. Between 2000 and 2007, the value rose from US$43.4 billion to US$69.4 billion.

But why would the South African government want FDI? Unquestionably, jobs are a compelling reason. South Africa has had one of the world's highest unemployment rates, estimated at 25.5 percent in 2006. Growth is another reason. South Africa's savings and investment rates have been too low to finance sufficient business expansion. The result was very sluggish growth during the 1990s.

A third reason is that foreign investment in state-owned companies usually improves the quality of their goods and services, a rationale that spurred South Africa to open its banking and telecom sectors to foreign investors. Finally, as a leading commodity exporter, South Africa is vulnerable to prolonged market downturns in developed countries; thus South African authorities reasoned that FDI would help diversify its economy.

To understand South Africa's attractiveness for FDI, it is necessary to briefly outline its recent history. Many businesspersons within and outside South Africa predicted that the 1994 end of apartheid (the system of minority white rule that lasted about 40 years and prevented South African blacks from fairly participating in the political, economic, and social affairs of the country) would lead to political instability and an antibusiness government. They speculated that newly elected politicians would take revenge against the whites who had oppressed them and against businesses that had been their collaborators. In this environment, foreign investors were harvesting their investments rather than adding to them.

Instead, the political changeover with the election of Nelson Mandela went smoothly, as have subsequent elections of his successor, Thabo Mbeki. Their ruling party, the African National Congress, has had a positive attitude toward business, especially toward foreign companies. They hoped that MNEs that had left South Africa during the apartheid era would return—for example, between 1986 and 1991, 235 of the 360 U.S. MNEs in South Africa left the country. At first, there was a "wait and see," but most have returned.

No one questions the enormous potential within South Africa. In 2007, it had almost 44 million people, an improving logistics infrastructure, advanced financial sector, a GDP per capita at PPP (2006) of $13,000, vast mineral wealth, and good access to more than 100 million people in southern Africa. (Map 12.2 shows South Africa's location.)

At the same time, there has been a rapid influx of foreign investment into South African portfolio equity funds due largely to an appreciating currency (rand) that has contributed to a high dollar return. The IMF described South Africa's macroeconomic framework as the best among emerging markets around the world. South Africa seemingly has built the foundation for sustainable business development within a stabilizing democracy—an ideal place for FDI.

However, since the beginning of the twenty-first century, FDI results for South Africa have been mixed. Between 2000 and 2005, the growth in South Africa's FDI stock was much higher than in any other African country. However, this growth was small in comparison with the growth in Brazil, China, and Mexico. Further, it has been disappointing in light of the high expectation that many had of postapartheid.

Nevertheless, the South African economy has transformed itself. Although commodities such as gold and platinum are still important, there is now a thriving capital-intensive manufacturing sector that exports, for example, BMWs, Mercedes, and Volkswagens. The problem of not attracting more FDI seems to be a mix of economic, risk, operational, incentive, image, and geographic challenges. We now look at each.

Generally, investors go where they see large markets and a history of sustainable growth. The former is evident in South Africa but the latter is not. The South African growth

MAP 12.2   South Africa: The Pros and Cons of Location

On the one hand, South Africa's location is obviously advantageous for serving the high-population market of southern Africa; on the other hand, it's a long way from the tip of Africa to the markets of the developed world.

Source: CIA Yearbook, 2002. www.cia.gov.

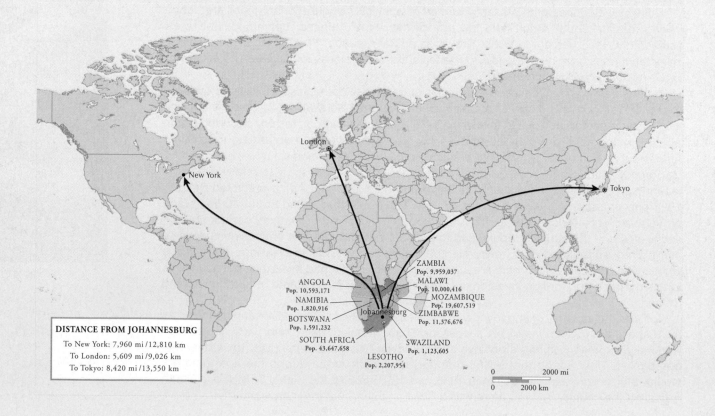

DISTANCE FROM JOHANNESBURG

To New York: 7,960 mi / 12,810 km
To London: 5,609 mi / 9,026 km
To Tokyo: 8,420 mi / 13,550 km

ZAMBIA
Pop. 9,959,037
MALAWI
Pop. 10,000,416
ANGOLA
Pop. 10,593,171
MOZAMBIQUE
Pop. 19,607,519
NAMIBIA
Pop. 1,820,916
ZIMBABWE
Pop. 11,376,676
Johannesburg
BOTSWANA
Pop. 1,591,232
SOUTH AFRICA
Pop. 43,647,658
SWAZILAND
Pop. 1,123,605
LESOTHO
Pop. 2,207,954

0   2000 mi
0   2000 km

rate, although improving since 2004, is due in good part to high world commodity prices that cannot likely be sustained. It is estimated that a sustained economic growth rate of 5 to 7 percent is needed to address its social problems adequately, and South African has not reached this.

Although South Africa has made considerable progress since 1994 in terms of households with access to clean water and use of electricity, households in formal housing, people attending schools, and development of port facilities, it still has problems. These include unemployment, continued inequality (although there is a rising black middle class), and declining population and life expectancy. For instance, the high incidence of AIDS reduced life expectancy in South Africa from 63 years in 1990 to 42 years in 2007. About half the population, mostly black, live below the poverty line. Complications arise from civil unrest and slow economic growth in much of southern Africa. These countries are important export markets. Turmoil there reduces earnings for South African export industries, thereby slowing the savings and investment needed to fund growth.

South Africa has enjoyed political stability since the fall of apartheid. Still, other political problems have created risks. The Corruption Perception Index rated South Africa as the third-least corrupt country in Africa, the 51st out of 166 countries ranked in 2006, and less corrupt than some EU countries. Although this ranking is not comparatively bad, the former South African president of the Associated Chambers of Commerce noted, "In the case of South Africa, the extent of perceived corruption makes for a lack of confidence which, in turn, has led to a sluggish rate of fixed investment in both the public and private sector."

There have also been personal safety issues. South Africa has the tenth highest crime rate in the world and the second highest murder rate of 62 countries compared. Protecting people and property adds a great deal of cost; firms typically have to spend between 5 to 10 percent of their budgets on additional security. Finally, instability in the region, particularly in Zimbabwe, threatens South Africa.

Foreign companies have often run into troubles in South Africa. Staffing is a recurring problem. The exodus of young, highly qualified whites has created shortages of skilled executives and labor. Some estimates put the shortfall of qualified technicians and managers at between 350,000 and 500,000. At the same time, South Africa has been strict at allowing skilled foreigners to work there. In response, Xerox has opened and operated a training program for technical and sales staff and has adopted a school in the predominantly black township of Thembisa. All in all, some companies have reasoned that effectively running a South African operation would demand more management time than is justified by the potential returns.

The image of South Africa has created other problems. Trying to convince an executive to leave a comparatively safer haven abroad to manage a new subsidiary in unruly Johannesburg has been hard. In addition, the financial emigration of some South African corporate giants—switching their home stock market listings to foreign bourses in an effort to distance themselves from the negative perceptions of corruption and crime in South Africa—has fanned suspicions.

Geography adds a final hurdle. The country is at the tip of a poor continent, making it hard to export and hard to buy imports at a low price. The three largest markets for South Africa are Japan, the United Kingdom, and the United States—all at a considerable distance. South Africa is so distant from developed countries that potential investors sometimes do not evaluate opportunities impartially.

Compounding physical distance are popular misconceptions. For example, a survey of corporate executives from around the world by South African officials concluded that one U.S. executive's remark, "We still see South Africa as one big game reserve," typified its challenge to attract foreign investment. Moreover, people abroad often assume that mining dominates South Africa's economy; actually, it accounts for less than 10 percent of GDP. Similarly, people think that most of the world's diamonds come from South Africa; actually, it is the world's fifth largest producer.

Nevertheless, some factors may bode well for future opportunities in South Africa. For example, the global geopolitical environment may be shifting in favor of Africa. Both Chinese and Indian companies have been turning more of their attention on South Africa as both a market and source of supplies. Further, the United States and the EU have argued that aid is necessary for African countries, lest they be havens for terrorist activities. As funds flow into Africa, South Africa may find more markets elsewhere in Africa and be the natural gateway for FDI that penetrates African markets. ∎

QUESTIONS

1. What are the costs and benefits to South Africa of having more foreign direct investment? Of having less?

2. How might a company try to weigh fairly the opportunities and risks of investing in South Africa?

3. If South Africa is to receive more foreign direct investment, how should it prioritize policies to attract it?

4. Assume you represent a non–South African company and are considering foreign expansion. What factors would you consider when comparing South Africa with other developing countries where you might locate? What about in terms of developed markets? What about in terms of other African markets?

SUMMARY

- Because companies seldom have sufficient resources to exploit all opportunities, two major considerations facing managers are which markets to serve and where to locate the production to serve those markets.

- Companies' decisions on market and production location are highly interdependent because companies often need to serve markets from local production and because they want to use existing production capacity.

- Scanning techniques aid managers in considering alternatives that might otherwise be overlooked. They also help limit the final detailed feasibility studies to a manageable number of those that appear most promising.

- Because each company has unique competitive capabilities and objectives, the factors affecting the choice of operating location will be slightly different for each. Nevertheless, a large number of companies consider comparative market potential indicators when seeking foreign sales and cost indicators when seeking foreign assets.

- Four broad categories of risk that companies may consider are political, monetary, natural disaster, and competitive.

- The amount, accuracy, and timeliness of published data vary substantially among countries. Managers should be particularly aware of different definitions of terms, different collection methods, and different base years for reports, as well as misleading responses.

- Companies frequently use several tools to compare opportunities and risk in various countries, such as grids that rate country projects according to a number of separate dimensions and matrices—for example, one on which companies plot opportunity on one axis and risk on another.

- When allocating resources among countries, companies need to consider how to treat reinvestments and divestments, the interdependence of operations in different countries, and whether they should follow diversification versus concentration strategies.

- Companies may reduce the risk of liability of foreignness by moving first to countries more similar to their home countries. Alternatively, they may contract with experienced companies to handle operations for them, limit the resources they commit to foreign operations, and delay entry to many countries until they are operating successfully in one or a few.

- Companies must develop location strategies for new investments and devise means of deemphasizing certain areas and divesting if necessary.

- Companies often evaluate entry to a country without comparing that country with other countries. This is because they may need to react quickly to proposals, to respond to competitive threats, and because multiple feasibility studies seldom are finished simultaneously.

KEY TERMS

concentration strategy (p. 474)   harvesting (or divesting) (p. 477)   liquidity preference (p. 462)
diversification strategy (p. 474)   imitation lag (p. 465)   oligopolistic reaction (p. 464)
first-mover advantage (p. 465)   liability of foreignness (p. 463)   spillover effect (p. 475)

ENDNOTES

1 *Sources include the following:* Carrefour, at www.carrefour.com (accessed June 11, 2007); "Business Crossroads: Carrefour," *The Economist,* March 17, 2007: 87; Eirmalas are Bani, "Carrefour Gives Priority to Locally-Made Products," *Business Times* [Malaysia], November 9, 1998: 3; "Carrefour Globalizes Sales," *Gazeta Mercantil Online* [Brazil], October 13, 1998: Business & Company News, n.p.; Michiyo Nakamoto, "Carrefour Sounds Alarm for Japan's Ailing Retail Market," *Financial Times,* December 8, 2000: 36; Rosabeth Moss Kanter, "Global Competitiveness Revisited," *Washington Quarterly* (Spring 1999): 39–58; "Global Strategy—Why Tesco Will Beat Carrefour," *JRetail Week,* April 6, 2001: 14; "Carrefour Closes Hong Kong Chain after Site Pitfalls," *JRetail Week,* September 1, 2000: 3; "Carrefour Beats Wal-Mart to Global Crown," *JRetail Week,* December 15, 2000: 5; "Carrefour Aims to Win Global Retail Battle," *MMR,* June 26, 2000: 60; "Hypermarkets for Britain," *The Economist,* July 3, 1976: 77; "French Retailer Abandons 'Hypermarkets' in U.S." *New York Times,* September 8, 1993: D4; "Strategies for Retail Globalisation," *Financial Times,* March 13, 1998: 4; Mark Albright, 'This Is Just Way Too Big': European-Style Hypermarkets Not as Hot in U.S.," *St. Petersburg* [FL] *Times,* February 12, 1990: 7; "AEON Acquires Carrefour's Japan Unit," *Japan Economic Newswire,* March 10, 2005; Robert Guy Matthews, "Problems in Carrefour's Home Market Sank CEO," *Wall Street Journal,* February 4, 2005: A1+; Dexter Roberts, Wendy Zellner, and Carol Matlack, "Let China's Retail Wars Begin," *Business Week Online,* January 17, 2005; Luc Vandevelde, "Carrefour n'a besoin de personne pour se développer," *Les Echos* [France], March 1, 2005: 32.

2 Shige Makino, Takehiko Isobe, and Christine M. Chan, "Does Country Matter?" *Strategic Management Journal* 25 (2004): 1027–43.

3 Bob Lutz, *GUTS: The Seven Laws of Business That Made Chrysler the World's Hottest Car Company* (New York: Wiley, 1998).

4 David Gonzalez, "Fried Chicken Takes Flight, Happily Nesting in U.S.," *New York Times,* September 20, 2002: A4; Joel Millman, "California City Fends Off Arrival of Mexican Supermarket," *Wall Street Journal,* August 7, 2002: B1+.

5 Don E. Schultz, "China May Leapfrog the West in Marketing," *Marketing News,* August 19, 2002: 8–9.

6 Makino, Isobe, and Chan, "Does Country Matter?"

7 Anil Khurana, "Strategies for Global R&D," *Research Technology Management* (March/April 2006): 48–59.

8 David Luchnow, "Missing Piece of the Mexican Success Story," *Wall Street Journal,* March 4, 2002: A11+.

9 Michael Peel, "Bitter-Sweet Confections of Business in Nigeria," *Financial Times,* November 20, 2002: 10.

10 Andrew Bartmess and Keith Cerny, "Building Competitive Advantage through a Global Network of Capabilities," *California Management Review* (Winter 1993): 78–103.

11 G. Bruce Knecht, "Going the Wrong Way Down a One-Way Street," *Wall Street Journal,* March 18, 2002: A1.

12 Alfredo J. Mauri and Arvind V. Phatak, "Global Integration as Inter-Area Product Flows: The Internationalization of Ownership and Location Factors Influencing Product Flows across MNC Units," *Management International Review* 41 (2001): 233–49.

13 Lisa Bannon, "As Holiday Season Approaches, Toy Shipments Are Imperiled," *Wall Street Journal,* October 4, 2002: A9.

14 Julian Birkinshaw, Pontus Braunerhjelm, and Ulf Holm, "Why Do Some Multinational Corporations Relocate Their Headquarters Overseas?" *Strategic Management Journal* 27 (2006): 681–700.

15 Nagesh Kumar, "Multinational Enterprises, Regional Economic Integration, and Export-Platform Production in the Host Countries: An Empirical Analysis for the U.S. and Japanese Corporations," *Weltwirtschaftliches Archive* 134:3 (1998): 450–83.

16 Anthony Rowley, "Investing in Japan," *Wall Street Journal,* June 7, 2007: A8; "Doors and Opportunities Open in Japan," *Financial Times,* June 7, 2007: 7.

17 World Bank, International Finance Corporation, *Doing Business in 2005* (Washington: The International Bank for Reconstruction and Development, 2005).

18 Hoon Park, "Determinants of Corruption: A Cross-National Analysis," *Multinational Business Review* 11:2 (2003): 29–48.

19 "Volkswagen Switches Work to Low-Cost Unit in Slovakia," *Financial Times,* December 19, 1995: 4.

20 John D. Daniels and James A. Schweikart, "Political Risk, Assessment and Management of," in Rosalie L. Tung, ed., *IEBM Handbook of International Business* (London: International Thomson Business Press, 1999): 502–14.

21 See Luciano Gremone and Ben Tsocanos, "Ongoing Political Risk in Venezuela Still Poses Challenges for Foreign Oil and Gas Companies," *Business News Americas,* February 14, 2007: 1; Farhan Bokhari, "Western Expatriates Give Way to Local Heroes,"

Financial Times, August 30, 2002: 8; Joseph T. Hallinan and Janet Adamy, "Chiquita Says It Paid Terrorists to Protect Workers in Colombia," *Wall Street Journal,* May 11, 2004: B10; Henri E. Cauvin, "Braving War and Graft, Coke Goes Back to Angola," *New York Times,* April 22, 2001: Sec. 3, 1+.

22 Marvin Zonis and Sam Wilkin, "Driving Defensively Through a Minefield of Political Risk," *Financial Times,* May 30, 2000: Mastering Risk, 8–10.

23 Chip Cummins, "Dirty Work," *Wall Street Journal,* June 7, 2007: 1+.

24 Much like options theory, theory of liquidity preference is associated with the work of Robert C. Merton, Myron S. Scholes, and Fisher Black. For good, succinct coverage, see John Krainer, "The 1997 Nobel Prize in Economics," *FRBSF Economic Letter* No. 98–05 (February 13, 1998).

25 United Nations Development Programme, *Reducing Disaster Risk: A Challenge for Development* (New York: United Nations, 2004).

26 Paul L. Knox and Sallie A. Marston, *Places and Regions in Global Context,* 3rd ed. (Upper Saddle River, NJ: Pearson Education, 2004), p. 120.

27 Robert A. Manning, "The 21st Century Will Be Asia's Century," *Pittsburgh Post-Gazette,* January 2, 2000: E1.

28 WHO, Public Health Mapping and GIS, Map Library, at http://gamapserver.who.int/mapLibrary/default.aspx (accessed June 11, 2007).

29 "A Threat Deadlier Than a Landmine," *Financial Times,* December 2, 2002: 10.

30 Amy Merrick and Ann Zimmerman, "Wal-Mart Bans Some Work Travel Due to SARS," *Wall Street Journal,* April 10, 2003: 36.

31 See Srilata Zaheer and Elaine Mosakowski, "The Dynamics of the Liability of Foreignness: A Global Study of Survival in Financial Services," *Strategic Management Journal* 18 (1997): 439–64; Stewart R. Miller and Arvind Parkhe, "Is There a Liability of Foreignness in Global Banking? An Empirical Test of Banks' X-Efficiency," *Strategic Management Journal* 23 (2002): 55–75.

32 Mikhail V. Gratchev, "Making the Most of Cultural Differences," *Harvard Business Review* (October 2001): 28–30.

33 Khanh T. L. Tran, "Blockbuster Finds Success in Japan," *Wall Street Journal,* August 19, 1998: A14; Cecile Rohwedder, "Blockbuster Hits Eject Button as Stores in Germany See Video-Rental Sales Sag," *Wall Street Journal,* January 16, 1998: B9A.

34 Jon A. Doukas and Ozgur B. Kan, "Does Global Diversification Destroy Firm Values?" *Journal of International Business Studies* 37 (2006): 352–71.

35 B. Kazaz, M. Dada, and H. Moskowitz, "Global Production Planning under Exchange-Rate Uncertainty," *Management Science* 51 (2005): 1101–9.

36 Edward B. Flowers, "Oligopolistic Reactions in European and Canadian Direct Investment in the United States," *Journal of International Business Studies* (Fall–Winter 1976): 43–55; Frederick Knickerbocker, *Oligopolistic Reaction and Multinational Enterprise* (Cambridge, MA: Harvard University, Graduate School of Business, Division of Research, 1973).

37 David Murphy and David Lague, "As China's Car Market Takes Off, the Party Grows a Bit Crowded," *Wall Street Journal,* July 3, 2002: A8; James Mackintosh and Richard McGregor, "Auto Industry," *Financial Times,* August 25, 2003: 13.

38 Hugh Pope, "Q: Why Are the World's IBMs Putting Down Roots in the Desert? A: Dubai," *Wall Street Journal,* January 23, 2001: A18; Lynn K. Mytelka and Lou Anne Barclay, "Using Foreign Investment Strategically for Innovation," paper presented at the Conference on Understanding FDI-Assisted Economic Development, University of Oslo, Norway (May 22–25, 2003).

39 See J. Myles Shaver and Fredrick Flyer, "Agglomeration Economies, Firm Heterogeneity, and Foreign Direct Investment in the United States," *Strategic Management Journal* 21 (2000): 1175–93; Philippe Martin and Gianmarco I. P. Ottaviano, "Growth and Agglomeration," *International Economic Review* 42 (2001): 947–68; and Edward E. Leamer and Michael Storper, "The Economic Geography of the Internet Age," *Journal of International Business Studies* 32 (2001): 641–65.

40 Philip Parker, "Choosing Where to Go Global: How to Prioritise Markets," *Financial Times,* November 16, 1998: Mastering Marketing, 7–8.

41 Joel Millman, "PriceSmart to Restate Results Due to an Accounting Error," *Wall Street Journal,* November 11, 2003: B9.

42 Jedrzej George Frynas, Kamel Mellah, and Geoffrey Allen Pigman, "First Mover Advantages in International Business and Firm-Specific Political Resources," *Strategic Management Journal* 27 (2006): 321–45; and Makino, Isobe, and Chan, "Does Country Matter?"

43 James Kynge, "Pyramid of Power behind Numbers Game," *Financial Times,* February 28, 2002: 6.

44 Chip Cumins, "Crude Theft," *Wall Street Journal,* April 13, 2005: A1+.

45 "Market Research," *Financial Times,* March 5, 2003: 9.

46 Moisés Naím, "The Five Wars of Globalization," *Foreign Policy* (January–February, 2003): 29–36.

47 "You're in Good Hands," at www.comebackalive.com/df/kidnapp/goodhand.htm (accessed June 12, 2007); "Five Britons Set Free by Nigerian Kidnapping Gang," June 12, 2007, at http://news.scotsman.com/international.cfm?id=917782007 (accessed June 12, 2007).

48 "Doing Business in Dangerous Places," *The Economist,* August 14, 2004: 11.

49 Mary Kissel, "U.S. Expats Deal with Terror Threat," *Wall Street Journal,* May 12, 2004: B4a, quoting Frank Holder, of Kroll, Inc.

50 "Global Terrorism Index," *The Economist,* August 30, 2003: 74, using data from the World Markets Research Centre.

51 Andrew Ward, "Terror Threat from Within Keeps America on High Alert," *Financial Times,* April 19, 2005: 3, quoting John Lewis.

52 Harry Hurt III, "Making the World Safer, One Client at a Time," *New York Times,* May 11, 2004: C12.

53 Igal Ayal and Jehiel Zif, "Marketing Expansion Strategies in Multinational Marketing," *Journal of Marketing* (Spring 1979): 84–94.

54 Makino, Isobe, and Chan, "Does Country Matter?"

55 Diane Summers, "Chunky Monkey Invasion," *Financial Times,* August 11, 1994: 7.

56 Susanna Voyle and James Drummond, "J. Sainsbury to Withdraw from Egypt," *Financial Times,* April 10, 2001: 23.

57 Nikki Tait, "Dana Set to Sell UK-Based Components Arm," *Financial Times,* November 29, 2000: 22.

58 Makino, Isobe, and Chan, " Does Country Matter?" Bernard Simon, "Goodyear Sells Its Last Plantation," Financial Times, December 1, 2004: 18.

59 See Jean J. Boddewyn, "Foreign and Domestic Divestment and Investment Decisions: Like or Unlike?" *Journal of International Business Studies* (Winter 1983): 28; Michelle Haynes, Steve Thompson, and Mike Wright, "The Determinants of Corporate Divestment in the U.K.," *Journal of Industrial Organization* 18 (2000): 1201–22; Jose Mata and Pedro Portugal, "Closure and Divestiture by Foreign Entrants: The Impact of Entry and Post-Entry Strategies," *Strategic Management Journal* 21 (2000): 549–62.

60 World Bank and International Finance Corporation, *Doing Business in 2005* (Washington, D.C.: The International Bank for Reconstruction and Development, 2005): 69.

61 Edna Fernandes, "India to Let Foreigners Invest in Newspapers," *Financial Times,* June 26, 2002: 6.

62 "Enron Assets Outside U.S. Go Up for Sale; Activity Seen in South Korea and India," *Wall Street Journal*, January 22, 2002: A6.

63 International Monetary Fund, *World Economic Outlook, September 2004* (Washington: International Monetary Fund, 2004): 143–49.

64 Deborah Hargreaves, "'Virtual' Staff Make Themselves at Home in Offices of the Future," *Financial Times*, May 14, 1999: 8.

65 Peter Hall, *Cities in Civilization: Culture, Technology, and Urban Order* (London: Weidenfeld & Nicholson, 1998).

66 David Aviel, "The Causes and Consequences of Public Attitudes to Technology: A United States Analysis," *International Journal of Management* 18 (2001): 166.

67 *Sources include the following:* "South Africa," *Financial Times*, June 5, 2007: special section; Faisal Ahmen, Rabah Arezki, and Norbert Funke, "The Composition of Capital Flows to South Africa," *Journal of International Development* 19 (2007): 275–94; Paula Green, "A Continent on the Cusp," *Global Finance* (May 2007): 20; Kupukile Mlambo, "Reviving Foreign Direct Investments in Southern Africa: Constraints and Policies," *African Development Bank* (2005): 552–79; Jon Jeter, "South Africa's Image Problem Deters Investors," *Washington Post*, October 17, 1999: A21; "FDI Revival Begins at Home," *Global News Wire*, South African Press Association (January 31, 2001); James Lamont, "South Africa Sees Rise in Investment," *Financial Times*, August 3, 2001: 7; "Small Mercies," *The Economist*, October 11, 2003: 52; "Emigration," *Financial Times*, April 13, 2004: 5; Wyndham Hartley and Farouk Chothia, "South Africa Politics: Less Risky," *EIU Newswire*, July 13, 2004; "South Africa Economy: Empowerment before Growth?" *EIU Newswire*, May 19, 2004; "Business on Hold?" *South African Privatisation*, June 26, 2004: 78; "Foreign Interest in South Africa Takes Off," *Funds International*, January 2005: 1; F. W. de Klerk, "An African First-World Country," *Wall Street Journal*, September 23, 2004: A14; "Africa: Turnaround in FDI Inflows Last Year," *UNCTAD Press Release*, September 22, 2004, at www.cia.gov/cia/publications/factbook/geos/sf.html.

13

Export and Import Strategies

Objectives

- To introduce the ideas of export and import

- To identify the elements of export and exporting strategies

- To compare direct and indirect selling of exporting

- To identify the elements of import and importing strategies

- To discuss the types and roles of third-party intermediaries

- To discuss the role of countertrade in international business

When one is prepared, difficulties do not come.

—*Ethiopian proverb*

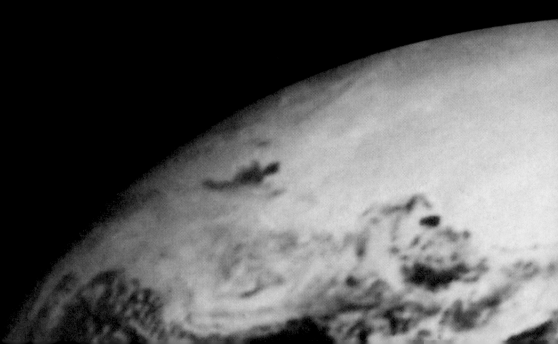

CASE: Grieve—A Small-Business Export Strategy

The biggest exporters, such as Boeing, Caterpillar, and General Electric, generate about 30 percent of all merchandise exports from the United States.[1] Their smaller shipments are usually much larger than the largest shipments of smaller companies. Still, small and medium-size enterprises (SME), companies with fewer than 250 workers, account for 97 percent of all U.S. exporters. In addition, SMEs account for more than

is found in every market segment, from commercial heat treating to drug discovery, used for paint baking to sterilizing and much more. The company began operations in 1949 with "one goal in mind . . . to create a line of industrial heat-processing equipment our customers could believe in." The company has always taken pride in offering complete custom-engineering design and manufacturing services.

MAP 13.1   The Association of South East Asian Nations (ASEAN)

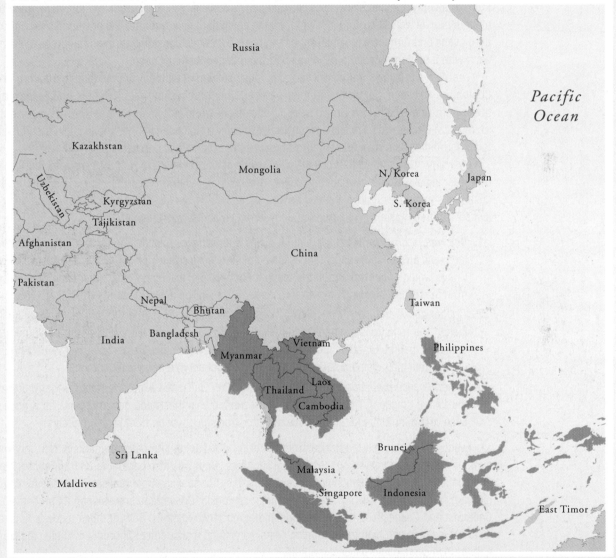

98 percent of the growth in the exporter population. And, in terms of volume, SMEs are responsible for at least half of all U.S. exports to 85 countries. One such SME is Grieve of Round Lake, Illinois.

Grieve manufactures laboratory and industrial ovens, furnaces, and heat processing systems. Grieve-built equipment

To this day, it believes it builds "ovens and furnaces for which there simply are no equals."

Since 1949, Grieve's primary business has been to design and manufacture laboratory and industrial ovens and furnaces for virtually all industries worldwide. Over time, Grieve has built core competencies in meeting any customer's particular requirements, officially aiming to be "more than manufacturers but, rather, problem solving professionals who take the time to understand your needs."

Presently, Grieve applies its knowledge and experience to building industrial ovens and furnaces ranging from routine heating applications to state-of-the-art systems that meet the rigid specifications of clean room, semiconductor, and pharmaceutical environments. The customized design and construction of each product goes hand in hand with rigorous testing. Then, before a unit is crated for shipment, management quality-checks more than 100 features. Grieve operates out of its 100,000-square-foot facility in Round Lake, Illinois, which houses its corporate headquarters, sales, engineering, research, and manufacturing divisions.

Improving responsiveness to customers led Grieve to expand its Web site, www.grievecorp.com, in 2006. Presently, the site showcases the company's capability in the design, manufacture, and delivery of standard, as well as custom, heat-processing equipment and systems. The site details over 400 standard ovens and furnaces; it displays the range of product customization through hundreds of examples, each with a photograph and a description of the unit and its application.

The Web site allows the viewer to index these custom equipment photographs by feature or style. Customers can then submit online their particular heat-processing requirements and receive a price quote from Grieve. Because Grieve sells its equipment worldwide through a network of manufacturer's representatives, its Web site allows a customer to enter a zip code into the "rep locator" area to get contact information. As a rule, Grieve representatives are experienced engineers.

Over time, Grieve ran into problems when some of its customers moved their manufacturing facilities overseas. Initially, Grieve continued to supply that customer with ovens or furnaces via exporting, but the customer's purchases gradually faded as it began sourcing from local providers. Despite more than a few lost sales, three reasons had dissuaded Grieve from proactively considering exports:

1. *The nature of its product.* Industrial ovens and furnaces, besides being relatively expensive, are large and bulky. Top management assumed the product's size would make shipping costs so high that Grieve would price itself out of the market. For example, shipping a fully automated furnace system from the factory in Round Lake to a customer in the Philippines cost about $41,000 in 2005.

2. *Doubts about chances of success abroad.* Management assumed Grieve, as a small business, lacked the resources needed to support a successful export program. Serving customers in the domestic market kept the company busy enough. They struggled to see how they could stretch their already thin management structure to develop and direct international operations.

3. *General concern about competition.* Grieve battled seasoned exporters from Germany, Japan, and the United Kingdom. These companies were fierce rivals that made good products for a good price. Even within the United States, Grieve ran into strong competition from local producers.

Eventually, Grieve felt it must confront the issue of pursuing international markets. Not only was the company losing customers overseas to local suppliers, but it was also beginning to experience increasing competition from foreign companies in the U.S. market. Top management realized it needed to respond to growing competition or risk its market position. In addition, Grieve regularly shipped its products to both California and Connecticut, its number-one and number-two markets. Both of these markets have strong local competition and high transportation costs, something management figured would give the company a step-up in serving international markets.

Keeping these issues in mind, Patrick Calabrese, Grieve's president, attended a one-day trade seminar that featured market analysis and trade reports from U.S. officials to countries in the Association of South East Asian Nations (ASEAN) (specifically, as seen in Map 13.1, Brunei Darussalam, Cambodia, Indonesia, Laos, Malaysia, Myanmar, the Philippines, Singapore, Thailand, and Vietnam). While listening to their presentation, he once again wondered whether or not it made sense to export to Asia.

By the time the final speaker spoke, Calabrese was confident there might be market opportunities for his firm in one of the world's fastest-growing regions. However, he was unfamiliar with the ASEAN region, a problem compounded by the company's lack of any sort of official sales offices or representatives in any of the ASEAN countries. He was also concerned about how his company would take on the British, German, and Japanese competition that had strong positions in those markets.

Grieve's marketing staff decided to sample potential interest in Asia by advertising in industry reports and trade publications that circulated in Southeast Asia, such as the *Asian Industrial Reporter, Asian Literature Showcase,* and *World Industrial Reporter.* To learn more about the market, Calabrese worked with a representative from the International Trade Administration of the Chicago Export Assistance Center. This center, like others in major metropolitan areas in the United States, is a one-stop shop ready to provide small or medium-size businesses with export assistance: Unlike large firms, SMEs especially depend on government export promotion programs. The center houses representatives of the U.S. Small Business Administration, the U.S. Department of Commerce, the U.S. Export-Import Bank, and other public and private organizations. Various representatives of the Chicago Export Assistance Center helped Calabrese plan his trip to Asia by arranging for interpreters at each stop on his itinerary and by coordinating meetings with various personnel at several U.S. embassies.

The goals of Calabrese's trip were to determine market potential and begin recruiting possible sales representatives. He had received inquiries from some distributors that were familiar with Grieve's product line but had not responded to them. However, Calabrese's staff had recently begun filing correspondences and sales contacts by country, rather than by their earlier system of sorting them by company name. Hence he had a head start on locating potential distributors and customers.

In addition, Calabrese tapped the U.S. Department of Commerce's Agent/Distributor Search to get leads on several other possible distributors. This service specifically helps small to medium-size exporters enlist the help of commercial specialists at U.S. embassies and consulates to search the market for qualified agents, distributors, and representatives. The trip was a huge success for Grieve. Interviews were held with 28 potential agents over 28 days, and exclusive agents were signed up in each country.

During his travels and discussions, Calabrese quickly learned he had to cut shipping costs. If not, the cost of transporting products from the United States to these markets would wipe out profits. Staff back in the United States began figuring out how to streamline packaging and started shopping among freight forwarders to find the best shipping rates. In addition, Calabrese's trip confirmed his sense of the need to visit potential customers in Asia personally rather than relying on the local sales representative. As he explains,

> The one thing that I found is that almost to an individual, [Asian customers] are very keen on a personal association. If I were to give anybody advice, I would never send a second-level individual. Never send a marketing manager or sales manager; I would send a top manager. If your company isn't too large to prohibit it, I would send the president or chairman.
>
> On the other end, you are talking to the owner of a small distributor or the president of a small manufacturing company, and you've got to meet [that person] on an equal level. My limited experience is [these people] are very cognizant of this; in other words, they are pretty much attuned to a president talking to a president. They also like to feel secure that they are dealing with someone who can make decisions.
>
> Another thing I found is that potential customers want to feel that you are financially secure and that you have sufficient funding to continue to work with them for a period of years, because it takes some time and some money on our end to get these people going. Follow-up is incredibly important. I heard all kinds of stories about American [businesspeople] who would come over and spend a day and talk to potential customers and leave [catalogs]. Then the first time the potential customers would send a fax asking for information, they didn't hear from them for two weeks, and that just turns them right off.

True to its tradition of engineering solutions, Grieve found ways to streamline its product. Still, Grieve struggled with high transport costs and significant competition from foreign companies as it worked to penetrate foreign markets. Throughout it all, top management stayed optimistic, confident they had a competitive product that people would buy. As Calabrese points out, "Our strength is that we are selling engineered products, using our 45 years of expertise to build something for them." Through his experiences in Southeast Asia, Calabrese learned some lessons about exporting successfully, specifically:

1. *Know your products well.*   Many people who go to Asia from the United States know little about their own products. In some cases, potential agents who have studied company brochures know more about the products than the company representative.

2. *Learn about the competition in the foreign market and the potential sale for your products.*   Keep an open mind: You may have to adjust your selling strategy, or even your product, to appeal to customers.

3. Jumpstart your brand image.

4. *Work hard.*   Too many foreign visitors want to spend a lot of time playing golf or seeing the sights.

5. *Build a strong response base back home.*   Most foreigners complain about poor factory backup, lengthy delays in getting correspondence answered, and delays in getting quotations.

6. *Arrange for your own transportation, and don't rely on the potential representative to solve your problems for you.*   That shows a lack of understanding of the local environment.

7. *Make someone at the home office the principal contact for the representative.*   People need someone who will answer questions and provide assistance.

8. *Learn the customs and business etiquette of the countries you visit.*   Once again, the U.S. Department of Commerce, among other government agencies, can provide assistance in this area.

9. *Have the authority to make decisions and commit the company.*   If you are going to meet with the top person in the representative organization, have the authority to make the same sorts of decisions.

10. *Be prepared.*   Before hopping on a plane, determine the right market for your company and think about how you'll service overseas customers.

Calabrese's initial foray overseas led to a new appreciation of the rewards and pitfalls of exporting. On balance, though, he realized export was no longer an option: Exporting had to become part of Grieve's strategy. Once he gained experience in Asian markets, he expanded his export activity to other countries. By 2007, Grieve listed Latin America/Caribbean, South America, Western Europe, Africa, Middle East, Europe, Canada, and Mexico as export markets. Although exporting has created challenges, it has also helped Grieve reach greater success.

Introduction

As our look at Grieve demonstrates, successful exporting is a challenging process. Once a company identifies the good or service it wants to sell, it must explore and assess market opportunities among the many options in the world (Table 13.1 lists both the top exporting and top importing countries in the world). Next, it must develop a production or service development strategy, prepare the goods or services for the market, determine the best means for transporting the goods or services, sell the goods or services, receive payment, and respond to service calls and warranty claims. Complicating matters is that the company must manage these activities while at the same time dealing with different cultures, market forces, financial systems, and legal requirements that show up when doing business in foreign markets.

Granted, a firm could try to go it alone. However, the planning required at each step persuades many companies, especially **small and medium-sized enterprises (SMEs)** with fewer than 250 employees that typically do not have export managers, to seek assistance. Some find it best to rely on specialists to move goods and services from one country to another, agents or distributors to sell the goods or services, banks to collect payment, and public agents to lend wisdom.

TABLE 13.1 The World's Trading Countries (in $ billions)

Top 25 Exporters			Top 25 Importers		
Rank	Country	Exports[*]	Rank	Country	Imports[**]
1	Germany	$ 1,361	1	United States	$ 1,987
2	European Union	1,330	2	European Union	1,466
3	China	1,221	3	Germany	1,121
4	United States	1,140	4	China	917.4
5	Japan	665.7	5	France	601.4
6	France	558.9	6	United Kingdom	595.6
7	Italy	474.8	7	Japan	571.1
8	Netherlands	465.3	8	Italy	483.6
9	Canada	440.1	9	Netherlands	402.4
10	United Kingdom	415.6	10	Canada	394.4
11	Korea, South	386.6	11	Hong Kong	371.3
12	Hong Kong	353.3	12	Korea, South	359.5
13	Russia	348.9	13	Spain	359.1
14	Belgium	328.1	14	Belgium	320.9
15	Singapore	317.6	15	Mexico	279.3
16	Mexico	267.5	16	Singapore	273.0
17	Spain	248.3	17	Russia	226.5
18	Taiwan	235.5	18	India	224.1
19	Saudi Arabia	215.0	19	Taiwan	214.3
20	Switzerland	201.0	20	Switzerland	189.6
21	Sweden	176.5	21	Austria	157.4
22	Malaysia	169.9	22	Sweden	157.2
23	Brazil	159.2	23	Turkey	156.9
24	Austria	158.3	24	Australia	152.7
25	United Arab Emirates	152.1	25	Poland	150.7

Source: CIA World Factbook. Retrieved February 4, 2008.

[*] The total U.S. dollar amount of merchandise exports on an f.o.b. (free on board) basis. Figures are calculated on an exchange rate basis.

[**] The total U.S. dollar amount of merchandise imports on a c.i.f. (cost, insurance, and freight) or f.o.b. (free on board) basis. Figures are calculated on an exchange-rate basis.

EXPORTING AND IMPORTING

Companies respond to many motivations when entering foreign markets. In this chapter, we focus on the issue of an export strategy (see Figure 13.1). Before beginning, we need to define two fundamental terms. In the broadest sense, **exporting** refers to the sale of goods or services produced by a company based in one country to customers that reside in a different country. **Importing** is the reverse: the purchase of goods or services by a company based in one country from sellers that reside in another. The idea of exporting manufactured goods presents a clear situation, as in the case of a German company manufacturing physical goods that are then shipped to customers in India, Brazil, or Russia.

Particular aspects of services present situations that can make it a bit tougher to define exporting and importing.[2] Engineering contractors, Bechtel, for example, are said to export services when they construct buildings, roads, utilities, airports, seaports, or other forms of infrastructure in a foreign country. Consultants such as McKinsey & Company export when they perform services for foreign clients. Investment banks such as Goldman Sachs export when they help a foreign company—say, Haier of China—arrange financing from global sources. They also assist customers in structuring foreign business acquisitions, such as Lenovo's acquisition of IBM's personal computer business.

FIGURE 13.1   Environmental Factors Influencing Export and Import Operations

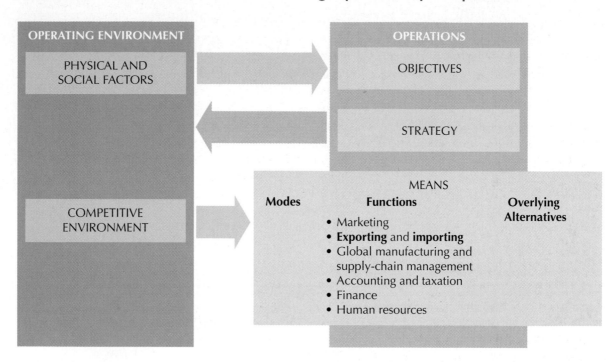

The opening of a Hyatt, McDonald's, or Starbucks in a foreign market, however, is not considered to be exporting but rather a foreign direct investment. The remainder of the chapter elaborates on these ideas, examining export and import strategies, the features of indirect versus direct selling in international markets, and the matter of countertrade.

Export Strategy

In Chapter 12, we showed that a company's choice of entry mode into a foreign market depends on different factors, such as the ownership advantages of the company, the location advantages of the market, and the internalization advantages that result from integrating transactions within the company's value chain.[3] In the following sections, we'll take a closer look at several of these factors as they pertain to export strategies.

ADVANTAGES TO CONSIDER

Ownership advantages are the firm's specific assets, international experience, and the ability to develop either low-cost or differentiated products within the context of its value chain. For instance, Samsung capitalizes on its ownership advantage through the development of sophisticated information technology; doing the same would be difficult for a new entrant to the market.

The location advantages of a particular market are a combination of market potential and investment risk. Internalization advantages are the benefits of retaining a core competency within the company and threading it through the value chain rather than opting to license, outsource, or sell it. Grieve, for example, could have explored the option of licensing its oven and furnace technology to local manufacturers in Asia. Instead, management preferred to maintain control over its core competencies and serve Asia through exports from its U.S. plant.

In general, companies that have low levels of ownership advantages either do not enter foreign markets or, if they do, they enter through low-risk modes such as exporting. Exporting requires a significantly lower level of investment than other modes of international expansion, such as FDI. As you might expect, the lower risk of export typically results in a

CONCEPT CHECK

In Chapter 12, we discuss some of the reasons why companies in a variety of industries find **exporting** the most attractive way to increase sales or acquire competitively useful assets in foreign markets. Here we use our opening case to show how one medium-size manufacturer used export operations to bolster its approach to creating **value**, especially in product design and distribution. Similarly, the opening case in Chapter 11 shows how a large apparel maker shaped its **strategy** for maximizing export potentials in configuring its **value chain**.

lower rate of return on sales than possible through other modes of international business. In other words, the usual return on export sales may not be tremendous, but neither is the risk.

Exporting allows managers to exercise operational control but does not provide them the option to exercise as much marketing control. An exporter usually resides far from the end consumer and often enlists various intermediaries to manage marketing and service activities.[4]

QUESTIONS TO ASK

The choice of exporting as an entry mode is not just a function of ownership, location, and internalization advantages. It also must fit the company's strategy. Companies typically consider these questions in evaluating the export option:

- What do we want to gain from exporting?
- Is exporting consistent with our other goals?
- Will exporting place demands on our key resources—management and personnel, production capacity, and financing—and, if so, how will we meet these demands?
- Does exporting help us leverage our core competency?
- Does exporting fit into the current configuration of our value chain?
- Can our existing coordination methods also deal with the managerial demands created by exporting?
- Are the projected benefits of exporting worth the costs? Would our resources be better used for developing new domestic business?[5]

These questions require managers to look at matters of global concentration, synergies, and strategic motivations. Global concentration, for instance, means that many global industries have only a few major players, and a company's strategy for penetrating a particular market might depend on the competition. If rivals are servicing markets by exporting, the company might also do well following the same strategy. However, if rivals have found ways to create superior value by servicing the local market through local production, the company might not be as successful in the future if it only exports.[6]

STRATEGIC ADVANTAGES OF EXPORTING

Principally, both service companies and manufacturers export to increase sales revenues. Many of the former, such as accountants, advertisers, lawyers, and consultants, export their services to meet the needs of clients working abroad. Companies that are capital and research intensive, pharmaceutical companies for example, export to achieve economies of scale by spreading their research, product development, and capacity expenditures over a larger sales area. Similarly, many companies that are not leaders in their domestic markets may more actively seek export sales as an indirect way to counter the volume advantage commanded by the market leader.

In Japan, Matsushita and Toyota are market leaders in consumer electronics and motor vehicles, respectively. Electronic manufacturers Sony and Sanyo, and automakers Nissan and Honda, lag behind the leaders and as such approach exports more aggressively. One advantage to these export sales is that it can alleviate the problem of excess capacity in the domestic market. Another reason some companies export rather than invest abroad is because of the perceived higher risk of operating internationally.

Diversification Exporting enables companies to diversify their activities, thereby developing the capacity to weather changes in the home market. As we saw in our opening case, for example, Grieve developed markets in Asia to expand its sales base and to reduce its heavy reliance on sales in the U.S. market. Because economic growth is not the same in every market, export diversification allows a company to use strong growth in one market to offset weak growth in another. Similarly, the company that develops more customers reduces its vulnerability to the loss of particular customers.

Exporting helps companies

- Expand sales.
- Achieve scale economies.
- Diversify sales.

CONCEPT CHECK

We explain in Chapter 1 that the attractiveness of **exporting** as a means of entering international business has been enhanced by several developments in export efficiency. We cite, for instance, the liberalization of the cross-border movement of resources and the development of services designed to support the export process. Here we observe that many of these developments have made exporting more attractive to a broader range of companies.

Case Review Note

The Role of Serendipity   It's appealing to depict the export process as a proactive strategy that management meticulously designs. However, research tells of accidental exporters who, responding to circumstances, enter overseas markets by chance and attain great success. Thus we need to address the role of **serendipity** as a catalyst for companies to begin exporting.

Edward Cutler is such a case. He's the owner and founder of Pennsylvania-based Squigle, a unique brand of toothpaste for people who cannot tolerate the harsh foaming agents commonly found in mass-produced toothpastes. After launching his toothpaste in 1998, Cutler focused on the U.S. market. News of the product's performance spread over the Internet, and Squigle began getting inquiries from people in Taiwan, Turkey, and elsewhere. One customer, a canker-sore sufferer in Britain, was so enthusiastic about the toothpaste that he began importing Squigle to England for sale there. That was good news for Cutler because it let him expand abroad at little cost or risk. Now he is eager to start exporting more product, explaining, "We're looking to sell overseas for the same reason the big companies do: Most of the world's population lies outside the United States."[7] Indeed, 95 percent of the world's consumers live outside of the United States. Hence, so if a U.S. business only sells domestically, it only reaches a small share of total potential customers.

Profit Potential   Lastly, one more strategic advantage of exporting is the potential of greater profitability. For several reasons, companies can sell their products at a greater profit abroad than at home. This often happens because the competitive environment in the foreign market is different, possibly because in that market, the product has no direct substitute or is in a different stage of its life cycle. A mature product at home often triggers extreme price competition, whereas a growth stage in foreign markets may permit premium prices.

Greater profitability also may come about because of different government actions at home and abroad that affect profitability, such as differences in the taxation of earnings or the regulation of prices. If, however, companies must divert efforts from domestic sales to service the greater demands of foreign markets, they may lack the resources to sustain their growth objectives.

CHARACTERISTICS OF EXPORTERS

Research on the characteristics of exporters consistently indicates the following:

- The probability of being an exporter increases with company size, as defined by sales revenues.

- *Export intensity,* the percentage of total revenues coming from export sales, is not positively correlated with company size. Rather, the greater the percentage of exports to total revenues, the greater the degree of export intensity.

- Exporting is engaged by both big and small companies. More than two-thirds of exporters have fewer than 20 employees.

Size   The first conclusion is that small companies can grow in the domestic market without having to export, but large companies must export if they are to increase sales.[8] And, yes, the largest companies, such as Sony, Boeing, and Nokia, are routinely the biggest exporters in their countries. Still, the data show that SMEs are progressively expanding their export capability. For instance, SMEs makes up about 88 percent of U.S. exporters, and they account for a fifth of the value of exports from the United States.[9]

Grieve, the subject of our opening case, is a good example. Although it's a small company in terms of total sales, Grieve's export revenues enhance its competitiveness and performance, and its export activity not only supports its overseas market share but also fortifies its competitive position in the United States. Others report similar effects; a study of Canadian companies found that the size of the firm was not the most important factor in determining a company's propensity to export, the number of countries it exported to, or its degree of export intensity.

Although the largest companies are the biggest exporters, small companies are also expanding their export capability.

Case Review Note

Perspective on Risk and Other Industry Factors Factors such as management's outlook on risk and industry factors are just as important as firm size. Managers who are more likely to take a risk are also more likely to engage in exporting. Small high-tech or highly specialized companies that operate in market niches with a global demand, as well as small companies that sell expensive capital equipment, are also highly inclined to export. Finally, companies are more likely to engage in exporting if they are operating in industries in which the leading companies are also exporters.[10]

STAGES OF EXPORT DEVELOPMENT

Several factors trigger exporting.[11] A company can export goods and services to related companies, such as subsidiaries, or it can export to independent customers. Sometimes a company exports its products to its related companies overseas, which then sell them to local consumers. Other times, a company exports semifinished goods that are used by its related companies as inputs in their manufacturing process. In many cases, however, the sale is to a third party, and in those situations, the exporter may sell directly to the buyer or indirectly via an intermediary.

Serendipity Revisited As we noted earlier, some companies begin exporting by serendipity rather than by design—an unsolicited sales order arrives in the mail, a contact is made at an industry conference, personal travel abroad alerts a manager to new options, and so on. The often unplanned stimulus to export, if not dealt with systematically, can create difficulties. Therefore, achieving the strategic advantages of exports depends on developing a sound yet insightful export strategy.

Three Phases of Export Development Figure 13.2 identifies the three phases of export development.[12] These phases have less to do with company size than with degree of export development—both big and small companies can be at any particular stage. Increasingly, we see more newly formed companies begin exporting sooner in their life cycle than ever before. A new generation of entrepreneurs and managers with a keen awareness of international business launches companies that are essentially "born global." That is, there is a growing trend for some firms to step straight onto the world stage, making exporting a primary goal from day one of operations.[13]

> The probability of being an exporter increases with the size of the company.

Uses of the Internet The flexibility and cost efficiencies of generating international sales via the Internet make these sorts of companies, as well as their more conventional counterparts, increasingly able to engage a range of export options. A company's Web site

> As companies move from initial to advanced exporting, they tend to export to more countries and expect exports to grow.

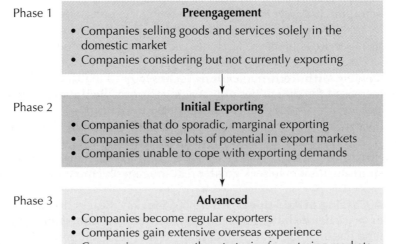

Phase 1	**Preengagement**
	• Companies selling goods and services solely in the domestic market • Companies considering but not currently exporting

Phase 2	**Initial Exporting**
	• Companies that do sporadic, marginal exporting • Companies that see lots of potential in export markets • Companies unable to cope with exporting demands

Phase 3	**Advanced**
	• Companies become regular exporters • Companies gain extensive overseas experience • Companies may use other strategies for entering markets

FIGURE 13.2
Phases of Export Development

As exporters gain greater experience and expertise, they often diversify their foreign markets, expanding operations to include countries that are farther away from home or countries whose business environments differ more significantly from that of the home country.

gives Internet users around the world instant access to the company's product line and even the ability to initiate sales directly.

For example, Evertek Computer Corporation, a small U.S. company, sells new and refurbished computers and parts. Evertek purchased an Internet-based program from the U.S. Commerce Department called BuyUSA.com, which helps it find buyers around the world. Within a year of starting to use BuyUSA.com, Evertek began selling in 10 new countries, with single purchases reaching up to $75,000.[14] In 2007, the company ships to clients in over 100 countries worldwide.

PITFALLS OF EXPORTING

Companies often see exporting as different—and far more difficult—from selling goods and services in their home market. Most companies, particularly smaller ones, prefer to concentrate on domestic rather than foreign markets, as seen in the fact that even though SMEs comprise 97 percent of all exporters in the United States, only less than 1 percent opt to export. Asked to explain, managers often cite a company's general familiarity with its own market along with reluctance to adjust its customary ways for trade regulations, cultural differences, and foreign-exchange situations. Again, this attitude shows up in reports that of the SMEs that do export, nearly two-thirds of them sell in only one foreign market.

Export veterans often recount that selling abroad comes with many challenges. Exporting strains resources, staff, and attention, and, as a result, it puts tough demands on management. Typically, potential exporters have a sense of the likelihood of needing to adjust their operations for different languages, cultures, and market demands.

Dealing with Financial Management   Similarly, most realize that exchange-rate fluctuations and transaction processes of export activity require more sophisticated financial management. Many companies struggle with the fact that export transactions may require them to help foreign customers obtain financing to buy the products.[15] If exporters fail to help foreign customers secure financing—whether in the form of trade credits, government-financed support, or bank guarantees—they risk losing the sale. Companies accustomed to providing financing in terms of the traditional 30- or 60-day trade-credit cycle in their home market are naturally reluctant to begin taking on the greater risk and complications of financing export transactions.

Dealing with Customer Demand   In addition, customers across the world are increasingly demanding a greater range of services from their vendors. "The new notch in the bar for us is the requests from our customers for additional services beyond the port of delivery," said the materials manager of Seco/Warwick Corp., a manufacturer of heat-treating furnaces. "In previous years, I would be responsible for cost, insurance, and freight (CIF) to the port of import, but now I'm often tasked with all aspects of the delivery to the customer's plant location. Now we're often involved in the installation and startup of the equipment, so we have service engineers and cranes waiting for the on-time delivery."[16]

Dealing with Communications Technology   Finally, communication technologies have increased the difficulties of managing exports. Before the Internet, exports were customarily arm's-length, ship-it-and-forget-it transactions. Contact with customers relied on hard-copy documents either faxed or sent overnight. This allowed for the luxury of a wide gap in time to deal with export issues, questions, and complaints. Presently, the ease of contacting vendors via e-mail or inexpensive voice-over-Internet-protocol (VoIP) spurs customers to seek greater real-time involvement in the details of the transaction.

A Catalog of Additional Stumbling Blocks   Rarely do new exporters not stumble once or twice before hitting their stride. Then, once up and running, just as rare is the exporter who has too much time or too many resources. Therefore, we can get a better sense of the elements of an export strategy by identifying the major difficulties that exporters face.

Aside from the problems common to international business, such as language and other cultural factors, exporters run into the following sorts of problems:[17]

- Failure to obtain qualified export counseling in developing a plan to guide export expansion
- Insufficient commitment by top management to overcome initial and ongoing difficulties
- Miscalculating the trade-off between a lean export department and the cost in delays or violations in export compliance
- Misestimating the complexity and costs of ocean shipping and customs clearance to export transactions
- Poor selection of overseas agents or distributors
- Chasing orders from around the world instead of establishing a base of profitable operations and manageable growth
- Neglecting export markets and customers when the domestic market booms
- Classifying products inaccurately according to the destination country's tariff schedule, thereby incurring a higher tax or slowing delivery
- Failure to treat international distributors on an equal basis with their domestic counterparts
- Unwillingness to modify products to meet other countries' regulations or cultural preferences
- Failure to print service, sales, and warranty messages in local languages
- Failure to consider use of an export management company or other marketing intermediary when the company lacks personnel to direct export
- Failure to prepare for disputes with customers

DESIGNING AN EXPORT STRATEGY

Designing an **export strategy** helps managers avoid making the mistakes just described. Figure 13.3 shows an international business transaction chain. A successful export (and import) strategy must evaluate elements of the **transaction chain.** To establish a successful export strategy, management must consider each of the following steps:

1. *Assess the company's export potential by examining its opportunities and resources.* The company needs to determine if there is a market for its goods and services. This task requires it to identify the degree to which it can potentially leverage its core competency into overseas sales. Next, it needs to make sure it has enough production capacity, or can quickly develop it, if success comes faster than expected.

2. *Obtain expert counseling on exporting.* Most governments provide assistance for their domestic companies, although the extent of commitment varies by country. As we saw in our opening case, the best place to start for small and medium-size U.S. companies like Grieve is the nearest export assistance center of the International Trade Administration (ITA) maintained by the U.S. Department of Commerce. Such assistance can be invaluable in helping an exporter get started. At Grieve, for example, Calabrese used information provided by the U.S. government to learn about Asian markets, plan business trips, and identify potential sales agents.

    Indeed, the U.S. government offers a wealth of information to exporters, most notably providing assistance and advice on the practical points of exporting. The U.S. government also offers many trade support services at www.export.gov, an official gateway to international trade support provided by agencies like the Commerce

CONCEPT CHECK

As straightforward as the concept of **exporting** may seem on the surface, we hasten here to reinforce a theme that we've touched upon throughout the book—namely, the fact that whether you're an entrepreneur or an **MNE**, exporting, like all modes of **international business**, is fraught with challenges. In Chapter 2, we highlight *behavioral barriers* to the smooth flow of international operations. In Chapter 3, for example, we discuss difficulties in complying with different *legal systems*, and Chapter 5 explores the pitfalls inherent in any effort to heed the imperatives of social *responsibility*. In Chapter 7, we describe the difficulties that arise in trying to capitalize on *government incentives*, and in Chapter 9, we explain some of the problems that arise in dealing with *foreign-exchange instruments*.

In designing an export strategy, managers must

- Assess export potential.
- Select a market or markets.
- Formulate and implement an export strategy.

Case Review Note

FIGURE 13.3
The International Transaction Chain

Between the point at which they negotiate an international sale and the point at which products have been shipped and received, both the exporter and the importer must handle a complex array of financial and distribution tasks. Each of these tasks is a link in the *transaction chain* forged by each firm's respective strategy for conducting international business. (Note, by the way, that financial transactions must be handled at every step in the process.)

Source: Export America, Vol. 1, November 1999, 17. Magazine published by the International Trade Administration of the U.S. Dept. of Commerce.

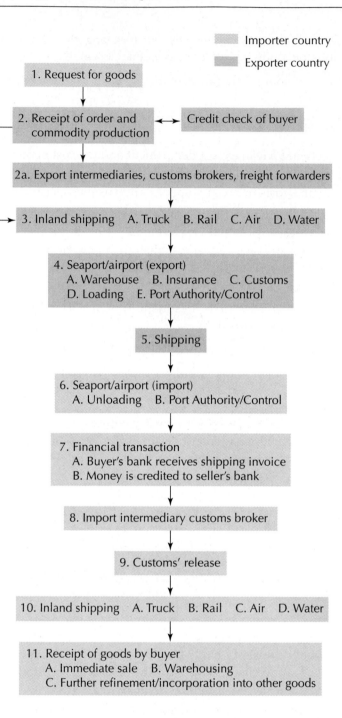

Legend: Importer country / Exporter country

1. Request for goods
2. Receipt of order and commodity production ←→ Credit check of buyer
2a. Export intermediaries, customs brokers, freight forwarders
3. Inland shipping   A. Truck   B. Rail   C. Air   D. Water
4. Seaport/airport (export)
   A. Warehouse   B. Insurance   C. Customs
   D. Loading   E. Port Authority/Control
5. Shipping
6. Seaport/airport (import)
   A. Unloading   B. Port Authority/Control
7. Financial transaction
   A. Buyer's bank receives shipping invoice
   B. Money is credited to seller's bank
8. Import intermediary customs broker
9. Customs' release
10. Inland shipping   A. Truck   B. Rail   C. Air   D. Water
11. Receipt of goods by buyer
    A. Immediate sale   B. Warehousing
    C. Further refinement/incorporation into other goods

Department, the State Department, and the Small Business Administration. Finally, personal help is available at the many export assistance centers run by various branches of the Commerce Department and the Small Business Administration. Finally, a few related avenues to explore:

• *Specialized Financial Assistance.* As a company's export plan increases in scope, it may seek specialized assistance from banks, lawyers, freight forwarders, export management companies, export trading companies, and others. For example, consider the challenge companies face in finding ways to help foreign customers get the necessary funds to buy their product. Exporters can supply several options to assist them. One such way is to have the buyer provide irrevocable letters of credit, covered in detail in Chapter 18, that are confirmed by a local bank and carry little collection risk.

• *Government Programs.*   Another option is to secure government payment guarantees from organizations, such as the Export-Import Bank of the United States (Ex-Im Bank), or purchase government-backed insurance, such as from the Federal Credit Insurance Association.

• *Agents.*   Finally, hiring an agent can make export a straightforward proposition. Instead of dealing with each individual order and making sure the product and paperwork are lined up, a company can rely on a distributor to oversee the transaction. As Edward Cutler, maker of Squigle toothpaste, reflects, "It is just easier to deal with distributors. We prefer to deal in master shippers of 144 tubes. We don't have to do anything then but slap a label on it."[18]

3. *Select a market or markets.*   The part of export strategy that trips up many companies, particularly smaller ones that are experimenting with export, is selecting a market. Small companies are often discouraged when their first forays abroad fail. Often, many follow hunches about foreign markets instead of applying the standards of sound business strategy that got their companies going in the first place. Entrepreneurs may overestimate the need for their product or service in a potential market. Likewise, it's tough to try to conquer customers from London to Lisbon in a day. Says one analyst, "Look at a few markets where you'll have success rather than trying to sell throughout Europe."[19]

A company can passively or actively select an export market. In the latter case, the company learns of markets by responding to requests from abroad that result from its occasional participation in local trade shows or its periodic advertisements in trade publications. Then, encouraged by the apparent interest and potential demand, the company can begin to investigate its export options. Recall from our opening case, for instance, that Grieve's Patrick Calabrese developed an interest in Southeast Asia as an export market at a trade seminar featuring the U.S. ambassadors to the countries of ASEAN.

A company also can determine which markets have products that are similar to its own and currently being exported. For example, the U.S. Census Bureau publishes extensive statistics on foreign trade activities and patterns that an exporter can use to identify markets for different types of exports. Similarly, the National Trade Data Bank (NTDB) provides specific industry reports for different countries. The NTDB is updated monthly. Other countries typically provide similar forms of assistance.

4. *Formulate and implement an export strategy.*   In this step, a company considers its export objectives (immediate and long term), the specific tactics it will use, the schedule of activities and deadlines that enable it to achieve its objectives, and the allocation of resources that allows it to accomplish the different activities. Then managers implement the strategy by getting the goods and services to foreign consumers.

A detailed export business plan is an essential element of an effective export strategy. Table 13.2 provides a sample of such a plan. Certainly, the development of the plan depends on the company, its outlook toward export markets, and its core competency. At small or medium-size companies, as we saw in our opening case, development of the plan usually commands the attention of top management. Larger companies might establish a separate export department. No matter the size of the particular company, research consistently shows that management commitment precedes a firm's success in export.[20]

The creation of an export department or, at the very least, appointment of a dedicated export manager, is a powerful indicator of top management's commitment. According to the import-export manager at BS&B Safety Systems LLC, "Change is constant in export shipping. Many companies need to know that if they hire a good export manager they'll end up saving all sorts of money on fees that the forwarders and third-party companies charge."[21]

CONCEPT CHECK

In detailing the concept of "The Firm as Value Chain" in Chapter 11, we define a **core competency** as a special outlook, skill, capability, or technology that creates unique **value** for a firm. Here we observe the need for would-be **exporters**, especially SMEs, to explore the opportunities for leveraging core competencies when they're designing export strategies.

TABLE 13.2   An Export Business Plan

In deciding if an export strategy is right for your business, you need to analyze its potential risks and benefits. According to many successful exporters, committing your assessment to a detailed business plan is a critical step in drawing up your strategy. Typically, your plan considers such factors as specific markets and how to deal with strategic and operational issues. The following list surveys, by key category, the issues that you need to explore.

1. **Executive Summary**
   - Key elements of the export plan
   - Description of business and target markets
   - Specification of management team
   - Summary of projections
2. **Company Description**
   - History
   - Goals and objectives
   - Core competency
   - Management
   - The export team
   - Company finances
3. **Product/Service Description**
   - Export opportunity
   - Fit of company's products in export market
   - Growth potential
   - Product strategy
4. **Foreign Marketplace Analysis**
   - Rationale for exporting
   - Rationale for targeted foreign market
   - Country profile
   - Industry profile
   - Competitor analysis
   - Specification of key assumptions
5. **Market Entry Strategies**
   - Form of operation
   - Indirect/direct exporting
   - E-commerce options
   - Target customer profile
   - Pricing strategies
   - Sales and promotion strategies
   - Logistics and transportation
6. **International Law**
   - Dispute resolution
   - Language consideration
   - Contract terms and conditions
   - Product liability considerations
   - Intellectual property protection
   - Sales agent and/or distributor agreements
   - Export/import regulations
7. **Financial Analysis**
   - Facility and equipment requirements
   - Sales forecast
   - Cost of goods sold
   - Projected international income statement
   - Projected international cash flow
   - Breakdown analysis
   - Financing requirements
   - Current financing sources
   - Tax consequences
8. **Risk Management**
   - Country risk
   - Commercial risk
   - Currency risk
   - Internal risk
   - Market risk
   - Political risk
9. **External Assistance**
   - Export America
   - U.S. Commerce Department
   - Census Bureau
   - Customs and Border Protection
   - www.export.gov
   - International Trade Administration
   - U.S. Export-Import Bank
   - National, regional, and local organizations
   - Cross-border trade consultancies
10. **Implementation Schedule**
    - Operational time line
    - Performance milestones
    - Contingency plans

Import Strategy

Thus far, we have talked mostly about exporters and exporting. In contrast, *importing* is the process of bringing goods and services into a country and results in the importer paying money to the exporter in the foreign country. Traditional goods imports are fairly straightforward. When Nissan North America ships a sedan from Nissan, Japan, to the U.S. market, it creates an import for the United States.

In addition, there is a variety of service imports. The German software company SAP is considered a service even though software usually comes in a physical package; in this case, it is classified as a service product. Foreign banks, such as the Royal Bank of Canada, that provide financial services to U.S. customers also create service imports.

TYPES OF IMPORTERS

Much less research, relative to the study of export strategies, is available about **import strategies**. However, research identifies three types of importers:

- Those that look opportunistically for any product around the world they can import. They might specialize in certain types of products—such as sports equipment or household items—but they are typically scanning the globe, looking for products that will generate profits for them.

- Those that look at foreign sourcing to get the highest-quality products at the lowest possible price. For instance, a small Utah-based company called ForEveryBody started out selling a variety of bath and body products. Soon, however, it branched out into decorative products for the home, so it identified manufacturers in China that could supply it with specific products for its stores.

- Those that use foreign sourcing as part of their global supply chain. Chapter 16 looks at how companies use this strategy.

Why Import? Generally, companies import for three reasons:

1. They can buy goods or services at lower prices from foreign suppliers.
2. The goods or services are of higher quality than similar goods produced locally.
3. The goods or services needed in their production processes are unavailable from local companies.

Essentially, an importer seeks lower-priced or better-quality supplies, materials, or components that help it improve its capability to create value.

STRATEGIC ADVANTAGES OF IMPORTS

There are two types of imports: those that provide industrial and consumer goods and services to individuals and companies that are not related to the foreign buyer and those that provide intermediate goods and services to companies that are part of the firm's global supply chain. Before continuing, it is useful to ask, "Why import in the first place?"

Specialization of Labor As we saw in earlier chapters, the specialization of labor makes export to and import from countries around the world more efficient than manufacturing every product in every country. As such, Nike buys shoes manufactured by companies located in several Asian countries, including Korea, Taiwan, China, Thailand, Indonesia, and Vietnam, because of their ability to make shoes for lower costs. It would be practically impossible to manufacture the same products in countries with high costs, sell them at a reasonable price, and still make a profit.

There are three types of importers:

- Those looking for any product around the world to import and sell.
- Those looking for foreign sourcing to get their products at the cheapest price.
- Those using foreign sourcing as part of their global supply chain.

There are two types of imports:

- Industrial and consumer goods to independent individuals and companies.
- Intermediate goods and services that are part of the firm's global supply chain.

CONCEPT CHECK

In discussing the "Theory of Comparative Advantage" in Chapter 6, we explain why product specialization results in greater overall efficiency, largely because of efficiencies pertaining to labor; specialization, for example, helps an economy generate excess production output that can be exchanged for otherwise unaffordable imports.

Global Rivalry   Similar situations exist in industries with a high degree of global competitive rivalry. Such industries, like consumer electronics and telecommunications, push the procuring company to try to combat import competition by switching to foreign suppliers whose components then enable it to lower the cost or boost the quality of its finished products. The automobile industry exemplifies this situation. Global competition in this industry spurs companies to seek out the highest-quality inputs for the lowest price wherever they happen to be made and then import them into the countries that house their factories.

Local Unavailability   Companies also import products that are unavailable in the local market. For example, North America imports bananas from tropical climates because the climate of North America is unsuitable for growing them. Simply put, North Americans would not enjoy fresh bananas were it not for imports. Similarly, a potential importer may seek new foreign products that complement its existing product lines, thereby giving it more ways to create value.

Diversification of Operating Risks   Finally, an importer, like an exporter, might try to diversify its operating risks by tapping international markets. In virtually every sort of industry structure, developing alternative suppliers usually makes a company less vulnerable to the dictates or fortunes of a single supplier. For example, many large customers of U.S. steelmakers, such as companies in the automobile industry, have diversified their steel purchases to include European, Chinese, and Korean suppliers. This strategy has reduced the risk of supply shortages for the U.S. automobile industry in case of a strike among U.S. steelworkers.

The Import Process

The import process mirrors the export process, involving both strategic and procedural issues. In fact, managers could straightforwardly adapt the export business plan in Table 13.2 (p. 500) to serve as the framework for an import business plan. Managers begin by studying potential markets, looking to pinpoint possible suppliers and potential policy situations. They then determine the legal ramifications of importing the products, both in terms of the products themselves and the countries from which they originate. Managers also evaluate the role of third-party intermediates, such as freight forwarders and customs agents, as well as arrange financing for the purchase.

IMPORT BROKERS

An import broker is an intermediary who helps an importer best navigate custom regulations.

Importing requires a certain degree of expertise in dealing with institutions and documentation. Not every company may command this proficiency. Consequently, a company may opt to hire an **import broker,** also known as a **customs broker,** to manage the process. An import broker provides access to several suppliers or producers as well as helps companies during price negotiation, arranging transportation and insurance, logistics support, and directing the return of damaged and rejected goods. Some import brokers have established foreign offices that are familiar with local cultures and business practices, including services to make sure the importers get quality products.

Broker Functions   Commonly, a broker or other import consultant can help an importer minimize import duties by performing the following functions:

- *Valuing products in such a way that they qualify for more favorable duty treatment.*   Different product categories have different duties. For example, finished goods typically have a higher duty than do parts and components.
- *Qualifying for duty refunds through drawback provisions.*   Some exporters use imported parts and components in their manufacturing process on which they paid a duty. In

the United States, the drawback provision allows domestic exporters to apply for a 99 percent refund of the duty paid on the imported goods, as long as they become part of the exporter's product.

- *Deferring duties by using bonded warehouses and foreign trade zones.*   Companies do not have to pay duties on imports stored in bonded warehouses and foreign trade zones until the goods are removed for sale or used in a manufacturing process.

- *Limiting liability by properly marking an import's country of origin.*   Because governments assess duties on imports based in part on the country of origin, a mistake in marking the country of origin could result in a higher import duty. For example, in the United States, if a product or its container is not properly marked when it enters the country, the product could be assigned a marking duty equal to 10 percent of the customs value. This would be in addition to the normal tariff.[22]

Import brokers may also help companies plow through paperwork that goes hand in hand with international trades. A broker obtains various government permissions and other clearances before forwarding the requisite paperwork to the carrier that is scheduled to deliver the goods to the importer. Import brokers in the United States are certified as such by the U.S. Bureau of Customs and Border Protection to perform the functions needed to transport products into the country.

CUSTOMS AGENCIES

When importing goods into any country, a company must be familiar with the customs operations of the importing country because once cargo reaches a port of entry, customs officials take control of the product for processing. In this context, "customs" are the country's import and export procedures and restrictions, not its cultural aspects.

Not surprisingly, countries vary greatly on the degree their **custom agencies** help or hinder international traders (see Table 13.3). For example, trading across Europe is becoming seamless, owing to the European Union and related free trade agreements. Thus Table 13.3 shows that several of the top-10 countries on the ease-of-trading list are European. Free trade pacts in other parts of the world are achieving similar effects. In contrast, prevalent custom practices in African and South Asian markets hamper exports and imports.

TABLE 13.3   Where the Trading Is Easy—and Where It's Not

Free trade agreements, particularly the EU, render trade much easier; the persistence of outmoded practices, notably in Africa, makes it much more difficult. Rankings reflect the average of a country's rankings on (1) number of documents and (2) length of time and overall cost required to complete an import or export transaction.

Easiest	Rank	Hardest	Rank
Hong Kong, China	1	Congo, Republic of the	166
Finland	2	Mali	167
Denmark	3	Zimbabwe	168
Singapore	4	Uzbekistan	169
Norway	5	Zambia	170
Estonia	6	Burundi	171
Germany	7	Kazakhstan	172
Canada	8	Kyrgyz Republic	173
Sweden	9	Niger	174
United Arab Emirates	10	Rwanda	175

Source: The International Bank for Reconstruction and Development/The World Bank, "Doing Business in 2007: How to Reform."

In the case of the United States, the responsibility of monitoring imports and exports lies with the Bureau of Customs and Border Protection. Notably, this unit is charged with the assessment and collection of all duties, taxes, and fees on imported merchandise, the enforcement of customs and related laws, and the administration of certain navigation laws and treaties. As a major enforcement organization, it also deals with smuggling operations and is increasingly involved in homeland security.[23]

Procedural Assistance An importer needs to know how to clear goods, what duties to pay, and what special laws exist regarding the importation of products. On the procedural side, when merchandise reaches the port of entry, the importer must file documents with customs officials, who assign a provisional value and tariff classification to the merchandise. The U.S. government has nearly 10,000 tariff classifications, and approximately 60 percent of them are subject to interpretation—that is, a particular product could fit more than one classification. It is almost an art form for companies to determine the tariff classification that will result in the lowest assessment.

When goods arrive at the border or port, customs officials examine them to determine whether there are any restrictions on their importation. If so, the goods may be rejected and prohibited from entering the country. If the goods are allowed to enter, the importer pays the duty and the goods are then released. The amount of the duty depends on the product's country of origin, the type of product, and other factors.

Efficiency Improvement Longer term, we see efforts by custom agents to improve the efficiency of export and import. Long delays, too many documents, and high administrative fees boost trade costs that increase domestic prices and restrict countries from trading. As such, custom agents are adopting new technologies and management systems.[24]

For example, improving risk management techniques and after-clearance audits allow countries to target customs inspections to higher-risk cargo. In Tanzania more than 90 percent of cargo is now risk-assessed before it arrives at Dar es Salaam. New risk management tools used in Nicaragua have reduced physical inspections to less than 10 percent of international trade shipments. After-clearance audits introduced in Egypt, Jordan, and Romania have allowed customs to release cargo to importers quickly, with the container contents verified after it reaches the warehouse. These successes trigger other initiatives, like uniform custom forms and electronic filing. Combined, they open up new markets for exporters and importers.

LOOKING TO THE FUTURE

The Technology of Trade

Advances in transportation and communications systems accelerate growth in trade by making it easier and cheaper for companies to reach international markets. The growing availability of electronic filing of cargo documents has reduced delays in many ports. Software that works in Hamburg or Sydney can also be used in Hong Kong and Seattle, further powered by simpler customs and transit forms that are increasingly standardized across countries. Consequently, the speed of trading is now greater than ever: Between January 2005 and April 2006 the time needed to comply with export-related requirements fell by nearly 1.5 days worldwide.

One of the Internet's strengths is its ability to help individuals all over the world engage each other easily and quickly. This, in turn, reduces many historically high transaction costs of international trade. Big MNEs have reaped rewards by advances in the electronic movement of information that enables companies to connect the flow of goods, funds, and information within an integrated system of different technologies. The real-time synchronization of their import and export activities has helped MNEs redefine the way they connect with their foreign suppliers and customers.

Unquestionably, big companies capture big rewards from innovations. Interestingly though, the technology of trade seems to offer bigger benefits to smaller companies. Indeed, technology increasingly makes it harder to tell the difference between an SME exporter and a large MNE. Historically, the latter had access to more capital, diverse markets, better systems, and economies of scale. Small exporters had to make do with shoestring budgets, getting by with whatever they could afford. Now, improving technologies create solutions and platforms that blur the distinction between the big company and the small company.

On one front, software helps SMEs exporters do things that were impossible just a few years ago. Said one executive, "There's been an explosion of collaborative business software in the past few years. It's created a total revolution in what small businesses are able to accomplish overseas."[25] Collaborative software lets the entrepreneurial exporter or importer with single-digit head counts establish close relationships with and keep close track on foreign vendors without traveling the world. For example, Edgar Blazona used to log 100,000 miles of air travel annually, visiting factories in the Far East. Now, Blazona uses two factories—one in Thailand and one in India—to make his products that are then imported into the United States. He depends on WebEx, a meeting and document-sharing program, to work in real time tandem with his overseas factories. Costing about $50 per month, this software cuts down on confusion, costly mistakes, and the need to ship designs overnight across the globe.

Other companies use similar programs to manage networks of overseas factories that once could be run only by big MNEs. China Manufacturing Network, for instance, relies on its 10-person staff in California to coordinate production of laboratory and industrial devices lasers among more than 90 independent factories in China, Malaysia, and Singapore. China Manufacturing uses NetSuite, an on-demand, scalable enterprise software product, to track activity in each factory, thereby letting it best determine where to place orders, monitor build rates, and manage inventory.

On another front, improvements in overnight shipping create a flexible and powerful platform to manage importing and exporting. At the least, growing availability of low-cost overnight shipping has robbed big firms of a long-running competitive advantage; SMEs also have the affordable ability to send products across the globe in less than a day. Now, the no-name, one-person exporter down the street from you, because of big-name shipping partners who span the globe, has many of the same logistics capabilities commanded by a large MNE.

Moreover, SMEs increasingly have as much if not a bit more shipping flexibility than big companies. The diffusion of supply chains throughout the world often creates logistics bottlenecks. Whether lost shipments, custom tie-ups, or out-of-sync links in the supply chain, holdups create delays that cost money. Unlike big companies that rely on their in-house systems, SMEs can tap an increasing range of sophisticated solution providers. Help is available from traditional intermediaries, like EMCs and ETCs, and emerging forms, so-called third-party logistics (or "3PLs"), like DHL, FedEx, and UPS. These companies develop state-of-the-art technology to help exporters understand their current trade practices, identify opportunities and risks, and convert vision to action.

These intermediaries, notably the 3PLs, command the system capabilities that enable international traders to do their jobs more efficiently. The 3PLs offer a rich menu of integration mechanisms, like online shipping and tracking information, which let the company and customer know when the shipments will reach customs. They also consolidate billing inclusive of all transportation, customs brokerage, duties, taxes, and package delivery services.

Finally, they have the capability to handle product returns, warranty claims, parts exchanges, and reverse logistics. A small international trader, therefore, can easily hire any of these sorts of firms to warehouse, truck, sail, fly, and deliver goods from factories in Asia to customers in Europe—all the while avoiding any sort of physical proximity of the goods. For example, South West Trading in Arizona, a family-owned start-up that markets yarns made from bamboo, corn, and soy fibers by fabric plants in China, had a long history of supply chain problems. UPS, through its Supply Chain Solutions program, enabled South West Trading to use the UPS facility in Shanghai to consolidate orders from various factories into one container, manage customs paperwork, and truck goods to the company's warehouse in Phoenix. The benefit to South West Trading's bottom line was immediate. The company once paid $9,400 to run four China-to-Arizona shipments per month; now its single monthly UPS shipment costs about $3,600 and reliably takes 21 days to travel.

Big or small, companies respond to these situations, confident that technology will create tools to let them jump the hurdles and capture the opportunities of international trade. Small companies in particular see the improving technology of trade. By decoupling the issues of firm size and performance, technology changes the game. Observed the CEO of China Manufacturing, "Our customers can't really tell how big we are. In a way, it's irrelevant. What matters is that we can get the job done."[26] ∎

IMPORT DOCUMENTATION

Generally, a great deal of paperwork is involved in the import business. The arrival of a shipment at a port requires the importer to file several documents with the port director to take title. For instance, importers typically receive products without purchasing them—that is, they take the title of ownership but without laying out any money. This arrangement requires two types of documents:

- Those that determine whether customs will release the shipment.
- Those that contain information for duty assessment and statistical purposes.

The specific documents that customs requires vary by country but usually include an entry manifest, a commercial invoice, and a packing list. For example, the exporter's commercial invoice contains information such as the country of origin, the port of entry to which the merchandise is destined, information on the importer and exporter, a detailed description of the merchandise including its purchase price, and the currency used for the sale.

Bureaucratic Impediments   An irony of growing globalization is the fact that inefficient importing due to delays, documents, and administrative fees remains a procedural challenge for many companies. Notwithstanding the success of the WTO, many rules and regulations hinder trade. For example, a Zambian trader noted, "My cargo of copper wire was held up in Durban, South Africa, for a week. The port authorities required proof that the wooden pallets on which the wire was loaded were free of pests. After some days the Ministry of Agriculture's inspector checked that the wood was fumigated, for a $100 fee."[27] More generally, priority ratings for various markets must sometimes be cleared by various government agencies; refusals come easily to officials worried about product shortages at home or political tension abroad.

These hindrances aren't likely to disappear anytime soon given the heightened importance of national economic agendas and international security concerns. Consequently, international traders navigate complex national, regional, and global trade agreements, all the while ensuring their compliance with pertinent regulations.

In the United States, homeland security issues have begun to match tariffs as areas of concern for importers. For example, the logistics manager at Schott North America points out, "The real danger to your supply chain these days isn't tariffs. . . . [I]t's that your containers are stuck down at the terminal in New York [harbor] waiting for inspection" by radiation detection instruments before receiving customs authorization to enter the United States.[28] Importers are increasingly turning to software programs' frequent updates of the latest regulations that affect international trade, including the expanding regulations issued by the Department of Homeland Security.

The Export Process

Exports may be one of two kinds:

- *Indirect exports* are sold to an independent intermediary in the domestic market, which then sells the product in the export market to the final consumer.
- *Direct exports* are goods and services sold to an independent intermediary outside of the exporter's home country, which then sells the product in the export market to the final consumer.

Generally, services are more likely to be sold in a direct fashion, whereas goods are exported both directly and indirectly. We now examine each approach.

INDIRECT SELLING

There is nothing mysterious about selling and buying goods indirectly. An exporter using **indirect selling** simply sells goods to or through an independent domestic intermediary in its home country. The intermediary then exports the products to customers in foreign markets. Indirect selling permits the exporter to use the same customer solicitation methods, terms and conditions of sale, packaging, shipping protocol, and credit and collection procedures for all customers, no matter whether they are down the street or around the world. The task and responsibility of dealing with the complications created by export sales are transferred to the export intermediary.

Export Intermediaries Figure 13.3 (p. 498) shows that exporters and importers use a variety of third-party intermediaries—companies that facilitate the trade of goods but are not related to either the exporter or the importer. **Export intermediaries** can range in size from specialized, small one-person operations to international trading companies with a globally dispersed staff. A company that exports or is planning to export must decide whether its internal staff will handle essential activities or if it will contract with other companies. Regardless of the choice, the following functions must occur:

- Stimulate sales, obtain orders, and do market research.
- Make credit investigations and perform payment-collection activities.
- Handle foreign traffic and shipping.
- Support the company's sales, distribution, and advertising.

A company's experience in export and import, along with the sophistication of its financial and management resources, influences its inclination for indirect selling. The challenge of preparing export and customs documents in the importing country, and identifying the best means of transportation, can quickly overwhelm the resources of any SME. In recourse, companies often turn to external specialists and intermediary organizations when they begin exporting operations. These companies have a range of skills, such as updated knowledge of trade laws, regulations, taxes, duties, insurance, and transportation.

In addition, if and when problems arise at the entry port due to technicalities in the law or glitches in the system, brokers can expedite resolution or, in more serious situations, represent their clients at trials and tribunals and deal directly with government officials. Many companies starting to export find that intermediaries offer an operationally easier and relatively risk-free approach.[29]

Increasingly, sophisticated exporters in the United States are seeing the increasing usefulness of trade intermediaries. Spurring this change has been growing security concerns stemming from the 9/11 attacks. Increasing government regulation regarding what can be shipped where and to whom has led to border delays and unexpected holdups.[30] Some companies delegate the tough job of keeping pace with the expanding body of Homeland Security regulations. Trade intermediaries, with the help of advanced software applications, have improved their expertise in customs compliance strategies, regulatory requirements, licensing requirements, and goods valuation and classification practices.

Exporters pay for the benefits provided by the intermediaries. Because the intermediaries expect to make a profit, the exporter has to reduce margins. In addition, the exporter forsakes control over aspects of its international sales, such as delivery schedules and customer service, to the intermediary. If control is a crucial concern, a company can opt to employ export intermediaries in any number of less comprehensive ways, including using them to provide short-term financing for the goods in transit or managing the conversion of national currencies.

These choices efficiently deal with the matters of financing sales and extending credit. The price for these services, depending on whether the intermediary is working on salary, commissions, or retainer plus commission, can be high.

EMCs and ETCs The major types of indirect intermediaries are the **export management company (EMC)**, the **export trading company (ETC)**, and export agents, merchants, or remarketers. The terms *EMC* and *ETC* are often used interchangeably,

CONCEPT CHECK
In Chapter 1, we suggest that **international business** is a challenging context for people who like to do everything themselves. For example, collecting information about foreign markets and cultures can get tough quickly. Consequently, some companies prefer to get help in finding information about the key factors in a country's *external environment.* In these sorts of cases, third-party intermediaries can be valuable sources of *knowledge* about such policies (e.g., trade laws, regulations, taxes).

especially for smaller intermediaries. Larger intermediaries, however, are almost always referred to as ETCs, or simply trading companies, because they deal with both exports and imports.

EXPORT MANAGEMENT COMPANIES   An EMC usually acts as the export arm of a manufacturer—although it can also deal in imports—and often uses the manufacturer's own letterhead in communicating with foreign sales representatives and distributors. The EMC's primary duty is to obtain orders for its clients' products through the selection of appropriate markets, distribution channels, and promotional campaigns. Additionally, it collects, analyzes, and furnishes credit information and advice regarding foreign accounts and payment terms.

The EMC may also take care of export documents, arrange transportation (including the consolidation of shipments among multiple clients to reduce costs), set up patent and trademark protection in foreign countries, and assist in establishing alternative forms of doing business, such as licensing or joint ventures.[31]

EMCs operate on a contractual basis, often as the agent for an exporter, and they provide exclusive representation in a well-defined foreign territory. Their contract with the company specifies pricing, credit and financial policies, promotional services, and method of payment. An EMC might operate on a commission basis for sales (unless it takes title to the merchandise) and charges a retainer for other services. EMCs usually concentrate on complementary and noncompetitive products so they can present a more complete product line to a limited number of foreign importers.

In the United States, most EMCs are small entrepreneurial ventures that tend to specialize by product, function, or market area. The Federation of International Trade Associations (FITA) estimates 600 to 1,000 EMCs are operating in the United States and each represents, on average, about 10 suppliers. This means that few U.S. companies use EMCs, although FITA believes that thousands more would benefit from doing so.[32]

Although EMCs perform an important function for companies, they are not the answer for all export situations. EMCs, for the most part, are relatively small and may have limited financial resources. Thus some may not be able to warehouse a company's product or to offer extended in-house financing to foreign customers. Inevitably, EMCs focus their efforts on those products that bring them the most profits. New lines, or those with limited potential, get overlooked or ignored.

Finally, and most worrisome, some companies fear that using an EMC will push them to relinquish control over crucial aspects of their foreign sales. Companies sometimes have no control over whom the EMC sells to, the selling price it charges, or the quality of promotional campaigns. Some companies have discovered that if an EMC does not actively promote their products, then they may be unable to do much to generate export sales. Therefore, manufacturers need to trade off their preference for control with the cost of directly managing export operations.[33]

EXPORT TRADING COMPANIES   In 1982, the U.S. government enacted the Export Trading Company Act, which removed some of the antitrust obstacles to the creation of ETCs in the United States. This legislation allowed the formation of ETCs by groups of competitors to market products jointly, without fear of antitrust action, as Dutch, Japanese, and British competitors have done for decades. By using ETCs without the legal barriers that constrained companies' export mobility, U.S. companies experienced increased international competitiveness with greater exports of U.S. goods and services.

Significantly, the legislation permitted banks to make equity investments in commercial ventures that qualified as ETCs, something that had previously been prohibited. Policymakers hoped that permitting banks to engage in commercial nonbanking transactions in the context of an ETC would encourage them to be more receptive to international trade transactions, thereby removing additional barriers that diminished the export interest and performance of U.S. companies.

EMCs operate on a contractual basis, usually as an agent of the exporter.

EMCs are not the perfect solution. Often they have few resources, devote too little attention, and assume too much control.

Operationally, the Federal Reserve Board approves these applications before the bank can start export operations. Many of the banks concentrate on customers in their geographic market and in parts of the world in which they already have a network in place. ETCs are important to banks because being able to invest in an ETC gives the banks access to more of the business than just the financing side.

An important distinction between ETCs and EMCs is that ETCs operate more on the basis of demand than of supply. ETCs are like independent distributors that match buyers with sellers and, as such, see their value creation as a function of finding out what foreign customers want and then identifying domestic suppliers. Therefore, rather than representing a single manufacturer, an ETC tries to work with as many manufacturers as it can to provide products to overseas customers. Effectively, ETCs operate as commissioned agents, charging the seller or the buyer a percentage of the value of the export while generally refusing to carry inventory in their own name or perform after-sale service activities.

> ETCs are like EMCs, but they tend to operate on the basis of demand rather than of supply. They identify suppliers who can fill orders in overseas markets.

> ETCs in the United States are exempt from antitrust provisions in order to allow them to collaborate with other companies to serve foreign markets.

Foreign Trading Companies   The only similarity between foreign trading companies and U.S. export trading companies is the designation "trading company." Exporters from Japan, Great Britain, the Netherlands, and several other traditional trading nations found long ago that wide-reaching trading companies could market and distribute products more efficiently than any single producer could. This, as noted earlier, was the basis for the legislation that permitted ETCs to operate in the United States. More recently, exporting companies from nontraditional trading countries, such as Argentina and Brazil, have applied this lesson to their own exporting strategies.

Not all countries have met with success. Japanese trading companies such as Mitsubishi, Mitsui, and Itochu are huge conglomerates with marketing, financial, and distribution arms that permit a truly global reach. In 1995, these three Japanese companies were the top three companies on *Fortune* magazine's list of the 500 largest global companies. By 2004, though, none of these three remained anywhere near the top, and all trading companies from Japan, Korea, Germany, and the like have tumbled as a result of new accounting rules that significantly lowered their revenues. Previously, foreign trading companies booked the gross value of their trades as revenue, but now they comply with U.S. Generally Accepted Accounting Principles and report transactions on a net basis.[34]

DIRECT SELLING

Competitive pressures to leverage core competencies and improve the performance of value chains push exporters to consider one of two things. The first option is to build a network of sales representatives, either salaried or commissioned, stationed in key markets around the world that deal with distributors, foreign retailers, or end users.

> Direct selling involves sales representatives, distributors, or retailers.

Direct Selling Through Distributors   A popular option for ambitious exporters is to develop their own international marketing capability, charging in-house sales personnel to monitor the actions and activities of foreign distributors. Exporters undertake **direct selling** to give them greater control over the marketing function and the opportunity to earn higher profits.

In the case of building a network of sales representatives, the company may transfer them exclusive rights to sell in a particular geographic area or may have them compete with other sales representatives who also represent the firm. It is far more common for sales representatives to have exclusive rights to a territory. For example, Grieve's sales representatives operate exclusively in their respective markets.

A distributor in a foreign country is a merchant who purchases the products from the manufacturer and sells them at a profit. Distributors usually carry a stock of inventory and service the product. They also usually deal with retailers rather than end users in the market.

Case Review Note

Evaluating Distributors   In evaluating potential distributors (and foreign sales representatives), companies consider the following issues:

- The size and capabilities of its sales force
- Its sales record
- An analysis of its territory
- Its current product mix
- Its facilities and equipment
- Its marketing policies
- Its customer profile
- Its promotional strategies

A company that has sufficient financial and managerial resources and decides to export directly rather than working through an intermediary has to build organizational capabilities. These capabilities may take any number of forms, ranging from a separate international division, to a separate international company, to full integration of international and domestic activities.

In addition, the company needs to fine-tune its control and coordination system to deal with the contingencies of exporting. The company that opts to manage export activities directly often develops an international sales force that is separate from its domestic counterpart with the view that foreign markets demand different types of expertise.

Direct Selling to Foreign Retailers and End Users   Exporters can also sell directly to foreign retailers. Usually, these products are limited to consumer lines. The growth of global retail chains, such as Wal-Mart and Ahold, facilitates the export of an increasing range of products directly to storefronts around the world. This trend gives existing exporters greater coverage and "born global" exporters, notably those emerging in China, immediate access to a wide market.[35] Exporters can also sell directly to end users. A good way to generate such sales is by printing catalogs or attending trade shows. They can also generate sales when foreign buyers see company brochures or respond to advertisements in trade publications.

An example of a company that sells directly to buyers is Cooley Distillery, the sole Irish-owned distiller of Irish whiskey. Cooley exports more than 80 percent of its production, up from about 25 percent in 1990. Cooley has a powerful customer list and sells in over 40 countries, including the top-25 retailers in Europe. In spite of this, Cooley has elected to sell the distillery, which means the customer takes title directly from Cooley and handles all the shipments. Cooley maintains a small bonded warehouse in the United Kingdom to handle just-in-time shipments to supermarket chains that order small quantities, but it generally lets the buyer handle shipping and storage in foreign markets.[36]

CONCEPT CHECK

In Chapter 2, we discuss ways in which the Internet has influenced political change in potential overseas markets; in Chapter 9, we explain the impact of electronic communications on the operations of **foreign-exchange markets**, and in Chapter 11, we emphasize the importance of e-commerce in configuring and coordinating both real and virtual **value chains**. Here we report on evidence that the Internet is reshaping export and import activity.

Direct Selling over the Internet   Electronic commerce is an important means by which companies, both big and small, trade internationally. E-commerce is especially vital to SMEs that can't afford to establish a sales network internationally. We already see Internet marketing growing among export companies in emerging countries as they use it to overcome some of the capital and infrastructure barriers of international markets. For example, exporters in Chile use extranets to communicate with importers around the world. Similarly, exporters in Costa Rica found online shops to be a good way of increasing product turnover with higher margins.[37] Others report that the Internet encourages the emergence of companies using virtual export channels to serve international markets.[38]

E-commerce has a range of features and functions. Research suggests it is easy to engage, provides faster and cheaper delivery of information, generates quick feedback on new products, improves customer service, accesses a global audience, levels the field of competition, and supports electronic data interchange (EDI) with both suppliers and customers.[39]

Finally, companies can expand their international trading by posting their home pages in different languages to target different audiences. In the case of industrial products, they can install software to track hits to their home page and then contact potential customers either through sales representatives or local distributors. In the case of consumer products, companies can sell their products directly to consumers worldwide.

> Internet marketing allows companies—both large and small—to engage in direct marketing quickly, easily, and cheaply.

Point Counterpoint

A Dirty Dilemma: Exporting Hazardous Waste

Point **Yes** Many people see export as a positive sum process: The more companies and countries export, the more they improve their performance, and consumers and companies worldwide that wish to import their products get what they want—a seemingly win-win situation for everyone. However, a dark side of exporting is beginning to emerge with regard to the trade of hazardous waste in the form of obsolete computer equipment. The volume of e-waste—trash composed of electronics equipment such as computers, monitors, cell phones, iPods, printers, and so on—is rising: For example, more than 63 million computers became obsolete in 2005 alone.[40] As shown in the major e-waste shipping routes (see Map 13.2), most is generated by industrialized nations and exported to developing countries.

Low labor costs, weak environmental regulations, and growing processing capacity have made Asia and Africa a high-tech dumping ground for everything from simple computer chips to the elaborate circuit boards that go into them.[41] In addition, tons of obsolete information technology ends up in shipping containers bound for China, Mali, India, and Bangladesh, among other countries. For example, some 500 containers of used electronic equipment enters Nigeria monthly, each one carrying about 800 computers, for a total of nearly 400,000 used computers. In these countries, rudimentary industries have sprung up to dismantle old computers, monitors, circuit boards, scanners, printers, routers, cell phones, and network cards for recycling.

Countries and companies see this export process as serving many goods. It gives them a way to meet growing social pressure to retain responsibility for the products they sell. More and more companies, such as Samsung, Mitsubishi, and Nokia, support corporate cradle-to-grave responsibility for obsolete cell phones. Today, honoring this obligation is nearly effortless as they export these products to other, particularly poorer, countries that have an interest in and infrastructure to recycle.

(continued)

Counterpoint **No** Many observers and institutions contend that growth in hazardous waste exports has created dangerous recycling industries in many countries. Electronic waste is a mixture of more than a thousand chemicals, including toxic metals (e.g., lead, barium, and mercury), acids, plastics, and chlorinated and brominated compounds. For example, an average computer monitor can contain as much as 8 pounds of lead, along with plastics laden with flame retardants and cadmium; the burning of electronic parts to separate copper, solder, or other metals from plastic coatings releases dioxins and other hazardous chemicals.

Most developing countries lack the regulatory codes or disposal infrastructure to safeguard the dangers of electronics recycling. For example, processing wastes from recycling commonly run off into municipal drains or simply drift outside the perimeter of the reclamation facility. Local air quality suffers as, for example, "circuit boards are burned after acid washing, spewing deadly smoke and exposing workers and people living around these facilities."[44] Ultimately, once local scrap shops finish disassembling equipment, their trash often goes into public landfills where the remaining toxins contaminate the environment.

Though severe, agrees Madhumita Dutta of Toxics-Link Delhi, a nongovernmental organization, these problems are far less disturbing than the problems created by the "appalling" working conditions in the typical recycling facility: "Everything from dismantling the computer to pulling out . . . parts of the circuit boards to acid washing boards to recover copper is done with bare hands without any protective gear or face protection."

What, then, of the premise of charity—that is, sending computer equipment from countries where it has little use to countries where it has tremendous use? Critics quickly shoot this down, asserting that U.S. businesses donate obsolete equipment to emerging markets to dodge high

(continued)

Disposal costs for hazardous waste in developing countries are a fraction of the cost of those in wealthier countries. As far back as 1988, disposal costs in these countries ranged from $2.50 to $50 per ton, compared with costs of $100 to $2,000 per ton in the United States, Japan, and the United Kingdom.[42] Although costs have increased in poorer countries, they have increased at a far greater rate in wealthier countries. Lower disposal costs in developing countries exist because of low or nonexistent environmental standards, less stringent laws, and absence of public opposition. Given these considerations, the economics of exporting hazardous waste from wealthy to poor countries is indisputable.

There are other benefits. Entrepreneurs in emerging markets create value for themselves and their countries by recovering, recycling, and reusing scarce resources. Copper, an increasingly valuable commodity, can represent nearly 20 percent of a mobile phone's total weight. Says Atul Maheshwar, owner of a mud-brick recycling depot in India, speaking of U.S. exports, "If your country keeps sending us the material, our business will be good."[43]

Much of the equipment being shipped to Asia and Africa is from recyclers in the United States who ship it abroad for repair, sale, or dismantling. Graham Wollaston of Scrap Computers, a recycler in Phoenix, claims there is a reuse for virtually every component of old electronic devices.

For example, old televisions are turned into fish tanks for Malaysia and a silicon glass shortage has created demand for old monitors, which are turned into new ones. "There's no such thing as a third-world landfill," Mr. Wollaston explains. "If you were to put an old computer on the street, it would be taken apart for the parts." Similarly, Luc Lateille of the Canadian firm BMP Recycling says that "we don't send junk—we only send the materials that they are looking for."

Certainly, some recyclers dump useless equipment around the world that then must be put into landfills. And, agree some, freedom from certifying the condition or destination of all the equipment creates the basis for opportunism. Despite these drawbacks, proponents of exporting hazardous waste maintain the system works—especially given the alternative. Regarding the latter, the U.S. Environmental Protection Agency (EPA) admits that "inappropriate practices" have occurred in the recycling industry but argues that stopping exports, besides possibly creating others problems, is not really an option. ●

recycling expenses. The Basel Action Network's report, "The Digital Dump: Exporting Reuse and Abuse to Africa," concludes that "too often, justifications of 'building bridges over the digital divide' are used as excuses to obscure and ignore the fact that these bridges double as toxic waste pipelines."

The majority of the equipment arriving in Lagos, the study reports, is unusable and neither economically repairable nor resalable. "Nigerians are telling us they are getting as much as 75 percent junk that is not repairable . . . [and] as a result, developing nations are carrying a disproportionate burden of the world's toxic waste from technology products."[45] Other data suggest this is a pervasive problem. Inspections of 18 European seaports in 2005 found that as much as 47 percent of waste destined for export, including e-waste, was illegal.[46]

Growing fear among developing countries has prompted them to address the spiraling amount of electronic wastes shipped to their countries. The Asia-Pacific Regional Scoping Workshop on the Environmentally Sound Management of Electronic Wastes proposes that manufacturers of electronic wastes should be responsible for hazardous materials at the end of the products' lives.[47] The group also recommends that countries set tougher standards to monitor, control, and certify cross-boundary shipments of electronic waste.

Others endorse worldwide compliance with the rule of the Basel Convention on the Transboundary Movement of Hazardous Wastes and Their Disposal, a UN treaty intended to limit the trade of hazardous waste. This treaty argues for aggressive measures, including an international ban on the export of any and all hazardous wastes, no matter whether for recovery, recycling, reuse, or final disposal. As of mid-2007, 166 countries had ratified the Basel Convention. The United States, which generates approximately 60 percent of the world's hazardous waste, is the only developed country in the world that has not endorsed this treaty.[48] ●

EXPORT DOCUMENTATION

Direct selling requires the exporter to comply with a battery of documents that regulate international trade. Duty rates, customs clearance, and entry processes differ for each country. Tariff classifications, value declaration, and duty management can create confusion and high costs. Customs and security initiatives have imposed new regulations on

MAP 13.2 Where E-Waste Gets Shipped (or Dumped)

When computers, cell phones, iPods, and other electronic equipment becomes obsolete, it's no longer an attractive commodity in such places as the United States, Japan, or the countries of the EU. It does, however, retain some value in developing countries, and that's exactly where, as exports, it usually ends up. Critics of the practice charge that the vast majority of so-called *e-waste* is also hazardous waste and that exporters are exploiting importers with low labor costs and lax environmental protections.

Source: Basel Action Network. Silicon Valley Toxics Condition.

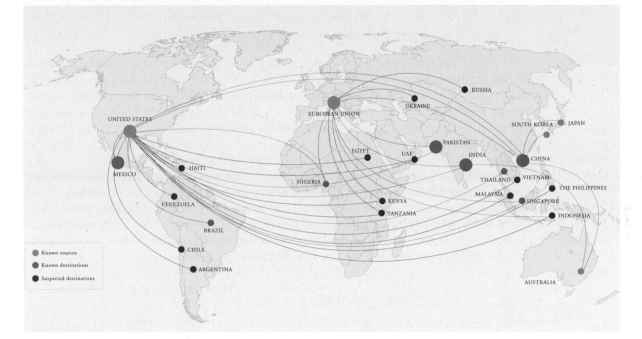

companies that complicate trading internationally. By sovereign right, each country determines whether domestic products or products transshipped through its borders can be exported to certain countries.

In the United States, an exporter consults the U.S. Department of Commerce to determine if its products can be shipped under a general license or if they must be exported under an individually validated license (IVL). For example, exports of certain high-tech products might be restricted for national security reasons, so an exporter must apply for an IVL to determine whether the exportation is permitted.

Key Documents Important documents for exporters include:

- A *pro forma invoice* is an invoice, like a letter of intent, from the exporter to the importer that outlines the selling terms, price, and delivery if the goods are actually shipped. If the importer likes the terms and conditions, it will send a purchase order and arrange for payment. At that point, the exporter can issue a commercial invoice.

- A *commercial invoice* is a bill for the goods from the buyer to the seller. It contains a description of the goods, the address of buyer and seller, and delivery and payment terms. Many governments use this form to assess duties.

- A *bill of lading* is a receipt for goods delivered to the common carrier for transportation, a contract for the services rendered by the carrier, and a document of title.

- A *consular invoice* is sometimes required by countries as a means of monitoring imports. Governments can use the consular invoice to monitor prices of imports and to generate revenue for the embassies that issue the consular invoice.

> Key export documents are pro forma invoice, commercial invoice, bill of lading, consular invoice, certificate of origin, shipper's export declaration, and export packing list.

- A *certificate of origin* indicates where the products originate and is usually validated by an external source, such as the chamber of commerce. It helps countries determine the specific tariff schedule for imports.

- A *shipper's export declaration* is used by the exporter's government to monitor exports and to compile trade statistics.

- An *export packing list* itemizes the material in each individual package, indicates the type of package, and is attached to the outside of the package. The shipper or freight forwarder, and sometimes customs officials, use the packing list to determine the nature of the cargo and whether the correct cargo is being shipped.

As you'd expect, these forms are comprehensive and somewhat cumbersome. Completing them accurately remains a difficulty. "Many loss-and-damage challenges stem in part from the sizeable percentage of exporters that use incorrect Incoterms," reported the FedEx Trade Network's Trade & Customs Advisory Services. (Incoterms is short for International Commercial Terms, the rules for the division of cost and risk in international sales transactions.) Proper Incoterms use helps exporters avoid disputes with their customers by clearly specifying each party's responsibilities.

Research also reports that many exporters do not classify their products accurately according to the tariff schedule of the country destination. For example, goods that arrive overseas with vague commercial invoice descriptions that don't match those of the importing country's tariff classification often end up classified under a catchall description, such as "machinery, other." A more precise description might incur a duty rate that is considerably lower than the rate for the catchall classification.

SOURCES OF REGULATORY ASSISTANCE

Making sense of the various forms of trade regulations and requirements is tough under the best of circumstances. Companies typically have many options from the private and public sectors to help them figure out the best option. As a case in point, our opening look at Grieve highlighted the export assistance provided by both the International Trade Administration of the Chicago Export Assistance Center and the Agent/Distributor Search program run by the U.S. Department of Commerce and easily accessible through the Internet portal www.export.gov. Potential exporters, therefore, can tap a wealth of public resources in the form of national, state, and local trade offices, to say nothing of freight forwarders, international banks, or general trade consultants. Table 13.4 profiles leading sources and the types of help they provide.

Federal, state, and local governments, seeing the benefits of international trade, aid the efforts of potential and active exporters and, to a lesser degree, protect the interests of struggling importers. Japan, for instance, relies on several offices, such as the Small and Medium Enterprise Agency, the Agency of Industrial Science and Technology, and the Ministry of International Trade and Industry. The latter, often referred to as MITI, develops policy and provides assistance to help Japanese companies trade internationally.

Programs in the United States give a sense of the financial help available to the international trader. The Ex-Im Bank and the Small Business Administration (SBA), for instance, help international traders get private sector loans to fund their export transaction financing needs. These federal agencies help arrange financing for manufacturing costs of goods for export or the purchase of goods or services. They also assist with foreign accounts receivable and standby letters of credit.

Similarly, most states and several cities fund and operate export financing programs, including preshipment and postshipment working-capital loans and guarantees, accounts receivable financing, and export insurance. The limited reserves of some states and cities force them to make their assistance contingent on the exporter's proof that they

---

CONCEPT CHECK

In Parts I and II (especially Chapters 1, 3, and 4), we underscore the fact that **international business** creates jobs, generates income, and expands national wealth. We pursue this theme in moving from Part II to Part III (Chapters 6–8) by showing how government action in fostering favorable economic environments and adopting pro-trade policies is instrumental in achieving these outcomes. Here we observe that, in order to reach such desirable economic goals, many governments go to great lengths to boost the ease and efficiency of **exporting** and **importing**.

In the United States, a number of institutions, most notably the Department of Commerce and its affiliates, help firms identify and realize export and import opportunities.

TABLE 13.4 Trade Information by Type and Source

If your company is thinking about getting into the export end of your business, various organizations and agencies offer assistance in making sense of the wealth of trade information.

U.S. Government Agencies	• Market demographics, product demand, and competition • Distribution channels and joint venture partners • U.S. customs, regulatory, and tax issues • Sales finance • Credit and insurance • Trade events, partners, and trade leads • Shipping documentation and requirements • Pricing, quotes, and negotiations
Trade Associations and Trade Groups	• Market demographics, product demand, and competition • Advertising and sales promotion alternatives • Distribution channels • Customs regulations and tax issues
Export Intermediaries	• Distribution channels • Host-country legal, accounting, and tax requirements • Sales finance • Credit and insurance • Logistics

do not risk losing much if the deal falls apart. An exporter need only provide proof of a letter of credit or sufficient credit insurance to satisfy this requirement. (Chapter 19 examines aspects of export financing.) In some situations, states and cities require the exporter to do part of the export deal within the jurisdiction of the funding authority. Often meeting this call for local content can be done by using local transportation facilities, such as an airport or seaport.

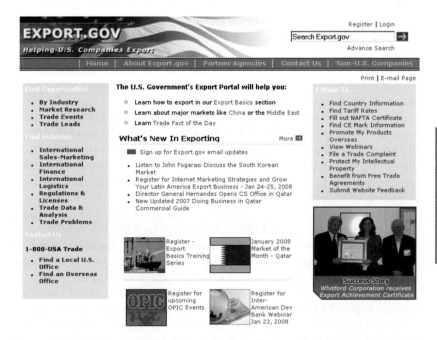

Export.gov is the gateway to an immense range of resources for international traders. Here both the aspiring and experienced exporter can find information, opportunities, and solutions for many aspects of international trade.

A foreign freight forwarder is an export or import specialist dealing in the movement of goods from producer to consumer.

FOREIGN FREIGHT FORWARDERS

Companies that want to sell directly to foreign customers but are reluctant to supervise the transport of goods from one country to another often hire a freight forwarder. Popularly known as the "travel agents of cargo," freight forwarders help exporters move shipments to foreign buyers. A **freight forwarder** is an agent for the exporter in moving cargo to an overseas destination.[49] The freight forwarder is used for both imports and exports for the simple reason that one company's exports are another company's imports.

Forwarder Functions   Today, the freight forwarder is the largest export intermediary in terms of value and weight of products transferred internationally. Generally, the services it offers are more limited than those of an EMC. Once an exporter makes a foreign sale, it hires a freight forwarder to arrange the best routing and means of transportation based on space availability, speed, and cost. The freight forwarder, therefore, finds the optimal path to move products from the manufacturing facility to the air or ocean terminal and then overseas.

In the same process, the forwarder secures space on planes or ships and in storage prior to shipment, reviews the letter of credit, obtains export licenses, pays consular fees, secures special documentation, and prepares required shipping documents. It also may advise on packing and labeling, purchase of transportation insurance, repacking of shipments damaged en route, and warehousing products. However, the freight forwarder does not take title to the goods or act as a sales representative in a foreign market. It simply deals with the preparation and transportation of goods.

Primary transportation modes include

- Surface freight (truck and rail), ocean freight, and airfreight.
- Intermodal transportation—the movement across different modes from origin to destination.

TRANSPORTATION OPTIONS   Freight forwarders, especially the smaller ones, sometimes specialize in a transportation mode—surface freight, ocean freight, and airfreight—and the geographical area served. Increasingly, however, freight forwarders handle many modes such as truck, rail, and airfreight.[50]

The movement of goods across different modes, from origin to destination, is known as **intermodal transportation.** Ocean freight is the cheapest way to move merchandise, and although the slowest, it predominates due to containerization. This particular transport mode is build on the platform of standard ISO containers (known as Shipping Containers or Isotainers) that can be loaded and sealed intact onto container ships, railroad cars, planes, and trucks. Containerization has revolutionized the efficiency of cargo shipping. Today, approximately 90 percent of nonbulk cargo worldwide moves by containers stacked on transport ships.

Forwarders help manufacturers get the best contract and help prepare the products for export. Exporters can load merchandise in a container for shipment overseas, or they can rely on a freight forwarder to consolidate their shipments with others. As we observed in our opening case, for example, Grieve's Patrick Calabrese shops for quotes from different freight forwarders when booking space on cargo ships.

Basic supply and demand for container space, in terms of the ports and the direction the goods travel, determine the shipping cost. For example, different rates apply to shipments from the United States to China and to shipments from China to the United States. Shipping one container of furniture (total volume weight 30,000 pounds or 13,607.91 kilos) from Philadelphia to Shanghai costs $2,643.82. The shipping charge for the same cargo, but from Shanghai to Philadelphia, is $4,389.47.[51]

Despite the cost advantage of containerization, the airfreight business thrives, given the needs for frequent shipments, lighter-weight shipments, and higher-value shipments. The trends toward global manufacturing, which we will discuss in Chapter 17, and contracting product life cycles have created a boom in airfreight traffic. As a result of these trends, airfreight sometimes is a more effective method of shipping than ocean freight.

Higher-value shipments are more likely to use airfreight as long as they are not too bulky because the exporter wants to get the product into the hands of the importer as soon as possible to collect on the sale. In most cases, the exporter will not be paid for the sale until delivery is complete. Federal Express and UPS have launched information campaigns targeted at small businesses to promote their shipping services. Indeed, both companies

Here we see the *Regina Maersk*, one of the world's largest container ships, heading into port. This leviathan of intermodal shipping can carry up to 6,000 twenty-foot equivalent (TEU) containers. In comparison, a train carrying that load would be nearly 25 miles (40 kilometers) long. Every day, surging international trade sets in motion more than 250 million-plus TEU containers from factories on through ports and ultimately to consumers worldwide.

have translated technology into a host of services in logistics, freight forwarding, customs clearance, technology, and finance that create trading opportunities for more companies.[52]

Forwarder Fees The freight forwarder usually charges the exporter a percentage of the shipment value, plus a minimum charge depending on the number of services provided. The forwarder also receives a brokerage fee from the carrier. Most companies, especially the SMEs, find it difficult to set up a full-time department to deal with freight issues and keep up with shipping regulations. Despite the costs of using a freight forwarder, it is usually less expensive for an exporter than providing the service internally. In addition, the forwarder can secure shipping space more easily because of its close relationship with carriers and consolidate shipments to obtain lower rates.

Countertrade

Currency is the preferred payment medium for any export or import transaction—it is easy, fast, and straightforward to transact. Sometimes, though, companies must adapt to the reality that buyers in many countries cannot provide it, either because their home country's currency is nonconvertible or the country does not have enough cash or sufficient lines of credit.

Sometimes companies and countries find it practically impossible to generate enough foreign exchange to pay for imports. In recourse, they devise creative ways to buy products. For example, Indonesia traded 40,000 tons of palm oil, worth about $15 million, with Russia in exchange for Russian Sukhoi fighter aircraft.[53] Similarly, Thailand and Indonesia signed a $40 million deal in which Indonesia would supply Thailand with an agricultural aircraft, train carriages, and fertilizer in exchange for Thai rice—no monies were or would be exchanged.[54]

On a more exotic note, Pepsi-Cola, which has the marketing rights for all Stolichnaya Vodka in the United States, delivers syrup that is paid for with Stolichnaya Vodka. Also, Pepsi took delivery of 17 submarines, a cruiser, a frigate, and a destroyer from the Russian government in payment for Pepsi products. In turn, Pepsi sold its "fleet" of 20 naval vessels for scrap steel, thereby paying for Pepsi products being moved to the Soviet Union.[55]

These trades, like others that fall under the umbrella term **countertrade**, illustrate that buyers and sellers often find creative ways of settling payment for imports and exports. Countertrade refers to any one of several different arrangements that parties negotiate so

Countertrade is when goods and services are traded for each other. It is used when a firm exports to a country whose currency creates barriers to efficient trade.

CONCEPT CHECK
Recall our discussions of poverty in Chapters 4 and 5. Here we point out that shortages of resources impoverish nations as well as individuals. Some countries, for example, struggle to acquire the foreign reserves they need to purchase goods from other nations. When they're unsuccessful in this effort, they often turn to such methods as **countertrade**. In Chapter 9, we show how and why companies conducting international business must deal with the implications of such economic conditions (e.g., exchange-rate and capital fluctuations) in foreign markets.

they can trade goods and services with limited or no use of currency. Technically, countertrade can be divided into two basic types: barter, based on clearing arrangements used to avoid money-based exchange, and buybacks, offsets, and counterpurchases, which are used to impose reciprocal commitments.[56]

Inefficiencies   Countertrade is an inefficient way of doing business; companies prefer the straightforward efficiency of cash or credit. In the case of countertrade, rather than simply consulting current foreign-exchange rates, buyers and sellers must enter complex and time-consuming negotiations to reach a fair value on the exchange—how many gallons of palm oil for how many planes, for example. In some situations, the goods sent as payment may be poor quality, packaged unattractively, or difficult to sell and service.

Also, there's a lot of room for price and financial distortion in countertrade deals given that nonmarket forces set the prices of these goods. Ultimately, countertrade and its variations threaten free market forces with protectionism and price-fixing that can complicate trade relations with other countries.

Benefits   The reality of international trade means that countertrade is often unavoidable for companies that want to do business in markets that have limited or no access to cash or credit. Complicating matters is the fact that as much as companies may dislike them, many emerging markets prefer countertrade to preserve their limited monetary assets, generate foreign exchange, and improve the balance of trade. In addition, countertrade helps emerging markets reduce their need to borrow working capital as well as let them access the technology and marketing expertise of MNEs.

More significantly, benefits beyond financing the immediate transaction do accrue to companies. Accepting countertrade shows a manager's good faith and flexibility in the face of onerous conditions. These sensitivities can position the firm to gain preferential access to emerging markets. Philosophically, the idea of countertrade fits with many countries' basic notions of business. For example, the idea of "barter and trade" is part of some African traditions' reluctance to conform to so-called Euro-centric methods of cash payment. Table 13.5 profiles leading types of countertrade.

It is difficult to gauge the size of the countertrade market due to inconsistent reporting and disclosure. The WTO estimates that countertrade accounts for around 5 percent of world trade, whereas the British Department of Trade and Industry has suggested as much as 15 percent. Various observers believe it to be closer to 30 percent, with east-west trade having been as high as 40 percent in some trading sectors of Eastern European and developing countries. No matter the absolute size, the fact that countertrade generally increases in economies that are experiencing economic problems makes it an enduring feature of international trade.

TABLE 13.5   Common Types of Countertrade

Barter	Transaction in which products are exchanged directly for products of equal value without the use of money as a means of purchase or payment.
Buyback	Transaction in which a supplier of capital or equipment agrees to be paid in future output generated by the investment. For example: The exporter of equipment to a chemical plant may be repaid with output from the factory to whose owner it "sold" the equipment.
Offset	Transaction in which an exporter sells products for cash and then helps the importer find opportunities to earn hard currency for payment. For example: Offsets are most common when big-ticket products (e.g., military equipment) are involved.
Switch Trading	Transaction (also known as a *swap* deal) in which one company sells to another its obligation to purchase something in a foreign country; so called because the arrangement often involves switching the documentation and destination of merchandise while it's in transit.
Counter purchase	Transaction in which a company that sells products to a foreign country promises to make a future purchase of a specific product made in that country; in short, a supplier agrees to purchase products from a foreign buyer as a condition of getting the buyer's order.

A Little Electronic Magic at Alibaba.com

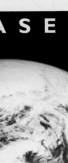

Electronic commerce, by making it easier and cheaper to trade internationally, is changing the way companies around the world do business.[57] Before the Internet, tracking down a product to import, or finding foreign customers to export to, were daunting challenges for the typical SME. These companies often had to rely on occasional trade shows, followed by expensive and time-consuming travels to foreign lands, to identify possible products, check on potential suppliers, or conduct primary market research.

An alternative for these companies was to contact directly consulates or embassies in foreign countries for support, either for promoting the export of their products or assisting with the import of goods. Although sounding straightforward, these were expensive options that commanded a lot of time from managers. Consequently, international trade was largely limited to those companies that could afford to attend expensive trade shows, publish costly brochures, travel internationally, and hire agents and export trading companies.

Today, the Internet provides a cost-effective way for SMEs, even those on a shoestring budget, to clear these hurdles. It has opened up a new era of business opportunities, making vital information, on any conceivable product and from virtually any market, accessible both readily and inexpensively. In addition, falling trade barriers, courtesy of the WTO, and more efficient logistics, from companies like FedEx, DHL, and UPS, offer an array of possibilities for import and export that has fueled the growth of global trade. The U.S. Small Business Administration estimates that the number of small businesses exporting goods or services tripled from 1994 through 2004. In terms of monetary flows, the value of exports from the United States grew from $731 billion in 2001 to $1.03 trillion in 2006 and imports grew from $1.14 trillion to $1.9 trillion over the same period.

Many companies are taking advantage of online technologies to start or expand international trade. They rely on the Internet as their primary channel for getting information, sourcing goods or services, finding suppliers, marketing their products, and tapping into new markets. In many cases, these companies build a virtual value chain online. International traders, both potential and practicing, have nearly infinite resources to tap into online. They can browse through catalog repositories, business-to-business (B2B) exchanges, electronic trade boards, trade journals, and virtual trade shows to find a product to import or a market for their export. Increasingly, as more firms throughout the world access the Internet, many entrepreneurs and trading companies use this technology as their primary way to develop their import and export business.

Recently, the emergence of country-specific portals and Web exchanges has accelerated this process. Replicating what eBay has done for consumer-to-consumer e-commerce, several sites have created online bazaars for international traders where exporters can lay out their wares and haggle with potential buyers from the far corners of the world. For instance, potential importers looking for products from South Korea can access www.koreatradeworld.com; those targeting India can check out www.trade-india.com; and those focusing on Europe need only visit www.bizeurope.com to tap into high-quality electronic trade boards. Also, if interested, one could shop the world at www.itrademarket.com.

One can track down country-specific business-to-business (B2B) exchanges for practically every country with a quick check of the open directory project at www.dmoz.org/Business/ E-Commerce/ Marketplaces. Although many sites exist, they share the goal of serving as a trade agency promoting a country's or region's commercial potential within the global community. This goal encourages sites to provide a variety of direct services to large and small international traders, such as trade consulting, export training, cybertrade infrastructures, international special exhibitions, virtual trade shows, and new trade strategies.

Conceptually, these sites are straightforward: They help move products from sellers in one place to buyers in another. But operationally, they represent powerful B2B Web sites that are changing the mechanics of import and export. These sites create flexible and dynamic platforms that let buyers and sellers of everything from bamboo toothpicks to farm tractors find each other and work out the terms of trade.

Besides introducing mom-and-pop shops from around the world to each other, these sites have opened up a vast and largely uncharted small-business hinterland in markets from Tibet to Patagonia. Long the unseen production sites for many pieces of the global economy, the only option for these small companies has been to trade within the context of global supply chains directed by large companies. Now, within the world of these new trade Web sites, they have the option to go straight to buyers and sellers. Consequently, these Web sites have reduced many of the barriers to international trade and, in the process, helped legions of small businesses become independent importers and exporters.

Like many parts of the global economy, this sort of e-commerce is having a big impact in China. Spearheading this effort is Alibaba, a Chinese Internet company that specializes in introducing manufacturers across China to buyers in China and beyond. Founded in 1999 by Jack Ma, who has been dubbed the father of the Chinese Internet, the company has translated its mission to make doing business easier into impressive accomplishments (see Figure 13.4).

Operationally, managers at Alibaba aim to enable an interactive community of millions to meet, chat, trade and work online through an integrated e-commerce framework composed of these resources:

- *Alibaba.com:* The world's largest online B2B marketplace for global and domestic China trade, reporting 3 million registered users from over 200 countries and territories.
- *Alisoft:* A leading provider of easy-to-use Web-based business software services for SMEs in China.
- *Yahoo! China:* A leading search engine and portal, acquired from Yahoo! Inc. in October 2005.
- *Taobao.com:* Literally "digging treasure," this is Asia's largest consumer e-commerce Web site.
- *Alipay:* China's leading online payment service.

Based in Hangzhou, about a two-hour drive south of Shanghai, Alibaba began operations with the goal of getting big by staying small. Jack Ma believes that his target customers are small businesses around the world—in his own words, "shrimps," not "whales." On a typical day, the online community doing business on Alibaba.com numbers hundreds of thousands of buyers and sellers, from more than 200 countries, seeking to initiate an import or export transaction. By 2007, Alibaba had 16 regional sales and service centers across the country, as well as corporate offices in Beijing, Hong Kong, the United States, and Europe, and listed more than 5,000 employees.

Acting as an online global trade fair, Alibaba enables smaller companies with import and export ambition but shoestring budgets to reach the global market. More specifically,

FIGURE 13.4 Alibaba: History and Milestones

Source: Alibaba Group, "Corporate Overview" (1999–2007), at www.alibaba.com (accessed October 26, 2007).

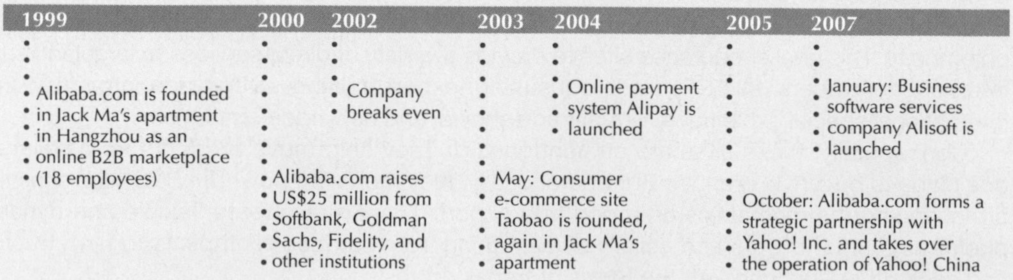

1999	2000	2002	2003	2004	2005	2007
Alibaba.com is founded in Jack Ma's apartment in Hangzhou as an online B2B marketplace (18 employees)	Alibaba.com raises US$25 million from Softbank, Goldman Sachs, Fidelity, and other institutions	Company breaks even		Online payment system Alipay is launched; May: Consumer e-commerce site Taobao is founded, again in Jack Ma's apartment		January: Business software services company Alisoft is launched; October: Alibaba.com forms a strategic partnership with Yahoo! Inc. and takes over the operation of Yahoo! China

most of Alibaba's users are SMEs in developing countries around the world. They are located in rural areas, as well as large cities, in countries such as Kyrgyzstan, Sierra Leone, and Peru.

Few of these companies are glamorous and high tech; most are low-tech companies making labor-intensive, scale-insensitive products. However, technology gives these companies the freedom to expand their market reach and grow their businesses—essentially, they can use Alibaba's infrastructure to survey and tap information on products and suppliers from over 30 different industries operating worldwide. Doing so lets SMEs, working from even the smallest apartment anywhere in the world, create a global business. Figure 13.5 illustrates the step-by-step mechanics of Alibaba.

The lure of Alibaba is undeniable: Importers around the world can request bids from Chinese manufacturers for a mind-boggling array of goods, such as cookware, poker chips, washing machines, or MP3 players. Also, product options are ever expanding. To this day, Alibaba has organized more than a thousand product categories, each with many subcategories. In addition, Alibaba offers new channels to trade services. For example, the classic home inventor in, say, Caracas or Chicago now has the option to design a product and then use Alibaba to find Chinese factories eager and able to manufacture and ship it to customers worldwide.

Operationally, buyers around the world use Alibaba to find potential suppliers that often have the lowest costs in the world, thereby eliminating the need to hire a representative in China to buy directly from the manufacturers on their behalf. So, for example, an enterprising company in Argentina looking to buy 500 DVD players can visit Alibaba.com, search among the dozens of potential suppliers, learn their terms of trade, contact the preferred vendor, and set the deal in motion. Said the cofounder of www.meetchina.com, a similar e-commerce site, "We want to make buying 1,000 bicycles from China as easy as buying a book from Amazon.com."

Historically, an importer often worried about being defrauded by an unknown supplier—that is, how does an importer from Buenos Aires find and trust a supplier in Guangzhou, half way around the world? Increasingly, as sites like Alibaba inject more transparency into the process of importing and exporting, buyers can worry less about fraud. Users of Alibaba,

FIGURE 13.5 How Alibaba.com Works

Alibaba.com acts as a marketing platform and meeting place for buyers and sellers.

Source: Alibaba Group, "Corporate Overview" (1999–2007) at www.alibaba.com (accessed January, 11, 2008).

The sourcing cycle

1. Discovery	Supplier Search RFI–Request for Information	1. Sellers post their products, trade leads, and build a company profile on Alibaba.com.
2. Negotiation	RFQ–Request for Quotation Supplier Selection	2. Buyers search products, trade leads and company listings, and can view video factory tours. Buyers can learn more about potential partners by examining their certifications and information provided by third-party credit companies.
3. Transaction	PO–Purchase Order	3. Buyers and sellers communicate and negotiate in a private and secure environment using My Alibaba's inquiry system and Alibaba's proprietary Trade Manager messaging software.
	Inspection Quality Assurance	4. All transactions are completed offline and outside of the Alibaba system.
	Insurance	
	Shipping Freight Forwarding	
	Tracking and Delivery	

like those on similar e-commerce sites, can post information about their companies on the site as well as access information about the reliability of other users.

Buyers also have the option to access Alibaba's basic screening and background checks on its registered users. Finally, they can access the seller's posted references, like one from the seller's bank, to verify the seller's status. Collectively, these data let the importer in Argentina cross-check potential trade partners in China, quickly getting a sense of their credibility and reliability.

This seemingly simple system of checks and balances is how Alibaba makes money. It offers a basic service of listing a company and its products on its Web site free of charge. It then generates revenue from the 85,000 members who pay $300 to $10,000 a year for services such as personalized Web pages, high-quality online introduction, and priority listing of products.

As it has in other parts of the business world, technology is creating opportunities for international traders. In the past, globalization gave a disproportionate amount of power and benefits to large companies. Rather than being overtaxed by the challenge of trading internationally, large companies could rely on their well-equipped international divisions to supervise imports and exports. Today, Internet and telecommunications advancements have spread trade opportunities throughout the world, both in wealthy nations as well as deep into developing countries. ■

QUESTIONS

1. List, in separate columns, the benefits and costs of using sites like Alibaba's to trade internationally. What does your analysis say to companies like Grieve (our opening case) as they think about their export strategy?

2. Is it reasonable to speculate that eventually most trade between SMEs might take place in the context of sites like Alibaba.com? If so, does that influence your inclination to consider importing and exporting?

3. Visit www.alibaba.com, www.trade-india.com, and www.europages.com. Compare and contrast these Web sites.

4. Visit www.alibaba.com, go to "Advanced Search," and enter the product you seek in the relevant box. Select required criteria and click on "Search." Review the list of companies that qualify and find a suitable one. Analyze this process for ease, usefulness, and potential value.

5. How transparent do sites like Alibaba.com make the import-export transaction? Would you still worry about fraud?

SUMMARY

- The probability of a company's becoming an exporter increases with company size, but the extent of exporting does not directly correlate with size.

- Companies export to increase sales revenues, use excess capacity, and diversify markets.

- Companies new to exporting (as well as some experienced exporters) make mistakes. One way to avoid mistakes is to develop a comprehensive export strategy that includes an analysis of the company's resources as well as its export potential. Companies can also improve the odds of success by working with an experienced export intermediary.

- As a company establishes its export business plan, it must assess export potential, obtain expert counseling, select a country or countries where it will focus its exports, formulate its strategy, and determine how to get its goods to market.

- Importers need to be concerned with strategic issues (import vs. buying domestically) and procedural issues (the steps needed to get goods into the country).

- Customs agencies assess and collect duties, as well as ensure compliance with import regulations.

- An import broker helps by valuing products to qualify for more favorable duty treatment, qualifying products for duty refunds through drawback provisions, deferring duties by using bonded warehouses and foreign trade zones, and limiting liability by properly marking an import's country of origin.

- Exporters may deal directly with agents or distributors in a foreign country or indirectly through third-party intermediaries, such as export management companies or other types of trading companies.

- Internet marketing is a form of direct exporting that allows companies to access export markets at low cost and with high impact.

- Trading companies perform many of the functions for which manufacturers lack the expertise. In addition, exporters use the services of other specialists, such as freight forwarders, to facilitate exporting. These specialists help an exporter with the complex documentation that accompanies exports.

- Government agencies in some countries, such as the Ex-Im Bank in the United States, provide assistance in terms of direct loans to importers, bank guarantees to fund an exporter's working capital needs, and insurance against commercial and political risk.

- Countertrade is any one of several different arrangements by which goods and services are traded for each other, either bilaterally or multilaterally, in exchanges that do not involve currency.

- Barter means trading goods or services for goods or services. Offsets are agreements by which the exporter helps the importer earn foreign exchange or the transfer of technology or production to the importing country.

KEY TERMS

countertrade (p. 517)
customs agencies (p. 503)
direct selling (p. 509)
exporting (p. 491)
export intermediaries (p. 507)
export management company
  (EMC) (p. 507)

export strategy (p. 497)
export trading company
  (ETC) (p. 507)
freight forwarder (p. 516)
import broker (customs broker) (p. 502)
importing (p. 491)
import strategy (p. 501)

indirect selling (p. 506)
intermodal transportation (p. 516)
small and medium-sized enterprise
  (SME) (p. 490)
serendipity (p. 494)
transaction chain (p. 497)

ENDNOTES

1 *Sources include the following:* Grieve Corp., at www.grievecorp.com; United States Census Bureau, *Profile of U.S. Exporting Companies, 2002–2003,* at www.census.gov/foreign-trade/aip/edbrel-0203.pdf; *Small & Medium-Sized Exporting Companies: Statistical Overview, 2003,* at www.ita.doc.gov/TD/Industry/OTEA/sme_handbook/SME_index.htm.

2 D. D. Chadee and J. Mattsson, "Do Service and Merchandise Exporters Behave and Perform Differently? A New Zealand Investigation," *European Journal of Marketing* 32 (1998): 830.

3 John H. Dunning, "The Eclectic Paradigm of International Production: Some Empirical Tests," *Journal of International Business Studies* (Spring 1988): 1–31.

4 Sanjeev Agarwal and Sridhar N. Ramaswami, "Choice of Foreign Market Entry Mode: Impact of Ownership, Location and Internalization Factors," *Journal of International Business Studies* 23:1 (1992): 2–5.

5 U.S. Department of Commerce, *Guide to Exporting, 1998* (Washington, DC: U.S. Department of Commerce and Unz & Co. Inc., November 1997), p. 3.

6 W. Chan Kim and Peter Hwang, "Global Strategy and Multinationals' Entry Mode Choice," *Journal of International Business Studies* 23:1 (1992): 32–35.

7 Mark Stein, "Export Opportunities Aren't Just for the Big Guys," *New York Times*, March 24, 2005.

8 Andrea Bonaccorsi, "On the Relationship Between Firm Size and Export Intensity," *Journal of International Business Studies* 23:4 (1992): 606.

9 Paul Magnusson, "The Split-Up That's Slanting the Trade Deficit," *Business Week*, June 7, 1999: 38.

10 Jonathan L. Calof, "The Relationship Between Firm Size and Export Behavior Revisited," *Journal of International Business Studies* 25:2 (1994): 367–87; James Obben and Phumzile Magagula, "Firm and Managerial Determinants of the Export Propensity of Small- and Medium-Sized Enterprises in Swaziland," *International Small Business Journal* 21:1 (2003): 73.

11 Paul Westhead, Mike Wright, and Deniz Ucbasaran, "International Market Selection Strategies Selected by 'Micro' and 'Small' Firms," *Omega* (February 2002): 51.

12 Leonidas C. Leonidou and Constantine S. Katsikeas, "The Export Development Process: An Integrative Review of Empirical Models," *Journal of International Business Studies* 27:3 (1996): 524–25.

13 O. Moen, "The Born Globals: A New Generation of Small European Exporters," *International Marketing Review*, April 30, 2002: 156.

14 U.S. Department of Commerce, "A San Diego Company Uses the Internet to Go Global," August 18, 2002, at www.usatrade.gov/website/website.nsf/WebBySubj/Main_WhatsNew081802.

15 "Congress Pushes More Export Financing for Small Business," *Associated Press*, September 5, 2006.

16 John Kerr, "Exporters Need to Connect with Customers," *Logistics Management*, March 1, 2006: 41.

17 "Most Common Mistakes of New-to-Export Ventures," *Business America*, April 16, 1984: 9.

18 Stein, "Export Opportunities Aren't Just for the Big Guys."

19 Benson Smith and Tony Rutigliano, *Discover Your Sales Strengths* (New York: Warner Business Books, 2003).

20 Paul Beamish et al., "The Relationship Between Organizational Structure and Export Performance," *Management International Review* 39:1 (1999): 51.

21 Kerr, "Exporters Need to Connect with Customers."

22 U.S. Department of the Treasury, U.S. Customs Service, *Importing into the United States* (Washington, DC: U.S. Government Printing Office, September 1991).

23 Because a practical discussion of importing procedures in every trading country of the world is impossible within this chapter, we focus on the matter of importing to the United States. We note that although U.S. import requirements and procedures provide a sufficient base for judging situations in other countries, a company must assess the importing regulations applicable to those countries in which they plan to engage. For an organizational chart of the U.S. Customs Bureau, including a roster of specific responsibilities, go to the home page of the U.S. Bureau of Customs and Border Protection, at www.customs.ustreas.gov.

24 The International Bank for Reconstruction and Development/The World Bank, "Doing Business in 2007: How to Reform."

25 Julie Sloane, Justin Martin, and Alessandra Bianchi, "Small Companies That Play Big," *FSB Magazine*, November 1, 2006, quoting Ram Iyer.

26 Sloane, Martin, and Bianchi, "Small Companies That Play Big," quoting Everette Phillips.

27 International Bank/World Bank, "Doing Business in 2007": 43.

28 Kerr, "Exporters Need to Connect with Customers."

29 Lee Li, "Joint Effects of Factors Affecting Exchanges Between Exporters and Their Foreign Intermediaries: An Exploratory Study," *Journal of Business & Industrial Marketing* (February–March 2003): 162–178.

30 Kerr, "Exporters Need to Connect with Customers."

31 See U.S. Department of Commerce, *Guide to Exporting, 1998*, p. 20; Philip MacDonald, *Practical Exporting and Importing*, 2nd ed. (New York: Ronald Press, 1959), pp. 30–40.

32 Courtney Fingar, "ABCs of EMCs," The Federation of International Trade Associations, July 2001, at http://fita.org/emc.html; Nelson T. Joyner, "How to Find and Use an Export Management Company," April 1999, at www.fita.org/aotm/0499.html.

33 "Basic Question: To Export Yourself or to Hire Someone to Do It for You?" *Business America*, April 27, 1987: 14–17.

34 Paola Hjelt, "The *Fortune* Global 500," *Fortune*, July 26, 2004: 159.

35 Jiang Jingjing, "Wal-Mart's China Inventory to Hit US$18B This Year," *China Business Weekly*, November 29, 2004 at www.chinadaily.com.cn/english/doc/2004–11/29/content_395728.htm.

36 John Daniels' interview with John Teeling, executive chairman of Cooley Distillery (2002).

37 Merlin Bettina, "Internet Marketing in Exports—A Useful Tool for Small Businesses," *Small Enterprise Development* (December 2004): 38.

38 Anna Morgan-Thomas and Susan Bridgewater, "Internet and Exporting: Determinants of Success in Virtual Export Channels," *International Marketing Review* 21:4 (2004): 393.

39 A. J. Campbell, "Ten Reasons Why Your Business Should Use Electronic Commerce," *Business America*, May 1998: 12–14.

40 J. Laurie Flynn, "Poor Nations Are Littered with Old PC's, Report Says," *New York Times*, October 24, 2005.

41 Helen Baulch, "Error: Dumping Does Not Compute," *Alternatives Journal*, Summer 2002: 2.

42 Zada Lipman, "A Dirty Dilemma: The Hazardous Waste Trade," *Harvard International Review* 23 (2002): 67.

43 Reported by Karl Schoenberger, "E-Waste Ignored in India," *Mercury News*, at www.ban.org/ban_news/ewaste_ignored_031228.html.

44 Baulch, "Error: Dumping Does Not Compute."

45 Basel Action Network, at www.ban.org/index.html, May 5, 2007; Flynn, "Poor Nations Are Littered with Old PC's."

46 "Where Does E-Waste End Up?" at www.greenpeace.org/international/campaigns/toxics/electronics/where-does-e-waste-end-up, May 5, 2007.

47 "E-Waste Importers," *Hazardous Waste Superfund Week*, December 23, 2002.

48 See "Secretariat of the Basel Convention, Competent Authorities," Membership List, April 18, 2005, at www.basel.int (accessed May 5, 2007). By definition, a "Competent Authority" means one governmental authority designated by a Party to be responsible within such geographic areas as the Party may think fit, for receiving the notification of a transboundary movement of hazardous wastes or other wastes, and any information related to it, and for responding to such a notification.

49 U.S. Department of Commerce, *Guide to Exporting, 1998*, p. 63.

50 Helen Richardson, "Freight Forwarder Basics: Contract Negotiation," *Transportation & Distribution*, May 1996; available in Lexis/Nexis News: CURNWS.

51 Estimates calculated May 15, 2007, at www.freight-calculator.com/apxocean.asp.

52 "UPS Unveils 'What Can Brown Do for You?' Ad Campaign,"
    Business First, February 7, 2002.

53 "Indonesia to Increase Sukhoi Planes to 16," *Xinhua General News
    Service* [China], April 9, 2005.

54 "Commodities: Thai Countertrade Deal Signed," Laksamana.net,
    June 10, 2002, at www.laksamana.net/printcfm?id=2893.

55 Dan West, "Countertrade—An Innovative Approach to
    Marketing," at www.barternews.com/approach_ marketing.htm
    (accessed May 15, 2007).

56 J. F. Hennart, "Some Empirical Dimensions of Countertrade,"
    Journal of International Business Studies 21 (1990):
    243–70.

57 ***Sources include the following:*** Various sources at www.Alibaba.com;
    Forbes Global, April 25, 2005: 30; Daniel Roth, "The Amazing Rise
    of the Do-It-Yourself Economy," *Fortune*, May 30, 2005: 45;
    TradeStats Express, at http://tse.export.gov (accessed July 1, 2007).
    John Heilemann, "Jack Ma Aims to Unlock the Middle Kingdom,"
    Business 2.0 Magazine, July 31, 2006.

14

Direct Investment and Collaborative Strategies

Objectives

- To clarify why companies may need to use modes other than exporting to operate effectively in international business

- To comprehend why and how companies make foreign direct investments

- To understand the major motives that guide managers when choosing a collaborative arrangement for international business

- To define the major types of collaborative arrangements

- To describe what companies should consider when entering into arrangements with other companies

- To grasp what makes collaborative arrangements succeed or fail

- To see how companies can manage diverse collaborative arrangements

If you can't beat them, join them.

—American proverb

CASE: The Fizz Biz: Coca-Cola

Sailin' round the world in a dirty gondola.

Oh, to be back in the land of Coca-Cola!

—Bob Dylan, *When I Paint My Masterpiece*

Although Dylan's "land of Coca-Cola" is the United States, more than 70 percent of Coca-Cola's (Coke's) sales are elsewhere.[1] Coca-Cola's brand is the world's most recognized; thus other companies, such as Murjani International for clothing, have paid Coca-Cola licensing fees for use of the logo on their products. Despite the popularity of the Coca-Cola name, you probably can name few of the more than 400 brand names the company uses globally within its five nonalcoholic drink segments: juice drinks, energy drinks, juices and juice drinks, soft drinks, and sports drinks. Here are just a few you might not recognize: Bonaqua Bonactive (Hong Kong), Jugos de Valle (Brazil and Mexico), Far Coast (Singapore), Mother (Australia), Multon (Russia), and Nanairo Acha (Japan). The company describes itself as a manufacturer, distributor, and marketer of nonalcoholic drinks.

A LITTLE HISTORY

Coca-Cola originated as a soda fountain drink in 1886, began bottling in 1894, commenced soda fountain sales in Canada and Mexico in 1897, and initiated its first foreign bottling plant in Panama in 1906. Coke continued to expand internationally during the 1920s and 1930s and even opened a foreign department in 1926. But its big international boost came during World War II. Recognizing that the war would bring a shortage of sugar, one of Coke's essential ingredients, its CEO announced on national radio that the company would ensure that all U.S. military personnel anywhere in the world could buy Coca-Cola at five cents a bottle. His propaganda message worked. Not only did Coca-Cola get all the sugar it wanted, even though U.S. households seldom found sugar in the grocery stores, it also got permission to build 64 bottling plants around the world during the war.

When the war ended, Coca-Cola was known almost everywhere, and returning service personnel had become loyal customers. In 1957, Coke celebrated having bottling operations in 100 countries when it launched a plant in the West African country of Sierra Leone. Former Coke CEO Roberto Goizueta said, "We were global when global wasn't cool." Today, Coke's network of more than 1,000 plants serves customers in about 200 countries and operates a fleet of delivery trucks five times larger than that of UPS. It has the largest share of the soft drink market, and more than 16,000 Coca-Cola beverages are consumed worldwide *every* second.

COLLABORATIVE ARRANGEMENTS

Joint Ventures: Suppliers

Although its product offerings and shrewd marketing are pillars of Coke's success, the company could not have reached its present position without "a little help from its friends." Coke buys from over 84,000 suppliers. It needs help in almost every aspect of its operations. For instance, in 1996 it formed a three-way joint venture for a facility in the former Soviet republic of Kyrgyzstan. The joint venture hired a Turkish turnkey operator (Fintraco Insaat ve Taahhut), which used 400 trucks just to carry supplies from Turkey, to build the plant.

In another example, Coca-Cola has paid to have a multipurpose exhibition and entertainment venue named the Coca-Cola Dome in Johannesburg, South Africa. The dome owner is the Sasol Pension Fund, which, in turn, pays Thebe Entertainment and Events a contractual fee for managing the facility. In sum, when operating both domestically and internationally, Coca-Cola uses a variety of collaborative operating forms, and it takes varying levels of ownership in operations that support its business. These vary by location, and many have changed over time in response to Coca-Cola's own objectives and competencies along with the environments within the countries where it operates.

The one area in which Coca-Cola maintains strict ownership control is in production of concentrate, thus ensuring that its "secret formula" does not fall into the hands of competitors.

Franchises: Bottlers

Coca-Cola sees its bottlers worldwide as the backbone of the company. These bottlers operate under franchise agreements in which each has exclusive rights to sell within a given territory. They not only bottle Coke beverages, but they also deliver them to such outlets as grocery stores and vending machines. They put up ad displays in stores and even make sure bottles are aligned correctly on supermarket shelves. In short, they know and respond well to their local markets. By turning activities over to the franchised bottlers, Coca-Cola can concentrate its efforts on what it feels it can do best. And these efforts help the profitability of bottlers.

What's in It for Bottlers?   So what do the bottlers get in return from Coca-Cola?

1. They get the results of Coca-Cola's innovation in developing new products, such as Coca-Cola Zero, and in developing ad campaigns that help sell Coca-Cola products worldwide. These have included such themes as "Coke side of life," "It's the real thing," "Things go better with Coca-Cola," and "I want to teach the world to sing."

2. They benefit from Coca-Cola's strict quality control, which includes procedures for and inspection of water purification and the mixing of syrup, concentrate, and carbonation. Quality control is important in that a slipup in one bottling plant can adversely affect sales in many countries as happened when 250 people in Belgium became ill from drinking contaminated Coke.

3. They get help in instituting work processes to increase their efficiency. Coca-Cola studies and compares bottlers, and because they are not in competition with each other, Coca-Cola shares information among them. Finally, last but not least, Coca-Cola makes the concentrate that all its bottlers must buy (at a hefty price).

The Franchise as Big Business?   Some of the franchisees are quite large and are themselves traded publicly. For example, Coca-Cola HBC is headquartered in Greece, has operating rights in 28 countries with a combined population of 550 million, and is traded on stock exchanges in Greece, the United Kingdom, Australia, and the United States. When franchise rights cover a large territory, the franchisees generally subfranchise to bottlers throughout their region.

Four of these large franchisees account for about 40 percent of Coca-Cola's worldwide sales. In each of these four, Coca-Cola has taken a significant minority ownership stake, ranging from 23 percent to 35 percent, which is sufficient to gain considerable influence in the operations. In some situations, however, Coca-Cola deals directly with a single bottler abroad, such as with the National Beverage Company, which has rights only in the Palestinian territory.

Ownership Options

Coca-Cola's ownership abroad varies substantially. For example within China, it wholly owns its concentrate plant but has joint ventures with various bottling plants. Coca-Cola's ownership in foreign bottling operations has become sufficiently significant that it has set up a Bottle Investment Group within the company. It has sometimes taken an equity position abroad, even a wholly owned one, to sustain production where it would like to sell. For instance, in the Philippines, Coca-Cola has bought some poorly performing bottlers that might otherwise have ceased production. Coke hopes to turn them around and then sell them. When entering the Vietnamese market, it did so with a local joint venture bottling partner that needed Coke's financial and marketing help. After the operation became viable, Coke sold its interest.

However, the ownership dynamics sometimes go the other way. For instance, Coca-Cola had a 35 percent interest in a joint venture with the Philippines' San Miguel. When San Miguel wanted to disengage itself to concentrate on its core businesses, Coca-Cola bought the remaining 65 percent.

Further, Coca-Cola has sometimes had to settle for a joint venture when it might have preferred full ownership. One case in point is India. Coca-Cola once left the market because of the Indian government's insistence on knowing Coke's concentrate formula. To return about 15 years later, the Indian government required Coca-Cola (and PepsiCo as well) to share ownership with an Indian company. Another case in point was when Coca-Cola wished to acquire Inca Kola, the largest soft drink company in Peru. The family owners of Inca Kola refused to sell the whole company, and Coke settled for a half ownership.

RED COUNTRIES VERSUS BLUE COUNTRIES

Whereas the two major U.S. political parties talk about red states and blue states, the two major global competitors in soft drinks refer to red countries (Coca-Cola) and blue countries (Pepsi) where each has the larger market share. These are shown on Map 14.1.

Although Coca-Cola still has the largest global share of soft drink sales, its position has been slipping; it fell from 57 percent to 53 percent between 2000 and 2006. It not only leads PepsiCo in most foreign markets, it depends much more on foreign sales than PepsiCo does. This is positive for Coke's future inasmuch as soft drink sales in the United States have been declining.

Competitive Markets and Product Lines   However, Pepsi is leading Coke in the two markets with the fastest growth potential, China and India. Not only are these the two most populated countries, but also their annual soft drink per capita consumption is low (e.g., 1.2 liters in China and 0.1 liters in India as compared with 31.3 liters in the United States and 20.2 liters in Brazil); thus there seems to be great potential for growth in those markets as the economies improve. This growth potential undoubtedly affected both companies' acceptance of operating terms in India that they may not have accepted elsewhere.

In addition, Coca-Cola must look at rivals other than PepsiCo. For instance, Cadbury Schweppes, whose products include 7 Up and Dr Pepper, has been gaining share at the expense of both Coke and Pepsi. RC did not enter the Philippines market until 2003 but had 30 percent of the Manila market by 2007.

The market for nonalcoholic drinks is changing. Whereas carbonated cola products once completely dominated the market, the growth, particularly in the United States, has been for bottled water, sports drinks, and specialty teas and coffees. In addition, people want a greater variety of carbonated soft drinks. One observer compared the change with that of television going from a few to a host of channels. New companies have been coming into the health and energy markets, and in aggregate their presence is formidable.

Coca-Cola has learned that it must widen its product line and doing so by simply adding cherry or vanilla flavoring to Coca-Cola is not enough. If Coca-Cola does not offer a larger variety of nonalcoholic drinks, it might lose exclusive sales to large customers, such as food franchisors and airlines. Coke's bottlers have also added production and distribution of products not available from Coke, such as Cadbury Schweppes' coffee latte drink, Cinnabon.

Collaboration as Expansion Strategy   Because of changes in the market, Coca-Cola has been expanding its product offerings in three ways:

- Developing new products
- Acquiring companies that have complementary products
- Gaining licenses to use brand names of other companies

Coke has been doing some of this broadening on its own and some in partnership with other companies. We've already discussed some of Coke's internal development of new products, such as Coca-Cola Zero and Cherry Coke. In addition, the company has gone so far as to test-market in Singapore, Toronto, and Oslo the opening of its own coffee shops. Its acquisitions have been widespread, including juice companies in Brazil and Russia and specialty water companies in Germany and the United States. It has a joint venture with Nestlé for tea products outside the United States and a joint venture with Cargill to develop a new sweetener to put into drinks. It is spending heavily on licensing ($901 million in 2006) for the production and sale of products using different trademarks. One of the most important license agreements is with Danone for various water brands including Sparkletts.

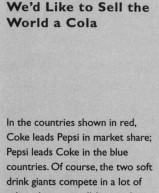

MAP 14.1
We'd Like to Sell the
World a Cola

In the countries shown in red, Coke leads Pepsi in market share; Pepsi leads Coke in the blue countries. Of course, the two soft drink giants compete in a lot of other places as well, but market share data are unavailable. Note that although red countries outnumber blue countries, the world's two most populous nations—China and India—are in the blue column. Data reflect sales of Coke/Diet Coke and Pepsi/Diet Pepsi only.

Source: Adapted from "I'd Like to Sell the World a Coke," *New York Times* (May 27, 2007), at www.nytimes.com (accessed November 5, 2007). Data from Euromonitor International and the Coca-Cola Co.

Introduction

Figure 14.1 shows that companies must choose an international operating mode to fulfill their objectives and carry out their strategies. In the preceding chapter, we discussed exporting and importing, which are the most common modes of international business. In fact, most companies would prefer to sell abroad by exporting, thus enabling them to produce within the familiar environments of their home countries rather than abroad.

Nevertheless, some compelling reasons make exporting and importing impractical. We first discuss these reasons. When companies depend on foreign production, they may own that production in whole or in part, develop the foreign operation or acquire it, and use some type of collaborative agreement with another company. We next explain the modes associated with each of these options and discuss the advantages and problems with each. We conclude the chapter by discussing management of these modes, particularly as foreign operations evolve over time.

Figure 14.2 shows the types of operating modes, categorized by whether the company has foreign ownership, whether the mode involves collaboration, and whether production is located in the home country versus a foreign country. The truly experienced MNE with a fully global orientation usually uses most of the operational modes available, selecting

them according to company capabilities, specific product, and foreign operating characteristics. Further, those modes may be combined. For example, Coca-Cola has a wholly owned concentrate plant in China as well as partially owned and franchised bottling plants there.

Why Exporting May Not Be Feasible

Companies may find more advantages by producing in foreign countries than by exporting to them. The advantages occur under six conditions:

1. When production abroad is cheaper than at home
2. When transportation costs to move goods or services internationally are too expensive
3. When companies lack domestic capacity
4. When products and services need to be altered substantially to gain sufficient consumer demand abroad
5. When governments inhibit the import of foreign products
6. When buyers prefer products originating from a particular country

FIGURE 14.1   Factors Affecting Operating Modes in International Business

Companies may conduct international business operations independently or in collaboration with other companies. The choice will be determined both by *external* factors in the firm's operating environment and by *internal* factors that include its objectives, strategies, and means of operation (e.g., such modes of international business as exporting, franchising, etc.).

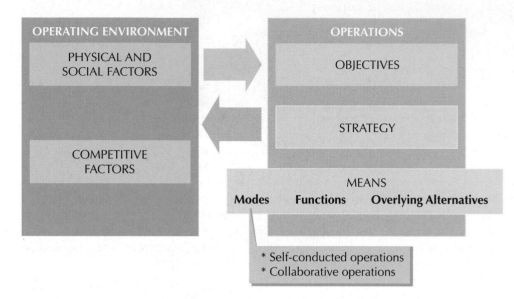

FIGURE 14.2   Foreign Expansion: Alternative Operating Modes

A firm may choose to operate globally either through *equity arrangements* (e.g., joint venture) or through *nonequity arrangements* (e.g., licensing). Exporting operations are conducted in the home country, while all other modes entail productions in foreign locations. The modes listed in the green boxes are *collaborative arrangements*. Note that, in any given location, a firm can conduct operations in multiple modes.

PRODUCTION OWNERSHIP	PRODUCTION LOCATION	
	Home country	Foreign country
Equity arrangements	a. Exporting	a. Wholly owned operations b. Partially owned with remainder widely held c. Joint ventures d. Equity alliances
Nonequity arrangements		a. Licensing b. Franchising c. Management contracts d. Turnkey operations

WHEN IT'S CHEAPER TO PRODUCE ABROAD

Although companies may have products or services that consumers abroad would like to buy, producing them within their home markets may be too expensive, especially if other companies can make reasonably similar substitutes at a lower cost. Hence competition requires that companies control their costs. For example, Turkey has been a growing market for the sale of automobiles. However, it is generally less expensive to produce them within Turkey than to export them to Turkey because producers can pay skilled labor and sophisticated engineers less than in their home countries. Further, Turks work more days per year and longer hours per day than workers from the home countries of U.S., Japanese, and European automakers. Thus these companies and many of their parts suppliers have established Turkish production to serve the Turkish market.[2]

WHEN TRANSPORTATION COSTS TOO MUCH

When companies add the cost of transportation to their production costs, they find that some products and services become impractical to export. Generally speaking, the farther the market from an existing production unit, the higher the transportation costs to that market.

Transportation raises costs so much that it becomes impractical to export some products.

Moreover, the higher the transportation costs relative to production costs, the more difficult for companies to develop viable export markets. For example, the international transportation cost for a soft drink is a high percentage of the manufacturing cost, so a sales price that includes both the manufacturing and transportation costs would have to be so high by exporting that soft drink companies would sell little by exporting to it.

This drawback, as we saw in our opening case, is among the reasons that Coca-Cola depends on local bottling plants. In fact, after Coke had successfully entered the Turkish market, it tried exporting from Turkey to Kyrgyzstan. The result, unfortunately, was a soft drink price of more than four times what it cost to buy a soft drink bottled in Kyrgyzstan itself—a price far too high for Kyrgyz consumers. (Nevertheless, such companies as Perrier have managed to find niche markets for exported bottled water that sells at high prices relative to production costs.)

Some services are impossible to export. Thus companies such as BP and McDonald's must have retail establishments abroad if they are to sell to foreign consumers because people are not going to send their cars to the United Kingdom to fill up their tanks with BP's petrol, nor will people fly to the United States just to buy a Big Mac.

However, products such as watches have low transportation costs relative to production costs. Because watch manufacturers lose few sales because of export transportation costs, companies such as Universal Genève and Seiko export watches from Switzerland and Japan, respectively, into the markets where they sell them.

WHEN DOMESTIC CAPACITY ISN'T ENOUGH

As long as a company has excess capacity, it may compete effectively in export markets despite high transport costs. This ability might occur if domestic sales cover fixed operating expenses, enabling the company to set foreign prices on the basis of variable rather than full (variable + fixed) costs. In fact, the company's average cost of production per unit goes down as foreign sales increase, but this cost decrease continues only as long as there is unused capacity.

Excess capacity
- *Usually leads to exporting rather than new direct investment.*
- *May be competitive because of variable cost pricing.*

Thus companies typically produce in one location from which they export before they establish plants in more than one country. For example, Volkswagen placed its first plant to build the new Beetle at its facilities in Mexico, which served global markets. However, when demand pushed that plant toward capacity, Volkswagen announced it would build a second plant in Europe to serve the European market.[3] The second plant freed Mexican capacity to serve nearby markets while reducing transportation costs for serving the European market.

WHEN PRODUCTS AND SERVICES NEED ALTERING

Companies often need to alter products to gain sufficient sales in a foreign market. This affects their production costs in two ways. First, they must make an additional investment, such as an automobile company's adding an assembly line to put steering wheels on the right as well as on the left. Second, they lose some of the economies from

Product alterations for foreign markets may lead to foreign production of the products.

large-scale production. In the process, their least-cost production locations may shift so they engage smaller-scale factories in the markets where they sell.

The more that products must be altered for foreign markets, the more likely that changes in production cost will create a need to shift some production to foreign markets. Whirlpool, for example, finds that most U.S. demand is for top-loading washing machines with large capacities using 110 electrical voltage, but most European demand is for front-loading washing machines (more efficient in using energy and water) with smaller capacity using 220 voltage.[4] Given the differences in product preferences, Whirlpool produces in both the United States and Europe.

WHEN TRADE RESTRICTIONS HINDER IMPORTS

CONCEPT CHECK

In Chapter 8, we explain why governments are currently reducing trade restrictions, whether through **bilateral integration** (in which two countries agree to cooperate), **regional integration** (in which a group of geographically related countries agrees to cooperate), or agreements reached by the **WTO**, which serves as a multilateral forum. Here we observe that importers still face certain regulatory restrictions, some of which are designed to encourage forms of direct investment.

Although governments have been reducing import barriers, they still restrict many imports. Thus companies may find they must produce in a foreign country if they are to sell there. For example, Volkswagen decided to build its Skoda models in India because of India's 121 percent duty on the imports.[5]

Managers must view import barriers along with other factors, such as the market size of the country imposing the barriers and the scale of technology used in production. For example, import trade restrictions have been highly influential in enticing automobile producers to locate in Brazil because of its large market. Similar restrictions by Central American countries have been ineffective because of their small markets. However, Central American import barriers on products requiring lower amounts of capital investment for production and, therefore, smaller-scale technology and markets (for example, pharmaceuticals) have been highly effective at enticing direct investment.

Removing trade restrictions among a group of countries also may attract direct investment, possibly because the expanded market may justify scale economies and possibly because the output from producing in a new location can be feasibly exported. For example, Israel has received an influx of high-tech direct investment to produce for markets in countries with which it has signed free trade agreements.[6]

WHEN COUNTRY OF ORIGIN BECOMES AN ISSUE

Consumers sometimes prefer domestically produced goods because of

- Nationalism.
- A belief that these products are better.
- A fear that foreign-made goods may not be delivered on time.

Government-imposed legal measures are not the only trade barriers to otherwise competitive goods. Consumer desires also may dictate limitations. Consumers may prefer to buy goods produced in their own country rather than another (perhaps because of nationalism).[7] If they feel strongly enough, they may even push for identification labels showing that goods are domestically produced (for instance, a green-and-gold logo for Australian-made products).[8] They may require labels showing where products are made, such as U.S. labeling of agricultural products, or preferences for domestic goods when governments make purchases, such as the state of Missouri's buy-American requirements.[9]

They may believe goods from a given country are superior, like German cars and French perfume, therefore preferring those countries' products.[10] They may also fear that service and replacement parts for imported products will be difficult to obtain. Adding to this need to invest directly is the global rise in just-in-time (JIT) manufacturing systems, which decrease inventory costs by having components and parts delivered as needed. These systems favor nearby suppliers who can deliver quickly.

In any of these cases, companies may find advantages in placing production where their output will have the best acceptance.

Noncollaborative Foreign Equity Arrangements

A company may or may not take ownership in the foreign facilities that provide products and services for them. It may simply contract with another company to produce or provide services on its behalf, or it may take some ownership equity in foreign operations, such as in warehousing, sales offices, or production facilities. Referring to Figure 14.2, you'll see there are four types of equity arrangements. In this section, we discuss two forms of foreign direct investment (FDI) that do not involve collaboration (wholly owned operations and partially owned with the remainder widely held). We also discuss the resources and methods for making FDI.

TAKING CONTROL: FOREIGN DIRECT INVESTMENT

For direct investment to take place, control must accompany the investment. Otherwise, it is a portfolio investment. If ownership is widely dispersed, then a small percentage of the holdings may be sufficient to establish control of managerial decision making. Generally, the more ownership a company has, the greater is its control over the decisions. However, governments often protect minority owners so that majority owners do not act against their interests. There are three primary reasons that spur companies to want a controlling interest: *internalization theory, appropriability theory,* and *freedom to pursue global objectives.* We now discuss each of these.

Internalization   Control through self-handling of operations (internal to the organization) is **internalization.**[11] This concept comes from *transactions cost theory,* which holds that companies should seek the lower cost between handling something internally and contracting another party to handle it for them. In actuality, a company may not easily find another company to handle something for it because, for example, it has a unique technology not easily understood by others. In other cases, self-handling may reduce costs for a number of reasons:

1. *Different operating units within the same company are likely to share a common corporate culture, which expedites communications.* For example, executives participating in a Thought Leadership Summit on Digital Strategies concluded that lack of trust and a common terminology and lack of shared knowledge are major obstacles to collaboration.[12]

2. *The company can use its own managers, who understand and are committed to carrying out its objectives.* For example, when GE acquired a controlling interest in the Hungarian company Tungsram, it was able to expedite control and changes because it put GE managers in key positions.[13]

3. *The company can avoid protracted negotiations with another company on such matters as how each will be compensated for contributions.* For example, the U.S. and Russian automakers GM and Avtovaz shut down production in their Russian joint venture while negotiating a rise in price for critical components that Avtovaz supplied to the operation.[14]

4. *The company can avoid possible problems with enforcing an agreement.* For example, Vidal Sassoon engaged in a long legal battle with Procter & Gamble over its claims that Procter & Gamble ceased support so it could boost its Pantene brand.[15]

Appropriability   The idea of denying rivals access to resources is called the **appropriability theory.**[16] Companies are reluctant to transfer vital resources—capital, patents, trademarks, and management know-how—to another organization. The company receiving these resources can use them to undermine the competitive position of the foreign company transferring them. For example, Chinese automakers such as SAIV, Dongfeng, and Changan have collaborative arrangements with major global auto competitors, such as GM, Volkswagen, Nissan, and Ford. They make no secret of their desire to learn from their partners so as to become global competitors in their own right.[17] As we pointed out in our opening case, on the other hand, Coca-Cola, though committed to a variety of collaborative operating forms with partners all over the world, steadfastly refuses to share ownership in the production of concentrate: The formula is simply too critical to the company's competitive viability.

Companies may want to operate through FDI to lessen the chance of developing competitors.

Case Review Note

Recall that, in discussing **global strategy** as a type of international strategy in Chapter 11, we explain why some companies treat the world as a single market, preferring to market standardized products to a specific global segment than to respond to the unique features that differentiate one market from another. Here we observe that the strategy of acquiring wholly owned subsidiaries supports a global international strategy.

Freedom to Pursue a Global Strategy   When a company has a wholly owned foreign operation, it may more easily have that operation participate in a global strategy. For example, if a U.S. company owned 100 percent of its Brazilian operation, it might be able to take actions that, although suboptimizing Brazilian performance, could deal more effectively with actual or potential competitors and customers globally—such as decreasing prices to an industrial customer in Brazil to gain that customer's business in Germany. Or it might standardize its product to gain global cost savings even though this might result in lost sales within Brazil. But if the company shared ownership in Brazil, either action might be detrimental to the other owners in Brazil. Because most countries have laws to protect minority shareholders' interests, sharing of ownership may restrict a company from implementing a global strategy.

HOW TO MAKE FDI

Foreign direct investment is usually an international capital movement. Although most FDI requires some type of international capital movement, an investor may transfer many other types of assets. For example, Westin Hotels has transferred very little capital to foreign countries. Instead, it has transferred managers, cost control systems, and reservations capabilities in exchange for ownership in foreign hotels. There are two ways companies can invest in a foreign country. They can either acquire an interest in an existing operation or construct new facilities—an option known as a *greenfield investment*. We now discuss the reasons for each.

Buying   Whether a company makes a direct investment by acquisition or start-up depends, of course, on which companies are available for purchase. The large privatization programs occurring in many parts of the world have put hundreds of companies on the market, and MNEs have exploited this new opportunity to invest abroad. For example, foreign companies, such as Vivendi from France, bought many British utility companies when they were privatized.[18]

The advantages of acquiring an existing operation include

- Adding no further capacity to the market.
- Avoiding start-up problems.
- Easier financing.

Why Buy?   There are many reasons for seeking acquisitions. One is that some vital resource may otherwise be difficult for the investor to secure, especially if the investor must have that resource to adapt and function successfully within the local environment.[19] For instance, an existing company may have personnel that the investor cannot easily hire at a good price on its own. By buying an existing company, the buyer gets not only labor and management but also an existing organizational structure. This combination may be particularly important if the company is making an FDI to augment its capabilities, such as to acquire knowledge.[20]

In addition, a company may gain the goodwill and brand identification important to the marketing of mass consumer products, especially if the cost and risk of breaking in a new brand are high. Recently, much Chinese investment in the United States has been by acquisition, seemingly because of Chinese companies' desire to secure well-known brand names that will help them sell.[21]

There are also financial considerations. A company that depends substantially on local financing rather than on the transfer of capital may find it easier to gain access to local capital through an acquisition. Local capital suppliers may be more familiar with an ongoing operation than with the foreign enterprise. In addition, a foreign company may acquire an existing company through an exchange of stock.

In other ways, acquisitions may reduce costs and risks—and save time. A company may be able to buy facilities, particularly those of a poorly performing operation, for less than the cost of new construction. If an investor fears that a market does not justify added capacity, acquisition enables it to avoid the risk of depressed prices and lower unit sales per producer that might occur if it adds one more producer to the market. Finally, by buying a company, an investor avoids inefficiencies during the start-up period and gets an immediate cash flow rather than tying up funds during construction.

Making Greenfield Investments Although acquisitions offer advantages, a potential investor will not necessarily be able to realize them. Companies frequently make foreign investments in sectors where there are few, if any, companies operating, so finding a company to buy may be difficult. In addition, local governments may prevent acquisitions because they want more competitors in the market and fear market dominance by foreign enterprises.

Even if acquisitions are available, they often don't succeed.[22] The acquired companies might have substantial problems. Personnel and labor relations may be both poor and difficult to change, ill will may have accrued to existing brands, or facilities may be inefficient and poorly located. Further, the managers in the acquiring and acquired companies may not work well together, particularly if the two companies are accustomed to different management styles and practices or if the acquiring company tries to institute many changes.[23] Finally, a foreign company may sometimes find local financing easier to obtain if it builds facilities, particularly if it plans to tap development banks for part of its financial requirements.

> Companies may choose to build if
>
> * No desired company is available for acquisition.
> * Acquisition will lead to carry-over problems.
> * Acquisition is harder to finance.

Why Companies Collaborate

The same reasons why companies establish collaborative arrangements for domestic operations carry over to their international operations as well. Recall from our opening case, for example, that Coca-Cola franchises most of its bottling operations in both the United States and foreign countries. The same rationale underlies the strategic choice in both cases—for reasons that we'll discuss in the next section. Companies also establish collaborative arrangements abroad for different reasons than they collaborate domestically. For example, one of the reasons that Coca-Cola established a joint venture in India was because Indian laws prohibited its gaining 100 percent ownership.

Figure 14.3 shows both the general and internationally specific reasons for collaborative arrangements.

ALLIANCE TYPES

Some different terms are used to describe alliances based on their objectives and where they fit in a firm's value chain. In terms of objectives, *scale alliances* aim at providing efficiency through the pooling of similar assets so that partners can carry out business activities in which they already have experience. For example, Coca-Cola and Procter & Gamble sought an alliance to gain economies in distribution through combining grocery sales of Coca-Cola's juices and Procter & Gamble's snacks.

Link alliances use complementary resources to expand into new business areas.[24] Keep in mind that each organization participating in a collaborative agreement has its own primary objectives for operating internationally and its own motives for collaborating. For example, GM entered a joint venture with Russian Avtovaz. GM wanted production of Avtovaz's low-priced vehicle to sell in developing countries, and Avtovaz wanted GM's financial and technical resources to make sport utility vehicles in Russia.

While we're on the subject, it's probably worthwhile to a quick look back at our opening case. In terms of its value chain, Coke's typical franchising arrangement with bottlers calls for a type of *vertical alliance* because each partner functions on a different level of the value chain. Its partnership with Inca Kola, in contrast, calls for a *horizontal alliance* because it extends Coca-Cola's operations on the same level of the value chain.

FIGURE 14.3   Collaborative Arrangements and International Objectives

A company may enter into a collaborative arrangement for the same *general* reason that it may enter into a domestic arrangement (e.g., to spread costs). In other cases, it may enter into a collaborative arrangement to meet objectives that are *specific* to its foreign-expansion strategies (e.g., to diversify geographically).

OBJECTIVES OF INTERNATIONAL BUSINESS
- Sales expansion
- Resource acquisition
- Risk minimization

MOTIVES FOR COLLABORATIVE ARRANGEMENTS
General
- Spread and reduce costs
- Specialize in competencies
- Avoid or counter competition
- Secure vertical and horizontal links
- Learn from other companies

MOTIVES FOR COLLABORATIVE ARRANGEMENTS
Specific to International Business
- Gain location-specific assets
- Overcome legal constraints
- Diversify geographically
- Minimize exposure in risky environments

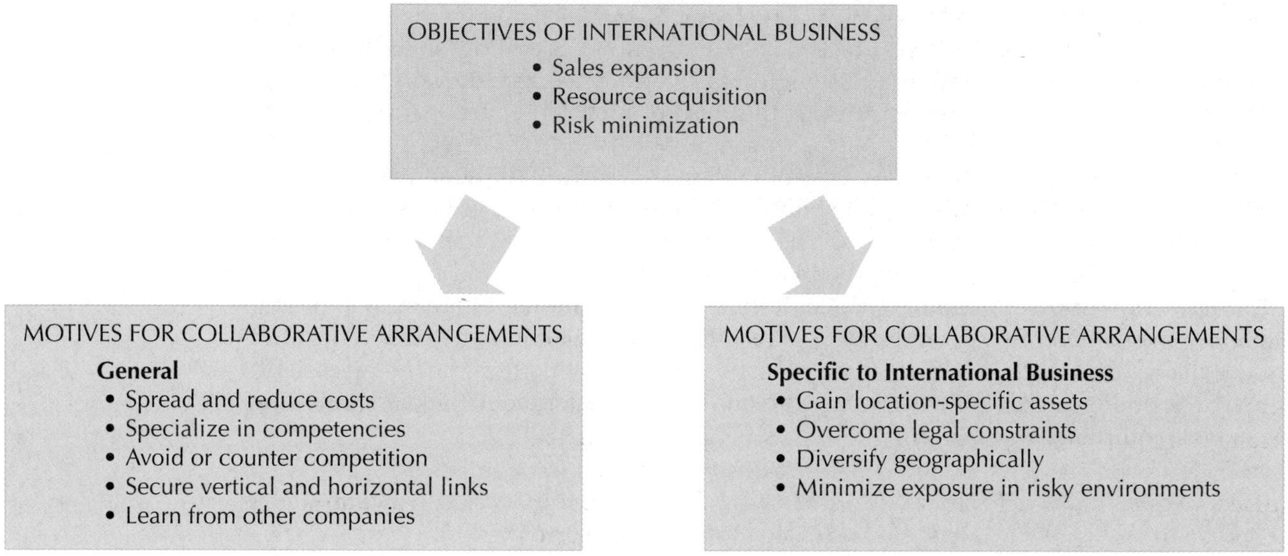

CONCEPT CHECK
We introduce the idea of the **value chain** in Chapter 11, where we explain how a company configures its global value chain by organizing a series of both primary and secondary activities—activities that naturally include the operations of its overseas partners. Needless to say, its global alliances must accommodate the structure of each firm's value chain.

Sometimes it's cheaper to get another company to handle work, especially:
- At small volume.
- When the other company has excess capacity.

Granting another company rights to an asset can yield a return on a product that does not fit the company's strategic priority based on its best competencies.

GENERAL MOTIVES FOR COLLABORATIVE ARRANGEMENTS

In this section, we explain the reasons that companies collaborate with other companies in either domestic or foreign operations: to spread and reduce costs, to allow them to specialize in their competencies, to avoid competition, to secure vertical and horizontal links, and to gain knowledge.

To Spread and Reduce Costs   To produce or sell abroad, a company must incur certain fixed costs. At a small volume of business, it may be cheaper for it to contract the work to a specialist rather than handle it internally. A specialist can spread the fixed costs to more than one company. If business increases enough, the contracting company then may be able to handle the business more cheaply itself. Companies should periodically reappraise the question of internal versus external handling of their operations.

A company may have excess production or sales capacity that it can use to produce or sell for another company. The company handling the production or sales may lower its average costs by covering its fixed costs more fully. Likewise, the company contracting out its production or sales (outsourcing) will not have to incur fixed costs that may otherwise be charged to a small amount of production or sales. Using this capacity also may reduce start-up time for the outsourcing company, thus providing earlier cash flow.

In addition, contracting companies may lack the resources to "go it alone." By pooling their efforts, they may be able to undertake activities that otherwise would be beyond their means. This is especially important for small and young companies.[25] But it is important for large companies when the cost of development and/or investment is very high. For example, the development cost of Disney's theme park in Hong Kong is so high it strains the capabilities of even a company as large as Disney. So the Hong Kong government shares ownership and costs.[26]

To Specialize in Competencies   The **resource-based view** of the firm holds that each company has a unique combination of competencies. A company may seek to improve its performance by concentrating on those activities that best fit its competencies, depending on other firms to supply it with products, services, or support activities for which it has lesser competency.

This concentration may be considered horizontally or vertically. Take horizontal. In our opening case, we saw that the Coca-Cola logo can be valuable for selling a variety of products, but Coke sees its competence as being nonalcoholic beverages; thus it licenses the production of clothes for which it lacks skills. Take vertical. Coca-Cola prefers to franchise its bottling so it can concentrate on innovative product and advertising development. However, a collaborative arrangement has a limited time frame, which may allow a company to exploit a particular product, asset, or technology itself at a later date if its core competencies change.

Case Review Note

To Avoid or Counter Competition   Sometimes markets are not large enough to hold many competitors. Companies may then band together so as not to compete. For example, approximately 30 communications carriers, including GTE, MCI, AT&T, and Cable and Wireless, have teamed to form New World, a broadband fiber-optic network connecting the United States with Latin America and the Caribbean.[27]

Companies may also combine resources to fight a leader in the market. For instance, Cisco joined six other companies to counter IBM's leadership. Another example was Coca-Cola and Danone's joint effort to challenge PepsiCo and Nestlé, the two companies with the largest market shares in U.S. bottled water sales.[28] Or companies may simply collude to raise everyone's profits. Only a few countries, mainly the United States, Canada, and those within the European Union, take substantial actions against the collusion of competitors.[29]

To Secure Vertical and Horizontal Links   There are potential cost savings and supply assurances from vertical integration. However, companies may lack the competence or resources necessary to own and manage the full-value chain of activities. For example, recall the LUKOIL case in Chapter 6. LUKOIL has abundant oil reserves but lacks final distribution skills so, in addition to making acquisitions abroad, it has established collaborative arrangements in countries that ensure markets for its petroleum.

Horizontal links may provide finished products or components. For finished products, there may be economies of scope in distribution, such as by having a full line of products to sell, thereby increasing the sales per fixed cost of a visit to potential customers. For example, Duracell, the biggest maker of consumer batteries, and Gillette, the biggest maker of razor blades, combine their sales forces in many parts of the world to gain economies of scope.[30]

One of the fastest growth areas for collaborative arrangements has been in industries with projects too large for any single company to handle—for example, new aircraft and communications systems. From such an arrangement's inception, different companies (sometimes from different countries) agree to take on the high cost and high risk of developmental work for different components needed in the final product. Then a lead company buys the components from the companies that did parts of the developmental work. A good example of this is the Boeing 787 aircraft, which involved components made by companies in eight different countries.[31]

To Gain Knowledge   Many companies, if they are open to new ideas and have the capacity to implement innovations, pursue collaborative arrangements to learn about a partner's technology, operating methods, or home market so their own competencies will broaden or deepen, making them more competitive in the future.[32] For example,

Chinese governmental authorities allow foreign companies to tap the Chinese market in exchange for their transference of technology. Sometimes each partner can learn from the other, a motive driving joint ventures between U.S. and European winemakers, such as the Opus One Winery owned by Constellation Brands' Robert Mondavi from the United States and Baron Philippe de Rothschild from France.[33]

INTERNATIONAL MOTIVES FOR COLLABORATIVE ARRANGEMENTS

In this section, we continue discussing the reasons why companies enter into collaborative arrangements, covering those reasons that apply only to international operations. Specifically, these reasons are to gain location-specific assets, overcome legal constraints, diversify geographically, and minimize exposure in risky environments.

To Gain Location-Specific Assets   Cultural, political, competitive, and economic differences among countries create barriers for companies that want to operate abroad. When they feel ill equipped to handle these differences, they may seek collaboration with local companies who will help manage local operations. For example, Wal-Mart first tried to enter the Japanese market on its own but gave up after having disappointing sales. It has since returned with a Japanese partner, Seiyu, which is more familiar with Japanese tastes and rules for opening new stores.[34]

In fact, most foreign companies in Japan need to collaborate with Japanese companies who can help in securing distribution and a competent workforce—two assets that are difficult for foreign companies to gain on their own there. For instance, non-Japanese pharmaceutical companies have had problems gaining Japanese distribution. Thus access to distribution was the primary reason that Merck (U.S.) teamed with the Japanese pharmaceutical company Chugai in Japan.[35]

To Overcome Governmental Constraints   Virtually all countries limit foreign ownership in some sectors. India is an example of a country that is particularly restrictive in that it sets maximum foreign percentage ownership in an array of industries.[36] In addition, India usually requires lengthy negotiations with governmental authorities to determine the terms of operations, and a savvy local partner can help the foreign investor. Thus companies may have to collaborate if they are to serve certain foreign markets.

Government procurement, particularly military procurement, is another area that may force companies to collaborate. In effect, governments may give preference to bids that include national companies. For example, Northrop Grumman from the United States teamed with Rolls-Royce in the United Kingdom to supply marine engines for both the British and U.S. navies.[37]

Protecting Assets   Collaboration can be a means of protecting an asset. Many countries provide little de facto protection for intellectual property rights such as trademarks, patents, and copyrights unless authorities are prodded consistently. To prevent pirating of these proprietary assets, companies sometimes have made collaborative agreements with local companies, which then monitor that no one else uses the asset locally.

In addition, some countries provide protection only if the internationally registered asset is exploited locally within a specified period. If a company does not use the asset within the country during that specified period, then whatever entity first does so gains the right to it. For example, Burger King did not use its name in time within the Australian market. Another company now uses it there, and Burger King sells its fare within Hungry Jack restaurants.[38]

In other cases, local citizens, known as trademark squatters, register rights to the unused trademarks. They then negotiate sales to the original owners when they do try to

---

Margin notes:

Legal factors may be

- Direct prohibitions against certain operating forms.
- Indirect (e.g., regulations affecting profitability).

Collaboration hinders nonassociated companies from pirating the asset, but it may aid pirating by the associated company.

enter the market. For example, a Russian company registered over 300 foreign trademarks, such as the trademark for Starbucks. Foreign companies then had to pay to regain their rights or go through lengthy court proceedings that could be even more expensive.[39]

To Diversify Geographically By operating in a variety of countries (geographic diversification), a company can smooth its sales and earnings because business cycles occur at different times within the different countries. Collaborative arrangements offer a faster initial means of entering multiple markets. Moreover, if product conditions favor a diversification rather than a concentration strategy, there are more compelling reasons to establish foreign collaborative arrangements. However, these arrangements will be less appealing for companies whose activities are already widely extended or those that have ample resources for such extension.

To Minimize Exposure in Risky Environments Companies worry that political or economic changes will affect the safety of assets and their earnings in their foreign operations. One way to minimize loss from foreign political occurrences is to minimize the base of assets located abroad—or share them. A government may be less willing to move against a shared operation for fear of encountering opposition from more than one company, especially if they are from different countries and can potentially elicit support from their home governments. Another way to spread risk is to place operations in a number of different countries. This strategy reduces the chance that all foreign assets will encounter adversity at the same time.

Collaborative arrangements allow for greater spreading of assets among countries.

CONCEPT CHECK

In discussing a firm's allocation of operational emphasis among countries in Chapter 12, we discuss the factors that contribute favorably to a geographic **diversification strategy:** namely, growth rate, sales stability, and program-control requirements are low in each market, competitive lead time is short, and spillover effects among markets are high.

The higher the risk managers perceive in a foreign market, the greater their desire to form collaborative arrangements in that market.

Types of Collaborative Arrangements

The forms of foreign operations differ in the amount of resources a company commits to foreign operations and the proportion of the resources located at home rather than abroad. Licensing, for example, may result in a lower additional capital commitment than a foreign joint venture will. Exporting places fewer resources abroad than foreign investment does.

Throughout this discussion, keep in mind that there are *trade-offs*. For example, a decision to take no ownership in foreign production, such as through licensing to a foreign company, may reduce exposure to political risk. However, learning about that environment will be slow, delaying (perhaps permanently) your reaping the full profits from producing and selling your product abroad.

Keep in mind also that when a company has a desired, unique, difficult-to-duplicate resource, it is in a good position to choose the operating form it would most like to use. However, when it lacks this bargaining strength, competition may force it to settle on a form that is lower on its priority list; otherwise, a competitor may preempt the market.

A further constraint facing managers is finding a desirable collaboration partner. For example, if the collaboration includes a transfer of technology, it may be impossible to find a local company familiar enough with the technology or having sufficiently similar values and priorities as the company transferring technology.[40] In effect, costs are associated with transferring technology to another entity, which include the time spent in cooperating to ensure that partners are cognizant of technologies, objectives, and means of implementing practices.[41]

Companies have a wider choice of operating form when there is less likelihood of competition.

SOME CONSIDERATIONS IN COLLABORATIVE ARRANGEMENTS

We have just discussed reasons for companies to enter collaborative arrangements. Before explaining the types of arrangements, we discuss two factors that influence managers' choice of one type of arrangement over another: their desire for control over foreign operations and their companies' prior foreign expansion.

Internal handling of foreign
operations usually means more
control and no sharing of profits.

Control   The more a company depends on collaborative arrangements, the more likely it is to lose control over decisions and their implementation, including those regarding quality, new product directions, and where to expand output. This is because each collaborative partner participates and favors its own performance rather than that of the network of the companies involved.

External arrangements also imply the sharing of revenues, a serious consideration for undertakings with high potential profits because a company may want to keep them all for itself. Such arrangements also risk allowing information to pass more rapidly to potential competitors. The loss of control over flexibility, revenues, and competition is an important consideration guiding a company's selection of forms of foreign operation.

Point Counterpoint

Should Countries Limit Foreign Control of Key Industries?

Point **Yes** I believe they should. A *key industry* is one that might affect a very large segment of the economy by virtue of its size or influence on other sectors. Thus I'm talking neither about foreign control of small investments nor about noncontrolling interest in large investments. In reality, foreign companies don't need to control key industries abroad to profit from them. By using collaborative agreements, they can obtain the foreign resources they need, such as technology, capital, export markets, and branded products. They can also profit by selling through collaborative arrangements.

Of course, each country should determine for itself what a key industry is, and, in fact, each does. For example, Mexico limits foreign control in its oil industry because it is such a dominant part of the Mexican economy. The United States is primarily concerned about security; thus the president can halt any foreign investment that endangers national security.

The United States also prohibits foreign control of television and radio stations because they could be used as instruments of foreign propaganda. It protects domestic transportation, a vital sector for national security, by prohibiting foreign control of domestic airlines and by preventing foreign airlines and ships from transporting passengers and cargo from one U.S. city to another.

The rationale for protecting key industries is supported by history, which shows that home governments have used powerful foreign companies to influence policies in the countries where they operate. During colonial periods, firms such as Levant and the British East India Company often acted as the political arm of their home governments.

More recently, home governments, especially the United States, have pressured their companies to leave certain areas (e.g., Libya, Nicaragua), not to pay taxes to a regime (e.g., Angola, Panama), and not to permit their subsidiaries to do business with certain countries (e.g., Cuba, North Vietnam),

Counterpoint **No** Although people make passionate arguments against foreign control of key industries, they don't convince me that such control leads to differences in companies' decisions or that limits on foreign ownership are in the best interests of people in host countries.

Are important decisions actually made outside the host countries? If so, are these decisions different from those that would be made by local companies? Certainly, companies make strategic global decisions at headquarters, but typically they depend on a good deal of local advice before making those decisions. Further, MNEs staff their foreign subsidiaries mainly with nationals of the countries where they operate, and these nationals make most routine decisions.

Regardless of the decision makers or ownership of companies, managers make decisions based on what they think is best for their companies' business, rather than based on some local socioeconomic agenda. At the same time, their decisions have to adhere to local laws and consider the views of their local stakeholders. Of course, MNEs sometimes make locally unpopular decisions, but so do local companies. In the meantime, governments can and do enact laws that apply both to local and international companies, and these laws can assure that companies act in the so-called local interest.

Although preventing foreign control of key industries may be well intentioned, the resultant local control may lead to the protection of inefficient performance. For instance, Mexican protection of its petroleum industry has led to high prices and poor service. Further, the key industry argument appeals to emotions rather than reason. That's why the arguments in the United States for security make little sense on close examination. For instance, there were no laws against foreign ownership of security-sensitive industries until 1989, well after the threats from the cold war had subsided. Although foreign propaganda through foreign ownership of even though the countries where the subsidiaries were located had trading relations with those countries.

At the same time, some companies are so powerful that they can influence their home-country governments to intercede on their behalf. Probably the most notorious example was United Fruit Company (UFC) in so-called banana republics, which persuaded the U.S. government to overthrow governments to protect its investments. Miguel Angel Asturias, a Nobel laureate in literature, referred to UFC's head as the "Green Pope" [who] "lifts a finger and a ship starts or stops. He says a word and a republic is bought. He sneezes and a president . . . falls. . . . He rubs his behind on a chair and a revolution breaks out."[42]

Whenever a company is controlled from abroad, that company's decisions can be made abroad. Such control means that corporate management abroad can make decisions about personnel staffing, export prices, and the retention and payout of profits. These decisions might cause different rates of expansion in different countries and possible plant closings with subsequent employment disruption in some of them.

Further, by withholding resources or allowing strikes, MNEs may affect other local industries adversely. In essence, the MNE looks after its global interests, which may not coincide with what is best for an operation in a given country. ●

radio and television stations is the rationale for ownership restrictions, there are no such restrictions on foreign ownership of U.S. newspapers. (Is this because people who read the news are presumed to be less swayed by propaganda?) In fact, Murdoch (Australian) and Thompson (Canadian) own many U.S. newspapers.

The protection of U.S. domestic transportation for security reasons is a sham, just to protect the U.S. shipbuilding industry and U.S. maritime employees. For instance, U.S. merchant flagships must employ only U.S. citizens as crews because of the vulnerability of putting a bomb on a ship in U.S. waters, but foreign flag carriers regularly use U.S. ports and foreigners can join the U.S. Navy.

The banana republic arguments are outdated and go back to *dependencia theory*, which holds that emerging economies have practically no power in their dealings with MNEs. Although this theory was popular in the 1970s and 1980s, it is largely out of vogue today.[43] More recent *bargaining school theory* states that the terms for a foreign investor's operations depend on how much the investor and host country need the other's assets.[44]

In effect, companies need countries because of their markets and resources. Countries need international companies because of their technology, capital, access to foreign markets, and expertise. Through a bargaining process, they come to an agreement or contract that stipulates what the MNE can and cannot do. Thus this agreement limits the absolute power of the MNE, even if it has 100 percent ownership.

I completely disagree that either countries or companies can necessarily gain the same through collaborative agreements as through foreign direct investment. Although collaborative agreements are often preferable, we have discussed the advantages from a company's standpoint of having wholly owned foreign operations. With wholly owned operations, companies are, therefore, less concerned about developing competitors and are more willing to transfer essential and valuable technology abroad. ●

Prior Expansion of the Company   When a company already has operations (especially wholly owned ones) in place in a foreign country, some of the advantages of contracting with another company to handle production or sales are no longer as important. The company knows how to operate within the foreign country and may have excess capacity it can use for new production or sales.

However, much depends on whether the existing foreign operation is in a line of business or performs a function that is closely related to the new product, service, or activity being initiated abroad. When there is similarity, as with production of a new type of office equipment when the company already produces office equipment, it is likely that the new production will be handled internally. In highly diversified companies or where operations are limited (such as when subsidiaries produce components only for the parent), the existing foreign facility may be handling goods or functions so dissimilar to what is being planned that it is easier to deal with an experienced external company.

LICENSING

Under a licensing agreement, a company (the licensor) grants rights to intangible property to another company (the licensee) to use in a specified geographic area for a specified period. In exchange, the licensee ordinarily pays a royalty to the licensor. The rights may be for an *exclusive license* (the licensor can give rights to no other company for the specified geographic area for a specified period of time) or nonexclusive (it can give away rights).

The U.S. Internal Revenue Service classifies intangible property into these five categories:

1. Patents, inventions, formulas, processes, designs, patterns
2. Copyrights for literary, musical, or artistic compositions
3. Trademarks, trade names, brand names
4. Franchises, licenses, contracts
5. Methods, programs, procedures, systems

Usually, the licensor is obliged to furnish technical information and assistance, and the licensee is obliged to exploit the rights effectively and to pay compensation to the licensor.

Major Motives for Licensing   Frequently, a new product or process may affect only part of a company's total output and then only for a limited time. The sales volume may not be large enough to warrant establishing overseas manufacturing and sales facilities. A company that is already operating abroad may be able to produce and sell at a lower cost and with a shorter start-up time, thus preventing competitors from entering the market. For the licensor, there is less risk of operating facilities and holding inventories. The licensee may find that the cost of the arrangement is less than if it developed the new product or process on its own.

For industries in which technological changes are frequent and affect many products, companies in various countries often exchange technology or other intangible property rather than compete with each other on every product in every market. Such an arrangement is known as *cross-licensing*. For example, Microsoft (U.S.) and LGE (South Korea) entered a technology-sharing, cross-licensing agreement for complementary computer technology.[45]

Payment Considerations   The amount and type of payment for licensing arrangements vary. Each contract is to be negotiated on its own merits. For example, the value to the licensee will be greater if potential sales are high. Potential sales depend, in turn, on such factors as the geographic scope of the sales territory, the length of time the asset will have market value, and the market experience of using the asset elsewhere.

Some developing countries set price controls on what licensees can pay or insist that licensees be permitted to export licensed goods. Their reasoning is that selling only to the local market results in small-scale production that spreads fixed costs inadequately and raises consumer prices. Licensors have countered that if licensees export, they should pay higher royalties because the companies could not sell an exclusive license to parties in other countries. MNEs also have argued that the development of process technologies for small-scale production in countries with small markets is often too costly but is done when economically feasible.

Putting a Price on Technology and Knowledge   Companies commonly negotiate a "front-end" payment to cover transfer costs when technology is involved. In addition, they usually charge fees based on actual or projected use, regardless of whether the transfer includes technology. Licensors of technology do this because it usually takes more than simply transferring *explicit* knowledge, such as through publications and reports. The move requires the transfer of *tacit* knowledge, such as through engineering, consultation, and adaptation. The licensee usually bears the transfer costs so the licensor is motivated to ensure a smooth adaptation. Of course, the license of some assets, such as copyrights, have much lower transfer costs.

Technology may be old or new, obsolete or still in use at home when a company licenses it. Many companies transfer technology at an early or even a developmental stage so products hit different markets simultaneously. This simultaneous market entry is important when selling to the same industrial customers in different countries and when global advertising campaigns can be effective. On the one hand, a licensee may be willing to pay more for a new technology because it may have a longer useful life. On the other hand, a licensee may be willing to pay less for a newer technology, particularly that in the development phase, because of its uncertain market value.

Selling to Controlled Entities   Although we think of licensing agreements as collaborative arrangements among unassociated companies, licenses are commonly given to companies owned in whole or part by the licensor. A license may be necessary to transfer intellectual property rights abroad because operations in a foreign country, even if 100 percent owned by the parent, usually are subsidiaries, which are separate companies from a legal standpoint. When a company owns less than 100 percent, a separate licensing arrangement may be a means of compensating the licensor for contributions beyond the mere investment in capital and managerial resources. (We noted in our opening case, for example, that Danone licensed its brand names to the joint venture that it established with Coca-Cola.)

Case Review Note

FRANCHISING

Franchising is a specialized form of licensing that originated centuries ago in which the franchisor not only sells an independent franchisee the use of the intangible property (usually a trademark) essential to the franchisee's business but also operationally assists the business on a continuing basis, such as through sales promotion and training. In many cases, the franchisor provides supplies, such as the concentrate Coca-Cola makes and sells to its bottlers.

Franchising includes providing an intangible asset (usually a trademark) and continually infusing necessary assets.

In another example, Domino's Pizza grants to franchisees the goodwill of the Domino's name and support services to get started, such as store and equipment layout information and a manager-training program. As part of the continual relationship, it offers economies and standardization through central purchasing, such as centrally purchasing mozzarella cheese in New Zealand to use worldwide.[46] In a sense, a franchisor and a franchisee act almost like a vertically integrated company because the parties are interdependent and each produces part of the product or service that ultimately reaches the consumer.

Today, franchising is most associated with the United States, although many international franchisors are from outside the United States. Franchising is most associated with fast food, but franchising exists in a huge array of businesses. A Danish company, Cryos International, even franchises sperm banks in about 40 countries and supplies the frozen sperm from donors in Denmark.[47] The fastest-growth businesses of U.S. foreign franchising have been food and business services because the U.S. market for these businesses is fairly mature.

Many types of products and many countries participate in franchising.

Franchisors once depended on trade shows a few times a year and costly visits to foreign countries to promote their expansion. However, because of the Internet, they now receive e-mailed requests for information around the clock, seven days a week.

Franchise Organization   A franchisor may penetrate a foreign country by dealing directly with franchisees or by setting up a *master franchise* and giving that organization (usually a local one) the rights to open outlets on its own or develop subfranchisees in the country or region. In the latter case, subfranchisees pay royalties to the master franchisee, which then remits some predetermined percentage to the franchisor. Coca-Cola handles most of its bottling franchising this way. Companies are most apt to use a master franchise system when they are not confident about evaluating potential franchisees and when it would be expensive to oversee and control franchisees' operations directly.[48]

If the franchisor is not well known to many local people, it may be difficult to convince them to make investments. People are usually willing to make investments in known franchises because the name is a guarantee of quality that can attract customers. It therefore is common for lesser-known franchisors to enter foreign markets with some company-owned outlets that serve as a showcase to attract franchisees.

> Franchisors face a dilemma:
>
> - The more standardization, the less acceptance in the foreign country.
> - The more adjustment to the foreign country, the less the franchisor is needed.

Operational Modifications   Securing good locations for franchises can be a major problem. Finding suppliers can add difficulties and expense. For example, McDonald's had to build a plant to make hamburger buns in the United Kingdom, and it had to help farmers develop potato production in Thailand.[49] Another concern for foreign franchise expansion has been governmental or legal restrictions that make it difficult to gain satisfactory operating permission.

Many franchise failures abroad result from the franchisor not developing enough domestic penetration first. Franchisors need to develop sufficient cash and management depth before considering foreign expansion. However, even a franchisor that is well established domestically may have difficulty in attaining foreign penetration, as evidenced by problems of Burger King in the United Kingdom, Wendy's in Australia, and Long John Silver's in Japan.

A dilemma for successful domestic franchisors is that their success comes from three factors: product and service standardization, high identification through promotion, and effective cost controls. When entering many foreign countries, franchisors may encounter difficulties in transferring these success factors. For example, for food franchising the standardization is important so consumers know what to expect and cost controls are maintained. But when a company enters a foreign country, the taste preferences may be different. In fact, even regionally within large countries, tastes may differ. In response to regional differences in China, Yum! Brands is offering regionally different food within its KFC and Pizza Hut outlets.[50]

At the same time, the more adjustments made to the host consumers' different tastes, the less a franchisor has to offer a potential franchisee. U.S. food franchisors' success in Japan is mostly due to that country's enthusiastic assimilation of Western products. Even so, food franchisors have had to make adjustments there. Wendy's sells a teriyaki burger, and Little Caesars has asparagus, potatoes, squid, and seaweed as pizza toppings.[51]

MANAGEMENT CONTRACTS

> Management contracts are used primarily when the foreign company can manage better than the owners.

One of the most important assets a company may have at its disposal is management talent, which it can transfer internationally, primarily to its own foreign investments. Management contracts are means by which a company may transfer such talent—by using part of its management personnel to assist a foreign company for a specified period for a fee. The company may gain income with little capital outlay. Contracts usually cover three to five years, and fixed fees or fees based on volume rather than profits are most common.

An organization usually pursues international management contracts when it believes a foreign company can manage its existing or new operation more efficiently than it can. For example, the British Airport Authority (BAA) has contracts to manage airports in Indianapolis (U.S.), Naples (Italy), and Melbourne (Australia) because it has developed successful airport management skills.[52]

With management contracts, the owners and host country get the assistance they want without foreign companies' control of the operations. In turn, the management company receives income without having to make a capital outlay. This pattern has been important in hotel operations where some governments have highly restricted foreign ownership and where some owners are basically knowledgeable about real estate rather than hotel operations. Further, evidence indicates that companies in international hotel chains favor management contracts over franchising when their brand reputation is low in a market and when quality and organizational competence are important to competitive advantage.[53]

TURNKEY OPERATIONS

Turnkey operations are a type of collaborative arrangement in which one company contracts with another to build complete, ready-to-operate facilities. Companies building turnkey operations are frequently industrial-equipment manufacturers and construction companies. They also may be consulting firms and manufacturers that decide an investment on their own behalf in the country is infeasible. The customer for a turnkey operation is often a governmental agency. Recently, most large projects have been in those developing countries that are moving rapidly toward infrastructure development and industrialization.

Turnkey operations are

- Most commonly performed by construction companies.
- Often performed for a governmental agency.

Contracting to Scale   One characteristic that sets the turnkey business apart from most other international business operations is the size of many of the contracts, frequently for hundreds of millions of dollars and into the billions. This means that a few very large companies—such as Bechtel (U.S.), Fluor (U.S.), Skanska (Sweden), and Hochtief (Germany)—account for a significant share of the international market. For example, Bechtel built a semiconductor plant for Motorola in China and a pipeline for BP in Algeria.[54] Smaller firms often serve either as subcontractors for primary turnkey suppliers or specialize in a particular sector, such as the handling of hazardous waste.

Making Contacts   The nature of these contracts places importance on hiring executives with top-level contacts abroad, as well as on ceremony and building goodwill, such as opening a facility on a country's independence day or getting a head of state to inaugurate a facility. Although public relations is important to gaining turnkey contracts, other

The photo shows a turnkey construction by Bechtel of an aluminum smelter for Alcoa in eastern Iceland.

factors—such as price, export financing, managerial and technological quality, experience, and reputation—are necessary to sell contracts of such magnitude.

Marshaling Resources   Many turnkey contracts are for construction in remote areas, necessitating massive housing construction and importation of personnel. Projects may involve building an entire infrastructure under the most adverse conditions, such as Bechtel's complex for Minera Escondida, which is high in the Andes. So turnkey operators must have expertise in hiring workers willing to work in remote areas for extended periods and in transporting and using supplies under very adverse conditions. One such area with adverse conditions has been Iraq, where large turnkey operations are being used for reconstruction.[55]

If a company holds a monopoly on certain assets or resources, such as the latest refining technology, other companies will find it difficult to compete to secure a turnkey contract. As the production process becomes known, however, the number of competitors for such contracts increases. Companies from developed countries have moved largely toward projects involving high technology, whereas companies from such countries as China, India, Korea, and Turkey can compete better for conventional projects for which low labor costs are important. For example, the Chinese companies China State Construction Engineering and Shanghai Construction Group have worked on a subway system in Iran, a railway line in Nigeria, an oil pipeline in Sudan, and office buildings in the United States.[56]

Arranging Payment   Payment for a turnkey operation usually occurs in stages as a project develops. Commonly, 10 to 25 percent comprises the down payment, with another 50 to 65 percent paid as the contract progresses, and the remainder paid once the facility is operating in accordance with the contract. Because of the long time frame between conception and completion, the company performing turnkey operations can encounter currency fluctuations and should cover itself through escalation clauses or cost-plus contracts.

Because the final payment is usually made only if the facility is operating satisfactorily, it is important to specify in a contract what constitutes "satisfactorily." For this reason, many companies insist on performing a feasibility study as part of the turnkey contract so they don't build something that, although desired by a local government, may be too large or inefficient. Inefficiency could create legal problems, such as determining who caused it, that hold up final payment.

JOINT VENTURES

Joint ventures may have various combinations of ownership.

A type of ownership sharing popular among international companies is the joint venture, in which more than one organization owns a company. Although companies usually form a joint venture to achieve particular objectives, it may continue to operate indefinitely as the objective is redefined. Joint ventures are sometimes thought of as 50/50 companies, but often more than two organizations participate in the ownership. Further, one organization frequently controls more than 50 percent of the venture. The type of legal organization may be a partnership, a corporation, or some other form permitted in the country of operation. When more than two organizations participate, the joint venture is sometimes called a **consortium**.

Possible Combinations   Almost every conceivable combination of partners may exist in an international joint venture as long as at least one of the partners is foreign. These include the following:

- Two companies from the same country joining together in a foreign market, such as NEC and Mitsubishi (Japan) in the United Kingdom
- A foreign company joining with a local company, such as Great Lakes Chemical (U.S.) and A. H. Al Zamil in Saudi Arabia

- Companies from two or more countries establishing a joint venture in a third country, such as that of Tata Motors (India) and Fiat (Italy) in Argentina
- A private company and a local government forming a joint venture (sometimes called a mixed venture), such as that of Petrobras (Brazil) with the Venezuela government-owned company PDVSA
- A private company joining a government-owned company in a third country, such as BP Amoco (private British-U.S.) and Eni (government-owned Italian) in Egypt

The more companies in the joint venture, the more complex is the management of the arrangement. For example, when the Australian government privatized Hazelwood Power Station, a British company (National Power), an Australian company (the Commonwealth Bank Group), and two U.S. companies (PacifiCorp and Destec Energy) bought the electric utility company. This involved four companies in the decision making. Figure 14.4 shows that as a company increases the number of partners and decreases the amount of equity it owns in a foreign operation, its ability to control that operation decreases.

Certain types of companies favor joint ventures more than others do. Companies that like joint ventures are usually new at foreign operations or have decentralized domestic decision making. Because these companies are used to extending control downward in their organizations, it is easier for them to do the same thing internationally.

EQUITY ALLIANCES

An **equity alliance** is a collaborative arrangement in which at least one of the collaborating companies takes an ownership position (almost always minority) in the other(s). You'll recall from our opening case, for instance, that Coke maintains significant ownership positions in the master franchise bottlers that account for a significant part of its overseas sales. In some cases, each party takes an ownership, such as by buying part of each other's shares or by swapping some shares with each other. For instance, Panama-based Copa and Colombia-based AeroRepublic took equity in each other.[57]

The purpose of the equity ownership is to solidify a collaborating contract, such as a supplier-buyer contract, so it is more difficult to break—particularly if the ownership is large enough to secure a board membership for the investing company. The airline industry epitomizes the use of equity alliances. We discuss the airline industry in the ending case of this chapter.

Equity alliances help solidify collaboration.

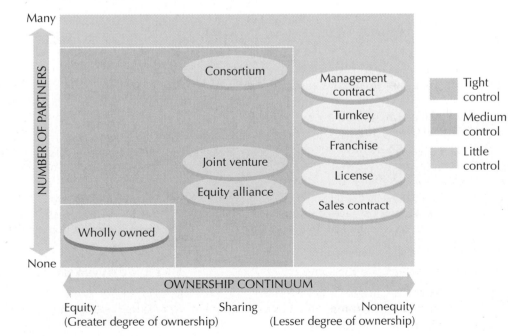

FIGURE 14.4
Collaborative Strategy and Complexity of Control

The more equity that a firm puts into a collaborative arrangement, coupled with the fewer partners that it takes on, the more control it will have over the foreign operations conducted under the arrangement. Note that nonequity arrangements typically entail at least one and often several partners.

Source: Adapted from Shaker Zahra and Galal Elhagrasey, "Strategic Management of International Joint Ventures," *European Management Journal* 12:1 (March 1994): 83–93. Reprinted with permission of Elsevier.

Problems with Collaborative Arrangements

Although collaborative arrangements have many advantages, some companies try to avoid them. Many arrangements develop problems that lead partners to renegotiate their relationships in terms of responsibilities, ownership, or management structure. In spite of new relationships, many agreements break down or are not renewed at the end of an initial contract period. For example, in the case of joint ventures, about half break up because one or all partners become dissatisfied with the venture. Often one partner buys out the other's interest so the operation continues as a wholly owned foreign subsidiary. In other breakups, companies agree to dissolve the arrangement or they restructure their alliance.

Figure 14.5 shows that joint venture divorce (and divorce from other collaborative arrangements) can be planned or unplanned, friendly or unfriendly, mutual or nonmutual. The major strains on collaborative arrangements are due to five factors:

- Relative importance to partners
- Divergent objectives
- Control problems
- Comparative contributions and appropriations
- Differences in culture[58]

In spite of our focus on these problems, we do not mean to imply there are no success stories. There are. For example, the joint venture between Xerox (U.S.) and Rank (U.K.) has performed well for a long period of time, and it even has a joint venture itself in Japan with Fuji Photo, which has also performed well.

RELATIVE IMPORTANCE

One partner may give more management attention to a collaborative arrangement than the other does. If things go wrong, the active partner blames the less active partner for its

FIGURE 14.5 How to Dissolve a Joint Venture

There's more than one way to dissolve a joint venture—and to influence the future of its erstwhile operations.

Source: Adapted from Manuel G. Serapio Jr. and Wayne F. Cascio, "End Games in International Alliances." *Academy of Management Executive* (May 1996): 67.

DIVORCE SCENARIOS	EXAMPLES	OUTCOMES	EXAMPLES
Planned vs.	General Motors (U.S.) and Toyota (Japan)	Termination by acquisition	Daewoo Motors (South Korea) and General Motors (U.S.)
Unplanned	AT&T (U.S.) and Olivetti (Italy)	Termination by dissolution	Meiji Milk (Japan) and Borden (U.S.)
Friendly vs.	Vitro (Mexico) and Corning (U.S.)		
Unfriendly	Coors Brewing Co. (U.S.) and Molson Breweries (Canada)	Termination by reorganization/ restructuring of the alliance	Matsushita Electric Industries Co. (Japan) and Solbourne Computer (U.S.)
Mutually agreed upon vs.	Ralston Purina (U.S.) and Taiyo Fishery (Japan)		
Disputed	Sover S.P.A. (Italy) and Suzhou Spectacles No. 1 Factory (China)		

lack of attention, and the less active partner blames the more active partner for making poor decisions. The difference in attention may be due to the different sizes of partners. For example, if the joint venture is between a large and a small company, the venture comprises a larger portion of operations for the small company than for the large one, so the small company may take more interest in the venture.

In addition, if there are disagreements that necessitate legal action for settlement, the smaller firm may be disadvantaged because it lacks the resources to fight the larger company. For example, Igen, a small U.S. firm, licensed its technology to Boehringer Mannheim of Germany, a company whose sales are more than 100 times those of Igen. When the two companies disagreed over royalty payments, Igen fought for four years and spent $40 million in legal fees (about the amount of one year's sales) to win a settlement of over a half billion dollars.[59] However, this example is unusual because most small companies cannot or will not fight a larger company so effectively.

DIVERGENT OBJECTIVES

Although companies enter into collaborative arrangements because they have complementary capabilities, their objectives may evolve differently over time. For instance, one partner may want to reinvest earnings for growth and the other may want to receive dividends. One partner may want to expand the product line and sales territory, and the other may see this as competition with its wholly owned operations. A partner may wish to sell or buy from the venture, and the other partner may disagree with the prices.

Finally, there may be different views about performance standards. For example, GM has a joint venture in Thailand with Fuji Heavy Industries to make and export vehicles to Opel in Germany and Subaru in Japan. Because of disagreements over quality, both companies perform inspections, which is time consuming and expensive. They have even argued over standards for paint jobs.[60]

QUESTIONS OF CONTROL

By sharing the assets with another company, one company may lose some control on the extent or quality of the assets' use. For example, the Israeli company Remedia, partly owned by the U.S. company H. J. Heinz, partnered with the German company, Humana Milchunion, to make baby formula. Humana Milchunion removed vitamin B_1 from the concentrate for the formula without notifying its partners. Thus the partners did not add the vitamin, causing the death of three infants.[61]

Some companies have well-known trademarked names that they license abroad for the production of some products they have never produced or had expertise with. For example, Pierre Cardin has licensed its label to hundreds of licensees in scores of countries. These licensees put the label on hundreds of products, from clothing to sheets and clocks to deodorants. Monitoring and maintaining control of so much diversity was so difficult that poor-quality Pierre Cardin–labeled products hurt the image of high-quality Pierre Cardin–labeled products. Pierre Cardin had to restructure its agreements and advertise heavily to reestablish the cachet of its name.[62] In today's world, problems in one country are quickly communicated to consumers in other countries.

In collaborative arrangements, even though control is ceded to one of the partners, both may be held responsible for problems. For example, in KFC's joint venture in China, the financial reporting to Chinese authorities was the Chinese partner's responsibility. However, China held both partners liable for tax evasion as a result of underreporting income.[63] Moreover, in joint ventures and management contracts, there are gray areas as to who controls employees. Further, employees may have anxieties about who is in charge. For example, in a proposed joint venture between Merrill Lynch, from the

United States, and UFJ, from Japan, a Japanese senior manager queried, "Who is going to be in charge—a Japanese or an American, or both?"[64]

When no single company has control of a collaborative arrangement, the operation may lack direction. At the same time, if one partner dominates, it must still consider the other company's interests.

COMPARATIVE CONTRIBUTIONS AND APPROPRIATIONS

One partner's capability of contributing technology, capital, or some other asset may diminish compared to its partner's capability over time. For example, in P&G's joint venture with Phuong Dong Soap & Detergent in Vietnam, P&G wanted to expand, but Phuong had neither the funds to expand nor the willingness to allow P&G to gain a larger ownership.[65] (Figure 14.6 shows how a poorly performing company may wish to ally with a well-performing one.)

In another case, one company may want to shift its strategic focus. In our opening case, for example, we report that a joint venture between Coca-Cola and P&G broke down because P&G shifted its product emphasis away from the food items assigned to the joint-venture agreement. The weak link may cause a drag on the collaborative arrangement, resulting in dissension between the partners.

FIGURE 14.6   Why Some Companies Don't Play Hard to Get

Source: © Copyright Chris Wildt, Cartoonstock.com.

"How does this sound: 'Single, nearly solvent company seeks relationship with like-minded, prosperous multinational.' "

In addition, one partner may be suspicious that the other is taking more from the operation (particularly knowledge-based assets) than it is. In almost all collaborative arrangements, there is a danger that one partner will use the other partner's contributed assets, enabling it to become a competitor. (Probably the only exception would be turnkey projects to build infrastructure.) In fact, there are many examples of companies "going it alone" after they no longer needed their partner, particularly if the purpose of the collaboration is to gain knowledge.

Similarly, the important contributions of one partner to the other may shift over time. For example, in transition economies, the importance of foreign investors' contributions in joint ventures with local companies shifts from marketing to knowledge as the transition economies gain experience.[66] Finally, it is difficult for companies that compete head-on within their core businesses in some markets to cooperate fully for the same core business in another market. In the case of joint ventures, both are apt to see substantial gains when each partner offers market expansion and technology to the other.

CULTURE CLASHES

Differences in Country Cultures   Companies differ by nationality in how they evaluate the success of their operations. For example, U.S. companies tend to evaluate performance on the basis of profit, market share, and specific financial benefits. Japanese companies tend to evaluate primarily on how an operation helps build its strategic position, particularly by improving its skills. European companies rely more on a balance between profitability and achieving social objectives.[67] These differences can mean that one partner is satisfied while the other is not. Anheuser-Busch attributed its joint venture breakup with Modelo (Mexican) to the fact that Modelo was run like a family business and was reluctant to share control.[68]

Finally, some companies don't like to collaborate with companies of very different cultures. In spite of these potential problems, joint ventures from culturally distant countries can survive because partners learn to deal with managers from different cultures.[69]

Differences in Corporate Cultures   In addition to national culture, differences in corporate cultures may also create problems within joint ventures. For example, one company may be accustomed to promoting managers from within the organization, whereas the other opens its searches to outsiders. One may use a participatory management style, and the other an authoritarian style. One may be entrepreneurial and the other risk averse. For this reason many companies develop joint ventures only after they have had long-term positive experiences with the other company through distributorship, licensing, or other contractual arrangements. However, as is the case with marriage, a positive prior relationship between two companies does not guarantee that partners will be well matched in a joint venture.[70] Compatibility of corporate cultures also is important in cementing relationships.

Managing Foreign Arrangements

If collaboration can better achieve the company's strategic objectives than "going it alone" can, the company should give little consideration to taking on duties itself. However, as the arrangement evolves, partners will need to reassess certain decisions. For example, a company's resource base may change compared to that of other companies, making collaboration either more or less advantageous.

In addition, the external environment changes. Perhaps a certain location becomes economically risky or its host government forbids foreign ownership in areas where the arrangement would like to do future business. Because of these changes, a company needs

The evolution to a different operating mode may

- Be the result of experience.
- Necessitate costly termination fees.
- Create organizational tensions.

CONCEPT CHECK

In discussing the many ways in which "Behavioral Influences" can affect relationships in **international business** in Chapter 2, we observe that there are substantial differences in the degrees of *trust* that people in different **cultures** extend to others. We go on to explain that when trust is high, managers tend to spend more time focusing on operational issues and less fussing over every little detail. Not surprisingly, the cost of doing business tends to be lower.

continually to reexamine the fit between collaboration and its strategy. Thus a company likely uses various modes of operations simultaneously because of its own capabilities, the specific products involved, and the characteristics of each foreign market.

We now discuss how companies change their operating forms, how they may find and negotiate with potential partners, and how they need to assess performance of collaborative arrangements.

DYNAMICS OF COLLABORATIVE ARRANGEMENTS

Companies' capabilities relative to specific locations may change over time and influence the form of operations undertaken. Collaboration with a local company provides the opportunity to learn from the local partner, enabling the company confidently to make a deeper commitment. However, the cost of switching from one form to another—for example, from licensing to wholly owned facilities—may be very high because of having to gain expertise from and possibly pay termination fees to another company.

Country Attractiveness and Operational Options   Figure 14.7 illustrates a type of matrix that relates country attractiveness with operating forms. The company should take a higher level of commitment, such as wholly owned operations, in the countries that appear in the top left corner of the matrix because those countries are not only very attractive, but they also fit with the companies' capabilities.

In the top right corner, the country attractiveness is also high, but the company has a weak competitive strength for those markets, perhaps because it lacks knowledge of how

FIGURE 14.7   Country Attractiveness/Company Strength Matrix

In a given scenario, a country in the upper-left-hand corner may be the most attractive place for a company to locate operations. Why? Because its market is well suited to the company's greatest competitive strength and thus to its highest level of commitment (e.g., establishing a wholly owned subsidiary). A country in the upper-right-hand corner also boasts an attractive market but poses a problem for a company whose competitive strengths don't quite match the opportunity (perhaps it has no experience in this particular market). It needn't forgo the opportunity, but it will probably prefer a joint venture or some other form of collaborative operation. Finally, note that because everything is subject to change—both a company's capabilities and the features of a country's market—firms try to be dynamic in their approach to potential operating modes.

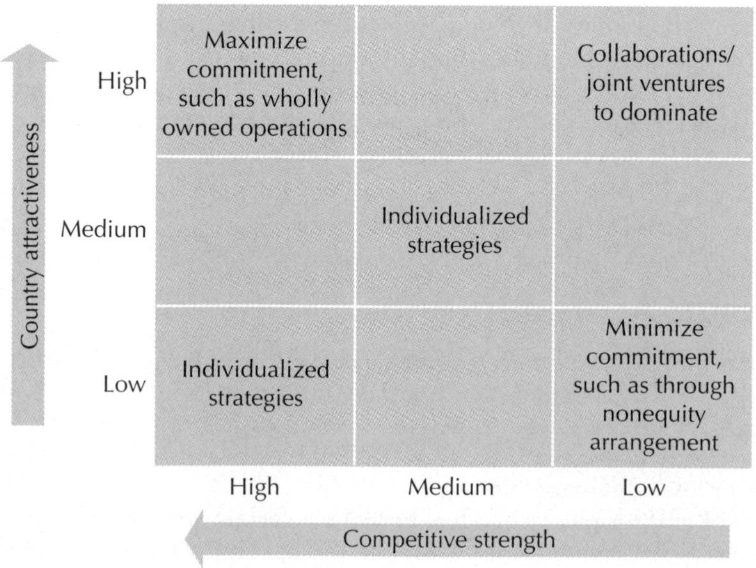

to operate therein. If the cost is not too high, the company might attempt to gain greater domination in those markets by partnering with another company whose assets are complementary.

A company might divest in countries in the bottom right corner or "harvest" by pulling out all possible cash it could generate while at the same time not replacing depreciated facilities. It could also engage in nonequity arrangements, thereby generating some income without the need to make investment outlays. In other areas, the company must analyze situations individually to decide which approach to take. These are marginal areas that require specific judgment.

Although this type of matrix may serve to guide decision making, managers must use it with caution. First, it is often difficult to separate the attractiveness of a country from a company's position. In other words, the country may seem attractive because of the company's fit with it. Second, some of the recommended actions take a defeatist attitude to a company's competitive position. There are simply many examples of companies that built competitive strength in markets that competitors had previously dominated or that built profitable positions without being the competitive leader.

Changing Conditions Tension may develop internally as a company's international operations change and grow because individuals may gain or lose responsibilities as control locations change. For example, moving from exporting to foreign production may reduce the size of a domestic product division. Various profit centers all may perceive they have rights to the sales in a country the company is about to penetrate. Legal, technical, and marketing personnel may have entirely different perspectives on contracts. Under these circumstances, a team approach to evaluating decisions and performance may work. A company also must develop means of evaluating performance by separating those things that are controllable and noncontrollable by personnel in different profit centers.

At the same time, evidence indicates that as companies enter more collaborative arrangements, they get better performance from them.[71] However, better performance is most associated with the use of similar types of collaborations from one place to another.[72] In essence, they may choose partners better and learn how to get better synergies between their partners and their own operations. At the same time, the way of effectively managing alliances has been undergoing significant changes; thus the knowledge gained from managing in one market may depreciate over time.[73]

FINDING COMPATIBLE PARTNERS

A company can seek out a partner for its foreign operations or it can react to a proposal from another company to collaborate with it. In either case, it is necessary to evaluate the potential partner not only for the resources it can supply but also for its motivation and willingness to cooperate.

A company can identify potential partners by monitoring journals, attending technical conferences, and developing links with academic institutions. It can also find partners by participating in social activities. After a company makes contact and builds rapport with managers of one local firm, those managers may offer introductions to managers in other firms.[74] A company can increase its own visibility by participating in trade fairs, distributing brochures, and nurturing contacts in the locale of potential collaboration—increasing the probability that other companies will consider it a partner.

The proven ability to handle similar types of collaboration is a key professional qualification. Because of a good track record, a partner may be able to depend more on trust rather than expensive control mechanisms to ensure that its interests will not be usurped. Once into a collaboration, partners may also be able to build partner trust through their actions in the collaborative arrangement.[75] But every company has to start somewhere. Without a proven track record, a company may have to negotiate harder with and make more concessions to a partner.

NEGOTIATING THE ARRANGEMENT

In technology agreements

- Seller does not want to give information without assurance of payment.
- Buyer does not want to pay without evaluating information.

The value of many technologies would diminish if they were widely used or understood. Contracts historically have included provisions that the recipient will not divulge this information. In addition, some sellers have held on to the ownership and production of specific components so recipients will not have the full knowledge of the product or the capability to produce an exact copy of it.

Many times, a company wants to sell techniques it has not yet used commercially. A buyer is reluctant to buy what it has not seen, but a seller that shows the work-in-process to the potential buyer risks divulging the technology. It has become common to set up preagreements that protect all parties.

Another controversial area of negotiation is the secrecy surrounding the financial terms of arrangements. In some countries, for example, governmental agencies must approve licensing contracts. Sometimes these authorities consult their counterparts in other countries regarding similar agreements to improve their negotiating position with MNEs. Many MNEs object to this procedure because they believe that contract terms between two companies are proprietary information with competitive importance and market conditions usually dictate the need for very different terms in different countries.

DRAWING UP THE CONTRACT

By transferring assets to a joint venture or intangible property rights to another company in a licensing agreement, a company undoubtedly loses some control over the asset or intangible property. A host of potential problems attends this lack of control and should be settled in the original agreement. At the same time, you need to develop sufficient rapport with partners so common sense, rather than the contract, is used to run the collaboration.[76]

A Few Specific Issues   Although it is impossible to anticipate all points of future disagreement and include coverage of them in a contract, provisions should address the following issues:

- Will the agreement be terminated if the parties don't adhere to the directives?
- What methods will be used to test for quality?
- What geographic limitations should be placed on an asset's use?
- Which company will manage which parts of the operation outlined in the agreement?
- What will be each company's future commitments?
- How will each company buy from, sell to, or otherwise use intangible assets that result from the collaborative arrangement?

Contracts should be spelled out in detail, but if courts must rule on disagreements both parties are apt to lose something in the settlement. Contract termination and formal settlement of disputes are costly and cumbersome. If possible, it is much better for parties to settle disagreements between themselves.

The ability to develop a rapport with the management of another company is an important consideration in choosing a partner. At the same time, national culture in terms of trust plays a part in how much a partner wants to cover within a contract. Thus, if parties from cultures with similar levels of trust come together, they are more likely able to agree on what must be incorporated in detailed contractual arrangements versus what must be left to trust.[77]

ASSESSING PERFORMANCE

Management also should estimate potential sales, determine whether the arrangement is meeting quality standards, and assess servicing requirements to check whether the other company is doing an adequate job. Mutual goals should be set so both parties understand what is expected, and the expectations should be spelled out in the contract.

In addition to the continual assessment of the partner's performance in collaborative arrangements, a company also needs to assess periodically whether the type of collaboration should change. For example, a joint venture may replace a licensing agreement. In some cases, even though a partner is doing what is expected, a company may assess that collaboration is no longer in its best interest. For instance, the company may decide that it wants a wholly owned FDI so it has greater freedom.

> When collaborating with another company, managers must
>
> • Continue to monitor performance.
> • Assess whether to take over operations.

LOOKING TO THE FUTURE

Why Innovation Breeds Collaboration

A half century ago, John Kenneth Galbraith wrote that the era of cheap invention was over and "because development is costly, it follows that it can be carried out only by a firm that has the resources associated with considerable size."[78] The statement seems prophetic in terms of the estimated billions of investment dollars needed to bring a new commercial aircraft to market, eliminate death from diseases, develop defenses against unfriendly countries and terrorists, guard against cyberspace intrusions, and commercialize energy substitutes for petroleum.

Moreover, markets must be truly global if high development costs are to be recouped. The sums companies need for developing and marketing these new inventions are out of reach of most companies acting alone. Of course, companies might become ever larger through internal growth or through mergers and acquisition. Although we have seen some examples of such growth, governments have nevertheless placed limits because of antitrust concern.

Furthermore, companies realize the cost of integrating a merged or acquired company can be very high. Therefore, collaborative arrangements will likely become even more important in the future. They are likely to involve both horizontal and vertical linkages among companies from many industries in many countries. However, some evidence indicates that collaborative arrangements slow the speed of innovation.[79] Thus large companies that have resources to go it alone may have advantages over small companies that do not.

Although some product developments require huge sums, most are much more modest. Nevertheless, companies lack all the product- and market-specific resources to go it alone everywhere in the world, especially if national differences dictate operating changes on a country-to-country basis. These situations present opportunities for alliances that employ complementary resources from different companies.

Collaborative arrangements will bring both opportunities and problems as companies move simultaneously to new countries and to contractual arrangements with new companies. For example, collaborations must overcome differences in a number of areas:

• Country cultures that may cause partners to obtain and evaluate information differently

• National differences in governmental policies, institutions, and industry structures that constrain companies from operating as they would prefer

• Corporate cultures that influence ideologies and values underlying company practices that strain relationships among companies

• Different strategic directions resulting from partners' interests that cause companies to disagree on objectives and contributions

• Different management styles and organizational structures that cause partners to interact ineffectively[80]

The more partners in an alliance, the more strained the decision-making and control processes. ■

CASE

Getting Airline Alliances Off the Ground

Map 14.2 shows the world's 20 largest airlines and the countries where they have their headquarters.[81] Most of the world's major airlines are in or have announced they will join an alliance whereby they combine routes, sales, airline terminal services, and frequent-flier programs. For example, by 2006, Air Canada, Air New Zealand, All Nippon Airways (ANA), Asiana, Austrian Airlines, bmi, LOT, Lufthansa, Scandinavian Airlines System (SAS), Singapore Airlines, South African Airways, Spanair, Swissair, TAP Portugal, Thai Airlines, United Airlines, and US Airways were in the Star Alliance.

In addition, many airlines hold ownership in other airlines. For example, KLM from the Netherlands has partial ownership of Northwest Airlines in the United States and Alitalia in Italy. Singapore Airlines owns 49 percent of Virgin Airlines in the United Kingdom. KLM and Air France have merged, although maintaining their separate identities.

Factors in Industry Arrangements

These alliances have blurred the competitive distinctions among the major international carriers. However, the airline industry is unique in that its need to form collaborative arrangements has been important almost from the start of international air travel because of regulatory, cost, and competitive factors. In recent years, this need has accelerated because of airlines' poor profit performance, due in part to a sluggish global economy, high oil prices, and concern about international terrorism.

Regulatory Factors

Countries have always seen airlines as key industries in which they want domestic service that is controlled by domestically owned companies. For example, the United States grants U.S.-based airlines the right to carry all passengers between domestic points, and it limits foreign ownership in U.S.-based airlines to 25 percent of voting stock and 49 percent of total equity.

Many countries have ensured national control through whole or partial government ownership of airlines. A 2005 report by the International Chamber of Commerce showed that in a survey of 150 airlines worldwide, 70 had majority government ownership and only 60 had no government-held shares. Many government-owned airlines are monopolies within their domestic markets, and many of these lose money but then receive government subsidies.

What Governments Can Regulate   Governments can further protect their airlines by regulating these activities:

- Which foreign carriers have landing rights
- Which airports and aircraft the carriers can use
- Frequency of flights
- Whether foreign carriers can fly beyond the country—for instance, the Japanese government restricted United from flying from the United States to Japan and then beyond to Australia
- Overflight privileges
- Fares they can charge

Countries agree on the restrictions and rights through treaties, usually to give equal treatment to each country's carriers. The International Air Transport Association (IATA) comprises nearly all the world's airlines. Given the extent of governmental ownership of airlines, governments comprise much of the membership. Today, IATA is mainly concerned with global safety standards. However, at times it has restricted competition on routes by requiring uniform fares, meal service, and baggage allowances.

MAP 14.2 Top 20 Passenger Airlines

These rankings are based on passenger miles flown—RPMs and RPKs—but other criteria may include operating profit, net profit, operating revenue, and fleet size. Not surprisingly, different criteria result in different rankings. *RPM* means *revenue passenger miles*: If an airline flies 100 passengers for 1,000 miles, it logs 100,000 RPMs. *RPK* is the same measurement in terms of kilometers.

Source: "Top 20 Largest Airlines in Terms of RPKs/RPMs," *Airlines.net*, at www.airlines.net (accessed August 20, 2007). Information based on 2005 operations.

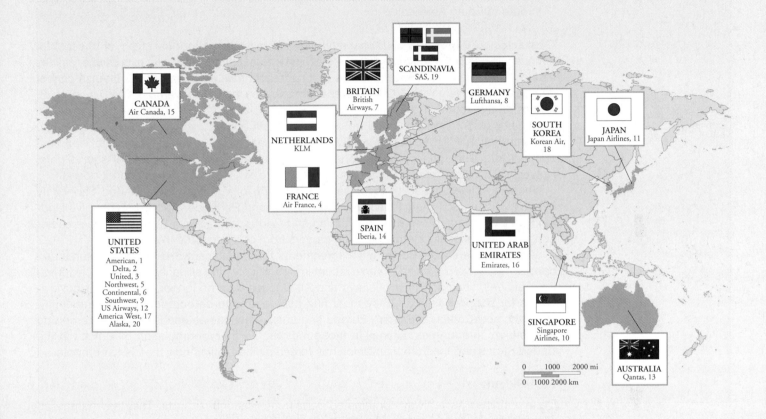

Why Governments Protect Airlines Five factors influence governments' protection of their airlines:

1. Countries believe they can save money by maintaining small air forces and relying on domestic airlines in times of unusual air transport needs. For example, the U.S. government used U.S. commercial carriers to help carry troops to Iraq.

2. In aviation's early days, airlines were heavily subsidized to carry mail overseas, and governments wanted to support their own fledgling companies rather than foreign ones. This consideration has shifted somewhat because mail subsidies no longer are very important internationally. For example, revenues from mail account for less than 0.5 percent of revenues for U.S. airlines.

3. Public opinion favors spending "at home," especially for government-paid travel. The public sees the maintenance of national airlines and the requirement that government employees fly on those airlines as foreign-exchange savings. (For example, when a U.S. resident uses a foreign airline internationally—say, Air France from New York to Paris—this is a service import for the United States.)

4. Airlines are a source of national pride, and aircraft (sporting their national flags) symbolize a country's sovereignty and technical competence. This national identification has been especially important for developing countries, whose airlines once were largely foreign owned. For example, the former PanAm controlled airlines in Brazil, Colombia,

Mexico, Panama, and Venezuela. As soon as countries were technically and financially capable, they developed national airlines and prohibited foreign ownership.

5. Countries have worried about protecting their airspace for security reasons. This is less of a concern today because foreign carriers routinely overfly a country's territory to reach inland gateways, such as British Air's flights between London and Denver. Further, overflight treaties are quite common, even among unfriendly nations. For example, Cubana overflies the United States en route to Canada, and American Airlines overflies Cuba en route to South America.

Obstacles to Expansion   National attitudes and regulations not only give rise to separate national airlines but also limit airlines' expansion internationally. With few exceptions, airlines cannot fly on lucrative domestic routes in foreign countries. For example, Lufthansa cannot compete on the New York to Los Angeles route because the U.S. government allows only U.S. airlines on that route.

Airlines also cannot easily control a flight network abroad that will feed passengers into their international flights. For example, Air France has no U.S. domestic flights to feed passengers into Chicago for connections to Paris, but American has scores of such flights. However, Air France has an advantage within France, where U.S. carriers cannot operate.

Finally, airlines usually cannot service pairs of foreign countries. United cannot fly between Brazil and Portugal because the Brazilian and Portuguese governments give landing rights on these routes only to Brazilian and Portuguese airlines. To avoid these restrictions, airlines must ally themselves with carriers from other countries.

Airlines have sought cooperative agreements to complement their route structures and capabilities. Privatization has been a recent impetus to forming alliances. For example, privatized airlines, such as British Airways and Air Canada, can no longer look to their governments for support. Instead, they must find new means to be competitive internationally. Similarly, privatization in Eastern Europe and Latin America has enabled foreign carriers to take stakes in countries' airlines in those regions. Further, deregulation of airlines in the United States and the European Union has forced airlines to find new means to compete.

Cost Factors

Certain airlines have always dominated certain international airports. They have amassed critical capabilities in those airports, such as baggage handlers and baggage-handling equipment. Sharing these capabilities with other airlines may spread costs. For example, KLM has long handled passenger check-in, baggage loading, and maintenance for a number of other airlines in Amsterdam.

Other contracts commonly cover the use of airport gates, ground equipment such as generators, and commissary services. Airlines also sometimes sublease aircraft to each other. When traffic on a route is low, airlines sometimes make market agreements to fly on alternate days. Or they may agree to share service in the same aircraft, which then has a dual-flight designation.

The high cost of maintenance and reservations systems has led to joint ventures. Swissair, Lufthansa, and Guiness Peat Aviation are partners in a maintenance center in Ireland. United, British Airways, US Airways, Swissair, Alitalia, and Air Canada share ownership in Covia, which operates and delivers the Apollo reservation system. United, US Airways, British Air, Alitalia, Swissair, KLM, Olympic, Austrian Airlines, AerLingus, Sabena, and TAP Air Portugal founded another reservation system, Galileo.

Competitive Factors

A number of airlines have established marketing agreements to complement their route structures. For example, Northwest handles KLM's operations in its Detroit facilities, and a high portion of KLM's traffic from Detroit to the Netherlands comes from Northwest's connections. The joint use of facilities within alliances may be the wave of the future because it is nearly impossible to add gates at the largest airports, and existing airlines own all the gates.

A problem with these marketing agreements is that the connections from one airline to another show up as separate route codes in reservations systems. These come up last on the screens of travel agents, and the agents tend to recommend the first scheduled flights they see. Further, when passengers see that they must change airlines, they worry about making those connections across great distances within ever-larger airline terminals.

This worry factor puts connections between two different airlines at a disadvantage to connections on the same airline. When KLM bought an interest in Northwest, the two airlines were able to secure the same route codes on their connecting flights. Northwest's ticket counters show KLM's logo as well. The alliance gives Northwest service to about 80 European cities. They have come as close as possible to a merger without actually making one.

Alliance Management

A problem in the proliferation of alliances is that relationships are intertwined among so many airlines, it's difficult to determine whether companies are competing, cooperating, or colluding. Management may find it increasingly hard to be cooperative, say, in joint maintenance agreements while trying to compete directly on some routes.

Government restrictions to prevent full mergers among airlines from different countries may be a blessing in some ways because corporate and national cultures may be difficult to mesh. For example, pilots at Air Canada are unionized, but those at Continental are not. Analysts conclude that the problems of combining unions after PanAm's acquisition of National was a major contribution to PanAm's eventual demise.

Other things simply may not mesh well in alliances. In the now defunct US Airways and British Airways agreement, British Airways was strong in connections from London to Europe and Asia. But US Airways' strength was at New York's LaGuardia Airport, which is purely domestic—most connecting passengers had to change airports. When Northwest and KLM allied, it was expected that KLM would help Northwest improve its service; however, the organizations could not work well in that effort because of entrenched Northwest employees who would not cooperate. ■

QUESTIONS

1. Discuss a question raised by the manager of route strategy of American Airlines: Why should an airline not be able to establish service anywhere in the world simply by demonstrating that it can and will comply with the local labor and business laws of the host country?
2. The president of Japan Air Lines has claimed that U.S. airlines are dumping air services on routes between the United States and Europe, meaning they are selling below their costs because of the money they are losing. Should governments set prices so carriers make money on routes?
3. What will be the consequences if a few large airlines or networks come to dominate global air service?
4. Some airlines, such as Southwest and Alaska Air, have survived as niche players without going international or developing alliances with international airlines. Can they continue this strategy?

SUMMARY

- Selling abroad by exporting home-country production may not be advantageous because of lower production costs abroad, high transport costs, the need to alter products substantially, protectionist barriers, lack of domestic capacity, and consumer preferences to buy from specific countries.

- Companies often prefer to operate with foreign direct investment, especially wholly owned, because such operations may lower their costs, lessen the possibility of developing competitors, and free them to follow global strategies.

- Some advantages of collaborative arrangements, whether a company is operating domestically or internationally, are to spread and reduce costs, allow a company to specialize in its primary competencies, avoid certain competition, secure vertical and horizontal links, and learn from other companies.

- Some motivations for collaborative arrangements that are specific to international operations are to gain location-specific assets, overcome legal constraints, diversify among countries, and minimize exposure in risky environments.

- The forms of foreign operations differ in how many resources a company commits and the proportion of resources committed at home rather than abroad. Collaborative arrangements reduce a company's commitment.

- Although the type of collaborative arrangement a company chooses should match its strategic objectives, the choice often means a trade-off among objectives.

- Licensing is granting another company the use of some rights, such as patents, copyrights, or trademarks, usually for a fee. It is a means of establishing foreign production and reaching foreign markets that may minimize capital outlays, prevent the free use of assets by other companies, allow the receipt of assets from other companies in return, and allow for income in some markets in which exportation or investment is not feasible.

- Franchising differs from licensing in that granting the use of intangible property (usually a trademark) is an essential asset for the franchisee's business and the franchisor assists in the operation of the business on a continuing basis.

- Management contracts are a means of securing income by managing a foreign operation while providing little capital outlay.

- Turnkey projects are contracts for construction of another company's operating facilities. These projects have been large and diverse, necessitating specialized skills and abilities to deal with top-level government authorities.

- Joint ventures are a special type of collaborative arrangement in which two or more organizations have equity in the venture. There are various combinations of owners, including governments and private companies and two or more companies from the same or different countries.

- Equity alliances occur when a company takes an equity position in the company with which it has a collaborative arrangement so as to solidify the collaborating contract.

- A common motive for jointly owned operations is to take advantage of complementary resources that companies have at their disposal.

- Problems occur in collaborative arrangements because partners place different levels of importance on and have different objectives for the venture, find a shared ownership arrangement difficult to control, worry that their partner is putting in too little or taking out too much from the operation, and misunderstand each other because of their different country or company cultures.

- Contracting for the outside management of a company's foreign business does not negate management's responsibility to ensure company resources are working. Management constantly needs to assess the other company's work.

- Companies may use different types of collaborative arrangements for their foreign operations in different countries or for different products. As diversity increases, coordinating and managing the foreign operations become more complex.

KEY TERMS

appropriability theory (p. 535)	equity alliance (p. 549)	resource-based view (of the firm)
consortium (p. 548)	internalization (p. 535)	(p. 539)

ENDNOTES

1 *Sources include the following:* The Coca-Cola Company, "Around the World" (2007), at www.thecoca-colacompany.com/ourcompany/aroundworld.html (accessed July 3, 2007); Andrew Martin, "Does Coke Need a Refill?" *New York Times,* May 27, 2007: Sec. 3, 1+; Leo Paul Dana, "Turkish Coca-Cola," *British Food Journal* 101:5/6 (1999): 468; "Coca-Cola Dome-Sasol Management Contract Renewed," at www.thebeexhibitions.co.za/press5.htm (accessed July 3, 2007); Sara Yin, "Coca-Cola Opens Concept Store," *Media,* December 1, 2006: 2; "Coca-Cola, Danone Create Joint Venture to Sell Bottled Water," *Wall Street Journal,* June 18, 2002: C18; "Coca-Cola, Nestlé Narrow Joint Venture," *Beverage Industry* 98:4 (2007): 6; Drake Weisert, "Coca-Cola in China: Quenching the Thirst of a Billion," *China Business Review* (July–August 2001), at www.chinabusinessreview.com/public/0107/weisert.html; Kevin Parker, "ERP and SOA at the Coca-Cola Company," *Manufacturing Business Technology* 25:5 (2007): 2; Betsy McKay, "Smaller Brands Hitch Brands with Coke Distributors," *Wall Street Journal,* January 29, 2007: B1; Betsy McKay, "More Fizz," *Wall Street Journal,* June 1, 2007: A1+; *Coca-Cola 2006 Annual Report.*

2 Hugh Pope, "Ford Forges Ahead with Turkey Plans," *Wall Street Journal,* July 24, 2000: A17+.

3 John Griffiths, "VW May Build Beetle in Europe to Meet Demand," *Financial Times,* November 11, 1998: 17.

4 Peter Marsh, "The World's Wash Day," *Financial Times,* April 29, 2002: 6.

5 "Skoda Brings New Luxury Car, Octavia," *The Statesman* (India), November 17, 2001, FT Asia Africa Intelligence Wire.

6 Aluf Benn, "Why Peace Doesn't Pay," *Foreign Policy* 124 (May–June 2001): 64–65.

7 Jill Gabrielle Klein, "Us versus Them, or Us versus Everyone? Delineating Consumer Aversion to Foreign Goods," *Journal of International Business Studies* 33:2 (2002): 345–63.

8 "Yes, You Can Help Our Balance of Payments," *The Daily Telegraph* (Sydney), June 4, 2005: 5.

9 Lynda V. Mapes, "Food Fight Ensues over Labeling," *Seattle Times,* April 25, 2002: A1; and Ken Leiser, "Toyota's Inroads with State Bypass 'Buy American' Law," March 6, 2002: A1.

10 John S. Hulland, "The Effects of Country-of-Brand and Brand Name on Product Evaluation and Consideration: A Cross-Country Comparison," *Consumer Behavior in Asia: Issues and Market Practice* (1999): 23–39.

11 *Internalization theory,* or holding a monopoly control over certain information or other proprietary assets, builds on earlier market-imperfections work by Ronald H. Coase, "The Nature of the Firm," *Economica* 4 (1937): 386–405. It has been noted by such writers as M. Casson, "The Theory of Foreign Direct Investment," Discussion Paper No. 50 (Reading, UK: University of Reading International Investment and Business Studies, November 1980); Alan M. Rugman, *Inside the Multinationals: The Economics of Internal Markets* (New York: Columbia University Press, 1981); David J. Teece, "Transactions Cost Economics and the Multinational Enterprise," Berkeley Business School International Business Working Paper Series, No. IB-3, 1985; B. Kogut and U. Zander, "Knowledge of the Firm and the Evolutionary Theory of the Multinational Corporation," *Journal of International Business Studies* 24:4 (1993): 625–45; and Peter W. Liesch and Gary A. Knight, "Information Internalization and Hurdle Rates in Small and Medium Enterprise Internationalization," *Journal of International Business Studies* 30:2 (1999): 383–96.

12 Eric M. Johnson, "Harnessing the Power of Partnerships," *Financial Times,* October 8, 2004: Mastering Innovation, 4.

13 Paul Marer and Vincent Mabert, "GE Acquires and Restructures Tungsram: The First Six Years (1990–1995)," *OECD, Trends and Policies in Privatization* III:1 (Paris: OECD, 1996), pp. 149–85; and their unpublished 1999 revision, "GE's Acquisition of Hungary's Tungsram."

14 James Mackintosh and Arkady Ostrovsky, "Partners Settle Lada Parts Dispute," *Financial Times,* February 21, 2006: 16.

15 Gary Gentile, "Hair Products," *Miami Herald,* September 3, 2004: 4C.

16 Stephen Magee, "Information and the MNC: An Appropriability Theory of Direct Foreign Investment," in Jagdish N. Bhagwati, ed., *The New International Economic Order* (Cambridge, MA: MIT Press, 1977), pp. 317–40; C. W. Hill, L. P. Hwang, and W. C. Kim, "An Eclectic Theory of the Choice on International Entry Mode," *Strategic Management Journal* 11 (1990): 117–18; Ashish Arora and Andrea Fosfuri, "Wholly Owned Subsidiary versus Technology Licensing in the Worldwide Chemical Industry," *Journal of International Business Studies* 31:4 (2000): 555–72.

17 Peter Wonacott, "Global Aims of China's Car Makers Put Existing Ties at Risk," *Wall Street Journal,* August 24, 2004: B1+; Norihiko Shirouzu and Peter Wonacott, "People's Republic of Autos," *Wall Street Journal,* April 18, 2005: B1+.

18 Andrew Taylor, "Overseas Groups Get on the UK Utility Map," *Financial Times,* June 17, 2002: 4.

19 Anne-Wil Harzing, "Acquisitions versus Greenfield Investments: International Strategy and Management of Entry Modes," *Strategic Management Journal* 23:3 (2002): 211–27.

20 Jaideep Anand and Andrew Delios, "Absolute and Relative Resources as Determinants of International Acquisitions," *Strategic Management Journal* 23:2 (2002): 119–34.

21 Geoff Dyer, Francesco Guerrera, and Alexandra Harney, "Chinese Companies Make Plans to Join the Multinational Club," *Financial Times,* June 23, 2005: 19.

22 One such indication is from a study by Alan Gregory, which is cited in Kate Burgess, "Acquisitions in US 'Disastrous' for British Companies," *Financial Times,* October 11, 2004: 18.

23 John Child, David Faulkner, and Robert Pitethly, *The Management of International Acquisitions* (Oxford: Oxford University Press, 2001); Peter Martin, "A Clash of Corporate Cultures," *Financial Times,* June 2–3, 2001: weekend section, xxiv.

24 Pierre Dussauge, Bernard Garrette, and Will Mitchell, "Asymmetric Performance: The Market Share Impact of Scale and Link Alliances in the Global Auto Industry," *Strategic Management Journal* 25 (2004): 701–11.

25 A. L. Zacharakis, "Entrepreneurial Entry into Foreign Markets: A Transaction Cost Perspective," *Entrepreneurship Theory & Practice* 22: 2 (1998): 23–39; Rodney C. Shrader, "Collaboration and Performance in Foreign Markets: The Case of Young High-Technology Manufacturing Firms," *Academy of Management Journal* 44:1 (2001): 45–60.

26 Rahul Jacob, "Hong Kong Banks on New Disney Park for Boost," *Financial Times,* August 31, 2001, 6.

27 "New World Ready to Build Caribbean Fiber System," *Fiber-Optics News,* June 26, 2000: 1.

28 Betsy McKay and Robert Frank, "Coke, Danone Discuss Joint Venture," *Wall Street Journal,* June 17, 2002: B5.

29 John M. Connor, "Global Antitrust Prosecutions of Modern International Cartels," *Journal of Industry, Competition and Trade* 4:3 (2004): 239.

30 Peter Marsh, "Profile Duracell," *Financial Times,* May 10, 1999: 27.

31 Doug Cameron, "Manufacturing Enters a New Era," *Financial Times*, June 18, 2007: 6.

32 Destan Kandemir and G. Tomas Hult, "A Conceptualization of an Organizational Learning Culture in International Joint Ventures," *Industrial Marketing Management* 34:5 (2005): 440.

33 Robert F. Howe, "The Fall of the House of Mondavi," *Business 2.0*, 6:3 (2005): 98.

34 Yumiko Ono and Ann Zimmerman, "Wal-Mart Enters Japan with Seiyu Stake," *Wall Street Journal*, March 15, 2002: B5.

35 "Merck and Chugai Form OTC Venture," *Financial Times*, September 19, 1996: 17; Michiyo Nakamoto, "Global Reach through Tie-Ups," *Financial Times*, April 30, 2002: health-care section, 3.

36 Peter Wonacott and Eric Bellman, "Foreign Firms Find Rough Passage to India," *Wall Street Journal*, February 1, 2007: A6.

37 "Northrop Grumman, Rolls-Royce Awarded Type 45 Destroyer Engine Contract," *Defense Daily International*, March 16, 2001: 1.

38 Julie Bennett, "Road to Foreign Franchises Is Paved with New Problems," *Wall Street Journal*, May 14, 2001: B10.

39 "H&M Wins Back Name in Russia," *Managing Intellectual Property* (April 2007): 1.

40 Peter J. Lane, Jane E. Salk, and Marjorie A. Lyles, "Absorptive Capacity, Learning, and Performance in International Joint Ventures," *Strategic Management Journal* 22 (2001): 1139–61.

41 Steven White and Steven Siu-Yun Lui, "Distinguishing Costs of Cooperation and Control in Alliances," *Strategic Management Journal* 26 (2005): 913–32.

42 Miguel Angel Asturias, *Strong Wind*, trans. Gregory Rabassa (New York: Delacorte Press, 1968), p. 112.

43 For an extensive treatise on the theory, see Robert A. Packenham, *The Dependency Movement: Scholarship and Politics in Development Studies* (Cambridge, MA: Harvard University Press, 1992). For some different national views of its validity, see Ndiva Kofele-Kale, "The Political Economy of Foreign Direct Investment: A Framework for Analyzing Investment Laws and Regulations in Developing Countries," *Law & Policy in International Business* 23:2/3 (1992): 619–71; Stanley K. Sheinbaum, "Very Recent History Has Absolved Socialism," *New Perspectives Quarterly* 13:1 (1996).

44 Ravi Ramamurti, "The Obsolescing 'Bargaining Model'? MNC-Host Developing Country Relations Revisited," *Journal of International Business Studies* 32 (2001): 23; Yadong Luo, "Toward a Cooperative View of MNC-Host Government Relations: Building Blocks and Performance Implication," *Journal of International Business Studies* 32 (2001): 401.

45 "Microsoft and LG Ink Broad Patent-Licensing Pact," *Wireless News*, June 10, 2007: 1.

46 Pierre Dussauge, "Domino's Pizza International, Inc.," Case #398–048–1 (Jouy-en-Josas, France: H.E.C., 1998).

47 Lizette Alvarez, "Spreading Scandinavian Genes, Without Viking Boats," *New York Times*, September 30, 2004: A4.

48 Fred Burton, Adam R. Cross, and Mark Rhodes, "Foreign Market Servicing Strategies of UK Franchisors: An Empirical Enquiry from a Transactions Cost Perspective," *Management International Review* 40:4 (2000): 373–400.

49 John K. Ryans, Jr., Sherry Lotz, and Robert Krampf, "Do Master Franchisors Drive Global Franchising?" *Marketing Management* 8:2 (1999): 33–38.

50 Janet Adamy, "Chinese Food the KFC Way," *Wall Street Journal Asian Edition*, October 20–22, 2006: 14–15.

51 Julie Bennett, "Product Pitfalls Proliferate in a Global Cultural Maze," *Wall Street Journal*, May 14, 2001: B11; Jane Wooldridge, "Fast Food Universe," *Miami Herald*, November 28, 2004: J1.

52 British Airport Authority, "International Airports" (2007), at http://www.baa.com/portal/page/Corporate%5EAbout+BAA%5EWho+does+what%5EInternational+airports/b0ccadc5c5c72010VgnVCM100000147e120a__/448c6a4c7f1b0010VgnVCM200000357e120a__/ (accessed July 6, 2007).

53 Chekitan S. Dev, M. Krishna Erramilli, and Sanjeev Agarwal, "Brands Across Borders," *Cornell Hotel and Restaurant Administration Quarterly* 43:6 (2002): 91–104.

54 Bechtel Corporation, "Projects" (2007), at http://www.bechtel.com/default_projects.htm (accessed October 30, 2007).

55 Glenn R. Simpson and Chip Cummins, "Fuel for the Fire," *Wall Street Journal*, April 14, 2004: A1+; Sheila McNulty, "Haliburton Boosted by Iraq Work," April 23–24, 2005: 8.

56 David Murphy, "Chinese Construction Companies Go Global," *Wall Street Journal*, May 12, 2004: B10.

57 Luis Zalamea, "AeroRepublica, Copa Offer Details of New Alliance," *Aviation Daily*, March 11, 2005: 5.

58 There are many different ways of classifying the problems. Two useful ways are found in Manuel G. Serapio, Jr., and Wayne F. Cascio, "End Games in International Alliances," *Academy of Management Executive* 10:1 (1996): 62–73; and Joel Bleeke and David Ernst, "Is Your Strategic Alliance Really a Sale?" *Harvard Business Review* (January–February 1995): 97–105.

59 Terrence Chea, "No Perfect Partnership," *Washington Post*, June 3, 2002: E1.

60 Gregory L. White, "In Asia, GM Pins Hope on a Delicate Web of Alliances," *Wall Street Journal*, October 23, 2002: A23.

61 Ramit Plushnick-Masti, "German Firm Faulted for Taking Vitamin Out of Baby Formula," *Miami Herald*, November 12, 2003: 19A.

62 William H. Meyers, "Maxim's Name Is the Game," *New York Times Magazine*, May 3, 1987: 33–35; Keith W. Strandberg, "EganaGoldpfeil Group Moves Forward with Pierre Cardin Watches," *National Jeweler*, October 1, 2002: 36.

63 Marcus W. Brauchli, "PepsiCo's KFC Venture in China Is Fined for Allegedly False Financial Reporting," *Wall Street Journal*, July 27, 1994: A10.

64 David Ibison, "Culture Clashes Prove Biggest Hurdle to International Links," *Financial Times*, January 24, 2002: 17.

65 Samantha Marshall, "P&G Squabbles with Vietnamese Partner," *Wall Street Journal*, February 27, 1998: A14.

66 H. Keven Steensma, Laslo Thiyani, Marjorie Lyles, and Charles Dhanaraj, "The Evolving Value of Foreign Partnerships in Transitioning Economies," *Academy of Management Journal* 48:2 (2005): 213–34.

67 Joel Bleeke and David Ernst, "The Way to Win in Cross-Border Alliances," *Harvard Business Review* (November–December 1991): 127–35.

68 Leslie Crawford, "Anheuser's Cross-Border Marriage on the Rocks," *Financial Times*, March 18, 1998: 16.

69 Seung Ho Park and Gerardo R. Ungson, "The Effect of National Culture, Organizational Complementarity, and Economic Motivation on Joint Venture Dissolution," *Academy of Management Journal* 40:2 (April 1997): 279–307; Harry G. Barkema, Oded Shenkar, Freek Vermeulen, and John H. J. Bell, "Working Abroad, Working with Others: How Firms Learn to Operate International Joint Ventures," *Academy of Management Journal* 40:2 (April 1997): 426–42, found survival differences only for differences in uncertainty avoidance.

70 Mike W. Peng and Oded Shenkar, "Joint Venture Dissolution as Corporate Divorce," *Academy of Management Executive* 16:2 (May 2002): 92–105.

71 Bharat Anand and Tarun Khanna, "Do Firms Learn to Create Value? The Case of Alliances," *Strategic Management Journal* 21:3 (March 2000): 295–315.

72 Anthony Goerzen and Paul W. Beamish, "The Effect of Alliance Network Diversity on Multinational Enterprise Performance," *Strategic Management Journal* 26 (2005): 333–54.

73 Rachelle C. Sampson, "Experience Effects and Collaborative Returns in R&D Alliances," *Strategic Management Journal* 26 (2005): 1009–31.

74 Anne Smith and Marie-Claude Reney, "The Mating Dance: A Case Study of Local Partnering Processes in Developing Countries," *European Management Journal* 15:2 (1997): 174–82.

75 Sanjiv Kumar and Anju Seth, "The Design of Coordination and Control Mechanisms for Managing Joint Venture–Parent Relationships," *Strategic Management Journal* 19:6 (June 1998): 579–99; T. K. Das and Bing-Sheng Teng, "Between Trust and Control: Developing Confidence in Partner Cooperation in Alliances," *Academy of Management Journal* 23:3 (July 1998): 491–512; Arvind Parkhe, "Building Trust in International Alliances," *Journal of World Business* 33:4 (1998): 417–37; Prashant Kale, Harbir Singh, and Howard Perlmutter, "Learning and Protection of Proprietary Assets in Strategic Alliances: Building Relational Capital," *Strategic Management Journal* 21:3 (March 2000): 217–37.

76 Africa Ariño and Jeffrey J. Reuer, "Designing and Renegotiating Strategic Alliance Contracts," *Academy of Management Executive* 18:3 (2004): 37–48.

77 Srilata Zaheer and Akbar Zaheer, "Trust Across Borders," *Journal of International Business Studies* 37:1 (2006): 21.

78 John Kenneth Galbraith, *American Capitalism* (Boston: Houghton Mifflin, 1952), pp. 91–92.

79 Eric H. Kessler, Paul E. Bierly, and Shanthi Gopalakrishnan, "Internal vs. External Learning in New Product Development: Effects of Speed, Costs and Competitive Advantage," *R & D Management* 30:3 (2000): 213–23.

80 These are adapted from Arvind Parkhe, "Interfirm Diversity, Organizational Learning, and Longevity in Global Strategic Alliances," *Journal of International Business Studies* 22:4 (1991): 579–601.

81 *Sources include the following:* Andrea Rothman, "U.S. to World: Airline Deals Hinge on Open Skies," *Business Week*, January 11, 1992: 46; Andrea Rothman, Seth Payne, and Paula Dwyer, "One World, One Giant Airline Market?" *Business Week*, October 5, 1992: 56; "All Aboard," *The Economist*, February 29, 1992: 78; "Wings Across the Water," *The Economist*, July 25, 1992: 62; Agis Salpukas, "Europe's Small Airlines Shelter Under Bigger Wings," *New York Times*, November 8, 1992: E4; "Code Breakers," *The Economist*, November 21, 1992: 78–79; Bridget O'Brian and Laurie McGinley, "Mixing of U.S., Foreign Carriers Alters Market," *Wall Street Journal*, December 21, 1992: B1; Bill Poling, "United, American Spar with USAir, BA over Proposed Deal," *Travel Weekly*, November 12, 1992: 49; Joan M. Feldman, "The Dilemma of 'Open Skies,'" *The New York Times Magazine*, April 2, 1989: 31; Philippe Gugler, "Strategic Alliances in Services: Some Theoretical Issues and the Case of Air-Transport Services," paper prepared for the Danish Summer Research Institute (DSRI), Denmark, August 1992; Martin Tolchin, "Shift Urged on Foreign Stakes in Airlines," *New York Times*, January 9, 1993: 17; Agis Salpukas, "The Big Foreign Push to Buy into U.S. Airlines," *New York Times*, October 11, 1992: F11; Robert Crandell, "When Less Really Means More," *Financial Times*, September 17, 1996: 17; Emma Tucker, "Commission to Approve Lufthansa-SAS Venture," *Financial Times*, January 16, 1996: 3; Scott McCartney, Diane Brady, Susan Carey, and Asra Q. Nomani, "U.S. Airlines' Prospects Are Grim on Expanding Access to Asian Skies," *Wall Street Journal*, September 25, 1996: A1; Michael Skapinker, "Austrian Air Switches Allegiance to Star Alliance," *Financial Times*, September 22, 1999: 9; Edward Alden and Michael Skapinker, "United Airlines–Lufthansa Join Battle for Air Canada," *Financial Times*, October 20, 1999: 1; Michael Skapinker, "Continental Chairman Calls for Creation of Third Air Alliance," *Financial Times*, October 5, 1998: 20; Michael Skapinker, "Passengers Not Convinced," *Financial Times*, November 19, 1998: business of travel section, p. iii; Michael Skapinker, "Boarding Business Class Now," *Financial Times*, July 9, 1998: 13; J. A. Donoghue, "Network Is Everything," *Air Transport World* 36:8 (August 1999): 9; Leonard Hill, "Global Challenger," *Air Transport World* 36:12 (December 1999): 52–54; Robert Gribben, "City," *The Daily Telegraph* (London), December 21, 1999: 29; Michael A. Taverna and John D. Morrocco, "Airlines Play Catch-Up in Partnership Game," *Aviation Week and Space Technology*, March 22, 1999: 70; Leonard Hill, "80 Years Young," *Air Transport World* 36:10 (October 1999): 44–47; "Star Alliance Welcomes Asiana, Lot and Spanair to Its Roster of World Class Airlines," *PR Newswire*, June 1, 2002; Shirene Shan, "Alliances Bring Benefit to Passengers," *New Straits Times Press* (Malaysia), May 14, 2002: Industry aviation section, p. 24; "Global Alliances Vulnerable to Shakeups in Four Areas," *Airline Financial News*, June 10, 2002; Kevin Done, "Air France–KLM Ahead on Savings," *Financial Times*, April 12, 2005: 30; www.iccwbo.org/home/statements_rules/statements/1995/state_aid.asp.

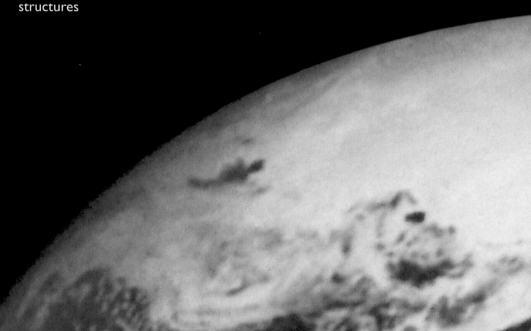

15

The Organization of
International Business

Objectives

- Profile the evolving understanding of the organization of international business

- Describe traditional and contemporary structures

- Study the systems used to coordinate and control operations

- Profile the role of organization culture

- Examine special situations in the organization of international business

Laws control the lesser man. Right conduct controls the greater one.

—Chinese proverb

CASE: Organizing "People, Values, and Environment" at Johnson & Johnson

The typical pharmaceutical company relies heavily on integration because its products are costly to develop and sensitive to scale economies.[1] Meanwhile, it often must be highly responsive to local market conditions, obtaining local government approval for each product in each country and establishing local sales and distribution systems. The parent company and its subsidiaries are involved in implementing the company's strategy. Building an organization that can meet this mission is truly a challenge. One standout organization that does so is Johnson & Johnson (J&J).

A LITTLE BACKGROUND

How J&J Grew

Since the start of its U.S. operations in 1886, J&J has evolved into the most broadly based health-care company in the world. International activity began in 1919 with J&J Canada. J&J now lists more than 250 operating companies across the world, sells products in more than 175 countries, generates annual global revenues of more than $53 billion, and employs about 123,000 people worldwide, with nearly 70,000 working in 57 countries outside the United States. Its steady success is renowned. It holds nearly 54,000 U.S. and foreign patents and is the world's leader in a broad segment of medical needs, such as adhesive bandages, contact lenses, prescription pharmaceuticals, and medical devices.

Through 2006, its annual sales had grown for 73 consecutive years. It has maintained profitability since going public in 1944, with 44 consecutive years of dividend increases. Not content to rest on its laurels, in early 2005, William Weldon, chairman of the board of directors and CEO, announced the stretch goal of $100 billion in sales in 2010. In 2006, J&J was named the most admired pharmaceutical company in the world and number six among all companies across all industries.

What J&J Sells

J&J develops, manufactures, and markets products to consumers and health-care professionals worldwide. It aims for industry leadership in its three core areas: pharmaceuticals, medical devices/professional, and consumer products. The pharmaceutical segment includes products in areas like anti-infective, cardiovascular, dermatology, immunology, and oncology. These products are distributed directly to retailers, wholesalers, and health-care professionals for prescription use by the general public.

The medical devices and diagnostics segment includes products distributed to wholesalers, hospitals, and retailers, used in the professional fields by physicians, nurses, therapists, hospitals, diagnostic laboratories, and clinics. The consumer segment manufactures and markets products used in the baby and child care, skin care, oral and wound care, and women's health-care fields, as well as nutritional and over-the-counter pharmaceutical products. These products, available without prescription, are marketed to the general public and sold to wholesalers and directly to independent and chain retail outlets throughout the world.

How J&J Is Run

J&J's Executive Committee manages all operations worldwide. Executive Committee members also chair worldwide Group Operating Committees (GOCs), composed of managers who represent key operations within the group, as well as management expertise in other specialized functions. GOCs oversee and coordinate the activities of domestic and international companies related to each of the consumer, pharmaceutical, and professional segments of the business. Each company is headed by a chairman, president, general manager, or managing director reporting either directly or through a line executive to a GOC.

DECENTRALIZED DECISION MAKING

Decentralized management is at the heart of J&J's organization, allowing managers who are physically closest to customers and competitors to make decisions. With few exceptions, each international subsidiary is managed by citizens of the country where it is located. Indeed, J&J's organizational structure is best described in terms of the configuration of its individual operating units. Map 15.1 shows the worldwide distribution of these units.

By design, each unit operates with substantial autonomy, commanding the freedom to act as it sees best given local market conditions. Decentralization, explains Ralph Larsen, CEO from 1989 to 2002, "gives people a sense of ownership and control—and the freedom to act more rapidly." His successor, William Weldon, concurs, adding, "The magic around J&J is decentralization." He expanded these ideas later, explaining:

The decentralized manner in which we operate our businesses marries the best qualities of smaller companies with entrepreneurial drive for growth and close proximity to customers with the resources,

**MAP 15.1
Johnson & Johnson:
Worldwide
Operations, 2007**

J&J maintains operations in virtually every part of the world. Numbers indicate the total of operating units in each country.

Source: Based on data from Johnson & Johnson, "Our Company: Family of Companies" (October 11, 2007), at www.jnj.com (accessed November 5, 2007).

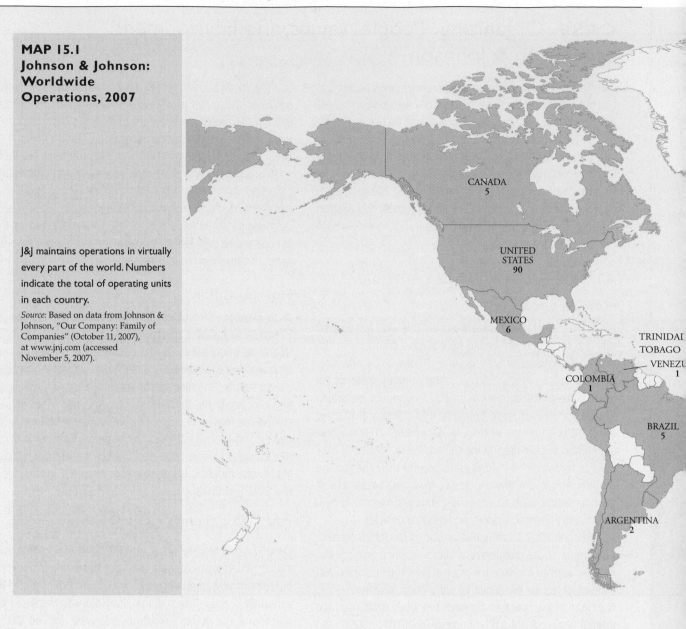

know how, and investment capital of a Fortune 500 company. This strategic approach gives us many advantages over a centralized operation. One is a strong sense of ownership, entrepreneurship, agility and accountability seldom seen in large multinational corporations. The leadership and employees of our 250 operating companies around the world are intensely competitive. We look to the leaders of our decentralized businesses to grow their businesses faster than their competitors. They are driven to innovate . . . [and] to bring greater value to the marketplace through internal discoveries, application of new science, technology, in-licensing and acquisition. We believe our decentralized approach to running the business yields better decisions—in the long run—for patients, health professionals and other customers, because the decision makers are close to the customers and are in a better position to understand their needs. Finally, our decentralized approach to managing the business is a tremendous magnet for talent, because it gives people room to grow and room to explore new ideas, thus developing their own skills and careers.

Essentially, this philosophy enables J&J to behave like 250 small, innovative, entrepreneurial firms, responding to the unique opportunities and threats in their local market yet still benefitting from the resources commanded and expertise generated by global operations.

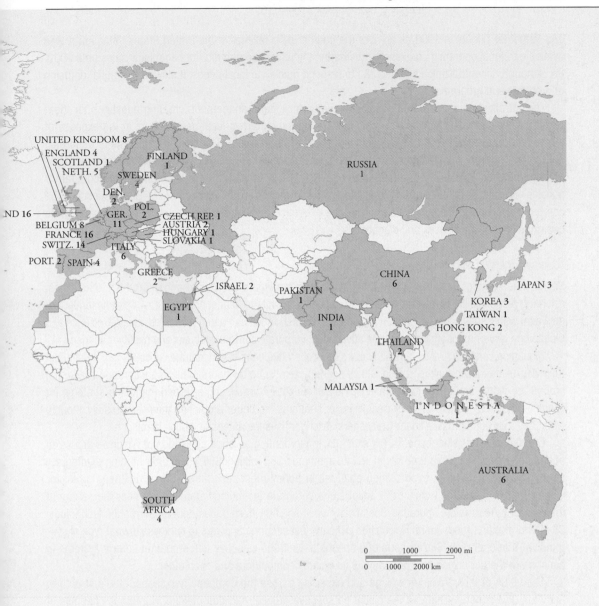

Supporting Subsidiaries

J&J entered new markets by adding subsidiaries through investment, alliance, or acquisition of another company, rather than with sweeping armies of home-office managers directed by headquarters-based generals. J&J provides full support to the new subsidiary and then waits for superior results. Its philosophy is that people who understand how the company creates value, have familiarity with the company's core competency, and are culturally familiar and physically close to the market ought to be running the local business. Thus, for example, baby oil managers in Italy decided how big a bottle to use, even if that bottle differed from the one sold in Germany, Japan, or Mexico.

The heads of J&J's foreign subsidiaries had once enjoyed so much autonomy that they were called "kings of their own countries." Headquarters would install some systems to coordinate and control activities among countries, often negotiating financial targets with the heads of the separate business units. It would then leave them to figure out how, given local market conditions, to best achieve those targets.

Competitive pressures pushing for global integration tested the company's commitment to decentralization, steadily creating friction between operating units and headquarters. Senior management concedes that decentralization resulted in inconsistent market development and duplication of efforts. For example,

J&J launched Tylenol in 1960 as an over-the-counter pain reliever in the United States. Although it was available to local operating units shortly thereafter, the Japanese unit did not begin local sales until 2000. So, although decentralization enabled J&J to respond quickly to local needs, it slowed the global diffusion of products and programs.

Decentralization also created agency dilemmas for local management, creating questions for them regarding their primary allegiance: simply put, should they improve local performance at the expense of global corporate objectives? This risk came into play in 2007 when J&J revealed that some of its foreign units made improper payments related to the sale of medical devices in two "small-market countries." Management did not disclose details of the payments but said they were "contrary to the company's policies" and "may fall within the jurisdiction of the Foreign Corrupt Practices Act." Simultaneously, the company announced the early retirement of the executive responsible for the units, the then worldwide chairman of medical devices and diagnostics.

Streamlining Coordination and Control

Senior management has streamlined the way country managers coordinate and control value activities, returning responsibility for certain activities from operating units to headquarters. The GOCs at headquarters now deal with issues common to many or all operating units, such as human resources, finance, science and technology, government affairs, corporate advertising, corporate communications, and quality management.

Managing certain activities at headquarters frees operating units to concentrate on issues that most affect their day-to-day performance. It also allows headquarters to better coordinate production and marketing around the world. Input from local managers is still sought in formulating a unified marketing strategy; for example, they may debate whether cleanliness or beauty is the better promotion theme. Ultimately, though, when J&J rolls out a product, country managers no longer have the automatic option to reject it.

Coordination has clear benefits. For example, implementing an updated version of Windows across all operating units at the same time saved J&J an estimated $80 million. Still, years after starting to integrate information technologies, even benign changes in policy meet resistance. Some business units, for instance, have argued that they can't adopt some corporate technology standards or bear their share of the cost for infrastructure upgrades. Specifically when she first started to integrate information technology, Chief Information Officer JoAnn Heisen had difficulty just securing answers to surveys on what type of systems were in operation. Similar sorts of problems have led to selective use of market control systems to benchmark the performance of operating units against competitors and each other.

The value of leveraging knowledge and expertise across the company has shaped J&J's structure. Early on, J&J aimed to improve the global perspective of local decision making. Numerous channels of communication and forums for discussion cut across the organization, encouraging and enabling far-flung units to share their ideas. Self-directed councils—of research, engineering, and operations directors, among others—meet regularly to swap ideas. Successful employees are rotated among various operating units and affiliates, sharing their expertise and collaborating with their new work group.

Building "FrameworkS"   J&J also developed "FrameworkS," a process that rotates employees through an ongoing dialogue with senior management on strategic topics applicable companywide. Plugged back into their worldwide networks, these employees then transfer information to their counterparts. Similarly, J&J reinforced planning at the business-unit level with initiatives on major issues such as biotechnology, the restructuring of the health-care industry, and globalization, challenging assumptions and introducing managers to better ways to coordinate value activities. Collectively, these efforts enable J&J to link and leverage its more than 250 centers of local resources and expertise.

THE CULTURE AND THE CREDO

J&J's organization culture is what former CEO Ralph Larsen referred to as the "glue that binds this company together." Since 1943, J&J has used a one-page ethical code of conduct, "Our Credo," to guide how it fulfills its business responsibilities (see Figure 15.1).

FIGURE 15.1
The J&J Credo

Originally spelled out in 1943, the J&J Credo has been updated over the years to reflect the changing market and strategic circumstances of J&J.

Source: Johnson & Johnson, "Our Company: Our Credo" (November 14, 2005), at www.jnj.com.

The Credo tells J&J managers worldwide who and what to care about and in what specific order. J&J's "first responsibility is to the doctors, nurses, patients, mothers and fathers who use our products and services." It addresses the needs of communities where J&J operates and the roles and duties of J&J employees. Notably, shareholders come last, long after suppliers and distributors. The Credo declares that shareholders will get a fair return if those other constituents get first priority: Essentially, the company holds that the business would be well served by putting the customer first. As declared on the title sheet of the 2006 *Annual Report*, the "Credo underscores J&J's personal responsibility to put the needs . . . of the people we serve first. It liberates our passion and deepens our commitment to delivering meaningful health innovations."

Translating the Credo

The Credo is available in 36 languages spreading across Africa, Asia-Pacific, Eastern Europe, Latin America, the Middle East, and North America. Executives worried that the language and attitude differences among these areas might distort the clear, shared understanding of the company's mission and objectives among its global workforce. Consequently, the company periodically surveys employees on how well J&J performs its Credo responsibilities. These assessments are returned to senior management, and where there are shortcomings, the company takes action. Lastly, the company continues to update some of the language of the Credo in recognition of new areas such as the environment and the balance between work and family. Despite these revisions, management believes the founding spirit of the Credo endures.

No matter the details of its particular structure, systems, and culture, J&J's leaders believe the basis of the company's continued success is building an organization that's flexible enough to exploit the knowledge and skills of each employee. Indeed, given the choice between staffing international operations with folks who would unquestionably implement top management orders or hiring local people who are entrepreneurial innovators, J&J regularly opted for the latter. Management reasoned that the costs of letting people on the front lines make their own decisions were trivial given the benefits of letting them capitalize on their initiative, develop their capabilities, and broaden their perspectives.

Decentralization has been, is, and will be the foundation of J&J's continued success. More pointedly, explained the CEO, "I am here to passionately protect the values of J&J. Our credo is value-based. It comes down to people, values, and environment."

Introduction

Organizing is the process of creating the structure, systems, and culture needed to implement the company's strategy.

Artfully engineering an organization that configures globally dispersed resources to meet the mandates of multinational operations is the frontier of international business. Although most international managers find it easier to decide what to do, many believe the basis of competitive advantage is devising an organization of such clarity that the intricate task of creating value while effectively mediating worldwide integration versus local differentiation is straightforward.[2] Therefore, this chapter examines how international companies build the organization to implement their chosen strategy.

Strategy as a Process   We begin with the notion that formulating the appropriate strategy for international business is just the first step of a long process. Essentially, an insightful strategy is a necessary though insufficient condition for long-term success. Instead, MNEs invest enormous energy into finding ways to implement their strategy effectively and efficiently.

This task inevitably turns managers' attention to the issue of how they should organize their international operations. J&J exemplifies this situation, showing the power of building an organization that takes a comprehensive view of integrating a network of decentralized national units, tailoring technology, human resources, reward systems, and information systems to coordinate and control value activities, and relying on its Credo to maintain a meaningful culture.

Throughout all these tasks, managers articulate what must be done to sustain the company's competitive advantage. They focus on how employees individually and collectively can contribute, how the company specifies and coordinates interdependencies among value activities, the means it would take to control situations that go awry, and the values and ideals that define its culture. As such, J&J gives a sense of the efforts managers make, arguably more than that given to fine-tuning their strategy, to build the organization that can implement their strategy.

Implementing strategy requires adept managers to build and run the necessary organization.

J&J also showcases the demanding variety of managerial activities that have to be performed both by people at headquarters and the local subsidiaries. Complicating this task is the fact that there are often numerous ways to tackle each activity. Many activities must be launched and supervised simultaneously, and many people in many operations in many countries are often resistant to change. Consequently, building an organization to implement the chosen strategy, as we see in Figure 15.2, presents managers with the tough job of integrating the efforts of many different people, teams, groups, and units into a smoothly functioning whole. Reports increasingly note, though, that while hard and time consuming, the payback of innovative organization design—in profits, costs, and risks—surpasses that of investments in product design and other conventional strategic initiatives.[3]

Change: The Critical Factor

How an MNE organizes its operations is one of the most provocative issues in international business. Perhaps no other topic in current management studies has undergone as much revision in the past few years. Indeed, it would not be overly dramatic to say that our ideas of the organization of international business are undergoing the sort of changes that require fundamentally reinterpreting many principles and practices.

FIGURE 15.2   Factors Affecting Organizing Operations

Organization refers to the activities through which a company builds the structures, systems, and culture that create a dynamic work environment. Organizing operations are designed to enable the firm to implement its chosen strategy.

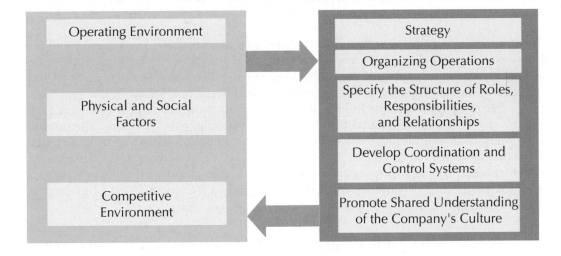

A Brief History of Approaches to Organizational Change   For generations, managers facing the task of building an organization could reasonably concern themselves with designing the system of lines and boxes that depicted its formal structure. Essentially, managers aimed to specify the formal arrangement of work within the company by specifying who did what job, who worked in which unit, who reported to whom, and who could make which decisions. The output of this effort was the company's formal structure. The company's structure basically instituted a system of control that largely relied on an arrangement of constraints and contracts to ensure compliance by all employees throughout the world.

Beginning with General Motors and DuPont in the early twentieth century, this general model performed well for many MNEs. However, preceding chapters have reported that various competitive pressures, industry conditions, and market opportunities spur MNEs to configure novel value chains. These configurations, in turn, create coordination and control challenges that can overwhelm the functionality provided by the formal specification of structure.

Indeed, some scholars advise that the very question of asking how an organization should be formally structured is anachronistic, given the realization of many MNEs that "reconfiguring the formal structure is a blunt and sometimes brutal instrument of change. A new structure creates new and presumably more useful managerial ties, but those can take months and often years to evolve into effective knowledge-generating and decision-making relationships."[4]

In times of rapid change, few MNEs have the luxury to await the emergence of "knowledge-generating and decision-making relationships." As a result, managers now question their customary approaches to organizing their companies, hoping to find ways to jump-start the development of and then sustaining these relationships.

Contemporary Approaches to Organizational Change   In the past few years, MNEs around the world have adopted radical programs to do so, as seen in widespread calls to downsize, delayer, restructure, reengineer, and reinvent the organization. Unquestionably, the structure of the company is a vital part of this reinterpretation. Today, however, managers elaborate on their idea of organization as a specification of boxes and lines with the integrated development of complementary systems and organization culture that supports their chosen strategy. Two sets of trends, one environmental, the other organizational, pressure managers to engage this challenge.

> Changes in the market environment and nature of work push managers to question how they organize work.

The Expansion of International Business   Regarding environmental trends, the first is the growth and diffusion of international business. Globalization has changed the opportunity set and efficiency frontier for companies. As we saw in Chapter 11, MNEs respond in kind, engaging unprecedented strategies that demand more sophisticated organizations—think of, for example, the cases of Zara and eBay.

The Importance of Knowledge as a Competitive Advantage   The second trend is a bit more subtle, involving the growing importance of knowledge as an engine of sustainable competitive advantage. More MNEs see the need to build the organization that accelerates the spread of ideas throughout their worldwide business.

The growing power of the Internet as an organization metaphor pushes managers to rethink many of their assumptions of how they get people to do their jobs. The Internet has emerged as a supremely efficient and effective global organization of knowledge, resources, and people. In the height of irony, however, the Internet itself has no formal organization, no board of directors, and no central administrator. The self-organizing and self-regulating capabilities of the Internet prompt the questioning of traditional notions of control.

> More sophisticated strategies involve activities that create new organizational requirements.

WORKPLACE ADJUSTMENTS   In addition, workplace trends are resetting organization standards for many companies. The speedily evolving nature of work is changing the conduct and context of employees' jobs, whether it takes place in the biggest headquarters or the smallest subsidiary. Most notably, employees working with computers, for example, create value through work that has astonishing variability, problem solving, and intellectual content. The flexibility of information technology means that, unlike earlier work environments, there are fewer jobs that senior managers can standardize in terms of the one best way to perform.

MANAGERIAL ADJUSTMENTS   Change in the nature of work has changed the nature of management. At the least, it is difficult and usually counterproductive to supervise workers charged with reasoning or problem-solving tasks. Moreover, the higher the level of manager in the hierarchy, historically, the more he or she knew about the various jobs in the company. Similarly, frontline employees at the subsidiary level presumably knew

> Here we see a class being conducted at the Toyota Technical Skills Academy. Some sessions are designed to teach auto maintenance techniques while others teach management skills. More importantly, these classes are part of the larger plan to inculcate the principles of the "Toyota Way" in the next generation of company leaders.

little more than their immediate responsibilities in the local marketplace. Today, employees who are closer to customers and competitors increasingly know as much, if not a bit more, about creating value as many managers back at headquarters. Senior executives, therefore, face growing pressure to empower employees around the world to make decisions and develop the basis of common ideas and ideals that ensure they will act in the best interests of the MNE.

Finally, competitive changes and performance expectations have changed the social contract between employee and organization. Employees' traditional concerns for security, pay, and benefits have expanded to greater interest in participating in decision making, devising solutions to unique problems, and receiving challenging assignments that improve their professional mobility.

ORGANIZING TODAY'S INTERNATIONAL BUSINESS

The enormity of environmental and workplace trends redefines the principles of the organization of international business. Companies now seek the complementary mix of structure, systems, and values that can build the organization needed to create value. Some companies, like Oticon in Sweden, Cisco in the United States, and Li Fung in Hong Kong, have engaged unprecedented formats. Rather than forcing employees into a conventional organization model, they build organizations that are flexible enough to leverage the knowledge and unique skills of employees.

Others, like Nestlé in Switzerland, Cemex in Mexico, and Infosys in India, have not abandoned their historic notions of organization. Instead, they have fine-tuned their organizations, trying to find a better combination of how to arrange the work environment, coordinate and control value activities, and create a common framework of values that encourages workers around the world to act creatively, responsibly, and entrepreneurially. These far more prevalent sorts of companies use a range of options to supplement their traditional organization, including cross-functional task forces, dual reporting relationships, informal networking, and incentive compensation tied to group performance.

The opening profile of J&J exemplifies this situation by highlighting that the organization of an international business is the totality of choices a company makes in its structure, systems, and culture. As we saw in Figure 15.2 (p. 573), this straightforward model helps us analyze the organizational capabilities a company needs to translate its ambitions into actions.

> Organization is defined by the formal structure, coordination and control systems, and the organization culture.

Organization: Structure, Framework, Systems, Values   Research on this general issue has applied many perspectives. Many studies use specialized terms, such as *organization context, architecture,* or *gestalt,* but they share the same premise: **Organization** within the international company is a function of how the company defines the formal structure that specifies the framework for work, develops the systems that coordinate and control what gets done, and cultivates a set of shared values and ideals among employees around the world.

This chapter looks at the components of organization in an international business. We begin by examining the idea of structure, move on to coordination and control systems, and culminate with a profile of how employees think, act, and behave in the context of organization culture. The chapter then closes with a discussion of the special situations in international business that shape how a company designs its organization.

> Structure is the formal arrangement of jobs within a company that specifies roles and relationships.

Organization Structure

Organization structure—the formal arrangement of roles, responsibilities, and relationships within an organization—is a powerful tool with which to implement strategy. Recall our profile of Zara in Chapter 11; managers believe that how they had designed their company was an instrumental aspect of its success. "Our structure," said Inditex CEO Jose Maria Castellano, "gives us tremendous advantages over our competition." International companies specify the structure that groups individuals and operational units in ways that managers believe best support the strategy of the firm. For example, if an MNE is pursuing a multidomestic strategy but designs a structure that delegates little responsibility to local subsidiaries, it will likely fail to implement its strategy.

Ultimately, a company's choice of structure depends on many factors, including the configuration of the company's value chain in terms of the location and type of foreign facilities, as well as the impact of international operations on total corporate performance. More immediately, two issues stand out: vertical differentiation, the matter of how the company balances centralization versus decentralization in decision making; and horizontal differentiation, the matter of how the company opts to divide itself into specific units to do specific jobs. We now look at each more closely.

VERTICAL DIFFERENTIATION: CENTRALIZATION VERSUS DECENTRALIZATION

Our discussion of strategy in Chapter 11 shows that every MNE faces the tough task of balancing global integration with local differentiation. This polarity can be expressed in many ways, such as efficiency versus effectiveness, standardization versus customization, or even science versus art. Irrespective of the terms used, the dilemma is the same: All companies must address who has what authority to make what decisions. For example, who makes factory location decisions? Where does the responsibility for product development and promotion lie? Do senior managers at the home office or the staff of local subsidiaries decide whom to hire and whom to fire? What are the responsibilities of foreign subsidiaries in terms of, how, when, and what they report to headquarters?

As we saw in our opening case, J&J's efforts to implement its strategy required that headquarters decide how much authority to delegate among various parties, including directors of subsidiaries, primary and support departments, operating plants, sales offices, distribution centers, and other units. In broad terms, determining where in the hierarchy the authority to make decisions stands is the issue of **vertical differentiation.** In practical terms, companies determine where in their hierarchy the authority to make decisions should go by working out the issue of centralization versus decentralization.

In some MNEs, top managers make all the decisions and lower-level managers and employees simply carry out their orders. At the other extreme are MNEs that push decision making down to the managers who are closest to the action, assigning them the responsibility to provide substantive input into the decision-making process or delegating them the authority to actually make decisions. The former companies are centralized, and the latter decentralized.

Differentiation means that the organization is composed of different units that work on different kinds of tasks.

Centralization Versus Decentralization in Organizational Design   For the MNE, the rule of thumb is that decisions made at the foreign-subsidiary level are considered decentralized, whereas those made above the foreign-subsidiary level are considered centralized. Table 15.1 shows that **centralization** and **decentralization** are based on different principles and beliefs, with each having its pros and cons for how a company designs its organization.

Centralization is the degree to which high-level managers, usually above the country level, make strategic decisions and pass them to lower levels for implementation.

We usually associate centralized decision making with an international or global strategy, decentralized decision making with a multidomestic strategy, and a combination of the two with a transnational strategy. The reason for choosing one over the other is partly a function of companies' attitudes. For example, the ethnocentric attitude one likely finds in an international company encourages it to develop core competencies in its home country and then supervise their transfer and use abroad. A polycentric attitude, of the sort found

TABLE 15.1   The Principles and Practice of Centralization and Decentralization

Centralization	Decentralization
Premise	**Premise**
Decisions should be made by senior managers who have the experience, expertise, and judgment to find the best course of action for the company	Decisions should be made by the employees who are closest to and most familiar with the situation
The effective configuration and coordination of the value chain depend on headquarters retaining authority over what happens	The effective configuration and coordination of the value chain depend on headquarters letting local managers deal with local market conditions
Centralized decision making ensures that operations in different countries help achieve global objectives	Decentralized decision making ensures that operations in different countries work toward achieving global objectives by meeting national goals
Advantages	**Advantages**
Facilitates coordination of the value chain	Decisions made by those who directly deal with customers, competitors, and markets
Ensures that decisions are consistent with strategic objectives	Encourages lower-level managers to exercise initiative
Gives senior executives the authority to direct major change	Motivates greater effort to do a better job by lower-level employees
Preempts duplicating activities across various subsidiaries	Enables more flexible response to rapid environmental changes
Reduces the risk that lower-level employees make costly, wrong decisions	Permits holding subsidiary managers more accountable for their unit's performance
Ensures consistent dealing with stakeholders—government officials, employees, suppliers, consumers, and the general public	
Disadvantages	**Disadvantages**
Discourages initiative among lower-level employees	Puts the organization at risk if many bad decisions are made at lower levels
Demoralized lower-level employees simply wait to be told what to do	Impedes cross-unit coordination and capture of strategic fits
Information flows from the top down, thereby preempting possible innovations from bottom-up information flow	Subsidiary will likely favor its own projects and performance at the expense of global or overall performance
Factors Encouraging More Centralization	**Factors Encouraging More Decentralization**
General environment and specific industry call for global integration and worldwide uniformity of products, purchases, methods, and policies	General environment and specific industry call for local responsiveness
Interdependent subsidiaries that share value activities or deal with common competitors and customers	Products, purchases, methods, and policies are suitable for local adaptation
Need for company to move its resources—capital, personnel, or technology—from one value activity to another	Economies of scale can be achieved via national production
Lower-level managers are not as capable or experienced at making decisions as upper-level managers	Lower-level managers are capable and experienced at making decisions
Decisions are important and the risk of loss is great	Decisions are relatively minor but must be made quickly
	Company is geographically dispersed
	Low need for foreign nationals to reach senior-level headquarters positions

Decentralization is the degree to which lower-level managers, usually at or below the country level, make and implement strategic decisions.

Decision making should occur at the level of the people who are most directly affected and have the most intimate knowledge about the problem.

in the company pursuing a multidomestic strategy like J&J, encourages it to decentralize decision making to foreign subsidiaries because headquarters believes that people on the spot know best what to do. The company pursuing a transnational strategy would actively balance the competing needs for centralization and decentralization, aiming for a sensitivity that enables it to deal simultaneously with global and local pressures.

The idea of centralization versus decentralization, though often represented as an either-or proposition, is in actuality marked by trade-offs, compromises, and exceptions. Simply put, as we saw with J&J, the locus of decision making is a long-running contest between managers at headquarters and those at the local subsidiary. If anything, this contest highlights the idea that an MNE is never completely centralized or decentralized. Few organizations could function effectively if all decisions were made by a select group of top managers. Nor, for that matter, could organizations function if all decisions were delegated to employees at the lowest levels.

HORIZONTAL DIFFERENTIATION: THE DESIGN OF THE FORMAL STRUCTURE

MNEs must horizontally differentiate their international operations—that is, managers must divide the company into discrete units that are assigned responsibility for specialized tasks. More specifically, **horizontal differentiation** describes how the company designs its formal structure to perform three functions:

- Specify the total set of organizational tasks
- Divide those tasks into jobs, departments, subsidiaries, and divisions so the work gets done
- Assign authority and authority relationships to make sure work gets done in ways that support the company's strategy

In traditional terms, MNEs resolved these issues on the basis of function, type of business, geographic area, or some combination of these three factors. We now examine the specific design standards of each.

Functional structures

- Group specialized jobs according to traditional business functions.
- Are popular among companies with narrow product lines.

Functional Structure   A **functional structure,** as depicted in Figure 15.3(a), is the ideal way to organize work when a company's products share a common technology and competitive pressures push for a global strategy. A functional structure helps managers maximize scale economies by arranging work responsibilities and relationships in the most efficient format. So, for example, this structure creates specific departments that group personnel in terms of traditional business functions—that is, production people work with other production people, marketing people work with other marketing people, finance works with other finance people, and so on.

Advantages and Disadvantages   Functional divisions are popular among companies with a narrow range of products, particularly if the production and marketing methods are undifferentiated among them, and where market change is more measured than erratic. For instance, oil and mineral extraction companies, such as ExxonMobil or British Petroleum, commonly use this structure.

A weakness of a functional structure is its inability to respond to environmental changes that require coordination between departments. This structure struggles to build the knowledge-generating and decision-making relationships that facilitate marketing people to coordinate their decisions with people in the production and finance departments. The vertical differentiation of a functional structure—a long chain of command that spans many levels of the hierarchy—often results in deliberate decision making that moves more slowly as the volume of data expands faster than the layers of the hierarchy can process it.

FIGURE 15.3 Common Organizational Structures for International Business

Though shown here in highly simplified forms, these five types of structure have been adopted by most companies that conduct international business. Remember, however, that many companies prefer mixed structures tailored to the particular circumstances and requirements of their chosen strategy.

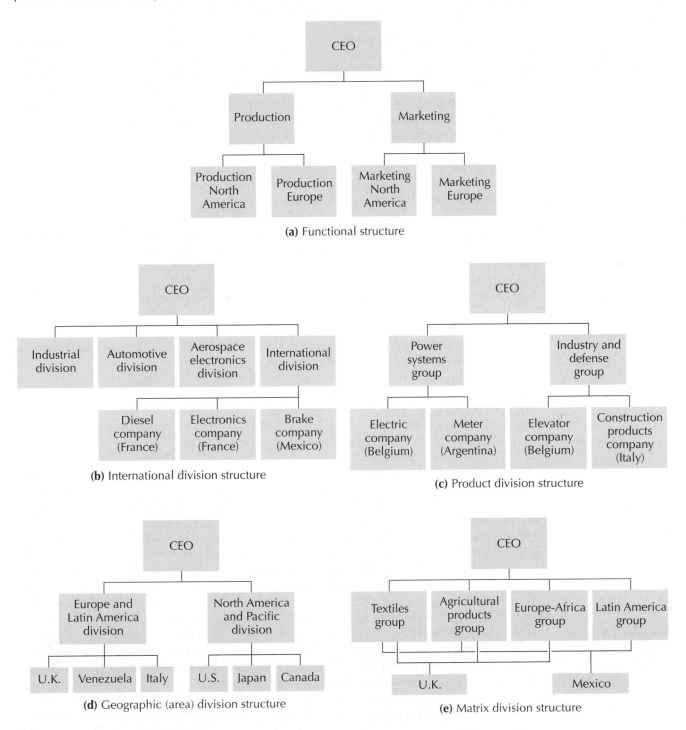

(a) Functional structure

(b) International division structure

(c) Product division structure

(d) Geographic (area) division structure

(e) Matrix division structure

Divisional structures

- Group units, products, customers, or geographic regions.
- Duplicate each function across all of the divisions.

Divisional Structure   Whereas executives specify roles and relationships in a functional structure in terms of inputs, they use the **divisional structure** format to specify them according to outputs. Each division in a company is assigned responsibility for a different set of products or markets. In theory, an MNE can opt for an international division, a global product structure, or a worldwide area structure.

International Division Structure   Grouping each international business activity into its own division puts internationally specialized personnel together to handle such diverse matters as export documentation, foreign-exchange transactions, and relations with foreign governments (Figure 15.3[b]). This structure's quick response to environmental changes enables the company to deal with several different markets. Also, this structure prevents duplication of these activities in more than one place in the organization.

An international division

- Creates a critical mass of international expertise.
- Often struggles to get resources from domestic divisions.

Domestic division managers are often evaluated on the basis of performance within the domestic divisions for which they are responsible. As such, they may withhold their products, personnel, technology, and other resources from international operations to boost their performance. An international division can preempt this tendency if it is large enough to enable personnel within the division to wield power within the larger organization.

The segmentation of an MNE into discrete divisions does frustrate its ability to exploit economies of scale or scope. Given the separation between domestic and foreign divisions, this structure is probably best suited for multidomestic strategies that demand little integration and standardization between domestic and foreign operations. Still, managers in an international division structure try to use methods like shared logistics or budget routines to achieve possible points of manufacturing integration or administrative coordination. Historically, this form of structure has been less popular among European MNEs relative to their U.S. counterparts largely because the latter depend much more on the domestic market.

Product Division Structure   Product divisions, as Figure 15.3(c) depicts, are probably the most popular among international companies today, largely because most companies' businesses involve a variety of diverse products.[5] For example, the merger of Moët Hennessy and Louis Vuitton created the world's largest luxury goods group, LVMH, which lists Christian Dior perfume, Tag Heuer watches, Louis Vuitton trunks, and Moët & Chandon champagne among its many brands. The dissimilarity among its many products led managers to split LVMH into five divisions, each focusing on a single product segment for its global market: wines and spirits; fashion and leather goods; perfumes and cosmetics; watches and jewelry; and selective retailing. Although there are overlaps in target markets, distribution channels, and supply chains, divisions tend to be independent.

As is true for the functional structure, the product division structure is well suited for a global strategy because both the foreign and domestic operations for a given product report to the same manager, who can find synergies between the two (e.g., by sharing information on the successes and failures of each one).

Product divisions are popular among international companies with diverse products.

Furthermore, a separate product group structure enhances a company's ability to sell or spin off certain product lines because they are not as interwoven with its other lines. Most likely, there will be duplicate functions and activities among the product divisions. Moreover, there is no formal means by which one product division can learn from another's international experience.

Finally, different subsidiaries from different product divisions within the same foreign country report to different groups at headquarters. For example, Figure 15.3(c) illustrates that the Belgian electric and elevator subsidiaries report to different headquarters divisions. So synergy could be lost within countries if different subsidiaries don't communicate with each other or with a common manager. Similarly, at one time in Westinghouse, one subsidiary was borrowing funds locally at an exorbitant rate while another unit in the same country had excess cash.

Geographic (Area) Division Structure   Companies are prone to using geographic divisions, as depicted in Figure 15.3(d), when they have large foreign operations that are not dominated by a single country or region (including the home country). This structure is more common to European MNEs than for U.S. MNEs; the latter tend to be dominated by their large domestic market. This sort of structure is useful when managers can gain economies of scale in production on a regional rather than on a global basis because of market size or the particular sorts of production technologies for the industry. Historically, this structure has been commonly associated with companies pursuing multidomestic strategies. This structure's degree of decentralization gives country managers leeway to adapt operations to local conditions.

A drawback of this structure is the potential for duplication of work among areas as the company locates similar value activities in several places rather than consolidating them in the most efficient place. For example, Nestlé had more than 500 factories in nearly 90 countries that sold its 8,000 brands to almost every country in the world. Consequently, headquarters in Switzerland struggled to determine the costs of raw materials its subsidiaries bought from suppliers from around the world. In an extreme case, each of Nestlé's more than 40 U.S. factories purchased raw materials independently. This lack of coordination, compounded by the fact that Nestlé used five different e-mail systems, meant that its U.S. factories were paying more than 20 different prices for vanilla to the same supplier.[6]

> Geographic divisions are popular when foreign operations are large and not dominated by a single country or region.

Matrix Structure   Some MNEs pursue strategies that try simultaneously to deal with competing pressures for global integration and local responsiveness. This choice requires designing a **matrix structure,** as depicted in Figure 15.3(e), one that simultaneously attains the benefits of functional and divisional structures. Rather than formally subordinating either integration or responsiveness, a matrix structure theoretically equips an MNE to gain the benefits of both in addition to preventing it from prematurely excluding one.

A matrix structure specifies that a subsidiary reports to more than one group (functional, product, or geographic). The basic premise is that making each group share responsibility for foreign operations will encourage each group to exchange information and resources more willingly.[7] For example, product-group managers must compete among themselves to ensure that R&D personnel attached to a functional group, such as production, develop technologies for their product groups. These product-group managers also must compete to ensure that their geographic counterparts pay enough attention to their product lines.

> A matrix organization
> * Institutes overlaps among functional and divisional forms.
> * Gives functional, product, and geographic groups a common focus.
> * Has dual-reporting relationships rather than a single line of command.

Advantages and Disadvantages   Product groups, functional groups, and geographic groups must all compete among themselves to obtain the resources others hold in the matrix. For example, the amount of resources needed to develop textile products in Mexico depends partly on the competition between Europe-Africa and Latin America groups and partly on the competition between textiles and the agricultural products groups for resources. Consequently, the matrix structure is a useful compromise when managers face difficulty integrating or separating foreign operations.

A matrix structure has drawbacks. It requires that groups compete for scarce resources, preferred operating methods, shares of reward, or shares of risk. Likely disputes among lower-level managers require that upper management step in to decide. Besides delaying the decision, upper management may favor a specific executive or group to the annoyance of the other group. As others in the organization see this happen, they may conclude the locus of power lies with a certain individual or group. In this case, group managers reason they are destined to lose, stop championing their group's unique needs, and thereby eliminate the multiple knowledge-generating and decision-making relationships that a matrix is supposed to engage.

WHAT ABOUT THE UNITY-OF-COMMAND PRINCIPLE?   Most notably, a matrix structure institutes a dual hierarchy that violates the **unity-of-command principle.** This principle holds that an unbroken chain of command and communication should flow from the senior executive to the worker on the factory floor. Often the resulting blurred lines of responsibilities and relationships within a matrix structure confuse the clarity of the chain of command.

In this situation, superiors may not monitor their subordinates because they wrongly assume someone else is doing so. For instance, managers in the Latin America group might ignore the day-to-day operations at the Mexican textile unit because they figure that their counterparts in the textile division are responsible for doing so. Meanwhile, managers in the textile division may wrongly assume that the Latin America group is overseeing its Mexican operations.

More specifically, the CEO of Dow Chemical, an early adopter of the matrix structure, explains, "We were an organization that was matrixed and depended on teamwork, but there was no one in charge. When things went well, we didn't know whom to reward; and when things went poorly, we didn't know whom to blame."[8] The misassumption that someone else was handling the responsibility has led some companies, like Dow Chemical, ABB, and Citibank, to return to structures that specify roles and relationships.[9]

Mixed Structure   In reality, the organizational charts of few MNEs neatly mimic a strictly functional, divisional, or matrix structure. This circumstance leads us to the final format— the **mixed structure**—that combines various functional, area, and product dimensions.

Because of growth dynamics, companies seldom, if ever, get all of their activities to correspond to the basic organizational structures described here. Most develop a mixed structure. For example, a recent acquisition might report to headquarters until it can be consolidated efficiently within an existing product division. Or circumstances regarding a particular function, product, or country might require it to be handled separately—that is, apart from the overall structure.

Similarly, changes in industry conditions, firm capabilities, and institutional environments often require structures to change at an uneven pace. For example, IBM's recent European reorganization aimed to "have decision-making staff closer to customers." This goal required that it reduce the scale of IBM's EMEA (Europe, Middle East, and Africa) headquarters, a major unit in place since the end of World War II, and move many of its responsibilities to two new, much smaller, hubs in Madrid and Zurich.[10]

Some operations may be wholly owned, thus enabling a denser network of communications to develop than in other operations where there is only partial or no ownership of the foreign operations. Further, the overall structure gives an incomplete picture of divisions in the organization.

CONTEMPORARY STRUCTURES

Some MNEs find that the preceding types of structures, typically referred to as traditional structures, provide an inadequate format to respond to the demands of their dynamic environments and complex strategies.[11] Specifically, there is a sense that increasing international activities, expanding internal relationships, rising expectations of foreign customers, and growing power of knowledge-based strategies create opportunities that exceed the range of traditional structures. Moreover, lower trade barriers and cheaper telecommunications and computing capabilities enable a globally dispersed labor force to collaborate more easily.

These changes push MNEs from the classic structure of separate businesses organized in different countries to a worldwide company that can divide and parcel out work to the most efficient locations. Or, in the words of the CEO of IBM, "work flows to the places where it will be done best; that is, most efficiently and to the highest quality."[12] Capitalizing on these opportunities spurs MNEs to conceive ways to arrange roles and responsibilities so more employees, particularly those on the front line, who deal more directly with resources and markets, have greater authority. Giving individuals freedom to make decisions positions them to do great things, as we saw in our opening profile of J&J. Thus the past few years have seen companies structure work in new ways that make them more locally responsive without sacrificing the potential of global integration.

Each firm's structure reflects its particular

- Administrative legacies.
- Executive preferences.
- Market circumstances.

CONCEPT CHECK

Recall from our discussion of "Types of Economic Systems" in Chapter 4 that a **mixed economy** combines some of the benefits of a free market with certain features that typify centrally planned systems. We note here that, interestingly, *mixed organizational structures* reflect a similar imperative to sacrifice purity to practicality; in particular, managers often customize "model" organizational configurations to accommodate the unique demands of their businesses and industries.

CONCEPT CHECK

In discussing "The Forces Behind Globalization" in Chapter 1, we explain how such factors as expanded technology, liberalized trade, and increased cross-national cooperation work to shape and reconfigure the external environment of **international business.** Here we emphasize that, in recognizing changes as opportunities, many companies experiment with organizational structures that will make them more responsive to environmental changes and business opportunities.

Case: IBM in Europe   IBM is a case in point.[13] Like many MNEs operating in Europe, IBM had pursued a multidomestic strategy supported by a geographic area structure that provided for a subsidiary for each country. IBM relied on a regional office in Paris to oversee its national subsidiaries and consolidate operations where possible.

Integration within the European Union in the 1990s pushed IBM to move more decision making from local subsidiaries to its regional office in the effort to develop a pan-European strategy that would achieve greater cross-national integration. Then, in 2005, IBM announced it would lay off up to 13,000 workers, mostly in Europe, and hire up to 14,000 workers in India. This was part of an ongoing evolution in its strategy of globalizing its operations by moving back-office work, like accounting, compliance, call support, and procurement, to low-cost locations.

Technological, regulatory, and competitive pressures pushed IBM to dismantle the national and regional fiefdoms it had established in each country in Europe in the post-war years in favor of hiring Indian software engineers who could work on projects anywhere in the world via the Internet. IBM reasoned that it no longer made sense to maintain traditional types of structures when it could, as its rivals had, adopt a leaner, global style of operation that let managers send work digitally across the Internet to where it could be done most efficiently. Dealing with the new realities of organizing international operations, IBM maintains the company is "still going to have deep roots locally, but we are increasingly globalizing our operations and processes."[14]

Removing Structural Boundaries   Examples of contemporary structures take on a range of names, such as *learning organization, virtual organization,* or *modular structure.* No matter the variations in the name, they all share the same premise: A structure should not be defined by, or limited to, the horizontal, vertical, or external boundaries that block the development of knowledge-generating and decision-making relationships in the company and would cause people to control, not share, information.

These ideas were popularized by Jack Welch, former chairman and CEO of General Electric, who wanted to eliminate vertical and horizontal boundaries within the company as well as break down barriers between the company and its customers, suppliers, and other stakeholders. In his words:

> *The simplest definition of what we are trying to create—what our objective is—is a boundaryless company, a company where the artificial barriers and walls people are forever building around themselves or each other—for status, security, or to keep change away—are demolished and everyone has access to the same information, everyone pulls in the same direction, and everyone shares in the rewards of winning—in the soul as well as in the wallet.*[15]

Contemporary structures, therefore, aim to have few to no boundaries between different vertical ranks and functions, different units in different geographic locations, and between the firm and its suppliers, distributors, joint-venture partners, strategic allies, and customers.

In practical terms, **boundaries** refer to the horizontal constraints that follow from having specific employees only do specific jobs in specific units and the vertical constraints that separate employees into specific levels of the hierarchy. Horizontal and vertical boundaries are characteristics of traditional structures. Effectively, each degree of specification in the hierarchy of a company in a traditional structure installs boundaries that block the movement of ideas. In response, contemporary structures call for loosely connected networks that self-organize and self-govern. Managers maximize information flows by minimizing the structure that gets in the way of people developing knowledge-generating and decision-making relationships.

Contemporary structures, for example, question the purpose and largely reject the features of traditional structures, like chains of command, formal departments, and precise reporting relationships. In their place, they champion notions of limitless spans of control, ad hoc teams, and self-organizing groups. We now profile leading examples of contemporary structures: the network and virtual organization.

Boundarylessness refers to eliminating vertical, horizontal, and external boundaries that hinder information flows.

FIGURE 15.4   Simplified Network Structure

At the center of the network structure is a core unit: Its function is to outsource value-adding activities for which it does not possess *core competencies*. The network itself consists of partner organizations that focus on areas in which they can deliver maximum value. Finally, there are the channels through which units communicate with other units. To manage the network, the core unit uses these channels to coordinate and integrate activities carried on throughout the system.

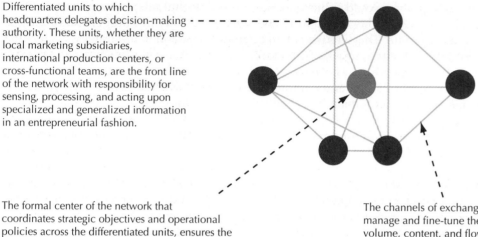

Differentiated units to which headquarters delegates decision-making authority. These units, whether they are local marketing subsidiaries, international production centers, or cross-functional teams, are the front line of the network with responsibility for sensing, processing, and acting upon specialized and generalized information in an entrepreneurial fashion.

The formal center of the network that coordinates strategic objectives and operational policies across the differentiated units, ensures the efficient flow of resources, supplies, components, and funds throughout the network, and effectively collects, sorts, and distributes the organization's accumulated wisdom, knowledge, and experiences.

The channels of exchange that manage and fine-tune the volume, content, and flow of hard and soft information. These linkages animate the network by setting paths of interaction, coordination, and integration between differentiated yet interdependent functional, area, and product units.

A network structure anchors a small core organization that outsources value activities to other firms.

Network Structure   An emergent structural option for managers is the **network structure,** in which a small core organization outsources value activities that it does not command a core competency to those that do (see Figure 15.4). This approach lets organizations focus on activities in which they create maximum value and contract out activities to those companies that can do them better than they do—or, as the saying goes, "Do what you do best and outsource the rest."

MNEs like Nike, L. L. Bean, and Cisco Systems emphasize their design skills and hire other MNEs, like Sanmina or Flextronics, to make their products. Similarly, many financial institutions, hotel chains, and credit card companies have found that they can create more value by offshoring call center functions to those companies that have a core competency in that activity.

A network structure helps MNEs to outsource activities, from manufacturing to service calls, while still maintaining a unifying sense of organization. That is, the relationship between the MNE and the companies in its network is not merely a matter of efficient ordering and order fulfillment processes that adhere to specific contractual parameters. Rather, the network structure promotes a web of relationships between the different companies in ways that let managers keep track of the work flow even though it is being done by other companies. Essentially, MNE partners with select suppliers and then develops specialized decision-making relationships that let the collectivity of companies jointly manage value activities.[16]

CONCEPT CHECK

The ideas of *networks* and *networking* are fundamental to discussions of **international business** in a variety of areas. In Chapter 7, for instance, we describe the kinds *of trade networks* formalized by the **WTO** and detail the various regional economic agreements designed to unite individual countries into integrated economic markets. In Chapter 9, we discuss the financial network composed of *global capital markets*, and in Chapter 14, we analyze the effort of companies to network with global partners by means of *collaborative alliances*.

The Japanese Keiretsu   Though a novel format for many MNEs today, variations of the network structure have been in play in other countries for many years. Japanese companies use the so-called *keiretsu* structure, basically an integrated collectivity of nominally independent companies in which each company owns a small percentage of others in the network. Many German companies are similarly intertwined, but there is no formal term to describe them.[17]

Keiretsus, as they work in Japan, rely on long-term personal relationships among executives in the different companies. The same directors often serve on more than one board. Sometimes *keiretsus* are vertical—for example, the network between Toyota and its parts suppliers. Sometimes they are horizontal and no single company dominates, as is the case with the Mitsubishi *keiretsu.*

Virtual Organization   A **virtual organization** is the antithesis of a traditional vertical hierarchy. Rather than seeking to control value chain activities through direct ownership of businesses, virtual organizations acquire resources or strategic capabilities by creating a temporary network of independent companies, suppliers, customers, and even rivals.

> A virtual organization is a temporary arrangement among partners that can be easily reassembled to adapt to market change.

This dynamic network, much like the sort we see developing at micro-multinationals, relies on information technology to create the links needed to share skills, costs, and access to one another's markets.[18] The inspiration for this structural approach largely comes from the film industry in which people from around the world are essentially "free agents" who move from project to project applying their skills—directing, talent search, costuming, makeup, set design—as needed.

Case: StrawberryFrog   Operationally, a virtual organization consists of a core of full-time employees that hires outside specialists to work on opportunities that arise. One example is StrawberryFrog, an international advertising agency. The peculiar name of this company was inspired by a rare amphibian with a red body and blue legs; its CEO explains that the nimble strawberry frog is the opposite of the existing "dinosaur agencies, established in the industrial age as monoliths, which have the greatest difficulty in adapting to the new era."[19]

> The flexibility of virtual structures means poorly performing partners can be simply replaced.

Competing with companies employing thousands, StrawberryFrog has just 100 people, known as "frogs," in its two offices—25 in New York and 75 in Amsterdam. It bulks up as needed by enlisting select freelancers from around the world.[20] Free of the overhead, constraints, and complexity of hierarchies, StrawberryFrog offers clients agility and cost-effectiveness. The company has leveraged its loosely coupled network to do work in Europe, Asia, and the United States for Mitsubishi, Sony Ericsson, Pfizer, Sprint, IKEA, MTV, and Research in Motion.

Finally, the use of temporary arrangements among members means that the virtual organization can quickly assemble and reassemble itself to meet a changing competitive environment.[21] Market mechanisms such as contracts, rather than hierarchy and authority, hold the virtual organization together; poorly performing companies are removed and replaced by better performing companies.

Some Pitfalls of Contemporary Structures   As we've already seen, hierarchies suffer from endemic limitations; so, too, do contemporary structures. Reports suggest that despite leaders championing decentralization, when push comes to shove, they intrude in decision making. Senior managers struggle with living by the promise not to intervene in a worker's stated rights to creative independence and self-direction. Reports further indicate that frequent managerial intervention erodes the credibility of this promise and creates motivational problems.

In some cases, contemporary organizations of various sorts have given way to more traditional structures.[22] More fundamentally, however, is the threat of hidden hierarchies lying latent in contemporary structures. One observer says, "I've been inside a lot of companies that espouse flat organizational structures and self-management. But when you really start looking at how things actually work, you find that there is in fact a hierarchy—just one that is not explicit."[23] Seemingly inevitable, workers are prone to organize around the rules, rewards, and punishments in the company, slowly creating a subtle, unspoken hierarchy even if officially there is none.

These difficulties and frustrations make the idea of a contemporary organization less appealing. However, few dispute the potential for innovation supported by a nonhierarchical organizational structure that encourages sharing, not controlling information, to say nothing of its elimination of boundaries that interfere with decision-making relationships. Companies, analysts argue, must rethink their hierarchical structures if they intended to unleash the power of their executives and to capture the opportunities of today's economy. Getting past the initial challenge of learning to do things in new ways is a frontier many companies face.

Moving forward, research finds, means overcoming barriers to adaptability that are "deeply rooted in the nature of organizations: inflexibility in the mental models of their managers; organizational complexity, driven by the demands of execution; and mismatches between current resources and future opportunities."[24] Ultimately, managers caught between the dilemma of a hierarchy or hyperarchy need to rethink what GE's former CEO, Jack Welch, has called an organization's "social architecture"—the bringing together of individual behavior, structure, and culture.

Point Counterpoint

Hierarchies or Hyperarchies?

Point Proponents of the classic hierarchy argue that this format is the enduring foundation for how managers across the world determine the optimal degrees of work specialization. They find hierarchy to be the best approach to departmentalization and building an efficient chain of command, while at the same time offering a functional span of control. They also believe it offers the ideal degree of rules, regulations, policies, procedures, and the right balance between centralization and decentralization. Indeed, many see hierarchy as the basis of the tried-and-true professional management model.

First developed in the 1920s by General Motors, DuPont, Sears, and Standard Oil, hierarchical structures, like functional, divisional, and matrix formats, have provided powerful frameworks that have guided the international expansions of thousands of companies from virtually every country in the world. The absolute clarity of decision making in a hierarchy—its bias toward extreme degrees of vertical and horizontal differentiation—enables companies to develop sophisticated planning systems, information systems, and control systems that allow top management to command and control operations. One of the great advocates of this hierarchy structure, Harold Geneen of ITT, believed it helped him in his quest "to make people as predictable and controllable as the capital resources that they're responsible for."[25]

Certainly, supporters of the long-proven authority of hierarchy recognize the implication of technological, regulatory, and competitive trends to organizational standards. They realize the environments of international business are changing and so, too, are companies' strategies and organizations. In response to this, rather than discard the principles of hierarchy, they reason that its strong foundation will lead to future success.

Counterpoint In contrast, some scholars herald the dawn of a new organizational form that helps companies identify and exploit opportunities ahead of their competitors. Many see the challenge lying in managing and analyzing the abundance of information flowing into the company.

Often hierarchy organizes information flows in ways that work against integrating all the pieces. Despite its best intentions, vertically designed structures, even with matrix and ad hoc overlays, slow information, make work more complex, and erode the efficiency of decision making.[27] Responding to the expanding data requires developing an organization that enables sharing throughout the company. While some refer to this sort of organization as a *social network,* and others call it a *peer-to-peer format,* the common term is *hyperarchy.*

Technically, a hyperarchy is "a large-scale, self-organizing community that sets free unusually high degrees of energy and engagement—despite the lack of clear or direct economic payoff for participants."[28] As such, a hyperarchy can unleash the intrinsic motivation of employees, thereby letting it get past hierarchy's tendency to stifle a worker's ability to adapt, innovate, and take calculated risks.

In a hyperarchy, "information flows along multiple and intermediate paths; this allows for multiple and overlapping points at which information can be sorted and interpreted. It makes it possible to process an abundance of information effectively."[29] A hyperarchy also provides a format that remedies the intrinsic limitation of the hierarchy as well as positions a company to better deal with the emerging environment of globalization.[30]

Perhaps the best-known hyperarchy is the Linux project, the vanguard of the broader open-source software movement in which program source code is given away to volunteers

Moreover, managers are redoubling their efforts to fortify this foundation by reengineering business functions and processes with the help of programs like total quality management, scenario and contingency planning, supply chain management, and Six Sigma. They believe these efforts clarify the division of work and differentiation of authority.[26]

On the flip side, defenders of hierarchy also point out that moving from the rhetoric of new forms of boundaryless structures to the day-to-day reality of coordinating and controlling international operations is a huge leap. Avoiding a steep, costly fall calls for common sense and thoughtful adjustment to the way organizations run. ●

who help fix bugs and design new features without any direct monetary compensation. Operationally, hyperarchy engages a battery of simple rules to increase transparency and symmetry of information. Because Linux programmers are able to see what others in the network are doing, everyone has an incentive to reciprocate when others share information with them. In the course of such sharing, participants build reputations, good or bad, throughout the community. Thus, reciprocity and reputation work together to establish trust as the primary transaction currency in hyperarchy.

The contest between hierarchies and hyperarchies will likely be determined by the environment in which companies operate within. In the end, the main purpose of structure is to arrange work so that a company can effectively implement its strategy. As such, some contend that the twenty-first century has ushered in a fundamental shift in our idea of organization. Now, markets reward companies that build an organization without boundaries that can support an energizing strategic purpose rather than precisely designing a structure that looks great on paper but falls apart in the stress-test of reality.

Finally, some point to events at Intel as possibly foreshadowing how the contest between hierarchies and hyperarchies might shake out. Andy Grove, CEO of Intel for many years, believes that an organizational structure must find ways to encourage and energize constructive confrontation in ways that let people agree and disagree but, ultimately, commit to the same goals. The challenge for management is to develop a structure that, as Grove reasons, enables them to "let chaos reign and then rein in chaos."[31] ●

Coordination and Control Systems

Thus far we've looked at the idea of structural differentiation—the vertical and the horizontal dimensions, or the lack thereof, found in a company's structure. Still, at the outset of the chapter, we noted that MNEs must also deal with the question of how to coordinate and control the activities that make up their value chains. Again, as we saw in the case of Zara and eBay in Chapter 11, MNEs are increasingly devising sophisticated strategies to create value. These strategies challenge managers to then build the coordination methods and control measures that complement the company's chosen organizational structure (and, as we see in the next section, the organization culture that shapes individual attitudes and actions). Research consistently reports that MNEs use several coordination and control tools to manage their value chains. We now profile each.

COORDINATION SYSTEMS

The importance of **coordination** follows from the reality of life in the MNE. The division of value activities across countries often leads different groups of managers and employees to develop different concerns and orientations. Depending on whether they are headquarters or subsidiary based, or working in primary or support value activities, employees tend to think and act in ways that are anchored in their immediate responsibilities. If unchecked, this tendency can lead employees in separate functions, subsidiaries, and countries to stop

CONCEPT CHECK

In Chapter 2, we note that managers deal with differences in the ways in which colleagues and subordinates (especially those from foreign **cultures**) respond when it comes to such issues as work motivation, relationship preferences, and other factors in workplace behavior. Here we observe that, in their efforts to accommodate these differences, global companies heed different behavioral practices and cultural orientations when deciding how to coordinate activities.

thinking about their counterparts. In turn, this makes it difficult for managers to develop the knowledge-generating and decision-making relationships that coordinate worldwide activities into an integrated whole. In extreme circumstances, people may deliberately or mistakenly act in self-serving ways to the detriment of the company. Without some means to coordinate what people do, the competitiveness of a value chain, no matter how brilliantly configured, will erode.

Approaches to Coordination   Managers tap several approaches to coordinate the operations of interdependent units and individuals. We now turn to three prevalent approaches to the process of coordination: *coordination by standardization*, *by plans*, and *by mutual adjustment*.

Coordination by Standardization
Companies with far-flung operations aim to establish a day-to-day infrastructure that prescribes many of the ways that employees do their jobs, work with one another, and deal with customers. A key motivation is the realization that a high degree of operational consistency helps the company leverage its core competency as well as brings the advantages of scale to its organization of activities. Therefore, MNEs specify routines that standardize many features of operations, ranging from the mundane, for instance dress and decorum that are spelled out in employee manuals, to the strategic, such as dealing with joint-venture partners or assessing potential markets.

Starbucks, for example, standardizes many features of its products, processes, and procedures to replicate the look, operations, and feel of the elusive atmosphere of its U.S. coffee shop concept to their thousands of shops around the world. Standardization, by prescribing how managers and workers do their jobs, installs the policies to coordinate decisions among units in the company.

Growing pressure to leverage innovations across value activities pushes many MNEs to expand standardization to also specify rules and regulations about how employees interact. Technically called formalization, this method of coordination aims to reduce the sorts of workplace uncertainty that complicate the exchange of ideas and resources. For example, formalizing distribution lists for production or marketing updates eliminates potential oversights in how the MNE collects, processes, and disseminates information.

An important assumption underlying coordination by standardization is that company rules and procedures apply to every situation in every unit in every country where it has operations. Regular exceptions to the rules undermine the authority of standardization and create points of uncertainty that impede coordination. Consequently, coordination by standardization is ideally suited for international or global strategies that champion constancy and predictability in industries that are more stable than volatile.

In the case of the international strategy, the intent to transfer, protect, and leverage core competencies spurs explicit specification of rules and regulations. In the case of the global strategy, the deep integration among typically consolidated value activities leaves little slack for surprises: Resources and components are needed at specific plants at specific times otherwise production grinds to a halt. Standardizing coordination methods—such as the structures for processing information—helps eliminate delays and mistakes.

Coordination by Plan
The fact that industry conduct, competitive dynamics, host-government attitudes, and many other factors differ among countries greatly complicates coordination by standardization. Some companies are more sensitive to this pressure than others, particularly those that create value by adapting operations to local conditions. Notably, MNEs following a multidomestic strategy, versus those following a geocentric strategy, are more likely to reason that coordination by standardization is not the best approach.

Coordination by standardization

- Sets universal rules and procedures that apply to units worldwide.
- Enforces consistency in performance of activities in geographically dispersed units.

Although diversity may preclude universal rules and procedures, it does not excuse managers of the responsibility of coordinating value activities. In such situations, the MNE may opt to establish objectives and schedules that give interdependent units greater discretion in developing coordination systems.

Relying on general objectives and detailed schedules, rather than rules and regulations, is the basis for coordination by plan. Provided they comply with the deadlines and targets of the plan, interdependent units have some latitude to adapt their operations. Effectively, a detailed planning document establishes a framework for the next quarter, quarters, or year that gives managers a blueprint for coordination.

Planning under the best of circumstances is tough in the MNE. Despite advances in communications technologies, some managers prefer to deal with their counterparts through face-to-face or voice-to-voice contact. Geographic distance and cultural divergence increase the time, expense, and possibility of error in cross-national communications.

More serious is the fact that no matter how carefully a project is planned, something may still go wrong; more poetically, "The best-laid plans of mice and men often go awry." Several conditions aggravate this situation, such as periodic disruptions, sensitivity to government regulations, and conflict with local partners. Combined, planning objectives and schedules may need to be revised, a tendency that constrains coordination.

Companies use a range of executive development and education programs to get people familiar with their preferred planning format and preempt the preceding threats. For example, many companies have adopted Six Sigma programs, a rigorous and disciplined process that utilizes data and statistical analysis to measure and improve a company's operational performance, practices, and systems. MNEs, like GE, Motorola, Allied-Signal, and DuPont, use Six Sigma to anchor their planning process. The ability of these programs to improve coordination by plan makes it so important that few question its purpose and most understand its procedures.

Each year, GE sends about 10,000 newly hired and longtime managers to its Leadership Development Center for a three-week course on the company's Six Sigma quality initiative. Other MNEs that rely on coordination by plan use related methods. They build teams with members from different countries to imagine scenarios on how the future may evolve.[32] Some locate international and domestic personnel in proximity to each other—for example, by placing the international division in the same building as the product divisions. Finally, others place foreign personnel on the board of directors and top-level committees to engage foreign viewpoints.

Coordination by Mutual Adjustment   Unlike the explicit features of standardization and planning, some MNEs coordinate value activities through a range of informal mechanisms. Basically, these mechanisms create ways for employees to engage fellow employees more often over matters of joint importance in a process called *coordination by mutual adjustment.*

For example, 3M has technology experts in more than 100 laboratories around the world that work in ways that support coordination of knowledge generation and decision making. Specifically, 3M's management uses techniques such as a Technical Council that is composed of the heads of the major labs. The council meets monthly and has a three-day annual retreat to discuss ways to improve cross-unit transfer of technology. In addition, management created a broader-based Technical Forum, composed of scientists and technical experts chosen as representatives, to facilitate grassroots communication among employees throughout its labs.[33] Both methods of interaction, by enabling the flexible exchange of ideas, create the capability that lets employees coordinate by mutual adjustment.

Certainly, MNEs that opt to encourage mutual adjustment also adopt a formal structure and install standardization and planning systems. However, they also see great value in engaging an adaptable approach to coordination that involves creating more opportunity and incentive for interdependent parties to work with one another.

Coordination by plan requires interdependent units to meet common deadlines and objectives.

CONCEPT CHECK

In Chapter 11, we explain that companies overcome a variety of "Operational Obstacles" in building communication channels among the links in their global **value chains.** In Chapter 12, we explain that, in deciding where to locate production operations, companies also consider the costs of moving information, materials, and products to and from product-development, supply, and distribution facilities. Here we recall that, not too long ago, problems related to both inefficient transportation and expensive communications hindered efforts to coordinate global activities. Today, however, improvements in these areas make *coordination by mutual adjustment* an increasingly practical option for more and more companies.

This approach can lead to many coordination mechanisms, such as developing teams from different countries to work on special projects of cross-national importance. Together they share viewpoints, giving divisions and subsidiaries credit for business resulting from cooperative efforts so they are encouraged to view activities broadly. They also establish liaisons among subsidiaries within the same country, so different product groups can both combine action on a given issue and rotate managers between domestic and international positions to encourage more engagement.

For instance, GE frequently transfers managers across divisional, business, or functional lines for lengthy tours of duty. Senior management believes that these sorts of transfers enable managers to develop relationships with colleagues in other parts of the company that, by weakening insular thinking and promoting idea sharing, make it possible to better coordinate operations. In summary, companies use coordination by mutual adjustment to give managers and workers the means to figure out jointly how to define a situation and devise a solution they see as vital to making the value chain work.

> Coordination by mutual adjustment requires managers to interact personally with counterparts.

Mutual adjustment is an effective coordination tool when an MNE faces new problems that cannot be defined with customary rules or procedures. MNEs also can preempt resistance to a particular initiative before it interferes with its strategy by getting employees on board before the launch. Still, coordination via mutual adjustment creates new challenges. Operationally, decisions can get bogged down in discussion as new viewpoints reset the debate.

More fundamentally, the premise of mutual adjustment resets the power of the organization. Headquarters must accept the notion that innovations, knowledge, and skills can arise anywhere within the firm's global network, not just at the center; as such, headquarters must adjust too.[34] The role of senior managers then moves from telling people what to do to facilitating what they do if they expect to transfer valuable innovations from a particular subsidiary to other parts of the organization.

CONTROL SYSTEMS

Every MNE, at some point, must decide how to regulate what people can and cannot do or else risk spinning out of control. Control systems are a fundamental part of a well-designed organization. Control is necessary because once an MNE adopts a strategy, it must ensure that employees implement it as planned. Operationally, this requires managers to build control systems that ensure employees do what needs to be done. Control takes precedence in the case of the latter: People are not performing properly; coordination problems are emerging; consequently, management takes steps to correct the situation.

An effective control system ensures that activities are completed in ways that attain the company's strategy. **Control systems** regulate the allocation and utilization of resources. In so doing, they facilitate the coordination process, no matter whether anchored in standardization, planning, or mutual adjustment routines. That being said, the criterion that determines the effectiveness of control systems is how well it compels actions that support the company's strategy. Finally, experiences at several companies, such as Barings Bank, Andersen Consulting, Parmalat, WorldCom, Enron, Citibank, Siemens, and Société Générale, show that the lack of controls or the wrong kinds of controls can cause irreparable damage.

Control Methods Methods of control include the following:

> Market control uses external market mechanisms to establish objective standards.

- *Market control*, whereby a MNE uses external market mechanisms, like price competition and relative market share, to establish internal performance benchmarks and standards. In this mode, headquarters evaluates each discrete unit of the organization, as in one of the 250 units of J&J, by looking at any number of market-based measures, such as percentage of total corporate profits each contributes. Control systems kick in when the unit fails to meet its target.

- *Bureaucratic control*, whereby a MNE uses centralized authority to install an extensive set of rules and procedures to govern a broad range of activities. Units that fail to comply with the policies and procedures trigger alarms that attract the attention of senior managers.

- *Clan control*, whereby a MNE relies on shared values among employees to idealize the preferred behaviors. Clan control encourages employees to identify strongly with the shared idea of what's important in the company. This identification then guides and controls how they do their job.

MNEs determine which sort of control system will work best with how they have configured and are trying to coordinate their value chain. For instance, companies following a global strategy tend to favor a mix of market controls, given that they can use considerable marketplace competition to evaluate the performance of their clearly specified and distinct products—such as computer chips or automobile tires.

In contrast, transnational companies tend to rely on clan control. The importance of open exchange among geographically diffuse people who are strongly encouraged to develop knowledge-generating and decision-making relationships fits well with less direct control tools. Ultimately, few MNEs rely on a single approach to control. Instead, they aim to design the control system that complements how the company has decided to coordinate its activities.

Control Mechanisms   MNEs use a range of control mechanisms to direct the activities of individuals toward the achievement of organizational goals. We now look at some of the principal mechanisms.

Reports   Reports, though sounding somewhat innocuous, are a powerful control mechanism. Headquarters needs timely reports to allocate resources, monitor performance, and reward personnel. Decisions on how to use capital, personnel, and technology continue without interruption, so reports must be frequent, accurate, and up-to-date. Headquarters uses reports to evaluate the performance of subsidiary personnel and reward and motivate them. These personnel adhere to reports and try to perform well on the tasks reported in them so they receive more rewards. They also seek feedback so they will know how well they are performing and can alter their performance accordingly.[35]

The intricacies of international business make reports an important element of control. For example, geographic distance often leads managers to standardize coordination methods. Similarly, headquarters often has less frequent contact with people in their foreign operations, which moves them to rely on extensive reports for control. MNEs often use reports to identify deviations from plans that could indicate problem areas. The focus of the reports may be to monitor short-term performance or longer-term indicators that match the company's strategy.

Information technology makes reports an even more attractive control mechanism. For example, most MNEs use ERP (enterprise resource planning) to monitor value activities, including product planning, parts purchasing, maintaining inventories, interacting with suppliers, providing customer service, and tracking orders. The resulting data give managers a remarkable control tool.

For instance, the Japanese retailer Ito-Yokado, which owns and operates the 7-Eleven convenience store franchise in Japan, has linked each store's automated cash registers into an ERP system that records sales and monitors inventory as well as schedules daily and weekly tasks for store managers. The ERP system tracks how often managers used the built-in analytical tools, graphs, and forecasts. Headquarters then tells those managers who have not checked in often enough to increase their participation.[36]

Finally, MNEs typically use reports for foreign operations that resemble those they use domestically. Managers reason that if reports have worked well domestically, they will also work well internationally. Moreover, standardizing the format of reports eliminates

Bureaucratic control emphasizes organizational authority and relies on rules and regulations.

Clan control uses shared values and ideals to moderate employee behavior.

Reports must be timely to allow managers to respond to their information.

the need to establish new types of reporting mechanisms, thereby leveraging corporate management's familiarity with the system. Lastly, and most powerfully, reports that share the same format permit better comparison of one operation with another.

Visits to Subsidiaries   Not all information exchange occurs through formalized written reports. Within many MNEs, especially those relying on coordination by adjustment and clan control, members of the corporate staff often visit subsidiaries to confer and socialize with local managers. Although this attention may alleviate misunderstandings, there are some "rules" for conducting visits properly.

On the one hand, if corporate personnel visit the tropical subsidiaries only when there are blizzards at home, the personnel abroad may perceive the trips as boondoggles. On the other hand, if a subsidiary's managers offer too many social activities and not enough analysis of operations, corporate personnel may consider the trip wasteful. Further, if visitors arrive only when the corporate level is upset about foreign operations, local managers may be overly defensive. Nevertheless, visits can serve the goal of controlling foreign operations because they enable the visitors to collect information and offer advice and directives.

Management Performance Evaluations   MNEs aim to evaluate subsidiary managers separately from their subsidiary's performance to avoid penalizing or rewarding them for conditions beyond their control. For example, headquarters may decide not to expand further in a country because of its slow growth and risky economic and political environment. Nonetheless, the company should still reward that country's managers for doing a good job in the face of adversity.

However, what is within a subsidiary manager's control varies from company to company (because of decision-making authority differences) and from subsidiary to subsidiary (because of local conditions). Take currency gains or losses. Who is responsible depends on whether working capital management decisions occur at headquarters or at the subsidiary level—and on whether there are instruments such as forward markets in a particular country that allow for hedging against currency value changes.

Another uncontrollable area is when headquarters managers make decisions that will optimize the company's performance, perhaps at the expense of a particular subsidiary. In addition, the normal profit-center records may well obscure the importance the subsidiary has within the total corporate entity.

One way to overcome the problems of evaluating performance is to look at the budget agreed on by headquarters and subsidiary managers. The budget covers the goals for each subsidiary that help the MNE achieve its objectives. This agreement enables the MNE to differentiate a subsidiary's worth and its management's performance.

Cost and Accounting Comparisons   Different costs among subsidiaries may prevent a meaningful comparison of their operating performance. For example, the ratio of labor to sales for a subsidiary in one country may be much higher than that for a subsidiary in another country, even though unit production costs may not differ substantially. So management must ensure that it is comparing relevant costs.

Different accounting practices can also create reporting and accountability problems. Most MNEs keep one set of books that are consistent with home-country principles and another to meet local reporting requirements. Headquarters needs to apply discretion in interpreting the data it uses to evaluate subsidiary performance, especially if it is comparing performance with competitors from other countries whose accounting methods differ.

Evaluative Measurements   Headquarters should evaluate subsidiaries and their managers on a number of indicators rather than emphasizing one. Financial criteria tend to dominate the evaluation of foreign operations and their managers, particularly when an MNE relies on plans to coordinate and a bureaucracy to control international operations.

> Companies aim to evaluate results in comparison to budgets but often find it hard to compare countries using standard operating ratios.

For instance, managers at British Petroleum's various divisions have some autonomy to run their units as they see fit provided they meet their budgets and comply with corporate guidelines.

Although many different criteria are important, the most important for evaluating both the operation and its management are "budget compared with profit" and "budget compared with sales value" because these immediately affect consolidated corporate figures. Many nonfinancial criteria are also important, such as market-share increase, quality control, and managers' relationship with host governments.

> A system that relies on a combination of measurements is more reliable than one that does not.

Information Systems   Corporate management often requires additional data to coordinate and control operations. Here are some examples of key needs:

- Information generated for centralized coordination, such as subsidiary cash balances and needs, so headquarters can move funds effectively.

- Information on external conditions, such as analyses of local political and economic conditions, so headquarters can plan where to expand and constrict operations.

- Information that can be used as feedback from parent to subsidiaries, such as R&D breakthroughs, so subsidiaries can compete more effectively.

- Information that subsidiaries can share so they can learn from each other and be motivated to perform as well as other subsidiaries.

- Information for external reporting needs, such as to stakeholders and tax authorities.

MNEs routinely face three problems in acquiring information: the cost of information compared to its value, redundant information, and information that is irrelevant. For example, much of the information useful to a subsidiary, such as whom to contact to clear items through customs, need not be reported to headquarters. To cope, companies periodically reevaluate the information sources they use.

Expanding global telecommunications, Internet links, and e-mail systems enable managers throughout the world to share information quickly and easily. On the one hand, this technology may permit more centralization because headquarters can more easily examine the global conditions and local performance, as we saw in the case of 7-Eleven in Japan. Recall, on the other hand, our opening case on J&J, where we discovered that local managers may become more autonomous because they have access to better local information than do managers in the home office.

Organization Culture

So far, we have looked at the roles that structure and systems play in defining the organization of a company. We now turn to the final element of this profile: the culture of the organization. In theory, one could look at organization culture in an applied fashion, specifying it as the way things get done in a company every day. Alternatively, we could follow the suggestion in Chapter 2 and adopt a more philosophical view, defining organization culture as a deeply embedded set of shared normative principles that guide action and serves as the standard to evaluate one's own and others' behaviors.

> Organization culture is the shared meaning and beliefs that shape how employees act.

We opt for a little of both, defining **organization culture** as the set of fundamental assumptions about the organization and its goals and practices that members of the company share. As such, organization culture is a system of shared values about what is important and beliefs about how the world works.

THE IMPORTANCE OF CULTURE

Historically, companies were sensitive to the idea that culture played some sort of role in the organization. However, several reasons have led managers to take an expansive view of organization culture, seeing it as a powerful tool that can be managed to encourage

CONCEPT CHECK

Recall our analysis of "The Comeback of Emerging Economies" in Chapter 4, where we suggest that this trend may herald an "inflection point" at which old strategic patterns of thought give way to new. Recall, too, our discussion of different national perspectives on *value creation* in Chapter 11, where we argue that such problems pose a specific challenge to managers charged with coordinating worldwide **value chain** operations. Here, we point out that solidifying a company's **organization culture** is an increasingly important means of anchoring innovative strategies.

and support the goals and behaviors that help the company achieve its strategy. Studies confirm a significant link between organization culture and the financial performance of a firm. Certain facets of organization culture, such as the values and principles of management, nature of the work climate and atmosphere, and traditions and ethical standards, are directly related to a company's financial performance.[37]

More generally, others report that culture is a critical component of a company's transition from "good" to "great" status. Technology, product development, and financial stewardship play principal roles in this transition. Still, most managers link the goal of becoming a great company to developing an organization culture that champions unwavering faith and passion, rigorous discipline and focus, clearly communicated and practiced core values and timeless principles, strong work ethics, and finding and promoting people with the right outlook.[38] In summary, great companies developed organization cultures that gave employees a consistent way to relate to their job, to each other, to customers, to shareholders, and to business partners.

It's likely that the importance of organization culture will increase in coming years. Earlier chapters highlighted growing pressures on companies to improve their global competitiveness. Later chapters detail many of the novel approaches companies use to do so—for instance, reconfiguring their value chains to streamline manufacturing processes or maximizing supply chain efficiencies with better coordination mechanisms.

These approaches have scant chance of producing sustainable benefits without an organization that has a complementary culture. Indeed, it is unwise for a company to undertake strategic moves that conflict with the values shared by managers and employees. Companies certainly could develop the set of constraints, controls, and contracts that compel employees to do their best. But this approach is costly and often counterproductive.

Key features of a company's organization culture include

- Values and principles of management.
- Work climate and atmosphere.
- Patterns of "how we do things around here."
- Traditions.
- Ethical standards.

Culture and Values   Successful companies develop an organization culture that instills in their employees degrees of enthusiasm and job involvement above and beyond that justified by economic rewards alone—"Objectives don't get you there. Values do," said Jack Welch of GE. Put simply, a strategy-supportive culture stimulate people to take on the challenge of realizing the company's vision, to do their jobs competently and with enthusiasm, and to collaborate with others.

In addition, a powerful organization culture lessens the need to regulate employees' behaviors with elaborate structures and systems. Therefore, the culture's capacity to build a high-performance organization puts the onus on managers to create the context that inspires this behavior. Or, put more directly, managers must build an organization that people don't want to just work for but want to belong to.

Moreover, in the event of poor performance, success will not follow from revising their formal structure to force changes in roles or revising systems to force change in interpersonal relationships. Rather, success will likely follow from reshaping the individual attitudes and actions of managers that then support the work ethic that triggers the individual-level behaviors of learning and collaboration.[39]

Finally, the shared values that make up organization culture influence what employees perceive, how they interpret, and what they do to respond to their world. At J&J, for example, the company anchors its ideas of value creation and strategic purpose in the principles of its Credo. Recall from our opening case that this manifesto champions—and clearly states—common values that embody the company's sense of its responsibilities to its stakeholders. The purpose of J&J's Credo is to ensure that, when they're confronted with opportunities or threats, employees and operating units have guidelines that reflect the organization culture and explain acceptable means of defining, analyzing, and resolving issues.

Case Review Note

Culture and the Value Chain   Even more practically, increasingly sophisticated value-chain configurations produce more interdependence among subsidiaries. Maximizing coordination and maintaining control of value activities spurs managers to contact their peers in other subsidiaries more frequently. Managers often set up cross-cultural teams to tackle issues common to foreign operations. These teams generally are composed of people chosen because of their expertise, not because of their positions, and they are made up of equals, not of a superior and subordinates. The ability of the team to reach consensus depends on the group members' enthusiasm as well as peer pressure within the groups, rather than on the control systems of structural devices.

An organization's culture often shapes the strategic moves it considers.

CHALLENGES AND PITFALLS

Rather than letting the organization's culture emerge naturally, companies increasingly develop and manage, just as they do with regard to their structure and systems, their set of shared values and beliefs. Still, MNEs run into difficulty managing their organization culture. Most immediately, managers from different countries often have values that differ from those endorsed by the company.

Complicating matters is the fact that people in an MNE often have slight exposure to the values held by senior managers. The severity of this problem is directly proportional to the importance of knowledge-generating and decision-making relationships to the MNE's competitiveness.[40] That is, convergent values ease the exchange of ideas between people from different countries, whereas different values tend to create boundaries and barriers.

MNEs also run into similar sorts of cultural conflicts that prevent cross-national teams, an increasingly popular management tool, from working well. For instance, at one company the U.S. managers complained that the U.K. managers were too bureaucratic, and the U.K. managers complained that the U.S. managers tried to reach decisions without thorough analysis.[41]

Against this backdrop are nagging questions about the performance impact of organization culture. Thus far, few organizations have been able to parlay it into high performance. A survey of 1,200 international executives found that "fewer than 10 percent of companies currently succeed at building high-performance cultures." This shortfall stands in sharp contrast to the fact that 9 in 10 CEOs acknowledge that "corporate culture is as important as a strategy for business success."[42] Finally, evidence suggests that mixing national cultures on teams does not necessarily improve performance.[43]

To overcome these challenges, many companies promote closer contact among managers from different countries. The aim is to convey a shared understanding of global goals and norms along with improving the transfer of ideas and best practices from one country to another.[44] For example, GE's Leadership Development Center runs courses for senior managers that sometimes focus on a single topic for up to a month. Classes pull managers from different businesses and different parts of the world.

Sharing Knowledge and Best Practices Besides spreading best practices throughout the organization, this sort of knowledge sharing improves managers' understanding of the company's culture.[45] Explained Jeffrey Immelt, chairman and CEO of General Electric, the company tries "very hard to provide a company, a set of values, and a culture that employees can be proud of, whether it be in Pittsfield, Paris, Shanghai, or London."[46]

Similarly, Mattel, the toy maker, has 25,000 employees in 36 countries and sells its products in 150 nations. Although you'd think selling the fun of toys would make for agreement on cultural ideals, differing ideas put up barriers to values and objectives. So, facing dissension throughout its global operations, the company launched a set of leadership programs at its Conference Leadership Center. The programs extend to facilities throughout the world through an e-learning system. Twice a year, the company holds a weeklong leadership program on global business growth for 35 directors and officers drawn from around the world.

CONCEPT CHECK

In Chapter 2, we classify "Company and Management Orientations" into *ethnocentric*, *polycentric*, and *geocentric* perspectives on adapting to foreign cultures. In Chapter 11, we suggest various ways in which these perspectives may affect a company's implementation of its strategy for conducting worldwide operations, whether *international*, *multidomestic*, *global*, or *transnational*. Here in putting some of these pieces together, we suggest that when they're organizationing operations, managers pay particular attention both to the company's global "orientation" and its fit with the environments in which it hopes to do business.

Dealing with critical issues facing Mattel has increased the knowledge of management worldwide, and now "global management is more closely aligned with the corporate strategies and goals," says the vice president of leadership development. "This, in turn, produces innovative and creative products, reduces costs, and improves employee satisfaction." Now employees are becoming "one Mattel company," rather than a number of companies operating separately.[47]

ORGANIZATION CULTURE AND STRATEGY

The principles and practices of organization culture vary with the requirements of the company's strategy (see Figure 15.5). For example, the company implementing a global strategy aims to develop a forceful culture that helps everyone around the world understand and accept a standard set of goals, priorities, and practices. Essentially, a global strategy's requirement to standardize value activities usually also requires standardizing employees' views about purposes and practices.

Alternatively, companies following a multidomestic strategy require people to share fewer common values and encourage greater variety in the local interpretation of corporate goals. Adapting value activities for local markets requires accepting more local autonomy, a requirement that rests on sensitivity to local outlooks and norms.

Despite specific differences, organization culture shares similar attributes across the different types of strategies. First, employees typically perceive an organization culture on the basis of what they see, hear, or experience within the company. Thus senior managers must establish and exemplify the set of assumptions about the company and the shared values and ideals. Top management's commitment to "walking the talk" compellingly influences an MNE's culture.

FIGURE 15.5
Strategy and Organizational Culture in International Business

The four strategies charted here correspond to the four types of MNE strategies that we introduced in Chapter 11. Recall, for example, that a company opting for a *global strategy* likely markets a standardized product for a specific global segment. Not surprisingly, then, it will design its *corporate culture* to help employees around the world accept and adopt a standardized set of goals and activities.

Pressure for Global Integration		
High	**GLOBAL** Strategic objectives: Productivity and efficiency Strategic emphasis: Integration, competitive advantage Dominant attribute: Standardized goal achievement, global competitiveness Leadership style: Production and achievement-oriented, decisive control orientation Bonding: Goal orientation, production, competition	**TRANSNATIONAL** Strategic objectives: Integration, responsiveness, learning Strategic emphasis: Innovation, ideas, and growth Dominant attribute: Innovation, creativity, dynamism, flexibility Leadership style: Innovator, risk affinitive, congruence between individual values and company goals Bonding: Flexibility, risk, entrepreneurship
Low	**INTERNATIONAL** Strategic objectives: Leverage core competencies Strategic emphasis: Control, stability, predictability Dominant attribute: Formal order, rules and regulations, uniformity Leadership style: Director, administrator, enforcer Bonding: Rules, policies and procedures, clear expectations	**MULTIDOMESTIC** Strategic objectives: Local responsiveness Strategic emphasis: Esprit de corps, commitment, consensus Dominant attributes: Cohesiveness, trust, affiliation Leadership style: Mentor, facilitator, coach, adaptability Bonding: Loyalty and tradition
	Low → High **Pressure for National Responsiveness**	

Second, even though individuals have different backgrounds, work at different organizational levels, or think about different ambitions, they tend to describe the company's culture in similar terms. Getting people who are likely to differ to share ideas and values spurs MNEs to forsake manipulating employees through traditional approaches of reward and punishment and adopt those that motivate them to accept and endorse "how things are done around here." Consequently, executives work hard to develop, communicate, and practice the values and ideals that encourage and sustain individual involvement.

Finally, *organization culture* is a descriptive term. It's concerned with how employees perceive their company, not with whether they think that what it does or aims to do is intrinsically right. Managers must develop the flexible processes that encourage and tolerate a range of interpretations and opinions as needed.

> Over time, organization culture varies with the type of strategy the company pursues.

LOOKING TO THE FUTURE

The Role and Rise of Corporate Universities

Many companies believe that instead of simply letting the organization's culture emerge naturally, managers must increasingly develop and monitor their shared values, just as they do with their structures and systems. This has led to a variety of new approaches, most notably, a boom in corporate universities—physical and "virtual" institutions that lead training efforts, facilitate learning, and help upgrade competencies.

In the past few years, there has been exponential growth in this strategy with the emergence of over a thousand new corporate universities. More specifically, corporate universities are growing by leaps and bounds in the United States, thriving in Europe, and making serious inroads in Asia. In the United States, for example, the number of corporate universities grew from around 400 in 1988 to more than 20,000 in 2007 and includes nearly half of the *Fortune* 500.[48]

Operationally, some are centrally located at headquarters, while others are sprinkled among offices at remote sites or are "virtual" universities, where employees learn via the Internet and interactive desktop videoconferencing. At the current pace of growth, the number of corporate universities will exceed the number of traditional universities by 2010. In a nutshell, the boom in corporate universities symbolizes the growing appreciation of the importance of proactively managing organization culture.

Corporate universities were originally created to teach employees practical skills and workplace systems. When the McDonald's Hamburger University in Illinois opened in the 1950s, its mission was to prepare people to run the day-to-day operations of a franchise. Today, "Training isn't just a nice thing to do anymore," reported the American Society for Training and Development. "Companies are now thinking of training as a strategic imperative."[49] Our upcoming profile of Infosys showcases a corporate university that aspires to embed newcomers in the organization that will use its processes and have a strategic understanding of its systems.

Others amplify this theme, confessing that their goal is to "inculcate everyone, from the clerical assistant to the top executive, in the culture and values that make the organization unique and special and to define behaviors that enable employees to 'live the values.'"[50] This goal of coupling executive learning to the company's strategy drives the recent and projected growth of the corporate university model. For example, the CEO of Unipart, a British auto parts maker, notes that his company's university "is at the very heart of the business" and a "key enabler for future growth of the business."[51] Like many other CEOs, he runs his own monthly course on the philosophy and principles of Unipart's approach to business.

When senior executives take on the hat of teacher, they can generate great benefits. The director of LVMH's university believes that putting top people into the teaching pit "gives them access to people they would never get access to. It is the role of our top senior executives to get a feel for what is going on."[52] Managers at LVMH gain similar benefits. Typically, they go though two-and-a-half-day forums that create networking opportunities. Then, when they return to their unit, if they run into a problem, they can more comfortably call someone for help. In addition, they pick up new management tools, often reporting that they return their divisions with six or seven new ideas. Finally, they return with a good idea of how the professional development stacks up with other folks in the company.

A growing mandate for corporate universities is integrating diverse workforces. Hiring more engineers in Mumbai or Sophia to help out people in Redmond

(continued)

makes great economic sense. Still, preempting a Tower of Babel requires the company to find ways to help people learn to work in global work groups. Done well, explains the vice president of Unisys University, corporate universities provide continual learning for employees in ways that align employees' learning with the strategy of the business and impact strongly on the culture of the organization.[53]

A recent change in the corporate university model is finding new ways to prepare future leaders of the company. The search for global leaders is seen as critical to current performance and future growth. Corporate universities design executive programs that engage high-potential executives on topics that impact the organization and industry. The scripted structure of a corporate university pushes executives to develop the insights and cultivate the personal relationships they might need to reshape their company. Monique Elliott of GE Capital Solutions, after a class at GE's corporate university, believes that, given that her fellow students are all GE employees, the experience is more rewarding because "[w]e all speak the same language, and we are comfortable in the GE culture."[54]

Some MNEs go so far as to build university sites around the world. Unisys, for example, has campuses in each of the five geographic areas where it has a large presence, namely, North America, Europe, the United Kingdom, Latin America, and Asia and the South Pacific. Many are enhancing their universities by utilizing e-learning tactics like live Webcasts, online chat and discussion groups, videoconferences, and interactive sessions to greatly expand accessibility.

Whether real or virtual, the growing power of corporate universities as agents of ideas may ultimately usher in a new crucible of company strategy. Some foresee a potential future whereby the corporate university becomes the strategic center for the company, formulating strategy rather than following it, while developing leadership that can build an organization that moves the company from where it is today to where it should be tomorrow. ■

CASE

Infosys: The Search for the Best and the Brightest

India produces about 300,000 engineering graduates each year, offering a fresh pool of candidates eager to work, often at a fraction of the cost of their global counterparts.[55] This advantage has proven decisively successful in catapulting India from a sleepy country to the forefront of the global offshore market. More specifically, India's offshoring sector, the world's largest and fastest growing, is dominated by its information technology (IT) services. By 2007, that sector employed nearly 1.5 million people and accounted for 7 percent of India's GDP. Growth is expected to accelerate; India's software services exports exceeded $31 billion in 2007 and are on target to reach $60 billion by 2010. Leading the charge is Infosys Technologies Limited (Infosys).

Infosys: An Introduction

Infosys, founded in Pune, India, in 1981, is presently headquartered in Bangalore, ground zero of the Indian offshoring industry. Infosys is a global technology services firm that defines, designs, and delivers IT-enabled, end-to-end business solutions that leverage technology for its clients in financial services, manufacturing, telecommunications, retail, utilities, logistics, and other industries. The company provides services in areas such as consulting, design, development, software reengineering, maintenance, systems integration, package evaluation, and implementation and infrastructure management. For example, it can offer integrated merchandising solutions as well as a Web-based broker-trading platform.

Historically, Indian software companies executed most of their software projects end to end at overseas locations. Infosys believes it can perform this function much more cost-efficiently if it has access to local talent—for example, application-development costs in India are a fifth that of

U.S. levels. Building an organization that can perform this function, said Narayana Murthy, the company's founder, will position the company to capitalize on the premise of globalization, namely, "sourcing capital from where it is cheapest, producing where it is most cost-effective, and selling where it is most profitable, all without being constrained by national boundaries."

The "Global Delivery Model"

Strategically, the company relies on its pioneering "Global Delivery Model" to develop and deliver software solutions. Infosys anchors its analysis in the value chain, disaggregating the various components into this Global Delivery Model. Once established, the model identifies how to carry out the bulk of code writing in Bangalore, with its qualified, productive, and efficient professionals housed among nine development centers in India, and then design and deliver end-to-end software solutions globally. Over time, Infosys has built additional capabilities to reinforce this model. One such accomplishment has been the stationing of on-site counterparts in more than 30 offices worldwide charged with implementation responsibilities and local customer relationship management.

Two Decades of Growth

Infosys grew modestly during its first decade, finishing 1991 with revenues of $3.89 million. The liberalization of the Indian economy in 1991, fueled by the growing adoption of free market principles, led to accelerated growth. Executives began to focus on global markets, supported by the promise of sophisticated and inexpensive communication technologies.

Infosys's revenues, under $2 million in 1983, increased to about $121 million by fiscal year 1998–99. By fiscal year 2007, the company's revenues passed $3.1 billion with a net income of $850 million. Along the way, employee head count grew from the original "founding seven" to more than 72,000 worldwide. Initial investors have been well rewarded, earning in mid-2007 an astounding 3,000 percent return on the initial public offering price in 1993.*

Stating (and Restating) a Mission Although a global juggernaut today, the company had humble beginnings. Murthy, along with six friends, began the idea of Infosys with a meeting in the bedroom of his small apartment, where they debated the mission of the company. After hours of discussion they resolved that their mission was not, he says, "to be the best, the biggest or the most profitable company, but to earn the respect of all our stakeholders. . . . My view was if we sought respect we'd automatically do the right thing by each of them. We'd satisfy our customers, be fair to our employees, and follow the finest principles with respect to investors . . . we would not violate laws, and, finally, we'd make a difference to society . . . [A]utomatically, you'll get revenues and profits and all that."

He goes on to say, "We started out as seven people in 1981, with $250. We had just one customer. . . . We never imagined we would come this far." And although many companies share this characteristic, the founding of Infosys is a legacy that the company fervently works to imbue in the organization today. This initial vision still infuses the company's current mission statement: "To achieve our objectives in an environment of fairness, honesty, and courtesy towards our clients, employees, vendors and society at large."

Being Smart as a Core Competency

As the saying goes, even the grandest vision depends on the success of the smallest details. The evolution and success of Infosys—it took the company 23 years to become a $1 billion company but only 23 months to double that—depends on the smallest components of their

---

*An investment of Rs. 9,500 (100 shares at an issue price of Rs. 95) in the initial public offering of Infosys in 1993 (Rs. 9,500 was approximately $300 according to the 1993 exchange rate) would, after adjusting for stock splits and bonuses, be worth Rs. 29,440,000 (approximately $665,235 in mid-2007).

organization. In the case of Infosys, senior executives, a small component themselves, gather knowledge of the company whose core competencies include human intellect and learning through a process of observation, data collection, analysis, and conclusion. Ably managed, knowledge can then be translated into pioneering software solutions.

More important, this knowledge is not archived in a static database. Rather it is encapsulated in the people the company hires to staff global operations. According to Murthy, "Our respect for our professionals can be summed up by our belief that the market capitalization of Infosys becomes zero after working hours end at 5 p.m., no matter what it was during the day. . . . It's our belief that the first duty of a corporation is to uphold respect and dignity for the individual."

Recruiting: Looking for "Learnability"

For a corporation growing as fast as Infosys, inspiring this vision in employees is a great challenge. In 2007, Infosys plans to recruit more than 25,000 workers. Here is where the company suffers an embarrassment of riches: In 2006, although entry-level jobs started out with annual salaries of about $5,000, more than 1.4 million people put in an application. Each applicant was required to pass an exam made up of math equations and logic puzzles designed to assess their aptitude for "learnability" (Infosys-speak for being a quick study). Few survived this screening—ultimately, Infosys hired 1 percent of its 1.4 million applicants.

Recruiting and hiring at this pace demands more than merely showing new employees to their desks. Infosys CEO Nandan Nilekani sums it up this way: "There aren't many companies growing like this. . . . Companies haven't been investing enough in people. Rather than train them, they let them go. Our people are our capital. The more we invest in them, the more they can be effective." To that end, Infosys devotes $65 of every $1,000 in revenue to training programs and educational initiatives, a sum that no competitor matches and most fall far short of.

Training: Preaching "Technical Evangelism"

Investment begins right off the bat. Even though the percentage of the applicants selected has excelled academically, they are still put through a 14-week boot camp. Specifically, each new hire attends a rigorous training program, taking classes from more than 150 instructors whom Infosys calls "technical evangelists." Rigorous course work includes analytical-thinking and problem-solving skills, principles of operating and database-management systems, networking, and instruction in team building, customer facing, business etiquette, and negotiation skills.

Throughout the program, the company goes to great lengths to communicate its values, systems, and processes with respects to C-Life (see Figure 15.6). More fundamentally, the training program addresses an aspect of the national Indian psyche. Says Murthy, "We have realized that our challenge is to take the reactive mind-set of Indian youngsters and change them into proactive problem-solving ones. By and large, because of our culture, family background, etc., we are reactive. To change that, we have to understand problem-solving as a science and an art. We have to understand algorithmic thinking."

FIGURE 15.6
The Concept of C-Life at Infosys

Source: Adapted from Infosys, "Vision and Mission" (2007), at www.infosys.com (accessed November 5, 2007).

Customer Delight	A commitment to surpassing our customers' expectations.
Leadership by Example	A commitment to set standards in our business and transactions and be an exemplar for the industry and our own teams.
Integrity and Transparency	A commitment to be ethical, sincere, and open in our dealings.
Fairness	A commitment to be objective and transaction-oriented, thereby earning trust and respect.
Pursuit of Excellence	A commitment to strive relentlessly, to constantly improve ourselves, our teams, our services, and products, so as to become the best.

For the average hardworking, stressed-out student, simply surviving the training program is no guarantee that he or she will "graduate," even after Infosys's total training costs of $5,000 per student. Completing the 14-week-class phase of the program earns the student a slot to take two three-hour comprehensive exams. The successful students then move from the status of "freshers" to "Infoscions."

Tapping a Global Labor Pool

In fall 2003, the company launched its Global Talent Program to recruit job candidates from around the world. The geographic distribution of Infosys's clients—18 countries account for 98 percent of the company's business—highlights the need to diversify its labor pool to ensure its capacity to deliver a high level of customer service. Infosys's goal is to hire individuals who understand the cultural nuances and languages of its vast client base. Karthik Sarman, associate vice president of human resources, emphasizes this point when he states, "A Japanese worker will tend to do better in Japan. It is a matter of being able to connect with clients on more than just the technical level."

New recruits are brought to India for a six-month training and orientation program, and then return to their home countries as local agents. The first cohorts of this program included 96 "Infoscions" from China and 78 from Mauritius. Presently, Infosys is enlisting 300 college graduates from the United States. The pursuit of talent beyond its home country's borders has proven successful—Infosys's employees represent 57 nationalities who speak 40 languages. Nevertheless, Sarman notes that "[t]he need for qualified talent will become more pressing as we continue to mature."

Looking to the Future

Thus far, maturity from a small start-up to a global juggernaut has gone well. Performance suggests that Infosys commands an insightful sense of how a company builds an organization to succeed in global markets. Despite its strong positioning, the company remains well aware that its past accomplishments do not guarantee future success, and it is ready to confront new challenges. Growing threats are evident in the evolution of offshoring where companies no longer rely on the combination of low-cost labor and brute code-writing skills to beat the competition.

The task at hand for Infosys, along with its rivals, is to move to increasingly more profitable, yet sophisticated, activities. Infosys knew that to stay ahead requires finding ways to integrate low-cost, high-quality software-development services with well-developed processes for managing large-scale projects in distributed locations. Early signs were promising—Airbus, for instance, had hired Infosys to design part of the intricate wing structure of the superjumbo A380 aircraft.

In addition, Infosys's profitability is attracting new rivals from around the world, as well as motivating its domestic competitors to work harder. Indeed, fast-moving global competitors, including Wipro, IBM, Tata Consultancy Services, Acccenture, Cisco, and Cognizant, were ramping up operations to offer higher-end offshoring solutions. The quest to stay at least one step ahead, if not two, of these rivals spurs Infosys to better deliver its existing services, as well as move to higher value-added activities.

Three Critical Challenges

This change, although part of the ongoing evolution of Infosys, does pose challenges. Asked to give his take on this challenge, Murthy identifies three enduring tests:

> Our biggest challenge is to become proactive problem-definers rather than be reactive problem-solvers. Right now, we solve problems our customers define. We need to be able to go to customers and say, "These are the problems we believe you will face, and here are some solutions." Our focus is on providing solutions leveraging IT. We need to help shape the design of the technology solutions and then implement those solutions. This is the biggest challenge we face—there's no doubt about that.

The second challenge is to become more and more and more multicultural. We have efforts under way to integrate people across various cultures. For instance, on large deals we make sure that people from different parts of the world contribute, on a collaborative basis, to prepare a proposal, to defend the proposal, and to execute the proposal. We also lay great emphasis on integrating leadership. We rotate selected managers from our operations every-where in the world through our Infosys Leadership Institute. But there is much more that we need to do. For instance, it has not been easy for us to transfer somebody from the United States to India. We are able to transfer people from the United States to Europe and from one function to another—from software development to sales and marketing, for instance. But transferring an employee from the United States to India is not easy.

Finally, the third challenge is to continue to retain the soul of a small organization in the body of a large organization. It will be tricky to balance the tension between scaling the organization as quickly as we have been doing against the need to maintain disciplined processes as well as an integrated multicultural organization.

Undoubtedly, this is a full set of challenges for any company. Infosys, ever humble but sincerely confident, believes it has built an organization that can successfully take these challenges head-on to, as its CEO, declares, "win in a flat world." ■

QUESTIONS

1. Can Infosys continue at this rate of growth in terms of sales and employees and still retain its founding values?
2. What organizational problems do you think will prove particularly troublesome to executives at Infosys?
3. Consider the options presented in the chapter regarding structural design, coordination and control, and corporate culture. Profile the interplay among these within Infosys.
4. What do you think was the key event in the organizational evolution of Infosys? What do you think the Infosys organization will look like in 2015?
5. Given what you have read, do you think you would like to work for Infosys? Why or why not?

SUMMARY

- The organization of international business is challenging because of the geographic and cultural distances that separate countries, the need to operate differently among countries, the large number of uncontrollable factors, the high uncertainty resulting from rapid change in the international environment, and problems in gathering reliable data in many places.

- Organization in the MNE is an integrated function of its formal structure, coordination and control systems, and the shared values that make up its culture.

- Prevailing environmental and workplace trends pressure managers to question their customary approaches to organizing their companies.

- Vertical differentiation is the matter of how the company balances the centralization versus the decentralization of decision making. Horizontal differentiation is the matter of how the company opts to divide itself into specific units to do specific jobs.

- The degree of centralization in a company is influenced by the pressures for global integration versus local responsiveness, the competence of headquarters versus subsidiary personnel, and decision importance, expediency, and quality expectations.

- Traditional structures, like the functional, divisional, and matrix formats, rely on hierarchical formats to specify the arrangement of roles, responsibilities, and relationships among employees.

- Contemporary structures, like the network or virtual formats, arrange work roles, responsibilities, and relationships in ways that eliminate the horizontal, vertical, or external boundaries that block the development of knowledge-generating and decision-making relationships.

- Firms engaging different strategies must develop different organizations to implement those strategies successfully. Firms engaging international, multidomestic, global, or transnational strategies need to tailor their structure, systems, and cultures to the demands of the strategy.

- No matter what sort of structure the MNE uses, it needs to develop coordination and control mechanisms to prevent duplication of efforts, to ensure that headquarters managers do not withhold the best resources from the international operations, and to include insights from anywhere in the organization.

- Coordination can take place via standardization, plans, and mutual adjustment. Standardization relies on specifying standard operating procedures; planning relies on general goals and detailed objectives; and mutual adjustment relies on frequent interaction among related parties.

- Companies exercise control through market, bureaucratic, and clan mechanisms. Market control relies on external market mechanisms, bureaucratic control relies on extensive rules and procedures, and clan control relies on shared values among all employees.

- Organization culture refers to the set of values and norms that is shared among employees. Values and norms express themselves as the behavior patterns or style of an organization that fellow employees encourage new employees to follow.

- MNEs opt to develop and manage, just as they do with regard to their structure and systems, their set of shared values and beliefs. The strategy the company is pursuing moderates the approaches and tools it uses.

KEY TERMS

boundaries (p. 583)
centralization (p. 576)
control systems (p. 590)
coordination (p. 587)
decentralization (p. 576)
divisional structure (p. 580)

functional structure (p. 578)
horizontal differentiation (p. 578)
matrix structure (p. 581)
mixed structure (p. 582)
network structure (p. 584)
organization (p. 575)

organization culture (p. 593)
organization structure (p. 575)
unity-of-command principal
  (p. 581)
vertical differentiation (p. 576)
virtual organization (p. 585)

ENDNOTES

1 *Sources include the following:* J&J 2006 Annual Report; www.jnj.com; "Profit Up at Johnson & Johnson," *New York Times,* January 24, 2007; Katharine Seelye, "J. & J. Says Improper Payments Were Made," *New York Times,* February 13, 2007.

2 "The Organization Man, Dead at 76," *Journal of Business Strategy* 18:6 (1997).

3 Lowell Bryan and Claudia Joyce, "Better Strategy through Organizational Design," *The McKinsey Quarterly* (May 2007).

4 Chris Bartlett and Sumantra Ghoshal, "Matrix Management: Not a Structure, a Frame of Mind," *Harvard Business Review* 68 (July–August 1990): 138–45.

5 Julian Birkinshaw, "The Structures behind Global Companies," *Financial Times,* December 4, 2000: Mastering Management section, 2–4.

6 "Nestlé Is Starting to Slim Down at Last," *Business Week,* October 27, 2003: 56–58; "Daring, Defying, to Grow," *The Economist,* August 7, 2004: 55–57.

7 John W. Hunt, "Is Matrix Management a Recipe for Chaos?" *Financial Times,* January 12, 1998: 10.

8 Richard Hodgetts, "Dow Chemical CEO Wiliam Stavropoulos on Structure," *Academy of Management Executive,* May 30, 1999: 30.

9 John Gapper and Nicholas Denton, "The Barings Report," *Financial Times,* October 18, 1995: 8.

10 "Axe to Fall Heavily at IBM, Unions Fear," *New York Times,* May 6, 2005.

11 The *strategy-structure-systems model* was first adopted by General Motors, DuPont, Sears, and Standard Oil in the 1920s. Not until the post–World War II era did many companies began to develop divisional structures that then led to the rapid adoption of diversification strategies. Some reason that the network structure and its variants will follow the same pattern, moving from the few in the early 2000s to the many over the ensuing decades.

12 "Hungry Tiger, Dancing Elephant: How India Is Changing IBM's World," *The Economist.* April 4, 2007.

13 Others pointed to W. L. Gore and its egalitarian workforce philosophy—no titles, workers collaborating in small teams, and no hiearchy fuels creativity and innovation: "We work hard at maximizing individual potential, maintaining an emphasis on product integrity and cultivating an environment where creativity can flourish," says CEO Terri Kelly. "A fundamental belief in our people and their abilities continues to be the key to our success, even as we expand globally." "It isn't a company for everyone," Brinton says. "It takes a special kind of person to be effective here—someone who is really passionate about sharing information, as opposed to controlling it."

14 Steve Lohr, "I.B.M. to Lay Off 10,000 to 13,000," *New York Times,* May 4, 2005: quoting Robert J. Moffat, IBM senior VP.

15 Statement from Jack Welch's Letter to Shareholders, "Boundarylessness Company in a Decade of Change," reported in GE's 1990 *Annual Report*.

16 Cisco, for instance, is essentially a research and development company that uses many outside suppliers and independent manufacturers to assemble the products it designs. Capitalizing on its core competency in design but still retaining in its outsourced production led Cisco to build a global network.

    Operationally, Cisco has entered into joint ownership arrangements with other companies to share production, distribution, and technology-development facilities. It contracts with other companies to share technology and relies on other companies to produce and distribute goods and components.

    Cisco organizes its many alliances with the communication technology that made Cisco successful. The company uses the Internet, e-mail, file sharing, and conferencing to link partners across corporate and national boundaries. More formally, the company designed the Cisco Connection and Cisco Internet Business Roadmap in order to give its partners easier communication and flexible relationships.

17 "A Tangled Web," *Financial Times,* June 12, 2001: Germany section, 7.

18 Sonny Ariss, Nick Nykodym, and Aimee Cole-Laramore, "Trust and Technology in the Virtual Organization," *SAM Advanced Management Journal* 67 (Autumn 2002): 22–26; William M. Fitzpatrick and Donald R. Burke, "Competitive Intelligence, Corporate Security and the Virtual Organization," *Advances in Competitiveness Research* 11 (2003): 20–46.

19 Scott Goodson, StrawberryFrog, "Special Report: Global Players," *Advertising Age,* January 26, 2004: S4; Juliana Koranteng, "Virtual Agency Goes Global via the Web," *AdAgeGlobal* 1 (2000): 46.

20 Theresa Howard, "Strawberry Frog Hops to a Different Drummer," *USA Today,* October 10, 2005.

21 Alf Crossman and Liz Lee-Kelley, "Trust, Commitment and Team Working: The Paradox of Virtual Organizations," *Global Networks: A Journal of Transnational Affairs* 4 (October 2004): 375–91; Philip J. Holt and James E. Lodge, "Merging Collaboration and Technology: The Virtual Research Organization," *Applied Clinical Trials* 12 (October 2003): 38–42.

22 Nicolai J. Foss. "Selective Intervention and Internal Hybrids: Interpreting and Learning from the Rise and Decline of the Oticon Spaghetti Organization," *Organization Science* 14 (May–June 2003): 331–50.

23 Patrick Kiger, "Hidden Hierarchies," *Workforce Management,* February 27, 2006: 24.

24 Eric Beinhocker, "The Adaptable Corporation," *The McKinsey Quarterly* 2 (2006).

25 Beaman, Karen, "An Interview with Christopher Bartlett," *Boundaryless HR: Human Capital Management in the Global Economy* (IHRIM Press, June 2002).

26 Darrell Rigby, "Bain & Company's 2005 Management Tools & Trends," at www.bain.com/management_tools (accessed August 2, 2005).

27 Bryan, Lowell and Claudia Joyce, "The 21st-Century Organization," *The McKinsey Quarterly* 3 (2005).

28 Loren Cary, "The Rise of Hyperarchies," *Harvard Business Review* (March 2004).

29 The Boston Consulting Group, "Reorganized Information Processing Vital to Improving U.S. Intelligence Capabilities," *BCG Media Releases,* at www.bcg.com/news_media/news_media_releases.jsp?id=928 (accessed May 6, 2007).

30 Adam Lashinsky, "Chaos by Design," *Fortune* (October 2, 2006); Geoffrey Colvin, "Managing in Chaos," *Fortune* (October 2, 2006).

31 More specifically, Grove reasoned: "Let chaos reign, then rein in chaos. Does that mean that you shouldn't plan? Not at all. You need to plan the way a fire department plans. It cannot anticipate fires, so it has to shape a flexible organization that is capable of responding to unpredictable events." (Michael E. Rock, "Case Example: Intel's Andy Grove," *CanadaOne* [2006], at www.canadaone.com/magazine/mr2060198.html [accessed October 31, 2007]).

32 Daniel Erasmus, "A Common Language for Strategy," *Financial Times,* April 5, 1999: Mastering Information Management section, 7–8.

33 Sumantra Ghoshal and Christopher Bartlett, "Changing the Role of Top Management: Beyond Structure to Process," *Harvard Business Review* 73 (January–February 1995): 93–94.

34 Jennifer Spencer, "Firms' Knowledge-Sharing Strategies in the Global Innovation System: Empirical Evidence from the Flat Panel Display Industry," *Strategic Management Journal* 23 (March 2003): 217–33.

35 Anil K. Gupta, Vijay Govindarajan, and Ayesha Malhotra, "Feedback-Seeking Behavior within Multinational Corporations," *Strategic Management Journal* 20 (March 1999): 205–22.

36 N. Shirouzu and J. Bigness, "7-Eleven Operators Resist System to Monitor Managers," *Wall Street Journal,* June 16, 1997: B1.

37 Eric Flamholtz and Rangapriya Kannan-Narasimhan, "Differential Impact of Cultural Elements in Financial Performance," *European Management Journal* 23 (February 2005): 50–65; Ursula Fairbairn, "HR as a Strategic Partner: Culture Change as an American Express Case Study," *Human Resource Management* 44 (Spring 2005): 79–84.

38 Jim Collins, *Good to Great: Why Some Companies Make the Leap . . . and Others Don't* (New York: HarperCollins, 2001). For example, on the importance of technology, Collins reports that "80 percent of the good-to-great executives—from more than 1400 companies over a 15 year span—we interviewed didn't even mention technology as one of the top five factors in the transition."

39 Ghoshal and Bartlett, "Changing the Role," 138–40.

40 Tatiana Kostova, "Transnational Transfer of Strategic Organizational Practices: A Contextual Perspective," *Academy of Management Review* 24 (1999): 308–24; Nitin Nohria and Sumantra Ghoshal, "Differentiated Fit and Shared Values: Alternatives for Managing Headquarters-Subsidiary Relations," *Strategic Management Journal* 15 (July 1994): 491–502. For a discussion of how capabilities improve with experience, see Andrew Delios and Paul Beamish, "Survival and Profitability: The Roles of Experience and Intangible Assets in Foreign Subsidiary Performance," *Academy of Management Journal* 44 (2001): 1028–38.

41 Alison Maitland, "Bridging the Culture Gap," *Financial Times,* January 28, 2002: 8.

42 Bain & Company, "Executives Are Taking a Hard Look at Soft Issues" (March 27, 2007), at www.bain.com/bainweb/publications/printer_ready.asp?id=25728 (accessed October 31, 2007).

43 P. Christopher Early and Elaine Mosakowski, "Creating Hybrid Team Cultures: An Empirical Test of Transnational Team Functioning," *Academy of Management Journal* 43 (2000): 26–49.

44 Dinker Raval and Bala Subramanianm, "Effective Transfer of Best Practices Across Cultures," *Competitiveness Review* (Summer–Fall 2000): 183.

45 John A. Byrne, "How Jack Welch Runs GE," *Business Week,* June 8, 1998: 90; Miriam Leuchter, "Management Farm Teams," *Journal of Business Strategy* (May 1998): 29–32; "The House That Jack Built," *The Economist,* September 18, 1999.

46 "In Search of Global Leaders: View of Jeffery Immelt, Chairman and CEO, General Electric," *Harvard Business Review,* August 1, 2003.

47 Leslie Gross Klaff, "Many People, One Mattel," *Workforce Management* (March 2004): 42–44.

48 Rebecca Knight, "Corporate Universities: Move to a Collaborative Effort," *Financial Times* (March 19, 2007).

49 Donna Fenn, "Corporate Universities for Small Companies," *Inc.com* (February 1999), at www.inc.com/magazine/ 19990201/730.html (accessed May 6, 2007).

50 Jeanne C. Meister, *Corporate Universities: Lessons in Building a World-Class Work Force* (New York: McGraw-Hill, 1998).

51 John Griffiths, "Unipart University," *Financial Times* (March 21, 2002).

52 Della Bradshaw, "LVMH," *Financial Times* (March 21, 2002).

53 Steve Trehern, "More Than Just Learning Process," *Financial Times* (March 21, 2002).

54 Knight, "Corporate Universities."

55 *Sources include the following:* Edward Luce, *In Spite of the Gods: The Strange Rise of Modern India* (New York: Doubleday, 2007); Julie Schlosser, "Harder Than Harvard," *Fortune*, March 17, 2006; "Virtual Champions," Survey: Business in India, *The Economist*, June 1, 2006; Anand Giridharadas, "India's Edge Goes Beyond Outsourcing," *New York Times*, April 4, 2007; Steve Hamm, "Passing the Baton at Infosys," *Business Week*, June 16, 2006; "Infosys' Murthy: Sharing a 'Simple Yet Powerful Vision,' " *Knowledge@Wharton* (May 23, 2001); Gautam Kumra and Jayant Sinha, "The Next Hurdle for Indian IT," *McKinsey Quarterly* (2003), Special edition: Global Directions; Subir Roy, "Infosys Builds a Realistic Terrain," *Rediff.com* (2005), at www.rediff.com/money/ 2005/jun/16spec.htm (accessed October 31, 2007); Gina Ruiz, "Infosys Technologies: Optimas Award Winner for Global Outlook," *Workforce Management*, March 26, 2007: 27.

16

chapter sixteen

Marketing Globally

May both seller and buyer see the benefit.

—*Turkish proverb*

Objectives

- To understand a range of product policies and the circumstances in which they are appropriate internationally

- To grasp the reasons for product alterations when deciding between standardized versus differentiated marketing programs among countries

- To appreciate the pricing complexities when selling in foreign markets

- To interpret country differences that may necessitate alterations in promotional practices

- To comprehend the different branding strategies companies may employ internationally

- To discern complications of international distribution and practices of effective distribution

- To perceive why and how emphasis in the marketing mix may vary among countries

CASE: Avon Calls on Foreign Markets

Avon, founded in 1886, is one of the world's oldest and largest manufacturers and marketers of beauty and related products.[1] Many are most familiar with Avon through its long-standing ad, "Ding dong, Avon calling," but the company has recently switched to "Hello Tomorrow" to change its image and better reflect the company's new marketing approaches.

WHERE OPPORTUNITY CURRENTLY KNOCKS

Avon is headquartered in the United States, but it makes over 70 percent of its sales outside its North American division. It seems to be selling everywhere—moisturizer to Inuits above the Arctic Circle and makeup delivered by canoe to residents of Brazil's Amazon region. It has its own sales operations in 63 countries and territories, and it distributes to another 51. However, Avon was 28 years old (an adult by human standards) before it ever ventured abroad, and then only to nearby Canada. Forty years later, a geriatric in human terms, it moved into its second foreign market, Venezuela.

Since 1990, Avon's international thrust has really accelerated. Most recently, Avon set up operations in Finland, Macedonia, Kazakhstan, Bosnia and Herzegovina, and Vietnam. Map 16.1 shows how Avon divides the world regionally and the portion of its business in each region.

Why Avon Went Global

So why has Avon put so much emphasis on international expansion in recent years? First, Avon forecast a slow growth potential in the U.S. market because there is virtually no remaining untapped market for cosmetics, fragrances, and toiletries. To grow rapidly in the United States would mean taking sales from competitors, and the U.S. beauty market is *very* competitive. If you doubt this, just try weaving through a large U.S. department store without being accosted and sprayed on.

Avon has preferred to put emphasis on less competitive markets, and its latest annual report even states that it expects U.S. "growth to be in line with that of the overall beauty market," which means its domestic sales will depend primarily on the population growth of women in the cosmetics-using age group. Even if there was a considerable untapped U.S. market, less than 5 percent of the world's population lives in the United States.

Second, you need to understand Avon's distribution system to appreciate why Avon worried about U.S. sales in the latter part of the twentieth century. Avon has always depended on direct selling by contracted independent salespersons (almost always women working part time and known as "Avon ladies" or "Avon representatives"), who sell to households by demonstrating products and giving beauty advice. These reps place sales orders with Avon and deliver orders to the customers once they receive them.

Historically, these direct sales have been the backbone of Avon's success. To begin with, direct selling offers Avon a cost savings advantage by enabling the company to maintain a smaller number of employees, keep its advertising budget low (the Avon ladies do much of the promotion), and avoid having to pay for shelf space in stores. The lower costs have facilitated Avon's maintenance of generally lower prices than those that competitors charge in department stores. Thus Avon has consistently maintained an image of good value for the money.

Direct selling also offers additional marketing advantages because word-of-mouth customers tend to be quite loyal to the Avon ladies they befriend. However, in the late twentieth century, the outlook for U.S. direct sales of any kind of product looked bleak. Droves of U.S. women were entering the workforce full time, which made them less receptive to door-to-door salespersons and less willing to spend time on makeup demonstrations and the arrangements for a later receipt of their purchases. Because of working full time, the pool of women seeking part-time employment seemed to be drying up.

Meanwhile, Back in the Home Market   Before we examine Avon's foreign market, let's look for a moment at what has actually transpired for Avon in the United States. In an effort to diversify from its direct sales model, Avon contracted to sell through Sears and JCPenney, retail chains whose images and customer bases are compatible with Avon's. However, by 2007 Avon was out of both because the two had changed their strategies by exiting almost completely out of the sale of cosmetics.

In an effort to combat the problem of house-to-house sales, Avon has allowed reps to open retail outlets, which are usually small kiosks in shopping malls. Further, Avon ladies have pretty much given up their old "ding dong" routines by selling instead to friends and family, colleagues at work, and through ads on their own Web sites. In the meantime, the prediction that the pool of part-time job seekers would dry up proved wrong. Between 1996 and 2005, the number of direct sellers in the United States for all companies increased from 8.5 million to 14.1 million, and sales value has increased proportionately.

MAP 16.1
Where Avon Sells
(and How Much)

Avon sells on every continent (except Antarctica) and derives most of its sales outside its home country. The labeled countries are where Avon has operations.

Source: Avon Products Inc., *Avon 2006 Annual Report,* at www.avoncompany. com (accessed November 6, 2007).

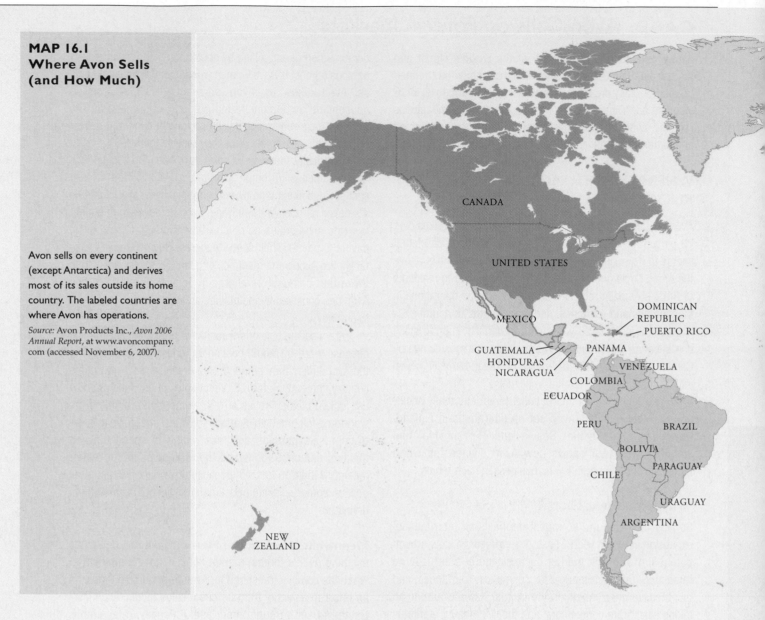

When the U.S. outlook looked gloomy, the outlook in foreign markets looked bright. For example, the lack of developed infrastructure in the rural areas of such countries as Brazil and the Philippines deters women from leaving their homes to shop for cosmetics. But in these countries, Avon ladies reach consumers in some of the most remote areas because there are ample numbers of potential Avon ladies.

For instance, Avon has 800,000 representatives in Brazil alone. In transitional economies, Avon's market entry coincided with pent-up demand from the period of centrally planned economic policies. Avon entered Ukraine, for instance, with free makeovers at meeting halls in nine major cities, which 240,000 people attended. In rapid-growth economies, such as Chile and Malaysia, Avon taps a growing middle-class market that can afford its products.

THE INTERNATIONAL STRATEGY

Global Products

As Avon moved internationally, it pretty much allowed its country managers to decide what products would sell in their markets. Either Avon's R&D unit in the United States or a local R&D unit would then develop them. These were largely produced within the country selling them and included such products

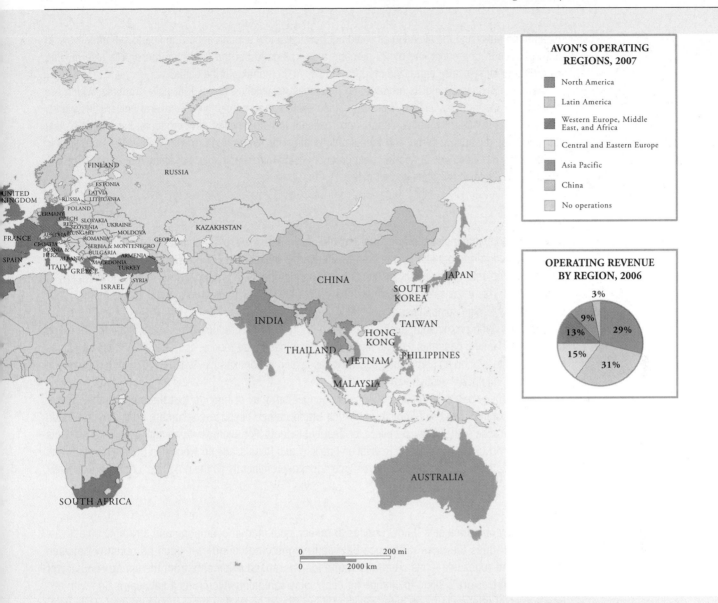

AVON'S OPERATING REGIONS, 2007

- North America
- Latin America
- Western Europe, Middle East, and Africa
- Central and Eastern Europe
- Asia Pacific
- China
- No operations

OPERATING REVENUE BY REGION, 2006

3%
9%
13%
15%
29%
31%

as a combination (moisturizer, sunscreen, and insect repellent) skin cream in Brazil, skin-lightening creams in parts of Asia, long-lasting citrus fragrances in Mediterranean countries, technology-driven skin products in Japan, health and wellness products in Argentina, and bigger bottles of personal care products in Spain.

Once products are developed, Avon disseminates the information to its facilities elsewhere. For example, Avon-Japan developed emulsion technologies to produce lotions and creams with lighter textures and higher hydration levels, and many Avon operations in other countries now use the process.

Some Pitfalls of Product Proliferation   On the one hand, this decentralization to fit the wants of local consumers has undoubtedly given consumers the products they want. On the other hand, it has come with costs. To begin with, the resultant product proliferation has increased manufacturing costs, which threatens Avon's strategy of maintaining a good profit margin while simultaneously offering customers a good value for their money.

Next, Avon has depended primarily on its catalogs to promote its products. For instance, it distributed about 600 million catalogs in 12 languages for 2007, which dwarfed the circulation of any commercial publication. However, with so many products—13,000 for the Mexican market alone—the catalogs became too bulky and the Avon ladies could not possibly know enough about the line to sell effectively. In 2006, Avon cut its product line by 25 percent, and it plans to cut the line even more. It is also moving toward more large-scale centralized production to save on manufacturing costs.

Although Avon is paring its product line, this does not imply a cutback in new products, which are important in the industry. In fact, Avon has signed exclusive agreements with several universities worldwide (such as in Australia, China, Japan, and Thailand) to help develop new products. For example, Asia has long been a leader in herbal and therapeutic treatments. Avon's venture with Chiang Mai University in Thailand has produced one of Avon's latest products using this Asian expertise, Anew Alternative, which is purported to diminish fine lines and wrinkles.

Global Branding

Avon now emphasizes global brands that include Anew, Rare Gold, beComing, and Far Away fragrances. Through standardized branding, Avon creates a uniform global quality image while saving costs by using uniform ingredients and packaging. Global branding also helps inform consumers that the company is international. This helps sales in countries such as Thailand, where consumers prefer to buy beauty products made by foreign companies.

Although Avon prominently displays its name on most of its products worldwide, some of its brand names differ among countries. For instance, when Avon has made foreign acquisitions, it has sometimes kept the successful brand name and goodwill it has acquired. For example, when Avon acquired Justine in South Africa, it kept the Justine name.

The company prints instructions in local languages but may or may not put the brand names in that language. It sometimes uses English or French brand names because consumers consider the United States and France high-quality suppliers for beauty products. For example, Avon sells skin care products called Rosa Mosqueta (in Spanish), Revival (in English), and Renaissage (in French) in Chile, Argentina, and Japan, respectively. In each case, the Avon logo appears prominently on the products' containers as well.

Global Pricing

Each country operation sets its own prices to reflect local market conditions and strategic objectives. However, at times the price difference between neighboring countries—such as recently between Colombia and Venezuela—has created demand for contraband shipments from the country with lower prices. The prices are subject to change for each sales campaign. Avon runs a new campaign with different special offers every two weeks in the United States and every three weeks abroad. The shortness of campaigns is helpful for adjusting prices in highly inflationary economies. However, recently Avon inaugurated a strategy of introducing two-tiered products that sell at different prices. The aim is to capture more upmarket sales while maintaining the existing clientele. For instance, it has contracted with Christian Lacroix to develop fragrances that will sell at a higher price than Avon's traditional ones.

Global Promotion

Although Avon's promotion is primarily through its brochures and catalogs, it has recently put more emphasis on advertising. In 2006, it increased its global advertising budget by 83 percent and then another 35 percent in 2007. It uses such media as broadcast and billboards and has four primary objectives:

- To sell newly launched products
- To accelerate sales in some of its fastest-growing markets, such as Russia
- To recruit reps in places like China
- To use a campaign called "Hello Tomorrow" to change the public perception of its products as unfashionable and outdated to stylish and modern

"Hello Tomorrow"   This campaign is Avon's first global ad campaign aimed at the image of its overarching Avon brand. Its prior global campaigns aimed at selling specific products. Despite the global campaign, some of Avon's ads vary by country. For instance, it sponsors a British TV drama about footballers' wives and one in Russia that includes a character who sells Avon products. Avon is also using celebrities to help sell its products. The Mexican film star Salma Hayek is the face of Avon. The Academy Award–winning actress Jennifer Hudson is the spokesperson for Imari fragrance. The baseball player Derek Jeter (yes, Avon does have *some* products for men too) has his name on a collection of skin care products.

Meeting the Needs of Women Worldwide   Perhaps Avon's most important campaign is to develop a global image as a company that supports women and their needs, a campaign that has generated favorable publicity in media reports. Building on this theme, Avon co-hosted the Global Summit for a Better Tomorrow at the United Nations during International Women's Day in 2007, and it gives annual Women of Enterprise Awards to leading women entrepreneurs. It also publicizes how being an Avon lady heightens the role of women, which has been particularly successful at attracting new reps in developing countries such as Malaysia and the Philippines.

Undoubtedly, Avon's biggest social responsibility projects are its work internationally in fighting breast cancer and domestic violence. Avon ladies disseminate information about breast cancer along with their promotion brochures and sell items to raise money for local needs. Avon is the largest corporate donor to breast cancer research. The fight against domestic violence is a newer Avon program. It is working through local organizations to prevent violence through education and to treat women who have been victims.

Global Distribution

Avon basically duplicates its distribution method in foreign countries, which means it sells to independent representatives (about 5.3 million worldwide) who have taken orders from customers they have either communicated with or visited. However, there are some variations. We have already discussed some of the changes in the United States. In Japan, there is a substantial mail-order business. In Argentina, Avon has beauty centers.

Probably the biggest deviation from direct selling occurred in China, the only single-country division in Avon's global network. In response to a 1998 Chinese law prohibiting house-to-house sales, Avon quickly opened about 6,000 beauty boutiques, lined up 9,000 independent stores to carry Avon, and opened 1,000 beauty counters. Thus Avon made its products available in virtually every corner of the country. In 2005, the Chinese government loosened its house-to-house sales regulations but with many restrictions, such as capping the commission for salespeople and preventing them from recruiting others to work on a shared commission plan.

Avon seeks to transfer successful practices in one country to other countries. To encourage the transfer of know-how, Avon brings marketing personnel from different countries together to share what it calls "best practices," and it passes on information from country to country. It also promotes competition among countries, such as the chairman's awards for country-level initiatives to improve sales, quality, and efficiency.

LOOKING TOWARD THE FUTURE

Avon has several challenges for the future. Although its direct sales method has been important in Avon's success, there are drawbacks to it. For one, customers cannot obtain a product whenever they want it. For another, reps report many returns because customers cannot always discern exact colors from catalogs. For another, it may be difficult for Avon to capture clientele in a higher-price category while maintaining the value-for-money clientele.

Avon anticipates that international operations will account for the bulk of its growth in the foreseeable future. Its products are still not available to a large portion of the world's women. It is operating in all four BRIC countries and is the market leader in two of them (Brazil and Russia).

Introduction

The Avon case points out that similar marketing principles are at work in domestic and foreign markets. In other words, regardless of where a company operates, it must have desirable products and services, inform people of their availability, and offer them at an acceptable price and accessible location that consumers favor. However, as we noted in the case, environmental differences may cause companies to apply these principles differently abroad, such as by offering product variations to correspond with local preferences, as Avon has done by adding an insect repellent to a skin cream for Brazil. Avon's experience also emphasizes the need to find the right balance between the benefits of local responsiveness and the efficiency gains of standardization.

As you read this chapter, keep in mind that whatever marketing approach a company takes abroad should be compatible with its overall aims and strategies. However, this does not imply that you must follow the same strategy for every one of your products or for every country. For example, cost leadership or differentiation may be more important for your product in some markets than in others. If you do choose to follow the same tactics globally, such as offering the same product to all countries, this may lead you to a mass market orientation in one country and a focused strategy in another. Finally, the degree of global standardization versus national responsiveness may vary within elements of the marketing mix, such as seeking maximum product standardization while promoting the product differently among countries.

Figure 16.1 shows the place of marketing within the functional operations in international business. We first discuss the application of different marketing strategies to international operations. Then we examine the elements within the marketing mix—product, pricing, promotion, branding, and distribution—and explain the major factors that managers need to consider for each of these when operating internationally. Finally, we discuss how emphasis within the marketing mix may need to vary to fit the conditions of each country where the company is selling.

CONCEPT CHECK

Recall that we devote an entire section of Chapter 11 to the issue of "Global Integration Versus Local Responsiveness." As we point out, when expanding into foreign markets, a company can save money by standardizing many of its policies and practices and—particularly if it's pursuing a **global strategy** of expansion— its products. Here we observe that a strategy of marketing *standardized products*— marketing the same or similar versions to specific global segments—falls at one end of the *global integration/local responsiveness* spectrum.

FIGURE 16.1   Marketing as a Means of Pursuing an International Strategy

Recall that we used Figure 14.1 to introduce the various *means* by which a company can pursue its international objectives and strategy. Among those *means* we included *functions*, and here we focus on one of the most important of those *functions: marketing.*

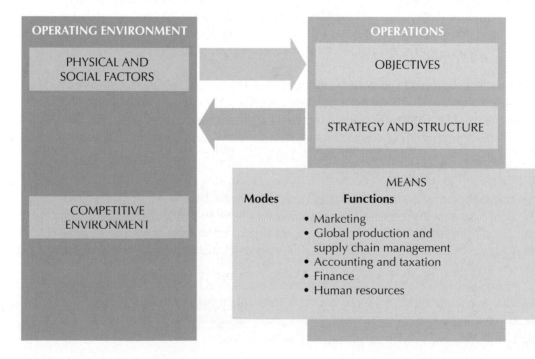

Marketing Strategies

Most marketing texts classify companies' marketing orientations, although there is some variation in the categories they use. We begin this section with discussion of the international application of these orientations. We conclude by explaining the concepts of market segmentation and targeting and how they relate both to the orientations and to all the elements of the marketing mix.

Overall international marketing strategies should depend on the company's

- Marketing orientation.
- Target market.

MARKETING ORIENTATIONS

This section highlights the international application of five common marketing orientations: *production, sales, customer, strategic marketing,* and *social marketing.*

Production Orientation   With production orientation, companies focus primarily on production—either efficiency or high quality—with little emphasis on marketing. There is little analysis of consumer needs; rather, companies assume customers want lower prices or higher quality. Although this approach has largely gone out of vogue, it is used internationally for certain cases:

- *Commodity sales,* especially those for which there is little need or possibility of product differentiation by country
- *Passive exports,* particularly those that serve to reduce surpluses within the domestic market
- *Foreign-market segments or niches* that may happen to resemble segments to which the product is aimed at home

Price is the most important factor in selling many commodities.

Commodity Sales   Companies sell many raw materials and agricultural commodities, such as grapes and tin, primarily on the basis of price because there is universal demand for the undifferentiated product. However, even for commodity sales, companies have realized that marketing efforts may yield positive international sales results. For example, the promotion of the Chiquita brand on bananas has helped increase global supermarket distribution in a glutted market.

In addition, oil producers, such as Petroven, LUKOIL, and Aramco, have bought branded gasoline-distribution operations abroad to help them sell an otherwise undifferentiated product. Commodity producers also put efforts into business-to-business marketing by providing innovative financing and ensuring timely, high-quality supplies.

CONCEPT CHECK

In explaining "Commodity Agreements" in Chapter 8, we define *commodities* as raw materials or primary products (e.g., crude petroleum, copper, coffee) that have entered into trade. Commodities account for about 25 percent of global merchandise trade.

Passive Exports   Many companies begin exporting very passively by filling unsolicited requests from abroad. At this point, they adapt their products very little, if at all, to foreign consumers' preferences. This practice suffices for many companies that view foreign sales as an accessory to domestic sales. In this situation, companies frequently export only if they have excess inventory they can't reasonably sell domestically. In fact, fixed costs are sometimes covered from domestic sales so they quote lower prices on exports as a means of liquidating inventories without disrupting the domestic market.

Passive sales occur when

- Advertising spills over.
- Foreign buyers seek new products.

Foreign Niches   A company may develop a product aimed at achieving a large share of its domestic market and then find there are consumers abroad who are willing to buy that product. For instance, a company may sell to a mass market at home and serve a niche market in foreign locations, such as Inca Kola, the largest-selling soft drink in Peru that has only small niche markets abroad—primarily to people who were consumers in Peru.

However, keep in mind that a niche market abroad may become a mass market, as is the case with Mexico's Corona beer. A company may also use a production orientation when selling in countries with only a small market potential. For example, in small

The unaltered domestic product may have appeal abroad.

- Because of spillover in product information from its home country.
- Through a simultaneous multicountry launch.
- By developing the product abroad.

developing countries, companies may make few product alterations because the market size does not justify the alteration expense. Furthermore, if competitors act likewise, there may be no pressure for product alterations. Companies may not even change plugs on exported electrical products to fit local sockets, leaving the job of conversion to local purchasers instead.

Sales Orientation   Internationally, sales orientation means a company tries to sell abroad what it can sell domestically and in the same manner on the assumption that consumers are sufficiently similar globally. A company may make this assumption erroneously because of its ethnocentricity or because it lacks sufficient information about the foreign market it wishes to serve.

This orientation differs from the production orientation because of its active rather than passive approach to promoting sales. However, there is much anecdotal evidence of foreign marketing failures because of assumptions that product acceptance will be the same as at home or that heavy sales efforts abroad can overcome negative foreign attitudes toward the product, its price, or method of distribution. Even so, there are successful examples of marketing abroad with little or no research on what foreign consumers want. Figure 16.2 offers a humorous twist on this point.

Of course, there are products other than commodities that need no adaptation on a country basis, such as razor blades, aircraft, and cameras. For other products, however, the greatest ability for a company to be successful with a sales orientation is to sell to countries where customs and traditions and customer characteristics are similar to those at home and where there is also a great deal of spillover in product information, such as between the United States and Canada.[2] A company may first develop the product for its home market. It may develop a new product to launch almost simultaneously in multiple countries, as Whirlpool did for high-capacity front-loading washing machines.[3] Or it may develop the product abroad and introduce it later to its home market, as Mars did with Whiskas, a cat food.

| A customer orientation takes geographic areas as given.

Customer Orientation   In a company that operates according to the sales orientation we just discussed, management usually is guided by answers to questions such as these: Should the company send some exports abroad? Where can the company sell more of product X? That is, the product is held constant and the sales location is varied.

In contrast, a customer orientation asks, What and how can the company sell in country A? In this case, the country is held constant and the product and method of marketing it are varied. This may occur, for example, when a company has already developed its sales in markets similar to its home country.

FIGURE 16.2   The Functionally Flexible Call Center

Sometimes you can sell products when and where conditions aren't particularly promising. For the most part, however, you need a well-conceived and well-implemented marketing program to facilitate the sale of just about any product.

Source: DILBERT © Scott Adams/Dist. by United Features Syndicate, Inc.

In addition, a company may want to penetrate markets in a given country because of the country's size, growth potential, proximity to home operations, currency or political stability, or any of a host of other reasons. In the extreme of this approach, a company would move to products completely unrelated to its existing product lines. Though an uncommon strategy, some companies have adopted it. For example, Chilena de Fosforos, a Chilean match producer, wanted to tap the Japanese market because of Japanese growth and size, competition within the Chilean market, and the promotional appeal of being able to say "We supply Japan." However, because the company was not price competitive in Japan for matches, it successfully entered the Japanese market by making chopsticks—a product that would use its poplar forest resources and wood-processing capabilities.[4] Or this orientation may lead a company to add products to its portfolio. In India, for instance, Avon sold a line of nutritional products as well as its core line of beauty products.[5]

As with a production orientation, a company using a customer orientation may do so passively. Increasingly, purchasing agents are setting product specifications and then seeking out contracts for the foreign manufacture of components or finished products. For example, the Hong Kong company Yue Yuen Industrial is the world's largest branded footwear manufacturer, making athletic shoes to the specifications of companies such as Nike, New Balance, and Adidas.[6] In such cases, the supplier depends on the buyer to determine what final customers want. The supplier is primarily concerned with promoting its production capabilities on a business-to-business basis by emphasizing its pricing and delivery of what it can make.

Strategic Marketing Orientation   Most companies committed to continual rather than sporadic foreign sales adopt a strategy that combines production, sales, and customer orientations. Companies that don't make changes to accommodate the needs of foreign customers may lose too many sales, especially if aggressive competitors are willing to make desired adaptations.

> The most common strategy is product changes as adaptations, done by degree.

Yet companies must consider their competencies; thus they tend to make marketing variations abroad without deviating very far from experience. For example, breweries such as Heineken, Stroh, Bass, and Lion, when faced with restrictions against alcoholic beverages in Saudi Arabia, have turned to sales of nonalcoholic beer (marketed as malt rather than beer), which is closely related to their managers' areas of expertise. The U.S. home builder Pulte Homes, in entering the Argentine market, kept the same floor plans and exterior look of its U.S. homes to gain economies of standardization, but it added bidets in the bathrooms and large rear patios to fit Argentine preferences.[7]

Social Marketing Orientation   Companies with social marketing orientations realize that successful international marketing requires serious consideration of potential environmental, health, social, and work-related problems that may arise when selling or making their products abroad. Such groups as consumer associations, political parties, and labor unions are becoming more globally aware—and vocal. They can quell demand when they feel a product in some way violates their concept of social responsibility.

> Companies consider effects on all stakeholders when selling or making their products.

Companies must increasingly consider not only how a product is purchased but also how it is made and disposed of and how it might be changed to be more socially desirable. Such considerations have led Coca-Cola to develop a vitamin-enriched beverage for Botswana and returnable glass containers for Argentina and Brazil.[8] They also led Avon to be the first cosmetic company to ban testing on animals.[9]

> Companies must decide on their target markets, which may include segments that exist in more than one country.

SEGMENTING AND TARGETING MARKETS

Although population and income may give a rough estimate of market size, there are few products that virtually the entire population can be convinced to consume with the same marketing mix. Thus, based on the orientations we have just discussed, companies must segment markets for their products and services and then decide which segment(s) to target and how.

CONCEPT CHECK

In the "Looking to the Future" box in Chapter 12, we touch upon the importance of *demographics* in the process whereby companies evaluate and select countries as locations for international operations. Many of the demographic data considered in international marketing decisions are the same. In addressing the question "Will Prime Locations Change?" for example, we point out that while populations in such high-income countries as Japan are declining, those in many developing countries are growing. We also describe some of the "Economic and Demographic Variables" that companies examine when considering the possibility of expanding sales in a foreign market.

The most common way of segmenting markets is through demographics, such as income, age, gender, ethnicity, and religion. Of course, these may be combined, such as identifying a segment that consists of women age 20 to 30 with incomes between $20,000 and $30,000 per year. Companies may further refine these segments by adding psychographics (attitudes, values, and lifestyles).

Three Approaches to Segmentation   Internationally, there are three basic approaches to segmentation.[10]

By Country   A company may decide, for example, to go for the time being only to the Japanese market because of its population size and purchasing power. It will then need to segment the Japanese market and decide whether to target a single versus multiple segments within Japan, whether to use the same marketing mix to sell to all segments, whether to tailor the products separately to each segment, and whether to vary the promotional and distribution separately for the different segments.

Although this approach may lead to success within Japan, it overlooks the possible similarities of various Japanese market segments with those in other countries. Thus there may be little opportunity of gaining economies through standardization that cut across countries.

By Global Segment   A company may identify some segments globally, such as segments based primarily on income. Thus each country may have some people within this same segment, but the proportional size of each segment will vary by country. Although this may bring about economies of standardization, a company may still need to prioritize by country of entry, may have to delay tapping bigger markets in some countries, and may face high entry costs in other countries where the targeted segment is small.

By Multiple Criteria   Finally, a company can combine these by looking first at countries as segments, second by identifying segments within each country, and third by comparing these within-country segments with those in other countries. Once a company makes this determination, it can determine similarities for targeting the most promising cross-country segments, gain efficiencies through standardization, and still tailor other aspects of its marketing mix—product offerings, promotion, branding, and distribution—so they are compatible with the needs of each country's market.

In effect, a company may hold one or more elements of these marketing functions constant while altering the others. For instance, Chanel aims its cosmetics sales to a segment that transcends national boundaries. It uses branding, promotion, pricing, and distribution globally, but it adapts the cosmetics to local ethnic and climatic norms.[11]

Mass Markets Versus Niche Markets   At the same time, most companies have multiple products and product variations that appeal to different segments in their home countries; thus they must decide which to introduce abroad and whether to target them to mass markets versus niche segments. Sales to a mass market may be necessary if a company is to gain sufficient economies in production and distribution.

For example, some foreign beer companies entered China with a focus strategy by concentrating on the premium sector. However, they failed in their analysis by not segmenting sufficiently by region. The market, although large enough in total size, is so dispersed that high distribution costs made it unprofitable.[12]

In contrast, General Motors (GM) has multiple automobile makes and models that it targets to different income segments. It entered the Chinese market only with its Buick models aimed at a high-income segment that is also highly dispersed. GM found a large enough market to gain production and distribution economies because distributing cars nationally is very different from distributing beer nationally.

Because the percentage of people who fall into any segment may vary substantially among countries, a niche market in one country may be a mass market in another. A company may be content to accept a combination of mass and niche markets; however, if it wishes to appeal to mass markets everywhere, it may need to change elements in its marketing program. For instance, U.S.-based Bell South managed successfully to reach a larger and more mass Venezuelan market by selling fewer minutes on phone cards. It added $4 phone cards to the $10 and $20 cards it customarily sold.[13]

Product Policies

Cost is a compelling reason for standardizing marketing as much as possible globally. When companies change any part of their marketing mix (product, price, promotion, brand, and distribution) to serve foreign markets, they incur additional costs of having to coordinate and control added diversity. Within the marketing mix, MNEs employ the highest degree of standardization in products because changes in products generally incur the most expense.[14] Nevertheless, product adaptations are common. We now consider the reasons for making product alterations for foreign markets, the costs of product alterations, the extent and mix of product lines, and product life cycle considerations.

WHY FIRMS ALTER PRODUCTS

We now examine the legal, cultural, and economic reasons for companies to alter their products to fit the needs of customers in different countries.

Legal Considerations Explicit legal requirements, usually meant to protect consumers, are the most obvious reason for altering products for foreign markets. If you don't comply with the law, you won't be allowed to sell.[15] Pharmaceuticals and foods are particularly subject to regulations concerning purity, testing, and labeling. Automobiles must conform to diverse safety, pollution, and fuel-economy standards.[16] In a seemingly bizarre ruling, China prohibited sales of the Cyndi Lauper song "I Drove All Night" because it sent an unsafe message to motorists.

Legal factors are usually related to safety or health protection.

When standards, such as for safety, differ among countries, companies may either conform to the minimum standards of each country or make and sell products to the highest global standard everywhere. The company must consider cost along with any ill will that may result by having lower standards in some countries. Critics have complained, for example, about companies' sales abroad—especially in developing countries—of such products as toys, automobiles, contraceptives, and pharmaceuticals that did not meet safety or quality standards elsewhere.

Packaging Requirements One of the more cumbersome product alterations for companies is adjusting to different laws on packaging, such as the placement of warning labels. For example, the EU requires such labeling on foods with 0.9 percent or more of bioengineered ingredients, but the United States has no warning-label requirements at all.[26] This difference has caused Unilever to use different types of oil (soy oil in the United States and vegetable oil in Europe) in its Hellmann's mayonnaise so as to avoid warning labels in Europe.[27]

Environmental-Protection Regulations Another problem concerns laws that protect the environment. Some countries prohibit certain types of containers, such as Denmark's ban on aluminum cans. Other countries restrict the volume of packaging materials to

Point Counterpoint

Should Home Governments Regulate Their Companies' Marketing in Developing Countries?

Point   Yes International companies sell products in developing countries that their home countries ban. They also freely advertise and promote products in developing countries for which there are restrictions in their home countries. If we have made a domestic decision not to sell these products because of their dangers, we have a moral obligation to prevent the same dangers abroad.

I know that my statement smacks of extraterritoriality. But let's face it, too many consumers in developing countries lack sufficient education and access to reliable information to make intelligent decisions. Further, they often have corrupt political leaders who do not look after their interests. Finally, we have some moral obligation to assure that these consumers spend on needs rather than on wants that our MNEs have created through clever promotion programs. If developed countries don't regulate to protect consumers in developing countries, no one will.

Companies also export products that don't meet quality standards at home. There are also examples of exporting dangerous products. For example, DDT is so dangerous to the environment that all developed countries have banned its use but not its production. Developed countries have pretty much abandoned the battery recycling business because of strict antipollution requirements to prevent lead poisoning that shows up only after the slow cumulative ingestion through the years. Thus companies export the batteries to developing countries that have either weak or weakly enforced pollution laws.[17]

Developed countries that sell tobacco have attempted to limit tobacco use through warning labels, restrictions on sales to minors, and prohibitions on smoking in certain public areas. The World Health Organization (WHO) estimates that tobacco is the leading cause of preventable death in the world, killing about 5 million people per year. As developed countries have taken more actions against tobacco, tobacco companies have increased their promotions in developing countries that now account for 70 percent of tobacco-related deaths.[18]

There are also examples of products that are suitable for most customers in developed countries but not for those in developing countries. The most famous case involved infant formula sales in developing countries, where infant mortality rates increased when bottle-feeding supplanted breastfeeding. Because of low incomes and poor education, mothers frequently overdiluted formula and gave it to their babies in unhygienic conditions. The governments of developing countries did little to stop the sales.

Counterpoint   No You paint a picture of consumers in developing countries as being incapable of making intelligent purchasing decisions. If this is true, which it may be or not, the answer is education rather than limiting people's choices by regulating international companies. In fact, there are many examples of behavior change, both by consumers and governments in developing countries, when they learn the facts. For instance, Thailand has restricted tobacco smoking in response to statistics showing that smoking is the leading cause of death among Buddhist monks.[22]

Your argument that products banned at home should not be sold abroad assumes the home government knows best, which may reflect a difference in morals rather than a problem of creating physical danger. For instance, some countries have banned the sale of the morning-after pill RU-486 on moral grounds. To ban sales in other countries, which accept a different morality, would seem to be cultural imperialism.

In addition, the conditions between rich and poor countries are sometimes so different that they need different regulations. Let's take your example of DDT exports. Developing countries realize its adverse long-term effect on the environment, but in the short term, many of these countries face a crisis from malaria. South Africa was persuaded to ban the use of DDT in three of its provinces in 1996 and turned, instead, to use of a different pesticide. The number of new malaria cases tripled by 2000, when South Africa renewed DDT spraying and brought the number of new cases down again.[23] DDT is simply the best way to kill the disease-carrying mosquitoes. Until there is some better solution, banning exports of DDT will do more harm than good.

Certainly, if one government has found a product dangerous, it should pass on this information to other governments; in terms of DDT and toxic materials exports, this is already being done.

It's true that tobacco companies are now promoting more heavily in developing countries. However, if, for example, the U.S. government was to limit Philip Morris's sales to or promotion of tobacco to those countries, their citizens would still be able to buy tobacco. Many developing countries have indigenous production of tobacco products. Many of the indigenous companies are even government-owned enterprises, such as the China National Tobacco Company. If Philip Morris were to curtail its advertising there, then smokers would simply buy from a different

Global publicity about the situation led WHO to pass a voluntary code to restrict formula promotion, but not sales, in developing countries. Critics hit Nestlé hardest because it had the largest share of infant formula sales in developing countries and because its name-identified products facilitated the organization of a boycott. The company ceased advertising that could discourage breastfeeding, limited free formula supplies at hospitals, and banned personal gifts to health officials.[19]

MNEs also pay too little attention to the needs of consumers in developing countries. Instead, they primarily develop products suitable to the needs of consumers in developed countries who can afford them. In some cases, these are superfluous products for low-income consumers, but MNEs introduce and promote them heavily there. Thus poor consumers end up buying them instead of spending their money on nutritional and health needs.

Take bottled water sold mainly in plastic bottles by such companies as Nestlé, Danone, Coca-Cola, and PepsiCo. It is often no better than tap water (in fact it often *is* tap water), but it sells for 10,000 times more. The bottles are thrown out and take 1,000 years to biodegrade. The crude oil used to make bottles just for the United States would fuel 100,000 cars per year.[20]

Furthermore, MNEs spend little to develop products to fit the needs of developing countries. Take pharmaceutical research. Only 10 percent of the global health research budget is spent on diseases that account for 90 percent of the global disease burden, mainly diseases that largely bypass developed countries.[21] Instead of spending heavily on life-threatening diseases like malaria, Chagas disease, and sleeping sickness, they spend on lifestyle treatments, such as penile erectile dysfunction and baldness. Surely we can find regulatory means to force companies to meet the real needs of developing countries rather than concentrating on selling dangerous and superfluous products there. ●

company, especially an already established company in the particular market.

I'm glad you brought up the infant formula situation because it shows the complexity of the issue we're discussing. Although there was a correlation between infant formula promotion and infant formula sales in developing countries, it is not clear that this promotion led to a decline in breastfeeding. Other factors also influenced the increase in bottle-feeding—specifically, more working mothers and fewer products and services being made in the home. Together, these factors led people to feed babies "home brews," but they were also often unsanitary. Promotion of infant formula may simply have persuaded them to give up the home brews in favor of the most nutritious breast milk substitute available.

Nevertheless, MNEs' curtailment of promotion when coupled with campaigns for mothers to breast-feed led to increases in breastfeeding. Thus the hard work by well-intentioned antiformula groups seemed to have worked. However, the HIV virus is transmitted through breast milk, which is a particular problem in southern Africa where many women are HIV/AIDS infected.[24] Now there are campaigns to get mothers not to breast-feed. This simply shows the futility of trying to legislate what is good for people.

In fact, how far can we go to try to protect people? For instance, in developed countries, obesity is a growing health problem. We're attacking it through education, the same way I said we should attack problems in developing countries. I can't imagine our banning sugars, fats, and carbohydrates or rationing the purchase of them. Certainly products such as soft drinks seem superfluous when people are ill nourished and in poor health. But there is no clear-cut means of drawing a line between people who can afford and people who can't afford these products. Furthermore, companies such as Coca-Cola have experimented with adding nutrition to products, but consumers have not been very receptive.

Companies *do* alter products to fit the needs of low-income people, everything from smaller packages to less sleek electrical appliances. Although you criticized pharmaceutical companies for not attacking their health needs, these same companies spend heavily to find solutions to health problems that attack both rich and poor people, such as cancer and diabetes.

However, pharmaceutical companies must recoup their expenses if they are to survive; thus they must concentrate on drugs for which they can be paid. Many governmental research centers and nonprofit foundations are better candidates for solving the developing countries' health problems. In fact, some of these are working jointly with pharmaceutical companies to find solutions.[25] ●

save resources and decrease trash. There also are differences in national requirements as to whether containers must be reusable and whether companies use packaging materials that must be recycled, incinerated, or composted.

Issues of Standardization   A recurring issue is the need to arrive at international product standards and eliminate some of the wasteful product requirements for alterations among countries. Although countries have reached agreement on some products (sprocket dimensions on movie film, technical standards on mobile phones, bar codes to identify products), other products (railroad gauges, power supplies, and electrical socket shapes) continue to vary. A global standard has usually resulted from companies' wanting to emulate a dominant producer, such as making personal computers that are IBM compatible.

In reality, there is both consumer and economic resistance to standardization, such as U.S. consumers' reluctance to adapt the metric system. Economically, a complete changeover would be more costly than simply educating people and relabeling. Containers would have to be redesigned and production retooled so that sizes would be in even numbers. (Would U.S. football have a first down with 9.144 meters to go?) Even for new products or those still under development, companies and countries are slow to reach agreement because they want to protect the investments they've already made. At best, international standards will come very slowly.

Indirect Legal Considerations   Marketing managers must also watch for the indirect legal requirements that may affect product content or demand. In some countries, companies cannot easily import certain raw materials or components, forcing them to construct an end product with local substitutes that may alter the final result substantially. Legal requirements such as high taxes on heavy automobiles also shift companies' sales to smaller models, thus indirectly altering demand for tire sizes and grades of gasoline.

Cultural Considerations   Religious differences obviously limit the standardization of product offerings globally; thus food franchise companies avoid sales of pork products in Islamic countries and meat of any kind in India. However, cultural differences affecting product demand are often not so easily discerned. For example, Toyota was initially unsuccessful in selling pickup trucks in the United States until it redesigned the interior with enough headroom for drivers to wear 10-gallon cowboy hats.[28] Volkswagen and Audi have extended the wheelbase for China to accommodate more passengers for weekend outings.[29] International food marketers alter ingredients (especially fat, sodium, and sugar) substantially to fit local tastes and requirements. For instance, a Kellogg's All-Bran bar has three times as much salt in the United States as in Mexico.

Economic Considerations
Income   If a country's average consumers have low incomes, too few of them may be able to buy a product the MNE sells domestically. The company therefore may have to design a cheaper model. For instance, several companies are competing with very inexpensive cars to sell in developing countries.[30] In some cases, consumers have so little extra cash that they buy personal items in small quantities as they need them. For these markets, Gillette sells razor blades and 3M sells scouring pads in smaller package sizes.[31]

Infrastructure   Even if a market segment has sufficient income to purchase the same product the company sells at home, differences in infrastructure may require product alterations. Developing countries generally have poorer infrastructures, and companies may gain advantages by selling products that will withstand rough terrain and utility outages.

Whirlpool sells washing machine models in remote areas of India that have rat guards to protect hoses, extra-strong parts to survive transportation on potholed roads, and heavy-duty wiring to cope with electrical ebbs and surges.[32] In Japan, the infrastructure for automobiles reflects crowded conditions and high land prices. Some U.S. automobile models are too wide to fit into elevators that carry cars to upper floors to be parked, and they cannot make narrow turns on back streets.

Income Distribution   Finally, differences in income distribution may affect demand for certain products. In countries where people with purchasing power typically have household servants, they may forgo purchasing laborsaving products. Whirlpool discovered this when trying to sell automatic washing machines in some markets. It bought "obsolete" technology from Korea so as to sell less automated two-tub machines in those markets.[33]

ALTERATION COSTS

Companies can usually reduce production and inventory costs substantially through product standardization. Nevertheless, as we have just demonstrated, there are sometimes compelling reasons to alter products for different national markets. Some product alterations are cheap to make yet have an important influence on demand. One such area is packaging, which is a common alteration exporters make because of legal and climatic requirements. Before making a decision, marketing managers should always compare the cost of an alteration with the cost of lost sales from no alterations.

One cost-saving strategy a company can use to compromise between uniformity and diversity is to standardize a great deal while altering some end characteristics. Whirlpool puts the same basic compressor, casing, evaporator, and sealant system in its refrigerators for all countries but changes such features as doors and shelves for different countries.[34]

CONCEPT CHECK
In Chapter 12, we list the factors that companies consider when "scanning" potential overseas locations to determine what conditions in the host country's environment are likely to affect the success of international operations. Under "Cost Considerations," we point out that poor internal *infrastructure* inflates operating costs and can in fact negate any cost savings afforded by low labor rates.

Some alterations cost less than others.

High-frequency stores in developing countries, including this one in Mexico, often hang products from the ceiling and attract customers who shop frequently because they cannot afford to buy in large quantities.

THE PRODUCT LINE: EXTENT AND MIX

Broadening the product line may gain distribution economies.

Most companies produce multiple products. It is doubtful that all of these products could generate sufficient sales in a given foreign market to justify the cost of penetrating that market. Even if they could, a company might offer only a portion of its product line, perhaps as an entry strategy.

Sales and Cost Considerations   In reaching product line decisions, marketing managers should consider the possible effects on sales and the cost of having one product as opposed to a family of products. Sometimes a company finds it must produce and sell some less lucrative products if it is to sell the more popular ones, such as sherry glasses to match crystal wine and water glasses. Or a company may be forced into a few short production runs to gain the mass market on other products.

If the foreign sales per customer are small compared to those in the domestic market, selling costs per unit may be higher because of the fixed costs associated with selling. In such a case, the company can broaden the product line it handles, either by grouping sales of several manufacturers or by developing new products for the local market that the same salesperson can handle. (But beware: As our opening case points out, the over-proliferation of Avon's product line resulted in problems both in selling and in cost of production and distribution.)

Product Life Cycle Considerations   There may be differences among countries in either the shape or the length of a product's life cycle. A product facing declining sales in one country may have growing or sustained sales in another. For example, cars are a mature product in Western Europe, the United States, and Japan. They're in the late growth stage in South Korea and in the early growth stage in India. At the mature stage, automobile companies must emphasize characteristics that encourage people to replace their still functional cars, such as by emphasizing lifestyle, speed, and accessories. In the early growth stage, they need to appeal to first-time buyers who worry about cost; thus they emphasize fuel consumption and price.[35]

Pricing Strategies

Within the marketing mix, companies place much importance on price. A price must be low enough to gain sales but high enough to guarantee the flow of funds required to carry on other activities, such as R&D, production, and distribution. The company's strategy on how to compete, such as through cost leadership versus product differentiation, also affects pricing decisions. The proper price will not only ensure short-term profits but also give the company the resources necessary to achieve long-term competitive viability.

POTENTIAL OBSTACLES IN INTERNATIONAL PRICING

Pricing is more complex internationally than domestically because of the following factors:

- Government intervention
- Market diversity
- Export price escalation
- Fluctuations in currency value
- Fixed versus variable pricing
- Relations with suppliers

Let's examine each of these factors.

Government Intervention   Every country has laws that affect the prices of goods at the consumer level. A government price control may set either maximum or minimum prices. Controls against lowering prices usually prevent companies from eliminating competitors to gain monopoly positions. Many countries also set maximum prices for numerous products, which can lower companies' profits.

The WTO, under its antidumping regulations, permits countries to establish restrictions against any import that comes in at a price below that charged to consumers in the exporting country. Although countries may not establish restrictions, the possibility that they will makes it more difficult for companies to differentiate markets through pricing.

Let's say a company wants to test sales in the foreign market. For example, Nestlé tested the U.K. market in this way by exporting for a year from Canada to see if enough of a market would develop to justify completing a frozen-food plant to make Lean Cuisine products. Nestlé used a test-marketing price that would equate more or less with what it would charge by producing the foods in the United Kingdom. To reach that price, it had to compensate for the high shipping costs and customs duties it had to pay during the test. Shipping such dishes as spaghetti bolognese in refrigerated ships and paying customs duties made the costs of the exported products much higher than their U.K. selling prices. However, the cost of this test was small compared to the value of the information gained and the amount of Nestlé's eventual commitment.

A company may also charge different prices in different countries because of competitive and demand factors. It may feel that prices can be kept high in the domestic market by restricting supply to that market. Excess production then can be sold abroad at a lower price, as long as that price covers variable costs and contributes to overhead. In this case, it is essentially following a production marketing strategy.

Market Diversity   Although a company can segment the domestic market and charge different prices in each segment in numerous ways, country-to-country variations create even more natural segments. For example, companies can sell few sea urchins or tuna eyeballs in the United States at any price, but they can export them to Japan, where they are delicacies. Levi's jeans often cost twice as much in the United Kingdom than in the United States.[36]

Pricing Tactics   In some countries, a company may have many competitors and thus little discretion in setting its prices. In other countries, it may have a near monopoly due either to the stage in the product life cycle or to government-granted manufacturing rights not held by competitors. In near-monopoly markets, a company may exercise considerable pricing discretion, using any of the following tactics:

- A **skimming strategy**—charging a high price for a new product by aiming first at consumers willing to pay the price, and then progressively lowering the price
- A **penetration strategy**—introducing a product at a low price to induce a maximum number of consumers to try it
- A **cost-plus strategy**—pricing at a desired margin over cost

Country-of-origin stereotypes also limit pricing possibilities. For example, exporters in developing economies often must compete primarily through low prices because of negative perceptions about their products' quality. But there are dangers in lowering prices in response to adverse stereotypes because a lower price may reduce the product image even further.

Diversity in buying on credit affects sales. Credit buying increases costs, which consumers in some countries are more willing to pay than are consumers in other countries. For example, in Japan consumers are more reluctant than in the United States to rely on consumer credit. Thus in Japan it is less possible than in the United States to use credit payments as a means of inducing the sale of goods. The tax treatment of interest payments also affects whether consumers will pay in cash or by credit.

Governmental price controls may
- Set minimum or maximum prices.
- Prohibit certain competitive pricing practices.

Consumers in some countries simply like certain products more and are willing to pay more for them.

Cash versus credit buying affects demand.

Price generally goes up by more than transport and duty costs.

Export Price Escalation   Another reason pricing is complex internationally is price escalation. If standard markups occur within distribution channels, lengthening the channels or adding expenses somewhere within the system will further increase the price to the consumer. For example, assume the markup is 50 percent and the product costs $1.00 to produce. The price to the consumer would be $1.50. However, if production costs were to increase to $1.20, the 50 percent markup would make the price $1.80, not $1.70 as might be expected.

Figure 16.3 shows price escalation in export sales, which occurs for two reasons:

1. Channels of distribution usually span greater distances and so exporters need to contract with organizations that know how to sell in foreign markets.

2. Tariffs and transport are additional costs that may be passed on to consumers.

There are two main implications of price escalation. Seemingly exportable products may turn out to be noncompetitive abroad if companies use cost-plus pricing—which many do.[37] To become competitive in exporting, a company may have to sell its product to intermediaries at a lower price to lessen the amount of escalation. It should determine what price will maximize profits.

Fluctuations in Currency Value   For companies accustomed to operating with one (relatively) stable currency, pricing in highly volatile currencies can be extremely troublesome. Marketing managers should make pricing decisions to assure the company of enough funds to replenish its inventory and still make a profit. Otherwise, it may be making a "paper profit" while liquidating itself—that is, what shows on paper as a profit may result from the company's failure to adjust for inflation while the merchandise is in stock. For example, during high inflationary periods, companies have to raise prices very frequently.[38] Recall that Avon puts out new brochures very frequently and uses the frequency as a basis for changing prices in such situations.

Two other pricing problems occur because of inflationary conditions:

1. The receipt of funds in a foreign currency that, when converted, buy less of the company's own currency than had been expected

2. The frequent readjustment of prices necessary to compensate for continual cost increases

In the first case, the company sometimes (depending on competitive factors and governmental regulations) can specify in sales contracts an equivalency in some hard currency. For example, a U.S. manufacturer's sale of equipment to a company in Uruguay

CONCEPT CHECK

In discussing "Export Strategy" in Chapter 13, we discuss the importance of *export intermediaries* in the international business *transaction chain* and explain their place in a carefully considered *export business plan*. In turning to "The Export Process," we describe the process of **indirect selling** and explain the central role of home-country intermediaries— independent companies that facilitate the international trade of goods.

FIGURE 16.3   Why Cost–Plus Pricing Pushes Up Prices

Let's say that a product is being exported from Country A and imported into Country B for purchase by consumers there. Let's also say that both the producer/exporter and the importer/distributor tack on 50% markups to the prices they pay for the product. If you add in the costs of transport and tariffs, the product is substantially more expensive in Country B than in Country A—perhaps too expensive to be sold competitively.

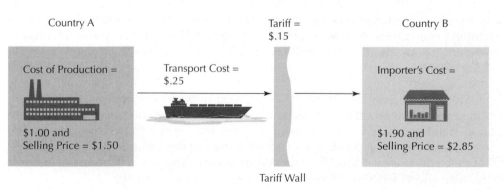

may specify that payment be made in dollars or in pesos at an equivalent price, in terms of dollars, at the time payment is made.

In the second case, frequent price increases make it more difficult for the company to quote prices in letters or catalogs. Perpetual price rises may even hamper what the company would otherwise prefer for distribution. For example, price increases in vending machine sales are frequently difficult because of the need to change machines and to come up with coins or tokens that correspond to the desired percentage increase in price.

Currency-value changes also affect pricing decisions for any product that has potential foreign competition. For example, when the U.S. dollar is strong, companies can sell non-U.S.-made goods more cheaply in the U.S. market because their price in dollars decreases. In such a situation, U.S. producers may have to accept a lower profit margin to be competitive. When the dollar is weak, however, foreign producers may have to adjust their margins downward.

When companies sell similar goods in multiple countries, price differences among them must not exceed by much the cost of bringing the goods in from a lower-priced country, or spillover in buying will occur. Ice cream manufacturers can vary their prices by a large percentage from country to country because the transportation costs compared to the product's price render large-scale movements across borders impractical. However, if the transportation costs compared to the product's price are low, consumers can feasibly buy abroad and import when prices vary substantially from country to country.

The Gray Market For example, automobile prices in Canada are typically much lower than those in the United States, so some Canadian distributors have been selling to U.S. customers where GM has not authorized them to sell. Recall, too, our opening case, where we explain that Avon delegates pricing discretion in foreign markets to in-country managers—a policy that leads occasionally to the importation into countries where prices are high of contraband products from countries where prices are lower. The selling and handling of goods through unofficial distributors, the **gray market,** can undermine the longer-term viability of the distributorship system, cause a company's operations in different countries to compete with each other, and prevent companies from charging what the market will bear in each country.

GM, therefore, has sought to prevent this gray market activity by disallowing warranty work on these vehicles by U.S. dealers and curtailing vehicle allocations to dealers involved in the gray market.[39] Some other companies try to keep prices fairly close among countries to prevent such movements. The courts in some countries uphold the right of companies to maintain prices through distributor agreements, but companies have to monitor compliance and can find enforcement difficult.[40] At the same time, attempts to maintain price differences among countries has been controversial, such as the higher prices U.S. consumers pay for prescription drugs. It has also become more difficult to maintain because consumers have more global information through the Internet.

Fixed Versus Variable Pricing MNEs often negotiate export prices, particularly to foreign distributors. Small companies, especially those from developing countries, frequently give price concessions too quickly, limiting their ability to negotiate on a range of marketing factors that affect their costs:

- Discounts for quantity or repeat orders
- Deadlines that increase production or transportation costs
- Credit and payment terms
- Service
- Supply of promotional materials
- Training of sales personnel or customers

CONCEPT CHECK

We define **foreign exchange** in Chapter 9 as the currency of one country denominated in the currency of another country or group of countries. We point out that most foreign-exchange transactions stem from the activities of commercial banks, but we also observe that **exporters** and **importers** are players on the foreign-exchange market and explain how such factors as **exchange rates** affect certain international business activities, especially the process of making overseas payments.

Case Review Note

There are country-to-country differences in

- Whether manufacturers set prices.
- Whether prices are fixed or bargained in stores.
- Where bargaining occurs.

TABLE 16.1   Negotiating Import-Export Prices

Exporters export because they want to sell their products in foreign markets, and pricing is a key factor in selling products profitably. MNEs and other veteran exporters have learned that negotiating prices—both their own and those of their import partners—is an effective way of considering all the factors that should go into pricing decisions.

The goal is to delay a pricing commitment while discussing a whole package of other commitments.

Importer's Reaction to Price Offer	Exporter's Response
1. Your offer is too expensive.	- Ask what is meant by too expensive.
	- Find out what is considered acceptable and on what basis.
	- Respond by providing justification.
	- Avoid lowering your price until you learn more about what the other party is looking for.
	- Find out if the objection is due to your price offer or if it reflects other factors.
	- Ask yourself, "If I'm too expensive, why are they negotiating with me?"
2. We don't have that kind of budget.	- Find out how large the budget is and for what time frame.
	- Explore whether your offer can fit within the overall budget by combining several budget lines.
	- Propose deferred payment schedules.
	- Confirm the order and postpone deliveries until a new budget is allocated.
	- Split your order into smaller units or miniorders to meet current budget limitations.
3. That's not what we are looking for.	- Ask what they are looking for, and insist on specifics.
	- Keep questioning until you understand the real needs.
	- Repackage your offer in light of the new information received.
4. Your offer is not competitive.	- Ask what "not competitive" means.
	- Find out if competitors' offers are comparable to yours.
	- Find weaknesses in other offers and emphasize your strengths.
	- Reformulate your offer by avoiding direct comparison with competition. Stress the unique features of your products/services.

Source: Claude Cellich, "Business Negotiations: Making the First Offer," *International Trade Journal* 2 (2000): 12–16. Reprinted by permission of Taylor and Francis Group LLC (www.taylorandfrancis.com).

Table 16.1 shows ways in which an exporter (or other marketers as well) may deal more effectively in price negotiations.

Custom influences price negotiations, such as the reluctance of German managers to take the time to bargain. Rather, they tend simply to say "thanks" and look for another provider.[41] The extent to which manufacturers can or must set prices at the retail level varies substantially by country. There is also substantial variation in whether, where, and for what products consumers bargain in order to settle on an agreed price. For instance, U.S. consumers commonly bargain for automobiles, real estate, and large orders of industrial supplies but not for grocery items. However, some automobile dealerships sell only on a fixed-price basis, and bargaining for smaller items is increasing because the Internet allows consumers to confront distributors with alternative prices they have obtained easily. In contrast, consumers in most developing countries commonly bargain for both large and small items but more likely in markets than in retail stores.[42]

Supplier Relations Dominant companies with clout can get suppliers to offer them lower prices, in turn enabling them to gain cost advantages over competitors. But if they buy locally they have this clout only where they have the dominance. Take dominant retailers. Wal-Mart, Marks & Spencer, and Carrefour have such clout in their domestic U.S., U.K., and French markets, respectively. However, they have been hard-pressed to gain the same advantage when entering the other's home market.

The Internet is also causing more companies to compete for the same business, especially when there are sales of largely undifferentiated materials. Thus many industrial buyers are claiming large price decreases through Internet buying. However, sellers can improve their positions by negotiating and by combining Internet communications with face-to-face communications.[43]

Promotion Strategies

Promotion is the presentation of messages intended to help sell a product or service. The types and direction of messages and the method of presentation may be extremely diverse, depending on the company, product, and country of operation.

THE PUSH-PULL MIX

Promotion may be categorized as **push,** which uses direct selling techniques, or **pull,** which relies on mass media. An example of push is Avon's direct selling of cosmetics; an example of pull is magazine advertisements for a brand of cigarettes. Most companies use combinations of both marketing strategies. Again, strategy at Avon provides a good example: In addition to having sales reps deliver brochures (a push tactic), Avon recently increased its advertising budget substantially (indicating a projected emphasis on pull tactics). For each product in each country, a company must determine its total promotional budget as well as the mix of the budget between push and pull.

Case Review Note

Factors in Push-Pull Decisions Several factors help determine the mix of push and pull among countries:

- Type of distribution system
- Cost and availability of media to reach target markets
- Consumer attitudes toward sources of information
- Price of the product compared to incomes

Generally, the more tightly controlled the distribution system, the more likely a company is to emphasize a push strategy because it requires a greater effort to get distributors to handle a product. This is true, for example, in Belgium, where most distributors are small and highly fragmented, forcing companies to concentrate on making their goods available.

Also affecting the push-pull mix is the amount of contact between salespeople and consumers. In a self-service situation, in which there are no salespersons to whom customers can turn for opinions on products, it is more important for the company to use a pull strategy by advertising through mass media or at the point of purchase.

Push is more likely when

- Self-service is not predominant.
- Advertising is restricted.
- Product price is a high portion of income.

SOME PROBLEMS IN INTERNATIONAL PROMOTION

Because of diverse national environments, promotional problems are extremely varied. For example, about 70 percent of India's population is rural, and many in rural areas are illiterate, poor, and without access to televisions and radios. Some mass consumer merchandisers such as Colgate-Palmolive, Unilever, Coca-Cola, and Pepsi are providing samples at religious pilgrimages that millions attend in the expectation that their subsequent word-of-mouth promotions will yield sales.[44]

In many countries, government regulations pose an even greater barrier. For example, Scandinavian television has long refused to accept commercials. Other countries may put legal constraints on what a company says, thus affecting the push-pull mix. For example, in the United States, pharmaceutical companies have been using more pull promotions even for prescription drugs. They talk about the product and brand in television ads and tell viewers to ask their physicians about it. European countries are more restrictive about mentioning the name of a drug. Thus Pfizer is advertising in Europe about the symptoms of erectile dysfunction and telling TV viewers to talk with their physicians about it; however, Pfizer never mentions its drug Viagra in these ads.[45]

Finally, the amount of consumer involvement in making a purchase decision varies by country because of income levels. When a product's price compared to consumer income is high, consumers usually will want more time and information before making a decision. Information is best conveyed in a personal selling situation, which fosters two-way communication. In developing economies, MNEs usually have to use more push strategies for mass consumer products because incomes are low compared to price.

Standardization: Pro and Con   The savings from using the same advertising programs as much as possible, such as on a global basis or among countries with shared consumer attributes, are not as great as those from product standardization. Nevertheless, they can be significant.

In addition to reducing costs, advertising standardization may improve the quality of advertising at the local level (because local agencies may lack expertise), prevent internationally mobile consumers from being confused by different images, and speed the entry of products into different countries. As we point out in our opening case, for example, Avon has in the past geared its global advertising campaigns toward the promotion of specific products. With its "Hello Tomorrow" campaign, however, the company has shifted its focus: Advertising messages are now designed to promote the image of the overarching Avon brand to a single target market all over the world.

However, globally standardized advertising usually means a program that is *similar* from market to market rather than one that is *identical* in each. For example, Apple used the same theme in its "Mac versus PC" ad series in the United States and in the United Kingdom, but it used U.S. TV personalities (John Hodgmann and Justin Long) for the U.S. version and U.K. TV personalities (David Mitchell and Robert Webb) for the U.K. version.[46]

Standardization usually implies using the same advertising agency globally. However, companies may differentiate campaigns among countries even if they use the same agency everywhere. By using the same agency, companies such as IBM, Colgate, and Tambrands have found they can take good ideas in one market and quickly introduce them into other markets because they need not worry about legal and ethical problems from having one agency copy what another has done. However, some companies, such as Procter & Gamble, prefer to use more than one agency to keep the agencies in a state of perpetual competition and to cover one agency's weak spots by drawing on the ideas of another agency.

Case Review Note

Advantages of standardized advertising include

- Some cost savings.
- Better quality at local level.
- Rapid entry into different countries.

A Few Related Issues   Finally, the issue of standardization in advertising raises problems in a few other areas—namely, *translation, legality,* and *message needs.*

TRANSLATION   When media reach audiences in multiple countries, such as MTV programs aired throughout most of Europe or satellite TV services throughout Latin America, ads in those media cannot be translated because viewers watch the same transmission. A problem of using multicountry media, however, is that the product may not be available everywhere that it is advertised.

When, however, a company is going to sell in a country with a different language, translation is usually necessary unless the advertiser is trying to communicate an aura of foreignness. Toyota did this in ads in the United States that were completely in French and Italian with subtitles.[47] The most audible problem in commercial translation is dubbing because words on an added sound track never quite correspond to lip movements. Marketing managers can avoid dubbing problems by creating commercials in which actors do not speak, along with a voice or print overlay in the appropriate language.

A growing type of dubbing in advertising involves product placement in movies and television shows. Because these shows are widely distributed internationally, a wide audience sees the placement. However, the product may not be available everywhere. Technology now permits the products to be removed and replaced for given markets. *Spider-Man 2* had Cadbury Schweppes's Dr Pepper logo on a refrigerator for U.S. screenings, but in Europe it had PepsiCo's Mirinda logo.[48]

On the surface, translating a message would seem to be easy. However, some messages, particularly plays on words, simply don't translate—even between countries that have the same language. The number of ludicrous but costly mistakes companies have made attest to translation difficulties. Sometimes what is an acceptable word or direct translation in one place is obscene, misleading, or meaningless in another. For example, the Milk Board's ad "Got milk?" comes out as "Are you lactating?" in Spanish.[49] In the same Apple commercial to which we referred earlier, the U.S. version used the word "doozy" and the U.K. version used the word "humdinger." Another problem is in choosing the language when a country has more than one. For example, in Haiti, a company might use Creole to reach the general population but French to reach the upper class.

LEGALITY   What is legal advertising in one country may be illegal elsewhere. The differences result mainly from varying national views on consumer protection, competitive protection, promotion of civil rights, standards of morality and behavior, and nationalism. For instance, China bans ads for feminine hygiene pads, hemorrhoid medications, and athlete's foot ointment during three daily mealtimes.[50] It also bans the use of pigs in ads because the use might offend its Muslim population.[51]

In terms of consumer protection, policies differ on the amount of deception permitted, what can be advertised to children, whether companies must list warnings on products of possible harmful effects, and the extent to which they must list ingredients. The United Kingdom and the United States allow direct comparisons with competitive brands (such as Pepsi versus Coca-Cola); the Philippines prohibits them. Only a few countries regulate sexism in advertising.

Some governments restrict the advertising of some products (such as contraceptives) because they feel they are in bad taste. Elsewhere, governments restrict ads that might prompt children to misbehave or people to break laws (such as advertising automobile speeds that exceed the speed limit) and those that show barely clad women. New Zealand banned a Nike ad in which a rugby team tackles the coach, as well as a Chanel ad in which the model said to her male lover before kissing him, "I hate you. I hate you so much I think I'm going to die from it, darling." In both cases, the ads were deemed to threaten violence.[52]

CONCEPT CHECK

In Chapter 2, we emphasize that although language practice *within* a culture serves as a "cultural stabilizer," the effort to apply language practices *across* cultures can have an entirely different effect. In discussing "Spoken and Written Language," we identify several reasons why internationally minded companies should be careful in translating a message conceived in one language into a message to be delivered in another. As for advertising in visual media, we also discuss a variety of potential pitfalls in "Silent Language"—nonverbal communication ranging from body language to the use of colors.

MESSAGE NEEDS   An advertising theme may not be appropriate everywhere because of national differences in how well consumers know the product and how they perceive it, who will make the purchasing decision, and what appeals are most important. For example, few Italians own dishwashers. Italian wives, who tend to stay home more than wives in most other European countries, feel that buying for the sake of convenience reduces cleanliness.

To counter this problem, a group of dishwasher manufacturers (Bosch, Electrolux, Reckitt, and Whirlpool) have teamed up to advertise that dishwashers clean better because they use hotter water.[53] Because of differences in economic level, Home Depot promotes its stores in the United States by appealing to hobbyists, whereas in Mexico it promotes the cost savings from the point of view of do-it-yourselfers.[54]

The reaction to how messages are presented may also vary. For example, Leo Burnett Worldwide produced a public service advertisement to promote checkups for breast cancer. It showed an attractive woman being admired in a sundress with a voice-over message, "If only women paid as much attention to their breasts as men do . . . " Japanese viewers found it a humorous way to draw attention to an important health issue, but French viewers found it offensive because there is nothing humorous about the issue.[55]

Given the increase in television transmission that reaches audiences in multiple countries, advertisers are being forced to find common themes and messages that will appeal to potential consumers in all the countries where their ads are viewed.

Branding Strategies

A *brand* is an identifying mark for products or services. When a company registers a brand legally, it is a trademark. A brand gives a product or service instant recognition and may save promotional costs. From the consumers' standpoint, a known brand conveys a perception of whether firms will deliver what they promise; however, the importance is more crucial in countries with strong cultural characteristics of uncertainty avoidance.[56]

Companies from many countries display their ads and logos wherever they operate. At the Plaza de la Republica in Buenos Aires, Argentina, the logos for such companies as Kodak (United States), Noblex (Germany), and Hitachi (Japan) are interspersed with ads for Argentine companies.

Because companies have spent heavily in the past to create brand awareness, *Business Week* magazine estimates that at least 100 global brands are worth at least a billion dollars. U.S. companies dominate the ownership of these brands, garnering 54 out of the 100 most valuable brands. Of the top dozen, U.S. companies own nine. These top-dozen brands in order are as follows: Coca-Cola, Microsoft, IBM, GE, Intel, Nokia (Finland), Disney, McDonald's, Toyota (Japan), Marlboro, Mercedes-Benz (Germany), and Citi.[57] The ending case in this chapter on Tommy Hilfiger emphasizes the importance of brand as a competitive device.

WORLDWIDE BRAND VERSUS LOCAL BRANDS

In addition to the same branding decisions that every producer has to make, international marketers must make a decision about whether to adopt a worldwide brand or to brand products for a variety of local markets. In this section, we discuss some of the ways in which the international environment affects this decision.

Some Problems with Uniform Brands Some companies, such as Sony, have opted to use the same brand and logo globally. This helps develop a global image, especially for customers who travel internationally. Other companies, such as Nestlé, associate many of their products under the same family of brands, such as the Nestea and Nescafé brands, to share these brands in their goodwill. Nevertheless, a number of problems are inherent in trying to use uniform brands internationally.

> Using the same brand name globally is hampered by
>
> • Language differences.
> • Acquisitions.

Language One problem is that brand names may carry a different association in another language. For example, GM renamed its Buick LaCrosse in Canada after it discovered the word was slang in Quebec for masturbation.[58] Coca-Cola tries to use global branding wherever possible but discovered that the word *diet* in Diet Coke had a connotation of illness in Germany and Italy. The brand is called Coca-Cola Light outside the United States. Big Boy put its customary statue (a boy with checkered overalls and cowlick curl) outside its restaurant in Thailand, and many Thais placed offerings at his feet because they thought it was Buddha.[59]

Pronunciation presents other problems because a foreign language may lack some of the sounds of a brand name or the pronunciation of the name may have a different meaning than the original. For example, Marcel Bich dropped the *h* from his name when branding Bic pens because of the fear of mispronunciation in English. Some locally popular soft drinks have unappetizing meanings when pronounced in English—Mucos (Japan), Pipi (Croatia), Pshitt (France), and Zit (Greece).

Different alphabets present still other problems. For example, consumers judge English brand names by whether the name sounds appealing; brand names in Mandarin and Cantonese need to have visual appeal as well because the Mandarin and Cantonese alphabets are pictograms. Such companies as Coca-Cola, Mercedes-Benz, and Boeing have taken great pains to ensure not only that the translation of their names is pronounced roughly the same as in English but also that the brand name is meaningful. For example, Coca-Cola is pronounced *Ke-kou-ke-le* in Mandarin and means tasty and happy. Google became Gu Ge in Mandarin because it means "harvest song" instead of "doggy" or "old hound," as the original name was being pronounced.[60] Furthermore, companies have sought names that are considered lucky in China, such as a name with eight strokes in it and displayed in red rather than blue. Similarly, the digit eight is overrepresented in product prices, such as ending a price with an eight.[61]

Brand Acquisition Much international expansion takes place through acquisition of companies in foreign countries that already have branded products. However, Sara Lee acquired various Brazilian coffee roasters and is now trying to consolidate them into a national brand because stretching the promotional budget over so many brands means that promotions are not as effective as they might be, given that less is spent on any one brand to build significant positive recognition.[62] Overall the portion of local brands to international brands is decreasing; however, there are many examples of strong local brands that companies cannot easily displace.[63]

Country-of-Origin Image   Companies should consider whether to create a local or a foreign image for their products. The products of some countries, particularly developed countries, tend to have a higher-quality image than do those from other countries.[64] There are also image differences concerning specific products from specific countries. For example, many Japanese believe that clothing made abroad is superior to that made in Japan. Thus Burberry has created separate labels for its products made in Japan and made in the United Kingdom (Burberry London brand). The British have a positive image of Australian wine; thus a young Australian winery sought a very Australian name, Barramundi, for its wine exports to the United Kingdom.[65]

> Images of products are affected by where they are made.

But images can change. Consider that for many years various Korean companies sold abroad under private labels or under contract with well-known companies. Some of these Korean companies, such as Samsung, now emphasize their own trade names and the quality of Korean products. At the same time, the Korean LG Group, best known for its Gold Star brand, has introduced a line of high-end appliances with a European-sounding name, LG Tromm.[66] At the same time, there is evidence that consumers have limited knowledge of the country of origin of most brands.[67]

In an innovative effort to create a British ice cream flavor along the lines of its American Cherry Garcia, Ben & Jerry's ran a contest for the best name and flavor. Cool Britannia won out over such entrants as Minty Python, Grape Expectations, Choc Ness Monster, and The Rolling Scones.[68]

One of the ongoing international legal debates concerns product names associated with location. The EU protects the names of many EU products, such as Roquefort and Gorgonzola cheeses, Parma ham, and Chianti wine. Starbucks has signed a licensing agreement with Ethiopia for use of the regional name Sidamo on one of its coffees.[69]

Generic and Near-Generic Names   Companies want their product names to become household words, but not so much that competitors can use trademarked brand names to describe their similar products. In the United States, the brand names Xerox and Kleenex are nearly synonymous with copiers and paper tissues, but they have nevertheless remained proprietary brands. Some other names that were once proprietary, such as cellophane, linoleum, and Cornish hens, have become **generic**—available for anyone to use.

> If a brand name is used for a class of product, the company may lose the trademark.

In this context, companies sometimes face substantial differences among countries that may either stimulate or frustrate their sales. For example, aspirin and Swiss army knives are proprietary names in Europe but generic in the United States, a situation that impairs European export sales of those products to the United States because U.S. companies can produce aspirin and Swiss army knives.

Distribution Strategies

A company may accurately assess market potential, design goods or services for that market, price them appropriately, and promote them to probable consumers. However, it will have little likelihood of reaching its sales potential if it doesn't make the goods or services conveniently available to customers. Companies need to place their goods where people want to buy them. For example, does a man prefer to buy shampoo in a grocery store, barbershop, drugstore, or some other type of outlet? At the same time, a company's system of distribution may give it strategic advantages not easily copied by competitors. Recall from our opening case, for instance, that Avon's strategy of selling directly through independent reps allows the company not only to save on certain costs but also to build customer loyalty through word-of-mouth advantages inherent in direct selling.

Distribution is the course—physical path or legal title—that goods take between production and consumption. In international marketing, a company must decide on the method of distribution among countries as well as the method within the country where final sale occurs. Companies may limit early distribution in given foreign countries by attempting to sell regionally before moving nationally. Many products and markets lend themselves to this sort of gradual development. In many cases, geographic barriers and poor internal transportation systems divide countries into very distinct markets. In other countries, very little wealth or few potential sales may lie outside the large metropolitan areas. In still others, advertising and distribution may be handled effectively on a regional basis.

We've already discussed operating forms for foreign-market penetration. In Chapter 13 we discuss distribution channels to move goods among countries and how the title to goods gets transferred. This section does not review these aspects of distribution; it discusses distributional differences and conditions within foreign countries that an international marketer should understand.

A company may enter a market gradually by limiting geographic coverage.

Does Geography Matter?

Is Necessity the Mother of Invention?

You've probably heard the saying that it is as "difficult as selling a refrigerator to Eskimos." Thus climate is a great influence on the demand for many products—clothes, sporting equipment, snow tires, air conditioners, and sunscreen, to name a few—and is a variable when identifying market segments. Furthermore, seasonal changes that occur at opposite times in the northern and southern hemispheres allow you to spread your sales more evenly during the year, such as by focusing ski sales in Switzerland during December through March and in Chile during June through September. This hemispheric difference may also cause you to make adjustments. Films aimed at a young audience sometimes debut months apart between the northern and southern hemispheres so as to be viewed during school vacation periods that correspond to the hot months.

Natural conditions—such as mountains, waterways, and deserts—create both barriers and expediencies to distribution. For example, countries can more easily build infrastructure where there are flat areas without obstructions; thus, other things being equal, these areas provide better internal distribution possibilities.

Emigration is largely clustered because people move where others of their ethnic group have gone before, thus forming subcultures. Understanding where these groups exist can help identify potential markets.[70] For instance, Guatemala's Pollo Campero, when entering the U.S. market, went first to Los Angeles, where there are more than a million Central Americans.

The distance between production and market affects pricing. Because transportation cost roughly correlates with distance, there is usually a higher cost to serve farther locations. This extra cost must either be passed on to consumers or absorbed by the selling company. In addition, if markets are close to each other, it is more difficult to maintain different price schedules between them because promotion likely reaches both markets and consumers will buy from the less expensive location. In fact, the closeness of most Canadians to the U.S. border has influenced Canadian stores to stay open longer and operate on more days, lest Canadians cross the border to buy in the United States.

Although geography does play a role in marketing, as people have more disposable income as well as knowledge about products from elsewhere this role has become less important. Thus people in tropical climates do buy winter clothes and skis because they travel to snowy areas for recreation. And there's even a market for refrigerators among the Eskimos. ●

DECIDING WHETHER TO STANDARDIZE

Within the marketing mix, MNEs find distribution one of the most difficult functions to standardize internationally for several reasons. Each country has its own distribution system, which an MNE finds difficult to modify because it is entwined with the country's cultural, economic, and legal environments. Nevertheless, many retailers are successfully moving internationally.

Some of the factors that influence how goods will be distributed in a given country are citizens' attitudes toward owning their own store, the cost of paying retail workers, legislation differentially affecting chain stores and individually owned stores, legislation restricting the operating hours and size of stores, the trust that owners have in their employees, the efficacy of the postal system, and the financial ability to carry large inventories.

For example, Hong Kong supermarkets, compared with those in the United States, carry a higher proportion of fresh goods, are smaller, sell smaller quantities per customer, and are located more closely to each other. This means that companies selling canned, boxed, or frozen foods encounter less demand per store in Hong Kong than in the United States. They would also have to make smaller deliveries because of store sizes and would have a harder time fighting for shelf space.

A few other examples should illustrate how distribution norms differ. Finland has few stores per capita because general-line retailers predominate there, whereas Italian distribution has a fragmented retail and wholesale structure. In the Netherlands, buyers' cooperatives deal directly with manufacturers. Japan has cash-and-carry wholesalers for retailers that do not need financing or delivery services. In Germany, mail-order sales are very important; not so in many developing countries that have less reliable delivery systems.

How do these differences affect companies' marketing activities? One soft drink company, for example, has targeted most of its European sales through grocery stores. However, the method for getting its soft drinks to those stores varies. In the United Kingdom, one national distributor has been able to gain sufficient coverage and shelf space so the soft drink company can concentrate on other aspects of its marketing mix. In France, a single distributor has been able to get good coverage in the larger supermarkets but not in the smaller ones; consequently, the soft drink company has been exploring how to get secondary distribution without upsetting its relationship with the primary distributor. In Norway, regional distributors predominate, so the soft drink company has found it difficult to effect national promotion campaigns. In Belgium, the company could find no acceptable distributor, so it has had to assume that function itself.

CHOOSING DISTRIBUTORS AND CHANNELS

We now compare why companies handle their own distribution or contract other companies to do it for them and discuss how they should choose outside distributors.

Is Internal Handling Feasible? When sales volume is low, it is usually more economical for a company to handle distribution by contracting with an external distributor. By doing so, however, it may lose a certain amount of control. However, small companies may lack the resources necessary to handle their own distribution.[71] Managers should reassess periodically whether sales and resources have grown to the point that they can handle distribution internally.

Circumstances conducive to the internal handling of distribution include not only high sales volume but also the following factors:

- When a product has the characteristic of high price, high technology, or the need for complex after-sales servicing (such as aircraft), the producer probably will have to deal directly with the buyer. The producer may simultaneously use a distributor within the foreign country that will serve to identify sales leads.

- When the company deals with global customers, especially in business-to-business sales—such as an auto-parts manufacturer that sells original equipment to the same automakers in multiple countries—such sales may go directly from the producer to the global customer.

- When the company views its main competitive advantage to be its distribution methods, such as some food franchisors, it eventually may franchise abroad but maintain its own distribution outlet to serve as a "flagship." Amway, Avon, and Tupperware are examples of companies that have successfully transferred their house-to-house distribution methods from the United States to their operations abroad. Dell Computer has successfully handled its own mail-order sales in Europe.

Which Distributors Are Qualified? A company usually can choose from a number of potential foreign distributors. These are some common criteria for selecting a distributor:

- The company's financial strength
- Its good connections
- Extent of its other business commitments
- Current status of its personnel, facilities, and equipment
- Its reliability as an honest performer
- Its image in relation to the product or service being sold

Some evaluation criteria for distributors include their

- *Financial capability.*
- *Connections with customers.*
- *Fit with a company's product.*
- *Other resources.*
- *Trustworthiness.*
- *Compatibility with product image.*

The distributor's financial strength is important because of the potential long-term relationship between company and distributor and because of the assurance that money will be available for such things as maintaining sufficient inventory. Good connections are particularly important if sales must be directed to certain types of buyers, such as governmental procurement agencies. They are also important in societies, such as China with its Confucianist heritage, where connections and mutual loyalty are often more important than product and price for making sales.[72]

The amount of other business commitments can indicate whether the distributor has time for the company's product and whether it currently handles competitive or complementary products. The current status of the distributor's personnel, facilities, and equipment indicates not only its ability to deal with the product but also how quickly start-up can occur. A distributor's history of reliance and image as a responsible business entity help enable trust as a means for enforcing performance.[73] This is especially important in some parts of the Middle East and Latin America where manufacturers cannot easily terminate agreements because of poor performance.

How Reliable Is After-Sales Service? Consumers are reluctant to buy products that may require spare parts and service in the future unless they feel assured these will be readily available in good quality and at reasonable prices. The more complex and expensive the product, the more important is after-sales servicing. When after-sales servicing is important, companies may need to invest in service centers for groups of distributors that serve as intermediaries between producers and consumers. Earnings from sales of parts and after-sales service sometimes may exceed that of the original product.

Spare parts and service are important for sales.

THE CHALLENGE OF GETTING DISTRIBUTION

Companies must evaluate potential distributors, but distributors must choose which companies and products to represent and emphasize. Both wholesalers and retailers have limited storage facilities, display space, money to pay for inventories, and transportation and personnel to move and sell merchandise, so they try to carry only those products that have the greatest profit potential.

Distributors choose which companies and products to handle. Companies

- *May need to give incentives.*
- *May use successful products as bait for new ones.*
- *Must convince distributors that product and company are viable.*

In many cases, distributors are tied into exclusive arrangements with manufacturers that impede new competitive entries. For example, for many years breweries in the United Kingdom owned the pubs, where they sold only their own beer. This forced Anheuser-Busch to enter the market strictly with supermarket sales. Currently, Japan is a country in which many manufacturers such as Shiseido, Toshiba, and Hitachi have arrangements with thousands of distributors to sell only their products.

In addition, any company that is new to a country and wants to introduce products that some competitors are already selling may meet difficulty in finding distributors to handle its brands. Even established companies sometimes find distribution difficult for their new products, although they have the dual advantage of being known and of being able to offer existing profitable lines only if distributors accept the new unproven products.

A company wanting to use existing distribution channels may need to analyze competitive conditions carefully to offer effective incentives for those distributors to handle the product. It may need to identify problems distributors have to gain their loyalty by offering assistance. Companies alternatively may offer other incentives such as higher profit margins, after-sales servicing, and promotional support—any of which may be offered on either a permanent or introductory basis. The type of incentive should also depend on the comparative costs within each market. In the final analysis, however, incentives will be of little help unless the distributors believe a company's products are viable. The company must sell the distributors on its products as well as on itself as a reliable company.

Of course, a company may use a combination of self-distribution and independent distributors. For instance, Kodak has done this very successfully in Russia. It handles some direct sales to big customers, such as LUKOIL, which it convinced to give cameras as gifts to employees rather than giving them books or bottles of vodka. Otherwise, it handles retail operations through distributors that it supports with extensive advertising, store decorations, rebate programs, and market research.[74] (In our chapter-closing case, we'll discuss the means by which Tommy Hilfiger developed brand recognition as a means of gaining distribution.)

Case Review Note

HIDDEN COSTS IN DISTRIBUTION

When companies consider launching products in foreign markets, they must determine what final consumer prices will be to estimate sales potential. Because of different national distribution systems, the cost of getting products to consumers varies widely from one country to another. Five factors that often contribute to cost differences in distribution are *infrastructure conditions, the number of levels in the distribution system, retail inefficiencies, size and operating-hour restrictions,* and *inventory stock-outs.*

In many countries, the roads and warehousing facilities are so poor that getting goods to consumers quickly, at a low cost, and with minimum damage or loss en route is problematic. For example in China, despite its market potential, companies find difficulty in transporting their products nationally because of poor roads and theft en route and from warehouses.[75]

Many countries have multitiered wholesalers that sell to each other before the product reaches the retail level. For example, national wholesalers sell to regional ones, who sell to local ones, and so on. Japan, although changing rapidly, has had many more levels of distribution than such countries as France and the United States. Because each intermediary adds a markup, they drive product prices up.

In some countries, particularly developing countries, low labor costs and a basic distrust by owners of all but family members result in retail practices that raise consumer prices. This distrust is evident in companies' preference for counter service rather than self-service. In the former, customers wait to be served and shown merchandise. A customer who decides to purchase something gets an invoice to take to a cashier's line to pay. Once the invoice is stamped as paid, the customer must go to another line to pick up the merchandise after presenting the stamped invoice. In some countries counter service is common for purchases as small as a pencil. The additional personnel add to retailing costs, and the added time people must be in the store means fewer people can be served in the given space. In contrast, most retailers in some (mainly economically developed) countries have equipment that improves the efficiency of handling customers and reports, such as electronic scanners, cash registers linked to inventory control records, and machines connecting purchases to credit-card companies.

Many countries, such as France, Germany, and Japan, have laws to protect small retailers. These effectively limit the number of large retail establishments and the efficiencies they bring to sales. Most countries have historic and present patchwork systems that limit days or hours of operations for religious purposes or to protect employees from having to work late at night or on weekends.[76] At the same time, the limits keep retailers from covering the fixed cost of their space over more hours, so these costs are passed on to consumers. Where retailers are small, there is little space to store inventory. Wholesalers must incur the cost of making small deliveries to many more establishments and sometimes may have to visit each retailer more frequently because of stock outages.

E-COMMERCE AND THE INTERNET

Estimates vary widely on the current and future number of worldwide online households and the electronic commerce generated through online sales. Nevertheless, they all indicate substantial growth. Table 16.2 shows one example of estimates of present and future Internet usage by region. As electronic commerce increases, customers worldwide can quickly compare prices from different distributors, which should drive prices down.

Opportunities Electronic commerce offers companies an opportunity to promote their products globally. However, it does not relieve them of the need to develop the marketing tools we have discussed throughout the chapter. For some products and services, such as airline tickets and hotel space, the Internet has largely replaced traditional methods of marketing. But even here, companies may need to adapt to country differences, such as providing access through different languages.[77] There are certainly

> The growth in online households creates new distributional opportunities and challenges in selling globally over the Internet.

TABLE 16.2 Internet Usage: The Global Picture, 2007

Note that regions with low penetration rates (e.g., the Middle East and Latin America and the Caribbean) show higher growth rates than well-penetrated regions. If this trend continues, the comparative numbers of users by region will change dramatically over the next few years.

World Regions	Population (2007 Est.)	Population % of World	Internet Usage	% Population (Penetration)	Usage % of World	Usage Growth 2000–2007
Africa	933,448,292	14.2%	33,421,800	3.6%	2.9%	640.3%
Asia	3,712,527,624	56.5%	409,421,115	11.0%	36.0%	258.2%
Europe	809,624,686	12.3%	319,092,225	39.4%	28.2%	203.6%
Middle East	193,452,727	2.9%	19,424,700	10.0%	1.7%	491.4%
North America	334,538,018	5.1%	230,987,282	69.0%	20.4%	113.7%
Latin America/Caribbean	556,606,627	8.5%	102,304,809	18.4%	9.0%	466.2%
Oceania/Australia	34,468,443	0.5%	18,756,363	54.4%	1.7%	146.2%
WORLD TOTAL	6,574,666,417	100.0%	1,133,408,294	17.2%	100.0%	214.0%

Source: Miniwatts Marketing Group, "Internet Usage Statistics: The Internet Big Picture," *Internet World Stats* (2007), at www.internetworldstats.com/stats.htm (accessed November 6, 2007).

many success stories. For example, the New Zealand company Tristyle International sells prefabricated housing. About 95 percent of its sales are export and 40 percent of its sales are through the Internet.[78]

The Internet also permits suppliers to deal more quickly with their customers. For example, Lee Hung Fat Garment Factory of Hong Kong supplies apparel to about 60 companies in Europe and now flashes picture samples of merchandise to them over the Web. Customers, such as Kingfisher of the United Kingdom, can tinker with the samples and transmit new versions back to Hong Kong so Lee Hung Fat produces exactly what the distributors want.[79]

Problems   Global Internet sales are not without problems. Many households, especially in developing countries, lack access to Internet connections. Therefore, if a company wants to reach mass global markets, it will need to supplement its Internet sales with sales using other means of promotion and distribution. A company also needs to set up and promote its Internet sales, which can be very expensive. Further, a switch to the Internet sales may upset existing distribution and, if unsuccessful, make future sales more difficult.[80]

A company cannot easily differentiate its marketing program for each country where it operates. The same Web advertisements and prices reach customers everywhere, even though different appeals and prices for different countries might yield more sales and profits. If the company makes international sales over the Internet, it must deliver what it sells expeditiously. This may necessitate placing warehouses and service facilities abroad, which the company itself may or may not own and manage.

Finally, the company's Internet ads and prices must comply with the laws of each country where the company makes sales. This is a challenge because a company's Web page reaches Internet users everywhere. Clearly, although the Internet creates new opportunities for companies to sell internationally, it also creates new challenges for them.

Managing the Marketing Mix

The difference between total market potential and companies' sales is due to gaps:

- Usage—less product sold by all competitors than potential.
- Product line—company lacks some product variations.
- Distribution—company misses geographic or intensity coverage.
- Competitive—competitors' sales not explained by product line and distribution gaps.

Although every element in the marketing mix—product, price, promotion, brand, and distribution—is important, the relative importance of one versus another may vary from place to place and over time. Thus management must monitor and adjust its marketing programs accordingly.

GAP ANALYSIS

Once a company is operating in a country and estimates that country's market potential, it must calculate how well it is doing there. A useful tool in this respect is **gap analysis,** a method for estimating a company's potential sales by identifying potential customers it is not serving adequately.[81] When sales are lower than the estimated market potential for a given type of product, the company has potential for increased sales.

Figure 16.4 is a bar showing four types of gaps: *usage, competitive, product line,* and *distribution.* To construct such a bar, a company first needs to estimate the potential demand for all competitors in the country for a relevant period, say for the next year or the next five years. This figure is the height of the bar. Second, a company needs to estimate current sales by all competitors, which is point A. The space between point A and the top of the bar is a *usage gap,* meaning this is the growth potential for all competitors in the market for the relevant period. Third, a company needs to plot its own current sales of the product, point B.

Types of Gaps   Finally, the company divides the difference between point A and point B into types of gaps based on its estimate of sales lost to competitors. The *distribution gap* represents sales lost to competitors who distribute where the company does not, such as

FIGURE 16.4 Gap Analysis

Why aren't sales as much as they could be? That's the question asked by a company's managers when they undertake *gap analysis.* The arrow at the top represents *total sales potential* for all competitors during a given period. The arrow at A indicates *actual sales.* Notice that there's a gap between the product's potential and actual sales—the so-called *usage gap.* But there are other gaps as well. The arrow bracketing points A and B, for example, designates all sales lost by the company to its competitors—the *gap,* that is, between what the company did sell and what it could have sold if, for a variety of reasons, it hadn't lost so many sales to competitors. Finally, remember that, in the real world, gap sizes will fluctuate.

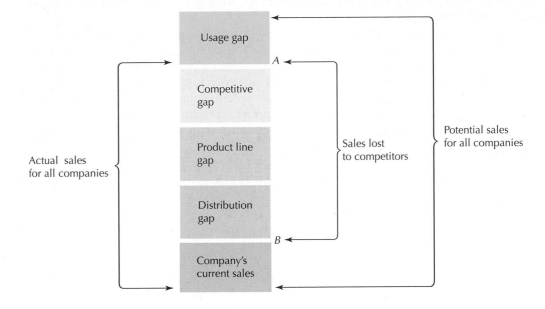

to additional geographic areas or types of outlets. The *product line gap* represents sales lost to competitors who have product variations the company does not have. The *competitive gap* is the remaining unexplained sales lost to competitors who may have a better image or lower prices.

Usage Gaps Companies may have different-sized gaps in different markets. The large chocolate companies have altered their marketing programs among countries because of their different gaps.[82] In some markets, they have found substantial usage gaps; that is, less chocolate is being consumed than would be expected on the basis of population and income levels. Industry specialists estimate that in many countries much of the population has never tasted chocolate. This has led companies to promote sales in those areas for chocolate in general.

The U.S. market shows another type of usage gap. Nearly everyone in this market has tried most chocolate products, but per capita consumption has fallen because of growing concern about weight. To increase chocolate consumption in general, Nestlé for a short time promoted chocolate as an energy source for the sports minded. Note, however, that building general consumption is most useful to the market leader. Nestlé, with U.S. chocolate sales below those of Mars and Hershey, actually benefited its competitors during the short-lived campaign.

Product Line and Distribution Gaps Chocolate companies also have found that they have product line gaps in some hot climates in the market for sweetened products. By developing new products, such as chocolate products that melt less easily, they have been able to garner a larger share of that market. In some markets, such as Ferrero Rocher in the United States, its emphasis in recent years has been on gaining more distribution in mainstream outlets.

Competitive Gaps   Finally, there are competitive gaps—sales by competitors that cannot be explained by differences between a company's own product line and distribution and those of the competitors. That is, competitors are making additional sales because of their prices, advertising campaigns, goodwill, or any of a host of other factors. In markets where per capita chocolate consumption is high, companies exert most of their efforts in gaining sales at the expense of competitors. For instance, Switzerland has the world's highest per capita chocolate consumption. In that market, such competitors as Migros, Lindt, and Nestlé's Cailler go head to head in creating images of better quality.[83]

Although gap analysis is primarily a means of prioritizing elements in the marketing mix within given countries, it is also possible to use the tool by aggregating needs among countries. For example, let's say that the product line gap is too small in a single country to justify the expenses of developing a specific new product, such as a heat-resistant chocolate bar. Nevertheless, the combined market potential among several countries for this product may justify the product and promotional developmental costs. Thus managers need to improve country-level performance along with enhancement of synergies among the countries where they operate.

LOOKING TO THE FUTURE

Marketing to the "Haves," the "Have-Nots" (and the "Have-Somes")

Most projections are that disparities between the "haves" and "have-nots" will grow in the foreseeable future, both within and among countries. Furthermore, because haves will be more educated and more connected to the Internet, they will be better able to search globally for lower prices for what they buy. Therefore, globally, the affluent segment will have even more purchasing power than their incomes indicate.

In addition, they will not likely forgo buying because of antimaterialistic sentiments. As these people's discretionary income increases, some luxury products will become more commonplace (partly because it will take fewer hours of work to purchase them), and seemingly dissimilar products and services (such as cars, travel, jewelry, and furniture) will compete with each other for the same discretionary spending. Because of better communications and rising educational levels of the haves, they will want more choices. However, these choices may not fall primarily along national lines. Rather, companies will identify consumer niches that cut across country lines.

At the other extreme, because of growing numbers of poor people with little disposable income, companies will have opportunities to develop low-cost standardized products to fit the needs of the have-nots. In reality,

low-income households collectively have considerable purchasing power, and it is a segment that MNEs have largely ignored. For instance, 680 million households have incomes of less than $6,000 per year in the 18 largest developing and transitional economies. They have roughly $1.7 trillion to spend, mainly on housing, food, health care, education, communications, finance charges, and consumer goods.[84] Thus companies will have conflicting opportunities—to develop luxury to serve the haves and to cut costs to serve the have-nots.

Despite the growing proportions of haves and have-nots, demographers project the actual numbers of people moving out of poverty levels and into middle-income levels will increase. This is largely because of population and income growth in some low-income countries, especially in Asia. Such a shift will likely mean that companies' sales growth in low-income countries will mainly be for products that are mature in industrial countries, such as telephones and household appliances.

Furthermore, with increased access to the Internet and lower barriers to trade, customers will be able to purchase goods from anywhere in the world. In the process, companies will find it more difficult to charge different prices in different countries. But they will be able to cut out intermediaries more effectively in the distribution of their products. ■

Tommy Hilfiger: Clothes Make the Man and Vice Versa

C hances are that when you think of Tommy Hilfiger, the first image that comes to your mind is a piece of clothing with a little red, white, and blue logo visibly displayed.[85] This logo has been a hallmark of Hilfiger's success since its beginning, and marketing has been the company's forte. The company is now privately owned and thus no longer publishes its financial information, but analysts estimate its annual sales to be about US$1.8 billion. Hilfiger also acquired the Karl Lagerfeld label, but our discussion centers on the brands using the Hilfiger name. Before we examine its international marketing practices, let's look for a moment at the company's description and history.

A Brief History

The early success of the Hilfiger brand was largely due to two men, the U.S. designer Tommy Hilfiger and the Indian textile magnate Mohan Murjani. Hilfiger began selling used jeans when he was still in high school and founded a retail company soon after for which he designed vests and sweaters, but this endeavor went bankrupt. He then began working as a freelance designer while opening a sportswear company, which bankrupted within a year.

Next he landed a regular job designing blue jeans for Jordache. In 1984, when Hilfiger was 33, Murjani sought him out to be a designer for Murjani International. Murjani had been one of the instrumental people in bringing about the designer blue jeans craze of the 1970s. Although he still owned the license for Gloria Vanderbilt jeans, he wanted to resurrect the jeans craze and develop a new brand of clothing by offering a line of slightly less preppy and less expensive clothes than those offered by Ralph Lauren that he thought would appeal to a young mass-appeal audience.

Sales success came quickly for the Hilfiger brand, but Murjani International faced financial problems. Murjani also had licenses to sell other clothing brands, such as Gloria Vanderbilt and Coca-Cola. In effect, it had difficulty separating its attention among its different brands, which it needed to sell to the same department stores. Hilfiger, Murjani, and two other investors bought out Murjani International in 1988, changed the name to Tommy Hilfiger, and moved the headquarters to Hong Kong, where one of the new owners had extensive connections for manufacturing the clothes throughout Asia. Tommy Hilfiger went public on the New York Stock Exchange in 1992. In 2006, the Apax Partner Fund in London took the company private again and moved the headquarters from Hong Kong to the Netherlands.

Hilfiger began only with a men's line, but its men's and women's clothing each account for about half of its sales. The company also had a line of children's wear that it discontinued in 2006 because of poor performance. Hilfiger began pushing internationally in 1996, and international sales now account for 49 percent of total sales. Europe alone accounts for 37 percent of sales. The expansion into Europe has been due largely to expansion problems in the United States, where clothing sales in general have been growing at less than 5 percent per year, much slower than in some foreign markets.

Promotion and Branding

Hilfiger's promotion and branding have been so intertwined that it is almost impossible to separate them. At the beginning, Murjani saw two primary needs: convince stores to stock a new brand and convince customers to want it. His approach turned out to be pure genius. Although his ad budget for the first year (1985) was US$1.4 million—quite small for selling in a mass consumer market, especially for an unknown brand—the ads were aimed strictly at getting Tommy Hilfiger's name known. He placed two-page ad spreads in leading magazines and newspapers *without* showing any clothes or any models. The ads included Hilfiger's face, the logo for the clothes, and words describing him as being on a par with such well-known designers as Ralph Lauren, Perry Ellis, and Calvin Klein.

The ads were so unusual that the brand received free publicity through write-ups in newspapers. Even Johnny Carson quipped about Hilfiger on his popular evening TV show. Within a short time, surveys in New York revealed that people thought of Hilfiger as one of the four or five most important designers. Department and specialty stores were willing to sell the clothes, and the logo-loving public was rushing to buy them. There was also some fortunate timing involved. The public was not only in love with a label, but also many young managers were eager to be seen in upscale sportswear during the newly popular casual Friday workdays.

Early on, Hilfiger received much publicity in newspaper and magazine columns globally that mentioned or showed celebrities wearing its clothes. These celebrities were certainly an eclectic group and included Bill Clinton, the Prince of Wales, Michael Jackson, Elton John, and Snoop Dogg. This fed into the image that Hilfiger clothes had cachet; thus the company's image was fairly well established abroad before the company expanded internationally.

Hilfiger first entered Europe by opening a retail store on London's upscale Bond Street. It had Kate Moss and Goldie Hawn for the opening. However, it overhyped its entry. The result was that retailers so wanted to carry Hilfiger that too much merchandise was available in stores, which led to discounting and a cheapening of the image the company wanted. Further, it led to look-alike merchandise using a similar brand name, such as Tommy Sport. Thus its first European store closed within a year. Since then, Hilfiger has gone more to celebrity advertising to help sell in the United Kingdom. These celebrities include the French soccer star Thierry Henry and the husband-wife team of entertainer David Bowie and supermodel Iman. Hilfiger is back with a flourishing store in London.

However, aside from celebrities, Hilfiger learned that the type of models it uses to sell its merchandise successfully in the United States does not work well in Europe. For example, its models for men's underwear in Europe, including those on point-of-purchase package displays, must be thinner and less muscular than those it uses in the United States. But it augments these thinner models by adding scantily clad seductive-looking women who stand behind the male models in the photos. Hilfiger also found that its average consumer in Germany was older than its average consumer in the United States, so it has dropped the Tommy Jeans name because it sounded too much like a teenage name.

Product and Price

Although early promotion with the brand name has been instrumental in Hilfiger's success, logo and image are not enough. From the start, Hilfiger clothes have been casual and of good quality. They are distinctive enough in color and shape so the public can usually distinguish a Hilfiger from clothing made by competitors.

Nevertheless, Hilfiger has encountered some negative reactions abroad to its image of being a U.S. brand. Although some U.S. clothing products have been well received abroad, such as jeans, most U.S. clothing brands—for example, Nautica, Gap, and North Face—have encountered problems in Europe. One of the key issues is that Europeans tend to see France and Italy as the centers of upscale fashions, which is hard for clothing brands from other countries to overcome.

In addition, Hilfiger has encountered some different national preferences. For example, in Germany, which is Hilfiger's largest European market, men don't mind paying $50 more than the highest-priced Hilfiger shirts in the United States, but they want them in a higher-quality cotton. Hilfiger has found throughout Europe that there is hardly any demand for the cotton sweaters so popular in the United States, so it has switched to wool sweaters. Hilfiger has adjusted to the European preference for slimmer-looking jeans and smaller logos on shirts. It has created a line of more luxury items, such as leather jackets and cashmere sweaters for the Italian market.

To make these changes, Hilfiger set up a design staff in Amsterdam in 2003 that has adapted the Hilfiger look to the European demands. Its CEO announced his plan to harmonize the products offered in the United States and Europe by moving upmarket in the United States and depending more on the European design team.

These product changes for Europe have increased production costs. Further, European operational costs are about three times those in the United States because of its more fragmented retail and wholesale system. On top of that, the margins to final consumers in Europe run from 50 percent to 100 percent higher than in the United States. The result is that prices for Hilfiger merchandise are much higher in Europe than in the United States.

Distribution

Hilfiger operates in three primary sectors: wholesale, retail, and licensing. Hilfiger has traditionally relied mainly in the United States on wholesaling to department stores, of which many have stand-alone Hilfiger departments within. By the 1990s, it sold through 1,800 department stores in the United States.

Hilfiger has stayed away from chains that are viewed as more lower end, such as JCPenney and Sears, but it does sell its outdated stock to discount chains T.J.Maxx and Marshall's. However, the U.S. department store market has become more difficult in recent years. First, the percentage of clothes sold in department stores has been declining. Second, consolidation has given department stores more clout in dealing with suppliers. Third, such large chains as Federated and Kohl's have been increasing and pushing their own-brand merchandise.

Hilfiger's retail sector includes about 600 company-owned or franchised stores globally. These include both outlets and full-priced stores. Direct retailing involves a bit of a balancing act. On one side, Hilfiger needs to expand its direct selling because of the department store trends. On the other side, this expansion risks alienating department stores that still remain its best U.S. customers.

The licensing sector is carried out in two types of situations. First, Hilfiger uses licensing to expand its line. For instance, other companies make such products as fragrances, sleepwear, umbrellas, bedding, and watches with the Hilfiger name on them. Second, Hilfiger licenses for production and sales in markets it cannot yet enter independently, such as Japan, the Middle East, and South America. As with any licensing contract, Hilfiger has to be careful that products and added products are complementary and that production and distribution in different markets are in line with the quality and image the company wants.

Distribution is perhaps the biggest difference that Hilfiger found when entering Europe. Because the company succeeded in the United States by first going into department stores, it put an early European emphasis on department stores as well. This led to its entry into such leading chains as Galeries Lafayette in France and El Corte Inglés in Spain.

But most European clothing sales are in small boutiques, so Hilfiger now sells in about 4,500 of them—much more than in the United States. Further, it has decentralized its showrooms, by opening 21 of them, so small retailers can visit them more easily. Finally, finding good competitive locations for its company-owned stores is problematic because space in prime locations opens infrequently.

The Future

Future growth for Hilfiger depends both on expansion internationally and revamping slow growth in the United States. Hilfiger's CEO, Fred Gehring, worries that so many changes for Europe create both a nonuniform image and an addition to costs. He has indicated there is no need to have two collections and thus a need to harmonize the two. Already, most new designs in the United States are coming from the European design team, which aims stylistically at basic American classics that are slightly more grown-up and sophisticated. ■

QUESTIONS

1. What factors have led to higher prices in Europe than in the United States for Hilfiger merchandise? What problems might Hilfiger encounter by having higher prices in Europe than in the United States?

2. Hilfiger's CEO would like to harmonize the European and U.S. collections by having Hilfiger move more upmarket in the United States. What problems might the company face in doing this? What might it do to make this strategy successful?

3. Make a list of clothing brands whose popularity has or has not sustained their popularity and quality/image over time. Why have they changed or not? Can Hilfiger find any keys for success from these experiences?

4. What strategies would you recommend for clothing companies outside France and Italy to overcome the positive images of "made in France" and "made in Italy"? What might Hilfiger do?

SUMMARY

- Although the principles for selling abroad are the same as those for selling domestically, the international businessperson must deal with a less familiar environment.

- International marketing strategies depend on companies' orientations, which include production, customer, strategic, and social.

- Companies need to decide which market segments to target. These segments may include different or similar groups from different countries. Once they make this determination, their product, branding, promotion, pricing, and distribution decisions should be compatible with the needs of their target markets.

- A standardized approach to marketing means maximum uniformity in products and programs among the countries in which sales occur. Although this approach minimizes expenses, most companies make changes to fit country needs to increase sales volume.

- A variety of legal, cultural, and economic conditions may call for altering products to capture foreign demand, but the cost of alteration relative to additional sales potential should be considered. In addition to determining when to alter products, companies also must decide how many and which products to sell abroad.

- Government regulations may directly or indirectly affect the prices that companies charge. International pricing is further complicated because of fluctuations in currency values, differences in product preferences, price escalation in exporting, and variations in fixed versus variable pricing practices.

- For each product in each country, a company must determine not only its promotional budget but also the mix between push and pull strategies and promotions. The relationship between push and pull should depend on the distribution system, cost and availability of media, consumer attitudes, and the product's price compared with incomes.

- Major problems for standardizing advertising among countries are translation, legality, and message needs.

- Global branding is hampered by language differences, expansion by acquisition, nationality images, and laws concerning generic names. Nevertheless, global brands help develop a global image.

- Distribution channels vary substantially among countries. The differences may affect not only the relative costs of operating but also the ease of making initial sales.

- Companies need to choose distributors carefully, both on the basis of their ability and on their trustworthiness. At the same time, companies have to sell themselves to get distributors to handle their products and services.

- Although the Internet offers new opportunities to sell internationally, using the Internet does not negate companies' needs to develop sound programs within their marketing mix.

- Gap analysis is a tool that helps companies determine why they have not met their market potentials for given countries and to decide what part of the marketing mix to emphasize.

KEY TERMS

cost-plus strategy (p. 623)
distribution (p. 633)
gap analysis (p. 638)

generic (p. 632)
gray market (p. 625)
penetration strategy (p. 623)

pull (p. 627)
push (p. 627)
skimming strategy (p. 623)

ENDNOTES

1 *Sources include the following:* Information came from Nanette Byrnes, "Avon: More than Cosmetic Changes," *Business Week,* March 12, 2007: 62; Jennie Rodriguez, "Direct Sales on the Rise," *Knight Ridder Tribune Business News,* February 25, 2007: 1; Barney Stokes, "Benchmark—Avon," *Marketing Week,* April 6, 2006: 33; Jessica Kiddle, "Cosmetic Enhancement," *The Scotsman,* March 22, 2007: 22; "Avon Launches First Global Ad Campaign," *Marketing Week,* March 8, 2007: 10; Mei Fong, "Avon Calling, But China Opens Door Only a Crack," *Wall Street Journal,* February 26, 2007: B1; "Avon Celebrates New Breed of Sales Leaders," *Manila Times,* May 13, 2007: n.p.; Mitchell Edgar, "Avon Celebrates Women's Day at U.N. Summit," *Women's Wear Daily,* March 9, 2007: 8; Umesh Pandey, "Avon Looks to Asia for Inspiration," *Knight Ridder Tribune Business News,* June 9, 2007: 1; Avon *Annual Reports* from 1995 through 2006; *Outlook* (Avon's monthly in-house magazine) from 1995 through 2002; and AVP–Q4 2004, Avon Products, Earning Conference Call, February 1, 2005.

2 Constantine S. Katsikeas, Saeed Damiee, and Marios Theodosiou, "Strategy Fit and Performance Consequences of International Marketing Standardization," *Strategic Management Journal* 27 (2006): 867–90.

3 "The World's Wash Day," *Financial Times,* April 29, 2002: 6.

4 Matt Moffett, "Learning to Adapt to a Tough Market, Chilean Firms Pry Open Door to Japan," *Wall Street Journal,* June 7, 1994: A10.

5 "Avon Beauty Plans Greater Mass Market Penetration," *Businessline,* April 22, 2003: 1.

6 Yue Yen Industrial (Holdings) Limited, "Welcome to Yue Yuen," at www.yueyuen.com (accessed June 22, 2007).

7 Evan Pérez, "A Bit of America Rises Near Old-World Buenos Aires," *Wall Street Journal,* January 16, 2002: B1.

8 Betsy McKay, "Drinks for Developing Countries," *Wall Street Journal,* November 27, 2001: B1+; McKay, "Coke's Heyer Finds Test in Latin America," *Wall Street Journal,* October 15, 2002: B4.

9 "Avon: Opportunity Knocks," *Brand Strategy,* April 5, 2005: 20.

10 Manoj K. Agarwal, "Developing Global Segments and Forecasting Market Shares: A Simultaneous Approach Using Survey Data," *Journal of International Marketing* 11:4 (2003): 56.

11 Rebecca Rose, "Global Diversity Gets All Cosmetic," *Financial Times,* April 10–11, 2004: W11.

12 Leslie T. Chang, "Nestlé Stumbles in China's Evolving Market," *Wall Street Journal,* December 8, 2004: A10.

13 Allen L. Hammond and C. K. Prahalad, "Selling to the Poor," *Foreign Policy* (May–June 2004): 30–37.

14 Katsikeas et al., "Strategy Fit."

15 "Music for the Masses," *Financial Times,* December 14, 2004: 9.

16 Milo Geyelin and Jeffrey Ball, "How Rugged Is Your Car's Roof?" *Wall Street Journal,* March 4, 2000: B1.

17 Bernardo V. Lopez, "Upshot," *BusinessWorld,* September 18, 2003: 1.

18 Garrett Mehl, Heather Wipfli, and Peter Winch, "Controlling Tobacco," *Harvard International Review* 27:1 (Spring 2005): 54–58.

19 "Cause for Concern with Nestlé in the Spotlight Again over Its Advertising Tactics," *Marketing Week,* February 11, 1999: 28–31.

20 Andrew Ward, "Global Thirst for Bottled Water Attacked," *Financial Times,* February 13, 2006: 3, referring to data from the Earth Policy Institute.

21 Sarah Houlton, "Drugs for Neglected Diseases," *Pharmaceutical Executive* 23:8 (2003): 28.

22 Mehl et al., "Controlling Tobacco."

23 Michael Finkel, "Bedlam in the Blood: Malaria," *National Geographic* (July 2007): 63.

24 Michael Waldholz, "Sparks Fly at AIDS Meeting over Breast-Feeding," *Wall Street Journal,* July 12, 2000: B2; Jolene Skordis and Nicoli Nattrass, "Paying to Waste Lives: The Affordability of Reducing Mother-to-Child Transmission of HIV in South Africa," *Journal of Health Economics* 21:3 (May 2002): 405.

25 Andrew Jack, "Anti-Malaria Drug to Sell at Cost Price," *Financial Times,* March 2, 2007: 3.

26 Scott Miller, "EU's New Rules Will Shake Up Market for Bioengineered Food," *Wall Street Journal,* April 16, 2004: A1.

27 Deborah Ball, Sarah Ellison, Janet Adamy, and Geoffrey A. Fowler, "Recipes Without Borders?" *Wall Street Journal,* August 18, 2004: B1+.

28 Norihiko Shirouzu, "Tailoring World's Cars to U.S. Taste," *Wall Street Journal,* January 15, 2001: B1.

29 Norihiko Shirouzu and Peter Wonacott, "People's Republic of Autos," *Wall Street Journal,* April 18, 2005: B1+.

30 John Reed, Amy Yee, and Joe Leahy, "India's Tata to Overtake Suzuki in Race for World's Cheapest Car," *Financial Times,* June 4, 2007: 13.

31 David A. Griffith, Aruna Chandra, and John K. Ryans, Jr., "Factors Influencing Advertising Message and Packaging," *Journal of International Marketing* 11:3 (2003): 30.

32 Keith Bradsher, "India Gains on China Among Multinationals," *International Herald Tribune,* June 12–13, 2004: 13.

33 Niraj Dawar and Amitava Chattopadhyay, "The New Language of Emerging Markets," *Financial Times,* November 11, 2000: Mastering Management section, 6.

34 "The World's Wash Day," *Financial Times*: 6.

35 Arvind Sahay, "Finding the Right International Mix," *Financial Times*, November 16, 1998: Mastering Marketing section, 2–3.

36 Brandon Mitchener, "Inexpensive Levi's May Soon Be Easier to Find in Britain," *Wall Street Journal*, April 6, 2001: A13.

37 Matthew B. Myers, "The Pricing of Export Products: Why Aren't Managers Satisfied with the Results?" *Journal of World Business* 32:3 (1997): 277–89.

38 Peter Rosenwald, "Surveying the Latin American Landscape," *Catalog Age* 18:2 (February 2001): 67–69.

39 Dave Guilford, "GM Takes Hard Line on Gray Market," *Automotive News*, July 22, 2002: 4.

40 Elin Dugan, "United States of America, Home of the Cheap and the Gray: A Comparison of Recent Court Decisions Affecting the U.S. and European Gray Markets," *The George Washington International Law Review* 33:2 (2001): 397–418.

41 Ana Campoy, "Think Locally," *Wall Street Journal*, September 27, 2004: R8.

42 C. Gopinath, "Fixed Price and Bargaining," *Businessline*, July 15, 2002: 1.

43 Claude Cellich, "FAQ . . . About Business Negotiations on the Internet," *International Trade Forum* 1 (2001): 10–11.

44 Rasul Bailay, "A Hindu Festival Attracts the Faithful and U.S. Marketers," *Wall Street Journal*, February 12, 2001: A18.

45 David Pilling, "Direct Promotion of Brands Gives Power to the Patients," *Financial Times*, April 30, 2001: iii; Sarah Ellison, "Viagra Europe Ads to Focus on Symptoms," *Financial Times*, March 22, 2000: B10.

46 Miho Inada, "Mac and PC's Overseas Adventures," *Wall Street Journal*, March 1, 2007: B1.

47 Eleftheria Parpis, "Say What?" *Adweek*, August 6, 2001: 16.

48 Charles Goldsmith, "Dubbing in Product Plugs," *Wall Street Journal*, December 6, 2004: B1+.

49 Rick Wartzman, "Read Their Lips," *Wall Street Journal*, June 3, 1999: A1.

50 Geoffrey A. Fowler, "China Cracks Down on Commercials," *Wall Street Journal*, February 19, 2004: B7A.

51 Gordon Fairclough and Geoffrey A. Fowler, "Pigs Get Ax in China TV Ads, in Nod to Muslims," *Wall Street Journal*, January 25, 2007: A1+.

52 Sally D. Goll, "New Zealand Bans Reebok, Other Ads It Deems Politically Incorrect for TV," *Wall Street Journal*, July 25, 1995: A12.

53 Deborah Ball, "Women in Italy Like to Clean but Shun the Quick and Easy," *Wall Street Journal*, April 25, 2006: A1+.

54 Andrew Ward, "Home Improvements Abroad," *Financial Times*, April 6, 2006: 8.

55 Sarah Ellison, "Sex-Themed Ads Often Don't Travel Well," *Wall Street Journal*, March 31, 2000: B7.

56 Tulin Erdem, Joffre Swait, and Ana Valenzuela, "Brands as Signals: A Cross-Country Validation Study," *Journal of Marketing* 70:1 (2006): 34; Desmond Lam, "Cultural Influence on Proneness to Brand Loyalty," *Journal of International Consumer Marketing* 19:3 (2006): 7.

57 "Top 100 Brands Scoreboard 2006" *Business Week Online* (2000–2007), at http://bwnt.businessweek. com/brand/2006 (accessed November 2, 2007).

58 "Embarrassed GM to Rename Car with Risqué Overtones," *Yahoo News Canada*, October 22, 2003.

59 Robert Frank, "Big Boy's Adventures in Thailand," *Wall Street Journal*, April 12, 2000: B1; Julie Bennett, "Product Pitfalls Proliferate in a Global Cultural Maze," *Wall Street Journal*, May 14, 2001: B11.

60 Mure Dickie, "Google Becomes Gu Ge in China," *Financial Times*, April 13, 2006: 19.

61 Lee Simmons and Robert M. Schindler, "Cultural Superstitions and the Price Endings Used in Chinese Advertising," *Journal of International Marketing* 11:2 (2003): 101.

62 Miriam Jordan, "Sara Lee Wants to Percolate Through All of Brazil," *Wall Street Journal*, May 8, 2002: A14+.

63 Isabelle Schuiling and Jean-Noël Kapferer, "Executive Insights: Real Differences Between Local and International Brands: Strategic Implications for International Marketers" *Journal of International Marketing* 12:4 (2004): 197.

64 Philip Kotler and David Gertner, "Country as Brand, Product, and Beyond: Place Marketing and Brand Management," *Journal of Brand Management* 9:4/5 (2002): 249–61; Keith Dinnie, "National Image and Competitive Advantage: The Theory and Practice of Country-of-Origin Effect," *Journal of Brand Management* 9:4/5 (2002): 396–98.

65 Gideon Rachman, "Christmas Survey: The Brand's the Thing," *The Economist*, December 18, 1999: 97–99.

66 Seah Park, "LG's Kitchen Makeover," *Wall Street Journal*, September 22, 2004: A19.

67 Saeed Samiee, Terrence A. Shimp, and Subash Sharma, "Brand Origin Recognition Accuracy: Its Antecedents and Consumers' Cognitive Limitations," *Journal of International Business Studies* 36 (2005): 379–97.

68 Tara Parker-Pope, "Minty Python and Cream Victoria? Ice Creams Leave Some Groaning," *Wall Street Journal*, July 3, 1996: B1.

69 Janet Adamy, "Starbucks, Ethiopia Agree on Licensing," *Wall Street Journal*, June 21, 2007: B6.

70 "Opportunities in Sub-Culture," *Businessline*, February 12, 2004: 1.

71 Oliver Burgel and Gordon C. Murray, "The International Market Entry Choices of Start-Up Companies in High-Technology," *Journal of International Marketing* 8:2 (2000): 33–62.

72 Gary F. Keller and Creig R. Kronstedt, "Connecting Confucianism, Communism, and the Chinese Culture of Commerce," *The Journal of Language for International Business* 16:1 (2005): 60–75.

73 S. Tamer Cavusgil, Seyda Deligonul, and Chun Zhang, "Curbing Foreign Distributor Opportunism: An Examination of Trust, Contracts, and the Legal Environment in International Channel Relationships," *Journal of International Marketing* 12:2 (2004).

74 Gary C. Anders and Danila A. Usachev, "Strategic Elements of Eastman Kodak's Successful Market Entry in Russia," *Thunderbird International Business Review* 45:2 (2003): 171.

75 James T. Areddy, "Solving China's Logistics Riddle," *Wall Street Journal*, October 15, 2003: A18+.

76 Marko Grunhagen, Stephen J. Grove, and James W. Gentry, "The Dynamics of Store Hour Changes and Consumption Behavior: Results of a Longitudinal Study of Consumer Attitudes Toward Saturday Shopping in Germany," *European Journal of Marketing* 37:11/12 (2003): 1801–19.

77 Rita Marcella and Sylvie Davies, "The Use of Customer Language in International Marketing Communication in the Scottish Food and Drink Industry," *European Journal of Marketing* 38:11/12 (2004): 1382.

78 *New Zealand Business* 18:11 (2004): 21–27.

79 Anil K. Gupta and Vijay Govindarajan, "The Rising Cost of Waiting," *CIO* 13:19 (2000): 54.

80 Moen Øystein, Iver Endresen, and Morten Gavlen, "Executive Insights: Use of the Internet in International Marketing: A Case Study of Small Computer Software Firms," *Journal of International Marketing* 11:4 (2003).

81 J. A. Weber, "Comparing Growth Opportunities in the International Marketplace," *Management International Review* 1

(1979): 47–54; Van R. Wood, John R. Darling, and Mark Siders, "Consumer Desire to Buy and Use Products in International Markets: How to Capture It, How to Sustain It," *International Marketing Review* 16:3 (1999): 231–42.

82 "Chocolate Makers in Switzerland Try to Melt Resistance," *Wall Street Journal*, January 5, 1981: 14; William Hall, "Swiss Chocolate Groups Aim to Keep Outlook Sweet," *Financial Times*, April 11–12, 1998: 23; William Hall, "Wraps Come Off Chocolate's Best-Kept Secret," *Financial Times*, June 5, 1998: 20; Stephanie Thompson, "Chocolate Gets Boost," *Advertising Age*, July 29, 2002: 12.

83 Haig Simonian, "Nestlé Enriches Its Choc Value," *Financial Times*, March 24, 2006: 9.

84 Allen L. Hammond and C. K. Prahalad, "Selling to the Poor," *Foreign Policy* (May/June 2004): 30–37.

85 *Sources include the following:* "Tommy Hilfiger: 2006 Company Profile Edition *Just-Style* (August 2006); "Business & Company Resource Center: Tommy Hilfiger," at http://iiiprxy.library.miami.edu:2309/servlet/BCRC?locID = Miami_richter&srchtp = cmp&c (accessed June 24, 2007); Teri Agins, "Costume Change," *Wall Street Journal*, February 2, 2007: A1 + ; Samantha Conti, "Hilfiger Signs French Soccer Star," *DNR*, December 11, 2006: 12; Miles Socha, "Tommy Takes Paris," *DNR*, October 23, 2006: 26; Socha, "Tommy's Latest Take," *WWD*, October 20, 2006: 1; Socha, *WWD* "Lagerfeld Supports Hilfiger Decision," *WWD*, July 25, 2006: 5; Julie Naughton, "Hilfiger and Lauder Aim for Perfect 10," *WWD*, June 23, 2006: 4; Lisa Lockwood, "CEO Says Tommy to Now Trade Up," *WWD*, May 11, 2006: 3; *Tommy Hilfiger 2004 Annual Report*; Krysten Crawford, "The Big Opportunity," *Business 2.0* 7:2 (2006): 94.

17

chapter seventeen

Global Manufacturing and Supply Chain Management

Objectives

- To describe the different dimensions of a global manufacturing strategy

- To examine the elements of global supply chain management

- To show how quality affects the global supply chain

- To illustrate how supplier networks function

- To explain how inventory management is a key dimension of the global supply chain

- To present different alternatives for transporting products along the supply chain from suppliers to customers

Right mixture makes good mortar.

—*English proverb*

CASE: Samsonite's Global Supply Chain

THE SAMSONITE STORY

Samsonite Corporation is a U.S.-based company that manufactures and distributes luggage all over the world.[1] The company was founded in 1910 in Denver, Colorado, and it took many years for it to become a global company. In 1963, Samsonite set up its first European operation in the Netherlands and later, in 1965, began production in Belgium. Shortly thereafter, it erected a joint-venture plant in Mexico to service the growing but highly protected Mexican market. By the end of the 1960s, Samsonite was manufacturing luggage in Spain and Japan as well. In addition to its manufacturing operations, Samsonite was selling luggage worldwide through a variety of distributors.

In the 1970s, business began to take off in Europe. In 1974, Samsonite developed its first real European product, called the Prestige Attaché, and business began to expand in the 1980s, Samsonite opened a new plant in France to manufacture the Prestige Attaché and other key products.

With the fall of the Iron Curtain in the early 1990s, Samsonite purchased a Hungarian luggage manufacturer and began to expand throughout Eastern Europe. During this same time period, Samsonite established several joint-venture companies throughout Asia, including China, to extend its reach there.

STRATEGIES FOR THE 1990s

The Quality Initiative

To establish products of high quality, Samsonite embarked on two different programs. The first was an internal program in which Samsonite conducted a drop test, a tumble test, a wheel test, and a handle test to determine if its products were strong

MAP 17.1 Where Samsonite Operates in Europe

The products that Samsonite sells in Europe are made at production facilities located in Europe. Six of these facilities are company owned, and one is a joint venture. In order to serve its European market, the company also maintains subsidiaries and retail outlets and deals with distributors and agents.

Italy, causing it to rival Germany as Samsonite's biggest market in Europe. Although the U.S. market began to turn to soft-side luggage in the 1980s, the European market still demanded hard-side luggage, so Samsonite developed a new hard-side suitcase for Europe called the Oyster case. Then soft-side luggage began to increase in importance, although Europe was still considered a hard-side market. In

enough and of sufficient quality for customers. The second program was two different, independent quality-assurance tests:

- The European-based ISO 9002 certification
- The GS Mark, which is the number-one government-regulated third-party product test mark (similar to brand) of Germany

The GS Mark, *Gepruefte Sicherheit* (translated "Tested for Safety"), is designed to help companies comply with European product liability laws as well as other areas of quality and safety. To enhance quality, Samsonite introduced state-of-the-art CAD-CAM machinery in its plants. Samsonite also introduced a manufacturing technique in which autonomous cells of about a dozen employees assembled a product from start to finish.

As you can see in Map 17.1, Samsonite has three company-owned production facilities and two headquarter offices in Europe. In addition, it has subsidiaries, joint ventures, retail franchises, distributors, and agents set up to service the European market. Although Samsonite initially serviced the European markets through exports, the transportation costs were high, and the demand for luggage soared in Europe, so Samsonite decided to begin production in Belgium in 1965.

SUPPLY CHAIN DECENTRALIZATION

In the early years, Samsonite had a decentralized supply chain, as illustrated in Figure 17.1, whereby it operated through different wholesale layers before it finally got the product to the retailers.

As Samsonite's business grew, management decided to centralize its supply chain so products were manufactured and shipped to a central European warehouse, which then directly supplied retailers upon request (see Figure 17.2). This centralized structure was put into place to eliminate the need to rely on wholesalers.

Samsonite had to worry about transporting manufactured products to the warehouse, storing them, and transporting them to the retailers in the different European markets. Samsonite invested heavily in information technology to link the retailers to the warehouse and thereby manage its European distribution system more effectively. Retailers would place an order with a salesperson or the local Samsonite office in their area, and the order would be transmitted to the warehouse and shipping company by modem.

The retail market in Europe began shifting at the turn of the new century, so Samsonite responded by opening franchised retail outlets in October 2002, beginning in Antwerp and spreading to other areas. As the vice president of marketing and sales put it, "We are anticipating a shift in the market, in which the traditional luggage channel will no longer be at the forefront and a wide new retail opportunity will emerge."

FIGURE 17.1
The Samsonite European Supply Chain (I): Decentralized, 1965–1974

For about a decade after it had first penetrated the European market, Samsonite shipped products from *factories* to *factory warehouses* and then to *national warehouses*. From there, products went to *wholesalers* and, at long last, to *retailers*. Needless to say, the system was cumbersome, lengthening the factory-to-retailer process and bumping up costs at every step of the way.

Source: F. De Beule and D. Van Den Bulcke, "The International Supply Chain Management of Samsonite Europe," Discussion Paper No. 1998/E/34 (Centre for International Management and Development, University of Antwerp, 1998), p. 13.

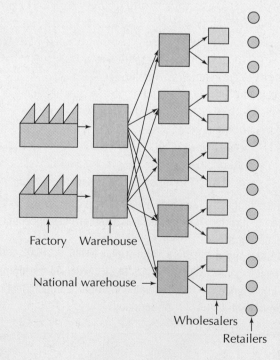

Factory   Warehouse

National warehouse →

Wholesalers

Retailers

FIGURE 17.2 The Samsonite European Supply Chain (II): Centralized, 1975–Mid-1980s

In the mid-1970s, Samsonite decided to streamline the cumbersome supply chain illustrated in Figure 17.1. For the next decade or so, the company shipped products from *factories* to a *central European warehouse*, which then shipped them, upon request, to *retailers* located across the continent.

Source: F. De Beule and D. Van Den Bulcke, "The International Supply Chain Management of Samsonite Europe." Discussion Paper No. 1998/E/34 (Centre for International Management and Development, University of Antwerp, 1998), p. 14.

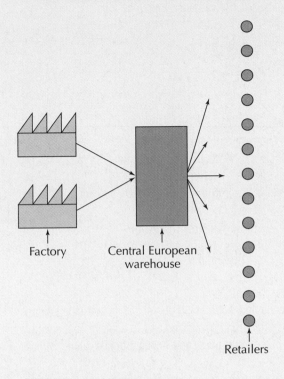

Factory   Central European warehouse   Retailers

R&D and Product Innovation

As noted earlier, Samsonite sold two basic types of suitcases: hard side and soft side. Most of the R&D was initially done in the United States, but the need to develop products for the European market led the company to establish R&D facilities in Europe. Samsonite invested heavily in R&D and in the manufacture of specialized machinery to help keep a competitive edge. To facilitate the transportation and storage of suitcases, Samsonite located its production facilities close to the centralized warehouse.

Soft-side luggage is less complex technologically, and Samsonite purchased Oda, the Belgium soft-side luggage company, to enter that market. Then it licensed its technology to other European companies. By the mid-1990s, 48 percent of Samsonite's sales came from hard-side luggage, 22 percent from soft side, and 30 percent from attaché cases and travel bags, some of which were hard side and some soft side. However, by fiscal 2000, soft-side luggage comprised 51 percent of European sales. In 2001 and 2002, sales of soft-side luggage continued to increase as a percentage, and hard-side luggage sales declined.

Outsourcing

As Samsonite expanded throughout the world, it continued to manufacture its own products and license production to other manufacturers. Then Samsonite entered into subcontract arrangements in Asia and Eastern Europe. In Europe, the subcontractors provide final goods as well as the subassemblies used in Samsonite factories. The trend to outsource more and more of its production has been steadily increasing. By 2007, Samsonite had shut down several of its plants in Europe and decreased internal manufacturing of soft-side luggage from 23 percent in 2004 to just 10 percent in 2007. Although it still produces the

FIGURE 17.3   The Samsonite European Supply Chain (III): Globalized, 1996–Present

As it expanded production throughout Europe, Samsonite was soon obliged to establish arrangements with subcontractors (who provided both final products and subassemblies). Because the company now had to coordinate outsourced goods and parts in addition to production from its own factories, it reconfigured its supply chain once again: Today, all products and parts, whether company produced or outsourced, go to a central European warehouse and, from there, straight to retailers.

Source: F. De Beule and D. Van Den Bulcke. "The International Supply Chain Management of Samsonite Europe," Discussion Paper No. 1998/E/34 (Centre for International Management and Development, University of Antwerp, 1998), p. 21.

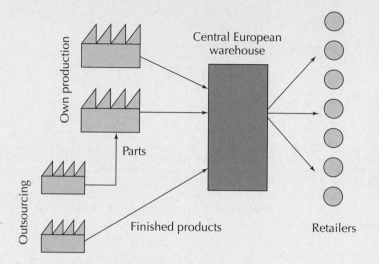

majority of its hard-side luggage internally, the company now sources 90 percent of its soft-side luggage from third-party manufacturers to consolidate its manufacturing capacities and to achieve cost savings. Figure 17.3 illustrates Samsonite's coordination of outsourced parts and finished goods, along with its own production.

Samsonite is a good example of the challenges a firm faces in determining how best to manage the supply chain from supplier to consumer. The greater the geographic spread of the company, the more challenging the management of the supply chain becomes.

Introduction

Our opening case illustrates a number of dimensions of the supply chain networks that link suppliers with manufacturers and customers. This chapter examines these different networks and how a company can manage the links most effectively to reach customers. As Figure 17.4 shows, global manufacturing and supply chain management is important in companies' international business strategies. Most companies agree that effective supply chain management is one of their most important tools in reducing costs and increasing revenues.[2]

As we discuss global supply chain management, we cover the following major issues: an *effective global manufacturing strategy*, the *role of information technology in global supply chain management*, *quality*, *supplier networks*, and *inventory management*, including the importance of effective transportation networks.

It's important to note that effective supply chain management is important for services as well as manufacturing. Our opening case on luggage-maker Samsonite traces developments in the supply chain strategy of a traditional manufacturing company. In our closing case, however, which deals with ePLDT Ventus, an offshore specialist in business process outsourcing, we show how critical it is for service companies to analyze their supply chain strategies in order to compete effectively on an international scale.

Case Review Note

FIGURE 17.4   Factors Influencing Supply Chain Management

Regardless of a company's particular strategies for conducting international operations, its ability to manage both global production and its global supply chain are crucial to its success.

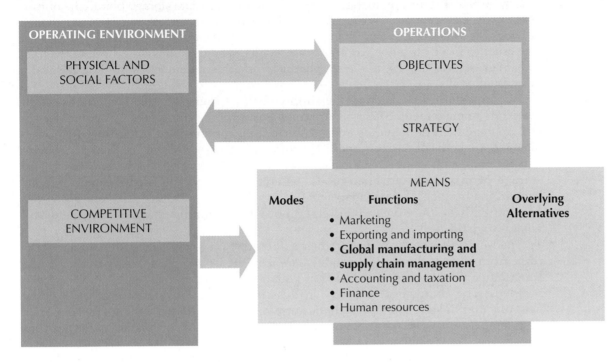

Even in the section of the chapter on global manufacturing strategy, the same issues apply to an effective global services strategy: cost minimization, dependability, quality, innovation, flexibility, and service locations.

WHAT IS SUPPLY CHAIN MANAGEMENT?

A company's **supply chain** encompasses the coordination of materials, information, and funds from the initial raw material supplier to the ultimate customer.[3] It is the management of the value-added process from the suppliers' supplier to the customers' customer.[4] In this chapter, we use supply chain management in its broadest definition, encompassing everything from supplier relationships to getting the product to the final consumer, with logistics as an important aspect of supply chain management.

Figure 17.5 illustrates the concept of a global supply chain. Suppliers can be part of the manufacturer's organizational structure, as would be the case in a vertically integrated company, or they can be independent of the company. The direct suppliers also

Supply chain—the coordination of materials, information, and funds from the initial raw material supplier to the ultimate customer.

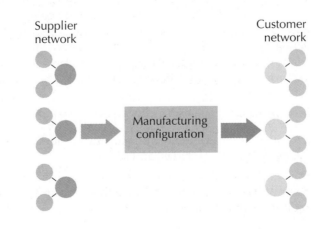

**FIGURE 17.5
The Global Supply Chain**

At every step in the process that transforms raw materials into finished products offered to consumers, a firm's global supply chain maintains connections between its *supplier network* (its suppliers and its suppliers' suppliers) with its *customer network* (its customers and its customers' customers).

have their networks. In a global context, the suppliers can be located in the country where the manufacturing or assembly takes place, or they can be located in one country and ship materials to the country of manufacture or assembly. The output of the suppliers can be shipped directly to the factory or to an intermediate storage point. The output of the manufacturing process can be shipped directly to the customers or to a warehouse network, as was the case with Samsonite. The output can be sold directly to the end consumer or to a distributor, wholesaler, or retailer, who then sells the output to the final consumer. As was the case in the supplier network, the output can be sold domestically or internationally.

> **Logistics (also called materials management)**—that part of the supply chain process that plans, implements, and controls the efficient, effective flow and storage of goods, services, and related information from the point of origin to the point of consumption in order to meet customers' requirements.

An important dimension of the supply chain is **logistics**, also sometimes called **materials management**. Materials management is inbound logistics or the movement and management of materials and products from purchasing through production to meet the demands of the consumer.[5] The difference between supply chain management and logistics is one of degree. Logistics focuses much more on the transportation and storage of materials and final goods, whereas supply chain management extends beyond that to include the management of supplier and customer relations. However, firms often have their own interpretation of what is supply chain management and what is logistics.

The MNEs that have excelled in their ability to manage their supply chain networks come from all over the world, including Apple in the United States, Tesco in the United Kingdom, Samsung in Korea, Nokia in Finland, Toyota in Japan, and AstraZeneca in Sweden.[6] The companies we study in this chapter are considered part of a global network that links together designers, suppliers, subcontractors, manufacturers, and customers. The supply chain network is quite broad, and the coordination of the network takes place through interactions between firms in the network.[7]

Global Manufacturing Strategies

Recall from our opening case that Samsonite initially exported to Europe but eventually set up manufacturing facilities in several European countries. We pointed out that Samsonite invested in Europe because of *location-specific advantages* (notably, hefty demand) and chose to enter the market through foreign direct investment in order to take advantage of its own *firm-specific assets* (especially an excellent product line and a solid manufacturing process). Finally, we emphasized Samsonite's strategic decision to internalize those advantages rather than sell them to an outside manufacturer.[8] Thus, although Samsonite entered into some licensing agreements and subcontracted some manufacturing, it initially kept most of its production, especially in high-end hard-side luggage, under its own control.

Although Samsonite engaged in its own manufacturing for the most part, it eventually subcontracted, or outsourced, manufacturing to other firms. Nike, for example, does not own any manufacturing facilities, but it subcontracts manufacturing to other companies. So Nike is basically a design and marketing company. Mattel does not own manufacturing facilities in China to manufacture Barbie dolls, but it subcontracts the manufacturing to a Hong Kong–based company that has investments in China. Some of the toys in McDonald's Happy Meals or Burger King meals are also subcontracted to a Hong Kong–based manufacturer that produces the toys in China.

FOUR KEY FACTORS IN MANUFACTURING STRATEGY

The success of a global manufacturing strategy depends on four key factors: *compatibility, configuration, coordination,* and *control.*[9]

> **Compatibility**—the degree of consistency between FDI decisions and a company's competitive strategy.

Compatibility   Compatibility in this context is the degree of consistency between the foreign investment decision and the company's competitive strategy. Direct manufacturing, for instance, made sense in Samsonite's case but not in Nike's. Here are some company strategies that managers must consider:

- *Efficiency/cost*—reduction of manufacturing costs
- *Dependability*—degree of trust in a company's products, its delivery, and price promises
- *Quality*—performance reliability, service quality, speed of delivery, and maintenance quality of the product(s)
- *Innovation*—ability to develop new products and ideas
- *Flexibility*—ability of the production process to make different kinds of products and to adjust the volume of output[10]

Efficiency/Cost Strategies *Cost-minimization strategies* and the drive for global efficiencies force MNEs to establish economies of scale in manufacturing, often by producing in areas with low-cost labor. This is one of the major reasons why many MNEs established manufacturing facilities in Asia, Mexico, and Eastern Europe.

OFFSHORE MANUFACTURING This type of foreign direct investment is known as **offshore manufacturing,** but clearly any manufacturing that takes place outside of a company's home country is considered "offshore." Offshore manufacturing escalated sharply in the 1960s and 1970s in the electronics industry as one company after another set up production facilities in the Far East, mostly in Taiwan and Singapore. Those locations were attractive because of low labor costs, the availability of cheap materials and components, and the proximity to markets. Even the athletic shoe market left the United States for Taiwan and Korea.

As wages rose in Korea, however, manufacturing began to shift to other low-cost countries—China, Indonesia, Malaysia, Thailand, and Vietnam. China particularly has become the hot spot for manufacturing and has even been termed by the *Wall Street Journal* as "the world's factory floor." Although reliable information does not exist for the average hourly wages in the country, data gathered by the U.S. Bureau of Labor Statistics place a rough estimate at 67 cents an hour—a number that includes both the pay rate and employer contributions for benefits and insurance. This rate contrasts sharply with the average of $23.65 earned by U.S. factory workers and even the $2.63 earned by workers in Mexico and the $4.54 earned in Poland.[11]

CONCEPT CHECK

In Chapter 11, we explain **value** as the underlying principle of *strategy*, defining it as "the measure of a firm's capability to sell what it makes for more than the costs incurred to make it." Here, while further refining our discussion of *strategy* to enumerate factors contributing to a successful strategy, we hasten to repeat our definition of **strategy** as "the efforts of managers to build and strengthen the company's competitive position within its industry *by creating value.*"

CONCEPT CHECK

In discussing the process of "Creating Value" in Chapter 11, we explain that a firm that aspires to a position of "Low-Cost Leadership" strives to be the low-cost producer in an industry *for a given level of quality.* This **strategy**, we observe, means that the firm adopts one of two tactics, both of which must be *compatible* with the structure of its **value chain**: (1) earning a profit higher than industry rivals by selling products *at* average industry prices or (2) capturing *market share* by selling products at prices *below* industry average.

Maquiladora workers make bras in Mexico. Offshore manufacturing by U.S. companies helps reduce costs by using low-cost workers in developing countries like Mexico.

Offshore manufacturing—any investment that takes place in a country different from the home country.

China's output is so large and wide ranging that it exerts deflationary pressure around the world on products such as textiles, TVs, furniture, auto parts, and mobile phones. It is now the world's fourth largest industrial base behind the United States, Japan, and Germany. Many MNEs set up operations in China in the 1980s to capitalize on China's huge population and growing demand.

As we indicate in our opening case, Samsonite is among the companies that have found it more cost-effective to manufacture products in China—and not just for the Chinese market, but for export to the rest of the world as well. Meanwhile, the Dutch company Philips Electronics produces some of its products solely in China and plans to make China its global supply base, from which it will export its products around the world.[12] Still other companies, such as U.S.-based Hewlett-Packard, Microsoft, and Motorola, have looked beyond simply outsourcing manufacturing to China and have established R&D centers within the country. IBM and General Motors are even using China as a global center for their companies' procurement operations.[13]

However, when employing a cost-minimization strategy, many companies overlook important elements—such as shipping distances, extra inventory, political and security risks, and the availability of skilled and educated workers—which causes them to underestimate the costs of outsourcing to low-wage countries. In other words, when making decisions to source abroad, companies should consider the total cost of facilitating the strategy, as opposed to merely the acquisition cost.

Total cost analysis—an in-depth assessment of the complete cost of a transaction that takes into account acquisition, ownership, and disposal costs.

TOTAL COST ANALYSIS   A *total cost analysis* takes into account the costs of ownership, such as storing and transporting inventory, and of disposal. In some instances, labor is such a small percentage of overall costs that employing cheap labor abroad does not effectively save the company money. For example, Nike decided to employ a small contractor in San Francisco to produce some of its made-to-order goods, in spite of its $15-per-hour rates that are 20 times those of the contractors in China. Nike determined that labor costs were a small portion of the total cost and that overhead costs, such as management of the flow of goods from halfway around the world and the risk of stock-outs and high inventories, were much more important considerations.[14]

In our closing case, however, we explain why companies like Ventus, a business process provider whose costs are due almost entirely to labor, is likely to be a very attractive option for many companies. Remember, however, that high turnover rates and expensive training costs often plague operations in low-wage areas and can in fact negate any potential cost savings.[15]

Dependability Strategies   Many other factors besides cost must also be taken into consideration. The growing customer demand for *dependability* and prompt deliveries has caused companies such as Dell to locate plants closer to customers rather than in low-wage areas. As the supply chain lengthens, there are risks of not being able to get components or finished goods to market on time. Thus shortening the distance in the supply chain can improve dependability.

Innovation and Quality Strategies   Many companies are also responding to the importance of *innovation* and *quality*. When companies invest abroad to take advantage of low-cost labor, they are not as concerned about innovation. However, as more and more companies establish R&D facilities abroad, they will be able to move beyond low-end manufacturing.

A major issue, though, is the issue of quality, which we discuss in more detail later in the chapter. If foreign operations can ensure high quality and contribute to innovation, companies will continue to set up operations abroad. However, after a decade-long trend of sourcing in low-cost countries like China, Japanese companies, such as Honda, Canon, and Sharp, are now relocating production back in their home country.

In 2006, Japanese companies registered to build 1,782 factories in Japan and only 182 abroad, compared to four years ago when 844 and 434, respectively, were built.

These Japanese companies have been responding to the need for access to Japan's pool of skilled workers, as well as its proximity to engineers, parts suppliers, and decision makers. They believe that to ensure innovation and quality, close communication between product development and manufacturing is essential.[16]

Flexibility Strategies The need for responsiveness or *flexibility* because of differences in national markets may result in regional manufacturing to service local markets. It may not be possible to produce all products in one location and ship them around the world. Wall's Unilever, for example, produces ice cream in China, and because of its local operations, it is able to develop products that are unique to the Chinese market, as well as produce its global brands, such as the Magnum Bar and the Cornetto.

However, it has found it can produce some of its global brands during the winter when demand is down and ship them to South Africa and Australia during their summer. This flexibility has enabled the company to utilize excess production facilities and reduce costs to markets outside of China.[17] However, differences in measurement systems, time zones, and problem-solving approaches can also add unnecessary complexity to the supply chain.

Changes in Strategy As a company's competitive strategies change, so too do its manufacturing strategies. In addition, MNEs may adopt different strategies for different product lines, depending on the competitive priorities of those products. For example, to reduce the cost and complexity of its products, the Finnish mobile-phone maker Nokia designs phones that contain fewer parts and bases its different models on the same basic components. This manufacturing strategy has allowed Nokia to maintain 16.8 percent profit margins on its low-end phones and 18.8 percent on its higher-end models, which are substantial in the highly competitive market for cellular phones.[18]

Toyota has always prided itself on high quality and has traditionally relied on manufacturing in Toyota City, Japan, where it is close to suppliers and can ensure high quality and adherence to its manufacturing strategy. However, Toyota has developed a family of vehicles based on a single low-cost platform that is targeted for emerging markets. To keep the prices for these vehicles low enough to compete in the developing world, Toyota has abandoned its traditional practice of sourcing key components from its Japanese plants and is instead locating factories for these parts in low-wage areas such as South America, Africa, and Southeast Asia, which has allowed the company to reduce the costs by 20 to 25 percent, although managers are concerned they may lose control over quality.[19]

Manufacturing Configuration Next, the company's managers need to determine the configuration of manufacturing facilities. The three basic configurations that MNEs consider as they establish a global manufacturing strategy are *centralized*, *regional*, and *multidomestic*.

Centralized Manufacturing Strategy The first configuration is to have *centralized manufacturing* that offers a selection of standard lower-priced products to different markets. That is basically a manufacture-and-export strategy. It is common for new-to-export companies to use this strategy, typically through their home-country manufacturing facilities. This is also important for expensive items where economies of scale in manufacturing are important and there is little need to localize the product for consumption in different markets, such as aircraft.

Regional Manufacturing Strategy The second configuration is the use of *regional manufacturing* facilities to serve customers within a specific region. That is what Samsonite did initially in Europe with its production facilities in Belgium and what Toyota is doing in its markets in developing countries.

Manufacturing configuration:

- Centralized manufacturing in one country.
- Manufacturing facilities in specific regions to service those regions.
- Multidomestic facilities in each country.

CONCEPT CHECK

In Chapter 11, in discussing "Configuration" as a factor in creating a **value chain,** we explain the importance of identifying the best "location economies"—those in which operations can be most effective given prevailing economic, political, and cultural conditions. We also analyze several factors that may influence a company's decisions in configuring its value chain (e.g., cost factors, **logistics, economies of scale**, buyers' needs).

CONCEPT CHECK

Recall from Chapter 11 our extended discussion of "Global Integration Versus Local Responsiveness" as an issue in *configuring* and *coordinating* a firm's **value chain.** We then proceed to explain how efforts to resolve this issue may contribute to the formulation of a **global strategy** or a **multidomestic strategy** for international operations. Here we analyze ways in which this same issue can put pressure on specific strategic decisions about the configuration of manufacturing facilities.

Multidomestic Manufacturing Strategy   Third, market expansion in individual countries, especially when the demand in those countries becomes significant, might argue for a *multidomestic approach* in which companies manufacture products close to their customers, using country-specific manufacturing facilities to meet local needs.[20] As we saw in our opening case, for example, Samsonite chose not to manufacture in every European country in which it marketed its products, but rather it segmented the broad European market into smaller areas supplied by seven well-placed manufacturing facilities. Unless the company has manufacturing facilities in every country where it is doing business, it must combine exporting with manufacturing. In reality, MNEs choose a combination of these approaches depending on their product strategies.

Countries often also specialize in the production of parts or final goods, a process known as *rationalization*. A good example can be borrowed from our opening case. In the 1980s, Samsonite opened a new factory in Hénin-Beaumont, France, specifically to manufacture Prestige Attaché and a few other products. In so doing, it was able to remove production of those products from its facility in Oudenaarde, Belgium, where it was then able to focus on its new Oyster product line. This strategy of specializing the manufacture of certain products in certain plants eventually made it feasible to export all production to a centralized European warehouse, from which Samsonite could then distribute its whole product line to retailers all over Europe.

> Coordination is linking or integrating activities into a unified system.

Coordination and Control   Coordination and control fit well together. *Coordinating* is the linking or integrating of activities into a unified system.[21] The activities include everything along the global supply chain from purchasing to warehousing to shipment. It is hard to coordinate supplier relations and logistics activities if those issues are not considered when the manufacturing configuration is set up.

Once the company determines the manufacturing configuration it will use, it must adopt a control system to ensure that company strategies are carried out. *Control* can be the measuring of performance so companies can respond appropriately to changing conditions. Another aspect of control structure is the organizational structure. Recall from our opening case, for example, that Samsonite established a European headquarters in Oudenaarde, Belgium, for the basic purpose of controlling all of its European activities—a strategy also designed to maximize the company's ability to respond to local and/or regional differences in a very large market.

CONCEPT CHECK

We define *control* in general as "the planning, implementation, evaluation, and correction of performance to ensure that organizational objectives are achieved." In explaining "Coordination and Control Systems" in Chapter 15, we explain that, regardless of its structure, the MNE must develop coordination and control mechanisms to prevent duplication of efforts, to coordinate resource allocation, and to ensure that companywide operations benefit from ideas generated anywhere in the organization.

Corporate management often requires additional data to coordinate and control operations. In Chapter 15, we discuss some of the key types of information supplied by IT.

Information Technology and Global Supply Chain Management

Earlier in the chapter, we defined global supply chain management and provided a simplified view of a global supply chain in Figure 17.5 (p. 653). A comprehensive supply chain strategy should include the following elements:

- Customer-service requirements
- Plant and distribution-center network design
- Inventory management
- Outsourcing and third-party logistics relationships
- Key customer and supplier relationships
- Business processes
- Information systems
- Organizational design and training requirements
- Performance metrics
- Performance goals[22]

In this section, we discuss *information systems* as a key part of the global supply chain management system. In the remainder of the chapter, we discuss *quality management, supplier networks,* and *inventory management,* which also includes transportation networks. Each of these areas relies on information technology to be effective.

Control systems, such as organizational structure and performance measurement systems, ensure that managers implement company strategies.

INFORMATION TECHNOLOGY

With competitive demands to produce high-quality products quickly and efficiently, manage inventory levels proficiently, communicate effectively with suppliers, and meet customer demand adequately, companies are coming to rely more and more on information technology (IT) to meet their needs. Nine out of 10 executives believe IT is an important source of competitive advantage,[23] reflected in the fact that global spending on IT exceeds $2.8 trillion a year and accounts for nearly 7 percent of GDP.[24]

A key to making the global supply chain work is a good information system.

Electronic Data Interchange (EDI)   The key to making a global information system work is information. As we note in our opening case, for example, Samsonite invested heavily in IT designed to speed up delivery time to retailers. In particular, the new technology made it possible for retailers or salespeople to trigger orders directly by contacting a central warehouse. Many companies use **electronic data interchange (EDI)** to link suppliers, manufacturers, customers, and intermediaries, especially in the food manufacturing and car-making industries, in which suppliers replenish in high volumes.

In a global context, EDI has been used to link exporters with customs to facilitate the quick processing of customs forms, thus speeding up the delivery of products across borders. Wal-Mart is known for its revolutionary use of EDI to connect its suppliers to its inventory ordering system.[25] Wal-Mart depends on over 61,000 suppliers located in 70 countries.[26] As noted in the Wal-Mart case in Chapter 8, Wal-Mart's information system was one of its competitive advantages in lowering costs and capturing market share in Mexico.

EDI (electronic data interchange)—the electronic linkage of suppliers, customers, and third-party intermediaries to expedite documents and financial flows.

However, EDI has some drawbacks. It is relatively limited and inflexible. It provides basic information but does not adapt easily to rapidly changing market conditions, a necessary condition in the global marketplace. It is relatively expensive to implement, so many small- and medium-size companies find it difficult to afford. Also, it is based on proprietary rather than on widely accepted standards, so systems tend only to be able to link together suppliers and their customers. In addition, it focuses more on the business-to-business value chain and does not deal effectively with end-use customers.[27]

Enterprise Resource Planning/Material Requirements Planning   The next wave of technology affecting the global supply chain was the implementation of information technology packages known as **enterprise resource planning (ERP).** Companies such as the German software giant SAP, Oracle, Baan, and PeopleSoft introduced software to integrate everything in the back office of the firm—the part of the business that dealt with the firm itself but not with the customer (known as the front office). ERP is essential for bringing together the information inside the firm and from different geographic areas, but its inability to tie in to the customer and take advantage of e-commerce has been a problem.

ERP (enterprise resource planning)—software that can link information flows from different parts of a business and from different geographic areas.

An extension of ERP is *material requirements planning* (MRP), a computerized information system that addresses complex inventory situations and calculates the demand for parts from the production schedules of the companies that use the parts. DENSO, the Japanese manufacturer of auto parts that is a major supplier to Toyota, uses MRP extensively because it not only manufactures parts for Toyota but for other auto companies as well. It uses MRP to calculate the demand for parts from the production schedules of the non-Toyota companies that it supplies.

MRP (material requirements planning)—computerized information system that addresses complex inventory situations and calculates the demand for parts from the production schedules of the companies that use the parts.

Radio Frequency ID (RFID)   A newer wave has recently been sweeping the technology scene in the form of *radio frequency ID (RFID),* a system that labels a product with an electronic tag that stores and transmits information regarding the product's origin, destination, and quantity. When electronic readers scan the tags, by means of radio waves, the data on the tags can be rewritten or captured and sent to a computer network database. The database collects, organizes, stores, and moves the data and is often used in conjunction with an ERP system.

This real-time information allows manufacturers, suppliers, and distributors to keep track of products and components throughout their manufacturing processes and transportation networks, resulting in increased efficiencies and more visibility along the supply chain. Although RFID is still in its infant stages, companies such as Wal-Mart and Procter & Gamble have credited it with saving them $8.3 billion and $400 million a year, respectively.[28] Its use in the Las Vegas airport to track luggage has resulted in more accurate sorting, better tracking, and fewer lost bags, a great boon to international travelers who frequent Las Vegas.[29]

E-Commerce   The next technological wave linking together the parts of the global supply chain is **e-commerce.** As an example, Dell Computer Corporation has a factory in Ireland that supplies custom-built PCs all over Europe. Customers can transmit orders to Dell via call centers or Dell's Web site. The company relays the demand for components to its suppliers. Trucks deliver the components to the factory and haul off the completed computers within a few hours.

All of this activity, of course, is made possible by the Internet. Wal-Mart, for example, moved its EDI-based infrastructure from traditional but expensive value-added networks (VANs) to the Internet. This has been good news for many of its 61,000 worldwide vendors. All of their transactions with Wal-Mart are now on the Web—a substantial cost savings over VANs for Wal-Mart and its vendors.[30]

Most experts agree that the Internet will revolutionize communications across all levels of the global supply chain, but it will occur at different speeds in different areas. The number of worldwide Internet users is rising—increasing from 420 million in 2000 to surpassing the 1 billion mark in 2005. It is predicted that the number of users will reach 2 billion by 2011.[31]

Extranets and Intranets   Dell has established an **extranet** for its suppliers—a linkage to Dell's information system via the Internet—so suppliers can organize production and delivery of parts to Dell when the company needs more parts. Dell uses the Internet to plug its suppliers into its customer database so they can keep track of changes in demand. It also uses the Internet to plug customers into the ordering process and allows them to track the progress of their order from the factory to their doorstep.[32]

The real attraction of the Internet in global supply chain management is that it not only helps to automate and speed up internal processes in a company through its **intranet** but also spreads efficiency gains to the business systems of its customers and suppliers.[33] The new technology wave using the Internet is that of **private technology exchange (PTX),** an online collaboration model that brings manufacturers, distributors, value-added resellers, and customers together to execute trading transactions and to share information about demand, production, availability, and more. PTXs will increase the efficiency of the supply chain and reduce costs for participants.

"The Digital Divide"   The challenge in global supply chain management is that some networks can be managed through the Internet, but others—particularly in emerging markets—cannot because of the lack of technology, especially high-speed access to the Internet. The use of the Internet varies by location and by industry. North America is at least five years ahead of some countries in Europe, especially Eastern Europe, but it is behind Asia, especially in some key infrastructures. Industries such as computing and electronics, aerospace and defense, and motor vehicles are blasting ahead; industrial equipment, food and agriculture, heavy industries, and consumer goods are lagging behind.

RFID (radio frequency ID)—a system that labels products with an electronic tag that stores and transmits information regarding the product's origin, destination, and quantity.

E-commerce—the use of the Internet to join together suppliers with companies and companies with customers.

Private technology exchange (PTX)—an online collaboration model that brings manufacturers, distributors, value-added resellers, and customers together to execute trading transactions.

CONCEPT CHECK

In discussing "Contemporary Approaches to Organizational Change" in Chapter 15, we observe that the Internet, which accelerates the spread of ideas throughout an organization, has become a "metaphor" for organization structure: In other words, as a supremely efficient and effective means of organizing global knowledge, resources, and people, the Internet has inspired many people to imagine new ways of effectively organizing a company's resources (especially its people). We also point out the ironic attractiveness of a self-regulating organizational model that features no formal organizational hierarchy.

This so-called digital divide has created difficulties for companies such as U.S.-based Newmont Mining Corporation. Newmont has struggled to implement its ordering and inventory management information system with its suppliers in Indonesia, who have to rent computers in different towns to even access the Internet and whose managers are former farmers who have never even used e-mail.[34] It is no coincidence that the leaders in e-commerce are those who have invested significant amounts of money over the years in IT—notably in the defense and motor vehicles industries.

It's clear from the preceding discussion that IT can help companies manage their global supply chains, but it has to be carefully integrated into the company's overall strategy. Because IT is highly technical as well as a support to the lines of business of a company, it is often difficult to align IT with the strategy of the firm. This is especially true in the international area where personnel in different countries may be used to their own IT systems and may have difficulty adopting a global IT format that will allow the firm to achieve some economies of scale as well as fully integrate IT in the firm's overall strategy.

Quality

An important aspect of all levels of the global supply chain is quality management, which is true for service as well as manufacturing companies. **Quality** is defined as meeting or exceeding the expectations of the customer. More specifically, it is the conformance to specifications, value, fitness for use, support (provided by the company), and psychological impressions (image).[35]

> Quality—meeting or exceeding the expectations of a customer.

For example, no one wants to buy computer software that has a lot of bugs. However, the need to get software to market quickly may mean getting the product to market as soon as possible and correcting errors later. In the airline industry, service is key. Some airlines, such as Singapore Air, have developed a worldwide reputation for excellence in service. That is a distinct competitive advantage, especially when trying to attract the business traveler.

Case: Car Quality Quality—or lack thereof—can have serious ramifications for a company. Ford Motor Company lost around $1 billion in 2001 because of faulty Firestone tires placed on its Ford Explorers. Because of this and other quality problems, Ford, General Motors, and DaimlerChrysler are taking a hard look at the way Japanese carmakers manufacture their cars with higher efficiency and fewer defects. As DaimlerChrysler puts it, we're "raiding Toyota Motor Corporation for quality expertise."

The American car companies, which have typically lagged behind the Japanese in quality, are learning to root out problems before assembly and bring each supplier into the design process earlier, hoping to spot component problems early. They are finding some success, particularly in their international plants. Ford's Brazil plant produces some of the best quality results of any of its factories.[36]

Each year, J.D. Power & Associates releases two different quality rankings on automobiles: the Initial Quality Study (IQS) and the Vehicle Dependability Study (VDS), which measures quality after three years of ownership. Although the Japanese automakers have long dominated the rankings, the 2007 results exhibited marked improvements for both American and European carmakers. Ford even outpaced Toyota with five top-model segment awards over Toyota's three. Nevertheless, Toyota still topped the overall rankings for both studies.[37]

ZERO DEFECTS VERSUS ACCEPTABLE QUALITY LEVEL

Quality can mean **zero defects,** an idea perfected by Japanese manufacturers who refuse to tolerate defects of any kind. Before the strong emphasis on zero defects, many companies operated according to the premise of **acceptable quality level (AQL).** This premise allowed an acceptable level of poor quality. It held that unacceptable products would be

> Zero defects—the refusal to tolerate defects of any kind.

dealt with through repair facilities and service warranties. This type of manufacturing/operating environment required buffer inventories, rework stations, and expediting. The goal was to push through products as fast as possible and then deal with the mistakes later. However, it is increasingly evident that AQL is inferior to zero defects, and global companies that take quality more seriously will beat the competition.[38]

THE DEMING APPROACH TO QUALITY MANAGEMENT

In the late 1970s, when Japanese companies began to outpace American companies seriously in their achievement of high-quality products and processes, a new emphasis was placed on actively managing the operations that affect quality. One of the contributors to this focus on *quality management*, and one of the people who trained the Japanese in quality was W. Edwards Deming.

Deming's 14 Points   To espouse the idea that the responsibility for quality resides within the policies and practices of managers, Deming developed several suggestions, which have come to be known as *Deming's 14 Points:*

1. Create constancy of purpose
2. Adopt a new philosophy
3. Cease mass inspection
4. End awarding business on the basis of price tag
5. Constantly improve the system
6. Institute training on the job
7. Improve leadership
8. Drive out fear
9. Break down barriers between departments
10. Eliminate slogans
11. Eliminate work standards
12. Remove barriers to pride
13. Institute education and self-improvement
14. Put everybody to work[39]

The emphasis on quality management has continued to provide a major source of competitive advantage and to play a major role for companies across the globe. However, just as different countries possess varying cultures, product preferences, and business practices, different regions of the world have approached the concept of quality management in different ways. The Japanese have long focused on lean production processes that eliminate waste and increase visibility, whereas the American approach has historically been more statistically based. The Europeans have opted to concentrate more on standards of quality.[40] These varying attitudes toward quality create a high level of complexity for multinational enterprises with global operations. As we will see, however, many of the best practices concerning quality have been perfected in Japan and are being used worldwide.

TOTAL QUALITY MANAGEMENT (TQM)

The Japanese approach to quality is **total quality management (TQM),** a process that stresses three principles: *customer satisfaction, continuous improvement,* and *employee involvement.*[41] The goal of TQM is to eliminate all defects. TQM often focuses on benchmarking world-class standards, product and service design, process design, and purchasing.[42]

The center of the entire process, however, is customer satisfaction, which to achieve may raise production costs. The difference between AQL and TQM centers on the attitude toward quality. In AQL, quality is a characteristic of a product that meets or exceeds engineering standards. In TQM, quality means a product is "so good that the customer wouldn't think of buying from anyone else."

TQM is a process of continuous improvement at every level of the organization—from the mailroom to the boardroom. It implies that the company is doing everything it can to achieve quality at all stages of the process, from customer demands to product design to engineering. For example, if management accounting systems are focused strictly on cost, they will preclude measures that could lead to higher quality. The key is to understand the company's overall strategy.

TQM does not use any specific production philosophy or require the use of other techniques, such as a just-in-time system for inventory delivery. TQM is a proactive strategy. Although benchmarking—determining the best processes used by the best companies—is an important part of TQM, using the best practices of other companies is not intended to be a goal. TQM means that a company will try to be better than the best.

Executives who have adopted the zero-defects philosophy of TQM claim that long-run production costs decline as defects decline. The continuous improvement process is also known as *kaizen*, which means identifying problems and enlisting employees at all levels of the organization to help eliminate the problems. The key is to make continuous improvement a part of the daily work of every employee.

TQM in a global setting is challenging because of cultural and environmental differences. In 1987, for instance, Samsonite entered into an agreement with a Hungarian manufacturer to supply low-end soft-side luggage. Unfortunately, a lack of advanced technology prevented the Hungarian firm from delivering products that satisfied Samsonite's world-class quality standards. As a result, Samsonite was forced to invest heavily in its Hungarian partner in order to get a supply of products that would satisfy even the low end of its European market.

> **TQM (total quality management)**—a process that stresses customer satisfaction, employee involvement, and continuous improvement of quality. Its goal is to eliminate all defects.

SIX SIGMA

A new management tool, Six Sigma, is starting to displace TQM as the corporate-reengineering tool of choice and strongly reflects the more statistical American approach to quality management. **Six Sigma** is a highly focused system of quality control that scrutinizes a company's entire production system. It aims to eliminate defects, slash product cycle times, and cut costs across the board. The Six Sigma process uses data and rigorous statistical analysis to identify "defects" in a process or product, reduce variability, and achieve as close to zero defects as possible. It involves driving toward six standard deviations between the mean and the nearest specification limit in any process—from manufacturing to transactional and from product to service.[43]

Motorola introduced Six Sigma in the 1980s, and it's been adopted by many MNEs, including General Electric, GlaxoSmithKline, and Lockheed Martin. Although some have accused the Six Sigma program of diverting attention away from customers and of squashing innovation, 82 of the 100 largest companies in the United States have embraced it.[44] It is unknown whether Six Sigma will eliminate the use of TQM, but for now, it is important for companies to explore both tools to determine the one that will better improve quality in the organization.[45]

> **Six Sigma**—a quality control system aimed at eliminating defects, slashing product cycle times, and cutting costs across the board.

QUALITY STANDARDS

There are three different levels of quality standards: *general-level, industry-specific,* and *company-specific.* The first level is a general standard, such as the Deming Award, which is presented to firms that demonstrate excellence in quality, and the Malcolm Baldrige National Quality Award, which is presented annually to companies that demonstrate quality strategies and achievements. However, even more important than awards is certification of quality.

Levels of quality standards:

- General level—ISO 9000, Malcolm Baldrige National Quality Award.
- Industry-specific level.
- Company level.

General-Level Standards The **International Organization for Standardization (ISO)** in Geneva was formed in 1947 to facilitate the international coordination and unification of industrial standards. From the beginning it has partnered with the IEC (International Electrotechnical Commission), which is the originator of global technical standards. It also collaborates with the International Telecommunications Union and the World Trade Organization. The ISO is an NGO and represents a network of standard setters in 158 countries throughout the world. It has established a total of 16,455 international quality standards.[46]

ISO 9000—a global set of quality standards intended to promote quality at every level of an organization.

ISO 9000 and ISO 14000 The two main families of standards issued by ISO are ISO 9000 and ISO 14000. ISO 9000 is concerned with quality management, or "what the organization does to enhance customer satisfaction by meeting customer and applicable regulatory requirements and continually to improve its performance in this regard."[47] ISO 14000 is concerned with environmental management and what the company does to improve its environmental performance.

ISO 9000 is a set of universal standards for a Quality Assurance system that is accepted around the world. The standards apply uniformly to companies in any industry and of any size. ISO 9000 is intended to promote the idea of quality at every level of an organization. Initially, it was designed to harmonize technical norms within the EU. Now it is an important part of business operations throughout Europe. In 2000, the ISO revised the standards and refers to them now as the ISO 9000:2000.

ISO 14000—a quality standard concerned with environmental management.

Basically, under ISO 9000:2000, companies must document how workers perform every function that affects quality and install mechanisms to ensure that they follow through on the documented routine. ISO 9000:2000 certification entails a complex analysis of management systems and procedures, not just quality-control standards. Rather than judging the quality of a particular product, ISO 9000:2000 evaluates the management of the manufacturing process according to standards it has created in 20 domains—from purchasing to design to training. A company that wants to be ISO certified must fill out a report and then be certified by a team of independent auditors.[48] The process can be expensive and time consuming. Each site of a company must be separately certified. The certification of one site cannot cover the entire company.

Most MNEs claim ISO certification, but as noted in a humorous way in Figure 17.6, ISO is not the solution to all quality issues. It has also been estimated that in places like China, as much as 40 percent of the ISO certifications are falsified.[49] However, ISO certification of suppliers will help companies to get more business, especially with European companies. When companies are choosing among different suppliers, it would be very beneficial for the supplier to have ISO certification.

U.S. companies that operate in Europe are becoming ISO certified to maintain access to the European market. When DuPont lost a major European contract to an ISO-certified

FIGURE 17.6 ISO 9000: A Good Reason to Take a Close Look at Your Internal Processes

Source: DILBERT reprinted by permission of United Feature Syndicate, Inc.

European company, it decided to become certified. By doing so, not only was DuPont able to position itself better in the European market, but it also benefited from the experience of going through ISO certification and focusing on quality in the organization. Some European companies are so committed to ISO certification that they will not do business with a supplier that is certified if its suppliers are not also ISO certified. They want to be sure that quality flows back to every level of the supply chain.

> Non-European companies operating in Europe need to become ISO certified in order to maintain access to that market.

Industry-Specific Standards   In addition to the general standards described earlier, there are industry-specific standards for quality, especially for suppliers, to follow. QS9000 is derived from ISO 9001, but it is more specific to the auto industry. Under the guidelines, suppliers must adapt their quality systems to meet the expectations of the automakers. QS9000 is required for any supplier of Ford, General Motors, and DaimlerChrysler.

Company-Specific Standards   Individual companies also set their own standards for suppliers to meet if they are going to continue to supply them. A good example centers on Samsonite's efforts to bring the output of its Eastern European suppliers up to its own quality standards. Toyota is another company that works aggressively with its suppliers to ensure delivery of high-quality parts based on what is acceptable to Toyota.

Supplier Networks

Global sourcing and production strategies can be better understood by looking at Figure 17.7. **Sourcing** is the firm's process of having inputs (raw materials and parts) supplied to it for the production process. Figure 17.7 illustrates the basic operating environment choices (the home country or any foreign country) by stage in the production process (sourcing of raw materials and parts and the manufacture and assembly of final products). Global sourcing is the first step in the process of materials management, which includes sourcing, inventory management, and transportation between suppliers, manufacturers, and customers.

> Sourcing—the process of a firm having inputs supplied to it from outside suppliers (both domestic and foreign) for the production process.

Ford, for example, assembles cars in Hermosillo, Mexico, and ships them into the United States for end-use consumers. The cars are designed by Mazda, a Japanese company, and use some Japanese parts. Ford can purchase parts manufactured in Japan and ship them to the United States for final assembly and sale in the U.S. market, or it can

FIGURE 17.7   Global Sourcing and Production Strategy

When a company wants to *source* raw materials, parts, or components as a function of its global strategy, it's faced with some key decisions. It may, for example, decide to source components at home, assemble them abroad, and then export the final product to the home market, to foreign markets, or to both.

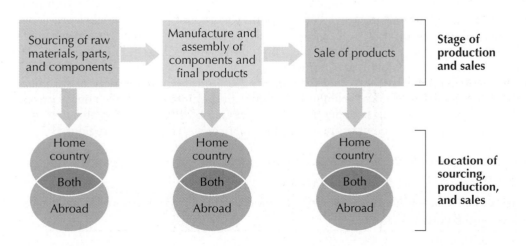

have Japanese- and U.S.-made parts shipped to Mexico for final assembly and sale in the United States and Mexico. For Mexican assembly, some of the parts come from the United States, some from Japan, and a small percentage from Mexico.

Case: A Loaf of Whole Grain White Bread   Although global sourcing is often linked with high-tech and complex products, it is a process that affects even the low-cost products we use and consume every day. A good example of this is U.S.-based Sara Lee's whole grain white bread. To make the bread, Sara Lee acquires ingredients from a variety of suppliers—nearly a third of them located in foreign countries. For example, it sources guar gum from India. Guar gum is used to keep the bread moist and is a powder that comes from the guar plant seed pods grown in India. Calcium propionate, a powdery mold inhibitor that is manufactured in several countries, is sourced in the Netherlands. Honey, used as a natural sweetener, is purchased from many suppliers, including from the United States, China, Vietnam, Brazil, Uruguay, India, Canada, Mexico, and Argentina. It sources from several different countries, including the United States, since U.S. supply can often run short. Flour enrichments to replenish the vitamins lost in the milling process are sourced in China. Due to consolidation in the industry, there are limited suppliers of flour enrichments. Beta-carotene, an artificial coloring used to provide color to the bread and crust, is sourced in Switzerland, although it is available in many countries. Vitamin D3 is sourced in China, and wheat gluten is sourced from suppliers in several countries, including France, Poland, Russia, the Netherlands, and Australia.[50]

> **Companies can manufacture parts internally or purchase them from external manufacturers.**

With its sources of ingredients spread all over the globe, Sara Lee must manage its supply chain carefully to ensure timeliness, safety, and quality. To accomplish this, Sara Lee has centralized its global ingredients purchasing, consolidating its previously scattered procurement operations into a single division known as the "nerve center," which is located at company headquarters. Purchasing specialists monitor weather patterns, commodity trends, and energy prices. They also communicate and work closely with Sara Lee's diverse base of suppliers, in some cases even investing money in their suppliers' operations to ensure they are complying with U.S. food safety standards.[51]

GLOBAL SOURCING

Companies can manufacture parts internally or purchase them from external (unrelated) manufacturers. Companies can also assemble their own products internally or subcontract to external companies, and the manufacture of parts and final assembly may take place in the company's home country, the country in which it is trying to sell the product, or a third country.[52]

> **Using domestic sources for raw materials and components allows a company to avoid problems with language differences, distance, currency, politics, and tariffs, as well as other problems.**

Sourcing in the home country enables companies to avoid numerous problems, including those connected with language differences, long distances and lengthy supply lines, exchange-rate fluctuations, wars and insurrections, strikes, politics, tariffs, and complex transportation channels. However, for many companies, domestic sources may be unavailable or may be more expensive than foreign sources. In Japan, foreign procurement is critical because nearly all of the country's uranium, bauxite, nickel, crude oil, iron ore, copper, coking coal, and approximately 30 percent of its agricultural products are imported. Japanese trading companies came into being expressly to acquire the raw materials needed to fuel Japan's manufacturing.

Procter & Gamble has also found that sourcing chemicals from a variety of suppliers abroad is necessary to provide flexibility in a global environment of volatile energy prices. By diversifying its chemicals supplier base, Procter & Gamble plans on being able to switch procurement between different suppliers as energy prices shift in different regions.[53]

Why Global Sourcing?   Companies pursue global sourcing strategies for a number of reasons:

> **Companies outsource abroad to lower costs and improve quality, among other reasons.**

- To reduce costs—due to less expensive labor, less restrictive work rules, and lower land and facilities costs
- To improve quality

- To increase exposure to worldwide technology
- To improve the delivery-of-supplies process
- To strengthen the reliability of supply by supplementing domestic with foreign suppliers
- To gain access to materials that are only available abroad, possibly because of technical specifications or product capabilities
- To establish a presence in a foreign market
- To satisfy offset requirements
- To react to competitors' offshore sourcing practices[54]

The reasons just given to engage in global sourcing are similar to the benefits to foreign direct investment discussed in Chapter 14. Whether the suppliers are company-owned or are independent companies, MNEs can take advantage of the location-specific advantages in foreign countries.

In some ways, however, global sourcing is more expensive than domestic sourcing. For example, transportation and communications are more expensive, and companies may have to pay brokers and agents fees. Given the longer length of supply lines, it often takes more time to get components from abroad, and lead times are less certain. This problem increases the inventory carrying costs and makes it more difficult to get parts to the production site in a timely manner. If imported components come in with errors and need to be reworked, the cost per unit will rise, and some components may have to be shipped back to the supplier.

Concerns That Come with Global Sourcing As noted, quality and safety are other concerns with global sourcing. This has been especially evident in the highly publicized recalls of tainted pet food and toothpaste, defective tires, and toys with traces of lead in their paint that were produced in China. Subsequent actions led Chinese regulators and inspectors to close 180 food plants and uncover more than 23,000 food safety violations,[55] forcing the Chinese government to admit that 20 percent of its consumer goods have failed safety inspections. Imagine being the firm that outsourced pet food from Chinese company Xuzhou Anying Biologic Technology Development Company, which resulted in the deaths of several dogs and cats and led to one of the biggest pet food recalls in U.S. history.[56] A situation like that could have irreversible effects on the image of a company whose Chinese supplier actions resulted in the deaths of pets.

China is not the only country producing substandard goods; black pepper with salmonella from India, filthy crabmeat from Mexico, mislabeled candy from Denmark, and produce with traces of illegal pesticides from the Dominican Republic have resulted in thousands of shipments halted by U.S. inspectors.[57] Such incidences have raised concerns over foreign-made products and accusations that quality and safety are being compromised to lower costs. The countries that churn out the cheapest products often lack adequate regulations, enforcement, and logistical infrastructure, leaving it up to the purchasing companies to ensure quality and safety.

MAJOR SOURCING CONFIGURATIONS

Vertical Integration **Vertical integration** occurs when the company owns the entire supplier network or at least a significant part of it. The company may have to purchase raw materials from outside suppliers, but it produces the most expensive parts itself. By integrating vertically, the company is able to reduce transaction costs (such as finding suppliers, selling output, negotiating contracts, monitoring contracts, and settling disputes with unrelated companies) by internalizing the different levels in the value chain.[58]

Industrial Clusters **Outsourcing** through industrial clusters is an alternative way to reduce transportation costs and transactions costs. Under clustering, buyers and suppliers locate in close proximity to facilitate doing business. For example, Dell Computer

---

Major outsourcing configurations:

- Vertical integration.
- Outsourcing through industrial clusters.
- Other outsourcing.

CONCEPT CHECK

In discussing "Noncollaborative Foreign Investments" in Chapter 14, we define **internalization** as control through "the self-handling of operations" (that is, by keeping them *internal* to the company). We point out the genesis of this concept in *transactions cost theory*, which holds that, when there's a decision to be made between handling something internally and contracting with someone else to handle it, companies should opt for the lower-cost alternative. As we suggest later in this chapter, *make or buy decisions* invite the application of this principle.

Corporation established an assembly operation in the Multimedia Supercorridor in Malaysia, where it is close to its key suppliers.

Japanese Keiretsus   The Japanese *keiretsus* are groups of independent companies that work together to manage the flow of goods and services along the entire value chain.[59] Toyota's highly coordinated supplier network is among the most successful and well known of the Japanese *keiretsus* and a good example of industrial clustering, almost bordering on vertical integration, because parts suppliers tend to set up shop close to Toyota's assembly operations, and Toyota usually has an ownership interest in the suppliers. However, recent changes in its global markets and price pressures resulting from the high cost of steel and the strong yen have caused the company to start looking beyond its closely knit supplier base in Japan. To meet its goal of cutting costs for buying car parts by 30 percent—an objective outlined in its "Construction of Cost Competitiveness for the 21st Century" program—Toyota is putting pressure on its *keiretsu* suppliers by benchmarking them to China's cheaper suppliers and by courting suppliers outside Japan. These outside suppliers are leaping at the chance of breaking into the supplier network of the world's second-largest automaker.[60]

> Make or buy—outsource or supply parts from internal production.

CONCEPT CHECK

As we explain in Chapter 14, the **resource-based view** of the firm holds that every company has a unique combination of competencies. Here we suggest that *make or buy decisions* may depend on the extent to which a firm embraces this view, which may prompt it to concentrate internally on those activities that best fit its competencies while depending on other firms to supply products, services, or support activities for which it has lesser competency.

> If MNEs outsource instead of source parts from internal production, they need to determine the degree of involvement with suppliers.

THE MAKE OR BUY DECISION

MNE managers struggle with a dilemma: Which production activities should be performed internally and which ones could be subcontracted to independent companies? That is the *make or buy decision*. In the case of subcontracting, companies also need to decide whether the activities should be carried on in the home market or abroad. A recent survey of the use of outsourcing by businesses reveals the importance of control measures. In spite of the cost savings, companies that struggle with outsourcing mention that a major issue is loss of operational control.[61]

In deciding whether to make or buy, MNEs could focus on those parts that are critical to the product and that they are distinctively good at making. They could outsource parts when suppliers have a distinct comparative advantage, such as greater scale, lower cost structure, or stronger performance incentives. They also could use outsourcing as an implied threat to underperforming employees: If they don't improve, the companies will move their business elsewhere.[62]

In determining whether to make or buy, the MNE needs to determine the design and manufacturing capabilities of potential suppliers compared to its own capabilities. If the supplier has a clear advantage, management needs to decide what it would cost to catch up to the best suppliers and whether it would make sense to do so.

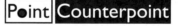

Should Firms Outsource Innovation?

Point   **Yes**   Yes, firms should outsource innovative processes if doing so will allow them to maintain their focus and to position themselves effectively in the increasingly competitive high-tech and electronics industries. Data show that more and more companies are coming to realize the advantages of doing so. Suppliers are taking on such responsibilities as designing and manufacturing prototypes, converting them into workable products, upgrading mature products, conducting quality tests, putting together

Counterpoint   **No**   No, companies should not outsource their research, design, and development functions. Recent trends have gone beyond outsourcing larger key components to outsourcing the R&D for entire lines of complete products! Many companies insist that although they may outsource some design and development work, they still keep core R&D in-house, but how do they know where to draw the line? How do they determine what is core intellectual property and what is commodity technology?

user manuals, and selecting parts vendors. For example, the designs of 65 percent of PC notebooks and those of 70 percent of PDAs are outsourced. Companies such as Dell, Motorola, and Philips are buying complete designs from Asian developers, and even Boeing is collaborating with an Indian company to develop software for its 787 Dreamliner jet.

Companies willing to outsource some of the R&D and the technological designs of their products can experience enormous cost savings. Although innovation is a key to remaining competitive, more and more companies are finding that their internal R&D teams aren't producing results that justify the large amount of investments put into them. Thus, in the face of demanding customers and relentless competition that put pressure on margins, these companies must find a way to reduce their costs or to increase their R&D productivity.

Outsourcing has proven to be a viable solution. Companies can save millions of dollars by simply buying designs rather than developing them in-house. For example, industry estimates indicate that using a predesigned platform for cell phones can reduce the costs of developing them from scratch—which takes approximately $10 million and 150 engineers—by 70 percent! Furthermore, demands by retailers and customers as well as the uncertainty of future market trends require companies to develop a range of product models, which is very costly. Third-party developers are better equipped to handle these costs because they can spread them over many buyers and have the expertise to develop a wide variety of models from a single basic design.

Outsourcing also allows companies to get their products on the market faster, and in the electronics and technology industries, where products become commodities in a matter of months, that speed becomes crucial to maintaining a competitive advantage. Hewlett-Packard claims that by working with partners and suppliers on designs it now takes 60 percent less time for it to get a new concept to the market. PalmOne has also reduced its product development time by months, decreased the number of defects by 50 percent, and increased its gross margins by 20 percent by outsourcing.

Critics worry that by outsourcing technology, companies are outsourcing their sources of competitive advantage, but outsourcing certain design and development processes allows these companies to better focus on their true core competencies. Few, if any, companies plan on completely eliminating their own R&D forces, and most insist that they will continue with the more proprietary R&D work. By shifting some of the less critical work to outside vendors, they will be able to focus more on the latest innovations and on the next-generation technologies that can truly serve to differentiate them.

The truth is that outsourcing turns intellectual property into commodity technology that becomes available to most anyone. By working with South Korean chipmakers to develop its DRAM memory chips, Toshiba allowed the technology behind these components to become commoditized, and it is now struggling to stay ahead of competitors.[63]

A company's competitive advantage often depends on trade secrets that set it apart from its rivals. Outsourcing innovation enhances the risk that a company will pass on these trade secrets and proprietary technologies to suppliers and partners, thereby fostering new competitors. Because suppliers rarely cooperate solely with one customer, the R&D they do for one can easily be transferred to another.

Such was the case for the Japanese company Sharp, which worked closely with its suppliers to develop a "sixth-generation" plant able to make much larger flat panels for televisions than "fifth-generation" plants were able to make. Unfortunately, its suppliers also work closely with Sharp's rivals, many of them Taiwanese companies, and not long after the completion of the plant, these competitors were constructing their own "sixth-generation" facilities. As a result, Sharp has started to take extra precautions, such as secretly rewriting software on some of the equipment it has purchased and fixing machinery in-house rather than having suppliers do it to keep vendors from knowing the problems that may exist in the equipment they have sold to competitors.[64]

There is also the risk that suppliers and partners will take what information and technology have been shared with them and become competitors themselves. After Motorola hired the Taiwanese company BenQ Corp. to design and manufacture mobile phones for it, the company began selling the phones under its own brand name in the highly competitive Chinese market, causing Motorola to terminate the contract.

Perhaps more important than giving rise to new competitors is losing competitive edge and the incentive to invest in new technology. Although some assert that outsourcing certain development and design work allows companies to focus more on new innovative technologies, in actuality, this outsourcing more often prompts companies to decrease the amount they invest in internal R&D and to become lazy in their pursuit of future breakthroughs, relying too much on suppliers to do the work for them. Jim Andrew, the senior vice president of Boston Consulting Group, warns, "If the innovation starts residing in the suppliers, you could incrementalize yourself to the point where there isn't much left."

High-tech and electronics companies that outsource their innovative processes risk losing the essence of their actual business, becoming mere marketing fronts for other companies. It also sends a bad message to investors, who might have difficulty finding the intrinsic value in a company that owns little true intellectual property and whose profits from

(continued)

No one company can manage everything in-house. Even the chief technology officer of Nokia—a company that once prided itself on developing almost everything on its own—has stated, "Nobody can master it all." In fact, a recent survey of global companies found that almost three-quarters of the respondents believed they could boost innovation dramatically by collaborating with outsiders, even competitors.[65] The companies that are going to survive in the future are those able to control a network of partners and suppliers efficiently and effectively around the world. ●

successful products are most likely simply being paid out in licensing fees to the companies that actually developed them.

Although much has been made of the outsourcing of manufacturing the past few decades, the outsourcing of innovation poses a potentially larger threat to high-tech firms that see it as a shortcut to cost savings. Looking to immediate cost savings as justification for outsourcing technology and innovation is shortsighted, and firms that do so will ultimately damage their competitive positions and lose viability as true players in their industries.[66]●

SUPPLIER RELATIONS

Supplier relationships are very important but sometimes complicated, especially for MNEs trying to manage supplier relationships around the world. The CEO of U.S.-based MNE John Deere stated,

> Our supplier partners have been at the heart of [our] effort to put superior value into our products . . . around the world and throughout the enterprise. Together with our suppliers and dealers, we are enriching the word "value" to include the very best design, quality, delivery, process and the very best cost, all at the same time. We know it has not been easy for suppliers and it still isn't! Following our example, suppliers have had to make major adjustments in how they do business. We've been pretty demanding on ourselves and others, but I'm confident . . . that by working together to aggressively reduce costs, increase quality, and improve delivery time, they've become stronger businesses, as well as stronger Deere suppliers. Like us, they too need a great business in order to sustain long-term success.[67]

Case: Toyota   If an MNE decides it must outsource rather than integrate vertically, it must determine how to work with suppliers. Toyota pioneered the Toyota Production System to work with unrelated suppliers. Toyota sends a team of manufacturing experts to each of its key suppliers to observe how the supplier organizes its factory and makes its parts. Then the team advises how to cut costs and boost quality. It is also common for Toyota to identify two suppliers for each part and have the suppliers compete aggressively with each other. The supplier that performs the best gets the most business. However, both suppliers know they will have an ongoing relationship with Toyota and will not be dumped easily.[68]

This is a good example of the close relationships that Japanese companies develop with their suppliers. It is very different from the arm's-length relationship that U.S. companies tend to have with their suppliers. Furthermore, Toyota has been able to reduce the number of supplier relationships it develops, which allows it to focus on a few key suppliers, promising to give them a lot of business if they perform up to Toyota standards.

In fact, the relationship between Toyota and its suppliers is often so close that when Toyota opens up production in foreign locations, its suppliers do so as well. One major Toyota supplier, DENSO, invested $1 million to establish a new plant in Tianjin, China, to produce car navigation systems for the Toyota plant located there. It did so partly to follow Toyota there but also because Toyota made it clear that DENSO had to match Chinese prices or lose their business. The best way for DENSO to protect its market was to move some production to China.

Case: JCPenney   The decision to work closely with suppliers requires a great deal of trust and oftentimes involves making drastic—sometimes risky—changes. However, such changes can provide large strategic advantages. Such is the case for JCPenney and its Hong Kong–based supplier of shirts, TAL Apparel Ltd. The retailer literally allows its supplier to take over some of its own processes. Rather than simply responding to orders sent to it from Penney, TAL tracks the retailer's sales data directly, running it through its personally designed computer program to determine the number of shirts to make, as well as their sizes, colors, and styles. These shirts are then shipped directly to individual JCPenney stores, completely bypassing the retailer's warehouses.

This cooperation has resulted in quicker merchandise turnovers and an inventory level of virtually zero—a significant improvement over the eight months' worth of inventory the retailer used to keep. TAL has also been allowed to handle market testing and the design of new shirt styles, which has given it the ability to respond more quickly and effectively to customer demands. With the leverage given it, TAL can roll out a new style in just four months.[69]

Not all customer–supplier relationships are as collaborative as those of Toyota and JCPenney, however. Sometimes large customers can use their strong market presence and buying power to place additional demands on suppliers. For many years, General Motors has placed heavy pressure on its U.S. suppliers to lower costs by certain set percentages each year and to then pass those cost savings on to GM via lower prices. Now, given GM's plans to shift important resources overseas to markets such as China, South Korea, and Europe over the next few years, some suppliers and management consultants working with GM have indicated that suppliers may be pressured to set up facilities in China to accommodate GM.[70]

The relationships MNEs establish with their suppliers are largely based on their individual competitive strategies, the nature of their products, the competitive environment they are facing, the capabilities of their suppliers, and the level of experience and trust they share with them. MNEs must consider these factors as they determine what kind of supplier relationship will best meet their needs.

THE PURCHASING FUNCTION

The purchasing agent is the link between the company's outsourcing decision and its supplier relationships. Just as companies go through stages of globalization, so does the purchasing agent's scope of responsibilities. Typically, purchasing goes through four phases before becoming "global":

1. Domestic purchasing only
2. Foreign buying based on need
3. Foreign buying as part of procurement strategy
4. Integration of global procurement strategy[71]

Phase 4 occurs when the company realizes the benefits that result from the integration and coordination of purchasing on a global basis and is most applicable to the MNE as opposed to, say, the exporter.

When purchasing becomes this global, MNEs often face the centralization/decentralization dilemma. Should they allow each subsidiary to make all purchasing decisions, or should they centralize all or some of the purchasing decisions? The primary benefits of decentralization include increased production facility control over purchases, better responsiveness to facility needs, and more effective use of local suppliers. The primary benefits of centralization are increased leverage with suppliers, getting better prices, eliminating administrative duplication, allowing purchasers to develop specialized knowledge in purchasing techniques, reducing the number of orders processed, and enabling purchasing to build solid supplier relationships.[72]

Major Sourcing Strategies   Companies pursue five major sourcing strategies as they move into phases 3 and 4 in the preceding list (foreign buying as part of procurement strategy and integration of global procurement strategy):

1. Assigning domestic buyer(s) for international purchasing
2. Using foreign subsidiaries or business agents
3. Establishing international purchasing offices
4. Assigning the responsibility for global sourcing to a specific business unit or units
5. Integrating and coordinating worldwide sourcing[73]

Global progression in the purchasing function:
- Domestic purchasing only.
- Foreign buying based on need.
- Foreign buying as part of a procurement strategy.
- Integration of global procurement strategy.

Sourcing strategies in the global context:
- Assign domestic buyers for foreign purchasing.
- Use foreign subsidiaries or business agents.
- Establish international purchasing offices.
- Assign the responsibility for global sourcing to a specific business unit or units.
- Integrate and coordinate worldwide sourcing.

These strategies move from the simple to the more complex. Companies start by using a domestic buyer and progress all the way to integrating and coordinating worldwide sourcing into the company's purchasing decisions so there is no difference between domestic and foreign sources.

Some companies are going even further than the last step and coordinating worldwide purchasing with competitor companies. Two automakers, Nissan and Renault, have been able to save millions of dollars in production costs by entering into joint purchasing agreements with each other. Approximately 40 percent of the parts the companies use in their vehicles are the same, and the two are looking to increase this amount to 70 percent to achieve further cost reductions.[74]

Figure 17.8 summarizes some of the key concepts in the preceding discussion in terms of selecting the best supplier. The key is for managers to select the best supplier, establish a solid relationship, and continuously evaluate the supplier's performance to ensure the best price, quality, and on-time delivery possible.

FIGURE 17.8   Global Sourcing: Assessing Your Strategy and Weighing Your Options

Source: Stanley E. Fawcett, "The Globalization of the Supply Environment," *The Supply Management Environment*, Vol. 2 (Tempe, AZ: Institute for Supply Management, 2000), p. 53. Reprinted by permission of the publisher.

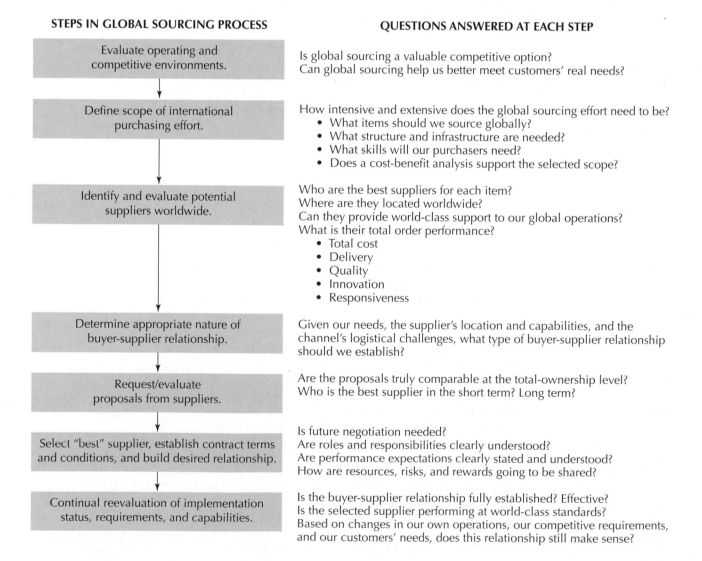

STEPS IN GLOBAL SOURCING PROCESS	QUESTIONS ANSWERED AT EACH STEP
Evaluate operating and competitive environments.	Is global sourcing a valuable competitive option? Can global sourcing help us better meet customers' real needs?
Define scope of international purchasing effort.	How intensive and extensive does the global sourcing effort need to be? • What items should we source globally? • What structure and infrastructure are needed? • What skills will our purchasers need? • Does a cost-benefit analysis support the selected scope?
Identify and evaluate potential suppliers worldwide.	Who are the best suppliers for each item? Where are they located worldwide? Can they provide world-class support to our global operations? What is their total order performance? • Total cost • Delivery • Quality • Innovation • Responsiveness
Determine appropriate nature of buyer-supplier relationship.	Given our needs, the supplier's location and capabilities, and the channel's logistical challenges, what type of buyer-supplier relationship should we establish?
Request/evaluate proposals from suppliers.	Are the proposals truly comparable at the total-ownership level? Who is the best supplier in the short term? Long term?
Select "best" supplier, establish contract terms and conditions, and build desired relationship.	Is future negotiation needed? Are roles and responsibilities clearly understood? Are performance expectations clearly stated and understood? How are resources, risks, and rewards going to be shared?
Continual reevaluation of implementation status, requirements, and capabilities.	Is the buyer-supplier relationship fully established? Effective? Is the selected supplier performing at world-class standards? Based on changes in our own operations, our competitive requirements, and our customers' needs, does this relationship still make sense?

Inventory Management

Whether a company decides to source parts from inside or outside the company or from domestic or foreign sources, it needs to manage the flow and storage of inventory. This is true of raw materials and parts sourced from suppliers, work-in-process and finished-goods inventory inside the manufacturing plant, and finished goods stored at a distribution center, such as the centralized European warehouse for Samsonite. As a Korean car manufacturer learned, if a company sources parts from a variety of suppliers from around the world, distance, time, and the uncertainty of the international political and economic environment can make it difficult for managers to determine correct reorder points for the manufacturing process.

Distance, time, and uncertainty in foreign environments cause foreign sourcing to complicate inventory management.

LEAN MANUFACTURING AND JUST-IN-TIME SYSTEMS

One reason why companies might hesitate when considering whether to source parts from foreign suppliers is because of *lean manufacturing* systems, "a productive system whose focus is on optimizing processes through the philosophy of continual improvement." It embodies the ideas of waste reduction and optimizing quality processes.[75] Because it relies on the efficiencies gained by reducing waste and defects, lean manufacturing is also closely tied to quality management.

Lean manufacturing—a productive system whose focus is on optimizing processes through the philosophy of continual improvement.

An important element of lean manufacturing is the just-in-time (JIT) inventory and purchasing system. "JIT systems focus on reducing inefficiency and unproductive time in the production process to improve continuously the process and the quality of the product or service."[76] The JIT system gets raw materials, parts, and components to the buyer "just in time" for use, sparing companies the cost of storing large inventories.

JIT—sourcing raw materials and parts just as they are needed in the manufacturing process.

That is what Dell hoped to accomplish in its Irish plant by having parts delivered just as they were to enter the production process and then go out the door to the consumers as soon as the computers were built. However, the use of JIT means that parts must have few defects and must arrive on time. That is why companies need to develop solid supplier relationships to ensure good quality and delivery times if JIT is to work and why industrial clustering is a popular way of linking more closely with suppliers.

Risks in Foreign Sourcing Foreign sourcing can create big risks for companies that use lean manufacturing and JIT because interruptions in the supply line can cause havoc. Foreign companies are becoming experts at meeting the requirements of JIT—ships that take two weeks to cross the Pacific dock within an hour of scheduled arrival, and factories are able more easily to fill small orders. However, because of distances alone, the supply chain is open to more problems and delays.[77]

It is hard to combine foreign sourcing and JIT production without having safety stocks of inventory on hand, which defeats the concept of JIT.

As we mentioned earlier in the chapter, companies such as Toyota that have set up manufacturing and assembly facilities overseas to service local markets have practically forced their domestic parts suppliers to move overseas as well to allow Toyota to continue with JIT manufacturing. That is why so many Japanese parts suppliers have moved to the United States and Mexico to be near their major customers.

A company's inventory management strategy—especially in terms of stock sizes and whether or not JIT will be used—determines frequency of needed shipments. The less frequent the delivery, the more likely the need to store inventory somewhere. Because JIT requires delivery just as the inventory is to be used, some concession must be made for inventory arriving from foreign suppliers. Sometimes that means adjusting the arrival time to a few days before use rather than a few hours. Kawasaki Motors Corp., U.S.A. carries a minimum of three days' inventory on parts coming from Japan, with an average inventory of five days.[78]

Kanban system—a system that facilitates JIT by using cards to control the flow of production through a factory.

The *Kanban* System   One system pioneered by Toyota to facilitate its JIT strategies is the *kanban system*. *Kanban* literally means "card" or "visible record" in Japanese. The *kanban* cards are used to control the flow of production through a factory. In the *kanban* system used by Toyota, components are shipped to a plant just before they need to go into production. They are kept in a bin that has a card attached to it identifying the quantity of items in the bin. When the assembly process begins, a production-order card signifies that a bin needs to be moved to the assembly line. When the bin is emptied, it is moved to a storage area and replaced with a full bin. The *kanban* card is removed from the empty bin and is used to order a replacement from the supplier.

FOREIGN TRADE ZONES

Foreign trade zones (FTZs)—special locations for storing domestic and imported inventory in order to avoid paying duties until the inventory is used in production or sold.

In recent years, **foreign trade zones (FTZs)** have become more popular as an intermediate step in the process between import and final use. FTZs are areas in which domestic and imported merchandise can be stored, inspected, and manufactured free from formal customs procedures until the goods leave the zones. The zones are intended to encourage companies to locate in the country by allowing them to defer duties, pay fewer duties, or avoid certain duties completely. Sometimes inventory is stored in an FTZ until it needs to be used for domestic manufacture. As noted earlier, one of the problems with JIT is the length of the supply line when relying on global sourcing, possibly causing either the buyer or the supplier to stockpile inventory somewhere until it is needed in the manufacturing process. One place to stockpile inventory is in a warehouse in an FTZ.

General-Purpose Zones and Subzones   FTZs can be general-purpose zones or subzones. A general-purpose zone usually is established near a port of entry, such as a shipping port, a border crossing, or an airport, and it usually consists of a distribution facility or an industrial park. It is used primarily for warehousing and distribution. A subzone usually is physically separate from a general-purpose zone but under the same administrative structure. It is usually located at a manufacturing facility. Since 1982, the major growth in FTZs has been in subzones rather than in general-purpose zones because companies have sought to defer duties on parts that are foreign sourced until they need to be used in the production process.

The major growth in subzones in the United States has been in the automobile industry, especially in the Midwest. Subzone activity is spreading to other industries, especially to shipbuilding, pharmaceuticals, and home appliances, and it is becoming more heavily oriented to manufacturing and assembly than was originally envisioned. Merchandise in U.S. FTZs may be assembled, exhibited, cleaned, manipulated, manufactured, mixed, processed, relabeled, repackaged, repaired, salvaged, sampled, stored, tested, displayed, and destroyed.[79]

In the United States, there are FTZ projects in 50 states and Puerto Rico, with another 60 pending cases for new zones and expansion. Over $300 billion a year in merchandise is handled in FTZs, and $19 billion is exported from FTZs each year.[80] FTZs in the United States have been used primarily as a means of providing greater flexibility as to when and how customs duties are paid. However, their use in the export business has been expanding.

The exports for which these FTZs are used fall into one of the following categories:

- Foreign goods transshipped through U.S. zones to third countries
- Foreign goods processed in U.S. zones and then transshipped abroad
- Foreign goods processed or assembled in U.S. zones with some domestic materials and parts, and then reexported

- Goods produced wholly of foreign content in U.S. zones and then exported
- Domestic goods moved into a U.S. zone to achieve export status prior to their actual exportation[81]

TRANSPORTATION NETWORKS

For a firm, the transportation of goods in an international context is extremely complicated in terms of documentation, choice of carrier (air or ocean), and the decision whether to establish its own transportation department or outsource to a third-party intermediary. Transportation is one of the key elements of a logistics system. The key is to link together suppliers and manufacturers on the one hand and manufacturers and final consumers on the other. Along the way, the company has to determine what its warehouse configuration will be. For example, McDonald's provides food items to its franchises around the world. It has warehouses in different countries to service different geographic areas.

Transportation links together suppliers, companies, and customers.

Case: Panalpina   Third-party intermediaries are an important dimension of transportation networks. Outsourcing of both manufacturing and other supply chain functions is becoming increasingly popular. For example, Panalpina is a Swiss forwarding and logistics services provider that focuses on intercontinental airfreight and sea freight, as well as other aspects of supply chain management. Using its main hub in Luxembourg to connect to 500 branches in 80 countries throughout the world, as well as to partners in another 60 countries, Panalpina seeks to simplify the complexity of its customers' supply chains by handling their transportation, distribution, customs brokerage, warehousing, and inventory control and also provides door-to-door transport insurance and real-time track and trace systems.[82]

Third-party intermediaries, such as Panalpina, are crucial in storing and transporting goods.

One company that Panalpina provides such services to is IBM and its operations in Latin America. Through its selected airfreight services provider, ASB-Air, and through

LOOKING TO THE FUTURE

Uncertainty and the Global Supply Chain

The chapter has emphasized two competing ideas: The first is that globalization has pushed companies to establish operations abroad or to outsource to foreign suppliers to reduce costs and be closer to markets. The second is that the longer the supply line, the greater the risk. Since September 11, 2001, the risks of longer supply lines have increased dramatically. At any time, global political events could completely disrupt a well-organized supply chain and put a company at risk.

Because some of Sara Lee's suppliers have consolidated (see p. 666), there are fewer options to purchase key ingredients for their products. What if no supplier could deliver, due either to political events or to safety or quality concerns? As the supply chain stretches and uncertainty increases, companies have to become much better at scenario building so viable contingencies are available. Maybe this means that companies will pursue more multidomestic strategies to insulate their foreign operations from other countries and allow them to be more responsive to local consumers.

However, as MNEs in the developed countries respond to competitive pressures to reduce costs, they will be forced to continue sourcing abroad, either in company-owned facilities or from third parties, at least until nobody can source abroad. That is probably a little extreme, but the important thing is to continue to look at the "what-ifs." What if there is no secure air or ocean transportation available to move goods? What if the goods can move, but there are delays? What if terrorists begin to use the global supply chain of legitimate companies to contaminate products or to move hazardous materials? Clearly the future is much more complicated, so let the manager beware. ∎

the management of its local branches, Panalpina coordinates vehicles to pick up IBM products in Europe and to transport them to its cargo hub in Luxembourg. From there, the goods travel by air to its cargo center in Miami. In Miami, products destined for various locations in South America are split and reconsolidated into pallets that are then loaded directly into Panalpina space-controlled aircraft and transferred to its own company warehouses operated by its own staff. The personnel in the warehouses complete all customs details, taking advantage of the on-site offices of customs authorities, and update the company's information systems with current status messages.

Once customs has been cleared, an electronic data transfer is sent to IBM while the goods are shipped to IBM warehouses. Panalpina maintains control of the goods throughout the entire process, using electronic documentation and tracking to maintain real-time data and to keep IBM informed. In this example, you can see all of the elements of the transportation networks that are so essential in international logistics.[83]

The logistics management that companies like Panalpina engage in is very detail oriented, requiring the ability to gather, track, and process large quantities of information. To be effective, logistics companies need to implement key technologies, including communications technologies, satellite tracking systems, bar-coding applications, and automated materials handling systems.[84]

CASE

Ventus and Business Process Outsourcing

by Professor Manuel Serapio

In 2007, ePLDT Ventus (Ventus), the voice business process outsourcing arm of Philippine Long Distance Telephone Company (PLDT), was deciding on what strategy to pursue to sustain the company's growth for the remainder of the decade.[85] Since the company's establishment in 2001, Ventus has grown to become the largest Filipino-owned call center in the Philippines, with over 6,000 employees, seven locations, and revenues in excess of $120 million.

Although the company enjoyed sustained growth, several issues are on the horizon. Should the company concentrate on the call center business or diversify from voice into the data segment of business process outsourcing? Should it continue to emphasize the U.S. market, as well as focus on a few customers that have made the company very successful, or should it diversify into new markets? Should the company grow organically or look into acquiring or partnering with other outsourcing providers in the Philippines and abroad? How should Ventus's management address emerging challenges facing the company, including a tightening labor market, increased cost pressures from a strengthening Philippine peso, and intensified rivalry among call center firms for both customers and employees?

The Philippine Call Center Industry

While India has attracted the world's attention as the global hub for call center outsourcing, the Philippines has quietly emerged as a leading provider of business process outsourcing, particularly in the call center industry. In 2006, the Philippines had more than 120 companies and over 145,000 people employed in the industry. It is estimated that the revenues booked by the Philippine call center industry have doubled every year since 2000. For example, the industry generated revenues of about $1.7 billion in 2005 compared to $800 million in 2004.

Figure 17.9 traces the evolution of business process outsourcing (including call centers) in the Philippines. Prior to 2000, the companies that primarily outsourced to the Philippines were shared services operations of multinational companies, such as IBM, Citibank, and Procter & Gamble. These companies provided internal services, such as back office support functions, transaction processing, and call center operations to their parent companies and international locations. Companies that established outsourcing facilities in the Philippines after 2000 include third-party providers and call centers, both foreign owned (e.g., Teletech, Convergys) and locally owned companies (e.g., Ventus).

Most recently, the Philippines has experienced a surge in the number of foreign companies that have established footprints in the Philippines, most notably Indian third-party outsourcing providers like Genpact and Daksh, and captive operations of multinational companies, such as Dell and HSBC. Map 17.2 additionally shows the concentration of outsourcing facilities in the Philippines, including locations of Ventus's call center facilities.

The rapid expansion of call center outsourcing in the Philippines is projected to continue into the next decade. The Business Processing Association/Philippines (BPAP) forecasts that call center revenues will increase threefold from $1.7 billion in 2005 to $5 billion in 2010. Similarly, the number of people employed by the call center industry in the Philippines is expected to increase from 145,000 to 500,000 people during the same period.

The Philippines has ranked in the top 10 in AT Kearney's global services location index since 2004. In 2005, AT Kearney ranked the Philippines fourth (up from sixth in 2004) in its global services location attractiveness index, behind India, China, and Malaysia and ahead of Singapore, Thailand, Czech Republic, Chile, and Canada. According to this index, the Philippines rated very favorably in terms of compensation competitiveness, infrastructure cost, and tax and regulatory costs.

In addition, the Philippines boasts a large, high-quality, college-educated and English-speaking labor pool. The country graduates over 400,000 students per year, with the large majority in the following areas: commerce- and business-related fields (114,000 students);

FIGURE 17.9   Evolution of the Business Process Outsourcing Industry in the Philippines

Ventus, the largest domestically owned call center in the Philippines, came on the scene between 2000 and 2003, when third-party providers and call centers began to enter the Philippine business process outsourcing industry. Prior to 2000, the industry included mostly *shared services operations* used by MNCs, and Indian-owned companies started to become major players in the middle of the decade. Today, the industry also includes many so-called captive operations—facilities for handling the tasks of parent firms.

Source: Adapted from Business Processing Association/Philippines, 2006.

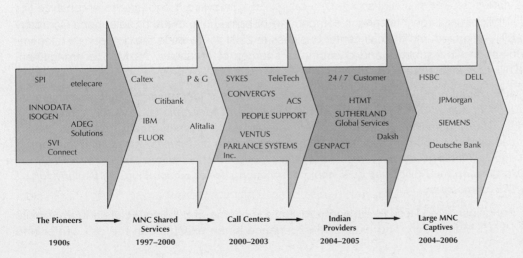

MAP 17.2   Key Outsourcing Locations in the Philippines

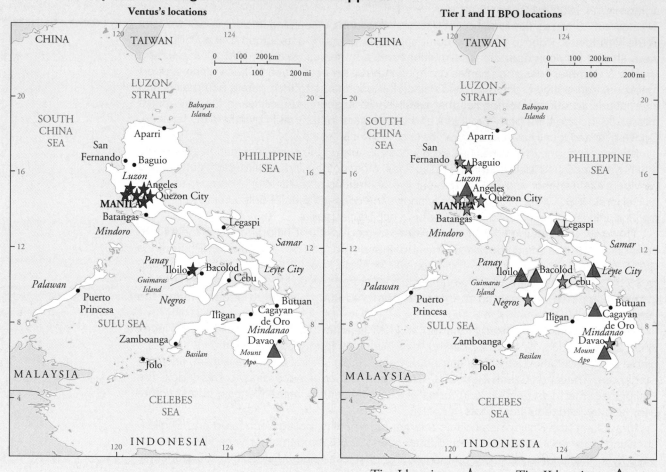

Tier-I locations - ☆   Tier-II locations - ▲

engineering, information technology, and computer sciences (90,000); and medical and allied/natural sciences (38,000). With these and other advantages, the Philippines in general and Ventus in particular are poised to solidify their position as a key provider of business process outsourcing and call center services in the global service supply chain.

The Ventus Story

The Philippines' largest telephone company—Philippine Long Distance Telephone Company (PLDT)—ventured into the call center business in 2001 to leverage the company's telecommunications investments and diversify its sources of revenues. As Manuel Pangilinan, PLDT's chairman, noted,

> With the continued decline in the settlement rates for long distance calls and given the fact that PLDT had already invested heavily in its fiber optic network (both international and domestic), it was a natural move for us to diversify downstream into the call center outsourcing business. Also, as globalization of services was gaining traction and with India taking the lead in this area, we thought that conditions were ripe for PLDT to position the Philippines as a viable destination site for outsourcing, particularly for U.S. companies.

Pangilinan hired Rose Montenegro to lead the charge of building a call center business for PLDT. Montenegro had extensive experience as an executive in the call center and business process outsourcing (BPO) business, having led pioneering service ventures at CitiBank and ABN AMRO in Asia. She quickly brought on board Albert Santos and Ken Brian Lamzon—two managers with strong backgrounds in running call center businesses for CitiBank and AIG.

Commercial operations in the call center business commenced in March 2002 with 50 full-time employees. At the end of 2006, the company had 6,200 employees in seven Philippine locations serving over a dozen customers. Prior to 2005, the company operated call centers for different customers under two major names and legal entities, Parlance and Vocativ. This was later merged into ePLDT Ventus to create a single global brand.

The company has been very successful in delivering value to its customers, both in terms of cost savings and other key metrics focusing on areas of their clients' value chain that are more likely to be outsourced instead of internalized. In general, customers sign up with Ventus because of the potential savings they could generate. On average, clients save between 25 and 33 percent of their fully loaded costs by outsourcing their call center operations to the Philippines.

However, most customers keep or expand their business for reasons other than cost savings. For example, Ventus helped a U.S. flower delivery company develop a call-handling system to meet the surge in customer calls during Mother's Day and Valentine's Day. Another customer, a major U.S. telecom company, noted that Ventus has consistently achieved one of the highest quality marks from among the various call center providers that it worked with in the United States and abroad. As a result, the company has transferred more business to Ventus.

Ventus views its business as providing high-value voice services to customers. As Montenegro explained,

> Ventus specializes in high value voice services; the company facilitates true customer service interaction where U.S. customers use the phone as a delivery/distribution channel. Our customer service representatives serve the most critical resource of our U.S. clients—their customers. We are the face and voice of the client to that U.S. customer and we only have 3–5 minutes to deliver on that moment of truth. Proficient English skills, not to mention the ability to listen, to probe, and to process customer needs are highly valued skills.

Factors in Ventus's Success

Ventus's success could be attributed to several factors. First, Ventus has benefited from the explosive growth of international outsourcing. For the past 10 years, companies from the United States and other industrialized countries have been outsourcing more of their call center operations and business processes to the Philippines, India, and other locations to cut costs, enhance quality, and remain competitive globally.

Second, Ventus has smartly leveraged the resources of the PLDT group of companies. These include telecom connectivity, redeploying underutilized PLDT assets (e.g., buildings and physical facilities), and the use of shared services. As such, Ventus has been able to employ a "model of building to market and to customer specifications" at a relatively faster speed and lower costs than its competitors. On average, Ventus can build, fit, and customize call center operations for customers within three to six months.

Moreover, Ventus has successfully leveraged its position as a member company of PLDT, the most profitable company in the Philippines, to attract employees to work for its call centers. Although Ventus does not pay the top wage rates in the industry, employees regard the company as a very stable and prestigious employer. Employees also enjoy the benefits of working for a large employer, such as excellent health benefits, pensions, performance bonuses, and profit sharing for management positions.

Third, Ventus is arguably one of the best led companies in the call center industry in the Philippines. At Ventus, Rose Montenegro, Albert Santos, and Ken Lamzon and the leadership team have created a culture that stresses professionalism, high-quality service, attention to customer needs, and a strong camaraderie among employees. The company has spared no expense on training and in building world-class facilities that provide customer service representatives an excellent work environment. As a case in point, the company commissioned English as a Second Language (ESL) teachers at a major California university to customize an "English for Filipinos" training module exclusively for Ventus's customer service representatives.

Reflecting the strength of its leadership and culture, Ventus has enjoyed one of the lowest turnover rates in the industry, both at the management and employee levels. For example, the leadership team that Montenegro has brought on board since the start of the company's commercial operations has remained largely intact.

Growing the Business

Growth in the call center outsourcing industry in the Philippines is expected to be robust for the next three to five years. PLDT's top management and Montenegro have set an aggressive growth target of over 10,000 seats by the end of 2008. The company's management has been contemplating a path that will take the business to its target without sacrificing service quality and risking expensive overhead. In this regard, the company has to address two key issues.

Expansion into the Data Segment

Although growth in the call center business is expected to be strong for the foreseeable future, the BPA/P projects an even stronger growth rate in the data segment of business process outsourcing. These include back-office transactions (e.g., finance/accounting/HR services), medical and legal transcription, animation, engineering design, software development, and digital content development and support. It is projected that the non–call center segment of business process outsourcing to the Philippines will increase from $1.5 billion in 2007 to over $7 billion in 2010.

As competition becomes more crowded and pricing pressures become more intense in the call center space, Ventus and PLDT's management have been looking for ways to provide higher value-added services that will continue to differentiate their company from competitors and accelerate the company's growth.

Expanding the company's presence into the data segment of BPO is one option on the table. However, venturing into the data segment business may be a double-edged sword. On the one hand, it provides Ventus with a platform for tapping into a fast-growing segment of outsourcing and gives the company an expanded suite of services that it could offer to customers who wish to outsource both voice and data services. On the other hand, running a data-based BPO is different from operating call centers because it requires different customer service specializations and entails different economics (e.g., cost and pricing).

In late 2006, PLDT closed on the acquisition of SPI Technologies, a leading global provider of medical and legal transcription and of publishing services. Although PLDT has no immediate plans of combining Ventus and SPI, Ray Espinosa, ePLDT's president and architect of the SPI acquisition, has been eager to create synergies between the two companies and to maximize PLDT's voice and data outsourcing capabilities. Should Ventus embark on its own diversification into data business process outsourcing or leave this segment to SPI? How can Ventus execute on such diversification without competing head on with SPI and sidetracking Ventus's management team from its highly successful call center business?

Market, Customer, and Geographic Diversification

Shortly after it commenced commercial operations, Ventus signed a marquee client, a major U.S. satellite provider. The client has been a driving force behind Ventus's early growth and to date accounts for the lion's share of the number of call center seats held by Ventus.

Like many Philippine-based call center providers, however, Ventus has been largely opportunistic with customer acquisitions. Until recently, the company did not have a sales presence in the United States. It had relied primarily on networking and customer referrals. The focus of the company's business is on inbound calls (customer service, technical support, and sales). The company serves a broad array of industry verticals, including satellite TV, electronics, retail, financial services, flower wire order, technology distribution, and others.

Ventus remains committed to the U.S. market and its current customers. However, it is struggling to determine the best path of growth for the business. These are some of the key issues the company is grappling with:

1. Should the company drive growth by continuing to expand the number of seats held by existing customers, or should it build a new pipeline of customers?

2. Should the company continue to be opportunistic and add new customers as they arise or should it specialize in and aggressively pursue fewer and more lucrative verticals, such as health care, financial services, and high technology?

3. As new markets emerge and grow, such as the Hispanic market in the United States and U.S. multinationals in China, should the company focus on these markets and customer segments? If so, should Ventus build new facilities or acquire or partner with companies near shore to the United States, such as in Mexico or Costa Rica?

Emerging Challenges

Although Ventus's management has set its sights on aggressively growing the business, it continues to have one eye keenly set on the emerging challenges that could derail the company's growth. Foremost among these is the prospect of a tightening labor market, making it more challenging for Ventus and other companies in the Philippines to attract and retain high-quality customer service representatives. The company has dealt with this issue by locating or planning to locate new facilities in second-tier or third-tier cities in the Philippines; solidifying relations with colleges and universities in Manila and the provinces, and shifting human resource responsibilities from PLDT's shared services to Ventus's own human resources department. An immediate priority for Ventus's leadership is to further enhance the company's reputation as an employer of choice in the call center industry.

Second, the Philippine peso (PHP) appreciated by about 8 percent from $1 = PHP 49.1460 to $1.00 = PHP 46.725 during the first half of 2007 and is projected to remain strong in the near term. Because Ventus invoices customers in dollars, it is likely that this will compress the company's profit margins. Finally, more companies have entered or have announced plans to expand their call center operations in the Philippines, including Indian third-party outsourcers and captive operations of U.S. multinational companies. This development portends increased competition for Ventus, both in the recruitment of employees and new customers. ∎

QUESTIONS

1. What factors explain the growth of the Philippine call center industry in general and ePLDT Ventus in particular? What current role(s) do business process outsourcers including call centers like Ventus play in the global supply chain for services? What additional roles can these outsourcers play in the future?

2. What will be the best path for growth for Ventus? Evaluate the various options discussed in the case. What path would you recommend Ventus take? Why?

3. How should Ventus address the emerging challenges that could potentially derail its growth? What other challenges are likely to emerge? How should Ventus deal with these additional challenges? It would be helpful to use the five-forces model discussed in Chapter 11 to analyze Ventus's strengths and weaknesses.

SUMMARY

- A company's supply chain encompasses the coordination of materials, information, and funds from the initial raw materials supplier to the ultimate customer.

- Logistics, or materials management, is that part of the supply chain process that plans, implements, and controls the efficient, effective flow and storage of goods, services, and related information from the point of origin to the point of consumption to meet customers' requirements.

- The success of a global manufacturing strategy depends on compatibility, configuration, coordination, and control.

- Cost-minimization strategies and the drive for global efficiencies often force MNEs offshore to low-cost manufacturing areas, especially in Asia and Eastern Europe.

- Three broad categories of manufacturing configuration are one centralized facility, regional facilities, and multidomestic facilities.

- The key to making a global supply chain system work is information. Companies are rapidly turning to the Internet as a way to link suppliers with manufacturing and eventually with end-use customers.

- Quality is defined as meeting or exceeding the expectations of customers. Quality standards can be general level (ISO 9000), industry specific, or company specific (AQL, zero defects, TQM, and Six Sigma).

- Total quality management (TQM) is a process that stresses customer satisfaction, employee involvement, and continuous improvements in quality while aiming for zero defects.

- Global sourcing is the process of a firm having raw materials and parts supplied to it from domestic and foreign sources.

- Domestic sourcing allows the company to avoid problems related to language, culture, currency, tariffs, and so forth. Foreign sourcing allows the company to reduce costs and improve quality, among other things.

- Under the make or buy decision, companies have to decide if they will make their own parts or buy them from an independent company.

- Companies go through different purchasing phases as they become more committed to global sourcing.

- When a company sources parts from suppliers around the world, distance, time, and the uncertainty of the international political and economic environment can make it difficult for managers to manage inventory flows accurately.

- Lean manufacturing and just-in-time systems focus on reducing inefficiency and unproductive time in the production process to continuously improve the process and quality of the product or service.

- The transportation system links together suppliers with manufacturers and manufacturers with customers.

KEY TERMS

acceptable quality level
   (AQL) (p. 661)
e-commerce (p. 660)
electronic data interchange
   (EDI) (p. 659)
enterprise resource planning
   (ERP) (p. 659)
extranet (p. 660)
foreign trade zones (FTZs) (p. 674)

International Organization for
   Standardization (ISO) (p. 664)
intranet (p. 660)
logistics (or materials management)
   (p. 654)
offshore manufacturing (p. 655)
outsourcing (p. 667)
private technology exchange
   (PTX) (p. 660)

quality (p. 661)
Six Sigma (p. 663)
sourcing (p. 665)
supply chain (p. 653)
total quality management
   (TQM) (p. 662)
vertical integration (p. 667)
zero defects (p. 661)

ENDNOTES

1 *Sources include the following:* F. De Beule and D. Van Den Bulcke, "The International Supply Chain Management of Samsonite Europe," Discussion Paper No. 1998/E/34, Centre for International Management and Development, University of Antwerp, 1998; "About Samsonite: History," *Samsonite: Life's a Journey* (2007), at www.samsonite.com/samsonite/about/history (accessed November 9, 2007); "Company Briefing Book," *Wall Street Journal*, January 27, 2000: www.wsj.com; *Samsonite Quarterly Report*, SEC Form 10-Q, 2002; "Samsonite to Be Sold," *New York Times*, July 6, 2007: C4; "Samsonite Fiscal Year 2007 Annual 10-K," Samsonite, January 31, 2007; "Samsonite Introduces POINT A Franchise Concept," *Samsonite: Life's a Journey* (October 1, 2002[?]ϑ, at www.samsonite.com/samsonite/?404=http://www.samsonite.com/global/globl_pressrelease_europ5.jsp.

2 "The Fourth Annual Global Survey of Supply Chain Progress," Computer Sciences Corporation (CSC) and *Supply Chain Management Review* (2006); Darrell Rigby, "Management Tools 2005," *Bain & Company*, 2005.

3 Deloitte & Touche, "Energizing the Supply Chain," *The Review*, January 17, 2000: 1.

4 Stanley Fawcett, "Supply Chain Management: Competing through Integration," in Tom L. Beauchamp and Norman E. Bowie, eds., *Ethical Theory and Business* (Upper Saddle River, NJ: Prentice Hall, 1993), p. 514.

5 Council of Supply Chain Management Professionals, "Supply Chain Management/Logistics Management Definitions" (2007), at www.cscmp.org/AboutCSCMP/Definitions/Definitions.asp (accessed August 28, 2007).

6 Kevin Reilly, "AMR Research Announces the 2007 Supply Chain Top 25," *AMR Research* (2007), at www.amrresearch.com/Content/View.asp?pmillid=20450 (accessed May 31, 2007).

7 Homin Chen and Tain-Jy Chen, "Network Linkages and Location Choice in Foreign Direct Investment," *Journal of International Business Studies* 29:3 (1998): 447.

8 For a discussion of firm-specific advantages, location-specific advantages, and internalization, see John H. Dunning, *International Production and the Multinational Enterprise* (London: Allen & Unwin, 1981); Peter Buckley and Mark Casson, *The Future of the Multinational Enterprise* (London: Macmillan Press, 1976); Peter Caves, "International Corporations: The Industrial Economics of Foreign Investment," *Economica* 56 (1971): 279–93.

9 Stanley E. Fawcett and Anthony S. Roath, "The Viability of Mexican Production Sharing: Assessing the Four Cs of Strategic Fit," *Urbana* 3:1 (1996): 29.

10 See S. C. Wheelwright, "Reflecting Corporate Strategy in Manufacturing Decisions," *Business Horizons* 21 (1978); S. C. Wheelwright, "Manufacturing Strategy: Defining the Missing Link," *Strategic Management Journal* 5 (1984): 77–91; Frank DuBois, Brian Toyne, and Michael D. Oliff, "International Manufacturing Strategies of U.S. Multinationals: A Conceptual Framework Based on a Four-Industry Study," *Journal of International Business Studies* 24:2 (1993): 313–14; Robert H. Hayes, Steven C. Wheelwright, and Kim B. Clark, *Dynamic Manufacturing* (New York: Free Press, 1988), 10–11.

11 U.S. Department of Labor, Bureau of Labor Statistics, "Table 2. Hourly Compensation Costs in U.S. Dollars" (November 30, 2006), at www.bls.gov/news.release/ichcc.t02.htm (accessed July 31, 2007).

12 Karby Leggett and Peter Wonacott, "Surge in Exports from China Gives a Jolt to Global Industry," *Wall Street Journal*, October 10, 2002: www.wsj.com.

13 Jim Hemerling, "China: Ready for the Next Sourcing Wave?" *BusinessWeek* (April 3, 2007), at www. businessweek.com/globalbiz/content/apr2007/gb20070403_362363.htm (accessed November 9, 2007).

14 See James P. Womack and Daniel T. Jones, "Lean Consumption: Locating for Lean Provision," *Harvard Business Review* (March 2005): 66–67 (online at http://64.233.169.104/search?q=cache:WD1mYdb8BQ8J: custom.hbsp.com/custom/LEANER0503C2005030461.pdf%3Bjessionid%3DSAMFE5NYVB-FAKAKRG WDSELQ+%22Harvard+Business+Review%22%2B%E2%80%9CLean+Consumption%22%2B%22Lean+ Provision%22&hl=en&ct=clnk&cd=1&gl=us [accessed November 9, 2007]).

15 Palu W. Beamish, "The High Cost of Cheap Chinese Labor," *Harvard Business Review* (June 2006): 23.

16 Yuka Hayashi, "Japan Adds Factories at Home," *Wall Street Journal*, June 12, 2007: A8.

17 Interview by author of Wall's Unilever personnel in Beijing, China, June 2006.

18 Jack Ewing, "Why Nokia Is Leaving Moto in the Dust," *BusinessWeek* (July 19, 2007), at www.businessweek.com/globalbiz/content/jul2007/gb20070719_088898.htm (accessed November 9, 2007).

19 Norihiko Shirouzu and Jathon Sapsford, "Heavy Load—For Toyota, a New Small Truck Carries Hopes for Topping GM," *Wall Street Journal*, May 12, 2005: A1.

20 Michael E. McGrath and Richard W. Hoole, "Manufacturing's New Economies of Scale," *Harvard Business Review* (May–June 1992): 94.

21 Fawcett and Roath, "The Viability of Mexican Production Sharing," 29.

22 Deloitte Consulting, "Energizing the Supply Chain: Trends and Issues in Supply Chain Management," 2000: www.dc.com.

23 Rigby, "Management Tools 2005."

24 "IT Investing for High Performance: A Global Survey of CIOs," *Accenture*, at www.accenture.com/Global/Research_and_Insights/By_Role/HighPerformance_IT/CIOResearch/ITInvestHPSurveyCIOs.htm (accessed July 31, 2007).

25 Richard Karpinski, "Wal-Mart Mandates Secure, Internet-Based EDI for Suppliers," *Internetweek.com* (September 12, 2002), at www.internetweek.com/supplyChain/INW20020912S0011.

26 R. Sridharan and Shamni Pande, "Surviving Wal-Mart," *Business Today* (July 29, 2007): 166.

27 "You'll Never Walk Alone," in "Business and the Internet: A Survey," *The Economist*, June 26, 1999: 11–12.

28 Bharatendu Srivastava, "Radio Frequency ID Technology: The Next Revolution in SCM," *Harvard Business Review* (November–December 2004): 60–68.

29 Scott McCartney, "A New Way to Prevent Lost Luggage," *Wall Street Journal*, February 27, 2007: D1.

30 Karpinski, "Wal-Mart Mandates Secure, Internet-Based EDI for Suppliers."

31 "Worldwide Internet Users Top 1 Billion in 2005," *Computer Industry Almanac Inc.* (January 4, 2006), at www.c-i-a.com/pr0106.htm (accessed November 9, 2007).

32 Check the Dell *Annual Report* for 2002 at www.dell.com, and as updated in subsequent *Reports*.

33 "You'll Never Walk Alone," 17.

34 Jeremy Wagstaff, "Digital Deliverance; Asia's Technology Conundrum," *Asian Wall Street Journal,* July 27, 2007: W8.

35 Lee J. Krajewski and Larry P. Ritzman, *Operations Management: Strategy and Analysis,* 4th ed. (Reading, MA: Addison-Wesley, 1996), pp. 141–42.

36 See "Detroit Is Cruising for Quality," *BusinessWeek* (September 3, 2001), at www.businessweek.com/magazine/content/01_36/b3747098.htm (accessed November 9, 2007); Todd Zaun et al., "Auto Makers Get More Mileage from Low-Cost Plants Abroad," *Wall Street Journal,* July 31, 2002: www.wsj.com.

37 J.D. Power & Associates Press Releases, "2007 Vehicle Dependability Study" and "2007 Initial Quality Study," at www.jdpower.com/cc/global/pr/search.asp (accessed July 31, 2007).

38 Hayes, Wheelwright, and Clark, *Dynamic Manufacturing,* 17.

39 S. Thomas Foster, *Managing Quality: Integrating the Supply Chain,* 3rd ed. (Prentice Hall, 2007), pp. 36–38.

40 Foster, *Managing Quality,* 70–90.

41 Krajewski and Ritzman, *Operations Management,* p. 140.

42 Krajewski and Ritzman, *Operations Management,* p. 156.

43 "Six Sigma Definition," at www.sixsigmasurvival.com/SixSigmaDefinition.html (accessed November 9, 2007).

44 Brian Hindo and Brian Grow, "Six Sigma: So Yesterday?" *Business Week,* June 11, 2007: 11.

45 PricewaterhouseCoopers, "Six Sigma and Internal Control" (2002), at www.pwcglobal.com/extweb/manissue.nsf/DocID/A09497E3D72ABCD085256B92005E627D.

46 International Organization for Standardization, "ISO in Figures for the Year 2006" (December 31, 2006), at www.iso.org/iso/en/aboutiso/isoinfigures/January2007-p2.html (accessed July 31, 2007).

47 International Organization for Standardization, "What Makes ISO 9000 and ISO 14000 So Special," www.iso.org/iso/en/aboutiso/introduction/index.html#twentytwo (accessed July 31, 2007).

48 See Jonathan B. Levine, "Want EC Business? You Have Two Choices," *Business Week,* October 19, 1992: 58; International Organization for Standardization, "ISO 9000:2000" (2007), at www.iso.org/iso/catalogue_detail?csnumber=21823 (accessed November 9, 2007).

49 Foster, *Managing Quality.*

50 Amy Schoenfeld, "A Multinational Loaf," *New York Times,* June 20, 2007, at www.nytimes.com/imagepages/2007/06/15/business/20070616_FOOD_GRAPHIC.html (accessed November 9, 2007).

51 Alexei Barrionuevo, "Globalization in Every Loaf," *New York Times* (June 16, 2007), at www.nytimes.com/2007/06/16/business/worldbusiness/16food.html?partner=rssnyt&emc=rss (accessed November 9, 2007).

52 Masaaki Kotabe and Glen S. Omura, "Sourcing Strategies of European and Japanese Multinationals: A Comparison," *Journal of International Business Studies* (Spring 1989): 120–22.

53 David Hannon, "Procter & Gamble Puts a New Spin on Global Chemicals Sourcing," *Purchasing* (February 15, 2007): 32C5.

54 Robert M. Monczka and Robert J. Trent, "Global Sourcing: A Development Approach," *International Journal of Purchasing and Materials Management* (Spring 1991): 3.

55 David Barboza, "Food-Safety Crackdown in China," *New York Times,* June 28, 2007: C1.

56 David Barvoza, "China Makes Arrest in Pet Food Case," *New York Times,* May 4, 2007.

57 Andrew Martin and Griff Palmer, "China Not Sole Source of Dubious Food," *New York Times,* July 12, 2007: C1.

58 R. D'Aveni and D. Ravenscraft, "Economies of Integration versus Bureaucracy Costs: Does Vertical Integration Improve Performance?" *The Academy of Management Journal* 37:5 (1994): 1167–1206; O. Williamson, "Vertical Integration and Related Variations on a Transaction-Cost Theme," in J. Stiglitz and G. Mathewson, eds., *New Developments in the Analysis of Market Structure* (Cambridge, MA: MIT Press, 1986); O. Williamson, *The Economic Institutions of Capitalism* (New York: The Free Press, 1985).

59 Russell Johnston and Paul R. Lawrence, "Beyond Vertical Integration—The Rise of the Value-Adding Partnership," *Harvard Business Review* (July–August 1988): 98.

60 Chester Dawson, "A 'China Price' for Toyota," *Business Week,* February 21, 2005: 50–51.

61 "Few Companies Use Outsourcing as Strategic Business Imperative," *Supply Chain Brain* (2002): www.supplychainbrain.com.

62 John McMillan, "Managing Suppliers: Incentive Systems in Japanese and U.S. Industry," *California Management Review* (Summer 1990): 38.

63 "Still Made in Japan." *Economist.com* (April 7, 2004) at www.economist.com/printedition/displayStory.cfm?Story_id=2571689 (accessed November 9, 2007).

64 "Still Made in Japan." *Economist.com.*

65 Rigby, "Management Tools 2005."

66 Adapted from Pete Engardio and Bruce Einhorn, "Outsourcing Innovation," *Business Week,* March 21, 2005: 84–94.

67 Robert W. Lane, "Competing Globally, Winning Locally," speech to the Waterloo Chamber of Commerce, (August 19, 2004), at www.deere.com/en_US/compinfo/speeches/2004/040819_lane.html.

68 Joseph B. White, "Japanese Auto Makers Help Parts Suppliers Become More Efficient," *Wall Street Journal,* September 10, 1991: 1.

69 Gabriel Kahn, "Invisible Supplier Has Penney's Shirts All Buttoned Up," *Wall Street Journal,* September 11, 2003: A1.

70 Lee Hawkins Jr., "GM Is Pushing Its U.S. Suppliers to Reduce Prices," *Wall Street Journal,* April 7, 2005: A2.

71 Monczka and Trent, "Global Sourcing: A Development Approach," 4–5.

72 Stanley E. Fawcett, "The Globalization of the Supply Environment," *The Supply Environment 2* (Tempe, AZ: NAPM, 2000).

73 Monczka and Trent, "Worldwide Sourcing": 17–18.

74 Guy Anderson, "Nissan Gearing Up for a Partnership," *Wall Street Journal,* December 8, 2004: 42.

75 Foster, *Managing Quality,* p. 87.

76 Krajewski and Ritzman, *Operations Management,* p. 732.

77 Gabriel Kahn, Trish Saywell, and Quenna Sook Kim, "Backlog at West Coast Docks Keeps Christmas Toys at Sea," *Wall Street Journal,* October 21, 2002: www.wsj.com.

78 Shawnee K. Vickery, "International Sourcing: Implications for Just-in-Time Manufacturing," *Production and Inventory Management Journal* (1989): 67.

79 International Trade Administration, "What Activity Is Permitted in Zones?" at http://ia.ita.doc.gov/ftzpage/index.html (accessed August 28, 2007).

80 Foreign-Trade Zones Board, "Information Summary: Current Statistics," (2007), at http://ia.ita.doc.gov/ftzpage/info/summary.html (accessed November 9, 2007).

81 John J. DaPonte Jr., "Foreign-Trade Zones and Exports," *American Export Bulletin* (April 1978).

82 Panalpina, "Company Information," (2005): www.panalpina.com/company.

83 Panalpina, "Transporting IBM Products to Latin America," (2005): www.panalpina.com/press/casestudies.

84 Fawcett, "The Globalization of the Supply Environment," 11.

85 *Sources include the following:* The Business Processing Association/Philippines and presentations by Mitch Locsin, executive secretary, 2006/2007; A. T. Kearney, *Global Services Location Index*, 2005 and 2007; *Philippine Outsourcing Review,* November 25, 2005; *Offshore Location Attractiveness Index: Making Offshoring Decisions,* 2004; personal interview with Manuel Pangilinan, chairman, PLDT, January 2007; personal interview with Rose Montenegro, president, ePLDT Ventus, January 2007.

The information on ePLDT Ventus and Philippine Long Distance Telephone Company is from the author's personal interviews and company sources/references. Adapted from the Business Processing Association/Philippines, 2006/2007. We would like to acknowledge Professor Manuel Serapio, Director of the Master of Science in International Business Program and Faculty Director of the Center for International Business Education and Research at the University of Colorado Denver, for writing the case.

18

International Accounting Issues

Even between parents and children, money matters make strangers.

—Japanese proverb

Objectives

- To examine the major factors influencing the development of accounting practices in different countries

- To examine the global convergence of accounting standards

- To explain how companies account for foreign-currency transactions and translate foreign-currency financial statements

- To discuss different forms of performance evaluation of foreign operations and how foreign exchange can complicate the budget process

- To explain how arbitrary transfer pricing can complicate performance evaluation and control

- To introduce the balanced scorecard as an approach to evaluating performance

CASE: Parmalat: Europe's Enron

In January 2002, a European magazine published an article titled "Enron: Could It Happen Here?" At the time the article was published, perhaps most people outside the United States would have answered "no" to that question.[1] In the wake of massive corporate frauds at Enron and WorldCom, there was a

created the Parmalat brand in 1963. Parmalat was the first Italian manufacturer of branded milk. In 1966, using packaging technology from Tetra Pak, Parmalat created its signature product, milk pasteurized at ultra high temperatures (UHT), giving milk a shelf life of over six months. UHT milk provided

MAP 18.1 Parmalat, Headquartered in Italy, Shows that Accounting Scandals Occur in European as Well as American Companies

feeling outside the United States that such scandals were "an American problem" caused by the more aggressive business environment and practices there. However, a family-owned Italian firm was about to show the world that massive corporate scandals can happen anywhere (Map 18.1).

A BRIEF BACKGROUND CHECK

After Calisto Tanzi inherited his father's company at age 22, he directed it into the production of dairy products in 1961 and

Parmalat with a technological competitiveness in the milk industry, placing Parmalat ahead of its competition. In 1970, the law permitted the sale of whole milk in grocery stores, removing the limitation of specialty milk shops. Parmalat quickly became the dominant milk supplier of Italy.

The "Champion's Milk"

Parmalat became known as the "champion's milk" after sponsoring the Ski World Cup and world champion Formula One race car driver Nicki Lauda in the 1970s. The company moved into new markets with the production of cheese, butter, and a variety of desserts near the end of the decade. As it increased in popularity, Parmalat also began international expansion through acquisitions in Germany and France, which marked the beginning of a global dairy empire.

The Pious Pioneer Sports Marketer

The author of such growth was Calisto Tanzi, an almost legendary figure in Italy. It was he who discovered the power of sports marketing to make Parmalat a famous brand. He had friends in important government positions who helped pass laws favoring Parmalat. A pious Catholic, Tanzi was a generous benefactor who sponsored the restoration of Parma's eleventh-century basilica and funded its professional soccer team. And he seemed modest about his achievements. He didn't smoke, drank little, and drove his own Lexus. Throughout Parmalat's expansion, Tanzi maintained a paternalistic approach to the business. "He would stand, for example, at the plant, spoon in hand, ready to taste the first sample each time a new yoghurt [flavor] was launched."

Going Public and Going Global

In 1989, the firm was acquired by a holding company and changed its name to Parmalat Finanziaria SpA. The milk giant showed healthy profits every year, and its balance sheet appeared strong with large amounts of cash on hand. This allowed Parmalat to go public in Italy and raise capital in the United States and other countries by selling shares and issuing bonds. The company used this new capital to expand into Latin America, where it dominated the dairy markets in Brazil, Argentina, Venezuela, and several other countries.

By the early 1990s, Parmalat was not only popular among grocery shoppers—investors and creditors deemed the firm a profitable business partner. Large international banks collected hefty fees by helping the company issue bonds, list stock in foreign markets, and raise capital to fund international acquisitions. As CFO Alberto Ferraris put it, "Outside my office, there was always a line of bankers, asking about new business." There was only one problem: The profits that Parmalat reported were only an illusion created by a set of accounting manipulations.

ACCOUNTING ISSUES

One of the most interesting aspects of Parmalat's case is the simplicity of its fraudulent accounting (which was not *quite* as simple as the scheme suggested in Figure 18.1). The purpose of the fraud was straightforward—to hide operating losses so as not to disappoint investors and creditors. The core of the scheme was double billing to Italian supermarkets and other retailers. By standard accounting procedures, every time product is shipped to a customer, a company records a receivable that it later expects to collect as cash. Because receivables count as sales revenue, Parmalat billed customers twice for each shipment, thus greatly enlarging its sales. The company used these inflated revenues as a means to secure loans from several international banks.

"Off-Balance-Sheet Financing"

By 1995, Parmalat was losing more than $300 million annually in Latin America alone. These continued operating losses caused company executives to search for more complex ways of masking the firm's true performance. Using a trick called "off-balance-sheet financing," executives set up three shell companies based in the Caribbean. These firms pretended to sell Parmalat products, and Parmalat would send them fake invoices and charge costs and fees to make the "sales" look legitimate. Then Parmalat would write out a credit note for the amount the subsidiaries supposedly owed it and take that to banks to raise money.

Off-balance-sheet financing was also used to hide debts. The company transferred over half of its liabilities to the books of small subsidiaries based in offshore tax havens such as the Cayman Islands. This allowed Parmalat to present a "healthy" balance sheet and a profitable income statement to investors and creditors by hiding large amounts of debt and overstating sales revenue. In 2002, Parmalat reported liabilities of close to $8 billion on its consolidated balance sheet. In reality, the company had roughly $14 billion in debt.

FIGURE 18.1
Top-Down Accounting

Source: www.businesscartoons.co.uk.

The Art of Milking Growth

Taking advantage of its image, Parmalat issued bonds in the United States and Europe, which were backed up by falsified assets, especially cash. "It was a reversal of logic," said the chief investigating magistrate after the scheme was discovered. Usually, companies take on debt to grow. But in Parmalat's case, "they had to grow to hide the debt." In other words, the company would obtain loans to pay off previous loans. Investigators report that without the accounting manipulations, the company would have reported operating losses every year between 1990 and 2003.

The circle of hiding operating losses by incurring increasingly larger amounts of debt eventually became hard to sustain. To perpetuate the fraud, Parmalat needed to continue incurring debt, paying interest on old debts with no real cash of its own, and finding new ways to create false sales. Alberto Ferraris, who was appointed CFO in March 2003, mentioned that "he couldn't understand why the company was paying so much to service its debt; the interest payments seemed far higher than warranted for the €5.4 billion in debt on the books."

By the late 1990s, auditors in Argentina and Brazil raised several red flags that pointed to problems with Parmalat's accounting. In early December 2003, the company failed to make a €150 million bond payment. This puzzled those familiar with the company because, according to the 2002 financial statements, Parmalat had plenty of cash on hand.

The fraud became public on December 19, 2003, when Grant Thornton, the company's auditor, made an interesting discovery. While auditing Bonlat, a fully owned subsidiary of Parmalat based in the Cayman Islands, the auditors contacted Bank of America to confirm a letter held by Bonlat in which Bank of America allegedly certified that the company had €3.95 billion in cash. Bank of America responded that such an account didn't exist. This finding led to a serious investigation into the financial position of Parmalat, which uncovered the accounting tricks described previously.

THE CONSEQUENCES

Parmalat filed for bankruptcy protection on December 24, 2003. CEO Calisto Tanzi resigned and was detained by Italian authorities three days later and sent to prison. He was subsequently confined to house arrest until September 27, 2004. Also accused of wrongdoing were Fausto Tonna, CFO during most of the period under investigation; Giovanni, Stefano, and Francesca Tanzi, brother, son, and daughter of Calisto Tanzi; and other key employees believed to have been involved in the scheme.

"If Convicted . . ."

Initially, it was thought that misstatements were created only to hide operating losses; however, more recent information has shown that the Tanzi family financially benefited from the fraud. For example, Calisto Tanzi revealed that $638 million was moved to "a family-owned tourism business." Two separate trials are occurring in regard to individuals associated with the Parmalat fraud. One trial, held in Milan, involves "Tanzi and 15 other people . . . accused of market manipulation, obstructing a regulator's investigation and falsifying audits. . . . If convicted in the Milan trial, Tanzi could face five years in prison, but he will also go on trial in Parma, where he is accused of bringing about Parmalat's bankruptcy by falsifying documents and [making] false statements. If convicted in that trial, he could be imprisoned for as long as 15 years."

Enrico Bondi was appointed by the government as CEO of Parmalat to direct recovery efforts. As part of his campaign, he has brought lawsuits against Grant Thornton and Deloitte, the auditors, for not performing the audit with proper care and not bringing their suspicions to the attention of management. Grant Thornton cut ties with its Italian practice after Parmalat's problems surfaced. In addition, Bondi is suing major international banks, such as Bank of America, Credit Suisse First Boston, Citigroup, and Deutsche Bank.

Lawsuits, Rounds I and II

The lawsuits accuse the banks of ignoring the fraud to obtain fees from doing business with Parmalat. As mentioned earlier, these banks were instrumental in helping the company raise capital to fund its international expansion. The banks and the auditors deny any wrongdoing and claim they were victims of the scheme. Citigroup Inc., UBS AG, Deustche Bank AG, and Morgan Stanley will be involved in the Milan trial for "failing to have procedures that would have prevented crimes that contributed to" Parmalat's failure. As of mid-June 2007, "Bondi . . . has collected almost $900 million in settlements in Italy and the United States."

Parmalat, in turn, has been sued by investors, banks, and other organizations. In the United States, the SEC filed a complaint against Parmalat on December 29, 2003, alleging that the company fraudulently raised money through bonds in the United States by overstating assets and understating liabilities. On July 30, 2004, Parmalat agreed to settle with the SEC without admitting or denying the claims. Parmalat won't be fined but has agreed to make changes to strengthen its board of directors and improve governance.

Restructuring

Besides the legal battles that have resulted from the fraud, Bondi's restructuring campaign calls for aggressive changes in Parmalat's organization. On March 29, 2004, the company announced it would narrow its focus to markets in Italy, Canada, Australia, South Africa, Spain, Portugal, Russia, and Romania and it would pull out of other regions. However, in May 2007, "Parmalat . . . agreed to sell its Spanish assets to Lacteos Siglo XXI." Latin American countries "with strong and profitable positions" such as Colombia, Nicaragua, and Venezuela would be retained. In addition, Parmalat would cut its workforce from 32,000 to less than 17,000, slash the number of brands from 120 to 30, and concentrate on "healthy lifestyle" products.

Repercussions in the Industry

Not only employees and investors were affected by the scandal. In the aftermath of the discovery, dairies across Europe and Latin America faced uncertainty about sales of their milk. For example, GLP of France was owed €1.25 million by Parmalat at the time of the bankruptcy announcement. A Hungarian cooperative, which sold 80 million liters of milk a year to Parmalat, was left wondering if it would be able to continue selling its milk. Brazil's dairy farmers asked their government to pressure the local unit of the Italian food company to make sure they got paid. In that country, Parmalat controlled 10 percent of the country's pasteurized milk market, a quarter of its long-life UHT milk market, and 40 percent of the market for long-life carton-packaged cream.

SO, WHAT HAPPENED?

In Europe, the Parmalat scandal created deep concern among authorities. The European Commission suggested it would like to strengthen auditing standards by insisting that member countries introduce accounting-oversight boards similar to those in the United States. Many organizations have proposed reforms to prevent another scandal of such magnitude. One of the areas of reform considered was more transparency in the bond market in Europe; in other words, bond-price disclosure. However, "the [European Commission] has indicated that it will allow traders to police themselves instead of requiring the same data about bonds as for stocks."

From an accounting perspective, Parmalat joined the ranks of other European companies by adopting International Financial Reporting Standards published by the International Accounting Standards Board and adopted by the European Commission for their consolidated financial statements, as noted in their December 31, 2006, annual report. In addition, Parmalat's independent auditors are now the global auditing firm, PricewaterhouseCoopers. The hope is that these two moves will help convince investors that Parmalat is moving in the right direction on the accounting side.

Plus a Little Corporate Misgovernance

However, even though these accounting moves were taken to help Parmalat recover, they are not enough. Although the fraud was perpetrated through a set of accounting tricks, several issues converged to allow such manipulations to happen. One of the clearest deficiencies at Parmalat was its corporate governance system. As a family-owned business, the company was tightly controlled by insiders, especially Calisto Tanzi, who held the positions of CEO and chairman of the board of directors.

Most of the other board members were family members or managers of Parmalat. This prevented the company from having a strong independent voice to stop the actions taken by management. In addition, Italian law allowed Parmalat to have two auditors instead of one. Grant Thornton was the main auditor, but Deloitte audited some of the subsidiaries, including Bonlat, where the fraud was uncovered. This arrangement made it more difficult for the auditors to have one clear, coherent picture of Parmalat's financial condition. As noted, neither of these auditors is used by Parmalat now. Finally, and perhaps most importantly, management integrity failed. In the end, a manager determined to commit fraud will most likely succeed even in a very good governance system.

In the aftermath of Parmalat's fraud, investigators were left wondering how a few accounting numbers could fool so many people. One thing, however, was clear: Europe now had its very own Enron.

Introduction

International business managers cannot make good decisions without relevant and reliable information about accounting (Figure 18.2), one of the functional areas that is critical for the operations of the MNE. Although accounting and information systems specialists provide such information, managers must also understand which data they need and the problems specialists face in gathering the data from different accounting systems around the world.

THE CROSSROADS OF ACCOUNTING AND FINANCE

The accounting and finance functions are closely related. Each relies on the other to fulfill its own responsibilities. The chief financial officer (CFO) of any company is responsible for procuring and managing the company's financial resources. This individual is usually one of the members of the top management team of a company. The CFO relies on the controller, or chief accountant, to provide the right information for making decisions.

In addition, the internal audit staff ensures that corporate policies and procedures are followed. They and the CFO and controller work closely with the external auditor to try to safeguard the assets of the business. (As you can see from our opening case on the Parmalat scandal, however, things can go wrong, especially when topmost management is willing to shirk its fiduciary responsibility and the external auditor may see a different sort of value in the company's assets.)

Case Review Note

FIGURE 18.2   Factors Influencing International Accounting

As a system for providing information that companies can *use*, accounting performs an essential *strategic function*. Recall that we used Figure 14.1 to introduce the various *means* by which a company can pursue its international strategy. Among those *means* we included *functions*, and here we focus on accounting as another of those functions.

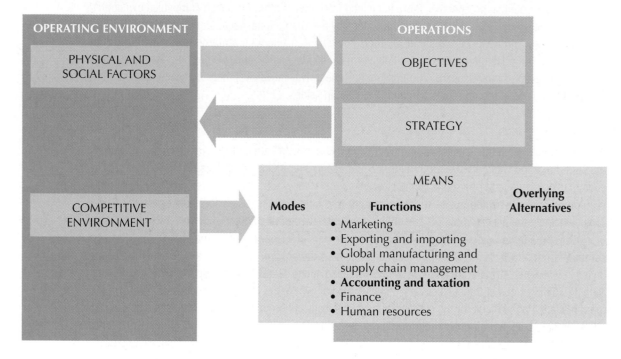

The actual and potential flow of assets across national boundaries complicates the finance and accounting functions. The MNE must learn to cope with differing inflation rates, exchange-rate changes, currency controls, expropriation risks, customs duties, tax rates and methods of determining taxable income, levels of sophistication of local accounting personnel, and local as well as home-country reporting requirements.

> The accountant is essential in providing information to financial decision makers.

What Does the Controller Control?   A company's controller collects and analyzes data for internal and external users. The overall objective of **accounting** is to provide information that management can use to make good decisions. It is, according to one useful account,

> *a service activity. Its function is to provide quantitative information, primarily financial in nature, about economic entities that is intended to be useful in making economic decisions—in making reasoned choices among alternative courses of action.*[2]

The role of the corporate controller has expanded beyond the traditional roles of management accounting. As Figure 18.3 indicates, the controller is part of the financial function of the firm. Some of the controller's typical responsibilities can be seen in Figure 18.3, although the exact duties and allocation among the finance staff, the controller, and the treasurer vary from company to company.

> The controller of an international company must be concerned about a broader range of issues dealing with corporate strategy than just accounting issues.

Today's controller is engaged in a variety of activities outside of the typical accounting and reporting functions that support the general strategy of the firm, such as managing the supply chain, evaluating potential acquisitions abroad, disposing of a subsidiary or a division, managing cash flow, hedging currency and interest rate risks, tax planning, internal auditing, and helping in the planning of corporate strategy. Today's accountant must have a much broader perspective of business in general—and international business in particular for the purposes of this book—than was the case even as recently as a decade ago (see Figure 18.4).

FIGURE 18.3 What the Controller Controls

We have our controller reporting to either a VP of Finance or a chief financial officer. Note that our controller's area of responsibility, like that of many contemporary controllers, is twofold: He or she oversees not only activities in accounting but those in financial management as well.

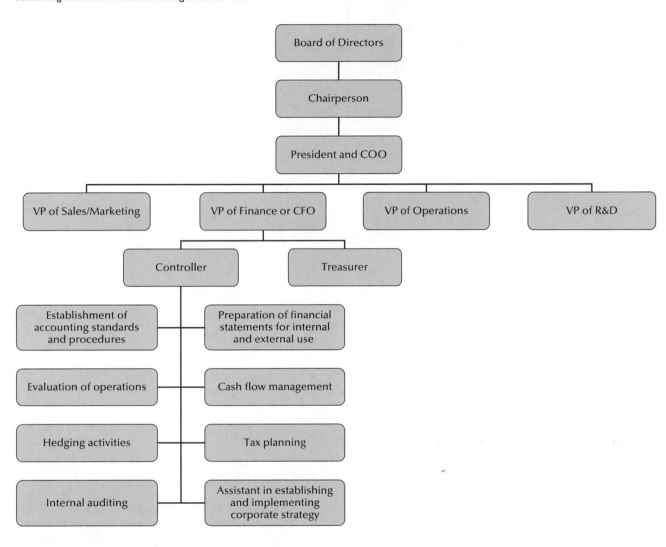

As noted in Chapter 15 and elaborated on in this chapter, foreign managers and subsidiaries are usually evaluated at headquarters on the basis of data generated in the company's reporting system that is set up and coordinated by the controller's office. The controller generates reports for internal consideration, local government needs, creditors, employees, suppliers, stockholders, and prospective investors. The controller handles the impact of many different currencies and inflation rates on the statements and should be familiar with different countries' accounting systems.

This chapter discusses some key accounting issues facing companies that do business abroad. Initially, we examine how accounting differs around the world and how global capital markets are forcing countries to consider converging their accounting and reporting standards as we attempt to move to one set of globally accepted standards. Then we examine some unique issues facing MNEs, such as accounting for foreign-currency transactions, translating foreign-currency financial statements, reporting on foreign operations to shareholders and potential investors, and evaluating the performance of foreign operations and managers.

Although our focus is on problems of MNEs, many of these issues affect any company doing business overseas, even a small importer or exporter. Foreign-currency

CONCEPT CHECK

We discuss **foreign-exchange rates** and the ways in which they affect the operations of an MNE in Chapter 9. Here we explain the responsibilities of the CFO in overseeing a company's closely related financial and **accounting** functions. As we'll see, financial management deals with the effects of exchange rates on such financial statement items as *receivables* and *payables*.

transactions, such as denominating a sale or purchase in a foreign currency, must be accounted for in the currency of the parent company, and this is true of both large and small firms and service firms as well as manufacturing firms.

Accounting for International Differences

Both the form and the content of financial statements are different in different countries.

One problem an MNE faces is that accounting standards and practices vary around the world. Financial statements in different countries are different in both form (or format) and content (or substance). For example, the balance sheets for U.S. companies are in this format:

$$\text{Assets} = \text{Liabilities} + \text{Shareholders' equity}$$

This format is known as the *balance format*. The balance sheet varies in the order of liquidity of the accounts presented. Some companies start with the least liquid assets (those that are harder to convert into cash quickly) and go to the most liquid assets, whereas other companies start with the most liquid assets (such as cash) and move to the least liquid assets (such as property, plant, and equipment). The former practice is very common among European companies, whereas the latter approach is used by U.S.-based companies.

The balance sheets for many European, especially British, companies are prepared in a different format known as the analytical format:

$$\text{Fixed assets} + \text{Current assets} - \text{Current liabilities} - \text{Noncurrent liabilities}$$
$$= \text{Capital and reserves}$$

Some of the terminology used in the presentation of the financial statements varies for companies around the world. In addition, some companies (i.e., U.S. companies) present only a set of consolidated financial statements, whereas other companies (i.e., European companies) present both parent company and group financial statements.

Some observers argue that differences in format are a minor matter, a problem of form rather than substance. In fact, however, the substance also differs because companies can measure assets and determine income differently in different countries.

ACCOUNTING OBJECTIVES

It's important for the accounting process to identify, record, and interpret economic events. Every country needs to determine the objectives of the accounting system it has put into place. According to the **Financial Accounting Standards Board (FASB),** the private-sector body that establishes accounting standards in the United States, financial reporting, the external reporting of accounting information, should provide information for three purposes:

- Investment and credit decisions
- Assessment of cash flow prospects
- Evaluation of enterprise resources, claims to those resources, and changes in them[3]

Who Uses Accounting Information?   To establish objectives, managers have to identify the major users of financial information. The **International Accounting Standards Board (IASB)** identifies the key users of accounting information represented in Figure 18.5.

It's important to identify users because a focus on different users might result in different financial information being reported. For example, because Germany's major users have historically been banks, accounting has focused more on the balance sheet, which contains a description of the company's assets. In the United States, however, because the major users are investors, accounting has focused more on the income statement. Investors see the income statement as an indication of the future success of the company, which affects the company's stock price (or share price) and its flow of dividends.

There is no consensus on whether there should be a uniform set of accounting standards and practices for all classes of users worldwide, but the general movement toward the development of accounting standards and practices is focused on financial information for investors.

> The accounting process identifies, records, and interprets economic events.

> The Financial Accounting Standards Board (FASB) sets accounting standards in the United States.

> The International Accounting Standards Board (IASB) is an international private-sector organization that sets accounting standards.

> Critical users of accounting information are investors, employees, lenders, suppliers and other trade creditors, customers, governments and their agencies, and the public.

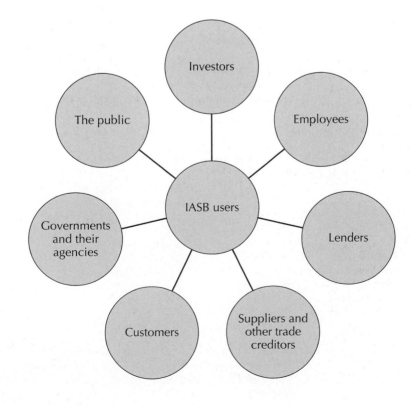

FIGURE 18.5
Who Uses Accounting Information?

Interestingly, key users differ from country to country. In Germany, the key readership of financial statements consists of bankers, who are interested primarily in asset valuation. In the United States, the key readership consists of investors, who want to know primarily how profitable a company is.

Source: Data from International Accounting Standards Committee Foundation, *A Guide through International Financial Reporting Standards (IFRSs®)* (London: IASCF, 2007), paragraph 9, p. 15.

CONCEPT CHECK

In discussing "Legal Issues in International Business" in Chapter 3, we survey the various ways in which local legal standards can affect foreign firms in *operational matters*—in the ways in which they function on a day-to-day basis. Naturally, these standards include **accounting** standards, and here we emphasize that attitudes toward—and, more importantly, regulations concerning—accounting practices vary widely from country to country. Remember, too, that although standard-setting bodies may be public or private organizations, policies such as those pertaining to **FASB** and **GAAP** are strongly influenced by local governments.

Case Review Note

FACTORS IN INTERNATIONAL ACCOUNTING PRACTICES

In Figure 18.6, we identify some of the forces leading to the development of accounting practices internationally. Although all of the factors shown in the figure are significant, their importance varies by country. For example, investors are influential in the United States and the United Kingdom, but creditors—primarily banks—have traditionally been more influential in Germany and Switzerland. Figure 18.6 is comprehensive because it focuses on *all* elements of the accounting process: national and international influences, users, regulators, auditors, and educators.

Taxation has a big influence on accounting standards and practices in Japan and France, but it is less important in the United States. Cultural issues cut across all countries and strongly influence the development of accounting. Certain international factors also have weight, such as former colonial influence and foreign investment. For example, most countries that are current or former members of the British Commonwealth have accounting systems similar to the United Kingdom's. Former French colonies use the French model, and so forth. Thus companies from those countries use standards and practices that are similar to companies from other countries in the same group.

The international public accounting firms, such as KPMG, Deloitte, PricewaterhouseCoopers, and Ernst & Young, are also important sources of influence because they transfer high levels of auditing practices worldwide. As we observed in our opening story on the Parmalat case, public accounting firms are also responsible for ensuring that proper accounting practices are followed and that publicly released financial statements accurately represent a firm's financial position.

FIGURE 18.6 Environmental Influences on Accounting Practices

Every aspect of the accounting process is influenced by a variety of internal and external factors, and they're all potentially important. Degree of importance will vary by country.

Source: Lee H. Radebaugh, "Environmental Factors Influencing the Development of Accounting Objectives, Standards and Practices—The Peruvian Case," *The International Journal of Accounting* 10:3 (1975): 41. © 1975. Reprinted by permission of Elsevier Science.

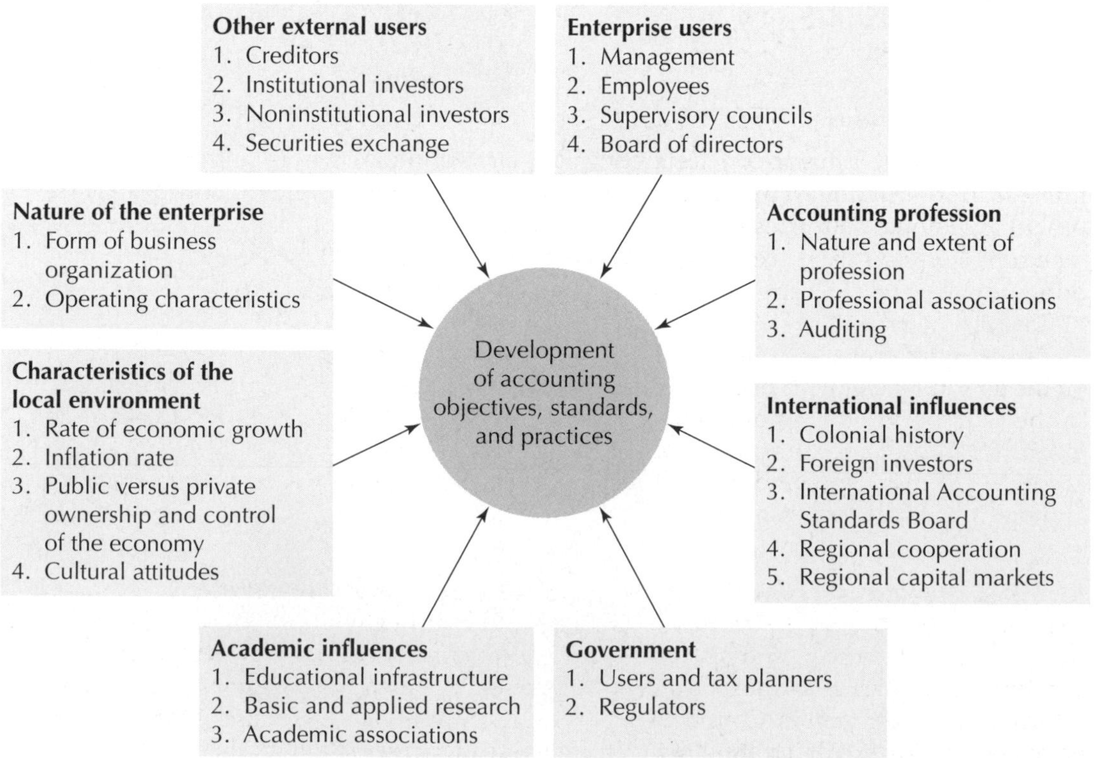

Other external users
1. Creditors
2. Institutional investors
3. Noninstitutional investors
4. Securities exchange
Enterprise users
1. Management
2. Employees
3. Supervisory councils
4. Board of directors
Nature of the enterprise
1. Form of business organization
2. Operating characteristics
Accounting profession
1. Nature and extent of profession
2. Professional associations
3. Auditing
Development of accounting objectives, standards, and practices
Characteristics of the local environment
1. Rate of economic growth
2. Inflation rate
3. Public versus private ownership and control of the economy
4. Cultural attitudes
International influences
1. Colonial history
2. Foreign investors
3. International Accounting Standards Board
4. Regional cooperation
5. Regional capital markets
Academic influences
1. Educational infrastructure
2. Basic and applied research
3. Academic associations
Government
1. Users and tax planners
2. Regulators

KPMG is one of the four largest public accounting firms in the world, offering auditing and tax services to multinational clients.

The Emergence of Convergence   These differences in accounting influences have resulted in differences in accounting standards and practices. However, the major development in accounting worldwide is now the issue of **convergence,** which implies that, through negotiations between the IASB and national standards setters, such as the FASB in the United States, we are moving closer to having the *International Financial Reporting Standards (IFRS)* of the IASB as the one set of accounting standards that can be used in capital markets. Before understanding the issue of convergence, however, we need to understand the underlying differences among countries, and culture is a key force.

Equity markets are an important source of influence on accounting in the United States and the United Kingdom. Banks are influential in Germany and Switzerland, and taxation is a major influence in Japan and France.

CULTURAL DIFFERENCES IN ACCOUNTING

A major source of influence on accounting standards and practices is culture. Of special interest to international investors are the differences in measurement and disclosure practices among countries—measurement meaning "how companies value assets, including inventory and fixed assets" and disclosure meaning "how and what information companies provide and discuss in their annual and interim reports for external users of financial data."

Much of the work on culture and accounting is initially based on Hofstede's research on the structural elements of culture, particularly those that most strongly affect behavior in the work situations of organizations and institutions.[4] Hofstede's work was then extended into the accounting area by Gray,[5] which resulted in classifying countries according to disclosure and measurement principles, specifically secrecy/transparency and optimism/conservatism.

The Secrecy–Transparency/Optimism–Conservatism Matrix   Figure 18.7 depicts the accounting practices of various groupings of countries within a matrix of the cultural values of secrecy–transparency and optimism–conservatism. With respect to accounting, secrecy and transparency indicate the degree to which companies disclose information to the public. Countries such as Germany, Switzerland, and Japan tend to have less disclosure (illustrating the cultural value of secrecy) than do the United States

CONCEPT CHECK

Chapter 2 is devoted to illustrating the many ways in which local culture shapes the environment in which **international business** is conducted from country to country. Here we point out that **culture** also affects differences in approaches to **accounting** systems and policies. In Chapter 2, we cite Gert Hofstede among the researchers who've studied national differences in managerial attitudes and preferences, and here we use applications of Hofstede's findings to studies of work-situation behavior as a means of shedding light on the effect of cultural differences on accounting standards and practices.

FIGURE 18.7   A Disclosure/Assessment Matrix for National Accounting Systems

The vertical axis reflects practices according to *transparency–secrecy*—the extent to which companies in a country disclose information to the public. The horizontal axis reflects practices according to *optimism–conservatism*—the degree of *caution* taken by companies when it comes to valuing assets and recognizing income. Note that, not surprisingly, transparency and optimism tend to go hand in hand, as do secrecy and conservatism.

Source: Lee H. Radebaugh and Sidney J. Gray, *International Accounting and Multinational Enterprises,* 5th ed. (New York: John Wiley & Sons, 2002). © 2002. Reprinted by permission of John Wiley & Sons.

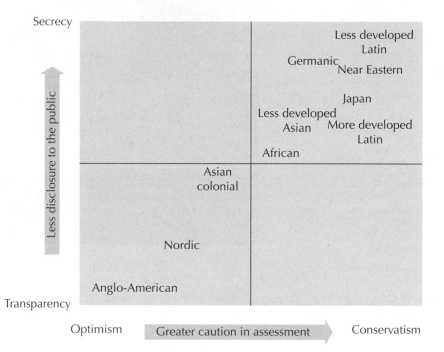

and the United Kingdom—both are Anglo-American countries—which are more transparent or open with respect to disclosure. By the same token, our opening case on the Parmalat scandal demonstrates that even companies that list on global exchanges, borrow money from the largest banks in the world, and turn their financial statements over to the best auditing firms in the world can insinuate secrecy into their corporate cultures.

Generally Accepted Accounting Principles   In addition, as companies from the upper-right quadrant of secrecy and conservatism utilize capital markets more extensively, they move closer to the Anglo-American mode. This is especially true of companies like Deutsche Bank and DaimlerChrysler, which adopted U.S. **Generally Accepted Accounting Principles (GAAP)** for reporting purposes as allowed under German law. As companies headquartered in the European Union and other countries throughout the world adopt International Financial Reporting Standards issued by the IASB, they should become more transparent and optimistic.

Culture influences measurement and disclosure practices:

- Measurement—how to value assets.
- Disclosure—the presentation of information and discussion of results.

Optimism and conservatism (in an accounting, not a political, sense) are the degree of caution companies exhibit in valuing assets and recognizing income—an illustration of the measurement issues mentioned earlier. Countries more conservative from an accounting point of view tend to understate assets and income, whereas optimistic countries tend to be more liberal in their recognition of income. Banks primarily fund French companies, as they do in Germany and Japan, and banks are concerned with liquidity. So French companies tend to be very conservative both when recording profits that keep them from paying taxes and when declaring dividends to pile up cash reserves to service their bank debt.

In contrast, U.S. companies want to show earnings power to impress and attract investors. British companies tend to be more optimistic in earnings recognition than U.S. companies, but U.S. companies are much more optimistic than continental European and

Japanese companies. The Asian financial crisis demonstrated that most Asian countries still fit squarely in the upper-right quadrant of measurement and disclosure. In particular, companies from Korea and Southeast Asia were guilty of a lack of transparency, which made it difficult for banks and investors to know where to lend and invest their money. They often put their money in Asian companies on the basis of relationships and reputation instead of good financial information.

CLASSIFYING ACCOUNTING SYSTEMS

Although accounting standards and practices differ significantly worldwide, we can still group systems used in various countries according to common characteristics. Figure 18.8 illustrates one approach to classifying accounting systems. It does not attempt to classify all countries, but it simply illustrates the concept using several developed Western countries. Although all major developed countries are moving to an accounting model that favors investors and thus is more similar to the micro-based countries at the bottom of Figure 18.8, understanding the macro tradition is essential to realize how difficult it is to converge accounting standards from different parts of the world.

From Macro-Uniform to Micro-Based Systems   The creators of Figure 18.8 have used the concept of natural science to classify countries, As you move from left to right, you move from the general to the specific. Macro-uniform systems are shaped more by government influence than are micro-based systems. The major accounting influences on

> Secrecy and transparency refer to the degree to which corporations disclose information to the public. Optimism and conservatism refer to the degree of caution companies display in valuing assets and recognizing income.

> British companies are optimistic when recognizing income. U.S. companies are slightly less optimistic. Japanese and continental European companies are even less optimistic than U.S. companies.

FIGURE 18.8   Development of Accounting Systems in the West

As a *class, macro-uniform accounting systems* have developed in countries with strong, codified legal systems. They're also shaped more heavily by government influences than are *micro-based accounting systems*, which, as a class, prevail in countries where accounting practices have developed in response to pragmatic business needs.

Source: From C. W. Nobes, "A Judgmental International Classification of Financial Reporting Practices," *Journal of Business Finance and Accounting* (Spring 1983). Reprinted by permission of Blackwell Publishing Ltd.

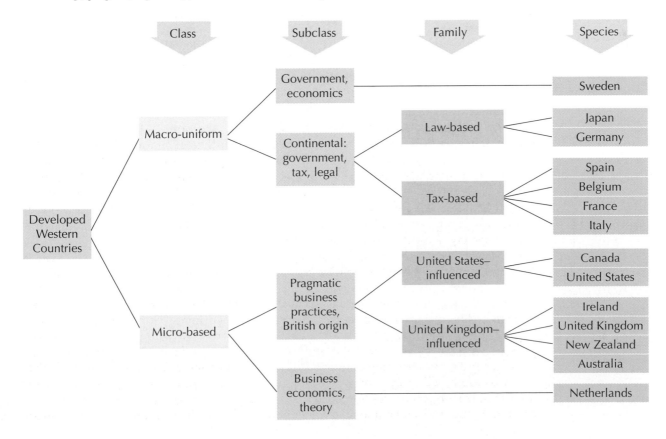

Macro-uniform accounting systems are shaped more by government influence, whereas micro-based systems rely on pragmatic business practice.

countries that fit into the macro-uniform category are a strong legal system, especially a codified legal system rather than a common law system, and tax law. These systems also tend to be more conservative and secretive about disclosure. Japan and Germany are legal-based systems, and Spain and France are tax-based systems. The former Soviet bloc countries and China would also fit in the macro category.

Note that Figure 18.8 identifies the traditions from which countries come, even though their measurement and disclosure practices are moving closer to the micro-based categories. These traditions are very much culturally and institutionally based and are slow to change completely.

Micro-based systems include features that support pragmatic business practice and have evolved from the British system. The United States is an example of a country that fits in the micro category. It exhibits more optimism and transparency than countries in the macro category, and it also relies less on legal and tax requirements than Germany, France, and Japan. The focus tends to be more on capital markets and less on banks and tax authorities.

Other countries that closely model the United States are Mexico and Canada, two members of NAFTA. The British model is also a micro-based model, but it relies even less on legal and tax influences than the United States. Current and former members of the British Commonwealth, such as the Bahamas, Australia, and New Zealand, also fit into this category.[6]

Strong Versus Weak Equity Markets   More recently, the developers of the *macro-uniform/micro-based* scheme for classifying accounting systems have updated it to distinguish among other factors, including *strong versus weak equity markets* (see Figure 18.9). This

CONCEPT CHECK

In discussing "Regional Economic Integration" in Chapter 8, we observe that the momentum toward cooperation in such blocs as the **EU** and **NAFTA** has spilled over into areas of **international business** that lie beyond the originally targeted terrain of trade and **tariffs**. Here we cite developments in such areas as accounting **convergence**—especially in the case of the EU—as particularly good examples of this phenomenon.

FIGURE 18.9   Classifying Accounting Systems According to Equity Market Strength

An *equity market* is pretty much the same thing as a *stock market*—a marketplace in which such *equity instruments* as stocks and bonds are traded. An equity market is *strong* when companies can rely on equity instruments to increase their capital bases. This version of accounting system schemes divides systems into two classes: those that have developed in nations where equity markets are strong and those that have developed in nations where equity markets are weak.

Source: Christopher Nobes and Robert Parker, *Comparative International Accounting*, 7th ed. (Harlow, England: FT Prentice Hall, 2002), p. 67.

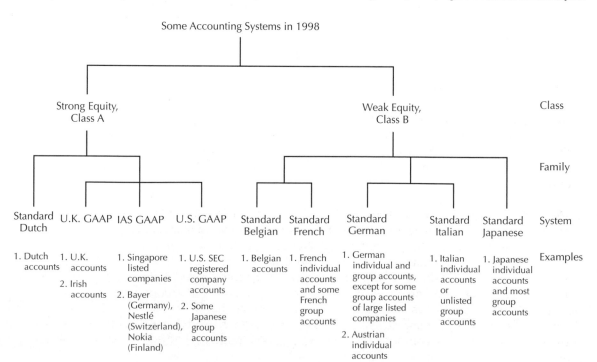

incorporates changes that are taking place internationally where some companies in countries such as Germany generate financial statements consistent with U.S. GAAP or IFRS.[7]

The shortcoming of both Figures 18.8 and 18.9 is that they do not include a large part of the world. However, companies from countries that have a weak equity market, which is true of most countries in Latin America, Asia, and Africa, tend to be more tax and legal oriented and fit in the weak equity part of Figure 18.9. Some companies from the developing countries list on a global stock market, such as the New York Stock Exchange, and they will be much more optimistic and transparent than if they had decided to stay in their local markets to raise capital.

> Countries can be distinguished between those with strong and weak equity market and shareholder orientations.

Differences in Financial Statements   The bottom line is that MNEs need to adjust to different accounting systems around the world, thus making the accounting function more complex and costly. The financial statements of a company, for example, include not only the statements themselves but also the accompanying footnotes. Companies that list on stock exchanges usually provide an income statement, a balance sheet, a statement of stockholder equity, a cash flow statement, and detailed footnotes as an important part of their annual report.

The financial statements of one country differ from those in another country in four major ways:

> Major reporting issues:
> - Language.
> - Currency.
> - Type of statements.
> - Financial statement format.
> - Extent of footnote disclosures.
> - Underlying GAAP on which the financial statements are based.

1. Language
2. Currency
3. Type of statements (including format and extent of footnote disclosure)
4. Underlying GAAP on which the financial statements are based

Differences in Language   As far as language goes, English tends to be the first choice of companies choosing to raise capital abroad. For example, the German company DaimlerChrysler issues financial statements in both German and English. The Swedish telecommunications company, Ericsson, provides its annual report in Swedish and English.[8]

Many companies also provide a significant amount of information on their home pages on the Internet in different languages. Managers can just click on the desired language button, and all the information is provided in that language. For example, Ericsson has a home page full of information for people all over the world. The company even has a link, www.ericsson.com.br, which gives financial information, as well as general information, in Portuguese for Brazilian readers. However, on its Brazilian link, it provides links to its annual report only in English and Swedish.

Differences in Currency   A second issue in classifying systems is currency. Companies around the world prepare their financial statements in different currencies. DaimlerChrysler presents its financial statements in euros. Ericsson presents its financial statements in Swedish kronor. Intel presents its financial statements in U.S. dollars.[9] In its 2006 annual report, Adidas discloses information on the firm's currency translation policies and gives exchange rates between the euro and the U.S. dollar, the British pound, and the Japanese yen.[10]

Differences in Types of Statements   Financial statement format is not a big issue, but it can be confusing for a manager to read a balance sheet prepared in an analytical format when the manager is used to seeing it in the balance format. A major area of difference is the use of footnotes. Footnote disclosures in the United States tend to be the most comprehensive in the world. For example, U.S. companies go into great detail describing the way certain information is determined as well as the detail behind the numbers. Greater transparency is synonymous with more extensive footnote disclosures. Companies that list on multiple stock exchanges, such as DaimlerChrysler, have extensive footnotes as well because they have to comply with the reporting requirements of the countries where they list.

Major approaches to dealing with accounting and reporting differences:

- Mutual recognition.
- Reconciliation to local GAAP.
- Recasting of financial statements in terms of local GAAP.

Differences in GAAP Usage   Finally, the most problematic area is that of differences in underlying GAAP. A major hurdle in raising capital in different countries is dealing with widely varying accounting and disclosure requirements. Although this problem is decreasing as more stock exchanges and countries allow the use of International Financial Reporting Standards, some countries care more about those differences than others.

THE PRINCIPLE OF MUTUAL RECOGNITION   Before the rise in importance of global capital markets, it was common for most countries to apply the principle of **mutual recognition.** That means that a regulator, such as the German stock exchange, would accept financial statements provided in the GAAP of a foreign issuer, such as U.S. GAAP by a U.S. company wanting to list securities in Germany. However, this practice is changing as European companies, and many others, are adopting International Financial Reporting Standards. DaimlerChrysler points out in its 2006 annual report that the consolidated financial statements through 2006 were prepared in U.S. GAAP, with other reports (according to IFRS and some German accounting rules) available on the company Web site. However, DaimlerChrysler now uses IFRS because it's a German company and must comply with EU regulations to use IFRS.

After December 31, 2008, firms domiciled outside of the EU will be required to use IFRS if they list on European exchanges.[11] The New York Stock Exchange and NASDAQ, however, require foreign registrants either to reconcile their home-country financial statements with U.S. GAAP or actually list in U.S. GAAP, the practice followed by DaimlerChrysler until 2007 when it implemented IFRS. In the United States, this reconciliation information is provided in a document called Form 20-F, which companies must file with the SEC.

INTERNATIONAL STANDARDS AND GLOBAL CONVERGENCE

Convergence is the process of bringing different national Generally Accepted Accounting Principles (GAAP) into line with International Financial Reporting Standards (IFRS) issued by the IASB.

Historically, U.S. GAAP has been the international standard because of the size of the major capital markets in the United States and the need for companies in locations all over the world to list on these exchanges to raise capital. As mentioned earlier, the SEC has allowed foreign registrants to list on the major U.S. stock exchanges as long as they reconcile their financial results with U.S. GAAP.

Despite the many differences in accounting standards and practices around the world, a number of forces are leading to convergence:

Major forces leading to convergence:

- Investor orientation.
- Global integration of capital markets.
- MNEs' need for foreign capital.
- Regional political and economic harmonization.
- MNEs' desire to reduce accounting and reporting costs.
- Convergence efforts of standards-setting bodies.

- A movement to provide information compatible with the needs of investors
- The global integration of capital markets, which means that investors have easier and faster access to investment opportunities around the world and, therefore, need financial information that is more comparable
- The need of MNEs to raise capital outside their home-country capital markets while generating as few different financial statements as possible
- Regional political and economic harmonization, such as the efforts of the EU, which affects accounting as well as trade and investment issues
- Pressure from MNEs for more uniform standards to allow greater ease and reduced costs in general reporting in each country
- The efforts of the IASB and national accounting standards-setting groups, such as the FASB in the United States, toward convergence of accounting standards throughout the world

The International Organization of Securities Commissions accepted a core set of accounting standards issued by the IASB in which securities regulators can be confident.

The New IASC   The International Accounting Standards Committee (IASC), the forerunner of the International Accounting Standards Board (IASB), was established in 1973 and has worked toward harmonizing accounting standards by issuing a set of International Accounting Standards (IAS). The turning point in the significance of IAS came in 1995 when the **International Organization of Securities Commissions (IOSCO)** announced publicly it would endorse IAS if the IASC developed a set of core standards acceptable to it. IOSCO is significant because it is composed of the stock market regulators of most of the stock markets in the world, including the SEC in the United States. In May 2000, the IASC completed a core set of standards acceptable to IOSCO, and the securities market regulators began the process of convincing their standards setters to adopt IFRS.

In March 2001, the IASC was reorganized into the International Accounting Standards Committee and the International Accounting Standards Board. The new IASC is the parent entity of the IASB, which assumed the major standards-setting functions of the old IASC.[12] A sister organization, the International Federation of Accountants, was established in 1977 at the same time the IASC was formed, and its major responsibilities are to deal with issues that affect accountants, such as ethics, auditing standards, educational requirements, certification requirements, and so on.

Trustees for the IASC foundation search for and appoint members of the IASB. The trustees come from countries all over the world, although the developing countries are not as represented as the developed countries are. Although the IASB members are not chosen for geographic reasons, they come from industrial countries where an investor orientation is widely established.[13]

International Financial Reporting Standards (IFRS)   When the IASB was organized, all of the old International Accounting Standards from the IASC were adopted, and the board then began to go through each standard to upgrade them. Then the board began to issue new standards, called **International Financial Reporting Standards (IFRS).** Thus when we use the term *IFRS*, we refer to the new standards as well as the old IAS.

> The IASB is attempting to harmonize accounting standards through issuing International Financial Reporting Standards (IFRS).

According to the IASB itself, its objectives are fourfold:

(a) [T]o develop, in the public interest, a single set of high quality, understandable and enforceable global accounting standards that require high quality, transparent and comparable information in financial statements and other financial reporting to help participants in the world's capital markets and other users make economic decisions; (b) to promote the use and rigorous application of those standards; (c) in fulfilling the objectives associated with (a) and (b), to take account of, as appropriate, the special needs of small and medium-sized entities and emerging economies; and (d) to bring about convergence of national accounting standards and International Accounting Standards and International Financial Reporting Standards to high quality solutions.[14]

THE EU AND THE IASC   To enhance the harmonization process, the EU supported the efforts of the IASB. In the spring of 2002, the EU directed its member countries to adopt International Accounting Standards, as set forth by the IASB, by 2005. The reason for choosing the IASB is that the EU can influence IASB standards because it is represented on the IASB, and the EU also avoids funding and developing a competing standards-setting body.[15]

> The EU and other countries have agreed to require IFRS for publicly listed companies.

Two major events greatly expanded the influence and effectiveness of the IASB. The first was the decision of the EU (and European Economic Area), Australia, and New Zealand to require all of their publicly listed companies to adopt IFRS in 2005 (2007 for New Zealand).

In the case of the EU, this meant that about 7,000 publicly listed companies started using IFRS for their consolidated financial statements in 2005.[16] An exception was given to companies like DaimlerChrysler using U.S. GAAP for their consolidated financial statements. They had until 2007 to convert from U.S. GAAP to IASB GAAP. The EU also extended the deadline for IFRS adoption for companies domiciled outside the EU that list on European stock exchanges until December 31, 2008.[17]

The acceptance of IFRS has not been an easy task for the EU due to a standard on accounting for financial derivatives that is heavily opposed by the French, especially the French banks.[18] In addition, it will take a few years to know just exactly how companies from different countries actually adopt the standards.

THE QUEST FOR CONVERGENT STANDARDS   The second is the decision of the FASB and IASB to adopt a process of convergence of accounting standards. In the past, the FASB and

IASB have not exactly competed with each other, but they have maintained a professional distance. That is no longer the case. In 2002, the FASB and the IASB reached "the Norwalk Agreement." In this agreement, "the two boards pledged to use their best efforts" to achieve several goals:

1. To make their existing financial reporting standards fully compatible as soon as is practicable; and
2. To coordinate their future work programmes to ensure that once achieved, compatibility is maintained."[19]

Now the FASB and IASB have joint projects to establish new standards, they are trying to eliminate existing differences in standards in a short-term convergence project for standards that should be easy to converge, and the FASB is explicitly considering the impact of IFRS on every standard it sets.[20]

THE EUROPEAN RESPONSE TO CONVERGENCE   This convergence process has been very unsettling to some Europeans, especially the French, because they feel the close cooperation of the two boards is making the new IFRS suspiciously similar to standards issued by the FASB. The fact that several Americans are on the IASB is further evidence to them that the board does not have a strong enough European presence and influence.

The board is examining a new constitution that will broaden representation of other countries on the foundation and the board, but the Europeans would like to see the IASB have a distinctly European flavor to establish standards that are more "European." This is another good example of how culture and tradition come into play, even though the standards are supposed to be for investors worldwide.

Initial reactions of various parties to the adoption of IFRS by European firms have been interesting. Although companies in EU countries adopted IFRS in 2005, various interpretations and applications of IFRS exist. Some companies use wide judgment in applying IFRS, and other use an adapted form of IFRS with changes or alternative interpretations based on individual country accounting treatments.

In addition, the EU's version of IFRS and the IASB's version of IFRS are different from each other. In our closing case, we'll examine the process by which Ericsson, a Swedish telecommunications company, has configured an EU version of IFRS as a means of responding to its particular needs in generating financial statements. Differences in opinion exist on how IFRS should be applied across borders, even within the European Union. The Accounting Regulatory Committee of the European Commission must "recommend endorsement" of the new standards and interpretations, which must then be followed by an adoption of the new standards and interpretations by the European Commission itself.[21]

Concerns have also arisen as to how the new rules will be enforced. If companies disclose that their financial statements have been issued according to IFRS, it is up to the independent external auditors to verify that companies are complying with IFRS. That principle implies the quality of the audit profession is the same worldwide, a dubious assumption. In Table 18.1, researchers Brown and Tarca (2005) classify the differences between actual and proposed enforcement/regulatory groups for four major European countries.

As Table 18.1 illustrates, France has the most restrictive/powerful regulatory body. We can also see traditional differences between the regulatory bodies of each country. For example, France's regulatory body is a government group, whereas the regulatory body in the United Kingdom is a private group. In addition, we can see the laissez-faire approach of the British in that they, as of 2003, did not have "proactive surveillance" as defined in Table 18.1, although a proposal for this practice came about in 2005.

From this chart, we can infer that differences in regulatory powers and structures may yield differences in the application of the accounting rules (IFRS). It will be interesting to observe just how IFRS are applied and enforced in countries where these standards have been adopted. Also, the adoption of IFRS in the EU is only applicable to companies

TABLE 18.1 Classifying European Regulatory Bodies

The table compares the bodies (both current and proposed) responsible for enforcing reporting and auditing practices in four different European countries. In France, for example, that body is a government agency with a broad range of both activities and powers. In the United Kingdom, on the other hand, responsibility is in the hands of a private-sector body whose activities and powers are more limited.

	France (COB)	United Kingdom (FRRP)	Germany (proposal)	Netherlands (proposal)
Enforcement body				
Type	Stock exchange regulator	Review panel	Review panel and government body	Stock exchange: regulator—AFM
Structure	Government body	Private sector	Government body and private sector	Government body
Date established	1967	1991	Before 2005	Before 2005
Activities				
Reactive investigation	Yes	Yes	Yes	Yes
Proactive surveillance	Yes	No (2003) Proposed (2005)	Yes	Yes
Issue accounting guidance statements	Yes	No	No	No
Provide pre-clearance	Yes	No	No	No
Powers				
Public statement	Yes	Yes	Yes	Yes
Levy line	Yes	No	To be decided	To be decided
Refer to courts for sanctions	Yes	Yes	Yes	Yes
De-list company	Yes	No	No	No

Source: From Philip Brown and Ann Tarca, "A Commentary on Issues Relating to the Enforcement of International Reporting Standards in the EU," *European Accounting Review* 14:1 (2005): 181–212. Reprinted by permission of the European Accounting Association and Routledge Journals, Taylor & Francis Group Ltd.

that are publicly traded. Private companies must still use local GAAP until the IASB can settle on standards for smaller, nonlisted companies, also referred to as *small- and medium-sized entities, or SMEs.*[22]

CONVERGENCE AND MUTUAL RECOGNITION The move to convergence adds an interesting twist to mutual recognition. Today's version of mutual recognition is that the United States might allow foreign issuers to list in the country using IFRS without reconciliation to U.S. GAAP. Recently, representatives of the SEC and the U.S. Treasury have made statements that support the mutual recognition of IFRS in the United States. The chairman of the SEC, Christopher Cox, on March 6, 2007, stated that "the Roadmap—an SEC plan addressing international convergence of accounting standards

> The SEC may soon allow U.S.-listed firms to report financial results using IFRS.

> . . . *commits us to eliminating the current U.S. GAAP reconciliation requirement, with the result that eligible firms listing on U.S. exchanges could choose whether to report under IFRS or U.S. GAAP. If an issuer chose IFRS, it would not be required to reconcile the differences with GAAP—just as today, issuers reporting under U.S. GAAP aren't required to reconcile the differences with IFRS.*[23]

Added U.S. Treasury Secretary Henry M. Paulson:

> *U.S. public markets should not be closed off to companies that adhere to high quality internationally accepted accounting standards. The Treasury Department is supportive of the SEC's action to eliminate the U.S. GAAP reconciliation requirement by 2009 of International Financial Reporting Standards reporting companies and the continued convergence of U.S. GAAP and IFRS.*[24]

In the past, some have been skeptical as to whether convergence between U.S. GAAP and IFRS would ever occur. Although not complete convergence of standards, recognition of IFRS in the United States, without reconciliation to U.S. GAAP, is certainly a large step in the direction of convergence.

Point Counterpoint

Should U.S. Companies Be Allowed to Close the GAAP?

Point **Yes** A major issue for investors around the world is obtaining reliable, comparable financial statement information for company evaluation and comparison. Investors, as well as creditors and other users, need reliable, comparable financial statement information to make well-informed decisions on a global basis. As the business world has shifted from being composed of domestic economies to a global economy, the need for a single set of financial reporting standards has never been greater.

U.S. GAAP and IFRS are the two most recognized sets of standards today and are steadily becoming nearly identical to each other. The combined efforts of the IASB and the FASB in their convergence project have brought the gap between IFRS and U.S. GAAP closer than ever before. The SEC should allow foreign firms that list on U.S. exchanges, as well as U.S. firms, to use IFRS for financial reporting. Not only would allowing IFRS to be used by U.S. companies make the United States more a part of the global economy, but also it would allow U.S. firms to raise more capital because investors in countries that use IFRS would be more familiar and able to keep up with the single, international set of standards.

In addition, allowing U.S. companies to use IFRS would benefit U.S. investors: They would become more familiar with the international standards and would feel more apt to invest in international companies. As the gap between IFRS and U.S. GAAP is becoming increasingly small or immaterial, the quality of the financial information presented under IFRS will not be lower than it has been under GAAP.

The "principles-based" approach of IFRS may actually enhance the quality of financial information and help the economy avoid some of the scandals that have occurred due to manipulation of loopholes in the more "rules-based" system that is U.S. GAAP. Principles-based accounting means that the standards-setter identifies key principles in a conceptual framework used to set standards and then tries to establish rules that are simple but conform to the key principles. A rules-based system is very legalistic with lots of detail and difficulty. ●

Counterpoint **No** It is unrealistic to assume that the European-based standards (IFRS) of the IASB would be appropriate for the unique environment that is the U.S. economy. The U.S. economy is the largest in the world and thus should have the most stringent financial reporting standards in the world. Many companies around the world continue to prepare their financial information in accordance with U.S. GAAP because it has been, historically, the most reliable set of standards in the world, designed to present information that is both relevant and reliable.

Allowing U.S. companies to use IFRS would impose tremendous costs on the U.S. economy. Publicly traded firms would need trained employees proficient in the application of IFRS. Accounting firms in the United States would be responsible for training their existing auditors in IFRS, hiring new employees and training them in IFRS, or hiring existing experts in IFRS. This training and/or hiring would impose tremendous burdens in both time and money on these important firms that would still be held responsible for meeting all of the rigorous standards of the Public Company Accounting Oversight Board (PCAOB) and the Sarbanes-Oxley Act of 2002.

The difference between IFRS and U.S. GAAP, although growing more insignificant, still exists. The standards are not directly comparable. This possible lack of comparability between financial statements presented in accordance with IFRS and those presented in accordance with U.S. GAAP could mean trouble for investors, who may have difficulty seeing the difference between the two sets of standards.

In addition, more than one set of IFRS seems to exist: (1) IFRS as issued by the IASB, (2) IFRS as adopted by the EU, and (3) IFRS as applied/adopted on an individual country basis. How will investors ascertain which set of IFRS are being used by various companies, and how will this information be comparable?

Finally, valuable invested money may leave the United States and be invested in foreign corporations not even listed in the country as U.S. investors become more expert in analyzing financial statements prepared in accordance with IFRS. Finally, more accounting scandals could result when U.S. companies use the more "principles-based" IFRS instead of the more "rules-based" U.S. GAAP because there is more room for interpretation and discretion when applying IFRS. ●

Transactions in Foreign Currencies

When a company operates outside the domestic market, it must concern itself with the proper recording and subsequent accounting of assets, liabilities, revenues, and expenses that are measured or denominated in foreign currencies. These transactions can result from the purchase and sale of goods and services as well as the borrowing and lending of foreign currency.

RECORDING TRANSACTIONS

Any time an importer has to pay for equipment or merchandise in a foreign currency, it must trade its own currency for that of the exporter to make the payment. Assume Sundance Ski Lodge, a U.S. company, buys skis from a French supplier for 28,000 euros when the exchange rate is $1.1000/euro. Sundance records the following in its books:

Purchases	5,500	
Accounts payable		5,500
€5,000 @ 1.1000		

If Sundance pays immediately, there's no problem. But what happens if the exporter extends 30 days' credit to Sundance? The original entry would be the same as the one here, but during the next 30 days, anything could happen. If the rate changed to $1.1500/euro by the time the payment was due, Sundance would record a final settlement as:

Accounts payable	5,500	
Foreign-exchange loss	250	
Cash		5,750

The merchandise stays at the original value of $5,500, but there is a difference between the dollar value of the account payable to the exporter ($5,500) and the actual number of dollars the importer must come up with to purchase the euros to pay the exporter ($5,750). The difference between the two accounts ($250) is the loss on foreign exchange and always recognized in the income statement.

The company that denominates the sale or purchase in the foreign currency (the importer in the current case) must recognize the gains and losses arising from foreign-currency transactions at the end of each accounting period, usually quarterly. In the example here, assume the end of the quarter has arrived and Sundance still has not paid the French exporter. The skis continue to be valued at $5,500, but the payable has to be updated to the new exchange rate of $1.1500/euro. The journal entry would be

Foreign-exchange loss	250	
Accounts payable		250

The payable now would be worth $5,750. If settlement was made in the month following the end of the quarter and the exchange rate remained the same, the final entry would be:

Accounts payable	5,750	
Cash		5,750

If the U.S. company were an exporter and anticipated receiving foreign currency, the corresponding entries (using the same information as in the example here) would be:

Accounts receivable	5,500	
Sales		5,500
Cash	5,750	
Foreign-exchange gain		250
Accounts receivable		5,500

> Foreign-currency receivables and payables give rise to gains and losses whenever the exchange rate changes. Transaction gains and losses must be included in the income statement in the accounting period in which they arise.

In this case, a gain results because the company received more cash than if it had collected its money immediately.

CORRECT PROCEDURES FOR U.S. COMPANIES

The procedures that U.S. companies must follow to account for foreign-currency transactions are found in Financial Accounting Standards Board Statement No. 52, "Foreign Currency Translation." Statement No. 52 requires companies to record the initial transaction at the spot exchange rate in effect on the transaction date and to record receivables and payables at subsequent balance sheet dates at the spot exchange rate on those dates. Any foreign-exchange gains and losses that arise from carrying receivables or payables during a period in which the exchange rate changes are taken directly to the income statement.[25] This is basically the same procedure required by the IASB as well in IAS 21.

> The FASB requires that U.S. companies report foreign-currency transactions at the original spot exchange rate and that subsequent gains and losses on foreign-currency receivables or payables be put on the income statement. The same procedure must be followed according to IFRS.

Translating Foreign-Currency Financial Statements

> Translation—the process of restating foreign-currency financial statements.

Even though U.S.-based MNEs receive reports originally developed in a variety of different currencies, they eventually must end up with one set of financial statements in U.S. dollars to help management and investors understand their worldwide activities in a common currency. The process of restating foreign-currency financial statements into U.S. dollars is called **translation.** The combination of all of these translated financial statements into one is **consolidation.** The same concept exists for other countries, such as a British-based MNE that has to come up with a set of financial statements in British pounds. For the sake of illustration, we use a U.S.-based MNE.

Translation in the United States is a two-step process:

> Consolidation—the process of combining the translated financial statements of a parent and its subsidiaries into one set of financial statements.

1. *Companies recast foreign-currency financial statements into statements consistent with U.S. GAAP.* This occurs because a U.S. company with a subsidiary in Brazil, for example, must keep the books and records in Brazil according to Brazilian GAAP. For consolidation purposes, however, the resulting financial statements have to be issued according to U.S. GAAP in format as well as content. As an example of content, Brazil might require that inventories be valued a certain way. For the U.S. consolidated financial statements, however, inventories must be valued according to U.S., not Brazilian, standards.

2. *Companies translate all foreign-currency amounts into U.S. dollars.* FASB Statement No. 52 describes how companies must translate their foreign-currency financial statements into dollars. All U.S. companies, as well as foreign companies that list on a U.S. exchange, must use Statement No. 52.

TRANSLATION METHODS

Statement No. 52 and IAS 21, the relevant translation standards issued by the FASB and IASB, are basically the same in how they require MNEs to translate their foreign-currency financial statements into the currency of the parent's country. For simplicity's sake, we continue to use the example of a U.S.-based MNE that must translate its foreign-currency financial statements into dollars. As noted earlier, the same would be true of a British MNE that must translate foreign-currency financial statements into British pounds. In the first case, the U.S.-based MNE would use FASB Statement 52, and in the second case, the British-based MNE would use IAS 21. The two standards yield the same result.

Two Methods: Current Rate and Temporal Both standards allow companies to use either of two methods in the translation process: the **current-rate method** (called the closing rate method by the IASB) or the **temporal method.** The method the company chooses depends on the **functional currency** of the foreign operation, which is the currency of the primary economic environment in which that entity operates.

For example, one of Coca-Cola's largest operations outside the United States is in Japan. The primary economic environment of the Japanese subsidiary is Japan, and the functional currency is the Japanese yen. The FASB identifies several factors that can help management determine the functional currency. Among the major factors are cash flows, sales prices, sales market data, expenses, financing, and transactions with other entities within the corporate group. For example, if the cash flows and expenses are primarily in the foreign operation's currency, that is the functional currency. If they are in the parent's currency, that is the functional currency.

If the functional currency is that of the local operating environment, the company must use the current-rate method. The current-rate method provides that companies translate all assets and liabilities at the current exchange rate, which is the spot exchange rate on the balance sheet date. All income statement items are translated at the average exchange rate, and owners' equity is translated at the rates in effect when the company issued capital stock and accumulated retained earnings.

If the functional currency is the parent's currency, the MNE must use the temporal method. The temporal method provides that only monetary assets (cash, marketable securities, and receivables) and liabilities are translated at the current exchange rate. The company translates inventory and property, plant, and equipment at the historical exchange rates (or the transaction rate according to IASB terminology), the exchange rates in effect when the assets were acquired. In general, the company translates most income statement accounts at the average exchange rate, but it translates cost of goods sold and depreciation expense, as well as owners' equity, at the appropriate historical exchange rates.

Because companies can choose the translation method—current rate or temporal method—that's most appropriate for a particular foreign subsidiary, they don't have to use one or the other for all subsidiaries. Coca-Cola operates in over 200 countries and uses 64 different functional currencies.[26] This practice is typical of most MNEs.

Figure 18.10 summarizes the selection of translation method, depending on the choice of functional currency. As in the preceding explanation, if the functional currency is the currency of the country where the foreign subsidiary is located, the current-rate method applies. If the functional currency is the reporting currency of the parent company, the temporal method applies.

Tables 18.2 and 18.3 show a balance sheet and income statement developed under both approaches to compare the differences in translation methodologies. The beginning balance in retained earnings for both methods is assumed to be $40,000. If the functional currency is the parent currency, the company uses the temporal method; if it is the local currency, the company uses the current-rate method. The following exchange rates are used to perform the translation process in Tables 18.2 and 18.3.

- $1.5000 Historical exchange rate when fixed assets were acquired and capital stock was issued
- $1.6980 Current exchange rate on December 31, 2007
- $1.5617 Average exchange rate during 2007
- $1.5606 Exchange rate during which ending inventory was acquired
- $1.5600 Historical exchange rate for cost of goods sold

Because the foreign currency was rising in value (strengthening) between the time when the capital stock was issued ($1.500) and the end of the year ($1.6980), the

The functional currency is the currency of the primary economic environment in which the entity operates.

The current-rate method applies when the local currency is the functional currency.

The temporal method applies when the parent's reporting currency is the functional currency.

FIGURE 18.10   Selecting a Translation Method

When an MNE receives reports from subsidiaries or branches located in different countries, the accounting department is faced with financial figures stated in different currencies. Accountants must *translate* these foreign-currency figures into amounts stated in the currency of the parent's home country. The *functional currency* may be either the currency of the economic environment in which the subsidiary or branch operates or the parent firm's currency, and the choice of functional currency will determine the *translation method* that the company will use.

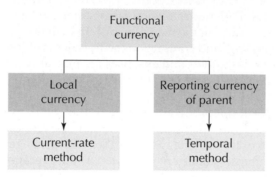

With the current-rate method, the translation gain or loss is recognized in comprehensive income rather than net income, and therefore it goes to owners' equity. With the temporal method, the translation gain or loss is recognized in the income statement.

balance sheet reflects a positive accumulated translation adjustment under the current-rate method. This is consistent with the idea that net assets were gaining value in a strong currency.

Disclosing Foreign-Exchange Gains and Losses   A major difference between the two translation methods is in the recognition of foreign-exchange gains and losses. Under the current-rate method, the gain or loss is called an *accumulated translation adjustment* and is taken to comprehensive income rather than net income, so it appears as a separate line item in owners' equity. This is important because the accumulated

TABLE 18.2   Translating Foreign Currency: The Balance Sheet

	Foreign Currency	Temporal Method Rate	Temporal Method Dollars	Current-Rate Method Rate	Current-Rate Method Dollars
Cash	20,000	1.6980	33,960	1.6980	33,960
Accounts receivable	40,000	1.6980	67,920	1.6980	67,920
Inventories	40,000	1.5606	62,424	1.6980	67,920
Fixed assets	100,000	1.5000	150,000	1.6980	169,800
Accumulated depreciation	(20,000)	1.5000	(30,000)	1.6980	(33,960)
Total	**180,000**		**284,304**		**305,960**
Accounts payable	30,000	1.6980	50,940	1.6980	50,940
Long-term debt	44,000	1.6980	74,712	1.6980	74,712
Capital stock	60,000	1.5000	90,000	1.5000	90,000
Retained earnings	46,000	*	68,652	*	77,481
Accumulated translation adjustment					12,507
Total	**180,000**		**284,304**		**305,640**

*Retained earnings is the U.S. dollar equivalent of all income earned in prior years retained in the business rather than distributed to shareholders plus this year's income. There is no single exchange rate used to translate retained earnings into dollars.

TABLE 18.3 Translating Foreign Currency: The Income Statement

	Foreign Currency	Temporal Method Rate	Temporal Method Dollars	Current-Rate Method Rate	Current-Rate Method Dollars
Sales	230,000	1.5617	359,191	1.5617	359,191
Expenses:					
Cost of goods sold	(110,000)	1.5600	(171,600)	1.5617	(171,787)
Depreciation	(10,000)	1.5000	(15,000)	1.5617	(15,617)
Other	(80,000)	1.5617	(124,936)	1.5617	(124,936)
Taxes	(6,000)	1.5617	(9,370)	1.5617	(9,370)
Translation gain (loss)	24,000		(9,633)		37,481
Net Income	**24,000**		**28,652**		**37,481**

translation adjustment does not affect earnings per share, a key figure that financial analysts monitor. From a cultural perspective, this points out how important net income is to U.S.-based companies, which rely on the stock market as a major source of funding. Under the temporal method, the gain or loss is taken directly to net income and thus affects earnings per share.

Management Accounting Issues

In the prior sections of the chapter, we discussed some important financial accounting issues that relate to preparing financial statements for external users, especially the stock markets. Now we turn to some important management accounting issues that MNEs must deal with, including *performance evaluation and control,* the *impact of transfer pricing on performance evaluation,* and the use of the *balanced scorecard* as a means of broadly evaluating performance.

PERFORMANCE EVALUATION AND CONTROL

In Chapter 15, we discussed the importance of using reports as a part of the control mechanism. The setting of strategic objectives usually requires managers to focus on choosing a suitable numeric target. Objectives can be quantified in terms of a particular budget number or financial ratio and seem to vary considerably from country to country. Possible targets include return on investment, sales, cost reduction, quality targets, market share, profitability, and budget to actual. There may also be environmental targets that companies are trying to reach, especially given that many companies must meet Kyoto Protocol goals for reducing greenhouse gas emissions.

The choice of target depends on the company, the home country, and the strategic intent—global versus multidomestic, sales versus cost minimization, and so forth. Sales or market share is particularly relevant for a unit that has no control over its input costs and whose primary purpose is to sell the goods of some other unit. Profitability, measured as a ratio or some other measure, is most appropriate for a fully fledged strategic business unit.

U.S.-based MNEs are more likely to use return on investment (ROI) as the most important measure of performance.[27] In a study of British MNEs, companies tended to use budget versus actual comparisons, followed by some form of ROI.[28] In a study of Japanese MNEs, where the culture is significantly different from what is found in the

Different measures are used to evaluate performance of foreign operations, including ROI, sales, cost reduction, quality targets, market share, profitability, and budget to actual.

CONCEPT CHECK

We introduce four "Types of Strategy," including **multidomestic** and **global**, in Chapter 11, explaining that MNEs develop **strategies** by analyzing international markets for growth opportunities, cost reductions, and risk diversification while trying to balance the competing demands of *global integration* and *local responsiveness*. Here we point out that, not surprisingly, *performance evaluation* targets must be consistent with a type of strategy. A firm with a *global strategy*, for example, works to maximize *integration*, centralizes the budgeting process, and probably targets *cost minimization* as one measure of performance.

United States and United Kingdom, it was found that sales were the most important criterion for performance evaluation.[29] As you can see, there are some major differences in selecting performance evaluation tools, and most MNEs use a variety of measures, not just one.

Performance Evaluation in the Budgeting Process   A complicating factor for MNEs is setting targets or budgets in different currencies. Either the budget will be set at headquarters in dollars (for a U.S.-based MNE) and then translated into local currency, or it will be set at the foreign location in the local currency and then translated into dollars for use at the headquarters. Either way, the MNE must deal with currency in the budgeting process.

Lessard and Lorange identify the different ways that firms can translate the budget from the local currency into the parent currency and then monitor actual performance.[30] Three different exchange rates are used in Table 18.4:

1. The actual exchange rate in effect when the budget was established
2. The rate that was projected at the time the budget was established in the local currency
3. The actual exchange rate in effect when the budgeted period actually takes place

The attractiveness of the first exchange rate is that it is an objective spot rate that actually exists on a given day. It is a reasonable rate to use in a stable environment, but it may be meaningless in an unstable foreign-exchange environment. The projected rate is an attempt on the part of management to forecast what it thinks the exchange rate will be for the budgeted time period. For example, management might project in November 2007 that the exchange rate between the U.S. dollar and the British pound will be $1.8600 during the first six months of 2008, so that would be the projected exchange rate used in the budgeting process. The actual exchange rate found in cell E-3 is an update of the exchange rate that was in effect when the budget was established. It provides the actual exchange rate in effect when the time period takes place.

TABLE 18.4   Exchange Rates and the Budget

The cells in the column headed "Rate Used to Track Performance" will vary according to the decisions made in the next three columns. If, for example, the exchange rate set for the budget is the "Actual Rate at Time of Budget" (*A-1*), then the "Rate Used to Track Performance"—the rate used to monitor the firm's performance for the budgetary period—will be the same. The cell labeled *A-3*, on the other hand, is a *projected* rate—what management *forecasts* the rate *will be* at the end of the budgetary period. To monitor performance, management will use the *actual* rate at the end of the budgetary period (*E-3*)—which may or may not conform to the rate forecast made at the beginning of the period.

Rate Used to Determine Budget	Rate Used to Track Performance to Budget		
	Actual Rate at Time of Budget	Projected Rate at Time of Budget	Actual Rate at End of Period
Actual Rate at Time of Budget	A-1	A-2	A-3
Projected Rate at Time of Budget	P-1	P-2	P-3
Actual Rate at Time of Period End (through updating)	E-1	E-2	E-3

Source: Donald R. Lessard and Peter Lorange, "Currency Changes and Management Control: Resolving the Centralization/Decentralization Dilemma," *Accounting Review* 52 (July 1977): 630.

These three exchange rates need to be considered for the establishment of the budget as well as the monitoring of performance. In cells A-1, P-2, and E-3, the exchange rate used to establish the budget and monitor performance is the same, so any variances will be due to price and volume, not the exchange rate. The value of P-2 over A-1 and E-3 is that it forces management to think initially of what its performance will be if the forecast is reasonably accurate. A-1 never takes into account what the exchange rate will be, and it does not attempt to reconcile the difference in the budget comparing the original rate with that of the actual rate. Given the instability in exchange rates, however, some would argue that a forecast exchange rate is no more accurate than any other exchange rate. E-3 does take into consideration what performance is at the actual exchange rate, but it does not force management to be forward thinking during the budget process.

A-3 and P-3 result in a variance that is a function of operating results and exchanges rate changes. Under A-3, the budget is established at the initial exchange rate, but actual performance is translated at the actual exchange rate. Thus there is an exchange rate variance that is the difference between the original and the actual rates. P-3 results in a variance that is the difference between what management thought the exchange rate would be and what it actually was at the end of the operating period. If management's forecast was reasonably accurate, P-3 should result in a very small foreign-exchange variance.

If the exchange rate between the parent and local currency is relatively stable, A-3 should also result in a relatively small foreign-exchange variance. However, it is important to realize that the use of A-3 and P-3 means that someone (usually local management) will be held accountable for exchange-rate variances.

Forecast Rates   As you can see in Table 18.5, the most widely used approaches for taking into consideration foreign exchange when comparing budget with actual performance for a sample of British MNEs are A-1, P-2, and P-3. The use of a *forecast rate* for setting budgets is by far the preferred approach. A forecast is usually made by the economists in the corporate treasury or in consultation with banks.

If the budget process is centralized, corporate treasury probably consults its lead money center bank or a couple of banks to get a consensus forecast of exchange

> When using a budget, management must select a currency to set the budget and a currency to evaluate performance.

> The most widely used approaches to translate budgets and compare with performance use forecasts of the exchange rate.

TABLE 18.5   Exchange Rates and the British MNE Budget

Note that among British MNEs, using *forecast* rates for setting budgets (*P-2* and *P-3*) is the preferred method. Both methods are also conducive to the use of *hedging strategies*—strategies, such as *forward contracts* and *options*, that allow companies to transfer risk to other parties.

| | Rate Used for Performance Evaluation | | | |
Rate Used to Determine Budget	Actual Rate at Time of Budget	Projected Rate at Time of Budget	Actual Rate at End of Budget Period	Total
Actual Rate at Time of Budget	A-1 10 Firms	A-2 0 Firms	A-3 4 Firms	14 Firms
Projected Rate at Time of Budget	P-1 0 Firms	P-2 16 Firms	P-3 11 Firms	27 Firms
Actual Rate at End of Budget Period	E-1 0 Firms	E-2 0 Firms	E-3 0 Firms	0 Firms
Total	10 Firms	16 Firms	15 Firms	

Source: Adapted from S. Demirag and Cristina De Fuentes, "Exchange Rate Fluctuations and Management Control in UK-Based MNCs: An Examination of the Theory and Practice," *European Journal of Finance* 5:3 (1999): 3–28.

rates. If the process is decentralized, the local operations probably consult one or more local banks for a consensus forecast of exchange rates. Given that most money center banks have operations worldwide, corporate treasury will receive forecasts from their money center bank's subsidiaries in countries where they have operations.

Hedging Strategies   Another interesting twist to using P-2 and P-3 is for companies that extensively use *hedging strategies*. In that case, the company may use a hedge rate instead of a forecast rate for setting budgets. Assume, for example, that a U.S.-based MNE decides to hedge its future balance sheet and income statement in Brazil by entering into forward contracts. Because management knows the forward rate, it could set its budget at the forward rate instead of a forecast rate from a bank. The variance would be the difference between the forward rate and the future spot rate.

TRANSFER PRICING AND PERFORMANCE EVALUATION

One of the additional elements of management of the multinational enterprise is **transfer pricing.** This refers to the pricing of goods and services that are transferred (bought and sold) between members of a corporate family—for example, parent to subsidiaries, between subsidiaries, from subsidiaries to parent, and so on. As such, internal transfers include raw materials, semifinished and finished goods, allocation of fixed costs, loans, fees, royalties for use of trademarks, copyrights, and other factors. In theory, such prices should be based on production costs, but in reality often they are not.

> Transfer pricing refers to prices on intracompany transfers of goods, services, and capital.

One of the important reasons for arbitrarily establishing transfer prices is taxation. However, taxation is only one of a number of reasons why internal transfers may be priced with little consideration for market prices or production costs. Companies may underprice goods sold to foreign affiliates so the affiliates can then sell them at prices that their local competitors cannot match. If tough antidumping laws exist on final products in the affiliate country, a company could underprice components and semifinished products to its affiliates. The affiliates could then assemble or finish the final product at prices that would have been classified as dumping prices had they been imported directly into the country rather than produced domestically.

> There are conflicting reasons for setting transfer prices that make it difficult for top management to select the correct price.

High transfer prices might be used to circumvent or significantly lessen the impact of national controls. A government prohibition on dividend remittances could restrict a firm's ability to maneuver income out of a country. However, overpricing the goods shipped to a subsidiary in such a country would make it possible for funds to be taken out. High transfer prices would also be of considerable value to a firm when it is paid a subsidy or earns a tax credit on the value of goods it exports. The higher the transfer prices on exported goods, the greater the subsidies earned or tax credit received.

High transfer prices on goods shipped to subsidiaries might be desirable when a parent wishes to lower the apparent profitability of its subsidiary. This might be desirable because of the demands of the subsidiary's workers for higher wages or greater participation in company profits; because of political pressures to expropriate high-profit, foreign-owned operations; or because of the possibility that new competitors might be lured into the industry by high profits.

There might also be inducements for having high-priced transfers go to the subsidiary when a local partner is involved, the inducement being that the increase in the parent company profits will not have to be split with the local partner. High transfer prices may also be desired when increases from existing price controls in the subsidiary's country are based on product costs (including high transfer prices for purchases).

TABLE 18.6   Factors Influencing High and Low Transfer Prices

Members of corporate families are constantly selling goods and services among themselves, and they can sometimes create competitive or financial advantages when determining the prices that they set on internally transferred goods and services. A wide range of factors can influence a parent company's decision to raise or lower prices charged to a subsidiary.

Conditions Conducive to *Low* Transfer Prices *from* Parent Company and *High* Transfer Prices *to* Parent Company	Conditions Conducive to *High* Transfer Prices *from* Parent Company and *Low* Transfer Prices *to* Parent Company
High ad valorem tariffs	Local partners
Corporate income tax rate lower than in parent's country	Pressure from workers to obtain greater share of company profit
Significant competition	Political pressure to nationalize or expropriate high-profit foreign firms
Local loans based on financial appearance of subsidiary	Restrictions on profit or dividend remittances
Export subsidy or tax credit on value of exports	Political instability
Lower inflation rate than in parent's country	Substantial tie-in sales agreements
Restrictions (ceilings) in subsidiary's country on the *value* of products that can be imported	Price of final product controlled by government but based on production cost
	Desire to mask profitability of subsidiary operations to keep competitors out

Source: Jeffrey S. Arpan, *Intracorporate Pricing: Non-American Systems and Views* (New York: Praeger, 1972).

Table 18.6 identifies the conditions in a subsidiary's country inducing either a high or a low transfer price on flows between affiliates and the parent. The challenge with setting an optimal transfer price is that there could be conflicting conditions in the local country. For example, a subsidiary could be in a country with a low corporate income tax rate, which calls for low transfer prices on goods shipped from the parent to the subsidiary to maximize profits at the subsidiary level, but with high political instability, which calls for high transfer prices to get money out of the country as quickly as possible.

THE BALANCED SCORECARD

The concept of the **balanced scorecard (BSC)** is another approach to performance measurement increasingly being used by companies, especially in the United States and Europe. Approximately 50 percent of *Fortune* 1000 companies in North America and about 40 percent in Europe use a version of the BSC, according to a recent survey by Bain & Co.[31] This approach endeavors to link more closely the strategic and financial perspectives of a business and takes a broad view of business performance.[32]

The BSC provides a framework to look at the strategies giving rise to value creation from the following perspectives:

> The balanced scorecard is an approach to performance measurement that closely links the strategic and financial perspectives of a business.

1. *Financial*—growth, profitability, and risk from the perspective of shareholders
2. *Customer*—value and differentiation from the customer perspective
3. *Internal business processes*—the priorities for various business processes that create customer and shareholder satisfaction
4. *Learning and growth*—the priorities to create a climate supporting organizational change, innovation, and growth

Although the focus is still ultimately on financial performance, the BSC approach reveals the drivers of long-term competitive performance. In simple terms, learning and growth help create more efficient business processes, which create value for customers, who reward

> Using the balanced scorecard helps management avoid using only one measure of performance.

the firm financially. The challenge is to clearly identify these drivers, to agree on relevant measures, and to implement the new system at all levels of the organization. The significant aspect about this measurement approach, however, is that it also creates a focus for the future because the measures used communicate to managers what is important.

Case: Internal Learning and Growth at IKEA   Although a firm's BSC is a proprietary strategic tool and generally not available to the general public, its principles are evident in the strategic decisions made by MNEs. IKEA, the Swedish firm, is a case in point. With strong roots in the Swedish culture and a centralized operating style, IKEA has grown to become the world's largest furniture retailer. The company uses a global strategy to spread a simple concept: to offer the broadest range of furniture at the lowest price possible.

IKEA's success begins with internal learning and growth by ensuring that all employees are trained in the cost-saving, hands-on, customer-focused mentality. This enables employees to focus on creating efficient processes that keep costs down. For example, the design team is constantly looking for new materials and suppliers to lower the cost of furniture without sacrificing quality.

Since its founding, IKEA has identified a customer base that would find value in low-cost, innovative furniture: young couples looking to furnish their first apartment. This strategic cohesiveness has rewarded the company with phenomenal growth. By the end of 2006, IKEA operated 237 stores in 35 countries, with sales of €17.7 billion. In 2005 and 2006 combined, it opened 36 new stores after opening 49 new stores between 1999 and 2004.[33]

Although the BSC offers the advantages of logically connecting financial performance with its nonfinancial drivers, establishing a coherent scorecard for an MNE has its challenges. For example, as IKEA grows, it faces different customer bases in different countries. IKEA must also ensure that its streamlined product line has appeal in its several markets of operation.

The cultural, geographic, and financial complexity of an MNE makes it challenging to establish a set of interrelated cause-and-effect performance measures. This task appears simpler for MNEs with global strategies like IKEA. However, multidomestic MNEs, such as Philips, the Dutch electronics company, have successfully implemented the BSC concept.

Perhaps the BSC helps solve many of the control and evaluation dilemmas presented throughout this chapter. Adequate use of the BSC helps managers avoid using only one measure of performance (such as ROI or sales growth) and forces them to link financial measures with the nonfinancial factors that drive them. In addition, subsidiaries are evaluated based on a coherent set of performance bases instead of just one base that may or may not be directly controlled by that subsidiary. Thus the BSC concept has been refined into a strategic management system, which replaces the traditional focus on the budget as the center for the management process.[34]

The crucial thing is to identify the most essential drivers for success and to look broadly as recommended in the BSC rather than to focus on a narrow financial measure. Then management must identify the most important metrics, or set of measurements, to identify how the company is performing.[35] This could be ROI, or it could also be the number of times a company is criticized for using call center employees who are not fluent in the target language of the customer.

Corporate Governance

The work of the controller is an important dimension in the overall corporate governance program that is put into place by a company. Corporate governance refers to the combination of external and internal mechanisms implemented to safeguard the assets of a company and protect the rights of the shareholders. Corporate governance is not a new concept, but corporate scandals in recent years have resulted in increased attention being given to corporate governance. A major problem at Parmalat, for example, was management collusion in diverting corporate resources into private family businesses, thus defrauding investors and creditors by means of improper accounting and reporting. In short, there was very little oversight of Parmalat's operations (and certainly none at the top).

EXTERNAL CONTROL MECHANISMS: THE LEGAL SYSTEM

An important external mechanism in corporate governance is the legal system. Countries like the United States have a very litigious environment that allows people to sue company management. Countries with a strong legal tradition, such as most developing countries, must have corporate governance practices put into law to ensure that companies will follow best practices.

Many countries, especially developing countries, have an underdeveloped and poorly functioning legal system that pays scant attention to corporate governance. Other countries have moved forward to institute corporate governance legislation. Mexico, for example, passed a law on corporate governance in 2000 to encourage more accurate financial reporting and more transparent disclosure practices by management.[36]

> Corporate governance is the external and internal factors designed to safeguard the assets of a company and protect the rights of shareholders.

The Sarbanes-Oxley Act in the United States   As a result of the corporate scandals in the United States, especially Enron, the U.S. government passed the Sarbanes-Oxley Act of 2002 (SOX), which resulted in strict reporting requirements for public firms in the United States and for foreign firms listing in the United States. In addition to the reporting requirements, SOX required stronger internal controls and tougher oversight on the part of the external auditors.

Satisfying this requirement has proved quite expensive for MNEs, especially those from other countries that list on the New York Stock Exchange (NYSE). As a result, many foreign MNEs have decided to exit the NYSE as a place to raise capital and others have decided against listing on the NYSE for the first time. Ericsson disclosed in its annual report that audit fees rose after 2002 when SOX had to be implemented, and their fees shifted as their main auditor was prohibited from engaging in certain types of consulting that it had done before SOX prohibited such activities.

> Corporate governance practices worldwide are partly a function of the legal environment in the countries where companies operate.

> The Sarbanes-Oxley Act of 2002 was passed in the United States to improve financial reporting and strengthen internal controls.

INTERNAL CONTROL MECHANISMS

Internal mechanisms refer to the management and ownership structure of the firm, and the role of the board of directors in overseeing the operations of the firm.[37] Large U.S.-based MNEs rely on the stock market as a major source of financing. Thus the firm's corporate governance system has to take into account how it protects investors and discloses information to the public.

Firms in developing countries tend to be family controlled with family members in key management positions and occupying important positions on the boards of directors. Voting rights for stocks tend to be in the hands of family members instead of outside investors. Thus the rights of minority owners are not protected very much in the absence of legal requirements. Firms from developing countries that list on foreign stock exchanges, however, have to conform more to corporate governance practices in the developed countries.

Boards of directors are now taking a stronger role worldwide, especially in the area of audit. It is more common to have an outside member of the board be responsible for the audit function, which is designed to improve the integrity of the financial reporting of the firm. The implementation of IFRS worldwide is important, but if companies don't implement strong corporate governance practices, investors will still not be safeguarded as much as they need to be.

LOOKING TO THE FUTURE

Will IFRS Become the Global Accounting Standard?

It's quite possible that IFRS will become the global accounting standard. With the adoption of IFRS by the EU, Australia, New Zealand, and others, nearly 100 countries in six continents will be requiring or permitting the use of IFRS for some or all domestic listed companies. From an accounting standpoint, the key question is this: "What will become the Coca-Cola of accounting standards—U.S. GAAP or IASB GAAP?" In other words, which will have the most recognized brand name in accounting standards?

IASB GAAP has a lot going for it, and its proponents are working hard to ensure it is accepted around the world. The IASB reaches through its board members and committees to various regions of the world by assignment to help them with adoption of or convergence with IFRS. The SEC simply sets guidelines and expects companies that wish to list in the United States to abide by these guidelines and laws.

IFRS are being set by collaboration with many of the major countries in the world, so they are the product of a great deal of negotiation, compromise, and broad-based input. They're appealing to the Europeans because they have a lot of influence in the development of its standards, and it is free of regulation by the U.S. SEC. In addition, as noted earlier, it has the backing of the EU. Finally, after 2008 the EU will no longer allow companies to list on European exchanges in U.S. GAAP. Before, a number of companies, even European companies, prepared their consolidated financial statements in U.S. GAAP so they could list in the United States as well as on European exchanges to raise capital because the European stock exchanges adopted the principle of mutual recognition. It was a lot easier to list in one set of standards instead of having to generate many different sets of financial statements.

By 2009, companies will have to list on European exchanges using IASB GAAP, and if they also want to list in the United States, they will have to list according to U.S. GAAP. However, at least the new IASB GAAP is modeled after the capital-markets orientation of the United Kingdom and the United States. At some point, it's possible that the United States will simply adopt IASB GAAP or allow it to be used for companies listing in there, eliminating the requirement for these firms to file a Form 20-F to reconcile results obtained under IFRS to those obtained under U.S. GAAP, which the SEC is working toward with its previously mentioned "Roadmap."

The major vote in favor of U.S. GAAP is that half of the world's stock market capitalization is located in the United States, and companies that want access to U.S. capital must play by U.S. rules. People in the United States have always felt their standards were the best in the world and it would be unfair for U.S. companies competing for cash in the U.S. market to allow foreign companies to list using IASB GAAP, which is perceived as more flexible and less comprehensive than U.S. GAAP. Foreign companies that want to list outside their national market typically look to the United States first and thus have to adopt U.S. reporting requirements.

An additional complication with combining or converging IFRS and U.S. GAAP is the Sarbanes-Oxley Act of 2002. This act requires companies to establish solid internal controls over financial reporting, limits the types of services that may be performed by primary auditors in addition to the financial statement audit, and requires the managers of publicly traded companies to assess internal controls and make a statement on this assessment, which must be examined and opined on by external auditors.

All of these requirements add additional costs to those already related to complying with U.S. GAAP. Although perhaps good for companies in the long term, as companies must establish effective controls over financial reporting, the initial costs of complying with the Sarbanes-Oxley Act of 2002 may be too great for some firms to consider listing on U.S. exchanges. In addition, the United States has strict laws on the granting of stock options to managers, and the U.S. market has a heightened sensitivity to wrongdoing because of recent accounting scandals, including Enron and WorldCom.

However, the convergence project between the FASB and IASB may solve some of these problems in the long run. To its credit, the IASB has expanded coverage of key topics and has narrowed the alternatives available to companies. The IASB has sold itself as based on *principles* rather than *rules*. U.S. GAAP is very rules based and complicated. However, the FASB and IASB are narrowing the differences in existing standards and developing new standards together. Now they jointly write new standards so even the wording is the same. In addition, public accounting firms and publicly traded companies have five years of experience in adopting the requirements of Sarbanes-Oxley. Maybe the future of accounting standards will be like a merger of Coca-Cola and Pepsi. ∎

Ericsson: The Challenges of Listing on Global Capital Markets and the Move to Adopt International Financial Reporting Standards

In 2002, the European Union mandated that its member countries adopt International Financial Reporting Standards (IFRS) as the basis for preparing and issuing consolidated financial statements beginning in 2005.[38] Ericsson, the Swedish MNE that supplies products and services to the world's largest mobile and fixed network operators, is a public limited liability company that must follow the Swedish Companies Act and the listing requirements of the Swedish Stock Exchange. In addition, it must comply with the listing requirements of the London Stock Exchange and NASDAQ in the United States because it lists securities on both stock exchanges. Given that Sweden is a member of the EU, Ericsson was required to adopt IFRS as of 2005, which is a change from its past practices. However, there are currently two sets of IFRS: (1) EU-approved IFRS and (2) IFRS as issued by the International Accounting Standards Board (IASB).

Should Ericsson adopt the full IFRS or just the more limited EU-approved IFRS? What are the implications of its decision on its listing on NASDAQ, and what are some of the other issues Ericsson has to face as a result of its decision to raise capital outside of its home market, Sweden?

A Little More About Ericsson

L. M. Ericsson was founded in Sweden in 1876 and is best known to the casual consumer through a Sony Ericsson joint venture that sells cellular handsets worldwide. However, it fits in the broader network of the communications equipment industry. Although Ericsson is known as one of Sweden's premier MNEs, it generates 29 percent of its sales in Western Europe; 28 percent in Central and Eastern Europe, the Middle East, and Africa; and 45 percent in Asia Pacific but only 9 percent each in Latin America and North America.

It issues stock in three major stock markets: Stockholm, London, and NASDAQ. Thus it raises capital from investors internationally and generates most of its sales outside of its native Sweden. In fact, only 3.6 percent of its sales are generated in Sweden, even though 58.4 percent of its assets and 29.9 percent of its employees are located there. Ericsson's major competitors are Nokia, Motorola, Cisco Systems, and Alcatel-Lucent, and it is considered to be the fourth largest company in the industry.

Before the Changeover to IFRS

Prior to the move to IFRS in 2005, Ericsson reported its financial results in compliance with Swedish GAAP—a bit of a mixture between Anglo-American accounting, which is driven by the capital markets, and Germanic accounting, which is driven by bank financing and taxation. Swedish reporting tends to be a little more transparent than German accounting but less transparent than Anglo-American accounting.

Issues of Transparency

One of the reasons why Swedish accounting has been less transparent is its orientation to creditors, government, and tax authorities. However, companies like Ericsson have had to become more transparent because of their desire to raise capital on foreign stock exchanges. In addition, because the Swedish Stock Exchange has become a focal point for listings by Nordic companies, the influential Swedish accounting profession has pushed for consolidated accounts to represent the needs of shareholders, whereas the parent company accounts have reflected Swedish legal requirements. Swedish accounting tends to be very conservative due to the importance of taxes to fund extensive social welfare programs and the tendency of the Swedish government to use tax policies to influence investment in areas deemed important to the government and its social objectives.

Sweden and the EU

Since Sweden entered the EU, Swedish accounting has evolved to incorporate EU accounting directives and philosophies. The Swedish government established an Accounting Standards Board (BFN) in 1976 to recommend accounting principles that fit within the framework of the Company Law. The Swedish Financial Accounting Council (RR) was established in 1991 to take over the role of the accounting profession in making recommendations on accounting practices, especially with respect to how to prepare an annual report according to the Annual Accounts Act.

The Swedish Stock Exchange has supported the efforts of the Accounting Council and the BFN, even though the recommendations of both bodies are voluntary and subject to the Company Law. However, the decision by the EU to require firms to use IFRS for consolidated financial statements takes precedence over everything for consolidated financial statements.

The Gap Between U.S. GAAP and Swedish GAAP

In its 2004 annual report, Ericsson still disclosed information according to the Swedish Company Law, although it knew by then it would have to adopt IFRS the following year. Because so many IFRS were still being finalized in 2004, it did not "early adopt" the new standards. In its Note on Accounting Policies, Ericsson stated that it prepared its consolidated and parent company financial statements "in accordance with accounting principles generally accepted in Sweden." However, it also mentioned that "these accounting principles differ in certain respects from generally accepted accounting principles in the United States (US GAAP)" and it gave a description of those differences in a later footnote in the report.

Even though it was trading shares on the London Stock Exchange, it did not make any reference to differences between Swedish GAAP and U.K. GAAP. This is because the London Stock Exchange does not require a reconciliation like the U.S. exchanges do.

Applying the Conservatism Index   In its Note to the Financial Statements detailing the differences between Swedish GAAP and U.S. GAAP, Ericsson mentions that the major differences are the treatment of capitalization of development expenses, provisions for restructuring, pension costs, hedge accounting, and goodwill. The overall difference in income is fairly significant. Using *Gray's conservatism index*, we can calculate the degree to which Ericsson's net income in 2004 was more or less conservative than U.S. income. We gain this information from Ericsson's Form 20-F, which provides a reconciliation from foreign GAAP to U.S. GAAP required by the SEC for U.S.-listed companies (see Table 18.7).

Given that Sweden is more driven by conservatism and tax issues, one would expect Swedish GAAP income to be more conservative than U.S. GAAP income. The index of conservatism for 2004 is computed as follows:

$$\text{Index} = 1 - \frac{\text{U.S. GAAP earnings} - \text{Swedish GAAP earnings}}{\text{U.S. GAAP earnings}}$$

or

$$\text{Index} = 1 - \frac{(14{,}386 - 19{,}024)}{14{,}386} = 1.3224$$

This result implies that Swedish GAAP income was less conservative than U.S. GAAP income. For example, under U.S. GAAP, the cost of developing new products must be expensed in the period it occurs, which lowers net income. In Sweden, development costs can be capitalized, which means they don't show up as expenses for the period, thus resulting in higher income. That was one of the largest adjustments for 2004, so Swedish net income had to be reduced by the amount of development costs amortized to get U.S. GAAP net income.

TABLE 18.7   Ericsson's Form 20-F: Net Income Reconciliation, 2004

Adjustment of Net Income	2004	2003	2002
Net income as reported per Swedish GAAP	19,024	−10,844	−19,013
U.S. GAAP adjustments before taxes:			
Pensions	−245	−840	412
Pension premium refund	—	—	47
Capital discount on convertible debentures	—	179	124
Goodwill amortization	475	1,636	1,064
Sale-leaseback	352	682	113
Hedging	−2,915	1,603	2,884
Capitalization of development costs for products			
to be sold	−2,606	−4,798	−4,018
for internal use	−131	−355	−922
Restructuring costs	−1,354	1,225	−1,240
Unrealized gains and losses on available-for-sale securities	−82	370	−370
Other	37	12	35
Tax effect of U.S. GAAP adjustments	1,831	533	966
Net income in accordance with U.S. GAAP	**14,386**	**−10,597**	**−19,918**
Earnings per share in accordance with U.S. GAAP			
Earnings per share per U.S. GAAP, basic	0.91	−0.68	−1.58
Earnings per share per U.S. GAAP, diluted	0.91	−0.68*	−1.58*
Average number of shares, basic per U.S. GAAP (million)	15,829	15,823	12,573
Average number of shares, diluted per U.S. GAAP (million)	15,855	15,831	12,684

*Potential ordinary shares are not considered when their conversion to ordinary shares would increase earnings per share.

Source: Telefonaktiebolaget LM Ericsson, *Ericsson Annual Report on Form 20-F 2004,* www.ericsson.com (accessed May 31, 2007).

In addition to these differences, Ericsson mentioned in its report that in 2004 it had adopted a new U.S. accounting standard issued by the FASB (FIN 46R—Consolidation of Variable Interest Entities) and that it planned to adopt two other U.S. standards and pronouncements in 2005 (SFAS 123R—Share Based Payments and SFAS 151—Inventory Costs). This is interesting because Ericsson already knew it was going to adopt IFRS the next year. Why, then, did it continue to adopt U.S. standards?

Impact of IFRS on Ericsson's Results

In the Note on Accounting Policies in its 2004 annual report, Ericsson disclosed that from 2005, it would prepare its financial statements according to IFRS. It also mentioned that the IFRS that were likely to have the greatest impact on income and shareholder's equity were standards regarding capitalization of development costs, business combinations, share-based payments, and financial instruments.

Conversion Costs

Ericsson estimated that the conversion to IFRS in 2005 would result in a difference of about SEK 1.5 billion for 2004 net income and a difference of SEK 5.7 billion for equity as of January 1, 2005. Net income under Swedish GAAP would have been SEK 17,539 million under IFRS, compared with SEK 19,024 million under Swedish GAAP. In addition, the recognition of cash on the balance sheet appears to be quite different under IFRS than it is under Swedish GAAP, with cash under IFRS being SEK 46.1 billion less than cash under Swedish GAAP. From Ericsson's Form 20-F report, one can also see that cash at the end of 2004 was the same under U.S. GAAP and IFRS.

Costs of implementing IFRS are difficult to gauge. Many countries implemented national regulations that attempted alignment with IFRS (e.g., Sweden). Thus costs of implementation may have been spread out over several years because companies knew that full IFRS implementation was drawing near. Ericsson's management notes the following in the 2004 annual report:

> Because Swedish GAAP, in recent years, has been adapted to IFRS to a high degree and as the rules for first time adopters allows certain exemptions from full retrospective restatements, the transition from Swedish GAAP to IFRS is expected to have a relatively limited effect on our financial statements. Furthermore, we believe the conversion to IFRS will align our reporting more closely with US GAAP.

After the Changeover to IFRS

As Ericsson studied the transition to IFRS, it had to decide if it wanted to adopt full IFRS or the EU-mandated IFRS, which was more limited in scope. Ericsson stated the following in its 2006 annual report:

> The consolidated financial reports as at and for the year ended December 31, 2006, have been prepared in accordance with International Financial Reporting Standards as endorsed by the EU, RR 30:05 Additional rules for Group Accounting and related interpretations by the Swedish Financial Accounting Standards Council (Redovisingsrådet) and the Swedish Annual Accounts Act. For the Company there is no difference between IFRS and IFRS endorsed by the EU, nor is RR 30:05 or the Swedish Annual Accounts Act in conflict with IFRS.

Note P1 to the Parent Company Financial Statements of Ericsson indicates that the parent company generally follows Swedish GAAP, with the following stipulation:

> The Parent Company, Telefonaktiebolaget LM Ericsson, adopted RR32 'Reporting in separate financial statements' from January 1, 2005. The adoption of RR32 has not had any effect on reported profit or loss for 2004 and 2005. The amended RR32:05 (from 2006) requires the Parent Company to use the same accounting principles as for the Group, i.e. IFRS to the extent allowed by RR32:05.

The Swedish MNE Electrolux, which lists on the Swedish Stock Exchange and trades in the United States through an American Depositary Receipt, states the following in its 2006 annual report:

> The consolidated financial statements are prepared in accordance with International Financial Reporting Standards (IFRS) as adopted by the European Union. Some additional information is disclosed based on the standard RR 30:05 from the Swedish Financial Accounting Standards Council. As required by IAS 1, Electrolux companies apply uniform accounting rules, irrespective of national legislation, as defined in the Electrolux Accounting Manual, which is fully compliant with IFRS. . . . The Parent Company's financial statements are prepared in accordance with the Swedish Annual Accounts Act and the standard RR 32:05 from the Swedish Financial Accounting Standards Council.

A careful reading of these statements indicates two things:

- The consolidated financial statements of some European companies are prepared on a different basis than parent company financial statements.
- More than one set of IFRS can be used by European companies for their consolidated financial statements: IFRS as adopted by the EU and IFRS as recommended by the IASB.

This dual standard in the EU is disturbing to the IASB.

Future Reconciliation to U.S. GAAP

As we noted in the chapter, companies may not have to file 20-F reports with the SEC in the future if the companies are in compliance with IFRS. Which set of IFRS will the SEC allow registrants to use: the EU version or the version endorsed and issued by the IASB? The EU is not allowing companies to list on European exchanges while preparing financial statements solely in conformance with U.S. GAAP after December 31, 2008. Thus, if firms want to disclose results in U.S. GAAP and list on European exchanges, they will have to report financial results in both U.S. GAAP and IFRS. The cost of using two reporting systems can be large for firms but may not be any larger than the cost currently incurred by firms that reconcile from IFRS to U.S. GAAP and from U.S. GAAP to IFRS today.

Ericsson's shares trade as "pink sheets" (securities traded over the counter—OTC—rather than on an exchange) and on NASDAQ. Because it lists in the United States, Ericsson has to prepare Form 20-F reports with the SEC. Interestingly, however, in its 2006 annual report, no reconciliation to U.S. GAAP is presented, whereas reconciliations were presented in the 2004 annual report. This change in presentation shows that the transition to IFRS is real and that companies in Europe, as well as shareholders, may consider IFRS to be at least as valid as U.S. GAAP.

Even though the reconciliation was not included in the 2006 annual report, Ericsson filed Form 20-F separately with the SEC for 2006. Table 18.8 illustrates that the difference between IFRS net income and U.S. GAAP net income was much less than that between Swedish GAAP net income and U.S. GAAP net income in 2004. ∎

TABLE 18.8   Ericsson's Form 20-F: Net Income Reconciliation, 2006

Adjustment of Net Income	2006	2005	2004
Net income attributable to stockholders of the parent company per IFRSs	26,251	24,315	17,539
U.S. GAAP adjustments before taxes:			
Pensions	−439	−64	−245
Sale-leaseback	93	191	352
Hedging	0	408	−2,915
Capitalization of development costs	−37	−78	−76
Restructuring costs	−4	120	−1,354
Unrealized gains and losses on available-for-sale securities	0	0	−82
Reversals of impairment losses	−31	−380	0
Other	93	56	82
Tax effect of U.S. GAAP adjustments	154	−73	1,085
Net income in accordance with U.S. GAAP	**26,080**	**24,495**	**14,386**
Earnings per share in accordance with U.S. GAAP			
Earnings per share per U.S. GAAP, basic	1.64	1.55	0.91
Earnings per share per U.S. GAAP, diluted	1.64	1.54	0.91
Average number of shares, basic per U.S. GAAP (million)	15,871	15,843	15,829
Average number of shares, diluted per U.S. GAAP (million)	15,943	15,907	15,855
Net income for the period from continuing operations according to U.S. GAAP	23,260	24,312	14,228
Net income for the period from discontinued operations according to U.S. GAAP	2,820	183	158
Total income for the period according to U.S. GAAP	26,080	24,495	14,386
Earnings per share from continuing operations basic	1.47	1.53	0.90
Earning per share from discontinued operations basic	0.17	0.02	0.01
Total earnings per share basic	**1.64**	**1.55**	**0.91**

Source: Telefonaktiebolaget LM Ericsson, *Ericsson Annual Report on Form 20-F 2006*, www.ericsson.com (accessed July 31, 2007).

1. What are the major sources of influence on Ericsson's accounting standards and practices?
2. What has been the impact on Ericsson's reporting of its listing on the London Stock Exchange? On NASDAQ?
3. What type of IFRS did Ericsson decide to disclose in its financial statements in 2006?
4. How would the adoption of IFRS affect Ericsson's index of conservatism in 2004? How does that compare with the index for conservatism according to U.S. GAAP? What was the index in 2006 for IFRS GAAP income reported by Ericsson and U.S. GAAP income disclosed to the SEC? What does that tell you about the convergence process?
5. Should Ericsson adopt full IFRS or IFRS as adopted by the EU? What difference does it make?

SUMMARY

- The MNE must learn to cope with differing inflation rates, exchange-rate changes, currency controls, expropriation risks, customs duties, tax rates and methods of determining taxable income, levels of sophistication of local accounting personnel, and local as well as home-country reporting requirements.

- A company's accounting or controllership function is responsible for collecting and analyzing data for internal and external users.

- Culture can have a strong influence on the accounting dimensions of measurement and disclosure. The cultural values of secrecy and transparency refer to the degree of disclosure of information. The cultural values of optimism and conservatism refer to the valuation of assets and the recognition of income. Conservatism results in the undervaluation of both assets and income.

- Financial statements differ in terms of language, currency, type of statements (income statement, balance sheet, etc.), financial statement format, extent of footnote disclosures, and the underlying GAAP on which the financial statements are based.

- Important users of financial statements that must be considered in determining accounting standards are investors, employees, lenders, suppliers and other trade creditors, customers, governments and their agencies, and the public.

- Some of the most important sources of influence on the development of accounting standards and practices are culture, capital markets, regional and global standards-setting groups, management, and accountants.

- The International Accounting Standards Board (IASB), an independent, privately funded accounting standards setter, is charged with developing a single set of high-quality, understandable, and enforceable global accounting standards. Standards developed by the IASB require transparent and comparable information in general-purpose financial statements.

- In cooperation with national accounting standards setters around the world, especially the Financial Accounting Standards Board (FASB) in the United States, the IASB hopes to achieve convergence in accounting standards.

- The possible elimination of the Form 20-F requirement for foreign companies listing in the United States and different methods of adopting IFRS are major issues that could affect the global convergence of accounting standards.

- When transactions denominated in a foreign currency are translated into dollars, all accounts are recorded initially at the exchange rate in effect at the time of the transaction. At each subsequent balance sheet date, recorded dollar balances representing amounts owed by or to the company that are denominated in a foreign currency are adjusted to reflect the current rate.

- Companies enter foreign-exchange gains and losses arising from foreign-currency transactions on the income statement during the period in which they occur. Companies enter gains and losses arising from translating financial statements by the current-rate method as a separate component of owners' equity. Companies enter gains and losses arising from translating according to the temporal method directly on the income statement.

- Many different performance evaluation measures are used for global operations, especially return on investment and budget compared with actual performance.

- In comparing budget with actual performance, MNEs need to decide which rate to use to translate the budget into the parent currency and in which currency to monitor results. Then the MNE must decide who is responsible for exchange-rate variances.

- MNEs may set arbitrary transfer prices to take advantage of tax differences between countries or to accomplish other corporate objectives, such as performance evaluation, profit manipulation, and so on.

- The balanced scorecard provides a framework to look at the strategies giving rise to value creation from the following perspectives: financial, customer, internal business processes, and learning and growth.

- Corporate governance refers to the combination of external and internal mechanisms implemented to safeguard the assets of a company and protect the rights of the shareholders. It involves improved financial disclosures and stronger internal controls with oversight by an independent board of directors.

KEY TERMS

accounting (p. 692)
balanced scorecard (BSC) (p. 715)
consolidation (p. 708)
convergence (p. 697)
current-rate method (p. 709)
Financial Accounting Standards Board (FASB) (p. 695)

functional currency (p. 709)
Generally Accepted Accounting Principles (GAAP) (p. 698)
International Accounting Standards Board (IASB) (p. 695)
International Financial Reporting Standards (IFRS) (p. 703

International Organization of Securities Commissions (IOSCO) (p. 702)
mutual recognition (p. 702)
temporal method (p. 709)
transfer pricing (p. 714)
translation (p. 708)

ENDNOTES

1 *Sources include the following:* Judith Burns, "Parmalat to Settle SEC Charges of Fraud for U.S. Bond Offering," *Wall Street Journal* (Europe), July 30, 2004; "The Pause After Parmalat," *The Economist*, January 17, 2004; Allessandra Galloni and Yaroslav Trofimov, "Tanzi's Power Games Helped Parmalat Rise, but Didn't Cushion Fall," *Wall Street Journal* (Europe), March 8, 2004; Michael Gray, Carlotta Amaduzzi, and Stephen Deane, "Corporate Governance Lessons from Europe's Enron: The Milk Sheikh Whose Dream Curdled," *The Guardian*, December 31, 2003; Peter Gumbel, "How It All Went So Sour," *Time* (Europe), November 29, 2004; Hoover's Online, "Parmalat," at www.hoovers.com (accessed April 19, 2005); Michelle Perry, "Enron: Could It Happen Here?" *Accountancy Age*, January 25, 2004; David Reilly and Allesandra Galloni, "Spilling Over: Banks Come Under Scrutiny for Role in Parmalat Scandal," *Wall Street Journal* (Europe), September 28, 2004; David Reilly and Matt Moffett, "Parmalat Inquiry Is Joined by Brazil," *Wall Street Journal* (Europe), January 7, 2004; Susannah Rodgers and Kenneth Maxwell, "Parmalat Fallout Hits Farmers; Dairies Worry About Their Future as Milk Seller Misses Payments," *Wall Street Journal* (Europe), January 15, 2004; Securities and Exchange Commission (SEC): *Complaint #18527* (29 December 2003); "Parmalat to Trim Key Operations in 10 Countries," *Wall Street Journal* (Europe), March 29, 2004; "How Parmalat Differs from U.S. Scandals," *Knowledge@Wharton* (January 28, 2004), at http://knowledge. wharton.upenn.edu (accessed November 15, 2007); Adrian Michaels, "Parmalat Case Leads to First Jail Sentences," *Financial Times*, June 29, 2005; Bruce Johnston and Caroline Muspratt, "Court Frees Daughter of Parmalat Founder," *The* [London] *Daily Telegraph*, March 9, 2004; "Daughter of Founder of Parmalat Is Freed," *Wall Street Journal* (Eastern Edition), March 9, 2004; Eric Sylvers, "In First Trial, Parmalat's Founder Charges That Banks Led Him Astray," *International Herald Tribune*, March 9, 2006; John Hooper, "Parmalat Fraudsters to Avoid Prison," *The Guardian*, June 29, 2005; Giada Zampano and Sabrina Cohen, "Parmalat Trial to Focus on Banks,"

Wall Street Journal (Eastern Edition), June 14, 2007; "Parmalat Settles Suits with Three Financial Firms," *International Herald Tribune,* June 19, 2007; "Parmalat SpA," *Wall Street Journal* (Europe), May 18, 2007; Steve Rothwell and Sebastian Boyd, "EU Backing Off Effort on Bond Transparency," *International Herald Tribune,* November 22, 2006.

2 "Basic Concepts and Accounting Principles Underlying Financial Statements of Business Enterprises," *Statement of the Accounting Principles Board No. 4* (New York: American Institute of Certified Public Accountants, 1970), paragraph 40; quoted in Earl K. Stice, James D. Stice, and K. Fred Skousen, *Intermediate Accounting,* 15th ed. (Thomson/Southwestern, 2004), p. 1.

3 Financial Accounting Standards Board, "Objectives of Financial Reporting by Business Enterprises," *Statement of Financial Accounting Concepts No. 1* (Stamford, CT: FASB, 1979), paragraphs 34–54.

4 Geert Hofstede, *Culture's Consequences: International Differences in Work-Related Values* (Beverly Hills: Sage, 1980); Hofstede and Michael H. Bond, "The Confucius Connection: From Cultural Roots to Economic Growth," *Organizational Dynamics* 16:4 (1988); Hofstede, *Cultures and Organizations* (Maidenhead, England: McGraw-Hill, 1991).

5 Sidney J. Gray, "Towards a Theory of Cultural Influence on the Development of Accounting Systems Internationally," *Abacus* (March 1998).

6 C. W. Nobes and R. H. Parker, eds., *Comparative International Accounting,* 6th ed. (Upper Saddle River, NJ: Prentice Hall, 2000).

7 Christopher Nobes and Robert Parker, *Comparative International Accounting,* 7th ed. (England: FT Prentice Hall, 2002).

8 Ericsson, *Ericsson Annual Report 2006,* at www.ericsson.com/ericsson/investors/financial_reports/annual_reports.shtml (accessed May 23, 2007).

9 Intel Corp., *Intel Annual Report 2006,* at http://media.corporate-ir.net/media_files/irol/10/101302/2006 IntelAnnualReport.pdf (accessed May 2007).

10 Adidas Group, *Annual Report 2006,* at www.adidas-group.com/en/investor/reports/annualreports/ar2006.asp (accessed July 27, 2007).

11 Deloitte Touche Tohmatsu, "International Financial Reporting Standards in Europe" (2007), at www.iasplus.com/restruct/euro2006.htm#dec2006 (accessed July 27, 2007).

12 International Accounting Standards Committee Foundation, "International Accounting Standards Board: About Us" at www.iasb.org/About+Us/About+Us.htm (accessed August 10, 2007).

13 For more details, including the members of the board and the organizational structure, go to the IASC Web site at www.iasb.org.

14 International Accounting Standards Committee Foundation, *A Guide Through International Financial Reporting Standards (IFRSs®)* (London: IASCF, 2007), p. 1.

15 "Uniform Rules for International Accounting Standards from 2005 Onwards," *European Parliament Daily Notebook,* March 12, 2002.

16 "Finance and Economics: Speaking in Tongues," *The Economist,* May 19, 2007: 77–78.

17 Deloitte Touche Tohmatsu, "International Financial Reporting Standards in Europe" (2007), at www.iasplus.com/restruct/euro2006.htm#dec2006 (accessed July 27, 2007).

18 Andrew Peaple, "Major Economies at Loggerheads over Global Accounting Rules," *Wall Street Journal* (Eastern Edition), February 8, 2004: C3.

19 Deloitte Touche Tohmatsu, *IFRSs and US GAAP: A Pocket Comparison* (London, 2007), p. 1.

20 FASB, Convergence with the International Accounting Standards Board."

21 Deloitte Touche Tohmatsu, "International Financial Reporting Standards in Europe" (2007), at www.iasplus.com/restruct/euro2007.htm (accessed July 27, 2007).

22 Deloitte Touche Tohmatsu, "IASB Agenda Project" (2007), at www.iasplus.com/agenda/sme.htm (accessed May 29, 2007).

23 Christopher Cox, "Speech by SEC Chairman: Chairman's Address to the SEC Roundtable on International Financial Reporting Standards" (U.S. Securities and Exchange Commission, Washington, DC, March 6, 2007), at www.sec.gov/news/speech/2007/spch030607cc.htm (accessed May 29, 2007).

24 U.S. Department of the Treasury, "Paulson Announces First Stage of Capital Markets Action Plan," *HP-408,* May 17, 2007, at www.treas.gov/press/releases/hp408.htm (accessed May 29, 2007).

25 FASB, "Foreign Currency Translation," *Statement of Financial Accounting Standards No. 52* (Stamford, CT: FASB, December 1981), pp. 6–7.

26 The Coca-Cola Company, Form 10-K (December 31, 2006), at http://ir.thecoca-colacompany.com/phoenix.zhtml?c=94566&p=irol-SECText&TEXT=aHR0cDovL2NjYm4u MTBrd2l6YXJkLmNvbS94bWwvZmlsaW5nLnhtb D9yZXBvPXRlbmsmaXBhZ2U9NDY5MjI3MiZhd HRhY2g9T04%3d (accessed July 27, 2007).

27 S. Robbins and R. Stobaugh, "The Bent Measuring Stick for Foreign Subsidiaries," *Harvard Business Review* (September–October 1973).

28 A. Appleyard, N. Strong, and P. Walton, "Budgetary Control of Foreign Subsidiaries," *Management Accounting (UK)* (September 1990): 44–45.

29 M. Shields, C. Chow, Y. Kato, and Y. Nakagawa, "Management Accounting Practices in the U.S. and Japan: Comparative Survey Findings and Research Implications," *Journal of International Financial Management and Accounting* 3:1 (1991): 61–77.

30 Donald Lessard and Peter Lorange, "Currency Changes and Management Control: Resolving the Centralization/Decentralization Dilemma," *Accounting Review* (July 1977).

31 A. Gumbus and B. Lyons, "The Balanced Scorecard at Phillips Electronics," *Strategic Finance* 84:5 (2002): 45–50.

32 R. Kaplan and D. P. Norton, "The Balanced Scorecard—Measures That Drive Performance," *Harvard Business Review* (January–February 1992): 71–79.

33 Inter IKEA Systems B.V., "Facts and Figures: Retail Facts" (2003–2007), at http://franchisor.ikea.com/showContent.asp?swfId=facts1 (accessed May/June 2007).

34 R. Kaplan and D. P. Norton, *The Strategy-Focused Organization* (Cambridge, MA: Harvard Business School Press, 2001).

35 Mark Hammer, "The 7 Deadly Sins of Performance Measurement and How to Avoid Them," *MIT Sloan Management Review* 40:3 (2007): 19–28.

36 Susan Machuga and Karen Teitel, "The Effects of the Mexican Corporate Governance Code on Quality of Earnings and Its Components," *Journal of International Accounting Research* 6:1 (Spring 2007).

37 D. K. Denis and J. J. McConnell, "International Corporate Governance," *Journal of Financial and Quantitative Analysis* 38:1 (2003): 1–36.

38 *Sources include the following:* Telefonaktiebolaget LM Ericsson, *Annual Report 2004* (2005), at www.ericsson.com/

ericsson/investors/financial_reports/2004/annual04/
ericsson_ar2004_complete_en.pdf (accessed May 31, 2007);
Ericsson, Form 20-F (March 23, 2005), at www.ericsson.com/
ericsson/investors/financial_reports/2004/20f.pdf
(accessed May 31, 2007); Electrolux, "Corporate Information,"
at www.electrolux.com/node60.aspx?year=2004
(accessed May 31, 2007); BMW Group, "Investor relations,"
at www.bmwgroup.com/e/nav/index.html?../

0_0_www_bmwgroup_com/home/home.html& source=overview
(accessed June 1, 2007); "Finance and Economics: Speaking in
Tongues," *The Economist*, May 19, 2007: 77–78; Ericsson, Form 20-F
(June 7, 2007), at www.sec.gov/Archives/edgar/data/
717826/000119312507131377/d20f.htm (accessed July 24, 2007);
Ericsson, Form 20-F (June 7, 2007), at www.ericsson.com/
ericsson/investors/financial_reports/2006/20f.pdf
(accessed July 31, 2007).

19

The Multinational Finance Function

Objectives

- To describe the multinational finance function and how it fits in the MNE's organizational structure

- To show how companies can acquire outside funds for normal operations and expansion, including offshore debt and equity funds

- To explore how offshore financial centers are used to raise funds and manage cash flows

- To explain how companies include international factors in the capital budgeting process

- To discuss the major internal sources of funds available to the MNE and to show how these funds are managed globally

- To describe how companies protect against the major financial risks of inflation and exchange-rate movements

- To highlight some of the tax issues facing MNEs

To have money is a good thing; to have a say over the money is even better.

—*Yiddish proverb*

CASE: GPS: In the Market for an Effective Hedging Strategy?

On April 10, 2000, U.S.-based Wells Fargo & Company and First Security Corporation announced they had signed a merger agreement of their banks in San Francisco and Salt Lake City, Utah, respectively.[1] Both banks, located in the West, were clearly positioning themselves to compete with each other, especially in the Utah market, which is composed of individuals,

Three key First Security personnel in the international banking area were Ali Manbeian, Jason Langston, and Ryan Gibbons, VP and Manager of the Foreign Exchange Department at First Security. On January 31, 2000, Manbeian had been promoted to VP and trade products manager in the International Banking Division, and Langston had been promoted to VP and foreign

MAP 19.1 **GPS, Headquartered in Utah, Started Local but Provides Foreign Exchange Services to Companies All Over the United States**

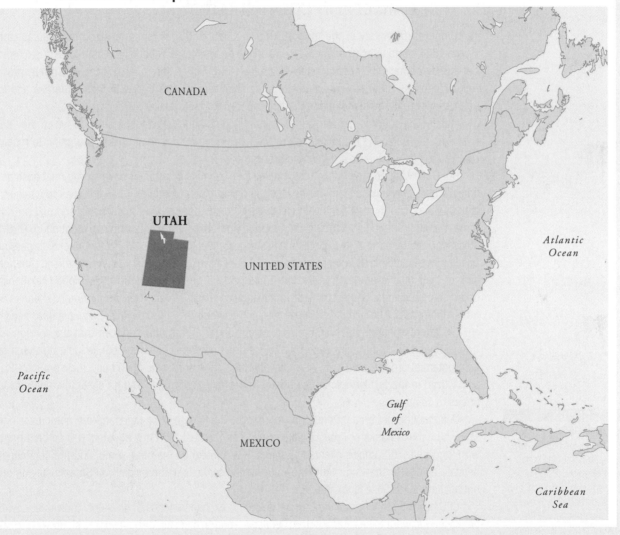

small businesses, middle market businesses, farmers and ranchers, and a few large corporate customers. Wells Fargo was operating in 22 states, whereas First Security was operating in seven states. Given the overlapping markets and client demographics, it was clear that services would be consolidated over the next several months.

exchange trader. All three had significant experience in international banking, and First Security Bank even had a trading room where they could provide foreign-exchange services and trade-related collections and payments for clients. With the merger, however, many of the more interesting businesses shifted to San Francisco, and the three could see the writing on the wall.

THE START-UP OF GPS

In 2002, with the help of some key investors, the three entrepreneurs formed Global Positioning Solutions Inc. (GPS) (Map 19.1). They realized there was a niche market in foreign exchange that was no longer being served in the Intermountain West, and they decided to strike out on their own with a business model they believed could be successful.

Bringing investors on board was essential to their success because they needed the necessary credit backing and reputation to enter the wholesale market. Without that financial backing, they wouldn't be able to access large clients and brokers. Jason Langston noted that, "90 percent of the transactions [we've] done in the past wouldn't have happened without these credible investors."

TARGET MARKET AND CLIENT STRATEGY

To compete effectively in the market, GPS decided to target medium-sized companies rather than *Fortune* 500 companies. They focused on serving companies that had significant foreign-exchange needs but that didn't have their own foreign-exchange team. With this in mind, they started out by providing the regular services that commercial banks offer. Their feeling was that with their expertise and low over-head, they would be able to outbid the larger banks for their business.

Initially, they offered the traditional inbound and outbound payments, areas in which they excelled at First Security Bank. These payments are the basic needs of companies that are going to receive or are required to pay invoices in a different currency.

But GPS was finding it difficult to obtain clients because companies have strong relationships with the banks where they have accounts. The first choice for most companies when it comes to foreign exchange is to use their commercial bank with which they already have a good relationship and that provides traditional banking services, including the inbound and outbound payments just mentioned. GPS financial advisers have overcome this obstacle with their competitors by visiting potential clients personally and building a relationship. It is more expensive as they travel to New York, Los Angeles, and other cities outside of the Rocky Mountain region, but it has paid off because they have developed relationships and obtained new clients. Some competitive advantages that GPS has over the commercial banks are lower transaction costs, 100 percent transparency, and customizing solutions to satisfy customer needs.

Commercial banks have so many different departments and services that the foreign-exchange transactions tend to be more expensive to meet the overhead. Also, the banks look at foreign exchange as a potential area to earn a lot of money, so they price aggressively to build their profits. GPS is more specialized in the foreign-exchange market and smaller so it can keep its costs low and pass on lower prices to companies.

Until the Internet brought more transparency to the foreign-exchange markets, companies often didn't know how much banks or brokers were making on the deal. GPS has adopted 100 percent transparency with its clients: GPS shows clients how much it will make on the deal, something the commercial banks hesitate doing. By showing clients the value-added services it is providing, GPS can justify its profits and not hesitate to disclose its model.

GPS has tried to focus on satisfying the foreign-exchange needs of its clients individually, whereas big banks tend to want to sell standardized services—one size fits all. GPS managers sit down with clients and discuss needs and strategies, and they come up with innovative solutions that result in more satisfactory foreign-exchange transactions. These strategies appear to be working. GPS has grown significantly since its inception.

Reuters and Bloomberg play an important role in the business of GPS. The company uses them because they have the most powerful analytical tools and real-time pricing. In spite of the high cost of subscribing to Reuters's and Bloomberg's services, GPS decided to go with both. In fact, the three partners have different preferences of which service they like the best. This has generated a friendly rivalry over the merits of Reuters versus Bloomberg. The two services provide real-time market information, analytics, and a trading platform. In addition, the services are essential as they try to price more complex foreign-exchange products such as options.

CONCEPT CHECK

We're concerned in this chapter with the *financial* aspects of **MNE** operations—in particular, with the ways in which MNEs gain access to *capital* in both local and global markets. Recall, however, our introduction of such global information providers as Reuters and Bloomberg in Chapter 9, where we refer to their role in furnishing *money center banks* with the data about **foreign exchange** that the banks pass on to client MNEs. Here, we hasten to reaffirm the importance of information and information flows in making not only **exchange-rate** transactions but a vast range of other decisions as well.

FUTURE CHALLENGES

Although GPS has never lost a client to another competitor, the future holds a number of challenges. The first challenge faces services. If GPS had stuck with its initial goal of providing traditional foreign-exchange services, it would have opened itself to significant competition with the banks and other market entrants, such as boutique firms that can focus only on the payments side in the small- and medium-sized market. So the key was in finding ways to move its clientele upstream with other value-added services. The problem was to decide what areas it should enter and where to find the expertise. What areas of corporate finance could GPS choose that would leverage its expertise in trading? All three of the founding members had banking backgrounds. Would that be enough as the company moved into new areas?

A second risk has to do with its target market. Given the merger and acquisition activity in the United States, could GPS continue to maintain its client base, or would its clients get bought out by larger firms, just as Wells Fargo snapped up First Security? If that was to happen, GPS would have to figure out how to sell its expertise to larger clients, possibly based outside of Utah with no experience or track record with GPS. That could force GPS to focus on other states or doing business with other companies.

A third risk is the potential of unfavorable new regulations. The regulatory environment of the foreign-exchange trade is intense and changes frequently. GPS will have to learn the new laws and regulations and adopt new policies and procedures to work in accordance with any new rules.

EXPANDED SERVICES: A KEY TO FUTURE GROWTH

As Manbeian, Langston, and Gibbons looked at their business, they realized the key to their future was to develop a broader base of services to their clients. As a result, they decided to focus on their strength—corporate foreign exchange—and to provide expanded services in global business risk management. The general idea of trading currencies to satisfy their initial core business of import and export transactions was simple. Some transactions went beyond exports and imports and involved derivatives to protect against future risks. With their connection to Reuters and Bloomberg, they had the capabilities necessary to enter into any transaction that the client needed.

But as they began to work with midmarket companies with operations around the world, they realized many of these companies were spending a lot of money making trades. As they analyzed the cash flows in different currencies, it was easy to see that as their clients' markets and the currencies in which they operated increased, they had to enter into more and more foreign-exchange transactions.

One of their clients, a large technology firm, was expanding internationally so rapidly that the growth was straining the capabilities of its finances to keep up with it. With hundreds of currency pairs and financial statements being generated in many different currencies and using several different functional currencies, the client was having a difficult time keeping on top of the complexities. GPS realized it could save its client a lot of money by netting its transactions. Instead of having each entity around the world settle its transactions with every other entity, GPS helped the firm set up a system that could reduce the number of times they had to exchange currency. As it did that, it reduced the costs of each transaction, an important source of revenue to the client's bank.

FXpert

GPS developed a proprietary software called FXpert to help its clients monitor foreign-exchange flows and determine how to save money on transactions. After identifying the timing and nature of the cash flows through a specialized audit, a GPS financial adviser proposes an effective hedging solution that GPS can provide. The solution might be as simple as reducing the number of foreign-currency transactions or as complex as hedging some of the exposures using forwards, options, or futures contracts. In addition to its software and trading expertise, GPS feels that one of its major strengths is its ability to provide a tailored solution.

The global risk management business also offers foreign accounts receivable review, global business consultation on global finance methods, dispute resolution on solving payment disputes, international loan packaging, and letters of credit. As it has developed these services, GPS has had to expand its expertise base to include an understanding of complex accounting rules on derivatives, complex financial hedging strategies, and software development.

Introduction

Why do you need to understand capital markets, cash management, and financial risk? Having a good product idea is not sufficient for success. MNEs need to get access to capital markets in different countries to finance expansion. Indeed, finance is integral to firms' international strategies, as Figure 19.1 shows. The small company involved in international business only tangentially may not be concerned about global capital markets, but it will probably still have to deal in foreign exchange through its commercial bank to settle payments for exports and imports. However, the MNE investing and operating abroad usually is concerned about access to capital in local markets as well as in large global markets.

This chapter examines external sources of debt and equity capital available to companies operating abroad as well as internal sources of funds that arise from intercompany links. The chapter also explores the international dimensions of the capital investment decision, global cash management, foreign exchange risk-management strategies, and international tax issues.

CONCEPT CHECK

It's worthwhile to make a quick comparison between Figure 19.2 and Figure 18.3, which focuses on the twofold responsibility of the company *controller*—overseeing activities in both accounting and financial management. Here, we focus on the responsibilities of the *treasurer*—controlling the company's cash payments and related financial functions, both domestic and foreign. As both figures show, the functions of the two offices fall under the overall responsibility of the *CFO* (or VP of Finance).

The Finance Function

One of the most important people on the management team is the chief financial officer (CFO). This chapter focuses on the CFO's most important global finance-related responsibilities. Figure 19.2 illustrates how the responsibilities of the CFO, controller, and treasurer fit into the organizational structure of the firm and especially how global financial management fits into the overall financial function.

The finance function in the firm focuses on cash flows, both short term and long term. The role of financial management is to maintain and create economic value or wealth by maximizing shareholder wealth—the market value of existing shareholders' common stock.[2] The management activities related to cash flows can be divided into these four major areas:

- *Capital structure*—determining the proper mix of debt and equity
- *Long-term financing*—selecting, issuing, and managing long-term debt and equity capital, including location (in the company's home country or elsewhere) and currency (the company's home currency or a foreign currency)

FIGURE 19.1   Factors Influencing Finance in International Business

Managing a company's finances, like conducting its marketing efforts or organizing its supply chain, is a function of implementing its strategies. The performance of this function is also subject to a variety of factors in the company's operating environment.

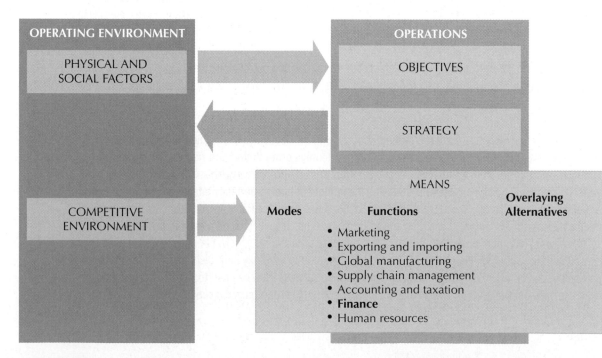

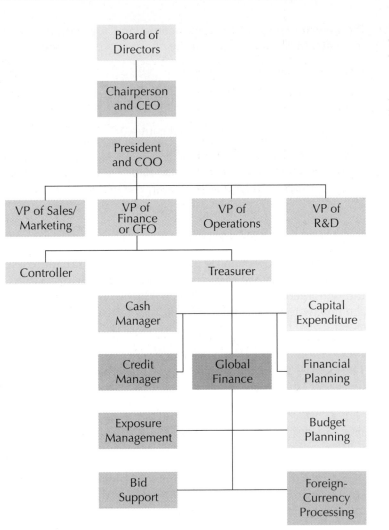

FIGURE 19.2
The Role of the Treasurer in the Financial Function

As a firm's chief accounting officer, the *controller* evaluates the financial results of business operations. The *treasurer* writes the checks—or, more precisely, controls the company's cash payments. The treasurer's department handles both domestic and foreign financial functions, including cash and exposure management, capital expenditure, and foreign-currency processing.

- *Capital budgeting*—analyzing investment opportunities
- *Working capital management*—managing the company's currency assets and liabilities (cash, receivables, marketable securities, inventory, trade receivables and payables, short-term bank debt)

In the following sections, we discuss these areas and also the impact of taxation on each of these decisions.[3]

> The corporate finance function acquires and allocates financial resources among the company's activities and projects. Four key functions are
> - Capital structure.
> - Long-term financing.
> - Capital budgeting.
> - Working capital management.

THE ROLE OF THE CFO

The CFO acquires financial resources and allocates them among the company's activities and projects. Acquiring resources (financing) means generating funds either internally (within the company) or from sources external to the company at the lowest possible cost. When GPS began, the founders needed outside investors with significant resources to fund the start-up as well as to lend credibility to potential clients. Allocating resources (investing) means increasing stockholders' wealth through the allocation of funds to different projects and investment opportunities.[4]

The CFO's Global Perspective The CFO's job is more complex in a global environment than in the domestic setting because of forces such as foreign-exchange risk, currency flows and restrictions, political risk, different tax rates and laws pertaining to the determination of taxable income, and regulations on access to capital in different markets. In the remainder of the chapter, we examine the following areas:

1. Overall capital structure
2. Global capital markets
3. Offshore financial centers
4. Capital budgeting in a global context
5. Internal sources of funds
6. Foreign-exchange risk management
7. Taxation of foreign-source income

Capital Structure

The CFO must determine the proper capital structure of the company—the mix between long-term debt and equity. Many companies start off with an initial investment and then grow through internally generated funds. However, when those sources are inadequate to fund continued growth into new markets, they have to decide the proper mix of debt and equity.

LEVERAGING DEBT FINANCING

Leverage—the degree to which a firm funds the growth of business by debt.

The degree to which a firm funds the growth of the business by debt is known as **leverage.** The weighted average cost of capital of a company is found as follows:

$$\begin{array}{l} Weighted \\ average \ \ cost \\ of \ capital \end{array} = \left[\begin{array}{l} After\text{-}tax \\ cost \ of \\ debt \end{array} \times \begin{array}{l} Proportion \\ of \ debt \\ financing \end{array}\right] + \left[\begin{array}{l} Cost \\ of \\ equity \end{array} \times \begin{array}{l} Proportion \\ of \ equity \\ financing \end{array}\right]$$

The amount of leverage used varies from country to country.

The degree to which companies use leverage instead of *equity capital*—known as stocks or shares—varies from country to country. Country-specific factors are a more important determinant of a company's capital structure than any other factor because companies tend to follow the financing trends in their own country and their particular industry within their country. Japanese companies, for example, are more likely to follow the capital structure of other Japanese companies than they are of U.S. or European companies. Leveraging is often perceived as the most cost-effective route to capitalization because the interest that companies pay on debt is a tax-deductible expense in most countries, whereas the dividends paid to investors are not.

When Is Leveraging *Not* the Best Option?   However, leveraging may not be the best approach in all countries for two major reasons. First, excessive reliance on long-term debt increases financial risk and thus requires a higher return for investors. Second, foreign subsidiaries of an MNE may have limited access to local capital markets, making it difficult for the MNE to rely on debt to fund asset acquisition.[5] In a study of foreign subsidiaries of U.S. MNEs, it was found that the debt-to-asset ratio of those studied averaged 0.545, which means that 54.5 percent of assets were funded by debt and 45.5 percent were funded by equity.[6]

Table 19.1 shows the debt-to-asset ratio on average for companies in a selected group of countries. Note the relatively higher reliance on equity capital by the U.K., U.S., and Canadian companies relative to companies from other countries in Europe and Asia, which tend to rely more on banks and family wealth. Recent research has confirmed that country-specific factors are important determinants of the capital structure of firms.[7]

FACTORS AFFECTING THE CHOICE OF CAPITAL STRUCTURE

Choice of capital structure depends on tax rates, degree of development of local equity markets, and creditor rights.

Many factors influence the choice of capital structure, both within a country and by MNEs with affiliates in different countries, such as local tax rates, the degree of development of local equity markets, and creditor rights. One study of the capital structure of foreign

TABLE 19.1   Selected Capital Structures

Because companies tend to follow financing practices that predominate in their own countries, country-specific factors are important in a firm's capital structure. Taxation is among such factors: If in a given country, for example, interest paid on debt is tax deductible and interest paid to shareholders is not, *leveraging*—funding growth by debt—may be regarded as more cost-effective than *equity financing*.

Country	Equity	Total debt	Long-term debt	Short-term debt
United Kingdom	68.3%	31.7%	N/A	N/A
United States	48.4	51.6	26.8%	24.8%
Canada	47.5	52.5	30.2	22.7
Germany	39.7	60.3	15.6	44.7
Spain	39.7	60.3	15.6	44.7
France	38.8	61.2	23.5	43.0
Japan	33.7	66.3	23.3	43.0
Italy	23.5	76.5	24.2	52.3

Source: Scott Besley and Eugene F. Brigham, *Essentials of Managerial Finance*, 13th ed. (Mason, OH: Thomson/South-Western, 2005), Chapter 9.

affiliates of U.S.-based MNEs found that local tax rates influenced the debt-to-equity ratios. Although a U.S.-based MNE, for example, might have a debt-to-equity ratio for the firm as a whole that is based on capital market expectations in the U.S. capital markets, its foreign affiliates have to be sensitive to local conditions. As noted in the study,

> Ten percent higher local tax rates are associated with 2.8 percent higher debt/asset ratios, with internal borrowing particularly sensitive to taxes. Multinational affiliates are financed with less external debt in countries with underdeveloped capital markets or weak creditor rights, reflecting significantly higher local borrowing costs. Instrumental variable analysis indicates that greater borrowing from parent companies substitutes for three-quarters of reduced external borrowing induced by capital market conditions. Multinational firms appear to employ internal capital markets opportunistically to overcome imperfections in external capital markets.[8]

In addition, different tax rates, dividend remission policies, and exchange controls may cause a company to rely more on debt in some situations and more on equity in others. It is important to understand that the different debt and equity markets discussed in this chapter have different levels of importance for companies worldwide.

Debt and the Asian Financial Crisis of 1997   One of the major causes of the Asian financial crisis in 1997 was that Asian companies relied too much on debt to fund their growth, especially bank debt. The lack of development of bond and equity markets in those countries forced companies to rely on bank debt for growth. Many of the Asian banks borrowed dollars from international banks and lent the money to local companies in local currencies, not dollars. At the time, many Asian countries pegged their currencies to the U.S. dollar, so the assumption was that if you borrow in dollars, it is the same as borrowing in the local currency. When the Asian currencies fell against the dollar, many of the banks could not service their loans and went into bankruptcy.

Some of the Asian companies that borrowed dollars directly from foreign banks couldn't generate enough local currency to pay off the debt, and they were brought close to bankruptcy. As a result, many companies were forced to exchange debt for equity, thereby losing some of their control or selling themselves outright to foreign investors who could pay off their dollar debt.[9] Argentine companies and banks also had a large amount of foreign debt, a factor that helped escalate its monetary crisis in 2002. Companies renegotiated contracts with their foreign lenders in an effort to restructure some of their loans.

A major cause of the Asian financial crisis of 1997 was excessive dollar bank debt.

DEBT MARKETS AS MEANS OF EXPANSION

An MNE that needs to raise capital through debt markets has a number of options. The local domestic debt market is the first source that a company will tap. This means Japan for Japanese companies, but it could also mean Japan for the Japanese subsidiary of a U.S. company. Nissan lists several types of long-term debt in its annual reports. In its 2005 annual report, it listed bonds in Japanese yen and U.S. dollars and listed notes in euros and U.S. dollars.[10]

Here's another example. In the early 1990s, Nu Skin, a direct seller of skin-treatment and personal-care products, embarked upon a program of expansion into Japan. In order to fund a portion of this expansion, the company borrowed capital in yen. As a result, its long-term debt ultimately included the long-term portion of Japanese yen–denominated 10-year notes issued to the Prudential Insurance Company of America in 2000. The notes bear interest at an effective rate of 3 percent per annum and are due October 2010, with annual principal payments that began in October 2004. As of December 31, 2006, the outstanding balance on the notes was 5.5 billion Japanese yen, or $46.6 million, $11.7 million of which was included in the current portion of long-term debt.[11]

MNEs have an advantage because they can tap local debt and equity markets, foreign debt and equity markets (such as the Eurodollar, Eurobond, and Euroequity markets), and internal funds from the corporate family. Most local companies are locked into local debt markets or possibly foreign debt markets, but they don't have the ability to raise funds as extensively as the local affiliates of MNEs do.

Companies can use local and international debt markets to raise funds.

Global Capital Markets

There are many reasons why currencies trade hands—for import and export transactions, foreign direct and portfolio investments, borrowing and lending money, and raising equity capital. Each country has its own debt and equity markets, but in this section, we look at the role of foreign debt and equity markets as sources of funds for MNEs.

Two major sources of funds external to the MNE's normal operations are debt markets and equity markets.

EUROCURRENCIES AND THE EUROCURRENCY MARKET

The **Eurocurrency market** is an important source of debt financing for MNEs to complement what they can find in their domestic markets. A **Eurocurrency** is any currency that is banked outside its country of origin. More specifically, a **Eurodollar** is a certificate of deposit in dollars in a bank outside of the United States. Most Eurodollar CDs are held in London, but they could be held anywhere outside of the United States. Currencies banked inside their country of origin are known as onshore currencies, and currencies banked outside their country of origin are known as offshore currencies. In essence, the Eurocurrency market is an offshore market.

A Eurocurrency is any currency banked outside its country of origin, but it is primarily dollars banked outside the United States.

A major advantage of the Eurodollar market is that it is not regulated by the U.S. Federal Reserve Bank, which is a real concern to "the Fed" because the market is offshore. The same is true for other currencies and their major regulators. The Eurocurrency market started with the deposit of U.S. dollars in London banks, and it was called the Eurodollar market. As other currencies entered the offshore market, the broader "Eurocurrency" name was adopted for market use.

Given the introduction of the euro as the new currency in Europe, the term *Eurocurrency* is now a little confusing, but the Eurocurrency market predates the euro, and the confusion isn't likely to go away. Eurocurrencies could be dollars or yen in London, euros in the Bahamas, or British pounds in Zurich. Eurodollars constitute a fairly consistent 65 to 80 percent of the Eurocurrency market. Dollars held by foreigners on deposit in the United States are not Eurodollars, but dollars held at branches of U.S. or other banks outside the United States are.

Major Sources of Eurocurrencies There are four major sources of Eurocurrencies:

- Foreign governments or individuals who want to hold dollars outside the United States
- Multinational enterprises that have cash in excess of current needs
- European banks with foreign currency in excess of current needs
- Countries such as Germany, Japan, and Taiwan that have large balance-of-trade surpluses held as reserves

The demand for Eurocurrencies comes from sovereign governments, supranational agencies such as the World Bank, companies, and individuals. Eurocurrencies exist partly for the convenience and security of the user and partly because of cheaper lending rates for the borrower and better yield for the lender.

Characteristics of the Eurocurrency Market Because the Eurocurrency market is a wholesale (companies and other institutions) rather than a retail (individuals) market, transactions are very large. Public borrowers such as governments, central banks, and public sector corporations are the major players. Although MNEs are involved in the Eurodollar market, the Eurodollar market has historically been an interbank market. Since the late 1990s, however, London banks have shifted to using nonbank customers for Eurodollar transactions. This was partly because of the introduction of the euro, the subsequent fall in foreign transactions, and consolidation in the banking sector.[12]

The Eurocurrency market is both short and medium term. Short-term borrowing is composed of maturities of less than one year. Anything from one to five years is considered a **Eurocredit,** which may be a loan, a line of credit, or another form of medium- and long-term credit, including **syndication,** in which several banks pool resources to extend credit to a borrower and spread the risk.

Interest Rates in the Eurocurrency Market A major attraction of the Eurocurrency market is the difference in interest rates compared with those in domestic markets. Of course, the domestic rates vary as well. Although the prime rate may not be the best surrogate for borrowing and lending rates, it is easy to find those numbers and use them as a basis of comparison. As of June 30, 2007, the prime rate was 8.25 percent in the United States, 4.00 percent in the euro zone, and 1.875 percent in Japan.[13] Because of the large transactions and the lack of controls and their attendant costs, Eurocurrency deposits tend to yield more than domestic deposits do, and loans tend to be cheaper than they are in domestic markets.

London Inter-Bank Offered Rate Traditionally, loans are made at a certain percentage above the **London Inter-Bank Offered Rate (LIBOR),** which is the deposit rate that applies to interbank loans within London. The LIBOR rates quoted on August 28, 2007, for Eurodollars were 5.50750 percent one month; 5.51000 percent three months; 5.42750 percent six months; 5.21250 percent one year. The rate for three-month Euro LIBOR was 4.723, which is lower than the Eurodollar LIBOR rate. This makes sense because the U.S. prime is higher than the Euro prime. However, it is very difficult to compare prime rates and the LIBOR rate because lending practices vary so much from country to country.

SUBPRIME LOANS Some financial firms lend money at rates above the prime rate, which are called *subprime loans* because the borrowers are below prime quality. These loans are made and then, at times, sold as securities by lenders to investors.[14] As variable-rate loans are made with rates below prime, problems can arise for debtors and for investors in these subprime loans as variable interest rates rise, as we found in 2007 when the housing market slumped in the United States.[15] Debtors could have a difficult time making their mortgage payments and the value of investments in subprime mortgages could decrease as debtors default.[16] This debt failure could in turn affect the market for commercial paper, a type of short-term loan, around the world.[17]

The amount of the interest rate above LIBOR that a borrower is charged all depends on the creditworthiness of the customer, and it must be large enough to cover expenses and build reserves against possible losses. Most loans are variable rate, and the rate-fixing period is generally six months, although it may be one or three months.

INTERNATIONAL BONDS

Many countries have active bond markets available to domestic and foreign investors. For example, Nissan raised money through bonds issued in Japan, the United States, and Europe. The bonds issued in yen are for ¥617 billion and mature (must be paid back) in 2007 at interest rates of 0.6 to 3.6 percent. The bonds issued in euros are for ¥17 billion and matured in 2006 at interest rates of 2.5 to 5.0 percent. Even though the domestic bond market dominates total bond issues, with the U.S. market offering the best opportunities, the international bond market still fills an important niche in financing.

One of the reasons why the bond (and stock) markets in the United States are so influential is because the companies of continental Europe and Japan still rely disproportionately on banks for finance—on average, banks constitute about 75 percent of corporate funding. That figure varies across Europe—from 70 percent in Germany and France to 80 percent in Spain, but it is much lower in Britain.[18] This situation may change, however, because banks across the world are tightening their loan outflows as a result of market collapses like the ones in Asia in 1997, and Argentina in 2002, and the subprime crisis in 2007.

Emerging bond markets have been growing more quickly than developed markets, but they are still only 5.6 percent of the total global bond market. Investors generally focus on purchasing foreign currency from emerging markets, but the bond market is four times as large as the currency market (i.e., $1,645 billion versus $432 billion). Emerging bond markets are gradually becoming an alternative source of funding for governments, corporations, and global fixed-income investors.[19]

Types of International Bonds

Foreign Bonds   **Foreign bonds** are sold outside of the borrower's country but denominated in the currency of the country of issue. For example, a French company floating a bond issue in Swiss francs in Switzerland would be selling a foreign bond. Foreign bonds typically make up about 18 percent of the international bond market. They also have creative names, such as Yankee bond (issued in the United States), Samurai bond (issued in Japan), Bulldog bond (issued in England), and Panda bond (issued in China).

> A foreign bond is one sold outside the country of the borrower but denominated in the currency of the country of issue. A Eurobond, also called a global bond, is a bond issue sold in a currency other than that of the country of issue.

Eurobonds   A **Eurobond** is usually underwritten (placed in the market for the borrower) by a syndicate of banks from different countries and sold in a currency other than that of the country of issue. A bond issue floated by a U.S. company in dollars in London, Luxembourg, and Switzerland is a Eurobond. Eurobonds make up approximately 75 percent of the international bond market.

Global Bonds   The **global bond,** introduced by the World Bank in 1989, is a combination of a domestic bond and a Eurobond—that is, it must be registered in each national market according to that market's registration requirements. It is also issued simultaneously in several markets, usually those in Asia, Europe, and North America. Global bonds are a small but growing segment of the international bond market.

What's So Attractive About the International Bond Market?   The international bond market is an attractive place to borrow money. For one thing, it allows a company to diversify its funding sources from the local banks and the domestic bond market and borrow in maturities that might not be available in the domestic markets. In addition, the international bond markets tend to be less expensive than local bond markets. However, not all companies are interested in global bonds or Eurobonds. Before the Asian financial crisis hit, Asian companies relied on their domestic banks more because of the ready availability of cheap loans. In addition, the companies and banks tended to develop a cozier relationship than might be the case with Western companies and banks.[20] However, the Asian financial crisis demonstrated the fundamental flaws in this strategy as banks went bankrupt and as companies were forced to face the fact that they couldn't generate enough funds to pay back the loans.

Although the Eurobond market is centered in Europe, it has no national boundaries. In contrast to most conventional bonds, Eurobonds are sold simultaneously in several financial centers through multinational underwriting syndicates and are purchased by an international investing public that extends far beyond the confines of the countries of issue.

U.S. companies first issued Eurobonds in 1963 as a means of avoiding U.S. tax and disclosure regulations. They're typically issued in denominations of $5,000 or $10,000, pay interest annually, are held in bearer form, and are traded over the counter (OTC), most frequently in London.[21] Any investor who holds a bearer bond is entitled to receive the principal and interest payments. In contrast, for a registered bond, which is more typical in the United States, the investor is required to be registered as the bond's owner to receive payments. An OTC bond is traded with or through an investment bank rather than on a securities exchange, such as the London Stock Exchange.

Case: Marks & Spencer: How Corporations Use Eurobonds   An example of a non–U.S. dollar Eurobond issue involves Marks & Spencer, the British retail company. In 2002, Marks & Spencer issued a £368.2 million Eurobond at a $6\frac{3}{8}$ percent fixed rate, which was stated to mature in 2011. Marks & Spencer then entered into an interest rate swap with another company in which it agreed to exchange its fixed rate obligation with a floating rate obligation.[22] An investment bank would have facilitated the swap. Marks & Spencer probably got a reasonably good Eurobond fixed interest rate because it is a British company and was issuing the bond in Eurosterling. The counterparty (the other company in the swap agreement) might have wanted a fixed rate obligation in sterling initially but couldn't get it for whatever reason, so it had to settle for a floating rate obligation.

As interest rates in Britain began to come down, it made sense for Marks & Spencer to enter into the swap to lower its overall interest charge. In a floating rate bond, the interest rate changes every six months, so as interest rates come down, the holder of the floating rate bond would end up paying lower interest to the bondholders. The holder of the floating rate bond might have wanted to trade to a fixed rate bond to eliminate the uncertainty of future interest rates and to lock in an attractive interest rate.

Another example of the use of the Eurobond market is with Gazprombank of Russia. In January 2004, Gazprombank placed a U.S. $300 million Eurobond issue with a maturity of 2008. Seventy percent of the issue went to European investors, 18 percent to offshore structures of investors from the United States, 5 percent to Asians, and 7 percent to other regions. This was one of many Eurobond issues made by Gazprombank, some denominated in dollars and some in euros. The deals were placed by JP Morgan Chase in London.[23]

Occasionally, Eurobonds may provide currency options, which enable the creditor to demand repayment in one of several currencies, thus reducing the exchange risk inherent in single-currency foreign bonds. More frequently, however, both interest and principal on Eurobonds are payable to the creditor in U.S. dollars. It is also possible to issue a Eurobond in one currency—say, the U.S. dollar—and then swap the obligation to another currency. (The process is similar to the interest-rate swap just described.) For example, a U.S. company with a subsidiary in Britain would generate large quantities of British pounds through normal operations, and it could use the pounds to pay off a British pound bond. If the U.S. company had issued Eurobonds in dollars in London, it could enter into a swap agreement through an investment bank to exchange its future dollar obligations with a British pound obligation and use the pound revenues to pay off the swapped obligation.

EQUITY SECURITIES AND THE EUROEQUITY MARKET

Another source of financing is *equity securities*, whereby an investor takes an ownership position in return for shares of stock in the company and the promises of capital gains—an appreciation in the value of the stock—and maybe dividends.

Access to Equity Capital   One way a company can easily and inexpensively get access to capital is through a private placement with a venture capitalist. In this case, a wealthy venture capitalist (or perhaps a venture-capital firm investing the money of one or several wealthy individuals) invests money in a new venture in exchange for stock.

Another source of demand for private placements is the corporate restructuring market in Europe. In recent years, European mergers have primarily taken place between firms in the same country, but mergers are now crossing national borders. Cross-European mergers have increased the demand for cash, and private placements have helped fill that demand.[24]

In addition to private placements, companies can access the *equity-capital market*, more commonly known as the *stock market*. Companies can raise new capital by listing their shares on a stock exchange, and they can list on their home-country exchange or on a foreign exchange. For example, Beijing-based China Techfaith Wireless Communication Technology Limited, a designer and manufacturer of mobile handsets, offered 8.73 million shares on an initial public offering (IPO) on NASDAQ on May 5, 2005. Its underwriters were Merrill Lynch, Lehman Brothers, and CIBC World Markets Corporation. Its shares listed at $16.27, and it raised $141.8 million.

Another example of an international IPO was the listing of Sistema on the London Stock Exchange in 2004. Sistema, the largest private sector consumer services company in Russia, issued a U.S. $1.56 billion offering in London, the largest ever Russian IPO on a public market anywhere. Sistema's offering comprised 1.8 million common shares in the form of 91.6 million Global Depositary Receipts (GDRs) with 50 GDRs representing one common share. Sistema needed access to equity dollars, which it was not able to raise inside Russia, so the Euroequity market in London was an obvious site for it to list. The growth in globalization has forced companies to look at equity markets as an alternative to debt markets and banks as a source of funds.

THE SIZE OF GLOBAL STOCK MARKETS

Map 19.2 identifies the 10 largest stock markets in developed countries and the 10 largest in emerging countries in terms of **market capitalization**—the total number of shares of stock listed times the market price per share. Note that the 10 largest are in the developed countries, with the largest in New York (including both the NYSE and NASDAQ), Tokyo, and London. In addition, we provide the market cap for the 10 largest emerging markets.

The numbers represent each specific stock market rather than all of the markets in the country. For example, the NYSE Group as a whole is listed as number one, but that does not include all stock markets in the United States. Note that the largest emerging market stock market is still smaller than the tenth largest developed country stock market on the map. Of course, there are other developed country stock markets that are smaller than some of the emerging market stock markets, but the map only includes the top 10 in each category.

These data only include domestic stocks and do not include foreign stocks listed on a domestic exchange. For example, on August 7, 2007, there were 428 non-U.S. issuers from 45 countries listed on the NYSE Euronext, but they were not included in the data for Map 19.2. Note, too, that the map contains separate data for NYSE and Euronext, but as pointed out in Chapter 9, they have merged to form NYSE Euronext.

Emerging Stock Markets   It's been interesting to track the development of the emerging stock markets. For many years, they were growing fairly rapidly. By 1998, however, the Asian financial crisis had clobbered the emerging stock markets, and they plunged to only 6.9 percent of total. That was followed by crises in Russia and Latin America. However, the emerging markets are growing again. In 2006, the market capitalization of emerging markets was about 12 percent of total market capitalization and climbing. A major event in the growth in the emerging markets is the rise of the stock market in Shanghai, which is now the largest in the emerging markets.

The three largest stock markets in the world are in New York, Tokyo, and London, with the U.S. markets controlling nearly half of the world's stock market capitalization.

MAP 19.2   Global Markets: Market Capitalization, 2006

Data reflect (domestic) *market capitalization*—total number of shares of stock listed multiplied by market price per share.

Source: World Federation of Exchanges, "Equity—1.1 Domestic Market Capitalization," www.world-exchanges.org (accessed August 28, 2007).

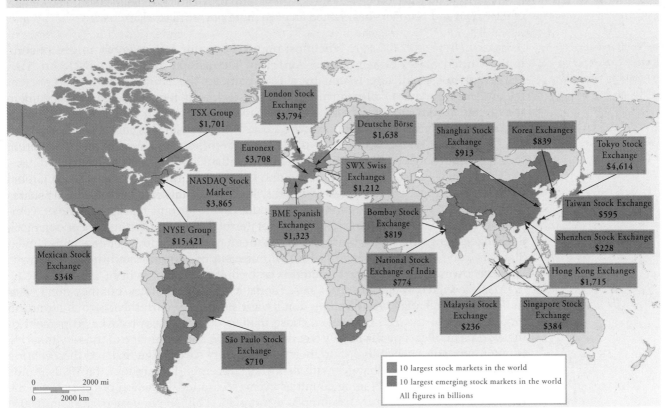

The Rise of the Euroequity Market   Another significant event in the past decade is the creation of the **Euroequity market,** the market for shares sold outside the boundaries of the issuing company's home country. Prior to 1980, few companies thought about offering stock outside the national boundaries of their headquarters country. Since then, hundreds of companies worldwide have issued stock simultaneously in two or more countries to attract more capital from a wider variety of shareholders. For example, when Daimler and Chrysler merged and issued global shares around the world, it did so on 21 different markets in eight different countries: Germany, the United States, Austria, Canada, France, Britain, Japan, and Switzerland.

> Euroequities are shares listed on stock exchanges in countries other than the home country of the issuing company.

The Trend Toward Delisting   However, the trend of listing on more than one exchange, which was popular in the 1990s, is beginning to reverse. More and more companies are reducing the number of exchanges on which their stocks are listed. For example, in March 2005, IBM announced it would remove its shares from the Tokyo Stock Exchange, after already removing its stock from exchanges in Vienna, Frankfurt, and Zurich. Investors are finding that the best price for stocks is usually in the home market of the company in which they are investing.

In addition, companies pay annual fees to list on exchanges, so if trading is light on a certain exchange, they can save money by listing on an exchange with heavier trading volume. Other reasons for delisting shares include weak market returns (fewer investors are putting their money into stocks) and increased regulation, such as the Sarbanes-Oxley Act in the United States. DaimlerChrysler still lists on 15 different stock exchanges in Germany, the United States, France, Japan, and Switzerland.

This trend toward delisting has affected even the NYSE. Following its recent corporate governance problems, the NYSE has decreased in popularity. However, it is still one of the most important stock exchanges in the world.[25] The U.S. market is important for U.S. and foreign companies looking for equity capital and is popular for Euroequity issues partly because of the market size and the speed with which offerings are completed. The large pension funds in the United States can buy big blocks of stock at low transaction costs. Pension fund managers regard foreign stocks as a good form of portfolio diversification. The merger of the NYSE and Euronext has created an even more powerful stock exchange.

AMERICAN DEPOSITARY RECEIPT   The most popular way for a Euroequity to get a listing in the United States is to issue an **American Depositary Receipt (ADR).** An ADR is a negotiable certificate issued by a U.S. bank in the United States to represent the underlying shares of a foreign corporation's stock held in trust at a custodian bank in the foreign country. ADRs are traded like shares of stock, with each one representing some number of shares of the underlying stock. For example, Toyota has listed ADRs on the NYSE since 1999 at a rate of two ADRs per common share of Toyota. They issue through a sponsored ADR facility operated by the Bank of New York as ADRs.

The United States is not the only market for Euroequities. There are also Global Depositary Receipts and European Depositary Receipts as illustrated in the earlier Sistema example, but the U.S. market dominates the depositary receipt market. However, compared to the NYSE, a much larger percentage of the total shares traded on the London Stock Exchange belongs to foreign companies even though the total trading volume in the United States is quite large. The creation of NYSE Euronext has complicated the comparisons because now the merger brings together six cash equities exchanges from five countries.

Many foreign corporations try to raise capital in the United States, but they don't want to list on an exchange because they don't want to comply with the onerous reporting requirements of the SEC. However, those that do so get access to over 50 percent of the world's market capitalization, a fact that is a significant advantage to those with a U.S. listing. Companies generally list on their home country's exchange first and then venture into the international exchanges with depositary receipts. Throughout the 1990s, funds raised from ADRs in developing countries averaged around $7 billion per year. Since the turn of the century, that figure has jumped to around $22 billion per year, peaking in 2000.[26]

Offshore Financing and Offshore Financial Centers

Companies can raise debt or equity funds in their domestic market or offshore. **Offshore financing** is the provision of financial services by banks and other agents to nonresidents. In its simplest form, this involves the borrowing of money from nonresidents and lending to nonresidents.[27] A good example of legitimate offshore financing is the use of the Eurodollar market. A U.S. company can raise Eurodollars in London by working with a bank to issue bonds or syndicate a loan.

WHAT'S AN OFC?

Offshore financial centers (OFCs) are cities or countries that provide large amounts of funds in currencies other than their own and are used as locations in which to raise and accumulate cash. Usually, the financial transactions are conducted in currencies other than the currency of the country and are thus the centers for the Eurocurrency market. An OFC could be defined as any financial center where offshore activity takes place, but a more practical definition of an OFC is a center where the bulk of financial center activity is offshore on both sides of the balance sheet, the transactions are initiated elsewhere, and the majority of the institutions involved are controlled by nonresidents.[28] OFCs can refer to any of the following:

- Jurisdictions that have relatively large numbers of financial institutions engaged primarily in business with nonresidents

- Financial systems with external assets and liabilities out of proportion to domestic financial intermediation designed to finance domestic economies

Bahamas Financial Centre. A woman walks past the Bahamas Financial Centre in Nassau, Bahamas, billed as the leading offshore financial center in the world. A growing number of wealthy Americans have begun moving their money to offshore accounts to avoid paying taxes. As a result, the Bahamas' thriving financial district contributes almost as much to the country's economy as the tourist industry.

- More popularly, centers that provide some or all of the following services: low or zero taxation (hence the term **tax-haven country)**; moderate or light financial regulation; banking secrecy and anonymity[29]

Offshore financial centers— cities or countries that provide large amounts of funds in currencies other than their own.

Characteristics of OFCs   Generally, the markets in these centers are regulated differently— and usually more flexibly—than domestic markets. These centers provide an alternative, (usually) cheaper source of funding for MNEs so they don't have to rely strictly on their own national markets. Offshore financial centers have one or more of the following characteristics:

OFCs offer low or zero taxation, moderate or light financial regulation, and banking secrecy and anonymity.

- A large foreign-currency (Eurocurrency) market for deposits and loans (in London, for example)
- A market that functions as a large net supplier of funds to the world financial markets (in Switzerland, for example)
- A market that functions as an intermediary or pass-through for international loan funds (in the Bahamas and the Cayman Islands, for example)
- Economic and political stability
- An efficient and experienced financial community
- Good communications and supportive services
- An official regulatory climate favorable to the financial industry, in the sense that it protects investors without unduly restricting financial institutions[30]

Operational Versus Booking Centers   These centers are either *operational centers*, with extensive banking activities involving short-term financial transactions, or *booking centers*, in which little actual banking activity takes place but in which transactions are recorded to take advantage of secrecy and low (or no) tax rates. In the latter case, individuals may deposit money offshore to hide it from their home-country tax authorities, either because the money is earned or to be used illegally—such as in the drug trade or to finance terrorist activities—or because the individual or company does not want to pay tax. London is an example of an operational center; the Cayman Islands is an example of a booking center.

Offshore financial centers can be operational centers or booking centers.

Although there are many offshore financial centers, the most important are Bahrain (for the Middle East), Brussels, the Caribbean (servicing mainly Canadian and U.S. banks), Dublin, Hong Kong, London, New York, Singapore, and Switzerland. London is a crucial center because it offers a variety of financial services in both debt and equity transactions and has a large domestic market; it also serves the offshore market. The Caribbean centers (primarily the Bahamas, the Cayman Islands, and the Netherlands Antilles) are essentially offshore locations for New York banks.

Switzerland has been a primary source of funds for decades, offering stability, integrity, discretion, and low costs. Singapore has been the center for the Eurodollar market in Asia (sometimes called the Asiadollar market) since 1968, thanks to its strategic geographic location, its strong worldwide telecommunications links, and government regulations that have facilitated the flow of funds. Hong Kong is critical because of its unique status with respect to China and the United Kingdom and its geographic proximity to the rest of the Pacific Rim. Bahrain, an island country in the Persian Gulf, is the financial center of petrodollars (dollars generated from the sale of oil) in the Middle East.

OFCs as "Tax Havens"   A major concern with OFCs is the tax avoidance dimension of their activities. The Organization for Economic Cooperation and Development (OECD) has been working closely with the major OFCs to ensure they are engaged in legal activity. Although not trying to tell the sovereign countries what their tax rates should be, the OECD is trying to eliminate harmful tax practices in these four areas:

1. The regime imposes low or no taxes on the relevant income (from geographically mobile financial and other service activities).

2. The regime is ring fenced (i.e., separated) from the domestic economy.

3. The regime lacks transparency; for example, the details of the regime or its application are not apparent or there is inadequate regulatory supervision or financial disclosure.

4. There is no effective exchange of information with respect to the regime.[31]

In 2000, the OECD identified 47 preferential tax regimes (in OECD countries) that were potentially harmful and began negotiating with the countries fostering these tax regimes to improve their practices. By the end of 2006, 21 of 47 preferential tax regimes had been "abolished," 13 had been "amended," and 13 were consider "not harmful."[32] As shown in the Parmalat case, however, policing needs to be done at the corporate level, not just the OFC level.

P•int Counterpoint

Should Offshore Financial Centers and Aggressive Tax Practices Be Eliminated?

P•int   **Yes** The problem with offshore financial centers (OFCs) is that they operate in a shroud of secrecy that allows companies to establish operations there that are used for illegal and unethical behavior. In December 2001, U.S. energy giant Enron filed for bankruptcy, resulting in one of the largest bankruptcies in corporate history. One of the contributors to Enron's problems was the creation of hundreds of subsidiaries in tax havens, including 662 in the Cayman Islands, 119 in Turks and Caicos, 43 in Mauritius, and 8 in Bermuda. The subsidiaries were used to pass off corporate debts, losses, and executive compensation.[33] The fondness of unscrupulous MNEs for OFCs only serves to underscore the venerable truth voiced in Figure 19.3.

Counterpoint   **No** Offshore financial centers are an efficient way for companies to use their financial resources more effectively. They are good locations for companies to establish finance subsidiaries that can raise capital for the parent company or its subsidiaries. They allow the finance subsidiaries to take advantage of lower borrowing costs and tax rates.

This type of activity is not illegal because the companies are still subject to home- and host-country laws and tax regulations. It is true that some transactions may be illegal, but most are not. The key to policing truly illegal activities, such as hiding drug money or engaging in corporate fraud like the Parmalat case in Chapter 18, is to improve transparency and reporting.

As pointed out in Chapter 18, Parmalat set up three shell companies based in the Caribbean to capture cash. The shell companies allegedly sold Parmalat products, and Parmalat sent them fake invoices and charged costs and fees to make the sales look legitimate. Then Parmalat would write out a credit note for the amount the subsidiaries supposedly owed it and take that to banks to raise money. Given the location of the subsidiaries, you would think the banks would have been suspicious, but Parmalat got away with these activities.

Off-balance-sheet financing was also used to hide debts. The company transferred over half of its liabilities to the books of small subsidiaries based in offshore tax havens such as the Cayman Islands. This allowed Parmalat to present a healthy balance sheet and a profitable income statement to investors and creditors by hiding large amounts of debt, understating interest expenses (thus overstating income), and overstating revenues for false bookings. Parmalat's actual debt was nearly double the amount that was disclosed to outsiders.

Terrorists and drug dealers also use OFCs to launder money. When the U.S. government went after the money of Osama bin Laden, it went after OFCs notorious for their secrecy. When a bank in the Bahamas refused to open its books to U.S. government investigators, the United States cut off the bank from the world's wire transfer systems. Within two hours, the bank changed policies.[34]●

Why shouldn't countries have the opportunity to attract business by offering tax haven status to MNEs? Many of these countries don't have other visible means of generating resources. They are too small to set up manufacturing operations, don't have a large enough population base to offer low-cost labor, and don't have natural resources they can sell. So what can they do? Companies and individuals need places to bank their wealth or raise capital, so the offshore financial centers have decided to use the theory of factor proportions discussed in Chapter 6 and develop the banking and financial infrastructure necessary to attract wealth. As long as they establish banking, privacy, and taxation laws that attract money, they should be allowed to do so.

Offshore financial centers don't rely on taxation to fund huge government expenditures, because they don't have a large military budget nor significant welfare costs. Is there anything wrong with not collecting large amounts of taxes? Some countries are upset that offshore financial centers offer a tax-free environment for revenues generated offshore, but that is the business of the countries. Nobody should force them to collect higher taxes just because the high-tax countries are at a disadvantage in attracting banking and other financial transactions. If countries want to charge high taxes on financial transactions, let them do so, but don't force the offshore financial centers to play their game.●

FIGURE 19.3   The Classic Lure of Offshore Tax Laxity

Source: John Morris, www.businesscartoons.co.uk

"Oh, what a tangled web we weave, when first we practise to deceive."

Capital Budgeting in a Global Context

The next international dimension of the financial function is the capital budgeting decision whereby the MNE determines which projects and countries will receive its capital investment funds. The parent company must compare the net present value or internal rate of return of a potential foreign project with that of its other projects around the world to determine the best place to invest its resources. The technique used to compare different projects is called *capital budgeting*.

> Capital budgeting—the process whereby MNEs determine which projects and countries will receive capital investment funds.

METHODS OF CAPITAL BUDGETING

Capital budgeting techniques:

• Payback period.
• Net present value of a project.
• Internal rate of return.

Payback Period   One approach to capital budgeting is to determine the **payback period** of a project, or the number of years required to recover the initial investment made. That is typically done by estimating the annual after-tax free cash flow from the investment, determining the present value of the future cash flow for each year, and then determining how many years it will take to recoup the initial investment.

Net Present Value   A second approach is to determine the **net present value (NPV)** of a project, which is defined as follows:

$$NPV = \sum_{t=1}^{n} \frac{FCF_t}{(1+k)^t} - IO$$

Where FCF_t = the annual free cash flow in time period t

k = the appropriate discount rate; that is, the required rate of return or cost of capital

IO = the initial cash outlay

n = the project's expected life

The required rate of return is the rate that the company must get from the project to justify the cost of raising the initial investment or at least maintaining the value of its common stock. If the NPV is positive, the project is also considered positive. If the NPV is negative, the company should not enter into the project.

MNEs need to determine free cash flows based on cash flow estimates and tax rates in different countries and an appropriate required rate of return adjusted for risk.

Internal Rate of Return   A third approach is to compute the internal rate of return (IRR) of the project and compare it with the required rate of return. The IRR is the rate that equates the present value of future cash flows with the present value of the initial investment. If the IRR is greater than the required rate of return, the investment is considered positive. However, the company then needs to compare the IRR with that of competing projects in other countries.

Several things are common about each of the methods. First, the firm needs to determine the free cash flows, which involves estimating cash flows as well as bringing into the equation different tax rates from different countries. Second, in the case of both NPV and IRR, the company needs to determine what the required rate of return is.

COMPLICATIONS IN CAPITAL BUDGETING

Several aspects of capital budgeting are unique to foreign project assessment:

• Parent cash flows must be distinguished from project cash flows. *Parent cash flows* refer to cash flows from the project back to the parent in the parent's currency. *Project cash flows* refer to the cash flows in local currency from the sale of goods and services. Will the decision be based on parent cash flows, project cash flows, or both?

CONCEPT CHECK

In the section on "Forecasting Exchange-Rate Movements" in Chapter 10, we point out the importance to MNEs of formulating general ideas of the timing, magnitude, and direction of exchange-rate movements. We also describe two approaches that companies can take to forecast exchange rates: **fundamental forecasting** (which bases external or internal decisions on a range of economic variables) and **technical forecasting** (which depends on specialists to analyze trends in **exchange rates** themselves).

• Remittance of funds to the parent, such as dividends, interest on loans, and payment of intracompany receivables and payables, is affected by differing tax systems, legal and political constraints on the movement of funds, local business norms, and differences in how financial markets and institutions function. In addition, tax systems affect free cash flows on the project, irrespective of the remittance issue.

• Differing rates of inflation must be anticipated by both the parent and subsidiary because of their importance in causing changes in competitive position and in cash flows over time.

• The parent must consider the possibility of unanticipated exchange-rate changes because of both their direct effects on the value of cash flows as well as their indirect effects on the foreign subsidiary's competitive position.

• The parent company must evaluate political risk in a target market because political events can drastically reduce the value or availability of expected cash flows.

- The terminal value (the value of the project at the end of the budgeting period) is difficult to estimate because potential purchasers from host, home, or third countries—or from the private or public sector—may have widely divergent perspectives on the value of the project. The terminal value is critical in determining the total cash flows from the project. The total cash outlay for the project is partially offset by the terminal value—the amount of cash the parent company can get from the subsidiary or project if it sells it eventually.[35]

Because of all the forces listed here, it's very difficult to estimate future cash flows, both to the subsidiary and to the parent company. There are two ways to deal with the variations in future cash flows. One is to determine several different scenarios and then determine the payback period, net present value, or internal rate of return of the project. The other is to adjust the hurdle rate, which is the minimum required rate of return that the project must achieve for it to receive capital. The adjustment is usually made by increasing the hurdle rate above its minimal level.

> Determine different cash flow scenarios or adjust the hurdle rate (the minimum required rate of return for a project).

Once the budget is complete, the MNE must examine both the return in local currency and the return to the parent in dollars from cash flows to the parent. Examining the return in local currency will give management a chance to compare the project with other investment alternatives in the country. However, cash flows to the parent are important because it is from these cash flows that dividends are paid to shareholders. If the MNE cannot generate a sufficient return to the parent in the parent's currency, it will eventually fall behind in its ability to pay shareholders and pay off corporate debt. Finally, the decision must be made in the strategic context of the investment, not just the financial context.

Internal Sources of Funds

Although the term *funds* usually means "cash," it is used in a much broader sense in business and generally refers to working capital—that is, the difference between current assets and current liabilities. From a general perspective, funds come from the normal operations of a business (selling merchandise or services) as well as from financing activities, such as borrowing money, issuing bonds, or issuing shares. Uses of funds are for the purchase of fixed assets, paying employees and purchasing materials and supplies, and investing in marketable securities or long-term investments.

> Funds are working capital, or current assets minus current liabilities.

Cash Flows and the MNE   Cash flows in an MNE are significantly more complex than for a company that operates in a strictly domestic environment. An MNE that wants to expand operations or needs additional capital can look not only to the domestic and international debt and equity markets but also to sources within itself. For an MNE, the complexity of internal sources is magnified because of the number of its subsidiaries and the diverse environments in which they operate.

Figure 19.4 shows a parent company that has two foreign subsidiaries. The parent, as well as the two subsidiaries, may be increasing funds through normal operations. These funds may be used on a companywide basis, perhaps through loans. The parent can loan funds directly to one subsidiary or guarantee an outside loan to the other. Equity capital from the parent is another source of funds for the subsidiary.

> Sources of internal funds are
> - Loans.
> - Investments through equity capital.
> - Intercompany receivables and payables.
> - Dividends.

Funds also can go from subsidiary to parent. The subsidiary could declare a dividend to the parent as a return on capital, or it could loan cash directly to the parent. If the subsidiary declared a dividend to the parent, the parent could lend the funds back to the subsidiary. The dividend would not be tax deductible to the subsidiary, but it would be included as income to the parent, and the parent would have to pay tax on the dividend. If the subsidiary loaned money to the parent, the interest paid by the parent would be tax deductible to the parent and would be taxable income to the subsidiary.

Merchandise, people (in the case of MNEs involved in services), and financial flows can travel between subsidiaries, giving rise to receivables and payables. Companies

FIGURE 19.4   How the MNE Handles Its Funds (I): Internal Funds

Funds consist of *working capital* that comes from normal business operations and that may be used to purchase assets and materials, to pay employees, and to make investments. If the company is an MNE, funds may come from either parent or subsidiary operations, or both, and can be used by the parent to support either its own operations or those of its subsidiaries.

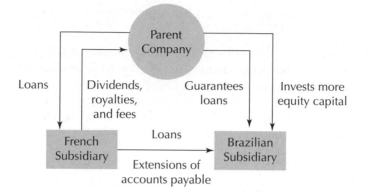

can move money between and among related entities by paying quickly, or they can accumulate funds by deferring payment. They also can adjust the size of the payment by arbitrarily raising or lowering the price of intercompany transactions in comparison with the market price, a transfer pricing strategy.

GLOBAL CASH MANAGEMENT

Effective cash management is a chief concern of the CFO, who must answer the following three questions to ensure effective cash management:

1. What are the local and corporate system needs for cash?
2. How can the cash be withdrawn from subsidiaries and centralized?
3. Once the cash has been centralized, what should be done with it?

> Cash budgets and forecasts are essential in assessing a company's cash needs.

The cash manager, who reports to the treasurer (as illustrated in Figure 19.2 on page 733), must collect and pay cash in the company's normal operational cycle and then must deal with financial institutions, such as commercial and investment banks, when generating and investing cash. Before the cash manager remits any cash into the MNE's control center—whether at regional or headquarters level—he or she must first assess local cash needs through cash budgets and forecasts. Because the cash forecast projects the excess cash that will be available, the cash manager will know how much cash can be invested for short-term profits.

> Dividends are a good source of intercompany transfers, but governments often restrict their free movement.

Once local cash needs are met, the cash manager must decide whether to allow the local manager to invest any excess cash or to have it remitted to a central cash pool. If the cash is centralized, the manager must find a way of making the transfer. A cash dividend is the easiest way to distribute cash, but government restrictions may interfere. For example, foreign-exchange controls may prevent the company from remitting as large a dividend as it would like. Cash also can be remitted through royalties, management fees, and repayment of principal and interest on loans.

> Multilateral netting—the process of coordinating cash inflows and outflows among subsidiaries so that only net cash is transferred, reducing transaction costs.

Multilateral Netting   An important cash-management strategy is **netting** cash flows internationally. For example, an MNE with operations in four European countries could have several different intercompany cash transfers resulting from loans, the sale of goods, licensing agreements, and so forth. In the illustration in Figure 19.5, for example, there are no fewer than seven different transfers among four subsidiaries. Among its special services, Global Positioning Services, the foreign-exchange company profiled in our opening case, helps clients determine their foreign currency cash flows and assists them in developing strategies to net cash flows by minimizing the number of their foreign-currency transactions.

Case Review Note

FIGURE 19.5   How the MNE Handles Its Funds (II): Multilateral Cash Flows

As the various subsidiaries of the MNE go about their business, cash can be transferred among them for a variety of reasons (e.g., in the form of loans or as proceeds from the sale of goods). Cash, of course, can flow in any direction, and if the MNE doesn't maintain some kind of cash-management center, each subsidiary must settle its accounts (receivables, payables, etc.) independently.

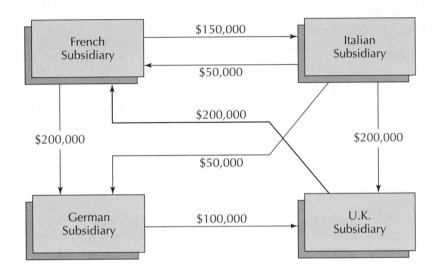

Table 19.2 identifies the total receivables, payables, and net position for each subsidiary. Rather than have each subsidiary settle its accounts independently with subsidiaries in other countries, many MNEs are establishing cash-management centers in one city (such as Brussels) to coordinate cash flows among subsidiaries from several countries.

Figure 19.6 illustrates how each subsidiary in a net payable position transfers funds to the central clearing account. The manager of the clearing account then transfers funds to the accounts of the net receiver subsidiaries. In this example, only four transfers need to take place. The clearing account manager receives transactions information and computes the net position of each subsidiary at least monthly. Then the manager orchestrates the settlement process. The transfers take place in the payor's currency, and the foreign-exchange conversion takes place centrally. For netting to work, the company needs to match its cash needs with software that can keep track of and transfer funds and banking relationships that allow money to be moved among corporate entities.

> Netting requires sophisticated software and good banking relationships in different countries.

TABLE 19.2   How the MNE Handles Its Funds (III): Net Positions

Assume that these data are from the same MNE as the one introduced in Figure 19.5. Because the company has no cash-management center, *net positions*—the difference between *total receivables* and *total payables*—must be determined on a subsidiary-by-subsidiary basis.

Subsidiary	Total Receivables	Total Payables	Net Position
French	250,000	350,000	(100,000)
German	250,000	100,000	150,000
Italian	150,000	300,000	(150,000)
U.K.	300,000	200,000	100,000

FIGURE 19.6
How the MNE Handles Its Funds (IV): Multilateral Netting

Dissatisfied with the process represented in Figure 19.5, our MNE has now established a cash-management center—a *clearing account* into which each subsidiary transfers its net cash. Naturally, the MNE may in turn distribute the total to support subsidiary operations.

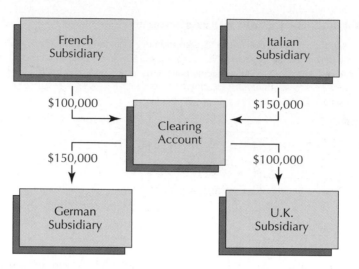

CONCEPT CHECK
Later in this chapter, we'll discuss *hedging strategies*—strategies by which companies can protect themselves from the losses to which they may be exposed in foreign-exchange transactions. Some of these strategies make use of the kinds of *foreign-exchange instruments* that we explain in Chapter 9, such as **forwards** (agreeing to exchange currency at a future date), **options** (agreeing to the right to trade currency at a later date), and **futures** (agreeing to trade currency at a particular price on a specific date).

Three types of foreign-exchange exposure—translation, transaction, economic or operational.

Translation exposure arises because the dollar value of the exposed asset or liability changes as the exchange rate changes.

Transaction exposure arises because the receivable or payable changes in value as the exchange rate changes.

Foreign-Exchange Risk Management

As illustrated earlier, global cash-management strategy focuses on the flow of money for specific operating objectives. Another important objective of an MNE's financial strategy is to protect against the foreign-exchange risks of investing abroad. The strategies that an MNE adopts to do this may mean the internal movement of funds as well as the use of one or more of the foreign-exchange instruments described in Chapter 9, such as options and forward contracts.

TYPES OF EXPOSURE

If all exchange rates were fixed in relation to one another, there would be no foreign-exchange risk. However, rates are not fixed, and currency values change frequently. Instead of infrequent one-way changes, currencies fluctuate often and both up and down. A change in the exchange rate can result in three different exposures for a company: *translation exposure, transaction exposure,* and *economic* or *operational exposure.*

Translation Exposure   Foreign-currency financial statements are translated into the reporting currency of the parent company (assumed to be U.S. dollars for U.S. companies) so they can be combined with financial statements of other companies in the corporate group to form the consolidated financial statements. **Translation exposure** occurs because exposed accounts—those translated at the balance sheet rate or current exchange rate—either gain or lose value in dollars when the exchange rate changes.

Consider the translation exposure example in Table 19.3 (Panel A) of a U.S. company with a subsidiary in Mexico. In this example, the Mexican subsidiary has 900,000 pesos in the bank. This is the question: What is the value of the cash *after* the exchange rate changes? The subsidiary still has pesos in the bank account; it's just that the dollar equivalent of the pesos has fallen, resulting in a loss. The gain or loss does not represent an actual cash flow effect because the pesos are only translated, not converted into dollars. In addition, reported earnings can either rise or fall against the dollar because of the translation effect, and this can affect earnings per share and stock prices.

Transaction Exposure   Denominating a transaction in a foreign currency gives rise to **transaction exposure** because the company has accounts receivable or payable in foreign currency that must be settled eventually. Consider the transaction exposure example of a U.S. exporter delivering merchandise to a British importer in Table 19.3 (Panel B). If the exporter were to receive payment in dollars, there would be no immediate impact on the exporter if the dollar/pound exchange rate changed. If payment were to be received in pounds, however, the exporter might incur a foreign-exchange gain or loss. In this case, because the pound

TABLE 19.3   The Effects of Foreign-Exchange Exposure

Panel A—Translation Exposure

A Mexican subsidiary reports cash in the bank of 900,000 pesos at a time when 9.5 pesos will buy U.S. $1; thus its U.S. parent translates the net in pesos into U.S. $94,737. When the exchange rate changes, however, and 10 pesos are required to buy U.S. $1, the total of 900,000 pesos must be retranslated from U.S. $94,737 into U.S. $90,000.

U.S. Company Bank Account in Mexico	900,000 pesos
Initial Exchange Rate	9.5 pesos/$
Initial Bank Account Worth	$94,737
Calculation: 900,000/9.5 = $94,737	
Subsequent Exchange Rate	10 pesos/$
Subsequent Bank Account Worth	$90,000
Calculation: 900,000/10 = $90,000	

Panel B—Transaction Exposure

If a U.S. company denominates its sales in dollars, it has no transaction exposure. If it denominates the sale in British pounds, the dollar value of the receivable rises or falls as the exchange rate changes, as illustrated below.

Total Price of Merchandise on Exporter's Books	$500,000
Initial Exchange Rate	1.9000 $/£
Initial Underlying Value of Sale	£263,158
Calculation: $500,000/1.9000 = £263,158	
Amount Received by Exporter	£263,158
Subsequent Exchange Rate	1.8800 $/£
Subsequent Payment Value of Collected Receivable	$494,737
Calculation: £263,158 × 1.8800 = $494,737	
Loss to the Exporter	$5,263
Calculation: $500,000 − $494,737 = $5,263	

Panel C—Economic (or Operating) Exposure

The transaction is the same as in Panel B, but this time the British importer must pay the U.S. exporter in dollars. The first calculation shows how many British pounds the importer must come up with to convert to dollars to pay the exporter. That amount is then marked up 10% for sale in the United Kingdom. The next calculation assumes that the British pound weakens to $1.8800 per pound, meaning that the importer has to come up with more pounds to convert to dollars to pay the exporter. The higher amount is then marked up by 10%, and we show how much more the importer would have to charge in the market and how much the importer's profit margin would be at the higher price. However, the economic exposure is that the importer may not be able to sell the products at a higher price, so there are two options. One is for the importer to sell the product for the same price as before and accept a lower profit margin (£23,517) or for the exporter to charge only $494,737, which would allow the importer to pay the same amount in British pounds as before the exchange-rate change and still be able to keep the price the same in the United Kingdom and earn the same profit margin as before. The difference between the last two calculations is that the importer suffers a drop in profits in the first case and the exporter suffers a drop in profits in the second case.

Total Price of Merchandise on Exporter's Books	$500,000
Initial Exchange Rate	1.9000 $/£
Initial Underlying Value of Sale	£263,158
Calculation: $500,000/1.9000 = £263,158	
Amount Charged by Importer After 10% Markup	£289,474
Subsequent Exchange Rate	1.8800 $/£
Subsequent Underlying Value of Sale	£265,957
Calculation: $500,000/1.8800 = £265,957	
Amount Charged by Importer After 10% Markup	£292,553
Difference in Sales Price Before and After Rate Change	£3,079
Profit to Importer If Importer Charges Higher Price	£26,596
Calculation: £292,553 − £265,957 = £26,596	
Profit to Importer If Importer Absorbs Cost Increase	£23,517
Calculation: £289,474 − £265,957 = £23,517	
Price Charged by Exporter for Constant Cost to Importer	$494,737
Calculation: £263,158 × 1.8800 = $494,737	

Economic, or operating, exposure arises from effects of exchange-rate changes on

- Future cash flows.
- The sourcing of parts and components.
- The location of investments.
- The competitive position of the company in different markets.

To protect assets from exchange-rate risk, management needs to

- Define and measure exposure.
- Establish a reporting system.
- Adopt an overall policy on exposure management.
- Formulate hedging strategies.

All three types of exposure must be monitored and measured separately.

Exchange-rate movements are forecast using in-house or external experts.

is falling in value, the exporter would receive fewer dollars from the sale after the change in the exchange rate. This would be an actual cash flow gain or loss to the exporter.

Economic (or Operating) Exposure   Economic exposure, also known as **operating exposure,** is the potential for change in expected cash flows. Economic exposure arises from the pricing of products, the sourcing and cost of inputs, and the location of investments. Pricing strategies have both an immediate and a long-term impact on cash flows. Consider the economic exposure example of the U.S. exporter and the British importer from Table 19.3 (Panel C). The first part of panel C shows what happens if the importer has to pay the exporter $500,000 for the merchandise. Because the pound is falling in value, the importer will have to convert more pounds into dollars to pay the exporter. Now, the *importer* can either sell the product at the original price and not earn as much profit or it can raise the price and hope that consumers will be willing to pay the higher price. The *exporter*, however, also has two choices. It can continue to sell the merchandise at the same price, or it can lower the price. If it lowers the price, it will incur a lower profit margin. If it continues to sell at the same price, the importer will have to pay more for the merchandise. Then the importer will have to decide what to do.

Another economic exposure decision involves how to make investment decisions. After three years of the euro strengthening against the dollar, BMW found itself in a very difficult situation in 2005 because its costs were generated in euros (most of its manufacturing facilities were in Europe), whereas its revenues in the United States were in dollars. Thus it was generating revenues in a weak currency and costs in a strong currency, severely affecting earnings. One of its economic considerations was to expand manufacturing operations in the United States to balance its revenues and expenses in the same currency.[36]

EXPOSURE-MANAGEMENT STRATEGY

To protect assets adequately against risks from translation, transaction, and economic exposure of exchange-rate fluctuations, management must do the following:

- Define and measure exposure
- Organize and implement a reporting system that monitors exposure and exchange-rate movements
- Adopt a policy assigning responsibility for minimizing—or hedging—exposure
- Formulate strategies for hedging exposure

Defining and Measuring Exposure   Most MNEs see all three types of exposure: translation, transaction, and economic. To develop a viable hedging strategy, an MNE must forecast the degree of exposure in each major currency in which it operates. Because the types of exposure differ, the actual exposure by currency must be tracked separately. For example, the translation exposure in Brazilian reals should be kept track of separately from the transaction exposure because the transaction exposure will result in an actual cash flow whereas the translation exposure may not. Thus the company generates one report on translation exposure and another on transaction exposure. The company may adopt different hedging strategies for the different types of exposure. Recall from our opening case that GPS has actually developed proprietary software, called FXpert, which not only conducts specialized audits of clients' foreign-exchange cash flows but proposes effective hedging strategies for improving them. Solutions may include such well-known hedging strategies as forwards, options, and futures contracts, but GPS has designed FXpert to tailor strategies to clients' specific needs.

A key aspect of measuring exposure is forecasting exchange rates. A company should estimate and use ranges within which it expects a currency to vary over the forecasting period by developing in-house capabilities to monitor exchange rates or using economists who also try to obtain a consensus of exchange-rate movements from the banks they deal with. Their concern is to forecast the direction, magnitude, and timing of an exchange-rate change.

Creating a Reporting System   Once the company has decided how to define and measure exposure and estimate future exchange rates, it must create a reporting system that will assist in protecting it against risk. To achieve this goal, substantial participation from foreign operations must be combined with effective central control. Foreign input is important to ensure that the information the company uses in forecasting is effective. As we'll see in our closing case, for example, Dell Computer has developed a system whereby hedging strategies are developed jointly by financial management at corporate headquarters and local management at its Brazilian production facility.

Because exchange rates move frequently, the company must obtain input from those who are attuned to the foreign country's economy. Central control of exposure protects resources more efficiently than letting each subsidiary and branch manage its own exposure. Each organizational unit may be able to define its own exposure, but the company also has an overall exposure. To set hedging policies on a separate-entity basis might not take into account the fact that exposures of several entities (that is, branches, subsidiaries, affiliates, and so on) could offset one another.

The reporting system should use both central control and input from foreign operations.

Management of an MNE should devise a uniform reporting system for all of its subsidiaries. The report should identify the exposed accounts the company wants to monitor, the amount of exposure by currency of each account, and the different time periods under consideration. Exposure should be separated into translation, transaction, and economic components, with the transaction exposure identified by cash inflows and outflows over time.

Once each basic reporting unit has identified its exposure, the data should be sent to the next organizational level for preliminary consolidation. The preliminary consolidation enables the region or division to determine exposure by account and by currency for each time period. The resulting reports should be routine, periodic, and standardized to ensure comparability and timeliness in formulating strategies. Final reporting should be at the corporate level, where top management can see the amount of foreign-exchange exposure. Specific hedging strategies can be taken at any level, but each level of management must be aware of the size of the exposure and the potential impact on the company.

Formulating Hedging Strategies   Once a company has identified its level of exposure and determined which exposure is critical, it can hedge its position by adopting operational and/or financial strategies, each with cost-benefit implications as well as operational implications. The safest position is a balanced position in which exposed assets equal exposed liabilities.

Hedging strategies can be operational or financial.

Operational Hedging Strategies   The use of debt to balance exposure is an interesting strategy. Many companies "borrow locally," especially in weak-currency countries, because that helps them avoid foreign-exchange risk from borrowing in a foreign currency and also balances off their exposed position in assets and earnings.

Companies in Argentina that borrowed dollars found themselves in serious trouble when the peso devalued against the dollar because they couldn't generate enough local currency revenues to pay off the higher debt. If they had borrowed in local currency, they would not have had the same problem. One problem with this strategy is that, because interest rates in weak-currency countries tend to be high, there must be a trade-off between the cost of borrowing and the potential loss from exchange-rate variations.

Operational strategies include
- *Using local debt to balance local assets.*
- *Taking advantage of leads and lags for intercompany payments.*

Protecting against loss from transaction exposure becomes complex. In dealing with foreign customers, it is always safest for the company to denominate the transaction in its own currency because it won't have any foreign-exchange exposure. The risk shifts to the foreign customer that has to come up with your currency. Or the company could denominate purchases in a weaker currency and sales in a stronger currency. If forced to make purchases in a strong currency and sales in a weak currency, it could resort to contractual measures such as forward contracts or options, or it could try to balance its inflows and outflows through astute sales and purchasing strategies.

A lead strategy means collecting or paying early. A lag strategy means collecting or paying late.

LEADS AND LAGS   Another operational strategy—leads and lags—protects cash flows among related entities, such as a parent and subsidiaries. A **lead strategy** means either collecting foreign-currency receivables before they are due when the foreign currency is expected to weaken or paying foreign-currency payables before they are due when the foreign currency is expected to strengthen. With a **lag strategy,** a company either delays collection of foreign-currency receivables if that currency is expected to strengthen or delays payables when the currency is expected to weaken. In other words, a company usually leads into and lags out of a hard currency and leads out of and lags into a weak currency.

Sometimes an operational strategy means shifting assets overseas to take advantage of currency changes. When the yen strengthened against the U.S. dollar, for example, Toyota shifted more of its manufacturing into the United States to take advantage of the cheaper dollar, something BMW is considering, as mentioned earlier. As long as the yen was strong, it was difficult to export from Japan to the United States, so companies could service U.S. demand through production in the United States, Canada, and Mexico.

Using Derivatives to Hedge Foreign-Exchange Risk

In addition to the operational strategies just mentioned, a company may hedge exposure through financial contracts such as forward contracts and options, also known as *derivatives*. The most common hedge is a forward contract.

Forward contracts can establish a fixed exchange rate for future transactions. Currency options can ensure access to foreign currency at a fixed exchange rate for a specific period of time.

Consider a U.S. exporter selling goods to a British manufacturer in the forward contract example from Table 19.4. At the time of the sale, the transaction is recorded on the exporter's books at $1.9 million, and a corresponding receivable is set up for the same amount. However, the exporter is concerned about the exchange risk. The exporter can enter into a forward contract, which will guarantee that the receivables convert into dollars at a rate of $1.8500 per pound, no matter what the actual future exchange rate is.

This is less than the company would have received without the forward contract and if the exchange rate had not changed. However, at least it was guaranteed the forward rate. Of course, the future spot rate could be $1.87000 per pound (more favorable than the forward rate), or $1.8000 per pound (less favorable than the forward rate), which would yield payouts of $1,870,000 and $1,800,000. The forward contract gives away possible future gains but limits future losses.

A foreign-currency option is more flexible than a forward contract because it gives its purchaser the right, but not the obligation, to buy or sell a certain amount of foreign currency at a set exchange rate within a specified amount of time. Consider a U.S. exporter selling merchandise to a British manufacturer in the foreign-currency example in Table 19.4. As explained in Chapter 9, the exporter can enter into an option with the writer of the option by paying a premium for the strike price, the price for which the exporter can exercise the option.

When the exporter receives the £1 million from the manufacturer, it must decide whether to exercise the option it purchased. If the exchange rate is above $1.9000, it will not exercise the option. The only thing lost is the $25,000 cost of the option, which is like insurance. However, if the exchange rate is below $1.9000—say, $1.8500—the exporter will exercise the option and trade pounds at the rate of $1.9000. The proceeds will be $1.9 million less the option cost of $25,000.

A good example of how companies use operational and financial hedging strategies is Coca-Cola. Because approximately 72 percent of Coke's "net operating revenues" in 2006 came from outside of the United States, foreign-currency changes can have a major impact on reported earnings. Coke manages its foreign-currency exposures on a consolidated basis, which allows it to net certain exposures from different operations around the world and also allows it to take advantage of natural offsets—for example, cases in which British pound receivables offset British pound payables. Coke "also use[s] derivative financial instruments to further reduce [its] net exposure to currency . . . fluctuations."[37] Coke uses forward-exchange contracts and currency options in several currencies, most notably the euro and Japanese yen, "to hedge . . . forecasted cash flows." In addition, Coke uses forward contracts to hedge "net investments in international operations."[38]

TABLE 19.4   Effects of Hedging Strategies

Panel A—Forward Contract

Having sold merchandise to a British importer worth £1,000,000 at an exchange rate of 1.9000 $/£, a U.S. exporter records a receivable of U.S. $1,900,000. But because the exporter is worried about the possibility of a decline in the value of the U.K. pound, it has entered into a *forward contract* stipulating that *regardless of any fluctuation in the value of the U.K. pound*, its receivable is payable at a rate of 1.8500 $/£.

Initial Sales Price (Pounds) with Payment Due in 90 Days	£1,000,000
Spot Exchange Rate	1.9000 $/£
Initial Sales Price (Dollars) with Payment Due in 90 Days	$1,900,000
Calculation: £1,000,000 × 1.9000 = $1,900,000	
Forward Rate	1.8500 $/£
Guranteed Amount Received by Using Forward Contract	$1,850,000
Calculation: £1,000,000 × 1.8500 = $1,850,000	
Possible Rate Greater Than Forward Rate	1.8700 $/£
Amount Received with Rate Greater Than Forward Rate	$1,870,000
Calculation: £1,000,000 × 1.8700 = $1,870,000	
Possible Rate Less Than Forward Rate	1.8000 $/£
Amount Received with Rate Less Than Forward Rate	$1,800,000
Calculation: £1,000,000 × 1.8000 = $1,800,000	

Panel B—Foreign-Currency Option

The case and companies are the same as in Panel A, but in this case the exporter—for a fee of $25,000—has taken out a *foreign-currency option* that permits it to sell the £1,000,000 that it receives in payment *at a specific rate (1.9000 $/£) within a specified period of time*. If the value of the U.K. pound slips to a rate of 1.8500 $/£, the exporter will exercise the option at 1.9000 $/£, thus receiving proceeds of U.S. $1,875,000 ($1,900,000 – $25,000). The final calculation shows the exporter's proceeds if the exchange rate should go *up* to 1.9500 $/£—in which case the exporter would decline the lower option rate of 1.9000 $/£.

Initial Sales Price (Pounds)	£1,000,000
Option Exchange Rate	1.9000 $/£
Initital Sales Price (Dollars)	$1,900,000
Calculation: £1,000,000 × 1.9000 = $1,900,000	
Option Cost	$25,000
Possible Future Exchange Rate (in the money)	1.8500 $/£
Possible Amount Received by Not Using Option	$1,850,000
Calculation: £1,000,000 × 1.8500 = $1,850,000	
Proceeds from Exercising Option	$1,875,000
Calculation: $1,900,000 − $25,000 = $1,875,000	
Possible Future Exchange Rate (out of the money)	1.9500 $/£
Possible Amount Received by Not Using Option	$1,950,000
Calculation: £1,000,000 × 1.9500 = $1,950,000	
Net Proceeds	$1,925,000
Calculation: $1,950,000 − $25,000 = $1,925,000	

Taxation of Foreign-Source Income

Tax planning is a crucial responsibility for the CFO because taxes can profoundly affect profitability and cash flow. This is especially true in international business. As complex as domestic taxation seems, it is simple compared to the intricacies of international taxation. The international tax specialist must be familiar with both the home country's tax policy on foreign operations and the tax laws of each country in which the international company operates.

Taxation has a strong impact on several choices:

- Location of operations
- Choice of operating form, such as export or import, licensing agreement, overseas investment

Tax planning influences profitability and cash flow.

- Legal form of the new enterprise, such as branch or subsidiary
- Possible facilities in tax-haven countries to raise capital and manage cash
- Method of financing, such as internal or external sourcing and debt or equity
- Capital budgeting decisions
- Method of setting transfer prices

INTERNATIONAL TAX PRACTICES

Differences in Tax Practices   Differences in tax practices around the world often cause problems for MNEs. Lack of familiarity with laws and customs can create confusion. In some countries, tax laws are loosely enforced. In others, taxes generally may be negotiated between the tax collector and the taxpayer—if they are ever paid at all.

Differences in Types of Taxes   Countries differ in terms of the types of taxes they have (income versus excise), the tax rates applied to income, the determination of taxable income, and the treatment of foreign-source income. Although we focus in this section on corporate income tax, excise taxes are another important source of income to governments. The value-added tax is an example of an excise tax used in Europe. It is a percentage levied on products at the point of sale in every stage of the value chain, and it is included in the final price of the product rather than added to the price as is the case with the sales tax in the United States. There are many other excise taxes, and the large number of taxes in some countries, like Brazil, are very confusing to both local and foreign investors.

Differences in GAAP   Variations among countries in GAAP can lead to differences in the determination of taxable income. In countries where tax laws allow companies to depreciate assets faster than accounting standards allow but where companies must use the same standards for tax and book accounting, higher depreciation expenses result in lower income and therefore lower taxes. Revenue recognition is also an important issue. Some countries tax income from worldwide revenues of MNEs, whereas others only recognize income from revenues generated in the domestic environment.

Differences in Tax Rates   Corporate tax rates also vary from country to country. Table 19.5 identifies the corporate tax rates of the OECD member countries. Note that central government corporate income tax rates range from a low of 8.5 percent in Switzerland to a high of 35 percent in Spain and the United States. However, the total corporate income tax burden includes subcentral government taxes (such as provincial or state and local taxes) as well as the central government corporate income tax.

Two Approaches to Corporate Taxation   Taxation of corporate income is accomplished through one of two approaches in most countries: the *separate entity approach*, also known as the *classical approach*, or the *integrated system approach*.

Separate Entity Approach   In the separate entity approach, which the United States uses, each separate unit—company or individual—is taxed when it earns income. For example, a corporation is taxed on its earnings, and stockholders are taxed on the distribution of earnings (dividends). The result is double taxation.

Integrated System Approach   Many other developed countries use an integrated system to eliminate double taxation. For example, Australia and New Zealand give a dividend credit to shareholders to shelter them from double taxation. That means that when shareholders report the dividends in their taxable income, they also get a credit for taxes paid on that income by the company that issued the dividend. That keeps the shareholders from paying tax on the dividend because the company has already paid a tax on it.

Germany used to have a split-rate system with two different tax rates on corporate earnings—one on retained earnings and one on distributed earnings. However, they

---

Margin notes:

Problems with different countries' tax practices arise from

- Lack of familiarity with laws.
- Loose enforcement.

With a value-added tax, each company pays a percentage of the value added to a product at each stage of the business process.

Corporate tax rates vary from country to country.

In the separate entity approach, governments tax each taxable entity when it earns income.

An integrated system tries to avoid double taxation of corporate income through split tax rates or tax credits.

TABLE 19.5   Corporate Income Tax Rates[1]

Country	Central Government Corporate Income Tax Rate[2]	Adjusted Central Government Corporate Income Tax Rate[3]	Subcentral Government Corporate Income Tax Rate[4]	Combined Corporate Income Tax Rate[5]	Targeted Corporate Tax Rates[6]
Australia[a]	30.0	30.0		30.0	Y
Austria	25.0	25.0		25.0	N
Belgium[b]	33.88 (33.0)	33.99		33.99	Y
Canada	22.1 (21.0)	22.1	14.0	36.1	Y
Czech Republic	24.0	24.0		24.0	Y
Denmark	28.0	28.0		28.0	N
Finland	26.0	26.0		26.0	N
France[c]	34.43	34.43		34.4	Y
Germany[d]	26.375 (25.0)	21.0	17.01	38.9	N
Greece	29.0	29.0		29.0	n.a.
Hungary[d]	18.0	16.0		16.0	Y
Iceland	18.0	18.0		18.0	N
Ireland	12.5	12.5		12.5	Y
Italy[e]	33.0	33.0		33.0	N
Japan	30.0	27.98	11.56	39.54	Y
Korea	25.0	25.0	2.5	27.5	Y
Luxembourg	22.88 (22.0)	22.88	7.5	30.4	Y
Mexico	29.0	29.0		29.0	Y
Netherlands	29.6	29.6		29.6	Y
New Zealand[a]	33.0	33.0		33.0	N
Norway	28.0	28.0		28.0	Y
Poland[g]	19.0	19.0		19.0	n.a.
Portugal[g]	25.0	25.0	2.5	27.5	Y
Slovak Republic	19.0	19.0		18.0	N
Spain	35.0	35.0		35.0	Y
Sweden	28.0	28.0		28.0	N
Switzerland[g]	8.5	6.69	14.64	21.3	N
Turkey	30.0	30.0		30.0	N
United Kingdom[a]	30.0	30.0		30.0	Y
United States[i]	35.0	32.7	6.6	39.3	Y

Key to abbreviations:

n.a.: Data not provided

Explanatory notes:

[1] This table shows "basic" (nontargeted) central, subcentral, and combined (statutory) corporate income tax rates. Where a progressive (as opposed to flat) rate structure applies, the top marginal rate is shown.

[2] This column shows the basic central government statutory (flat or top marginal) corporate income tax rate measured gross of a deduction (if any) for subcentral tax. Where surtax applies, the statutory corporate rate exclusive of surtax is shown in round brackets( ).

[3] This column shows the basic central government statutory corporate income tax rate (inclusive of surtax [if any]), adjusted (if applicable) to show the net rate where the central government provides a deduction in respect of subcentral income tax.

[4] This column shows the basic subcentral (combined state/regional and local) statutory corporate income tax rate, inclusive of subcentral surtax (if any).

[5] This column shows the basic combined central and subcentral (statutory) corporate income tax rate given by the adjusted central government rate plus the subcentral rate.

[6] This column indicates whether targeted (nonbasic) corporate tax rates exist (e.g., with targeting through a special statutory corporate tax rate applied to qualifying income, or through a special deduction determined as a percentage of qualifying income).

Country-specific footnotes:

[a] For Australia, New Zealand, and the United Kingdom, all with a noncalendar tax year, the rates shown are those in effect as of 1 July, 1 April and 5 April respectively.

[b] These are the rates applying to income earned in 2000, to be paid in 2001. The rates include surcharges, but does not include the local business tax (*Taxe professionnelle*) or the turnover-based solidarity tax (*Contribution de Solidarité*). More information on the surcharges is included as a comment.

[c] The rates include the regional trade tax (*Gewerbesteuer*) and the surcharge.

(Continued)

TABLE 19.5   Corporate Income Tax Rates (continued)

d The rates does not include the turnover-based local business tax.

e These rates do not include the regional business tax (*Imposta Regionale Sulie Attività Produttive: IRAP*).

f Source for the information: KPMG's Corporate Tax Rate Survey.

g Adjusted central and subcentral tax rates are calculated by the Swiss Federal Tax Administration (see "Quels taux effectifs et nominaux d'imposition des sociétés en Suisse pour le calcul des coins fiscaux. Le procédé de la déduction fiscale en Suisse").

h The subcentral rate is a weighted average state corporate marginal income tax rate.

Source: Organization for Economic Cooperation and Development, *OECD Tax Data Base* (2007), www.oecd.org (accessed August 30, 2007).

replaced the split rate system with an overall lower corporate tax rate on earnings. Also, individuals are only taxed on 50 percent of the dividends they receive.[39]

Taxation of foreign-source income depends on the country where the parent company is domiciled. It is common for most developed countries to tax companies on their worldwide income and give them a credit for foreign corporate income taxes paid. That is not true everywhere, however. Hong Kong companies, for example, pay tax only on Hong Kong–source income, and their tax rate is only 17.5 percent. As we will see later, U.S. companies are taxed on foreign-source income if dividends are remitted to the United States. However, Hong Kong companies do not have to pay tax on foreign-source income, even if remitted to Hong Kong.[40] That is a characteristic of "tax-haven" countries.

TAXING BRANCHES AND SUBSIDIARIES

To illustrate the complexities of taxing foreign-source income, let's look at how U.S.-based companies tax earnings from a *foreign branch* and a *foreign subsidiary*.

| Foreign branch income (or loss) is directly included in the parent's taxable income.

The Foreign Branch   A foreign branch is an extension of the parent company rather than an enterprise incorporated in a foreign country. Any income the branch generates is taxable immediately to the parent, whether or not cash is remitted by the branch to the parent as a distribution of earnings. However, if the branch suffers a loss, the parent is allowed to deduct that loss from its taxable income, reducing its overall tax liability.

| Tax deferral means that income is not taxed until it is remitted to the parent company as a dividend.

The Foreign Subsidiary   Whereas a branch is a legal extension of a parent company, a foreign corporation is an independent legal entity set up in a country (incorporated) according to the laws of incorporation of that country. When an MNE purchases a foreign corporation or sets up a new corporation in a foreign country, that corporation is called a *subsidiary* of the parent. Income earned by the subsidiary is either reinvested in the subsidiary or remitted as a dividend to the parent company.

Subsidiary income is either taxable to the parent or tax deferred—that is, it is not taxed until it is remitted as a dividend to the parent. Which tax status applies depends on whether the foreign subsidiary is a *controlled foreign corporation* (*CFC*—a technical term in the U.S. tax code) and whether the income is active or passive.

| In a CFC, U.S. shareholders hold more than 50 percent of the voting stock.

The Controlled Foreign Corporation   A **controlled foreign corporation (CFC),** from the standpoint of the U.S. tax code, is any foreign corporation that meets the following condition: More than 50 percent of its voting stock is held by "U.S. shareholders." A U.S. shareholder is any U.S. person or company that holds 10 percent or more of the CFC's voting stock. Any foreign subsidiary of an MNE would automatically be considered a CFC from the standpoint of the tax code. However, a joint-venture company abroad that is partly owned by the U.S.-based MNE and partly by local investors might not be a CFC if the U.S. MNE does not own more than 50 percent of the stock of the joint-venture company.

Table 19.6 shows how this might work. Foreign corporation A is a CFC because it is a wholly owned subsidiary of a U.S. parent company (U.S. Person V). Foreign corporation B also is a CFC because U.S. Persons V, W, and X each own 10 percent or more of the voting

TABLE 19.6 Controlled Foreign Corporations

To qualify as a *controlled foreign corporation (CFC)*, more than 50% of a company's voting shares must be held by U.S. shareholders. A *U.S. shareholder* must be a U.S. person or company holding at least 10% of the corporation's voting shares. Foreign Corporation B qualifies as a **CFC** because the combined shares of U.S. Persons V, W, and X, each consisting of at least 10%, add up to 75% of the total.

	Percentages of the Voting Stock		
Shareholder	Foreign Corporation A	Foreign Corporation B	Foreign Corporation C
U.S. Person V	100%	45%	30%
U.S. Person W		10	10
U.S. Person X		20	8
U.S. Person Y			8
Foreign Person Z		25	44
Total	**100%**	**100%**	**100%**

stock, which means they qualify as U.S. shareholders and their combined voting stock is more than 50 percent of the total. This situation might exist if three U.S. companies partnered together with a foreign partner to establish a joint venture overseas.

Such collaborative arrangements are not uncommon, especially in telecommunications and high-tech industries. Foreign corporation C is not a CFC because even though U.S. Persons V and W qualify as U.S. shareholders, their combined stock ownership is only 40 percent. U.S. Persons X and Y do not qualify as U.S. shareholders because their individual ownership shares are only 8 percent each. When Enron set up its shell companies in tax-haven countries, it was careful to not own more than 50 percent of the stock so it could avoid having to include the debt in those operations in its consolidated income.[41]

Active Versus Passive Income If a foreign subsidiary qualifies as a CFC, the U.S. tax law requires the U.S. investor to classify the foreign-source income as active income or Subpart F (or passive) income. **Active income** is derived from the direct conduct of a trade or business, such as from sales of products manufactured in the foreign country. **Subpart F income**, or **passive income**, which is specifically defined in Subpart F of the U.S. Internal Revenue Code, comes from sources other than those connected with the direct conduct of a trade or business, generally in tax-haven countries. Subpart F income includes the following:

Active income is derived from the direct conduct of a trade or business. Passive income (also called Subpart F income) usually is derived from operations in a tax-haven country.

- *Holding company income*—income primarily from dividends, interest, rents, royalties, and gains on sale of stocks.

- *Sales income*—income from foreign sales corporations that are separately incorporated from their manufacturing operations. The product of such entities is manufactured outside and sold for use outside the CFC's country of incorporation, and the CFC has not performed significant operations on the product.

- *Service income*—income from the performance of technical, managerial, or similar services for a company in the same corporate family as the CFC and outside the country in which the CFC resides.

Subpart F income usually derives from the activities of subsidiaries in tax-haven countries such as the Bahamas, the Netherlands Antilles, Panama, and Switzerland. The U.S. government treats any country whose income tax is lower than that of the United States as a tax-haven country. The tax-haven subsidiary may act as an investment company, a sales agent or distributor, an agent for the parent in licensing agreements, or a

FIGURE 19.7
The Tax-Haven Subsidiary as Holding Company

A U.S. company has established a *tax-haven subsidiary* as a *holding company* in an offshore location. As such, the offshore subsidiary owns shares in three foreign subsidiaries called *grandchild subsidiaries*. The offshore holding company generates *holding company income* that's recorded by the U.S. parent company as *Subpart F income*.

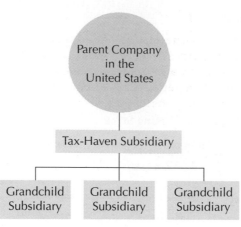

holding company of stock in other foreign subsidiaries that are called grandchild—or second-tier—subsidiaries. This setup is illustrated in Figure 19.7. In the role of a holding company, its purpose is to concentrate cash from the parent's foreign operations into the low-tax country and to use the cash for global expansion.

Different rules regarding the tax status and deferability of income are in effect for non-CFCs, CFCs, and foreign branches.

Determining a Subsidiary's Income   Figure 19.8 illustrates how the tax status of a subsidiary's income is determined. All non-CFC income—active and Subpart F—earned by the foreign corporation is deferred until remitted as a dividend to the U.S. shareholder (the parent company in this example). In contrast, a CFC's active income is tax deferred to the parent, but its Subpart F income is taxable immediately to the parent as soon as the CFC earns it.

If a foreign branch earns the income, it is immediately taxable to the parent company, whether it is active or Subpart F. There is an exception, however. If the foreign-source income is the lower of $1 million or 5 percent of the CFC's gross income, none of it is treated as Subpart F income. At the other extreme, if the foreign-source income is more than 70 percent of total gross income, all of the corporation's gross income for the tax year is treated as Subpart F income.

Finally, foreign-source income subject to high foreign taxes is not considered Subpart F income if the foreign tax rate is more than 90 percent of the maximum U.S. corporate income tax rate. Assuming a corporate tax rate of 35 percent in the United States, that means a parent would not have to consider any income as Subpart F income that is earned in a country with a corporate tax rate greater than 31.5 percent (90 percent $\times$ 35 percent).[42]

FIGURE 19.8   The Tax Status of U.S.-Owned Foreign Subsidiaries

Both CFC and Subpart F provisions are designed to prevent U.S. firms from establishing tax-haven subsidiaries for the purpose of investing *passive income* indefinitely—and thus earning tax-free income. Basically, these provisions tax income just as if it had been remitted to the U.S. parent at the time when it was earned.

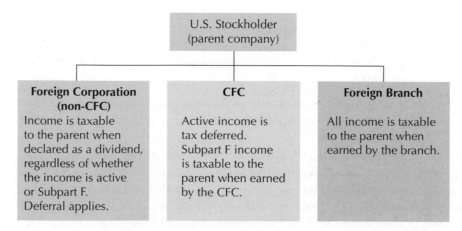

TRANSFER PRICES

As noted in Chapter 18, a major tax challenge as well as an impediment to performance evaluation is the extensive use of transfer pricing in international operations. Because the price is between related entities, it is not necessarily an **arm's-length price**—that is, a price between two companies that do not have an ownership interest in each other. The assumption is that an arm's-length price is more likely than a transfer price to reflect the market accurately.

> A transfer price is a price on goods and services one member of a corporate family sells to another.

Transfer Prices and Taxation   Companies establish arbitrary transfer prices primarily because of differences in taxation between countries. For example, if the corporate tax rate is higher in the parent company's country than in the subsidiary's country, the parent could set a low transfer price on products it sells the subsidiary to keep taxable profits low in its country and high in the subsidiary's country. The parent also could set a high transfer price on products sold to it by the subsidiary.

The OECD is very concerned about the way companies manipulate transfer prices to minimize their tax liability worldwide. Its recommendation is that to determine the tax liability in each country, an arm's-length price should be applied, and it has issued guidelines on the matter. The OECD Center for Tax Policy and Administration meets periodically to discuss a wide range of tax issues, including the adoption of sound transfer pricing policies. The OECD issued guidelines on transfer pricing in 1979 and updated the policies in 1995 to give guidance on how to tell if a transfer between independent firms is similar to a transfer within a group and different transfer pricing methods that could be used.[43]

> The OECD has set transfer pricing guidelines to eliminate the manipulation of prices and, therefore, taxes for MNEs.

Companies can get into disputes with different tax jurisdictions over transfer pricing policies. GlaxoSmithKline (GSK), the British pharmaceutical company, settled a transfer pricing dispute with the U.S. Internal Revenue Service (IRS) in 2006 by paying $3.1 billion in federal, state, and local taxes and interest, slightly less than the $5 billion the IRS was seeking and nearly half of GSK's operating cash flow. The IRS contends that GSK charged its U.S. affiliate too little for marketing services provided by the affiliate, which meant that U.S. earnings were low, resulting in lower taxes collected in the United States. The dispute arose over whether GSK should have paid for the marketing services at cost or at the price it would have paid an independent third party. These are complex issues that leave companies open to significant financial risks if they don't price services or products correctly.[44]

DOUBLE TAXATION AND TAX CREDIT

Every country has a sovereign right to levy taxes on all income generated within its borders. However, MNEs run into a problem when they earn income taxed in the country where the income is earned and where it might also be taxed in the parent country as well. This could result in double taxation.

In U.S. tax law, a U.S. MNE gets a credit for income taxes paid to a foreign government. For example, when a U.S. parent recognizes foreign-source income (such as a dividend from a foreign subsidiary) in its taxable income, it must pay U.S. tax on that income. However, the U.S. IRS allows the parent company to reduce its tax liability by the amount of foreign income tax already paid. It is limited by the amount it would have had to pay in the United States on that income.

> The IRS allows a tax credit for corporate income tax U.S. companies pay to another country. A tax credit is a dollar-for-dollar reduction of tax liability and must coincide with the recognition of income.

Assume, for example, that U.S. MNE A earns $100,000 of foreign-source income on which it paid $40,000 (40 percent tax rate) on that income in the foreign jurisdiction. If that income is considered taxable in the United States, Company A would have to pay $35,000 in income taxes (35 percent tax rate). In the absence of a tax credit, Company A would have paid a total of $75,000 in income tax on the $100,000 of income, a 75 percent tax rate.

The IRS, however, allows Company A to reduce its U.S. tax liability by a maximum of $35,000—what it would have paid in the United States if the income had been earned there. If Company A's subsidiary had paid $20,000 in foreign income tax (a 20 percent tax rate), it would be able to claim the entire $20,000 as a credit because it was less than the U.S. liability of $35,000. Company A will pay a total of $35,000 in corporate income tax on its foreign-source income—$20,000 to the foreign government and $15,000 to the U.S. government.

Tax Treaties: Eliminating Double Taxation   The primary purpose of tax treaties is to prevent international double taxation or to provide remedies when it occurs. The United States is an active participant in over 60 different tax treaties.[45] The general pattern between two treaty countries is to grant reciprocal deductions on dividend withholding and to exempt royalties and sometimes interest payments from any withholding tax.

> The purpose of tax treaties is to prevent double taxation or to provide remedies when it occurs.

The United States has a withholding tax of 30 percent for owners (individuals and corporations) of U.S. securities issued in countries with which it has no tax treaty. However, interest on portfolio obligations and on bank deposits is normally exempted from withholding. When a tax treaty is in effect, the U.S. rate on dividends generally is reduced to 5 to 15 percent, and the tax on interest and royalties is either eliminated or is reduced to 5 to 10 percent.

Other countries have similar tax treaty provisions as does the United States. Members of the EU are a little different. Using France as an example, the French subsidiary of an EU parent company does not pay withholding tax on dividends paid to the parent. In most other cases, the French tax treaties are 0/10/15 percent, depending on the country. The average withholding tax on dividends to nontreaty countries is 33 percent.[46]

LOOKING TO THE FUTURE

Technology and Cash Flows

As companies drive down costs to increase their profitability and market value, they will need to reduce borrowing costs. Greater emphasis will be placed on moving corporate cash worldwide to take advantage of differing rates of return. In addition, companies will need to perfect their strategies for issuing bonds at the cheapest price possible and minimizing their tax bills worldwide.

However, the United States has been clamping down on tax minimization schemes and attacking the providers of such schemes, such as law firms and public accounting firms, as well as going after the corporate clients that are adopting such schemes. As companies establish strategies to take advantage of tax havens, they need to make sure they are very careful to avoid strategies that will turn them into the next Enron or Parmalat. The move to drive down costs can't come at the expense of the future viability of the company.

The explosion of information and technology and the growing number and sophistication of hedging instruments (financial derivatives such as options and forwards) will significantly influence the cash-management and hedging strategies of MNEs in the future. Advances in information systems will continue to enable companies to get information more quickly and cheaply.

In addition, electronic data interchange (EDI) will allow them to transfer information and money instantaneously worldwide. Companies will significantly reduce paper flow and increase the speed of delivery of information and funds, enabling them to manage cash and to use intercompany resources much more effectively than before. Consequently, companies will reduce not only the cost of producing information but also interest and other borrowing costs.

Investment and commercial banks will continue to develop new derivative instruments that will help companies hedge their currency and interest rate exposures in the short and long term. However, new standards in accounting for derivative financial instruments by the FASB and IASB will force companies to mark most derivatives to market and recognize gains and losses in income. In spite of the tightening of accounting standards, derivatives will be a big help to companies as they attempt to hedge their cash flows and protect against the erosion of earnings in an unstable financial environment.

The OECD, the IMF, and the EU are three institutions that will help countries narrow their tax differences and crack down on the transfer of money for illegal purposes. Although illegal financial transfers have occurred for years, especially due to drug trafficking, the attacks on 9/11 and subsequent moves to track down money laundering by Osama bin Laden and other terrorists have created a more urgent need to reform the global financial system. This will continue to narrow the options of companies to move funds, but that isn't a bad idea. ■

Dell Mercosur: Getting Real in Brazil

CASE

Todd Pickett, CFO of Dell Mercosur, was facing the end of 2002 with conflicting predictions of the value of the Brazilian currency, the real, and what to do to hedge Dell's operation in Brazil.[47] Although Pickett was concerned about Dell's exposure in the other Mercosur countries, especially Argentina, Brazil was clearly the largest concern.

The year 2002 began with the shocks resulting from the Argentine financial crisis that started at the end of 2001, and it ended with the election in October of Luiz Inácio Lula da Silva, known simply as Lula, as the president of Brazil. Lula, the leader of the Workers' Party and a longtime leftist politician, had held the lead throughout the year. The markets were skeptical of Lula's potential leadership, a factor that caused the real to weaken from 2.312 reals per U.S. dollar at the end of 2001 to a record 4 reals to one U.S. dollar at one point just prior to the election. After the election, the real began to strengthen somewhat, as noted in Figure 19.9 below, but Pickett had to base his strategies on whether the real would continue to strengthen or would weaken again.

A Little Background

U.S.-based computer company Dell was founded in 1984 by Michael Dell. In 2002, at the time of the case, Dell was operating in 34 countries with 36,000 employees, of which about 14,400 are outside the United States, and recorded $32 billion in sales. In the previous five years, Dell had expanded beyond PCs to servers, storage, and communications equipment. Most PC manufacturers have claimed poor results since the technology bubble burst in 2000—IBM left the industry in 2000 and Compaq and HP merged in 2001 in hopes of boosting their competitive position. Unlike its competitors, Dell had thrived in the previous few years, moving from a market share of 12 percent to 15 percent in 2001, the number-one spot in the industry.

Fiscal 2002, however, was one of the toughest years to date in the PC industry. Because of the softening of the global economy and the events of 9/11, demand for PCs was down sharply. Dell responded with an aggressive price strategy and reduced costs through workforce reductions and facility consolidations. Although global industry shipments fell in 2002 by 5 percent, Dell's unit shipments increased by 15 percent, thus enabling Dell to retain its number-one position.

Dell bases its success on its build-to-order, direct sales model. Dell has eliminated resellers and retailers and sells directly to the customer by phone or over the Internet. Dell

FIGURE 19.9   The Brazilian Real and the U.S. Dollar: Exchange Rate, 1995–2007

Source: Based on "Brazilian Reals to 1 USD," *x-rates.com* (1995–2007), www.x-rates.com (accessed November 26, 2007).

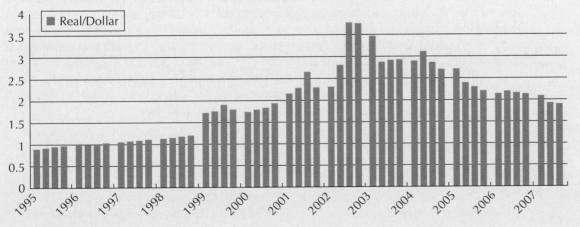

customizes every computer to the customer's needs and waits to build the computer until it is ordered. As a result, Dell requires little inventory (four days on average) and is able to deliver the newest technology to its customers. Costs are kept to a minimum compared with its competitors because it has no costly retail outlets and little inventory.

Dell began assembling computers in Round Rock, Texas, in 1985 and moved to global production in the following order:

1990: Opened manufacturing plant in Ireland
1996: Opened manufacturing plant in Malaysia
1998: Opened manufacturing plant in China
1999: Opened manufacturing plants in Tennessee and Brazil

According to the company's 2002 Form 10K:

Sales outside the United States accounted for approximately 35% of the Company's revenues in fiscal year 2002. The Company's future growth rates and success are dependent on continued growth and success in international markets. As is the case with most international operations, the success and profitability of the Company's international operations are subject to numerous risks and uncertainties, including local economic and labor conditions, political instability, unexpected changes in the regulatory environment, trade protection measures, tax laws (including U.S. taxes on foreign operations), and foreign currency exchange rates.

Dell in Brazil

Dell's production facility in Brazil is in Eldorado do Sul, close to Porto Alegre, the capital of Rio Grande do Sul, the southernmost state in Brazil. In addition, its call center in Brazil, which is similar to Dell's call center in Bray, Ireland, services both Brazil and Argentina. Its Brazilian manufacturing facility, which consists of 100,000 square feet of leased property, is the smallest of its facilities outside the United States, but the potential in Brazil and Argentina is huge, and Dell is planning further expansion.

Because of the tariff-free provisions of Mercosur and the close proximity of Dell's manufacturing facilities in the south of Brazil, Dell is well positioned to service all of Mercosur with its Brazilian manufacturing operations. In fiscal year (FY) 2002, it held a 4.5 percent market share in Brazil, behind HP/Compaq, IBM, and a Brazilian company. However, it was rapidly moving up to third place in the market and growing quickly.

Although Dell is divided into products and customers, it is managed generally geographically. Terry Kahler, the general manager of Dell Mercosur, reports to Rosendo Parra, the vice president of the Americas/International Group in Austin, Texas. Pickett works very closely with Kahler to decrease currency risk and meet budget targets in dollars, but he reports directly to the CFO staff in Austin to coordinate hedging strategies.

Dell's revenues in Brazil are denominated in reals, and most of its operating costs are also denominated in reals. However, about 97 percent of Dell's manufacturing costs in Brazil are denominated in U.S. dollars because Dell imports parts and components from the United States. Most general and administrative costs are in U.S. dollars. It translates its financial statements according to the current-rate method, which means that assets and liabilities are translated into dollars at the current exchange rate, and revenues and expenses are translated at the average exchange rate for the period. Because of business development loans from the Brazilian government, Dell's net exposed asset position in Brazil is quite small, but it is subject to foreign-exchange gains and losses as the rate changes.

How Dell Hedges Its Bets

In its Form 10K for FY 2002, Dell states its foreign-currency hedging strategy as follows:

The Company's objective in managing its exposure to foreign currency exchange rate fluctuations is to reduce the impact of adverse fluctuations on earnings and cash flows

Sharing in growth: Reforms in Brazil have raised regulatory standards, helping to attract vast amounts of capital from foreign investors.

associated with foreign currency exchange rate changes. Accordingly, the Company utilizes foreign currency option contracts and forward contracts to hedge its exposure on forecasted transactions and firm commitments in most of the foreign countries in which the Company operates. The principal currencies hedged during fiscal 2002 were the British pound, Japanese yen, euro, and Canadian dollar. The Company monitors its foreign currency exchange exposures to ensure the overall effectiveness of its foreign currency hedge positions. However, there can be no assurance the Company's foreign currency hedging activities will substantially offset the impact of fluctuations in currency exchange rates on its results of operations and financial position.

The Company uses purchased option contracts and forward contracts designated as cash flow hedges to protect against the foreign currency exchange risk inherent in its forecasted transactions denominated in currencies other than [the] U.S. dollar. Hedged transactions include international sales by U.S. dollar functional currency entities, foreign currency denominated purchases of certain components, and intercompany shipments to certain international subsidiaries. The risk of loss associated with purchased options is limited to premium amounts paid for the option contracts. The risk of loss associated with forward contracts is equal to the exchange rate differential from the time the contract is entered into until the time it is settled. These contracts generally expire in 12 months or less.

The Company also uses forward contracts to economically hedge monetary assets and liabilities, primarily receivables and payables that are denominated in a foreign currency. These contracts are not designated as hedging instruments under generally accepted accounting principles, and, therefore, the change in the instrument's fair value is recognized currently in earnings and is reported as a component of investment and other income (loss), net. The change in the fair value of these instruments represents a natural hedge as their gains and losses offset the changes in the underlying fair value of the monetary assets and liabilities due to movements in currency exchange rates. These contracts generally expire in three months or less.

Based on these general statements of principle, Dell's strategy is to hedge all foreign-exchange risk, which is a very aggressive hedging strategy. Because there is no options market for Brazilian reals, Pickett uses forward contracts to hedge the foreign-exchange risks in Brazil.

Corporate financial management monitors currency movements worldwide and provides support to Pickett's Brazilian financial-management group in terms of currency forecasts and hedging strategies. Within the broad strategy approved by corporate finance, the Brazilian group establishes a strategy and then works with corporate on specific execution of the strategy.

The Two-Part Strategy

There are two key parts to the strategy. One has to do with forecasting exposure, and the other has to do with designing and executing the strategy to hedge the exposure. Although the balance sheet exposure is not material, it still must be forecast and is partly a function of the cash flows generated by revenues. Because the revenue side is more difficult to forecast, Pickett hedges about 80 percent of forecasted revenues.

However, the Dell team in Brazil has become very adept at forecasting revenues and in executing a strategy to reach its target forecast. The team works hard on identifying the challenges in reaching its target and in devising policies to overcome those challenges. Its execution strategies vary widely quarter by quarter, and the management team has become very good at meeting its targets by working closely together and being flexible. Pickett and Kahler work closely together daily to execute their strategy.

The second key to the strategy is designing and executing the hedging strategy. Because revenues vary every day, Pickett does not enter into contracts all at once. Instead, he works with corporate finance to enter into contracts in different amounts and different maturities depending on when it expects to generate the operating revenues. Revenues are generally lower at the beginning of the quarter and are always higher in the last week or two of the quarter, so he enters into contracts accordingly.

Timing is a crucial issue. The gain or loss on a forward contract is the difference in exchange rates between when the contract is entered into and when it is settled. The key is to unwind (or settle) the contracts while the rate is still favorable. Pickett noted that if Dell began to unwind the contracts in the last week or two of the quarter instead of the last day or two of the quarter, it could get much more favorable foreign-exchange gains. His strategy was so successful that in some quarters, Dell was generating more financial income than operating income.

Although Pickett and his finance team have some flexibility in designing and implementing strategy, corporate finance keeps in close touch, depending on their forecasts of the exchange rate and the strategy that Dell Brazil is following. Corporate finance uses a consensus forecast of exchange rates that is provided by a group of banks, but banks have different scenarios. For example, in the last quarter of 2002, corporate was relying on bank forecasts that the real would revalue even more by the end of the year.

Pickett's dilemma was that his gut feeling was telling him the real would actually fall instead of rise. That would indicate a different hedging strategy. He was resisting entering into hedges while corporate was pressuring him to do just that. But he was closely watching the forward market, and when it began to move, he decided it was time to enter into the contracts. He was also considering entering into operating strategies that would provide natural hedges for Dell in Brazil. But who knows what will happen to Brazil if Lula, Brazil's new president, loses fiscal control of the ninth largest economy in the world, resulting in another round of inflation and a falling currency? Dell has significant market opportunities in Mercosur, but the financial risks will make for exciting times in the years to come. ∎

QUESTIONS

1. Given how Dell translates its foreign-currency financial statements into dollars, how would a falling Brazilian real affect Dell Mercosur's financial statements? What about a rising real?
2. Dell imports about 97 percent of its manufacturing costs. What type of exposure does that create for it? What are its options to reduce that exposure?
3. Describe and evaluate Dell's exposure management strategy.

4. Build a graph on the value of the real against the dollar by quarter since the third quarter of 2002 using the spot rate at the end of each quarter. What has happened to the value of the real? Based on the change in the exchange rate, how would you evaluate Dell's hedging philosophy and strategy?

5. What are some programs or strategies that management of Dell Mercosur could implement to provide it with operational hedges?

SUMMARY

- The corporate finance function deals with the acquisition of financial resources and their allocation among the company's present and potential activities and projects.

- CFOs need to be concerned with the international dimensions of the company's capital structure, capital budgeting decisions, long-term financing, and working capital management.

- Country-specific factors are the most important determination of a company's capital structure.

- Two major sources of funds external to the MNE's normal operations are debt markets and equity markets.

- A Eurocurrency is any currency banked outside its country of origin, but it is primarily dollars banked outside the United States.

- A foreign bond is one sold outside the country of the borrower but denominated in the currency of the country of issue. A Eurobond, also called a global bond, is a bond issue sold in a currency other than that of the country of issue.

- Euroequities are shares listed on stock exchanges in countries other than the home country of the issuing company. Most foreign companies that list on the U.S. stock exchanges do so through American Depositary Receipts, which are financial documents that represent a share or part of a share of stock in the foreign company. ADRs are easier to trade on the U.S. exchanges than are foreign shares.

- Offshore financial centers such as Bahrain, the Caribbean, Hong Kong, London, New York, Singapore, and Switzerland deal in large amounts of foreign currency and enable companies to take advantage of favorable tax rates.

- When deciding to invest abroad, MNE management must evaluate the cash flows from the local operation as well as the cash flows from the project to the parent. The former allows management to determine how the project stacks up with other opportunities in the foreign country, and the latter allows management to compare projects from different countries.

- The major sources of internal funds for an MNE are dividends, royalties, management fees, loans from parent to subsidiaries and vice versa, purchases and sales of inventory, and equity flows from parent to subsidiaries.

- Global cash management is complicated by differing inflation rates, changes in exchange rates, and government restrictions on the flow of funds. A sound cash-management system for an MNE requires timely reports from affiliates worldwide.

- Management must protect corporate assets from losses due to exchange-rate changes. Exchange rates can influence the dollar equivalent of foreign-currency financial statements, the amount of cash that can be earned from foreign-currency transactions, and a company's production and marketing decisions.

- Foreign-exchange risk management involves defining and measuring exposure, setting up a good monitoring and reporting system, adopting a policy to assign responsibility for exposure management, and formulating strategies for hedging exposure.

- Companies can enter into operational or financial strategies for hedging exposures. Operational strategies include balancing exposed assets with exposed liabilities, using leads and lags in cash flows, and balancing revenues in one currency with expenses in the same currency. Financial strategies involve using forward contracts, options, or other financial instruments to hedge an exposed position.

- International tax planning has a strong impact on the choice of location for the initial investment, the legal form of the new enterprise, the method of financing, and the method of setting transfer prices.

- Countries differ in terms of the types of taxes they have (income versus excise), the tax rates applied to income, the determination of taxable income, and the treatment of foreign-source income.

- Tax deferral means that the income a foreign subsidiary earns is taxed only when it is remitted to the parent as a dividend, not when it is earned.

- A controlled foreign corporation (CFC) must declare its Subpart F income as taxable to the parent in the year it is earned, whether or not it is remitted as a dividend.

- A tax credit allows a parent company to reduce its tax liability by the direct amount its subsidiary pays a foreign government on income that must be taxed by the parent company's government.

- The purpose of tax treaties is to prevent international double taxation or to provide remedies when it occurs.

KEY TERMS

active income (p. 759)
American Depositary Receipt (ADR) (p. 742)
arm's-length price (p. 761)
controlled foreign corporation (CFC) (p. 758)
economic (or operating) exposure (p. 752)
Eurobond (p. 738)
Eurocredit (p. 737)
Eurocurrency (p. 736)

Eurocurrency market (p. 736)
Eurodollar (p. 736)
Euroequity market (p. 741)
foreign bonds (p. 738)
global bond (p. 738)
leverage (p. 734)
lag strategy (p. 754)
lead strategy (p. 754)
London Inter-Bank Offered Rate (LIBOR) (p. 737)
market capitalization (p. 740)

net present value (NPV) (p. 746)
netting (p. 748)
offshore financial centers (p. 742)
offshore financing (p. 742)
payback period (p. 746)
Subpart F (or passive) income (p. 759)
syndication (p. 737)
tax-haven country (p. 743)
transaction exposure (p. 750)
translation exposure (p. 750)

ENDNOTES

1 *Sources include the following:* "People on the Move," *Deseret News*, January 31, 1999: M02; Wells Fargo New Release, "Wells Fargo & Company and First Security Corporation Agree to Merge," April 10, 2000, at www.wellsfargo.com/press/firstsec20000410?year=2000 (accessed November 20, 2007); interviews with Ali Manbeian and Jason Langston; company literature.

2 Arthur J. Keown, John D. Martin, J. William Petty, and David F. Scott, Jr., *Financial Management,* 10th ed. (Upper Saddle River, NJ: Pearson Prentice Hall, 2005), p. 5.

3 Based on David K. Eiteman, Arthur I. Stonehill, and Michael H. Moffett, *Multinational Business Finance,* 10th ed. (Reading, MA: Addison-Wesley, 2003), p. 3.

4 Keown et al., *Financial Management,* p. 290.

5 "Theory versus the Real World," *Finance & Treasury,* April 26, 1993: 1.

6 Mihir A. Desai, C. Fritz Foley, and James R. Hines, Jr., "A Multinational Perspective on Capital Structure Choice and Internal Capital Markets," *Journal of Economic Literature* (October 2003).

7 Abe de Jong, Rezaul Kabir, and Thuy Thu Nguyen, "Capital Structure around the World: The Roles of Firm- and Country-Specific Determinants" (November 2006). EFA 2006 Zurich Meetings, at SSRN, http://ssrn.com/abstract=890525 (accessed November 20, 2007).

8 De Jong et al., "Capital Structure Around the World."

9 Henry Sender, "Financial Musical Chairs," *Far Eastern Economic Review,* July 29, 1999: 30–36.

10 Nissan, "Short-Term Borrowings and Long-Term Debt," *Nissan Annual Report* (2005), 69, at www. nissan-global.com/EN/IR/LIBRARY/AR/2005/index.html (accessed May 22, 2007).

11 Nu Skin Enterprises Inc., *Nu Skin Form 10-K/A* (2006), p. 58, at www.nuskinenterprises.com/en/library/pdf/sec-filings/2006/10KA_03–17–06.pdf (accessed May 22, 2007).

12 Patrick McGuire, "A Shift in London's Eurodollar Market," *BIS Quarterly Review* (September 2004): 67.

13 "International Rates," *Wall Street Journal Online* (accessed August 28, 2007).

14 Ben White and Victoria Kim, "Lehman to Shut Down Subprime Unit," *Financial Times,* August 22, 2007, at www.ft.com/cms/s/2caa76fa-50de-11dc-8e9d-0000779fd2ac,dwp_uuid=d355f29c-d238–11db-a7c0–000b5df10621.html (accessed August 27, 2007).

15 "US Senator Sees Sub-Prime Crisis Getting Worse Before Better," *Yahoo! News,* at http://news.yahoo.com/s/afp/20070820/pl_afp/marketsfinanceus (accessed August 27, 2007).

16 "US Senator Sees Sub-Prime Crisis Getting Worse Before Better," *Yahoo! News.*

17 "EuroLinks Daily View: Why German Banks Face an Especially Tight Squeeze," online edition, *Wall Street Journal Online: Sunday Edition (Eastern Edition)* (August 19, 2007): ProQuest. E-mailed August 25, 2007; viewed August 27, 2007.

18 "Europe's American Dream," *The Economist,* November 21, 1998: 71.

19 "Global Financial Stability Report," *International Monetary Fund* (September 2002): 48.

20 "An Offer They Can Refuse," *Euromoney* (February 1995): 76.

21 Anant Sundaram, "International Financial Markets," in Dennis E. Logue, ed., *Handbook of Modern Finance* (New York: Warren, Gorham, Lamont, 1994), pp. F3–F4.

22 "Financial Review," *Marks & Spencer Annual Report and Financial Statements* (2002): www2. marksandspencer.com/thecompany/ investorrelations/annualreport/ fin_review.shtml.

23 "Gazprombanks's Eurobonds," at www.gazprombank.ru/eng/ corporate/securities/eurobonds/ index.wbp (accessed May 24, 2005).

24 "Private Equity Stirs Up the Pot," *Euroweek* (October 1999): 27–34.

25 Aaron Lucchetti and Craig Karmin, "Intensity to Be a 'Global' Stock Has Waned," *Wall Street Journal,* May 10, 2005: C1.

26 International Monetary Fund, "Global Financial Stability Report: Market Development and Issues" (September 2002), 56, at www.imf.org/External/Pubs/FT/GFSR/2002/03/index.htm.

27 IMF Monetary and Exchange Affairs Department, "IMF Background Paper: Offshore Financial Centers," June 23, 2000.

28 "IMF Background Paper: Offshore Financial Centers."

29 "IMF Background Paper: Offshore Financial Centers."

30 "How the Heavyweights Shape Up," *Euromoney* (May 1990): 56.

31 Organization for Economic Cooperation and Development (OECD), "Project on Harmful Tax Practice: The 2004 Progress Report," March 22, 2004.

32 Organization for Economic Co-operation and Development, "Committee on Fiscal Affairs Releases Outcome of Review of Preferential Tax Regimes in OECD Countries," at www.oecd.org/ document/31/0,3343,en_2649_33745_37446047_1_1_1_1,00.html; OECD, "The OECD'S Project on Harmful Tax Practices: 2006 Update on Progress in Member Countries," at www.oecd.org/ dataoecd/1/17/37446434.pdf (accessed June 15, 2007).

33 David Cay Johnston, "How Offshore Havens Helped Enron Escape Taxes," *New York Times,* January 18, 2002.

34 Lucy Komisar, "Funny Money," *Metroactive News & Issues,* January 24, 2002, at www.metroactive.com/papers/sonoma/01.24.02/ offshorebanking-0204.html (accessed June 7, 2005).

35 Eiteman et al., *Multinational Business Finance.*

36 Stephen Power, "BMW's Profit Softened in Quarter," *Wall Street Journal,* May 4, 2005: A12.

37 The Coca-Cola Company, *Coca-Cola Annual Report 2006,* 14, at http://ir.thecoca-colacompany.com/phoenix.zhtml?c= 94566&p=IROL-sec&control_selectgroup=Annual%20Filings (accessed July 13, 2007).

38 The Coca-Cola Company, *Coca-Cola Annual Report 2006,* 65.

39 Deloitte Touche Tohmatsu, "Germany Snapshot: Individual Tax," at www.deloittetaxguides.com/index.asp?layout= countrySnapshotDtt&country_id=1360000136 (accessed August 30, 2007).

40 Deloitte Touche Tohmatsu, "Hong Kong Snapshot: Corporate Tax," www.deloittetaxguides.com/index.asp?layout= countrySnapshotDtt&country_id=1560000156 (accessed August 30, 2007).

41 Johnston, "How Offshore Havens Helped Enron Escape Taxes."

42 William H. Hoffman et al., *West Federal Taxation: Corporations, Partnerships, Estates, and Trusts* (Cincinnati: South-Western, 2002), section 9, p. 33.

43 OECD, *Transfer Pricing Guidelines for Multinational Enterprises and Tax Administrations* (OECD Publishing, June 18, 2001), p. 254.

44 Ronald Fink, "Haven or Hell," *CFO Magazine* (March 2004); Helen Shaw, "Transfer Students," *CFO Magazine* (April 2007), at www.cfo.com/article.cfm/8885626/c_8910395?f=insidecfo (accessed August 30, 2007).

45 Deloitte Touche Tohmatsu, "Foreign Income and Tax Treaties," in *United States of America International Tax and Business Guide,* at www.deloittetaxguides.com (accessed August 30, 2007).

46 Deloitte Touche Tohmatsu, "Foreign Income and Tax Treaties," in *France International Tax and Business Guide,* at www.deloittetaxguides.com (accessed August 30, 2007).

47 *Sources include the following:* Author interview with Todd Pickett (2002); Dell Computer Corp., *Form 10-K,* 2002 (April 28, 2003), at http://phx.corporate-ir.net/phoenix.zhtml?c=101133&p= irol-sec&control _selectgroup=Annual%20Filings (accessed November 20, 2007); Michael Schrage, "The Dell Curve," *Wired Magazine* (July 2002): www.wired.com/wired/archive/10.07/dell.

Human Resource Management

Objectives

- To discuss the importance of human resource management in international business

- To profile principal types of staffing policies used by international companies

- To explain the qualifications of international managers

- To examine how MNEs select, prepare, compensate, and retain managers

- To profile MNEs' relations with organized labor

If you are planning for a year, plant grain. If you are planning for a decade, plant trees. If you are planning for a century, plant people.

—Chinese proverb

CASE: Go or No Go: Your Career?

Chairman and CEO of General Electric, Jeffrey Immelt,[1] once declared that

> *a good global company does three things: It's a global sales company—meaning it's number one with customers all over the world, whether in Chicago or Paris or Tokyo. It's a global products company, with technologies, factories, and products made for the world, not just for a single region. And, most important, it's a global people company—a company that keeps getting better by capturing global markets and brains.*

WHAT DO PEOPLE DO IN INTERNATIONAL BUSINESS?

The issue of a person's role in international business is an increasingly critical one. International companies have been moving people around for centuries, seeking to capture many of the benefits that follow from putting the right person into the right job at the right place at the right time. Now, more than ever, companies engaged in international business must do so. The success of globalization, by increasing trade, capital, and investment flows across nations, has created many operating units worldwide. The growth in emerging economies such as the BRICs has intensified these trends. Together, they support the notion that if you are going to be successful, you have to be global.

In a borderless marketplace, economic patterns and business practices in one region can determine the fate of a company on the other side of the globe. Increasingly, being a corporate leader demands an international background. "You have to have an intuitive sense of how the world works and how people behave. . . . There is no substitute for personal experience," says Paul Laudicina, vice president of A. T. Kearney. Daniel Meiland, executive chairman of Egon Zehender International, a large international executive search firm, offers this assessment:

> *[T]he world is getting smaller, and markets are getting bigger. In my more than 25 years in the executive search profession, we've always talked about the global executive, but the need to find managers who can be effective in many different settings is growing ever more urgent. In addition to looking for intelligence, specific skills, and technical insights, companies are also looking for executives who are comfortable on the world stage.*

The Expatriate Manager

International companies often use expatriates (someone sent by their company from his or her home country to live and work in another country) to run their foreign operations. Some MNEs, such as FedEx, use few expatriates; others, like Royal Dutch Shell and Toyota, use many. Unfortunately, little guidance is available for MNEs when dealing with the multitude of human resource management issues. The most fundamental of these are why, when, and where we should use expatriates to staff foreign operations. Other issues to consider are the practical matters of selecting the right expatriate, making sure the employee gets the right predeparture preparation, designing the right compensation package to motivate performance, and determining the right way to reintegrate that employee back into the home company on the completion of the tour of duty abroad.

The benefits of overseas success and costs of overseas failure move companies like Honeywell to identify and develop potential candidates years before their possible assignment to a foreign unit. Early on, Honeywell briefs potential expatriates on their cross-cultural skills and prescribes training paths that deal with possible points of culture shock. Manfred Fiedler, vice president of human resources, describes the process: "We give them a horizon, a perspective and, gradually, we tell them they are potentially on an international path. . . . We want them to develop a cross-cultural intellect, what we call 'strategic accountability.'" To this end, Honeywell might advise an employee to network with people who have already worked abroad, study another language, or informally explore areas where he or she might struggle while living in another country.

Things to Consider Before Expatriating Yourself

Laying the foundation for a possible career in international business takes time. Many factors have to be considered, from career progression to the stresses of living outside one's comfort zone. Many people who have worked overseas note that early challenges are not always obstacles. These challenges force them to look at situations in a different way. Working internationally compels employees to develop richer management repertoires than those used while working in their home nation.

Consider Joan Pattle, a Microsoft marketing manager who worked at corporate headquarters in Seattle for three years before accepting a post as product manager for direct marketing in Britain. While in the United States, Pattle had been

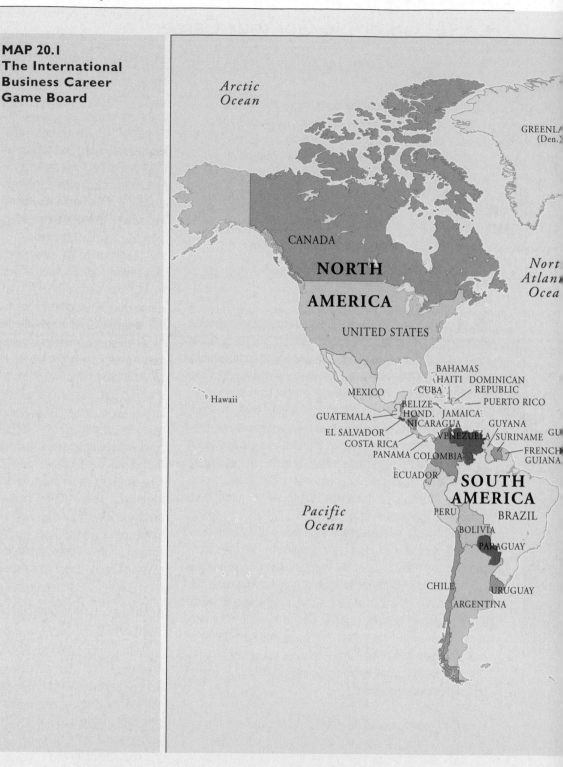

**MAP 20.1
The International
Business Career
Game Board**

in charge of direct marketing. Her U.K. job came with much wider responsibilities: "At home, my job was very strictly defined. I basically had to know everything about managing a database. But when I got to London, I was also in charge of direct marketing and press relations. I was exposed to a much broader set of experiences."

Similarly, Laura Anderson, a spokeswoman for Intel Corp. explained that her two assignments in Hong Kong exposed her to a side of the company's business and media relations she had never experienced before. In China, a flashy fashion show helped showcase Intel technology, and the press responded with strong coverage. There, unlike in the United States, a special show wrapped around a core-product marketing event is key to attracting media interest. That, and several other Asian media relations encounters, opened Anderson's eyes during her short-term Hong Kong assignments. "For me," she says, "it was a tremendous growth experience."

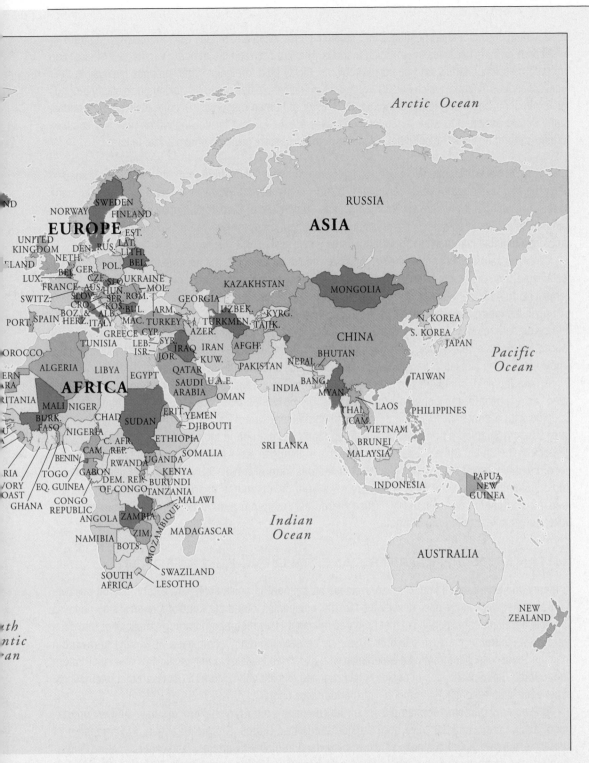

Along these lines, McKinsey & Company, a global management consulting firm, found that an expatriate who has technical competence is now a given but that

> [g]lobal market pioneers must have a particular mind-set. . . . When you look behind the success stories of leading globalizers, you find companies that have learned how to think differently from the herd. They seek out different information, process it in a different way, come to different conclusions, and make different decisions. Where others see threats and complexity, they see opportunity. Where others see a barren landscape, they see a cornucopia of choices.

Still, an international assignment is risky for both managers and the companies. For many foreign executives, cultural clashes, language difficulties, murky business practices, and a harsh environment rule out anything beyond a short posting. Other problems arise when a company asks an executive to transfer to second- or third-tier cities in emerging markets. The gap between life at home versus "over there" can create professional, family, and personal problems. Richly paid foreigners often produce jealousy in their local colleagues. Alibaba, which has 30 expatriates in Hangzhou, has made disclosing one's salary grounds for termination, according to Jin Jianhang, its director of human resources. Despite their best intentions, many people assigned to work in foreign companies are not cut out for dealing with a new and complex foreign culture; this has the potential of leading to the expensive problem of expatriate failure.

Coming Home   Eventually, most managers return home. One would think this would be a snap—pack the bags, say good-bye to colleagues, board the plane, and return to a hero's welcome. In many cases, everything but the hero's welcome happens. Tom Schiro of Deloitte & Touche observed that "some companies just send somebody overseas and forget about them for two years." To combat this potential problem, continual communication with the home unit is essential.

Likewise, careful career planning can make a world of difference when it's time to return. For example, following a four-year assignment in Tokyo, Bryan Krueger returned to a promotion to president of Baxter Fenwal North America. When he left to start his job in Tokyo, his company did not guarantee him a promotion upon his return. So, while away, he kept up-to-date with the goings-on at headquarters. Krueger credited his smooth return to his intensive networking. During his stint in Tokyo, he returned to the United States four to five times a year to see colleagues and friends. As he explains, "I was definitely proactive. Anyone who's not is doing himself a disservice. I made a conscious effort to stay in touch, and it paid off."

On the flip side, companies may be unable to entice some expatriates to return home. While overseas, an expatriate can achieve remarkable levels of compensation, responsibility, and prestige. Coupled with a penchant for living abroad, an international career can prove irresistible. For example, after stints in Singapore and London, a Morgan Stanley expatriate in India muses, "I still don't want to go back to the United States. It's a big world—lots of things to see." But he goes on to say that international business travel "is perhaps the most dangerous form of travel. Tourists wouldn't consider flying into a Colombian war zone for a week, yet folks from oil, computer, pharmaceutical, agricultural and telecom companies do it regularly." Once there, just frequenting good hotels and restaurants with colleagues makes them prime targets.

INTERNATIONAL EXPERIENCE AND YOUR CAREER TRAJECTORY

In theory, the professional impact of an overseas assignment to one's career trajectory may be positive, neutral, or negative. In the past, despite the fact that companies touted the value of foreign assignments as valuable development experiences that prepared managers for greater corporate responsibilities, the odds were on a neutral or negative outcome. This may be because many companies were slow to reward a manager's successful international experience with expanded leadership responsibilities upon their return home. Today, the globalization of business has changed this situation. More CEOs assert that international experience is an essential feature of a high-performance career.

At Procter & Gamble, for example, 39 of the company's top 44 global officers have had an international assignment, and 22 were born outside the United States. Giorgio Siracusa, P&G manager of human resource's global business services, believes that global awareness and experience are "ingredient[s] you must have if you aspire to be a global player in the long term." This globalization has spurred MNEs like Samsung, AstraZeneca, and Dow Chemical to see multinational experience as being just as essential as multifunctional and multiproduct experiences in reaching the upper echelons of the company. Data confirm this trend; for example, 80 percent of FTSE 100 CEOs had experience with international assignments.

More pointedly, Daniel Meiland conjectures, "If you look ahead five to ten years, the people with the top jobs in large corporations, even in the United States, will be those who have lived in several cultures and who can converse in at least two languages. Most CEOs will have had true global exposure, and their companies will be all the stronger for it."

Introduction

The challenge of putting the right person into the right job in the right place at the right time for the right compensation takes us to the front lines of international business. From opening markets to returning home, international business careers take any number of directions. At the center is the individual facing challenges that often lead to surprising opportunities. The contest between challenges and opportunities is the spirit of a career in international business.[2] This chapter looks at the role of the individual in international business, paying particular attention to facets of human resource management as they apply to managers in the MNE.

Human resource management refers to activities necessary to staff the organization.

WHAT IS HRM?

Human resource management (HRM) refers to the activities that a company, whether solely domestic or thoroughly global, takes to staff its organization. Opening and operating a business demands that companies determine their human resource needs, hire people to meet those needs, motivate them to perform well, upgrade their skills so they can move on to more challenging tasks, and, ultimately, retain them.[3]

This chapter, building on the themes introduced in Chapter 11 and applied since to various value chain activities, looks at HRM from the perspective that successful companies staff their operations with people who can leverage their core competencies while dealing with pressures for local responsiveness and global integration. This premise emphasizes that the various HRM activities, like discrete activities in the company's value chain, perform best when managers link them to the strategy of the firm (see Figure 20.1).

HRM and the Global Company   HRM is more difficult for the international company than its domestic counterparts. Complications arise from political, cultural, legal, and economic differences between countries—to say nothing of the struggle of traveling the

FIGURE 20.1   Factors Influencing HRM in International Business

Managing a company's human resources, like managing its finances, marketing efforts, and supply chain, is a function of implementing its strategies. In this case, it's a matter of putting the right person in the right job in the right place at the right time for the right compensation.

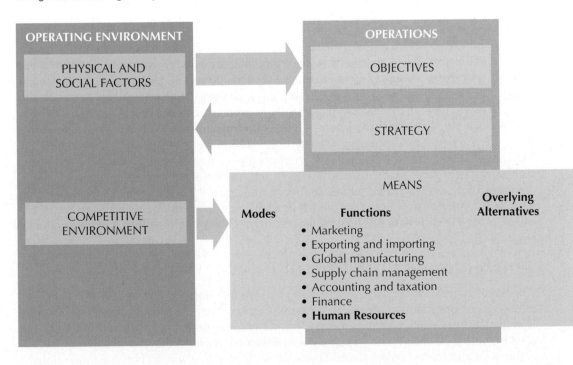

FIGURE 20.2
Have Career, Will Travel

Source: From *Punch Magazine.*
Reprinted by permission.

"I've never actually met him—as soon as he's over the jet lag, it's time for another trip in search of overseas markets."

HRM is more difficult for the international company than its domestic counterpart due to

• Environmental differences.
• Organizational challenges.

world (see Figure 20.2). For example, leadership styles and management practices vary from country to country.[4] These differences can cause difficulties between people at different units, say, headquarters and a local subsidiary. More worrisome, these differences can turn a great manager at home into an ineffective one in foreign markets.

Similarly, labor markets vary in the mix of workers, costs, and productivity. As we saw in Chapter 3, local labor laws often require a company to change its workplace standards and hiring practices. Finally, dual career and family obligations make it tough to convince executives to leave the home office to join a foreign subsidiary. Consequently, companies develop recruitment, training, compensation, transfer, and retention programs to persuade, prepare, and provide incentives for executives to work abroad.

Global HRM as Competitive Advantage   One wonders why companies and people put up with these aggravations. The short answer is that in the face of globalization they must. The long answer is that in the face of globalization, insightfully dealing with these challenges creates competitive advantages. Both answers highlight the mandate for HRM: Develop the means and methods to build, develop, and retain the cadre of managers that will lead an international company to greater performance.

This chapter discusses how international companies use HRM processes to meet this mandate. We begin by discussing the role that HRM plays in supporting the strategy the MNE has chosen to create value.[5] We then profile those HRM activities that move the company's personnel plans from ambition to action, namely, the selection, development, compensation, and retention of international managers.[6] The chapter concludes with a look at the relationship between the MNE and labor, examining the implication of the linkages among international labor relations, management action, and firm strategy.

The Strategic Function of International HRM

Anecdotes suggest and research confirms a powerful relationship between HRM processes, management productivity, and strategic performance.[7] We noted in Chapter 11 that Jeffrey Immelt, CEO and chairman of General Electric, believes success is "truly about people, not about where the buildings are. You've got to develop people so they are prepared for leadership jobs and then promote them. That's the most effective way to become more global."

Furthermore, as we saw in our opening case, Immelt adds that "a good global company" is "a global people company"—one that's as much interested in global brainpower as it is in global markets. Similarly, the former chairman of Unilever, discussing how the world is changing and what management can do to respond, reasons, "The single most important issue for us has been, and will continue to be, organization and people."[8]

When HRM Is Strong   Research confirms that superior human resources sustains high productivity, competitive advantage, and value creation. The Human Capital Index, synthesized from the practices of 2,000 companies, found that superior human resource practices positively correlated with a firm's financial returns and were a leading indicator of increased shareholder value.[9]

Significantly, analysis found a notable pattern of causality: Superior HRM was a stronger determinant of a firm's financial performance, in contrast to the thesis that superior financial outcomes lead companies to develop superior HRM practices. Or, to paraphrase Jeffrey Immelt, creating value is "truly about people, not about where the buildings are." Others report similar effects, finding that the interaction between the firm's strategy and its HRM processes accounts for more variation in its performance than simply looking at the primary effects of HRM.[10]

When HRM Is Weak   The irony of this situation is that we often hear companies trumpet "Our people are our most important asset." Still, more than a few employees can relay tales that when push came to shove, companies failed to honor this pledge. Research finds similar effects, confirming that many international companies do not match rhetoric to reality. For instance, later parts of the chapter discuss the odd fact of what happens to executives when they return home from their overseas assignment—more than half leave their company within a year due to their dissatisfaction with how their companies rewarded and recognized their foreign accomplishments.

Study of HRM at more than 300 multinationals reports that developing and managing human resources is one of the weakest capabilities in most firms.[11] There is even the suggestion that although many companies believe they understand the cost of their international assignments, "only a few are in a position to measure the specific expense, resulting value, and, ultimately, return on investment from such postings."[12] In contrast, companies that improved the strategic performance of their HRM practices increased their market value by as much as 30 percent.[13] In summary, then, research reports that executives acknowledge that the effectiveness of human resource practices materially affects firm performance, but many fail to achieve their HRM goals.

Although the MNE whose HRM policies support its strategy can create superior value, many MNEs struggle to develop effective HRM policies.

STRATEGIZING HRM

The gap between rhetoric and reality of the value of human resources has led to the necessity of changing how companies staff operations. Now HRM must hire, develop, reward, and retain people whose performance improves the productivity of the firm's core competencies within the context of how it has configured and coordinated its value chain. The odds that a company successfully engages its chosen strategy is influenced by how well it staffs the right person in the right job in the right place at the right time for the right salary.

Our earlier look at the types of strategies that international businesses follow provides a way to elaborate this view. Chapter 11 discussed four strategies pursued by an MNE: The *international strategy* and its quest to leverage core competencies abroad, the *multidomestic strategy* and its quest to maximize the local responsiveness of its foreign operations, the *global strategy* and its quest to maximize global integration, and the *transnational strategy* and its quest to optimize all three tasks simultaneously.

Case: Transnational Strategy at GE   The type of strategy that MNEs pursue has explicit HRM requirements. A company makes its strategic ambitions mere speculations if it does not build the human resources needed to achieve them. For example, GE uses a transnational strategy. Getting to this point has taken the company more than two decades. Beginning in the 1980s, GE focused on globalizing its markets to tighten its cost structure (the international strategy). In the late 1980s, the company moved to globalizing its material sources to get higher-quality inputs for lower prices (the global strategy). Then, in the mid-1990s, it began trying to globalize its intellect, seeking, learning, and transferring ideas throughout its global operations (the transnational strategy).

At each stop along the way to its current transnational strategy, GE rethought its HRM philosophy to make sure it had the human capital to achieve its strategy. The key to its international strategy was staffing people who could optimize location economics and scale effects; the key to its global strategy was staffing people with the outlook to manage global scanning and supply chains; and the key to its transnational strategy has been staffing people around the world who can develop, transfer, and receive ideas. At each stage in GE's evolution, its HRM aligned the processes of employee selection, development, and compensation policies to support its strategy.

A vital part of GE's HRM evolution has been its use and expectations of expatriates. Jeffrey Immelt explains, "When I first joined General Electric [in 1982], globalization meant training the Americans to be global thinkers. So Americans got the expat assignments. We still have many Americans living around the world, and that's good, but we shifted our emphasis in the late 1990s to getting overseas assignments for non-Americans. Now you see non-Americans doing new jobs, big jobs, important jobs at every level and in every country." GE's sophisticated use of expatriates has created a cadre of international managers with the expertise to manage its core competency in developing and diffusing powerful ideas around the world.

GE's success in international business, like that of many other companies we profile throughout this chapter, highlights the standard for HRM in an MNE: staffing the manager with the necessary qualifications to the job that best supports and sustains the company's strategy.

An expatriate is an employee who leaves her or his native country to live and work in another.

Taking the Expatriate Perspective   As with preceding chapters, we apply an executive perspective to study HRM in the MNE. Technically, executives in the MNE are one of three classes: *locals, citizens of the countries in which they're working,* or *expatriates.* A local is hired by the MNE in his or her home country to staff the local operations. An **expatriate** (or *expat*) is temporarily sent to work in a country other than his or her legal residence. By definition, an expatriate is either a **home-country national**—a citizen of the country where the company is headquartered—or a **third-country national**—a citizen of neither the country where they work nor the headquarters country but a third country (for example, a Swedish citizen running the Brazilian operation for an Australian company).

A third-country national is an employee who is a citizen of neither the home nor the host country.

Trends in Expatriate Assignment   Recently, there has been a burst in worldwide demand for expatriates.[14] Growing demand follows from the emergence of developing countries as high-growth markets coupled with the growing difficulty in finding skilled locals for start-up operations or in replacing expatriates in existing units. Staffing globalization, so to speak, has led to redefining the mechanics of expatriate assignments.

The central concept of an expatriate is someone who leaves his or her home country to work abroad. However, precise classification of an expatriate, like the sort we note above, is no longer quite so straightforward. Historically, an expatriate was typically posted to a particular host country for a three- to five-year assignment with the ultimate plan of returning to the home country. Now, surveys report that most international assignments are much shorter. A decade ago, a little more than 10 percent of international assignments were scheduled for one year or less; today, 80 percent or more run that short.[15] "Short-term assignments are popular because they are generally more cost-effective than long-term assignments and they allow companies to transfer skill sets quickly and easily," said one analyst.[16]

Traditionally, expatriates were midlevel executives being developed for higher levels of responsibility. As such, companies saw an international assignment as a midcareer stepping-stone for its future leadership. Now, some companies are changing their traditional profile of an expatriate in terms of age, targeting younger employees who are single, more mobile, and less resistant to change or older employees whose children have grown and whose partners may be more willing to move.

In addition, the changing workplace of globalization elevates the usefulness of third-country nationals.[17] When companies establish lead operations abroad, such as headquarters for a product division, third-country nationals often have the competencies needed for the foreign assignments. Moreover, the move toward short-term assignments boosts the appeal of third-country nationals—a banker living in London yet working for a U.S. headquartered firm, for instance, may spend Monday through Friday working in Zurich and then return home for the weekend.

The rise of emerging markets has added a final twist to our evolving ideas of expatriates. Historically, companies selected expatriates from the pool of executives in richer countries and sent them to staff operations in developing countries. Now, well-educated executives from leading emerging economies are being sent straightaway to the richer ones and are becoming ideal local candidates for many European or American firms. Hired directly into the home-country headquarters to learn the ropes, they then return to head operations in their home market, typically replacing an expatriate.

Changes in the global environment continue to change our ideas of how best to staff globalization. The mechanics of expatriate assignments will continue to evolve. Notwithstanding these changes, staffing the thousands of home offices and foreign affiliates around the world means international companies must find and move managers between national operations. And on the matter of simply finding qualified managers, surveys report growing worries among senior human resource managers about companywide talent shortages. Companies around the world are finding it harder than ever to recruit the future leaders of their organizations.[18] As such, we see enduring permanence to the anchor of HRM in the international company: Finding people to fill international jobs begins with how the MNE defines its staffing policies.

DEVELOPING STAFFING POLICIES

For MNEs, the issue of staffing policies centers on the decision of whether to run their international operations with local workers in the host nation, expatriates sent from the home country, or third-country nationals. Research spotlights three types of frameworks as they sort through these staffing questions: the ethnocentric approach, the polycentric approach, and the geocentric approach.

First, however, a quick caveat: As you review each type, keep in mind there is no theoretically superior approach. Each one has strengths and weaknesses that shape how it anchors staffing policies.

Ethnocentric Approach   An ethnocentric staffing policy reflects the belief that the principles and practices used by the home-office country are superior to those used by companies in other nations. Thus, given its success in the home market, there is little need to adapt principles and practices when transferred to foreign markets.[19] This staffing policy leads companies to fill expatriate slots with executives from the home office.

Advantages of the Ethnocentric Approach   As you can see in Table 20.1, several benefits support this approach.

TRANSFERRING CORE COMPETENCIES   MNEs that link firm performance to how well they transfer core competencies are keen to adopt an ethnocentric approach. Specifically, a firm earns success in its home market doing something exceptional. A legacy of success leads companies to see their business methods as the best way to do things. In such situations,

Companies are sensitive to the congruence between the values held by an employee and those of its organizational culture.

CONCEPT CHECK

In discussing "Company and Management Orientations" in Chapter 2, we introduce *polycentrism, ethnocentrism*, and *geocentrism* as three "attitudes or orientations" that companies and their managers may take toward foreign cultures. Here, in explaining the ways in which these "attitudes or orientations" can affect a specific function of a company's global **strategy**—its *staffing policies*—we note that these approaches reflect the decisions of individual managers as well as those of MNEs.

Three perspectives anchor a MNE's staffing policy:

- Ethnocentric.
- Polycentric.
- Geocentric.

TABLE 20.1   Seven Good Reasons to Staff Foreign Operations with Expatriates

This list endorses the *ethnocentric approach* to staffing international operations, which holds that home-country practices and principles are more effective than those of host countries.

Command and control	Familiarity with the way decisions are made and things get done at headquarters means that expatriates can be counted on to transfer home-country procedures to foreign operations.
Local talent gaps	In the face of a shortage of qualified local candidates, along with a particular need to transfer specialized technologies, staffing overseas operations with highly skilled expatriates makes sense.
Social integration	Putting expatriates in positions around the world helps spread the word about underlying corporate policies and practices.
Ownership structure	Deploying expatriate managers to foreign joint-venture operations solidifies a company's ownership interest in the venture.
Local implementation	Because the process of transferring policies and practices is prone to breakdown, it's a good idea to have expatriate managers on hand to solve problems.
High turnover among locals	Because expatriates are less likely to leave the company than local employees—even highly skilled professionals—they're less likely to leak proprietary information in the event they change companies.
Management development	The international exposure and experience gained by expatriates adds to a company's fund of knowledge about international-business strategies and practices.

companies aim to sustain their success when expanding and operating overseas by controlling the transfer and regulating the use of their core competencies. Firms that are sensitive to leveraging their core competency in foreign markets believe an ethnocentric staffing policy works well on two levels: the matters of transfer and protection.

Regarding transfer, staffing overseas operations with people from the home country goes a long way to ensuring that the firm's core competency makes it overseas as planned.[20] This is vital when the core competency is difficult to articulate, specify, or standardize—such as Apple's product-design expertise. Posting a home-country manager to foreign operations, therefore, puts the company's core competency under the direction of the home-country manager who commands the hands-on knowledge that made the company successful in the first place.

The HSBC Group long epitomized this model. For generations, virtually all its top bosses were drawn from a tight-knit cadre of elite expatriates who, in going from one foreign position to another, carried what an executive at HSBC calls "the DNA of the organisation."[21] Regarding protection, companies are keen to safeguard their core competency. With it, the firm prospers; without it, the firm fails. This stark reality leads headquarters to entrust control of the company's "crown jewels" to those who they believe will unconditionally protect them—fellow colleagues at headquarters.

> An ethnocentric staffing approach fills key management positions with home-country nationals.

COUNTERING COGNITIVE DISSONANCE   Finally, earlier chapters noted the challenge of operating in unusual markets. Companies often use an ethnocentric staffing approach to reduce the degree of *cognitive dissonance*—the incompatibility between home-country and host-country attitudes—they face as they expand internationally. Relying on people familiar with proven workplace methods and labor procedures helps companies cope with the stress of foreign situations.

For example, Wipro, an Indian technology company, employs 54,000 people in 35 countries, more than 11,000 of them working outside India. Of these, more than 90 percent are Indian, and a large share are middle-level managers. Wipro sends many Indians abroad given their familiarity with its intense around-the-clock schedules. "We sprinkle Indians in new markets to help seed and set up the culture and intensity," says Sanjay Joshi, chief executive of global programs. Sometimes, an ethnocentric staffing policy is practically impossible. Host governments, alert to the importance of developing and employing local workers, prefer foreign subsidiaries to hire locals. They often use immigration laws or workplace regulations to push the MNE to do so.

Drawbacks of the Ethnocentric Approach   As the adage goes, "Vices are simply virtues taken to extreme." The same is often said about an ethnocentric staffing approach. Force-fitting foreign operations with a standardized staffing policy risks pounding circular pegs into square slots. Eventually, a company can make its foreign operations mirror the outward appearance of the home office. However, putting people in foreign settings does not automatically imbue new attitudes; it can also create high costs and lost opportunities.

Predictably, companies have excellent reasons when asked why they rely only on home-country nationals to run their international operations. They believe there is no shortage of brainpower in a particular country, just a shortage of people with the right mix of technical skills, experience with their particular business methods, and trustworthiness. This limitation can prove detrimental, effectively blinding the company to different, possibly better, ways of doing things.

Ethnocentric staffing policies can also leave local managers and workers unmotivated and demoralized. An assumption of the ethnocentric view—that all the smart, capable people live within a 20-mile radius of headquarters—sends the message to subsidiary personnel that headquarters do not value them. Unless a foreign assignment is intended to develop an expatriate, local employees will likely resent someone coming from a foreign country who they see as no more qualified than they are. Unchecked, resentment can lower productivity and increase turnover.

Polycentric Approach   A polycentric outlook holds that staffing policies ought to adapt to differences between operations in the home and host countries. A polycentric staffing policy sees the effectiveness of the business practices of foreign markets as equivalent to those in the home country. This approach motivates the company to staff each operation from headquarters in the home country to each foreign subsidiary with people from the local environment—Chinese run the China operations, Mexicans run the Mexico operations, Austrians run the Austria operations, and so on. Therefore, a polycentric staffing approach is a key feature of the multidomestic strategy. It is, for the record, inappropriate for a company whose strategy requires that it configure value chains to exploit location economies or coordinate value chains to leverage core competencies worldwide.

> A polycentric staffing policy uses host-country nationals to manage local subsidiaries.

Advantages of the Polycentric Approach   As Table 20.2 shows, staffing foreign operations with locals has several advantages. As we saw in our case profile of Johnson & Johnson (J&J) in Chapter 15, its management believes that staffing local operations with local managers is the most effective policy. Specifically, the CEO of J&J explained,

> *[o]ur decentralized approach to running the business yields better decisions—in the long run—for patients, health professionals and other customers, because the decision-makers*

TABLE 20.2   Six Good Reasons to Staff Foreign Operations with Local Managers

This list endorses the *polycentric approach* to staffing international operations, which holds that employing local managers at local operations is the most advantageous policy.

Cost containment	For a slew of reasons ranging from tax equalization to housing allowances, an expatriate compensation package can be several times more than either a home-country base salary or the salary required to hire a local manager.
Nationalism	Host countries—especially those that aren't well disposed to foreign-controlled operations—often prefer local managers who can be trusted to put local interests above a foreign firm's global objectives.
Management development	Consistently awarding top jobs to expatriates makes it harder for a company to attract, motivate, and retain local employees.
Employee morale	Local workers often prefer to work for local managers.
Expatriate failure rates	The unavoidable failure of some expatriates may ultimately take a toll on the company in terms of unsatisfactory performance, sidetracked careers, and deflated morale.
Product issues	Because they're arguably more astute at interpreting and dealing with local conditions, local managers are better able than expatriates to adjust operations accordingly.

are close to the customers and are in a better position to understand their needs. Finally, our decentralized approach to managing the business is a tremendous magnet for talent, because it gives people room to grow and room to explore new ideas, thus developing their own skills and careers.[22]

POLITICAL CONSIDERATIONS   From a different perspective, local managers are politically astute choices. That is, the host country that is suspicious of foreign-controlled operations will typically see local managers as "better citizens" because they presumably put local interests ahead of global objectives. This local image may play a role in employee morale as well. Many subsidiary employees prefer to work for someone from their own country.[23] Too, there are impediments to using expatriates, such as licensing requirements that prevent companies from using expatriate accountants and lawyers.

ECONOMIC CONSIDERATIONS   The economics of staffing international operations is a compelling motivation for a polycentric staffing approach. Hiring local managers eliminates the often exorbitant expense of sending people from the home office. A general rule of thumb is that the cost of an expatriate is three times the expatriate's annual salary for every year of the assignment; it is nearly impossible to nail down total cost due to the range of variables that go into the calculation. Still, data report that an international assignment costs companies an average of $311,000 per year.[24] Adding indirect expenses also boosts this sum; on average, expatriates are supported by twice as many HR professionals (1 HR professional to 37 expats) versus staff not on international assignment (1 HR professional to 70 managers).

Pressed to control the cost of expatriate assignments, human resource managers often respond by hiring locals. For example, HSBC Group had more than 1,000 expats five years ago out of 312,000 worldwide employees. It now has about 380 expatriates, drawn from 33 nations. Today, HSBC prefers to fill foreign slots with local executives largely because of the higher costs that expatriates impose.

CONSIDERATIONS OF EFFICIENCY AND EFFECTIVENESS   In addition, HSBC, like J&J, reasons that local managers should perform better, sooner, given their finer understanding of local customers, markets, and institutions. Other companies echo this view. For instance, when operating outside the United States, Microsoft tries to hire foreign nationals. As then COO Robert Herbold explained: "You want people who know the local situation, its value system, the way work gets done, the way people use technology in that particular country, and who the key competitors are. . . . If you send someone in fresh from a different region or country, they don't know those things."[25] More philosophically, Bill Gates, chairman of Microsoft, reasons a polycentric policy is a moral obligation of international business, declaring that when staffing an international office, "It sends the wrong message to have a foreigner come over to run things."[26]

Drawbacks to the Polycentric Approach   Operationally, a polycentric staffing policy leads companies to transfer authority to locals to run the subsidiary. Difficulties can arise on issues of accountability and allegiance. Accountability issues emerge when subsidiaries evolve into quasi-autonomous operations that depend less and less on the home office for resources.

Furthermore, host-country nationals in charge of a subsidiary tend to see their primary allegiance to their local colleagues and country, rather than the distant home office. In theory, local managers balance the competing demands of making sense of events from a local and home office view. In practice, however, they may believe national concerns take precedence.[27]

Compounding this situation is a subtle drawback of a polycentric staffing policy—namely, the potential disengagement of local staff from the parent company. By definition and design, a polycentric staffing policy creates few opportunities to work outside one's own country. This outcome constrains the international mobility of host-country

> Using host-country managers helps local motivation and morale but at the possible cost of a gap with global operations because of problems with accountability and allegiance.

nationals. As a result, there may be little incentive for local managers to understand commercial and cultural practices in other markets. Left standing, these differences can isolate national subsidiaries. Consequently, headquarter's policy to staff local operations with locals may mutate the goal of a global company into the reality of a loose federation of largely independent country operations.

Geocentric Approach Moving from a multidomestic company to a global or transnational company lessens the need to have home-country or host-country managers supervise local activities. Unlike the ethnocentric and polycentric variations, therefore, a geocentric staffing policy is not tied to a particular home or host nation. Instead, it scans the world looking for the best people for key jobs throughout the organization, regardless of their nationality. Jeffrey Immelt of GE, explaining the company staffing policy, says, "It's more important to find the best people, wherever they may be, and develop them so that they can lead big businesses, wherever those may be." A geocentric policy enables the MNE to build the requisite cadre of international executives who can move between countries and cultures without forfeiting their effectiveness.[28]

Advantages: Geocentric Staffing and Core Competencies A geocentric staffing policy is instrumental to companies pursing a global and, especially, a transnational strategy. Both types of strategies rely on learning opportunities around the world to generate ideas that enhance their core competencies. As the CEO of Schering-Plough explains, "Good ideas can come from anywhere . . . the more places you are, the more ideas you will get. And the more ideas you get, the more places you can sell them and the more competitive you will be. Managing in many places requires a willingness to accept good ideas no matter where they come from—which means having a global attitude."[29]

Others, seeing the power of ideas to refine and create new core competencies, adopt a geocentric orientation. For instance, Fujio Mitarai, president of Canon Inc., observes, "Until recently, everything we did overseas was an extension of what we were doing in Japan. From now on, we want to give birth to new value abroad. We want to make the best of the different kinds of expertise available in different countries."

Drawbacks to the Geocentric Approach A geocentric staffing policy is hard to develop and costly to maintain. Difficulty follows from the need to keep a sense of who you are and still be able to understand the views of a diverse range of people. For instance, the aggressively multinational composition of senior management that results from geocentric staffing policies arguably reduces cultural myopia and enhances local responsiveness. The gap between theory and reality, however, can be big. For example, the investment bank J. P. Morgan Chase employs more than 50 nationalities in its London office.[30]

Making sense of all outlooks that potentially bear on a decision can prove overwhelming. If done poorly, geocentrism can erode the sense of common purpose. Like the Tower of Babel, the clarity of the task can get lost in a hodgepodge of differences. Similarly, the logistics of geocentrism are costly. Exposing people to different ideas in diverse places is expensive. Training and relocation costs escalate when frequently transferring high-priced managers from country to country. Too, problems emerge when the higher pay and prestige enjoyed by managers placed in the company's global executive vanguard trigger resentment.

Determining an Approach: Pros and Cons Table 20.3 summarizes the merits and shortcomings of the three staffing approaches. Broadly speaking, an ethnocentric approach is congruent with an international strategy, a polycentric approach is congruent with a multidomestic strategy, and a geocentric approach is congruent with global and transnational strategies. In reality, companies may use elements of each staffing policy, given particular opportunities and constraints, changes in configuration or coordination of their value chains, or the preferences of leadership.[31] Nonetheless, companies tend to champion the staffing policy that is most congruent with their current standard of

A geocentric staffing policy seeks the best people for key jobs throughout the organization, regardless of their nationality.

Economic factors, decision-making routines, and legal contingencies complicate a geocentric staffing policy.

CONCEPT CHECK

A quick comparative review of Table 20.1 (which endorses the *ethnocentric* approach to global staffing) and Table 20.2 (which endorses the *polycentric* approach) demonstrates a principle that we develop throughout this book: Although most of us are prone to look for a "one best way" of doing things, it's seldom a promising approach in any area, including that of formulating **international business strategy**. We first point out the shortcomings of our three "Staffing Policies" when we introduce them in Chapter 2 as three "Company and Management Orientations." We explain **international**, **multidomestic**, and **global strategies** in Chapter 11.

TABLE 20.3   Comparing Approaches to Staffing Foreign Operations

Types of *staffing approaches* are described in this chapter. For more detailed discussions of categories of *strategic appropriateness—international, multidomestic,* and *global* and *transnational—*see Chapter 11.

Staffing Approach	General Assumptions	Strategic Appropriateness	Advantages	Drawbacks
Ethnocentric	Presumes that the leadership ideals, management values, and workplace practices of one's company are superior to those in foreign companies Headquarters makes key decisions and foreign subsidiaries follow commands	International	Leverages a company's core competence Gives people a strong point of perspective Development of the senior management team	Can inspire belief that one's company is intrinsically better at everything Can promote cultural arrogance and illiteracy May blind managers to innovations in other countries
Polycentric	Accepts the importance of adapting to differences, real or imaginary, between the home and host countries Headquarters makes broad strategic decisions that local units adapt to their marketplace	Multidomestic	Helps people see the special virtues of a particular nation Operationally the least expensive. Eases adapting to the local market's workplace norms Placates host governments and promotes local staff development	Complicates value chain coordination Isolates country operations Reduces incentive to engage an international perspective Potential for quasi-autonomous country operations
Geocentric	All nations are created equal and possess inalienable characteristics that are neither superior nor inferior but simply there Headquarters and subsidiaries collaborate to identify, transfer, and diffuse best practices	Global and Transnational	Adept way to deal with different people in different counties Leverages powerful ideas worldwide Opens learning opportunities	Tough to develop, costly to run, hard to maintain Contrary to many nations' market development plans Difficult to find qualified expatriates

value creation, as exemplified by GE's aim to staff people who will "globalize the intellect of the company" and its corresponding engagement of a geocentric staffing policy.

Few MNEs question the need for expatriates. Translating this belief into a cadre of high-performance expatriates requires MNEs to find those people who are prepared for an international assignment, devise ways to motivate them to perform well, and capitalize on their new skills and improved outlook when they are ready for their next job. Therefore, we turn now to the matters of expatriate selection, development, compensation, and repatriation.

Managing Expatriates

Some people enjoy the thrill of living and working abroad. Others, however, prefer not to work in a foreign country, particularly if they perceive an assignment as long term or dangerous. In our opening case, for example, we heard from a Morgan Stanley expatriate who's worked in Britain, Singapore, and India. He remains excited about the prospect of seeing the "big world" but admits that international business travel isn't always the safest activity.

Case Review Note

Screening executives to find those with the greatest inclination and highest potential for a foreign assignment is the process of expatriate selection. This process, always difficult, is increasingly so given growing concerns about companywide talent shortages and the difficulty of recruiting future business leaders.[32] Consequently, few MNEs have the luxury of a large cadre of mobile and experienced expatriates to call on as needed. Again, recall our opening case, where we found that, in order to maximize the probability of success and minimize the possibility of failure, Honeywell starts looking at potential expatriate candidates years before they'll actually be posted to overseas positions.

SELECTING EXPATRIATES

Two factors complicate this situation. First, there is no specific set of technical indicators that consistently distinguishes a good versus poor expatriate. In addition, it is a persistent challenge to judge a potential expatriate's adaptability to foreign places, people, and processes. However, the overriding need of expatriates to run international operations, coupled with the severe cost of expatriate failure, strongly encourages thorough selection processes. Therefore, selecting the right expatriates pushes MNEs to assess their talent pool with a range of indicators. Despite efforts to rely on psychoanalytic testing or in-depth interviews, objective measures are ready, but usually rough, estimators. In recourse, companies look for people with skills and outlooks in the matters of *technical competence*, *adaptiveness*, and *leadership ability*.

Technical Competence Corporate managers, expatriates, and local staff routinely agree that technical competence, usually indicated by past job performance, is the biggest determinant of success in foreign assignments.[33] At the least, an expatriate must command the functional skills to do the job and, if necessary, understand how to transfer or tailor them to foreign situations.[34] Managers commonly have had several years' worth of work experience before a company sends them abroad. This tendency also reflects the fact that expatriate selections are usually made by line managers based on the candidate's operational track record. Moreover, many companies translate a record of outstanding technical competence into the self-confidence needed to do well abroad.

This tendency is changing somewhat—recall that some companies are seeking younger or older employees to staff international slots. For the former, companies are willing to trade performance track records for long-term potential. For example, PricewaterhouseCoopers (PWC), a global accounting and auditing firm with about 145,000 employees, started a Life Experience Abroad Programme (LEAP) to accelerate international assignments. LEAP begins by identifying promising workers (those who show an interest in living abroad and who have a flair for foreign languages) who have been at the firm for three or four years. The program calls for posting them abroad for several years with the goal of returning for senior leadership roles. PWC plans to have 5,000 LEAP staff working in 30 countries, effectively doubling the company's expatriate head count.

Adaptiveness Performance data show that effective expatriates possess adaptive characteristics. Thus MNEs routinely evaluate a possible expatriate in terms of three sets of adaptive characteristics:

Self-Maintenance These qualities, such as personal resourcefulness, are useful precisely because things do not always go as planned. Companies struggle to identify this characteristic. Like many MNEs, the selection process at HSBC uses tests, interviews, and exercises. Still, its CEO explains, "We don't look so much at what or where people have studied but rather at their drive, initiative, cultural sensitivity, and readiness to see the world as their oyster. Whether they've studied classics, economics, history, or languages is irrelevant. What matters are the skills and qualities necessary to be good, well-rounded executives in a highly international institution operating in a diverse set of communities."[35]

CONCEPT CHECK

In Chapters 2, 3, and 4, we analyze the *environments—cultural, political/legal, economic*—in which **international business** is conducted, and in each case, we emphasize the effects of *variability* in these environments and the extent to which environmental variables make it impossible to set absolute "standards" for handling the challenges of operating internationally. Here, we observe that these same differences make it hard to set standards for expatriate selection. Moreover, experiences in handling these differences shape the ways in which companies and managers identify the "optimal" mix of skills and perspectives that they want in expatriates.

Technical competence often is the strongest determinant of who is selected for an international assignment.

Adaptiveness refers to a person's potential for

- Self-maintenance and personal resourcefulness.
- Developing satisfactory relationships.
- Interpreting the immediate environment.

Satisfactory Relationships with Host Nationals   These characteristics include flexibility and tolerance. Whether called *cultural empathy, others-orientation,* or simply *leadership,* this orientation enhances an expatriate's ability to interact with new people. Research reports that two factors play vital roles in this process: the ability of an expatriate to develop sincere, honest friendships with foreign nationals and the expatriate's willingness to use the host-country language.

Sensitivity to Host Environments   Valuable qualities include the skills and sensitivities that help one to interpret the immediate environment in ways that reject stereotypes, preconceptions, and unrealistic expectations.[36] Better interpreting how colleagues, customers, and competitors in the local market see events goes far to working well in a different country.

> Top managers in subsidiaries usually assume a greater range of leadership roles and broader duties than do managers of similar-size home-country operations.

Leadership Ability   Increasingly, companies see personal leadership as a key to an expatriate's success.[37] Expatriates often find themselves as senior managers at foreign subsidiaries that are usually much smaller than the parent but nevertheless still require top-level leadership duties. Communication skills, motivation, self-reliance, courage, risk taking, and diplomacy become essential qualities for success.

Successful expatriates often command, in descending order of importance, optimism (believes future challenges can be overcome), drive (has passion to succeed), adaptability (handles ambiguity well), foresight (imagines the future), experience (has seen and done a great deal), resilience (recovers quickly from failure), sensitivity (adjusts management style to cultural differences), and organization (plans ahead, follows through).[38] As we saw in our opening case, Microsoft's Joan Pattle found that working abroad gave her an opportunity to wear an extra hat or two. At home, her job in direct marketing required basically some know-how in handling a database. When she got to Britain, she took on some new responsibilities that came with the job of brand manager, including press relations. Success depends on understanding cultural differences in problem solving, motivation, use of power, and consensus building, as well as being able to make sense of trade rules and regulations, business practices, and joint ventures.

EXPATRIATE FAILURE

> Expatriate failure is operationally costly and professionally detrimental.

Despite the best laid plans of mice and men, as the saying goes, things often go astray. MNEs experience this situation when they select their best and brightest managers, send them to a foreign market, pay them well, and watch them fail. **Expatriate failure** can be narrowly defined as a manager's premature return home due to poor job performance; broadly defined, it's the failure of an MNE's selection policies to find individuals who will succeed abroad. However it's defined, it's an enduring concern among MNEs. In the 1980s, research reported that between 16 and 40 percent of all American employees sent abroad to more developed countries returned from their assignments early, and almost 70 percent of employees sent to emerging markets returned home early. Recent surveys indicate that today less than 10 percent of expatriates fail to complete their assignments abroad.[39]

> The improving sophistication of MNE selection procedures has reduced the rate of expatriate failure.

The Costs of Failure   The fall in the rate of expatriate failure testifies to the improving sophistication of selection processes. Still, few see this drop as cause to stop and celebrate. The financial and personal costs of expatriate failure, no matter how infrequent, are destructive. The average cost per failure can be as high as three times the expatriate's annual domestic salary plus the cost of relocation.[40] The direct costs of each failure can easily reach $1 million when one adds the time and money spent in selection, visits to the location before the executive moves, and the expatriate's lost productivity as things fall apart. Finally, an incalculable cost is the personal implications of professional failure to the formerly high-performing executive's self-confidence and leadership potential.

Preventing Failure   Firms try to identify the causes of expatriate failure and develop preemptive training and preparation programs. Assessments of expatriate failure have focused on the expatriate's technical expertise, ability to cope with greater responsibilities overseas, challenges of the new environment, personal or emotional problems, and ability of the expatriate's spouse to adjust to the foreign environment. The growing sophistication of HRM has reduced the rates of expatriate failure due to insufficient technical expertise. Today, rare is the foreign assignment that fails because HRM did not identify the person as technically incompetent prior to his or her departure.

Dealing with Adjustment and Stress   Other causes of expatriate failure have proven more intractable. Traditionally, attention has focused on the expatriate's adjustment to the new environment as the best predictor of failure.[41] The inability of an expatriate to adjust to the foreign assignment has consistently been linked to his or her inadequate cultural sensitivities and skills. Recently, companies have turned their attention toward the adjustment difficulties for the spouse and family.[42]

Research shows, for example, that a foreign assignment is usually more stressful for the family than for the expatriate. Consequently, the leading cause of expatriate failure is the inability of a spouse and children to adapt to the host nation: "If the family starts to unravel, the employee will at some time start to unravel, too."[43] Abrupt separation from friends, family, and career isolate the spouse and children. In recourse, they often look to the working spouse or parent for more companionship and support. Almost always, the working spouse has less time because of the new job. This often fans family stress, which then affects the expatriate's work performance.

Employers experiment with ways to bypass this risk. More executives are sent on short-term, "commuter" assignments where they need not uproot their families. Also, moves to send younger or older expats speaks to this threat: The younger are more likely single, and the older have grown children and partners less resistant to change.[44]

TRAINING EXPATRIATES

Companies recognize the need to prepare expatriates for their overseas assignment. Although easily said, many companies struggle to deal with these issues systematically. The HRM departments of most companies typically have lots of employee data. However, most profile employees' technical capabilities and accomplishments. Far less data profile their adaptive capabilities, willingness to accept foreign assignments, geographic preferences, or foreign-language qualifications.[45]

Focusing on Adaptiveness and Related Characteristics   This data gap largely reflects the MNE's historic preoccupation of linking expatriate selection to technical competence. This leads MNEs to direct training efforts toward improving their employees' technical skills and generally leaving it up to the individual to develop his or her adaptive competencies. Achieving the latter are those managers who have an interest in international careers to travel abroad, study world events, and seek people of different ethnicities, cultures, and nationalities.[46] When eventually posted as expatriates, these executives often perform well, thereby encouraging more companies, as we saw with our opening look at Honeywell, to prepare expatriates for overseas assignments with cross-cultural training.

Many MNEs prepare potential expatriates by developing their general understanding of a country, cultural sensitivity, and practical skills prior to their departure. As we observed in our opening case, for instance, Honeywell begins training potential expatriates early and focuses on cross-cultural skills, including those necessary for dealing with culture shock. Let's take a closer look at each of these issues.

General Country Understanding   The most common predeparture training is an informational briefing about the way things work in the host country. Topics typically include politics, economics, features of the workplace, and lifestyle options.[47] Some companies follow this training with a refresher course about six months after expatriates arrive in a foreign country.

A leading cause of expatriate failure is the inability of a spouse to adapt to the host country.

CONCEPT CHECK
We explain in this chapter why the challenge of preparing people for overseas assignments can lead to corporate head scratching at the most experienced MNEs. We hasten to point out, however, that MNEs know where to look for solutions—most of which depend on *information*. In Chapters 2 through 10, for example, we explain the kind of information necessary to make decisions about foreign markets; in Chapters 11 through 15, we discuss the kind of information that's needed to makes decisions about international operations. Here, we observe that data on employees is simply another source of the information necessary for selecting and preparing people for expatriate assignments.

Training and predeparture preparations can lower the probability of expatriate failure. Increasingly, preparation activities include the spouse.

Case Review Note

Cultural Sensitivity   Cultural training aims to sensitize the expatriates to see the opportunity of working with host-country nationals, encouraging them to keep an open mind to different ideas, attitudes, and beliefs. Exposure to other nations and cultures, the reasoning goes, is the best preparation for dealing with **culture shock**—a soon-after-arrival dissatisfaction with the host culture which, if not dealt with, may deteriorate into homesickness, irritability, arrogance, and disdain.

Because developing the cultural sensitivity to rise above culture shock doesn't always come naturally, preparing expatriates requires helping them see their biases. Therefore, some companies encourage expatriates to undergo cultural training to foster an appreciation for the host country's culture. For instance, a survey of 200 multinational firms found that 60 percent provide cross-cultural training for international assignments. Once in the host country, employees and their families are typically on their own.[48]

Practical Skills   Practical training aims to familiarize the expatriate and family with the routines of life in the host country. The sooner the family develops a useful pattern of schooling, socializing, and shopping, the greater the odds that they will survive culture shock. Expatriates can do a number of things to help themselves adjust to foreign locations, such as socializing with local community groups and expatriate associations. Also, before they depart, managers can seek information from people who have positive memories of their expatriate experiences and can offer practical wisdom on a successful transition.

MNEs usually anchor training programs to transfer specific information about the host country as well as improve the executive's cultural sensitivity.

Trends in Training   Despite the usefulness of preparation programs, reports suggest that most managers receive little to no training prior to their departure. Indeed, many expatriates prepare for their assignment on the flight to their new home country, scanning various reports and resources. Usually, companies blame the urgency of the situation for this deficiency, noting there is not enough time for an executive to take a familiarization trip to the host country, let alone a crash course on its history, culture, politics, economy, religion, and business environment. Typically, the home office sees the performance of the foreign operations deteriorating or the fading of key opportunity and believes it must dispatch help immediately.

Two Approaches: Specialized Knowledge Versus Cultural Sensitivity   More commonly, MNEs often fail to train their potential expatriates for international responsibilities due to uncertainty about the best way to do so. Companies generally opt either to transfer specific and specialized knowledge about the foreign environments or develop interpersonal awareness and adaptability in the context of intensive cultural sensitivity training. The former approach tends to reduce some of the fear of dealing with the unknown. In contrast, the latter approach tends to make people more receptive to and tolerant of foreign environments. However, the awareness of a difference does not necessarily imply a willingness to adapt to it, particularly if it is a cultural variation. Although either approach generally helps a person adjust better than those who get no training, there appears to be no significant difference in the relative effectiveness of the approaches.[49]

Broader, More Sophisticated Programs   Finally, increasingly sophisticated strategies spur MNEs to engage more of their employees in general international development. The need to generate, transfer, and adopt ideas from wherever they originate to wherever they add value, particularly compelling for the MNEs pursuing a global or transnational strategy, means preparing all employees to do so. Also, MNEs with an international or multidomestic strategy face pressures, given growing globalization, to help more employees understand worldwide operations and opportunities. In response, MNEs use development programs to help employees overcome their hesitancy.

MNEs of all sorts see the value of including international business components once reserved for expatriates in development programs for all employees—irrespective of whether the person plans to work abroad. Examples include Mattel's and Infosys's regional training centers, where managers from several countries convene to examine specific topics; Procter & Gamble's training on globalization issues; and programs at Honda of America to teach foreign languages and cultural sensitivity.

CONCEPT CHECK

In Chapter 11, we explain the concept of "The Firm as Value Chain" and discuss several **strategies** by which a company may pursue **value**—strategies by which it seeks to strengthen the competitive position that it's staked out to maximize its ability to sell what it makes for more than it costs to make it. Here we observe that a firm's strategy directly shapes who it selects to staff its value chain worldwide.

Point Counterpoint

Learning a Foreign Language—Still Useful?

Point **Yes** When asked about the importance of their foreign-language needs for employees, human resource managers regularly respond that foreign-language competency adds professional and personal value.[50] Surveys report that managers who learn one or more foreign languages find ways to make innovative contributions to their company. Operationally, the effort to speak the local language, no matter how poorly, sends a subtle but important cultural message. The American Council on the Teaching of Foreign Languages posits that "[j]ust making an effort to say a few words in the native tongue can make a good impression . . . [as it] sends a subliminal message that 'we are equal.'"[51]

Even if the expatriate is far from fluent, a willingness to communicate in the language of the host country can help build rapport with local employees, thereby improving the manager's effectiveness. Proponents of language skills also point out that countries have different cultural and business expectations that can only be deciphered through the local language. Thus the expatriate who decides not to learn the local language risks only partial inclusion in the local business environment.

Cross-cultural illiteracy can also lead to exclusion from influential business networks, complicate relations and negotiations with local officials, and make it a struggle to chat with local colleagues.[52] Finally, working abroad is itself a challenge; language limitations can make it further isolating.[53] For example, Microsoft's Joan Pattle noted that her inability to speak Turkish made her seven-month stint in Istanbul very lonely. "You can't really mix with the locals . . . [or] use local transportation because you can't read any of the signs."[54] Clearly, this indicates the benefits of knowing at least something about the local language and culture.

Against this backdrop, proponents of foreign language competency maintain that one of the important things about learning another language is its potential to be a personally enriching experience. The study of another culture often triggers insights and clarifies perspectives of one's own history, society, and values. In addition, grasping an understanding of the local language and culture proves valuable when confronting the consequences of globalization. Growing networks of international cooperation and exchange depend on people who possess foreign-language proficiency.

Moreover, if not for enrichment, some say learning a foreign language will soon be a competitive necessity. The growing spread of English competency worldwide means that an English speaker today will lose the competitive

(continued)

Counterpoint **No** Some people interpret the widespread and growing prevalence of English throughout the world as a sign that language training for expatriates is unnecessary. English ably performs as the language of world business—it is quickly becoming the *lingua franca* of the world and, for a growing number of people, a practical alternative to their native language. Nearly a quarter of the world's population speaks some English. That includes around 400 million who speak it as their mother tongue and about the same number who speak it fluently as a second language. In general, as shown in Chapter 2, the English language accounts for a much larger portion of world output than for the portion of native speakers in the world—although English is spoken by only 6 percent of the world's population, English *speakers* account for 42 percent of world output.

This trend is highlighted by the situation in Western Europe, where more than half the people in the European Union (EU) claim to be reasonably conversant in English. Many envision developing their English further; a survey of 16,000 people living in the EU found that more than 70 percent agreed with the statement: "Everybody should speak English." Similar trends show up in India. In 2005, India had the world's largest English-speaking and English-understanding population. It now has the the second-largest "fluent" English-speaking population, after the United States. It expects to have the world's largest number of English speakers within a decade.

While English is not an official language in many countries, it is currently the language most often taught around the world as a second language. In the EU, English is the top foreign language studied by schoolchildren (89 percent), followed by French (32 percent), German (18 percent), and Spanish (8 percent).[55] Nearly 200 million students in China are learning English in school, and more than a fifth of Japanese 5-year-olds attend classes in English conversation. Countries from Chile to Mongolia aim to become bilingual in English in the next decade or two. English was added to the Mexican primary-school curriculum in 2006; children there are learning English along with 200,000 teachers.[56] Collectively, with 2 billion people speaking or studying English today, we are on the verge of a massive diffusion of English competency.[57]

The prevalence of English is best seen by the predominance of English on the Internet, both in terms of English language content and the English language itself. Its predominance makes it increasingly possible to conduct business all over the world using only the English interface

(continued)

advantage that once came with being among the relatively few native Anglophones who could speak the most useful language of the business world. Now, bilinguals or multilinguals will offer the same that English monoglots can but with richer language skills and possibly broader international perspectives.

Ultimately, this line of discussion always triggers the question: Which foreign language should one study? Presently, growth in expatriate positions is moving rapidly from Western Europe and North America to the booming BRIC countries. As MNEs struggle to place expatriates in these high-growth markets, for instance, proficiency in these languages will likely translate into job opportunities and salary premiums. Finally, entrepreneurs may look around their hometown and go for fast-growing languages such as Spanish, Mandarin, or Arabic. ●

of one's preferred browser.[58] Furthermore, reports that more than 80 percent of home pages on the Web are in English reinforce the likelihood of English as a *lingua franca* of the Internet. On a related front, the growing sophistication of translation software makes foreign language competency a moot point for those who prefer using their local language on the Internet.

Many managers have responded in kind. *The Economist*, for example, reports that just under half of employers rate language skills as important—a tendency that many link to the laborious struggle to master a foreign language. Others report that language competency is ranked well behind technical competencies, leadership skills, and career development but ahead of motivation for working abroad, previous success abroad, and overall business vision in gauging the suitability of a candidate for international assignments.[59] Increasingly, English is the working language of a growing number of international companies.

Finally, some say language is a misleading proxy of an expatriate's cultural sensitivity and general ability to perform in foreign markets. The CEO of Schering-Plough, for example, notes that "I've met many people who speak three or four languages yet still have a very narrow view of the world. At the same time, I've come across people who speak only English but have a real passion and curiosity about the world and who are very effective in different cultures."[60] This view suggests that the debate concerning the overall value of learning a foreign language is far from over. ●

COMPENSATING EXPATRIATES

> Compensation must neither overly reward nor unduly punish a person for accepting a foreign assignment.

If a U.S. MNE transfers its finance manager who is making $150,000 per year in Philadelphia to China, where the going rate is $100,000 per year, what should the manager's salary be? Or if a Chinese finance manager is transferred to the United States, what pay should the company offer? Should it compensate in dollars or yuans? Which set of fringe benefits should apply?

These are a few of the many questions a company faces when it posts people to its foreign operations. Managing an international workforce means HRM must deal with differing pay levels, benefits, and prerequisites. On the one hand, HRM must prevent the already high costs of an expatriate assignment from spiraling out of control—companies in the United States spend nearly $1.3 million per expatriate during the course of a typical three-year foreign assignment.[61] On the other hand, HRM must pay people enough to motivate them to work hard and get the family to move.

The Pay-Performance Link   All things being equal, therefore, compensation can determine the likelihood and success of expatriate assignments. Pay them too little, and people decline to go or, if they do go, eventually regret it. Pay them too much, then costs escalate, returns fall short, and pay inequities fan dissension. Further complicating the pay-performance link is the weak to nonexistent correlation between higher pay for expatriates and improved performance. Rather, data show that the higher the pay, the longer assignments tend to last; some employees, quite content to prolong a munificent financial existence abroad, see little incentive to return.[62]

The task, then, is clear: Devise a compensation package that gets people to go, lets them maintain their standard of living, reflects the responsibility of the foreign assignment, and ensures that after-tax income will not fall as a result of the foreign assignment.

Types of Compensation Plans   Many MNEs, especially in the United States, apply the **balance sheet compensation plan** to manage their expatriate accounts.[63] The approach develops a salary structure that equalizes purchasing power across countries so expatriates have the same living standard in their foreign posting that they had at home—no matter which country their assignment takes them.[64] The principle of equalization presumes that expatriates should neither overly prosper nor unduly suffer merely because their companies assigned them work abroad. In addition, the balance sheet approach outlines how the company provides financial incentives that offset qualitative differences between assignment locations.

> The most common approach to expatriate pay is the balance sheet approach.

There are three common methods of implementing a balance sheet compensation plan:

Home-Based Method   This method bases the expatriate's compensation on the salary of a comparable job in his or her home city. This method, by preserving equity with home-country colleagues, treats the expatriate's compensation as if the person had never left home. This method simplifies the expatriate's eventual return. The home-based method is the most prevalent expatriate compensation plan with 66 percent of companies using it for long-term and 75 percent for short-term assignments.

Headquarters-Based Method   This approach sets the expatriate's salary in terms of the salary of a comparable job in the city where the MNE has its headquarters. For example, if a Boston-headquartered MNE posted expatriates to its offices in London, Santiago, and Jakarta, it would give each expatriate a salary structured in terms of Boston pay rates. This plan recognizes the disruption of a foreign assignment and makes sure an expatriate can live as she or he had in the home country.

Host-Based Method   Sometimes called *destination pricing* and *localization*, this method bases an expatriate's compensation on the prevailing pay scales in the locale of the foreign assignment. Basically, an expatriate starts with a salary equivalent to that of a local national with similar responsibilities and then adds whatever foreign-service premiums, extra allowances, home-country benefits, and taxation compensation were negotiated. This method is not as personally lucrative as the home- or headquarters-based methods. Essentially, it pays an expatriate less to reduce tension between the expatriate and his or her colleagues in the host country due to extreme variation in pay for similar jobs.

HRM executives compare the features of their compensation plans with those offered by other companies. They rely on data from firms that specialize in international compensation as well as estimates of cost-of-living differences.[65]

Key Aspects of Expatriate Compensation   Table 20.4 illustrates a typical expatriate compensation package. Expatriates negotiate their compensation package in terms of a base salary, a foreign-service premium, allowances of various types, fringe benefits, tax differentials, and benefits. We now look more closely at each.

Base Salary   An expatriate's base salary normally falls in the same range as the base salary for the comparable job in the home country. It is paid in either the home-country currency or in the local currency.

Foreign Service Premium   A *foreign service premium*, often called a *mobility premium*, is a cash incentive to compensate individuals for the inconveniences of moving to a new country, living away from family and friends, dealing with the day-to-day challenges of a new culture, new language, new workplace practices, and the reality that they will ultimately have to disrupt their life upon return. Long-terms assignments typically qualify for mobility premium; few short-term assignments do.

TABLE 20.4   What Does an Expatriate Cost?

Numbers reflect the following scenario: A Seattle-based company will assign a senior executive to run a wholly owned subsidiary in Tokyo. Back in the United States, this executive, who has a working spouse and two children, earns an annual income of $150,000. A quick look at the balance sheet gives us a good idea of the outlay that will be needed to compensate this executive in the overseas posting.

Direct Compensation Costs	
Base salary	$ 150, 000
Foreign-service premium	25, 000
Goods and services differential	120, 000
Housing	97, 000
U.S. (hypothetical) taxes	(38, 000)
Company-Paid Costs	
Education (schooling for two children)	30, 000
Japanese income taxes	115, 000
Transfer moving costs	47, 000
Miscellaneous costs (i.e., shipping and storage; home sale or property management fees; cultural, practical, and language training; preassignment orientation trip, destination assistance)	85, 000
Working spouse allowance	75, 000
Annual home leave (airfare for four, hotel, and meals)	15, 000
Additional health insurance, pension supplements, evacuation coverage	20, 000

Allowances   Sending an executive on an international assignment creates expensive logistics and considerable stress. Companies adjust the total compensation package with a variety of allowances that help reduce the difficulties the executive and his or her family face.

COST-OF-LIVING ALLOWANCES   Expatriates receive a cost-of-living allowance (sometimes called a goods-and-services differential) to nullify the risk that they will suffer a decline in their standard of living due to the exorbitant expense of a particular city (London or Tokyo) or nation (Switzerland).[66] Some companies reduce the cost-of-living differential over time, reasoning that as expatriates adapt to their environment, they should adopt local purchasing practices—for example, buying vegetables from a neighborhood market instead of using imported packaged goods.[67]

HOUSING ALLOWANCES   A housing allowance ensures the expatriate will duplicate his or her customary quality of housing—a key concern when asked to move from midpriced Salt Lake City to high-priced Shanghai. Housing costs also vary substantially because of crowded conditions that raise land prices as well as shortages of homes that are acceptable to expatriates.[68] Westerners pay steep premiums in some parts of Asia to rent accommodations with Western-style bathrooms and kitchens.[69]

SPOUSE ALLOWANCES   A spouse allowance partly funds an expatriate's spouse's effort to find work and take cross-cultural training programs. In some cases, this allowance will offset the loss in income due to the spouse's forsaking his or her job.[70] About a quarter of MNEs provide spouses of expatriates with job-search assistance, often through networks with other companies.[71] For example, Kodak tries to find employment for spouses; when it cannot, it pays for a partial loss in income.

A spouse allowance also deals with the hardship created by potential changes in total family income and status. In the home country, all members of the family may be able to work, whereas when they go abroad, only the expatriate may have the legal right to do so; host governments seldom grant people other than the transferred employee permission to work. Therefore, the spouse or companion of an expatriate may have to either give up employment or be separated from the partner. About half of large U.S. companies include spouse support in their international assignments policy.

HARDSHIP ALLOWANCES A hardship allowance (sometimes called "combat pay") goes to expatriates assigned to difficult environments or dangerous locations—especially for long-term assignments. Living conditions in certain settings pose severe hardships, such as harsh climatic or health conditions, or expose the expatriate to security threats.[72] For instance, expatriate personnel of many MNEs, given their high profiles, have been targeted for kidnapping and assault. Companies have had not only to rethink their hardship allowances but also purchase ransom insurance, provide training programs on safety for expatriates and families, pay for home alarm systems and security guards, and assess their legal liability regarding employee safety.[73]

Where conditions are less severe, expatriates may encounter living conditions that are substandard to those at home, thus qualifying for a hardship allowance. Lastly, expatriates also receive miscellaneous allowances, such as a travel allowance that lets an expatriate and his or her family travel home periodically or an education allowance to finance the expatriate's children's access to a private education in the event that host-country public schools are unsuitable.

TRENDS IN ALLOWANCES Overall, companies are offering fewer allowances. First, more individuals see international assignments as a chance to develop business skills and leadership qualities. These people are then more willing to go abroad for less financial reward. In addition, foreign assignments have "gone from being special and unique, with piles of money thrown at them, to being an everyday part of the company."[74] Cost-reduction techniques include reducing benefits and allowances (many companies with operations in Europe now treat the continent as if it were one country) and cutting "hardship" allowances for posts that were once difficult but no longer are, such as a post to Prague or Mumbai. Pressure to reduce pay and perks will continue, both for cost control as well as a growing supply of skilled employees from developing countries who are eager to work worldwide.

Fringe Benefits Firms typically provide expatriates the same level of medical and retirement benefits abroad that they received at home rather than those customarily granted in the host country. However, most companies expand these benefits to deal with local contingencies, such as bearing the cost of transferring ill expatriates or family members to suitable medical facilities.

Tax Differentials The objective of compensation adjustments is to ensure that expatriates' after-tax income and, presumably, their motivation, will not suffer because of the costs created by foreign assignment. Because taxes are usually assessed on the adjustments that companies make to the expatriate's base salary, companies must adjust even further upward if the foreign tax rate is higher than that in the home country. Tax equalization has become a costly component of expatriate compensation. If there is no reciprocal tax treaty between the expatriate's home country and host country, then he or she may be legally obligated to pay income tax to both governments. In such situations, the MNE ordinarily pays the expatriate's tax bill in the host country.

Complications Posed by Nationality Differences In addition to over 1,700 expatriates stationed in more than 50 countries, Unilever has 20,000-plus managers spread over 90 countries.[75] Should Unilever pay executives in different countries according to the prevailing standards in each country, or should it equalize pay for each position on a global basis? Figuring out how to pay managers in different countries is complicated by

MNEs often provide additional compensation or more fringe benefits to employees who work in remote or dangerous areas.

CONCEPT CHECK
Recall our discussion, in Chapter 1, of "The Forces Driving Globalization," in which we identify several factors contributing to the emergence of more and stronger "interdependent relationships" among people from different parts of the world. We point out that the importance of these relationships has already begun to shrink the physical and cultural distances that separate countries. Here we suggest that this trend—the convergence of cultures, politics, and markets—has also begun to make the prospect of moving from one country to another a more common and attractive career arc (resulting in companies reducing incentives to take overseas assignments).

Companies struggle to determine the proper degree to which they should equalize pay for the same job done in different countries.

legal, cultural, and regulatory factors. As companies employ expatriates from home and third countries, compensation issues grow more complicated.

These problems are pressing for companies with a geocentric staffing policy. Both the global and transnational strategies depend on developing a cadre of international managers that likely includes different nationalities. The issue then emerges whether all managers who perform the same job but in different locations should be paid the same salary. For a Finnish transnational like Nokia, this would require compensating its foreign nationals, no matter where they worked, in terms of Finnish salary levels. If Nokia opts not to develop an equitable standard, it will likely result in the "underpaid" members of the international cadre resenting their higher-paid counterparts.

Firms applying ethnocentric or polycentric staffing policies, though largely immune to these problems, also must systematize their compensation programs. If not, then they may pay someone more than necessary to persuade them to go abroad, given the unequal conditions among countries. More worrisome, disparities in pay packages for people doing the same jobs can distort the motivation of home- or host-country managers and impede a sense of unanimity among different parts of the global operations. As you'll recall from our opening case, the problem of disgruntling pay comparisons is taken so seriously at Alibaba that expatriate employees in China are warned that disclosing salaries may be grounds for termination. Finally, even though the company with an ethnocentric or polycentric staffing policy may have few expatriates today, likely growth in its international activities will make it increasingly cumbersome to administer foreign compensation packages on a case-by-case basis.

Presently, there is little consensus on how to deal with these issues. A decade ago, salaries for similar jobs varied substantially among countries, as did the relationships of salaries within the corporate hierarchy. Today, more MNEs apply a global framework to their pay and benefit programs while adapting them to regional standards to offer consistency in their reward practices worldwide but differentiations for performance-based pay by country and region based on regulatory and cultural differences. Figure 20.3 highlights some of these changes, showing the makeup of pay packages for CEOs by company nationality.

CEOs in the United States enjoy the largest and most comprehensive pay packages, both in terms of base compensation and total remuneration. CEOs in France, Germany, Italy, Switzerland, and the United Kingdom also command higher levels of total compensation than their peers elsewhere. This model is inspiring emulation; Asian and Latin American companies are instituting similar pay practices, particularly the use of performance-based pay that ties compensation to business results.

Differences persist. Long-term incentives, such as options on restricted stock, are popular in the United States but not in Germany. However, German managers often receive compensation that U.S. managers do not, such as housing allowances and partial payment of salary outside Germany, neither of which is taxable. Similarly, countries with aggressive personal income tax rates spur employees to ask for pay plans that reduce taxable base salaries in favor of tax-exempt fringe benefits. Ultimately, as companies from more countries become more multinational, they compete globally for executive talent. Likewise, local firms must tailor compensation to retain executives. Therefore, convergence in compensation practices is the order of the day.

Total compensation as well as forms of compensation varies substantially among countries.

REPATRIATING EXPATRIATES

HRM aims to build a staffing process that creates a cycle of events, beginning with the selection of the right expatriate, the delivery of the appropriate type of predeparture preparation, the design of a motivating compensation package, and the means of **repatriation**—that is, the process of easing the ultimate reintegration of the expatriate into the home company on completion of a successful tour of duty. Success at each stage supports a self-sustaining system whereby returning expatriates share their knowledge with colleagues and persuade other high-performing executives also to work abroad.

FIGURE 20.3   The Components of CEO Compensation

Like frontline workers, CEOs receive *base pay* plus compensation in other forms, such as *benefits* and *perquisites*— "perks." The model for CEO pay favored in North America and many European countries—a model of performance-based pay that ties compensation to business results—is becoming more prevalent in Asia and Latin America as well. Figures here represent percentages of total remuneration.

Source: HR Services, "Pay Components 2005—Chief Executive Officer," *Managing Global Pay and Benefits* (Towers Perrin, 2005–2006), www.towersperrin.com (accessed November 28, 2007).

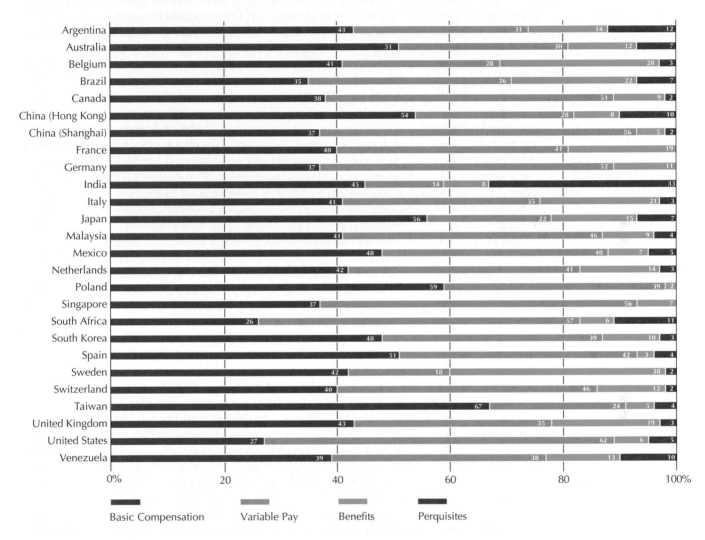

Evidence suggests the system works—for some. Nearly one in four expatriates who returns home gets promoted in his or her first year of repatriation. However, many do not land promotions and some of these former high flyers quit the company within a year of their return. Therefore, expatriates often face a different scenario that threatens the HRM system.[76]

As a rule, MNEs worry more about preparing and paying workers for the foreign assignment than supporting them when they return. In addition, although statistics show that 85 percent of organizations regard reintegration as important, only 20 percent acknowledge they manage it effectively.[77] Consequentially, returning home can deteriorate into a disappointing part of the expatriate assignment.

A survey of repatriated executives who had successfully completed their overseas assignment found more than a third held temporary assignments three months after returning home, nearly 80 percent felt their new job was a demotion from their foreign assignment, and more than 60 percent felt they did not have opportunities to transfer

> Returning home from a foreign assignment is fraught with difficulties.

> Repatriation tends to cause dissonance in many areas, most notably
> - Financial.
> - Work.
> - Social.

their international expertise to their new job.[78] Worse still, 15 percent of international assignees resigned within 12 months of completing their international posting. In general, expatriates face repatriation stress in three areas: change in personal finances, readjustment to the home-country corporate structure, and readjustment to life at home.

Changes in Personal Finances

Changes in personal finances can be dramatic on a manager's return home. Most expatriates enjoy rich benefits during their foreign assignment; many live in exclusive neighborhoods, send their children to prestigious schools, employ domestic help, socialize with elites, and still save a good amount. Returning home to a reasonable compensation plan with far fewer perks and privileges is often demoralizing.

Readjustment to Home-Country Corporate Structure

Readjustment to home-country corporate structure poses problems on several levels. Returning expatriates may find that their previous peers have been promoted above them, they have less autonomy as they return to being a "little fish in a big pond," and they struggle to rejoin the office network. As a result, they return to a company that doesn't quite know what to do with them and often sees them with market knowledge and technical skills that aren't quite on the cutting edge. In these situations, resentment builds within repatriated executives as they typically feel they've grown professionally during their overseas post, worked hard, sacrificed much for the company, and expect praise and promotion.

> The principal cause of repatriation frustrations is finding the right job for someone to return to.

More often than not, the opposite happens. One study found that some 60 to 70 percent of repatriated expatriates did not know what their position would be when they returned home, and about 60 percent said their companies were vague about the repatriation process, their pending jobs, and future career progression within the company. Compounding these tendencies is the sad fact that, for many expatriates, being out of sight overseas turns out to be truly out of mind back home, amplifying the fear that "companies station people abroad and then forget about them. If anything, advancement is even more difficult for the expat when he returns to headquarters, having missed out on opportunities to network with top management."[79]

MNEs reply that the issue of repatriation puts them between a rock and a hard place: An office does not sit vacant while the manager goes abroad for a few years; cost cutting, mergers, and acquisitions often mean they cannot be kept; and permitting the repatriated employee to bump his or her "replacement" on return is unfair. Still, data indicate that expatriates are likely to stay if the company gives them chances to apply their expertise.[80] Increasingly, companies push expatriates to take more responsibility for their return. More than a third require that employees take home leave and visit the home office before they finish their international assignment.

Readjustment to Life at Home

Readjusting to life at home can be stressful.[81] Troubles emerge as returning expatriates and their families experience "reverse culture shock." Upon return, managers and their families often find they need to relearn some of what they once took for granted. Meantime, children may struggle to fit into the local school system while spouses may feel isolated or out of touch with the career or friends they once again left behind.

Managing Repatriation

Companies are not blind to the problems of repatriation. Moreover, ignoring them is not an option—the greater the difficulties that confront returning expatriates, the more difficult it becomes to convince others to take foreign assignments. In recourse, MNEs experiment with a range of remedies. HRM executives advocate providing expatriates with advance notice of when they will return, more information about their possible new jobs, placement in jobs that leverage their foreign experiences, housing assistance, reorientation programs, periodic visits to headquarters while working abroad, and enlisting a formal headquarters mentor to watch over their interests while they are abroad.[82]

Some companies, like Dow Chemical, make written guarantees that repatriated employees will return to jobs at least as good as those they left behind. Other companies integrate foreign assignments into career planning and develop mentoring programs to look after the expatriates' domestic interests. Abbott Laboratories tries to keep its repatriate turnover rate less than 10 percent by focusing on career development. It also cautions workers before they leave the United States to expect the adjustment of returning home to be just as tough as going abroad and encourages them to stay in touch.

Some MNEs make the manager who originally sponsored an expatriate also responsible for finding his or her protégé a job on return. For example, Avaya protects its investment with at-home mentors who keep in touch with expatriates abroad and help them make a transition to a new position when they return in the simple belief that Avaya "has invested in this person. To leave him overseas or to lose him to another company is a waste of money."[83]

Some companies try to resolve the less obvious hardships of repatriation. Monsanto deals with reverse culture shock by formally addressing the social expectations of returning expatriates and giving them an opportunity to showcase their new knowledge in a debriefing session. Similarly, Viacom has set up a "comprehensive expatriate administrative tracking program" that includes specific health and retirement benefits tailored to the needs of those who have undertaken more than one consecutive overseas posting.[84]

Despite these efforts, statistics show that many expatriates are unhappy on their return. Pressed to pinpoint where repatriation begins to break down, the principal culprit is the challenge of finding the right job for someone to return to. One report concludes, "People who have spent two years working in different ways across varied markets and cultures are not always happy to return to the same desk and the same prospects. In this vacuum of direction, many have a career 'wobble,' then leave via a recruitment market in which their experience is seen as increasingly valuable."

Personal career management, therefore, is as vital to being selected for a foreign assignment as triumphantly returning home. Recall from our opening case the experience of Baxter Fenwall's Bryan Krueger, who accepted a four-year assignment in Tokyo without any guarantees of a promotion when he got home. As we saw, Krueger was conscientiously "proactive," networking avidly, keeping up with events at headquarters, and returning to the United States several times a year. The lesson here is that expatriates can't rely on the company to safeguard their career interests. A passive approach is hazardous, especially because expatriates often hear too late about possible promotion opportunities back home.[85] Instead, while abroad, they must navigate the repatriation process with a keen sense of its positive and negative aspects.

International Labor Relations

In each country in which an MNE operates, managers deal with groups of workers whose approach to the workplace reflects the local sociopolitical environment. This environment affects whether they join labor unions, how they collectively bargain, and what they want from companies. Expectedly, differences prevail across countries in how labor and management view each other.

When there is little mobility between the two groups (generally, children of laborers become laborers, and children of managers become managers), explicit class difference exists between the managers who run the MNE and the workers they hire and fire. Labor may perceive itself in a class struggle that echoes the divisions of Marx's conception of the proletariat versus the bourgeoisie. Labor-MNE relations in these countries, such as Brazil, the United Kingdom, and France, tend to be a zero-sum game—labor wins only when the MNE loses and vice versa.

In contrast, labor groups in many countries take a less confrontational approach. They are more inclined to follow the advice of their labor leaders and try to negotiate win-win solutions.[86] Unions in these countries often rely on national legislation rather than workplace activism to check the power of the MNE. Moreover, labor's agenda may be based in a broader sensitivity of general work conditions in the country—that is, a rising tide lifts all boats—rather than specific conditions at a specific MNE.

Usually, the HRM function of an MNE deals with these situations, taking charge of the company's relations with labor both within a particular country as well as within the global context. Operationally, HRM monitors and manages a range of workplace issues that fall under the broad umbrella of international labor relations. HRM aims to integrate its efforts with the straightforward standard of how, why, and where might organized labor constrain how the MNE configures or coordinates its value chain. HRM then supports the company's leadership in developing options to preempt, neutralize, or deal with these situations so they do not interfere with its basis for creating value.

> Collective bargaining refers to negotiations between labor union representatives and employers to reach agreement on a work contract.

The intensity of these concerns varies with the type of strategy an MNE pursues. Companies pursuing an international or global strategy, given their heightened sensitivities to exploiting location economies, consolidating operations, and protecting the transfer and use of core competencies, are sensitive to labor's actions. The multidomestic and transnational companies, given their greater degrees of local responsiveness, command more flexibility to adapt operations to labor's concerns without unduly sacrificing their value creation capabilities. Still, no matter what type of strategy the firm pursues, the enduring power of organized labor on both a country-to-country basis, as well as internationally, spurs MNEs to develop beneficial relations.

Against this backdrop, we now consider three aspects of international labor relations. First, we discuss how labor commonly represents the motives and means of MNEs; we then turn to the methods and successes of labor's responses to MNEs, and we close with a look at trends that moderate the relationship between MNEs and labor.

HOW LABOR LOOKS AT THE MNE

Complaints about the effects of globalization usually are lodged by employees whose companies have shifted work to other countries, leaving behind fewer jobs and lower wages. An ongoing debate is whether the MNE, through the power of its globally dispersed value chain, systematically weakens the rights and roles of labor. Critics argue that

> Labor unions, in defending their rights and expressing their views, occasionally take to the streets to show solidarity and gain public support. Here we see labor union members, armed with banners calling for higher pay and better working conditions, marching through Paris, France.

MNEs do so precisely because the multinationality of their product and resource flows let them manipulate markets and governments for gains that labor must ultimately bear.

A case in point. When the Disney Company was planning an amusement park for Europe, it began by pitting several countries against each other in the effort to get the best possible investment incentives. It eventually narrowed it down to alternative sites in France and Spain; ultimately, the company chose a site just outside of Paris. Labor's reaction was immediate. A representative of the Confédération Générale du Travail (General Confederation of Labour—CGT) of France contended that the Disney Company had used the threat of locating in Spain to drive a tough bargain with government officials. Specifically, he asserted that "Disney put Barcelona and the French site in competition and, as a result of this bidding war, the French government won the contract at the expense of many laws and many hard-won social rights."[87]

The MNE's Advantages   Once MNEs get their local operations up and running, labor contends they can hold out longer than workers in negotiating a solution to a strike. Furthermore, labor contends that MNEs can easily move value activities from one country to another in the effort to exploit less restrictive labor conditions. Complicating these situations is the complexity of the globally dispersed value chains of MNEs. Labor often lacks the information to verify MNEs' claims about products and profits as well as estimate their capacity to meet workers' demands. We now review these rationales.

Product and Resource Flows   Presumably, in the event of a strike in Country X, an MNE can divert output from its facilities in other countries and sell it to the consumers in Country X, thereby reducing the need to settle the strike. Moreover, because each country may comprise only a small percentage of an MNE's total worldwide sales, profits, and cash flows, a strike in one country may minimally affect its global performance. Given these circumstances, an MNE faces little pressure to resolve labor tensions. Therefore, an MNE's ability to threaten dire consequences in the event of a strike, and then hold out longer, gives it an advantage in collective bargaining with labor.

In their defense, managers point out that an MNE can supply customers in the strike-afflicted country only if it has excess capacity and produces an identical product in more than one country. Even if it meets these preconditions, an MNE would still confront the transport and tariff costs that led it to establish multiple production facilities in the first place. If the MNE partially owns the struck operation, partners or even minority stockholders may balk at financing a lengthy work stoppage.

Furthermore, if the idle facilities produce components needed for integrated production in other countries, then a strike may have far-reaching effects. For example, a strike at one GM facility in the United States prevented GM's Mexican plants from getting parts needed for assembly operations. Moreover, Mexican laws against layoffs meant GM had to maintain its Mexican workers on the payroll, thus adding pressure on GM to settle the strike.[88] In summary, there appear to be limited advantages of international diversification to enable an MNE to escape conflict with labor.

Value Activity Switching   MNEs often threaten to move value activities to other countries to extract wage reductions or work concessions from their employees. This tactic presses unions to accept lower compensation, fewer benefits, and poorer workplace conditions in favor of job security. For example, Daimler-Benz's German workers agreed to accept lower wages after the company procured agreements from French, Czech, and British labor to work for less.

This trend has gained greater visibility in the context of the offshoring of jobs. MNEs counter that this rationale partially represents the situation. Unquestionably, relocating production activities is plausible when a company has facilities in more than one country; at other times they would seem more plausible when different companies own facilities in different countries. For example, suppose a Canadian company competes with Brazilian imports. If Canadian workers demand and get substantial wage increases

---

Labor claims it is disadvantaged in dealing with MNEs because

- It is hard to get full data on MNEs' global operations.
- MNEs can manipulate investment incentives.
- They can easily move value activities to other countries.
- Ultimate decision making occurs in another country.

CONCEPT CHECK

We begin in Chapter 1 by showing how "The Forces Driving Globalization" have resulted in a raft of new **international business strategies** designed to respond to those forces. In Chapter 17, we discuss the emergence of several sophisticated strategies for **supply chain** management, many of which will no doubt affect such labor-related concerns as wage rates and job security in both home- and host-country markets. Here we suggest that, in light of such developments, the tension between labor and MNE management is likely to be strained even further in the future.

that result in higher product prices, the Brazilian competitor will likely seize the opportunity to build Canadian market share at the expense of the Canadian company and its workers. However, suppose the Brazilian company also owns the facility in Canada. The Brazilian management would have to weigh the cost-saving advantages of moving its production from Canada to Brazil against the losses it would incur in Canada by discarding its facilities there.

Operational Scale and Complexity   Observers claim it is difficult for labor unions to deal with MNEs because of the global scale of their value chains and the difficulties in interpreting how they coordinate value activities. Both issues are complicated by the difficulty labor has in identifying the location of decision making and in interpreting financial data for the typical MNE. These ambiguities mean that labor is often at the mercy of decision makers and resources that are far removed from their country. Labor therefore argues that MNEs who command such positions are more likely to impose arbitrarily stringent antilabor policies in the event of workplace activism.

Workers, especially with the assistance of unions, examine MNEs' financial data to determine MNEs' ability to meet their demands. Interpreting these data is a difficult task because of disparities among managerial, tax, and disclosure requirements in home and host countries. Moreover, labor has been apprehensive that MNEs might manipulate transfer prices to give the appearance that a given subsidiary cannot meet labor demands.

MNEs reply that these concerns overemphasize their ability to increase compensation and deemphasize the more important issue of going-wage rates in both the industry and geographic area. Although MNEs may report complex data, at least one set of financial statements must satisfy local authorities. By definition, this set should be no more difficult to interpret than that reported by a purely domestic company. In terms of transfer pricing, the MNE that sets artificial levels to aid in a particular collective bargaining situation creates distortions and possible problems elsewhere. Specifically, if an MNE understates profits in one country, it would have to overstate them elsewhere, which would then put it at a disadvantage in collective bargaining in that country.

HOW LABOR RESPONDS TO THE MNE

Labor tries to strengthen its bargaining power through cross-national cooperation.

Workers have responded to the power of the MNEs through several actions. First and foremost, workers have organized unions to fight, via collective bargaining with management, for higher pay, better benefits, greater job security, and improved working conditions. Unions' bargaining power is derived largely from their ability to threaten to disrupt production, either by a strike or some other form of work protest—most commonly, through a slowdown in the pace of work or the refusal to work overtime. This threat is credible, however, only insofar as management has no alternative but to employ workers who are not members of the union.

Labor's Options   Unions engage several tactics to counter MNEs' bargaining power. Internationally, unions cooperate in a range of ways, sharing information, assisting bargaining units in other countries, and dealing simultaneously with MNEs.[89] The most common international cooperation among unions is exchanging information on an MNE's local policies and activities. This sort of collaboration helps determine the validity of the company's local claims as well as helps it reference precedents from other countries on bargaining issues.

Exchanging Information   International confederations of unions, trade secretariats made up of related unions in a single industry or a complex of related industries, and company councils that include representatives from an MNE's plants around the world can exchange information. More specifically, a European work council (EWC) represents a company's employees throughout the European Union. Through an EWC, a company informs and consults with workers on such issues as its current national, regional, and global performance as well as its strategies so the employees understand likely staffing, business, and market changes.

Coordinating Activities Labor groups in one country may support their counterparts in other countries in the view that coordinating union action across countries disrupts the coordination of a MNE's value chain. Popular measures include refusing to work overtime to supply a market normally served by striking workers' production, sending financial aid to workers in other countries, and disrupting work in their own countries. For example, French workers pledged to disrupt work at Pechiney in support of striking workers in the company's U.S. facilities.

Calling upon Transnational Institutions Finally, labor appeals to any number of transnational institutions to assist their efforts to check the power of MNEs. The International Labor Organization (ILO), for example, was founded in 1919 on the premise that the failure of any country to adopt humane labor conditions impedes other countries' efforts to improve their own conditions. Several associations of unions from different countries support similar ideals. These associations include various international trade secretariats representing workers in specific industries—for example, the International Confederation of Free Trade Unions (ICFTU), the World Federation of Trade Unions (WFTU), and the World Confederation of Labour (WCL).

These organizations' activities, along with the general enhancement of worldwide communications, publicize the different labor conditions among countries. Among the newsworthy reports have been legal proscriptions against collective bargaining in Malaysia, wages below minimum standards in Indonesia, and the use of forced labor and child labor in some emerging markets. Upon publicizing such conditions, these organizations then champion economic and political sanctions to provoke change.[90] Similarly, various codes of conduct on industrial relations, such as those issued by the OECD, ILO, and EU, influence the labor practices of MNEs. Although the codes are voluntary, an MNE's compliance, or lack thereof, has symbolic significance to consumers and governments.

THE LABOR STRUGGLE: BARRIERS TO INTERNATIONAL UNANIMITY

National unions regularly endorse calls for international cooperation with fellow organizations. Offsetting calls for unanimity is a stark reality of globalization, namely, that national unions are locked in a zero-sum game of competing with each other to attract investment and jobs from MNEs. Consequently, when push comes to shove, there has been little enthusiasm among workers to support their counterparts in another country.

Labor may be at a disadvantage in MNE negotiations because the

- Country bargaining unit is only a small part of MNE activities.
- MNE may continue serving customers with foreign production or resources.

Different Country-Specific Goals For example, Canada and the United States have long shared a common union membership in the belief that united they stood, divided they fell. Still, there are ongoing moves among Canadian workers to form unions independent of those in the United States. One Canadian organizer summarized this attitude explaining, "An American union is not going to fight to protect Canadian jobs at the expense of American jobs." The logic is that international unions will adopt policies favoring the bulk of their membership, which in any joint Canadian-U.S. relationship is bound to be American.

Even when labor in one country helps labor in another, it likely aims to achieve its own specific goals. For example, a union representing U.S. tomato pickers helped its Mexican counterpart negotiate a stronger collective agreement that limited the local workplace power of both domestic and foreign companies. This change then dissuaded the Campbell Soup Company from moving operations to Mexico. As a result of such competition between national unions, cooperation is difficult to establish.

Different Structures and Ideals   Further impeding international unanimity among unions is the fact that unions largely evolved independently in each country. As a result, the demography, structure, ideals, and goals of unions vary from country to country. For example, the percentage of workers in unions is much higher in some countries than in others.

Furthermore, some organized workers in France, Portugal, and Great Britain belong to Communist unions whose view of the intrinsic class conflict of collective bargaining with MNEs clashes with the more moderate views of unions elsewhere in Germany, the Netherlands, Scandinavia, and Switzerland. Cross-national differences in unions' agendas extend to a host of comparatively more mundane matters like wage rates and workers' preferences. For example, Spanish workers are more willing to work on weekends than are German workers.

Different Collective Bargaining Methods   Unions in different countries prefer different methods of collective bargaining. As such, MNEs in a given country may deal with one or several unions that, depending on the situation, represent workers in many industries, in many companies within the same industry, or in only one company. If it represents only one company, the union may represent all plants or just one plant. In Sweden, bargaining tends to be highly centralized; employers from numerous companies in different industries deal together with a federation of trade unions. In Germany, employers from associations of companies in the same industries bargain jointly with union federations.

Different Approaches to Reconciling Labor Tension   Approaches to reconcile labor tension differ from country to country. The use of mediation by an impartial party is mandatory in Israel but voluntary in the United States and the United Kingdom. Among countries that have mediation practices, diverse attitudes prevail. For example, there is much less enthusiasm for it in India than in the United States. Not all differences are settled through changes either in legislation or through collective bargaining. Other means are the labor court and the government-chosen arbitrator. For example, wages in many Austrian industries are arbitrated semiannually. These sorts of ideological and operational gaps have made sustained cross-national cooperation difficult for unions.

Regulatory Difficulties   Lastly, organized labor has met with limited success in getting national and international bodies to regulate MNEs. National agencies have helped workers gain better access to the intricacies of the MNEs' decision-making process. Most notably, legislation in some countries, particularly in northern Europe, gives labor the legal right to participate in the management of companies.

Codetermination   The principle of **codetermination** emphasizes cooperative decision making within firms that benefits both the workers and the company.[91] Despite some voluntary moves toward codetermination, most examples have been mandated by the government. Labor has persuaded government officials, particularly in Western Europe, to require companies to comply with worker-friendly plant closure prenotification requirements. In addition, international agencies like the ILO, EU, and OECD have adopted codes of conduct for multinational firms in their relations with labor. These guidelines, from the view of labor, fail to regulate MNEs. For instance, there are early examples of workers deterring investment outflows, acquisitions, and plant closures. Still, the fact that these conduct codes lack any enforcement capability means they have had an inconsistent effect on companies' international business decisions and activities.

LOOKING TO THE FUTURE

Which Countries Will Have the Jobs of the Future?

As capital, technology, and information grow more mobile among countries and companies, human resource development increasingly explains competitive differences. Consequently, companies' access to and retention of more qualified personnel grow more important as they face the challenge of recruiting and retaining highly skilled, highly valued workers.

Demographers are nearly unanimous in projecting that populations will grow much faster in emerging economies (China being the notable exception) than in the wealthier countries—at least through 2030. At the same time, the number of retirees as a percentage of the population in the wealthier countries will grow as people live longer and retire earlier. People will also need to be educated for more years to get better jobs. Overall, these trends indicate that there will be fewer people to do productive work within the wealthier countries. These countries are already trying to adjust, engaging in a range of education and training programs.[92] Still, these programs have many social and economic consequences to which MNEs must adapt.

One adjustment might be for wealthier countries to encourage emigration from emerging economies that struggle to generate enough jobs for their swelling workforce. In Canada, the United States, and parts of Western Europe, there has been a long-term migration of foreign workers, both legally and illegally, from emerging economies. This entry generates assimilation costs within wealthier countries and a brain drain from emerging economies when their highly qualified people leave for other countries. Some, however, suggest that emigration benefits everyone by encouraging brain circulation among wealthier and emerging economies.[93]

An increasing number of U.S. success stories from Taiwan, China, Korea, and India are returning to their native homes to start companies. Nonetheless, times of economic downturns will likely see unemployed workers in the wealthier countries blame foreign workers for their plight. Under this scenario, companies will have to spend more time getting work permits and integrating different nationalities into their workforces.

Another potential adjustment in wealthier countries is the continued push toward adopting robotics and other laborsaving equipment.[94] Although this may help solve some of the shortages in workers, it will inevitably escalate companies' need for workers who command higher skill levels. Less-educated members of the workforce will likely be unemployable, forced to take lesser-paying jobs in the service sector or to compete with immigrants for less appealing jobs. Gaps between haves and have-nots may widen within wealthier countries as well as between those countries and emerging economies. In this scenario, have-nots may pressure governments to push companies to shift technological development away from laborsaving priorities.

A third possible adjustment is the acceleration of business migration to emerging economies to tap rich supplies of inexpensive productive labor. At the same time, emerging economies may devise ways to support brain circulation or, if unsuccessful, to halt the process of brain drain. Either approach will shift more entry-level production jobs from wealthier countries to their emerging counterparts.[95] If successful, managers who return to their countries will likely shift many low-skilled jobs to their home market. Governments in wealthier countries will then face the tough problem of what to do with underqualified workers who face deteriorating job prospects.[96] ■

TRENDS IN MNE–LABOR RELATIONS

The relationship between labor and MNEs is an intrinsic facet of international business. Two trends, one from the perspective of labor, the other from MNEs, will define the next stage of their relationship.

As Table 20.5 shows, union membership as a portion of the total workforce has been falling in most countries for the past few decades. Several trends drive this decline.

- *Increase in white-collar workers as a percentage of total workers.* White-collar workers see themselves more as managers than as laborers, and thus they are less inclined to join a union.

- *Increase in service employment in relation to manufacturing employment.* There is more variation in service assignments than in manufacturing, so workers believe their situations differ from that of their co-workers.

TABLE 20.5 Trends in Trade Union Membership, 1970–2003

Trade union membership—union membership as a proportion of employed wage and salary earners—is declining in most countries. Note that most of the exceptions are in Scandinavia.

	Percentage of Workforce in Trade Unions					Percentage Change
	1970	1990	1993	1998	2003	1970–2003
Australia	50	41	38	28	23	−27.3
Austria	63	47	43	38	35*	−27.4
Belgium	42	54	55	55	55*	+13.3
Canada	32	33	33	29	28	−3.2
Denmark	60	75	77	76	70	+10.1
Finland	51	73	81	78	74	+22.8
France	22	10	10	8	8	−13.4
Germany	32	31	32	26	23	−9.4
Ireland	53	51	48	42	35	−17.9
Italy	37	39	39	36	34	−3.3
Japan	35	25	24	23	20	−15.4
Republic of Korea	13	18	15	12	11	−1.4
The Netherlands	37	24	26	25	22	−14.2
New Zealand	55	51	35	22	22*	−33.1
Norway	57	59	58	56	53	−3.5
Spain	n/a	13	18	16	16	n/a
Sweden	68	81	84	82	78	+10.3
Switzerland	29	24	23	22	18**	−11.1
United Kingdom	45	39	36	30	29	−15.5
United States	24	16	15	13	12	−11.1

Note:* = 2002; ** = 2001.

Sources: Jelle Visser, "Union Membership Statistics in 24 Countries," *Monthly Labor Review* 129 (2006): 38–49; David G. Blanchflower, "International Patterns of Union Membership," *British Journal of Industrial Relations* 45 (March 2007): 1–28.

- *Rising portion of women in the workforce.* Traditionally, women have been less inclined to join unions.

- *Rising portion of part-time and temporary workers.* Such workers do not see themselves in the job long enough for a union to help them much.

- *Trend toward smaller average plant size.* More direct interactions between workers and managers align their interests, thereby harmonizing outlooks.

- *Decline in the belief in collectivism among younger workers.* Few of today's younger workers have suffered economic deprivation; hence they question the value of collective solutions.[97]

The overall decline in union membership is a long-running trend, although there are exceptions. Unions in Sweden, for instance, have maintained their strength because they have forged cooperative relationships with flagship companies like Electrolux and Volvo to improve corporate competitiveness and to share the rewards from the success. Still, the harsh reality is that the power of unions is a function of the size of their membership rolls. Continuing decline in membership foreshadows unions with weaker negotiation positions and less incentive for cooperation with counterparts in other countries.

On the flip side, MNEs are developing HRM policies and practices that fortify their power. Historically, irrespective of the strategy that companies pursued, most MNEs decentralized labor relations responsibilities to the HRM manager in foreign subsidiaries. Practicality, rather than bold insight, motivated this policy. Country-to-country variability in labor laws, union structure, workplace attitudes, and collective bargaining processes created a complex situation that continually changed. Most MNEs reasoned that headquarters was poorly positioned and prepared to manage worldwide labor relations effectively. In recourse, they delegated the task to local managers.

This outlook is giving way to a trend toward greater coordination and control of global labor policies by the senior leadership of MNEs. Coordinating globally dispersed value chains spurs headquarters to preempt disruptions by sporadic workplace activism. Moreover, companies whose value creation is sensitive to labor costs no longer can delegate labor relations to a range of local managers. Integrating global operations spurs MNEs also to integrate labor relations. Growing attention to and integration of their labor relations creates powerful advantages for MNEs. They increasingly sharpen their understanding of how to use the threat of production switching or resource redirection to strengthen their collective bargaining positions.

> Falling union membership in many countries foreshadows lower bargaining power for labor, whereas the effort of MNEs to develop integrated labor relations across countries increases their bargaining power.

Tel-Comm-Tek (TCT)

C A S E

In January 2007, Mark Hopkins of Tel-Comm-Tek (TCT) India, a company headquartered in the United States, announced his resignation and intention to return to the United States.[98] At the time, he was the managing director of the Indian subsidiary of TCT. During his tenure, Hopkins witnessed a dramatic increase in growth, which he had a hand in; his importance to the company was evident. After his announcement, TCT immediately began a search for his replacement.

TCT: A Brief Introduction

TCT manufactures a variety of small office equipment in nine different countries. It distributes and sells products such as copying machines, dictation units, laser printers, and paper shredders worldwide, most recently reporting sales in more than 70 countries. TCT has sold and serviced products in India since the early 1980s even though it lacks its own in-country manufacturing facility. Originally, it hired independent importers to sell its products. It soon realized that generating higher sales required setting up its own operations. In 1992, it opened a sales office in New Delhi. Map 20.2 profiles India.

Today, TCT is poised to expand its Indian operations, mainly based on reports of significantly higher sales and profitability from its sales operation. Another factor in this bid to expand is the strategic importance of the Indian subsidiary, which is now at the forefront of TCT's corporate family. Sales are dramatically increasing as the Indian economy, driven by a boom in the information technology sector, posts double-digit growth.

India: The Next Big Industrial Power?

Some see India developing into the world's next big industrial power, a projection that is leading many global companies to increase their operations in the country. For example, IBM, a long-time customer of TCT, increased its Indian staff from literally a handful to 53,000 employees between the mid-1990s and 2007 through a series of acquisitions and investments. Moreover, internal company analysis indicates that the economic growth rate for the overall economy, along with the sectors that TCT specifically serves, could boost total sales of the Indian subsidiary past those in the company's home market.

MAP 20.2   India

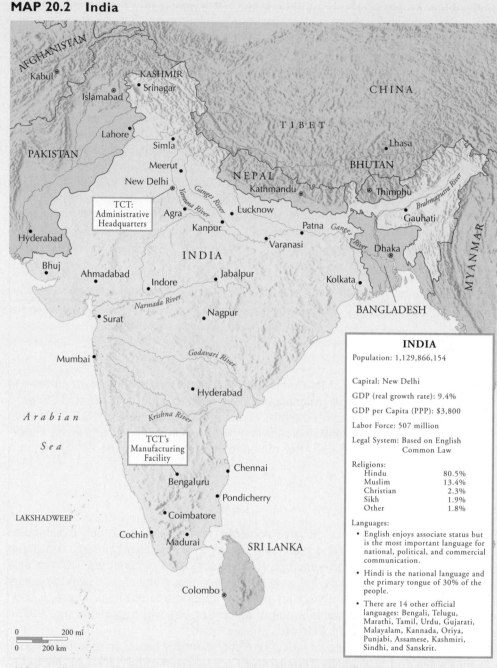

INDIA

Population: 1,129,866,154

Capital: New Delhi

GDP (real growth rate): 9.4%

GDP per Capita (PPP): $3,800

Labor Force: 507 million

Legal System: Based on English
            Common Law

Religions:
Hindu	80.5%
Muslim	13.4%
Christian	2.3%
Sikh	1.9%
Other	1.8%

Languages:

• English enjoys associate status but is the most important language for national, political, and commercial communication.

• Hindi is the national language and the primary tongue of 30% of the people.

• There are 14 other official languages: Bengali, Telugu, Marathi, Tamil, Urdu, Gujarati, Malayalam, Kannada, Oriya, Punjabi, Assamese, Kashmiri, Sindhi, and Sanskrit.

U.S.-based Tel-Comm-Tek (TCT), which makes small office equipment in 9 countries and sells in more than 70, opened an Indian sales office in the capital of New Delhi in 1992 and broke ground on a manufacturing plant in Bengaluru in 2008. India appears to be an excellent point from which TCT can supply sales locations throughout Asia, and the company expects that total sales through its Indian subsidiary will eventually surpass total sales in the United States.

Source: Central Intelligence Agency, "India," *The World Factbook 2007*, www.cia.gov (accessed November 28, 2007).

Expansion: Pros

Improved Infrastructure   Also shaping TCT India's expansion plans is the ongoing improvement in India's transportation infrastructure. Improvement in highways, railways, and seaports promises to improve the efficiency of product movement both in and out of the country. Completed successfully, management at TCT envisions making the local subsidiary a vital link in TCT's increasingly sophisticated supply chain. Presently, TCT's supply chain integrates input suppliers, production, and wholesalers in the United States and Europe. Long-term plans indicate the need to incorporate supply points throughout Asia.

Democratic Traditions   India's independence in 1947 institutionalized a strong democratic tradition of accountability, transparency, and individual freedom. Progress on the economic front was even more dynamic. From 1947 through 1990, India's decision to have a centrally planned economy led to the infamous "License Raj," a situation marked by elaborate licenses, regulations, and bureaucracy that were required to set up business. In 1991, India began a transition toward a free market economy with the intended demise of the License Raj. This transition, an ongoing process, has helped stabilize the economic environment and boost India's attractiveness as a manufacturing site, but India's business environment continues to pose many challenges.

Expansion: Cons

Problematic Legal Environment   The Indian legal environment, although endorsing the principles of the rule of law, continues to struggle with pervasive corruption. The primary driver of corruption, in many observers' eyes, is the country's vast bureaucracy, a legacy of the previous centrally planned economy. Partial success in dismantling the License Raj has resulted in a civil administration that influences many aspects of economic life. Western high-tech companies often run into problems with intellectual property violation. Patent infringement and business process piracy are not uncommon.

Outmoded Labor Laws   The legal system creates other complications. For example, India's labor laws, little changed since they were enacted after independence in 1947, make it difficult to lay off employees even if a company's fortunes hit hard times or the economy slows. Consequently, companies are reluctant to hire workers given the risk of being unable to fire them if need be. Necessary terminations are extremely difficult to execute and often involve extensive negotiations and settlements. "[C]ompanies think twice, 10 times, before they hire new people," said Sunil Kant Munjal, the chairman of the Hero Group, one of the world's largest manufacturers of inexpensive motorcycles.

Anticompetitive Legislation   In addition, some legislation bars companies with more than 100 employees from competing in many industries. These laws are aimed at protecting small enterprises operating in many villages scattered throughout India, often at the expense of larger-scale operations. Another challenge is high tariffs. These were put in place long ago to promote domestic production and still apply to many classes of imports, including some that are inputs into products manufactured by TCT. Finally, some of India's labor laws discourage flexibility; for example, companies are prohibited from allowing manufacturing workers to clock more than 54 hours of overtime in any three-month period, even if the workers are willing to do so.

TCT Moves Forward

In late 2007, TCT began building its first factory in Bengaluru, the center of India's Silicon Valley (see Map 20.2). The plant will make a full range of laser printers, from entry level to high end. The first production run took place in June 2008. Logistically, TCT plans initially to supply the factory with components from its manufacturing facilities in Europe and the United States. Eventually, management plans to find local suppliers or backward integrate into the local production of those components.

The scale of the production operation requires 150 to 200 production workers. TCT anticipates no problems in hiring a skilled labor force given other companies' success stories. For example, in 2005, the South Korean conglomerate LG looked to staff 458 assembly-line jobs at its new Indian factory. It required each applicant to have at least 15 years of education—a condition that translates into having both high school and technical college certification. Seeking a young workforce, the company also decided that no more than 1 percent of the workers could have any prior work experience. Despite these restrictions, 55,000 people qualified for interviews.

TCT enlisted a U.S. engineering firm to supervise construction of its plant in Bengaluru. Upon completion, TCT will "turn over the key" to the on-site factory director, a U.S. expatriate sent specifically to run the completed plant. This director reports directly to TCT's U.S. headquarters on production and quality control matters. He or she will report to TCT India's managing director in New Delhi, the position now vacant, on all other matters, such as accounting, supply chain logistics, finance, and labor relations. The managing director of TCT India, in turn, will report to the Asian Regional Office at TCT's U.S. headquarters.

Selecting a Managing Director

As in the past, TCT prefers to fill executive vacancies by promotion from within the company. TCT uses a mix of home-, host-, and third-country nationals to staff management positions in foreign countries. In addition, TCT often rotates its managers among its foreign and U.S. locations. Headquarters sees international experience as an important factor in determining who to promote.

The Candidates   Following procedure, the Asian Regional Office charged a selection committee to nominate the new managing director for TCT India. The committee identified six candidates:

Tom Wallace   A 30-year TCT veteran, Wallace is knowledgeable and experienced in the technical and sales aspects of the job. He has supported some supply chain initiatives in the U.S. market. Although he has never worked abroad, he has toured the company's foreign operations and always expressed interest in an expatriate position. His superiors typically rate his performance as proficient. He will retire in about four-and-a-half years. He and his wife speak only English. Their children are grown and live with their own families in the United States.

Presently, Wallace supervises a U.S.-based operation that is about the size of that in India's new factory. However, the merger of Wallace's unit with another TCT division will eliminate his current position within six months.

Brett Harrison   Harrison, 40, has spent 15 years with TCT running both line activities as well as supervising staff. His superiors consider him highly competent and poised to move into upper-level management within the next few years. For the past three years, he has worked in the Asian Regional Office and has regularly toured TCT's Southeast Asian operations.

Both he and his wife have traveled to India several times in the last 20 years and are well acquainted with its geography, politics, customs, and outlooks. The Harrisons personally know many U.S. expatriates in the Bengaluru region. Their children, ages 14 and 16, have also vacationed in India with their parents. Mrs. Harrison is a midlevel executive with a multinational pharmaceuticals company that presently does not have an Indian operation.

Atasi Das   Born in the United States, Das joined TCT 12 years ago after earning her M.B.A. from a university in New England. At 37, she has successfully moved between staff and line positions with broader responsibilities in strategic planning. For two years, she was the second in command of a product group that was about half the size of the expanding Indian operations. Her performance regularly earns excellent ratings. Currently, she works on a planning-staff team based at TCT headquarters.

When she originally joined TCT, she noted that her ultimate goal was to be assigned international responsibilities, and she pointed to her undergraduate major in international management as evidence of her long-term plan. She recently reiterated her interest in international responsibilities, seeing it as an essential career step. She speaks Hindi and is unmarried. Her parents, who now live in the United States, are first-generation immigrants from India. Several family members and relatives live in Kashmir and Punjab, northern states of India.

Ravi Desai   Desai, 33, is currently an assistant managing director in the larger Asian operation. He helps oversee production and sales for the Southeast Asian markets in Singapore, Malaysia, and China. A citizen of India, he has spent his 10 years with TCT working in operational slots throughout Southeast Asia.

He holds an M.B.A. from the prestigious Indian Institute of Management. Some in TCT see him as a likely candidate to direct the Indian operation eventually. He is married with four children (ages 2 to 7) and speaks English and Hindi well. His wife, also a native of India, neither works outside the home nor speaks English.

Jalan Bukit Seng   Seng, 38, is the managing director of TCT's assembly operation in Malaysia. A citizen of Singapore, Seng has worked in either Singapore or Malaysia his entire life. However, he did earn undergraduate university and M.B.A. degrees from leading universities in the United States. He is fluent in Singapore's four official languages—Malay, English, Mandarin, and Tamil—and sees himself learning other languages as needed.

His performance reviews, both with respect to the Malaysia plant and other TCT plant operations around the world, have consistently been positive, with an occasional ranking of excellent. Seng is unmarried, but he is close to extended family members who live in Singapore and Malaysia.

Saumitra Chakraborty   At 31, Chakraborty is the assistant to the departing managing director in India. He has held that position since joining TCT upon graduating from a small private university in Europe four years earlier. Unmarried, he consistently earns a job performance rating of competent in operational matters and distinctive in customer relationship management. Although he excels in employee relations, he lacks direct-line experience. Still, he has successfully increased TCT India's sales, somewhat owing to his personal connections with prominent Indian families and government officials, along with his skillfulness in the ways of the Indian business environment. Besides speaking India's main languages of English and Hindi fluently, Chakraborty speaks Kannada (the local language of Bengaluru). ■

QUESTIONS

1. Which candidate should the committee nominate for the assignment? Why?
2. What challenges might each candidate encounter in the position?
3. How might TCT go about minimizing the challenges facing each candidate?
4. Should all candidates receive the same compensation package? If not, what factors should influence each package?
5. What recommendations can you offer to help a company facing this sort of decision that will enable it to balance professional and personal characteristics?
6. Returning to material covered in Chapter 15, specifically that dealing with the idea of a matrix organization, do you see any benefit to appointing two of the individuals described here to the post? Operationally, one individual would be in charge of internal affairs, and the other would manage external affairs. What might be the likely benefits and problems with this arrangement?

SUMMARY

- Research and anecdotes show that the MNE whose HRM policies support its chosen strategy creates superior value. Still, many MNEs struggle to develop effective HRM policies.

- The top-level managers of foreign subsidiaries normally perform much broader duties than do domestic managers with similar cost or profit responsibilities. They must resolve communications problems, usually with less staff support, between corporate headquarters and subsidiaries.

- Three perspectives describe how companies set about staffing their international operations, namely the ethnocentric, polycentric, and geocentric approaches. Companies may use elements of each staffing policy, but one approach predominates.

- An ethnocentric staffing approach fills foreign management positions with home-country nationals. A polycentric staffing policy uses host-country nationals to manage local subsidiaries.

A geocentric staffing policy seeks the best people for key jobs throughout the organization, regardless of their nationality.

- Although executives transferred from headquarters to local operations are more likely to best understand the company's core competencies, an ethnocentric staffing can result in a narrow perspective in foreign markets.

- MNEs often employ more locals than expatriate managers because the former better understand local operations and demand less compensation.

- Hiring locals rather than expatriates demonstrates that opportunities are available for local citizens, shows consideration for local interests, avoids the red tape of cross-national transfers, and is usually cheaper.

- The selection of an individual for an expatriate position is largely influenced by the candidate's technical competence, adaptiveness, and leadership ability.

- MNEs transfer people abroad to infuse technical competence and home-country business practices, to control foreign operations, and to develop managers' business skills.

- Training and predeparture preparations often includes general country orientation, cultural sensitivity, and practical training.

- MNEs that transfer personnel abroad should consider their technical competencies, how well the people will be accepted, how well they will adapt to local conditions, and how to treat them when they return home from their foreign assignment.

- Training and predeparture preparations usually reduce the odds of expatriate failure. Increasingly, preparation activities include the expatriate's spouse or partner.

- Key international training functions include building a global awareness among managers in general and equipping managers to handle the specific challenges of a foreign assignment.

- Expatriate failure, narrowly defined, is the manager's premature return home due to poor job performance. Broadly defined, it is the failure of the MNE's selection policies to find individuals who will succeed abroad.

- When transferred abroad, an expatriate's compensation usually is increased because of hardships and differences in cost of living. Transfers to remote areas typically carry higher premiums.

- The compensation of an expatriate must neither overly reward nor unduly punish a person for accepting a foreign assignment. Generally, most MNEs use the balance sheet approach to manage this dilemma.

- Repatriation, the act of returning home from a foreign assignment, has many difficulties. The principal cause of repatriation frustrations is finding the right job for the expatriate to return to.

- A country's sociopolitical environment largely determines the type of relationship between labor and management and affects the number, representation, and organization of unions. Generally, the overall attitude in a country affects how labor and management view each other and how labor will try to negotiate better working conditions.

- International organizations pressure companies to follow internationally accepted labor practices wherever they operate, regardless of whether the practices conflict with the norms and laws of the host countries.

- International cooperation among labor groups in a concerted effort to confront MNEs is minimal. Labor groups' initiatives include information exchanges, simultaneous negotiations or strikes, and refusals to work overtime to supply the market in a struck country.

- Organized labor has, to slight success, formed international labor agreements and strategies to offset MNEs' bargaining power.

- Labor contends that it is disadvantaged in dealing with MNEs because it is hard to get full data on MNEs' global operations, MNEs can manipulate investment incentives, MNEs can easily move value activities to other countries, and MNEs often make key decisions in another country.

KEY TERMS

balance sheet compensation plan (p. 791)
codetermination (p. 802)
culture shock (p. 788)
expatriate (778)

expatriate failure (p. 786)
home-country national (p. 778)
human resource management
  (HRM) (p. 775)

repatriation (794)
third-country national (p. 778)

ENDNOTES

1 *Sources include the following:* "In Search of Global Leaders: View of Jeffery Immelt, Chairman and CEO, General Electric," *Harvard Business Review,* August 1, 2003; Barbara Ettorre, "A Brave New World," *Management Review* 82:4 (1993): 10–16; Mark Larson, "More Employees Go Abroad as International Operations Grow," *Workforce Management,* June 1, 2006; Jane Fraser and Jeremy Oppenheim, "What's New About Globalization?" *The McKinsey Quarterly* 2 (1997): 168–79; "Go East, My Son," *The Economist,* August 10, 2006; "China's Recruitment Market Is Booming," *The Economist,* September 21, 2006; Sandra Jones, "Going Stateside: Once the Overseas Hitch Is Over, Homeward-Bound Expats Hit Turbulence," *Crain's Chicago Business,* July 24, 2000; Barry Newman, "Expat Archipelago," *Wall Street Journal,* December 12, 1995: A1; Robert Pelton, "The World's Most Dangerous Places," *Harper Resource* (2003); Joe Sharkey, "Global Economy Is Leading to More Dangerous Places," *New York Times,* April 19, 2005; Mark Schoeff Jr., "P&G Places a Premium on International Experience," *Workforce Management,* April 10, 2006: 28; Elizabeth Marx, "Route to the Top, 2006," Cranfield University School of Management (2007), at www.som.cranfield.ac.uk/som/news/story.asp?id=329; "In Search of Global Leaders," *Harvard Business Review,* August 1, 2003.

2 Paula Caligiuri and Victoria Di Santo, "Global Competence: What Is It, and Can It Be Developed through Global Assignments?" *Human Resource Planning* 24 (September 2001): 27–36; Mark Morgan, "Career-Building Strategies: It's Time to Do a Job Assessment: Are Your Skills Helping You Up the Corporate Ladder?" *Strategic Finance* 83 (June 2002): 38–44.

3 Hoon Park, "Global Human Resource Management: A Synthetic Approach." *The Journal of International Business and Economics* (2002).

4 William Judge, "Is a Leader's Character Culture-Bound or Culture-Free? An Empirical Comparison of the Character Traits of American and Taiwanese CEOs," *Journal of Leadership Studies* 8 (Fall 2001): 63–79.

5 Keith Brouthers, "Institutional, Cultural and Transaction Cost Influences on Entry Mode Choice and Performance," *Journal of International Business Studies* 33 (Summer 2002): 203–22.

6 Ben Kedia, Richard Nordtvedt, and Liliana M. Perez, "International Business Strategies, Decision-Making Theories, and Leadership Styles: An Integrated Framework," *Competitiveness Review* 12 (Winter–Spring 2002): 38–53.

7 Sully Taylor, Schon Beechler, and Nancy Napier, "Toward an Integrative Model of Strategic International Resource Management," *Academy of Management Review* 21 (1996): 959–85, discuss these models in the context of multidomestic and a combination of global and transnational strategies.

8 Globesmanship," *Across the Board* 27 (January–February 1990): 26, quoting Michael Angus.

9 Watson Wyatt Worldwide, "Human Capital Index: Human Capital as a Lead Indicator of Shareholder Value," at www.watsonwyatt.com/research/resrender.asp?id=w-488&page=1 (accessed November 27, 2007).

10 See, for example, N. Khatri, "Managing Human Resource for Competitive Advantage: A Study of Companies in Singapore," *International Journal of Human Resource Management* 11:2 (2000): 336.

11 R. Coleman, "HR Management Lags Behind at World Class Firms," *CMA Management* (July–August, 2002).

12 Mercer LLC, "International Assignments Increasing, Mercer Survey Finds," May 16, 2006, at www.mercerhr. com/summary.jhtml?idContent=1222700 (accessed November 27, 2007).

13 "Human Capital: A Key to Higher Market Value," *Business Finance* (December 1999): 15.

14 "Travelling More Lightly," *The Economist,* June 22, 2006.

15 Leslie Klaff, "Thinning the Ranks of the Career Expats," *Workforce Management* (October 2004): 84–87.

16 Yvonne Sonsino, reported in "Travelling More Lightly." See also Mercer LLC, "International Assignments Increasing."

17 Calvin Reynolds, "Strategic Employment of Third Country Nationals: Keys to Sustaining the Transformation of HR Functions," *Human Resource Planning* 20 (March 1997): 33–50.

18 Adrian Wooldridge, "The Battle for the Best," *The Economist: The World in 2007.*

19 Chi-fai Chan and Neil Holbert, "Marketing Home and Away: Perceptions of Managers in Headquarters and Subsidiaries," *Journal of World Business* 36 (Summer 2001): 205.

20 Tsun-yan Hsieh, Johanne Lavoie, and Robert Samek, "Are You Taking Your Expatriate Talent Seriously?" *The McKinsey Quarterly* (Summer 1999): 71.

21 "Travelling More Lightly."

22 William C. Weldon, "Chairman's Letter: To Our Shareholders," *Annual Report 2006* (Johnson & Johnson, 2007), at http://jnj.v1.papiervirtuel.com/report/2007030901 (accessed November 27, 2007).

23 Vijay Pothukuchi, Fariborz Damanpour, Jaepil Choi, Chao C. Chen, and Seung Ho Park, "National and Organizational Culture Differences and International Joint Venture Performance," *Journal of International Business Studies* 33 (Summer 2002): 243–66.

24 PricewaterhouseCoopers LLP and Cranfield School of Management, "Measuring the Value of International Assignments" (November 9, 2006), at www.som.cranfield.ac.uk/som/news/story.asp?id=329.

25 Jeremy Kahn, "The World's Most Admired Companies," *Fortune,* October 11, 1999: 267.

26 Kahn, "The World's Most Admired Companies."

27 David Ahlstrom, Garry Bruton, and Eunice S. Chan, "HRM of Foreign Firms in China: The Challenge of Managing Host Country Personnel," *Business Horizons* 44 (May 2001): 59.

28 "High-Tech Nomads: These Engineers Work as Temps on Wireless Projects All Over the World," *Time,* November 26, 2001: B20; Ben L. Kedia and Ananda Mukherji, "Global Managers: Developing a Mindset for Global Competitiveness," *Journal of World Business* 34 (Fall 1999): 30.

29 "In Search of Global Leaders: View of Fred Hassan, Chairman and CEO, Schering-Plough," *Harvard Business Review,* August 1, 2003.

30 Astrid Wendlandt, "The Name Game Is a Puzzle for Expats at Work," *Financial Times,* August 15, 2000: 3.

31 *The type of ownership* of its foreign operations influences an MNE's staffing policy. Expatriates transferred abroad to a foreign joint venture, for example, may find themselves in ambiguous situations, unsure of whom they represent and uncertain of whether they report to both partners or to the partner that transferred them. Typically, MNEs insist on using their own executives when they're concerned that local personnel may make decisions in their own interest rather than that of the joint venture.

32 Wooldridge, "The Battle for the Best."

33 Susan Schneider and Rosalie Tung, "Introduction to the International Human Resource Management Special Issue," *Journal of World Business* 36 (Winter 2001): 341–46.

34 Caligiuri and Di Santo, "Global Competence"; Hsieh et al., "Are You Taking Your Expatriate Talent Seriously?"

35 "In Search of Global Leaders: View of Stephen Green, Group CEO, HSBC," *Harvard Business Review,* August 1, 2003.

36 Sunkyu Jun, James Gentry, and Yong Hyun, "Cultural Adaptation of Business Expatriates in the Host Marketplace," *Journal of International Business Studies* 32 (Summer 2001): 369; J. Stewart Black and Mark Mendenhall, "Cross-Cultural Training Effectiveness: A Review and a Theoretical Framework for Future Research," *Academy of Management Review* 15 (January 1990): 117.

37 *The New International Executive Business Leadership for the 21st Century* (Harvard Business School and Amrop International, 1995); reported in Andrew Crisp, "International Careers Made Easy," *The European,* March 24, 1995: 27.

38 Hsieh et al., "Are You Taking Your Expatriate Talent Seriously?"

39 John D. Daniels and Gary Insch, "Why Are Early Departure Rates from Foreign Assignments Lower Than Historically Reported?" *Multinational Business Review* 6:1 (1998): 13–23.

40 Data provided by National Foreign Trade Council. Maria L. Kraimer, Sandy Wayne, and Renata Jaworski, "Sources of Support and Expatriate Performance: The Mediating Role of Expatriate Adjustment," *Personnel Psychology* 54 (Spring 2001): 71.

41 Margaret Shaffer, David Harrison, K. Matthew Gilley, and Dora Luk, "Struggling for Balance amid Turbulence on International Assignments: Work-Family Conflict, Support and Commitment," *Journal of Management* 27 (January–February 2001): 99; Chris Moss, "Expats: Thinking of Living and Working Abroad?" *The Guardian,* October 19, 2000: 4.

42 "Expat Spouses: It Takes Two," *Financial Times,* March 1, 2002; "Travelling More Lightly."

43 Diane E. Lewis, "Families Make, Break Overseas Moves," *Boston Globe,* October 4, 1998: 5D.

44 Klaff, "Thinning the Ranks of the Career Expats."

45 D. Ones and C. Viswesvaran, "Relative Importance of Personality Dimensions for Expatriate Selection: A Policy Capturing Study," *Human Performance* 12 (1999): 275–94.

46 Chris Brewster, "Making Their Own Way: International Experience Through Self-Initiated Foreign Assignments," *Journal of World Business* 35 (Winter 2000): 417; Vesa Suutari, Kerr Inkson, Judith Pringle, Michael B. Arthur, and Sean Barry, "Expatriate Assignment versus Overseas Experience: Contrasting Models of International Human Resource Development," *Journal of World Business* 32 (1997): 351–68.

47 Valerie Frazee, "Send Your Expats Prepared for Success," *Workforce* 78 (March 1999): S6.

48 Larson, "More Employees Go Abroad as International Operations Grow."

49 P. Christopher Earley, "Intercultural Training for Managers: A Comparison of Documentary and Interpersonal Methods," *Academy of Management Journal* 30:4 (1987): 685–98; Sharon Leiba-O'Sullivan, "The Distinction between Stable and Dynamic Cross-Cultural Competencies: Implications for Expatriate Trainability," *Journal of International Business Studies* 30 (Winter 1999): 709.

50 C. Panella, "Meeting the Needs of International Business: A Customer Service-Oriented Business Language Course," *The Journal of Language for International Business* 9:1 (1998): 65–75; Marianne E. Inman, "How Foreign Language Study Can Enhance Career Possibilities" (Washington DC: ERIC Clearinghouse on Languages and Linguistics, 1987), at www.ericdigests.org/pre-927/career.htm (accessed November 27, 2007); C. Randlesome and A. Myers, "Cultural Fluency: Results from a UK and Irish Survey," *Business Communication Quarterly* 60:3 (1997): 9–22.

51 Tanya Mohn, "All Aboard the Foreign Language Express," *New York Times,* October 11, 2000.

52 Stephen Baker, "Catching the Continental Drift: These Days, English Will Suffice for Americans Working in Europe," *Business Week,* August 14, 2001.

53 Christopher Cole, "Bridging the Language Gap: Expatriates Find Learning Korean Key to Enjoying a More Satisfying Life," *The Korea Herald,* August 16, 2002.

54 Melinda Ligos, "The Foreign Assignment: An Incubator, or Exile?" *New York Times,* October 22, 2000.

55 European Commission, "Languages of Europe" (July 18, 2007), *Education and Training,* at http://europa.eu. int/comm/education/policies/lang/languages/index_en.html#Most%20taught%20languages (accessed November 27, 2007).

56 "They All Speak English," *The Economist,* December 13, 2006.

57 "Global Spread of English Poses Problems for UK," *People's Daily Online,* February 18, 2006.

58 Amy Sitze, "Language of Business: Can E-Learning Help International Companies Speak a Common Language?" *Online Learning,* March 2002: 19–23.

59 PricewaterhouseCoopers, *International Assignments: European Policy and Practice* (1997), available at www.pwcglobal.com/extweb/ncsurvres.nsf.

60 "In Search of Global Leaders: View of Fred Hassan, Chairman and CEO, Schering-Plough," *Harvard Business Review,* August 1, 2003.

61 Estimate reported in the second annual study of expatriate issues, conducted from January through March 2002, sponsored by CIGNA International Expatriate Benefits; the National Foreign Trade Council, an association of multinational companies that supports open international trade and investment; and WorldatWork, at www.prnewswire.com/micro/CI9 (accessed September 2, 2005).

62 "Measuring the Value of International Assignments."

63 Carolyn Gould, "What's the Latest in Global Compensation?" *Global Workforce* (July 1997).

64 Geoffrey W. Latta, "Expatriate Policy and Practice: A Ten-Year Comparison of Trends," *Compensation and Benefits Review* 31:4 (1999): 35–39, quoting studies by Organization Resources Counselors.

65 Towers Perrin and CIGNA, for example, specialize in international compensation. In addition, companies rely on estimates of cost-of-living differences—even if they're imperfect. MNEs commonly use such sources as the U.S. State Department's cost-of-living index, published yearly in *Labor Developments Abroad,* the UN *Monthly Bulletin of Statistics,* and surveys by the *Financial Times,* P-E International, Business International, and the Staff Papers of the International Monetary Fund.

66 This practice, however, appears to be disappearing, especially for assignments in so-called world capitals like New York, London,

and Tokyo, in which many executives are interested and where there is (relatively) little "deprivation." In addition, the number and nature of "hardships" resulting from foreign assignments are in decline, particularly as advances in transportation and communications enable expatriates to keep in closer contact with home countries; the openness of economies allows them to buy familiar goods and services; and the general level of housing, schooling, and medical services increasingly meets their needs.

67 A U.S. family based in China, for example, commonly spends more money to get the same goods than they would buy back home. Why? Because they simply prefer Western items that must be imported and have thus been subjected to high tariffs. Expatriates often obtain food and housing at rates higher than going local rates because they don't know the language well, where to buy, or how to bargain.

68 "Home Away from Home: Expatriate Housing in Asia," *The Korea Herald*, May 2, 2002.

69 "Tokyo Tops in H.K. Survey on Living Cost for Expatriates," *Japan Economic Newswire*, January 24, 2002.

70 Alison Maitland, "A Hard Balancing Act: Management of Dual Careers," *Financial Times*, May 10, 1999: 11.

71 Valerie Frazee, "Expert Help for Dual-Career Spouses," *Workforce* 78 (March 1999): S18.

72 Judy Clark, "Added Global Risks Impact Security Planning for Oil, Gas Expat Workers," *The Oil and Gas Journal*, April 2002: 32–37.

73 Roberto Ceniceros, "Precautions, Training Can Lessen Risk of Kidnapping," *Business Insurance* 35 (May 14, 2001): 26.

74 Mercer LLC, "International Assignments Increasing."

75 Gould, "What's the Latest in Global Compensation?"

76 "New Survey Suggests Ways to Maximize Expatriate Performance and Loyalty," *Internet Wire*, March 27, 2001. Estimates reported at 2001 National Foreign Trade Council's International HR Management Symposium. See also Leslie Gross Klaff, "The Right Way to Bring Expats Home," *Workforce* 81 (July 2002): 40–44; Jeff Barbian, "Return to Sender: Companies That Fail to Effectively Manage Employees Returning from a Foreign Assignment May Find Their Investments Permanently Hitting the Road," *Training* 39 (January 2002): 40–43.

77 PricewaterhouseCoopers LLP and Cranfield School of Management, "Understanding and Avoiding Barriers to International Mobility," *Geodesy* (October 2005), at www.pwc.extweb/pwcpublications.nfs/docid/ 7ACA93FA424E80E88525121E006E82C/$file/geodesy.pdf (accessed November 27, 2007).

78 J. S. Black and H. B. Gregersen, "The Right Way to Manage Expats," *Harvard Business Review* (March–April 1999): 52–62.

79 "In Search of Global Leaders: View of Daniel Meiland, Executive Chairman, Egon Zehender International," *Harvard Business Review* (August 1, 2003).

80 GMAC Relocation Services, "Minimizing Expatriate Turnover," at http://64.233.169.104/search?q=cache:FexXDu5unOcJ: www.gmacglobalrelocation.com/insight_support/grts/ 2002_GRTS.pdf+%22Minimizing+Expatriate+Turnover%22%2BG MAC&hl=en&ct=clnk&cd=3&gl=us (accessed May 15, 2007).

81 Mila Lazarova and Paula Caligiuri, "Retaining Repatriates: The Role of Organizational Support Practices," *Journal of World Business* 36 (Winter 2001): 389–402.

82 Linda K. Stroh, Hal B. Gregersen, and J. Stewart Black, "Closing the Gap: Expectations Versus Reality Among Repatriates," *Journal of World Business* 33 (1998): 111–124; Klaff, "The Right Way to Bring Expats Home."

83 Klaff, "The Right Way to Bring Expats Home."

84 C. Reidy, "Corporate Synergy Leads Way in Constructing Effective Retirement and Health Benefits," *IBIS Review* (January 1996): 16–17.

85 Iris I. Varner and Teresa M. Palmer, "Successful Expatriation and Organizational Strategies," *Review of Business* 23 (Spring 2002): 8–12; Jan Selmer, "Practice Makes Perfect? International Experience and Expatriate Adjustment," *Management International Review* 42 (January 2002): 71–88.

86 Bruce E. Kaufman, "Reflections on Six Decades in Industrial Relations: An Interview with John Dunlop," *Industrial and Labor Relations Review* 55 (January 2002): 324–49.

87 Jean-Louis Chaumet, CGT Labor Representative, "Euro-Disney News Profile," *ABC News*, March 29, 1992.

88 Neil Templin, "GM Strike Hits Mexican Output as Talks on Settlement Resume," *Wall Street Journal*, March 20, 1996: A3.

89 Robert A. Senser, "Workers of the World: It's Time to Unite," *Commonweal*, September 22, 2000: 13; Julie Kosterlitz, "Unions of the World Unite: European and American Unions Working Together," *National Journal* 30 (1998): 1134.

90 Ans Kolk and Rob van Tulder, "Child Labor and Multinational Conduct: A Comparison of International Business and Stakeholder Codes," *Journal of Business Ethics* 36 (2002): 291–302.

91 John Addison, "Nonunion Representation in Germany," *Journal of Labor Research* 20:1 (Winter 1999): 73–91.

92 The Annecy Symposium, "The Future of Work, Employment and Social Protection," *International Labour Review* 140 (Winter 2001): 453–75.

93 Anna Saxenian, "Brain Circulation: How High-Skill Immigration Makes Everyone Better Off," *Brookings Review* 20 (Winter 2002): 28–32; Moises Naim, "The New Diaspora: New Links Between Emigrés and Their Home Countries Can Become a Powerful Force for Economic Development," *Foreign Policy* (July–August 2002): 96–98.

94 Mark Poster, "Workers as Cyborgs: Labor and Networked Computers," *Journal of Labor Research* 23 (Summer 2002): 339–54.

95 "We Must Halt the Brain-Drain," *Africa News Service*, December 17, 2001.

96 "The Poorest Are Again Losing Ground," *Business Week*, April 23, 2001: 130.

97 Nancy Mills, "New Strategies for Union Survival and Revival," *Journal of Labor Research* 22 (Summer 2001): 599.

98 *Sources include the following:* Central Intelligence Agency, "India" (November 15, 2007), *The World Factbook 2007*, at www.cia.gov/cia/publications/factbook/geos/in.html; Library of Congress, "A Country Study: India," *Country Studies* (November 8, 2005), at http://memory.loc.gov/frd/cs/ intoc.html; "Country Profile: India" (July 26, 2007), *bbc.co.uk*, at http://news.bbc.co.uk/1/hi/world/ south_asia/ country_profiles/1154019.stm; Keith Bradsher, "A Younger India Is Flexing Its Industrial Brawn," *New York Times*, September 1, 2006; "Hungry Tiger, Dancing Elephant," *The Economist*, April 4, 2007; "Virtual Champions, Survey: Business in India," *The Economist*, June 1, 2006.

Glossary

Absolute advantage: A theory first presented by Adam Smith, which holds that because certain countries can produce some goods more efficiently than other countries, they should specialize in and export those things they can produce more efficiently and trade for other things they need.

Acceptable quality level (AQL): A concept of quality control whereby managers are willing to accept a certain level of production defects, which are dealt with through repair facilities and service centers.

Acquired advantage: A form of trade advantage due to technology rather than due to the availability of natural resources, climate, etc.

Acquired group memberships: Affiliations not determined by birth, such as religions, political affiliations, and professional and other associations.

Active income: Income of a CFC that is derived from the active conduct of a trade or business, as specified by the U.S. Internal Revenue Code.

Ad valorem duty: A duty (tariff) assessed as a percentage of the value of the item.

ADR: *See* American Depositary Receipt.

Advance import deposit: A deposit prior to the release of foreign exchange, required by some governments.

AFTA: *See* ASEAN Free Trade Area.

Agglomeration: A theory that competitive companies may gain efficiencies by locating near each other.

American Depositary Receipt (ADR): A negotiable certificate issued by a U.S. bank in the United States to represent the underlying shares of a foreign corporation's stock held in trust at a custodian bank in the foreign country.

American terms: The practice of using the direct quote for exchange rates.

Andean Community (CAN): A South American form of economic integration involving Bolivia, Colombia, Ecuador, Peru, and Venezuela.

APEC: *See* Asia Pacific Economic Cooperation.

Appropriability theory: The theory that companies will favor foreign direct investment over such nonequity operating forms as licensing arrangements so that potential competitors will be less likely to gain access to proprietary information.

Arbitrage: The process of buying and selling foreign currency at a profit that results from price discrepancies between or among markets.

Arm's-length price: A price between two companies that do not have an ownership interest in each other.

Ascribed group memberships: Affiliations determined by birth, such as those based on gender, family, age, caste, and ethnic, racial, or national origin.

ASEAN: *See* Association of South East Asian Nations.

ASEAN Free Trade Area (AFTA): A free-trade area formed by the ASEAN countries on January 1, 1993, with the goal of cutting tariffs on all intrazonal trade to a maximum of 5 percent by January 1, 2008.

Asia Pacific Economic Cooperation (APEC): A cooperation formed by 21 countries that border the Pacific Rim to promote multilateral economic cooperation in trade and investment in the Pacific Rim.

Association of South East Asian Nations (ASEAN): A free-trade area involving the Asian countries of Brunei, Indonesia, Malaysia, the Philippines, Singapore, and Thailand.

Authoritarianism: A system of government in which leaders are not subjected to the test of free elections.

Balance of payments: Statement that summarizes all economic transactions between a country and the rest of the world during a given period of time.

Balance-of-payments deficit: An imbalance of some specific component within the balance of payments, such as merchandise trade or current account, that implies that a country is importing more than it exports.

Balance-of-payments surplus: An imbalance in the balance of payments that exists when a country exports more than it imports.

Balance of trade: The value of a country's exports less the value of its imports ("trade" can be defined as merchandise trade, services, unilateral transfers, or some combination of these three).

Balance on goods and services: The value of a country's exports of merchandise trade and services minus imports.

Balanced scorecard: An approach to performance measurement that endeavors to more closely link the strategic and financial perspectives of a business and take a broad view of business performance.

Bank for International Settlements (BIS): A bank in Basel, Switzerland, that facilitates transactions among central banks; it is effectively the central banks' central bank.

Bargaining theory: A theory holding that the negotiated terms for foreign investors depend on how much investors and host countries need each other's assets.

Barriers to entry: Factors that make it difficult or costly for firms to enter an industry or market.

Barter: The exchange of goods for goods or services instead of for money.

Base currency: The currency whose value is implicitly 1 when a quote is made between two currencies; for example, if the Brazilian real is trading at 1.9 reals (reais) per dollar, the dollar is the base currency and the real is the quoted currency.

Basic balance: The net current account plus long-term capital within a country's balance of payments.

Bid (buy) rate: The amount a trader is willing to pay for foreign exchange.

Bilateral integration: A form of integration between two countries in which they decide to cooperate more closely together, usually in the form of tariff reductions.

BIS: *See* Bank for International Settlements.

Black market: The foreign-exchange market that lies outside the official market.

Booking center: An offshore financial center whose main function is to act as an accounting center in order to minimize the payment of taxes.

Born-global company: A company that starts out with an international focus, often because of the founder(s) international experience.

Brain drain: A condition where countries lose potentially productive resources when educated people leave.

Branch (foreign): A foreign operation of a company that is not a separate entity from the parent that owns it.

Bretton Woods Agreement: An agreement among IMF countries to promote exchange-rate stability and to facilitate the international flow of currencies.

Broker (in foreign exchange): Specialists who facilitate transactions in the interbank market.

Buy local legislation: Laws that are intended to favor the purchase of domestically sourced goods or services over imported ones, even though the imports may be a better buy.

Buybacks: Counterdeliveries related to, or originating from, an original export.

CACM: *See* Central American Common Market.

Canada-U.S. Free Trade Agreement: An agreement, enacted in 1989, establishing a free-trade area involving the United States and Canada.

Capital account: A measure of transactions involving previously existing rather than currently produced assets.

Capitalism: An economic system characterized by private ownership, pricing, production, and distribution of goods.

Caribbean Community and Common Market (CARICOM): A customs union in the Caribbean region.

Caribbean Free Trade Association (CARIFTA): *See* Caribbean Community and Common Market.

CARICOM: *See* Caribbean Community and Common Market.

Central American Common Market (CACM): A customs union in Central America.

Central American Free Trade Association-DR (CAFTA-DR): A free trade association between the United States and the CACM countries plus the Dominican Republic.

Central bank: A government "bank for banks," customarily responsible for a country's monetary policy.

Centralization: The situation in which decision making is done at the home office rather than at the country level.

Centrally planned economy (CPE): *See* Command economy.

Certificate of origin: A shipping document that determines the origin of products and is usually validated by an external source, such as a chamber of commerce; it helps countries determine the specific tariff schedule for imports.

Chaebol: Korean business groups that are similar to *keiretsu* and also contain a trading company as part of the group.

Civil law system: A legal system based on a very detailed set of laws that are organized into a code; countries with a civil law system, also called a codified legal system, include Germany, France, and Japan.

Civil liberties: The freedom to develop one's own views and attitudes.

Cluster effects: The cluster effect is the effect of buyers and sellers of a particular good or service congregating in a certain place and hence inducing other buyers and sellers to relocate there as well.

Code of conduct: A set of principles guiding the actions of MNEs in their contacts with societies.

Codetermination: A process by which both labor and management participate in the management of a company.

Codified legal system: *See* Civil law system.

Collaborative arrangement: A formal, long-term contractual agreement among companies.

Collective bargaining: The process of negotiation between employers (or their representatives) and a union on wages and other employment conditions.

Collectivism: System that puts emphasis on collective goals as opposed to individual goals.

Command economy: An economic system in which the political authorities make major decision regarding the production and distribution of goods and services.

Commercial bill of exchange: An instrument of payment in international business that instructs the importer to forward payment to the exporter.

Commercial law: The body of rules applied to commercial transactions; derived from the practices of traders rather than from jurisprudence.

Commodity: A product that is difficult to differentiate from those of competitors, such as raw materials and agricultural output.

Common law system: A legal system based on tradition, precedent, and custom and usage, in which the courts interpret the law based on those conventions; found in the United Kingdom and former British colonies.

Common market: A form of regional economic integration in which countries abolish internal tariffs, use a common external tariff, and abolish restrictions on factor mobility.

Communism: A form of totalitarianism initially theorized by Karl Marx in which the political and economic systems are virtually inseparable.

Communist totalitarianism: A version of collectivism advocating that socialism can be achieved only through a totalitarian dictatorship.

Communitarian paradigm: The government defines needs and priorities and partners with business in a major way.

Comparable access argument: Companies and industries often argue that they are entitled to the same access to foreign markets as foreign industries and companies have to their markets.

Comparative advantage: The theory that there is global efficiency gains from trade if a country specializes in those products that it can produce more efficiently than other products regardless of whether other countries can produce those products even more efficiently.

Competitive advantage: The strategies, skills, knowledge, resources or competencies that differentiate a business from its competitors.

Compound duty: A tax placed on goods traded internationally, based on value plus units.

Concentration strategy: A strategy by which an international company builds up operations quickly in one or a few countries before going to another.

Confirmed letter of credit: A letter of credit to which a bank in the exporter's country adds its guarantee of payment.

Conservatism: A characteristic of accounting systems that implies that companies are hesitant to disclose high profits or profits that are consistent with their actual operating results; more common in Germanic countries.

Consolidation: An accounting process in which financial statements of related entities, such as a parent and its subsidiaries, are combined to yield a unified set of financial statements; in the process, transactions among the related enterprises are eliminated so that the statements reflect transactions with outside parties.

Consortium: The joining together of several entities, such as companies or governments, in order to strengthen the possibility of achieving some objective.

Constitutional law: Law that is created and changed by the people.

Consumer price index (CPI): A measure of the cost of typical wage-earner purchases of goods and services expressed as a percentage of the cost of these same goods and services in some base period.

Consumer sovereignty: The freedom of consumers to influence production through the choices they make.

Contract: Formal document that specifies conditions of an exchange and details rights and obligations of involved parties.

Control: The planning, implementation, evaluation, and correction of performance to ensure that organizational objectives are achieved.

Controlled foreign corporation (CFC): A foreign corporation of which more than 50 percent of the voting stock is owned by U.S. shareholders (taxable entities that own at least 10 percent of the voting stock of the corporation).

Convergence: Efforts by the FASB and IASC to move toward a common global set of accounting standards.

Coordination: Linking or integrating activities into a unified system.

Core competency: Those functions of value creation in which the firm is most competent.

Corporate culture: The common values shared by employees in a corporation, which form a control mechanism that is implicit and helps enforce other explicit control mechanisms.

Corporate social responsibility: An expression used to describe what some see as a company's obligation to be sensitive to the needs of "all" of its stakeholders in its business operations and produce an overall positive impact on society.

Correspondent (bank): A bank in which funds are kept by another, usually foreign, bank to facilitate check clearing and other business relationships.

Cost-of-living adjustment: An increase in compensation given to an expatriate employee when foreign living costs are more expensive than those in the home country.

Cost-plus strategy: The strategy of pricing at a desired margin over cost.

Council of the European Union: One of the five major institutions of the European Union; made up of the heads of state of each of the EU members.

Counterfeiting: The unauthorized copying or imitating of an item which is later passed on as an original.

Countertrade: A reciprocal flow of goods or services valued and settled in monetary terms.

Country of origin effect: A condition where consumers may prefer to buy goods produced in one country rather than another usually because of quality perceptions or because of nationalism.

Country-similarity theory: The theory that a company will seek to exploit opportunities in those countries most similar to its home country because of the perceived need to make fewer operating adjustments.

Country size theory: The theory that larger countries are generally more self-sufficient than smaller countries.

Creolization: The process by which some, but not all, elements of an outside culture are introduced.

Criminal law: Body of laws dealing with crimes against the public and members of the public.

Cross-licensing: The exchange of technology by different companies.

Cross rate: An exchange rate between two currencies used in the spot market and computed from the exchange rate of each currency in relation to the U.S. dollar.

Cultural collision: A condition that occurs when divergent cultures come in contact with each other.

Cultural diffusion: The cultural changes that occur when different cultures come in contact with each other.

Cultural distance: The degree to which countries differ from each other as measured by different cultural factors; the greater the difference, the greater the distance.

Cultural imperialism: Cultural change by imposition.

Culture: The specific learned norms of a group's attitudes, values, and beliefs.

Culture shock: A generalized trauma one experiences in a new and different culture because of having to learn and cope with a vast array of new cues and expectations.

Currency swaps: The exchange of principal and interest payments.

Current-account balance: Exports minus imports of goods, services, and unilateral transfers.

Current-rate method: A method of translating foreign-currency financial statements that is used when the functional currency is that of the local operating environment.

Custom broker: Act on behalf of the importer to clear goods through customs and deliver the items to the importer's warehouse or final destination.

Customary law system: A legal system anchored in the wisdom of daily experience or great spiritual or philosophical traditions.

Customer orientation: A customer orientation asks: What and how can the company sell in country A? In this case, the country is held constant and the product and method of marketing it is varied.

Customs union: A form of regional economic integration that eliminates internal tariffs among member nations and establishes common external tariffs.

Customs valuation: The value of goods on which customs authorities charge tariffs.

Decentralization: The situation in which decisions tend to be made at lower levels in a company or at the country-operating level rather than at headquarters.

Demand conditions: Includes three dimensions: the composition of home demand (or the nature of buyer needs), the size and pattern of growth of home demand, and the internationalization of demand.

Democracy: A political system that relies on citizens' participation in the decision-making process.

Dependencia theory: The theory holding that developing countries have practically no power when dealing with MNEs.

Derivative: A foreign-exchange instrument such as an option or futures contract that derives its value from the underlying currency.

Derivatives market: Market in which forward contracts, futures, options, and swaps are traded in order to hedge or protect foreign-exchange transactions.

Devaluation: A formal reduction in the value of a currency in relation to another currency; the foreign-currency equivalent of the devalued currency falls.

Developed country: High-income country. Also called industrial country.

Developing country: A low income country, also known sometimes as an emerging country.

Differentiation: A business strategy in which a company tries to gain a competitive advantage by providing a unique product or service, or providing a unique brand of customer service.

Digitization: The conversion of paper and other media in existing collections to digital form.

Direct quote: A quote expressed in terms of the number of units of the domestic currency given for one unit of a foreign currency.

Direct selling: A sale of goods by an exporter directly to distributors or final consumers rather than to trading companies or other intermediaries in order to achieve greater control over the marketing function and to earn higher profits.

Disclosure: The presentation of financial information and discussion of results.

Diversification strategy: A term used in international business to describe a strategy whereby a company moves rapidly into many markets and gradually increases its commitments within each one.

Divesting: Reduction in the amount of investment.

Divisional structures: An organization that contain separate divisions based around individual product lines or based on the geographic areas of the markets served.

Draft: An instrument of payment in international business that instructs the importer to forward payment to the exporter.

Dumping: The underpricing of exports, usually below cost or below the home-country price.

Duty: A government tax (tariff) levied on goods shipped internationally. Also called tariff.

Dynamic effects of integration: The overall growth in the market and the impact on a company of expanding production and achieving greater economies of scale.

EC: *See* European Community.

E-commerce: The use of the Internet to join together suppliers with companies and companies with customers.

Economic Community of West African States (ECOWAS): A form of economic integration among certain countries in West Africa.

Economic exposure (operational exposure): The foreign-exchange risk that international businesses face in the pricing of products, the source and cost of inputs, and the location of investments.

Economic Freedom Index: The Economic Freedom Index is the systematic measurement of economic freedom in countries throughout the world. The survey is sponsored by the Heritage Foundation and Wall Street Journal.

Economic integration: The abolition of economic discrimination between national economies, such as within the EU.

Economic system: The system concerned with the allocation of scarce resources.

Economics: A social science concerned chiefly with the description and analysis of the production, distribution, and consumption of goods and services.

Economies of scale: The lowering of cost per unit as output increases because of allocation of fixed costs over more units produced.

Economies of scope: Decreases in average total cost made possible by increasing the range of goods produced.

Effective tariff: The real tariff on the manufactured portion of developing countries' exports, which is higher than indicated by the published rates because the ad valorem tariff is based on the total value of the products, which includes raw materials that would have had duty-free entry.

EFTA: *See* European Free Trade Association.

Electronic data interchange (EDI): The electronic movement of money and information via computers and telecommunications equipment.

Embargo: A specific type of quota that prohibits all trade.

Emerging economy: Countries with developing economies, often experiencing rapid growth and offering lucrative investment opportunities, but also characterized by political instability and high risk.

EMS: *See* European Monetary System.

Enterprise resource planning (ERP): Software that can link information flows from different parts of a business and from different geographic areas.

Equity alliance: A situation in which a cooperating company takes an equity position (almost always a minority) in the company with which it has a collaborative arrangement.

ERP: *See* Enterprise resource planning.

Essential-industry argument: The argument holding that certain domestic industries need protection for national security purposes.

Ethnocentric staffing: A staffing approach in which all key management positions, whether in the home country or abroad, are filled by home country nationals.

Ethnocentrism: A belief that one's own group is superior to others; also used to describe a company's belief that what worked at home should work abroad.

Eurobond: A bond sold in a country other than the one in whose currency it is denominated.

Eurocredit: A loan, line of credit, or other form of medium- or long-term credit on the Eurocurrency market that has a maturity of more than one year.

Eurocurrency: Any currency that is banked outside of its country of origin.

Eurocurrency market: An international wholesale market that deals in Eurocurrencies.

Eurodollars: Dollars banked outside of the United States.

Euroequity market: The market for shares sold outside the boundaries of the issuing company's home country.

European Central Bank (ECB): Established July 1, 1998, the ECB is responsible for setting the monetary policy and for managing the exchange-rate system for all of Europe since January 1, 1999.

European Commission: One of the five major institutions of the EU;

composed of 27 women and men, one from each EU country. The president is chosen by EU governments and endorsed by the European Parliament. The commissioners do not represent their home country governments, and they serve as an executive branch for the EU.

European Community (EC): The predecessor of the European Union.

European Court of Justice: The court of the European Union. The Court is an appeals court and ensures interpretation and application of EU treaties. One of the five major institutions of the EU; composed of one member from each country in the EU and serves as a supreme appeals court for EU law.

European Economic Community (EEC): The predecessor of the European Community.

European Free Trade Association (EFTA): A free-trade area among a group of European countries that are not members of the EU.

European Monetary System (EMS): A cooperative foreign-exchange agreement involving many members of the EU and designed to promote exchange-rate stability within the EU.

European Monetary Union: An agreement by participating European Union member countries that consists of three stages coordinating economic policy and culminating with the adoption of the euro.

European Parliament: One of the five major institutions of the EU; its representatives are elected directly in each member country.

European terms: The practice of using the indirect quote for exchange rates.

European Union (EU): A form of regional economic integration among countries in Europe that involves a free-trade area, a customs union, and the free mobility of factors of production that is working toward political and economic union.

Exchange rate: The price of one currency in terms of another currency.

Eximbank: *See* Export-Import Bank.

Exclusive license: The licensor can give rights to no other company for the specified geographic area for a specified period of time.

Expatriate compensation: The process of setting the appropriate level of direct and indirect benefits to motivate someone to accept and perform an international job assignment.

Expatriate failure: The premature return of expatriate manager to the home country.

Expatriates: Noncitizens of the country in which they are working.

Experience curve: The relationship of production-cost reductions to increases in output.

Explicit knowledge: Knowledge that can be passed to others through published reports.

Export-Import Bank (Eximbank): A U.S. federal agency specializing in foreign lending to support exports.

Export-led development: An industrialization policy emphasizing industries that will have export capabilities.

Export license: A document that grants a government permission to ship certain products to a specific country.

Export management company (EMC): A company that buys merchandise from manufacturers for international distribution or sometimes acts as an agent for manufacturers.

Export processing zone (EPZ): An area in which companies can import and process virtually without paying duties or taxes as long as the output is exported.

Export strategy: Specification of the key issues that shape the success of an export venture.

Export tariff: A tax on goods leaving a country.

Export trading company (ETC): A form of trading company sanctioned by U.S. law to become involved in international commerce as independent distributors to match up foreign buyers with domestic sellers.

Exports: Goods or services leaving a country.

Exposure: A situation in which a foreign-exchange account is subject to a gain or loss if the exchange rate changes.

Expropriation: The taking over of ownership of private property by a country's government.

Extended family: A family situation which includes family members of several generations or family members which stretches out horizontally, including aunts, uncles, cousins, etc.

External environment: The physical and competitive factors in a country that influence a company's international strategy.

Externalities: External economic costs related to a business activity.

Extranet: The use of the Internet to link a company with outsiders.

Extraterritoriality: The extension by a government of the application of its laws to foreign operations of companies.

Factor mobility: The movement of factors of production such as labor and capital from one location to another.

Factor-proportions theory: The theory that differences in a country's proportionate holdings of factors of production (land, labor, and capital) explain differences in the costs of the factors and that export advantages lie in the production of goods that use the most abundant factors.

Fairness argument: Like the comparable access argument, domestic companies contend that they should have the same access to foreign markets as foreign companies have to their markets.

FASB: *See* Financial Accounting Standards Board.

Fascism: A system of government that promotes extreme nationalism, repression, anticommunism, and is ruled by a dictator.

Fatalism: A belief that events are fixed in advance and that human beings are powerless to change them.

Favorable balance of trade: An indication that a country is exporting more than it imports.

FCPA: *See* Foreign Corrupt Practices Act.

FDI: *See* Foreign direct investment.

Financial Accounting Standards Board (FASB): The private-sector organization that sets financial accounting standards in the United States.

First-mover advantage: A cost-reduction advantage due to economies of scale attained through moving into a foreign market ahead of competitors.

Fisher Effect: The theory about the relationship between inflation and interest rates; for example, if the nominal interest rate in one country is lower than that in another, the first country's inflation should be lower so that the real interest rates will be equal.

Flag of convenience: The use of a shipping company registration within a country offering low taxes and few rules on employment practices.

Floating currency: A currency whose value responds to the supply of and demand for that currency.

Floating exchange rate: An exchange rate determined by the laws of supply and demand and with minimal government interference.

Foreign bond: A bond sold outside of the borrower's country but denominated in the currency of the country of issue.

Foreign Corrupt Practices Act (FCPA): A law that criminalizes certain types of payments by U.S. companies, such as bribes to foreign government officials.

Foreign direct investment (FDI): An investment that gives the investor a controlling interest in a foreign company.

Foreign exchange: Checks and other instruments for making payments in another country's currency.

Foreign-exchange control: A requirement that an individual or company must apply to government authorities for permission to buy foreign currency above some determined threshold amount.

Foreign investment: Direct or portfolio ownership of assets in another country.

Foreign Investment Advisory Service (FIAS): A division of the International Finance Corporation that can make recommendations to countries as to the feasibility of attracting companies to invest locally.

Foreign portfolio investment: An investment abroad without controlling a foreign company.

Foreign sales corporation (FSC): A special type of corporation established by U.S. tax law that can be used by a U.S. exporter to shelter some of its income from taxation.

Foreign service premium: A cash allowance given to an employee who agrees to transfer to a foreign location. Also called International Adjustment Allowance or International Assignment Premium.

Foreign trade zone (FTZ): A government-designated area in which goods can be stored, inspected, or manufactured without being subject to formal customs procedures until they leave the zone.

Forward contract: A contract between a company or individual and a bank to deliver foreign currency at a specific exchange rate on a future date.

Forward discount: *See* Discount.

Forward premium: *See* Premium.

Forward rate: A contractually established exchange rate between a foreign-exchange trader and the trader's client for delivery of foreign currency on a specific date.

Franchising: A specialized form of licensing in which one party (the franchisor) sells to an independent party (the franchisee) the use of a trademark that is an essential asset for the franchisee's business and also gives continual assistance in the operation of the business.

Freedom House: An organization that attempts to classify countries according to political and economic freedom.

Freely convertible currency: *See* Hard currency.

Free trade agreement: An agreement between countries that has the goal of abolishing all tariffs between member countries.

Free trade area (FTA): A form of regional economic integration in which internal tariffs are abolished, but member countries set their own external tariffs.

Freight forwarder: A company that facilitates the movement of goods from one country to another.

Fringe benefit: Any employee benefit other than salary, wages, and cash bonuses.

FTZ: *See* Foreign trade zone.

Functional currency: The currency of the primary economic environment in which an entity operates.

Functional division: An organizational structure in which each function in foreign countries (e.g., marketing or production) reports separately to a counterpart functional group at headquarters.

Functional structure: An organization that is structured according to functional areas of business.

Fundamental forecasting: A forecasting tool that uses trends in economic variables to predict future exchange rates.

Future orientation: An orientation where people invest for the future and delay instant gratification.

Futures contract: An agreement between two parties to buy or sell a particular currency at a particular price on a particular future date, as specified in a standardized contract to all participants in that currency futures exchange.

FX swap: A simultaneous spot and forward transaction.

G7 countries: *See* Group of 7.

G8 countries: See Group of 8.

GAAP: *See* Generally Accepted Accounting Principles.

Gap analysis: A tool used to discover why a company's sales of a given product are less than the market potential in a country; the reason may be a usage, competition, product line, or distribution gap.

GATT: *See* General Agreement on Tariffs and Trade.

General Agreement on Tariffs and Trade (GATT): A multilateral arrangement aimed at reducing barriers to trade, both tariff and nontariff ones; at the signing of the Uruguay round, the GATT was designated to become the World Trade Organization (WTO).

Generally Accepted Accounting Principles (GAAP): The accounting standards accepted by the accounting profession in each country as required for the preparation of financial statements for external users.

Generic names: Formerly trademarked names that have become part of the public domain.

Generic products: Any of a class of products, rather than the brand of a particular company; also relates to pharmaceutical products which have lost patent protection and can be sold by an company under a name that is different from the original branded name.

Geocentric: Operations based on an informed knowledge of both home and host country needs.

Geocentric staffing: The staffing approach where the company assigns the best people to key jobs throughout the global operation, regardless of nationality.

Geocentrism: An attempt to bring together home and host country needs.

Geographic division structure: An organizational structure in which a company's operations are separated for reporting purposes into regional areas.

Global bond: A combination of domestic bond and Eurobond that is issued simultaneously in several markets and that must be registered in each national market according to that market's registration requirements.

Global company: A company that integrates operations located in different countries.

Global integration: The unification of distinct national economic systems into one global market.

Globalization: The broadening set of interdependent relationships among people from different parts of a world that happens to be divided into nations. The term sometimes refers to the integration of world economies through the reduction of barriers to the movement of trade, capital, technology, and people.

Global sourcing: The acquisition on a worldwide basis of raw materials, parts, and subassemblies for the manufacturing process.

Global strategy: A strategy that management uses to focus on increasing profitability by achieving cost reductions from experience curves and location economies. Licensors with the use of improvements made on the technology originally licensed.

Gray market: The handling of goods through unofficial distributors.

Green GNP: The measurement of national output that attempts to take into account various effects on the environment and natural resources.

Gross domestic product (GDP): The total of all economic activity in a country, regardless of who owns the productive assets.

Gross national income (GNI): Formerly referred to as Gross National Product.

Gross national product (GNP): The total of incomes earned by residents of a country, regardless of where the productive assets are located.

Group of 7 (G7): A group of developed countries that periodically meets to make economic decisions; this group consists of Canada, France, Germany, Italy, Japan, the United Kingdom, and the United States.

Group of 8 (G8): The Group of 7 (G7) plus Russia.

GSP: *See* Generalized System of Preferences.

Hard currency: A currency that is freely traded without many restrictions and for which there is usually strong external demand; often called a freely convertible currency.

Hardship allowance: A supplement to compensate expatriates for working in dangerous or adverse conditions.

Harvesting: Reduction in the amount of investment. Also known as divestment.

Hedge: To attempt to protect foreign-currency holdings against an adverse movement of an exchange rate.

Heterarchy: An organizational structure in which management of an alliance of companies is shared by so-called equals rather than being set up in a superior-subordinate relationship.

Hierarchy of needs theory: A well-known motivation theory stating that there is a hierarchy of needs and that people must fulfill the lower-order needs sufficiently before they will be motivated by the higher-order ones.

High-context culture: A culture in which most people consider that peripheral and hearsay information is necessary for decision making because such information bears on the context of the situation.

Home country: The country in which an international company is headquartered.

Home-country nationals: Expatriate employees who are citizens of the country in which the company is headquartered.

Horizontal alliance: An alliance of companies that produce similar products, as opposed to a vertical alliance which links together different elements of the value chain from raw materials to final consumption.

Horizontal differentiation: How the company specifies, divides, and assigns the set of organizational tasks.

Host country: Any foreign country in which an international company operates.

Human development index: A measurement of human progress introduced by the United Nations Development Programme that combines indicators of purchasing power, education, and health.

Human Resource Management: The primary staffing function of the organization. It includes the activities of human resources planning, recruitment, selection, performance appraisal, compensation, and retention.

Hyperinflation: A rapid increase (at least 1 percent per day) in general price levels for a sustained period of time.

IASB: *See* International Accounting Standards Board.

Idealism: Trying to determine principles before settling small issues.

Ideology: The systematic and integrated body of constructs, theories, and aims that constitute a society.

IFE: *See* International Fisher Effect.

IMF: *See* International Monetary Fund.

Imitation lag: A strategy for exploiting temporary monopoly advantages by moving first to those countries most likely to develop local production.

Import broker: An individual who obtains various government permissions and other clearances before forwarding necessary paperwork to the carrier that will deliver the goods from the dock to the importer.

Import deposit requirement: Government requirement of a deposit prior to the release of foreign exchange.

Import documentation: The various categories of documents required in international trade transactions.

Import licensing: A method of government control of the exchange rate whereby all recipients, exporters, and others who receive foreign exchange are required to sell to the central bank at the official buying rate.

Import strategy: Specification of the key issues that shape the success of an import venture.

Import substitution: An industrialization policy whereby new industrial development emphasizes products that would otherwise be imported.

Imports: Goods or services entering a country.

Income distribution: A description of the fractions of a population that are at various levels of income.

Indirect quote: An exchange rate given in terms of the number of units of the foreign currency for one unit of the domestic currency.

Indirect selling: A sale of goods by an exporter through another domestic company as an intermediary.

Individualism versus collectivism index: A study comparing national preferences toward dependence on the organization for fulfilling leisure time, improving skills, and receiving benefits, along with preferences for personal decision making.

Individualistic paradigm: Minimal government intervention in the economy.

Industrial country: High-income country. Also known as developed country.

Industrial organization: Industrial organization is the field of economics that studies the behavior of firms, the structure of markets and of their interactions.

Industrial policy: Strong intervention by the government in the nature and direction of the economy.

Industrialization argument: A rationale for protectionism that argues that the development of industrial output should come about even though domestic prices may not become competitive on the world market.

Industry structure: The makeup of an industry: its number of sellers and their size distribution, the nature of the product, and the extent of barriers to entry.

Infant-industry argument: The position that holds that an emerging industry should be guaranteed a large share of the domestic market until it becomes efficient enough to compete against imports.

Inflation: A condition where prices are going up.

Innovation: A new idea, method or device that, in creating a new product or process, creates competitive advantage.

Intellectual property: Property in the form of patents, trademarks, service marks, trade names, trade secrets, and copyrights.

Intellectual property rights: Ownership rights to intangible assets, such as patents, trademarks, copyrights, and know-how.

Interbank market: The market for foreign-exchange transactions among commercial banks.

Interbank transactions: Foreign-exchange transactions that take place between commercial banks.

Intermodal transportation: The transportation of freight in a container or vehicle, using multiple modes of transportation (rail, ocean vessel, and truck), without any handling of the freight itself when changing modes.

Internalization: Control through selfhandling of foreign operations, primarily because such control is less expensive to deal with in the same corporate family than to contract with an external organization.

International Accounting Standards Board (IASB): The international private-sector organization that sets financial accounting standards for worldwide use.

International business: All business transactions involving private companies or governments of two or more countries.

International division structure: A structure whereby the company creates a division that is responsible for its international activities.

International Financial Reporting Standards (IFRS): A set of accounting standards often known by the older name of International Accounting Standards (IAS). They are issued by the International Accounting Standards Board (IASB).

International Fisher Effect (IFE): The theory that the relationship between interest rates and exchange rates implies that the currency of the country with the lower interest rate will strengthen in the future.

International law: The regulations resulting from treaties among countries.

International Monetary Fund (IMF): A multigovernmental association organized in 1945 to promote exchange-rate stability and to facilitate the international flow of currencies.

International Organization of Securities Commissions (IOSCO): An international organization of securities regulators that supports the efforts of the IASB to establish comprehensive accounting standards.

International Strategy: The effort of managers to create value by transferring core competencies from the home market to foreign markets in which local competitors lack those competencies.

Intranet: The use of the Internet to link together the different divisions and functions inside a company.

Investment incentives: Governmental inducements, such as lower taxes, to entice companies to invest in the country.

Invisible hand: The reliance on market forces independent of government policies to allocate resources.

IOSCO: *See* International Organization of Securities Commissions.

Irrevocable letter of credit (L/C): A letter of credit that cannot be canceled or changed without the consent of all parties involved.

Islamic law: A system of theocratic law based on the religious teachings of Islam. Also called Muslim law.

ISO 9000: A quality standard developed by the International Standards Organization in Geneva that requires companies to document their commitment to quality at all levels of the organization.

Jamaica Agreement: A 1976 agreement among countries that permitted greater flexibility of exchange rates, basically formalizing the break from fixed exchange rates.

JIT: *See* Just-in-time manufacturing.

Joint venture: An investment in which two or more companies share the ownership.

Just-in-time (JIT) manufacturing system: A system that reduces inventory costs by having components and parts delivered as they are needed in production.

Kaizen: The Japanese process of continuous improvement, the cornerstone of TQM.

Keiretsu: A corporate relationship linking certain Japanese companies, usually involving a noncontrolling interest in each other, strong high-level personal relationships among managers in the different companies, and interlocking directorships.

Key industry: Any industry that might affect a very large segment of a country's economy or population by virtue of its size or influence on other sectors.

Kinesics: Body language; the way people walk, touch, and move their bodies.

Labor market: The mix of available workers and labor costs available to companies.

Labor union: An association of workers intended to promote and protect the welfare, interests, and rights of its members, primarily by collective bargaining.

LAFTA: *See* Latin American Free Trade Association.

Lag strategy: An operational strategy that involves either delaying collection of foreign-currency receivables if the currency is expected to strengthen or delaying payment of foreign-currency payables when the currency is expected to weaken; the opposite of a lead strategy.

Laissez-faire: The concept of minimal government intervention in a society's economic activity.

Latin American Free Trade Association (LAFTA): A free-trade area formed by Mexico and the South American countries in 1960; it was replaced by ALADI in 1980.

Latin American Integration Association (ALADI): A form of regional economic integration involving most of the Latin American countries.

Law: A binding custom or practice of a community.

Lead strategy: An operational strategy that involves either collecting foreign-currency receivables before they are due when the currency is expected to weaken or paying foreign-currency payables before they are due when the currency is expected to strengthen; the opposite of a lag strategy.

Lean Manufacturing: A production system whose focus is on optimizing processes through the philosophy of continual improvement.

Learning curve: A concept used to support the infant-industry argument for protection; it assumes that costs will decline as workers and managers gain more experience.

Letter of credit (L/C): A precise document by which the importer's bank extends credit to the importer and agrees to pay the exporter.

Liability of foreignness: Foreign companies' lower survival rate in comparison to local companies for many years after they begin operations.

Liberal Democracy: A system of government characterized by universal adult suffrage, political equality, majority rule, and constitutionalism.

Liberal trade: A government policy of minimal influence on international trade and investment.

LIBOR: *See* London Inter-Bank Offered Rate.

License (import or export): Formal or legal permission to do some specified action; a government method of fixing the exchange rate by requiring all recipients, exporters, and others that receive foreign exchange to sell it to the central bank at the official buying rate.

Licensing agreement: Agreement whereby one company gives rights to another for the use, usually for a fee, of such assets as trademarks, patents, copyrights, or other know-how.

Link alliance: An alliance that uses complementary resources to expand into new business areas.

Liquidity preference: A theory that helps explain capital budgeting and, when applied to international operations, means that investors are willing to take less return in order to be able to shift the resources to alternative uses.

Locals: Citizens of the country in which they are working.

Location economies: Cost advantages from performing a value creation activity at the optimal location for that activity.

Location-specific advantage: A combination of factor and demand conditions, along with other qualities, that a country has to offer domestic and foreign investors.

Logistics (materials management): That part of the supply chain process that plans, implements, and controls the efficient, effective flow and storage of goods, services, and related information from the point of origin to the point of consumption, to meet customers' requirements; sometimes called materials management.

London Inter-Bank Offered Rate (LIBOR): The interest rate for large interbank loans of Eurocurrencies.

London International Financial Futures Exchange (LIFFE): An exchange dealing in futures contracts for several major currencies. Now part of NYSE Euronext.

London Stock Exchange (LSE): A stock exchange located in London and dealing in Euroequities.

Low-context culture: A culture in which most people consider relevant only information that they receive firsthand and that bears very directly on the decision they need to make.

Low-cost leadership: The strategy whereby the organization aims to be the lowest cost producer in its industry.

Maastricht (Treaty of): The treaty approved in December 1991 that was designed to bring the EU to a higher level of integration and is divided into the Economic Monetary Union (EMU) and a political union.

Management contract: An arrangement whereby one company provides management personnel, who perform general or specialized management functions to another company for a fee.

Maquiladora: An industrial operation, originally developed between the United States and Mexico but now used in other geographic areas, in which components may be shipped duty free, assembled, and then re-exported.

Market capitalization: A common measure of the size of a stock market, which is computed by multiplying the total number of shares of stock listed on the exchange by the market price per share.

Market economy: An economic system in which resources are allocated and controlled by consumers who "vote" by buying goods.

Market environment: The environment that involves the interactions between households (or individuals) and companies in the allocation of resources, free from government ownership or control.

Masculinity-femininity index: An index comparing countries' norms on empathy for successful achievers versus the unfortunate, preference for being better than others versus being on a par with them, belief that it's better "to live to work" versus "to work to live," preference for performance and growth versus quality of life and the environment, and belief that gender roles should be different versus similar.

Master franchise: A franchise agreement that is given to one franchisee in a country to establish franchises in many different areas, possibly the entire country.

Materials management: *See* Logistics.

Matrix division structure: An organizational structure in which foreign units report (by product, function, or area) to more than one group, each of which shares responsibility over the foreign unit.

Mercantilism: An economic philosophy based on the beliefs that a country's wealth is dependent on its holdings of treasure, usually in the form of gold, and that countries should export more than they import in order to increase wealth.

Merchandise exports: Goods sent out of a country.

Merchandise imports: Goods brought into a country.

Merchandise trade balance: The part of a country's current account that measures the trade deficit or surplus; its balance is the net of merchandise imports and exports.

MERCOSUR: A major subregional group established by Argentina, Brazil, Paraguay, and Uruguay, which spun off from ALADI in 1991 with the goal of setting up a customs union and common market. Venezuela has applied for membership.

MFN: *See* Most-favored-nation.

Mixed economy: An economic system characterized by some mixture of market and command economies and public and private ownership.

Mixed legal system: A legal system that emerges when two or more legal systems function in a country.

Mixed structure: A structure that integrates various aspects of the other forms of structures.

MNE: *See* Multinational enterprise.

Modes of operations: Different ways of doing business internationally, such as through exports/imports, foreign direct investment, joint ventures, licensing agreements, etc.

Monochronic culture: A culture in which most people prefer to deal with situations sequentially (especially those involving other people), such as finishing with one customer before dealing with another.

Most-favored-nation (MFN): A GATT requirement that a trade concession that is given to one country must be given to all other countries.

Multidomestic strategy: Emphasizing the need to be responsive to the unique conditions prevailing in different national markets.

Multifiber Arrangement (MFA): An agreement between textile and fiber producing and consuming countries that gave producers a quota of delivery to the consuming countries. This was disbanded by the WTO.

Multinational corporation (MNC): A synonym for multinational enterprise.

Multinational enterprise (MNE): A company that has an integrated global philosophy encompassing both domestic and foreign operations or a company with operations in more than one country; sometimes used simultaneously with multinational corporation or transnational corporation.

Multiparty Democracy: Multiparty system in which three or more political parties have the capacity to gain control of government separately or in coalition.

Multiple exchange-rate system: A means of foreign-exchange control whereby the government sets different exchange rates for different transactions.

Mutual recognition: The principle that a foreign registrant that wants to list and have its securities traded on a foreign stock exchange need only provide information prepared according to the GAAP of the home country.

National competitive advantage theory: The theory that countries have a competitive advantage in certain industries because of market conditions, factor conditions, firm strategy and structure, firm rivaly, and/or government forces.

National responsiveness: Readiness to implement operating adjustments in foreign countries in order to reach a satisfactory level of performance.

Natural advantage: Climatic conditions, access to certain natural resources, or availability of labor, which gives a country an advantage in producing some product.

Neomercantilism: The approach of countries that apparently try to run favorable balances of trade in an attempt to achieve some social or political objective.

Net capital flow: Capital inflow minus capital outflow, for other than import and export payment.

Net export effect: Export stimulus minus export reduction.

Net present value: The sum of the present values of the annual cash flows minus the initial investment.

Netting: The transfer of funds from subsidiaries in a net payable position to a central clearing account and from there to the accounts of the net receiver subsidiaries.

Network organization: A situation in which a group of companies is interrelated and in which the management of the interrelation is shared among so-called equals.

Nontariff barriers: Barriers to imports that are not tariffs; examples include administrative controls, "Buy America" policies, and so forth.

Nontradable goods: Products and services that are seldom practical to export, primarily because of high transportation costs.

Normal trade relations: A privilege that replaced the most-favored-nation clause and is granted to official members of the WTO.

Normativism: A theory stating that universal standards of behavior (based on people's own values) exist that all cultures should follow, making nonintervention unethical.

North American Free Trade Agreement (NAFTA): A free trade agreement involving the United States, Canada, and Mexico that went into effect on January 1, 1994, and will be phased in over a period of 15 years.

Nuclear family: A family consisting of parents and children.

OAU: *See* Organization of African Unity.

OECD: *See* Organization for Economic Cooperation and Development.

Offer rate: The amount for which a foreign-exchange trader is willing to sell a currency.

Official reserves: A country's holdings of monetary gold, Special Drawing Rights, and internationally acceptable currencies.

Offset trade: A form of countertrade in which an exporter sells goods for cash but then helps businesses in the importing country to find opportunities to earn hard currency.

Offshore financial centers: Cities or countries that provide large amounts of funds in currencies other than their own and are used as locations in which to raise and accumulate cash.

Offshore financing: The provision of financial services by banks and other agents to nonresidents.

Offshoring (offshore manufacturing): The process of shifting production to a foreign country.

Oligopolistic reaction: The process in oligopoly industries for competitors to emulate each other, such as going to the same locations.

OPEC: *See* Organization of Petroleum Exporting Countries.

Operational centers: Offshore financial centers that perform specific functions, such as the sale and servicing of goods.

Opinion leader: One whose acceptance of some concept is apt to be emulated by others.

Opportunity-risk matrix: An investment matrix that compares the opportunities of investing in a country with the risks and is a tool that companies can use to determine where to invest.

Optimism: A characteristic of an accounting system that implies that companies are more liberal in recognition of income.

Optimum-tariff theory: The argument that a foreign producer will lower its prices if an import tax is placed on its products.

Option: A foreign-exchange instrument that gives the purchaser the right, but not the obligation, to buy or sell a certain amount of foreign currency at a set exchange rate within a specified amount of time.

Organization of African Unity (OAU): An organization of African nations that is more concerned with political than economic objectives.

Organization culture: The values, beliefs, business principles, traditions, ways of doing things, and nature of internal work environment within a company.

Organization for Economic Cooperation and Development (OECD): A multilateral organization of industrialized and semi-industrialized countries that helps to formulate social and economic policies.

Organization of Petroleum Exporting Countries (OPEC): A producers' alliance among 12 petroleum-exporting countries that attempt to agree on oil production and pricing policies.

Organization structure: The formal arrangement of roles, responsibilities, and relationships within an organization.

Outright forward: A forward contract that is not connected to a spot transaction.

Outsourcing: Where one company contracts with another company to perform certain functions, including manufacturing and back office operations. May be done in or close to the company's home country (nearshoring) or in another country (offshoring).

Overseas Private Investment Corporation (OPIC): A U.S. government agency that provides insurance for companies involved in international business.

Over-the-counter (OTC) market: Trading in stocks, usually of smaller companies, that are not listed on one of the stock exchanges; also refers to how government and corporate bonds are traded, through dealers who quote bids and offers to buy and to sell "over the counter."

Par value: The benchmark value of a currency, originally quoted in terms of gold or the U.S. dollar and now quoted in terms of Special Drawing Rights.

Parliamentary Democracy: A system of government where the people exercise their political power by electing representatives to parliament to make laws.

Passive income: Income from investments in tax-haven countries or sales and services income that involves buyers and sellers in other than the tax-haven country, where either the buyer or the seller must be part of the same organizational structure as the corporation that earns the income; also known as Subpart F income.

Patent: A right granted by a sovereign power or state for the protection of an invention or discovery against infringement.

Payback period: The number of years required to recover the initial investment made.

Peg: To fix a currency's exchange rate to some benchmark, such as another currency.

Penetration strategy: A strategy of introducing a product at a low price to induce a maximum number of consumers to try it.

Philadelphia Stock Exchange (PHLX): An exchange in the United States that trades foreign-currency options.

Piracy: The unauthorized duplication of goods protected by intellectual property law.

PLC: *See* Product life cycle theory.

Pluralistic societies: Societies in which different ideologies are held by various segments rather than one ideology being adhered to by all.

Political freedom: The right to participate freely in the political process.

Political ideology: The body of constructs (complex ideas), theories, and aims that constitute a sociopolitical program.

Political risk: Potential changes in political conditions that may cause a company's operating positions to deteriorate.

Political science: A discipline that helps explain the patterns of governments and their actions.

Political system: The system designed to integrate a society into a viable, functioning unit.

Polycentric staffing: A staffing policy whereby a company relies on host country nationals to manage operations in their own country, while parent-country nationals staff key positions at corporate headquarters.

Polycentrism: Characteristic of an individual or organization that feels that differences in a foreign country, real and imaginary, great and small, need to be accounted for in management decisions.

Polychronic culture: A culture in which most people are more comfortable dealing simultaneously with multiple situations facing them.

Porter diamond: A diagram showing four conditions—demand (conditions); factor endowments (conditions); related and supporting industries; and firm strategy, structure, and rivalry—that usually must all be favorable for an industry in a country to develop and sustain a global competitive advantage.

Portfolio investment: An investment in the form of either debt or equity that does not give the investor a controlling interest.

Post Christian society: A term describing northern European countries that do not adhere strongly to any religion, but which hold strong Christian values because of centuries of profound religious influence.

Poverty: The condition of being poor or deprived of material belongings.

Power distance: A measurement of preference for consultative versus autocratic styles of management.

PPP: *See* Purchasing-power parity.

Pragmatism: Settling small issues before deciding on principles.

Premium (in foreign exchange): The difference between the spot and forward exchange rates in the forward market; a foreign currency sells at a premium when the forward rate exceeds the spot rate and when the domestic currency is quoted on a direct basis.

Price escalation: The process by which the lengthening of distribution channels increases a product's price by more than the direct added costs, such as transportation, insurance, and tariffs.

Principles-based accounting: A system of accounting that identifies key principles in a conceptual framework and establishes simple rules that conform to the key principles.

Private Technology Exchange (PTX): An online collaboration model that brings manufacturers, distributors, value-added resellers, and customers together to execute trading transactions and to share information about demand, production, availability, and more.

Privatization: Selling of government-owned assets to private individuals or companies.

Process technology: Technology of the production process rather than the product itself.

Product division structure: An organizational structure that assigns global responsibilities to each product division.

Productivity: Output per unit of input, usually measured either by labor productivity or by total factor productivity.

Product life cycle (PLC) theory: The theory that certain kinds of products go through a cycle consisting of four stages (introduction, growth, maturity, and decline) and that the location of production will shift internationally depending on the stage of the cycle.

Product technology: Technology related to the specific product, such as plasma screens for a television set.

Production network: A company's network where R&D may be done in one country, production in another, and finance in another.

Production orientation: A marketing strategy based on producing products at the lowest cost possible and providing them to consumers everywhere, irrespective of consumer preferences or differences.

Property rights: The legal rights to use goods, services, or resources.

Protectionism: Government restrictions on imports and occasionally on exports that frequently give direct or indirect subsidies to industries to enable them to compete with foreign production either at home or abroad.

Protestant ethic: A theory that there is more economic growth when work is viewed as a means of salvation and when people prefer to transform productivity gains into additional output rather than into additional leisure.

Pull promotion: A promotion strategy that sells consumers before they reach the point of purchase, usually by relying on mass media.

Purchasing power: What a sum of money actually can buy.

Purchasing power parity (PPP): A theory that explains exchange-rate changes as being based on differences in price levels in different countries. Also, the number of units of a country's currency to buy the same products or services in the domestic market that U.S.$1 would buy in the United States.

Push promotion: A promotion strategy that involves direct selling techniques.

Quality: Meeting or exceeding the expectations of a customer.

Quantity controls: Government limitations on the amount of foreign currency that can be used for specific purposes.

Quota: A limit on the quantitative amount of a product allowed to be exported from or imported into a country.

Quoted currency: The currency whose value is not the base currency when an exchange rate is quoted for two currencies.

Rationalization: *See* Rationalized production.

Rationalized production: The specialization of production by product or process in different parts of the world to take advantage of varying costs of labor, capital, and raw materials.

Reciprocal quote: The reciprocal of the direct quote. Also known as the indirect quote.

Regional integration: A form of integration in which a group of countries located in the same geographic proximity decide to cooperate.

Relativism: A theory stating that ethical truths depend on the groups holding them, making intervention by outsiders unethical. The belief that behavior has meaning and can be judged only in its specific cultural context.

Repatriation: An expatriate's return to his or her home country.

Representative democracy: A type of government in which individual citizens elect representatives to make decisions governing the society.

Resource-based view of the firm: A perspective that holds that each company has a unique combination of competencies.

Retaliation: A situation in which one country restricts imports from another country in response to that country's restrictions against its exports.

Return on investment (ROI): The amount of profit, sometimes measured before and sometimes after the payment of taxes, divided by the amount of investment.

Revaluation: A formal change in an exchange rate by which the foreign-currency value of the reference currency rises, resulting in a strengthening of the reference currency.

Reverse culture shock: The experience of culture shock when returning to one's own country that is caused by having accepted what was experienced abroad.

Revocable letter of credit: A letter of credit that can be changed by any of the parties involved.

Royalties: Payments for the use of intangible assets.

Rule of law: The principle that every member of a society, even a ruler, must follow the law.

Rule of man: Notion that the word and whim of one man are law.

Rules-based accounting: A legalistic accounting system filled with specific details in an attempt to address as many potential contingencies as possible.

Sales orientation: A company tries to sell abroad what it can sell domestically and in the same manner on the assumption that consumers are sufficiently similar globally.

Sales representative (foreign): A representative that usually operates either exclusively or nonexclusively within an assigned market and on a commission basis, without assuming risk or responsibility.

Scale alliance: An alliance where firms aim at providing efficiency through the pooling of similar assets so that partners can carry out business activities in which they already have experience.

Scanning: Examining a variety of variables for different countries that may affect foreign investment alternatives.

SDR: *See* Special Drawing Right.

Secrecy: A characteristic of an accounting system that implies that companies do not disclose much information about accounting practices; more common historically in Germanic countries.

Secular totalitarianism: A dictatorship not affiliated with any religious group or system of beliefs.

Securities and Exchange Commission (SEC): A U.S. government agency that regulates securities brokers, dealers, and markets.

Separate entity approach: A system for taxation of corporate income in which each unit is taxed when it receives income, with the result being double taxation.

Service exports: Internationally paid earnings other than those derived from exporting tangible goods.

Service imports: Internationally paid earnings other than those derived from importing tangible goods.

Services: International earnings other than those on goods sent to another country. Also referred to as invisibles.

Services account: The part of a country's current account that measures travel and transportation, tourism, and fees and royalties.

Settlement: The actual payment of currency in a foreign-exchange transaction.

Sight draft: A commercial bill of exchange that requires payment to be made as soon as it is presented to the party obligated to pay.

Silent language: The wide variety of cues other than formal language by which messages can be sent.

Single European Act: A 1987 act of the EU (then the EC) allowing all proposals except those relating to taxation, workers' rights, and immigration to be adopted by a weighted majority of member countries.

Six Sigma: A highly focused system of quality control that uses data and rigorous statistical analysis to identify "defects" in a process or product, reduce variability, and achieve as close to zero defects as possible.

Skimming strategy: Charging a high price for a new product by aiming first at consumers willing to pay that price and then progressively lowering the price.

Small Business Administration (SBA): A governmental agency that aids, counsels, assists, and protects the interests of small business concerns.

Smithsonian Agreement: A 1971 agreement among countries that resulted in the devaluation of the U.S. dollar, revaluation of other world currencies, a widening of exchange-rate flexibility, and a commitment on the part of all participating countries to reduce trade restrictions; superseded by the Jamaica Agreement of 1976.

Social Democracy: The political ideology of socialism, including values of a representative government, and private property.

Social stratification: The ranking of individuals in a society.

Socialism: A system based on public ownership of the means of production and distribution of wealth.

Societal marketing orientation: Successful international marketing requires serious consideration of potential environmental, health, social, and work-related problems that may arise when selling or making their products abroad.

Society: A broad grouping of people having common traditions, institutions, and collective activities and interests; the term nation-state is often used in international business to denote a society.

Soft currency: *See* Weak currency.

Sogo shosha: Japanese trading companies that import and export merchandise.

Sourcing strategy: The strategy that a company pursues in purchasing materials, components, and final products; sourcing can be from domestic and foreign locations and from inside and outside the company.

Special Drawing Right (SDR): A unit of account issued to countries by the International Monetary Fund to expand their official reserves bases.

Specialization: A result of free trade policies that causes countries to concentrate on producing and exporting those products for which they have the greatest advantage and importing those for which they have less advantage.

Specific duty: A duty (tariff) assessed on a per-unit basis.

Speculation: The buying or selling of foreign currency with the prospect of great risk and high return.

Speculator: A person who takes positions in foreign exchange with the objective of earning a profit.

Spillover effects: Situations in which the marketing program in one country results in awareness of the product in other countries.

Spot market: The market in which an asset is traded for immediate delivery, as opposed to a market for forward or future deliveries.

Spot rate: An exchange rate quoted for immediate delivery of foreign currency, usually within two business days.

Spot transactions: Foreign exchange transactions involving the exchange of currency the second day after the date on which the two foreign-exchange traders agree to the transaction.

Spread: In the forward market, the difference between the spot rate and the forward rate; in the spot market, the difference between the bid (buy) and offer (sell) rates quoted by a foreign-exchange trader.

Stakeholders: The collection of groups, including stockholders, employees, customers, and society at large, that a company must satisfy to survive.

Standardization: The procedure of maintaining methods and equipment as constant as possible.

Static effects of integration: The shifting of resources from inefficient to efficient companies as trade barriers fall.

Stereotype: A standardized and oversimplified mental picture of a group.

Strategic alliance: An agreement between companies that is of strategic importance to one or both companies' competitive viability.

Strategic intent: An objective that gives an organization cohesion over the long term while it builds global competitive viability.

Strategic marketing orientation: Most companies committed to continual rather than sporadic foreign sales adopt a strategy that combines production, sales, and customer orientations.

Strategic plan: An organization's process of defining its strategy, or direction, and making decisions on allocating its resources to pursue this strategy, including its capital and people.

Strategic trade policy: The identification and development of target industries to be competitive internationally.

Strategy: The means companies select to achieve their objectives.

Subpart F income: Income of a CFC that comes from sources other than those connected with the active conduct of a trade or business, such as holding company income.

Subsidiary: A foreign operation that is legally separate from the parent company, even if wholly owned by it.

Subsidies: Direct assistance from governments to companies to make them more competitive.

Supply chain: The coordination of materials, information, and funds from the initial raw material supplier to the ultimate customer.

Swap: A simultaneous spot and forward foreign-exchange transaction.

Syndication: Cooperation by a lead bank and several other banks to make a large loan to a public or private organization.

Tacit knowledge: Knowledge imbedded in people, which usually can be transferred only on a person-to-person basis rather than through printed material.

Tariff: A government tax levied on goods, usually imports, shipped internationally.

Tax credit: A dollar-for-dollar reduction of tax liability that must coincide with the recognition of income.

Tax deferral: Income is not taxed until it is remitted to the parent company as a dividend.

Tax-haven countries: Countries with low income taxes or no taxes on foreign-source income.

Tax-haven subsidiary: A subsidiary of a company established in a tax-haven country for the purpose of minimizing income tax.

Tax treaty: A treaty between two countries that generally results in the reciprocal reduction on dividend withholding taxes and the exemption of taxes or royalties and sometimes interest payments.

Technical forecasting: A forecasting tool that uses past trends in exchange rates themselves to spot future trends in rates.

Temporal method: A method of translating foreign-currency financial statements used when the functional currency is that of the parent company.

Terms currency: Exchange rates are quoted as the number of units of the terms currency per base currency.

Terms of trade: The quantity of imports that can be bought by a given quantity of a country's exports.

Theocratic totalitarianism: A dictatorship led by a religious group.

Third-country nationals: Expatriate employees who are neither citizens of the country in which they are working nor citizens of the country where the company is headquartered.

Tied aid and loans: Aid and loans given by one government to another on the condition that the recipient country spend the money on products from the donor country.

Time draft: A commercial bill of exchange calling for payment to be made at some time after delivery.

TNC: *See* Transnational company.

Total cost analysis: The process of determining monetary value based on acquisition costs, maintenance costs, and disposal costs.

Total quality management (TQM): The process that a company uses to achieve quality, where the goal is elimination of all defects.

Totalitarianism: A political system characterized by the absence of widespread participation in decision making.

TQM: *See* Total quality management.

Trade creation: Production shifts to more efficient producers for reasons of comparative advantage, allowing consumers access to more goods at a lower price than would have been possible without integration.

Trade diversion: A situation in which exports shift to a less efficient producing country because of preferential trade barriers.

Trade Related Aspects of Intellectual Property Rights (TRIPS): A provision from the Uruguay round of trade negotiations requiring countries to agree to enforce procedures under their national laws to protect intellectual property rights.

Trade sanctions: Tariffs and non-tariff barriers levied on another country, usually for political reasons.

Trademark: A name or logo distinguishing a company or product.

Transaction cost theory: As applied to international business, the choice of operating based on the relative cost of doing business with a company's owned operations versus doing business with an independent company.

Transaction exposure: Foreign-exchange risk arising because a company has outstanding accounts receivable or accounts payable that are denominated in a foreign currency.

Transfer price: A price charged for goods or services between entities that are related to each other through stock ownership, such as between a parent

and its subsidiaries or between subsidiaries owned by the same parent.

Translation: The restatement of foreign-currency financial statements into U.S. dollars.

Translation exposure: Foreign-exchange risk that occurs because the parent company must translate foreign-currency financial statements into the reporting currency of the parent company.

Transnational: (1) An organization in which different capabilities and contributions among different country-operations are shared and integrated; (2) multinational enterprise; (3) company owned and managed by nationals from different countries.

Transnational company (TNC): A company owned and managed by nationals in different countries; also may be synonymous with multinational enterprise.

Transnational strategy: A strategy that attempts to take advantage of corporate strengths across national boundaries; it is very interdependent.

Transparency: A characteristic of an accounting system that implies that companies disclose a great deal of information about accounting practices; more common in Anglo-Saxon countries (United States, United Kingdom).

TRIPS: *See* Trade Related Aspects of Intellectual Property Rights.

Turnkey operation: An operating facility that is constructed under contract and transferred to the owner when the facility is ready to begin operations.

Uncertainty avoidance: A cultural trait where individuals are uncomfortable with uncertainty and prefer structure to independence.

Underemployed: Those people who are working at less than their capacity.

Unfavorable balance of trade: An indication of a trade deficit—that is, imports are greater than exports. Also called deficit.

Unilateral transfer: A transfer of currency from one country to another for which no goods or services are received; an example is foreign aid to a country devastated by earthquake or flood.

United Nations (UN): An international organization of countries formed in 1945 to promote world peace and security.

United Nations Conference on Trade and Development (UNCTAD): A UN body that has been especially active in dealing with the relationships between developing and industrialized countries with respect to trade.

U.S.-Canada Free Trade Agreement: *See* Canada-U.S. Free Trade Agreement.

U.S. terms: *See* American terms.

Value-added tax (VAT): A tax that is a percentage of the value added to a product at each stage of the business process.

Value chain: The collective activities that occur as a product moves from raw materials through production to final distribution.

VAT: *See* Value-added tax.

Vertical alliance: An alliance that links together elements in the value chain backward and forward, such as back to raw materials and forward to final distribution.

Vertical integration: The control of the different stages as a product moves from raw materials through production to final distribution.

Virtual manufacturing: Subcontracting the manufacturing process to another firm.

Virtual organization: A form of company that acquires strategic capabilities by creating a temporary network of independent companies, suppliers, customers, and even rivals.

Visible exports: *See* Merchandise exports.

Visible imports: *See* Merchandise imports.

Voluntary export restraint (VER): A negotiated limitation of exports between an importing and an exporting country.

Weak (or soft) currency: A currency that is not fully convertible. However, even a hard currency can be weak relative to another currency because of the relative exchange rates over time.

WIPO: *See* World Intellectual Property Organization.

World Bank: A multilateral lending institution that provides investment capital to countries.

World Intellectual Property Organization (WIPO): A multilateral agreement to protect patents.

World Trade Organization (WTO): A voluntary organization through which groups of countries negotiate trading agreements and which has authority to oversee trade disputes among countries.

WTO: *See* World Trade Organization.

Zero defects: The elimination of defects, which results in the reduction of manufacturing costs and an increase in consumer satisfaction.

Zero-sum game: A situation in which one party's gain equals another party's loss.

Photo Credits

Company Index and Trademarks

Page references with "f" refer to figures, page references with "m" refer to maps, and page references with "n" refer to endnotes cited by number.

Name Index

Page references with "f" refer to figures, page references with "n" refer to notes cited by number, and page references with "t" refer to tables.

Subject Index

Page references with "f" refer to figures, page references with "m" refer to maps, page references with "n" refer to endnotes cited by number, and page references with "t" refer to tables.